Canon LEAGUE

FOOTBALL PLAYERS' RECORDS

1946-1984

Compiled by Barry J. Hugman

NEWNES BOOKS

Published 1984 by Newnes Books, a Division of The Hamlyn Publishing
Group Limited
84–88 The Centre, Feltham, Middlesex, England
and distributed for them by
The Hamlyn Publishing Group Limited
Rushden, Northants, England

ISBN 0 600 37318 5

Typeset by Gee Graphics Ltd

Printed in Great Britain by
Butler & Tanner Ltd, Frome and London

Photographic acknowledgements

The publishers gratefully acknowledge the following sources for photographs
used in the biographical sections throughout the book:
Associated Sports Photography, Leicester – George Herringshaw; Barnsley
Chronicle; Colorsport, London; Graham Hind; Syndication International,
London; Greg Szpurko.

Contents

Acknowledgements

Once again a special thank you must go to Michael Featherstone, who has continued to make sterling efforts in tracing the missing player birthdates required; with great success.

Alan Platt took responsibility for the sub-editing where his expertise was seen to great effect and is also in the process of co-ordinating post-war club audits for future volumes against the Football League appearance records of which the following have been completed:

Charlton Athletic *Morley Farrer*
Tottenham H. *Michael Featherstone*
Carlisle United *Keith Wild*
Leicester City *Dave Smith*
Peterborough United *Mick Robinson*
West Ham United *John Powles*
Manchester City *John Maddocks*
Hull City *Doug Lamming*
W.B.A. *Tony Matthews*
Brighton & H.A. *Nigel Bishop*
Everton *Gordon Smailes*

Blackburn Rovers *Harry Berry*
Aldershot *Jack Rollin*
Barnsley *Granville Firth*
Fulham *Dennis Turner*
Chelsea *Ian Rennie*
Liverpool *Allan Twells*
Torquay United *John Lovis*
Cambridge United ⎫
Wigan Athletic ⎬ *Clubs*
Wimbledon   ⎪
Hereford United ⎭

Tony Pullein was kind enough to provide the audited Football League goals for the season, which was highly valued.

Thanks are also in order to Mr Graham Kelly of the Football League, who again put the mass of records at my disposal with a special mention to Mike Foster, Lloyd Bell, Debbie Singleton and Carol Eaton, who made life easier with their assistance.

Thanks, too, to Gordon Taylor of the Professional Footballers Association for his help and understanding. John Beckwith must also be mentioned for his invaluable help at a crucial stage of the book.

Finally, thanks again to my wife Jennifer, with help from daughter Debbie, son Gareth and Daniel Kitchener for spending many hours typing and assembling the work into requisite order.

Preface

Once again it gives me great pleasure to produce a 'Football League Players' Records,' only this time under the Canon label and with an additional three seasons added to the original version. The work again takes in every player who made at least one appearance in league soccer since the war, even as a substitute, right up to the end of the 1983/84 season. Use has been made of my personal records library, Football League appearance ledgers, club programmes, local newspapers and a whole host of club statisticians who delight in recreating the records of the players they remember so well.

Where club appearance audits do not exist, Football League records were used, a facility kindly made available by Mr Graham Kelly, the Secretary of the Football League. Once again birth dates of players play a significant role in the make-up of the book, with amazingly only 100 missing from a possible 15,000; if there are any ex-players or relations who can help provide that missing information it will be warmly received.

The work has been updated for the pleasure and information of all: the older reader may reflect on names from the past and the younger on the names of today. Whether your own post-war heroes wore heavy boots and baggy shorts or still do wear streamlined shirts decorated with fancy strip and a sponsor's name, they are all included in this book. I hope you enjoy reading it.

Barry J. Hugman, June 1984

Key to Reading the Entries

Statistical Section

Players' Names	Surname shown first, followed by leading Christian name plus any initials.
Birthplace	Any birthplace outside of the United Kingdom and the Republic of Ireland is indicated by name of country.
Birthdate	Day/Month/Year
Previous Club	Prior to joining Football League, includes Non-League/Amateur/Scottish League/Junior Leagues/Foreign Leagues etc.

APP	=	Apprentice signing
JNRS	=	Junior (players signed prior to 17th birthday or direct from school/college)
TR	=	Transfer (including free transfers)
L	=	Loan transfer (only where appearances have been made).

League Club	All clubs who have held league status since 1946/7
Date Signed	Professional signing date – month/year (Loan transfer date shown if player is later signed permanently).

*	=	Pre-war signing
+	=	Wartime signing
N/C	=	Non-contract
N/L	=	Non-League
AM	=	Amateur

Seasons Played	Years stated are for the earliest period of a season, ie 1946 means season 1946/47.
Career Record	Does not include League appearances made prior to 1946/47. Under the 'Sub' heading an oblique stroke (/) indicates that the player in question played in the period when substitutes were allowed, but made no substitute appearances.
Remarks Column	Shows playing positions, ie (F) = Forward, (D) = Defender, (G) = Goalkeeper, (M) = Midfield, (IF) = Inside Forward, (FB) = Full Back, (HB) = Half Back, (WH) = Wing Half, (W) = Winger, (CF) = Centre Forward.
	Shows International Honours down to schoolboy levels as at 2 June 1984, ie EI = Eire, E = England, NI = Northern Ireland, S = Scotland, W = Wales.
	A black spot (●) indicates that further details and a picture appear in the biographical sections of the book.
General Note	Players' records shown span Football League careers only.

Biographical Sections

Biographies of well-known long service players, leading goalscorers and International players who have represented their countries on many occasions.

The biographies are spread alphabetically through the main statistical pages, which carry cross-references to biographies.

Players' Records and Biographies 1946–84

Including appearance records for every League player making at least one appearance (including as a substitute) between 1946 and 1984.

Biographical notes with photographs are included in batches for players with distinguished League careers based on such data as a large number of appearances, long service with one club, goal scoring feats, International records, etc.

Players Names	Birthplace	Date	Previous Club	League Club	Date Signed	Seasons Played	Apps	Sub	Gls	
AAS, Einar J.	Norway	12.10.55	Bayern Munich	Nottingham F.	03.81	1980-81	20	1	1	(D) NORWEGIAN INT.
ABBISS, Keith D.	Hatfield	26.04.32	Hitchin T.	Brighton & H.A.	10.57	1959-60	19		3	(IF)
ABBLEY, Steve G.	Liverpool	19.03.57	Parks F.C.	Swindon T.	10.79	1979-81	14	9	0	(F)
ABBOTT, Gregory	Coventry	14.12.63	APP	Coventry C.	01.82					(D)
			TR	Bradford C.	09.82	1982-83	41	5	3	
ABBOTT, John	Winsford	25.05.43	Winsford U.	Crewe Alex.	07.62	1961-64	4		0	(HB)
ABBOTT, Peter	Rotherham	01.10.53	APP	Manchester U.	10.70					(F)
			TR	Swansea C.	02.74	1973-75	34	7	3	
			TR	Crewe Alex.	08.76	1976	27	4	8	
			TR	Southend U.	07.77	1977-78	26	1	4	
ABBOTT, Ron	London	02.08.53	APP	Q.P.R.	07.71	1973-78	32	14	4	(D)
ABBOTTS, John	Stoke	10.10.24		Port Vale	05.49	1950	3		0	
ABRAHAMS, Laurie	Stepney	03.04.53	Barking	Charlton Ath.	05.77	1977	12	4	2	(F)
ABREY, Brian	Hendon	25.04.39	JNRS	Chelsea	10.56					(WH)
			TR	Colchester U.	05.61	1961	38		2	
ABTHORPE, John	Nottingham	19.01.33	Wolves(AM)	Notts.Co.	AM	1955	5		3	(CF)
ACKERLEY, Ernie	Manchester	23.09.43	JNRS	Manchester U.	10.60					(CF) Brother of Stan
			TR	Barrow	04.63	1962-63	53		12	
ACKERLEY, Stan	Manchester	12.07.42	JNRS	Manchester U.	11.59					(FB)
			TR	Oldham Ath.	06.61	1961	2		0	
ACKERMAN, Alf A.E.	S. Africa	05.01.29	Clyde	Hull C.	07.50	1950	34		21	(CF)●
			TR	Norwich C.	08.51	1951-53	67		30	
			TR	Hull C.	10.53	1953-54	58		28	
			TR	Derby Co.	03.55	1954-56	36		21	
			TR	Carlisle U.	11.56	1956-58	96		62	
			TR	Millwall	01.59	1958-60	82		33	
ACKERMAN, Antony	Islington	20.02.48	West Ham U.(AM)	Orient	10.66	1966-67	4	/	0	(CH)
ACLAND, Mike	Sidcup	04.06.35		Gillingham	AM	1956	2		0	(F)
A'COURT, Alan	Rainhill	30.09.34	Prescot Cables	Liverpool	09.52	1952-62	354		61	(OL)E.-S/E. F.LGE REP/
			TR	Tranmere Rov.	10.64	1964-65	50	/	11	E.U23-7
ACRES, Basil D.J.	Brantham	27.10.26	Brantham	Ipswich T.	09.50	1951-59	217		6	(FB)
ACTON, Alec E.	Leicester	12.11.38	Leicester C.(AM)	Stoke C.	01.56					(HB)
			Brush Sports	Stockport Co.	08.58	1958-59	9		0	
ADAM, Charlie	Glasgow	22.03.19	Strathclyde	Leicester C.	*	1946-50	158		22	(OL)
			TR	Mansfield T.	07.52	1952-54	94		7	
ADAM, Jim	Paisley	22.04.31	Penilee U.	Leeds U.	06.51					(IF)
			TR	Mansfield T.	08.54	1954	39		12	
ADAM, Jim	Glasgow	13.05.31		Aldershot	AM	1950	1		0	(OL)
			Spennymoor	Luton T.	07.53	1953-58	137		22	
			TR	Aston Villa	08.59	1959-60	24		3	
			TR	Stoke C.	07.61	1961	22		7	
ADAMS, Anthony A.	Romford	10.10.66	APP	Arsenal	01.84	1983	3	/	0	(D)
ADAMS, Brian	Tottenham	18.05.47	Chelsea(APP)	Milwall	08.64	1964-65	15	/	0	(HB)
ADAMS, Chris J.	Hornchurch	06.09.27	Romford	Tottenham H.	11.48	1951-52	6		1	(OL)
			TR	Norwich C.	12.52	1952-54	28		3	
			TR	Watford	03.54	1953-55	75		5	
ADAMS, Don F.	Northampton	15.02.31		Northampton T.	05.51	1951-55	24		7	(CF)
ADAMS, Ernie R.	Dagenham	17.01.48	APP	Arsenal	01.65					(G)
			TR	Colchester U.	07.67	1967-68	48	/	0	
			TR	Crewe Alex.	07.69	1969-71	112	/	0	
			TR	Darlington	07.72	1972	25	/	0	
ADAMS, Ernie W.	Willesden	03.04.22		Preston N.E.	*					(F)
			TR	Q.P.R.	09.47	1947-49	5		0	
ADAMS, Francis	Liverpool	08.02.33	Bury Amats.	Bury	01.56	1956-61	169		0	(G)
			TR	Chester C.	07.63	1963	8		0	
			TR	Tranmere Rov.	02.64					
ADAMS, George	Falkirk	16.10.26	Chelmsford	Orient	05.49	1949	4		0	
			Bath C.	Crystal Palace	03.54					
ADAMS, George R.	Hackney	28.09.47	JNRS	Chelsea	09.65					(CF)
			TR	Peterborough U.	07.66	1966-67	13	3	2	
ADAMS, Graham	Torrington	01.03.33		Plymouth Arg.	01.58	1957	1		0	(FB)
ADAMS, Jim A.	Stoke	02.08.37		Port Vale	06.56	1957	1		0	(HB)
			TR	Crewe Alex	08.60					
ADAMS, Laurie	Barnet	14.02.31		Watford	07.52	1951	1		0	(IF)
ADAMS, Mick R.	Sheffield	08.11.61	APP	Gillingham	11.79	1979-82	85	7	4	(D)E.YTH.INT.
			TR	Coventry C.	07.83	1983	16	1	1	
ADAMS, Mike A.	Banwell	20.02.65	APP	Bristol Rov.	02.83	1982	0	1	0	(D)
ADAMS, Rex	Oxford	13.02.28	Oxford C.	Blackpool	06.48	1948-50	16		1	(OR)
			TR	Oldham Ath	06.53	1953	23		2	

Players Names	Birthplace	Date	Previous Club	League Club	Date Signed	Seasons Played	Apps	Sub	Gls	
ADAMS, Rod	Bath	15.09.45	Frome T.	Bournemouth	06.66	1966-68	15	2	4	(F)
ADAMS, Steve	Windsor	18.06.58	APP	Q.P.R.	07.75					(M)
			TR	Millwall	'07.77	1977	1	/	0	
			Windsor & Eton	Cambridge U.	03.78	1977-78	1	2	0	
ADAMS, Vince	Chesterfield	16.10.46	APP	Arsenal	10.63					(HB)E.SCH.INT.
			TR	Chesterfield	11.65	1965-66	14	2	1	
ADAMS, William H.	Arlecdon	08.01.19		Tottenham H.	*					
			TR	Carlisle U.	06.46	1946	33		1	
			Cheltenham	Workington	N/L	1951	3		0	
ADAMS, William V.	Plymouth	10.05.21	Plymouth U.	Plymouth Arg.	*	1946	1		0	
ADAMSON, David	Chester-le-street	07.05.51	Durham C.	Doncaster Rov.	07.70	1970-71	28	/	0	(FB)
ADAMSON, Henry	Kelty	27.06.24	Jeanfield Swifts	Notts. Co.	08.46	1947-55	233		5	(WH)
ADAMSON, Jim	Ashington	04.04.29	Ashington	Burnley	01.47	1950-63	425		17	(WH)EF LGE REP.●
ADAMSON, Keith	Houghton-le-Spring	03.07.45	Tow Law	Barnsley	03.66	1965-66	7	/	0	(F) Brother of Terry
ADAMSON, Terry	Houghton-le-Spring	15.10.48	APP	Sunderland	11.65					(FB)
			TR	Luton T.	07.66	1966	2	/	0	
			TR	Hartlepool U.	07.67	1967	1	/	0	
ADCOCK, Anthony C.	Bethnal Green	27.03.63	APP	Colchester U.	08.81	1980-83	99	15	48	(F)
ADDINALL, Albert	Paddington	30.01.21		Q.P.R.	*	1946-52	149		59	(CF)
			TR	Brighton & H.A.	01.53	1952-53	60		31	
			TR	Crystal Palace	07.54	1954	12		2	
ADDISON, Colin	Taunton	18.05.40	JNRS	York C.	05.57	1957-60	87		27	(CF)
			TR	Nottingham F.	01.61	1960-66	159	/	61	
			TR	Arsenal	09.66	1966-67	27	1	9	
			TR	Sheffield U.	12.67	1967-70	93	1	22	
			TR	Hereford U.	N/L	1972-73	23	/	1	
ADDY, Mike	Knottingley	20.02.43	JNRS	Leeds U.	05.62	1962	2		0	(F)
			TR	Barnsley	06.64	1964-66	50	1	5	
ADEY, Arthur	Glasgow	01.03.30	B. Auckland	Doncaster Rov.	09.50	1950-53	48		10	(CF)
			TR	Gillingham	07.54	1954	7		1	
			TR	Bradford P.A.	10.54	1954	13		4	
ADKINS, Nigel H.	Birkenhead	11.03.65	APP	Tranmere Rov.	03.83	1982-83	14	/	0	(G)
ADLINGTON, Terry	Blackwell	21.11.35	Blackwell C.W.	Derby Co.	12.55	1956-60	36		0	(G)
			TR	Torquay U.	06.62	1962-65	148	/	0	
AGAR, Roy F.	Islington	01.04.36	Barnet	Swindon T.	AM	1955-56	12		0	(IF) E.AMAT.INT.
AGBOOLA, Reuben O.	London	30.05.62	APP	Southampton	04.80	1980-83	80	1	0	(D)
AGNEW, David G.	Belfast	31.03.25	Crusaders	Sunderland	01.50	1950	1		0	(G) N.I.AMAT.INT.
AGNEW, David Y.	Kilwinning	04.08.39	JNRS	Leicester C.	08.58					(FB)
			TR	Scunthorpe U.	06.61	1961	1	/	0	
			TR	Notts. Co.	06.62	1962-66	85	/	1	
AGNEW, John	Stockton	27.06.35		Sheffield Wed.	11.53					
			TR	Darlington	08.54	1954-55	24		4	
AGNEW, Paul	Lisburn	15.08.65		Grimsby T.	02.84	1983	1	/	0	(D)
AGNEW, Steve M.	Shipley	09.11.65	APP	Barnsley	11.83	1983	0	1	0	(F)
AHERNE, Tom	Limerick	26.01.19	Belfast Celtic	Luton T.	03.49	1948-56	266		0	(FB)N.I.-4/EI-16
AIKEN, Tom	Ballymena	18.03.46	Ballymena	Doncaster Rov.	11.67	1967-68	12	1	1	(OL)N.I.AMAT.INT.
AIMSON, Paul	Macclesfield	03.08.43	JNRS	Manchester C.	08.60	1961-63	16		4	(CF)
			TR	York C.	07.64	1964-65	77	/	43	
			TR	Bury	03.66	1965-66	30	1	11	
			TR	Bradford C.	09.67	1967	23	/	11	
			TR	Huddersfield T.	03.68	1967-68	34	4	13	
			TR	York C.	08.69	1969-72	133	9	55	
			TR	Bournemouth	03.73	1972	7	2	2	
			TR	Colchester U.	08.73	1973	3	1	2	
AINDOW, Roger	Liverpool	23.10.46		Southport	07.69	1968-70	52	7	4	(IF)
AINGE, Ron. P.	Pontardawe	05.08.20	Llanelli	Newport Co.	10.46	1946	5		0	(W)
AINSCOUGH, John	Adlington	26.03.26	Astley Bridge	Blackpool	08.49	1950-53	7		0	(CH)
AINSCOW, Alan	Bolton	15.07.53	APP	Blackpool	07.71	1971-77	178	14	28	(M)E.YTH.INT.
			TR	Birmingham C.	07.78	1978-80	104	4	16	
			TR	Everton	08.81	1981-82	24	4	3	
			L	Barnsley	11.82	1982	2	/	0	
AINSLEY, George	Sth. Shields	15.04.15	Bolton W.(*)	Leeds U.	*	1946-47	30		13	(CF)*Sunderland
			TR	Bradford P.A.	11.47	1947-48	44		30	
AINSWORTH, Alphonso	Manchester	31.07.13	Oldham Ath.(+)	New Brighton	*	1946-47	41		9	(IF)*Manchester U./d.1975
AINSWORTH, David	Bolton	28.01.58	APP	Rochdale	01.76	1975	0	2	0	(F)
AINSWORTH, John				New Brighton	AM	1946	4		3	(F)
AIRD, Jock	Glencraig	18.02.26	Jeanfield Swifts	Burnley	08.48	1949-54	132		0	(FB) S-4/

Players Names	Birthplace	Date	Previous Club	League Club	Date Signed	Seasons Played	Career Record Apps	Sub	Gls	
AIREY, Carl	Barnsley	06.02.65	APP	Barnsley	02.83	1982-83	30	8	5	(F)
			L	Bradford C.	10.83	1983	4	1	0	
AIREY, Jack	Blackburn	28.11.37		Blackburn Rov.	01.59	1958-59	3		1	(CF)
AITCHISON, Barry G.	Colchester	15.11.37	JNRS	Tottenham H.	01.55					(F)
			TR	Colchester U.	08.64	1964-65	49	1	7	
AITCHISON, Peter	Netteswell	19.09.31		Colchester U.	10.51	1951-54	18		2	(F)
AITKEN, Andy	Edinburgh	21.08.34	Hibernian	W.B.A.	09.59	1959-60	22		2	(F)
AITKEN, Charlie	Edinburgh	01.05.42	Edinburgh Th.	Aston Villa	08.59	1960-75	558	2	13	(FB)S.U23-3/●
AITKEN, George B.	Dalkeith	13.08.28	Edinburgh Th.	Middlesbrough	06.46	1951-52	17		0	(CH)
			TR	Workington	07.53	1953-59	262		3	
AITKEN, George C.	Lochgelly	28.05.25	T. Lanark	Sunderland	11.51	1951-58	244		3	(WH) S-8/
			TR	Gateshead	03.59	1958-59	58		0	
AITKEN, Glen	Woolwich	30.09.52	Chelsea (AM)	Gillingham	12.72	1972-74	19	4	0	(D)E.YTH.INT.
			TR	Wimbledon	N/L	1977	11	/	1	
AITKEN, Peter G.	Cardiff	30.06.54	APP	Bristol Rov.	07.72	1972-79	230	4	3	(D)
			TR	Bristol C.	11.80	1980-81	41	/	1	
			TR	York C.	02.82	1981	18	/	2	
				Bournemouth	N/C	1982	1	/	0	
AITKEN, William	Dumfries	11.01.51	APP	Oldham Ath.	01.68	1968	1	/	0	(F)
AIZLEWOOD, Mark	Newport	01.10.59	APP	Newport Co.	10.77	1957-77	35	3	1	(D)W.U21-2/W.SCH.INT.
			TR	Luton T.	04.78	1978-81	90	8	3	
			TR	Charlton Ath.	11.82	1982-83	53	/	2	
AIZLEWOOD, Steve	Newport	09.10.52	JNRS	Newport Co.	01.70	1968-75	191	6	17	(D)W.SCH.INT.
			TR	Swindon T.	03.76	1975-78	111	1	10	Brother of Mark
			TR	Portsmouth	07.79	1979-83	175	/	13	
AKERS, Vic	London	24.08.46	Bexley U.	Cambridge U.	07.71	1971-74	122	7	5	(FB)
			Tooting & M	Watford	07.75	1975	22	/	0	
ALBERRY, William E.	Doncaster	21.07.22		Doncaster Rov.	*					d.1978
			TR	Leeds U.	05.46					
			TR	Hull C.	04.47	1946	1		0	
ALBESON, Brian	Oldham	14.12.46	JNRS	Bury	05.65	1965	/	1	0	(FB)E.YTH.INT.
			TR	Darlington	07.67	1967-70	136	2	2	
			TR	Southend U.	07.71	1971-73	109	1	9	
			TR	Stockport Co.	03.74	1973-74	54	/	1	
ALBISTON, Arthur R.	Edinburgh	14.07.57	APP	Manchester U.	07.74	1974-83	264	6	5	(D)S.U21-5/S.SCH.INT./S-6
ALBURY, William	Portsmouth	10.08.33	JNRS	Portsmouth	10.51	1956-57	23		0	(WH)
			TR	Gillingham	07.59	1959	38		12	
ALCOCK, Terry	Hanley	09.12.46	APP	Port Vale	09.64	1963-66	112	/	0	(D)
			TR	Blackpool	08.67	1967-75	190	6	21	
			L	Bury	02.72	1971	6	/	1	
			L	Blackburn Rov.	12.76	1976	3	/	1	
			TR	Port Vale	02.77	1976-77	4	/	0	
			TR	Halifax T.	09.77	1977	14	/	2	
ALDECOA, Emilio G.	Spain	30.11.22	Wolverhampton W. (*)	Coventry C.	*	1946	29		0	SPANISH INT.
ALDERSON, Brian	Dundee	05.05.50	Lochee Harp	Coventry C.	07.70	1970-74	116	11	29	(F)S.U23-1
			TR	Leicester C.	07.75	1975-77	87	3	9	
ALDERSON, Kevin	Shildon	21.08.53	APP	Darlington	APP	1970	1	/	0	(CH)
ALDERSON, Stuart	Bishop Auckland	15.08.48	Evenwood	Newcastle U.	08.65	1966	3	/	0	(F)
			TR	York C.	06.67	1967	17	2	5	
ALDERTON, Jim H.	Wingate	06.12.24	JNRS	Wolverhampton W.	*	1946	11		0	(WH)
			TR	Coventry C.	10.47	1947-51	62		0	
ALDIS, Peter B.	Birmingham	11.04.27	Hay Green	Aston Villa	05.49	1950-58	262		1	(FB)
ALDOUS, Stan E.R.	Northfleet	10.02.23	Gravesend	Orient	07.50	1950-57	302		3	(CH)
ALDREAD, Paul	Mansfield	06.11.46	JNRS	Mansfield T.	12.63	1965-66	10	1	3	(F)
ALDRED, Arthur	Atherton	27.08.19		Aston Villa	07.46					
			TR	Walsall	05.48	1948	11		1	
ALDRIDGE, John W.	Liverpool	18.09.58	Sth.Liverpool	Newport Co.	04.79	1979-83	159	11	67	(F)
			TR	Oxford U.	03.84	1983	5	3	4	
ALDRIDGE, Norman	Walsall	23.02.21	Foxford FC	W.B.A.	05.46	1946	1		0	(FB)
			TR	Northampton T.	06.48	1948	2		0	
ALDRIDGE, Steve P.	Armthorpe	02.11.57	APP	Sheffield U.	12.75					(F)
				Doncaster Rov.	N/C	1980	1	/	0	
ALEKSIC, Milija	Newcastle-under-Lyme	14.04.51	Stafford Rgrs.	Plymouth Arg.	02.73	1973-75	32	/	0	(G)
			TR	Luton T.	12.76	1976-78	77	/	0	
			TR	Tottenham H.	12.78	1978-81	25	/	0	
			L	Luton T.	11.81	1981	4	/	0	
ALESINOYE, Martin	Middlesbrough	01.10.55	Barnsley(AM)	Doncaster Rov.	10.75	1975	13	1	1	(IF)
ALEXANDER, Alan	Cumbernauld	01.11.41		Bradford P.A.	07.59	1961	5		0	(G)
ALEXANDER, Alex	Glasgow	28.09.24	New Brighton(AM)	Tranmere Rov.	10.47	1946-48	23		3	

Players Names	Birthplace	Date	Previous Club	League Club	Date Signed	Seasons Played	Apps	Sub	Gls	
ALEXANDER, Angus C.	Arbroath	10.01.34	JNRS	Burnley	01.51					(F)
			TR	Southport	07.57	1957	14		1	
			TR	Workington	02.58	1957-58	49		4	
			TR	York C.	06.59	1959	7		0	
ALEXANDER, Anthony A.	Reading	08.02.35	JNRS	Reading	08.52	1952-55	11		2	(F)
				Crystal Palace	08.60					
ALEXANDER, Dennis L.	Nottingham	19.02.35	JNRS	Nottingham F.	06.55	1955-56	20		4	(F)
			TR	Brighton & H.A.	03.58					
			TR	Gateshead	10.58	1958	18		1	
ALEXANDER, Ian	Glasgow	26.01.63	Leicester Juv.	Rotherham U.	10.81	1981-82	5	6	0	(F)
ALEXANDER, John E.	Liverpool	03.10.55	Ulysses	Millwall	07.77	1976-77	10	5	2	(F)
			TR	Reading	10.78	1978-80	22	3	9	
			TR	Northampton T.	08.81	1981	21	1	4	
ALEXANDER, Phil J.	Slough	04.09.62	Wokingham	Norwich C.	08.81	1982	0	1	0	(D)
ALISON, Jimmy	Peebles	11.10.23	Falkirk	Manchester C.	12.49	1949-50	19		1	(OR)
			TR	Aldershot	07.52	1952-56	171		9	
ALLAN, Alex (Sandy)	Forfar	29.10.47	Rhyl	Cardiff C.	03.67	1967-69	8	/	1	(F)
			TR	Bristol Rov.	03.70	1969-72	51	7	18	
			L	Swansea C.	03.73	1972	6	2	1	
ALLAN, Jim	Inverness	10.11.53	APP	Swindon T.	07.71	1971-83	371	/	0	(G)
ALLAN, John	Amble	26.09.31		Barnsley	01.49	1951-52	11		0	(G)
ALLAN, John	Stirling	22.03.31	T.Lanark	Bradford P.A.	02.59	1958-60	72		51	(F)
			TR	Halifax T.	03.61	1960	10		1	
ALLANSON, Gary E.	Hull	06.03.65	APP	Doncaster Rov.	03.83	1981-82	11	2	0	(D)
ALLARDYCE, Sam	Dudley	19.10.54	APP	Bolton W.	11.71	1973-79	180	4	21	(D)
			TR	Sunderland	07.80	1980	24	1	2	
			TR	Millwall	09.81	1981-82	63	/	2	
			TR	Coventry C.	09.83	1983	28	/	1	
ALLATT, Vernon	Hednesford	28.05.59	Hednesford	Walsall	11.79					(F)
			TR	Halifax T.	11.79	1979-82	93	5	14	
			TR	Rochdale	08.83	1983	40	/	8	
ALLAWAY, Jim	Bristol	23.04.22		Bristol Rov.	12.46	1946	4		0	
			TR	Bristol C.	09.47					
ALLCHURCH, Ivor J.	Swansea	16.10.29	Plasmark	Swansea C.	05.47	1949-58	330		124	(IF) W-68/●
			TR	Newcastle U.	10.58	1958-61	143		46	Brother of Len
			TR	Cardiff C.	08.62	1962-64	103		39	
			TR	Swansea C.	07.65	1965-67	116	2	42	
ALLCHURCH, Len	Swansea	12.09.33	JNRS	Swansea C.	10.50	1951-60	272		49	(OR) W-11/W.SCH.INT.●
			TR	Sheffield U.	03.61	1960-64	123		32	
			TR	Stockport Co.	09.65	1965-68	131	/	16	
			TR	Swansea C.	07.69	1969-70	70	3	11	
ALLCOCK, Frank E.	Nottingham	07.09.25	Beeston B.	Nottingham F.	*					(CH)
			TR	Aston Villa	08.46					
			Cheltenham	Bristol Rov.	06.52	1953-55	58		0	
ALLCOCK, Ken	Kirkby-in-Ashfield	24.04.21	Notts.Co.(AM)	Mansfield T.	04.47	1947	1		0	(CF)
ALLCOCK, Terry	Leeds	10.12.35	JNRS	Bolton W.	12.52	1953-57	31		9	(IF)
			TR	Norwich C.	03.58	1957-68	334	5	87	
ALLDER, Doug S.	Hammersmith	30.12.51	APP	Millwall	10.69	1969-74	191	11	10	(M)E.YTH.INT.
			TR	Orient	07.75	1975-76	34	7	0	
			TR	Torquay U.	08.77					
			TR	Watford	09.77	1977	1	/	0	
			TR	Brentford	10.77	1977-79	68	20	2	
ALLDIS, Gilbert	Birkenhead	26.01.20		Tranmere Rov.	*	1946-48	73		4	(F)
			TR	New Brighton	07.50	1950	12		0	
ALLEN, A. Robert	Bromley	11.10.16	Brentford(*)	Northampton T.	*	1946	5		0	(FB)*Orient/Fulham/
			TR	Colchester U.	N/L	1950	29		1	Doncaster Rov.E.SCH.INT.
ALLEN, Adrian	Preston	23.03.34	Preston N.E.(AM)	Southport	AM	1954	6		0	(OR)
ALLEN, Anthony	Stoke	27.11.39	JNRS	Stoke C.	11.56	1957-69	414	3	2	(LB) E-3/E.U23-7/●
			TR	Bury	10.70	1970-71	29	/	0	EF LGE REP/E.YTH.INT.
ALLEN, Brynley W.	Gilfach Goch	28.03.21	Swansea C.(*)	Cardiff C.	*	1946-47	41		18	(IF) W-2
			TR	Newport Co.	10.47	1947	26		7	
			TR	Cardiff C.	08.48	1948	17		4	
			TR	Reading	05.49	1949	26		12	
			TR	Coventry C.	02.50	1949-52	88		26	
ALLEN, Clive D.	London	20.05.61	APP	Q.P.R.	09.78	1978-79	43	6	32	(F)E.U21-3/E.YTH.INT./
			TR	Arsenal	06.80					E.SCH.INT.
			TR	Crystal Palace	08.80	1980	25	/	9	Son of Les
			TR	Q.P.R.	06.81	1981-83	83	4	40	
ALLEN, Dennis	Dagenham	02.03.39	JNRS	Charlton Ath.	08.56	1957-60	5		1	(IF) Brother of Les
			TR	Reading	06.61	1961-69	331	4	84	
			TR	Bournemouth	08.70	1970	17	/	3	
ALLEN, Derek	Wombwell	14.07.46	JNRS	Rotherham U.	11.65	1965	1		0	(HB)
ALLEN, Derek A.	Luton	08.04.30	Alton T.	Luton T.	01.52	1954	1		0	(F)
			TR	Watford	06.56	1956	6		1	

Players Names	Birthplace	Date	Previous Club	League Club	Date Signed	Seasons Played	Apps	Sub	Gls	
ALLEN, Frank	Shirebrook	28.06.27		Chesterfield	03.51	1951-52	3		0	(HB)
			TR	Mansfield T.	07.53	1953-54	6		0	
ALLEN, George	Birmingham	23.01.32	Coventry C.(AM)	Birmingham C.	11.52	1953-61	134		0	(FB)
			TR	Torquay U.	01.62	1961-64	133		0	
ALLEN, Geoff	Newcastle	10.11.46	JNRS	Newcastle U.	02.64	1963-68	22	/	1	(IF) E.YTH.INT.
ALLEN, Graham F.	Walsall	20.08.32		Walsall	AM	1953	1		1	(F)
ALLEN, Herbert	Nottingham	27.10.24	Beeston B.C.	Nottingham F.	*	1947	1		0	(FB)
			TR	Notts. Co.	08.49	1951-53	30		0	
ALLEN, John	Coventry	24.04.55	Hinckley A.	Leicester C.	08.78					(F)
			TR	Port Vale	06.80	1980-	18	/	4	
ALLEN, John	Mancot	14.11.64	APP	Chester C.	11.81	1981-83	67	12	5	(F)W.SCH.INT.
ALLEN, John C.	Elderslie	27.01.32	Beith J.	Q.P.R.	09.52	1953	1		1	(F)
			TR	Bournemouth	07.54	1954-55	52		11	
ALLEN, Keith	I.O.W.	09.11.43	Ryde	Portsmouth	12.62					(F)
			TR	Grimsby T	05.64	1964	6		1	
			TR	Stockport Co.	06.65	1965-66	49	/	16	
			TR	Luton T.	03.67	1966-69	128	9	36	
			TR	Plymouth Arg.	07.70	1970-72	74	5	10	
ALLEN, Ken R.	Thornaby	12.01.49		Hartlepool U.	AM	1968	7	/	0	(G)
			Bath C.	Bournemouth	08.78	1978-82	152	/	0	
			Peterborough N/C	Torquay U.	03.84	1983	11	/	0	
ALLEN, Kevin	Ryde IOW	22.03.61	JNRS	Bournemouth	08.79	1979	1	/	0	(D)
ALLEN, Les W.	Dagenham	04.09.37	Briggs Spts	Chelsea	09.54	1956-59	44		11	(CF)E-U23-1/
			TR	Tottenham H.	12.59	1959-64	119		47	E.F. LGE REP.
			TR	Q.P.R	07.65	1965-68	123	5	54	
ALLEN, Mark S.	Newcastle	18.12.63	APP	Burnley	12.81	1981	0	2	1	(F)
			TR	Tranmere Rov.	08.83	1983	6	4	0	
ALLEN, Mike	Sth. Shields	30.03.49	APP	Middlesbrough	05.66	1967-71	32	3	1	(D)
			TR	Brentford	10.71	1971-78	223	10	11	
ALLEN, Paul K.	Aveley	28.08.62	APP	West Ham U.	08.79	1979-83	111	3	3	(M)E.YTH.INT.
ALLEN, Peter C.	Hove	01.11.46	Tottenham H.(AM)	Orient	07.65	1965-77	423	7	28	(M)
			TR	Millwall	03.78	1977-78	16	2	0	
ALLEN, Peter M.	Bristol	08.10.34		Bristol C.	07.53	1954	1		0	(CH)
ALLEN, Reg	Marylebone	03.05.19	Corona F.C.	Q.P.R.	*	1946-49	152		0	(G) E.F.LGE REP.
			TR	Manchester U.	06.50	1950-52	75		0	
ALLEN, Robert	Belfast	16.01.39	Denbigh T.	Wolverhampton W.	09.57					(IF)
			TR	Coventry C.	06.59	1960-61	25		2	
ALLEN, Robert H.A.	Shepton Mallet	05.12.16		Notts. Co.	*	1946	1		0	
			TR	Bristol C.	11.46	1946	1		0	
ALLEN, Ronald L.	Birmingham	22.04.35	JNRS	Birmingham C.	05.53					(HB)
			TR	Lincoln C.	07.58	1958-60	60		1	
ALLEN, Ronnie	Fenton	15.01.29	JNRS	Port Vale	*	1946-49	123		34	(CF)E-5/E'B'-2/
			TR	W.B.A.	03.50	1949-60	415		208	E.F.LGE REP.●
			TR	Crystal Palace	05.61	1961-64	100		34	
ALLEN, Russell	Birmingham	09.01.54	Arsenal (APP)	W.B.A.	05.71					(F) Son of Ronnie Allen
			TR	Tranmere Rov.	07.73	1973-77	137	19	44	
			TR	Mansfield T.	07.78	1978-80	99	17	18	
ALLEN, William	Newburn	22.10.17	Chesterfield (*)	York C.	*	1946-49	130		23	(WH)
			TR	Scunthorpe U.	06.50	1950-51	64		1	
ALLEYNE, Andy	Barbados	19.05.51	Newbury T.	Reading	11.72	1972-75	46	2	2	(FB)
ALLINSON, Ian J.R.	Hitchin	01.10.57	APP	Colchester	10.75	1974-82	291	17	69	(F)
			TR	Arsenal	10.83	1983	7	2	0	
ALLISON, John	Stannington	31.07.22	Blyth Spartans	Chesterfield	04.47					(OL)
			Blyth Spartans	Reading	01.49	1948-49	29		4	
			TR	Walsall	06.50	1950-51	47		1	
ALLISON, John A.	Cramlington	09.08.32	Blyth Spartans	Chesterfield	05.55	1957-60	32		0	(HB)
ALLISON, John J.	Consett	17.11.13	Workington	Barnsley	*					d.1971
			TR	Hartlepool U.	09.46	1946	13		0	
ALLISON, Ken	Edinburgh	06.01.37	Cowdenbeath	Darlington	07.63	1963-65	75	/	39	(F)
			TR	Lincoln C.	02.66	1965-66	41	1	12	
ALLISON, Malcolm	Dartford	05.09.27	Charlton Rov.	Charlton Ath	*	1949	2		0	(CH)
			TR	West Ham U.	02.51	1950-57	238		10	
ALLISON, Tom	Fencehouses	20.02.21	South Hetton	Darlington	09.46	1946	6		0	(W)
ALLISTER, John G.	Edinburgh	30.06.27	Tranent J.	Chelsea	07.49	1951-52	4		1	(IF)
			Aberdeen	Chesterfield	06.58					
ALLMAN, George	Stockport	23.07.30		Stockport Co.	05.50	1950-51	7		1	(F)
			TR	Chester C.	07.55	1955-56	49		14	
ALLSOP, Norman	West Bromwich	01.11.30	Hednesford	W.B.A.	05.48					(IF)
			TR	Walsall	10.53	1953	9		0	
ALLSOP, William	Ripley	29.01.12	Port Vale(*)	Halifax T.	*	1946	37		0	(FB)*Bolton W.

Players Names	Birthplace	Date	Previous Club	League Club	Date Signed	Seasons Played	Apps	Sub	Gls	
ALLUM, Albert	Notting Hill	15.10.30		Brentford	10.52					(F)
				Q.P.R.	06.57	1957	1		0	
ALSOP, Gilbert	Frampton Court	10.09.08	Ipswich T.(*)	Walsall	*	1946	7		2	(CF)*Bath C./Coventry C./ Walsall/W.B.A.
ALSTON, Adrian	Preston	06.02.49	Safeways (Australia)	Luton T.	08.74	1974-75	26	3	8	(F)Brother of Alec
			TR	Cardiff C.	10.75	1975-76	44	4	16	
ALSTON, Alec	Preston	26.02.37	Netherfield	Preston N.E.	05.55	1957-62	102		26	(IF)
			TR	Bury	03.63	1962-65	86	/	22	
			TR	Barrow	09.65	1965-66	46	1	14	
ALTY, Colin	Preston	23.10.44	JNRS	Preston N.E.	10.61	1962	1		0	(IF)
			TR	Southport	06.64	1964-69	184	7	22	
AMBLER, Roy	Wakefield	02.12.37	JNRS	Leeds U.	12.54					(IF)
			TR	Shrewsbury T.	01.59	1958-60	29		8	
			TR	Wrexham	05.61	1961-62	21		13	
			TR	York C.	11.62	1962	12		3	
			TR	Southport	07.63	1963	11		0	
AMBROSE, A. Leroy	W. Indies	26.06.60	Croydon	Charlton Ath.	08.79	1979-81	28	5	1	(F)
AMES, Ken	Canford	17.09.33	JNRS	Portsmouth	09.50	1953	2		0	(CF) E.SCH.INT
AMES, Percy	Bedford	13.12.31	Bedford Ave	Tottenham H.	05.51					(G)
			TR	Colchester U.	05.55	1955-64	397		0	
AMES, Trevor	Poole	14.12,62	Aston Villa (APP)	Hereford U.	10.80	1980-81	5	3	0	(F)
			TR	Crystal Palace	10.81					
AMOR, William	Pewsey	06.11.19	Huntleys	Reading	AM	1947-51	66		12	(OL) E.AMAT.INT.
AMOS, Keith	Walton-on-Thames	13.01.32	JNRS	Arsenal	05.52					(G)
			TR	Aldershot	08.54	1955-57	77		0	
			TR	Fulham	08.58					
AMPHLET, Ray	Manchester	25.09.22	Guildford C.	Cardiff C.	04.48					
			TR	Newport Co.	04.49	1949	13		0	
AMPOFO, Chris J.K.	Paddington	06.10.63	APP	West Ham U.	10.81					(D)
			TR	Aldershot	08.83	1983	4	/	0	
ANDERS, Harry	St. Helens	28.11.26	St. Helens	Preston N.E.	+	1947-52	69		4	(OL)
			TR	Manchester C.	03.53	1952-54	32		4	
			TR	Port Vale	07.56	1956	3		0	
			TR	Accrington St.	06.57	1957-59	114		18	
			TR	Workington	07.60	1960	7		1	
ANDERS, Jimmy	St. Helens	08.03.28	St. Helens	Preston N.E.	+					(IF) Brother of Harry
			TR	Brentford	09.48	1949-50	12		0	
			TR	Bradford C.	06.51	1951-52	51		11	
			TR	Rochdale	07.53	1953-56	125		28	
			TR	Bradford P.A.	09.56	1956	20		4	
			TR	Accrington St.	01.57	1956-59	129		30	
			Buxton	Bradford P.A.	09.60	1960-61	39		8	
			TR	Tranmere Rov.	11.61	1961	8		1	
ANDERSON, Alex	Glasgow	08.01.22	Hearts	Rochdale	02.48	1947	4		0	(G) L.O.I REP.
			Dundalk	Southport	11.49	1949-50	21			
ANDERSON, Alex F.	Monifieth	15.11.21	Forfar Ath.	Southampton	11.49	1949-51	20		0	(FB)
			TR	Exeter C.	06.52	1952	6		0	
ANDERSON, Alex O.W.	Aucht'muchty	20.02.30	Newburgh J.	Southend U.	04.50	1950-62	451		6	(FB)●
ANDERSON, Arthur	Edinburgh	21.12.39	Falkirk	Millwall	09.59	1960-61	73		0	(HB)
			TR	Scunthorpe U.	07.62	1962	6		0	
ANDERSON, Ben	Aberdeen	18.02.46	Peterlee	Blackburn Rov.	03.64	1964-67	21	7	7	(F)
			TR	Bury	07.68	1968-69	51	2	4	
			Cape Town C.	Crystal Palace	11.73	1973	11	/	1	
ANDERSON, Chris	Aberdeen	30.08.25	Aberdeen	Hartlepool U.	09.46	1946	2		0	(RH)
ANDERSON, Chris S.	Glasgow	28.02.28	Lochore	Blackburn Rov.	08.50	1950-51	13		1	(OR)
			TR	Stockport Co.	06.53	1953	34		0	
			TR	Southport	07.54	1954	28		0	
ANDERSON, Colin R.	Newcastle	26.04.62	APP	Burnley	04.80	1980-81	3	3	0	(F)
			Nth. Shields	Torquay U.	10.82	1982-83	79	2	9	
ANDERSON, Darren I.	Merton	06.09.66	Coventry C.(APP)	Charlton Ath.	03.84	1983	1	/	0	(M)
ANDERSON, Des	Edinburgh	08.01.38	Hibernian	Millwall	06.61	1961-63	46		1	(WH) S.SCH.INT.
ANDERSON, Doug E.	Hong Kong	29.08.63	Port Glasgow	Oldham Ath.	09.80	1981-83	4	5	0	(F)
ANDERSON, Edward	Glasgow	23.09.17	Stirling A.	Rochdale	03.48	1947	1		0	(FB) Brother of Alex
ANDERSON, Edward W.	Newcastle	17.07.11	Chester C.(*)	Tranmere Rov.	*	1946-47	42		0	(WH)*Jarrow/ Wolverhampton W./Torquay U. West Ham U./d.1979
ANDERSON, Eric	Manchester	12.03.31		Liverpool	12.51	1952-56	73		22	(IF)
			TR	Barnsley	07.57	1957	9		1	
ANDERSON, Gary L.	Bow	20.11.55	APP	Tottenham H.	12.72					(FB)
			TR	Northampton T.	03.75	1974-75	14	/	0	

Players Names	Birthplace	Date	Previous Club	League Club	Date Signed	Seasons Played	Apps	Sub	Gls	
ANDERSON, Geoff T.	Sheerness	26.11.44	APP	Birmingham C.	12.62	1963	1	/	0	(F)
			TR	Mansfield T.	05.64	1964-65	44	/	13	
			TR	Lincoln C.	07.66	1966	44	/	6	
ANDERSON, J. Des	Templepatrick	11.09.40	Glenavon	Exeter C.	08.62	1962-65	142	2	1	(HB)N.I.AMAT.INT.
			TR	Chesterfield	07.66	1966-67	9	/	0	
ANDERSON, Jim	Felling	23.07.13	Q. of South	Brentford	+					(LB) *Blyth Spartans/
			TR	Carlisle U.	09.46	1946	10		0	Wigan Ath/Darlington
ANDERSON, Jim M.	Glasgow	25.12.32		Bristol Rov.	04.53	1954-56	24		0	(HB)
			TR	Chester C.	06.57	1957-59	62		0	
ANDERSON, John	Dublin	07.11.59	APP	W.B.A.	11.77					(D)EI-5/EI.U21-1
			TR	Preston N.E.	08.79	1979-81	47	4	0	
			TR	Newcastle U.	09.82	1982-83	72	2	1	
ANDERSON, John	Salford	11.10.21	JNRS	Manchester U.	*	1947-48	33		1	(WH)
			TR	Nottingham F.	10.49	1949-50	40		1	
ANDERSON, John	Barrhead	08.12.29	Arthurlie	Leicester C.	12.48	1948-58	261		0	(G) S-1/S'B'-1
			TR	Peterborough U.	07.60					
ANDERSON, John C.	Dundee	08.05.15	Stobswell	Portsmouth	*					(CF)
			TR	Aldershot	06.46	1946	4		1	
ANDERSON, John E.	Newcastle	07.06.31	Langold C.W.	Grimsby T.	05.54	1955	3		0	(FB)
			TR	Crystal Palace	08.58					
ANDERSON, John H.	Renfrew	11.01.37	Johnstone Burgh	Stoke C.	01.57	1957-60	24		2	(F)
ANDERSON, John L.	Glasgow	05.04.28	Partick T.	Northampton T.	06.53	1953	14		3	(IF)
			TR	Exeter C.	07.54	1954	7		0	
			Dundee	Wrexham	06.56	1956-58	98		27	
			TR	Rochdale	07.59	1959	27		6	
			TR	Chester C.	07.60	1960	17		2	
			TR	Wrexham	08.61	1961	1		0	
ANDERSON, John R.	Newcastle	09.11.24		Middlesbrough	+	1947	1		0	(G) Brother of William R.
			Blackhall C.W.	Crystal Palace	10.51	1951-52	38		0	
			TR	Bristol Rov.	03.53	1952-53	10		0	
			TR	Bristol C.	04.54	1954-58	106		0	
ANDERSON, Norman	Hebburn	30.11.30	Reyrolles	Gateshead	03.51	1953-55	19		2	(F)
ANDERSON, Percy	Cambridge	22.09.30	Cambridge U.	W.B.A.	09.51					(IF)
			TR	Stockport Co.	07.53	1953	1		0	
ANDERSON, Peter T.	London	31.05.49	Hendon	Luton T.	02.71	1970-75	178	3	34	(M)
			Tampa Bay	Sheffield U.	09.78	1978	28	2	12	
			Tampa Bay	Millwall	12.80	1980-82	30	2	4	
ANDERSON, Peter D.	Plymouth	11.09.32	Astor Inst.	Plymouth Arg.	07.50	1952-62	241		41	(OL)
			TR	Torquay U.	12.62	1962-64	77		18	
ANDERSON, Phil	Portadown	05.01.48	Portadown	Bury	05.66	1966-69	5	4	1	(IF)
ANDERSON, Robert	Newton Heath	11.08.28		Leicester C.	+	1946-47	19		2	
ANDERSON, Robert	Aberdeen	21.01.37		Chesterfield	08.59	1959	4		0	(OR)
ANDERSON, Robert J.	Portsmouth	23.02.36	Chesterfield Tube	Mansfield T.	09.56	1956-59	41		3	(F)
ANDERSON, Robert L.	Derry	23.04.26	Ulsterville	Doncaster Rov.	11.49	1950-51	3		0	(FB)
ANDERSON, Ron J.	Gateshead	03.07.22		Bury	+	1946	2		0	(IF)
			TR	Crystal Palace	05.47					
ANDERSON, Sammy	Manchester	11.01.36		Oldham Ath.	08.54	1955-56	6		0	(FB)
ANDERSON, Stan	Horden	27.02.34	JNRS	Sunderland	03.51	1052-63	402		31	(WH)E-2/E.U23-4/
			TR	Newcastle U.	11.63	1963-65	81	/	13	E.SCH.INT.●
			TR	Middlesbrough	11.65	1965	21	/	1	
ANDERSON, Terry K.	Woking	11.03.44	APP	Arsenal	08.61	1962-64	25		6	(OR) E.YTH.INT./
			TR	Norwich C.	02.65	1964-73	218	18	16	d.1980
			L	Colchester U.	02.74	1973	4	/	0	
			TR	Scunthorpe U.	09.74	1974	10	/	0	
			TR	Crewe Alex.	11.74	1974	4	/	0	
			TR	Bournemouth	01.75					
			TR	Colchester U.	08.75	1975	13	3	0	
ANDERSON, Thomas	Edinburgh	24.09.34	Q. of South	Watford	12.56	1956-57	52		12	(F) S.SCH.INT.
			TR	Bournemouth	06.58	1958	5		1	
			TR	Q.P.R.	11.58	1958	11		3	
			TR	Torquay U.	07.59	1959	9		4	
			TR	Stockport Co.	06.60	1960-61	60		17	
			TR	Doncaster Rov.	11.61	1961	16		3	
			TR	Wrexham	03.62	1961-62	12		3	
			Hellas	Barrow	12.63	1963	11		3	
			Hellas	Watford	12.64	1964-65	21	/	2	
			Australia	Orient	07.67	1967	8	1	0	
ANDERSON, Trevor	Belfast	03.03.51	Portadown	Manchester U.	10.72	1972-73	13	6	2	(F)NI-22/NI.U21-1
			TR	Swindon T.	11.74	1974-77	128	3	34	
			TR	Peterborough U.	12.77	1977-78	49	/	6	
ANDERSON, Viv A.	Nottingham	29.08.56	APP	Nottingham F.	08.74	1974-83	323	5	15	(D)E-11/E.U21-1/ E.F.LGE REP.
ANDERSON, William	Lochore	06.11.26	Hibernian	Southend U.	05.54	1954-55	16		1	(IF)

Players Names	Birthplace	Date	Previous Club	League Club	Date Signed	Seasons Played	Career Record Apps	Sub	Gls	
ANDERSON, William			Dundee	Millwall	+	1946-7	30		8	
ANDERSON, William B.	Sunderland	28.03.35	Silksworth J.	Barnsley	09.52	1955	6		0	(HB)
			TR	Hartlepool U.	02.56	1955-60	179		11	
ANDERSON, William R.	Ponteland	20.09.27	Throckley Welfare	Newcastle U.	02.47	1946	1		0	(G)
ANDERSON, Willie J.	Liverpool	24.01.47	APP	Manchester U.	02.64	1963-66	7	/	0	(M)
			TR	Aston Villa	01.67	1966-72	229	2	36	
			TR	Cardiff C.	02.73	1972-76	122	4	12	
ANDERTON, John	Skelmersdale	07.02.33	JNRS	Everton	03.51					(FB)
			TR	Torquay U.	07.54	1954-57	40		2	
ANDERTON, Sylvan	Reading	23.11.34	JNRS	Reading	06.52	1952-58	155		19	(WH)
			TR	Chelsea	03.59	1958-61	76		2	
			TR	Q.P.R.	01.62	1961	4		0	
ANDREW, George	Glasgow	24.11.45	Possilpark	West Ham U.	09.63	1966	2	/	0	(HB)
			TR	Crystal Palace	07.67					
ANDREW, Matt	Johnstone	05.01.22		Bristol C.	10.74					(HB)
			TR	Swansea C.	08.48	1948-50	4		0	
			TR	Workington	06.51	1951	22		0	
			TR	Q.P.R.	09.52					
ANDREW, Ron E.H.	Ellesmere Port	05.01.36	Ellesmere Port	Stoke C.	05.54	1957-63	115		1	(CH)
			TR	Port Vale	06.64	1964	8	/	1	
ANDREWS, Cecil J.	Alton	01.11.30	/	Portsmouth	01.49					(WH)
			TR	Crystal Palace	06.26	1952-55	104		11	
			TR	Q.P.R.	06.56	1956-57	58		1	
ANDREWS, Derek	Bury	14.12.34		Rochdale	03.55	1955	22		4	(IF)
ANDREWS, George	Dudley	23.04.42		Luton T.	01.60					(F)
			Gornal Ath.	Cardiff C.	10.65	1965-66	43	/	21	
			TR	Southport	02.67	1966-69	115	2	39	
			TR	Shrewsbury T.	11.69	1969-72	123	1	50	
			TR	Walsall	01.73	1972-76	156	3	38	
ANDREWS, Glen	Dudley	11.02.45	JNRS	Manchester U.	09.63					(FB)
			TR	Wolverhampton W.	07.66					
			TR	Bradford P.A.	09.67	1967-8	47	2	6	
ANDREWS, Ian E.	Nottingham	01.12.64	APP	Leicester C.	12.82	1983	2	/	0	(G)
			TR	Swindon T.	01.84	1983	1	/	0	
ANDREWS, Jimmy P.	Angus	01.02.27	Dundee	West Ham U.	11.51	1951-55	114		21	(OL)
			TR	Orient	06.56	1956-58	35		8	
			TR	Q.P.R.	06.59	1959-61	82		15	
ANDREWS, John E.	York	03.02.50	Moor Lane YC	York C.	AM	1968	11	/	0	(G)
ANDREWS, Les	Dudley	29.10.53	JNRS	Wolverhampton W.	09.72					(F)
			L	Scunthorpe U.	03.74	1973	7	2	1	
ANDREWS, Percy	Alton	12.06.22		York C.	09.47	1947-54	175		0	(LB)
ANDRUSZEWSKI, Manny	Eastleigh	04.10.55	APP	Southampton	10.73	1974-79	82	1	3	(D)
			Tampa Bay	Aldershot	08.82	1982	25	2	0	
ANGELL, Peter F.	Chalvey	11.01.32	Slough T.	Q.P.R.	07.53	1953-64	418	/	37	(WH) d.1979
ANGUS, John	Amble	02.09.38	JNRS	Burnley	09.55	1956-71	438	/	3	(FB)E-1/E.U23-7/ E.F.LGE REP/E.YTH.INT.●
ANGUS, John	Newcastle	12.03.09	Wolverhampton W.(*)	Exeter C.	*	1947	3		0	(FB)*Scunthorpe U./ Uncle of John/d.1965
ANGUS, Mike A.	Middlesbrough	28.10.60	JNRS	Middlesbrough	08.78	1979-81	35	2	1	(D)
			L	Scunthorpe	09.82	1982	20	/	2	
			TR	Southend	08.83					
			L	Darlington	03.84	1983	13	/	7	
ANSELL, Barry	Birmingham	29.09.47		Aston Villa	10.67	1967	2	/	0	(FB)
ANSELL, William	Bletchley	04.08.21	Bletchley Wks	Northampton T.	03.48	1947-51	131		0	(G)
ANSLOW, Stan T.	Hackney	05.05.31	Eton Manor	Millwall	03.51	1951-58	130		12	(FB)
ANTHONY, Tom H.	Hounslow	16.08.43	JNRS	Brentford	12.61	1962	33		1	(FB)
			TR	Coventry C.	08.65					
			TR	Millwall	11.65					
ANTIC, Radomir	Yugoslavia	22.11.49	Real Zaragoza	Luton T.	07.80	1980-83	54	46	9	(M)YUGOSLAV INT.
ANTONIO, George	Whitchurch	20.10.14	Oswestry T.	Stoke C.	*	1946	16		5	(CF)
			TR	Derby Co.	03.47	1946-47	18		2	
			TR	Doncaster Rov.	10.48	1948-49	34		7	
			TR	Mansfield T.	10.49	1949-50	67		2	
APPLEBY, Jim P.	Shotton	15.06.34	Wingate W.	Burnley	02.53	1956	1		0	(HB)
			TR	Blackburn Rov.	02.58	1958-61	2		0	
			TR	Southport	10.61	1961	13		0	
			TR	Chester C.	06.62	1962	1		0	
APPLEBY, Robert	Warkworth	15.01.40	Amble W.	Middlesbrough	05.57	1959-66	99	/	0	(G)
APPLETON, Colin H.	Scarborough	07.03.36	Scarborough	Leicester C.	03.54	1954-65	277	/	19	(WH) E.F.LGE REP.
			TR	Charlton Ath.	06.66	1966	28	/	1	
			TR	Barrow	08.67	1967-68	40	4	1	

Players Names	Birthplace	Date	Previous Club	League Club	Date Signed	Seasons Played	Apps	Sub	Gls	
APPLETON, Tom H.	Stanley	09.06.36	Annfield Plain	Burnley	08.54					(F)
			TR	Gateshead	08.58	1958	26		0	
			TR	Accrington St.	06.59					
APPLETON, Ron	Cleator Moor	24.09.32		Workington T.	02.53	1952	3		0	(W)
ARBER, Robert L.	Poplar	13.01.51	APP	Arsenal	03.68					(FB)
			TR	Orient	07.70	1971-72	31	/	0	
ARBLASTER, Brian	London	06.06.43	JNRS	Sheffield U.	07.62					(G)
			TR	Chesterfield	12.64	1964-66	55	/	0	
			TR	Scunthorpe U.	06.67	1967	10	/	0	
			TR	Barnsley	05.68	1967-73	111	/	0	
ARCHELL, Graham	London	08.02.50	JNRS	Orient	11.67	1967-68	5	2	0	(F)
ARCHER, John	Biddulph	18.06.41	JNRS	Port Vale	07.58	1959-60	10		3	(IF)
			TR	Bournemouth	07.61	1961-65	139	/	37	
			TR	Crewe Alex.	09.66	1966-67	59	/	14	
			TR	Huddersfield T.	01.68	1967	7	2	0	
			TR	Chestefield	05.69	1969-71	116	/	22	
ARCHER, John G.	Whitstable	09.04.36	Whitstable T.	Grimsby T.	04.54	1954	10		0	(G)
ARCHER, Phillip	Rotherham	25.08.52	Sheffield U.(APP)	Reading	08.71	1971	12	5	0	(FB)
ARCHER, Ron	Barnsley	03.09.33	JNRS	Barnsley	09.50	1951-55	27		0	(WH)E.SCH.INT
ARCHER, Trevor	Barnsley	16.01.35	JNRS	Barnsley	05.53	1954	1		0	(HB)
ARCHER, William	Scunthorpe	05.02.14	Lincoln(+)	Doncaster Rov.	+	1946-47	14		0	(CH)
ARCHIBALD, Murray J.	Carron	19.03.17		Wrexham	+	1946	1		0	
ARCHIBALD, Steve	Glasgow	27.09.56	Aberdeen	Tottenham H.	05.80	1980-83	128	3	58	(F)S-23/S.U21-5
ARDILES, Osvaldo C.	Argentine	03.08.52	Huracan	Tottenham H.	07.78	1978-83	150	1	13	(M)ARGENTINE INT.●
ARDRON, Wally	Rotherham	19.09.18	Denaby U.	Rotherham U.	*	1946-48	122		94	(CF) d.1978●
			TR	Nottingham F.	07.49	1949-54	183		123	
ARENTOFT, Preben	Denmark	01.11.42	Morton	Newcastle U.	03.69	1968-70	46	4	2	(IF)
			TR	Blackburn Rov.	09.71	1971-73	94	/	3	
ARGUE, Jimmy	Glasgow	27.11.17	Birmingham C.(*)	Chelsea	*	1946	1		1	(IF)*St. Rochs./d.1978
ARINS, Anthony F.	Chesterfield	26.10.58	APP	Burnley	07.76	1978-79	29	/	2	(D)
			TR	Leeds U.	05.80	1981	0	1	0	
			TR	Scunthorpe	11.81	1981	20	/	1	
ARKWRIGHT, Ian	Shafton	18.09.59	APP	Wolverhampton W.	09.77	1978	3	1	0	(F)
			TR	Wrexham	03.80	1979-83	104	2	10	
			L	Torquay U.	03.84	1983	2	/	0	
ARMES, Ivan	Lowestoft	06.04.24	Brooke Moor	Norwich C.	11.46	1946-49	61		1	(HB)
			TR	Exeter C.	12.51	1951-52	14		2	
ARMFIELD, Jimmy C.	Blackpool	21.09.35	JNRS	Blackpool	09.54	1954-70	568	/	6	(FB)E-43/E.U23-9/ E.F.LGE REP.●
ARMITAGE, Ken J. (now Fenton)	Sheffield	23.10.20	Gainsborough	Orient	+	1946	7		0	(CH) d.1952
			TR	Oldham Ath.	07.47	1947	5		0	
ARMITAGE, Lewis G.	Hull	15.12.21		Rotherham U.	+	1946-47	15		9	(F)
			TR	Grimsby T.	01.48	1947	8		2	
ARMITAGE, Stan	Woolwich	05.06.19		Q.P.R.	06.46	1946	2		0	
ARMSTRONG, Adam	Blackpool	06.06.25	Petershill	Chesterfield	09.49	1949	1		0	(OL)
ARMSTRONG, Dave T.	Mile End	09.11.42	Hornchurch	Millwall	12.65	1965-67	13	6	0	(F)
			TR	Brighton & H.A.	09.68	1968-69	38	6	6	
ARMSTRONG, David	Durham	26.12.54	APP	Middlesbrough	01.72	1971-80	357	2	59	(M)E.U23-4/E-3
			TR	Southampton	08.81	1981-83	124	/	38	
ARMSTRONG, Derek	Carlisle	16.03.39		Blackpool	08.58	1958	1		0	(OL)
			Morecambe	Carlisle U.	08.61	1961	1		0	
ARMSTRONG, Eric	Hebburn	25.05.21	Cramlington	West Ham U.	01.47	1947	1		0	(WH) d.1975
ARMSTRONG, Gary S.	London	02.01.58		Gillingham	01.76	1975-79	82	4	2	(D)
			TR	Wimbledon	03.80	1979-81	71	/	0	
			Finland	Gillingham	N/C	1983	7	1	0	
ARMSTRONG, George	Hebburn	09.08.44	JNRS	Arsenal	08.61	1961-76	490	10	53	(W)E.U23-5/E.YTH.INT.●
			TR	Leicester C.	09.77	1977-78	14	1	0	
			TR	Stockport Co.	09.78	1978	34	/	0	
ARMSTRONG, Gerry	Belfast	23.05.54	Bangor	Tottenham H.	11.75	1976-80	65	19	10	(F)NI-53
			TR	Watford	11.80	1980-82	50	26	12	
ARMSTRONG, Jimmy	Ulverston	14.09.43	APP	Barrow	12.60	1960-62	17		2	(F)
			TR	Chesterfield	07.63	1963	7			
ARMSTRONG, Joe	Brighton	16.11.31		Southend U.	11.52					(IF)
			TR	Barrow	07.53	1953-57	104		33	
			TR	Workington	03.58	1957-58	25		10	
ARMSTRONG, Joe M.	Newcastle	29.01.39	Leslie B.C.	Leeds U.	05.57					(HB)
			TR	Gateshead	07.59	1959	22		9	
ARMSTRONG, John	Airdrie	05.09.36	Bellshill	Barrow	03.58	1957-58	21		0	(G)
			TR	Nottingham F.	11.58	1958-62	20		0	
			TR	Portsmouth	02.63	1962-66	79	/	0	
			TR	Southport	08.67	1967-70	86	/	0	

Players Names	Birthplace	Date	Previous Club	League Club	Date Signed	Seasons Played	Apps	Sub	Gls	
ARMSTRONG, Keith T.	Corbridge	11.10.57	JNRS	Sunderland	01.75	1977	7	4	0	(F)
			L	Newport Co.	08.78	1978	3	1	0	
			L	Scunthorpe	10.78	1978	0	1	0	
			Oulu	Newcastle U.	06.79					
ARMSTRONG, Ken	Bradford	03.06.24	Bradford Rov.	Chelsea	12.46	1947-56	362		25	(WH)E-1/E'B'-3/ E.F.LGE REP.
ARMSTRONG, Ken C.	Bridgnorth	31.01.59	Kilmarnock	Southampton	06.83	1983	26	/	0	(D)
			L	Notts. Co.	03.84	1983	10	/	0	
ARMSTRONG, Robert	Newcastle	01.07.38		Darlington	07.59	1959	1		0	(F)
ARMSTRONG, Terry	Barnsley	10.07.58	APP	Huddersfield T.	07.76	1976-78	36	4	2	(D)
			TR	Port Vale	02.81	1980-83	109	3	12	
ARMSTRONG, Tom	Carlisle	27.02.20	Holme Head	Carlisle U.	08.46	1946	3		0	(FB)
ARNELL, Alan	Chichester	25.11.33	Worthing	Liverpool	03.54	1953-60	68		33	(CF)
			TR	Tranmere Rov.	02.61	1960-62	68		34	
			TR	Halifax T.	07.63	1963	14		6	
ARNISON, Joe	S. Africa	27.06.24	Glasgow Rgrs.	Luton T.	08.48	1948-50	44		19	(CF)
ARNOLD, Eric	Lowestoft	13.09.22	Lowestoft T.	Norwich C.	09.47	1947-51	13		0	(FB)
ARNOLD, James A.	Stafford	06.08.50	Stafford Rgrs.	Blackburn Rov.	06.79	1979-80	58	/	0	(G)
			TR	Everton	08.81	1981-83	48	/	0	
			L	Preston N.E.	10.82	1982	6	/	0	
ARNOLD, John W.L.	London	06.12.54	APP	Charlton Ath.	03.73	1972-73	1	4	0	(F)
ARNOLD, Rodney J.	Wolverhampton	03.06.52	APP	Wolverhampton W.	06.70					(G)
			TR	Mansfield T.	02.71	1970-83	440	/	0	
ARNOLD, Steve	Crewe	05.01.51	APP	Crewe Alex.	01.69	1968-70	13	2	0	(HB)
			TR	Liverpool	09.70	1970	1	1	0	
			L	Southport	01.72	1971	16	/	3	
			L	Torquay U.	09.72	1972	2	1	1	
			TR	Rochdale	06.73	1973	37	3	1	
ARNOTT, John	Sydenham	06.09.32	Beckenham	West Ham U.	07.54	1953-54	6		2	(CF)
			TR	Shrewsbury T.	08.55	1955	30		6	
			TR	Bournemouth	07.56	1956-61	173		21	
			TR	Gillingham	08.62	1962-67	184	2	2	
ARNOTT, Kevin W.	Bensham	28.09.58	APP	Sunderland	09.76	1976-81	132	1	16	(M)
			L	Blackburn Rov.	11.81	1981	17	/	2	
			TR	Sheffield U.	06.82	1982-83	53	/	7	
			L	Blackburn Rov.	11.82	1982	11	1	1	
			L	Rotherham U.	03.83	1982	9	/	2	
ARNOTT, William	Edinburgh	29.05.35		Crewe Alex.	12.57	1957	7		0	
ARROWSMITH, Alf	Manchester	11.12.42	Ashton U.	Liverpool	09.60	1961-67	42	6	20	(CF)
			TR	Bury	12.68	1968-69	45	3	11	
			TR	Rochdale	06.70	1970-71	41	6	14	
ARROWSMITH, Brian	Barrow	02.07.40	Vickers Spts	Barrow	10.61	1961-70	376	2	2	(FB)
ARTHUR, David R.	Wolverhampton	09.03.60	APP	W.B.A.	03.78	1981	2	1	0	(D)
			TR	Walsall	08.82	1982	8	1	0	
ARTHUR, Jackie	Edenfield	14.12.17		Everton	+					(OR)*Stockport Co.
			TR	Chester C.	05.46	1946	24		3	
			TR	Rochdale	04.47	1946-53	169		25	
ARUNDEL, Frank	Plymouth	20.02.39	JNRS	Plymouth Arg.	08.56	1956	4		0	(F)
			TR	Torquay U.	07.59	1959-60	6		0	
ASH, Micky	Sheffield	04.09.43	APP	Sheffield U.	11.60	1963	3		1	(F)E.YTH.INT./
			TR	Scunthorpe U.	09.65	1965-66	48	2	7	E.SCH.INT.
ASHALL, George H.	Killamarsh	29.09.11	Wolverhampton W.(*)	Coventry C.	*	1946-47	25		6	(OL)*Frickley Col./ E.F.LGE REP.
ASHALL, Jim	Normanton	13.12.33	JNRS	Leeds U.	10.51	1955-60	89		0	(FB)
ASHCROFT, Charles	Chorley	03.07.26	Chorley	Liverpool	05.46	1946-54	87		0	(G) E'B'-1
			TR	Ipswich T.	06.55	1955	7		0	
			TR	Coventry C.	06.57	1957	19		0	
ASHCROFT, Lew	Flint	10.07.21	Flint T.	Tranmere Rov.	+	1946	20		4	
ASHCROFT, William	Liverpool	01.10.52	JNRS	Wrexham	10.70	1970-77	196	23	72	(F)
			TR	Middlesbrough	09.77	1977-81	139	20	21	
ASHE, Armour D.	Paisley	14.10.25	St. Mirren	Stockport Co.	06.53	1953	2		0	(FB) d.1968
			TR	Accrington St.	09.53	1953-57	162		0	
			TR	Gateshead	11.57	1957-58	54		1	
			TR	Southport	07.59	1959	14		2	
ASHE, Norman J.	Bloxwich	16.11.43	APP	Aston Villa	05.61	1959-60	5		0	(OR) E.YTH.INT./
			TR	Rotherham U.	03.63	1962	6		1	E.SCH.INT.
ASHENDEN, Russell E.	Sth. Ockenden	04.02.61	APP	Northampton T.	02.79	1978-79	6	12	0	(D)
ASHER, Sid J.	Portsmouth	24.12.30	JNRS	Portsmouth	08.48					(CF)
			Hastings U.	Northampton T.	11.56	1956	21		11	
ASHER, Tom	York	21.12.36	Wolverhampton W.(AM)	Notts.Co.	07.54	1957-58	31		4	(F) E.SCH.INT.

Players Names	Birthplace	Date	Previous Club	League Club	Date Signed	Seasons Played	Apps	Sub	Gls	
ASHFIELD, George	Manchester	07.04.34		Stockport Co.	09.51					(CH)
			TR	Aston Villa	03.54	1955-57	9		0	
			TR	Chester C.	02.59	1958	5		0	
ASHLEY, John	Clowne	10.06.31	Frickley Col.	York C.	10.50	1950	9		0	(G)
ASHMAN, G. Allan	Rotherham	30.05.28	Sheffield U.(AM)	Nottingham F.	+	1948-49	13		3	(CF) Brother of Yorks/
			TR	Carlisle U.	06.51	1951-57	207		98	Worc. Cricketer
ASHMAN, Ron	Whittlesey	19.05.26	Whittlesey	Norwich C.	+	1947-63	590		55	(WH)●
ASHMORE, Alf	Sheffield	11.09.37		Sheffield U.	08.57	1957	1		0	(G)
			TR	Bradford C.	07.61	1961	9		0	
			TR	Chesterfield	10.62	1962	2		0	
ASHMORE, Arthur	Goldthorpe	11.08.46	Frickley Col.	Doncaster Rov.	11.66	1966-67	3	/	0	(HB)
ASHTON, Derek	Worksop	04.07.22		Wolverhampton W.	+					
			TR	Aston Villa	05.46	1946-48	8		0	
ASHTON, John	Reading	04.07.54	JNRS	Reading	01.75	1971-74	10	3	1	(F)
ASHTON, Ken J.	Irlam	12.12.36	Bolton W.(AM)	Stockport Co.	09.56	1957-61	39		0	(FB)
ASHTON, Roger	Llanidloes	16.08.21		Wrexham	+					(G)
				Cardiff C.	04.48	1947	1		0	
			Bath C.	Newport Co.	12.49	1949-50	11		0	
ASHURST, Jack	Coatbridge	12.10.54	APP	Sunderland	10.71	1972-79	129	11	4	(D)
			TR	Blackpool	10.79	1979-80	53	/	3	
			TR	Carlisle U.	08.81	1981-83	117	/	2	
ASHURST, Len	Liverpool	10.03.39	Prescot Cables	Sunderland	12.57	1958-69	404	6	4	(FB) E.U23-1/
			TR	Hartlepool U.	03.71	1970-72	42	4	2	E.YTH.INT.●
ASHWORTH, Alec	Southport	01.10.39	JNRS	Everton	05.57	1957-59	12		3	(IF)
			TR	Luton T.	10.60	1960-61	63		20	
			TR	Northampton T.	07.62	1962	30		25	
			TR	Preston N.E.	06.63	1963-65	42	1	14	
ASHWORTH, Barry	Stockport	18.08.42	Bangor	Southend U.	07.63	1963-64	31		5	(FB)
			TR	Hartlepool U.	03.65	1964-65	45	/	4	
			TR	Tranmere Rov.	07.66	1966	21	/	3	
			TR	Chester C.	08.67	1967-69	116	2	9	
ASHWORTH, Fred	Oldham	26.01.28		Blackburn Rov.	10.48					
			TR	Shrewsbury T.	11.51	1951-52	56		1	
ASHWORTH, Ian	Blackburn	17.12.58	APP	Manchester U.	12.75					(F)
			TR	Crewe Alex.	07.79	1979	7	6	0	
ASHWORTH, Joe	Huddersfield	06.01.43	JNRS	Bradford P.A.	01.60	1961	3		0	(WH)
			TR	York C.	05.62	1962-64	57		0	
			TR	Bournemouth	06.65	1965-66	60	/	2	
			TR	Southend U.	07.67	1967	36	/	2	
			TR	Rochdale	07.68	1968-71	133	/	3	
			TR	Chester C.	12.71	1971	5	/	0	
			TR	Stockport Co.	06.72	1972	14	/	0	
ASHWORTH, John	Nottingham	04.07.37	Wealdstone	Portsmouth	AM	1962	1		0	(CH) E.AMAT.INT.
ASHWORTH, Philip	Burnley	14.04.53	Nelson	Blackburn Rov.	01.75					(F)
			TR	Bournemouth	09.75	1975	30	1	2	
			TR	Workington	07.76	1976	38	1	7	
			TR	Southport	08.77	1977	22	2	9	
			TR	Rochdale	07.78	1978	9	2	0	
			TR	Portsmouth	09.79	1979	3	1	4	
			TR	Scunthorpe	07.80	1980	14	9	3	
ASKEW, William	Limley	02.10.59	APP	Middlesbrough	10.77	1979-81	10	2	0	(M)
			Gateshead	Hull C.	09.82	1982-83	65	4	7	
ASKEY, Colin	Stoke	03.10.32	JNRS	Port Vale	10.49	1949-57	200		23	(OR)
			TR	Walsall	07.58	1958-61	83		12	
			TR	Mansfield T.	06.62	1962-63	30		2	
ASPDEN, Ray	Horwich	06.02.38	Bolton W.(AM)	Rochdale	05.55	1955-65	298	/	2	(CH)
ASPIN, Neil	Gateshead	12.04.65	APP	Leeds U.	10.82	1981-83	36	/	1	(D)
ASPINALL, John	Birkenhead	15.03.59		Tranmere Rov.	10.82	1982-83	73	4	19	(M)
ASPINALL, John	Ashton-under-Lyne	27.04.16		Bolton W.	+	1946-49	14		0	*Oldham Ath.
ASPINALL, Wayne	Wigan	10.12.64	APP	Wigan Ath.	06.83	1983	7	/	0	(D)
ASPREY, William	Wolverhampton	11.09.36	JNRS	Stoke C.	09.53	1953-65	304	/	23	(FB)
			TR	Oldham Ath.	01.66	1965-67	80	/	3	
			TR	Port Vale	12.67	1967-68	30	1	0	
ASQUITH, Beaumont	Painthorpe	16.09.10	Manchester U.(+)	Barnsley	+	1946-47	38		5	(IF)*Barnsley/
			TR	Bradford C.	09.48	1948-49	31		4	d.1977
ASTALL, Gordon	Horwich	22.09.27	Southampton(AM)	Plymouth Arg.	11.47	1947-53	188		43	(OR) E-2/E'B'-1/
			TR	Birmingham C.	10.53	1953-60	235		60	E.F.LGE.REP.
			TR	Torquay U.	07.61	1961-62	33		10	
ASTBURY, Mike J.	Leeds	22.01.64	APP	York. C.	01.82	1980-83	25	/	0	(G)
ASTBURY, Tom	Buckley	09.02.20	Mold Alex.	Chester C.	+	1946-54	302		38	(RH)
ASTLE, Jeff	Eastwood	13.05.42	JNRS	Notts. Co.	10.59	1961-64	103		32	(CF) E-5/E.F.LGE REP.●
			TR	W.B.A.	09.64	1964-73	290	2	137	

Players Names	Birthplace	Date	Previous Club	League Club	Date Signed	Seasons Played	Career Record Apps	Sub	Gls	
ASTON, Alf J.	Newport	29.07.30	JNRS	Newport Co.	08.48	1947-50	6		1	(OL)
ASTON, John (Snr)	Manchester	03.09.21	JNRS	Manchester U.	+	1946-53	253		29	(FB) E-17/E.F.LGE REP.
ASTON, John (Jnr)	Manchester	28.06.47	APP	Manchester U.	06.63	1964-71	139	17	25	(F)E.U23-1
			TR	Luton T.	07.72	1972-77	171	3	31	
			TR	Mansfield T.	09.77	1977	24	7	4	.
			TR	Blackburn Rov.	07.78	1978-79	12	3	2	
ASTON, Philip	Measham	13.05.24	Measham Imp.	Walsall	12.51	1951	10		0	(WH) E.AMAT.INT.
ASTON, Stan	Nuneaton	10.05.40	Burton A.	Hartlepool U.	12.66	1966-67	20	1	0	(HB)
ASTON, W. Vivien	Coseley	16.10.18		Bury	*	1946-47	6		0	(FB)
			TR	Oldham Ath.	07.48	1948-51	30		1	
			TR	Chester C.	01.52					
ATHERSYCH, Russ	Sheffield	21.09.62	APP	Chesterfield	09.80	1981-82	11	9	0	(F)
ATHERTON, Dewi	Bangor	06.07.51	JNRS	Blackburn Rov.	07.68	1968-70	9	1	0	(HB)
ATHERTON, Frank G.	Horwich	18.06.34	Bury Amats	Bury	09.55	1955-64	327		13	(WH)
			TR	Swindon T.	12.64	1964-65	31	/	0	
			TR	Bury	01.66	1965	7	/	0	
ATHERTON, Jim G.	Queensferry	02.04.23		Wrexham	AM	1947-48	18		0	(G) W.AMAT.INT.
ATKIN, John M.	Scunthorpe	14.02.48		Scunthorpe U.	09.69	1969-74	116	5	0	(HB)
ATKINS, Arthur	China	21.02.25	Paget Rgrs.	Birmingham C.	11.48	1949-53	97		0	(CH)
			TR	Shrewsbury T.	06.54	1954	16		0	
ATKINS, Dennis	Bradford	08.11.38	JNRS	Huddersfield T.	12.55	1959-66	194	/	0	(FB)
			TR	Bradford C.	03.68	1967-70	108	/	0	
ATKINS, Ian L.	Birmingham	16.01.57	APP	Shrewsbury T.	01.75	1975-81	273	5	58	(M)
			TR	Sunderland	08.82	1982	36	1	4	
ATKIN, John M.	Scunthorpe	14.02.48		Scunthorpe U.	09.69	1969-74	116	5	0	(HB)
ATKINS, Robert G.	Leicester	16.10.62	Leicester C.(APP)	Sheffield U.	07.82	1982-83	21	3	3	(D)
ATKINS, Trevor A.J.	Exeter	17.08.41	JNRS	Exeter C.	08.58	1957-59	3		3	(F)
ATKINS, William	Bingley	09.05.39	Birmingham G.P.O.	Aston Villa	05.58					(F)
			TR	Swindon T.	06.59	1959-64	75		27	
			TR	Halifax T.	08.65	1965-66	74	/	34	
			TR	Stockport Co.	03.67	1966-68	92	/	37	
			TR	Portsmouth	04.69	1968-69	11	/	2	
			TR	Halifax T.	11.69	1969-72	123	2	37	
			TR	Rochdale	12.72	1972-73	25	/	7	
			TR	Darlington	09.73	1973-74	41	3	12	
ATKINSON, Brian	Sheffield	16.11.34		Sheffield U.	06.53					(HB)
			TR	Halifax T.	06.56	1956-58	67		0	
ATKINSON, Brian H.	Saffron Walden	15.04.34	B. Stortford	Watford	06.54	1955-56	20		0	
ATKINSON, Charles	Hull	17.12.32	Marist O.B.	Hull C.	05.50	1953-55	37		2	(OR)
			TR	Bradford P.A.	07.56	1956-63	344		50	
			TR	Bradford C.	06.64	1964	16		1	
ATKINSON, Charles B.C.	Haswell	05.05.38		Hartlepool U.	12.58	1959-63	47		0	(HB)
ATKINSON, David	Hull	03.04.51	APP	Hartlepool U.	APP	1968	8	/	1	(F)
			TR	Charlton Ath.	05.69					
ATKINSON, Fred	Newcastle	24.08.19		Gateshead	+	1946-48	32		6	
ATKINSON, Graham	Liverpool	17.05.43	Aston Villa(AM)	Oxford U.	N/L	1962	18		4	(F)
			Cambridge U.	Oxford U.	12.64	1964-73	304	4	71	
ATKINSON, Harold	Liverpool	28.07.25		Tranmere Rov.	+	1946-54	185		95	(CF)
			TR	Chesterfield	07.55					
ATKINSON, Hugh A.	Dublin	08.11.60	APP	Wolverhampton W.	11.78	1979-81	38	8	3	(M)EIU21-1
				Exeter C.	01.84	1983	28	/	1	
ATKINSON, Ian	Carlisle	19.12.32		Carlisle U.	06.51	1952-56	122		52	(IF)
			TR	Exeter C.	07.57	1957	7		2	
ATKINSON, John E.	Durham	20.12.13	Washington	Bolton W.	*	1946-47	30		0	(CH)
			TR	Brighton & H.A.	05.48	1948-49	51		0	
ATKINSON, Paul	Chester-le-Street	19.01.66	APP	Sunderland	11.83	1983	7	1	1	(M)
ATKINSON, Paul G.	Pudsey	14.08.61	APP	Oldham Ath.	08.79	1979-82	139	4	11	(F)E.YTH.INT.
			TR	Watford	07.83	1983	8	3	0	
ATKINSON, Peter	Middlesbrough	13.09.24	Billingham	Hull C.	04.47	1946-47	6		0	(G) d.1972
ATKINSON, Peter	Gainsborough	14.12.49		Rotherham U.	05.69	1969	3	/	0	(FB)
ATKINSON, Peter	Spilsby	20.09.29	Walsall YMCA	Walsall	11.49	1949-51	2		0	(G)
ATKINSON, Ron	Liverpool	18.03.39	BSA Tools	Aston Villa	05.56					(WH) Brother of Graham
			TR	Oxford U.	N/L	1962-71	382	1	12	
ATKINSON, Trevor	Barnsley	19.11.28	Hull Amats.	Hull C.	05.46	1946	2		0	(OL)
			TR	Barnsley	08.48					
ATKINSON, Trevor J.	Bishop Auckland	23.11.42	Spennymoor	Darlington	11.63	1963-68	137	4	3	(CH)
			TR	Bradford P.A.	01.69	1968-69	59	1	6	
ATKINSON, Walter	Gateshead	31.08.20	Hexham Hrts.	Norwich C.	01.49	1951	1		0	(HB)
ATKINSON, William	Sunderland	21.12.44	APP	Birmingham C.	03.62					(F)
			TR	Torquay U.	06.64	1964	19		7	

Players Names	Birthplace	Date	Previous Club	League Club	Date Signed	Seasons Played	Career Record Apps	Sub	Gls	
ATTHEY, Nick	Newcastle	08.05.46	APP	**Walsall**	07.63	1963-76	431	10	17	(M)
ATTLEY, Brian R.	Cardiff	27.08.55	APP	Cardiff C.	08.73	1974-78	73	6	1	(F)
			TR	Swansea C.	02.79	1978-81	83	6	6	
			TR	Derby Co.	02.82	1981-83	54	1	1	
			L	Oxford U.	03.83	1982	5	/	0	
ATWELL, Reg	Oakengates	23.03.20	Denaby U.	West Ham U.	*	1946	4		0	(WH) E.F.LGE REP./
			TR	Burnley	10.46	1946-54	245		9	Father played for
			TR	Bradford C.	10.54	1954	24		0	Shrewsbury T.
ATYEO, P. John	Dilton	07.02.32	Westbury U.	Portsmouth	AM	1950	2		0	(IF)E-6/E.U23-2/E'B'-3
			TR	Bristol C.	06.51	1951-65	597		315	E.F.LGE REP./E.YTH.INT.●
AUGUSTE, Joseph	Trinidad	24.11.65		Exeter C.	N/C	1983	7	3	0	(F)
AULD, R. (Bertie)	Glasgow	23.03.38	Glasgow Celtic	Birmingham C.	05.61	1961-64	125		26	(IF)S-3/S.LGE REP.
AULD, Walter	Bellshill	09.07.29	Bellshill Ath.	Middlesbrough	12.50	1950	2		1	(OL)
AUSTIN, J. Frank	Stoke	06.07.33	JNRS	Coventry C.	07.50	1952-62	303		2	(WH) E.SCH.INT.
			TR	Torquay U.	01.63	1962-63	24		0	
AUSTIN, Roy L.	Islington	26.03.60	Millwall (APP)	Doncaster Rov.	08.78	1978	3	/	0	(F)
AUSTIN, Terry	Isleworth	01.02.54	JNRS	Crystal Palace	06.72					(F)
			TR	Ipswich T.	05.73	1974-75	10	9	1	
			TR	Plymouth Arg.	10.76	1976	58	/	18	
			TR	Walsall	03.78	1977-78	44	3	19	
			TR	Mansfield T.	03.79	1978-80	84	/	31	
			TR	Huddersfield T.	12.80	1980-82	39	3	10	
			TR	Doncaster Rov.	09.82	1982	30	4	5	
			TR	Northampton T.	08.83	1983	42	1	11	
AVERY, Roger	Cambridge	17.02.61	APP	Cambridge	02.79	1977	0	1	0	(F)
AVEYARD, Walter	Sheffield	11.06.18	Denaby U.	Sheffield Wed.	*	1946	4		3	(IF)
			TR	Birmingham C.	04.47	1947	7		3	
			TR	Port Vale	06.48	1948-51	103		26	
			TR	Accrington St.	03.52	1951-52	24		4	
AVIS, Vernon	London	24.10.35	JNRS	Brentford	11.52	1953-60	19		0	(FB)
AVRAMOVIC, Radojko	Yugoslavia	29.11.49	N.K. Rijeka	Notts. Co.	08.79	1979-82	149	/	0	(G)
			TR	Coventry C.	09.83	1983	18	/	0	
AYLOTT, Steve J.	Ilford	03.09.51	APP	West Ham U.	06.70					(F)
			TR	Oxford U.	04.71	1971-75	143	11	8	
			TR	Brentford	07.76	1976-77	6	1	0	
AYLOTT, Trevor	London	26.11.57	APP	Chelsea	07.76	1977-79	26	3	2	(F)
			TR	Barnsley	11.79	1979-81	93	3	26	
			TR	Millwall	08.82	1982	32	/	5	
			TR	Luton T.	03.83	1982-83	32	/	10	
AYRE, Colin	Ashington	14.03.56	APP	Newcastle U.	09.73					(F)
				Torquay U.	09.76	1976	2	/	0	
AYRE, Robert W.	Berwick	26.03.32	Chippenham	Charlton Ath.	07.52	1952-57	110		48	(OR) E.U.23-2
			TR	Reading	05.58	1958-59	57		24	
AYRE, William	Crookhill	07.05.52	Scarborough	Hartlepool U.	08.77	1977-80	141	/	27	(D)
			TR	Halifax T.	01.81	1980-81	63	/	5	
			TR	Mansfield T.	08.82	1982-83	67	/	7	
AYRES, Fred	Stoke	17.07.26		Crewe Alex.	11.48	1948	2		0	(CF)
AYRES, Harry	Redcar	10.03.20		Fulham	07.46	1946-48	36		8	(WH)
			TR	Gillingham	06.50	1950-54	136		2	
AYRES, Ken E.	Oxford	15.05.56	APP	Manchester U.	06.73					(F) E.SCH.INT.
			TR	Crystal Palace	11.73	1974	3	3	0	
AYRIS, John P.	Wapping	08.01.53	APP	West Ham U.	10.70	1970-76	41	16	1	(F)E.YTH.INT.
AYRTON, Neil	Lewisham	11.02.62	Maidstone	Portsmouth	12.79	1980	1	1	0	(F)
AYTON, Jimmy	Barrhead	15.10.23	T. Lanark	Leicester C.	10.48	1948-50	8		1	(IF)
			TR	Shrewsbury T.	06.51	1951	25		1	

Players Names	Birthplace	Date	Previous Club	League Club	Date Signed	Seasons Played	Apps	Sub	Gls	
BABER, John	London	10.10.47	Charlton Ath.(APP)	Southend U.	09.66	1966-70	72	10	18	(F)
BABES, John	Lurgan	20.11.29	Glentoran	Arsenal	01.48					(RB)
			TR	Scunthorpe U.	09.50	1950-51	9		0	
BACCI, Alf	Bedington	15.07.22	W.Sleekburn	Chesterfield	08.50	1950-51	6		2	(IF)
BACKOS, Des P.	S. Africa	13.11.50	L.Angeles Aztecs	Stoke C.	10.77	1977	1	1	0	(F)
BACON, Cyril	Hammersmith	09.11.19	Hayes	Orient	06.46	1946-49	118		3	(WH)
			TR	Brentford	08.50					
BACON, Ron A.S.	Fakenham	04.03.35	Holt	Norwich C.	12.55	1955-57	41		6	(F)
			TR	Gillingham	05.58	1958-60	129		15	
BACUZZI, Dave R.	London	12.10.40	Eastbourne	Arsenal	05.59	1960-63	46		0	(FB)E.YTH.INT./
			TR	Manchester C.	04.64	1964-65	56	1	0	Son of Joe
			TR	Reading	09.66	1966-69	107	/	1	
BACUZZI, Joe	London	25.09.16	Tufnell Park	Fulham	*	1946-55	213		1	(FB)
BADDELEY, Kevin	Swindon	12.03.62	APP	Bristol C.	03.80	1980	1	/	0	(D)
			TR	Swindon T.	06.81	1981-83	89	1	2	
BADES, Brian	Blackburn	03.07.39		Accrington St.	02.60					(F)
			TR	Chester C.	08.63	1963	15		1	
BADGER, Colin A.	Rotherham	16.06.30		Rotherham U.	11.50	1950	2		0	(F)
BADGER, Len	Sheffield	08.06.45	APP	Sheffield U.	08.62	1962-75	457	1	7	(D) E. U23-13/E.F.LGE./●
			TR	Chesterfield	01.76	1975-77	46	/	0	REP./E.YTH.INT./ E.SCH.INT.
BADHAM, Jack	Birmingham	31.01.19	Muntz St.YC	Birmingham C.	05.46	1947-56	173		4	(FB)
BADMINTON, Roger	Portsmouth	15.09.47		Brighton & H.A.	07.66	1966	1	/	0	(WH)
BAGNALL, Reg	Brinsworth	22.11.26	Rotherham U.(AM)	Notts. Co.	+	1946-47	8		0	
BAILEY, Alf			Darwen	Walsall	AM	1953	1		0	
BAILEY, Anthony	Winsford	03.12.39		Crewe Alex.	06.60	1959	3		0	(F)
BAILEY, Anthony D.	Burton	23.09.46	Burton A.	Derby Co.	09.70	1971	1	/	0	(D)
			TR	Oldham Ath.	01.74	1973-74	26	/	1	
			TR	Bury	12.74	1974-78	124	7	1	
BAILEY, Danny S.	Leyton	21.05.64	APP	Bournemouth	APP	1980	1	1	0	(M)
				Torquay U.	N/C	1983	1	/	0	
BAILEY, David	Worksop	11.01.57	JNRS	Chesterfield	01.76	1975	1	/	1	(F)
BAILEY, Dennis	Biddulph	24.09.35	JNRS	Bolton W.	09.53	1956	1		0	(F)
			TR	Port Vale	08.58	1958	1		0	
BAILEY, E. Jack	Bristol	17.06.21	B.A.C.	Bristol C.	+	1946-56	334		0	(LB)
BAILEY, Gary R.	Ipswich	09.08.58	Witts Univ. (S.A.)	Manchester U.	01.78	1978-83	226	/	0	(G) E.U21-16
BAILEY, George	Doncaster	31.10.58	APP	Manchester U.	11.75					(D) E.SCH.INT
			L	Doncaster Rov.	02.78	1977	3	/	0	
BAILEY, Graham	Stoke	08.12.34		Port Vale	03.55	1955	2		0	
BAILEY, Graham T.	Dawley	22.03.20	Donnington W.	Huddersfield T.	*	1946	33		0	(FB)
			TR	Sheffield U.	03.48	1947-48	20		0	
BAILEY, Ian C.	Middlesbrough	20.10.56	APP	Middlesbrough	10.74	1975-81	140	5	1	(D)
			L	Doncaster Rov.	11.76	1976	9	/	0	
			L	Carlisle U.	02.77	1976	7	/	1	
			L	Bolton W.	11.81	1981	5	/	0	
			TR	Sheffield Wed.	08.82	1982	35	/	0	
BAILEY, John A.	Liverpool	01.04.57	APP	Blackburn Rov.	07.75	1975-78	115	5	1	(D)
			TR	Everton	07.79	1979-83	155	/	3	
BAILEY, John S.	Oxford	30.07.50	APP	Swindon T.	08.68	1967	0	2	0	(F)
BAILEY, Malcolm	Halifax	07.05.37		Bradford P.A.	04.58	1957-58	10		1	(F)
			TR	Accrington St.	10.60	1960	2		0	
BAILEY, Malcolm	Stoke	14.04.50	JNRS	Port Vale	05.67	1968	2	/	0	(FB)
BAILEY, Mike A.	Wisbech	27.02.42	JNRS	Charlton Ath.	03.59	1960-65	151	/	20	(M) E-2/E.U23-5/●
			TR	Wolverhampton W.	03.66	1965-76	360	1	19	E.F.LGE. REP.
			Minnesota Kicks	Hereford U.	08.78	1978	13	3	1	
BAILEY, Neil	Billinge	26.09.58	APP	Burnley	07.76					(F)
			TR	Newport Co.	09.78	1978-83	129	5	7	
			TR	Wigan Ath.	10.83	1983	16	7	1	
BAILEY, Ray	St. Neots	16.05.44	Bedford T.	Gillingham	05.66	1966-70	154	6	7	(WH)Northants Cricketer
			TR	Northampton T.	10.71	1971	1	/	0	
BAILEY, Roy N.	Epsom	26.05.32	JNRS	Crystal Palace	06.49	1949-55	118		0	(G) Father of Gary
			TR	Ipswich T.	03.56	1955-64	315		0	
BAILEY, Steve J.	Bristol	12.03.64	APP	Bristol Rov.	03.82	1981	15	1	1	(M)
BAILEY, Terry	Stoke	18.12.47	Stafford Rgrs.	Port Vale	08.74	1974-77	161	4	26	(M)
BAILEY, W. Craig	Airdrie	06.07.44	Kirkintilloch	Brighton & H.A.	12.61	1962	4		1	(F)
BAILIE, Colin J.	Belfast	31.03.64	APP	Swindon T.	04.82	1981-83	64	1	4	(D)
BAILLIE, Doug	Drycross	27.01.37	Airdrie	Swindon T.	03.56	1955	1		0	(CH)S.U23-2/S.SCH.INT.

Players Names	Birthplace	Date	Previous Club	League Club	Date Signed	Seasons Played	Apps	Sub	Gls	
BAILLIE, Joe	Dumfries	26.02.29	Glasgow Celtic	Wolverhampton W.	12.54	1954	1		0	(FB)S.F.LGE REP.
			TR	Bristol C.	06.56	1956-57	23		0	
			TR	Leicester C.	06.57	1957-59	75		0	
			TR	Bradford P.A.	06.60	1960	7		1	
BAILY, Eddie F.	Clapton	06.08.25	JNRS	Tottenham H.	+	1946-55	296		64	(IL)E-9/E'B'-3/
			TR	Port Vale	01.56	1955-56	24		8	E.F.LGE REP.
			TR	Nottingham F.	10.56	1956-58	68		15	
			TR	Orient	12.58	1958-59	29		3	
BAIN, Alex	Edinburgh	22.01.36	Motherwell	Huddersfield T.	08.57	1957-58	29		11	(F)
			TR	Chesterfield	02.60	1959	18		9	
			Falkirk	Bournemouth	08.61	1961	8		4	
BAIN, Jimmy A.	Blairgowrie	14.12.19	Gillingham	Chelsea	+	1946	9		1	(OL)
			TR	Swindon T.	05.47	1947-53	236		40	
BAIN, John	Glasgow	23.06.57	APP	Bristol C.	07.74	1976-78	5	1	0	(M)
			L	Brentford	02.77	1976	17	1	1	
BAIN, John	Calderbank	20.07.46	Clarkston	Bury	07.63	1964-66	9	2	0	(FB)
BAIN, William C.	Alloa	16.11.24	Dunfermline	Hartlepool U.	08.50	1950	2		0	(F)
BAINBRIDGE, Ken V.	Barking	15.01.21		West Ham U.	+	1946-49	80		16	(OL)
			TR	Reading	06.50	1950-52	89		32	
			TR	Southend U.	02.53	1952-54	78		24	
BAINBRIDGE, Peter E.	York	30.01.58	Middlesbrough (APP)	York C.	11.77	1977-78	9	/	0	(D)
			TR	Darlington	08.79	1979	16	/	0	
BAINBRIDGE, Robert	Acomb	22.02.31		York C.	05.54	1954	3		1	
BAINBRIDGE, Terry	Hartlepool	23.12.62	Henry Smith Y.C.	Hartlepool U.	10.82	1981-83	34	3	1	(D)
BAINBRIDGE, William	Gateshead	09.03.22	Ashington	Manchester U.	+					(IR)
			TR	Bury	05.46	1946	2		1	
			TR	Tranmere Rov.	11.48	1948-53	168		63	
BAINES, John R.	Colchester	25.09.37	Colchester Cas.	Colchester U.	01.60	1960-62	4		0	(CF)
BAINES, Peter C.	Australia			Wrexham	05.46	1946	6		2	(IF)
			TR	Crewe Alex.	11.46	1946	7		0	
			TR	Hartlepool U.	06.47	1947	9		1	
			TR	New Brighton	10.47	1947	2		0	
BAINES, Steve J.	Newark	23.06.54	APP	Nottingham F.	07.72	1972	2	/	0	(D)
			TR	Huddersfield T.	07.75	1975-77	113	1	10	
			TR	Bradford C.	03.78	1977-79	98	1	17	
			TR	Walsall	07.80	1980-81	47	1	5	
			L	Bury	12.81	1981	7	/	0	
			TR	Scunthorpe U.	08.82	1982	37	1	1	
			TR	Chesterfield	07.83	1983	45	/	2	
BAINES, Stan N.	Leicester	28.07.20	Leicester C.(*)	Northampton T.	07.46	1946	1		0	
BAIRD, Doug H.	Falkirk	26.11.35	Partick Th.	Nottingham F.	09.60	1960-62	32		0	(RB)S.U23-1/
			TR	Plymouth Arg.	10.63	1963-67	147	1	1	S.F.LGE REP.
BAIRD, Henry	Belfast	17.08.13	Manchester U.(*)	Huddersfield T.	*					(WH)N.I.-1/IRISH
			TR	Ipswich T.	06.46	1946-51	216		6	LGE REP./*Linfield
BAIRD, Hugh	Monkland	14.03.30	Airdrie	Leeds U.	06.57	1957-58	45		22	(CF) S-1
BAIRD, Ian J.	Southampton	01.04.64	APP	Southampton	04.82	1982-83	15	2	3	(F)
			L	Cardiff C.	11.83	1983	12	/	6	
BAIRD, J.A. Gordon	Basford	14.01.24	N. Houghton	Mansfield T.	11.46	1946-47	11		0	(WH)
BAIRD, Sammy	Denny	13.05.30	Clyde	Preston N.E.	06.54	1954	15		2	(IF)S-7/S.F.LGE REP.
BAIRSTOW, David	Bradford	01.09.51	JNRS	Bradford C.	12.71	1971-72	10	7	1	(F)Yorks.Cricketer
BAKER, Alan R.	Tipton	22.06.44	APP	Aston Villa	07.61	1960-65	92	1	13	(IF)E.YTH.INT./E.SCH.INT.
			TR	Walsall	07.66	1966-70	128	8	31	
BAKER, Charles	Turners Hill	06.01.36	R.A.F.	Brighton & H.A.	05.60	1960-62	81		0	(G)
			TR	Aldershot	07.64	1964-65	28	/	0	
BAKER, Clive	Doncaster	05.07.34		Doncaster Rov.	08.52					(F)
			TR	Halifax T.	08.55	1955-58	58		22	
			TR	Southport	07.59					
BAKER, Clive E.	Nth. Walsham	14.03.59	JNRS	Norwich C.	07.77	1977-80	14	/	0	(G)
BAKER, Cliff H.	Bristol	11.01.24	Coalpit Hth.	Bristol Rov.	01.47	1946	5		2	(OR)
BAKER, Colin W.	Cardiff	18.12.34	Cardiff Nomads	Cardiff C.	03.53	1953-65	293	1	18	(WH)W-7/W.U23-1
BAKER, Darren S.	Wednesbury	28.06.65	JNRS	Wrexham	08.83	1982-83	18	6	1	(M)W.SCH.INT.
BAKER, David F.	London	15.05.39	JNRS	Q.P.R.	04.57	1960	2		0	(WH)
BAKER, David H.	Penzance	21.10.28	Brush Spts.	Nottingham F.	10.49	1949	3		0	(CH)
BAKER, Doug G.	London	08.04.47	APP	Arsenal	05.64					(F)
			TR	Millwall	06.66	1966	4	1	1	
BAKER, Frank	Stoke	22.10.18	JNRS	Stoke C.	*	1946-49	81		11	(IL)
BAKER, Gerald	Sth. Hindley	22.04.39	JNRS	Bradford P.A.	01.57	1957-60	16		0	(FB)

Players Names	Birthplace	Date	Previous Club	League Club	Date Signed	Seasons Played	Apps	Sub	Gls	
BAKER, Gerry A.	U.S.A.	11.04.38	Larkhall Th.	Chelsea	06.55					(CF)Brother of Joe
			St. Mirren	Manchester C.	11.60	1961-62	37		16	
			Hibernian	Ipswich T.	12.63	1963-67	135	/	58	
			TR	Coventry C.	11.67	1967-69	27	6	5	
			L	Brentford	10.69	1969	8	/	2	
BAKER, Gerrard	Wigan	16.09.38	Wigan Ath.	Nottingham F.	12.59					(FB)
			TR	York C.	07.63	1963-68	214	/	7	
BAKER, Graham	Southampton	03.12.58	APP	Southampton	12.76	1977-81	111	2	22	(M) E.U21-2
			TR	Manchester C.	08.82	1982-83	63	/	12	
BAKER, Joe	Liverpool	17.07.40	Torino	Arsenal	08.62	1962-65	144	/	93	(CF)E-8/E.U23-6/S.
			TR	Nottingham F.	03.66	1965-68	116	1	41	SCH.INT
			TR	Sunderland	07.69	1969-70	39	1	12	
BAKER, Keith	Oxford	15.10.56	APP	Oxford U.	11.74					(G)E.SCH.INT.
			L	Grimsby T.	08.75	1975	1	/	0	
BAKER, Kieron	Isle of Wight	29.10.49	Fulham (AM)	Bournemouth	07.67	1969-77	217	/	0	(G)
			L	Brentford	02.73	1972	6	/	0	
			TR	Ipswich T.	08.78					
BAKER, Mark	Swansea	26.04.61	JNRS	Swansea C.	09.78	1978-79	3	8	2	(F)
BAKER, Peter R.	Walthamstow	24.08.34	Tottenham H.(AM)	Sheffield Wed.	11.54	1957	11		0	(FB)Cousin of Peter R.B.
			TR	Q.P.R.	03.61	1960-62	25		0	
BAKER, Peter R.B.	Hampstead	10.12.31	Enfield	Tottenham H.	10.52	1952-64	299		3	(FB)
BAKER, Roy V.	Bradford	08.06.54		Bradford C.	07.74	1972-74	39	7	11	(F)
BAKER, Steve	Newcastle	02.12.61	APP	Southampton	12.79	1980-83	21	/	0	(D)
			L	Burnley	02.84	1983	10	/	0	
BAKER, T. George	Maerdy	06.04.36	JNRS	Plymouth Arg.	10.53	1954-59	78		16	(F)W.U23-2
			TR	Shrewsbury T.	06.60	1960-61	52		5	
BAKER, Tom A.	Charlton	09.08.39		Bristol Rov.	10.56	1962	1		0	(WH)
BAKER, William	Penrhiwceiber	03.10.20	Troedyrhiw	Cardiff C.	*	1946-54	290		5	(LH)W-1/W.SCH.INT.
			TR	Ipswich T.	06.55	1955	20		0	
BAKES, Martin S.	Bradford	08.02.37	JNRS	Bradford C.	02.54	1953-58	72		7	(OL)
			TR	Scunthorpe U.	06.59	1959-62	77		5	
BAKEWELL, Herbert	Barnsley	08.03.21	JNRS	Barnsley	*					(G)
			TR	Newport Co.	09.46	1946	8		0	
B'ALAC, Peta J.	Exeter	09.12.53	APP	Plymouth Arg.	12.71	1971-72	40	/	0	(G)
			L	Hereford U.	08.73	1973	2	/	0	
			L	Swansea C.	09.73	1973	4	/	0	
BALCOMBE, Steve W.	Bangor	02.09.61	APP	Leeds U.	10.79	1981	1	/	1	(F)W.U'21-1
BALDERSTONE, J. Chris	Huddersfield	16.11.40	JNRS	Huddersfield T.	05.58	1959-64	117		23	(IF)Leic/Yorks
			TR	Carlisle U.	06.65	1965-74	369	7	67	Cricketer●
			TR	Doncaster Rov.	07.75	1975	38	1	1	
BALDIE, Doug W.	Scoon	16.04.21		Bristol Rov.	+	1946-47	8		4	(F)+Luton T.
BALDRIDGE, Robert	Sunderland	26.11.32	Hendon S.C.	Gateshead	02.57	1956-59	59		22	(F)
BALDRY, William J.	Luton	09.07.56	Luton T.(AM)	Cambridge U.	06.76	1975-77	27	/	0	(D)
BALDWIN, George	Islington	26.07.21		Gillingham	08.51	1951	1		0	
BALDWIN, Harry	Saltley	17.07.20	W.B.A.(*)	Brighton & H.A.	+	1946-51	164		0	(G)*Sutton T.
			Kettering	Walsall	12.53	1953-54	37		0	
BALDWIN, Jimmy J.	Blackburn	12.01.22		Blackburn Rov.	+	1946-49	88		0	(WH)
			TR	Leicester C.	02.50	1949-55	180		4	
BALDWIN, Tommy	Gateshead	10.06.45	Wrekenton	Arsenal	12.62	1964-66	17	/	6	(F) E.U23-2
			TR	Chelsea	09.66	1966-74	182	5	74	
			L	Millwall	11.74	1974	6	/	1	
			L	Manchester U.	01.75	1974	2	/	0	
			Gravesend	Brentford	N/C	1977	4	/	1	
BALL, Alan	Farnworth	12.05.45	APP	Blackpool	05.62	1962-65	116	/	41	(M) E-72/E.U23-8/●
			TR	Everton	08.66	1966-71	208	/	66	E.F.LGE.REP.
			TR	Arsenal	12.71	1971-76	177	/	45	
			TR	Southampton	12.76	1976-79	132	/	9	
			Vancouver W.	Blackpool	07.80	1980	30	/	5	
			TR	Southampton	03.81	1980-82	63	1	1	
			TR	Bristol Rov.	01.83	1982	17	/	2	
BALL, Donald	Barnard Castle	14.06.62	APP	Darlington	08.80	1979-81	57	3	2	(D)
BALL, Geoff	Nottingham	02.11.44	JNRS	Nottingham F.	02.63	1964-65	3	/	0	(FB)
			TR	Notts.Co.	11.67	1967-71	111	1	0	
BALL, J. Alan	Farnworth	23.09.24		Southport	+	1946	2		0	(IF)
			TR	Birmingham C.	05.47					Father of Alan/
			TR	Southport	02.48	1947-49	40		10	d.1982
			TR	Oldham Ath.	07.50	1950	7		0	
			TR	Rochdale	02.52	1951	5		1	
BALL, Joe H.	Walsall	04.04.31	Walsall W'd.	Ipswich T.	08.51	1951-52	30		2	(W)
			TR	Aldershot	06.54	1954-55	31		6	
BALL, John	Wigan	13.03.25	Wigan Ath.	Manchester U.	03.48	1947-49	22		0	(RB)E.F.LGE REP.
			TR	Bolton W.	09.50	1950-57	200		2	

Players Names	Birthplace	Date	Previous Club	League Club	Date Signed	Seasons Played	Apps	Sub	Gls
BALL, John A.	Brighton	16.07.23	JNRS	Brighton & H.A.	+	1946-52	113		0 (G)
BALL, Keith	Walsall	26.10.40		Walsall	01.59	1958-61	11		0 (G)
			Worcester C.	Walsall	05.65	1966-67	35		0
			TR	Port Vale	11.68	1968-71	130	/	0
			Stourbridge	Walsall	11.72	1972	2	/	0
BALL, Kevin A.	Hastings	12.11.64	Coventry C.(APP)	Portsmouth	05.84	1983	1	/	0 (D)
BALL, S. Gary	St. Austell	15.12.59	APP	Plymouth Arg.	12.77	1979	0	1	0 (F)
			TR	Lincoln C.	10.79	1979	3	/	0
BALLAGHER, John	Dukinfield	21.03.36	Stalybridge	Sheffield Wed.	02.57	1958	3		0 (IF)
			TR	Doncaster Rov.	02.61	1960-61	41		13
			TR	Gillingham	08.62	1962-63	40		10
BALLANTYNE, John	Newburn	16.09.27		West Ham U.	05.46				
			TR	Hartlepool U.	07.50	1950-51	13		0
			TR	Millwall	08.53				
BALLARD, Edgar A.	Brentford	16.06.20	Brentford(AM)	Orient	+	1946	26		1 (FB)
			TR	Southampton	06.47	1947-50	45		0
			TR	Orient	08.52				
BALMER, J. Mike	Hexham	25.05.46	APP	Leicester C.	01.64				(HB)
			TR	Halifax T.	05.65	1965-66	28	/	9
BALMER, John	Liverpool	06.02.16	Colton	Liverpool	*	1946-51	166		63 (IF)
BALOGUN, Jesilimi	Nigeria	27.03.31	Skegness	Q.P.R.	09.56	1956	13		3 (F)
BALSOM, Cliff G.	Torquay	25.03.46	APP	Torquay U.	03.64	1963	4		0 (FB)
			TR	Swindon T.	06.64				
BALSOM, Mike J.C.	Bridport	09.09.47	JNRS	Exeter C.	08.65	1966-73	274	2	9 (HB)
BAMBER, J. David	St. Helens	01.02.59	Manchester Univ.	Blackpool	09.79	1979-82	81	5	28 (F)
			TR	Coventry C.	06.83	1983	18	1	3
			TR	Walsall	03.84	1983	9	1	3
BAMBRIDGE, Keith	Rawmarsh	01.09.35		Rotherham U.	02.55	1955-62	161		16 (OL)
			TR	Darlington	12.64	1964	6		0
			TR	Halifax T.	03.65	1964-65	8	1	1
BAMBRIDGE, Steve	London	27.05.60	APP	Aldershot	05.78	1976	0	2	0 (F)
BAMFORD, Harry C.	Bristol	08.02.20	Bristol C.(AM)	Bristol Rov.	+	1946-58	487		5 (FB)d.1958●
BAMFORD, Harry F.	Kingston	08.04.14	Ealing CYC	Brentford	+				d.1949
			TR	Brighton & H.A.	06.46	1946	8		0
BANCROFT, Paul	Derby	10.09.64	APP	Derby Co.	09.82				(F)
			L	Crewe Alex.	01.83	1982	21	/	3
BANFIELD, Neil A.	London	20.01.62	APP	Crystal Palace	08.79	1980	2	1	0 (D) E.SCH.INT./E.YTH.INT.
				Orient	N/C	1983	6	/	0
BANHAM, Roy	Nottingham	30.10.36	JNRS	Nottingham F.	11.53	1955-56	2		0 (HB)
			TR	Peterborough U.	N/L	1960-61	16		0
BANJO, Tunji	Kennington	19.02.60	APP	Orient	03.77	1977-81	20	7	1 (M)
BANKS, Alan	Liverpool	05.10.38	Rankin Boys	Liverpool	05.58	1958-60	8		6 (IF)
			Cambridge C.	Exeter C.	10.63	1963-65	85	/	48
			TR	Plymouth Arg.	06.66	1966-67	19	/	5
			TR	Exeter C.	11.67	1967-72	161	13	57
BANKS, Eric	Workington	07.04.50	JNRS	Workington	09.68	1967-72	26	3	1 (F)
BANKS, Francis	Hull	21.08.45	JNRS	Southend U.	10.62	1963-65	4	/	0 (D)
			TR	Hull C.	09.66	1967-75	284	4	7
			TR	Southend U.	03.76	1975-77	75	/	0
BANKS, George E.	Wednesbury	28.03.19	Brownhills Ath.	W.B.A.	*				(F)
				Mansfield T.	11.47	1947-48	62		21
BANKS, Gordon	Sheffield	20.12.37	Rawmarsh	Chesterfield	09.55	1958	23		0 (G)E-73/E.U23-2/
			TR	Leicester C.	05.59	1959-66	293	/	0 E.F.LGE REP.●
			TR	Stoke C.	04.67	1966-72	194	/	0
BANKS, Ian	Mexborough	09.01.61	APP	Barnsley	01.79	1978-82	158	6	36 (M)
			TR	Leicester C.	06.83	1983	22	4	3
BANKS, Ken	Wigan	19.10.23	Wigan Ath.	Southport	+	1946-51	118	/	5 (HB)
BANKS, Ralph	Farnworth	28.06.20	S. Liverpool	Bolton W.	+	1946-52	107		0 (FB)Brother of Tommy
			TR	Aldershot	01.54	1953-54	43		1
BANKS, Tommy	Farnworth	10.11.29	JNRS	Bolton W.	10.47	1947-60	233		2 (FB)E-6/E.F.LGE REP
BANNAN, Tommy N.	Lanark	13.04.30	Airdrie	Wrexham	06.51	1951-54	158		55 (CF)
			TR	Lincoln C.	06.55	1955-56	67		19
			TR	Wrexham	08.57	1957-58	68		23
			TR	Barrow	08.59	1959-60	45		15
BANNER, Arthur	Sheffield	28.06.18	Doncaster Rov.(*)	West Ham U.	*	1946-47	26		0 (FB)
			TR	Orient	02.48	1947-52	165		1
BANNERMAN, Telford	Coupar Angus	17.09.24	Blairgowrie J.	New Brighton	01.49	1948-50	33		3 (F)
BANNISTER, Bruce	Bradford	14.04.47	JNRS	Bradford C.	08.65	1965-71	199	9	60 (F)
			TR	Bristol Rov.	11.71	1971-76	202	4	80
			TR	Plymouth Arg.	12.76	1976	24	/	7
			TR	Hull C.	06.77	1977-79	79	6	20

Players Names	Birthplace	Date	Previous Club	League Club	Date Signed	Seasons Played	Apps	Sub	Gls	
BANNISTER, Eddie	Preston	02.06.20	Oaks Fold	Leeds U.	05.46	1946-49	44		1	
			TR	Barnsley	07.50	1950	32		0	
BANNISTER, Garry	Warrington	22.07.60	APP	Coventry C.	05.78	1978-80	17	5	3	(F)E.U'21-1
			TR	Sheffield. Wed.	08.81	1981-83	117	1	55	
BANNISTER, Jack	Chesterfield	26.01.42	JNRS	W.B.A.	08.59	1959-62	9		0	(HB)
			TR	Scunthorpe U.	06.64	1964	9		0	
			TR	Crystal Palace	07.65	1965-68	119	3	7	
			TR	Luton T.	10.68	1968-70	79	3	0	
			TR	Cambridge U.	05.71	1971-73	28	4	0	
BANNISTER, Jim H.	Chesterfield	01.02.29		Chesterfield	12.50					(FB)
			TR	Shrewsbury T.	06.52	1952-57	238		2	
			TR	Northampton T.	07.58	1958	24		0	
			TR	Aldershot	08.59	1959-60	85		0	
BANNISTER, Keith	Sheffield	13.11.30	JNRS	Sheffield U.	05.48					(HB)E.YTH.INT.
			TR	Birmingham C.	08.50	1952-53	21		0	
			TR	Wrexham	07.55	1955	14		0	
			TR	Chesterfield	12.55	1955	21		1	
			TR	Norwich C.	07.56	1956	7		0	
BANNISTER, Keith	Sheffield	27.01.23		Sheffield Wed.	+	1946-52	75		0	(FB)
			TR	Chesterfield	06.53	1953	17		0	
BANNISTER, Neville	Brierfield	21.07.37	JNRS	Bolton W.	07.54	1955-60	26		4	(OR)
			TR	Lincoln C.	03.61	1960-64	74		16	
			TR	Hartlepool U.	08.64	1964	41		8	
			TR	Rochdale	07.65	1965	17	1	2	
BANNISTER, Paul	Stoke	11.10.47		Port Vale	04.65	1964-67	12	/	2	(F)
BANNON, Eamonn J.	Edinburgh	18.04.58	Hearts	Chelsea	01.79	1978-79	25	/	1	(M) S-6 S.U21-7/S.SCH. INT./S.LGE.REP
BANNON, Ian	Bury	03.09.59	APP	Rochdale	09.77	1976-69	112	10	0	(D)
BANNON, Paul A.	Dublin	15.11.56	Bridgend T.	Carlisle U.	02.79	1978-83	127	12	45	(F)
			L	Darlington	10.83	1983	2	/	0	
			TR	Bristol Rov.	01.84	1983	11	/	3	
BANOVIC, Yakka	Yugoslavia	12.11.56	Heidelberg	Derby Co.	09.80	1981-83	35	/	0	(G) YUGOSLAVIA INT.
BANTON, Dale C.	Kensington	15.05.61	APP	West Ham U.	05.79	1979-81	2	3	0	(M)
			TR	Aldershot	08.82	1982-83	90	1	43	
BANTON, Geoff	Ashton-under Lyne	16.03.57	Bolton W. (APP)	Plymouth Arg.	05.75	1976	6	1	0	(D)
			TR	Fulham	07.78	1978-81	37	1	3	
BARBER, Dave E.	Wombwell	06.12.39	JNRS	Barnsley	06.58	1957-60	82		4	(WH)E.YTH.INT.
			TR	Preston N.E.	06.61	1961-63	38		2	
BARBER, Eric	Dublin	18.01.42	Shelbourne	Birmingham C.	03.66	1965-66	3	1	1	(F) N.I.-2
BARBER, Eric	Stockport	25.03.26		Sheffield U.	02.47					(F)
				Bolton W.	03.50					
			TR	Rochdale	04.51	1950-51	17		2	
BARBER, Fred	Ferryhill	26.08.63	APP	Darlington	08.81	1982-83	58	/	0	(G)
BARBER, John M.	Lichfield	09.10.29	Arsenal	Swansea C.	08.50	1950	4		0	(OL)
			TR	Walsall	07.51	1951	6		0	
BARBER, Keith	Luton	21.09.47	Dunstable	Luton T.	04.71	1970-76	142	/	0	(G)
			TR	Swansea C.	07.77	1977	42	/	0	
			L	Cardiff C.	09.78	1978	2	/	0	
BARBER, Len	Stoke	03.07.29	Bury(AM)	Port Vale	06.47	1949-54	47		12	(CF)
BARBER, Mike J.	Kensington	24.08.41	Arsenal(AM)	Q.P.R.	12.59	1960-62	63		11	(OL)
			TR	Notts. Co.	07.63	1963-64	33		3	
BARBER, Phil A.	Tring	10.06.65		Crystal Palace	02.84	1983	8	1	2	(F)
BARBER, William	Watford	09.09.39	JNRS	Watford	03.57	1956-59	25		0	(WH)
			TR	Aldershot	08.62	1962	1		0	
BARCLAY, John M.	Mid Calder	08.09.21		Bournemouth	12.47	1947-48	5		2	(CF)
BARCLAY, Robert	Perth	03.11.22		Preston N.E.	+					
				Stockport Co.	08.48	1948	1		0	
BARCLAY, William	Larkhall	11.07.24	Motherwell	Bury	03.49	1948-49	17		0	(OL)
BARDSLEY, David J.	Manchester	11.09.64	APP	Blackpool	11.82	1981-83	45	/	0	(D)
			TR	Watford	11.83	1983	25	/	0	
BARDSLEY, Leslie	Stockport	08.08.25	Linfield	Bury	04.48	1947-54	200		2	(WH) +Manchester C.
			TR	Barrow	09.55	1955	21		0	
BARGH, George W.	Garstang	27.05.10	Chesterfield(+)	Bury	09.46	1946	1		0	(IR)*Preston N.E./Sheff. Wed./ Bury
BARHAM, Mark	Folkestone	12.07.62	APP	Norwich C.	04.80	1979-83	109	6	12	(M) E.YTH.INT./E-2
BARK, Robert	Stranraer	27.01.26	Q. of South	Barrow	04.48	1948	1		0	
BARKAS, Sam	Wardley	29.12.09	Bradford C.(*)	Manchester C.	*	1946	3		0	(FB)E-5/E.F.LGE REP.
BARKAS, Tom	South Shields	27.03.12	Bradford C.(*)	Halifax T.	*					(FB)*Washington Col./
			TR	Rochdale	09.46	1946-47	44		17	Brother of Sam
			TR	Stockport Co.	11.47	1947-48	44		18	(Ned/Frank pre-war)
			TR	Carlisle U.	02.49	1948	14		5	

Players Names	Birthplace	Date	Previous Club	League Club	Date Signed	Seasons Played	Career Record Apps	Sub	Gls	
BARKE, John L.	Nuncargate	16.12.12	Sheffield U.*	Mansfield T.	*	1946	32		0	(WH)*Scunthorpe U./d.1976
BARKER, A. Mick	Bishop Auckland	23.02.56	APP	Newcastle U.	03.73	1974-78	21	2	0	(D)
			TR	Gillingham	01.79	1978-79	64	/	2	
			B. Auckland	Hartlepool U.	09.82	1982-83	59	1	1	
BARKER, Donald	Long Eaton	17.06.11	Bradford P.A.(*)	Millwall	*					(IF)
			TR	Brighton & H.A.	07.46	1946	14		4	
BARKER, Geoff	Hull	7.02.49	JNRS	Hull C.	03.67	1968-70	29	1	2	(D)
			L	Southend U.	12.70	1970	25	/	0	
			TR	Darlington	07.71	1971-74	151	/	6	
			TR	Reading	02.75	1974-76	51	1	2	
			TR	Grimsby T.	07.77	1977-78	66	/	1	
BARKER, Gordon	Leeds	06.07.31	B.Auckland	Southend U.	12.54	1954-58	57		9	(F)Essex Cricketer
BARKER, Jeffrey	Scunthorpe	16.10.15	Aston Villa(*)	Huddersfield T.	+	1946-47	67		0	(FB)*Scunthorpe
			TR	Scunthorpe U.	06.50	1950-51	73		1	
BARKER, John	Huddersfield	04.07.48	APP	Scunthorpe U.	07.66	1965-74	261	2	6	(F) Son of Jeffrey
BARKER, Keith	Stoke	22.02.49		Cambridge U.	N/L					(G)
			TR	Barnsley	03.71	1971	9	/	0	
BARKER, Len	Salford	26.03.24		Stockport Co.	01.48	1948-50	39		12	(F)
BARKER, Ritchie	Derby	23.11.39	Burton A.	Derby Co.	10.67	1967-68	30	7	12	(IF)
			TR	Notts. Co.	12.68	1968-70	99	13	37	
			TR	Peterborough U.	09.71	1971	36	/	9	
BARKER, Robert C.	Kinglassie	01.12.27	Kelty Rgrs	W.B.A.	+	1948	14		2	(OL)
			TR	Shrewsbury T.	08.50	1950	25		1	
BARKER, Simon	Farnworth	04.11.64	APP	Blackburn Rov.	11.82	1983	28	/	3	(M)
BARKER, Tom H.	Tyldesley	12.01.36	Boothstown	Southport	12.57	1957-58	35		4	(F)
BARKER, William	Stoke	31.05.24		Stoke C.	10.48	1949	1		0	(F)
BARKS, Edwin	Ilkeston	01.09.21	Heanor T.*	Nottingham F.	*	1946-48	66		5	(WH)
			TR	Mansfield T.	01.49	1948-54	212		6	
BARLEY, Derek C.	Highbury	20.03.32	Maidenhead U.	Arsenal	12.51					(F)E.YTH.INT./
			TR	Q.P.R.	05.53	1953	4		0	Son of pre-war player
			TR	Aldershot	07.54	1954	2		0	
BARLEY, Peter J.	Scunthorpe	25.04.36	Leeds U.(AM)	Scunthorpe U.	10.53	1953	5		0	(G)
BARLOW, Colin	Manchester	14.11.35	Tarporley B.C.	Manchester C.	12.56	1957-62	179		76	(OR)
			TR	Oldham Ath.	08.63	1963	6		1	
			TR	Doncaster Rov.	08.64	1964	3		0	
BARLOW, Frank	Mexborough	15.10.46	JNRS	Sheffield U.	09.65	1965-71	116	5	2	(WH)E.SCH.INT.
			TR	Chesterfield	08.72	1972-75	140	1	3	
BARLOW, Harry	Manchester	28.10.23	Manchester C.(AM)	Crewe Alex.	+	1946-50	29		1	(CH)
BARLOW, Herbert	Kilnhurst	22.07.16	Wolverhampton W.(*)	Portsmouth	*	1946-49	90		29	(IF)*Barnsley
			TR	Leicester C.	12.49	1949-51	42		9	
			TR	Colchester U.	07.52	1952-53	60		16	
BARLOW, Peter	Colchester	09.01.50	APP	Colchester U.	01.68	1966-68	18	3	4	(F) Son of Herbert
			TR	Workington	02.69	1968-69	41	1	11	
			TR	Hartlepool U.	07.70	1970	8	3	0	
BARLOW, Philip D.	Shipley	19.12.46	Guiseley	Bradford C.	07.66	1966	15	1	0	(HB)
			TR	Lincoln C.	08.67	1967	5	/	0	
BARLOW, Ray J.	Swindon	17.08.26	Garrards F.C.	W.B.A.	+	1946-59	403		31	(WH) E-1●
			TR	Birmingham C.	08.60	1960	5		0	
BARMBY, Jeff	Hull	15.01.43	Selby T.	York C.	AM	1962-63	2		0	(CF)
BARNARD, Arthur	Mossley	20.06.32	Astley & T.Col.	Bolton W.	11.51	1954-55	2		0	(G)
			TR	Stockport Co.	07.56	1956-58	53		0	
			TR	Southport	09.59	1959	42		0	
BARNARD, Chris L.	Cardiff	01.08.47	APP	Southend U.	08.65	1965	4	4	0	(F)
			TR	Ipswich T.	07.66	1966-69	18	2	0	
			TR	Torquay U.	10.70	1970-71	29	4	2	
			TR	Charlton Ath.	01.72	1971	0	1	0	
BARNARD, Geoff	Southend	23.03.46	JNRS	Norwich C.	09.63	1964-66	6	/	0	(G)
			TR	Scunthorpe U.	07.68	1968-74	265	/	0	
			Scarborough	Scunthorpe	09.76	1976	6	/	0	
BARNARD, H. Mike	Portsmouth	08.07.33	Gosport Bor.	Portsmouth	08.51	1953-58	116		24	(IF) Hants Cricketer
BARNARD, Leigh	Worsley	29.10.58	APP	Portsmouth	08.77	1977-81	71	8	8	(M)
			L	Peterborough U.	03.82	1981	1	3	0	
			TR	Swindon U.	07.82	1982-83	81	1	11	
BARNARD, Ray S.	Middlesbrough	06.04.33	JNRS	Middlesbrough	04.50	1951-59	113		0	(FB) E.SCH.INT.
			TR	Lincoln C.	06.60	1960-62	43		0	
BARNES, Bernard	Plymouth	25.12.37	Bideford	Plymouth Arg.	01.55	1956-57	4		1	(F)
BARNES, Colin	Luton	28.05.57	Barnet	Torquay U.	08.83	1983	35	/	8	(F)
BARNES, David	London	16.11.61	APP	Coventry C.	05.79	1979-81	9	/	0	(D) E. YTH. INT.
			TR	Ipswich T.	05.82	1982-83	16	1	0	
BARNES, David O.	Kingston	17.12.62	APP	West Ham U.	09.80	1980-83	13	9	3	(F)
BARNES, Eric	Wythenshawe	29.11.37		Crewe Alex.	07.58	1957-69	347	2	1	(CH)

Players Names	Birthplace	Date	Previous Club	League Club	Date Signed	Seasons Played	Apps	Sub	Gls	
BARNES, John C.B.	Jamaica	07.09.63	Sudbury Court	Watford	07.81	1981-83	116	1	34	(F)E.U'21-2/E-9
BARNES, Ken	Birmingham	06.03.29	Stafford Rgrs.	Manchester C.	05.50	1951-60	258		18	(WH)E.F.LGE REP./
			TR	Wrexham	05.61	1961-64	132		24	Father of Peter S.
BARNES, Mike F.	Reading	17.09.63	APP	Reading	09.81	1980-83	29	5	2	(D)
BARNES, Peter	St. Albans	29.06.38	JNRS	Watford	03.57	1960-61	10		0	(HB)
BARNES, Peter S.	Manchester	10.06.57	APP	Manchester C.	08.74	1974-78	108	7	15	(W) E.-20/E.U21-9/
			TR	W.B.A.	07.79	1979-80	76	1	23	E.YTH.INT./E.F.LGE.REP.
			TR	Leeds U.	08.81	1981	30	/	1	
			Real Betis	Leeds U.	08.83	1983	25	2	4	
BARNES, Ron	Bolton	21.02.36	JNRS	Blackpool	05.54	1956-58	9		0	(OR)
			TR	Rochdale	06.59	1959-60	91		6	
			TR	Wrexham	07.61	1961-63	88		24	
			TR	Norwich C.	08.63	1963	21		1	
			TR	Peterborough U.	07.64	1964-65	39		6	
			TR	Torquay U.	01.66	1965-68	110	4	25	
BARNES, Walley	Brecon	16.01.20	Portsmouth(AM)	Arsenal	+	1946-55	267		11	(FB)W-22/d.1975
BARNES, William	Dumbarton	16.03.39	Glencairn	Bradford C.	04.58	1958-60	59		0	(FB)
			Scarborough	Bradford P.A.	09.66	1966-67	53	/	0	
BARNETT, Alan	Croydon	04.11.34	Croydon Amats.	Portsmouth	09.55	1955-57	25		0	(G)
			TR	Grimsby T.	12.58	1958-62	116		0	
			TR	Exeter C.	07.63	1963-65	57	/	0	
			TR	Torquay U.	06.66					
BARNETT, Dave	London	24.09.51	APP	Southend U.	09.69	1968-72	48	9	0	(HB)
BARNETT, Gary L.	Stratford	11.03.63	APP	Coventry C.	01.81					(M)
			TR	Oxford U.	07.82	1982-83	36	5	9	
			L	Wimbledon	02.83	1982	5	/	1	
BARNETT, Geoff C.	Northwich	16.10.46	APP	Everton	05.64	1965-67	10	/	0	(G)E.YTH.INT./E.SCH.INT.
			TR	Arsenal	10.69	1969-75	39	/	0	
BARNETT, Graham	Stoke	17.05.36		Port Vale	06.56	1958-59	49		35	(F)
			TR	Tranmere Rov.	03.60	1959-60	32		11	
			TR	Halifax T.	08.61	1961	32		9	
BARNETT, Tom	Muswell Hill	12.10.36	Chatham	Crystal Palace	12.58	1958-60	14		2	(OL)
BARNEY, Vic C.	London	03.04.22	Oxford C.	Reading	09.46	1946-48	45		12	
			TR	Bristol C.	10.48	1948	28		2	
			TR	Grimsby T.	06.49	1949	7		0	
BARNEY, Vic R.	Oxford	18.11.47	APP	Bristol Rov.	12.65	1966-69	30	1	3	(HB)Son of Vic. C.
BARNSLEY, Geoff R.	Bilston	09.12.35	JNRS	W.B.A.	12.52	1954	1		0	(G)
			TR	Plymouth Arg.	06.57	1957-60	131		0	
			TR	Norwich C.	05.61	1961	8		0	
			TR	Torquay U.	12.62	1963	6		0	
BARNWELL, John	Newcastle	24.12.38	B.Auckland	Arsenal	11.56	1956-63	138		23	(WH)E.U.23-1/E.YTH.INT.
			TR	Nottingham F.	03.64	1963-69	174	8	22	
			TR	Sheffield U.	04.70	1970	9	/	2	
BARON, Kevin P.	Preston	19.07.26	Preston N.E.(AM)	Liverpool	+	1947-53	141		31	(IF)d.1971
			TR	Southend U.	05.54	1954-58	138		47	
			TR	Northampton T.	09.58	1958	25		4	
			Gravesend	Aldershot	07.60	1960	6		0	
BARR, Hugh	Ballymena	17.05.35	Linfield	Coventry C.	07.62	1962-63	47		15	(CF) N.I.-3/N.I.SCH.INT.
BARR, John M.	Bridge-o-Weir	09.09.17	T. Lanark	Q.P.R.	+	1946	4		0	(CH)
BARRASS, Malcolm W.	Blackpool	13.12.24	Ford Motors	Bolton W.	+	1946-56	329		25	(CH)E-3/E.F.LGE REP./
			TR	Sheffield U.	09.56	1956	18		0	Son of pre-war player
BARRATT, Alf G.	Kettering	13.04.20	Northampton T.(*)	Leicester C.	+	1947-48	4		0	(WH)
			TR	Grimsby T.	07.50	1950	24		0	
			TR	Southport	07.51	1951-55	197		0	
BARRATT, Harry	Headington	25.12.18	Herberts Ath.	Coventry C.	*	1946-51	165		11	(WH)Son of pre-war player
BARRATT, Les E.	Windermere	13.08.45	APP	Barrow	08.62	1962-63	10		0	(F)
			TR	Grimsby T.	07.64	1964	4		1	
			TR	Southport	07.65	1965	9	1	0	
BARRELL, Les	Colchester	30.08.32		Colchester U.	12.56	1956	4	1	0	(F)
BARRETT, Arthur H.	Liverpool	21.12.27	JNRS	Tranmere Rov.	+	1946	1		0	(CH)
BARRETT, C. Roger	Doncaster	19.10.46	Doncaster U.	Doncaster Rov.	10.68	1968	1	/	0	(IF)
BARRETT, Colin	Stockport	03.08.52	Cheadle Heath N.	Manchester C.	05.70	1972-75	50	3	0	(D)
			TR	Nottingham F.	03.76	1975-78	64	5	4	
			TR	Swindon T.	06.80	1980	3	/	0	
BARRETT, G. Tom	Salford	16.03.34	JNRS	Manchester U.	08.52					(F)
			TR	Plymouth Arg.	07.57	1957-58	26		1	
			TR	Chester C.	07.60	1960-61	41		2	
			TR	Oldham Ath.	09.61					
BARRETT, Jim G.	London	05.11.30	JNRS	West Ham U.	02.49	1949-54	85		24	(IF)Son of ex West
			TR	Nottingham F.	12.54	1954-58	105		64	Ham U. player
			TR	Birmingham C.	10.59	1959	10		4	
			TR	West Ham U.	08.60					

Players Names	Birthplace	Date	Previous Club	League Club	Date Signed	Seasons Played	Apps	Sub	Gls	
BARRETT, John	Birmingham	26.03.31	JNRS	Aston Villa	07.49					(HB) E.YTH.INT
			TR	Scunthorpe U.	06.54	1954-55	17		0	
				Bradford P.A.	10.59					
BARRETT, Ken B.	Bromsgrove	05.05.38	Stoke Wks	Aston Villa	02.57	1958	5		3	(F)
			TR	Lincoln C.	06.59	1959-62	17		4	
BARRETT, Les	London	22.10.47	JNRS	Fulham	10.65	1965-76	421	2	74	(F) E.U23-1
			TR	Millwall	10.77	1977	8	/	1	
BARRETT, Mike J.	Bristol	12.09.59	Shirehampton	Bristol Rov.	10.79	1979-83	119	10	18	(F)
BARRETT, Ron H.	Maidenhead	22.07.39	Maidenhead	Grimsby T.	08.58	1958	3		0	(F)
BARRIE, John	Blantyre	17.05.25	Thorniewood	Cardiff C.	07.48					
			TR	Tranmere Rov.	11.48	1948-50	14		3	
BARRITT, Ron	Huddersfield	15.04.19	Wombwell	Doncaster Rov.	01.49	1948-49	13		6	(OR)
			Frickley Col.	Leeds U.	04.51	1951	6		1	
			TR	York C.	07.52	1952	5		0	
BARRON, Jim (Snr)	Blyth	19.07.13	Blackburn Rov.(*)	Darlington	06.46	1946	23		0	(G) d.
BARRON, Jim (Jnr)	Durham	19.10.43	Newcastle W.E.	Wolverhampton W.	11.61	1963-64	8	/	0	(G)
			TR	Chelsea	04.65	1965	1	/	0	
			TR	Oxford U.	03.66	1965-69	152	/	0	
			TR	Nottingham F.	07.70	1970-73	155	/	0	
			TR	Swindon T.	08.74	1974-76	79	/	0	
			TR	Peterborough U.	08.77	1977-80	21	/	0	
BARRON, Paul	London	16.09.53	Slough T.	Plymouth Arg.	07.76	1976	44	/	0	(G)
			TR	Arsenal	07.78	1978-79	8	/	0	
			TR	Crystal Palace	08.80	1980-82	90	/	0	
			TR	W.B.A.	12.82	1982-83	62	/	0	
BARRON, Roger W.	Northampton	30.06.47	APP	Northampton T.	07.65	1967-68	17	/	0	(G) Son of William
BARRON, William	Houghton-le-Spring	26.10.17	Charlton Ath.(*)	Northampton T.	*	1946-50	154		0	(FB) *Wolverhampton W. Lancs/Northants Cricketer
BARROW, Graham	Chorley	13.06.54	Altrincham	Wigan Ath.	07.81	1981-83	110	1	18	(M)
BARROWCLIFFE, Geoff	Ilkeston	18.10.31	Ilkeston T.	Derby Co.	10.50	1951-65	475	/	36	(FB)●
BARROWCLOUGH, Stewart	Barnsley	29.10.51	APP	Barnsley	11.69	1969	9	/	0	(M) E.U23-5
			TR	Newcastle U.	08.70	1970-77	201	18	20	
			TR	Birmingham C.	05.78	1978	26	3	2	
			TR	Bristol Rov.	07.79	1979-80	60	1	14	
			TR	Barnsley	02.81	1980-82	46	6	1	
			TR	Mansfield T.	08.83	1983	36	2	10	
BARRY, Kelvin A.	Woolwich	13.09.30	JNRS	Charlton Ath.	12.47	1952	3		0	(OL)
BARRY, Kevin	Newcastle	09.01.61	Nottingham F.(APP)	Darlington	09.79	1979-80	18	/	0	(G)
BARRY, Mike J.	Hull	22.05.53	APP	Huddersfield T.	06.70	1970-72	21	5	0	(F) W.U23-1
			TR	Carlisle U.	05.73	1973-76	73	8	10	
			TR	Bristol Rov.	09.77	1977-78	46	1	3	
BARRY, Patrick P.	Southampton	25.10.20		Southampton	+					(FB)
			Hyde U	Blackburn Rov.	05.48					
			TR	Bournemouth	05.50	1950	4		0	
BARRY, Roy	Edinburgh	19.09.42	Dunfermline	Coventry C.	10.69	1969-72	82	1	2	(CH)
			TR	Crystal Palace	09.73	1973-74	41	1	1	
BARTHOLOMEW, Henry	Motherwell	18.01.20	Motherwell	Exeter C.	05.47	1947-48	66		7	(HB)
			TR	Bournemouth	08.49					
			TR	Newport Co.	06.50	1950	3		0	
BARTLETT, Frank	Chester-le-Street	08.11.30	Blackhall C.W.	Barnsley	08.50	1952-62	296		68	(HB)
			TR	Halifax T.	07.63	1963	21		4	
BARTLETT, Fred L.	Reading	05.03.13	Q.P.R.(*)	Orient	*	1946-47	37		0	(CH)
BARTLETT, Gordon	London	03.12.55	APP	Portsmouth	12.73	1974	0	2	1	(F)
BARTLETT, Kevin F.	Portsmouth	12.10.62	APP	Portsmouth	11.80	1980-81	0	3	0	(F)
BARTLETT, Paul	Grimsby	17.01.60	APP	Derby Co.	12.77	1977-79	7	6	0	(F)
BARTLETT, Terry R.	Cleethorpes	30.08.48	JNRS	Grimsby T.	AM	1967	1	/	0	(OR)
BARTLEY, Anthony	Stalybridge	08.03.38	Stalybridge	Bolton W.	09.56					(OL)
			Stalybridge	Bury	11.58	1958-64	117		24	
			TR	Oldham Ath.	09.64	1964-65	48	2	13	
			TR	Chesterfield	07.66	1966	12	/	3	
BARTLEY, Danny R.	Paulton	03.10.47	APP	Bristol C.	10.64	1965-72	92	8	7	(F) E.YTH.INT.
			TR	Swansea C.	08.73	1973-79	195	4	8	
			TR	Hereford U.	03.80	1979-82	112	2	7	
BARTLEY, John R.	London	15.09.58	Welling U.	Millwall	10.80	1980-81	39	1	8	(F)
BARTON, Anthony E.	Sutton	08.04.37	JNRS	Fulham	05.54	1953-58	51		8	(OR) E.SCH.INT
			TR	Nottingham F.	12.59	1959-61	22		1	
			TR	Portsmouth	12.61	1961-66	129	1	34	
BARTON, C. Reg	Chester	04.03.42		Chester C.	07.63	1961-64	14		0	(G)
BARTON, D. Roger	Jump	25.09.46	APP	Wolverhampton W.	10.63					(F)
			TR	Lincoln C.	07.64	1964-65	38	/	0	
			TR	Barnsley	07.66	1966-68	52	2	3	

Players Names	Birthplace	Date	Previous Club	League Club	Date Signed	Seasons Played	Apps	Sub	Gls	
BARTON, David	B. Auckland	09.05.59	APP	Newcastle U.	05.77	1977-81	101	1	5	(D)
			L	Blackburn Rov.	08.82	1982	8	/	1	
			TR	Darlington	02.83	1982-83	49	/	3	
BARTON, Doug. J.	Islington	31.07.27	Fords Spts.	Reading	02.49	1950-52	10		1	(FB)
			TR	Newport Co.	01.53	1952-53	23		0	
BARTON, Frank	Barton	22.10.47	APP	Scunthorpe U.	08.65	1964-67	92	/	26	(F) E.YTH.INT
			TR	Carlisle U.	01.68	1967-71	161	4	22	
			TR	Blackpool	07.72	1972	18	/	1	
			TR	Grimsby T.	06.73	1973-75	123	/	15	
			TR	Bournemouth	06.76	1976	66	/	13	
			TR	Hereford U.	01.78	1977-78	22	/	3	
			TR	Bournemouth	09.78	1978	22	/	2	
BARTON, John B.	Wigan	27.04.42	JNRS	Preston N.E.	05.59	1958-65	48	/	0	(G)
			TR	Blackburn Rov.	06.66	1966-71	68	/	0	
BARTON, John S.	Birmingham	24.10.53	Worcester C.	Everton	12.78	1978-80	18	2	0	(D)
			TR	Derby Co.	03.82	1981-83	68	1	1	
BARTON, Ken R.	Caernarvon	20.09.37	JNRS	Tottenham H.	10.56	1960-63	4		0	(FB) W.SCH.INT.
			TR	Millwall	09.64					d.1982
			TR	Luton T.	12.64	1964	11		0	
BARTON, Les	Rochdale	20.03.20		Bolton W.	09.46					(HB)
			TR	New Brighton	08.49	1949-50	65		1	
BARTON, Peter	Barrow	03.04.51	APP	Barrow	04.69	1968	2	/	0	(G)
BARTRAM, Per	Denmark	08.01.44	Morton	Crystal Palace	08.69	1969	8	2	2	(IF)
BARTRAM, Sam	Simonside	22.01.14	Boldon CW	Charlton Ath.	*	1946-55	397		0	(G) d.1981●
BASEY, Phil	Cardiff	27.08.48	JNRS	Brentford	06.66	1966	2	/	0	(OL)
BASFORD, John	Crewe	24.07.25		Crewe Alex	04.48	1948-53	146		52	(IF)
			TR	Chester C.	01.54	1953	10		1	
BASON, Brian	Epsom	03.09.55	APP	Chelsea	09.72	1972-76	18	1	1	(M) E.SCH.INT
			TR	Plymouth Arg.	09.77	1977-80	127	3	10	
			TR	Crystal Palace	03.81	1980-81	25	2	0	
			L	Portsmouth	01.82	1981	9	/	0	
			TR	Reading	08.82	1982	41	/	0	
BASSETT, David	Watford	04.09.44	Walton & Hersham	Wimbledon	N/L	1977	35	/	0	(M) E.AMAT.INT
BASSETT, George R.	Birmingham	12.05.43		Coventry C.	08.61	1961	1		0	(F)
BASSETT, Graham R.	Sunderland	06.10.64	Sunderland(APP)	Hartlepool U.	08.83	1983	4	3	0	(F)
			TR	Burnley	03.84					
BASSETT, William	Brithdir	08.06.12	Cardiff C.(*)	Crystal Palace	+	1946-48	70		0	(WH)*Aberaman
BASSHAM, Alan J.	Kensington	03.10.33	JNRS	Brentford	10.51	1953-57	43		0	(FB) E.SCH.INT
BASTIN, Cliff S.	Exeter	14.03.12	Exeter C.(*)	Arsenal	*	1946	6		0	(OL)E-21/E.F.LGE REP/E.SCH.INT.
BATCH, Nigel	Huddersfield	09.11.57	Derby Co. (APP)	Grimsby T.	07.76	1976-83	274	/	0	(G)
BATCHELOR, Edward	Rugby	04.08.30	JNRS	Wolverhampton W.	10.47					(WH)
			TR	Swindon T.	08.50	1950-54	89		0	
BATEMAN, Albert	Wortley	13.06.24	Oxspring B.C.	Huddersfield T.	+	1946-48	73		14	(OR)
BATEMAN, Arthur	Audley	12.06.18		Crewe Alex.	+	1946	3		0	
BATEMAN, Colin	Hemel Hempstead	22.10.30	Hemel H.T.	Watford	03.53	1954-57	51		0	(FB) Brother of Ernie
BATEMAN, Ernie	Hemel Hempstead	05.04.29	Hemel H.T.	Watford	03.52	1955-56	22		0	(F)
BATER, Phil T.	Cardiff	26.10.55	APP	Bristol Rov.	10.73	1974-80	211	1	2	(D) W.U21-2
			TR	Wrexham	09.81	1981-82	73	/	1	
			TR	Bristol Rov.	09.83	1983	30	2	1	
BATES, Alan J.W.	Swindon	14.04.20	Chippenham	Swindon T.	11.52	1952	1		0	
BATES, Anthony N.	Blidworth	06.04.38	Blidworth Col	Notts. Co.	07.59	1958	1		0	(CF)
BATES, Brian F.	Stapleford	04.12.44		Notts.Co.	07.66	1963-68	125	3	15	(F)
			TR	Mansfield T.	07.69	1969	20	1	3	
BATES, Don	Brighton	10.05.33	Lewes	Brighton & H.A.	11.50	1957	20		1	(WH) Sussex Cricketer
BATES, Edric	Thetford	03.05.18	Norwich C.(*)	Southampton	*	1946-52	173		62	(IF)
BATES, Ernie	Huddersfield	10.06.35	Deighton YMCA	Huddersfield T.	08.55					(IL)
			TR	Bradford P.A.	05.57	1957-58	44		0	
BATES, George R.	Sheffield	21.11.23	Shardlows	Sheffield Wed.	+					
			TR	Darlington	07.46	1946	3		0	
BATES, John	Newcastle	28.04.42	Consett	Hartlepool U.	03.66	1965	11	/	0	(OR)
BATES, Keith	Huddersfield	01.09.33	Bradley Rgrs	Halifax T.	AM	1956	1		0	(IL)
BATES, Mark	Walsall	25.04.65	APP	Walsall	05.83	1982-83	6	/	0	(D)
BATES, Mick J.	Doncaster	19.09.47	APP	Leeds U.	09.64	1966-75	106	16	4	(M)
			TR	Walsall	06.76	1976-77	84	1	4	
			TR	Bradford C.	06.78	1978-79	54	2	1	
			TR	Doncaster Rov.	06.80	1980	3	1	0	

Players Names	Birthplace	Date	Previous Club	League Club	Date Signed	Seasons Played	Apps	Sub	Gls	
BATES, Phil (Chic)	W. Bromwich	28.11.49	Stourbridge	Shrewsbury T.	05.74	1974-77	160	/	45	(F)
			TR	Swindon T.	01.78	1977-79	50	13	15	
			TR	Bristol C.	03.80	1979-80	26	3	4	
			TR	Shrewsbury T.	12.80	1980-83	98	11	18	
BATES, William H.	Eaton Bray	13.01.22	Waterlows	Luton T.	+	1946	1		0	(OR)
				Watford	07.48	1948	13		1	
BATEY, N. Robert	Greenhead	18.10.12	Preston N.E.(*)	Leeds U.	+	1946	8		0	(WH) *Carlisle U.
			TR	Southport	06.47	1947	29		0	
BATHGATE, Syd	Aberdeen	20.12.19	Parkvale	Chelsea	09.46	1946-52	135		0	(FB) d.1962
BATSON, Brendon M.	W. Indies	06.02.53	APP	Arsenal	06.71	1971-73	6	4	0	(D)
			TR	Cambridge U.	01.74	1973-77	162	1	6	
			TR	W.B.A	02.78	1977-82	172	/	1	
BATT, Vic T.	Dorking	13.03.43	JNRS	Reading	08.61	1961-62	15		0	(F)
BATTY, Fred R.	W.Stanley	20.12.34	Stanley U.	Bradford P.A.	01.56	1955-58	56		0	(FB) Brother of Ron
BATTY, Mike	Manchester	10.07.44	APP	Manchester C.	07.61	1962-64	13		0	(WH)
BATTY, Paul W.	Edlington	09.01.64	APP	Swindon T.	01.82	1982-83	78	2	5	(M)
BATTY, Ron R.	Lanchester	05.10.25	East Tanfield Col.	Newcastle U.	+	1948-57	161		1	(FB) d.1971
			TR	Gateshead	03.58	1957-58	40		0	
BATTY, Stan G.	Tottenham	14.02.17	Aston Villa(*)	Newport Co.	+	1946-47	60		3	(IF) *Finchley
BATTYE, John	Scissett	19.05.26	JNRS	Huddersfield T.	+	1949-57	71		1	(FB)
			TR	York C.	07.59	1959	17		0	
BAUGH, John R.	Uganda	23.02.56	Luton T.(AM)	Exeter C.	07.77	1976-77	20	/	0	(G)
BAULD, Phil	Glasgow	20.09.29	Clyde	Plymouth Arg.	06.53					(HB)
			TR	Aldershot	07.54	1954	3		0	
BAVERSTOCK, Ray	Southall	03.12.63	APP	Swindon T.	12.81	1982	17	/	0	(D)
BAVIN, John	S.Ferriby	25.05.21	Arbroath	Tranmere Rov.	AM	1948	2		0	(FB)
BAXTER, Jim	Glasgow	29.09.39	Glasgow Rgrs.	Sunderland	05.65	1965-67	87	/	10	(WH)S-34/S.U23-1/
			TR	Nottingham F.	12.67	1967-68	47	1	3	S.F.LGE REP.●
BAXTER, Jim C.	Hill of Beath	08.11.25	Dunfermline	Barnsley	+	1946-51	224		56	(IF) Cousin of
			TR	Preston N.E.	07.52	1952-58	245		65	William C. Cunningham
			TR	Barnsley	07.59	1959	26		4	
BAXTER, Larry R.	Leicester	24.11.31		Northampton T.	03.52	1952-53	18		1	(IF)
			TR	Norwich C.	11.54	1954	5		0	
			TR	Gillingham	10.55	1955-57	50		7	
			TR	Torquay U.	09.57	1957-61	164		22	
BAXTER, Mike J.	Birmingham	30.12.56	APP	Preston N.E.	12.74	1974-80	209	1	17	(D)
			TR	Middlesborough	08.81	1981-83	122	/	7	
BAXTER, Paul A.	Hackney	22.04.64	Tottenham H.(APP)	Crystal Palace	09.81	1981	1	/	0	(D)
BAXTER, Robert D.	Redcar	04.02.37	Bo'Ness	Darlington	11.59	1959-61	67		30	(WH)
			TR	Brighton & H.A.	06.61	1961-66	195	/	6	
			TR	Torquay U.	07.67	1967-68	58	4	6	
			TR	Darlington	07.69	1969	41	1	1	
BAXTER, Stuart W.	Wolverhampton	16.08.53	APP	Preston N.E.	10.71	1972-74	34	7	1	(D) Son of William/
			Dundee	Stockport Co.	12.76	1976	4	/	0	Brother of Mike J.
BAXTER, William A.	Nottingham	06.09.17		Nottingham F.	*	1946	7		0	(CH)
			TR	Notts. Co.	10.46	1946-53	140		0	
BAXTER, William A.	Edinburgh	23.0439	Broxburn Ath.	Ipswich T.	06.60	1960-70	409	/	21	(CH)●
			TR	Hull C.	03.71	1970-71	20	1	0	
			L	Watford	10.71	1971	11	/	0	
			TR	Northampton T.	06.72	1972	41	/	4	
BAXTER, William	Methil	21.09.24	JNRS	Wolverhampton W.	+	1948-53	43		1	(WH)
			TR	Aston Villa	11.53	1953-56	98		6	
BAYLEY, Tom K.	Wednesbury	25.06.21		Wrexham	08.47	1947	6		0	(G) + Walsall
BAYLISS, Ron	Belfast	20.09.44		Reading	02.65	1964-67	34	1	1	(HB)
			TR	Bradford C.	07.68	1968-69	35	4	0	
BAYLY, Martin J.	Dublin	14.09.66	APP	Wolverhampton W.	APP	1983	7	/	0	(M)
BAYNHAM, John	Rhondda	21.04.18	Brentford(AM)	Orient	+	1946/47	60		7	(OL)
			TR	Swindon T.	08.48	1948	4		1	
BAYNHAM, Ron L.	Birmingham	10.06.29	Worcester C.	Luton T.	11.51	1952-64	388		0	(G)E-3/E'B'-1/E.F.LGE REP./1 outfield appearance.
BAZLEY, John A.	Runcorn	04.10.36	Bangor C.	Oldham Ath.	10.56	1956-61	130		19	(F)
BEACH, Doug F.	Watford	02.02.20	Sheffield Wed.(+)	Luton T.	+	1946	23		0	(FB)
			TR	Southend U.	07.47	1947-48	41		0	
BEACOCK, Gary	Scunthorpe	22.01.60	Sheffield U. (APP)	Grimsby T.	05.80	1980-82	10	6	0	(F)
			TR	Hereford U.	08.83	1983	13	1	3	
BEADNELL, William	Sunderland	24.01.33	Burnley(AM)	Chesterfield	06.50					(CF)
				Middlesbrough	05.53					
			TR	Southport	05.54	1954-55	63		8	
BEAL, Phil	Godstone	08.01.45	APP	Tottenham H.	01.62	1963-74	330	3	1	(D) E.YTH.INT.
			TR	Brighton & H.A.	07.75	1975-76	9	1	0	
			Memphis Rogues	Crewe Alex.	08.79	1979	4	/	0	

Players Names	Birthplace	Date	Previous Club	League Club	Date Signed	Seasons Played	Apps	Sub	Gls	
BEALE, John M.	Portsmouth	16.10.30	JNRS	Portsmouth	08.48	1951-52	14		1	(WH)
BEAMAN, Ralph W.	Willenhall	14.01.43		Walsall	12.60	1961	1		0	(F)
BEAMENT, Roger	Croxley	28.09.37	Croxley BC	Watford	AM	1956	1		0	(G)
BEAMISH, Ken	Bebbington	25.08.47	JNRS	Tranmere Rov.	07.66	1965-71	176	1	49	(F)
			TR	Brighton & H.A.	03.72	1971-73	86	10	27	
			TR	Blackburn Rov.	05.74	1974-76	86	/	18	
			TR	Port Vale	09.76	1976-78	84	1	29	
			TR	Bury	09.78	1978-79	49	/	20	
			TR	Tranmere Rov.	11.79	1979-80	57	2	15	
			TR	Swindon T.	08.81	1981	1	1	0	
BEAN, Alan	Doncaster	17.01.35	JNRS	Blackburn Rov.	04.52	1952-54	2		0	(HB)
BEAN, Alf S.	Lincoln	25.08.15	Lincoln Corries	Lincoln C.	*	1946-48	101		9	(WH)
BEAN, Ron E.	Crayford	10.04.26	Gravesend	Gillingham	N/L	1951	3		0	(G)
BEANEY, William R.	Southampton	29.05.54	APP	Southampton	06.72	1972-74	2	1	0	(FB)
BEANLAND, Anthony	Bradford	11.01.44	APP	Blackpool	01.62					(FB)
			TR	Southport	07.62	1962-65	142	/	3	
			TR	Southend U.	03.66	1965-66	57	/	3	
			TR	Wrexham	07.67	1967-68	84	/	5	
			TR	Bradford P.A.	06.69	1969	29	2	1	
BEARD, Malcom	Cannock	03.05.42	JNRS	Birmingham C.	05.59	1960-70	350	1	27	(WH) E.YTH.INT.
			TR	Aston Villa	07.71	1971-72	5	1	0	
BEARDALL, Jim T.	Whitefield	18.10.46		Blackburn Rov.	03.68	1967-68	4	2	1	(F)
			TR	Oldham Ath.	05.69	1969	21	1	10	
BEARDS, Alan	Normanton	19.10.32	Whitwood J.	Bolton W.	10.50	1950-53	14		2	(OL)
			TR	Swindon T.	03.54	1953-54	21		4	
			TR	Stockport Co.	07.55	1955	5		0	
BEARDSHAW, E. Colin	South Hetton	26.11.12	Stockport Co.(*)	Bradford C.	*					(FB) *Gateshead/d.1977
			Cork	Southport	10.48	1948-50	61		0	
BEARDSLEY, Don T.	Alyth	23.10.46	APP	Hull C.	11.64	1966-72	128	2	0	(FB)
			L	Doncaster Rov.	03.72	1971	10	/	0	
			TR	Grimsby T.	08.73	1973-74	65	/	0	
BEARDSLEY, Peter	Newcastle	18.01.61	Wallsend B.C.	Carlisle U.	08.79	1979-81	93	11	22	(F)
			Vancouver W.	Manchester U.	09.82					
			Vancouver W.	Newcastle U.	09.83	1983	34	1	20	
BEARPARK, Ian H.	Stonehouse	13.01.39	Stonehouse	Bristol Rov.	08.60	1960	2		0	(G)
BEARRYMAN, Henry	London	26.09.24	JNRS	Chelsea	+					(WH)
			TR	Colchester U.	N/L	1950-53	174		3	
BEASANT, David	Willesden	20.03.59	Edgware T.	Wimbledon	08.79	1979-83	174	/	0	(G)
BEASLEY, Albert	Stourbridge	27.07.13	Huddersfield T.(*)	Fulham	+	1946-49	153		13	(OL) E-1
			TR	Bristol C.	08.50	1950-51	66		5	*Stourbridge/Arsenal
BEASON, Malcolm L.	Dulwich	01.12.55	APP	Crystal Palace	08.73					(IF)
			TR	Orient	09.75	1975	0	1	0	
BEATON, William	Dunfermline	30.09.35	Dunfermline	Aston Villa	10.58	1958	1		0	(G)
BEATTIE, Andy	Aberdeen	11.08.13	Inverurie	Preston N.E.	*	1946	25		0	(FB) S-7/d.1983
BEATTIE, Andy H.	Liverpool	09.02.64	APP	Cambridge U.	02.82	1983	21	/	0	(M)
BEATTIE, Bradley	Torquay	20.08.57	APP	Torquay U.	APP	1973-74	2	2	0	(IF)
BEATTIE, George	Aberdeen	16.06.25		Southampton	08.47	1947	1		0	(IF)
			Gloucester C.	Newport Co.	09.50	1950-52	113		24	
			TR	Bradford P.A.	07.53	1953-54	53		16	
BEATTIE, Robert	Kilmarnock	24.01.16	Kilmarnock	Preston N.E.	*	1946-53	191		32	(IF) S-1
BEATTIE, Richard S.	Glasgow	24.10.36	Glasgow Celtic	Portsmouth	08.59	1959-61	122		0	(G)S.U23-3/S.F.LGE REP.
			TR	Peterborough U.	06.62	1962	10		0	
BEATTIE, T. Kevin	Carlisle	18.12.53	APP	Ipswich T.	07.71	1972-80	225	3	24	(D) E-9/E.YTH.INT.
			TR	Colchester U.	N/C	1982	3	1	0	
			TR	Middlesborough	11.82	1982	3	1	0	
BEATTIE, Thomas	Sheepwash	12.03.21	Morpeth T.	Gateshead	01.47	1946-47	20		4	(CF)
BEAUMONT, Alan	Liverpool	09.01.27		Chester C.	04.49	1948	5		0	(FB)
BEAUMONT, Frank	Barnsley	22.12.39	JNRS	Barnsley	12.57	1957-61	107		37	(IF) E.YTH.INT.
			TR	Bury	09.61	1961-63	68		12	
			TR	Stockport Co.	09.64	1964-65	52	3	4	
BEAVEN, Ken H.	Bovingdon	26.12.49	APP	Luton T.	APP	1967	1	/	0	(F)
BEAVON, Cyril	Barnsley	27.09.37	JNRS	Wolveshampton W.	12.54					(FB) E.YTH.INT.
			TR	Oxford U.	N/L	1962-68	271	2	7	Father of Stuart
BEAVON, David G.	Nottingham	08.12.61	APP	Notts. Co.	12.79	1980	5	/	0	(F)
			TR	Lincoln C.	11.81	1981-82	7	1	0	
			TR	Northampton T.	03.83	1982	2	/	0	
BEAVON, M. Stuart	Wolverhampton	30.11.58	APP	Tottenham H.	07.76	1978-79	3	1	0	(M) Son of Cyril
			L	Notts. Co.	12.79	1979	6	/	0	
			TR	Reading	07.80	1980-83	152	7	22	

Players Names	Birthplace	Date	Previous Club	League Club	Date Signed	Seasons Played	Apps	Sub	Gls	
BEBBINGTON, Peter	Oswestry	13.10.46	Oswestry T.	Leicester C.	10.65					(FB)
			TR	Barrow	11.67	1967-68	51	1	3	
			TR	Stockport Co.	07.69	1969	16	1	1	
BEBBINGTON, R. Keith	Nantwich	04.08.43	JNRS	Stoke C.	08.60	1962-65	99	2	17	(W)
			TR	Oldham Ath.	08.66	1966-71	237	/	38	
			TR	Rochdale	07.72	1972-73	57	3	6	
BECK, John A.	Edmonton	25.05.54	APP	Q.P.R.	05.72	1972-75	32	8	1	(M)
			TR	Coventry C.	06.76	1976-78	60	9	6	
			TR	Fulham	10.78	1978-81	113	1	13	
			TR	Bournemouth	09.82	1982-83	59	1	7	
BECKERS, Peter	Dundee	03.10.47	Craigmore Th.	Grimsby T.	11.64	1964	1		0	(F)
BECKETT, Roy W.	Stoke	20.03.28	JNRS	Stoke C.	+	1950-53	14		1	(HB)
BECKETT, William	Liverpool	04.07.15		Watford	+	1946	7		1	*New Brighton/
			TR	Northampton T.	06.47					Bradford C.
BEDFORD, N. Brian	Ferndale	24.12.33		Reading	04.54	1954	3		1	(CF)●
			TR	Southampton	07.55	1955	5		2	
			TR	Bournemouth	08.56	1956-58	75		32	
			TR	Q.P.R.	07.59	1959-64	258		163	
			TR	Scunthorpe U.	09.65	1965-66	37	/	23	
			TR	Brentford	09.66	1966	21	/	10	
BEDSON, Ray A.	Newcastle-under-Lyme	04.02.29		Crewe Alex.	08.52	1953	2		0	(HB)
BEE, Frank E.	Nottingham	23.01.27	Nottm.F.(AM)	Sunderland	06.47	1947	5		1	(W)
			TR	Blackburn Rov.	03.49	1948	4		0	
BEEBY, Oliver	Leicester	02.10.34		Leicester C.	05.53	1955	1		0	(FB) E.YTH.INT.
			TR	Notts.Co.	06.59	1959	13		0	
BEECH, Cyril	Tamworth	12.03.25	Merthyr Tydfil	Swansea C.	08.49	1949-53	133		34	(OL) Brother to Gilbert
			TR	Newport Co.	07.55	1955-56	39		8	
BEECH, Gilbert	Tamworth	09.01.22	Merthyr Tydfil	Swansea C.	11.49	1949-57	157		1	(FB)
BEECH, Harry	Kearsley	07.01.46	JNRS	Bolton W.	06.64	1965-66	14	1	0	(HB)
			TR	Southport	07.67	1967	2	2	0	
BEECH, Ken	Stoke	18.03.58	APP	Port Vale	01.76	1974-80	169	6	17	(M)
			TR	Walsall	08.81	1981-82	78	1	5	
			TR	Peterborough	08.83	1983	38	/	3	
BEEL, William J.L.	Leominster	23.08.45	APP	Shrewsbury T.	07.63	1962-63	3	/	0	(G)
				Birmingham C.	01.65	1964	1		0	
BEER, Alan	Swansea	11.03.50	West End	Swansea C.	02.71	1970-71	10	4	3	(F) W.AMAT.INT
			Weymouth	Exeter C.	11.74	1974-77	114	/	52	
BEER, Colin	Exeter	15.08.36	Exbourne	Exeter C.	05.56	1956-57	5		2	(CF)
BEESLEY, Colin	Stockton	06.10.51	APP	Sunderland	01.69	1968	0	3	0	(F)
BEESLEY, Mike	High Beech	10.06.42	JNRS	West Ham U.	10.59	1960	2		1	(IF)
			TR	Southend U.	08.62	1962-64	79		34	
			TR	Peterborough U.	07.65	1965-66	23	2	3	
			TR	Southend U.	08.67	1967-70	121	14	11	
BEESTON, Thomas	Gateshead	26.04.33		Gateshead	AM	1956	1		0	(G)
BEGG, Jim A.	Dumfries	14.02.30	Auchinleck T.	Liverpool	04.52					(G)
			TR	Bradford P.A.	08.53	1953-54	10		0	
BEIGHTON, Graham	Sheffield	01.07.39	Firthbrown Tools	Sheffield Wed.	03.59					(G)
			TR	Stockport Co.	06.61	1961-65	137	/	0	
			TR	Wrexham	01.66	1965	23	/	0	
			TR	Barnsley	10.67					
BEKKER, John	Cardiff	24.12.51	Bridgend T.	Swansea C.	07.75	1974-75	16	6	4	(F)
BELCHER, Jim. A.	Stepney	31.10.32	JNRS	Orient	03.50					(WH)
			Snowdown Col.	West Ham U.	08.52					
			TR	Crystal Palace	06.54	1954-57	128		20	
			TR	Ipswich T.	05.58	1958-59	27		0	
			TR	Brentford	07.61	1961	30		1	
BELFIELD, Mike R.	London	10.06.61		Wimbledon	03.80	1979-82	16	8	5	(F)
BELFITT, Rod	Doncaster	30.10.45	Retford T.	Leeds U.	07.63	1964-71	57	19	17	(IF)
			TR	Ipswich T.	11.71	1971-72	40	/	13	
			TR	Everton	11.72	1972	14	2	2	
			TR	Sunderland	10.73	1973-74	36	3	4	
			L	Fulham	11.74	1974	6	/	1	
			TR	Huddersfield T.	02.75	1974-75	34	/	8	
BELFON, Frankie	Wellingborough	18.02.65	JNRS	Northampton T.	04.82	1981-83	38	10	10	(F)
BELL, Alex S.	Ayr	13.03.31	Partick Th.	Exeter C.	08.54	1954-57	40		0	(G)
			TR	Grimsby T.	07.58	1958	8		0	
BELL, Andy D.	Taunton	06.05.56		Exeter C.	07.79	1979	2	1	0	(CF)
BELL, Anthony W.	North Shields	27.02.55	APP	Newcastle U.	03.73	1974	1	/	0	(G)
BELL, Arthur	Sedgefield	05.03.31	Hylton Col.J.	Barrow	08.50	1950	1		0	
BELL, Barry	Woolwich	09.04.41	JNRS	Millwall	10.58	1958	1		0	(CF)
BELL, Charlie	Sheffield	21.03.45	JNRS	Sheffield U.	01.64	1966	3	/	1	(WH)
			TR	Chesterfield	06.68	1968-72	149	3	11	

Players Names	Birthplace	Date	Previous Club	League Club	Date Signed	Seasons Played	Apps	Sub	Gls	
BELL, Colin	Heselden	26.02.46	Horden C.W.	Bury	07.63	1963-65	82	/	25	(M) E-48/E.U23-2/●
			TR	Manchester C.	03.66	1965-78	393	1	117	E.F.LGE.REP.
BELL, Colin	Horsley	24.03.26	Holbrook FC	Derby Co.	09.46	1950-54	78		2	(WH)
BELL, David	Corbridge	24.12.09	Derby Co.(*)	Ipswich T.	*	1946-49	146		1	(FB)*Newcastle U.
BELL, David J.	Carlisle	13.09.39	JNRS	Carlisle U.	03.57	1958	1		1	(HB)
BELL, Derek M.	Wyberton	30.10.56	Derby Co. (APP)	Halifax T.	05.75	1975-78	104	8	21	(F)
			L	Sheffield Wed.	03.76	1975	5	/	1	
			TR	Barnsley	10.78	1978-79	45	1	20	
			TR	Lincoln C.	11.79	1979-82	69	14	33	
			TR	Chesterfield	08.83	1983	15	2	3	
			TR	Scunthorpe U.	01.84	1983	19	/	5	
BELL, Derek S.	Newcastle	19.12.63	APP	Newcastle U.	12.81	1981-82	3	1	0	(M)
BELL, Eric J.	Bedington	13.02.22	Blyth Spartans	Blackburn Rov.	+	1946-56	323		9	(WH) E.F.LGE.REP.
BELL, Eric	Manchester	27.11.29		Bolton W.	11.49	1950-57	102		1	(WH)E'B'2/E.F.LGE.REP.
BELL, Ernie	Hull	22.07.18		Aldershot	+					(IF)*HullC/Mansfield T.
			TR	Hull C.	08.46	1946	5		1	d.1968
BELL, Gary	Stourbridge	04.04.47	Lower Gornal	Cardiff C.	02.66	1966-73	222	2	10	(D)
			L	Hereford U.	03.74	1973	8	/	0	
			TR	Newport Co.	08.74	1974-77	126	/	5	
BELL, George W.	South Shields	26.03.37	St. Marys B.C.	Doncaster Rov.	05.55	1955	1		0	(F)
			Frickley Col.	Cardiff C.	03.59					
BELL, Graham	Middleton	30.03.55	Chadderton	Oldham Ath.	12.73	1974-78	166	4	9	(M) E.YTH.INT.
			TR	Preston N.E.	03.79	1978-82	140	3	9	
			L	Huddersfield T.	11.81	1981	2	/	0	
			TR	Carlisle U.	08.83	1983	11	3	0	
			TR	Bolton W.	02.84	1983	20	/	1	
BELL, Harold	Liverpool	22.11.24	JNRS	Tranmere Rov.	+	1946-59	595		11	(CH)●
BELL, Henry D.	Sunderland	14.10.24	Hylton Col.	Middlesbrough	+	1946-54	289		9	(WH)
			TR	Darlington	09.55	1955-58	125		19	
BELL, Ian	Middlesbrough	14.11.58	APP	Middlesbrough	12.76	1977-80	10	/	1	(F)
			TR	Mansfield T.	07.81	1981-82	82	2	12	
BELL, Jackie	Evenwood	17.10.39	JNRS	Newcastle U.	11.56	1957-61	111		8	(WH)
			TR	Norwich C.	07.62	1962-64	48		3	
			TR	Colchester U.	06.65	1965	7	/	0	
BELL, Joe	Sunderland	28.07.24	Stockton	Chesterfield	05.46	1947-48	38		0	(FB)+Sunderland
			TR	Coventry C.	06.49	1949-51	10		0	
BELL, John A.	Edinburgh	25.04.36	Stirling A.	Swindon T.	07.60	1960-61	31		2	(HB)
BELL, John H.	Morpeth	29.08.19		Gateshead	+	1946-49	50		0	
BELL, Norman	Sunderland	16.11.55	AP.	Wolverhampton W.	11.73	1975-81	58	22	17	(CF)
			TR	Blackburn Rov.	11.81	1981-83	57	4	10	
BELL, Peter	Grangemouth	10.04.35	Gairdoch J.	Plymouth Arg.	07.54	1955	1		0	(HB)
BELL, Robert	Glasgow	20.03.35	Partick Th.	Plymouth Arg.	11.55	1955	1		1	(F) S.SCH.INT.
			Partick Th.	Carlisle U.	06.59	1959	1		0	
BELL, Robert C.	Cambridge	26.10.50	Tottenham H.(APP)	Ipswich T.	09.67	1968-71	32	/	1	(D)
			TR	Blackburn Rov.	09.71	1971	2	/	0	
			TR	Crystal Palace	09.71	1971-73	31	/	0	
			L	Norwich C.	02.72	1971	3	/	0	
			S. Africa	York C.	02.77	1976	5	/	0	
BELL, Robert Mc.	Ayr	16.09.34	Ayr U.	Watford	05.57	1957-64	269		2	(FB)
BELL, Sid E.	Stepney	08.01.20		Southend U.	+	1946-47	15	/	0	(LB)
BELL, Stan W.G.	West Ham	28.10.23		Southend U.	07.48	1948	3	/	0	
BELL, Steve	Middlesbrough	13.03.65	APP	Middlesbrough	05.82	1981-83	64	4	10	(F)E.YTH.INT.
BELL, Terry	Nottingham	01.08.44		Nottingham F.	08.64					(F)
			TR	Manchester C.	10.64					
			TR	Portsmouth	11.64					
			Nuneaton	Hartlepool U.	07.66	1966-69	113	6	34	
			TR	Reading	03.73	1969-72	82	5	20	
			TR	Aldershot	07.73	1973-77	112	12	49	
BELL, Tom A.	Crompton	30.12.23	Mossley	Oldham Ath.	12.46	1946-51	168		0	(FB) Father of Graham
			TR	Stockport Co.	08.52	1952	31		0	
			TR	Halifax T.	07.53	1953-55	117		1	
BELL, Tom H.	W. Stanley	14.06.24	Hammersmith U.	Millwall	AM	1948	1		0	
BELL, William G.	Manchester	16.06.53	Hyde U.	Rochdale	N/C	1974	5	1	0	(IF)
BELL, William J.	Johnstone	03.09.37	Queens Pk.	Leeds U.	07.60	1960-67	204	/	15	(FB)S-2/S.AMAT.INT.
			TR	Leicester C.	09.67	1967-68	49	/	0	
			TR	Brighton & H.A.	07.69	1969	44	/	1	
BELLAMY, Arthur	Blackhill	05.04.42	JNRS	Burnley	06.59	1962-71	205	12	30	(F)
			TR	Chesterfield	07.72	1972-75	133	/	12	
BELLAMY, Gary	Worksop	04.07.62	APP	Chesterfield	06.80	1980-83	105	3	1	(D)

Players Names	Birthplace	Date	Previous Club	League Club	Date Signed	Seasons Played	Apps	Sub	Gls	
BELLAS, William J.	Liverpool	21.05.25	Notts. Co.(+)	Nottingham F.	05.46					(CH)
			TR	Southport	10.48	1948-50	88		0	
			TR	Grimsby T.	07.51	1951	5		0	
BELLETT, Wally R.	Stratford	14.11.33	Barking	Chelsea	09.54	1955-58	35		1	(FB) E.YTH.INT
			TR	Plymouth Arg.	12.58	1958-59	41		1	
			Chelmsford C.	Orient	01.61					
			TR	Chester C.	07.61	1961	11		1	
			TR	Wrexham	07.62	1962	2		0	
			TR	Tranmere Rov.	07.63					
BELLIS, Alf	Ellesmere Port	08.10.20	Burnells IW	Port Vale	*	1946-47	55		14	(OL)
			TR	Bury	01.48	1947-50	95		18	
			TR	Swansea C.	08.51	1951-52	43		11	
			TR	Chesterfield	08.53	1953	13		3	
BELLIS, Tom G.	Mold	21.04.19		Wrexham	*	1946-48	81		1	
BELLOTTI, Derek C.	London	25.12.46	Bedford T.	Gillingham	07.66	1966-69	35	/	0	(G)
			TR	Charlton Ath.	10.70	1970-71	14	/	0	
			TR	Southend U.	11.70	1970-73	77	/	0	
			TR	Swansea C.	05.74	1974	19	/	0	
BEMROSE, Frank E.	Caistor	20.10.35	Caistor	Grimsby T.	AM	1958-60	2		0	(OL)
BENCE, Paul I.	Littlehampton	21.12.48	APP	Brighton & H.A.	05.67	1967	0	1	0	(D)
			TR	Reading	06.68	1968-69	12	1	2	
			TR	Brentford	07.70	1970-76	238	6	6	
			L	Torquay U.	11.76	1976	5	/	0	
BENJAFIELD, Brian	Barton-on-Sea	02.08.60		Bournemouth	01.79	1978	2	/	0	(M)
BENJAMIN, Ian T.	Nottingham	11.12.61	APP	Sheffield U.	05.79	1978-79	4	1	3	(M) E.YTH.INT.
			TR	W.B.A.	08.79	1980	1	1	0	
			TR	Peterborough U.	08.82	1982-83	77	3	14	
BENJAMIN, Tristran	W. Indies	01.04.57	APP	Notts. Co.	03.75	1974-83	208	15	4	(D) E.YTH.INT.
BENN, Alf	Leeds	26.01.26		Leeds U.	01.47					
			TR	Southport	07.48	1948	3		0	
			TR	Halifax T.	09.49					
BENNETT, Albert	Durham	16.07.44	Chester Moor	Rotherham U.	10.61	1961-64	108		64	(CF) E.U23-1/E.YTH.INT.
			TR	Newcastle U.	07.65	1965-68	85	/	22	
			TR	Norwich C.	02.69	1968-70	54	1	15	
BENNETT, Allan	Stoke	05.11.31	JNRS	Port Vale	05.49	1948-56	123		9	(OL) E.YTH.INT.
			TR	Crewe Alex.	09.57	1957	10		0	
BENNETT, David A.	Manchester	11.07.59	JNRS	Manchester C.	08.78	1978-80	43	9	9	(F)
			TR	Cardiff C.	09.81	1981-82	75	2	18	
			TR	Coventry C.	07.83	1983	32	2	6	
BENNETT, David M.	Southampton	05.03.39	JNRS	Arsenal	05.56					(F) E.SCH.INT.
			TR	Portsmouth	06.58					
			TR	Bournemouth	12.60	1960-61	12		2	
BENNETT, David P.	Oldham	26.04.60	Manchester C. (APP)	Norwich C.	08.78	1978-83	64	7	9	(F)
BENNETT, Des	Doncaster	30.10.63	APP	Doncaster Rov.	APP	1980-81	0	2	0	
BENNETT, Don	Wakefield	18.12.33	JNRS	Arsenal	08.51					(FB) Middlesex Cricketer/
			TR	Coventry C.	09.59	1959-61	73		0	E.YTH.INT
BENNETT, Edgar W.	Stoke	29.03.29	Vauxhall M.	Luton T.	09.52	1953	1		0	(OR)
BENNETT, Edward E.	Kilburn	22.08.25	Southall	Q.P.R.	AM	1948	2		0	(G) E.AMAT.INT.
			Southall	Watford	12.53	1953-55	81		0	
BENNETT, Gary E.	Manchester	04.12.61	Ashton U.	Manchester C.	09.79					(D)
			TR	Cardiff C.	09.81	1981-83	85	2	11	
BENNETT, George F.	Durham	16.03.38	JNRS	Burnley	04.55					(FB)
			TR	Barnsley	01.60	1959-60	24		0	
BENNETT, Harry	Liverpool	16.05.49	JNRS	Everton	03.67	1967	2	1	0	(HB)
			TR	Aldershot	01.71	1970-72	77	12	7	
			TR	Crewe Alex.	07.73	1973	28	2	1	
BENNETT, John	Rotherham	15.05.49	APP	Rotherham U.	APP	1965	1	/	0	(OL)
BENNETT, John G.	Liverpool	21.03.46	APP	Liverpool	04.63					(HB)
			TR	Chester C.	06.66	1966-68	72	3	0	
BENNETT, Ken E.	Wood Green	02.10.21	Tottenham H.(+)	Southend U.	06.46	1946-47	50		10	(IF)
			TR	Bournemouth	06.48	1948	19		1	Brother of Les
			TR	Brighton & H.A.	06.50	1950-52	101		37	
			TR	Crystal Palace	07.53	1953	17		2	
BENNETT, Lawson H.	Darwen	28.08.38	Darwen	Accrington St.	05.59	1958-60	29		2	(F)
BENNETT, Les D.	Wood Green	10.01.18	JNRS	Tottenham H.	+	1946-54	272		102	(IF)
			TR	West Ham U.	12.54	1954-55	26		3	
BENNETT, Martyn	Birmingham	04.08.61	APP	W.B.A	08.78	1978-83	95	1	4	(D) E.SCH.INT
BENNETT, Mike	Bolton	24.12.62	APP	Bolton W.	01.80	1979-82	62	3	1	(D)E.YTH.INT
			TR	Wolverhampton W.	06.83	1983	6	/	0	
			TR	Cambridge U.	03.84	1983	11	/	0	
BENNETT, Paul	Liverpool	30.01.61	Everton (APP)	Port Vale	09.78	1980-82	28	2	1	(M)

Players Names	Birthplace	Date	Previous Club	League Club	Date Signed	Seasons Played	Career Record Apps	Sub	Gls	
BENNETT, Paul R.	Southampton	04.02.52	APP	Southampton	11.69	1971-75	116	/	1	(D)
			TR	Reading	07.76	1976-78	105	/	3	
			TR	Aldershot	08.79	1979-81	112	1	2	
BENNETT, Peter	Plymouth	29.11.39		Exeter C.	08.59	1959-60	6		5	(F)
BENNETT, Peter L.	Hillingdon	24.06.46	APP	West Ham U.	07.63	1963-70	38	4	3	(M) E.SCH.INT.
			TR	Orient	10.70	1970-78	195	4	13	
BENNETT, Richard	Northampton	16.02.45	Wellingborough	Peterborough U.	08.63	1963-64	4		0	(WH) E.YTH.INT.
BENNETT, Robert	Harrow	29.12.51	Staines	Southend U.	06.72	1972	1	/	0	(CF)
			L	Scunthorpe U.	10.73	1973	2	1	0	
BENNETT, Ron	Hinckley	08.05.27		Wolverhampton W.	+					(F)
			TR	Portsmouth	07.48	1949-51	8		1	
			TR	Crystal Palace	01.52	1951-52	27		5	
			TR	Brighton & H.A.	07.53	1953	3		0	
BENNETT, Stan T.	Birmingham	18.09.44	APP	Walsall	09.62	1963-74	377	8	12	(CH)
BENNETT, Tom	Chesterfield	27.11.25		Chesterfield	06.46					(G)
			TR	Mansfield T.	08.47	1947	1		0	
BENNETT, Walter H.	Doncaster	15.12.18	Mexborough	Barnsley	*	1946-47	37		22	(F)
			TR	Doncaster Rov.	01.48	1947-49	39		14	
			TR	Halifax T.	01.50	1949	7		1	
BENNING, Mike D.	Watford	03.02.38	JNRS	Watford	09.56	1958-61	98		11	(F)
BENNION, John R.	Burnley	02.04.34		Burnley	01.52					(HB)
			TR	Hull C.	06.57	1957-59	35		1	
			TR	Stockport Co.	07.60	1960	26		1	
			TR	Barrow	07.61	1961-62	16		0	
BENNION, Stan	Chester	09.02.38		Wrexham	10.59	1959-62	52		18	(F)
			TR	Chester C.	06.63	1963	19		3	
BENNYWORTH, Ian R.	Hull	15.01.62	APP	Hull C.	01.80	1979	1	/	0	(D)
BENSKIN, Dennis W.	Nottingham	28.05.47	JNRS	Notts.Co.	AM	1965	4	/	1	(OL)
BENSON, Joe R.	Misterton	07.01.33		Scunthorpe U.	09.55	1955	2		0	
BENSON, John	Arbroath	23.12.42	JNRS	Manchester C.	07.61	1961-63	44	/	0	(D)
			TR	Torquay U.	06.64	1961-70	233	7	7	
			TR	Bournemouth	10.70	1970-73	85	8	0	
			TR	Exeter C.	03.73	1972	4	/	0	
			TR	Norwich C.	12.73	1973-74	29	2	0	
			TR	Bournemouth	01.75	1974-78	56	1	0	
BENSON, Ron	Acomb	26.03.25		York C.	10.47	1949	21		3	
BENT, Geoff	Salford	27.09.32	JNRS	Manchester U.	04.51	1954-56	14		0	(FB) d.1958
BENT, Graham W.	Ruabon	06.10.45	Aston Villa(APP)	Wrexham	12.63	1963-64	10		2	(F) W.SCH.INT
BENTALL, Charles E.	Helmsley	28.01.22		York C.	+	1946	1		0	d.1947
BENTHAM, Alan	Liverpool	12.09.40	JNRS	Everton	11.57					(FB)E.SCH.INT
			TR	Southport	06.60	1960-61	25		1	
BENTHAM, John J.	Pontefract	03.03.63	APP	York C.	03.81	1981	22	1	0	(D)
BENTHAM, Stan J.	Leigh	17.03.15	Wigan Ath.	Everton	*	1946-48	60		4	(IF)
BENTLEY, Alf	Aylesham	28.10.31	Snowdown Col.	Coventry C.	10.55	1955-56	29		0	(G)
			TR	Gillingham	08.58	1958-61	13		0	
BENTLEY, Anthony	Stoke	20.12.39	JNRS	Stoke C.	12.56	1958-60	44		17	(F)
			TR	Southend U.	05.61	1961-70	378	3	14	
BENTLEY, David A.	Worksop	30.05.50	APP	Rotherham U.	07.67	1966-73	243	7	13	(F)
			L	Mansfield T.	09.72	1972	1	3	1	
			TR	Chesterfield	06.74	1974-76	53	2	1	
			TR	Doncaster Rov.	08.77	1977-79	87	2	4	
BENTLEY, John	Liverpool	17.02.42	JNRS	Everton	11.59	1960	1		0	(F)
			TR	Stockport Co.	05.61	1961-62	49		5	
BENTLEY, Keith	Hull	27.07.36		Hull C.	11.57	1957	4		0	(IF)
BENTLEY, Roy F.T.	Bristol	17.05.24	JNRS	Bristol C.	+					(CF)E-12/E'B'-1/
			TR	Newscastle U.	06.46	1946-47	48		21	E.F.LGE REP.●
			TR	Chelsea	01.48	1947-56	324		128	
			TR	Fulham	09.56	1959-60	143		23	
			TR	Q.P.R	06.61	1961-62	45		0	
BENTLEY, William J.	Stoke	21.10.47	APP	Stoke C.	10.64	1965-68	44	4	1	(D) E.YTH.INT./E.SCH.INT
			TR	Blackpool	01.69	1968-76	289	7	10	
			TR	Port Vale	07.77	1977-79	92	3	0	
BERESFORD, John T.	Sunderland	02.01.43		Hartlepool U.	AM	1966	3	/	0	(WH)
BERESFORD, John W.	Sheffield	25.01.46	APP	Chesterfield	01.63	1962-64	53		11	(HB)
			TR	Notts.Co.	05.65	1965-66	49	1	13	
BERESFORD, Philip	Hollingwood	30.11.44		Chesterfield	01.64	1963	7		3	(F)
BERESFORD, Reg	Chesterfield	29.06.25	Hardwick Col.	Notts.Co.	+	1946	10		1	(OR)
BERESFORD, Reg H.	Walsall	03.06.21		Aston Villa	*					
			TR	Birmingham C.	09.46					
			TR	Crystal Palace	08.48	1948	7		1	
BERMINGHAM, Alan	Liverpool	11.09.44	Skelmersdale	Wrexham	06.67	1967-70	115	3	2	(FB)

Players Names	Birthplace	Date	Previous Club	League Club	Date Signed	Seasons Played	Apps	Sub	Gls	
BERNARD, Mike P.	Shrewsbury	10.01.48	APP	Stoke C.	01.65	1965-71	124	12	6	(M) E.U23-3/E.YTH.INT
			TR	Everton	04.72	1972-76	139	8	8	
			TR	Oldham Ath.	07.77	1977-78	6	/	0	
BERRY, Dave	Newton-le-Willows	01.06.45	JNRS	Blackpool	09.63					(HB)
			TR	Chester C.	07.64	1966	0	1	0	
BERRY, George F.	West Germany	19.11.57	APP	Wolverhampton W.	12.75	1976-81	124	/	4	(D) W-5
			TR	Stoke C.	08.82	1982-83	35	4	5	
BERRY, John A.	Manchester	27.08.65		Torquay U.	N/C	1983	1	/	0	(D)
BERRY, Johnny J.	Aldershot	01.06.26	Aldershot YMCA	Birmingham C.	+	1947-51	103		5	(OR)E-4/E'B'-1/
			TR	Manchester U.	08.51	1951-57	247		37	E.F.LGE REP.
BERRY, Les	Plumstead	04.05.56	APP	Charlton Ath.	03.74	1975-83	320	5	11	(D)
BERRY, Mike J.	Newbury	14.02.55	APP	Southampton	02.73	1974	2	/	0	(FB)
BERRY, Neil	Edinburgh	06.04.63	APP	Bolton W.	03.81	1981-83	19	7	0	(D)
BERRY, Norman	Bury	15.08.22		Bury	AM	1946-47	23		6	
BERRY, Paul	Grays	15.11.35	JNRS	Chelsea	04.53	1956-57	3		0	(CH)
BERRY, Paul A.	Oxford	08.04.58	APP	Oxford U.	07.77	1976-81	98	12	20	(F)
BERRY, Peter	Aldershot	20.09.33	JNRS	Crystal Palace	08.51	1953-57	151		25	(F) Brother of Johnny
			TR	Ipswich T.	05.58	1958-59	38		6	
BERRY, Steve A.	Liverpool	04.04.63	APP	Portsmouth	01.81	1981-82	26	2	2	(M)
			L	Aldershot	03.84	1983	5	2	0	
BERRY, Tom	Clayton-le-Moor	31.03.22	Gt.Harwood	Hull C.	05.47	1947-57	276		1	(CH)
BERRY, William	Mansfield	04.04.34	Langwith Col.	Mansfield T.	03.56	1956	10		1	(F)
BERTOLINI, Jack	Stirling	21.03.34	Stirling Alb.	Workington	01.53	1952-57	181		35	(FB)
			TR	Brighton & H.A.	07.58	1958-65	258	/	12	
BERTRAM, Jim T.	Whitehaven	03.02.53	Carlisle U.(APP)	Workington	AM	1971	0	1	0	
BERTSCHIN, Christian	Kensington	07.09.24	Ilford	Reading	08.47	1947-48	12		1	
BERTSCHIN, Keith	Enfield	25.08.56	Barnet	Ipswich T.	10.73	1975-76	19	13	8	(F)E.U21-3/E.YTH.INT
			TR	Birmingham C.	07.77	1977-80	113	5	29	
			TR	Norwich C.	08.81	1981-83	107	2	27	
BESAGNI, Remo	Italy	22.04.35		Crystal Palace	10.52	1952	2		0	(F)
BEST, Clyde	Bermuda	24.02.51	Bermuda	West Ham U.	03.69	1969-75	178	8	47	(CF)
BEST, David	Wareham	06.09.43	JNRS	Bournemouth	10.60	1960-66	230	/	0	(G)●
			TR	Oldham Ath.	09.66	1966-68	98	/	0	
			TR	Ipswich T.	10.68	1968-73	168	/	0	
			TR	Portsmouth	02.74	1973-74	53	/	0	
			TR	Bournemouth	07.75	1975	2	/	0	
BEST, George	Belfast	22.05.46	JNRS	Manchester U.	05.63	1963-73	361	/	137	(F)NI-37●
			L	Stockport Co.	11.75	1975	3		2	
			L.Angeles Aztecs	Fulham	09.76	1976-77	42	/	8	
			Golden Bay	Bournemouth	03.83	1982	5	/	0	
BEST, John B.	Liverpool	11.07.40	JNRS	Liverpool	05.58					(HB)
			TR	Tranmere Rov.	08.60	1960	7		0	
BEST, Tom H.	Milford Haven	23.12.20	Merthyr Tydfil	Chester C.	07.47	1947-48	40		14	(F)
			TR	Cardiff C.	10.48	1948-49	28		10	
			TR	Q.P.R.	12.49	1949	12		3	
BEST, William	Glasgow	07.09.43	Pollok	Northampton T.	07.62	1963-67	38	2	11	(F)
			TR	Southend U.	01.68	1967-72	225	1	106	
			TR	Northampton T.	09.73	1974-77	201	2	37	
BESWICK, Ivan	Manchester	02.01.36		Manchester U.	10.54					(FB)
			TR	Oldham Ath.	08.58	1958-60	46		0	
BESWICK, Keith	Cardiff	03.02.43	Cardiff Corries	Millwall	01.62	1962	12		0	(G)
			TR	Newport Co.	08.64	1964-66	58	/	0	
BETMEAD, Harry	Grimsby	11.04.12	Ray Cross	Grimsby T.	*	1946	34		0	(CH) E-1
BETT, Fred	Scunthorpe	05.12.20	Scunthorpe U.	Sunderland	*					(F)
			TR	Coventry C.	05.46	1946-48	28		11	
			TR	Lincoln C.	09.48	1948	14		2	
BETTANY, Colin D.	Leicester	15.06.32	Leicester C.(AM)	Crewe Alex.	08.53	1953-54	29		6	(FB)
			TR	Birmingham C.	06.55					
			TR	Torquay U.	04.57	1957-65	335	/	4	
BETTANY, John W.	Laughton	16.12.37	Thurcroft	Huddersfield T.	09.60	1960-64	59		6	(WH)
			TR	Barnsley	03.65	1964-69	194	4	24	
			TR	Rotherham U.	06.70	1970	16	/	1	
BETTERIDGE, Ray M.	Redditch	11.08.24	Loughboro College	W.B.A.	11.48	1949-50	5		0	(IF)
			TR	Swindon T.	07.51	1951-53	108		23	
			TR	Chester C.	03.54	1953	8		1	
BETTS, Anthony	Derby	31.10.53		Aston Villa	03.72	1974	1	3	0	(F) E.YTH.INT.
			L	Southport	12.74	1974	8	1	1	
			TR	Port Vale	10.75	1975	1	/	0	

Players Names	Birthplace	Date	Previous Club	League Club	Date Signed	Seasons Played	Apps	Sub	Gls	
BETTS, Eric	Coventry	27.07.25		Mansfield T.	+	1946	19		5	(OL)
			TR	Coventry C.	08.47					
			Nuneaton	Walsall	05.49	1949	30		3	
			TR	West Ham U.	04.50	1950	3		1	
			Nuneaton	Rochdale	10.51	1951-52	52		7	
			TR	Crewe Alex.	02.53	1952-53	25		5	
			TR	Wrexham	10.53	1953-55	53		21	
			TR	Oldham Ath.	02.56	1955-56	26		5	
BETTS, J. Barry	Barnsley	18.09.32	JNRS	Barnsley	11.50	1952-56	59		0	(FB)
			TR	Stockport Co.	11.57	1957-59	112		3	
			TR	Manchester C.	06.60	1960-63	101		5	
			TR	Scunthorpe U.	08.64	1964	7		0	
BETTS, Mike	Barnsley	21.09.56	APP	Blackpool	10.73	1975	4	3	0	(D) Twin brother of Stuart
			Northwich Vic.	Bury	N/C	1980	1	/	0	
BETTS, Stuart	Barnsley	21.09.56	APP	Blackpool	10.73					(F)
				Halifax T.	09.76					
			TR	Crewe Alex.	N/C	1977	2	/	0	
BEVAN, Brian E.	Exeter	20.03.37	Bridgwater	Bristol C.	02.56	1957-59	2		0	(F)
			TR	Carlisle U.	03.60	1959-60	27		2	
			TR	Millwall	02.61	1960	3		0	
BEVAN, Paul P.	Shrewsbury	20.10.52	APP	Shrewsbury T.	10.70	1970-72	67	5	1	(D)
			TR	Swansea C.	08.73	1973-74	77	2	5	
			TR	Crewe Alex.	07.75	1975-79	170	2	7	
BEVANS, Stan	Kingsley	16.04.34	JNRS	Stoke C.	04.51	1950-54	15		1	(F)
BEVIS, David R.	Southampton	27.06.42	JNRS	Ipswich T.	08.59	1963-65	6	/	0	(G)
BEVIS, William	Warsash	29.09.18	Portsmouth(*)	Southampton	*	1946	14		6	(OR) *Gosport Bor.
BEWLEY, David G.	Bournemouth	22.09.20	Wolverhampton W. (AM)	Fulham	+	1946-48	15		1	(FB) E.SCH.INT.
			TR	Reading	03.50	1949-50	11		1	
			TR	Fulham	11.50					
			TR	Watford	05.53	1953-55	113		1	
BEYNON, Edgar R.	Swansea	03.05.40		Wrexham	07.59	1959	1		0	(FB)
BEYNON, Edwin, R	Aberdare	17.11.24		Wrexham	01.47	1946-51	72		22	(FB) W.SCH.INT.
			TR	Shrewsbury T.	10.51	1951-54	91		6	
BICKERSTAFFE, John	St. Helens	08.11.18	Peasley Cross	Bury	+	1946-48	27		0	
			TR	Lincoln C.	12.48	1948-50	12		0	
			TR	Halifax T.	09.51	1951-52	37		0	
BICKLE, Mike	Plymouth	25.01.44	St. Austell	Plymouth Arg.	12.65	1965-71	170	9	71	(F)
			TR	Gillingham	11.71	1971-72	32	/	7	
BICKLES, David	West Ham	06.04.44	APP	West Ham U.	07.61	1963-66	24	1	0	(HB) E.YTH.INT.
			TR	Crystal Palace	10.67					
			TR	Colchester U.	09.68	1968-69	68	/	3	
BICKNELL, Jack	Edington	16.12.31	Retford T.	Walsall	02.54	1953	3		0	(IL)
BICKNELL, Charlie	New Topton	06.11.05	Bradford C.(*)	West Ham U.	*	1946	19		1	(FB) *Chesterfield
BICKNELL, Roy	Doncaster	19.02.26	JNRS	Wolverhampton W.	+					(CH)
			TR	Charlton Ath.	05.47	1947-48	7		0	
			TR	Bristol C.	06.49	1949-50	21		0	
			TR	Colchester U.	06.52	1952-53	25		0	
BICKNELL, Steve J.	Rugby	28.11.59	APP	Leicester C.	12.76	1976	6	1	0	(M)
			TR	Torquay U.	08.78	1978	0	3	0	
BIELBY, Paul A.	Darlington	24.11.56	APP	Manchester U.	11.73	1973	2	2	0	(M)E.YTH.INT.
			TR	Hartlepool U.	11.75	1975-77	74	19	8	
			TR	Huddersfield T.	08.78	1978	29	2	5	
BIELBY, Terry	Doncaster	24.11.43	JNRS	Doncaster Rov.	01.61	1960	1		0	(FB)
BIGGINS, Brian	Ellesmere Port	19.05.40	JNRS	Chester C.	06.57	1957-58	5		0	(G)
BIGGINS, Graham W.	Chapeltown	10.03.58	Rotherham U.(AM)	Doncaster Rov.	07.77	1977	2	/	0	(G)
BIGGINS, Steve J.	Walsall	20.06.54	Hednesford	Shrewsbury T.	12.77	1977-81	140	6	41	(F)
			TR	Oxford U.	07.82	1982-83	43	9	20	
BIGGINS, Wayne	Sheffield	20.11.61	APP	Lincoln C.	11.79	1980	8	/	1	(F)
			Matlock	Burnley	02.84	1983	20	/	8	
BIGGS, Alf G.	Bristol	08.02.36	JNRS	Bristol Rov.	02.53	1953-60	214		74	(CF)●
			TR	Preston N.E.	07.61	1961-62	49		22	
			TR	Bristol C.	10.62	1962-67	210	/	100	
			TR	Walsall	03.68	1967-68	23	1	9	
			TR	Swansea C.	11.68	1968	16	/	4	
BIGGS, Anthony	Greenford	17.04.36	Hounslow	Arsenal	08.56	1957-58	4		1	(CF) E.AMAT.INT.
			TR	Orient	12.58	1958-59	4		1	
BILCLIFF, Ray	Blaydon	24.05.31	Spen. Jnrs	Middlesbrough	05.49	1951-60	182		0	(FB)
			TR	Hartlepool U.	01.61	1960-63	118		0	
BILEY, Alan	Leighton Buzzard	26.02.57	Luton T.(APP)	Cambridge U.	07.75	1975-79	160	5	75	(F)
			TR	Derby Co.	01.80	1979-80	47	/	19	
			TR	Everton	07.81	1981	16	3	3	
			L	Stoke C.	03.82	1981	8	/	1	
			TR	Portsmouth	08.82	1982-83	83	/	39	
BILL, Roger J.	Creswell	17.05.44	Chelsea (AM)	Reading	09.62	1962	4		0	(OR)

Players Names	Birthplace	Date	Previous Club	League Club	Date Signed	Seasons Played	Apps	Sub	Gls	
BILLINGHAM, John	Daventry	03.12.14	Bristol C.(*)	Burnley	*	1946-48	77		28	(CF) *Northampton T.
			TR	Carlisle U.	09.49	1949-50	64		17	
			TR	Southport	03.51	1950-54	150		37	
BILLINGHAM, Peter A.	Pensnett	08.10.38	JNRS	Walsall	10.55	1955-59	98		9	(WH)
			TR	W.B.A.	05.60	1960	7		0	
BILLINGS, John	Doncaster	30.03.44	JNRS	Doncaster Rov.	05.61	1962-64	18		4	(F)
BILLINGTON, Brian	Leicester	28.04.51	Leicester C.(AM)	Notts.Co.	10.69	1969	4	3	0	(F)
BILLINGTON, Charlie	Chesterfield	08.11.27		Aldershot	12.46	1946-55	210		11	(CH)
			TR	Norwich C.	01.56	1955-56	22		0	
			TR	Watford	07.57	1957	14		0	
			TR	Mansfield T.	06.58	1958	1		0	
BILLINGTON, Hugh J.R.	Ampthill	24.02.16	Waterlows	Luton T.	*	1946-47	60		35	(CF)
				Chelsea	03.48	1947-50	83		28	
BILLINGTON, Stan	Wallasey	23.02.37	JNRS	Everton	06.55					(HB) E.YTH.INT.
			TR	Tranmere Rov.	07.60	1960-63	93		0	
BILLINGTON, Wilf F.	Blackburn	28.01.30		Blackburn Rov.	04.48					(G)
			TR	Workington	07.54	1954-57	52		0	
BIMPSON, J. Louis	Rainford	14.05.29	Burscough	Liverpool	01.53	1952-59	96		37	(CF)
			TR	Blackburn Rov.	11.59	1959-60	22		5	
			TR	Bournemouth	02.61	1960	11		1	
			TR	Rochdale	08.61	1961-62	54		15	
BINCH, David	Doncaster	10.05.56		Doncaster Rov.	07.76	1975-76	3	2	0	(D)
BINES, Henry M.	Cardiff	17.05.30		Swindon T.	08.50	1950-51	6		0	(HB)
BING, Doug	Broadstairs	27.10.28	Margate	West Ham U.	01.51	1951-54	28		3	(OR)
BING, Tommy	Broadstairs	24.11.31	Margate	Tottenham H.	09.54	1957	1		0	(F)
BINGHAM, John G.	Ripley	23.09.49	Charlton Ath.(APP)	Manchester C.	10.67					(W)
			TR	Oldham Ath.	07.69	1969	16	1	3	
			TR	Mansfield T.	08.70	1970-71	18	3	0	
			L	Chester C.	03.72	1971	7	/	1	
			TR	Stockport Co.	07.72	1972	16	4	3	
BINGHAM, William L.	Belfast	05.08.31	Glentoran	Sunderland	11.50	1950-57	206		45	(W)N.I.-56/IRISH LGE REP.●
			TR	Luton T.	07.58	1958-60	87		27	
			TR	Everton	10.60	1960-62	86		25	
			TR	Port Vale	08.63	1963-64	40		6	
BINGHAM, William P.	Swindon	12.07.22		Swindon T.	08.46	1946-47	20		0	
BINGLEY, Walter	Sheffield	17.04.30	Eccleshall M.W.	Bolton W.	04.48	1949-54	6		0	(FB)
			TR	Sheffield Wed.	05.55	1955-57	38		0	
			TR	Swindon T.	01.58	1957-59	101		0	
			TR	York C.	08.60	1960-62	130		5	
			TR	Halifax T.	07.63	1963-64	63		1	
BINKS, Martin J.	Romford	15.09.53	Orient(APP)	Colchester U.	05.72	1972	10	/	0	(HB)
			TR	Cambridge U.	01.73	1972	1	/	0	
BINNEY, Fred	Plymouth	12.08.46	Launceston	Torquay U.	10.66	1967-69	24	10	10	(F)
			TR	Exeter C.	02.69	1968-73	177	/	90	
			TR	Brighton & H.A.	05.74	1974-76	68	2	35	
			TR	Plymouth Arg.	10.77	1977-79	67	4	39	
			TR	Hereford U.	01.80	1979-81	21	6	6	
BINNIE, Laurie	Falkirk	17.12.17	Camelon J.	Chesterfield	+					(WH)
			TR	Mansfield T.	11.46	1946	19		0	
BINNS, Eric	Halifax	13.08.24	Huddersfield T.(AM)	Halifax T.	05.46	1946	6		1	(FB)
			Goole T.	Burnley	03.49	1952-54	15		0	
			TR	Blackburn Rov.	05.55	1955-56	23		0	
BIRBECK, Joe	Gateshead	15.04.32	Evenwood	Middlesbrough	04.53	1953-58	38		0	(LH)
			TR	Grimsby T.	07.59	1959	18		0	
BIRBECK, John D.	Lincoln	01.10.32	Spilsby F.C.	Lincoln C.	01.52	1954	2		0	(FB)
BIRBECK, Ken	Manchester	14.05.28		Accrington St.	AM	1948	1		0	d.1978
BIRCH, Alan	W. Bromwich	12.08.56	APP	Walsall	08.73	1972-78	158	13	23	(M)
			TR	Chesterfield	07.79	1979-80	90	/	35	
			TR	Wolverhampton W.	08.81	1981	13	2	0	
			TR	Barnsley	02.82	1981-82	43	1	11	
			TR	Chesterfield	08.83	1983	30	2	5	
			TR	Rotherham U.	03.84	1983	14	/	10	
BIRCH, Brian	Salford	18.11.31	JNRS	Manchester U.	05.49	1949-51	11		4	(IF) E.YTH.INT.
			TR	Wolverhampton W.	03.52	1951	3		1	
			TR	Lincoln C.	12.52	1952-54	56		15	
			TR	Barrow	06.56	1956-58	60		27	
			TR	Exeter C.	09.58	1958-59	19		2	
			TR	Oldham Ath.	01.60	1959-60	35		10	
			TR	Rochdale	03.61	1960	10		0	
BIRCH, Brian	Southport	09.04.38	JNRS	Bolton W.	04.55	1954-63	165		23	(OR) E.YTH.INT./E.SCH.INT.
			TR	Rochdale	07.64	1964-65	60	1	6	
BIRCH, Cliff	Newport	01.09.28	Ebbw Vale	Norwich C.	12.46	1949	5		3	(OR)
			TR	Newport Co.	10.50	1950-53	143		28	
			TR	Colchester U.	06.54	1954	12		3	
BIRCH, Harry	Crieff	11.01.14	Bangor(NI)	Barrow	+	1946	26		2	(FB)

Players Names	Birthplace	Date	Previous Club	League Club	Date Signed	Seasons Played	Career Record Apps	Sub	Gls	
BIRCH, J. Walter	Ecclesfield	05.10.17	Huddersfield T.(+)	Rochdale	+	1946-52	244		10	(CH)Son of Arnold (pre-war/player
BIRCH, Jeff	Sheffield	21.10.27	Scarborough TR	Sheffield U. York C.	09.47 10.49	1949	7		1	
BIRCH, Jim V.	Ashover	25.10.27	Greenoside	Huddersfield T. Halifax T.	+ 08.48	1948	3		1	
BIRCH, Ken J.	Birkenhead	31.12.33	JNRS TR	Everton Southampton	08.51 03.58	1955-57 1957-58	43 33		1 3	(WH)
BIRCH, Paul	Birmingham	20.11.62	APP	Aston Villa	07.80	1983	22	/	2	(M)
BIRCH, Trevor	W.Bromwich	20.11.33	Accles & P. TR	Aston Villa Stockport Co.	01.52 11.60	1954-59 1960-61	22 43		1 0	(WH)
BIRCH, Trevor N.	Ormskirk	16.02.58	APP TR TR	Liverpool Shrewsbury T. Chester C.	12.75 03.79 07.80	1978-79 1980	23 30	2 1	4 0	(F)
BIRCH, William	Southport	20.10.44	APP TR	W.B.A. Crystal Palace	04.63 06.63	1963-64	6		0	(F)
BIRCHALL, Paul	Liverpool	03.09.57	Everton (AM)	Southport	03.77	1976-77	16	3	1	(M)
BIRCHAM, Bernard	Durham	31.08.24	JNRS TR TR TR	Sunderland Chesterfield Grimsby T. Colchester U.	+ 11.46 06.48 07.50	1949 1950	8 7		0 0	(G)
BIRCHAM, Clive	Herrington	07.09.39	JNRS TR	Sunderland Hartlepool U.	09.56 02.60	1958-59 1959-62	28 105		2 15	(F)
BIRCHENALL, Alan	E. Ham	22.08.45	TR TR TR L TR Memphis Rogues TR TR	Sheffield U. Chelsea Crystal Palace Leicester C. Notts Co. Notts Co. Blackburn Rov. Luton T. Hereford U.	06.63 11.67 06.70 09.71 03.76 09.77 09.78 03.79 10.79	1964-67 1967-69 1970-71 1971-76 1975 1977 1978 1978-79 1979	106 74 41 156 5 28 17 9 11	1 1 / 7 / / 1 1 /	31 20 11 12 0 0 0 0 0	(F) E.U23-4
BIRCUMSHAW, Anthony	Mansfield	08.02.45	APP TR	Notts. Co. Hartlepool U.	02.62 07.66	1960-65 1966-70	148 180	/ 3	1 11	(FB)
BIRCUMSHAW, Peter	Mansfield	29.08.38	JNRS TR TR	Notts.Co. Bradford C. Stockport Co.	07.56 06.62 06.63	1956-61 1962 1963	72 27 17		40 7 4	(OL) Brother of Tony
BIRD, John C.	Doncaster	09.06.48	Doncaster U. TR TR TR	Doncaster Rov. Preston N.E. Newcastle U. Hartlepool U.	03.67 03.71 08.75 07.80	1967-80 1970-75 1975-79 1980-83	48 166 84 135	2 / 3 1	3 9 5 15	(D)
BIRD, John F.	Rumney	21.11.40	JNRS TR	Newport Co. Swansea C.	11.57 07.67	1957-66 1967	260 8	/ /	5 0	(WH) W.SCH.INT.
BIRD, Ken	Norwich	25.09.18	Wolverhampton W.(*)	Bournemouth	*	1946-52	232		0	(G) E.SCH.INT.
BIRD, Kevin	Doncaster	07.08.52	Doncaster Rov.(AM) TR	Mansfield T. Huddersfield T.	07.72 08.83	1972-82 1983	362 1	5 /	55 0	(D) Brother of John
BIRD, Ron P.	Erdington	27.12.41	JNRS TR TR TR TR	Birmingham C. Bradford P.A. Bury Cardiff C. Crewe Alex.	01.59 06.61 10.65 02.66 07.71	1961-65 1965 1965-70 1971	129 13 97 19	/ / 10 1	39 3 24 0	(OL) E.YTH.INT.
BIRKETT, Cliff	Newton-le Willows	17.09.33	JNRS TR	Manchester U. Southport	10.50 06.56	1950 1956	9 14		2 4	(OR) E.SCH.INT.
BIRKETT, Ron	Warrington	21.07.27	TR TR TR	Manchester C. New Brighton Oldham Ath. Accrington St.	+ 01.47 08.48 07.49	1946-47 1948 1949	8 4 14		0 0 2	
BIRKETT, Wilf	Warrington	26.06.22	Haydock TR TR TR	Everton Southport Shrewsbury T. Southport	+ 11.46 07.52 07.53	1946-51 1952 1953	162 20 15		0 0 0	(G) Brother of Ron
BIRKS, Graham	Sheffield	25.01.42	JNRS TR TR TR	Sheffield Wed. Peterborough U. Southend U. Chester C.	01.60 05.64 01.66 10.69	1962 1964-65 1965-69 1969-71	4 34 138 71	/ 1 2	0 0 1 0	(FB)
BIRMINGHAM, Charles	Liverpool	24.08.22	Everton(AM)	Tranmere Rov.	08.46	1946	2		1	(IF)
BIRSE, Charles D.V.	Dundee	26.10.16	Hibernian	Watford Northampton T.	05.46 07.47	1946	7		0	(WH)
BIRTLES, Garry	Nottingham	27.07.56	Long Eaton TR TR	Nottingham F. Manchester U. Nottingham F.	03.77 10.80 09.82	1976-80 1980-81 1982-83	87 57 58	/ 1 1	32 11 22	(F) E.-3/E.U21-2
BISHOP, Ian W.	Liverpool	29.05.65	APP L	Everton Crewe Alex.	06.83 03.84	1983 1983	0 4	1 /	0 0	(M)
BISHOP, Peter	Sheffield	04.01.44	JNRS TR	Sheffield U. Chesterfield	04.63 05.65	1965-70	78	3	8	(F) E.YTH.INT.

Players Names	Birthplace	Date	Previous Club	League Club	Date Signed	Seasons Played	Apps	Sub	Gls	
BISHOP, Ray	Hengoed	24.11.55	Cheltenham	Cardiff C.	01.77	1977-80	92	10	25	(F)
			TR	Newport Co.	02.81	1980-81	8	10	2	
			TR	Torquay U.	08.82	1982-83	33	7	8	
BISHOP, Sid H.	Tooting	08.04.34	Chertsey	Orient	06.52	1953-64	296		4	(CH)
BISHTON, Dennis R.	Windsor	22.09.50	APP	Reading	09.68	1968	2	/	0	(RB)
BISSELL, Steve J.	Birmingham	08.10.58	Nottingham F.(APP)	Blackpool	09.78	1978	1	/	0	(F)
BISSET, Tom	Croydon	21.03.32	Redhill	Brighton & H.A.	01.53	1952-60	115		5	(FB)
BITHELL, Brian	Winsford	05.10.56	APP	Stoke C.	10.73	1976	16	1	0	(D)
			L	Port Vale	09.77	1977	2	/	0	
			TR	Wimbledon	12.77	1977	6	/	0	
BLACK, Alan	Glasgow	04.06.43	Dumbarton	Sunderland	08.64	1964-65	4	2	0	(FB)
			TR	Norwich C.	09.66	1966-73	171	4	1	
BLACK, Andy	Stirling	23.09.17	Hearts	Manchester C.	06.46	1946-49	139		48	(CF)S-3/S.F.LGE.REP.
			TR	Stockport Co.	08.50	1950-52	94		38	
BLACK, Ian H.	Aberdeen	27.03.24	Aberdeen	Southampton	12.47	1947-49	97		0	(G) S-1/
			TR	Fulham	08.50	1950-57	263		1	
BLACK, John	Helensburgh	10.11.57	APP	Wolverhampton W.	12.75	1977-78	5	1	0	(F)
			TR	Bradford C.	01.80	1979-82	50	5	13	
			TR	Hereford U.	08.83	1983	8	1	0	
BLACK, John	Blackburn	04.11.45	APP	Arsenal	02.63					(G) W.SCH.INT.
			TR	Swansea C.	12.64	1964-65	15	/	0	
BLACK, Neville	Ashington	19.06.31	Pegswood	Newcastle U.	09.49					(F)
			TR	Exeter C.	01.53	1952	4		0	
			TR	Rochdale	07.53	1953-55	62		13	
BLACKADDER, Fred	Carlisle	13.01.16	Queens Pk.	Carlisle U.	AM	1946	1		0	*Carlisle U.(AM)
BLACKBURN, Alan	Pleasley	04.08.35	JNRS	West Ham U.	08.53	1954-57	15		3	(F)
			TR	Halifax T.	11.57	1957-60	124		35	
BLACKBURN, Colin	Dalton	16.01.61	JNRS	Middlesbrough	12.79	1980	1	/	0	(F)
BLACKBURN, Derek	Wakefield	05.07.31		Burnley	06.53					(HB)
			TR	Chesterfield	06.54					
			Ossett T.	Swansea C.	01.57	1957	2		0	
BLACKBURN, Edwin	Houghton-le-Spring	18.04.57	APP	Hull C.	09.74	1974-79	68	/	0	(G)
			TR	York C.	04.80	1980-81	76	/	0	
			TR	Hartlepool U.	01.83	1982-83	61	/	0	
BLACKBURN, Keith	Manchester	17.07.40	Bolton W. (AM)	Portsmouth	07.59	1960-63	34		8	(F)
BLACKBURN, Ken A.	Wembley	13.05.51	APP	Brighton & H.A.	05.69	1968	1	/	1	(F)
BLACKER, Jim	Leeds	10.08.45	JNRS	Bradford C.	01.63	1963-64	21		0	(FB)
BLACKHALL, Mark C.	Upney	17.11.60	APP	Orient	11.78	1981-82	12	6	1	(F)
BLACKHALL, Ray	Ashington	19.02.57	APP	Newcastle U.	08.74	1974-77	26	11	0	(D)
			TR	Sheffield W.	08.78	1978-81	115	/	1	
			IK Tord	Mansfield T.	11.82	1982	15	/	0	
BLACKHALL, Sid	Ashington	25.09.45	APP	Bradford P.A.	10.62	1963	1		0	(F)
BLACKLAW, Adam	Aberdeen	02.09.37	JNRS	Burnley	10.54	1956-66	318	/	0	(G)S-3/S.U23-2/
			TR	Blackburn Rov.	07.67	1067-69	96	/	0	S.SCH.INT.
			TR	Blackpool	06.70	1970	1	/	0	
BLACKLER, Martin J.	Swindon	14.03.63	APP	Swindon T.	03.81	1982	8	1	0	(M)
BLACKLEY, Arthur	Carlisle	31.01.39	JNRS	Chelsea	10.56					(W)
			TR	Carlisle U.	11.60	1960-61	38		7	
BLACKLEY, John H.	Falkirk	12.05.48	Hibernian	Newcastle U.	10.77	1977-78	46	/	0	(D)S-7/S.U23-4
			TR	Preston N.E.	07.79	1979-81	51	2	0	
BLACKMAN, Ron H.	Portsmouth	02.04.25	Gosport Bor.	Reading	03.47	1946-53	218		156	(CF)●
			TR	Nottingham F.	06.54	1954	11		3	
			TR	Ipswich T.	07.55	1955-57	27		12	
BLACKMORE, Clayton G.	Neath	23.09.64	APP	Manchester U.	09.82	1983	1	/	0	(F)W.U'21-3
BLACKSHAW, William	Ashton-under-Lyne	06.09.20	Manchester C.(*)	Oldham Ath.	07.46	1946-48	67		22	(IF)
			TR	Crystal Palace	07.49	1949-50	32		5	
			TR	Rochdale	02.51					
BLACKWELL, Paul	Mancot	13.01.63	JNRS	Chester C.	09.81	1981-83	80	5	3	(M)
BLACKWELL, Wilf	Maltby	19.11.26		Portsmouth	10.47					(OL) d.1959
			TR	Mansfield T.	08.48					
			TR	Aldershot	06.50	1950	1		0	
BLACKWOOD, John S.D.	Ayr	25.01.35	Girvan J.	Accrington St.	AM	1958-59	4		1	(F)
			TR	York C.	11.59					
BLACKWOOD, Robert	Edinburgh	20.08.34	Hearts	Ipswich T.	06.62	1962-64	62		11	(F) S.F.LGE REP.
			TR	Colchester U.	05.65	1965-67	104	1	6	
BLADEN, Don	Hemsworth	21.05.45	APP	Rotherham U.	APP	1962	1		0	(OR)
			TR	Barnsley	07.63					
BLADES, Paul A.	Peterborough	05.01.65	APP	Derby Co.	12.82	1982-83	10	/	0	(D) E.YTH.INT.
BLAGG, Edward A.	Worksop	09.02.18	Netherton	Nottingham F.	*	1946-47	54		0	Notts Cricketer/
			TR	Southport	11.48	1948	11		0	d. 1976

Players Names	Birthplace	Date	Previous Club	League Club	Date Signed	Seasons Played	Apps	Sub	Gls	
BLAIN, Jimmy D.	Liverpool	09.04.40	JNRS	Everton	05.59					(IF)●
			TR	Southport	02.60	1959-62	127		40	
			TR	Rotherham U.	12.62	1962-63	23		2	
			TR	Carlisle U.	04.64	1964-65	41	/	7	
			TR	Exeter C.	10.65	1965-73	311	9	14	
BLAIR, Andy	Bedworth	18.12.59	AP.	Coventry C.	10.77	1978-80	90	3	6	(M)S.U21-5
			TR	Aston Villa	08.81	1981-83	24	10	0	
			L	Wolverhampton W.	10.83	1983	10	/	0	
BLAIR, Doug	Sheffield	26.06.21		Blackpool	+					(IF) Brother of Jim A.
			TR	Cardiff C.	08.47	1948-53	201		28	
BLAIR, Jim	Glasgow	06.01.18	Cardiff C.(AM)	Blackpool	*	1946	27		4	(IF) S-1
			TR	Bournemouth	10.47	1947-49	80		8	
			TR	Orient	12.49	1949-52	107		25	
BLAIR, Jim	Calderbank	13.01.47	St. Mirren	Norwich C.	09.72	1972-73	3	3	0	(F)
BLAIR, Ken	Dublin	28.09.52	JNRS	Derby Co.	06.70					(M)
			TR	Halifax T.	10.74	1974-75	42	1	4	
			L	Stockport Co.	02.76	1975	7	/	0	
			TR	Southport	08.76	1976	17	/	0	
BLAIR, Ron	Coleraine	26.09.49	Coleraine	Oldham Ath.	10.66	1966-69	74	2	1	(M) NI-5/NI.SCH.INT.
			TR	Rochdale	03.70	1969-71	66	5	3	
			TR	Oldham Ath.	08.72	1972-80	285	10	22	
			TR	Blackpool	08.81	1981	35	1	3	
			TR	Rochdale	08.82	1982	3	/	0	
BLAKE, Anthony, J.	Crofton Hill	26.02.27	Rubery O.F.C.	Birmingham C.	01.49	1949	3		0	(FB)
			TR	Gillingham	07.52	1952	10		1	
BLAKE, Jim B.	Manchester	05.05.66	JNRS	Rochdale	N/C	1983	2	/	0	(D)
BLAKE, Noel L.	Jamaica	12.01.62	Sutton Coldfield	Aston Villa	08.79	1979-81	4	/	0	(D)
			L	Shrewsbury T.	03.82	1981	6	/	0	
			TR	Birmingham C.	09.82	1982-83	71	/	5	
BLAKE, Russell T.	Colchester	24.07.35		Colchester U.	04.56	1955-60	57		8	(F)
BLAKEMAN, Allan	Oldham	02.11.37	Ashton U.	Rotherham U.	05.58	1958	2		0	(F)
			TR	Workington	01.59	1958	14		8	
BLAKEMAN, Alec G.	Headington	11.06.18	Oxford C.	Brentford	05.46	1946-48	42		7	
			TR	Sheffield U.	11.48	1948	5		0	
			TR	Bournemouth	02.49	1948-49	25		8	
BLAKEY, David	Newburn	22.08.29	Chevington	Chesterfield	05.47	1948-66	613	/	20	(CH)●
BLAKIE, Jim S.	Reston	09.12.26		Barrow	08.50	1950	9		1	(F)
BLAMPEY, Stuart	Hull	13.06.51	JNRS	Hull C.	08.68	1969-74	61	9	1	(HB)
BLANCHFLOWER, Jackie	Belfast	07.03.33	JNRS	Manchester U.	03.50	1951-57	104		26	(CH) N.1.-12/N.I.SCH.INT.
BLANCHFLOWER, R. Danny	Belfast	10.02.26	Glentoran	Barnsley	04.49	1948-50	68		2	(WH) N.1.-56/IRISH
			TR	Aston Villa	03.51	1950-54	148		10	& E.F. LGE REPS./●
			TR	Tottenham H.	12.54	1954-63	337		15	Brother of Jackie
BLANT, Colin	Rawtenstall	07.10.46	Rossendale U.	Burnley	08.64	1966-69	46	6	7	(D)
			TR	Portsmouth	04.70	1970-71	64	/	1	
			TR	Rochdale	07.72	19172-73	51	/	0	
			TR	Darlington	01.74	1973-75	89	/	0	
			TR	Grimsby T.	08.76	1976	9	/	0	
			TR	Workington	11.76	1976	21	/	0	
BLATCHFORD, Pat J.	Plymouth	28.12.25	Saltash	Plymouth Arg.	11.48	1948-50	19		2	(OL)
			TR	Orient	08.51	1951-52	59		8	
BLEANCH, Norman	Heddon	19.08.40	Willington	West Ham U.	02.60					(F)
			TR	Southend U.	07.61	1961	3		0	
			TR	Bradford P.A.	11.61	1961	9		3	
BLEARS, Brian T.	Prestatyn	18.11.33		Chester C.	07.54	1954-55	2		0	
BLEASDALE, David G.	St. Helens	23.03.65	Liverpool(APP)	Preston N.E.	08.83	1983	4	1	0	(M)
BLENKINSOP, Tom W.	Blyth	13.05.20	W. Auckland	Grimsby T.	*	1946-47	74		10	(CH) E.F.LGE REP.
			TR	Middlesbrough	05.48	1948-52	98		0	
			TR	Barnsley	11.52	1952	4		0	
BLICK, Mike R.	Berkeley	20.09.48	APP	Swindon T.	09.66	1964-70	7	/	0	(HB)
BLINCOW, Ernie	Walsall	09.11.21	W.B.A.(AM)	Walsall	AM	1946	1		0	
BLISSETT, Gary P.	Manchester	29.06.64	JNRS	Crewe Alex.	08.83	1983	20	2	3	(F)
BLISSETT, Luther	Jamaica	01.02.58	JNRS	Watford	07.75	1975-82	222	24	95	(F)E.U'21-4/E-14
BLIZZARD, Les W.B.	Acton	13.03.23		Q.P.R.	+	1946	4			(CH)
			TR	Bournemouth	05.47	1947	1		0	
			Yeovil T.	Orient	07.50	1950-56	221		12	
BLOCHEL, Joe E.	Chalfont-St. Giles	03.03.62	APP	Southampton	03.80					(F)
			L	Wimbledon	01.82	1981	6	/	1	
BLOCK, Mike	Ipswich	28.01.40	JNRS	Chelsea	02.57	1957-61	37		6	(OR) E.YTH.INT.
			TR	Brentford	01.62	1961-65	146	/	30	
			TR	Watford	10.66	1966	11	2	2	

Players Names	Birthplace	Date	Previous Club	League Club	Date Signed	Seasons Played	Career Record Apps	Sub	Gls	
BLOCKLEY, Jeff	Leicester	12.09.49	APP	Coventry C.	06.67	1968-72	144	2	6	(D) E-1/E.U23-10/
			TR	Arsenal	10.72	1972-74	52	/	1	E.F.LGE.REP.
			TR	Leicester C.	01.75	1974-77	75	1	2	
			TR	Notts. Co.	06.78	1978-79	57	2	5	
BLONDEL, Fred	Lancaster	31.10.23	Morecambe	Bury	07.46	1946	1		0	(IF)
BLOOD, John F.	Nottingham	02.10.14	Notts. Co.(*)	Exeter C.	+	1946-47	38		1	(FB)
BLOOMER, Brian Mc.	Cleethorpes	03.05.52	Brigg T.	Scunthorpe U.	08.78	1978	3	4	1	(F)
BLOOMER, Jimmy	Rutherglen	10.04.26	Strathclyde	Hull C.	02.48	1947	4		2	(IF)
			TR	Grimsby T.	07.49	1949-54	109		41	
BLOOMER, Jimmy	Glasgow	22.08.47	JNRS	Grimsby T.	11.64	1965-68	48	4	0	(FB)
BLOOMFIELD, Edward	Wisbech	28.06.32		Carlisle U.	05.55	1953-55	5		1	
			TR	Southport	07.56	1956	2		0	
BLOOMFIELD, Jimmy H.	Kensington	15.02.34	Hayes	Brentford	10.52	1952-53	42		5	(IF) E.U23-2/
			TR	Arsenal	07.54	1954-60	210		54	E.F. LGE REP./
			TR	Birmingham C.	11.60	1960-63	122		26	d.1983
			TR	Brentford	06.64	1964-65	44	/	4	
			TR	West Ham U.	10.65	1965	9	1	0	
			TR	Plymouth Arg.	09.66	1966-67	25	/	1	
			TR	Orient	03.68	1967-68	43	1	3	
BLOOMFIELD, Ray	Kensington	15.10.44	JNRS	Arsenal	11.61					(W) E.YTH.INT./E.SCH.INT.
			TR	Aston Villa	08.64	1964-65	4	/	0	
BLOOMFIELD, William	Kensington	25.08.39	JNRS	Brentford	08.56	1956-57	3		0	(F)
BLOOR, Alan	Stoke	16.03.43	JNRS	Stoke C.	03.60	1961-76	384	4	17	(D) E.YTH.INT
			TR	Port Vale	06.78	1978	5	1	1	
BLOOR, Mike	Wrexham	25.03.49	Newport FC	Stoke C.	04.67					(FB)
			TR	Lincoln C.	05.71	1971/72	71	2	0	
			TR	Darlington	08.73	1973	7	/	0	
BLOOR, Robert	Stoke	08.07.32		Crewe Alex.	01.54	1953-54	25		1	
BLORE, Reg	Wrexham	18.03.42	JNRS	Liverpool	05.59	1959	1		0	(CF) W.U23-4
			TR	Southport	07.60	1960-63	139		55	
			TR	Blackburn Rov.	11.63	1963-65	11	/	0	
			TR	Oldham Ath.	12.65	1965-69	176	5	19	
BLOSS, Philip K.	Colchester	16.01.53	APP	Colchester U.	04.71	1970-72	32	2	2	(M)
BLOWMAN, Peter	Billingham	12.12.49		Hartlepool U.	11.67	1967-69	56	7	15	(F)
BLOXHAM, Jim A.	N. Coughton	02.07.23	Ollerton Col.	Hull C.	10.47	1947-49	33		2	(W)
BLUCK, David	India	31.01.30		Aldershot	AM	1951	1		0	(LH)
BLUE, Archie	Glasgow	08.04.40	Hearts	Exeter C.	07.61	1961	34		6	(CF)
			TR	Carlisle U.	07.62	1962	2		1	
BLUNDELL, Alan	Birkenhead	18.08.47	APP	Tranmere Rov.	08.65	1965-66	3	/	0	(HB)
BLUNSTONE, Frank	Crewe	17.10.34	JNRS	Crewe Alex.	01.52	1951-52	48		12	(OL)E-5/E.U23-5/
			TR	Chelsea	03.53	1952-63	317		47	E.F.LGE REP./E.YTH.INT
BLUNT, David	Goldthorpe	29.04.49		Bradford P.A.	AM	1967	2	/	0	(IF)
			TR	Chester C.	06.68					
BLUNT, Edwin	Tunstall	21.05.18	Bury(*)	Northampton T.	*	1946-48	59		1	(WH)*Port Vale
			TR	Accrington St.	07.49	1949	9		1	
BLY, Terry G.	Fincham	22.10.35	Bury T.	Norwich C.	08.56	1956-59	56		31	(CF)●
			TR	Peterborough U.	06.60	1960-61	88		81	
			TR	Coventry C.	07.62	1962	32		25	
			TR	Notts.Co.	08.63	1963-64	29		4	
BLY, William	Newcastle	15.05.20	Walkers Temp.	Hull C.	*	1946-59	394		0	(G) d.1982
BLYTH, Jim A.	Perth	02.02.55	APP	Preston N.E.	10.72	1971	1	/	0	(G) S-2
			TR	Coventry C.	10.72	1975-81	151	/	0	
			L	Hereford U.	03.75	1974	7	/	0	
			TR	Birmingham C.	08.82	1982	14	/	0	
BLYTH, John W.	Edinburgh	26.05.47		Halifax T.	05.67	1966-67	5		0	(HB)
BLYTH, Mel	Norwich	28.07.44	Gt.Yarmouth	Scunthorpe U.	11.67	1967	27	/	3	(D)
			TR	Crystal Palace	07.68	1968-74	213	3	9	
			TR	Southampton	09.74	1974-76	104	1	7	
			L	Crystal Palace	11.77	1977	6	/	0	
			Margate	Millwall	11.78	1978-80	75	/	0	
BLYTHE, John A.	Darlington	31.01.24		Darlington	06.46	1946-48	17		0	(CH)
BLYTHE, John D.	Deighton	21.07.47		Hartlepool U.	AM	1969	1	1	0	(CF)
BOAG, Jim	Blairhall	12.11.37	Bath C.	Exeter C.	10.62	1962	2		0	(G)
BOAM, Stuart W.	Kirkby	28.01.48	Kirkby B.C.	Mansfield T.	07.66	1966-70	175	/	2	(D)●
			TR	Middlesbrough	06.71	1971-78	320	/	14	
			TR	Newcastle U.	08.79	1979-80	69	/	1	
			TR	Mansfield T.	07.81	1981-82	11	4	1	
			TR	Hartlepool U.	N/C	1982	1	/	0	
BOARDMAN, George	Glasgow	14.08.43	Queens Pk.	Shrewsbury T.	06.63	1963-68	173	4	49	(IF) S.AMAT.INT.
			TR	Barnsley	06.69	1969-72	123	3	14	

Players Names	Birthplace	Date	Previous Club	League Club	Date Signed	Seasons Played	Career Record Apps	Sub	Gls	
BODAK, Peter J.	Birmingham	12.08.61	APP	Coventry C.	05.79	1980-81	30	2	5	(F)
			TR	Manchester U.	08.82					
			TR	Manchester C.	12.82	1982	12	2	1	
BODEL, Andy C.	Clydebank	12.02.57	APP	Oxford U.	02.75	1975-79	128	/	11	(D)
BODELL, Norman	Manchester	29.01.38		Rochdale	09.56	1958-62	81		1	(F)
			TR	Crewe Alex.	05.63	1963-66	108	1	2	
				Halifax T.	10.66	1966-67	36	/	0	
BODEN, John G.	Grimsby	04.10.26	Skegness T.	Lincoln C.	04.50	1949-50	3		2	(OR)
BODEN, Ken	Thrybergh	05.07.50	Bridlington	Doncaster Rov.	N/C	1976	1	/	0	(M)
BODIN, Paul J.	Cardiff	13.09.64	Newport Co. (N/C)	Cardiff C.	08.82	1982-83	53	4	3	(D)
BODLE, Harold	Doncaster	04.10.20	Rotherham U.(*)	Birmingham C.	*	1946-48	94		31	(IF)
			TR	Bury	03.49	1948-51	119		40	
			TR	Stockport Co.	10.52	1952	29		6	
			TR	Accrington St.	08.53	1953-56	94		13	
BOERSMA, Phil	Liverpool	24.09.49		Liverpool	09.68	1969-75	73	10	17	(F)
			L	Wrexham	03.70	1969	3	2	0	
			TR	Middlesbrough	12.75	1975-76	41	6	3	
			TR	Luton T.	08.77	1977-78	35	1	8	
			TR	Swansea C.	09.78	1978	15	3	1	
BOGAN, Tommy	Glasgow	18.05.20	Glasgow Celtic	Preston N.E.	10.48	1948	11		0	(IF) S.F.LGE REP.
			TR	Manchester U.	08.49	1949-50	29		7	
			Aberdeen	Southampton	12.51	1951-52	9		2	
			TR	Blackburn Rov.	08.53	1953	1		0	
BOGIE, Malcolm	Edinburgh	26.12.39	Hibernian	Grimsby T.	07.63	1963	1		0	(W)S.SCH.INT
			TR	Aldershot	07.64	1964	2		1	
BOLAM, Tom E.	Newcastle	08.07.24		Barrow	08.50	1950-51	35		0	(CH)
BOLDER, Robert	Dover	02.10.58	Dover T.	Sheffield Wed.	03.77	1977-82	196	/	0	(G)
			TR	Liverpool	08.83					
BOLLAND, Gordon	Boston	12.08.43	JNRS	Chelsea	08.60	1961	2		0	(IF)
			TR	Orient	03.62	1961-63	63		19	
			TR	Norwich C.	03.64	1963-67	104	1	29	
			TR	Charlton Ath.	11.67	1967-68	9	2	2	
			TR	Millwall	10.68	1968-74	239	5	62	
BOLLANDS, John F.	Middlesbrough	11.07.35	South Bank	Oldham Ath.	05.53	1954-55	23		0	(G)
			TR	Sunderland	03.56	1955-59	61		0	
			TR	Bolton W.	02.60	1959	13		0	
			TR	Oldham Ath.	09.61	1961-65	131	/	0	
BOLTON, Ian R.	Leicester	13.07.53	Birmingham C.(APP)	Notts Co.	03.72	1971-76	61	9	4	(D)
			L	Lincoln C.	08.76	1976	1	/	0	
			TR	Watford	08.77	1977-83	231	1	28	
			TR	Brentford	12.83	1983	14	/	1	
BOLTON, John	Lesmahagow	26.10.41	Raith Rov.	Ipswich T.	07.63	1963-65	69	/	2	(HB)
BOLTON, Joe	Birtley	02.02.55	APP	Sunderland	02.72	1971-80	264	9	11	(D)
			TR	Middlesbrough	07.81	1981-82	59	/	1	
			TR	Sheffield U.	08.83	1983	45	/	1	
BOLTON, Lyall	Gateshead	11.07.32	Windy Nook J.	Sunderland	08.50	1955-56	3		0	
BOLTON, Ron	Rotherham	01.09.21		Rotherham U.	+	1948-54	150		0	(G)
BOLTON, Ron	Golborne	21.01.38	Crompton Rov.	Bournemouth	04.58	1958-65	199	/	31	(WH)
			TR	Ipswich T.	10.65	1965-67	21	/	0	
			TR	Bournemouth	09.67	1967-68	61	4	17	
BOND, Anthony	Preston	27.12.13		Accrington St.	05.46	1946	29		4	(OR)
BOND, Dennis J.	Walthamstow	17.03.47	APP	Watford	03.64	1964-66	93	/	17	(M)E.YTH.INT./
			TR	Tottenham H.	03.67	1966-70	20	3	1	E.SCH.INT
			TR	Charlton Ath.	10.70	1970-72	70	5	3	
			TR	Watford	02.73	1972-77	178	1	20	
BOND, Graham C.	Torquay	30.12.32		Torquay U.	09.51	1953-60	134		47	(F)
			TR	Exeter C.	10.60	1960	9		4	
			Weymouth	Torquay U.	10.61	1961	5		1	
BOND, J. Ernie	Preston	04.05.29	Leyland Motors	Manchester U.	12.50	1951-52	20		4	(F)
			TR	Carlisle U.	09.52	1952-58	191		24	
BOND, John F.	Colchester	17.12.32	Colchester Cas.	West Ham U.	03.50	1951-64	381		32	(FB) E.F.LGE REP.●
			TR	Torquay U.	01.66	1965-68	129	1	12	
BOND, Kevin J.	London	22.06.57	Bournemouth (APP)	Norwich C.	07.74	1975-80	137	5	12	(D) Son of John
				Seattle Sounders	Manchester C.	09.81	1981-83	105	2	10	
BOND, Len A.	Ilminster	12.02.54	APP	Bristol C.	09.71	1970-76	30	/	0	(G)
			L	Exeter C.	11.74	1974	30	/	0	
			L	Torquay U.	10.75	1975	3	/	0	
			L	Scunthorpe U.	12.75	1975	8	/	0	
			L	Colchester U.	01.76	1975	3	/	0	
			TR	Brentford	08.77	1977-79	122	/	0	
			TR	Exeter C.	10.80	1980-83	138	/	0	
BONDS, William A.	Woolwich	17.09.46	APP	Charlton Ath.	64.9	1964-66	95	/	1	(D) E.U23-2●
			TR	West Ham U.	05.67	1967-83	601	1	45	

Players Names	Birthplace	Date	Previous Club	League Club	Date Signed	Seasons Played	Career Record Apps	Sub	Gls	
BONE, Jim	Bridge of Allan	22.09.49	Partick Th.	Norwich C.	03.72	1971-72	39	/	9	(CF) S-2/S.U23-3
			TR	Sheffield U.	02.73	1972-73	30	1	9	
BONE, John	Hartlepool	19.12.30	Wingate T.	Sunderland	05.51	1954-56	11		0	(CH)
BONER, David	Queensferry	12.10.41	JNRS	Everton	10.58					(F) S.SCH.INT.
			Raith Rov.	Mansfield T.	07.63	1963	12		1	
BONETTI, Peter	Putney	27.09.41	JNRS	Chelsea	05.59	1959-78	600	/	0	(G)E.-7/E.U23-12/E.F.LGE. REP.●
BONNAR, Pat	Ballymena	27.11.20	Belfast Celtic	Barnsley	08.49	1949	6		1	(OL) IRISH LGE REP./
			TR	Aldershot	06.50	1950-52	62		20	1 appearance in goal for Aldershot
BONNELL, Arnold	Barnsley	23.03.21	JNRS	Barnsley	*	1946-47	7		0	
			TR	Rochdale	07.48	1948	5		0	
BONNER, Bernard	Motherwell	22.07.27	Airdrie	Wrexham	02.52	1951	1		0	(CF)
BONNYMAN, Phil	Glasgow	06.02.54	Hamilton Acad.	Carlisle U.	03.76	1975-79	149	3	26	(M)
			TR	Chesterfield	03.80	1979-81	98	1	25	
			TR	Grimsby T.	08.82	1982-83	67	2	4	
BONSON, Joe	Barnsley	19.06.36	JNRS	Wolverhampton W.	07.53	1956	10		4	(CF)
			TR	Cardiff C.	11.57	1957-59	72		37	
			TR	Scunthorpe U.	06.60	1960-61	52		11	
			TR	Doncaster Rov.	02.62	1961	14		4	
			TR	Newport Co.	06.62	1962-64	99		47	
			TR	Brentford	06.64	1964-65	35	/	13	
			TR	Lincoln C.	01.66	1965-66	45	1	16	
BOOK, Anthony	Bath	04.09.35	Bath C.	Plymouth Arg.	08.64	1964-65	82	/	3	(FB)● Brother of Kim
			TR	Manchester C.	07.66	1966-73	242	2	4	
BOOK, Kim	Bath	12.02.46	Frome T.	Bournemouth	07.67	1967-68	2	/	0	(G)
			TR	Northampton T.	10.69	1969-71	78	/	0	
			L	Mansfield T.	09.71	1971	4	/	0	
			TR	Doncaster Rov.	12.71	1971-73	84	/	0	
BOOKER, Ken	Sheffield	03.03.18	Dronfield	Chesterfield	*	1946-51	182		4	(CH)
			TR	Shrewsbury T.	07.52	1952	9		0	
BOOKER, Mike	Barnsley	22.10.47	APP	Barnsley	10.65	1966	0	1	0	(FB) E.SCH.INT.
			TR	Bradford P.A.	06.68	1968	11	2	0	
BOOKER, Robert	Watford	25.01.58	Bedmond Social	Brentford	10.78	1978-83	120	27	27	(F)
BOORN, Alan	Folkestone	11.04.53	Coventry C.(AM)	Brighton & H.A.	12.72	1972	2	/	0	(HB) E.YTH.INT.
BOOT, Eddie	Loughton	13.10.15	Sheffield U.(*)	Huddersfield T.	*	1946-51	223		3	(WH) *Denaby U.
BOOT, Micky C.	Leicester	17.12.47	APP	Arsenal	12.64	1966	3	1	2	(F) E.SCH.INT.
BOOTH, Anthony J.	Biggin Hill	20.06.61		Charlton Ath.	03.79	1978-79	2	6	0	(F)
BOOTH, Colin	Manchester	30.12.34	JNRS	Wolverhampton W.	01.52	1954-59	78		26	(IF) E.U23-1
			TR	Nottingham F.	10.59	1959-61	87		39	
			TR	Doncaster Rov.	08.62	1962-63	88		57	
			TR	Oxford U.	07.64	1964-65	48	/	22	
BOOTH, David	Barnsley	02.10.48	JNRS	Barnsley	05.67	1967-71	161	3	8	(D)
			TR	Grimsby T.	06.72	1972-77	199	1	7	
BOOTH, David C.	Manchester	25.10.62	JNRS	Stockport Co,	04.80	1979-80	20	8	4	(M)
BOOTH, Dennis	Stanley Common	09.04.49	APP	Charlton Ath.	04.66	1966-70	67	10	5	(M)
			TR	Blackpool	07.71	1971	12	/	0	
			TR	Southend	03.72	1971-73	77	1	1	
			TR	Lincoln C.	02.74	1973-77	162	/	9	
			TR	Watford	10.77	1977-79	97	3	2	
			TR	Hull C.	05.80	1980-83	121	1	2	
BOOTH, Grenville V.	Chester	02.04.25	JNRS	Chester C.	08.48	1948	8		0	
BOOTH, Ken K.	Blackpool	22.11.34	JNRS	Blackpool	01.52	1954-56	2		1	(F)
			TR	Bradford P.A.	05.57	1957-58	46		14	
			TR	Workington	06.59	1959	30		13	
			TR	Southport	07.60	1960	26		7	
BOOTH, Ray	Wrexham	05.09.49	JNRS	Wrexham	10.67	1966-68	5	/	0	(F)
BOOTH, Sam	Shotts	20.04.26	Derry C.	Exeter C.	08.51	1951-53	64		0	(WH)
			TR	Bradford C.	07.54	1954	15		0	
BOOTH, Tommy	Manchester	09.11.49	JNRS	Manchester C.	08.67	1968-81	380	2	25	(D)U.23-4
			TR	Preston N.E.	10.81	1981-83	73	/	2	
BOOTH, W. Sammy	Hove	07.07.20		Cardiff C.	+					*Port Vale
			TR	Brighton & H.A.	08.47	1947-48	28		6	
BOOTH, Wilf	Mapplewell	26.12.18	Wombwell Ath.	Halifax T.	12.47	1947	5	2	(F)	
BOOTHMAN, Jim	Great Harwood	02.12.20		Oldham Ath.	+	1946-47	44		0	
BOOTHWAY, John	Manchester	04.02.19	Manchester C.(+)	Crewe Alex.	+	1946	11		5	(CF)
			TR	Wrexham	10.46	1946-49	95		55	
BOOTLE, William	Ashton	09.01.26		Manchester C.	+	1948-49	5		0	(F)
				Crewe Alex.	03.54	1953-54	14		4	
BOROTA, Petar	Yugoslavia	05.03.52	Partizan Belgrade	Chelsea	03.79	1978-81	107	/	0	(G) YUGOSLAV. INT.
BORROWS, Brian	Liverpool	20.12.60	JNRS	Everton	04.80	1981-82	27	/	0	(D)
			TR	Bolton W.	03.83	1982-83	53	/	0	

Players Names	Birthplace	Date	Previous Club	League Club	Date Signed	Seasons Played	Career Record Apps Sub Gls		
BORTHWICK, Cyril	Romford	02.11.32	JNRS	Fulham	08.50	1951	1		0
BORTHWICK, Gary	Slough	30.11.55	Barnet	Bournemouth	03.78	1977-79	66	8	4 (D)
BORTHWICK, John R.	Hartlepool	24.03.64	Owton M.S.C.	Hartlepool T.	N/C	1982-83	9	2	0 (F)
BORTHWICK, Walter	Edinburgh	04.04.48	Morton	Brighton & H.A.	05.67	1966	1	/	0 (IF)
BOSLEM, William	Manchester	11.01.58		Rochdale	09.76	1975-77	42	3	1 (D)
BOSSONS, Percy L.	Crewe	10.01.24	West Ham(AM)	Crewe Alex.	06.46	1946-48	34		2 (LB) d.1950
BOSTOCK, Ben R.	Mansfield	19.04.29	JNRS	Crystal Palace	05.46	1948	3		0
BOSWELL, Allan	Walsall	08.08.43	JNRS	Walsall	08.60	1961-62	66		0 (G)
			TR	Shrewsbury T.	08.63	1963-68	223	/	0
			TR	Wolverhampton W.	09.68	1968	10	/	0
			TR	Bolton W.	10.69	1969-70	51	/	0
			TR	Port Vale	08.72	1972-73	86	/	0
BOSWELL, Jimmy	Chester	13.03.22	Chester C.(AM)	Gillingham	N/L	1950-57	342		6 (WH)
BOTHAM, Ian T.	Heswall	24.11.55		Scunthorpe U.	N/C	1979-83	7	2	0 (F) Somerset/England Cricket Captain
BOTTIGLIERI, Antonio	Gillingham	29.05.62	APP	Gillingham	04.80	1979-81	5	4	0 (F)
BOTTOM, Arthur E.	Sheffield	28.02.30	JNRS	Sheffield U.	04.47	1948-53	24		7 (CF)
			TR	York C.	06.54	1954-57	137		91
			TR	Newcastle U.	01.58	1957-58	11		10
			TR	Chesterfield	11.58	1958-59	34		6
BOTTOMS, Mike C.	Harrow	11.01.39	Harrow T.	Q.P.R.	07.60	1960	2		0 (F)
			TR	Oxford U.	N/L				
BOUGHEN, Paul	South Kirkby	17.09.49	APP	Barnsley	10.67	1968-70	3	5	0 (HB)
BOULD, Steve A.	Stoke	16.11.62	APP	Stoke C.	11.80	1981-83	50	4	2 (D)
			L	Torquay U.	10.82	1982	9	/	0
BOULTER, David A.	London	05.10.62	APP	Crystal Palace	07.80	1981	16	/	0 (D)
BOULTON, Clint W.	Stoke	06.01.48	APP	Port Vale	08.65	1964-71	244	/	11 (D)
			TR	Torquay U.	11.71	1971-78	260	2	35
BOULTON, Colin D.	Cheltenham	12.09.45	Cheltenham P.C.	Derby Co.	08.64	1964-77	273	/	0 (G)
			L	Southampton	09.76	1976	5	/	0
			N. York Cosmos	Lincoln C.	07.80	1980	4	/	0
BOULTON, Frank P.	Chipping Sodbury	12.08.17	Arsenal(*)	Derby Co.	*				(G) *Bath C.
			TR	Swindon T.	08.46	1946-49	97		0
BOULTON, Ralph	Grimsby	22.07.23		Grimsby T.	04.48	1947-48	3		0
BOURNE, Albert	Golborne	30.09.34		Manchester C.	08.52				(F)
			TR	Oldham Ath.	06.58	1958-59	35		9
BOURNE, George F.	Stoke	05.03.32		Stoke C.	06.50	1952-55	100		1 (FB)
BOURNE, Jeff A.	Burton	19.06.48	Burton A.	Derby Co.	02.71	1970-76	35	14	9 (F)
			TR	Crystal Palace	03.77	1976-77	32	/	10
			Atlanta Chiefs	Sheffield U.	09.79	1979	25	1	11
BOURNE, Richard A.	Colchester	09.12.54	JNRS	Colchester U.	04.73	1971-72	3	1	0 (D)
			Bath C.	Torquay U.	06.79	1979-81	64	4	7
BOUSTON, Bryan	Hereford	03.10.60	APP	Hereford U.	10.78	1977	4	2	0 (D)
BOVINGTON, Eddie	Edmonton	23.04.41	JNRS	West Ham U.	05.59	1959-67	138	/	1 (WH)
BOWDEN, John	Manchester	25.08.21	JNRS	Oldham Ath.	+	1946-48	72		1 (HB)
BOWDEN, John	Stockport	21.01.63	JNRS	Oldham Ath.	01.80	1981-83	60	7	5 (M)
BOWDEN, Peter W.	Liverpool	23.07.59	JNRS	Doncaster Rov.	08.77	1976-78	22	6	1 (D)
BOWEN, Daniel	Llanwonno	16.11.21	Treharris	Scunthorpe U.	07.50	1950	5		0 (F)
BOWEN, David L.	Maesteg	07.06.28		Northampton T.	07.47	1047-48	12		0 (WH) W-19/
			TR	Arsenal	07.50	1950-58	146		2 Father of Keith
			TR	Northampton T.	07.59	1959	22		1
BOWEN, Keith	Northampton	26.02.58	JNRS	Northampton T.	N/C	1976-81	61	4	25 (F) W.SCH.INT.
			TR	Brentford	09.81	1981-82	42	9	9
			TR	Colchester U.	03.83	1982-83	59	/	15
BOWEN, R. Mark	Neath	07.12.63	APP	Tottenham H.	12.81	1983	6	1	0 (D)W.SCH.INT./W.YTH.INT./W.U'21-2
BOWEN, Tom H.	W. Bromwich	21.08.24		W.B.A.	+				(OR) Father played for
			TR	Newport Co.	07.46	1946-479	37		6 Walsall
			TR	Walsall	07.50	1950-52	94		7
BOWER, Ken	Huddersfield	18.03.26		Darlington	01.47	1946-48	75		35 (CF)
			TR	Rotherham U.	07.49	1949	27		11
BOWERING, Mike	Hull	15.11.36		Hull Co.	09.58	1958-59	45		7 (OL)
			TR	Chesterfield	06.60	1960	17		1
BOWERS, Ian	Stoke	16.01.55	JNRS	Stoke C.	06.73	1974-77	35	4	2 (D)
			L	Shrewsbury T.	03.78	1977	6	/	0
			TR	Crewe Alex.	07.79	1979-83	170	5	2
BOWERS, John	Leicester	14.11.39	Derby Corries	Derby Co.	02.57	1959-65	65	/	18 (F)Son of pre-war
			TR	Notts. Co.	06.66	1966	5		0 international
BOWEY, Keith A.	Newcastle	09.05.60	APP	Blackpool	03.78	1978-79	3	/	1 (M)

Players Names	Birthplace	Date	Previous Club	League Club	Date Signed	Seasons Played	Apps	Sub	Gls	
BOWERY, Herbert	W. Indies	29.10.54	Worksop T.	Nottingham F.	01.75	1975-76	2	/	2	(M)
			L	Lincoln C.	02.76	1975	2	2	1	
BOWGETT, Paul	Hitchin	17.06.55	Letchworth	Tottenham H.	02.78					(D)
			TR	Wimbledon	03.79	1978-79	41	/	0	
BOWIE, Jim D.	Aberdeen	09.08.24	Park Vale	Chelsea	+	1947-50	76		18	(IF)
			TR	Fulham	01.51	1950-51	33		7	
			TR	Brentford	03.52	1951	9		0	
			TR	Watford	07.52	1952-55	124		39	
BOWIE, Jim M.	Howwood	11.10.41	Arthurlie	Oldham Ath.	07.62	1962-71	331	3	38	(IF)
			TR	Rochdale	10.72	1972	1	2	0	
BOWKER, Keith	W. Bromwich	18.04.51	APP	Birmingham C.	08.68	1970-72	19	2	5	(F)
			TR	Exeter C.	12.73	1973-75	110	/	38	
			TR	Cambridge U.	05.76	1976	12	5	1	
			L	Northampton T.	12.76	1976	4	/	0	
			TR	Exeter C.	08.77	1977-79	93	9	28	
			TR	Torquay U.	08.80	1980-81	50	3	9	
BOWLER, Gerry C.	Derry	08.06.19	Distillery	Portsmouth	08.46	1946-48	8		0	(CH) N.1.-3
			TR	Hull C.	08.49	1949	38		0	
			TR	Millwall	06.50	1950-54	165		0	
BOWLES, Jack C.	Cheltenham	04.08.14	Accrington St.(*)	Stockport Co.	*	1946-52	235		0	(G)
BOWLES, Paul M.A.	Manchester	31.05.57	APP	Crewe Alex.	05.75	1974-79	174	4	20	(D) Cousin of Stan
			TR	Port Vale	10.79	1979-80	98	/	8	
			TR	Stockport Co.	06.82	1982-83	66	1	0	
BOWLES, Stan	Manchester	24.12.48	APP	Manchester C.	01.67	1967-69	15	2	2	(M)E-5/E.F.LGE.REP.
			L	Bury	07.70	1970	5	/	0	
			TR	Crewe Alex.	09.70	1970-71	51	/	18	
			TR	Carlisle U.	10.71	1971-72	33	/	12	
			TR	Q.P.R.	09.72	1972-79	255	/	70	
			TR	Nottingham F.	12.79	1979	19	/	2	
			TR	Orient	07.80	1980-81	46	/	7	
			TR	Brentford	10.81	1981-83	80	1	16	
BOWMAN, Andy	Pittenweem	07.03.34	JNRS	Chelsea	06.51	1953	1		0	(WH) S.SCH.INT.
			Hearts	Newport Co.	08.61	1961-62	69		7	
BOWMAN, Richard D.	Lewisham	25.09.54	APP	Charlton Ath.	03.73	1972-76	93	3	7	(M)
			TR	Reading	12.76	1976-80	194	/	30	
			TR	Gillingham	08.81	1981-82	26	/	6	
BOWMAN, Robert C.C.	Motherwell	21.10.20	Kilmarnock	New Brighton	01.49	1948	18		0	
BOWRON, Ken	Newcastle	10.04.39	Berwick Rgrs.	Workington	12.65	1965-66	8	1	2	(F)
BOWSTEAD, Peter	Cambridge	10.05.44	Cambridge U.	Oxford U.	10.62	1962-63	8		2	(F)
BOWTELL, Steve J.	London	02.12.50	APP	Orient	01.68	1967-71	7	/	0	(G) E.YTH.INT./E.SCH.INT.
BOWYER, Frank	Chesterton	10.04.22	JNRS	Stoke C.	*	1947-59	398		138	(IF)
BOWYER, Ian	Ellesmere Port	06.06.51	APP	Manchester C.	08.68	1968-70	42	7	13	(M)
			TR	Orient	06.71	1971-72	75	3	18	
			TR	Nottingham F.	10.73	1973-80	222	17	49	
			TR	Sunderland	01.81	1980-81	15	/	1	
			TR	Nottingham F.	01.82	1981-83	104	2	11	
BOXALL, Alan R.	Woolwich	11.05.53	Barton T.	Scunthorpe U.	08.80	1980-83	50	4	1	(D)
			TR	Chesterfield	11.83	1983	4	1	0	
BOXLEY, Jack	Cradley	31.05.31	Stourbridge	Bristol C.	10.50	1950-56	195		34	(OL)
			TR	Coventry C.	12.56	1956-59	90		17	
			TR	Bristol C.	08.60	1960	12		0	
BOXSHALL, Danny	Bradford	02.04.20	Salem Ath.	Q.P.R.	+	1946-47	30		14	(CF)
			TR	Bristol C.	05.48	1948-49	52		10	
			TR	Bournemouth	07.50	1950-51	51		8	
			TR	Rochdale	07.52	1952-53	11		3	
BOYCE, Ron W.	West Ham	06.01.43	JNRS	West Ham U.	05.60	1960-72	275	7	21	(IF) E.YTH.INT./E.SCH.INT.
BOYD, Brian G.	Carlisle	04.01.38	JNRS	Carlisle U.	12.58	1955-58	6		0	
BOYD, Gordon	Glasgow	27.03.58	Glasgow Rgrs.	Fulham	05.78	1978	1	2	0	(F) S.SCH.INT
			Glasgow Rgrs.	Barnsley	06.80	1980	1	1	0	
			TR	Scunthorpe U.	03.82	1981	10	1	0	
BOYD, Jack	Consett	10.04.25	Medomsley BC	Sunderland	+					(FB)
			TR	W.B.A.	06.48	1948	1		0	
BOYD, John	U.S.A.	10.09.26	Gloucester C.	Bristol C.	12.50	1950-51	31		6	(OR)
BOYD, John R.	Lothian	07.03.26		Newport Co.	03.47	1947	1		0	(CH)
BOYD, Len A.	Plaistow	11.11.23	Ilford	Plymouth Arg.	+	1946-48	78		5	(WH) E'B'-1/
			TR	Birmingham C.	01.49	1948-55	246		14	
BOYD, Stuart	Workington	22.12.54	JNRS	Workington	AM	1973	1	2	0	(RB)
BOYD, Wiliam	Bellshill	18.10.58	APP	Hull C.	10.77					(G)S.YTH.INT.
			TR	Doncaster Rov.	02.80	1979-83	104	/	0	
BOYDEN, Joe	Willenhall	12.02.29	JNRS	Walsall	12.48	1952	4		0	

Players Names	Birthplace	Date	Previous Club	League Club	Date Signed	Seasons Played	Apps	Sub	Gls	
BOYER, Phil J.	Nottingham	25.01.49	APP	Derby Co.	11.66					(F)E-1/E.U23-2●
			TR	York C.	07.68	1968-70	108	1	27	
			TR	Bournemouth	12.70	1970-73	140	1	46	
			TR	Norwich C.	12.74	1973-76	115	1	34	
			TR	Southampton	08.77	1977-80	138	/	49	
			TR	Manchester C.	11.80	1980-82	17	3	3	
BOYES, Ken	York	04.02.35	Scarborough	York C.	10.55	1957-65	53	/	2	(HB)
BOYES, Walter	Sheffield	05.01.13	W.B.A.(*)	Everton	*	1946-48	17		4	(OL) E-3/E.F.LGE.REP./
			TR	Notts. Co.	08.49	1949	3		1	*Woodhouse M.U./
			TR	Scunthorpe U.	08.50	1950	13		2	d.1960
BOYLAN, Anthony	W. Hartlepool	19.02.50	B. Auckland	Hartlepool U.	AM	1969-71	11	1	0	(M)
BOYLE, David W.	North Shields	24.04.29		Newcastle U.	10.47					(F)
			Berwick Rgrs.	Barnsley	03.51					
			TR	Crewe Alex.	06.52	1952-53	25		3	
			TR	Chesterfield	07.54	1954-55	42		10	
			TR	Bradford C.	07.56	1956-60	92		13	
BOYLE, Henry	Glasgow	22.04.24	Murton CW	Southport	07.47	1947-49	87		0	(FB)
			TR	Rochdale	06.50	1950-55	175		0	
BOYLE, Ian R.	Barnsley	07.12.53	APP	Barnsley	01.72	1972-73	19	2	0	(FB)
BOYLE, John	Motherwell	25.12.46	JNRS	Chelsea	08.64	1964-73	188	10	10	(WH)
			L	Brighton & H.A.	09.73	1973	10	/	0	
			TR	Orient	12.73	1973-74	18	/	0	
BOYLE, Terry	Ammanford	29.10.58	APP	Tottenham H.	11.75					(D) W.SCH.INT./W.2/W.U21-1
			TR	Crystal Palace	01.78	1977-80	24	2	1	
			L	Wimbledon	10.81	1981	5	/	1	
			TR	Bristol C.	10.81	1981-82	36	1	0	
			TR	Newport Co.	11.82	1982-83	73	1	1	
BOYLEN, David	Manchester	26.10.47	Ryder Brow B.C.	Grimsby T.	07.65	1966-77	370	13	33	(M)
BRABROOK, Peter	E. Ham	08.11.37	JNRS	Chelsea	03.55	1954-61	251		47	(OR) E-3/E.U23-9/
			TR	West Ham U.	10.62	1962-67	167	/	33	E.F.LGE.REP/E.YTH.INT.
			TR	Orient	07.68	1968-70	68	2	6	
BRACE, Robert L.	Edmonton	19.12.64	APP	Tottenham H.	12.82	1983	0	1	0	(F)
BRACE, Stewart	Taunton	21.09.42	Taunton T.	Plymouth Arg.	11.60	1962-64	8		0	(W)
			TR	Watford	09.65	1965	16	/	4	
			TR	Mansfield T.	07.66	1966-67	55	1	25	
			TR	Peterborough U.	11.67	1967-68	22	1	6	
			TR	Grimsby T.	10.68	1968-73	205	1	82	
			TR	Southend U.	10.73	1973-75	106	6	37	
BRACEWELL, Ken	Colne	05.10.36		Burnley	04.57					(FB)
			TR	Tranmere Rov.	05.59	1959-60	28		1	
			Canada	Lincoln C.	11.63	1963-64	12		1	
			Margate	Bury	12.66	1966	1	/	0	
			Canada	Rochdale	03.68	1967	5	/	0	
BRACEWELL, Paul W.	Stoke	19.07.62	APP	Stoke C.	02.80	1979-82	123	6	5	(M)E.U'21-12
			TR	Sunderland	07.83	1983	38	/	4	
BRACK, Alistair	Aberdeen	27.01.40		Cardiff C.	09.61	1962	1		0	(FB)
BRADBURY, Allen	Barnsley	23.01.47	APP	Barnsley	01.65	1964-69	68	1	9	(WH)
				Hartlepool U.	01.71	1970	7	/	0	
BRADBURY, Barry	Rochdale	05.08.52	Matthew Moss	Rochdale	08.72	1972-73	12	3	0	(FB)
BRADBURY, Terry E.	London	15.11.39	JNRS	Chelsea	07.57	1960-61	29		1	(WH) E.SCH.INT.
			TR	Southend U.	09.62	1962-65	160	1	19	
			TR	Orient	06.66	1966	25	2	0	
			TR	Wrexham	06.67	1967-68	77	1	4	
			TR	Chester C.	06.69	1969-70	90	/	2	
BRADBURY, William	Matlock	03.04.33	JNRS	Coventry C.	05.55	1951-54	24		7	(F)
			TR	Birmingham C.	11.54	1954-55	3		2	
			TR	Hull C.	10.55	1955-59	178		82	
			TR	Bury	02.60	1959-60	18		4	
			TR	Workington	11.60	1960	23		5	
			TR	Southport	08.61	1961	11		2	
BRADD, Les	Buxton	05.11.47	Earl Sterndale	Rotherham U.	03.66	1967	3	/	0	(F)
			TR	Notts. Co.	10.67	1967-77	381	17	125	
			TR	Stockport Co.	08.78	1978-80	116	1	31	
			TR	Wigan Ath.	07.81	1981	57	6	25	
			L	Bristol Rov.	12.82	1982	1	/	1	
BRADER, Alec	Horncastle	06.10.42	Horncastle U.	Grimsby T.	09.61	1960	2		0	(F)
BRADFORD, David W.	Manchester	22.02.53	APP	Blackburn Rov.	08.71	1971-73	58	6	3	(M)
			TR	Sheffield U.	07.74	1974-76	54	6	3	
			L	Peterborough U.	10.76	1976	4	/	0	
			TR	W.B.A.	02.77					
			Washington Dips	Coventry C.	10.81	1981	6	/	1	
BRADFORD, Geoff R.	Bristol	18.07.27	Soundwell	Bristol Rov.	05.49	1949-63	461		245	(IF) E-1●
BRADFORD, Lewis	Gresley	24.11.16	Kilmarnock	Bradford C.	10.46	1946-48	68		1	(CH)*Preston N.E.
			TR	Newport Co.	11.48	1948	24		0	
BRADLEY, Brendan	Derry	07.06.50	Finn Harps	Lincoln C.	07.72	1972	31	/	12	(IF)

Players Names	Birthplace	Date	Previous Club	League Club	Date Signed	Seasons Played	Career Record Apps	Sub	Gls	
BRADLEY, Charles	York	15.05.22		York C.	+	1946	10		2	
BRADLEY, David	Manchester	16.01.58	APP	Manchester U.	01.75					(D) E.SCH. INT.
			L	Wimbledon	03.78	1977	7	/	0	
			TR	Doncaster Rov.	08.78	1978-79	67	/	5	
			TR	Bury	08.80	1980	8	/	0	
BRADLEY, David H.	Bolton	06.12.53	Silcoms	Workington	09.75	1975	8	/	1	(IF)
BRADLEY, Don J.	Clipstone	11.09.24	Clipstone Col.	W.B.A.	+					(FB)
			TR	Mansfield T.	08.49	1949-61	385		5	
BRADLEY, George J.	Maltby	07.01.17	Rotherham U.(*)	Newcastle U.	*					(WH) *Maltby
			TR	Millwall	09.46	1946-49	74		2	
BRADLEY, Gordon	Scunthorpe	20.05.25	Scunthorpe U.	Leicester C.	+	1946-49	69		0	(G)
			TR	Notts. Co.	02.50	1950-57	192		1	
BRADLEY, Gordon	Easington	23.11.33	Stanley U.	Bradford P.A.	01.56	1955-56	18		1	(HB)
			TR	Carlisle U.	09.57	1957-60	129		3	
BRADLEY, Jim	Greenock	21.03.27	T. Lanark	Shrewsbury T.	07.52	1952	1		0	
BRADLEY, John	Hemsworth	27.11.16	Chelsea *	Southampton	+	1946-47	49		22	(IF) *Huddersfield T./
			TR	Bolton W.	10.47	1947-50	87		19	Swindon T.
			TR	Norwich C.	11.50	1950-51	6		0	
BRADLEY, Keith	Ellesmere Port	31.01.46	APP	Aston Villa	06.63	1964-71	116	7	2	(WH)
			TR	Peterborough U.	11.72	1972-75	106	3	0	
BRADLEY, Lee	Manchester	27.05.57	APP	Stockport Co.	08.75	1975	39	1	4	(D)
			TR	Halifax T.	10.76	1976-78	62	10	4	
BRADLEY, Noel	Manchester	17.12.57	St. Roberts B.C.	Manchester C.	11.78					(D)
			L	Bury	03.80	1979	9	/	0	
			TR	Bury	08.81	1981	15	3	1	
			TR	Chester	08.82	1982	27	4	4	
BRADLEY, Peter K.	Donnington	18.03.55	APP	Shrewsbury T.	07.73	1973	3	/	0	(WH)
BRADLEY, Ron	Wolverhampton	24.04.39	JNRS	W.B.A.	06.56	1962	13		0	(WH) E.YTH.INT.
			TR	Norwich C.	07.64	1964-65	4	/	0	
BRADLEY, Warren	Hyde	20.06.33	B. Auckland	Manchester U.	11.58	1958-61	63		20	(OR) E-3/E.AMAT.INT.
			TR	Bury	03.62	1961-62	13		1	
BRADLEY, William	Glasgow	26.06.37	Ayr U.	Hartlepool U.	07.63	1963-65	100	/	15	(F)
BRADSHAW, Alan	Blackburn	14.09.41	JNRS	Blackburn Rov.	07.63	1962-64	11		2	(M)
			TR	Crewe Alex.	05.65	1965-72	287	7	50	
BRADSHAW, George F.	Southport	10.03.13	Doncaster Rov.(*)	Bury	*	1946-49	78		0	(G)*New Brighton/Everton/
			TR	Oldham Ath.	07.50					Arsenal
BRADSHAW, George H.	Clay Cross	24.03.20	Newstead Col.	Chesterfield	+	1947	7		1	(CF)
BRADSHAW, Paul	Sheffield	02.10.53	APP	Burnley	10.70	1974-76	11	2	2	(F) E.YTH.INT./E.SCH.INT
			TR	Sheffield Wed.	09.76	1976-77	62	2	9	
BRADSHAW, Paul W.	Altrincham	28.04.56	APP	Blackburn Rov.	07.73	1973-77	78	/	0	(G)E.U21-4/E.YTH.INT
			TR	Wolverhampton W.	09.77	1977-83	200	/	0	
BRADY, Liam	Dublin	13.02.56	APP	Arsenal	08.73	1973-79	227	8	43	(M) EI-45
BRADY, Pat	Dublin	11.03.36	Home Farm	Millwall	01.59	1958-62	145		1	(FB) Brother of Ray/Liam
			TR	Q.P.R.	07.63	1963-64	61		0	
BRADY, Paul J.	Marston Wood	26.03.61	APP	Birmingham C.	08.78					(D)
			TR	Northampton T.	08.81	1981-82	49	2	3	
			TR	Crewe Alex.	02.83	1982-83	42	1	1	
BRADY, Ray	Dublin	03.06.37	Home Farm	Millwall	07.57	1957-62	166		4	(CH) E1-6
			TR	Q.P.R.	07.63	1963-65	89	/	0	
BRAGG, Wally L.	London	08.07.29	JNRS	Brentford	01.47	1946-56	161		6	(HB)
BRAHAN, Mel E.	London	03.12.26	Walthamstow	Orient	AM	1955	1		0	(CH)
BRAITHWAITE, Robert M.	Belfast	24.02.37	Linfield	Middlesbrough	06.63	1963-66	67	1	12	(W) N.I.-10/N.I.SCH.INT.
BRAITHWAITE, Ron S.	Ash Vale	09.04.31		Crystal Palace	08.49	1952	3		0	(HB)
BRAMHALL, John	Warrington	20.11.56	JNRS	Tranmere Rov.	07.76	1976-81	164	6	7	(D)
			TR	Bury	03.82	1981-83	100	/	12	
BRAMHALL, Neil	Blackpool	16.10.65	APP	Blackpool	10.83	1982	0	3	0	(F)
BRAMLEY, Arthur	Mansfield	25.03.29	Bentinck Col.	Mansfield T.	10.49	1949-52	19		0	(G) Brother of Ernest
BRAMLEY, Ernest	Mansfield	29.08.20	Bolsover Col.	Mansfield T.	*	1946-47	32		1	(RB)
BRAMLEY, J. Stuart	Scunthorpe	19.04.46	APP	Scunthorpe U.	04.64	1964-66	35	/	3	(F)
			TR	Plymouth Arg.	08.67					
BRAMWELL, John	Ashton	01.03.37	Wigan Ath.	Everton	04.58	1958-59	52		0	(FB)
			TR	Luton T.	10.60	1960-64	187		1	
BRANAGAN, Keith G.	Fulham	10.07.66	JNRS	Cambridge U.	08.83	1983	1	/	0	(G)
BRANAGAN, Ken F.	Salford	27.7.30	N.Salford B.C.	Manchester C.	11.48	1950-59	196		3	(FB)
			TR	Oldham Ath.	10.60	1960-65	177	/	5	
BRANAGAN, Jim P.S.	Barton	03.07.55	JNRS	Oldham Ath.	07.73	1974-76	24	3	0	(D) Son of Ken
			Cape Town C.	Huddersfield T.	11.77	1977-78	37	1	0	
			TR	Blackburn Rov.	10.79	1979-83	190	1	3	

Players Names	Birthplace	Date	Previous Club	League Club	Date Signed	Seasons Played	Apps	Sub	Gls	
BRAND, Andrew S.	Edinburgh	08.11.57	APP	Everton	11.75	1975-76	2	/	0	(G)
			L	Crewe Alex.	02.77	1976	14	/	0	
			L	Crewe Alex.	08.78	1978	1	/	0	
			TR	Hereford T.	05.80	1980-81	54	/	0	
			L	Wrexham	11.82	1982	1	/	0	
				Blackpool	N/C	1983	3	/	0	
BRAND, Ken R.	Whitechapel	28.04.38	Eton Manor	Millwall	09.56	1956	13		0	(FB)
BRAND, Ralph L.	Edinburgh	08.12.36	Glasgow Rgrs.	Manchester C.	08.65	1965-66	20	/	2	(CF)S-8/S.U23-1/S.F.LGE
			TR	Sunderland	08.67	1967-68	31	/	7	REP./S.SCH.INT.
BRAND, Ray E.	Islington	02.10.34	Hatfield	Millwall	10.51	1955-60	150		8	(CH)
			TR	Southend U.	08.61	1961-62	22		9	
BRANDER, George M.	Aberdeen	01.11.29	Raith Rov.	Newcastle U.	03.52	1952	5		2	(W)
BRANDON, Ken A.	Birmingham	08.02.34	Kingstanding BC	Swindon T.	AM	1952	4		0	(OL)
				Chester C.	07.54	1953-55	39		7	
			TR	Leicester C.	07.56					
			TR	Darlington	06.58	1958	16		1	
BRANFOOT, Ian	Gateshead	26.01.47	Gateshead	Sheffield Wed.	07.65	1966-69	33	3	0	(D)
			TR	Doncaster Rov.	12.69	1969-72	156	/	5	
			TR	Lincoln C.	07.73	1973-77	166	/	11	
BRANNAN, Peter	Bradford	07.04.47		Bradford P.A.	02.69	1968-69	38	4	2	(F) Son of Robert
BRANNAN, Robert	Bradford	27.08.24		Bradford C.	09.47	1947-48	11		2	
BRANSTON, Terry G.	Rugby	25.07.38		Northampton T.	10.58	1960-66	244	2	2	(CH)
			TR	Luton T.	06.67	1967-70	101	2	9	
			TR	Lincoln C.	09.70	1970-72	99	1	1	
BRASS, Robert A.	Middlesbrough	09.11.43	JNRS	Middlesbrough	06.62					(HB)
			TR	Hartlepool U.	10.64	1964-65	27	1	0	
			TR	Darlington	09.66					
BRASTED, Gordon	Burnham	30.06.33	Burnham Ramblers	Arsenal	12.53					(CF)
			TR	Gillingham	07.56	1956	5		4	
BRATLEY, Anthony	Grimsby	30.04.39		Grimsby T.	08.57	1958	2		0	(FB)
BRATT, Harold	Salford	08.10.39	JNRS	Manchester U.	11.57					(HB) E.SCH.INT.
			TR	Doncaster Rov.	05.61	1961-62	54		0	
BRAY, Geoff C.	Chatham	30.05.51	Erith & Belvedere	Oxford U.	07.71	1972-74	22	11	6	(F)
			TR	Swansea C.	07.75	1975-76	43	3	20	
			TR	Torquay U.	11.76	1976	7	/	2	
BRAY, George	Oswaldtwistle	11.11.18	Gt.Harwood	Burnley	*	1946-51	207		8	(WH) Brother of Manchester C. player
BRAY, Ian M.	Neath	06.12.62	APP	Hereford U.	12.80	1981-83	63	3	3	(F)
BRAY, John	Rishton	16.03.37	JNRS	Blackburn Rov.	03.54	1959-64	153		2	(FB)
			TR	Bury	04.65	1965	32	/	0	
BRAY, Wayne	Bristol	17.11.64	APP	Bristol C.	11.81	1981-82	28	1	2	(M)
BRAYTON, Barry J.	Carlisle	29.09.38		Carlisle U.	01.60	1959-66	158	/	34	(F)
			TR	Workington	02.67	1966-67	43		8	
BRAZIER, Colin	Birmingham	06.06.57	Alvechurch	Wolverhampton W.	08.75	1976-81	69	9	2	(D)
			Jacksonville	Birmingham C.	09.82	1982	10	1	1	
			TR	Lincoln C.	04.83	1982	9	/	0	
			TR	Walsall	08.83	1983	45	/	2	
BRAZIL, Alan	Glasgow	15.06.59	APP	Ipswich T.	05.77	1977-82	143	11	70	(F) S-13/S.U'21-8
			TR	Tottenham H.	03.83	1982-83	29	2	9	
BRAZIL, Gary W.	Tunbridge Wells	19.09.62	Crystal Palace (APP)	Sheffield U.	08.80	1980-83	33	23	7	(F)
BREAKER, Tim S.	Bicester	02.07.65	APP	Luton T.	05.83	1983	2	/	0	(M)
BREAKS, Eddie	Halifax	29.12.19		Halifax T.	07.48	1948-54	179		1	(FB)
BREARS, Paul	Oldham	25.09.54	Oldham Ath.(AM)	Rochdale	08.73	1973-75	26	1	0	(HB)
BRECKIN, John	Sheffield	27.07.53	APP	Rotherham U.	11.71	1971-82	405	4	8	(D)
			L	Darlington	10.72	1972	4	/	0	
			TR	Bury	02.83	1982	17	/	0	
			TR	Doncaster Rov.	08.83	1983	17	1	0	
BREMNER, Desmond G.	Aberchider	07.09.52	Hibernian	Aston Villa	09.79	1979-83	166	4	8	(M) S-1/S.U23-9
BREMNER, Kevin J.	Banff	07.10.57	Keith	Colchester U.	10.80	1980-82	89	6	31	(F) Brother of Des
			L	Birmingham C.	10.82	1982	3	1	1	
			L	Wrexham	12.82	1982	4	/	1	
			L	Plymouth Arg.	01.83	1982	5	/	1	
			TR	Millwall	02.83	1982-83	58	1	21	
BREMNER, William J.	Stirling	09.12.42	JNRS	Leeds U.	12.59	1959-76	585	1	92	(M) S-54/S.U23-4/●
			TR	Hull C.	09.76	1976-77	61	/	6	S.SCH.INT
			TR	Doncaster Rov.	N/C	1979-81	2	3	0	
BRENEN, Albert	South Shields	05.10.15	South Shields	York C.	*	1946-50	190		7	
BRENNAN, Bryan	Halifax	25.05.33	JNRS	Stockport Co.	06.50	1950	4		0	E.SCH.INT.
BRENNAN, Frank	Anathill	23.04.24	Airdrie	Newcastle U.	05.46	1946-55	318		3	(CH) S-7
BRENNAN, Harry	Derby	17.11.30		Shrewsbury T.	12.53	1953-54	19		3	

Players Names	Birthplace	Date	Previous Club	League Club	Date Signed	Seasons Played	Apps	Sub	Gls	
BRENNAN, Ian	Easington	25.03.53	APP	Burnley	10.70	1979-79	173	2	11	(D)
			TR	Bolton W.	12.80	1980-81	16	1	0	
BRENNAN, Jim	Downpatrick	29.02.32	Glentoran	Birmingham C.	06.52					(FB)
			TR	Swindon T.	06.54	1954-55	17		1	
BRENNAN, Malcolm	Manchester	11.11.34		Crewe Alex.	12.52	1956	1		0	
BRENNAN, Mark R.	Rossendale	04.10.65	APP	Ipswich T.	04.83	1983	19	/	1	(M)
BRENNAN, Matt	Glasgow	03.01.43	St. Rochs	Luton T.	06.62	1962	4		1	(IF)
BRENNAN, Mike	Salford	17.05.52	APP	Manchester C.	12.69	1970-72	1	2	0	(CF)
			L	Stockport Co.	02.72	1971	18	/	3	
			TR	Rochdale	10.73	1973-74	35	2	4	
BRENNAN, Pat J.	Dublin	01.03.24	Shelbourne	Brighton & H.A.	08.48	1948-50	45		0	(HB)
BRENNAN, Ray J.	Blackpool	13.11.44	Wolverhampton W.(AM)	Blackburn Rov.	07.62					(F)
			TR	Barrow	03.64	1963-64	46		10	
			TR	Norwich C.	07.65					
BRENNAN, Robert A.	Belfast	14.03.25	Distillery	Luton T.	10.47	1947-48	69		22	(IF)N.I.-5/IRISH LGE. REP.
			TR	Birmingham C.	.07.49	1949	39		7	
			TR	Fulham	06.50	1950-52	73		13	
			TR	Norwich C.	07.53	1953-59	222		44	
BRENNAN, Seamus	Manchester	06.05.37	JNRS	Manchester U.	04.55	1957-69	290	1	3	(FB) EI-19
BRENNAN, Steve A.	Mile End	03.09.58	APP	Crystal Palace	02.76	1976-77	2	1	1	(M)
			TR	Plymouth Arg.	08.78	1978	6	/	0	
BRENT, Peter	Staveley	18.11.37	JNRS	Chesterfield	01.55	1959	2		0	(HB)
BRETHERTON, Tom	Chorley	09.04.20	Leyland M.	Accrington St.	02.47	1946	4		0	(IR)
BRETT, David S.	Chester	08.04.61		Chester C.	N/C	1983	24	5	2	(M)
BRETT, Ron A.	Stanford-le-Hope	04.09.37	JNRS	Crystal Palace	09.54	1955-58	36		12	(CF) d.1962
			TR	West Ham U.	06.59	1959-60	12		4	
			TR	Crystal Palace	03.62	1961	8		1	
BRETTELL, Ray L.	Strood	22.08.35		Doncaster Rov.	AM	1960	8		1	(IF)
BREWER, Anthony P.	Edmonton	20.05.32	JNRS	Millwall	10.49	1950-57	48		0	(G)
			TR	Northampton T.	12.57	1958-60	87		0	
BREWSTER, George W.	Barlborough	19.10.25	Retford T.	Bristol C.	09.49	1949-50	13		3	(F)
BREWSTER, John R.	Creswell	19.08.42		Sheffield U.	05.61					(HB)
			TR	Torquay U.	08.64	1964-65	21	/	2	
BREWSTER, William C.	Kinglassie	04.08.33	Dundonald B.	Chelsea	08.51					(G)
			TR	Southend U.	08.55	1955	2		0	
BRICE, Gordon H.J.	Bedford	04.05.24	Bedford St. C.	Luton T.	+	1946	13		0	(CH) Northants Cricketer
			TR	Wolverhampton W.	05.47	1947	12		0	
			TR	Reading	03.48	1947-52	198		8	
			TR	Fulham	12.52	1952-55	87		1	
BRICKLEY, Dennis	Bradford	09.09.29	Huddersfield T.(AM)	Bradford P.A.	08.49	1950-56	169		17	(OR) E.YTH.INT.
BRIDDON, Sam	Alfreton	26.07.15	Brentford (*)	Swansea C.	+	1946	18		0	(LH) d.1975
BRIDGE, M. Jack	Great Wakering	30.05.32	JNRS	Southend U.	08.50	1952-55	54		3	(HB)
BRIDGER, Dave J.	Hartley Wintney	08.11.41	JNRS	Reading	03.62	1962-64	10		0	(CH)
BRIDGES, Barry	Norwich	29.04.41	JNRS	Chelsea	05.58	1958-65	174	2	80	(CF) E-4/E.F.LGE.REP./
			TR	Birmingham C.	05.66	1966-68	83	/	36	E.YTH.INT./E.SCH.INT.●
			TR	Q.P.R.	08.68	1968-70	72	/	32	
			TR	Millwall	09.70	1970-71	77	/	27	
			TR	Brighton & H.A.	09.72	1972-73	56	10	14	
BRIDGES, Ben	Hull	03.02.37	JNRS	Hull C.	07.57	1957	1		0	(F)
BRIDGES, Bernard	Doncaster	28.02.59	JNRS	Scunthorpe U.	07.76	1976-77	22	1	0	(D)
BRIDGES, Harold	Burton	30.06.15	Manchester C.(*)	Tranmere Rov.	+	1946-47	33		9	(IL)
BRIDGETT, John	Walsall	10.04.29	JNRS	W.B.A.	05.46					(F)
			TR	Walsall	08.50	1950-54	108		18	
BRIDGETT, Ray	Nottingham	05.04.47	JNRS	Nottingham F.	05.64	1967-69	2	2	0	(FB)
BRIDGEWOOD, Gerry	Stoke	17.10.44	APP	Stoke C.	10.61	1960-68	90	4	6	(F)
			TR	Shrewsbury T.	02.69	1968-72	112	3	7	
BRIEN, William R.	Stoke	11.11.30		Port Vale	05.51	1953	1		0	(HB)
BRIER, John	Halifax	03.04.41	JNRS	Burnley	06.58					(WH)
			TR	Halifax T.	08.61	1961-65	78	2	0	
BRIERLEY, Keith	Dewsbury	14.12.51		Halifax T.	08.70	1969-72	52	4	11	(CF)
BRIERLEY, Ken	Ashton-under-Lyne	03.04.26	Range Boilers	Oldham Ath	+	1946-47	58		5	(OL)
			TR	Liverpool	02.48	1947-52	60		8	
			TR	Oldham Ath	03.53	1952-54	67		5	
BRIGGS, Alec M.	Sheffield	21.06.39	JNRS	Bristol C.	04.57	1959-69	348	2	1	(FB)
BRIGGS, Charlie E.	Newtown	04.04.11	Bradford P.A.(*)	Halifax T.	*					(G) *Guildford/
			Clyde	Rochdale	05.47	1946-47	12		0	Crystal Palace
			TR	Chesterfield	12.47					
BRIGGS, Gary	Leeds	08.05.48	APP	Middlesbrough	05.77					(D)
			TR	Oxford U.	01.78	1977-83	265	2	9	

Players Names	Birthplace	Date	Previous Club	League Club	Date Signed	Seasons Played	Apps	Sub	Gls	
BRIGGS, George H.	Shotton	27.2.23	Shotton Col.	Crystal Palace	11.47	1948-54	146		4	(CH)
BRIGGS, John	Barnsley	27.10.24	Huddersfield T.(AM)	Gillingham	N/L	1950-52	52		14	(F)
BRIGGS, John C.	Salford	24.11.18	Darwen	Accrington St.	+	1946-49	135		1	*Rochdale/
			TR	Southport	03.50	1949	3		0	E.SCH.INT
BRIGGS, Malcolm	Sunderland	14.09.61	APP	Birmingham C.	08.79	1978	0	1	0	(F)
BRIGGS, Max	Norwich	09.09.48	JNRS	Norwich C.	12.67	1968-73	127	8	0	(F)
			TR	Oxford U.	02.74	1973-77	94	3	1	
BRIGGS, Steve	Leeds	02.12.46	JNRS	Leeds U.	10.65					(CF)
			TR	Doncaster Rov.	02.69	1968-72	114	7	34	
BRIGGS, Tom H.	Chesterfield	27.11.23		Plymouth Arg.	+					(CF) E'B'-1/d.1984●
			TR	Grimsby T.	05.47	1947-50	116		77	
			TR	Coventry C.	01.51	1950-51	11		7	
			TR	Birmingham C.	09.51	1951-52	50		22	
			TR	Blackburn Rov.	12.52	1952-57	194		140	
			TR	Grimsby T.	03.58	1957-58	19		9	
BRIGGS, Tom R.	Rotherham	11.05.19		Huddersfield T.	+	1946-49	45		0	(CH)
			TR	Crewe Alex.	12.49	1949-55	202		2	
BRIGGS, W. Ronnie	Belfast	29.03.43	JNRS	Manchester U.	03.60	1960-61	9		0	(G)
			TR	Swansea C.	05.64	1964	27		0	
			TR	Bristol Rov.	06.65	1965-67	35	/	0	
BRIGGS, Walter	Middlesbrough	29.11.22	Cochranes	Middlesbrough	05.47	1946-47	2		0	(G)
			TR	Southport	06.48	1948	4		0	
			TR	Hartlepool U.	09.49	1949-51	45		0	
BRIGGS, Wilson W.	Gorebridge	15.05.42	Arniston Rov.	Aston Villa	08.59	1961.62	2		0	(FB)
BRIGHAM, Harry	Selby	19.11.14	Frickley Col.	Stoke C.	*	1946	12		0	(RB)
			TR	Nottingham F.	11.46	1946-47	35		2	
			TR	York C.	07.48	1948-49	56		5	
BRIGHT, David	Prudhoe	24.12.46		Sunderland	08.65					(FB)
			TR	Preston N.E.	08.67	1968	1	/	0	
			TR	Oldham Ath.	03.69	1968-69	19	/	0	
BRIGHT, Gerry	Northampton	02.12.34		Northampton T.	08.57	1956-57	4		0	
BRIGHT, Mark A.	Stoke	06.06.62	Leek T.	Port Vale	08.82	1981-83	18	11	10	(F)
BRIGHT, Stewart L.	Colchester	13.10.57	APP	Colchester U.	10.75	1975-76	23	2	0	(D)
BRIGNALL, Steve J.C.	Ashford	12.06.60	APP	Arsenal	05.78	1978	0	1	0	(D)
BRIGNULL, Phil A.	Stratford	02.10.60	APP	West Ham U.	09.78	1978	0	1	0	(D) E.SCH.INT.
			TR	Bournemouth	08.81	1981-83	119	/	10	
BRILEY, Les	Lambeth	02.10.56	APP	Chelsea	06.74					(M)
			TR	Hereford U.	05.76	1976-77	60	1	2	
			TR	Wimbledon	02.78	1977-79	59	2	2	
			TR	Aldershot	03.80	1979-83	157	/	3	
BRIMACOMBE, Anthony	Plymouth	06.08.39	Barnet	Plymouth Arg	AM	1965-67	15	2	0	(IF)
BRIMS, Don	Auchendinny	08.01.34	Motherwell	Bradford P.A.	05.58	1958-59	76		3	(HB)
BRINDLE, John J.	Blackburn	12.07.17	Rochdale	Chelsea	+					d.1975
			TR	Rochdale	08.47	1947	2		0	
			TR	New Brighton	03.48	1947	9		3	
BRINDLE, William	Liverpool	29.01.50	APP	Everton	08.67	1967	1	/	0	(HB)
			TR	Barnsley	05.70	1970	0	1	0	
BRINDLEY, John	Ashbourne	02.06.31		Chesterfield	12.53	1953	1		0	
BRINDLEY, John C.	Nottingham	29.01.47	JNRS	Nottingham F.	02.64	1965-69	7	8	0	(D) E. YTH. INT./E.SCH.INT.
			TR	Notts. Co.	05.70	1970-75	221	2	0	
			TR	Gillingham	07.76	1976	19	1	1	
BRINE, Peter K.	London	18.07.53	APP	Middlesbrough	09.70	1972-77	59	21	6	(F)
BRINTON, Ernie J.	Bristol	26.05.08	Newport Co. (*)	Aldershot	08.46	1946	12		0	(LH) *Bristol C.
BRINTON, John V.	Avonmouth	11.07.16	Newport Co. (*)	Derby Co.	*					(W)*Bristol C.
			TR	Stockport Co.	07.46	1946-47	58		9	Brother of Ernie
			TR	Orient	08.48	1948	4		1	
BRISCOE, James P.	Swinton	14.10.23	JNRS	Sheffield Wed.	08.46	1946	5		3	(CF)
BRISCOE, James E.R.	Clockface	23.04.17	Hearts	Northampton T.	09.46	1946-48	53		17	(OR) *Preston N.E./d.1981
BRISCOE, John	Huddersfield	31.05.47		Barnsley	10.66	1966-67	11	/	5	(F)
BRISLEY, Terry W.	Stepney	04.07.50	APP	Orient	07.68	1967-74	133	9	10	(M)
			L	Southend U.	03.75	1974	8	/	0	
			TR	Millwall	07.75	1975-77	106	1	15	
			TR	Charlton Ath.	01.78	1977-78	44	4	5	
			TR	Portsmouth	07.79	1979-80	55	/	13	
BRISSETT, Trevor A.	Stoke	02.01.61	JNRS	Stoke C.	04.78					(D)
			TR	Port Vale	05.80	1980-81	47	8	0	
			TR	Darlington	08.82	1982	10	2	0	
BRISTOW, George A.	Chiswick	25.06.33	JNRS	Brentford	07.50	1950-60	244		9	(HB) Father of Guy
			TR	Q.P.R.	05.61					
BRISTOW, Guy	Kingsbury	23.10.55	APP	Watford	07.73	1974-76	18	5	1	(D) Son of George

Players Names	Birthplace	Date	Previous Club	League Club	Date Signed	Seasons Played	Apps	Sub	Gls	
BRITT, Martin C.	Leigh	17.01.46	APP	West Ham U.	01.63	1962-65	20	/	6	(CF) E.YTH.INT.
			TR	Blackburn Rov.	03.66	1965	8	/	0	
BRITTAN, Colin	Bristol	02.06.27	Bristol O.B.	Tottenham H.	10.48	1950-57	40		1	(WH)
BRITTEN, Martyn E.	Bristol	01.05.55	APP	Bristol Rov.	05.73	1974-76	17	3	2	(M)
			TR	Reading	08.77	1977-78	6	2	0	
BRITTON, Ian	Dundee	19.05.54	APP	Chelsea	07.71	1972-81	253	10	33	(M)
			Dundee U.	Blackpool	12.83	1983	29	1	9	
BRITTON, Jim	Salford	27.05.20		Bradford P.A.	+	1946	1		0	
			TR	Rochdale	12.47	1947-48	20		0	
BROAD, Ron	Sandbach	18.08.33	Congleton T.	Crewe Alex.	AM	1955	6		0	(OL)
BROADBENT, Albert H.	Dudley	20.08.34	Dudley T.	Notts. Co.	03.52	1953-54	31		11	(OL)
			TR	Sheffield Wed.	07.55	1955-57	80		17	
			TR	Rotherham U.	12.57	1957-58	48		13	
			TR	Doncaster Rov.	06.59	1959-61	100		20	
			TR	Lincoln C.	11.61	1961-62	38		4	
			TR	Doncaster Rov.	01.63	1962-65	106		19	
			TR	Bradford P.A.	10.65	1965-66	55	/	11	
			TR	Hartlepool U.	02.67	1966-67	25	/	3	
			TR	Rotherham U.	03.68					
BROADBENT, Peter F.	Ellerington	15.05.33	JNRS	Brentford	05.50	1950	16		1	(IR)E-7/E.U23-1/E'B'-1/
			TR	Wolverhampton W.	02.51	1950-64	453		127	E.F.LGE REP.●
			TR	Shrewsbury T.	01.65	1964-65	68	/	7	
			TR	Aston Villa	10.66	1966-68	60	1	2	
			TR	Stockport Co.	10.69	1969	31	/	1	
BROADFOOT, Joe	Lewisham	04.03.40	JNRS	Millwall	01.58	1958-63	225		60	(OR)
			TR	Ipswich T.	10.63	1963-65	96	/	19	
			TR	Northampton T.	11.65	1965	17	/	1	
			TR	Millwall	07.66	1966	26	/	5	
			TR	Ipswich T.	02.67	1966	4	1	0	
BROADHURST, Brian W.	Sheffield	24.11.38	Hallam	Chesterfield	10.61	1961	7		0	(F)
BROADHURST, Kevin	Dewsbury	03.06.59	APP	Birmingham C.	03.77	1976-83	148	6	10	(D)
			L	Walsall	11.79	1979	3	/	0	
BROADIS, Ivor A.	Poplar	18.12.22	Tottenham H.(AM)	Carlisle U.	08.46	1946-48	91		52	(IF)E-14/E.F.LGE REP.
			TR	Sunderland	02.49	1948-51	79		25	
			TR	Manchester C.	10.51	1951-53	74		10	
			TR	Newcastle U.	10.53	1953-54	42		17	
			TR	Carlisle U.	07.55	1955-58	159		32	
BROADLEY, Les	Goole	10.08.30	Goole T.	Scunthorpe U.	08.52	1952	5		2	(CF)
BROADLEY, Pat J.	Croy	13.05.26	Sligo	Oldham Ath.	06.51	1951	6		0	
BROCK, Kevin S.	Middleton Stoney	09.09.62	APP	Oxford U.	09.79	1979-83	144	11	19	(M) E.SCH.INT./E.U'21-3
BROCKBANK, Andrew	Haverigg	23.09.61	APP	Blackpool	12.79	1979-82	32	4	1	(M)
BROCKEN, Budde J.P.	Holland	12.09.57	Willem II	Birmingham C.	08.81	1981	17	/	0	(M)
BROCKLEHURST, John F.	Bolton	15.12.27	Stalybridge	Accrington St.	05.52	1952	34		0	(HB)
			Heywood	Bradford P.A.	08.54	1954-55	47		1	
BRODDLE, Julian R.	Laughton	01.11.64	APP	Sheffield U.	11.82	1981	1	/	0	(F)
			TR	Scunthorpe U.	08.83	1983	9	4	1	
BRODERICK, Mortimer	Cork	01.09.23	Cork	Sheffield U.	08.50	1950	2		0	EI.F.LGE REP.
BRODIE, Chic T.	Duntocher	22.02.37	Partick Avondale	Manchester C.	03.54					(G)
			TR	Gillingham	07.57	1957	18		0	S.SCH.INT.
			TR	Aldershot	07.58	1958-60	95		0	
			TR	Wolverhampton W.	02.61	1960	1		0	
			TR	Northampton T.	09.61	1961-63	87		0	
			TR	Brentford	11.63	1963-70	201	/	0	
BRODIE, Eric	Edinburgh	08.11.40	Dundee U.	Shrewsbury T.	06.63	1963-67	181	4	24	(WH)
			TR	Chester C.	05.68	1968-69	43	1	4	
			TR	Tranmere Rov.	10.69	1969-71	80	3	4	
BRODIE, John	Ashington	08.09.47	Whitley Bay	Carlisle U.	12.67	1967-68	8	1	0	(D)
			TR	Bradford P.A.	06.69	1969	43	/	0	
			TR	Port Vale	01.71	1970-76	175	4	2	
BRODIE, Murray	Glasgow	26.09.50	Cumbernauld U.	Leicester C.	10.69	1969	3	/	2	(F)
			TR	Aldershot	09.70	1970-82	450	11	84	
BROGAN, Dave	Glasgow	11.01.39	St.Anthonys	Luton T.	09.60	1960	4		0	(F)
BROGAN, Frank A.	Glasgow	03.08.42	Glasgow Celtic	Ipswich T.	06.64	1964-69	201	2	58	(W) Brother of Jim
			TR	Halifax T.	11.71	1971-72	25	2	6	
BROGAN, Jim	Glasgow	05.06.44	Glasgow Celtic	Coventry C.	08.75	1975	28	/	0	(FB)S-4/S.F.LGE REP.
BROGDEN, Lee	Leeds	18.10.49	Ashley Rd F.C.	Rotherham U.	12.67	1967-71	79	8	16	(W)
			TR	Rochdale	03.72	1971-73	48	9	7	
BROLLS, Norman	Wigtown	26.09.33	T. Lanark	Bradford P.A.	06.56	1956	11		0	
BROLLY, Mike	Kilmarnock	06.10.54	JNRS	Chelsea	10.71	1972-73	7	1	1	(M) S.SCH.INT
			TR	Bristol C.	06.74	1974-75	27	3	2	
			TR	Grimsby T.	09.76	1976-78	246	8	27	
			TR	Derby Co.	08.82	1982	41	1	4	
			TR	Scunthorpe U.	08.83	1983	40	1	5	

Players Names	Birthplace	Date	Previous Club	League Club	Date Signed	Seasons Played	Apps	Sub	Gls	
BROLLY, Tom H.	Belfast	01.06.12	Sheffield Wed.(*)	Millwall	*	1946-49	94		2	(RH)*Glenavon/N.I.-4.
BROMAGE, Russell	Stoke	09.11.59	APP	Port Vale	11.77	1977-83	222	7	10	(M)
			L	Oldham Ath.	10.83	1983	2	/	0	
BROMILOW, Geoff W.	Farnworth	14.09.45		Bolton W.	AM	1968	3	2	0	(IF)
BROMILOW, George J.	Southport	04.12.31	Northern Nomads	Southport	AM	1955-58	84		37	(IF) E.AMAT.INT./E.YTH.INT./ Son of famous player
BROMLEY, Brian	Burnley	20.03.46	APP	Bolton W.	03.63	1962-68	164	1	25	(IF) E.YTH.INT.
			TR	Portsmouth	11.68	1968-71	88	1	3	
			TR	Brighton & H.A.	11.71	1971-73	47	3	3	
			TR	Reading	09.73	1973-74	13	1	1	
			L	Darlington	02.75	1974	3	/	0	
BROMLEY, Tom C.	West Bromwich	30.04.33	Swan Village	Walsall	AM	1953	13		1	(IF)
BROOK, Daryl	Holmfirth	19.11.60	APP	Huddersfield T.	11.78	1978	1	/	0	(M)
BROOK, Harold	Sheffield	15.10.21		Sheffield U.	+	1946-53	229		89	(CF)
			TR	Leeds U.	07.54	1954-47	102		46	
			TR	Lincoln C.	03.58	1957	4		1	
BROOK, Lewis	Halifax	27.07.18	Northowran	Huddersfield T.	*	1946	6		1	(CF)
			TR	Oldham Ath.	03.48	1947-56	189		14	
BROOKE, Gary J.	Bethnal Green	24.11.60	APP	Tottenham H.	10.78	1980-83	48	21	14	(M)
BROOKE, Maurice	Thurcroft	04.06.25	Buxton	Stockport Co.	01.51	1950	1		0	(F)
BROOKES, Colin	Barnsley	02.01.42	JNRS	Barnsley	05.59	1959-60	46		5	(F). E.SCH.INT
			TR	W.B.A.	06.61					
			TR	Peterborough U.	06.62					
			TR	Southport	07.63	1963	20		2	
BROOKES, Eric	Mapplewell	03.02.44	JNRS	Barnsley	04.61	1960-68	324	1	1	(FB) E.YTH.INT./ E.SCH.INT.
			TR	Northampton T.	07.69	1969-70	81	/	1	
			TR	Peterborough U.	06.71	1971-72	41	1	1	
BROOKES, John	Stalybridge	18.10.44		Sheffield Wed.	09.64					(F)
			TR	Southport	07.65	1965	14	/	5	
			TR	York C.	08.66	1966	1	/	0	
			Cleveland	Stockport Co.	08.70	1970	18	2	3	
BROOKES, Stan K.	Doncaster	02.02.53	APP	Doncaster Rov.	02.71	1971-76	230	5	7	(D)
BROOKES, William A.	Dudley	19.04.31	Churchfield	W.B.A.	05.49	1953-56	19		0	(WH)
BROOKFIELD, Anthony	Southport	11.04.59	JNRS	Southport	N/C	1976-77	14	5	1	(M)
BROOKIN, William J.	Tilehurst	14.06.19		Newport Co.	08.46	1946	2		0	(G)
BROOKING, Trevor D.	Barking	02.10.48	APP	West Ham U.	05.66	1967-83	521	7	88	(M) E-47/E.U23-1/ E.YTH.INT./E.F.LGE.REP./ E.SCH.INT.●
BROOKS, Anthony	Ince	12.03.44	APP	Blackpool	03.62					(F)
			TR	Preston N.E.	08.62					
				Bury	08.63	1963	1		0	
			TR	Stockport Co.	06.64	1964	2		0	
BROOKS, Harry	Tibshelf	02.06.15	Doncaster Rov.(*)	Aldershot	+	1946-47	23		14	(CF)
BROOKS, John	Stoke	08.03.27		Stoke C.	12.46	1950	2		0	(HB)
BROOKS, John T.	London	23.08.47	APP	Q.P.R.	08.65					(G)
			TR	Ipswich T.	12.66					
			TR	Northampton T.	10.67	1967	1	/	0	
BROOKS, Johnny	Reading	23.12.31	JNRS	Reading	04.49	1949-52	46		6	(IF) E-3/ Father of Shaun
			TR	Tottenham H.	02.53	1952-59	166		46	
			TR	Chelsea	12.59	1959-60	46		6	
			TR	Brentford	09.61	1961-63	83		36	
				Crystal Palace	01.64	1963	7		0	
BROOKS, Norman H.	Reading	28.05.20	Huntleys	Reading	AM	1946	1		0	d.1973
BROOKS, Shaun	London	09.10.62	APP	Crystal Palace	10.79	1979-83	47	7	4	(M)E.SCH.INT./E.YTH. INT./Son of John
			TR	Orient	10.83	1983	33	3	9	
BROOKS, Steve M.	Liverpool	18.06.55	Marine	Southport	02.77	1976-77	65	/	3	(D)
			TR	Hartlepool U.	07.78	1978-79	62	1	2	
BROOKS, Tom W.	Wallsend	02.02.48	APP	Lincoln C.	02.65	1965-70	98	9	1	(HB)
BROOME, Frank H.	Berkhamsted	11.06.15	Berkhamsted	Aston Villa	*	1946	1		0	(CF) E-7
			TR	Derby Co.	09.46	1946-49	112		45	
			TR	Notts.Co.	10.49	1949-52	105		35	
			TR	Brentford	07.53	1953	6		1	
			TR	Crewe Alex.	10.53	1953-54	36		16	
BROOMFIELD, Des	Hove	06.10.21		Brighton & H.A.	01.47	1946-47	20		0	(HB)
BROOMFIELD, Ian L.	Bristol	17.12.50	APP	Bristol C.	08.68	1968-72	17	3	2	(F)
			TR	Stockport Co.	12.72	1972-74	22	5	1	
			S. Africa	Workington	10.75	1975	3	/	0	
BROOMFIELD, John	Crewe	06.06.34		Crewe Alex.	AM	1956	1		0	
BROOMHALL, Keith L.	Stoke	21.05.51	APP	Port Vale	APP	1968	1	1	0	(FB)
BROPHY, Hubert	Dublin	02.09.48	Shamrock Rov.	Crystal Palace	07.66	1966	0	1	0	(F) NI.AMAT.INT.

Players Names	Birthplace	Date	Previous Club	League Club	Date Signed	Seasons Played	Apps	Sub	Gls	
BROTHERSTON, Noel	Belfast	18.11.56	APP	Tottenham H.	04.74	1975	1	/	0	(M)NI-25/NI.U21-1
			TR	Blackburn Rov.	07.77	1977-83	241	6	32	
BROUGH, Neil K.	Daventry	22.12.65	APP	Northampton T.	APP	1983	3	2	0	(M)
BROUGHTON, Edward	Bradford	09.02.25		Bradford C.	+					(OR)
			TR	New Brighton	07.47	1947	4		0	
			TR	Crystal Palace	08.48	1948-52	96		6	
BROWN, Alan	Lewes	11.12.37	Portslade	Brighton & H.A.	09.58	1960-61	7		2	(HB)
			TR	Exeter C.	01.62	1961	11		3	
BROWN, Alan	Easington	22.05.59	APP	Sunderland	07.76	1976-81	87	26	21	(F)
			L	Newcastle	11.81	1981	5	/	3	
			TR	Shrewsbury	08.82	1982-83	65	/	15	
			TR	Doncaster Rov.	03.84	1983	9	/	2	
BROWN, Alan D.	Leven	12.10.26	E. Fife	Blackpool	12.50	1950-56	157		68	(IF)S-14/S.F.LGE REP.
			TR	Luton T.	02.57	1956-60	151		52	
			TR	Portsmouth	03.61	1960-62	69		8	
BROWN, Alan W.	Corbridge	26.08.14	Huddersfield T.(*)	Burnley	+	1946-48	88		0	(CH)*Spen Black/
			TR	Notts.Co.	10.48	1948	13		0	E.F.LGE REP.
BROWN, Albert E.	Bristol	04.03.34	Exeter U.	Crystal Palace	08.56	1957	3		0	(HB)
			TR	Q.P.R.	07.59					
BROWN, Albert R.	Smenthan	14.08.17	Nottingham F.(*)	Wrexham	+	1946	24		3	
			TR	Mansfield T.	07.47	1947	16		2	
BROWN, Alex	Glasgow	15.08.30	Partick Th.	Preston N.E.	06.57					(FB)
			TR	Carlisle U.	06.58	1958-60	104		0	
BROWN, Alex D.	Grangemouth	24.03.39	Partick Th.	Everton	09.63	1963-70	174	35	9	(FB) S.F.LGE REP.
			TR	Shrewsbury T.	05.71	1971	21	/	0	
			TR	Southport	07.72	1972	17	2	0	
BROWN, Alex R.	Sale	28.02.27		Mansfield T.	11.46	1946	5		0	
BROWN, Alistair	Musselburgh	12.04.51	JNRS	Leicester C.	04.68	1968-71	93	8	32	(F)
			TR	W.B.A.	03.72	1971-82	254	24	72	
			TR	Crystal Palace	03.83	1982	11	/	2	
			TR	Walsall	08.83	1983	37	1	13	
BROWN, Andrew	Coatbridge	19.02.15	Cardiff C.(*)	Torquay U.	*	1946	3		0	(LB) d.1973
BROWN, Andy L.	Liverpool	17.08.63	JNRS	Tranmere Rov.	N/C	1982	1	/	0	(D)
BROWN, Anthony	Oldham	03.10.45	APP	W.B.A.	10.63	1963-79	561	12	217	(F) E-1/E.F.LGE.REP.●
			TR	Torquay	10.81	1981-82	38	7	11	
BROWN, Anthony J.	Bradford	17.09.58	Thackley	Leeds U.	03.83	1982-83	23	/	1	(D)
BROWN, Brian D.	Shoreditch	10.09.49	APP	Chelsea	11.66					(FB)
			TR	Millwall	03.68	1968-74	187	5	6	
BROWN, Cyril	Ashington	25.05.18		Sunderland	+					(WH)
			TR	Notts.Co.	08.46	1946	13		5	
			TR	Rochdale	08.48	1948-50	61		10	
BROWN, David	Wallasey	21.10.63		Tranmere Rov.	N/C	1982	1	/	0	(D)
BROWN, David J.	Hartlepool	28.01.57	Horden C.W.	Middlesbrough	02.77	1977	10	/	0	(G)
			L	Plymouth Arg.	08.79	1979	5	/	0	
			TR	Oxford U.	10.79	1979-80	21	/	0	
			TR	Bury	09.81	1981-83	100	/	0	
BROWN, Dennis J.	Reading	08.02.44	JNRS	Chelsea	06.62	1963	10		1	(IF)
			TR	Swindon T.	11.64	1964-66	90	/	38	
			TR	Northampton T.	02.67	1966-68	41	5	10	
			TR	Aldershot	07.69	1969-74	237	8	56	
BROWN, Doug	Airdrie	21.03.58	Clydebank	Sheffield U.	03.79	1978-79	17	8	2	(F)
BROWN, Edward	Preston	28.02.26		Preston N.E.	08.48	1948-50	36		6	(CF)●
			TR	Southampton	09.50	1950-51	57		32	
			TR	Coventry C.	03.52	1951-54	85		50	
			TR	Birmingham C.	10.54	1954-58	158		74	
			TR	Orient	01.59	1958-60	63		27	
BROWN, Edward A.C.	St. Pancras	04.10.27		Brenford	02.50					
				Torquay U.	08.50					
			TR	Aldershot	08.53	1953	3		0	
BROWN, Ernie	Stockport	30.05.23	Manchester C.(+)	Aldershot	06.46	1946	12		0	(LH)
			TR	Accrington St.	08.49	1949	2		0	
BROWN, Ernie C.	South Shields	03.02.21	South Shields	Newcastle U.	+					
			TR	Southend U.	02.47	1946-47	5		0	
				Hartlepool U.	01.51					
BROWN, Fred	Leyton	06.12.31	Leytonstone	Aldershot	06.52	1952-54	107		0	(G)
			TR	W.B.A.	05.55	1955-57	11		0	
			TR	Portsmouth	06.58	1958-59	18		0	
BROWN, George	Longcroft	12.01.32	Stenhousemuir	Crewe Alex.	06.57	1957	38		0	(G)
BROWN, George			Airdrie	Southport	04.51	1950	1		0	
BROWN, George	Sheffield	18.10.34	JNRS	Liverpool	10.51					(RH)E.SCH.INT.
			TR	Chesterfield	05.53	1953-54	66		5	
BROWN, George D.	Airdrie	08.05.28	Clyde	Bradford P.A.	07.56	1956	17		2	

Players Names	Birthplace	Date	Previous Club	League Club	Date Signed	Seasons Played	Apps	Sub	Gls	
BROWN, Gordon	Dunfirmline	04.02.32		Blackburn Rov.	04.51					(F)
			TR	Newport Co.	08.55	1955-58	138		13	
			TR	Gillingham	06.59	1959-60	67		13	
BROWN, Gordon	Ellesmere Port	30.06.33	JNRS	Wolverhampton W.	09.51					(F)
			TR	Scunthorpe U.	12.52	1952-56	154		71	
			TR	Derby Co.	01.57	1956-59	53		20	
			TR	Southampton	03.60	1959-60	8		2	
			TR	Barrow	07.61	1961-63	39		16	
			TR	Southport	01.64	1963	4		1	
BROWN, Gordon A.	East Kilbride	07.12.65	APP	Rotherham U.	12.83	1983	1	/	0	
BROWN, Gordon S.	Worksop	21.03.29	JNRS	Nottingham F.	12.46					(CF)
			TR	York C.	06.50	1950-57	322		26	
BROWN, Graham C.	Matlock	21.03.44		Millwall	12.64					(G)
			Crawley T.	Brighton & H.A.	02.66					
			Crawley T.	Watford	08.68					
			Crawley T.	Mansfield T.	08.69	1969-73	142	/	0	
			TR	Doncaster Rov.	07.74	1974-75	53	/	0	
			TR	Swansea C.	09.76	1976	4	/	0	
			TR	Southport	12.76					
			Portland Timbers	York C.	08.77	1977-79	69	/	0	
			TR	Rotherham U.	02.80	1979-80	31	/	0	
			TR	Mansfield T.	N/C	1981	1	/	0	
BROWN, Graham F.	Leicester	05.11.50	APP	Leicester C.	03.70	1969	0	1	0	(F)
BROWN, Harry T.	Kingsbury	09.04.24	Q.P.R.(+)	Notts .Co.	+	1946-48	93		0	(G) d.1982
			TR	Derby .Co.	10.49	1949-50	37		0	
			TR	Q.P.R.	08.51	1951-55	187		0	
			TR	Plymouth Arg.	08.56	1956-57	66		0	
			TR	Exeter C.	09.58					
BROWN, Henry S.	Kirkcaldy	23.05.18	Reading(*)	Wolverhampton W.	*					(IL)*Hibs/Darlington/
			TR	Hull C.	05.46	1946	22		0	Chesterfield/Plymouth Arg. d.1963
BROWN, Hugh	Carmyle	07.12.21	Partick Th.	Torquay U.	11.50	1950-51	55		0	(WH)S-3/S.F.LGE.REP.
BROWN, Irvin	Lewes	20.09.35	JNRS	Brighton & H.A.	10.52	1957	3		0	(HB)
			TR	Bournemouth	09.58	1958-62	65		2	
BROWN, James	Cumnock	16.02.24	Motherwell	Chesterfield	05.48	1948	5		2	(CF)
			TR	Bradford C.	11.48	1948	20		11	
			Q.of South	Carlisle U.	09.50	1950-51	15		9	
BROWN, James	Manchester	05.10.35		Rochdale	04.57	1956-60	52		4	(OR)
BROWN, James B.	Stirling	07.06.39	Dumbarton	Darlington	09.60	1960-62	11		0	(HB)
BROWN, James G.	Coatbridge	11.05.52	Albion Rov.	Chesterfield	12.72	1972-73	47	/	0	(G) S-1/S.U23-4
			TR	Sheffield U.	03.74	1973-77	170	/	0	
			Washington Dips	Cardiff C.	12.82	1982	3	/	0	
			Kettering	Chesterfield	07.83	1983	40	/	1	
BROWN, James K.	Wallyford	03.10.43	APP	Aston Villa	10.70	1969-74	72	4	2	(M)
			TR	Preston N.E.	10.75	1975-77	64	/	3	
			Greece	Portsmouth	02.80	1979	5	/	0	
BROWN, Jeremy	Newport	13.06.61	APP	Newport Co.	06.78	1978	2	1	0	(F)
BROWN, Joe	Cramlington	26.04.29	JNRS	Middlesbrough	+	1949-50	11		0	(WH)
			TR	Burnley	08.52	1952	6		0	
			TR	Bournemouth	06.54	1954-59	215		5	
			TR	Aldershot	07.60	1960	5		0	
BROWN, Joe S.	Port Sunlight	07.05.20	Port Sunlight	Chester C.	09.47	1946-47	15		2	(OL)
BROWN, John	Wadebridge	29.07.40	Wadebridge	Plymouth Arg.	10.60	1960-62	8		2	(F)
			TR	Bristol Rov.	07.63	1963-67	157	/	34	
BROWN, John	Edinburgh	06.03.40	Dunbar	Colchester U.	09.61	1962	1		0	(HB)
BROWN, John	Belfast	08.11.14	Coventry C.(*)	Birmingham C.	*					(OR)N.I.-10*Belfast Celtic
			Barry T.	Ipswich T.	05.48	1948-50	98		25	Wolverhampton W.
BROWN, John C.	Bradford	30.12.47	APP	Preston N.E.	03.65	1966-74	67	/	0	(G)
			L	Stockport Co.	11.70	1970	26	/	0	
			TR	Stockport Co.	07.75	1975	15	/	0	
			TR	Wigan Ath.	N/L	1978-81	93	/	0	
BROWN, John L.	Crook	23.03.21	Stanley U.	York C.	02.48	1947-49	21		0	
BROWN, John M.			Queens.Pk	Shrewsbury T.	AM	1953	5		3	(CF)
BROWN, John T.	Edinburgh	02.04.35	T. Lanark	Tranmere Rov.	01.61	1960-61	33		0	(FB) S.SCH.INT.
			TR	Hartlepool U.	07.62	1962-63	68		10	
BROWN, Keith	Liverpool	19.10.57	East Villa	Southport	N/C	1976	4	/	0	(D)
BROWN, Keith	Hucknall	01.01.42	JNRS	Notts.Co.	01.59	1958	8		4	(F) E.SCH.INT.
			TR	Rotherham U.	07.59					
BROWN, Keith	Grimsby	23.09.54	Nottingham F.(APP)	Grimsby T.	10.73	1973-75	32	7	5	(IF)
BROWN, Keith G.	Coseley	16.07.54	JNRS	Walsall	07.73	1973-74	8	2	0	(FB)
BROWN, Keith J.	Bournemouth	29.01.42	Pokesdown	Bournemouth	09.60	1963-64	15		0	(FB)
BROWN, Keith T.	Bristol	28.09.59	Bristol St.George	Bristol Rov.	10.77	1978-80	4	3	0	(F)

Players Names	Birthplace	Date	Previous Club	League Club	Date Signed	Seasons Played	Apps	Sub	Gls	
BROWN, Ken	Forest Gate	16.02.34	Neville U.	West Ham U.	10.51	1952-66	386	/	4	(CH) E-1
			TR	Torquay U.	05.67	1967-68	40	2	1	
BROWN, Ken G.	Barnsley	21.03.52	APP	Barnsley	04.70	1969-77	267	9	24	(F)
			TR	Bournemouth	06.78	1978-79	29	3	4	
BROWN, Ken J.	Coventry	18.10.33		Coventry C.	01.56	1956	2		0	
			Corby T.	Nottingham F.	11.56					
			TR	Bournemouth	07.57	1957	6		1	
			TR	Torquay U.	07.58	1958	8		1	
BROWN, Laurie	Shildon	22.08.37	B.Auckland	Darlington	AM	1958	3		0	(CH) E.AMAT.INT.
			B.Auckland	Northampton T.	10.60	1960	33		21	
			TR	Arsenal	08.61	1961-63	101		2	
			TR	Tottenham H.	04.63	1963-65	62	/	3	
			TR	Norwich C.	09.66	1966-68	80	1	2	
			TR	Bradford P.A.	12.68	1968-69	36	/	1	
BROWN, Malcolm	Salford	13.12.56	APP	Bury	10.75	1973-76	10	1	0	(D)
			TR	Huddersfield T.	05.77	1977-82	256	/	16	
			TR	Newcastle U.	08.83					
BROWN, Mick	Walsall	11.07.39	JNRS	Hull C.	10.58	1959-65	8	/	0	(FB)
			TR	Lincoln C.	07.67	1967	39	/	0	
BROWN, Mick J.	Slough	11.04.44	APP	Fulham	09.61	1961-62	4		0	(F)
			TR	Millwall	02.65	1964-66	47	5	11	
			TR	Luton T.	07.67	1967-68	9	5	2	
			TR	Colchester U.	10.68	1968-69	47	5	12	
BROWN, Mick J.L.	Swansea	27.09.51	APP	Crystal Palace	09.69					(HB) W.SCH.INT.
			TR	Brighton & H.A.	06.73	1973	5	3	1	
			L	Brentford	09.73	1973	3	/	0	
BROWN, Monty	Grimsby	07.09.43	JNRS	Scunthorpe U.	07.63	1964-65	20	/	6	(F)
BROWN, Neil R.	Sheffield	16.01.66	APP	Chesterfield	11.83	1983	5	/	0	(D)Twin brother of Philip J.
BROWN, Owen J.	Liverpool	04.09.60	JNRS	Liverpool	11.78					(F)
			TR	Carlisle U.	06.80	1980	4	/	2	
			TR	Tranmere Rov.	08.81	1981	29	8	8	
			TR	Crewe Alex.	08.82	1982	1	/	0	
			TR	Tranmere Rov.	10.82	1982-83	47	9	12	
BROWN, Peter	Hemel Hempstead	01.09.61	Chelsea (APP)	Wimbledon	08.80	1980-81	53	2	3	(D)
BROWN, Peter B.	Andover	13.07.34	JNRS	Southampton	01.52	1953-57	16		3	(F)
			TR	Wrexham	07.58	1958-59	33		9	
BROWN, Philip	Hartlepool	30.05.59		Hartlepool	07.78	1979-83	169	6	7	(M)
BROWN, Philip J.	Sheffield	16.01.66	APP	Chesterfield	10.83	1982-83	16	1	6	(F)
BROWN, R. Berry	West Hartlepool	06.09.27		Manchester U.	08.46	1947-48	4		0	(G)
			TR	Doncaster Rov.	01.49	1948	4		0	
				Hartlepool U.	08.51	1951-55	125		0	
BROWN, Ralph	Ilkeston	26.02.44	APP	Aston Villa	03.61					(F)
			TR	Notts. Co.	05.62	1962	18		3	
BROWN, Ray M.	Carlisle	11.02.28	Queens Pk	Notts. Co.	08.51	1951	7			
BROWN, Robert	Glasgow	09.08.24	Camerons	Derby Co.	10.47					(IF)
			TR	Southend U.	07.48	1948-49	12		0	
			TR	Shrewsbury T.	07.50	1950-52	104		41	
			TR	Barnsley	07.53	1953-56	121		55	
			TR	Rotherham U.	09.56	1956-57	41		13	
BROWN, Robert	Bristol	14.05.49	APP	Bristol Rov.	06.67	1968-71	28	7	4	(IF)
			L	Newport Co.	03.70	1969	8	1	0	
BROWN, Robert	Motherwell	02.12.31	Motherwell	Workington	05.56	1956-67	418	1	2	(FB)
BROWN, Robert	Workington	23.11.55		Workington	08.74	1974-76	44	/	0	(D)
BROWN, Robert C.	Plymouth	24.11.53	JNRS	Chelsea	08.72					(F)
			TR	Sheffield Wed.	08.74	1974-75	17	5	3	
			L	Aldershot	02.76	1975	3	2	0	
BROWN, Robert H.	Streatham	02.05.40	Barnet	Fulham	AM	1960-61	8		4	(CF) E.AMAT.INT.
			TR	Watford	11.61	1961-62	28		10	
			TR	Northampton T.	12.63	1963-66	51	/	22	
			TR	Cardiff C.	10.66	1966-67	50	/	24	
BROWN, Robert J.	Great Yarmouth	07.11.15	Gorleston	Charlton Ath.	*					(IL)
			TR	Nottingham F.	05.46	1946-47	46		17	
			TR	Aston Villa	10.47	1947-48	30		9	
BROWN, Roger W.	Tamworth	12.12.52	A.P. Leamington	Bournemouth	02.78	1977-78	63	/	3	(D)
			TR	Norwich C.	07.79	1979	16	/	0	
			TR	Fulham	03.80	1979-83	141	/	18	
			TR	Bournemouth	12.83	1983	23	/	2	
BROWN, Ron	Sunderland	26.12.44	Whitley Bay	Blackpool	11.65	1965-70	54	7	13	(F)
			TR	Plymouth Arg.	02.71	1970-72	31	5	3	
			TR	Bradford C.	09.72	1972-74	90	7	11	
BROWN, Ron	Ballymoney	20.03.23	Linfield	Plymouth Arg.	+					(F) brother to Gerry/Cecil
			TR	Hull C.	03.47	1946	7		3	pre-war Wolves players
BROWN, Roy	Bradford	17.06.32	Gainsborough	Doncaster Rov.	05.53	1953-56	26		6	(F)

Players Names	Birthplace	Date	Previous Club	League Club	Date Signed	Seasons Played	Career Record Apps	Sub	Gls	
BROWN, Roy	Stockton	10.06.25	Stockton W.E.	Darlington	01.47	1946-55	159		20	(FB)
			TR	Hartlepool U.	08.56					
BROWN, Roy E.	Hove	05.10.45	APP	Tottenham H.	10.62	1966	1	/	0	(G)
			TR	Reading	07.68	1968-69	63	/	0	
			TR	Notts. Co.	07.70	1970-74	113	/	0	
				Mansfield T.	N/C	1975	1	/	0	
BROWN, Roy H.	Stoke	20.12.23	JNRS	Stoke C.	+	1946-52	70		14	(CF)
			TR	Watford	07.53	1953-57	143		41	
BROWN, Stan	Lewes	15.09.41	JNRS	Fulham	05.59	1960-72	348	5	16	(WH)
			L	Brighton & H.A.	10.72	1972	9	/	0	
			TR	Colchester U.	12.72	1972	23	/	0	
BROWN, Stephen F.	Northampton	06.07.66	JNRS	Northampton T.	N/C	1983	0	1	0	
BROWN, Steve A.J.	Peckham	13.07.52	APP	Millwall	06.70	1970-74	47	21	3	(F)
BROWN, Tom	Galashiels	07.06.29	Annbank J.	Ipswich T.	07.52	1952-55	84		10	(F)
			TR	Walsall	06.56	1956-57	39		8	
BROWN, Tom	Troon	26.10.19	Glenathon	Ipswich T.	*	1946-50	111		0	(G) Brother to 2 pre-war players
BROWN, Tom	Leven	17.11.33	Newburgh	Lincoln C.	04.56	1957	3		0	(HB)
BROWN, Tom E.	Throckley	08.09.35	JNRS	Middlesbrough	04.53	1954-57	44		0	(FB)
BROWN, Tom H.	Liverpool	08.05.30	S.Liverpool	Doncaster Rov.	02.51	1951-53	86		1	(HB) E.YTH.INT.
			TR	Swansea C.	12.55	1955-58	69		0	
BROWN, Tom G.	Cowdenbeath	11.08.24	Worcester C.	Portsmouth	10.46	1947	17		1	(IF)
			TR	Watford	08.49	1949-53	108		11	
BROWN, Tom L.	Glenbuck	17.04.21	Hearts	Milwall	+	1946-48	67		7	(WH)
			TR	Charlton Ath.	10.48.	1948-49	34		1	
			TR	Orient	08.50	1950-52	98		5	
BROWN, W. Dewis	Rotherham	04.06.19		Stockport Co.	+	1946-49	65		15	(F)
			TR	Rotherham U.	08.50	1951	1		0	
BROWN, Walter S.	Oakengates	08.02.21	Oakengates	Walsall	*	1946-47	19		4	(IF)
BROWN, William	Kilsyth	21.02.29	Bridgeton Wav.	Reading	02.50					(CF)
			TR	Exeter C.	08.51	1951	6		0	
BROWN, William	Murton	27.03.28	Murton C.W.	Gateshead	09.50	1950-57	214		7	(HB)
BROWN, William	Falkirk	05.02.50	JNRS	Burnley	02.67	1968	0	1	0	(F)
			TR	Carlisle U.	07.69	1969	16	3	8	
			L	Barrow	09.69	1969	6	/	1	
			TR	Newport Co.	08.70	1970-74	166	2	49	
			L	Hereford U.	03.74	1973	9	/	6	
			TR	Brentford	11.74	1974	16	/	9	
			TR	Torquay U.	03.75	1974-77	137	2	46	
BROWN, William			Forfar Ath.	Accrington St.	08.53	1953	6		2	
BROWN, William C.	Barking	24.04.20	Romford	Orient	08.46	1946	2		1	(CF)
BROWN, William D.	Dundee	08.10.31	Dundee	Tottenham H.	06.59	1959-65	222	/	0	(G)S-28/S'B'-1/S.F.LGE REP.
			TR	Northampton T.	10.66	1966	17	/	0	
BROWN, William F.	Larkhall	20.10.22	Larkhall Th.	Preston N.E.	+	1946-49	40		0	(FB)
			Q.of South	Grimsby T.	06.51	1951-57	264		1	
BROWN, William H.	Choppington	11.03.09	W.Stanley	Middlesbrough	*					(WH)
			TR	Hartlepool U.	06.46	1946-47	80		0	
BROWN, William I.	Clydebank	25.11.38	St. Mirren	Accrington St.	08.59	1959	29		0	(G)
			TR	Chester C.	06.60	1960	41		0	
BROWN, William I.	London	06.09.09	Huddersfield T.(*)	Brentford	*	1946	8		0	(WH)*Luton T.
			TR	Orient	05.47	1946-47	26		0	
BROWN, William T.	Dagenham	07.02.43		Southampton	09.60					(CF)
			TR	Charlton Ath.	07.61					
			Bedford T.	Gillingham	02.66	1965-67	104	1	33	
			TR	Portsmouth	06.68	1968	8	/	2	
			TR	Brentford	07.69	1969	4	/	0	
BROWNBILL, Derek	Liverpool	04.02.54	JNRS	Liverpool	02.72	1973	1	/	0	(F)
			TR	Port Vale	02.75	1974-76	84	8	13	
			TR	Wigan Ath.	09.78	1978-79	32	16	8	
BROWNE, Robert J.	Londonderry	09.02.12	Derry C.	Leeds U.	*	1946	19		0	(WH) N.I.-6/IRISH LGE REP.
			TR	York C.	08.47	1947	5		0	
BROWNE, Steve L.	London	21.06.64	APP	Charlton Ath.	06.82	1981	0	1	0	(F)
BROWNING, Len J.	Leeds	30.03.28	JNRS	Leeds U.	08.46	1946-51	97		43	(CF)
			TR	Sheffield U.	11.51	1951-53	65		25	
BROWNLEE, Tom C.	Carnwath	21.05.35	Broxburn	Walsall	09.56	1957-58	30		14	(IF)
			TR	York C.	12.58	1958	9		2	
			TR	Workington	06.59	1959-60	25		2	
			Netherfield	Bradford C.	01.65	1964-65	25	/	15	
BROWNLIE, John	Caldercruix	11.03.52	Hibernian	Newcastle U.	08.78	1978-81	124	/	2	(D) S-7/S.U23-5
			TR	Middlesbrough	08.82	1982	12	/	0	
BROWNLOW, Jackie M.	Belfast	18.06.16	Gravesend	Ipswich T.	05.46	1946	1		0	
				Hartlepool U.	10.48	1948	3		0	

Players Names	Birthplace	Date	Previous Club	League Club	Date Signed	Seasons Played	Apps	Sub	Gls	
BROWNSWORD, N. Jack	Campshall	15.05.23	Frickley Col.	Hull C.	09.46	1946	10		0	(FB)●
			TR	Scunthorpe U.	N/L	1950-64	595		50	
BRUCE, Alex R.	Dundee	23.12.52	APP	Preston N.E.	05.70	1971-73	55	7	22	(F) S.U23-1
			TR	Newcastle U.	01.74	1973-75	16	4	3	
			TR	Preston N.E.	08.75	1975-82	288	13	135	
			TR	Wigan Ath.	08.83	1983	32	4	7	
BRUCE, Robert	Belfast	14.10.28	Larne	Leicester C.	03.50					(IF)
				Orient	11.51	1951	1		0	
BRUCE, Steve R.	Durham	31.12.60	APP	Gillingham	10.78	1979-83	203	2	28	(D)
BRUCK, Dietmar J.	Germany	19.04.44	APP	Coventry C.	05.62	1960-70	182	8	7	(FB)
			TR	Charlton Ath.	10.70	1970-71	54	2	0	
			TR	Northampton T.	06.72	1972-73	41	/	0	
BRUNFIELD, Peter	Treeton	05.09.44		Chesterfield	07.64	1964	1		0	(HB)
BRUNSKILL, Joe	Carlton	22.04.32	Newcastle U.(AM)	Sunderland	04.50					(F)
			TR	Oldham Ath.	05.54	1954	12		2	
BRUNT, Geoff R.	Nottingham	24.11.26	JNRS	Notts.Co.	09.49	1949-53	29		1	(WH)
BRUNT, Malcolm E.	Sheffield	05.12.46	Sheffield Wed.(AM)	Chesterfield	07.66	1966	7	/	0	(G)
BRUSH, Paul	London	22.02.58	APP	West Ham U.	04.77	1977-83	126	7	0	(D)
BRUTON, David E.	Gloucester	31.10.52	APP	Bristol C.	07.71	1971-72	16	1	0	(D)
			TR	Swansea C.	08.73	1973-78	185	8	19	
			L	Newport Co.	02.77	1976	6	/	1	
			TR	Newport Co.	10.78	1978-80	79	3	9	
BRUTON, Mike	Gloucester	06.05.58	Gloucester C.	Newport Co.	08.79	1979	3	6	1	(F) Brother of David
BRYAN, Ernie N.	Hawarden	06.06.26	JNRS	Chester C.	+	1948	1		0	
BRYAN, Peter	Oxford	30.04.44	Botley Minors	Oxford U.	N/L	1962-65	18		0	(HB)
BRYAN, Peter A.	Birmingham	22.06.43		Middlesbrough	08.61	1964	4		0	(HB)
			TR	Oldham Ath.	07.65	1965	11	1	0	
BRYANT, Eric	Birmingham	18.11.21		Mansfield T.	05.46	1946-47	36		17	(CF)
			Yeovil T.	Plymouth Arg.	10.49	1949-50	11		4	
			TR	Orient	07.51	1951	12		1	
BRYANT, Jeff S.	Redhill	27.11.53		Fulham	03.73					(D) E.YTH.INT.
			Walton & Hersham	Wimbledon	N/L	1977-78	70	3	9	
			TR	Bournemouth	06.79	1979	16	/	2	
BRYANT, Steve P.	Islington	05.09.33	APP	Birmingham C.	07.71	1974-75	34	2	1	(D)
			L	Sheffield Wed.	08.76	1976	2	1	0	
			TR	Northampton T.	12.76	1976-78	95	2	5	
			TR	Portsmouth	03.79	1978-81	111	/	5	
			TR	Northampton T.	03.82	1981	10	/	0	
BRYCELAND, Tommy	Greenock	01.03.39	St. Mirren	Norwich C.	09.62	1962-69	253	1	49	(IF) S.SCH.INT.
			TR	Oldham Ath.	03.70	1969-71	66	1	10	
BRYDON, Ian F.	Edinburgh	22.03.27	St.Johnstone	Darlington	09.53	1953	1		0	(F)
			TR	Accrington St.	11.53	1953-54	27		20	
			TR	Bradford P.A.	06.55	1955	12		3	
BUCHAN, Alistair, R.	Aberdeen	27.05.26	Hunslet	Rochdale	02.51	1950-53	106		3	(WH)
BUCHAN, George	Aberdeen	02.05.50	Aberdeen	Manchester U.	05.73	1973	0	3	0	(F) Brother of Martin
			TR	Bury	08.74	1974-75	57	8	6	
BUCHAN, Martin	Aberdeen	06.03.49	Aberdeen	Manchester U.	03.72	1971-82	376	/	4	(D)S-34/S.U23-3●
			TR	Oldham Ath.	08.83	1983	24	/	0	
BUCHAN, Tom	Edinburgh	06.12.15	Woodhall Th.	Blackpool	*	1946-47	12		0	(WH)
			TR	Carlisle U.	08.49	1949	30		0	
BUCHAN, William R.M.	Grangemouth	17.10.14	Glasgow Celtic	Blackpool	*	1946-47	31		13	(IF) S.F.LGE REP.
			TR	Hull C.	01.48	1947-48	40		12	
			TR	Gateshead	11.49	1949-51	88		16	
BUCHANAN, Cameron	Holytown	31.07.28	JNRS	Wolverhampton W.	+					(F)
			TR	Bournemouth	08.49	1949-54	83		19	
			TR	Norwich C.	10.56	1956	3		0	
BUCHANAN, David	Newcastle	23.06.62	APP	Leicester C.	06.79	1978-82	24	9	7	(F) E.YTH.INT
			L	Northampton T.	10.82	1982	3	2	2	
			TR	Peterborough U.	08.83	1983	13	3	4	
BUCHANAN, John	Dingwall	19.09.51	Ross Co.	Northampton T.	11.70	1970-74	104	10	25	(F)
			TR	Cardiff C.	10.74	1974-81	217	14	54	
			TR	Northampton T.	09.81	1981-82	66	3	4	
BUCHANAN, John	Edinburgh	03.01.35	Raith Rov.	Newport Co.	08.61	1961	31		8	(F)
BUCHANAN, John	Falkirk	09.06.28	Clyde	Derby Co.	02.55	1954-56	32		13	(F)
			TR	Bradford P.A.	12.57	1957-62	163		65	
BUCHANAN, Peter S.	Glasgow	13.10.15	Chelsea(*)	Fulham	+	1946	19		1	(IF)*Wishaw J./S-1
			TR	Brentford	08.47	1947-48	74		13	
BUCHANAN, William	Glasgow	29.07.24	Motherwell	Carlisle U.	07.49	1949	9		0	(FB)
			TR	Barrow	10.49	1946-55	242		0	
BUCK, Alan	Colchester	25.08.46	JNRS	Colchester U.	07.64	1964-68	38	1	0	(G)

Players Names	Birthplace	Date	Previous Club	League Club	Date Signed	Seasons Played	Apps	Sub	Gls	
BUCK, Anthony	Oxford	18.08.44	Seaford B.C.	Oxford U.	N/L	1962-67	30	5	6	(F)
			TR	Newport Co.	12.67	1967-68	49	/	18	
			TR	Rochdale	02.69	1968-72	73	12	29	
			L	Bradford C.	01.72	1971	3	/	0	
			TR	Northampton T.	01.73	1972-73	16	1	3	
BUCK, David C.	Colchester	25.08.46	JNRS	Colchester U.	05.65	1965	0	1	0	(WH)
BUCK, George W.	Abingdon	25.01.41	JNRS	Reading	01.58	1958-60	32		3	(CF)
			TR	Stockport Co.	07.62	1962	3		0	
BUCKINGHAM, Colin M.	Plymouth	12.08.43	APP	Plymouth Arg.	08.61	1962-65	16	/	0	(WH)
			TR	Exeter C.	09.65	1965-66	30	/	0	
BUCKINGHAM, Vic F.	Greenwich	23.10.15	JNRS	Tottenham H.	*	1946-48	93		0	(WH)
BUCKLAND, Mark C.	Cheltenham	18.08.61	A.P.Leamington	Wolverhampton W.	02.84	1983	13	2	0	(D)
BUCKLE, Edward W.	Southwark	28.10.24		Manchester U.	+	1946-49	20		6	(LF)
			TR	Everton	11.49	1949-54	97		31	
			TR	Exeter C.	07.55	1955-56	65		10	
BUCKLEY, Alan P.	Mansfield	20.04.51	APP	Nottingham F.	04.68	1971-72	16	2	1	(F) Cousin of Ambrose
			TR	Wallsall	08.73	1973-78	241	/	125	
			TR	Birmingham C.	10.78	1978	24	4	8	
			TR	Walsall	07.79	1979-83	160	16	49	
BUCKLEY, Ambrose	Brinsley	31.01.09	Doncaster Rov.(+)	Stockport Co.	+	1946	11		0	(LB)*Fulham/d.1968
BUCKLEY, Frank L.	Lichfield	11.05.22		Notts.Co	+					(HB)
			TR	Crystal Palace	11.46	1947-50	69		0	
BUCKLEY, Gary	Manchester	03.03.61	APP	Manchester C.	04.78	1980	4	2	0	(M)
			TR	Preston N.E.	10.81	1981-82	27	7	2	
				Bury	N/C	1983	8	1	0	
BUCKLEY, Glen	Wigan	31.08.60	Preston N.E.(N/C)	Wigan Ath.	N/C	1979	1	/	0	(F)
BUCKLEY, Ian	Oldham	08.10.53	APP	Oldham Ath.	12.71	1971	5	/	0	(D) E.YTH. INT.
			L	Rochdale	02.74	1973	6	/	0	
			TR	Stockport Co.	08.75	1975-76	55	10	2	
			Durban C.	Cambridge U.	11.77	1977-80	51	6	2	
BUCKLEY, Mike J.	Manchester	04.11.53	APP	Everton	06.71	1971-77	128	7	10	(M) E.723-1/E.YTH.INT./
			TR	Sunderland	08.78	1978-82	117	4	7	
			TR	Hartlepool U.	N/C	1983	6	/	0	
			TR	Carlisle U.	09.83	1983	24	1	2	
BUCKLEY, Pat M.	Leith	12.08.46	T. Lanark	Wolverhampton W.	02.64	1964-67	27	1	8	(F)
			TR	Sheffield U.	01.68	1967-70	9	6	2	
			TR	Rotherham U.	06.72	1972	1	2	0	
BUCKLEY, Steve	Brinsley	16.10.53	Burton A.	Luton T.	04.74	1974-77	123	/	9	(D) Brother of Alan P.
			TR	Derby Co.	01.78	1977-83	231	/	13	
BUGG, Alec	Needham Market	27.11.48	JNRS	Ipswich T.	06.67	1968-69	4	/	0	(G)
			L	Bournemouth	02.70	1969	4	/	0	
BUICK, Joe L.	Broughty Ferry	01.07.33	Broughty Ath.	Lincoln C.	10.55	1955-61	31		3	(HB)
BUIST, Jim G.	Falkirk	19.06.18	Dundee	New Brighton	08.46	1946	21		6	(F)
			TR	Plymouth Arg.	06.47	1948	1		0	
BUKOVINA, John F.	Barnsley	02.02.64	APP	Barnsley	02.82					(F)
			TR	Doncaster Rov.	N/C	1983	1	/	0	
BUKOWSKI, Dave J.	Northampton	02.11.52	APP	Northampton T.	11.71	1971-72	10	1	0	(CH)
BULCH, Robert S.	Newcastle	01.01.33	Washington	Notts. Co.	03.53	1955-57	27		1	(WH)
			TR	Darlington	06.58	1958-59	44		1	
			TR	Hartlepool U.	11.60					
BULL, Mike F.	Twickenham	03.04.30		Brentford	09.48	1952	3		0	(F)
			TR	Swindon T.	06.53	1953-54	69		15	
BULL, William H.	Birmingham	01.04.26		Coventry C.	03.48	1948	1		0	
BULLESS, Brian	Hull	04.09.33	JNRS	Hull C.	10.50	1952-63	327		29	(FB)
BULLIMORE, Alwyn A.	Norwich	22.10.33	JNRS	Norwich C.	10.53	1955-56	3		0	(WH)
BULLIONS, Jim L.	Stirling	12.03.24	Chesterfield(AM)	Derby Co.	+	1946-47	17		0	(WH)
			TR	Leeds U.	11.47	1947-49	34		0	
			TR	Shrewsbury T.	09.50	1950-53	131		2	
BULLIVANT, Terry P.	London	23.09.56	APP	Fulham	05.74	1974-79	94	7	2	(F)
			TR	Aston Villa	11.79	1979-81	10	3	0	
			TR	Charlton Ath.	07.82	1982	30	/	3	
			TR	Brentford	07.83	1983	24	/	1	
BULLOCK, Mike E.	Stoke	02.10.46	APP	Birmingham C.	10.63	1963-66	27	/	10	(F)E.SCH.INT./
			TR	Oxford U.	06.67	1967-68	58	1	15	Brother of Peter
			TR	Orient	10.68	1968-75	267	10	64	Uncle of Simon
			TR	Halifax T.	02.76	1975-78	98	8	19	
BULLOCK, Norman	Nuneaton	26.03.32	Coton Villa	Aston Villa	09.49					(F)
			TR	Chester C.	07.52	1952-59	187		40	

Players Names	Birthplace	Date	Previous Club	League Club	Date Signed	Seasons Played	Apps	Sub	Gls	
BULLOCK, Peter L.	Stoke	17.11.41	JNRS	Stoke C.	11.58	1957-61	44		14	(IF) E.YTH.INT./
			TR	Birmingham C.	03.62	1961-64	27		3	E.SCH.INT.
			TR	Southend U.	02.65	1964-65	11	/	2	
			TR	Colchester U.	10.65	1965-67	94	1	33	
			TR	Exeter C.	07.68	1968	14	/	2	
			TR	Walsall	12.68	1968	7	/	0	
BULLOCK, Simon J.	Stoke	28.09.62	Stoke C.(APP)	Halifax T.	09.80	1980-81	15	2	1	(F)
BULLOCK, Steve	Stockport	05.10.66	JNRS	Oldham Ath.	N/C	1983	0	1	0	
BULMER, Peter	Liverpool	31.08.65	APP	Chester C.	09.83	1982-83	19	14	1	(M)
BUMPSTEAD, Dave J.	Rainham	06.11.35	Tooting & M.	Millwall	06.58	1957-61	85		7	(IF) E.AMAT.INT.
			TR	Bristol Rov.	12.61	1961-63	40		0	
BUMSTEAD, Charles H.	Croydon	08.01.22		Millwall	+	1946-47	12		0	(G)
			TR	Crystal Palace	08.48	1948-51	53		0	
BUMSTEAD, John	Rotherhithe	27.11.58	APP	Chelsea	03.78	1978-83	159	6	20	(M)
BUMSTEAD, Ray G.	Ringwood	27.01.36	Ringwood	Bournemouth	05.58	1958-69	412	2	55	(OR)
BUNCE, Fred	Watford	16.02.38	JNRS	Watford	10.55	1955-62	149		34	(F) E.YTH.INT.
BUNCLARK, Cyril	Rotherham	27.03.31		Rotherham U.	11.53	1954	2		1	(F)
BUNKELL, Ray K.	Edmonton	18.09.49	APP	Tottenham H.	06.67					(F)E.YTH.INT.
			TR	Swindon T.	06.71	1971-73	52	4	3	
			TR	Colchester U.	12.73	1973-79	117	12	9	
BUNN, Frank S.	Birmingham	06.11.62	APP	Luton T.	05.80	1980-83	35	4	4	(M)
BUNNER, Harry	Manchester	18.09.36	Bury Amats.	Bury	04.57	1957-64	106		0	(HB)
			TR	Stockport Co.	04.65	1965	3	/	0	
BUNTING, Ben	Rochdale	14.02.23	Rochdale(AM)	Oldham Ath.	08.46	1946-47	32		0	(FB)
BURBANKS, William E.	Bentley	01.04.13	Denaby U.	Sunderland	*	1946-47	46		10	(OL)d.1983
			TR	Hull C.	06.48	1948-52	143		21	
			TR	Leeds U.	07.53	1953	13		1	
BURBECK, Ron T.	Leicester	27.02.34	JNRS	Leicester C.	05.52	1952-55	3		0	(F) E.YTH.INT.
			TR	Middlesbrough	10.56	1956-62	138		24	
			TR	Darlington	08.63	1963	18		1	
BURCKITT, John D.	Coventry	16.12.46	JNRS	Coventry C.	07.64	1964	5		0	(FB)E.YTH.INT.
			L	Bradford C.	03.67	1966	9	/	0	
			TR	Walsall	06.68					
BURDEN, Brian	W.Stockwith	26.11.39		Lincoln C.	03.61	1960	1		0	(G)
BURDEN, Ian	Bradford	27.05.44	Poppleton Rd.	York C.	AM	1965	3	/	2	(CF)
BURDEN, Tommy D.	London	21.02.24	Wolverhampton W.(+)	Chester C.	+	1946-47	82		40	(IF)●
			TR	Leeds U.	07.48	1948-54	244		13	
			TR	Bristol C.	10.54	1954-60	231		19	
BURDESS, John	Easington	10.04.46	APP	Oldham Ath.	04.64	1963-64	3		0	(F)
BURGESS, Albert C.	Birkenhead	21.09.19	Bromborough	Bolton W.	*	1946-47	5		3	(IF)
			TR	Chester C.	10.48	1948-51	111		64	
			TR	Crystal Palace	09.51	1951-52	47		40	
			TR	York C.	07.53	1953	33		14	
BURGESS, David J.	Liverpool	20.01.60	JNRS	Tranmere Rov.	10.81	1981-83	136	/	1	(D)
BURGESS, Eric R.C.	Edgware	27.10.44	APP	Watford	07.62	1963-64	3		0	(FB)
			TR	Torquay U.	07.65	1965-67	73	1	0	
			TR	Plymouth Arg.	07.68	1968-69	14	1	0	
			Plymouth C.	Colchester U.	12.70	1970-71	46	1	9	
BURGESS, Mike R.	Canada	17.04.32		Bradford P.A.	08.52					(IF)
			TR	Orient	07.53	1953-55	32		12	
			TR	Newport Co.	02.56	1955-56	24		7	
			TR	Bournemouth	06.57	1957-60	109		34	
			TR	Halifax T.	07.61	1961-62	34		3	
			TR	Gillingham	03.63	1962-65	109	1	2	
			TR	Aldershot	11.65	1965	6	/	0	
BURGESS, Robert B.	Glasgow	01.04.27	T. Lanark	Walsall	AM	1953	2		1	
BURGESS, W.A. Ron	Cwm	09.04.17	Cwm Villa	Tottenham H.	*	1946-53	280		14	(WH)W-32/E.F.LGE REP.●
			TR	Swansea C.	08.54	1954-55	47		1	
BURGESS, Walter	Golborne	19.06.21	Coleraine	Halifax T.	11.46	1946	13		2	(IF)
BURGIN, Andy	Sheffield	06.03.47	APP	Sheffield Wed.	03.64	1964	1		0	(FB)
			TR	Rotherham U.	08.67	1967	9	/	0	
			TR	Halifax T.	12.68	1968-74	243	/	9	
			TR	Blackburn Rov.	09.74	1974-75	45	/	1	
BURGIN, Edward	Sheffield	29.04.27	Alford T.	Sheffield U.	03.49	1949-56	281		0	(G) E'B'-2●
			TR	Doncaster Rov.	12.57	1957	5		0	
			TR	Leeds U.	03.58	1958-60	58		0	
			TR	Rochdale	01.61	1960-65	207	/	0	
BURGIN, Eric	Sheffield	04.01.24		Sheffield U.	12.46					Yorks Cricketer
			TR	York C.	05.49	1949-50	24		0	
BURGIN, Terry	Nottingham	09.10.38		Reading	11.59	1960	2		0	(CF)
BURGIN, Trevor	Darfield	28.08.43	Wombwell	Bradford P.A.	07.67	1967	12	5	0	(HB)
BURKE, Charles	Arran	13.09.21	Ardeer Rec.	Bournemouth	+	1946	25		7	(RH)

Players Names	Birthplace	Date	Previous Club	League Club	Date Signed	Seasons Played	Career Record Apps Sub Gls		
BURKE, David I.	Liverpool	06.08.60	APP	Bolton W.	08.77	1978-80	65	4	1	(D) E.YTH.INT.
			TR	Huddersfield T.	06.81	1981-83	127	/	2	
BURKE, John	Motherwell	10.08.62	Motherwell	Sheffield U.	07.80					(D) S.SCH.INT.
			TR	Exeter C.	N/C	1982	3	/	0	
			TR	Chester C.	N/C	1983	3	/	0	
BURKE, John J.	Dublin	28.06.11	Chester C.(*)	Millwall	*	1946	9		0	(G)
			TR	Gillingham	N/L	1950	5		0	
BURKE, Marshall	Glasgow	26.03.59	APP	Burnley	03.77	1977-79	22	2	5	(F) S.SCH.INT.
			TR	Leeds U.	05.80					
			TR	Blackburn Rov.	12.80	1980-81	34	5	7	
			TR	Lincoln C.	10.82	1982-83	49	1	7	
			L	Cardiff C.	12.83	1983	3	/	0	
BURKE, Nick W.G.	Burnham	03.09.50	APP	Bristol C.	APP	1966	0	1	0	
BURKE, Peter	Rotherham	26.04.57	APP	Barnsley	08.75	1974-76	35	/	1	(D)
			TR	Halifax T.	03.78	1977-79	79	6	9	
			TR	Rochdale	07.80	1980-81	68	/	2	
BURKE, Peter J.	Galway	01.02.12	Luton T.(+)	Southport	07.46	1946	1		0	(CH)*Prescott Celtic/ Oldham Ath./Norwich C.
BURKE, Richard	Ashton	28.10.20	JNRS	Blackpool	*					(RB)
			TR	Newcastle U.	12.46	1946	15		0	
			TR	Carlisle U.	08.47	1947-48	78		8	
BURKE, Robert G.	Ballymena	05.11.34	Albertville U.	Burnley	09.55	1955	19		5	(IF)
			TR	Chester C.	06.58					
BURKE, Ronnie S.	Marske	13.08.21	St.Albans	Manchester U.	08.46	1946-48	28		16	(CF)
			TR	Huddersfield T.	06.49	1949-51	27		6	
			TR	Rotherham U.	03.53	1952-54	73		54	
			TR	Exeter C.	06.55	1955-56	41		14	
BURKE, Steve J.	Nottingham	29.09.60	APP	Nottingham F.	03.78					(F) E.YTH.INT.
			TR	Q.P.R.	09.79	1979-83	43	24	5	
			L	Millwall	10.83	1983	7	/	1	
BURKE, Tom	Greenock	18.10.39	Clyde	Barnsley	02.63	1962	1		0	(F)
BURKETT, Jack W.	Edmonton	21.08.42	JNRS	West Ham U.	10.59	1961-67	141	1	4	(FB)
			TR	Charlton Ath.	06.68	1968-69	8	/	0	
BURKINSHAW, George A.	Barnsley	01.10.22	Woolley Col.	Barnsley	+					d.1982
			TR	Carlisle U.	09.46	1946	25		0	
			TR	Barnsley	06.47					
			TR	Bradford C.	11.48	1948	12		0	
BURKINSHAW, Keith	Higham	23.06.35	Denaby U.	Liverpool	11.53	1954	1		0	(WH)
			TR	Workington	12.57	1957-64	293		9	
			TR	Scunthorpe U.	05.65	1965-67	107	1	3	
BURKITT, John O.	Wednesbury	19.01.26	Darlaston	Nottingham F.	05.47	1948-61	464		14	(WH)●
BURLEIGH, Martin S.	Newcastle	02.02.51	Willington	Newcastle U.	12.68	1970-73	11	/	0	(G)
			TR	Darlington	10.74	1974	30	/	0	
			TR	Carlisle U.	06.75	1975-76	26	/	0	
			TR	Darlington	08.77	1977-78	71	/	0	
			TR	Hartlepool U.	10.79	1979-81	84	/	0	
BURLEY, George E.	Cumnock	03.06.56	APP	Ipswich T.	06.73	1973-83	351	/	6	(D) S.SCH.INT./ S-11/S.U21-5
BURLISON, Robert L.	Newcastle	29.03.20	Horden CW	Charlton Ath.	+	1946	1		0	
BURLISON, Tom H.	Edmondsley	23.05.36	JNRS	Lincoln C.	12.53					(WH)
			TR	Hartlepool U.	07.57	1957-63	148		5	
			TR	Darlington	08.64	1964	26		2	
BURLURAUX, Don	Skelton	08.06.51	JNRS	Middlesbrough	07.68	1970-71	4	1	0	(W)
			L	York C.	12.71	1971	3	/	1	
			TR	Darlington	07.72	1972-74	105	7	13	
BURMAN, Anthony P.	London	03.06.58	Q.P.R. (APP)	Charlton Ath.	12.76	1976-77	16	3	3	(M)
BURN, John H.	South Shields	21.01.30		Chelsea	10.48					(G)
			TR	Chesterfield	08.50					
			TR	Carlisle U.	06.55	1955	26		0	
BURN, Ralph G.	Alnwick	09.11.31		Northampton T.	08.50	1950	1		0	(WH)
			TR	Crewe Alex.	07.54	1954	1		0	
BURNETT, Alf P.	Aberdeen	23.07.22	Dundee	Barrow	12.46	1946-49	87		32	(F)
			TR	Lincoln C.	11.49	1949	4		1	
BURNETT, Dennis	Southwark	27.09.44	JNRS	West Ham	10.62	1965-66	48	2	0	(D)
			TR	Millwall	08.67	1967-73	257	/	3	
			TR	Hull C.	10.73	1973-74	46	/	2	
			L	Millwall	03.75	1974	6	/	2	
			TR	Brighton & H.A.	09.75	1975-76	41	3	1	
BURNETT, George G.	Liverpool	11.02.20	JNRS	Everton	*	1946-50	47		0	(G)
			TR	Oldham Ath.	10.51	1951-54	100		0	
BURNETT, John	Market Rasen	24.06.39	Gainsborough	Grimsby T.	07.58	1958	1		0	
BURNETT, William J.	Pelaw	01.03.26	Wardley Welf.	Grimsby T.	07.46	1947	10		0	(OR)
			TR	Hartlepool U.	11.48	1948-53	193		17	

Players Names	Birthplace	Date	Previous Club	League Club	Date Signed	Seasons Played	Career Record Apps	Sub	Gls	
BURNS, Anthony	Edenbridge	27.03.34	Tonbridge	Arsenal	03.63	1964-65	31	/	0	(G)
			TR	Brighton m& H.A.	07.66	1966-68	54	/	0	
			TR	Charlton Ath.	03.69	1968-69	10	/	0	
			Durban U.	Crystal Palace	10.73	1974-77	90	/	0	
			L	Brentford	01.77	1976	6	/	0	
			TR	Plymouth Arg.	08.78	1978	8	/	0	
BURNS, Barry	Doncaster	19.06.37	Dunscroft	Rotherham U.	10.54	1957	5		4	(F)
BURNS, David	Ellesmere Port	12.11.58	APP	Chester C.	10.76	1976-81	66	12	1	(D)
BURNS, Derek G.	Bournemouth	23.01.50	APP	Bournemouth	02.68	1968	3	1	0	(HB)
BURNS, Eric O.	Newton Stewart	08.03.45	APP	Bradford P.A.	03.62	1963-65	27	2	3	(F)
			TR	Barnsley	08.66	1966	3	/	0	
BURNS, Francis	Glenboig	17.10.48	JNRS	Manchester U.	10.65	1967-71	111	10	6	(D)S-1/S.U23-1/
			TR	Southampton	06.72	1972	20	1	0	S.SCH.INT.
			TR	Preston N.E.	08.73	1973-80	271	2	9	
BURNS, Francis J.	Workington	11.11.24	Wolverhampton W.(AM)	Swansea C.	+	1946-51	172		9	(WH)
			TR	Southend U.	07.52	1952-54	88		14	
			TR	Crewe Alex.	11.56	1956-57	30		7	
BURNS, Kenny	Glasgow	23.09.53	APP	Birmingham C.	07.71	1971-76	163	7	45	(D) S-20/S.U23-2●
			TR	Nottingham F.	07.77	1977-81	137	/	13	
			TR	Leeds U.	10.81	1981-83	54	2	2	
			L	Derby Co.	03.83	1982	6	1	1	
			TR	Derby Co.	02.84	1983	11	/	0	
BURNS, Kinear	Isle of Man	24.09.23		Tranmere Rov.	09.46	1946	14		4	(OR)
			TR	Southport	11.47	1947	5		0	
BURNS, Leo F.	Manchester	03.08.32		Oldham Ath.	09.53	1955	4		0	
BURNS, Les	Shepherds Bush	22.06.44	Carshalton	Charlton Ath.	03.67	1966-67	8	/	0	(HB)
BURNS, Michael E.	Blackpool	21.12.46	Skelmersdale	Blackpool	05.69	1969-73	174	5	53	(F)E.AMAT. INT.
			TR	Newcastle U.	07.74	1974-77	143	2	39	
			TR	Cardiff C.	08.78	1978	6	/	0	
			TR	Middlesbrough	10.78	1978	58	3	24	
BURNS, Michael T.	Leeholm	07.06.08	Preston N.E.(*)	Ipswich T.	*	1946-51	115		0	(G)*Chilton Col./
										Newcastle U./d. 1982
BURNS, Neil J.	Bellshill	11.06.45	Bethesda	Mansfield T.	11.65	1965-66	7	4	1	(F)
BURNS, Oliver H.	Larkhall	16.05.14	Q.of South	Burnley	*					
			TR	Oldham Ath.	10.46	1946	25		4	
			TR	Halifax T.	09.47	1947	27		5	
BURNS, Peter	Ulverston	17.04.31	Askam U.	Barrow	02.52	1951	8		2	(CF)
BURNSIDE, David G.	Bristol	10.12.39	JNRS	W.B.A.	02.57	1957-62	127		39	(IF)E.U23-1/E.YTH.INT.
			TR	Southampton	10.62	1962-64	61		22	
			TR	Crystal Palace	12.64	1964-66	52	4	8	
			TR	Wolverhampton W.	09.66	1966-67	38	2	5	
			TR	Plymouth Arg.	03.68	1967-70	105	/	14	
			TR	Bristol C.	12.71	1971	1	/	0	
			TR	Colchester U.	03.72	1971	13	/	0	
BURRELL, Gerry	Belfast	06.09.26	St.Mirren	Huddersfield T.	12.53	1953-55	59		9	(OL)
			TR	Chesterfield	07.56	1956-57	51		4	
BURRELL, Lester F.	Brighton	08.08.17	Margate	Crystal Palace	+	1946-47	19		4	
				Ipswich T.	05.48					
BURRIDGE, Peter J.	Harlow	30.12.33	Barnet	Orient	04.58	1958-59	6		2	(IF)
			TR	Millwall	08.60	1960-61	87		58	
			TR	Crystal Palace	06.62	1962-65	114	/	42	
			TR	Charlton Ath.	11.65	1965-66	42	2	4	
BURRIDGE, John	Workington	03.12.51	APP	Workington	01.70	1968-70	27	/	0	(G)
			TR	Blackpool	04.71	1970-75	134	/	0	
			TR	Aston Villa	09.75	1975-76	65	/	0	
			L	Southend U.	01.78	1977	6	/	- 0	
			TR	Crystal Palace	03.78	1977-79	88	/	0	
			TR	Q.P.R.	12.80	1980-81	39	/	0	
			TR	Wolverhampton W.	08.82	1982-83	74	/	0	
BURROWS, Adrian M.	Sutton	16.01.59		Mansfield T.	05.79	1979-81	77	1	6	(D)
			TR	Northampton T.	08.82	1982-83	88	/	4	
BURROWS, Alan	Thorne	20.10.41	Stockport Co.(AM)	Blackpool	05.59	1959	1		0	(HB)
BURROWS, Arthur	Stockport	04.12.19	JNRS	Stockport Co.	*	1946	4		1	
				Accrington St.	03.48	1948	9		0	
BURROWS, David	Bilsthorpe	07.04.61	APP	Lincoln C.	04.79	1978	1	/	0	(F)
BURROWS, Frank	Larkhall	30.01.44	Raith Rov.	Scunthorpe U.	06.65	1965-67	106	/	4	(D)
			TR	Swindon T.	07.68	1968-76	294	4	9	
			L	Mansfield T.	03.74	1973	6	/	0	
BURROWS, Harry	St.Helens	17.03.41	JNRS	Aston Villa	03.58	1959-64	146		53	(OL) E.U23-1
			TR	Stoke C.	03.65	1964-71	239	6	69	
			TR	Plymouth Arg.	08.73	1973-74	18	1	3	

Players Names	Birthplace	Date	Previous Club	League Club	Date Signed	Seasons Played	Apps	Sub	Gls	
BURROWS, Philip	Stockport	08.04.46	JNRS	Manchester C.	07.64					(D)
			TR	York C.	06.66	1966-73	333	4	14	
			TR	Plymouth Arg.	07.74	1974-75	81	/	2	
			TR	Hereford T.	08.76	1976-79	110	/	2	
			L	Gillingham	10.77	1977	5	/	0	
BURSELL, John C.	Hull	16.01.35	JNRS	Hull C.	11.52	1952	1		2	(F) d.1973
BURT, Jim H.L.	Harthill	05.04.50	Whitburn B.	Leicester C.	06.67					(FB)
			TR	Aldershot	09.70	1970-71	22	2	0	
			TR	Northampton T.	07.72	1972	16	5	0	
			TR	Rochdale	09.73	1973	4	/	0	
BURTENSHAW, Charles E.	Portslade	16.10.22	Southwick	Luton T.	01.48	1948-49	10		1	(OR) Brother of Steve/
			TR	Gillingham	N/L	1950-51	28		5	William
BURTENSHAW, Steve	Portslade	23.11.35	JNRS	Brighton & H.A.	11.52	1952-66	237	/	3	(WH)
BURTENSHAW, William F.	Portslade	13.12.25	Southwick	Luton T.	08.48	1948-49	2		0	(IR)
			TR	Gillingham	N/L	1950/51	39		7	
BURTON, Alan R.	Aldershot	11.01.39	Wimbledon	Aldershot	01.61	1960-69	225	5	44	(W)
BURTON, Alwyn D.	Chepstow	11.11.41	JNRS	Newport Co.	12.58	1958-60	53		8	(WH)W-9/W.U23-5/
			TR	Norwich C.	03.61	1960-62	57		8	W.SCH.INT
			TR	Newcastle U.	06.63	1963-71	181	7	6	
BURTON, Brian B.	Nottingham	28.12.32		Nottingham F.	07.51	1954	1		0	(F)
BURTON, Ernie	Sheffield	02.09.21		Sheffield Wed.	11.47					(OR) Father of Ken O.
			TR	York C.	08.48	1948	3		0	
BURTON, Ken	Sheffield	11.02.50	APP	Sheffield Wed.	05.67	1968-71	55	1	2	(D)
			L	Peterborough U.	03.73	1972	3	1	0	
			TR	Chesterfield	07.73	1973-78	234	3	6	
			TR	Halifax T.	08.80	1980	26	1	1	
BURTON, Roy	Wantage	13.03.51		Oxford U.	09.70	1971-82	397	/	0	(G)
BURTON, Sam	Swindon	10.11.26		Swindon T.	+	1946-61	463		0	(G)●
BURVILL, Glen	Camden Town	26.10.62	APP	West Ham U.	09.80					(M)
			TR	Aldershot	08.83	1983	33	5	12	
BUSBY, David E.	Paddington	27.07.56	APP	Brighton & H.A.	08.74	1973-74	1	2	0	(F)
BUSBY, Martin G.	Slough	24.03.53	APP	Q.P.R.	07.70	1970-76	71	7	6	(F)E.YTH.INT.
			L	Portsmouth	02.76	1975	6	/	1	
			TR	Notts. Co.	10.76	1976-77	37	/	4	
			TR	Q.P.R.	09.77	1977-79	56	10	11	
			L	Burnley	02.80	1979	4	/	1	
BUSBY, Viv	Slough	19.06.49	Wycombe W.	Luton T.	01.70	1969-72	64	13	16	(F) Brother of Martin
			L	Newcastle U.	12.71	1971	4	/	2	
			TR	Fulham	08.73	1973-76	114	4	29	
			TR	Norwich C.	09.76	1976-77	22	/	11	
			TR	Stoke C.	11.77	1977-79	33	17	9	
			L	Sheffield U.	01.80	1979	3	/	1	
			Tulsa R.	Blackburn Rov.	02.81	1980	8	/	1	
			TR	York C.	N/C	1982-83	9	10	4	
BUSH, Brian	Bristol	25.04.25	Soundwell	Bristol Rov.	10.47	1947-54	114		19	(OR)
BUSH, Terry D.	Ingoldsthorpe	29.01.43	JNRS	Bristol C.	02.60	1960-69	147	15	44	(F)
BUSH, Tom W.	Shirpheel	22.02.14		Liverpool	*	1946	3		0	(CH) d.1969
BUSHBY, Alan	Doncaster	15.01.32		Scunthorpe U.	08.52	1952-58	218		10	(HB) d.1967
			TR	Rochdale	07.59	1959-60	67		0	
BUSHBY, Dennis	Bournemouth	25.12.33		Bournemouth	11.57	1957	6		0	(WH)
BUSHBY, Tom W.	Shildon	21.08.14	Portsmouth(+)	Southampton	09.46	1946	3		0	(CH)*Southend U.
BUSHELL, Alan	Burnley	04.09.32	Wood Top FC	Accrington St.	AM	1952	8		1	
BUTCHER, John	Newcastle	27.05.56	JNRS	Blackburn Rov.	03.76	1976-81	104	/	0	(G)
			TR	Oxford U.	07.82	1982	16	/	0	
			L	Halifax T.	09.82	1982	5	/	0	
			L	Bury	12.83	1983	11	/	0	
BUTCHER, Reg	Liverpool	13.02.16	Reading(*)	Chester C.	*	1946-49	132		1	*Aston Villa
BUTCHER, Terry I.	Singapore	28.12.58	JNRS	Ipswich T.	08.76	1977-83	203	/	10	(D)E-24/E.U21-7
BUTLER, Barry	Stockton	30.07.34	South Bank	Sheffield Wed.	09.52	1953-54	26		1	(CH) d.1966
			TR	Norwich C.	07.57	1957-65	303	/	3	
BUTLER, David	Stockton	23.03.45	Stockton	Workington	11.64	1964-70	195	4	7	(FB)
			TR	Watford	11.70	1970-75	168	/	2	
BUTLER, David J.	Wolverhampton	01.09.62	APP	Wolverhampton W.	04.80					(F)
			TR	Torquay U.	12.81	1981	5	1	0	
BUTLER, David J.	Wednesbury	30.03.53	APP	W.B.A.	04.71					(F)
			TR	Shrewsbury T.	06.73	1973	5	5	0	
			L	Workington	03.74	1973	10	/	0	
BUTLER, Dennis A.	Macclesfield	24.06.44	JNRS	Bolton W.	06.61	1962-67	61	4	11	(W) Nephew of famous
			TR	Rochdale	02.68	1967-72	152	4	39	Billy Butler
BUTLER, Dennis G.	Reading	04.08.52	APP	Reading	05.70	1969-70	6	3	0	(WH)

Players Names	Birthplace	Date	Previous Club	League Club	Date Signed	Seasons Played	Apps	Sub	Gls	
BUTLER, Dennis M.	Fulham	07.03.43	JNRS	Chelsea	06.60	1961-62	18		0	(FB)
			TR	Hull C.	06.63	1963-69	215	2	0	
			TR	Reading	12.69	1969-73	170	/	1	
BUTLER, Ernie	Middlesbrough	28.08.24	Stockton	Southend U.	08.48	1948-51	36		3	(OR)
			TR	Darlington	06.53	1953	6		0	
BUTLER, Ernie A.	Box	13.05.19	Bath C.	Portsmouth	*	1946-52	222		0	(G)
BUTLER, Geoff	Middlesbrough	29.09.46	APP	Middlesbrough	05.64	1965-67	54	1	1	(D)
			TR	Chelsea	09.67	1967	8	1	0	
			TR	Sunderland	01.68	1967-68	1	2	0	
			TR	Norwich C.	10.68	1968-75	151	2	1	
			TR	Bournemouth	03.76	1975-80	118	1	1	
			TR	Peterborough U.	N/C	1981	39	/	0	
BUTLER, Ian	Darton	01.02.44	APP	Rotherham U.	08.61	1960-64	101	/	28	(OL) E.YTH.INT.
			TR	Hull C.	01.65	1964-72	300	5	66	
			TR	York C.	08.73	1973-74	43	3	2	
			L	Barnsley	10.75	1975	5	/	1	
BUTLER, Joe	Newcastle	07.02.43	JNRS	Newcastle U.	09.60	1963	3	/	0	(D)
			TR	Swindon T.	08.65	1965-75	355	5	17	
			TR	Aldershot	08.76	1976-77	31	8	0	
BUTLER, John	Dawley	16.10.20	Dawley	Shrewsbury T.	08.50	1950-53	58		8	(OL)
BUTLER, John E.	Liverpool	07.02.62	Prescot Cables	Wigan Ath.	01.82	1981-83	79	3	7	(D)
BUTLER, John H.	Birmingham	10.03.37	Eastwood Col.	Notts.Co.	10.57	1958-61	111		0	(CH)
			TR	Chester C.	05.62	1962-67	220	2	0	
BUTLER, John P.	Salford	07.09.64	APP	Blackpool	11.82	1981-82	4	1	0	(M)
BUTLER, Ken	Whitburn	23.08.36		Hartlepool U.	01.60	1959-60	20		1	(F)
BUTLER, Malcolm P.	Belfast	06.08.13	Bangor	Blackpool	*					(FB) N.I.-1
			TR	Accrington St.	07.47	1947	32		0	
BUTLER, Mike A.	Barnsley	27.01.51	Worsboro Br.	Barnsley	07.73	1972-75	118	2	57	(F)
			TR	Huddersfield T.	03.76	1975-77	73	6	21	
			TR	Bournemouth	07.78	1978-79	68	1	19	
			TR	Bury	08.80	1980-81	80	2	15	
BUTLER, Paul J.	Stockton	09.06.64	APP	Wolverhampton W.	06.82	1982-83	1	10	0	(F)
			L	Hereford U.	01.84	1983	16	/	2	
BUTLER, Peter	Nottingham	03.10.42	JNRS	Notts.Co.	11.60	1961-65	44	/	0	(G)Brother of John H.
			TR	Bradford C.	08.66	1966	17	/	0	
BUTLER, Stan	Stellington	07.01.19	Scunthorpe U.	W.B.A.	*	1946	3		0	(OL)
			TR	Southport	07.47	1947	4		0	
BUTLER, Tom	Atherton	28.04.18	Oldham Ath.(*)	Middlesbrough	+					(IR)*Macclesfield/
			TR	Oldham Ath.	08.46	1946	30		3	Bolton W.
			TR	Accrington St.	07.47	1947-52	217		26	
BUTLER, Walter G.	Birmingham	07.02.23	Derby Co.(+)	Port Vale	06.46	1946-50	128		0	(FB)
BUTLIN, Barry	Rosliston	09.11.49	JNRS	Derby Co.	01.67	1966-72	6	/	0	(F)
			L	Notts. Co.	01.69	1968-69	29	1	13	
			TR	Luton T.	11.72	1972-74	56	1	24	
			TR	Nottingham F.	10.74	1974-76	71	3	17	
			L	Brighton & H.A.	09.75	1975	5	/	2	
			L	Reading	01.77	1976	5	/	1	
			TR	Peterborough U.	08.77	1977-78	64	/	12	
			TR	Sheffield U.	08.79	1970-80	50	3	12	
BUTT, Len	Wilmslow	26.08.10	Huddersfield T.(*)	Blackburn Rov.	*	1946	10		0	(IF)*Wilmslow/
			TR	York C.	01.47	1946-47	25		2	Stockport Co./
			TR	Mansfield T.	10.47	1947	14		4	Macclesfield
BUTT, Robert	Chester	27.03.46	JNRS	Wrexham	AM	1964	3		0	(W)
BUTTERFIELD, Jack	Barnsley	30.08.22		Burnley	+	1947	3		0	(RB)
BUTTERWORTH, Aiden J.	Leeds	07.11.61	JNRS	Leeds U.	05.80	1980-83	54	10	15	(M) E.SCH.INT
BUTTERWORTH, David	Bristol	04.05.37	Guildford C.	Exeter C.	12.57	1957-59	27		0	(HB)
BUTTERWORTH, Ian S.	Crewe	25.01.65	APP	Coventry C.	08.81	1981-83	61	7	0	(D)
BUTTLE, Steve	Norwich	01.01.53	Ipswich T.(APP)	Bournemouth	08.73	1973-76	136	3	12	(M)
BUTTRESS, Mike D.	Peterborough	23.03.58	APP	Aston Villa	02.76	1976-77	1	2	0	(M)
			TR	Gillingham	03.78	1977-78	5	2	0	
BUXTON, Ian R.	Cromford	17.04.38	JNRS	Derby Co.	03.59	1959-67	142	1	42	(IF) Derbyshire Cricketer
			TR	Luton T.	09.67	1967-68	46	1	14	
			TR	Notts. Co.	07.69	1969	4	1	1	
			TR	Port Vale	12.69	1969	16	2	6	
BUXTON, Mike	Corbridge	29.05.43	JNRS	Burnley	06.60	1962-67	16	3	0	(FB)
			TR	Halifax T.	06.68	1968-70	35	/	0	
BUXTON, Steve C.	Birmingham	13.03.60	JNRS	Wrexham	07.78	1977-83	93	16	21	(F)
BYATT, Dennis J.	Hillingdon	08.08.58	APP	Fulham	05.76					(D)
			TR	Peterborough U.	07.78	1978	2	1	0	
			TR	Northampton T.	06.79	1979-80	46	1	3	
BYCROFT, Sid	Lincoln	19.02.12	Grantham	Doncaster Rov.	*	1946-51	211		1	(CH)

Players Names	Birthplace	Date	Previous Club	League Club	Date Signed	Seasons Played	Apps	Sub	Gls	
BYERS, Richard	Haltwhistle	19.11.51	Hadrians Paints	**Workington**	AM	1971	1	/	0	(CF)
BYRNE, Anthony	Rathdowny	02.02.46	JNRS	**Millwall**	08.63	1963	1	/	0	(D)EI-14
			TR	**Southampton**	08.64	1966-73	81	14	3	
			TR	**Hereford T.**	08.74	1974-76	54	1	0	
			TR	**Newport Co.**	03.77	1976-78	80	/	1	
BYRNE, Gerry	Glasgow	10.04.57	APP	**Cardiff C.**	04.75	1977-78	11	4	0	(D)
BYRNE, Gerry	Liverpool	29.08.38	JNRS	**Liverpool**	08.55	1957-68	273	1	2	(FB) E-2/E.U23-1
BYRNE, Joe				**Workington**	AM	1952	2		0	(G)
BYRNE, John	Newton	20.05.39	Pollok J.	**Preston N.E.**	03.58					(OL)
			Q. of South	**Tranmere Rov.**	05.61	1961	27		4	
			Hibernian	**Barnsley**	11.63	1963-64	69		13	
			TR	**Peterborough U.**	07.65	1965-67	106	1	28	
			TR	**Northampton T.**	12.67	1967-68	40	/	4	
BYRNE, John F.	Manchester	01.02.61	APP	**York C.**	01.79	1979-83	157	8	52	(F)
BYRNE, John J.	W. Horsley	13.05.39	JNRS	**Crystal Palace**	05.56	1956-61	202		85	(IF) E-11/E.U23-7/●
			TR	**West Ham U.**	03.62	1961-66	156	/	79	E.YTH.INT.
			TR	**Crystal Palace**	02.67	1966-67	36	/	5	
			TR	**Fulham**	03.68	1967-68	16	2	2	
BYRNE, John J.A.	Wallasey	24.03.49	Cammell Laird	**Tranmere Rov.**	AM	1968	1	/	0	(OR)
BYRNE, Pat J.	Dublin	15.05.56	Shelbourne	**Leicester C.**	07.79	1979-80	31	5	3	(M)
BYRNE, Roger W.	Manchester	08.02.29	Ryder Brow BC	**Manchester U.**	03.49	1951-57	245		17	(FB) E-33/E'B'-3/E.F.LGE REP./d.1958●
BYRNE, William	Newcastle	22.10.18		**Port Vale**	05.46	1946	15		2	
			TR	**Crewe Alex.**	07.47	1947-48	18		1	
BYROM, John	Blackburn	28.07.44	JNRS	**Blackburn Rov.**	08.61	1961-65	106	2	45	(F)E.YTH.INT.
			TR	**Bolton W.**	06.66	1966-75	298	8	113	
			TR	**Blackburn Rov.**	09.76	1976	15	1	6	
BYROM, Ray	Blackburn	02.01.35		**Accrington St.**	01.56	1957-58	8		1	(F)
			TR	**Bradford P.A.**	12.58	1958-60	70		14	
BYROM, Tom	Upton	17.03.20	Heswall	**Tranmere Rov.**	+	1946	3		0	(WH)
BYROM, William	Blackburn	30.03.15	Burnley (+)	**Q.P.R.**	+					(FB)
			TR	**Rochdale**	06.46	1947-47	30		0	
BYRON, Gordon F.	Prescot	04.09.53	APP	**Sheffield Wed.**	07.71					(WH)
			TR	**Lincoln C.**	08.74	1974	3	3	0	
BYWATER, Noel L.	Lichfield	08.02.20		**Huddersfield T.**	+					(G)
			TR	**Luton T.**	09.46	1946	19		0	
			TR	**Rochdale**	12.47	1947-48	34		0	

ALF ACKERMAN (Hull C./Norwich C./Hull C./Derby Co./Carlisle U./Millwall)
Ackerman was a South African forward who made a name in the Scottish League with Clyde before crossing the border to Hull City. After scoring 21 goals in 34 games he moved on to Norwich and then back to Hull before transferring to Derby County in March 1955, in a vain attempt to help the "Rams" avoid relegation, this time to Division Three. By now becoming a real wanderer, Alf answered Carlisle's call and then went to Millwall before returning home.

JIMMY ADAMSON (Burnley)
One of the finest wing halves of his day, Adamson was unfortunate in never gaining a coveted England cap. He played for the Football League, and was recognised for sterling services to soccer with the player of the year award in 1962, following the losing Cup Final for Burnley against Spurs. He signed for the "Clarets" in 1947, not making his debut until 1950/1; actually he started out as an inside forward. An ever present asset in the 1959/60 Burnley Championship winning side, he played over 400 games before acting as coach to England's World Cup team in Chile 1962, bowing out of League soccer a season later.

CHARLIE AITKEN (Aston Villa)
A great discovery by the Villa, Aitken was spotted playing with the Scottish juniors Edinburgh Thistle and signed pro in 1959. He made his first appearance in the last match of the 1960/1 season, going on to gain under 23 honours very quickly. He became a reliable full back of great quality; one of the players Villa used as a cornerstone for their return to the big League after dropping out in 1967. He gained a Third Division medal, and two seasons later saw Villa back in the First Division as Second Division runners up, before leaving the game, after playing more than any other player in the history of the club.

IVOR ALLCHURCH (Swansea C., Newcastle U., Cardiff C., Swansea C. & Wales)
One of the great names in post war soccer, Allchurch was a tall, blond, lovely ball player, very fast with perceptive dribbling skill, unorthodox in his approach. It wasn't until national service had been completed that Ivor returned to the "Swans" ready to embark on a brilliant future as a highly sought after inside forward. Winning his first cap for Wales at the age of 20, he played a further 26 consecutive games over six years before Newcastle took him to St. James' Park in October 1958 to £27,000, plus a player. He went back home to Cardiff for £15,000 in August 1962, staying three seasons before going back to Swansea. He scored over 250 League goals in an exceptional career.

LEN ALLCHURCH (Swansea C., Sheffield U. & Wales/Stockport Co./Swansea C.)
Younger brother of the brilliant Ivor, Len followed him to Swansea, signing pro October 1950. He played mainly at outside right, although he often moved inside. Being in the shadows of a famous brother could not have made it easy, but Len battled on, finally making the Welsh National side in 1955 against Ireland. He played in the Second Division for the Town, as the club then was, before being transferred to Sheffield United in March 1961, just in time to help them gain promotion into the top League. He played over 100 games for Stockport County, his next side, before coming back to the Vetch Field for his final "Swansong".

RONNIE ALLEN (Port Vale/W.B.A. & England/Crystal Palace)
Allen was taken to the Hawthorns from Port Vale for a fee of £18,000 in March 1950, after playing for the Potteries team since the age of 17. He was predominantly an outside right, but although slight and only 5ft 8in was converted successfully to centre forward. He struck up great partnerships, first with Johnny Nicholls and then Derek Kevan, scoring every one game out of two. He played for England in 1952 as well as collecting a Cup winners medal along with other honours. A beautiful ball player, he loved to work behind his own lines, creating chances for others. He finished with Crystal Palace after helping them to promotion from the Third Division in 1963/4.

TONY ALLEN (Stoke C. & England/Bury)
A brilliant blond-haired player, Allen signed for the home town side on reaching 17. He settled down very quickly as a left back showing great qualities; he was very stylish, accurate, precise in his kicking. Before reaching his 20th birthday, England had called for the youngster to follow up his under 23 honours with a full cap. He was a member of the Stoke City side which gained promotion to Division One in 1962/3. He moved to Bury before going to play in South Africa in 1972.

ALEX ANDERSON (Southend U.)
One of the Scottish contingent at Roots Hall, Anderson made his debut in 1950/1, settling down as a consistent left back of character. He became, upon playing 451 League games, the United record appearance holder, which is still in keeping. In season 1951/2 he was an ever present player of the Southend rearguard, also figuring in the Cup run to fifth round, the club finally being eliminated by Sheffield United in a close game. Nicknamed "Sandy" by the fans for obvious reasons, he gave the "Shrimpers" great service until finishing in 1962/3.

STAN ANDERSON (Sunderland & England/Newcastle U./Middlesbrough)
A north east local product playing for England schoolboys before making his debut for Sunderland in the 1952/3 season, Anderson became a hard tackling constructive wing half, thoroughly dependable. Seemingly set for high honours he played four times for England under 23s, but after being sent off against Bulgaria full International recognition was slow in coming. After eventually gaining two England caps in 1961/2, Stan made the short journey to neighbouring Newcastle for a fee of £35,000, later playing the rest of 1965/6 season out with Middlesbrough. His play developed over the years, taking on a craggy consistency which was directly related to the playing environment.

JOHN ANGUS(Burnley & England)
Angus was taken by Burnley from an Amble boys' club on amateur terms in 1954, and became professional on his 17th birthday in September 1955. He made his First Division debut in season 1956/7 as a right back, giving early warnings that he was one to take due note of. Becoming a polished defender, he graduated from youth honours and under 23s to an England cap in 1961 against Austria in Vienna. He won a League Championship medal in 1960 which was followed by a losing Cup Final against the well nigh invincible Spurs during their glory years. A loyal team member, John played as a Burnley regular for over 15 years before bowing out finally in 1971/2.

OSVALDO ARDILES (Tottenham H. & Argentina).
Ardiles was sensationally signed for Spurs in July 1978 for £325,000, after being a key player in the Argentinian side that lifted the World Cup. When coming to White Hart Lane 'Ossie' did not speak very good English, but his soccer style was unmistakably that of a master. Ardiles and his compatriot, Villa, who signed at the same time, made all the difference to the younger players in the side, with the heady days of several years ago being rekindled. Ardiles achieved a major ambition when collecting a winners medal from the 1981 F.A. Cup Final classic against Manchester City and the following season he assisted Spurs as losing finalists in the League Cup as well as the F.A. Cup semi-finals, before being recalled to the Argentina team. He came back after injury to collect a U.E.F.A. Cup winners medal after the victory over Anderlecht in 1984.

WALLY ARDRON (Rotherham U./Nottingham F.)
One of the most coveted of the early post war centre forwards Ardron made his debut for United before the war, after signing from Denaby United. He was a most prodigious accumulator of goals in a career that was held up by the war, preventing what would surely have been one of the biggest tallies ever. He was transferred to Forest in July 1949, for the obvious purpose of getting the ball in the opponent's net, which Wally did with monotonous regularity, scoring 217 post war goals out of 305 matches played. A part time footballer, he worked on the railways during the week, and was a keen all round sportsman.

JIMMY ARMFIELD (Blackpool & England)
A stylish defener, Armfield came to the fore with the local club after assisting a nearby church team. Following a brilliant display in the 1962 World Cup Finals in Chile, Jimmy was voted the finest right back in the World. The overlap was his speciality and he could rightly stake a claim to being the originator of the modern technique, although others would doubtless argue the point. He had become by now an England regular, setting up at one stage a sequence of 37 consecutive games. Highly composed, efficient to the last and above all constructive, he played just short of 600 League games before retiring and going on to football management with Bolton, then Leeds United.

GEORGE ARMSTRONG (Arsenal/Leicester C./Stockport Co.)
A little left winger from the North East who Arsenal snapped up in August 1961, Armstrong went on to give the "Gunners" sterling service, covering nearly 500 League games, before joining Leicester City in 1977. A specialist taker of corner kicks, he was perpetual motion in action, buzzing here, there and everywhere, a constant thorn to any defence. He gained England under 23 honours, but surprisingly did not follow up with full caps. He is memorably associated with the Arsenal "Double" side of 1970/1 after winning an European Fairs Cup medal the previous year. His final season of League soccer was 1978/9 with Stockport County.

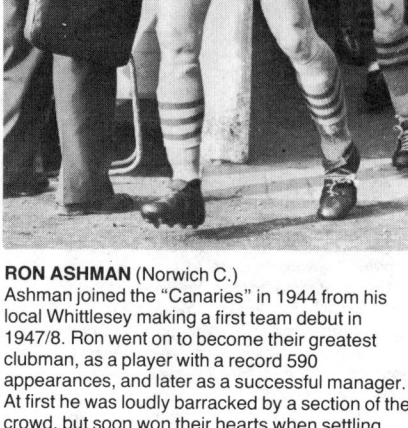

RON ASHMAN (Norwich C.)
Ashman joined the "Canaries" in 1944 from his local Whittlesey making a first team debut in 1947/8. Ron went on to become their greatest clubman, as a player with a record 590 appearances, and later as a successful manager. At first he was loudly barracked by a section of the crowd, but soon won their hearts when settling down as resident left half. He would surely regard the fabulous Cup run of 1958/9 season as the high spot of a long career, when he captained Norwich to the semi-finals, failing by a whisker to get to Wembley.

LEN ASHURST (Sunderland/Hartlepool U.)
A Liverpool born full back Ashurst made the trip to the North East following fine performances with Prescott Cables, after being rejected by a famous local club. At Roker Park he followed up youth honours with an England under 23 cap; being steady, constructive, with good recovery. He was expected to go even further still. With Sunderland, Len played Second Division football until 1964, when the club finally gained promotion after several near misses. The most notable occasion was in the 1962/3 season when Chelsea pipped Sunderland on goal average mainly due to a Tommy Harmer goal at Roker. He moved to Hartlepool, eventually becoming manager, following Brian Clough's trail a few years earlier.

JEFF ASTLE (Notts Co./W.B.A. & England)
Nearly 6ft tall, Astle was a Notts County prodigy, making his debut for them in 1961/2. Particularly good in the air, he became very useful on the deck as well, using brains instead of brawn more than often. Albion saw him as the man around whom they could build up front, bringing him to the Hawthorns in September 1964. His career was highlighted at club level by success in the Football League Cup and then climaxed by the winning F.A. Cup Final against Everton in 1968, during which a tremendous rasping goal from Jeff himself decided the issue. He played five times in all for England without scoring, but he scored nearly 150 goals with Albion.

JOHN ATYEO (Bristol C. & England)
A tall striding youngster who played two games for Pompey as an amateur in 1950/1, whilst studying for surveying exams, Atyeo also played rugby at county level. On completion of certain exams, John turned pro with Bristol City, going on to complete 15 seasons with them, playing nearly 600 League games and scoring over 300 goals. An extremely powerful goal scoring machine, relishing tough tackling, no quarter taken, none given, he won a Third Division South medal in 1955. One of the few players from a lower division to represent England, John played at all levels of Internationals except schoolboy. He retired in May 1966 and qualified as a teacher at Warminster.

LEN BADGER (Sheffield U./Chesterfield)
A brilliant full back prospect when arriving on the soccer scene in 1962/3 with local club Sheffield United, Badger was also a member of the England mini World Cup winning side that achieved such prestige that year. In setting up a very effective partnership with Bernard Shaw, Len became one of the youngest captains in the club's history after becoming a regular in season 1964/5. Over a period of 11 seasons he missed only 30 League matches – a tremendous record of consistency, which was matched by keen positional play, adroit tackling and a passion to use the flank to its full advantage. He finished his career at Chesterfield.

MIKE BAILEY (Charlton Ath. & England/Wolverhampton W./Hereford U.)
Bailey was a product of Charlton juniors, signing for the London club on leaving school, and very quickly developing into a really tough tackling, ambitious wing half who surprisingly played only twice for England in the early 1960s. Wolves, trying to recapture former glories, saw him as the man to lead them from the Second Division wilderness back into the big time, a mission accomplished in 1966/7. Injury apart, Mike was a regular for 11 seasons before trying his luck in the U.S.A., later coming back into League soccer as player manager with Hereford United. A first-class player in his heyday, he would have graced any side in the country.

CHRIS BALDERSTONE (Huddersfield T./Carlisle U./Doncaster Rov.)
A tall, constructive forward, Balderstone started out with Huddersfield Town in the late 1950s, joining Carlisle United in June 1965, when chances of playing in the First Division seemed to have passed him by. Extremely adept at set pieces in the modern game, with a highly proficient left foot, he scored over 90 League goals. He achieved his ambition of First Division soccer when Carlisle made it in 1972. He also played county cricket with Yorkshire and Leicestershire, on one occasion battling until 6.30 p.m., being driven away to play soccer for Doncaster Rovers an hour later, and returning the next day to complete a century.

ALAN BALL (Blackpool, Everton, Arsenal & England/Southampton/Blackpool/Southampton/Bristol Rov.).
A 5ft 6in tall, redhaired midfield terrier of a player, Ball started out on the right wing for Blackpool in 1962 and had been a victorious member of the famous World Cup side before signing for Everton in August 1966 at a fee of £110,000. With the "Toffees", he collected a Championship medal in 1970, later signing for Arsenal in December 1971 for £220,000. He played for Southampton until going to Blackpool as player-manager in July 1980, where unfortunately things did not go to plan, and he finished the season back at the Dell. The son of an ex-professional player, the little dynamo was earmarked for stardom as a youngster and his career certainly vindicated that early promise.

HARRY BAMFORD (Bristol Rov.)
Extremely versatile, Bamford played in at least six different positions before finally settling down at full back. He retired when nearing the age of 40, still being a giant in stature but with "Father Time" relentlessly closing in. He created quite a stir when it was discovered that he practised ball control by dribbling around the racing pigeons he owned. Notching up close on 500 League appearances, which, were it not for wartime, would have been considerably more, Harry was a real Bristolian clubman.

GORDON BANKS (Chesterfield/Leicester C., Stoke C. & England)
Picked up by Chesterfield from Rawmarsh Welfare, Banks learned the rudiments of the game with them, spending three years before making his debut in the "Spireites" goal. At the end of his first playing season was transferred to Leicester City, going on to play for England in 1963, the first of 73 caps. He was signed by Stoke City for £50,000 in 1967, thus allowing Peter Shilton to gain experience in the Leicester goal. He became acknowledged as one of the World's great keepers, using tremendous powers of concentration and great technique. Gordon's playing career was ended prematurely following a car accident in 1972, but he will be remembered as one of the England World Cup winners in 1966 for many years to come, as well as for the exceptional goal minding ability he showed.

RAY BARLOW (W.B.A. & England/Birmingham C.)

A tall, blond, attacking left half, Barlow, after waiting many years in the shadows, finally won an England cap against Ireland in 1954. He was one of the best wing halves of that period, with a long stride and terrific shot. Converted from inside forward, championing the long pass, Ray Barlow was almost "Buchanesque" in style and technique. Often playing up front, he was always a danger within shooting distance. He signed for neighbours Birmingham when finishing a career that was really incomplete due to a distinct lack of further International honours, although he was the proud possessor of a 1954 F.A. Cup winning medal against Preston.

SAM BARTRAM (Charlton Ath.)

Bartram must be the greatest goalkeeper never to be capped for England. Red haired and imposing, it was unthinkable that Charlton could ever be without the services of their net minder supreme for over 20 years. He originally came to them from Boldon Colliery. In his younger days, Sam was an outfield player, who four days after leaving school, received a letter saying he had been picked to play for England schools. Working in the pits, he took up goalkeeping when the colliery's regular keeper was injured and became an immediate success. But for the interruption of the League programme he would have played maybe a further 200 games.

GEOFF BARROWCLIFFE (Derby Co.)

Signed from Ilkeston Town in October 1950, Barrowcliffe was predominantly a full back, but was also used at centre forward when the need arose. Making his debut in the First Division during season 1950/1, he was hailed as one of Derby County's best local discoveries for a long time. He was a member of the County side that dropped from the First to Third Division North within three seasons, but he gained a medal when missing only one game when helping the "Rams" back into Division Two in 1956/7. He was a reliable defender who could play his way out of defence with fair distribution allied to trusty clearances.

BILLY BAXTER (Ipswich T./Hull C./Northampton T.)

Only 5ft 8in, Baxter was a wing-cum-centre half who attracted a lot of attention over the border when playing for juniors Broxborn Athletic, being snapped up in June 1960 by Ipswich Town. Making the first team almost immediately, he won a Division Two medal in his first season, followed by a First Division medal the next year when Ipswich, under Alf Ramsey, remarkably won the League title. He was a member of the side relegated in 1963/4 but he again helped Ipswich win promotion in 1967/8 as Champions, when he was supreme at the heart of defence. He finally moved to Hull City and then Northampton, being loaned to Watford for just under a dozen games, on route. He made up for his lack of inches with skill.

JIM BAXTER (Sunderland & Scotland/Nottingham F.)

"Slim Jim", as he was often called because of 5ft 10in pencil slim build, Baxter was one of the most brilliant Scots players to come over the border, and that he never really settled is now history. One of the most talked about personalities of the game, he was signed by Sunderland from Glasgow Rangers in May 1965 for £85,000, before moving on to Forest in December 1967. He played less than 50 games before being given a free transfer in the summer of 1969. He played 34 times for Scotland, where he had begun with Raith Rovers before going to Ibrox Park. He is remembered at his best as a classic passer of the ball, constructive and cool, turning defence into attack.

BRIAN BEDFORD

(Reading/Southampton/Bournemouth/ Q.P.R./Scunthorpe U./Brentford)

A bustling centre forward with terrific shooting ability, Bedford really came into his own with Q.P.R., who secured his transfer from Bournemouth for only £750. Beginning with Reading in April 1954, he moved to Southampton a year later, and in two seasons at Dean Court scored 32 goals in 75 games. After he had scored over 150 goals with the Rangers, Scunthorpe saw him as the man to bolster their attack after dropping into the Third Division. He again scored on a high percentage ratio, but was surprisingly transferred to Brendford after just over one year with the "Irons" He finished his League career at Griffin Park.

COLIN BELL (Bury/Manchester C. & England)
A perpetual motion player Bell became a great all rounder, before having to leave the game rather prematurely through injuries after winning 48 England caps and promising to control the National side's midfield for years to come. He was discovered by Second Division Bury when playing for Horden Colliery Welfare and made quite a reputation before joining Manchester City in a then club record £45,000 deal. He was effectively the key member of the City side which won the Football League, F.A. Cup, European Cup Winners Cup and League Cup within four highly successful years. Standing nearly 6 ft. tall, well built, he stood out mainly for exceptional non-stop running, playing just short of 400 games for the City.

ROY BENTLEY (Bristol C./Newcastle U./Chelsea & England/Fulham/Q.P.R.)
One of the finest roving centre forwards, Bentley was truly brilliant in the air, excellent on the ground, strongly built, and had a fierce shot in either boot. He was originally an inside forward with his home town club Bristol City, moving to Newcastle for £8,000 before the post-war League programme had commenced. Never really settling down in the North East, Roy joined Chelsea in January 1948 for £11,000. But he was recognized by England during 1949, and went on to play in the World Cup in Brazil. He captained Chelsea to their only Championship title in 1954/5, but found it a bitter pill to swallow when the club in September 1956 allowed him a transfer. Fulham and then Q.P.R. were very happy to use Roy's qualities in a conversion to centre back.

GEORGE BEST (Manchester U., Fulham & N. Ireland/Bournemouth).
Undoubtedly the greatest individual player of the modern British football period, Best's outstanding ball control and scoring talents made him the most exciting man in the game. He was only 17 years four months old when making his First Division debut for Manchester United in 1963 and he later played for Northern Ireland whilst still a month short of his 18th birthday. The peak of career came in 1968, when he won the British and European footballer of the year awards after gaining a European Cup winners medal to go with two Championship winning medals. Apart from brief displays with Fulham and Bournemouth, he now plays his soccer in the U.S.A. During a brilliant career, which unfortunately expired before his full talent was exploited, he won 37 full caps, and scored nearly 150 League goals.

HAROLD BELL (Tranmere Rov.)
A local wartime discovery for the Rovers, Bell settled down at centre half on the resumption of League football. He created a tremendous record by not missing a single game during nine post war seasons and 401 League appearances. Tranmere built their post-war team around him before Harold was tried up front. Deciding to retire at the end of the 1959/60 season, he had put together 595 games spread over 14 seasons, but it is his consecutive appearance record which is hardly likely to be beaten.

DAVID BEST (Bournemouth/Oldham Ath./ Ipswich T./Portsmouth/Bournemouth)
A brilliant young local goalkeeper, Best came through the junior ranks, making his debut for Bournemouth in 1960/1, displacing old favourite Tommy Godwin. He soon became a great hero at Dean Court, playing nearly 250 League games before signing for Oldham. After two years at Boundary Park, he was transferred for £15,000 to Ipswich Town. Custodian of the Portman Road goal for over five years, he eventually left for Portsmouth before finishing in League soccer with his first club, Bournemouth. The only time he played in the First Division was with Ipswich, and it was at Stamford Bridge against Chelsea that the amazing goal that never was, passing through the side netting, was awarded against Best and the East Anglians.

ALF BIGGS (Bristol Rov./Preston NE./Bristol Rov. Walsall/Swansea C.)
A home grown centre-cum-inside forward, extremely popular with the locals, Biggs made his debut in 1953/4 and was soon amongst the goals. He was 6ft 1in tall and well built: extremely effective in and around the penalty area. Preston saw him as being an answer to their goal shortages and completed the transfer for £18,000 in July 1961. However, after a season at Deepdale where he topped their goal charts, Alf returned once again to Rovers in order to help them regain the Second Division status lost the previous season. Scoring around 100 goals in just over 200 games was what the doctor ordered, but Rovers' League status was unaffected and in March 1968 he left, seeing out his footballing career with first Walsall and then Swansea.

BILLY BINGHAM (Sunderland, Luton T, Everton, Port Vale & Ireland)
Bingham was a wonderful tricky winger, who played 56 times for his country. After an outstanding display for the Irish League against the Football League in 1950, Sunderland paid a big fee to Glentoran in bringing his elusive talents to Roker Park. He played over 200 games before being transferred for £15,000 in July 1958 to Luton Town, very quickly receiving a losing F.A. Cup Final medal from the game against Forest. In October 1960, big spenders Everton gave the Hatters £20,000 along with John Bramwell and Alex Ashworth to bring the little wizard to Goodison, where he would weave his magic spell over that enthusiastic crowd. Before going into League management, Billy helped Port Vale prepare for a return to Divison Three.

RONNIE BLACKMAN (Reading/Nottingham F./Ipswich T.)
Born in Hampshire, Blackman played for Gosport Borough before Reading stepped in to sign this powerful six footer who could score goals regularly. In the Third Division South, Blackman scored over 150 League goals after becoming a regular in the 1948/9 season. Particularly good in the air and the possessor of a strong shot, Nottingham Forest saw him as a ready made replacement for Wally Ardron, who was ready to hang up his boots. A season later saw him transferred to Ipswich under Alf Ramsey, who was beginning Football League management with the Town. He left the League scene during 1957/8 after scoring in a very high proportion of games played.

JIMMY BLAIN (Everton/Southport/Rotherham U. /Carlisle U./Exeter C.)
Blain started out with Everton as a winger-cum-inside forward before finishing his League career with Exeter City as a left back some 15 years later. With Everton he did not get a chance to shine, moving on to Southport in February 1960, where he missed only a couple of games in two and a half years. Eventually he found himself down in the West Country with Exeter City, where he played 300 League games for the "Grecians." He really had the ability to make his mark as a goalscorer, but was too versatile to stablilise.

DAVID BLAKEY (Chesterfield)
A great stout hearted pivot, Blakey, between 1947 and 1967, notched up record appearances for his only League club after being signed from Chevington juniors. Most of his football was played in the Third and Fourth Divisions, although his debut in 1948/9 was in the Second Division, that status being lost by Chesterfield in 1951. He was well built and imposing, standing over 6ft and it was a sad day for the "Spireites" when he finally hung up his boots.

DANNY BLANCHFLOWER (Barnsley, Aston Villa, Tottenham H. & N. Ireland)
Barnsley paid Glentoran £6,500 for Blanchflower, a fine, constructive wing half of the classic mould, in April 1949, and in March 1951 the Villa enticed "Danny Boy" to Villa Park. With a fantastic ability to run the game, it wasn't until Danny joined Spurs in 1954 for £30,000 that his stage was really set. He captained Ireland through to the last eight of the 1958 World Cup following the player of the year award, which was again won in 1961. By this time Spurs had found the missing formula, with Blanchflower skippering them through the wonderful "double" campaign of 1960/1. After many honours, too numerous to mention, he retired in 1963/4 for a new career in journalism.

TERRY BLY (Norwich C./Peterborough U./ Coventry C./Notts. Co.)
One of the most prolific goalscorers of the lower Leagues, Bly was a hard boned 6ft tall youngster when signed by Norwich City from local Eastern Counties League side Bury Towrl. He was allowed to move to Peterborough United, scoring 52 goals from 46 games in his first season, 1960/1, which became a post-war scoring record. The next season he got another 30 goals for the "Posh" before Coventry City bought him. With the "Sky Blues" in 1962/3 he scored 25 goals in 30 games before surprisingly going to Notts County at the end of that season. Somehow the ability to find the net with the same reularity deserted him, possibly due to injuries and constant heavy marking.

STUART BOAM (Mansfield T./Middlesbrough/Newcastle U./Mansfield T.)
A 6ft 1in tall centre half, Boam was found in local junior football by Mansfield Town. He missed only ten games over four seasons whilst at the Field Mill ground, showing great potential at the heart of defence. Middlesbrough recognised this when signing him in June 1971 to form a vital partnership with Willie Maddren, which was vindicated when the 'Boro gained promotion back into the First Division in 1973/4. Before joining Newcastle United in August 1977, Stuart had played nearly 500 League games. Briefly he went into League management with Mansfield, before coming back as a non-contract player with Hartlepool U.

BILLY BONDS (Charlton Ath/West Ham U.)
An extremely competitive half back and captain, Bonds leads by inspiration as the driving force in face of all opposition. He was an apprentice at the Valley where he played just short of 100 League matches before joining West Ham in May 1967 for a bargain by today's standards, £50,000. He has twice led the "Hammers" at Wembley in collecting two winning F.A. Cup medals, but has yet to play for his country. Instrumental in helping the "Hammers" back to the First Division, with a runaway title victory during season 1980/1, he also played well in two wonderful League Cup Final games, when the Cup was claimed by Liverpool at the second attempt.

TONY BOOK (Plymouth Arg./Manchester C.)
Book's is one of the great romance stories of the modern football era. He was plucked out of obscurity with Bath City when working as a bricklayer at the age of 29. He became a great success at full back with Argyle; lanky and effective, very resourceful when going forward, quick in recovery. Malcolm Allison and Joe Mercer saw in Tony the man to lead Manchester City to glory and purchased him in July 1966. The rest is history: Football League Champions 1967/8, F.A. Cup 1968/9, European Cup Winners Cup 1969/70, Football League Cup 1969/70. The footballer of the year award in 1969 – an honour shared with the legendary Dave MacKay – was the icing on Book's football career.

JOHN BOND (West Ham U./Torquay U.)
A classy, strong full back, Bond became a regular with the Hammers in the early 1950s, after being spotted with junior side Colchester Casuals. He was able to turn in sterling performances at centre forward when needed, scoring many valuable goals, mainly in the 1957/8 season, when he helped the club gain promotion back to the top sector. Recognised by the Football League in representative matches, he did not quite make the full International standard. He moved to Torquay United in January 1966, after gaining an F.A. Cup winners medal against Preston in 1963/4. His son Kevin followed him into League soccer as an apprentice, turning pro for Norwich City in 1974.

PETER BONETTI (Chelsea & England)
Nicknamed "The Cat", son of a Swiss born restauranteur, Peter Bonetti came to the forefront when in 1959/60 Chelsea found themselves without a first team available keeper. The 17-year-old youth side choice was drafted in against Manchester City, who were fielding their new signing Denis Law. Unfortunate to be in the wings of the great Gordon Banks, he collected only seven England caps, but with Chelsea was a great hero of many victories, notably the 1970 Cup Final where, after the first replay since 1912, the "Blues" beat Leeds United. He made 600 League appearances, also winning a European Cup Winners Cup medal before taking his family to the Isle of Mull, where he occasionally turned out for Scottish League sides.

PHIL BOYER (Derby Co./York C./Bournemouth/Norwich C. & England/Southampton/Manchester C.).
Boyer started out with Derby County, but moved on to York City without even getting a first team game at the Baseball Ground. It was with the "Minster Men" that he first formed the famous scoring partnership with another reject, Ted McDougall, where initially the smaller man, only 5ft 8in, was rather overshadowed by the Scot in goalscoring feats. In playing later for Bournemouth, Norwich and Southampton, Boyer followed McDougall in setting up their formidable partnership. Whilst with Norwich he succeeded in gaining an England cap against Wales in 1976. Transferred to Manchester City to link up once again with Manager John Bond in November 1980, he was unlucky to have missed the 1981 F.A. Cup Final due to injury.

GEOFF BRADFORD (Bristol Rov. & England)
An inside-cum-centre forward, the scorer of many a hat trick, Bradford was originally a failed half back. He started out with a local junior side before turning pro at the age of 22 with Bristol Rovers, after being turned down by Blackburn Rovers. A hustling six-footer, Bradford, in a 15 year span, scored over 250 League goals. He recovered from a broken leg, which followed other serious injuries, to win an England cap in 1955. This outstanding feat was all the more meritorious as the Rovers were not in the top flight. A great friendly rivalry existed between Geoff and the other goalscoring Bristolian from the opposite side of the city, John Atyeo.

BILLY BREMNER (Leeds U. & Scotland/Hull C.)
A small, redhaired, veritable human dynamo, with fiery temperament to match, Bremner is currently the manager of Doncaster Rovers. He made his debut as a 17-year-old winger alongside Don Revie for Leeds United against Chelsea in 1960, eventually becoming a key player in the club's great successes under his former partner. Numerous honours include two Championships and an F.A. Cup winners medal, as well as two European Fairs Cup triumphs, in 1968 and 1971. He had many setbacks in his career, notably losing three F.A. Cup Finals from four played, but he had the satisfaction of appearing for Scotland on 54 occasions. He was player of the year in 1970.

BARRY BRIDGES (Chelsea & England/Birmingham C./Q.P.R./Millwall/Brighton &HA)
A sprint champion who joined Chelsea after winning International soccer honours at school, Bridges came to the fore in Tommy Docherty's young side of the early 1960s, being a perfect foil to Bobby Tambling as well as scoring regularly himself. He was the centre of controversy, which led to him being sold to Birmingham, when the "Doc" dropped Barry to allow the young Peter Osgood to play regularly. By then he had already won four England caps. Although scoring consistently with a succession of clubs after leaving City, he never again commanded the attention he received at the Bridge. He was one of the fastest players ever on a soccer pitch.

TOMMY BRIGGS (Plymouth Arg./Grimsby T./Coventry C./Birmingham C./Blackburn Rov./Grimsby T.)
A great stout hearted centre forward Briggs would never let the Argyle forget his free transfer to Grimsby in 1947, for in 1951, after scoring 77 goals, he was transferred to Coventry for £20,000, and by 1950 had represented England "B". Quickly moving on to Birmingham, still scoring, but not very happy, it wasn't until he arrived at Blackburn that Tommy recaptured his real deadliness near the goal. In six seasons he scored 140 League goals. Tommy had originally been a discovery of Pat Glover, the great Grimsby/Welsh International, and it was back with the "Mariners" that he finished his playing career at age 35.

PETER BROADBENT (Brentford/Wolverhampton W. & England/Shrewsbury T./Aston Villa/Stockport Co.)
A brilliant teenage prodigy, who eventually became a mercurial long service player, Broadbent was snapped up by Brentford from his home town club Dover, and quickly became a first teamer before Wolves took him to Molineux for £10,000 on advice from George Poyser, who had earlier discovered him. A clever, thoughtful inside forward, adept in setting up chances for others, Broadbent flourished with the Wolves and was one of the key players of the 1950s and early 1960s. Honours were abundant for both Peter and the club: Football League Champions three times, F.A. Cup winners in 1959/60 versus Blackburn, several England appearances as the famous Wolves went on the rampage. In 1965 he joined Shrewsbury, then briefly went back to the First Division with Villa before finishing at Stockport County.

TREVOR BROOKING (West Ham U. & England)
A fine midfielder, Brooking started out as a professional with the "Hammers" in May 1966, after coming through the apprentice ranks, and he became recognised as an outstanding craftsman. Noted for precision passing, deft touches, with immaculate crosses to near and far posts alike, he was one of the exponents of the set piece in the modern game. He played for England many times, adding to Football League and junior International honours. He twice played in an F.A. Cup Final at Wembley, firstly when helping West Ham to defeat Fulham in the second all-London Final in 1975 and again in 1980, this time scoring the only goal of the match in the defeat of Arsenal.

EDDIE BROWN (Preston NE./Southampton/Coventry C./Birmingham C./Orient)

Brown, one of the great "clowns" of the modern game, caused havoc to many opposing defences with roving tactics allied to energetic speed. He nearly entered the church, finally chose playing to praying, as a centre forward for Preston just after the war. He moved to Southampton in part exchange for Charlie Wayman, and then to Coventry before becoming the speediest man on the books at Birmingham. One of his many quirks was occasionally shaking hands with the corner flags after scoring, which he did often. He scored seven times in the "Blues" 1955/6 Cup run which culminated in losing to Manchester City at Wembley in the famous Bert Trautmann Final. He joined Orient in 1959 still enjoying every moment.

TONY BROWN (W.B.A. & England/Torquay U.).

A real hot shot, Brown scored 217 League goals before going off to finish his soccer days in the U.S.A., and finally Torquay. Joining Albion straight from school, Tony developed into a dynamic inside forward who possessed the ability to take on defences in all out assault. He collected only one England cap; strange reward indeed for many positive club displays, during which he gained an F.A. Cup winners medal from the 1968 defeat of Everton. In a 17-year career he became the proud possessor of both W.B.A.'s appearance and goalscoring records.

JACK BROWNSWORD (Hull C./Scunthorpe U.)

Brownsword gave wonderful service to the "Irons" after joining them from Hull City whilst they were still in the Midland League. He played less than a dozen games in the first post-war season at Boothferry Park, after being secured from Frickley, before going on to play just short of 600 games in 15 seasons at Scunthorpe. He was one of the finest club servants in the history of the game. Being rather on the short side at only 5ft 8in for a full back, he made up for this discrepancy with incisiveness and speed, coupled with all round manoeuverability.

MARTIN BUCHAN (Manchester U. & Scotland/Oldham Ath.)

Born and bred in Aberdeen, Buchan captained the local side at the age of 20 in winning the Scottish Cup Final of 1970. When he was transferred to Manchester United in March 1972, it cost a then club record fee of £125,000 to secure the young man's services. A regular performer and skipper since that occasion, he became recognised as one of the top quality defensive players of the modern game. He led United back to the First Division in 1974/5 after the traumatic drop into the Second, and to three F.A. Cup Finals in four years, gaining a winners medal in 1977 against Liverpool. Holder of over 30 Scottish International caps, he signed for Oldham Athletic in August 1983.

TOMMY BURDEN (Chester C./Leeds U./Bristol C.)

Starting with Major Buckley at Molineux during the war, Burden soon moved on to Chester where he began to build a reputation. Leeds United were not slow in noting his progress at either wing half or inside forward and they signed him in July 1948. He soon became captain and played nearly 250 games before moving again, this time to Bristol City in 1954, where he stayed until 1961. Predominantly a maker rather than taker of chances, Tommy picked up a Third Division South medal whilst at Ashton Gate.

RON BURGESS (Tottenham H. & Wales/Swansea C.)

Burgess learnt his football in the slag heaps of South Wales, playing for the local Cwm Villa, before Spurs signed him just before the outbreak of war. Dark haired before prematurely going bald, and aggressive, he inspired by example. He was an automatic choice from both Wales and Tottenham, playing for Great Britain against the Rest of Europe in 1947. He captained the great Spurs side which won in successive seasons the First and Second Division Championships in the early 1950s. Ron went back home to Swansea in August 1954, becoming player-manager, not again to play for his native Wales.

TED BURGIN (Sheffield U./Doncaster Rov./Leeds U./Rochdale)
A dark haired acrobat of a goalie who for a long time was on the brink of International honours, Burgin eventually had to settle for two England "B" appearances. Whilst playing for Alford Town in Lincs, he wrote to Sheffield United for a trial before signing in March 1949. He was a regular at United until the advent of the brilliant young Allan Hodgkinson, whose early displays soon warranted a regular first team place. Not happy to be a long term understudy, the once prospective International goalkeeper moved to Doncaster Rovers and a few months later, in March 1958, to Leeds. He later went on to Rochdale and gave sterling service.

JACK BURKITT (Nottingham F.)
Signed originally as a centre half, from Wednesbury, Burkitt settled down at wing half, becoming one of the most consistent players in the club's history. A top class constructive player, he would have surely played for his country if with a more fashionable side. On becoming captain, he led Forest into the First Division and crowned his career by taking them to Wembley, beating Luton Town in the 1959 F.A. Cup Final.

KENNY BURNS (Birmingham C., Nottingham F. & Scotland/Leeds U./Derby Co.)
Burns started out life with Birmingham City, mainly as an effective striker, but seemingly his career was held up, mostly by disciplinary actions rather than ability. In July 1977 the Nottingham Forest management duo, in preparing for First Division action, signed Kenny, promptly converting him to central defence alongside Larry Lloyd. Forest confounded the critics, and their new signing collected a Championship medal when missing only one match, and he also gained the player of the year award. These honours were followed by two European Cup winning medals in succession to add to his collection of 20 Scottish caps. More recently both Leeds and Derby saw him as the defender to bolster their defensive systems.

SAM BURTON (Swindon T.)
Burton was a long service goalminder at Swindon, signing in 1945 as a part timer after working in the mines. He gained a reputation for waving his hands and arms at any opposing penalty taker, which must have been rather distracting. Tall and well built, Sam played all the post-war seasons up until 1962, helping to bring along the Town's promising youngsters being blooded in the late 1950s. Sam also helped to score a goal for Bristol Rovers against his own side when taking a goal clearance which struck his centre half Ted Batchelor on the back of the head, the ball flying into the Swindon goal.

JOHNNY BYRNE (Crystal Palace, West Ham U. & England/Crystal Palace/Fulham)
Known as "Budgie", Byrne was capped by England when playing Third Division soccer with the Palace, being transferred soon after to West Ham in March 1962 for £58,000 plus a player, a then record between British clubs. Mainly at inside forward, Johnny was more than dangerous when in sight of the goal, having great skill and not requiring a large amount of space to manoeuvre the ball into a shooting chance. He was part of West Ham's F.A. Cup Final winning side against Preston in 1963/4, later being transferred back to the Palace, but staying only a year before signing off with Fulham. He played for England 11 times, and will be remembered for his great skill in setting up chances either for himself or others.

ROGER BYRNE (Manchester U. & England)
Byrne came to Old Trafford at the age of 20, as an outside left before being converted to the left back position, in which his natural speed was a great asset. He won the first of his 33 England caps against Scotland in 1954, and was by now already captaining the famous "Busby Babes". Intelligent play was his forte; the team obviously benefited, becoming under his captaincy a great side. Three Football League Championship medals were attained, before he and his team mates were struck down in the Munich air disaster – Roger losing his life. He was probably at the peak of his career, in a position to lead the United towards all available honours.

Players Names	Birthplace	Date	Previous Club	League Club	Date Signed	Seasons Played	Career Record Apps	Sub	Gls	
CABRIE, David	Port Glasgow	03.06.18	St.Mirren	Newport Co.	05.46	1946	9		0	
CADDEN, Joe Y.	Glasgow	13.04.20	Brooklyn W.	Liverpool	07.48	1950	4		0	(CH)
			TR	Grimsby T.	02.52	1952	1		0	
			TR	Accrington St.	06.53	1953	17		0	
CADE, David	Hemsworth	29.09.38	Doncaster Rov.(AM)	Barnsley	05.57					(F) E.SCH.INT.
			TR	Bradford P.A.	07.59	1959	1		0	
CAHILL, Paul G.	Liverpool	29.09.55	APP	Coventry C.	01.73					(D)E.YTH.INT.
			TR	Portsmouth	02.75	1974-77	95	2	2	
			L	Aldershot	01.78	1977	2	/	0	
			California S.	Tranmere Rov.	10.78	1978	5	/	0	
			TR	Stockport Co.	02.79	1978	3	/	0	
CAHILL, Tom	Glasgow	14.06.31	Vale of Leven	Newcastle U.	12.51	1952-53	4		0	(FB)
			TR	Barrow	08.55	1955-64	283		3	
CAIN, Jim P.	Fishburn	29.12.33	Stockton	Bristol C.	05.57					(HB)
			South Shields	Hartlepool U.	08.60	1960-61	30		0	
CAINE, Brian	Nelson	20.06.36	Accrington St.(AM)	Blackpool	02.57	1957	1		0	(G)
			TR	Coventry C.	09.59	1960	1		0	
			TR	Northampton T.	07.61					
			TR	Barrow	10.61	1961-63	109		0	
CAINE, William G.	Barrow	01.07.27	Barrow R.C.	Barrow	07.52	1951-54	12		0	(CH)
CAIRNEY, Charles	Blantyre	21.09.26	Glasgow Celtic	Orient	10.50	1950	4		0	(RH)
			Barry T.	Bristol Rov.	07.53	1953-54	14		1	
CAIRNEY, Jim	Glasgow	13.07.31	Shawfield J.	Portsmouth	09.49					(HB)
			TR	York C.	07.56	1956-57	53		0	
CAIRNS, Colin	Alloa	17.09.36	Camelon J.	Southend U.	02.58	1958	2		0	(F)
CAIRNS, John G.	Newcastle	13.04.22		Hartlepool U.	03.48	1947-49	16		2	
CAIRNS, Kevin W.	Preston	29.06.37	Dundee U.	Southport	08.62	1962-67	203	2	1	(FB)
CAIRNS, Robert L.	Choppington	25.12.27	Sunderland(AM)	Gateshead	09.48	1948-56	141		0	(FB) d.1958
CAIRNS, Robert S.	Annathill	27.05.29	Ayr. U.	Stoke C.	12.53	1953-60	175		9	(WH)
CAIRNS, Ron	Chopwell	04.04.34	Consett	Blackburn Rov.	09.53	1955-58	26		7	(F)
			TR	Rochdale	06.59	1959-63	194		66	
			TR	Southport	07.64	1964	34		13	
CAIRNS, William H.	Newcastle	07.10.12	Newcastle U.(*)	Gateshead	+					(CF) *Stargate
			TR	Grimsby T.	05.46	1946-53	221		119	
CAKEBREAD, Gerry	Acton	01.04.36	JNRS	Brentford	06.55	1954-63	348		0	(G) E.YTH.INT.
CALDER, William	Glasgow	28.09.34	Port Glasgow	Leicester C.	08.55	1958	3		0	(CF)
			TR	Bury	05.59	1959-63	174		67	
			TR	Oxford U.	11.63	1963-66	66	1	28	
			TR	Rochdale	11.66	1966	7	1	1	
CALDERBANK, G. Ray	Manchester	08.02.36	Hyde U.	Rochdale	AM	1953	1		0	
CALDERWOOD, Colin	Glasgow	20.01.65		Mansfield T.	03.82	1981-83	56	3	1	(D)
CALDERWOOD, Jim	Glasgow	28.02.55	APP	Birmingham C.	07.72	1972-79	135	10	4	(D)S.U23-1
			L	Cambridge U.	11.79	1979	8	/	0	
CALDWELL, Anthony	Salford	21.03.58	Horwich RMI	Bolton W.	06.83	1983	32	1	19	(F)
CALDWELL, David L.	Clydebank	07.05.32	Aberdeen	Rotherham U.	05.60	1960	1		0	(FB)
CALDWELL, David W.	Aberdeen	31.07.60	Inverness Caley	Mansfield T.	06.79	1979-83	126	11	48	(F)
CALDWELL, Terry	Sharlston	05.12.38	JNRS	Huddersfield T.	06.57	1959	4		0	(WH) E.YTH.INT.
			TR	Leeds U.	12.59	1959-60	20		0	
			TR	Carlisle U.	07.61	1961-69	340	4	1	
			TR	Barrow	07.70	1970-71	29	1	0	
CALEB, Graham S.	Oxford	25.05.45	APP	Luton T.	05.63	1963-64	20		0	(HB)
CALLACHAN, Ralph	Edinburgh	29.04.55	Hearts	Newcastle U.	02.77	1977	9	/	0	(M)
CALLAGHAN, Chris	Sandbach	25.08.30		Crewe Alex.	12.52	1953-56	45		0	(FB)
CALLAGHAN, Ernie	Birmingham	21.01.10	Atherstone	Aston Villa	*	1946	10		0	(RB) d.1972
CALLAGHAN, Fred	Parsons Green	19.12.44	APP	Fulham	08.62	1963-73	290	4	9	(FB)
CALLAGHAN, Henry	Glasgow	20.03.29	Kirkintilloch	Ipswich T.	09.54	1954	1		0	(OL)
CALLAGHAN, Ian	Liverpool	10.04.42	JNRS	Liverpool	03.60	1959-77	636	4	49	(M)E-4/E.U23-4
			TR	Swansea C.	09.78	1978-79	76	/	1	E.F.LGE REP.●
			Cork Hibs.	Crewe Alex.	10.81	1981	15	/	0	
CALLAGHAN, Nigel	Singapore	12.09.62	APP	Watford	07.80	1979-83	135	6	24	(W)E.U'21-9
CALLAGHAN, Robert	Glasgow	05.10.31	Duntocher H.	Scunthorpe U.	08.55	1955	19		6	(F)
			TR	Barrow	10.56	1956-57	40		10	
CALLAGHAN, William	Glasgow	07.02.30	Gt.Perth J.	Ipswich T.	07.52	1952-54	21		6	(IR)
CALLAGHAN, William A.	Glasgow	09.12.41	Dumbarton	Barnsley	08.64	1964	16		0	(OR)
CALLAGHAN, William F.	Ebbw Vale	26.02.24	Frickley Col.	Aldershot	06.49	1949	1		0	
CALLAN, Dennis	Merthyr Tydfil	27.07.32	Troedyrhw	Cardiff C.	07.52	1955	1		0	
			L	Exeter C.	05.54	1954-57	40		0	
CALLAN, Francis	Belfast	24.05.35	Dundalk	Doncaster Rov.	11.57	1957-58	28		6	(F)

Players Names	Birthplace	Date	Previous Club	League Club	Date Signed	Seasons Played	Career Record Apps	Sub	Gls	
CALLAND, Albert	Durham	10.09.29		Torquay U.	03.50	1951-53	24		11	(F)
CALLAND, Edward	Durham	15.06.32		Torquay U.	09.52	1952-56	47		22	(CF) Brother of Albert/Ralph
			TR	Exeter C.	07.57	1957-59	106		49	
			TR	Port Vale	08.60	1960	12		3	
			TR	Lincoln C.	07.61	1961	7		3	
CALLAND, Ralph	Durham	05.07.16	Charlton Ath.(*)	Torquay U.	+	1946-53	207		14	(FB)
CALLENDER, Jack	W. Wylam	02.04.23	JNRS	Gateshead	+	1946-57	470		41	(WH) Brother of Tom
CALLENDER, Norman	Newburn	09.06.24		Darlington	06.46	1946-48	27		1	(RH)
CALLENDER, Tom S.	W. Wylam	20.09.20	Lincoln C.(*)	Gateshead	+	1946-56	439		61	(CH) E.SCH.INT.
CALLOWAY, Laurie	Birmingham	19.06.45	APP	Wolverhampton W.	10.62					(IF)
			TR	Rochdale	07.64	1964-66	160	/	4	
			TR	Blackburn Rov.	03.68	1967-69	17	7	1	
			TR	Southport	08.70	1970	45	/	7	
			TR	York C.	06.71	1971-72	54	1	3	
			TR	Shrewsbury T.	12.72	1972-74	77	5	3	
CALOW, Charlie J.	Belfast	30.09.31	Cliftonville	Bradford P.A.	06.52	1952	1		0	(G) N.I.AMAT.INT.
CALVER, John	Blackburn	22.09.38	JNRS	Burnley	09.55					(HB)
			TR	Southport	07.61	1961	2		0	
CALVERLEY, Alf	Huddersfield	24.11.17		Huddersfield T.	+					(OL)
			TR	Mansfield T.	06.46	1946	30		1	
			TR	Arsenal	03.47	1946	11		0	
			TR	Preston N.E.	07.47	1947	13		0	
			TR	Doncaster Rov.	12.47	1947-52	142		11	
CALVERT, Cliff A.	York	21.04.54		York C.	07.72	1972-75	62	5	0	(D)E.YTH.INT.
			TR	Sheffield U.	09.75	1975-78	78	3	5	
CALVERT, Joe W.	Bullcroft	03.02.07	Bristol Rov.(*)	Leicester C.	*	1946-47	38		0	(G)
			TR	Watford	02.48	1947	5		0	
CALVERT, Steve	Barrow	02.04.52	JNRS	Barrow	AM	1971	22	/	4	(WH)
CAMDEN, Chris E.	Birkenhead	28.05.63	Poulton Vic.	Chester C.	12.83	1983	9	/	2	(F)
CAMERON, Alex	Leith	05.10.43	Hibernian	Oldham Ath.	05.64	1964	15		0	(FB)
CAMERON, Daniel	Dundee	09.11.53	APP	Sheffield Wed.	07.71	1973-75	31	/	1	(D)
			L	Colchester U.	02.75	1974	5	/	0	
			TR	Preston N.E.	04.76	1975-80	120	2	0	
CAMERON, Daniel P.	Dublin	16.06.22	Shelbourne	Everton	07.48	1948	1		0	
CAMERON, David	Glasgow	10.03.36	Glencairn	Bradford C.	04.58	1958	7		2	(F)
CAMERON, Duncan	Lanark	01.02.36		Swindon T.	09.56	1956-57	2		0	
CAMERON, Hugh G.	Blantyre	01.02.27	Clyde	Torquay U.	05.48	1948-50	120		17	(OR)
			TR	Newcastle U.	04.51	1951	2		0	
			TR	Bury	03.52	1951-53	29		1	
			TR	Workington	11.53	1953-55	54		4	
CAMERON, Jack	Dumbarton	07.03.31	Dumbarton	Hartlepool U.	11.53	1953-59	175		0	(FB)
CAMERON, John	Greenock	29.11.29	Motherwell	Bradford P.A.	07.56	1956	3		0	
CAMERON, Robert	Greenock	23.11.32	Pt. Glasgow	Q.P.R.	06.50	1950-58	254		56	(IF) S.SCH.INT.
			TR	Leeds U.	07.59	1959-61	58		8	
			TR	Southend U.	10.63	1963	3		0	
CAMERON, Rod	Newcastle	11.04.39		Bradford C.	08.57	1958	1		0	(FB)
CAMERON, Stuart J.	Liverpool	28.11.66	JNRS	Preston N.E.	N/C	1983	1	/	0	(G)
CAMMACK, Steve R.	Sheffield	20.03.54	APP	Sheffield U.	05.71	1971-75	21	15	5	(F)E.YTH.INT.
			TR	Chesterfield	01.76	1975-78	95	18	21	
			TR	Scunthorpe U.	09.79	1979-80	84	/	27	
			TR	Lincoln C.	07.81	1981	18	/	6	
			TR	Scunthorpe U.	03.82	1981-83	89	1	46	
CAMP, Steve	Manchester	08.02.54	Leatherhead	Fulham	09.75	1975-76	4	1	0	(F)
			TR	Peterborough U.	08.77	1977	6	1	1	
CAMPBELL, Alan	Belfast	11.09.44	Coleraine	Grimsby T.	10.70	1970-72	84	3	0	(FB)
CAMPBELL, Alan J.	Arbroath	21.01.48	JNRS	Charlton Ath.	02.65	1965-70	196	2	28	(M)S.U23-1
			TR	Birmingham C.	10.70	1970-75	169	6	12	
			TR	Cardiff C.	03.76	1975-80	165	2	2	
			TR	Carlisle U.	11.80	1980-81	29	2	2	
CAMPBELL, Charles	Oban	27.02.28		Oldham Ath.	11.49	1949	2		0	
CAMPBELL, Daniel	Manchester	03.02.44	Droylsden	W.B.A.	11.62	1965-67	8	/	0	(CH)
			U.S.A.	Stockport Co.	01.69	1968-69	31	/	3	
			TR	Bradford P.A.	03.70	1969	10	/	1	
CAMPBELL, Dave	Wrexham	18.02.47	JNRS	Wrexham	07.65	1964-67	41	2	7	(F)
CAMPBELL, Dave A.	Edinburgh	02.11.58	JNRS	Charlton Ath.	06.77	1975-79	71	5	3	(D)
CAMPBELL, Don	Bootle	19.10.32	JNRS	Liverpool	11.50	1953-57	47		2	(FB) E.YTH.INT.
			TR	Crewe Alex.	07.58	1958-61	149		1	
			TR	Gillingham	09.62	1962-63	29		0	

Players Names	Birthplace	Date	Previous Club	League Club	Date Signed	Seasons Played	Career Record Apps	Sub	Gls	
CAMPBELL, Dougald	Kirkintilloch	14.12.22		Q.P.R.	03.48					(F)
			TR	Crewe Alex.	07.49	1949	34		0	
			TR	Barrow	08.50	1950-51	30		3	
			TR	Grimsby T.	10.51	1951	6		0	
CAMPBELL, Frank	Oundell	23.12.50	JNRS	Grimsby T.	03.68	1968	4	1	0	(HB)
CAMPBELL, A. Glen	Leyland	26.02.65	APP	Preston N.E.	02.83	1982	1	/	0	(G)
CAMPBELL, Jim	Thornton Hill	11.11.22		Charlton Ath.	+	1946-57	255		1	(FB)
CAMPBELL, Jim			Leicester C.(+)	Walsall	10.46	1946-47	15		1	
CAMPBELL, Jim C.	St. Pancras	11.04.37	Maidenhead	W.B.A.	10.55	1957-58	31		9	(OR)
			TR	Portsmouth	07.59	1959-61	50		13	
			TR	Lincoln C.	05.62	1962-63	63		15	
CAMPBELL, John	Dumbarton	22.09.34	Motherwell	Chesterfield	08.59	1959	1		0	(FB)
CAMPBELL, John	W. Wylam	23.07.28		Gateshead	11.49	1949-55	183		48	(OL)
CAMPBELL, John J.	Liverpool	17.03.22	Liverpool (+)	Blackburn Rov.	+	1946-55	224		19	(WH)
			TR	Oldham Ath.	07.56	1956	26		5	
CAMPBELL, John P.	Belfast	28.06.23	Belfast Celtic	Fulham	03.49	1949-52	63		4	(OL)N.I.-2/IRISH LGE.REP./ d.1968
CAMPBELL, Joseph	Glasgow	28.03.25	Glasgow Celtic	Orient	07.49	1949	5		1	(IF)
			TR	Gillingham	09.50	1950	12		2	
CAMPBELL, Les	Wigan	26.07.35	Wigan Ath.	Preston N.E.	06.53	1953-59	64		6	(OL)
			TR	Blackpool	07.60	1960	11		0	
			TR	Tranmere Rov.	06.61	1961-63	99		9	
CAMPBELL, Paul J.	Newcastle	07.10.64	Gateshead	Hartlepool U.	10.83	1983	1	2	0	(M)
			TR	Burnley	03.84					
CAMPBELL, Phil A.	Barnsley	16.10.61	APP	Sheffield Wed.	10.79	1980	0	1	0	(F)
CAMPBELL, Robert	Glasgow	28.06.22	Falkirk	Chelsea	05.47	1947-53	188		36	(OR) S-5/
			TR	Reading	08.54	1954-57	95		12	
CAMPBELL, Robert	Liverpool	23.04.37	JNRS	Liverpool	05.54	1958-60	24		2	(WH) E.YTH.INT.
			Wigan Ath.	Portsmouth	11.61	1961-65	60	1	2	
			TR	Aldershot	07.66	1966	2	3	0	
CAMPBELL, Robert M.	Belfast	13.09.56	APP	Aston Villa	01.74	1973-74	7	3	1	(F)NI.-2
			L	Halifax T.	02.75	1974	14	1	0	
			TR	Huddersfield T.	04.75	1975-76	30	1	9	
			TR	Sheffield U.	07.77	1977	35	2	11	
			TR	Huddersfield T.	09.78	1978	7	/	3	
			TR	Halifax T.	10.78	1978	19	3	3	
			Brisbane C.	Bradford C.	12.79	1979-82	147	1	76	
			TR	Derby Co.	08.83	1983	11	/	4	
			TR	Bradford C.	11.83	1983	32	/	9	
CAMPBELL, Roy	Congleton	19.10.34		Crewe Alex.	12.55	1955-56	14		0	(HB)
CAMPBELL, Tom	Glasgow	20.02.35	Dundee U.	Tranmere Rov.	06.61	1961	4		0	(F)
CAMPBELL, William	Belfast	02.07.44	Distillery	Sunderland	09.64	1964-65	5		0	(F) N.I.-6/N.1.U23-3
CAMPBELL, Winston R.	Sheffield	09.10.62	APP	Barnsley	10.80	1979-83	53	4	5	
			L	Doncaster Rov.	01.83	1982	3	/	0	
CANDLIN, Maurice H.	Jarrow	11.11.21	Partick Th.	Northampton T.	02.49	1949-52	138		1	(CH)
			TR	Shrewsbury T.	07.53	1953-54	69		2	
CANN, Ralph	Sheffield	17.11.34		Mansfield T.	05.57	1957	2		0	(WH)
CANNELL, Paul	Newcastle	02.09.53	JNRS	Newcastle U.	07.72	1973-77	47	1	13	(F)
			Washington Dips.	Mansfield T.	01.82	1981-82	29	1	4	
CANNELL, Stuart	Doncaster	31.12.58	Bentley Vic.	Doncaster Rov.	08.78	1977-78	22	4	0	(D)
CANNING, L. Danny	Pontypridd	21.02.26	Abercynon	Cardiff C.	+	1946-47	80		0	(G)
			TR	Swansea C.	01.49	1948-50	47		0	
			TR	Nottingham F.	07.51	1951	5		0	
			Yarmouth	Newport Co.	08.55					
CANNING, Larry	Cowdenbeath	01.11.25	Paget Rgrs.	Aston Villa	10.47	1948-53	39		3	(RH) BBC Broadcaster
			Kettering	Northampton T.	06.56	1956	2		0	
CANNON, Jim	Coatbridge	19.03.27	T. Lanark	Darlington	06.56	1956	12		1	
CANNON, Jim A.	Glasgow	02.10.53	APP	Crystal Palace	10.70	1972-83	404	3	22	(D)
CANOVILLE, Paul K.	Hillingdon	04.03.62	Hillingdon Bor.	Chelsea	12.81	1981-83	34	8	9	(F)
CANTELLO, Len	Newton Heath	11.09.51	APP	W.B.A.	10.68	1968-78	297	4	13	(M)E.U23-8/E.YTH.INT.
			TR	Bolton W.	06.79	1979-81	89	1	3	
			Altrincham	Hereford U.	N/C	1982	1	/	0	
			TR	Bury	N/C	1982	8	1	1	
CANTWELL, Noel	Cork	28.02.32	Cork	West Ham U.	09.52	1952-60	248		11	(FB) E.I.-36
			TR	Manchester U.	11.60	1960-66	123		6	
CANVIN, Cyril E.	Hemel Hempstead	22.01.24	Apsley FC	Orient	03.47	1946	3		0	d.1950
CAPE, John P.	Carlisle	16.11.10	Q.P.R.(*)	Carlisle U.	10.46	1946	3		0	(OR)*Carlisle U./Newcastle U./ Manchester U.
CAPEL, Fred J.	Manchester	14.01.27	Goslings	Chesterfield	06.48	1949-56	284		18	(FB)
CAPEL, John E.	Newport	31.03.37		Newport Co.	12.55	1955	3		0	(OR) W.SCH.INT.

Players Names	Birthplace	Date	Previous Club	League Club	Date Signed	Seasons Played	Apps	Sub	Gls	
CAPEL, Maurice J.	Crewe	15.02.35		Crewe Alex.	07.56	1955-56	6		0	
CAPEL, Tom A.	Manchester	27.06.22		Manchester C.	+	1946-47	9		2	(IF) Brother of Fred
			TR	Chesterfield	10.47	1947-48	62		27	
			TR	Birmingham C.	06.49	1949	8		1	
			TR	Nottingham F.	11.49	1949-53	154		69	
			TR	Coventry C.	06.54	1954-55	36		20	
			TR	Halifax T.	10.55	1955	7		1	
CAPEWELL, Ron	Sheffield	26.07.29		Sheffield Wed.	03.50	1952-53	29		0	(G)
			TR	Hull C.	07.54	1954	1		0	
CAPPER, John	Wrexham	23.07.31	JNRS	Wrexham	11.49	1952-54	48		0	(HB)
			Headington	Lincoln C.	01.56	1955-58	21		0	
			TR	Chester C.	09.59	1959-60	37		0	
CAPSTICK, Albert L.	South Kirkby	02.01.28	Fleetwood	Accrington St.	08.48	1948	2		0	(IF)
CARBERRY, Bert	Glasgow	16.01.31	Avondale	Norwich C.	01.49	1953-54	6		0	(WH)
			Bedford T.	Gillingham	07.56	1956	1		0	
			TR	Port Vale	07.57	1957	29		0	
			TR	Exeter C.	08.58					
CARBERRY, Larry	Liverpool	18.01.36	Bootle	Ipswich T.	05.56	1956-64	257		0	(FB)
			TR	Barrow	07.65	1956-66	17	/	0	
CARDEW, Norman	South Shields	07.11.38	South Shields	Darlington	AM	1965	6	/	0	(IF)
CARDWELL, Louis	Blackpool	20.08.12	Blackpool(*)	Manchester C.	*	1946	2		0	(CH)
			Netherfield	Crewe Alex.	10.47	1947-48	25		0	
CAREY, Johnny J.	Dublin	23.02.19	St.James Gate	Manchester U.	*	1946-52	256		7	(FB) EI-29/N.I.-7●
CAREY, Peter R.	Barking	14.04.33	Barking	Orient	10.57	1956-59	34		2	(WH)
			TR	Q.P.R.	07.60	1960	15		1	
			TR	Colchester U.	11.60	1960	10		0	
			TR	Aldershot	08.61	1961-62	48		0	
CAREY, Richard	Paisley	19.11.27	Cowdenbeath	Southport	07.49	1949	1		0	(WH)
CARGILL, David A.	Arbroath	21.07.36	JNRS	Burnley	07.53	1953-55	5		0	(OL)
			TR	Sheffield Wed.	09.56	1956-57	10		0	
			TR	Derby Co.	04.58	1958-60	56		8	
			TR	Lincoln C.	12.60	1960	9		0	
CARGILL, Jim	Alyth	22.09.45	JNRS	Nottingham F.	09.62	1964-65	2	/	0	(G) S.SCH.INT.
			TR	Notts. Co.	07.66	1966	10	/	0	
CARLESS, Eric F.	Barry	09.09.12		Cardiff C.	*					Glamorgan Cricketer
			TR	Plymouth Arg.	12.46	1946	4		0	
CARLIN, Pat	Dunscroft	17.12.29	Dunscroft	Bradford P.A.	07.53	1953	6		0	(RB)
CARLIN, Willie	Liverpool	06.10.40	JNRS	Liverpool	05.58	1959	1		0	(IF) E.YTH.INT./
			TR	Halifax T.	08.62	1962-64	95		32	E.SCH.INT.
			TR	Carlisle U.	10.64	1964-67	92	1	21	
			TR	Sheffield U.	09.67	1967-68	36	/	3	
			TR	Derby Co.	08.68	1968-70	89	/	14	
			TR	Leicester C.	10.70	1970-71	31	/	1	
			TR	Notts. Co.	09.71	1971-73	57	3	2	
			L	Cardiff C.	11.73	1973	22	/	1	
CARLINE, Peter	Chesterfield	02.03.51	JNRS	Chesterfield	09.70	1970	2	/	0	(WH)
CARLING, Terry	Otley	26.02.39	Dawsons	Leeds U.	11.56	1960-61	5		0	(G)
			TR	Lincoln C.	07.62	1962-63	84		0	
			TR	Walsall	06.64	1964-66	101	/	0	
			TR	Chester C.	12.66	1966-70	199	/	0	
CARLSON, George E.	Liverpool	27.07.25		Tranmere Rov.	09.47	1947-48	2		0	
CARLTON, David G.	London	02.11.52	APP	Fulham	12.69	1971-72	5	4	0	(M)
			TR	Northampton T.	10.73	1973-76	99	5	6	
			TR	Brentford	10.76	1976-79	138	2	7	
			TR	Northampton T.	09.80	1980-81	76	/	1	
CARMICHAEL, Jack	Newcastle	11.11.48	Possilpark J.	Arsenal	11.66					(D)
			TR	Peterborough U.	01.71	1970-79	331	21	5	
			N. Eng. Teamen	Swindon T.	09.80					
			N. Eng. Teamen	Peterborough U.	N/C	1982	5	1	0	
CARNABY, Brian	Plymouth	14.12.47	Bexley U.	Reading	07.72	1972-76	136	9	10	(M)
CARNEY, Len F.	Liverpool	30.05.15	Collegiate OB	Liverpool	AM	1946-47	6		1	
CARNEY, Steve	Wallsend	22.09.57	Blyth Spartans	Newcastle U.	10.79	1979-83	119	9	0	(D)
CAROLAN, Joe	Dublin	08.09.37	Home Farm	Manchester U.	02.56	1958-60	66		0	(FB) EI-2
			TR	Brighton & H.A.	12.60	1960-61	33		0	
CAROLIN, Brian	Ashington	06.12.39		Gateshead	08.57	1957-59	17		0	(HB)
CARPENTER, Tom A.	Carshalton	11.03.25	Harrow T.	Watford	11.50	1950	4		0	(G)
CARR, Cliff P.	London	19.06.64	APP	Fulham	06.82	1982-83	42	5	5	(D)
CARR, Dave	Aylesham	31.01.57	APP	Luton T.	07.75	1976-78	39	4	0	(M)
			TR	Lincoln C.	07.79	1979-82	165	3	4	
			TR	Torquay U.	08.83	1983	34	/	0	
CARR, Dave	Wheatley Hill	19.01.37	Spennymoor	Darlington	05.57	1957-61	132		42	(IF)
			TR	Workington	07.62	1962-64	108		47	
			TR	Watford	02.65	1964-65	10	/	3	

Players Names	Birthplace	Date	Previous Club	League Club	Date Signed	Seasons Played	Apps	Sub	Gls	
CARR, Derek H.	Mansfield	01.09.27	Lockheed F.C.	Birmingham C.	02.48	1949	3		0	(CF)
CARR, Edward M.	Wheatley Hill	03.10.17	Arsenal(*)	Huddersfield T.	+	1946	2		0	(CF) *Margate
			TR	Newport Co.	10.46	1946-49	98		47	
			TR	Bradford C.	10.49	1949-52	93		49	
			TR	Darlington	08.53	1953	7		0	
CARR, Everton D.	W. Indies	11.01.61	APP	Leicester C.	01.79	1978-80	11	1	0	(D)
			TR	Halifax T.	08.81	1981-82	49	4	0	
			TR	Rochdale	03.83	1982	9	/	0	
CARR, Frank J.	Maltby	21.04.19	Rotherham U.(+)	York C.	08.46	1946	7		3	(OR)
CARR, John W.	S.Africa	10.06.26	S.Africa	Huddersfield T.	10.50	1950	1		0	(F)
CARR, John	Lanark	12.01.24	Clyde	Gillingham	N/L	1950	11		2	(F)
CARR, Kevin	Ashington	06.11.58	Burnley (N/C)	Newcastle U.	07.76	1977-83	149	/	0	(G)
CARR, Lance L.	S. Africa	18.02.10	Liverpool(*)	Newport Co.	*					
			TR	Bristol Rov.	08.46	1946	41		9	
CARR, Peter	Darlington	25.08.51	APP	Darlington	08.69	1967-72	131	4	1	(D)
			TR	Carlisle U.	11.72	1972-77	202	2	1	
			N. Eng. Teamen	Hartlepool U.	10.79	1979	22	/	0	
CARR, Peter	Rawmarsh	16.11.60	APP	Rotherham U.	11.78	1978-81	31	5	3	(M)
CARR, Stan R.	Southport	01.06.26	Brockhouse	Southport	+					(FB)
				New Brighton	08.48	1948	1		0	
CARR, W. Graham	Newcastle	25.10.44	JRNS	Northampton T.	08.62	1962-67	84	1	0	(HB) E.YTH.INT.
			TR	York C.	06.68	1968	32	1	1	
			TR	Bradford P.A.	07.69	1969	42	/	2	
CARR, Willie M.	Glasgow	06.01.50	APP	Coventry C.	07.67	1967-74	245	7	32	(M)S-6/S.U23-4●
			TR	Wolverhampton W.	03.75	1974-81	231	6	21	
			TR	Millwall	08.82	1982	8	/	1	
CARRICK, M. David	Ramshaw	05.12.46	APP	Wolverhampton W.	12.64					(IF)
			TR	Wrexham	07.66	1966-67	20	4	3	
			Altrincham	Port Vale	01.69	1968	14	2	0	
			Witton A.	Preston N.E.	11.73	1973	0	2	0	
			TR	Rochdale	03.74	1973-74	25	1	4	
CARRICK, Willie F.	Dublin	26.09.52	APP	Manchester U.	09.70					(G)
			TR	Luton T.	07.72	1972	4	/	0	
CARRINGTON, Andy	Grimsby	14.11.36		Grimsby T.	09.55	1959-60	4		0	(HB)
CARRODUS, Frank	Manchester	31.05.49	Altrincham	Manchester C.	11.69	1969-73	33	9	1	(M)
			TR	Aston Villa	08.74	1974-78	151	/	7	
			TR	Wrexham	12.79	1979-81	97	/	6	
			TR	Birmingham C.	08.82	1982	7	1	0	
			TR	Bury	10.83	1983	31	3	1	
CARROLL, Alf	Bradford	06.03.20		Bradford C.	03.48	1948-49	28		0	
CARROLL, John			Limerick	West Ham U.	05.48	1948	5		0	(CF)
CARROLL, Joseph	Radcliffe	06.01.57		Oldham Ath.	07.75	1975	3	1	0	(F)
			TR	Halifax T.	09.76	1976-78	76	6	14	
CARROLL, Mick	Aberdeen	10.09.52	Liverpool (APP)	Grimsby T.	03.71	1970	0	1	0	(F) S.SCH.INT.
CARROLL, Mike	Blaydon	04.10.61	Whickham	Chesterfield	09.81	1981-82	5	1	1	(F)
CARROLL, Tom	Dublin	18.08.42	Cambridge C.	Ipswich T.	07.66	1966-71	115	2	2	(FB) E1-17
			TR	Birmingham C.	10.71	1971-72	38	/	0	
CARRUTHERS, Alex N.	Loganlea	12.05.14	Falkirk	Rochdale	05.46	1946	13		4	(OR)*Falkirk/Bolton W./d.1977
CARRUTHERS, Eric	Edinburgh	22.02.53	Hearts	Derby Co.	01.75	1976	0	1	0	(F)
CARRUTHERS, John P.	Dumfries	02.08.26		Carlisle U.	07.49	1949	2		0	(OR)
			TR	Workington	07.51	1951	3		0	
CARSON, Alec M.	Corby	12.11.42	JNRS	Northampton T.	11.59	1960-61	8		0	(HB)
			TR	Aldershot	05.63	1963-64	5		0	
CARTER, Brian	Weymouth	17.11.38	Weymouth	Portsmouth	01.56	1957-60	46		0	(IF)
			TR	Bristol Rov.	07.61	1961	4		0	
CARTER, Don F.	Middle Norton	11.09.21	Stourbridge	Bury	*	1946-47	56		27	(F)
			TR	Blackburn Rov.	06.48	1948	2		0	
			TR	New Brighton	11.48	1948-50	104		19	
CARTER, Geoff	Moulton	14.02.43	JNRS	W.B.A.	02.60	1959-64	25		3	(OL)
			TR	Bury	07.66	1966	4	/	0	
			TR	Bradford C.	08.67	1967	1	/	0	
CARTER, Horatio S.	Sunderland	21.12.13	Sunderland (*)	Derby Co.	+	1946-47	63		34	(IF) E-13/E.F.LGE.REP./●
			TR	Hull Co.	04.48	1947-51	136		56	E.SCH.INT./Derby Cricketer
CARTER, Joe				Notts. Co.	+					(G)
			TR	Hull C.	06.46	1946	5		0	*Walsall
			TR	Bournemouth	03.47					
			TR	Bradford C.	08.48					
CARTER, Les A	Farnborough	24.10.60	APP	Crystal P.	11.77	1980	1	1	0	(F)E.SCH.INT.
			TR	Bristol C.	02.82	1981	16	1	0	

Players Names	Birthplace	Date	Previous Club	League Club	Date Signed	Seasons Played	Apps	Sub	Gls	
CARTER, Mike	Warrington	18.04.60	APP	Bolton W.	07.77	1979-81	37	12	8	(M)
			L	Mansfield T.	03.79	1978	18	/	4	
			L	Swindon T.	03.82	1981	4	1	0	
			TR	Plymouth Arg.	08.82	1982	6	6	1	
			TR	Hereford T.	03.83	1982	10	/	0	
CARTER, Ray	Chester	01.05.51	JNRS	Chester C.	09.71	1971-73	56	6	0	(F)
			TR	Crewe Alex.	07.74	1974	26	/	3	
CARTER, Ray H.	West Heathly	01.06.33	Brixham	Torquay U.	08.58	1958-59	3		1	(F)
			TR	Exeter C.	10.60	1960-62	106		50	
CARTER, Roger F.	Great Yarmouth	11.10.37	Gorleston	Aston Villa	12.55					(WH)
			TR	Torquay U.	07.60	1960	5		0	
CARTER, Roy	Torpoint	19.02.54	Falmouth	Hereford U.	04.75	1974-77	64	7	9	(M)
			TR	Swindon T.	12.77	1977-82	193	7	34	
			TR	Torquay U.	10.82	1982-83	27	/	8	
			L	Bristol Rov.	12.82	1982	4	/	1	
			TR	Newport Co.	09.83	1983	37	2	4	
CARTER, Sid	Chesterfield	28.07.16	Macclesfield	Mansfield T.	*	1946	13		3	(CF)
CARTER, Stan A.	Exeter	06.09.28	Heavitree U.	Exeter C.	11.49	1950-51	2		0	(CH)
CARTER, Steve C.	Gt. Yarmouth	23.04.53	APP	Manchester C.	08.70	1970-71	4	2	2	(F)
			TR	Notts. Co.	02.72	1971-78	172	16	21	
			TR	Derby Co.	08.78	1978-79	32	1	0	
			TR	Bournemouth	08.82	1981-83	42	4	1	
CARTER, Wilf	Wednesbury	04.10.33	JNRS	W.B.A.	01.51	1951-56	57		12	(IF)●
			TR	Plymouth Arg.	03.57	1957-63	252		133	
			TR	Exeter C.	05.64	1964-65	48	/	6	
CARTER, William J.	Woking	14.09.45	JNRS	Orient	10.64	1965-66	27	3	3	(WH)
CARTLIDGE, David	Leicester	09.04.40	JNRS	Leicester C.	10.57					(F)
			TR	Bradford C.	06.61	1961	6		3	
			TR	Chester C.	11.61	1961-62	20		0	
CARTWRIGHT, Ian J.	Birmingham	13.11.64	APP	Wolverhampton W.	09.82	1982-83	23	2	1	(M)
CARTWRIGHT, John	Northampton	05.11.40	JNRS	West Ham U.	11.57	1959-60	4		0	(IF) E.YTH.INT.
			TR	Crystal Palace	05.61	1961-62	11		1	
CARTWRIGHT, Les	Aberdare	04.03.52	JNRS	Coventry C.	08.71	1973-76	50	18	3	(M) W-7/W.U23-4
			TR	Wrexham	06.77	1977-81	111	4	6	
			TR	Cambridge U.	03.82	1981-83	47	6	1	
			L	Southend U.	09.83	1983	2	2	0	
CARTWRIGHT, Mick	Birmingham	09.10.46		Coventry C.	08.65	1965	1	/	0	(FB)
			TR	Notts. Co.	06.67	1967-68	15	1	0	
			L	Bradford C.	11.67	1967	1			
CARTWRIGHT, Peter	Newcastle	23.08.57	Nth. Shields	Newcastle U.	06.79	1979-82	57	8	3	(M)
			L	Scunthorpe U.	12.82	1982	2	2	1	
			TR	Darlington	03.83	1982-83	48	2	5	
CARTWRIGHT, William	Malpass	11.06.22		Tranmere Rov.	+	1946-47	9		1	
CARTY, Steve F.	Dunfermline	12.01.34	Blair Hall	Crewe Alex.	05.57	1956-59	37		0	(FB)
CARVER, David F.	Rotherham	16.04.44	APP	Rotherham U.	01.62	1961-64	83		0	(FB)
			TR	Cardiff C.	01.66	1965-72	210	1	1	
			L	Swansea C.	12.72	1972	3	/	0	
			TR	Hereford U.	08.73	1973	14	/	0	
			TR	Doncaster Rov.	03.74	1973-74	29	1	0	
CARVER, Gerry	Leigh Court	27.06.35	JNRS	Notts. Co.	08.52	1953-65	279	1	10	(WH)
CASCARINO, Anthony G.	St. Pauls Cray	01.09.62	Crockenhill	Gillingham	01.82	1981-83	89	10	31	(F)
CASE, Jimmy	Liverpool	18.05.54	Sth. Liverpool	Liverpool	05.73	1974-80	170	16	23	(M)E.U23-1
			TR	Brighton & H.A.	08.81	1981-83	103	/	10	
CASE, Norman	Prescott	01.09.25	Ards	Sunderland	10.49	1949-50	4		2	(CF) IRISH LGE REP.
			TR	Watford	12.50	1950	10		3	
			TR	Rochdale	02.52	1951	2		0	
CASEY, Gerry	Birkenhead	25.08.41	Holyhead T.	Tranmere Rov.	08.67	1967-69	49	3	5	(HB)
CASEY, Len	London	24.05.31	Leyton	Chelsea	02.54	1955-58	34		0	(WH)
			TR	Plymouth Arg.	12.58	1958-60	45		0	
CASEY, Paul	W. Germany	06.10.61	APP	Sheffield U.	06.79	1979-81	23	2	1	(M)
CASEY, Terry D.	Swansea	05.09.43	JNRS	Leeds U.	10.60	1961	3		0	(HB)
CASEY, Tom	Belfast	11.03.30	Bangor	Leeds U.	05.49	1949	4		0	(WH) N.1-12
			TR	Bournemouth	08.50	1950-51	66		1	
			TR	Newcastle U.	08.52	1952-57	116		8	
			TR	Portsmouth	07.58	1958	24		1	
			TR	Bristol C.	03.59	1958-62	122		9	
CASHLEY, Ray	Bristol	23.10.51	JNRS	Bristol C.	09.70	1970-80	227	/	1	(G)
			L	Hereford U.	01.81	1980	20	/	0	
				Bristol Rov.	08.82	1983	27	/	0	
CASHMORE, Norman	Aldershot	24.03.39	Woking	Aldershot	07.63	1964	7		0	(HB)
CASKEY, William	Belfast	12.10.53	Glentoran	Derby Co.	09.78	1978-79	26	2	3	(F)NI-7
CASLEY, John E.	Torquay	27.04.26		Torquay U.	06.47	1947	1		0	(G)

Players Names	Birthplace	Date	Previous Club	League Club	Date Signed	Seasons Played	Apps	Sub	Gls	
CASPER, Frank	Barnsley	09.12.44	APP	Rotherham U.	07.62	1962-66	101	1	26	(CF) E.F.LGE REP.
			TR	Burnley	06.67	1967-75	230	7	74	
CASSELL, Jim	Manchester	23.04.47		Bury	07.70	1970	2	1	0	(IF)
CASSELLS, Keith B.	London	10.07.57	Wembley T.	Watford	11.77	1978-80	6	6	0	(F)
			L	Peterborough U.	01.80	1979	8	/	0	
			TR	Oxford U.	11.80	1980-81	43	2	13	
			TR	Southampton	03.82	1981-82	13	6	4	
			TR	Brentford	02.83	1982-83	42	4	17	
CASSIDY, Andy D.	Leeds	01.03.59	Sunderland (AM)	Stockport Co.	08.78	1977-78	5	/	0	(G)
CASSIDY, Francis J.A.	Watford	20.08.64	APP	Watford	09.82					(M)
			L	Plymouth Arg.	02.84	1983	1	/	0	
CASSIDY, Jim T.	Glasgow	01.12.43	E.Stirling	Oxford U.	07.63	1963	5		0	(FB)
			TR	Barrow	03.65	1964	5		0	
CASSIDY, Laurie	Manchester	10.03.23		Manchester U.	02.47	1947-51	4		0	(F)
			TR	Oldham Ath.	07.56	1956	4		1	
CASSIDY, Nigel	Sudbury	07.12.45	Lowestoft	Norwich C.	07.67	1967-68	2	1	0	(IF)
			TR	Scunthorpe U.	12.68	1968-70	88	/	35	
			TR	Oxford U.	11.70	1970-73	113	3	33	
			TR	Cambridge U.	03.74	1973-75	52	2	13	
CASSIDY, Tommy	Belfast	18.11.50	Coleraine	Newcastle U.	10.70	1970-79	170	10	22	(M)NI-24
			TR	Burnley	07.80	1980-82	70	2	4	
CASSIDY, William	Gateshead	30.06.17	Close Wks	Gateshead	*	1946-52	83		3	(WH)
CASSIDY, William P.	Hamilton	04.10.40	Glasgow Rgrs.	Rotherham U.	08.61	1961-62	28		1	(IF)
			TR	Brighton & H.A.	11.62	1962-66	113	5	26	
			Detroit Cougars	Cambridge U.	07.70	1970	27	4	6	
CASWELL, Brian L.	Wednesbury	14.02.56	APP	Walsall	09.73	1972-83	354	11	17	(D)
CASWELL, Peter D.	Leatherhead	16.01.57	APP	Crystal P.	08.75	1976-77	3	/	0	(G)
			TR	Crewe Alex.	08.78	1978	22	/	0	
CATER, Ron	Fulham	02.02.22	Leytonstone	West Ham U.	+	1946-49	63		0	(WH)
			TR	Orient	06.51	1951	4		0	
CATERER, Brian	Hayes	23.01.43	Chesham U.	Brentford	AM	1968	1	/	0	
CATLEUGH, George C.	Horden	11.06.32	Nuneaton	Watford	05.54	1954-64	293		14	(IF)
CATLEY, Jack W.	Grimsby	16.03.45	JNRS	Grimsby T.	07.62	1962	2		0	(F)
CATON, Thomas	Liverpool	06.10.62	APP	Manchester C.	10.79	1979-83	164	1	8	(D)E.SCH.INT./E.YTH.INT.
			TR	Arsenal	12.83	1983	26	/	0	E.U'21-14
CATON, William C.	Stoke	11.09.24	JNRS	Stoke C.	+	1947-49	22		2	(HB)
			TR	Carlisle U.	04.50	1949-51	64		16	
			TR	Chesterfield	10.52	1952	7		0	
			Worcester C.	Crewe Alex.	07.54	1954	38		8	
CATTERICK, Harry	Darlington	26.11.19	Cheadle Heath	Everton	*	1946-51	59		18	(CF)
			TR	Crewe Alex.	12.51	1951-52	24		11	
CATTLIN, Chris	Milnrow	25.06.46	Burnley (AM)	Huddersfield T.	08.64	1964-67	59	2	1	(D)E.U23-1
			TR	Coventry C.	03.68	1967-75	213	4	0	
			TR	Brighton & H.A.	06.76	1976-78	95	1	1	
CATTRELL, Gordon	Sunderland	18.12.54	APP	Leeds U.	01.72					(WH) E.SCH.INT.
			TR	Darlington	08.73	1973-75	96	6	5	
CAUGHTER, Alan	Bangor	19.02.46		Chester C.	08.69	1969	1	/	0	(FB)
CAULFIELD, Graham	Leeds	18.07.43	Frickley Col.	York C.	AM	1966	9	/	2	(CF)
			TR	Bradford C.	AM	1967	1	/	0	
CAVANAGH, Irvin	Rochdale	31.07.24		Bury	05.48	1949	1		0	
CAVANAGH, Tommy H.	Liverpool	29.06.28		Preston N.E.	08.49					(IF)
			TR	Stockport Co.	01.50	1949-51	32		2	
			TR	Huddersfield T.	05.52	1952-55	93		29	
			TR	Doncaster Rov.	05.56	1956-58	119		16	
			TR	Bristol C.	07.59	1959	24		6	
			TR	Carlisle U.	06.60	1960	34		4	
CAVE, Mick	Weymouth	28.01.49	Weymouth	Torquay U.	07.68	1968-70	106	8	17	(F)
			TR	Bournemouth	07.71	1971-73	91	8	17	
			L	Plymouth Arg.	03.72	1971	8	/	4	
			TR	York C.	08.74	1974-76	94	2	13	
			TR	Bournemouth	02.77	1976-77	42	/	3	
CAVEN, John B.	Kirkintilloch	06.07.34	Kirmarnock	Brentford	10.57	1957-58	7		1	(F)
			Airdrie	Brighton & H.A.	03.62	1961-62	10		0	
CAVENER, Phillip	Sth. Shields	02.06.61	APP	Burnley	05.79	1979-82	55	13	5	(F)
			L	Bradford C.	03.83	1982	9	/	2	
				Gillingham	N/C	1983	4	6	1	
CAWSTON, Mervyn	Norwich	04.02.52	APP	Norwich C.	07.69	1970	4	/	0	(G)E.SCH.INT.
			L	Southend U.	08.74	1974	10	/	0	
			L	Newport Co.	01.76	1975	4	/	0	
			TR	Gillingham	05.76	1976	19	/	0	
			Chicago Stings	Southend U.	08.78	1978-83	189	/	0	
			TR	Stoke C.	03.84					

Players Names	Birthplace	Date	Previous Club	League Club	Date Signed	Seasons Played	Apps	Sub	Gls	
CAWTHORNE, Graham J.	Doncaster	30.09.58	Harworth C.W.	Grimsby T.	11.79	1979	1	/	0	(D)
			TR	Doncaster Rov.	03.82	1981-82	33	/	1	
CEGIELSKI, Wayne	Bedwellty	11.01.56	APP	Tottenham H.	05.73					(D)W.U21-2
			L	Northampton T.	03.75	1974	11	/	0	
			Schalke 04	Wrexham	09.76	1976-81	112	11	0	
			TR	Port Vale	08.82	1982-83	82	1	4	
CHADBOURNE, William	Mansfield	29.10.22		Mansfield T.	04.47	1946-47	10		5	(F)
CHADWICK, Clifton	Bolton	26.01.14	Oldham Ath.(*)	Middlesbrough	*					(OR)*Fleetwood
			TR	Hull C.	09.46	1946	23		7	
			TR	Darlington	07.47	1947	37		5	
CHADWICK, Dave E.	India	19.08.43	JNRS	Southampton	10.60	1961-65	24	/	2	(W)
			TR	Middlesbrough	07.66	1966-69	100	3	3	
			TR	Halifax T.	01.70	1969-71	95	/	15	
			TR	Bournemouth	02.72	1971-73	29	7	4	
			L	Torquay U.	12.72	1972	10	/	0	
			TR	Gillingham	09.74	1974	35	/	3	
CHADWICK, Frank R.	Blackburn	09.11.27	JNRS	Blackburn Rov.	06.46	1948-52	11		1	(HB)
			TR	York C.	07.55					
CHADWICK, Fred W.	Manchester	08.09.13	Newport Co.(*)	Ipswich T.	*	1946	6		2	
			TR	Bristol Rov.	07.47	1947	6		1	
CHADWICK, Graham	Oldham	08.04.42	JNRS	Manchester C.	03.62	1962-63	12		0	(HB)
			TR	Walsall	08.64	1964	9		0	
			TR	Chester C.	07.65	1965-66	11	1	0	
CHADWICK, Harold				Grimsby T.	+					
				Tranmere Rov.	03.48	1947-48	9		0	
CHADWICK, Keith M.	Stoke	10.03.53	JNRS	Port Vale	09.73	1973-75	29	12	7	(WH)
CHALK, Steve R.	Southampton	15.10.57	APP	Bournemouth	02.76	1975-77	11	/	0	(G)
			TR	Charlton Ath.	06.78					
CHALKLIN, Geoff	Swindon	01.10.56	APP	Swindon T.	01.76	1975	3	/	0	(CF) E.SCH.INT.
CHALLIS, Roger L.	Rochester	03.08.43	JNRS	Gillingham	07.61	1960-62	9	/	0	(FB) E.YTH.INT.
			TR	Crewe Alex.	08.64	1964	3		0	
CHALLIS, Stan. M.	Lympstone	22.04.18	Lympstone FC	Exeter C.	+	1946	4		1	(OL)
CHALMERS, Len	Corby	04.09.36	Corby T.	Leicester C.	01.56	1957-65	171	/	4	(FB)
			TR	Notts.Co.	07.66	1966-67	51	/	1	
CHAMBERLAIN, Alec F.R.	Ely	20.06.64	JNRS	Ipswich T.	07.81					(G)
			TR	Colchester U.	08.82	1982-83	50	/	0	
CHAMBERLAIN, Derek C.	Nottingham	06.01.33	Parliament St.M.	Aston Villa	11.53					(FB)
			TR	Mansfield T.	11.56	1956-57	43		0	
			TR	York C.	07.58					
CHAMBERLAIN, Glyn	Chesterfield	29.07.57	APP	Burnley	11.74					(D)
			TR	Chesterfield	12.76	1976-78	17	1	0	
			TR	Halifax T.	08.81	1981	35	/	0	
CHAMBERLAIN, Ken R.	S. Africa	30.06.26	Parkhill S.A.	Charlton Ath.	10.51	1952-56	42		0	(CH)
CHAMBERLAIN, Mark V.	Stoke	19.11.61	APP	Port Vale	04.79	1978-81	90	6	17	(W)E.SCH.INT./E-4/E.U'21-3
			TR	Stoke C.	08.82	1982-83	76	1	13	
CHAMBERLAIN, Neville	Stoke	22.01.60	APP	Port Vale	02.78	1977-82	133	8	33	(F) Brother of Mark
			TR	Stoke C.	09.82	1982-83	6	/	0	
			L	Newport Co.	11.83	1983	6	/	2	
			L	Plymouth Arg.	03.84	1983	7	4	3	
CHAMBERLAIN, Peter M.	Liverpool	30.06.35		Leicester C.	09.56					(F)
			TR	Swindon T.	06.57	1957-62	80		6	
			TR	Aldershot	10.62	1962-64	46		1	
CHAMBERLAIN, Trevor	Edmonton	11.07.34	JNRS	Fulham	07.51	1954-64	183		59	(OL) E.YTH.INT./ E.SCH.INT.
CHAMBERS, Brian M.	Newcastle	31.10.49	JNRS	Sunderland	08.67	1970-72	53	10	5	(M)E.SCH.INT.
			TR	Arsenal	06.73	1973	1	/	0	
			TR	Luton T.	02.74	1974-76	73	3	9	
			TR	Millwall	07.77	1977-78	54	5	9	
			TR	Bournemouth	07.79	1979-80	39	3	7	
			TR	Halifax T.	03.81	1980	10	/	0	
CHAMBERS, David M.	Barnsley	06.06.47	APP	Rotherham U.	06.65	1965-67	21	5	4	(F) Brother of Phil
			Cambridge U.	Southend U.	10.68	1968-70	51	6	5	
			TR	York C.	03.71	1970-71	8	8	1	
CHAMBERS, John F.	Birmingham	07.10.49	APP	Aston Villa	10.66	1968	1	1	0	(F)
			TR	Southend U.	07.69	1969	6	1	0	
CHAMBERS, Philip M.	Barnsley	10.11.53	APP	Barnsley	11.71	1970-83	436	1	8	(D)E.SCH.INT./Brother of David
CHAMPELOVIER, Les	Kensington	23.04.33	Hayes	Brighton & H.A.	AM	1957	1		0	(IF) E.AMAT.INT.
CHANDLER, Frank E.J.	Hythe	02.08.12	Swindon T.(*)	Crewe Alex.	*	1946	13		0	(IL)*Reading/Blackpool
CHANDLER, Jeff	Hammersmith	19.06.59	APP	Blackpool	08.76	1977-78	31	6	7	(F)EI-2/EI.U21-1
			TR	Leeds U.	09.79	1979-80	21	5	2	
			TR	Bolton W.	10.81	1981-83	113	3	20	

Players Names	Birthplace	Date	Previous Club	League Club	Date Signed	Seasons Played	Apps	Sub	Gls	
CHANDLER, Ray	Bath	14.08.31	Bristol C.(AM)	Bristol Rov.	06.53	1953-54	12		0	(G)
			TR	Swindon T.	06.56	1956-58	35		0	
CHANDLER, Ricky D.	Bristol	26.09.61	APP	Bristol C.	10.78	1980-82	57	4	12	(M)E.SCH.INT.
CHANDLER, Robin A.S.	Luton	19.12.42	JNRS	Luton T.	12.61	1960-64	13		0	(F) E.SCH.INT.
CHANNON, Mick R.	Orcheston	28.11.48	APP	Southampton	12.65	1965-76	388	4	155	(F)E-46/E.U23-9
			TR	Manchester C.	07.77	1977-79	71	1	24	E.F.LGE REP.●
			TR	Southampton	09.79	1979-81	119	/	27	
			TR	Newcastle U.	09.82	1982	4	/	1	
			TR	Bristol Rov.	10.82	1982	4	5	0	
			TR	Norwich C.	12.82	1982-83	54	3	8	
CHAPMAN, Daryl M.	Kenilworth	17.09.63	JNRS	Derby Co.	07.82					(F)
			N/C	Crewe Alex.	N/C	1982	3	3	2	
CHAPMAN, Eddie	East Ham	03.08.23	Romford	West Ham U.	+	1948	7		3	(IF)
CHAPMAN, Edwin	Blackburn	02.05.19	Accrington St.(*)	Oldham Ath.	+					(F)d.1976
			TR	Stockport Co.	08.46	1946	9		3	
CHAPMAN, George	West Bromwich	08.10.20	Donisthorpe FC	W.B.A.	*					(IL)
			TR	Brighton & H.A.	07.46	1946-47	43		12	
CHAPMAN, Harry	Liverpool	04.03.21	Kidderminster	Aston Villa	02.47	1947	6		0	(WH)
			TR	Notts.Co.	03.49	1948-50	53		1	
CHAPMAN, John	Sacriston	24.05.45	Stockton	Workington	02.63	1963-65	28	/	1	(FB)
			TR	Reading	06.66	1966-68	102	1	2	
			TR	Stockport Co.	07.69	1969-71	89	3	5	
CHAPMAN, Ken A.	Coventry	25.04.32	JNRS	Blackpool	08.49					(IL)
			TR	Crewe Alex.	07.53	1953	24		8	
			TR	Bradford C.	07.54	1954	26		4	
CHAPMAN, Ken F.	Grimsby	16.11.48	Louth U.	Grimsby T.	AM	1969	7	1	0	(OL)
CHAPMAN, Lee R.	Lincoln	05.12.59	JNRS	Stoke C.	06.78	1979-81	95	4	34	(F)E.U21-1
			L	Plymouth Arg.	12.78	1978	3	1	0	
			TR	Arsenal	08.82	1982-83	15	8	4	
			TR	Sunderland	12.83	1983	14	1	3	
CHAPMAN, Les	Oldham	27.09.48	High Barn	Oldham Ath.	01.67	1966-69	75	1	9	(M)
			TR	Huddersfield T.	09.69	1969-74	120	13	8	
			TR	Oldham Ath.	12.74	1974-78	186	1	11	
			TR	Stockport Co.	05.79	1979	32	/	1	
			TR	Bradford C.	02.80	1979-82	137	2	3	
			TR	Rochdale	06.83	1983	44	1	0	
CHAPMAN, Neville	Cockfield	15.09.41	JNRS	Middlesbrough	11.58	1961-66	51	1	0	(HB)
			TR	Darlington	09.67	1967-68	31	1	0	
CHAPMAN, Paul C.	Cardiff	28.09.51	APP	Plymouth Arg.	10.69	1969	2	2	0	(HB)
CHAPMAN, Phil. E.	Chasetown	27.11.25	Cannock T.	Walsall	09.48	1948-50	62		36	(CF)
CHAPMAN, Reg	Eccles	14.06.28	Hereford U.	Crewe Alex.	05.50	1950-51	21		1	(F)
CHAPMAN, Reg F.J.	Shepherds Bush	07.09.21		Q.P.R.	+	1946-52	98		2	(CH)
CHAPMAN, Robert	Wednesbury	18.08.46	JNRS	Nottingham F.	08.63	1963-76	347	12	17	(D)
			TR	Notts. Co.	08.77	1977	42	/	0	
			TR	Shrewsbury T.	07.78	1978-79	36	1	6	
CHAPMAN, Roger A.	Balby	20.11.44		Rotherham U.	07.65	1964	2		0	(G)
			TR	Doncaster Rov.	12.65	1965	5	/	0	
CHAPMAN, Roy C.	Birmingham	18.03.34	Kynoch Wks	Aston Villa	02.52	1953-57	19		7	(IF)d.1983●
			TR	Lincoln C.	11.57	1957-61	105		45	
			TR	Mansfield T.	08.61	1961-64	136		77	
			TR	Lincoln C.	01.65	1964-66	69	1	31	
			TR	Port Vale	08.67	1967-68	77	1	38	
			TR	Chester C.	06.69	1969	9	/	3	
CHAPMAN, Sammy E.	Belfast	16.02.38	Shamrock Rov.	Mansfield T.	10.56	1956-57	63		26	(WH) N.I.'B'-1
			TR	Portsmouth	02.58	1957-61	48		10	
			TR	Mansfield T.	12.61	1961-63	105		15	
CHAPMAN, Stuart	Newcastle	06.05.51	APP	Port Vale	07.69	1966-69	4	2	0	(F)
CHAPMAN, Vernon	Leicester	09.05.21		Leicester C.	+	1946	1		0	
			TR	Orient	07.47	1947-48	31		7	
CHAPPELL, Larratt	Sheffield	19.12.30	JNRS	Barnsley	05.49	1952-58	218		95	(CF)
			TR	Doncaster Rov.	08.59	1959-60	34		5	
CHAPPELL, Les A.	Nottingham	06.02.47	APP	Rotherham U.	02.65	1965-67	109	2	36	(M)
			TR	Blackburn Rov.	05.68	1968	7	/	0	
			TR	Reading	07.69	1969-74	193	8	81	
			TR	Doncaster Rov.	12.74	1974-75	57	1	10	
			TR	Swansea C.	07.76	1976-77	65	2	5	
CHARD, Philip J.	Corby	16.10.60	Nottingham F. (JNRS)	Peterborough U.	01.79	1978-83	128	19	17	(M)
CHARLES, Clive M.	Bow	03.10.51	APP	West Ham U.	06.70	1971-73	12	2	0	(D)E.YTH.INT./
			TR	Cardiff C.	03.74	1973-76	75	2	5	Brother of John
CHARLES, Jeremy M.	Swansea	26.09.59	APP	Swansea C.	01.77	1976-83	224	23	53	(F)W.U21-2/W14/
			TR	Q.P.R.	11.83	1983	10	2	5	Son of Mel
CHARLES, John W.	West Ham	20.09.44	APP	West Ham U.	05.62	1962-69	117	1	1	(FB) E.YTH.INT./
										Brother of Clive

Players Names	Birthplace	Date	Previous Club	League Club	Date Signed	Seasons Played	Apps	Sub	Gls	
CHARLES, Mel	Swansea	14.05.35	Leeds U.(AM)	Swansea C.	05.52	1952-58	233		69	(WH) W-31/W.U23-1/●
			TR	Arsenal	04.59	1959-61	60		26	Brother of W. John
			TR	Cardiff C.	02.62	1961-64	81		24	
			Portmadoc	Port Vale	02.67	1966	7	/	0	
CHARLES, Robert	Southampton	26.12.41	JNRS	Southampton	04.59	1959-60	26		0	(G) E.YTH.INT./E.SCH.INT.
CHARLES, Steve	Sheffield	10.05.60	Sheffield Univ.	Sheffield U.	01.80	1979-83	110	11	9	(M)
CHARLES, W. John	Swansea	27.12.31	JNRS	Leeds U.	01.49	1948-56	297		151	(CF) W-38/●
			Juventus	Leeds U.	08.62	1962	11		3	
			Roma	Cardiff C.	08.63	1963-65	65	1	19	
CHARLESWORTH, Arnold	Sheffield	06.07.30	Boston U.	W.B.A.	03.52					(IF)
			TR	Rotherham U.	08.53					
			TR	York C.	04.54	1954	1		0	
CHARLESWORTH, Stan	Conisbrough	10.03.20	Wath W.	Grimsby T.	*	1946	1		0	(CH)
			TR	Barnsley	12.46	1946	7		0	
CHARLESWORTH, Terry	Scunthorpe	13.07.33		Scunthorpe U.	08.56	1952-56	19		0	(G)
CHARLTON, Harry	Gateshead	22.06.51	APP	Middlesbrough	07.68	1970-74	8	2	0	(F)
			L	Hartlepool U.	01.76	1975	2	1	0	
			TR	Chesterfield	03.76	1975-76	17	4	0	
			Buxton	Darlington	08.79	1979-81	69	3	4	
CHARLTON, Jack	Ashington	08.05.35	JNRS	Leeds U.	05.52	1952-72	629	/	70	(CH)E-35/E.F.LGE REP.●
										Brother of Robert
CHARLTON, John A.				Gateshead	AM	1949	1		0	(G)
CHARLTON, Kevin	Birmingham	12.09.54	APP	Wolverhampton W.	09.72					(G)
			TR	Bournemouth	12.73	1973-74	21	/	0	
			TR	Hereford U.	06.75	1975-77	52	/	0	
CHARLTON, Robert	Ashington	11.10.37	JNRS	Manchester U.	10.54	1956-72	604	2	198	(IF)E-106/E.U23-6/
			TR	Preston N.E.	05.74	1974	38	/	8	E.F.LGE REP./
										E.YTH.INT./E.SCH.INT.●
CHARLTON, Stan	Exeter	28.06.29	Bromley	Orient	11.52	1952-55	151		1	(FB)E.AMAT.INT./
			TR	Arsenal	11.55	1955-58	99		0	Son of Exeter C. player
			TR	Orient	12.58	1958-64	216		0	(pre-war)
CHARLTON, Wilf S.	Blyth	12.09.33	JNRS	Huddersfield T.	11.50					(WH)
			TR	Southport	07.54	1954-56	109		7	
			TR	Tranmere Rov.	06.57	1957-60	92		4	
CHARNLEY, Derek	Doncaster	07.05.54		Scunthorpe U.	02.73	1972-75	28	10	3	(F)
CHARNLEY, Ray	Lancaster	29.05.35	Morecambe	Blackpool	05.57	1957-67	363	/	193	(CF) E-1●
			TR	Preston N.E.	12.67	1967	23	/	4	
			TR	Wrexham	07.68	1968	19	1	5	
			TR	Bradford P.A.	01.69	1968-69	59	/	15	
CHARTER, Ray	Ashton	10.01.50	APP	Blackburn Rov.	01.68	1969-70	13	5	0	(FB)
			TR	Stockport Co.	07.71	1971-73	87	4	2	
CHASE, Charles T.	Steyning	31.01.24	Brighton & H.A.(AM)	Watford	09.46	1946-47	15		1	(IF)
			TR	Crystal Palace	07.48	1948-49	55		2	
CHATHAM, Alec	Glasgow	07.07.36		Barrow	12.58	1958	1		0	(CF)
CHATHAM, Ray H.	London	20.07.24	JNRS	Wolverhampton W.	+	1946-53	76		0	(CH)
			TR	Notts. Co.	01.54	1953-58	128		4	
CHATTERLEY, Lew	Birmingham	15.02.45	APP	Aston Villa	02.62	1962-70	149	5	25	(D)E.YTH.INT.
			L	Doncaster Rov.	03.71	1970	9	/	0	
			TR	Northampton T.	09.71	1971	23	/	2	
			TR	Grimsby T.	02.72	1971-73	72	1	15	
			TR	Southampton	03.74	1973-74	7	2	0	
			TR	Torquay U.	02.75	1974-76	55	2	10	
CHATTERTON, Nick	Norwood	18.05.54	JNRS	Crystal Palace	08.73	1973-78	142	9	31	(M)
			TR	Millwall	11.78	1978-83	210	4	49	
CHAYTOR, Ken	Trimdon	18.11.37	JNRS	Oldham Ath.	11.54	1954-59	77		20	(IF)
CHEADLE, Reg G.	Stoke	17.10.29	JNRS	Port Vale	11.46	1947	1		0	
CHEADLE, Tom	Stoke	08.04.19	N.Staffs Regt.	Port Vale	05.46	1946-56	332		14	(CH)
			TR	Crewe Alex.	07.57	1957-58	37		0	
CHEESEBROUGH, Albert	Burnley	17.01.35	JNRS	Burnley	01.52	1951-58	140		36	(IF) E.U23-1
			TR	Leicester C.	06.59	1959-62	122		40	
			TR	Port Vale	07.63	1963-64	57		13	
			TR	Mansfield T.	07.65	1965-66	24	/	0	
CHEESLEY, Paul M.	Bristol	20.10.53	APP	Norwich C.	10.71	1972-73	10	3	1	(F)
			TR	Bristol C.	12.73	1973-76	61	3	20	
CHEETHAM, Hugh D.	Manchester	03.02.58	APP	Crewe Alex.	01.76	1975-78	90	6	0	(F)
			TR	Reading	07.79	1979-80	10	2	0	
CHEETHAM, Roy A.J.	Eccles	02.12.39	JNRS	Manchester C.	12.56	1957-67	128	4	4	(HB)
			Detroit Coug.	Charlton Ath.	10.68					
				Chester C.	12.68	1968-71	122	2	8	
CHEETHAM, Tom	Liverpool	08.12.50		Southport	12.69	1969-70	24	2	4	(F)
CHEETHAM, Tom M.	Newcastle	11.10.10	Brentford(*)	Lincoln C.	+	1946-47	47		31	(CF) *Q.P.R.

Players Names	Birthplace	Date	Previous Club	League Club	Date Signed	Seasons Played	Apps	Sub	Gls	
CHENEY, Dennis	Coalville	30.06.24	JNRS	Leicester C.	+	1947-48	2		0	(CF)
			L	Watford	02.48	1947	18		5	
			TR	Bournemouth	10.48	1948-53	157		47	
			TR	Aldershot	06.54	1954-55	53		19	
CHENHALL, John C.	Bristol	23.07.27	Colston Sports	Arsenal	+	1951-52	16		0	(FB)
			TR	Fulham	07.53	1953-57	91		0	
CHERRY, Rex A.	Sheffield	11.11.33		Gillingham	03.53	1952-53	10		4	(CF)
CHERRY, Steve R.	Nottingham	05.08.60	APP	Derby Co.	03.78	1979-83	77	/	0	(G)E.YTH.INT.
			L	Port Vale	11.80	1980	4	/	0	
CHERRY, Trevor	Huddersfield	23.02.48	JNRS	Huddersfield T.	07.65	1966-71	184	2	10	(D)E-27/E.F.LGE REP●
			TR	Leeds U.	06.72	1972-82	393	6	24	
			TR	Bradford C.	12.82	1982-83	72	/	0	
CHESSELL, Sam	Shirebrook	09.07.21	Welbeck Col.	Mansfield T.	+	1946-53	257		6	(FB)
CHESTERS, Colin W.	Crewe	21.11.59	APP	Derby Co.	11.77	1977-78	6	3	1	(F) One app. in goal
			TR	Crewe Alex.	09.79	1979-81	52	9	6	for Crewe Alex.
CHEW, Jackie	Blackburn	13.05.20	Blackburn Rov.(AM)	Burnley	+	1946-53	226		40	(OR)
			TR	Bradford C.	06.54	1954	36		4	
CHEW, John	Longton	25.11.15	Luton T.(+)	Port Vale	+	1946	9		0	
CHI-DOY-CHEUNG	Hong Kong	30.07.41	Hong Kong	Blackpool	10.60	1960-61	2		1	(F)
CHIEDOZIE, John	Nigeria	18.04.60	APP	Orient	04.77	1976-80	131	14	20	(W)
			TR	Notts. Co.	08.81	1981-83	110	1	15	
CHILCOTT, Ken	Rhondda	17.03.20	Eastville U.	Bristol C.	*	1946-48	37		4	(OR)
CHILDS, (Bert) A.R.	Liverpool	25.09.30	Northern Nomads	Liverpool	AM	1953	2		0	(FB)E.AMAT.INT.
CHILDS, Gary P.C.	Birmingham	19.04.64	APP	W.B.A.	02.82	1981-83	2	1	0	(M) E.YTH.INT.
			TR	Walsall	10.83	1983	27	3	2	
CHILTON, Allenby C.	South Hylton	16.09.18	Seaham Col.	Manchester U.	*	1946-54	352		3	(CH)E-2
			TR	Grimsby T.	03.55	1954-56	63		0	
CHILTON, Chris R.	Sproatley	25.06.43	JNRS	Hull C.	07.60	1960-71	415	/	195	(CF)●
			TR	Coventry C.	09.71	1971	26	1	3	
CHILTON, Fred	Washington	10.07.35	Unsworth Col.	Sunderland	05.53	1955-57	4		0	(FB)
CHILVERS, Geoff T.	Sutton	31.01.25	Sutton U.	Crystal Palace	+	1948-53	118		1	(HB)E.SCH.INT.
CHILVERS, Gordon M.	Norwich	15.11.33	Fordhouses BC	Walsall	04.52	1951-57	123		0	(G)
CHINAGLIA, Giorgio	Italy	24.01.47	APP	Swansea C.	04.65	1964-65	4	1	1	(CF)ITALIAN INT.
CHIPPENDALE, Brian A.	Bradford	29.10.64	Bradford C.(APP)	York C.	10.83	1983	0	4	0	
CHISHOLM, Gordon W.	Glasgow	08.04.60	APP	Sunderland	04.78	1978-83	160	4	9	(D)
CHISHOLM, Jack R.	London	09.10.24	JNRS	Tottenham H.	+	1947	2		0	(CH)
			TR	Brentford	10.47	1947-48	49		1	d.1977/
			TR	Sheffield U.	03.49	1948-49	21		1	Middlesex Cricketer
			TR	Plymouth Arg.	12.49	1949-53	175		2	
CHISHOLM, Ken M.	Glasgow	12.04.25	Partick T.	Leeds U.	01.48	1947-48	40		18	(IF)
			TR	Leicester C.	01.49	1948-49	42		17	
			TR	Coventry C.	03.50	1949-51	67		35	
			TR	Cardiff C.	03.52	1951-53	63		13	
			TR	Sunderland	01.54	1953-55	77		34	
			TR	Workington	08.54	1956-57	39		15	
CHISHOLM, Wilf	Hebburn	23.05.21	Newcastle U.(AM)	Grimsby T.	09.46	1946-50	91		0	(G)
CHISNALL, J. Phil	Manchester	27.10.42	JNRS	Manchester U.	11.59	1961-63	35		8	(IF)E.U23-1/E.SCH.INT.
			TR	Liverpool	04.64	1964	6		1	
			TR	Southend U.	08.67	1967-70	137	5	28	
			TR	Stockport Co.	09.71	1971	30	/	2	
CHISWICK, Peter	London	19.09.29	JNRS	West Ham U.	07.47	1953-54	19		0	(G)
			TR	Gillingham	07.56	1956	14		0	
CHITTY, Wilf S.	Walton-on-Thames	10.07.12	Plymouth Arg.(*)	Reading	+	1946-47	23		7	(OL)*Woking/Chelsea
CHIVERS, Gary P.S.	Stockwell	15.05.60	APP	Chelsea	08.78	1978-82	128	5	4	(D)
			TR	Swansea C.	08.83	1983	10	/	0	
			TR	Q.P.R.	02.84					
CHIVERS, Martin	Southampton	27.04.45	JNRS	Southampton	09.62	1962-67	173	1	97	(F)E-24/E.U23-17/
			TR	Tottenham H.	01.68	1967-75	268	10	118	E.F.LGE REP.●
			Servette	Norwich C.	07.78	1978	11	/	4	
			TR	Brighton & H.A.	03.79	1978-79	4	1	1	
CHMILOWSKYJ, Roman	Bradford	19.04.59	JNRS	Halifax T.	AM	1976	1	/	0	(G)
CHOLERTON, William	Derby	01.01.49	APP	Derby Co.	12.66	1966	1	/	0	(FB)
			TR	Mansfield T.	08.68					
CHOULES, Len G.	Orpington	29.01.32	Sutton U.	Crystal Palace	05.51	1952-61	260		2	(HB)
CHRISTIE, Derek H.M.	Bletchley	15.03.57	APP	Northampton T.	03.75	1973-78	116	22	18	(F)
			TR	Cambridge U.	11.78	1978-83	132	6	19	
CHRISTIE, Frank	Scone	17.02.27		Liverpool	+						(F)
			Forfar	Liverpool	03.49	1949	4		0	
CHRISTIE, John A.	Fraserburgh	26.09.29	Ayr. U.	Southampton	01.51	1950-58	197		0	(G)
			TR	Walsall	06.59	1959-62	102		0	

Players Names	Birthplace	Date	Previous Club	League Club	Date Signed	Seasons Played	Apps	Sub	Gls	
CHRISTIE, Trevor	Newcastle	28.02.59	APP	Leicester C.	12.76	1977-78	28	3	8	(F)
			TR	Notts. Co.	06.76	1979-83	158	29	64	
CHRISTOPHER, Paul A.	Poole	19.06.54	APP	Bournemouth	01.71					(F)
			TR	Mansfield T.	07.73	1973	7	1	1	
CHUNG, (Sammy) Cyril	Abingdon	16.07.32	Headington	Reading	11.51	1953-54	32		12	(IF)
			TR	Norwich C.	01.55	1954-56	47		9	
			TR	Watford	06.57	1957-64	220		21	
CHURCH, Gary	Pontefract	20.9.44	Great Preston Jnrs.	Bradford P.A.	07.62	1963	4		0	(HB)
			TR	Bournemouth	08.65					
CHURCH, John	Lowestoft	17.09.19	Lowestoft	Norwich C.	*	1946-49	97		15	(OL)
				Colchester U.	07.50	1950-53	118		20	
CHURCHILL, Trevor	Barnsley	20.11.23	Sheffield U. (AM)	Reading	09.46	1946	10		0	(G)
			TR	Leicester C.	08.47					
			TR	Rochdale	01.49	1948-52	110		0	
			TR	Swindon T.	05.53	1953	11		0	
CHURCHOUSE, Gary	Wembley	01.02.57	Windsor & Eton	Charlton Ath.	03.79	1978-79	13	5	0	(M)
CHURMS, Dennis J.	Rotherham	08.05.31	Spurley Hey.	Rotherham U.	04.50	1953-55	15		0	(IF)
			TR	Coventry C.	06.56	1956	10		2	
			TR	Exeter C.	03.57	1956-57	44		8	
CINI, Joe	Malta		Floriana	Q.P.R.	AM	1959	7		1	(OR)
CITRON, Gerry C.	Manchester	08.04.35	Corinthian Cas.	Chester C.	AM	1959	2		0	(IF)
CLACK, Frank E.	Witney	30.03.12	Brentford(+)	Bristol C.	+	1946-48	67		0	(G)*Witney/Birmingham C.
CLAMP, Eddie	Coalville	14.09.34	JNRS	Wolverhampton W.	04.52	1953-61	214		23	(WH)E-4/E.F.GLE REP./
			TR	Arsenal	11.61	1961-62	22		1	E.SCH.INT
			TR	Stoke C.	09.62	1962-63	50		2	
			TR	Peterborough U.	10.64	1964	8		0	
CLAMP, Eddie	Burton	13.11.22	Gresley Rov.	Derby Co.	11.47	1948	1		0	(G)
			TR	Oldham Ath.	07.49	1949	3		0	
CLAMP, Martin	Coventry	31.01.48	JNRS	Coventry C.	01.66					(G)
				Plymouth Arg.	07.68	1969	8	/	0	
CLANCY, John P.	Perivale	05.07.49	Tottenham H.(APP)	Bristol C.	03.67					(F)
			TR	Bradford P.A.	07.67	1967-68	52	4	2	
CLAPHAM, Graham L.	Lincoln	23.09.47	APP	Newcastle U.	09.65					(F)
			TR	Shrewsbury T.	08.67	1967-71	73	15	5	
			TR	Chester C.	01.72	1971-72	37	4	7	
CLAPHAM, Keith	Fareham	09.09.52	Bournemouth (APP.)	Exeter C.	07.72	1972-76	79	12	0	(M)
CLAPTON, Danny R.	London	22.07.34	Leytonstone	Arsenal	08.53	1954-61	207		26	(OR)E-1/E.F.LGE REP.
			TR	Luton T.	09.62	1962	10		0	
CLAPTON, Dennis E.	London	12.10.39	JNRS	Arsenal	08.58	1959-60	4		0	(CF) E.YTH.INT./
			TR	Northampton T.	08.61	1961	1		0	Brother of Danny
			TR	Orient	09.62					
CLARE, Jimmy E.	Islington	06.11.59	APP	Chelsea	08.78	1980	0	1	0	(F)
			TR	Charlton Ath.	08.81					
CLARK, Albert H.	Ashington	24.07.21	North Shields	Newcastle U.	01.48	1948	1		0	(WH)
CLARK, Alex	Lanark	28.10.56	Airdrie	West Ham U.	06.82	1982	26	/	7	(F)
CLARK, Ben	North Shields	14.04.33		Sunderland	08.50					(WH)
			Yeovil T.	Derby Co.	05.54	1954-57	16		0	
			TR	Barrow	02.59	1958-63	202		7	
CLARK, Brian	Bristol	13.01.43	JNRS	Bristol C.	03.60	1960-66	194	/	83	(F)Son of Don
			TR	Huddersfield T.	10.66	1966-67	29	4	11	
			TR	Cardiff C.	02.68	1967-72	178	4	75	
			TR	Bournemouth	10.72	1972-73	28	2	12	
			TR	Millwall	09.73	1973-74	66	5	16	
			TR	Cardiff C.	05.75	1975	19	2	1	
			TR	Newport Co.	08.76	1976-78	72	8	18	
CLARK, Clive	Leeds	19.12.40	JNRS	Leeds U.	01.58					(OL) E.U23-1
			TR	Q.P.R.	08.58	1958-60	58		7	
			TR	W.B.A.	01.61	1960-68	300	1	80	
			TR	Q.P.R.	06.69	1969	7	1	1	
			TR	Preston N.E.	01.70	1969-72	71	1	9	
			TR	Southport	07.73	1973	7	1	1	
CLARK, David G.	Ilford	19.01.38	Leyton	Orient	12.61	1961-62	4		0	(CH)
CLARK, Derek	Newcastle	10.08.31	Durham FC	Lincoln C.	12.51	1951	4		1	(IR)
CLARK, Derek B.	Leyburn	27.12.35		Darlington	03.55	1954-55	5		1	
CLARK, Don F.	Bristol	25.10.17	N.Bristol O.B.	Bristol C.	*	1946-50	110		68	(CF)
CLARK, Frank	Highfield	09.09.43	Crook T.	Newcastle U.	11.62	1963-74	388	1	0	(D)E.F.LGE REP./
			TR	Nottingham F.	07.75	1975-78	116	1	1	E.AMAT.INT./E.YTH.INT.
CLARK, Graham J.	Aberdeen	20.01.61	APP	Sheffield U.	10.78					(D)S.SCH.INT.
			TR	Darlington	08.79	1979	6	/	0	
CLARK, Harry	Sunderland	11.09.34		Sunderland	05.56	1956	6		0	(F)
CLARK, Harry	Cloughdene	30.03.13	Manchester C.(AM)	Accrington St.	+					(OL)
			TR	Gateshead	06.46	1946	23		1	

Players Names	Birthplace	Date	Previous Club	League Club	Date Signed	Seasons Played	Apps	Sub	Gls	
CLARK, Harry M.	Newcastle	29.12.32		Darlington	07.51	1950-56	142		20	(IF)
			TR	Sheffield Wed.	10.57	1957	1		0	
			TR	Hartlepool U.	08.58	1958-60	118		43	
CLARK, James D.	Dornoch	01.05.23	Aberdeen	Exeter C.	08.48	1948-52	95		5	(FB)
			L	Bradford C.	09.52	1952	6		0	
CLARK, Jonathan	Swansea	12.11.58	APP	Manchester U.	11.75	1976	0	1	0	(M)W.SCH.INT./W.U21-2
			TR	Derby Co.	09.78	1978-80	48	5	3	
			TR	Preston N.E.	08.81	1981-83	52	/	5	
CLARK, Joseph T.	Bermondsey	02.03.20	Gravesend	Orient	+	1946	18		0	(FB)
CLARK, Neville	Gateshead	09.10.30	Chilton Col.	Grimsby T.	12.48					(RH)
				Sunderland	12.49					
			TR	Hartlepool U.	08.53	1953	2		0	
CLARK, Paul P.	Benfleet	14.09.58	APP	Southend U.	07.76	1976-77	29	4	1	(M)E.YTH.INT./
			TR	Brighton & H.A.	11.77	1977-80	69	10	9	E.SCH.INT.
			L	Reading	10.81	1981	2	/	0	
			TR	Southend U.	08.82	1983	48	3	1	
CLARK, Peter J.	Doncaster	22.01.38	JNRS	Wolverhampton W.	03.55					(HB)
			TR	Doncaster Rov.	07.59	1959	14		8	
			TR	Mansfield T.	06.60	1960	2		0	
			Hednesford	Stockport Co.	08.65	1965	21	/	2	
			TR	Crewe Alex.	07.66	1966	2	/	0	
CLARK, Ron	Clarkston	21.05.32	Kilmarnock	Gillingham	07.56	1956-57	33		5	(F)
			TR	Oldham Ath.	06.58	1958	4		0	
CLARK, Steve	Baldock	20.09.64	APP	Cambridge U.	09.82	1983	16	/	0	(D)
CLARK, Tom H.	Luton	05.10.24	Vauxhall M.	Aston Villa	04.47					(IF) Surrey Cricketer/
			TR	Walsall	05.48	1948	9		2	d.1981
CLARK, Willie	Larkhall	25.02.32	Petershill	Q.P.R.	02.54	1953-55	95		32	(CF)
CLARKE, A. Robert	Liverpool	13.10.41		Chester C.	10.61	1961-62	30		4	(F)
CLARKE, Alan	Houghton Regis	10.04.42	JNRS	Luton T.	10.61	1961-62	9		0	(HB)
CLARKE, Alan F.	Crayford	02.12.52	APP	Charlton Ath.	07.71	1971	2	/	0	(G)
			L	Bristol Rov.	09.71	1971	1	/	0	
			TR	Exeter C.	02.73	1972-73	16	/	0	
CLARKE, Alan J.	Willenhall	31.07.46	APP	Walsall	08.63	1963-65	72		41	(F)E-19/E.U23-6/●
			TR	Fulham	03.66	1965-67	85		45	
			TR	Leicester C.	06.68	1968	36	/	12	
			TR	Leeds U.	07.69	1969-77	270	3	110	
			TR	Barnsley	06.78	1978-79	47		15	
CLARKE, Alf	Hollinwood	23.08.26	Stalybridge	Crewe Alex.	02.48	1947-48	22		12	(CF) 1 appearance in goal
			TR	Burnley	12.48	1948-51	24		6	for Halifax T.
			TR	Oldham Ath.	08.52	1952-53	43		10	
			TR	Halifax T.	03.54	1953-55	71		22	
CLARKE, Ambrose	Liverpool	10.09.45		Everton	06.64					(WH)
			TR	Southport	01.66	1965-70	193	5	4	
			TR	Barrow	07.71	1971	45	1	0	
CLARKE, Chris E.	Battersea	11.12.46	Chelsea(APP)	Millwall	12.63	1964-65	19	/	4	(F)
			TR	Watford	08.66	1966	1	1	0	
CLARKE, Colin	Penilee	04.04.46	Arthurlie J.	Arsenal	10.63					(D)
			TR	Oxford U.	07.65	1965-77	443	1	18	
			L. Angeles Aztecs	Plymouth Arg.	09.78	1978	35	/	3	
CLARKE, Colin J.	Newry	30.10.62	APP	Ipswich T.	10.80					(F)
			TR	Peterborough U.	07.81	1981-83	76	6	18	
			L	Gillingham	03.84	1983	8	/	1	
CLARKE, David A.	Nottingham	03.12.64	APP	Notts. Co.	12.82	1982-83	29	7	0	(D) E.YTH INT.
CLARKE, David A.	Derby	25.09.46	Derby Co.(AM)	Nottingham F.	05.64					(F)
			TR	Notts.Co.	07.66	1966	23	1	0	
CLARKE, David L.	Newcastle	24.07.49	N.Felham BC	Newcastle U.	06.67					(G)
			TR	Doncaster Rov.	08.69	1969	3	/	0	
			L	Darlington	03.70	1969	11	/	0	
CLARKE, Dennis	Stockton	18.01.48	APP	W.B.A.	02.65	1966-68	19	2	0	(FB)
			TR	Huddersfield T.	01.69	1968-73	172	/	3	
			TR	Birmingham C.	09.73	1973-74	14	/	0	
CLARKE, Derek	Willenhall	19.02.50	APP	Walsall	12.67	1967	6	7	2	(F)Brother of
			TR	Wolverhampton W.	05.68	1968-69	2	3	0	Alan/Frank/Kelvin/Wayne
			TR	Oxford U.	10.70	1970-75	172	7	35	
			TR	Orient	08.76	1976-78	30	6	6	
			L	Carlisle U.	10.78	1978	0	1	0	
CLARKE, Don L.	Poole	29.06.31		Cardiff C.	08.54					(F)
			TR	Brighton & H.A.	06.55	1955	2		0	
CLARKE, Doug	Bolton	19.01.34	Darwen	Bury	02.52	1953-55	37		16	(OR)●
			TR	Hull C.	11.55	1954-64	368		80	
			TR	Torquay U.	07.65	1965-67	116	4	21	
CLARKE, Frank J.	Willenhall	15.07.42	Willenhall	Shrewsbury T.	11.61	1961-67	189	/	77	(F)
			TR	Q.P.R.	02.68	1967-69	67	/	17	
			TR	Ipswich T.	03.70	1969-72	62	4	14	
			TR	Carlisle U.	08.73	1973-77	121	5	30	

Players Names	Birthplace	Date	Previous Club	League Club	Date Signed	Seasons Played	Apps	Sub	Gls	
CLARKE, Fred J.	Crewe	03.01.31		Crewe Alex.	11.51	1953-54	3		0	(HB)
CLARKE, Fred R.G.	Banbridge	04.11.41	Glenavon	Arsenal	11.60	1961-64	26		0	(FB)
CLARKE, Gary	Boston	06.11.60	APP	Bristol Rov.	11.78	1978-79	6	5	0	(F)
CLARKE, George E.	Ipswich	25.04.21		Ipswich T.	11.46	1946-52	34		1	(HB)
CLARKE, Gerry	Barrow Hill	04.01.36	Oaks Fold	Chesterfield	03.55	1954-67	382	1	20	(FB)
CLARKE, Graham	Nottingham	11.08.35		Southampton	06.53	1957-58	3		0	(FB)
CLARKE, Harry	Sunderland	26.11.60	Middlesbrough (N/C)	Hartlepool T.	08.79	1981	5	2	1	(M)
CLARKE, Harry A.	Woodford	23.02.23	Lovells Ath.	Tottenham H.	03.49	1948-56	295		4	(CH) E-1/E'B'-1
CLARKE, Ike	Tipton	09.01.15	T.E.Wesley	W.B.A.	*	1946-47	49		20	(CF)
			TR	Portsmouth	11.47	1947-52	116		49	
CLARKE, James	West Bromwich	07.12.23		Nottingham F.	05.47	1947-53	18		0	(FB)
CLARKE, James H.	Broomhill	27.03.21	Rotherham U.(*)	Darlington	+	1946	19		17	(CF) *Goole T.
			TR	Leeds U.	02.47	1946	14		1	
			TR	Darlington	11.47	1947-48	37		25	
			TR	Hartlepool U.	11.49	1949	6		1	
			Stockton	Darlington	09.52	1952	14		12	
CLARKE, Jeff	Pontefract	18.01.54		Manchester C.	01.72	1974	13	/	0	(D)
			TR	Sunderland	06.75	1975-81	178	3	6	
			TR	Newcastle U.	08.82	1982-83	53	/	1	
CLARKE, John L.	Northampton	23.10.46	JNRS	Northampton T.	07.65	1966-74	228	5	1	(WH) E.YTH.INT.
CLARKE, Kelvin L.	Wolverhampton	16.07.57	APP	Walsall	07.75	1974-78	4	5	0	(D)
CLARKE, Kevin	Drogheda	29.04.23	Drogheda	Barrow	+	1946	13		1	
CLARKE, Kevin N.	Santry	03.12.21	Drumcondra	Swansea C.	11.48	1948-51	10		0	(HB) E1-2/L.O.I. REP.
CLARKE, Malcolm M.G.	Clydebank	29.06.44	Johnstone Burgh	Leicester C.	07.65	1965	0	1	0	(F)
			TR	Cardiff C.	08.67	1967-68	43	2	5	
			TR	Bristol C.	07.69	1969	2	1	0	
			TR	Hartlepool U.	07.70	1970-71	29	4	0	
CLARKE, Mick	Sheffield	28.11.44	APP	Sheffield U.	01.62					(HB)
			TR	Aldershot	06.64	1964	5		0	
			TR	Halifax T.	07.65	1965-66	50	1	1	
CLARKE, Norman F.	Birmingham	31.10.34	JNRS	Aston Villa	07.53	1954	1		0	(F) E.YTH.INT.
			TR	Torquay U.	07.56	1956-58	55		0	
CLARKE, Norman S.	Antrim	01.04.42	Ballymena	Sunderland	02.62	1962	4		0	(F) N.1.U23-2
CLARKE, Paul S.	Chesterfield	25.09.50	APP	Liverpool	10.67					(HB) E.SCH.INT.
			TR	Rochdale	08.69	1969-71	10	1	0	
CLARKE, Peter A.	Bolton	06.07.49	JNRS	Bolton W.	06.69	1970	13	/	0	(G)
			TR	Stockport Co.	07.71	1971-74	49	/	0	
CLARKE, Ray C.	Hackney	25.09.52	APP	Tottenham H.	10.69	1972	0	1	0	(F)E.YTH.INT.
			TR	Swindon T.	06.73	1973	11	3	2	
			TR	Mansfield T.	08.74	1974-75	91	/	52	
			Bruges	Brighton & H.A.	10.79	1979	30	/	8	
			TR	Newcastle U.	07.80	1980	14	/	2	
CLARKE, Roy J.	Newport	01.06.25	JNRS	Cardiff C.	+	1946	39		11	(OL) W-22
			TR	Manchester C.	04.47	1946-57	349		73	Brother of William A.
			TR	Stockport Co.	09.58	1958	25		5	
CLARKE, Stuart A.	Torquay	25.01.61	JNRS	Torquay U.	02.78	1978	4	1	0	(M)Son of Doug
CLARKE, Tom	Ardrossan	12.04.46	Airdrie	Carlisle U.	07.70	1971-74	23	/	0	(G)
			TR	Preston N.E.	07.75	1975	3	/	0	
CLARKE, W. John	Bargoed	26.12.40	Bargoed YMCA	Newport Co.	05.59	1959-61	12		0	(G)
CLARKE, Wayne	Wolverhampton	28.02.61	APP	Wolverhampton W.	03.78	1977-83	129	19	30	(F)E.YTH.INT./E.SCH.INT.
CLARKE, William A.	Newport	17.04.23		Ipswich T.	AM	1946	3		0	(WH) W.AMAT.INT.
CLAXTON, Tom	Rochdale	17.10.44	Burnley(AM)	Bury	03.63	1963-68	97	4	3	(F)
CLAY, John H.	Stockport	22.11.46	APP	Manchester C.	05.64	1967	1	1	0	(F)
CLAYPOLE, Anthony	Weldon	13.02.37	JNRS	Northampton T.	03.54	1956-61	116		1	(FB)
CLAYTON, Eddie	London	07.05.37	Eton Manor	Tottenham H.	12.57	1957-67	88	4	20	(IF)
			TR	Southend U.	03.68	1967-69	70	3	16	
CLAYTON, Gordon	Wednesbury	03.11.36	JNRS	Manchester U.	11.53	1956	2		0	(G) E.YTH.INT./E.SCH.INT.
			TR	Tranmere Rov.	11.59	1959-60	4		0	
CLAYTON, John	Elgin	20.08.61	APP	Derby Co.	12.78	1978-81	21	3	4	(F)
			Hong Kong	Chesterfield	06.83	1983	25	8	5	
CLAYTON, John M.	St.Asaph	28.03.37	JNRS	Everton	06.55					(HB)
			TR	Southport	07.59	1959-60	32		3	
CLAYTON, Ken	Preston	06.04.33	JNRS	Blackburn Rov.	05.50	1952-58	73		0	(WH) Brother to Ronnie
CLAYTON, Lewis	Barnsley	07.06.24	Monkton Ath.	Barnsley	+	1946	24			(WH)
			TR	Carlisle U.	09.46	1946	24		0	
			TR	Barnsley	06.47	1948-49	15		0	
			TR	Q.P.R.	08.50	1950-53	90		5	
			TR	Bournemouth	05.55	1955-56	40		1	
			TR	Swindon T.	06.57	1957-58	35		2	

Players Names	Birthplace	Date	Previous Club	League Club	Date Signed	Seasons Played	Apps	Sub	Gls	
CLAYTON, Paul S.	Dunstable	04.01.65	APP	Norwich C.	01.83	1983	3	4	0	(M)
CLAYTON, Ronnie	Preston	05.08.34	JNRS	Blackburn Rov.	08.51	1950-68	577	2	14	(WH)E-35/E'B'-1/ E.U-23-6/E.FLGE REP.●
CLAYTON, Ron	Hull	18.01.37	Hereford U.	Arsenal	01.58					(F)
			TR	Brighton & H.A.	09.58	1958-59	14		3	
CLAYTON, Roy	Dudley	18.02.50	Warley	Oxford U.	08.69	1969-72	49	5	7	(IF)
CLEARY, George	Bedford	14.05.48	Kettering T.	Cambridge U.	12.75	1975	5	3	0	(WH)
CLEARY, William	Middlesbrough	20.04.31		Sunderland	05.49					(WH)
			TR	Norwich C.	05.52	1953-55	18		0	
			Wisbech T.	Port Vale	11.57	1957	8		0	
CLEEVELY, Nigel	Cheltenham	23.12.45		Derby Co.	07.64	1964-66	14	1	3	(F)
CLEGG, Anthony	Bradford	08.11.65	APP	Bradford C.	11.83	1983	2	/	0	(D)
CLEGG, Don	Huddersfield	02.06.21		Huddersfield T.	+	1946-47	3		0	(G)
			TR	Bury	07.48	1948-49	15		0	
			TR	Stoke C.	06.50	1950	2		0	
CLEGG, Malcolm B.	Leeds	09.04.36	Bradford Rov.	Bradford P.A.	AM	1957	6		0	(CF)
CLELAND, Peter	Birmingham	08.05.32	Worcester C.	Norwich C.	08.58	1958	4		0	(F)
CLELLAND, Crawford	U.S.A.	03.12.30	Aberdeen	Plymouth Arg.	06.55	1955	2		0	(IF)
CLELLAND, David	Netherburn	18.03.24		Arsenal	08.46					(OR)
			TR	Brighton & H.A.	01.48	1947	8		1	
			TR	Crystal Palace	09.49	1949	2		0	
			Weymouth	Scunthorpe U.	07.50	1950	16		8	
CLEMENCE, Ray	Skegness	05.08.48	Notts. Co. (AM)	Scunthorpe U.	08.65	1965-66	48	/	0	(G)E-61/E.U23-4
			TR	Liverpool	06.67	1969-80	470	/	0	E.F.LGE REP.●
			TR	Tottenham H.	08.81	1981-83	105	/	0	
CLEMENT, Dave T.	Battersea	02.02.48	JNRS	Q.P.R.	07.65	1966-78	402	3	22	(D)E-5/E.YTH.INT./d.1982
			TR	Bolton W.	06.79	1979-80	33	/	0	
			TR	Fulham	10.80	1980	17	1	0	
			TR	Wimbledon	10.81	1981	9	/	2	
CLEMENTS, Andy P.	Swindon	11.10.55	APP	Bolton W.	07.74	1977	1	/	0	(D)
			L	Port Vale	02.77	1976	2	1	0	
			TR	York C.	11.77	1977-80	146	2	6	
CLEMENTS, Dave	Larne	15.09.45	Portadown	Wolverhampton W.	01.63					(WH)N.I.-48/N.I.U23-3/
			TR	Coventry C.	07.64	1964-71	226	2	26	N.I.AMAT.INT.●
			TR	Sheffield Wed.	08.71	1971-73	78	/	0	
			TR	Everton	09.73	1973-75	81	4	6	
CLEMENTS, Ken H.	Manchester	09.04.55	JNRS	Manchester C.	07.75	1975-78	116	3	0	(D)
			TR	Oldham Ath.	09.79	1979-83	181	1	2	
CLEMENTS, Paul	Greenwich	07.11.46	Skelmersale	Oldham Ath.	06.71	1971-72	32	3	0	(IF)E.AMAT.INT
CLEMENTS, Stan F.	Portsmouth	25.06.23	Gosport Bor.	Southampton	+	1946-54	115		1	(CH)
CLEMPSON, Frank	Salford	27.05.30		Manchester U.	09.48	1949-52	15		2	(IF)
			TR	Stockport Co.	02.53	1952-58	246		36	
			TR	Chester C.	07.59	1959-60	67		7	
CLEWLOW, Sid J.	Wallasey	08.11.19	New Brighton(*)	Wolverhampton W.	+					
			TR	New Brighton	08.46	1946	1		0	
CLEWS, Malcolm D.	Tipton	12.03.31	JNRS	Wolverhampton W.	03.48	1951	1		0	(F)
			TR	Lincoln C.	02.54	1953-54	7		0	
CLIFF, Eddie	Liverpool	30.09.51	APP	Burnley	10.68	1970-72	21	/	0	(M)
			TR	Notts. Co.	09.73	1973	5	/	0	
			L	Lincoln C.	10.74	1974	3	/	0	
			Chicago Stings	Tranmere Rov.	09.76	1976-78	44	6	4	
			TR	Rochdale	09.79	1979-80	25	1	0	
CLIFF, John G.	Middlesbrough	07.11.46	APP	Middlesbrough	11.63					(F)
			TR	Halifax T.	07.66	1966	1	/	0	
CLIFF, Philip	Rotherham	20.11.47	JNRS	Sheffield U.	11.62	1966-69	16	6	5	(CF)
			TR	Chesterfield	02.71	1970-72	30	1	2	
CLIFTON, Brian	Whitchurch	15.03.34		Southampton	02.53	1957-62	112		35	(WH)
			TR	Grimsby T.	10.62	1962-65	104	/	5	
CLIFTON, Bryan	Bentley	13.02.39		Doncaster Rov.	10.58	1958	2		0	
CLIFTON, Henry	Marley Hill	28.05.14	Newcastle U.(*)	Grimsby T.	+	1946-48	69		23	(IL) *Chesterfield
CLINCH, Peter	Coventry	15.10.50	APP	Oxford U.	08.69	1969	2	/	0	(HB)
CLINTON, Tommy J.	Dublin	13.04.26	Dundalk	Everton	03.48	1948-53	73		4	(FB)EI-3
			TR	Blackburn Rov.	04.55	1955	6		0	
			TR	Tranmere Rov.	06.56	1956	9		0	
CLISH, Colin	Newcastle	14.01.44	JNRS	Newcastle U.	01.61	1961-63	20		0	(FB)
			TR	Rotherham U.	12.63	1963-67	130	/	4	
			TR	Doncaster Rov.	02.68	1967-71	99	1	4	
CLISH, Tommy P.	Wheatley Hill	19.10.32	Wheatley Hill	West Ham U.	09.53					(G)
			TR	Darlington	07.55	1955-57	52		0	

Players Names	Birthplace	Date	Previous Club	League Club	Date Signed	Seasons Played	Career Record Apps	Sub	Gls	
CLISS, Anthony	March	22.09.59	JNRS	Peterborough	08.77	1977-82	65	20	11	(F)Nephew of David
			TR	Crewe Alex.	12.82	1982-83	66	1	7	
CLISS, David	Enfield	15.11.39	JNRS	Chelsea	11.56	1957-61	24		1	(IF)E.YTH.INT.
CLOSE, D. Brian	Rawden	24.02.31	JNRS	Leeds U.	02.49					(IF)E.YTH.INT./
			TR	Arsenal	08.50					Yorks/Somerset/
			TR	Bradford C.	10.52	1952	6		2	England Cricker
CLOUGH, Brian H.	Middlesbrough	21.03.35	Gt.Broughton	Middlesbrough	05.53	1955-60	213		197	(CF)E-2/E.U23-3/E'B'-1/
			TR	Sunderland	07.61	1961-64	61		54	E.F.LGE REP.●
CLOUGH, James K.	Newcastle	30.08.18	Seaton Burn	Southport	*	1946	40		9	(OL)
			TR	Crystal Palace	09.47	1947-48	68		12	
			TR	Southend U.	05.49	1949	34		7	
			TR	Barrow	07.50	1950	17		3	
CLOVER, William	Bracknell	19.02.20		Reading	+	1946-49	44		4	(FB)
CLOWES, John A.	Alton (Staffs)	05.11.29		Stoke C.	06.59	1950	2		2	(F)
			TR	Shrewsbury T.	06.52	1952-53	11		2	
			Wellington	Stoke C.	08.55	1955	2		0	
CLUGSTON, James E.	Belfast	30.10.34	Distillery	Liverpool	01.52					(F) N.I.SCH.INT.
			Glentoran	Portsmouth	01.57	1956	1		0	
CLUNIE, James R.	Kirkcaldy	04.09.33	St.Mirren	Bury	07.65	1965	10	/	0	(CH)
CLUROE, Malcolm	Nottingham	06.02.35		Nottingham F.	11.54	1954	1		0	(F)
CLUTTON, Nigel G.	Chester	12.02.54		Chester C.	N/C	1977	1	/	0	(F)
CLYDESDALE, William M.	Fallin	14.09.35	Aberdeen	Hartlepool U.	08.60	1960	14		0	(FB)
COADY, Mike L.	Dipton	01.10.58	APP	Sunderland	07.76	1976-79	4	2	0	(D)
			TR	Carlisle U.	07.80	1980-81	48	3	1	
COAK, Tim D.T.	Southampton	16.01.58	APP	Southampton	01.76	1976-77	4	/	0	(D)
COAKLEY, Tom	Bellshill	02.05.47	Motherwell	Arsenal	05.66	1966	9	/	1	(OR)
COATES, David P.	Newcastle	11.04.35	Shiney Row	Hull C.	10.52	1956-59	61		13	(IF)
			TR	Mansfield T.	03.60	1959-63	161		17	
			TR	Notts.Co.	07.64	1964-66	66	/	1	
COATES, Frank	Farrington	16.04.22	Leyland Motors	Blackburn Rov.	+					(CF)
				Accrington St.	01.48	1947	4		0	
COATES, John A.	Southport	03.06.44	Burscough	Southport	02.65	1964	5	/	0	(G)
			TR	Chester C.	08.66	1966	1	/	0	
			TR	Tranmere Rov.	02.67					
			Morecambe	Southport	N/C	1976	16	/	0	
COATES, John A.	Limehouse	13.05.20		Crystal Palace	AM	1946	4		0	
COATES, Ralph	Hetton-le-Hole	26.04.46	APP	Burnley	06.63	1964-70	214	2	26	(M)E-4/E.U23-8/
			TR	Tottenham H.	05.71	1971-77	173	15	14	E.F.LGE REP.
			TR	Orient	10.78	1978-80	76	/	12	
COATSWORTH, Fred W.	Lincoln	05.07.48	JNRS	Scunthorpe U.	07.65	1965-66	15		2	(F)
COATSWORTH, John	Newcastle	21.05.35	Crook T.	Gateshead	03.57	1956	16		4	
COBB, William W.	Newark	29.09.40	Ransome & M	Nottingham F.	09.59	1960-62	30		5	(WH)
			TR	Plymouth Arg.	10.63	1963-64	31		0	
			TR	Brentford	10.64	1964-66	69	2	23	
			TR	Lincoln C.	11.66	1966-67	67	/	10	
COCHRAN, Albert G.	Ebbw Vale	26.11.39	Ilford	Plymouth Arg.	09.59					(G)
			TR	Orient	07.60	1960	1			
COCHRANE, Alan	Belfast	16.03.56	APP	Shrewsbury T.	03.74	1973-74	3	/	0	(CF)
COCHRANE, Colin	Sutton-in-Ashfield	26.08.21		Mansfield T.	09.47	1947	1		0	
COCHRANE, David	Portadown	14.08.20	Portadown	Leeds U.	*	1946-50	144		24	(OR)N.1.-12
COCHRANE, George N.	Glasgow	27.02.31	Arthurlie	New Brighton	07.50	1950	2		0	(F)
COCHRANE, Hugh	Glasgow	09.02.43	Dundee U.	Barnsley	08.63	1963	5		0	(IF)
COCHRANE, James	Brierley Hill	26.10.35	JNRS	Birmingham C.	10.52	1952-53	3		1	(F)
			TR	Walsall	06.58	1958	6		1	
COCHRANE, James K.	Glasgow	14.01.54	Drumchapel	Middlesbrough	05.71	1973	3	/	0	(D)
			TR	Darlington	02.75	1974-79	222	1	5	
			TR	Torquay U.	08.80	1980	16	/	0	
COCHRANE, John	Bellshill	27.04.59	APP	Preston N.E.	02.77	1976-78	3	2	2	(F)
COCHRANE, John J.	Belfast	11.05.44	JNRS	Brighton & H.A.	10.61	1961-62	14		3	(F)
			TR	Exeter C.	08.63	1963	2		0	
COCHRANE, Terry	Killyleagh	23.01.53	Coleraine	Burnley	10.76	1976-78	62	5	13	(W)NI-26
			TR	Middlesbrough	10.78	1978-82	96	15	7	
			TR	Gillingham	10.83	1983	34	/	6	
COCKBURN, Henry	Ashton	14.09.23	Goslings FC	Manchester U.	+	1946-54	243		4	(WH) E-13/E'B'-1/
			TR	Bury	10.54	1954-55	35		0	E.F.LGE REP.
COCKBURN, Keith	Barnsley	02.09.42	JNRS	Barnsley	11.66	1966	1	/	0	(F)
			TR	Bradford P.A.	07.68	1968	16	/	1	
			TR	Grimsby T.	01.69	1968-69	14	4	2	

Players Names	Birthplace	Date	Previous Club	League Club	Date Signed	Seasons Played	Apps	Sub	Gls	
COCKBURN, William R.	Shotton	03.05.37	Murton J.	Burnley	08.55					(HB)
			TR	Gillingham	06.60	1960-61	62		1	
COCKELL, David J	Ashford	01.02.39	Hounslow T.	Q.P.R.	08.60	1960-61	9		0	(HB)
COCKER, Les	Stockport	13.03.24		Stockport Co.	08.47	1946-52	173		42	(CF) d.1979
			TR	Accrington St.	08.53	1953-57	122		49	
COCKER, Les J.	Wolverhampton	18.09.39	JNRS	Wolverhampton W.	06.58	1960	1		0	(WH) E.YTH.INT.
COCKERILL, Ron	Sheffield	28.02.35	JNRS	Huddersfield T.	05.52	1955-57	40		1	(WH)
			TR	Grimsby T.	08.58	1958-67	294	1	27	
COCKERILL, Glen	Grimsby	25.08.59	Louth U.	Lincoln C.	11.76	1976-79	65	6	10	(F)
			TR	Swindon T.	12.79	1979-80	23	3	1	
			TR	Lincoln C.	08.81	1981-83	114	1	25	
			TR	Sheffield U.	03.84	1983	10	/	1	
COCKRAM, Allan C.	Kensington	08.10.63	APP	Tottenham H.	01.81	1983	2	/	0	(M)
COCKROFT, Hubert	Barnsley	21.11.18		Bradford C.	05.46	1946	27		0	(LH) +Barnsley/brother of Joe
			TR	Halifax T.	07.47	1947	10		1	
			Peterborough	Bradford C.	05.50					
COCKROFT, Joe	Barnsley	20.06.11	West Ham U.(*)	Sheffield Wed.	+	1946-48	87		2	(WH)*Wombwell/
			TR	Sheffield U.	11.48	1948	12		0	Rotherham U./Gainsborough
COCKROFT, Vic H.	Birmingham	25.02.41	JNRS	Wolverhampton W.	12.59					(FB) E.YTH.INT.
			TR	Northampton T.	07.62	1962-66	45	1	1	
			TR	Rochdale	06.67	1967	42	/	0	
COCKS, Alan W.	Burscough	07.05.51	APP	Chelsea	04.69					(CF)
			L	Brentford	01.70	1969	11	/	2	
			TR	Southport	07.70	1970	24	1	7	
CODD, Ronnie W.	Sheffield	03.12.28	Meynell Y.C.	Bolton W.	03.50	1950-53	31		5	(CF)
			L	Sheffield Wed.	03.53	1952	2		0	
			TR	Barrow	10.54	1954-55	45		11	
CODDINGTON, John W.	Worksop	16.12.37	JNRS	Huddersfield T.	01.55	1955-66	332	/	17	(CH)
			TR	Blackburn Rov.	06.67	1967-69	72	/	3	
			TR	Stockport Co.	01.70	1969-70	52	/	0	
COE, Norman C.	Pentrecwyth	06.12.40	JNRS	Arsenal	08.58					(G)
			TR	Northampton T.	07.60	1960-65	58	/	0	
COEN, Laurie	Lowestoft	04.12.14	W.B.A.(*)	Coventry C.	*	1946-47	17		1	(OL) E.SCH.INT./d.1972/ *Milford Haven
COFFEY, Mike J.J.	Liverpool	29.09.58	APP	Everton	07.76					(M)
			TR	Mansfield T.	07.78	1978	2	1	0	
COFFILL, Peter T.	Romford	14.02.57	APP	Watford	02.75	1975-77	56	7	6	(F)
			TR	Torquay U.	11.77	1977-80	101	21	11	
			TR	Northampton T.	07.81	1981-82	64	5	3	
COFFIN, Geoff W.	Chester	17.08.24	JNRS	Chester C.	05.47	1947-54	151		35	(CF)
COGGINS, Phil R.	Bristol	10.07.40		Bristol C.	10.58	1959	4		0	(F)
			TR	Bristol Rov.	07.60	1960	3		0	
COGLAN, Alan	Barrow	14.12.36	JNRS	Barrow	04.54	1953-61	51		0	(G)
COHEN, Avi	Egypt	14.11.56	Macabbi T.A.	Liverpool	07.79	1979-80	16	2	1	(D)ISRAEL INT.
COHEN, George R.	Kensington	22.10.39	JNRS	Fulham	10.56	1956-68	409	/	6	(FB)E-37/E.U23-8/ E.F.LGE REP.●
COHEN, Jacob	Israel	25.9.56	Macabbi T.A.	Brighton & H.A.	10.80	1980	3	3	0	(D)ISRAEL INT.
COKER, Ade O.	Nigeria	19.05.54	APP	West Ham U.	12.71	1971-73	9	1	3	(F)
			L	Lincoln C.	12.74	1974	6	/	1	
COLBOURNE, Neil	Swinton	25.08.56	Hyde U.	Rochdale	N/C	1979	1	/	0	(G)
COLBRIDGE, Clive	Hull	27.4.34	Hull C.(AM)	Leeds U.	05.52					(OL)
			TR	York C.	05.55	1955-57	37		4	
			TR	Workington	09.57	1957-58	46		8	
			TR	Crewe Alex.	10.58	1958	29		8	
			TR	Manchester C.	05.59	1959-61	62		12	
			TR	Wrexham	02.62	1961-64	108		33	
COLDRICK, Graham G.	Newport	06.11.45	APP	Cardiff C.	11.62	1963-69	91	5	2	(WH) W.U23-2/W.SCH.INT.
			TR	Newport Co.	03.70	1969-74	156	1	10	
COLDWELL, G. Cecil	Sheffield	16.01.29	Norton Woodseats	Sheffield U.	09.51	1951-66	409	1	2	(FB)●
COLE, G. Doug	Hessal	02.07.16	Sheffield U.(*)	Chester C.	+	1946-47	20		0	d.1959
COLE, James E.	Wrexham	14.08.25	Wrexham(AM)	Bolton W.	05.47					
			TR	Chester C.	08.49	1949	1		0	
COLE, Mike E.	Ilford	09.06.37	Harwich & P.	Norwich C.	08.56	1955-57	3		0	(FB)
COLE, Roy	Barnsley	08.12.53	APP	Barnsley	12.71	1971-73	6	/	0	(HB)
COLEMAN, Anthony G.	Liverpool	02.05.45	Stoke C.(APP)	Tranmere Rov.	10.62	1962-63	8		0	(W)
			TR	Preston N.E.	05.64	1964	5		1	
			Bangor C.	Doncaster Rov.	11.65	1965-66	58	/	11	
			TR	Manchester C.	03.67	1966-69	82	1	12	
			TR	Sheffield Wed.	10.69	1969	25	1	2	
			TR	Blackpool	08.70	1970	17	/	0	
			Durban C.	Southport	11.73	1973	22	1	1	
			TR	Stockport Co.	06.74	1974-75	28	2	3	

Players Names	Birthplace	Date	Previous Club	League Club	Date Signed	Seasons Played	Apps	Sub	Gls	
COLEMAN, Dave J.	Colchester	27.03.42	Harwich & P.	Colchester U.	11.61	1961-62	2		1	(F)
COLEMAN, Edward P.	Middlesbrough	23.09.57	APP	Middlesbrough	09.75	1975	1	/	0	(F)
			L	Workington	03.77	1976	10	2	1	
COLEMAN, Geoff J.	Bedworth	13.05.36	Bedworth T.	Northampton T.	05.55	1955-58	18		0	(FB)
COLEMAN, Gordon	Nottingham	11.02.54	Padstow Y.C.	Preston N.E.	09.73	1973-82	248	21	25	(M)
			TR	Bury	08.83	1983	24	5	0	
COLEMAN, John	Nottingham	03.03.46	JNRS	Nottingham F.	03.63					(HB)
			TR	Mansfield T.	08.66	1966-67	43	1	1	
			TR	York C.	07.68	1968	8	3	3	
COLEMAN, Keith	Washington	24.05.51	APP	Sunderland	06.68	1971-72	49	/	2	(D)
			TR	West Ham U.	09.73	1973-76	96	5	0	
			R. Malines	Darlington	07.79	1979	25	/	0	
COLEMAN, Neville J.	Prescott	29.01.30	Gorleston.	Stoke C.	01.55	1953-58	114		46	(OR)
			TR	Crew Alex.	02.59	1958-60	73		16	
COLEMAN, Phil	Woolwich	08.09.60	APP	Millwall	08.78	1978-80	23	13	1	(D)
			TR	Colchester U.	02.81	1980-83	82	4	6	
			L	Wrexham	09.83	1983	17	/	2	
COLES, Arthur	Crediton	28.01.14	Copplestone	Exeter C.	*	1946-48	14		0	(CH)
COLES, David A.	Wandsworth	15.06.64	APP	Birmingham C.	04.82					(G)
			TR	Mansfield T.	03.83	1982	3	/	0	
			TR	Aldershot	08.83	1983	45	/	0	
COLEY, William E.	Wolverhampton	17.09.16	Bournemouth(*)	Torquay U.	*	1946	19		0	(WH) *Wolverhampton W.
			TR	Northampton T.	08.47	1947-50	105		7	
			TR	Exeter C.	07.51	1951	8		0	
COLFAR, Ray	Liverpool	04.12.35	Sutton U.	Crystal Palace	11.58	1958-60	41		6	(OL)
			Cambridge U.	Oxford U.	N/L	1962-63	18		4	
COLGAN, Walter	Castleford	03.04.37	Ashley Rd FC	Q.P.R.	07.54	1957-58	3		0	(FB)
COLL, Iam A.	Carrick	16.12.29		Accrington St.	08.49	1949-50	13		0	
COLLARD, Ian	Hetton-le-Hole	31.08.47	APP	W.B.A.	11.64	1964-68	63	6	7	(IF)
			TR	Ipswich T.	05.69	1969-74	82	9	5	
			L	Portsmouth	09.75	1975	1	/	0	
COLLARD, J. Bruce	Hetton-le-Hole	21.08.53	APP	W.B.A.	05.71					(IF) Brother to Ian
			TR	Scunthorpe U.	07.73	1973	21	1	0	
COLLETT, Ernie	Sheffield	17.11.14	Oughtibridge	Arsenal	*	1946	6		0	(WH)
COLLIER, Alan	Markyate	24.03.38	JNRS	Luton T.	05.55	1958-60	10		0	(G) E.YTH.INT./E.SCH.INT.
COLLIER, Austin	Dewsbury	24.07.14	Mansfield T.(*)	York C.	+	1946	10		0	(FB) *Frickley Col.
			Q. of South	Rochdale	04.47	1946-47	6		0	
			TR	Halifax T.	11.47	1947	1		0	
COLLIER, David	Colwyn Bay	02.10.57	APP	Shrewsbury T.	10.75	1974-76	20	/	4	(D)
			TR	Crewe Alex.	08.77	1977	24	2	1	
COLLIER, Gary B.	Bristol	04.02.55	APP	Bristol C.	11.72	1972-78	193	/	3	(D)
			TR	Coventry C.	07.79	1979	2	/	0	
COLLIER, Geoff	Blackpool	25.07.50	Macclesfield	Notts. Co.	07.73	1973	0	3	0	(F)
COLLIER, Graham R.	Nottingham	12.09.51	APP	Nottingham F.	03.69	1969-70	13	2	2	(F)
			TR	Scunthorpe U.	07.72	1972-76	155	6	19	
			TR	Barnsley	08.77	1977	22	2	2	
			Buxton	York C.	09.78	1978	5	/	0	
COLLIER, Jim	Stockport	24.08.52	APP	Stockport Co.	03.70	1968-73	99	5	11	(F)
COLLINDRIDGE, Colin	Borough Green	15.11.20		Sheffield U.	*	1946-49	142		52	(OL)
			TR	Nottingham F.	08.50	1950-53	151		45	
			TR	Coventry C.	06.54	1954-55	34		6	
COLLINGWOOD, Graham	Barnsley	08.12.54	APP	Barnsley	08.73	1973-74	12	2	0	(WH)
COLLINS, Albert D.	Chesterfield	15.04.23	JNRS	Chesterfield	+	1946	8		0	(F)
			TR	Halifax T.	11.46	1946-47	44		10	
			TR	Carlisle U.	02.48	1947-48	20		3	
			TR	Barrow	12.48	1948-49	55		7	
			TR	Bournemouth	08.50	1950	5		1	
			TR	Shrewsbury T.	08.51	1951	9		2	
			TR	Accrington St.	07.52	1952	17		2	
COLLINS, Andy	Carlisle	20.10.58	Carlisle Spartans	Carlisle U.	09.77	1977-81	47	7	1	(D)
COLLINS, Anthony N.	Kensington	19.03.26		Sheffield Wed.	11.47					(OL)
			TR	York C.	07.49	1949	10		1	
			TR	Watford	08.50	1950-52	90		2	
			TR	Norwich C.	07.53	1953-54	29		2	
			TR	Torquay U.	07.55	1955-56	89		17	
			TR	Watford	07.57	1957	17		3	
			TR	Crystal Palace	11.57	1957-58	54		14	
			TR	Rochdale	06.59	1959-60	48		4	
COLLINS, Ben V.	Kislingbury	09.03.28	JNRS	Northampton T.	04.48	1948-58	213		0	(CH)

Players Names	Birthplace	Date	Previous Club	League Club	Date Signed	Seasons Played	Apps	Sub	Gls	
COLLINS, Doug	Newton	28.08.45	Rotherham U.(APP)	Grimsby T.	06.63	1963-68	94	6	11	(M)
			TR	Burnley	09.68	1968-75	172	14	18	
			TR	Plymouth Arg.	05.76	1976	22	1	2	
			TR	Sunderland	03.77	1976-77	4	2	0	
			Tulsa R.	Rochdale	01.79	1978	6	2	0	
COLLINS, George G.	Barry	06.08.35	Ton Pentre	Bristol Rov.	06.60	1960	3		1	(F)
COLLINS, Glyn	Hereford	18.01.46		Brighton & H.A.	AM	1965	2	/	0	(G)
COLLINS, Graham F.	Bury	05.02.47		Rochdale	09.65	1965-66	17	1	0	(F)
COLLINS, James	Ayr	21.12.37	Lugar B.C.	Tottenham H.	06.56	1961	2		0	(IF)
			TR	Brighton & H.A.	10.62	1962-66	199	2	44	
COLLINS, James K.	Colne	07.11.23	Derby Co.(AM)	Barrow	09.47	1947-54	295		52	(WH)
			TR	Chester C.	07.55	1955-56	48		11	
COLLINS, James P.	Urmston	27.12.66	Crystal Palace(APP)	Oldham Ath.	N/C	1983	0	1	0	
COLLINS, Jeremy D.	Plymouth	21.12.61	APP	Plymouth Arg.	01.80	1980-81	4	/	0	(M)
			Falmouth	Torquay U.	08.83	1983	6	/	0	
COLLINS, John J.	Manchester	30.01.45	JNRS	Blackburn Rov.	02.63					(FB)
			TR	Stockport Co.	01.64	1963-65	83	/	1	
COLLINS, John L.	Rhymney	21.01.49	APP	Tottenham H.	03.66	1965-67	2	/	0	(D)W.U.23-7/W.SCH.INT.
			TR	Portsmouth	05.71	1971-73	71	3	0	
			TR	Halifax T.	08.74	1974-75	82	/	1	
			TR	Sheffield W.	07.76	1976	7	/	0	
			TR	Barnsley	12.76	1976-79	129	1	1	
COLLINS, John W.	Chiswick	10.08.42	JNRS	Q.P.R.	08.59	1959-66	174	1	43	(IF)
			TR	Oldham Ath.	10.66	1966	20	1	8	
			TR	Reading	08.67	1967-68	82	3	29	
			TR	Luton T.	08.69	1969-70	40	2	10	
			TR	Cambridge U.	02.71	1970-72	93	4	16	
COLLINS, Ken	Pontypridd	11.10.33	Ynysybwl	Fulham	05.52	1955-58	32		0	(FB)
COLLINS, Kevin	Birmingham	21.07.64	Boldmere-St. Michael	Shrewsbury T.	01.84	1983	1	/	0	(D)
COLLINS, Lyn	Skewen	30.04.48		Newport Co.	06.66	1966-67	16	5	0	(FB)
COLLINS, Mike A.	S. Africa	27.07.53	JNRS	Wolverhampton W.	08.71					(F)
			Stafford R.	Swindon T.	07.73	1973	2	4	0	
COLLINS, Mike J.A.	Bermondsey	01.02.38	JNRS	Luton T.	03.55	1959-61	8		0	(HB)
COLLINS, Peter M.	Chelmsford	29.11.48	Chelmsford	Tottenham H.	01.68	1968-72	77	6	4	(CH)
COLLINS, R. Mike	Middlesbrough	08.06.33	Redcar	Chelsea	11.51	1953	1		0	(G)
			TR	Watford	07.57	1957-58	43		0	
COLLINS, Robert L.	Winchester	12.08.39	Winchester C.	Newport Co.	AM	1962	1		0	(G)
COLLINS, Robert Y.	Glasgow	16.02.31	Glasgow Celtic	Everton	09.58	1958-61	133		42	(IF)S-31/S.F.LGE.REP.●
			TR	Leeds U.	03.62	1961-66	149	/	24	
			TR	Bury	02.67	1966-68	74	1	5	
			Morton	Oldham Ath.	10.72	1972	6	1	0	
COLLINS, Ron D. (Sam)	Bristol	13.01.23		Bristol C.	+	1946-47	14		2	(IF)●
			TR	Torquay U.	06.48	1948-57	355		203	
COLLINS, Steve M.	Stamford	21.03.62	APP	Peterborough U.	08.79	1978-82	92	2	1	(D)
			TR	Southend U.	08.83	1983	36	/	0	
COLLINS, Terry	Penrhiwceiber	08.01.43	Ton Pentre	Swansea C.	03.67	1967	1	/	0	(F)
COLLINS, William H.	Belfast	15.02.20	Belfast Celtic	Luton T.	02.48	1947-48	7		0	(WH)
			TR	Gillingham	N/L	1950	13		0	
COLLINSON, Cliff	Middlesbrough	03.03.20	Urmston B.C.	Manchester U.	09.46	1946	7		0	(G)
COLLINSON, Les	Hull	02.12.35		Hull C.	09.56	1956-66	296	1	14	(WH)
			TR	York C.	02.67	1966-67	35	/	2	
COLLINSON, Roger	Rawmarsh	05.12.40	Doncaster Rov.(AM)	Bristol C.	10.58	1959-60	50		1	(FB)E.YTH.INT./E.SCH.INT.
			TR	Stockport Co.	07.61	1961	2		0	
COLMAN, Eddie	Salford	01.11.36	JNRS	Manchester U.	11.53	1955-57	85		1	(WH) d.1958
COLOMBO, Don	London	26.10.28	Barking	Portsmouth	03.53					(OL)
			TR	Walsall	12.53	1953	20		1	
COLQUHOUN, Eddie	Prestonpans	29.03.45	JNRS	Bury	03.62	1963-66	81	/	2	(D)S-9
			TR	W.B.A.	02.67	1966-68	46	/	1	
			TR	Sheffield U.	10.68	1968-77	360	3	21	
COLQUHOUN, John	Stirling	03.06.40	Stirling A.	Oldham Ath.	08.61	1961-64	163		32	(IF)
			TR	Scunthorpe U.	06.65	1965-68	149		25	
			TR	Oldham Ath.	11.68	1968-69	68	2	6	
COLRAIN, John	Glasgow	04.02.37	Clyde	Ipswich T.	06.63	1963-65	55	1	18	(F) S.U23-1
COLVAN, Hugh	Port Glasgow	24.09.25	Hibernian	Rochdale	02.48	1947	1		0	(IL)
COLVILLE, Henry	Kirkcaldy	12.02.24	E. Fife	Chester C.	08.47	1947	4		1	
COLVILLE, Robert J.	Nuneaton	27.04.63		Oldham Ath.	02.84	1983	4	/	1	(F)
COMERFORD, Pat	Chester-le-Street	30.11.25		Shrewsbury T.	07.52	1952	7		0	(WH)

Players Names	Birthplace	Date	Previous Club	League Club	Date Signed	Seasons Played	Apps	Sub	Gls	
COMLEY, Len G.	Swansea	25.01.22		Swansea C.	+	1946-47	28		7	(F)
			TR	Newport Co.	10.48	1948-50	76		29	
			TR	Scunthorpe U.	03.51	1950	12		5	
COMMON, Alan R.	Ashington	16.12.54	W.B.A.(APP)	Stockport Co.	07.73	1973	2	1	0	(FB)
COMMONS, Mike	Doncaster	18.05.40	Wath.W.	Lincoln C.	05.58	1959-60	2		1	(CF)
			TR	Workington	07.61	1961-63	74		36	
			TR	Chesterfield	07.64	1964	10		1	
COMNY, Oliver	Mulraney	13.11.39		Huddersfield T.	05.59	1960-62	3		0	(IF) EI-5
			TR	Petersborough U.	05.64	1964-71	251	11	34	
COMPTON, Denis C.S.	Hendon	23.05.18	Hampstead T.	Arsenal	*	1946-49	32		10	(OL)Famous Middlesex/ England Cricketer/ Brother of Les H.
COMPTON, John F.	Poplar	27.08.37	JNRS	Chelsea	02.55	1955-59	12		0	(FB)
			TR	Ipswich T.	07.60	1960-63	111		0	
			TR	Bournemouth	07.64	1964	27		1	
COMPTON, Les H.	Woodford	12.09.12	Hampstead T.	Arsenal	*	1946-51	186		0	(CH)E-2/E.F.LGE REP./ Famous Middlesex Cricketer
COMPTON, Paul D.	Stroud	06.06.61	Trowbridge	Bournemouth	10.80	1980-82	64	/	0	(D)
			TR	Aldershot	12.83	1983	13	/	0	
			TR	Torquay U.	02.84	1983	16	/	2	
COMPTON, Roy	London	08.11.54	Millwall(APP)	Swindon T.	03.73	1973	4	2	0	(F)
COMPTON, Terry	Bristol	28.11.31	JNRS	Bristol C.	12.48	1951-57	44		0	(CH)
COMSITIVE, Paul T.	Southport	25.11.61	JNRS	Blackburn Rov.	10.79	1980-82	3	3	0	(D)
			L	Rochdale	09.82	1982	9	/	2	
			TR	Wigan Ath.	08.83	1983	29	/	2	
CONBOY, Frank J.A.	Marylebone	05.09.47	APP	Chelsea	07.65					(FB)
			TR	Luton T.	10.66	1966	19	/	1	
CONDE, Jim	Creswell	19.07.44	JNRS	Wolverhampton W.	05.62					(F)
			TR	Scunthorpe U.	06.63	1963	4		1	
CONDIE, Jim	Hamilton	24.07.26	Kilsyth Rgrs.	Walsall	12.47	1947-49	49		2	(W)
CONEY, Dean H.	Dagenham	18.09.63	APP	Fulham	05.81	1980-83	112	1	27	(F)
CONLEY, Brian J.	Thurnscoe	21.11.48	APP	Sheffield U.	01.66					(D)
			TR	Bradford P.A.	12.68	1968-69	11	2	0	
CONLEY, Joe J.	Whitstable	27.09.20		Torquay U.	+	1946-50	156		72	(F)
CONLON, Bryan	Shildon	14.01.43		Newcastle U.	05.61					(CF)
				Darlington	08.64	1964-67	70	3	27	
			TR	Millwall	11.67	1967-68	40	1	14	
			TR	Norwich C.	12.68	1968-69	29	/	8	
			TR	Blackburn Rov.	05.70	1970-71	43	2	7	
			L	Crewe Alex.	01.72	1971	4	/	1	
			TR	Cambridge U.	03.72	1971-72	17	1	3	
			TR	Hartlepool U.	09.72	1972-73	38	3	3	
CONN, Alfie	Kirkcaldy	05.04.52	Glasgow Rgrs.	Tottenham H.	07.74	1974-76	35	3	6	(M)S-2/S.U23-3/
			Hearts	Blackpool	03.81	1980	3	/	0	Son of Scots Int.
CONNACHAN, Eddie	Prestonpans	27.08.35	Dunfermline	Middlesbrough	08.63	1963-65	95	/	0	(G)S-2/S.F.LGE REP.
CONNAUGHTON, John	Wigan	23.09.49	APP	Manchester U.	10.66	1971	3	/	0	(G)E.YTH.INT.
			L	Halifax T.	09.69	1969	3	/	0	
			L	Torquay U.	10.71	1971	22	/	0	
			TR	Sheffield U.	10.72	1973	12	/	0	
			TR	Port Vale	06.74	1974-79	191	/	0	
CONNEALLY, Martin P.	Lichfield	02.02.62	APP	Walsall	02.80	1980	3	/	0	(G)
CONNELL, Jim D.	Blackburn	24.05.51	Blackburn Rov.(APP)	Bury	02.68	1969	9	/	2	(F)
CONNELL, Peter M.	East Kilbride	26.11.27	Morton	Northampton T.	05.51	1951	13		0	(FB)
CONNELL, Roger	Wembley	08.09.46	Walton & Hersham	Wimbledon	N/L	1977-78	30	2	14	(F)E.AMAT.INT.
CONNELL, Tom E.	Newry	25.11.57	Coleraine	Manchester U.	08.78	1978	2	/	0	(D)
CONNELLY, Edward	Dumbarton	09.12.16	Newcastle U.(*)	Luton T.	*	1946-47	38		8	(IF) *Rosslyn J.
			TR	Orient	06.48	1948-49	32		5	
			TR	Brighton & H.A.	10.49	1949	6		1	
CONNELLY, John	St.Helens	18.07.38	St.Helens	Burnley	11.56	1956-63	216		85	(OR)E-20/E.U23-1/
			TR	Manchester U.	04.64	1964-66	79	1	22	E.F.LGE REP.●
			TR	Blackburn Rov.	09.66	1966-69	148	1	36	
			TR	Bury	06.70	1970-72	128	/	37	
CONNELLY, Mike	Stainforth	08.09.38	JNRS	Doncaster Rov.	AM	1956	3		0	(W)
			TR	Wolverhampton W.	09.59					
			TR	Stockport C.	11.60	1959-60	6		0	
CONNER, Richard J.	Jarrow	13.08.31		Newcastle U.	01.50					(WH)
			South Shields	Grimsby T.	08.52	1953-58	185		8	
			TR	Southampton	07.59	1959-60	78		2	
			TR	Tranmere Rov.	07.61	1961	4		0	
			TR	Aldershot	07.62	1962	6		0	
CONNOLLY, John	Glasgow	13.06.50	St. Johnstone	Everton	03.72	1971-75	105	3	16	(M)S-1/SU23-2
			TR	Birmingham C.	09.76	1976-77	49	8	9	
			TR	Newcastle U.	05.78	1978-79	42	7	10	

Players Names	Birthplace	Date	Previous Club	League Club	Date Signed	Seasons Played	Career Record Apps Sub Gls	
CONNOLLY, Pat J.	Newcastle under-Lyme	27.07.41		Crewe Alex.	01.61	1960-62	9	3 (CF)
			Macclesfield	Colchester U.	07.64	1964	21	6
CONNOR, David	Manchester	27.10.45	JNRS	Manchester C.	11.62	1964-71	130 11	10 (FB)
			TR	Preston N.E.	01.72	1971-72	29 /	0
			TR	Manchester C.	03.74			
CONNOR, Harry	Liverpool	26.12.29	Marine Crosby	Stoke C.	AM	1952-53	3	2 (F)
CONNOR, James	Sunderland	28.11.38	Stanley U.	Darlington	AM	1965	2 /	0 (OL)
CONNOR, James T.	Stockport	31.01.59	JNRS	Stockport Co.	02.79	1978	1 1	0 (D)
CONNOR, John	Ashton-under-Lyne	01.02.14	Mossley	Bolton W.	*			(FB)
			TR	Tranmere Rov.	06.47	1947-48	46	3
CONNOR, John	Stockport	15.05.65	JNRS	Stockport Co.	N/C	1981	1 /	0 (G)
CONNOR, John F.	Maryport	25.07.34		Huddersfield T.	10.52	1954-60	85	10 (CH)
			TR	Bristol C.	10.60	1960-70	353 1	10
CONNOR, John T.	Todmorden	21.12.19	Albion Rov.	Ipswich T.	+	1946	12	4 (CF)●
			TR	Carlisle U.	12.46	1946-47	39	12
			Ards	Rochdale	12.48	1948-50	81	42
			TR	Bradford C.	04.51	1950-51	14	7
			TR	Stockport Co.	10.51	1951-56	206	132
			TR	Crewe Alex.	09.56	1956	27	4
CONNOR, Kevin	Radcliffe	12.01.45		Rochdale	01.66	1965-66	21 3	1 (HB)
CONNOR, Robert	Bradford	13.10.25	Salts	Bradford C.	11.49	1949-50	28	0 (G)
			TR	Wrexham	07.51	1951-53	77	0
CONNOR, Terry F.	Leeds	09.11.62	APP	Leeds U.	11.79	1979-82	83 13	19 (F)E.YTH.INT.
			TR	Brighton & H.A.	03.83	1982-83	45 2	14
CONNORS, John J.	Stockton	21.08.27		Darlington	03.48	1947-51	65	0 (HB)
CONROY, Gerry	Dublin	02.10.46	Glentoran	Stoke C.	03.67	1967-78	244 27	49 (F)EI-26
			Hong Kong	Crewe Alex.	01.80	1979-80	37 /	5
CONROY, Richard	Bradford	29.07.27	Sevain House	Bradford C.	+	1948-52	159	0 (CH)
			TR	Bradford P.A.	10.53	1953-55	57	0
CONROY, Richard M.	Bradford	26.04.19	Fulham (*)	Accrington St.	+	1946-48	87	1
			TR	Scunthorpe U.	09.50	1950	1	0
CONROY, Robert B.	Twechar	20.06.29	Ashfield J.	Bury	10.51	1955-61	217	2 (FB)
			TR	Tranmere Rov.	07.62	1962-64	103	1
CONROY, Steve	Chesterfield	19.12.56	APP	Sheffield U.	10.73	1977-82	104 /	0 (G)E.SCH.INT.
			TR	Rotherham U.	N/C	1982	5 /	0
			TR	Rochdale	06.83	1983	46 /	0
CONSTANTINE, Jim	Ashton	16.02.20	Rochdale (+)	Manchester C.	+	1946	18	12 (CF)
			TR	Bury	08.47	1947	32	14
			TR	Millwall	05.48	1948-51	141	75
CONSTANTINE, David	Dukinfield	02.02.57	Hyde U.	Bury	02.79	1978-81	67 3	2 (D)
CONWAY, Andy	South Shields	17.02.23	North Shields	Hull C.	06.47	1947-48	6	5 (CF)
			TR	Stockport Co.	07.50			
CONWAY, Chris	Dundee	23.07.28	Ayr U.	Bury	09.54	1954-55	44	0 (G)
CONWAY, James	Motherwell	27.08.40	Glasgow Celtic	Norwich C.	05.61	1961-63	42	12 (CF) S.SCH.INT.
			TR	Southend U.	10.63	1963-64	32	9
CONWAY, James P.	Dublin	10.08.46	Bohemians	Fulham	05.66	1966-75	311 4	67 (F(EI-19/EI.AMAT.INT.
			TR	Manchester C.	08.76	1976	11 2	1
CONWAY, John	Dublin	11.07.51	Bohemians	Fulham	08.71	1971-74	30 8	6 (F) Brother of Jim P.
CONWAY, John G.	Gateshead	24.01.31		Gateshead	05.53	1953-54	4	0 (F)
CONWAY, Mike D.	Sheffield	11.03.56	APP	Brighton & H.A.	09.74	1972-73	1 1	1 (F)
			TR	Swansea C.	12.75	1975-77	56 5	11
CONWAY, Tom	Stoke	07.11.33	JNRS	Port Vale	05.51	1955	15	4 (F)
CONWELL, Anthony	Bradford	17.01.32	JNRS	Sheffield Wed.	02.49	1953-54	44	0 (FB)
			TR	Huddersfield T.	07.55	1955-58	102	2
			TR	Derby Co.	06.59	1959-61	98	1
			TR	Doncaster Rov.	07.62	1962-63	35	0
COOK, Anthony	Bristol	08.10.29	Clifton St.V.	Bristol C.	01.50	1952-63	320	0 (G)
COOK, Anthony J.	Crewe	26.12.61		Crewe Alex.	N/C	1981	2 1	0 (M)
COOK, Charles	Cheltenham	28.01.37	Gloucester C.	Bristol C.	02.57	1956-57	2	0 (FB)
COOK, Jeff W.	Hartlepool	14.03.53	Hellenic	Stoke C.	10.77	1977-80	22 8	5 (F)
			L	Bradford C.	02.79	1978	8 /	1
			L	Plymouth Arg.	12.79	1979	4 3	5
			TR	Plymouth Arg.	10.81	1981-82	54 1	21
			TR	Halifax T.	08.83	1983	25 5	6
COOK, John A.	Iron Acton	27.06.29	JNRS	Bristol Rov.	09.46	1946	2	0
COOK, Les	Blackburn	11.11.24	JNRS	Blackburn Rov.	+	1946-48	76	0 (FB) E.SCH.INT.
			TR	Coventry C.	07.49	1949-53	87	0
COOK, Malcolm	Glasgow	24.05.43	Motherwell	Bradford P.A.	07.63	1963-64	45	2 (HB)
			TR	Newport Co.	07.65	1965	30 2	0

Players Names	Birthplace	Date	Previous Club	League Club	Date Signed	Seasons Played	Apps	Sub	Gls	
COOK, Maurice	Berkhamsted	10.12.31	Berkhamsted	Watford	05.53	1953-57	206		68	(CF)
			TR	Fulham	02.58	1957-64	221		89	
			TR	Reading	05.65	1965	12	/	2	
COOK, Mike	Enfield	09.04.51	Orient (AM)	Colchester U.	07.69	1969-83	609	4	21	(D)●
COOK, Mike J.	Belmont	25.01.50	APP	Crystal Palace	02.68	1967	1	/	0	(F)
			TR	Brentford	08.69	1969	16	4	4	
COOK, Peter	Hull	01.02.27	Kingston W.	Hull C.	06.46	1946-47	5		0	(CH) d.1960
			Scarborough	Bradford C.	05.49	1949	1		0	
			TR	Crewe Alex.	08.50	1950-52	45		7	
COOK, Reuben	Gateshead	09.03.33	Tow Law	Arsenal	11.51					(WH)
			TR	Orient	01.56	1956	2		0	
COOK, Robert K.	Letchworth	13.06.24	Letchworth	Reading	03.48					(F)
			TR	Tottenham H.	07.49	1949	3		0	
			TR	Watford	08.51	1951-52	54		8	
COOK, Trevor	Blidworth	02.07.56	APP	Mansfield T.	07.74	1973	1	/	0	(F)
COOKE, Alan				Crewe Alex.	08.55	1955	8		0	
COOKE, Barry A.	Wolverhampton	22.01.38	Erdington	W.B.A.	05.55					(WH) E.YTH.INT.
			TR	Northampton T.	07.59	1959-61	58		1	
COOKE, Charlie	Fife	14.10.42	Dundee	Chelsea	04.66	1966-72	204	8	15	(M)S-16/S.U23-4/
			TR	Crystal Palace	10.72	1972-73	42	2	0	S.F.LGE REP.
			TR	Chelsea	01.74	1973-77	85	2	7	
COOKE, David	Birmingham	29.11.46	JNRS	Wolverhampton W.	07.65					(FB)
			TR	Stockport Co.	07.68	1968	3	/	0	
COOKE, Edward J.	Barnsley	18.03.42	JNRS	Port Vale	06.60	1960-63	7		0	(G)
COOKE, Gordon C.	Crewe	31.05.28	JNRS	Crewe Alex.	05.48	1948	2		0	
COOKE, Harry W.	Whittington	07.03.19	Bournemouth (*)	Luton T.	+	1946-52	211		4	(FB)
			TR	Shrewsbury T.	07.53	1953	4		0	
			TR	Watford	07.54	1954	12		0	
COOKE, Joe	W. Indies	15.02.55	APP	Bradford C.	05.72	1971-78	184	20	62	(D)
			TR	Peterborough U.	01.79	1978	18	/	5	
			TR	Oxford U.	08.79	1979-80	71	1	13	
			TR	Exeter C	06.81	1981	17	/	3	
			TR	Bradford C.	01.82	1981-83	61	1	6	
COOKE, John	Salford	25.04.62	APP	Sunderland	11.79	1979-83	38	11	4	(F)
COOKE, Peter C.	Northampton	15.01.62	JNRS	Northampton T.	07.80	1980	4	1	1	(F)
COOKE, Richard E.	Islington	04.09.65	APP	Tottenham H.	05.83	1983	9	/	1	(M)
COOKE, Robert L.	Rotherham	16.02.57	APP	Mansfield T.	08.76	1976-77	7	8	1	(F)
			Grantham	Peterborough U.	05.80	1980-82	115	/	51	
			TR	Cambridge U.	02.83	1982-83	46	3	8	
COOKE, Terry A.	Wrexham	21.02.62	APP	Chester C.	02.80	1980-82	37	12	11	(F)
COOKE, Wilf H.	Crewe	05.10.15	Fulham (+)	Crewe Alex.	+	1946	12		2	*Bradford C./+ Leeds U.
COOLE, William	Manchester	27.01.25		Mansfield T.	01.48	1947-53	183		36	(OR)
			TR	Notts. Co.	10.53	1953-55	42		5	
			TR	Barrow	07.56	1956-58	56		3	
COOKSON, Jim	Liverpool	22.08.27		Everton	+					(FB)
			TR	Southport	08.49	1949-51	55		1	
COOLING, Roy	Barnsley	09.12.21	Mitchells M.W.	Barnsley	+	1946	6		3	(CF)
			TR	Mansfield T.	09.47	1947-49	65		15	
COOMBES, Jeff	Rhondda	01.04.54	APP	Bristol Rov.	04.72	1972-74	10	1	1	(IF) W.SCH.INT.
COOMBS, Frank H.	East Ham	24.04.25	Dartford	Bristol C.	06.49	1949	24		0	(G)
			TR	Southend U.	06.50	1950	20		0	
			TR	Colchester U.	07.51	1951-53	38		0	
COOP, Jim (Yates)	Horwich	17.09.27		Sheffield U.	05.46	1947-48	9		1	(OL)
			TR	York C.	07.49	1949-50	12		4	
COOP, Mick A.	Leamington	10.07.48	APP	Coventry C.	01.66	1966-80	412	12	18	(D)●
			L	York C.	11.74	1974	4	/	0	
			TR	Derby Co.	07.81	1981	17	1	0	
COOPER, Adrian S.J.	Reading	16.01.57	APP	Reading	07.73	1973-75	14	/	2	(HB) E.SCH.INT.
COOPER, Arthur	Etruria	16.03.21	Shelton St Marks	Port Vale	+	1946	4		0	(LH)
COOPER, Charles	Farnworth	14.06.41	JNRS	Bolton W.	05.59	1960-68	79	5	0	(FB)
			TR	Barrow	07.69	1969-70	54	/	0	
COOPER, Doug	Middlesbrough	18.10.36	JNRS	Middlesbrough	10.53	1954-56	4		0	(F)
			TR	Rotherham U.	01.59	1958	13		5	
			TR	Hartlepool U.	08.60	1960	16		6	
COOPER, Fred	London	18.11.34	JNRS	West Ham U.	12.51	1956-57	4		0	(FB) E.SCH.INT.
COOPER, Gary S.	Horwich	15.02.55	Horwich RMI	Rochdale	12.73	1973-76	81	10	14	(F)
			TR	Southport	08.77	1977	13	7	5	
COOPER, George	Kingswinford	01.10.32	Brierley Hill	Crystal Palace	01.55	1954-58	69		27	(FB)
			TR	Rochdale	01.59	1958-59	34		9	
COOPER, Graham	Huddersfield	22.05.62		Huddersfield T.	N/C	1983	3	/	1	(M)

Players Names	Birthplace	Date	Previous Club	League Club	Date Signed	Seasons Played	Apps	Sub	Gls	
COOPER, Ian L.	Bradford	21.09.46	JNRS	Bradford C.	08.66	1965-76	442	1	4	(D)
COOPER, James	Blackpool	13.01.28	Fleetwood	Accrington St.	06.52	1952	7		1	
COOPER, James E.	Chester	19.01.42	JNRS	Chester C.	09.59	1959-61	91		17	(F)
			TR	Southport	06.62	1962	28		7	
			TR	Blackpool	07.63	1963	4		0	
			TR	Mansfield T.	05.64	1964	7		3	
			TR	Crewe Alex.	07.65	1965	6	/	0	
COOPER, James T.	Glasgow	28.12.39	Airdrie	Brighton & H.A.	08.62	1962-63	41		6	(F)
			TR	Hartlepool U.	07.65	1965	19	/	1	
COOPER, Joe	Reddish	16.02.18	Blackpool(*)	Crewe Alex.	+	1946	3		0	(WH)
COOPER, Joe	Gateshead	15.10.34	Winlaton Mill	Newcastle U.	09.52	1953-57	6		0	(HB)
COOPER, Leigh V.	Reading	07.05.61	APP	Plymouth Arg.	05.79	1979-83	172	/	16	(M)
COOPER, Len A.	Lower Gornal	11.05.36	JNRS	Wolverhampton W.	05.53					(OL) E.YTH.INT.
				Walsall	02.56	1955	5		2	
COOPER, Mark D.	Watford	05.04.67	APP	Cambridge U.	APP	1983	1	1	0	(M)
COOPER, Neil	Aberdeen	12.08.59	Aberdeen	Barnsley	01.80	1979-81	57	3	6	(D)S.SCH.INT.
			TR	Grimsby T.	03.82	1981-83	47	/	2	
COOPER, Paul D.	Brierley Hill	21.12.53	APP	Birmingham C.	07.71	1971-73	17	/	0	.(G)
			TR	Ipswich T.	03.74	1973-83	339	/	0	
COOPER, Paul T.	Birmingham	12.07.57	APP	Huddersfield T.	08.75	1976	2	/	0	(D)
			TR	Grimsby T.	07.77	1977	3	/	0	
COOPER, Richard D.	London	07.05.65	APP	Sheffield U.	05.83	1982	1	1	0	(F)
COOPER, Ron	Peterborough	28.08.38	JNRS	Peterborough U.	N/L	1963-67	132	/	1	(FB)
COOPER, Steve B.	Birmingham	22.06.64	Moor Green	Birmingham C.	11.83					(F)
			L	Halifax T.	12.83	1983	7	/	1	
COOPER, Steve M.	Basingstoke	14.12.55	Stourbridge	Torquay U.	03.78	1977-83	219	15	76	(F)E.YTH.INT.
COOPER, Terry	Castleford	12.07.44	APP	Leeds U.	07.62	1963-74	239	10	7	(D)E-20
			TR	Middlesbrough	03.75	1974-77	105	/	1	
			TR	Bristol C.	07.78	1978	11	/	0	
			TR	Bristol Rov.	08.79	1979-81	53	6	0	
			TR	Doncaster Rov.	11.81	1981	20	/	0	
			TR	Bristol C.	08.82	1982-83	38	21	0	
COOPER, Terry	Cwmbran	11.03.50	JNRS	Newport Co.	07.68	1967-69	64	4	1	(D)
			TR	Notts. Co.	07.70	1971-72	3	6	0	
			L	Lincoln C.	12.71	1971	3	/	0	
			TR	Lincoln C.	08.72	1972-78	265	2	12	
			L	Scunthorpe U.	11.77	1977	4	/	0	
			TR	Bradford C.	06.79	1979-80	47	1	2	
			TR	Rochdale	08.81	1981	35	/	2	
COOPER, William G.E.	York	02.11.17	Halifax T.(AM)	Bradford C.	09.46	1946-47	7		4	(F) d.1978
COOTE, Ken A.	Paddington	19.05.28	Wembley T.	Brentford	05.49	1949-63	513		14	(WH)●
COPE, Anthony	Doncaster	17.01.41	JNRS	Doncaster Rov.	09.58	1958-59	8		0	(IF)
COPE, Ron	Crewe	05.10.34	JNRS	Manchester U.	10.51	1956-60	93		2	(CH) E.SCH.INT.
			TR	Luton T.	08.61	1961-62	28		0	
COPELAND, Mick	Newport	31.12.54	JNRS	Newport Co.	07.73	1973	3	1	0	(FB)
COPELAND, Edward	Hetton-le-Hole	19.05.21	Easington Col.	Hartlepool U.	+	1946-47	38		9	(OR)
COPELAND, Phil	Workington	16.09.36		Workington	02.57	1960-62	11		0	(CH)
COPESTAKE, Oliver	Mansfield	01.09.21		Mansfield T.	+	1946	32		8	d.1953
COPLEY, Dennis I.	Misterton	21.12.21	Norwich C.(AM)	Lincoln C.	09.46	1946	1		0	(IF)
COPLEY, Gary	Rotherham	30.12.60	APP	Barnsley	N/C	1978	1	/	0	(G)
COPP, Len J.H.	Aberystwyth	07.10.40	JNRS	Leeds U.	10.57					(F)
			TR	Shrewsbury T.	07.58	1960	2		1	
			TR	Bristol C.	07.61					
COPPELL, Steve	Liverpool	09.07.55	Liverpool Univ.	Tranmere Rov.	01.74	1973-74	35	3	10	(F)E.U23-1/E-42
			TR	Manchester U.	02.75	1974-82	320	2	53	E.F.LGE REP.●
CORBETT, Alex M.	Saltcoats	20.04.21	Ayr U.	New Brighton	07.46	1946-47	58		0	(G)
			TR	Hull C.	01.48	1947	8		0	
			Weymouth	Hartlepool U.	07.53	1953	7		0	
CORBETT, Anthony	Wolverhampton	28.04.40	JNRS	Wolverhampton W.	05.59					(HB) E.YTH.INT.
			TR	Shrewsbury T.	07.60	1960-61	8		0	
CORBETT, Arthur B.	Birmingham	17.08.28	Sutton T.	Walsall	12.49	1949-50	24		5	(WH)
CORBETT, David F.	Marshfield	15.04.40		Swindon T.	08.58	1958-61	68		3	(OR)
			TR	Plymouth Arg.	02.62	1961-66	85	/	8	
CORBETT, George	N.Walbottle	11.05.25		Sheffield Wed.	+					(FB)
			Spennymoor	W.B.A.	03.51	1951	1		0	
			TR	Workington	07.53	1953	9		0	
CORBETT, John T.	Bow	09.01.20	Swansea C.(+)	Crystal Palace	09.46	1946	1		1	(F) +Hartlepool U.
CORBETT, Norman G.	Falkirk	23.06.19	Hearts	West Ham U.	*	1946-49	128		2	(WH)
CORBETT, Pat A.	Hackney	12.02.63	APP	Tottenham H.	10.80	1981-82	3	2	1	(D) E.YTH.INT.
			TR	Orient	08.83	1983	43		1	

Players Names	Birthplace	Date	Previous Club	League Club	Date Signed	Seasons Played	Apps	Sub	Gls	
CORBETT, Peter	Preston	05.03.34		Preston N.E.	06.56					(G)
			TR	Workington	08.57	1957-58	11		0	
			TR	Oldham Ath.	07.59	1959	10		0	
CORBETT, Robert	Newburn	16.03.22	Throckley Welfare	Newcastle U.	+	1946-51	46		1	(FB)
			TR	Middlesbrough	12.51	1951-56	92		0	
			TR	Northampton T.	08.57	1957	8		1	
CORBETT, William	Wolverhampton	29.07.20	Cardiff C.(+)	Doncaster Rov.	+	1946-47	37		0	(LB)
			TR	Bristol C.	06.48	1948	1		0	
CORBETT, William R.	Falkirk	31.08.22	Glasgow Celtic	Preston N.E.	06.48	1948	19		0	
			TR	Leicester C.	08.49	1949	16		0	
CORBIN, Kirk	W. Indies	12.03.55	Wokingham	Cambridge U.	01.78	1978	3	/	0	(D)
CORBISHLEY, Colin	Stoke	13.06.39		Port Vale	10.59	1960-61	11		0	(WH)
			TR	Chester C.	08.62	1962-64	83		11	
CORDELL, John G.	Walsall	06.12.28	Walsall Star	Aston Villa	09.49	1951-52	5		0	(G)
			TR	Rochdale	05.53	1953-54	16		0	
CORDICE, Neil A.	Amersham	07.04.60	Flackwell Heath	Northampton T.	07.78	1978	4	4	1	(F)
CORDJOHN, Barry	Oxford	05.09.42	JNRS	Charlton Ath.	06.60					(FB)
			TR	Aldershot	07.63					
			TR	Portsmouth	07.64	1964	14		0	
CORE, John	Ripponden	29.03.29		Halifax T.	AM	1949-53	29		14	(CF)
CORFIELD, Ernie	Wigan	18.01.31	JNRS	Bolton W.	04.48	1949-51	6		0	(IF)
			TR	Stockport Co.	07.53	1953	2		0	
CORISH, Robert	Liverpool	13.09.58	JNRS	Derby Co.	08.76	1977	0	1	0	(F)
CORK, Alan G.	Derby	04.03.59	JNRS	Derby Co.	07.77					(F)
			L	Lincoln C.	09.77	1977	5	/	0	
			TR	Wimbledon	02.78	1977-83	198	2	94	
CORK, David	Doncaster	08.10.59	APP	Manchester U.	10.76					(M)
			TR	Doncaster Rov.	08.78	1978-79	9	/	1	
CORK, David	Doncaster	28.10.62	APP	Arsenal	06.80	1983	5	2	1	(M)
CORKHILL, Robert	Barrow	20.11.43	Holker COB	Barrow	07.64	1963-64	8		1	(OL)
CORKHILL, William	Belfast	23.04.10	Cardiff C.(*)	Notts. Co.	+	1946-51	99		0	(WH)*Northern Nomads/Notts Co. d.1978/1 appearance in goal
CORMACK, Peter	Edinburgh	17.07.46	Hibernian	Nottingham F.	03.70	1969-71	74	/	15	(M)S-9/S.U23-5/S.
			TR	Liverpool	07.72	1972-75	119	6	21	S.F.LGE REP./S.
			TR	Bristol C.	11.76	1976-79	59	8	15	AMAT.INT.
CORNER, Brian	Glasgow	06.01.61	APP	Fulham	01.79	1980	1	2	0	(D)
CORNER, Norman	Horden	16.02.43	Horden CW	Hull C.	08.62	1963-66	5	/	4	(IF)
			TR	Lincoln C.	10.67	1967-68	44	1	12	
			TR	Bradford C.	01.69	1968-71	105	5	16	
CORNES, Stuart	Usk	04.03.60	APP	Hereford U.	01.78	1977-81	91	2	3	(D)
CORNFIELD, Allen H.	Dudley	19.12.40	Gornal	Shrewsbury T.	11.59	1959-61	9		0	(F)
CORNOCK, Walter B.	Australia	01.01.21	Hereford U.	Rochdale	11.47	1947	1		0	(G) +Oldham Ath./ Leics. Cricketer
CORNWELL, Ellis	Coppull	14.11.13	Rochdale(+)	Accrington St.	+	1946	5		0	(FB) +Chorley
CORNWELL, Kevin	Birmingham	10.12.41	Banbury T.	Oxford U.	07.62	1962-63	25		10	(F)
CORNWELL, John A.	Bethnal Green	13.10.64	APP	Orient	10.82	1981-83	71	2	10	(M)
CORR, John	Glasgow	18.12.46	Possilpark J.	Arsenal	07.65					(OR)
			TR	Exeter C.	07.67	1967-70	75	8	19	
CORR, Pat M.	Derry	31.03.27	Coleraine	Burnley	10.51	1951	3		0	(WH) IRISH F.LGE REP./ N.I.AMAT.INT.
CORR, Peter J.	Dundalk	26.06.23	Dundalk	Preston N.E.	04.47	1946	3		0	(OR) EI-4
			TR	Everton	08.48	1948-49	24		2	
CORRIGAN, Frank	Liverpool	13.11.52	Ormskirk	Blackpool	08.72					(M)
			TR	Walsall	07.73	1973	1	/	0	
			Northwich Vic.	Wigan Ath.	N/L	1978-80	113	3	12	
CORRIGAN, Joe	Manchester	18.11.48	Sale F.C.	Manchester C.	01.67	1968-82	476	/	0	(G)E-9/E.U23-1/E.U21-3●
			Seattle Sounders	Brighton & H.A.	09.83	1983	36	/	0	
CORTHINE, Peter A.	Highbury	19.07.37	Leytonstone	Chelsea	12.57	1959	2		0	(IF)
			TR	Southend U.	03.60	1959-61	73		24	
COSSLETT, Mike P.	Barry	17.04.57	Barry T.	Newport Co.	02.78	1977-78	2	/	0	(D)
COSTELLO, John	Prestonpans	23.05.20		Southend U.	08.52					(FB)
			TR	Barrow	07.53	1953	6		0	
COSTELLO, Matt	Airdrie	04.08.24	N.Steventon	Chesterfield	05.49	1949-51	18		2	(OR)
			TR	Chester C.	07.52	1952	9		2	
COSTELLO, Mortimer	Dagenham	08.07.36	Leyton	Aldershot	AM	1956	28		7	(FB)
			TR	Southend U.	05.57	1957-64	250		15	
COTHLIFF, Harold	Liverpool	24.03.16		Torquay U.	*	1946-47	23		1	
COTON, Anthony P.	Tamworth	19.05.61	Mile Oak Rov.	Birmingham C.	10.78	1980-83	87	/	0	(G)
COTON, Paul S.	Birmingham	09.02.49	APP	Walsall	02.67	1966	1	/	0	(FB)

Players Names	Birthplace	Date	Previous Club	League Club	Date Signed	Seasons Played	Career Record Apps	Sub	Gls	
COTTAM, John E.	Worksop	05.06.50	APP	Nottingham F.	04.68	1970-75	92	3	4	(D)
			L	Mansfield T.	11.72	1972	2	/	1	
			L	Lincoln C.	03.73	1972	1	/	0	
			TR	Chesterfield	08.76	1976-78	120	/	7	
			TR	Chester C.	07.79	1979-81	117	3	1	
COTTEE, Anthony R.	West Ham	11.07.65	APP	West Ham H.	09.82	1982-83	40	7	20	(F)
COTTINGTON, Brian A.	London	14.02.65	APP	Fulham	02.83	1983	0	1	0	(M)
COTTON, Fred	Halesowen	12.03.32		Crystal Palace	08.56	1956	4		0	
COTTON, John	Stoke	02.03.30		Stoke C.	05.52	1952-53	3		0	(FB)
			TR	Crewe Alex.	10.55	1955	14		0	
COTTON, Roy W.	Fulham	14.11.55	JNRS	Brentford	AM	1973	1	1	0	(F)E.YTH.INT.
			TR	Orient	07.74	1975	0	3	0	
			TR	Aldershot	07.76	1977	5	/	0	
COTTON, Russell	Wellington	04.04.60	APP	Colchester U.	04.78	1977-81	33	4	1	(M)
COTTON, Terry	Swansea	25.01.46	Ammanford	Swansea C.	05.70	1968-70	12	1	1	(IF) W.AMAT.INT.
COUCH, Alan	Neath	15.03.53	JNRS	Cardiff C.	08.70	1971-72	7	4	0	(F)
COUCH, Geoff. R.	Crowle	03.04.53	Crowle	Scunthorpe U.	03.78	1977-79	22	4	5	(F)
COUGHLIN, Dennis M.	Houghton-le-Spring	26.11.37	Durham C.	Barnsley	10.57					(HB)
			Yeovil	Bournemouth	03.63	1962-65	86	2	41	
			TR	Swansea C.	08.66	1966-67	39	1	11	
			L	Exeter C.	03.68	1967	13	/	2	
COUGHLIN, Jim	Cheltenham	26.07.53		Hereford U.	03.77	1976	1	1	1	(F)
COUGHLIN, Russell	Swansea	15.02.60	APP	Manchester C.	03.78					(M)W.SCH.INT.
			TR	Blackburn Rov.	03.79	1978-80	22	2	0	
			TR	Carlisle U.	10.80	1980-83	114	16	13	
COULL, George	Dundee	10.08.35	Dundee Downfield	Millwall	08.56	1956	6		1	(WH)
COULSON, William	North Shields	14.01.50	Consett T.	Newcastle U.	09.71					(IF)
			TR	Southend U.	10.73	1973-75	51	1	4	
			L	Aldershot	02.75	1974	3	/	0	
			L	Huddersfield T.	11.75	1975	2	/	0	
			L	Darlington	01.76	1975	11	2	1	
COUPE, Joe N.	Carlisle	15.07.24	Swift Rovers	Carlisle U.	09.47	1948-50	31		0	(FB)
			TR	Rochdale	10.51	1951	8		0	
			TR	Workington	10.52	1952	6		0	
COUPLAND, Joe	Glasgow	10.04.20	Ayr U.	Bradford C.	08.50	1950-51	18		0	(FB)
			TR	Carlisle U.	07.52	1952-53	3		0	
COURT, Colin	Ebbw Vale	03.09.37	JNRS	Chelsea	09.54					(OL) W.SCH.INT.
			TR	Torquay U.	05.59	1959-60	27		5	
COURT, Colin	Winchester	25.03.64	Andover	Reading	N/C	1981	1	/	0	(G)
COURT, David J.	London	01.03.44	APP	Arsenal	01.62	1962-69	167	7	17	(WH)
			TR	Luton T.	07.70	1970-71	50	2	0	
			TR	Brentford	08.72	1972	8	4	1	
COURT, Harold J.	Tirphil	13.06.19		Cardiff C.	*					
			Dundee	Swindon T.	06.50	1950	16		2	
COUSANS, W.Eric	Doncaster	10.09.29	Goole T.	Walsall	08.54	1954	4		1	(F)
			TR	Gillingham	09.55	1955	2		0	
COUSINS, Harry	Chesterfield	25.09.07	Chesterfield (*)	Swindon T.	*	1946	9		0	(WH) d.1981
COUSINS, Ken F.	Bristol	06.08.22	Brislingten	Bristol C.	+	1946	3		0	(G)
COUTTS, Roger	Barrow	18.12.44	Walney Rov.	Barrow	10.65	1964	2		0	(CF)
COWAN, Don	Durham	17.08.31		Darlington	11.52	1952-53	17		0	(G)
COWAN, Ian	Falkirk	27.11.44	Dunfermline	Southend U.	07.70	1970	3	/	0	
COWAN, Jimmy C.	Paisley	16.06.26	Morton	Sunderland	06.53	1953	28		0	(G)S-25/S.F.LGE REP./ d.1968
COWAN, John	Belfast	08.01.49	Crusaders	Newcastle U.	02.67	1969-72	6	3	0	(IF) N.1-1/
			Drogheda	Darlington	08.75	1975	10	/	0	
COWANS, Gordon S.	Durham	27.10.58	APP	Aston Villa	09.76	1975-82	247	9	41	(M)E.YTH.INT./E.U21-5/E-7
COWDRILL, Barry J.	Birmingham	03.01.57	Sutton C.T.	W.B.A.	04.79	1979-83	49	2	0	(D)
COWELL, G. Robert	Trimdon	05.12.22	Blackhall C.W.	Newcastle U.	+	1946-54	289		0	(FB)
COWEN, John M.	Lewisham	01.12.44	APP	Chelsea	10.62					(G) E.YTH.INT.
			TR	Watford	10.64	1964-66	17	/	0	
COWIE, Andrew D.	Motherwell	11.03.13	Aberdeen	Swindon T.	07.48	1948-50	89		4	(FB)
COWIE, George A.	Buckie	09.05.61	APP	West Ham U.	08.78	1981-82	6	2	0	(M)
COWLEY, Carl	London	10.07.65	APP	Millwall	10.82	1983	2	1	0	(D)
COWLEY, Frank	London	28.11.57	Sutton U.	Derby Co.	08.77					(F)
			TR	Wimbledon	02.78	1977-78	5	3	0	
COWLING, Chris	Scunthorpe	19.09.62	APP	Scunthorpe U.	12.79	1979-83	94	13	18	(F)
COWLING, David R.	Doncaster	27.11.58	Mansfield T.(APP)	Huddersfield T.	08.77	1978-83	224	5	34	(F)
COWSILL, Charlie	Farnworth	05.05.29		Bury	05.50					
				Workington	11.51	1951	1		0	

Players Names	Birthplace	Date	Previous Club	League Club	Date Signed	Seasons Played	Apps	Sub	Gls	
COX, Alan W.	Liverpool	18.03.21		Tranmere Rov.	+	1946-47	8		1	(OR)
COX, Albert E.H.	Treeton	24.06.17	Woodhouse Mill	Sheffield U.	*	1946-51	180		5	(FB)
			TR	Halifax T.	07.52	1952-53	53		1	
COX, Brian R.	Sheffield	07.05.61	APP	Sheffield Wed.	02.79	1978-80	22	/	0	(G)
			TR	Huddersfield T.	03.82	1981-83	82	/	0	
COX, David	Dukinfield	16.09.36	Oldham Ath.(AM)	Stockport Co.	10.55	1956-57	8		4	(F)
COX, Freddie J.A.	Reading	01.11.20	JNRS	Tottenham H.	*	1946-48	89		13	(OR) d.1973
			TR	Arsenal	09.49	1949-52	79		8	
			TR	W.B.A.	07.53	1953	4		1	
COX, Geoff	Arley	30.11.34	JNRS	Birmingham C.	12.51	1952-56	35		3	(WH)
			TR	Torquay U.	12.57	1957-66	260	1	62	
			TR	Plymouth Arg.	09.67					
COX, Graham P.	London	30.04.59	APP	Brentford	04.77	1976-77	4	/	0	(G)
COX, Keith	Heanor	26.01.36	Heanor T.	Charlton Ath.	04.54	1956-58	14		0	(HB)
COX, Mark L.	Birmingham	04.10.59	APP	Lincoln C.	09.77	1976-77	3	2	0	(F)
			TR	Doncaster Rov.	09.78	1978	10	5	3	
COX, Maurice	Torquay	01.10.59	JNRS	Torquay U.	01.80	1978-81	49	13	13	(F) Son of Geoff
			TR	Huddersfield T.	N/C	1982	3	1	2	
COX, Ron B.	Foleshill	02.05.19	JNRS	Coventry C.	+	1946-51	29		0	(HB)
COX, Sam	Mexborough	30.10.20	Denaby U.	W.B.A.	05.48	1948	2		0	(FB)
			TR	Accrington St.	07.51	1951	43		0	
			TR	Scunthorpe U.	07.52	1952	3		0	
COXHILL, David	Northfields	10.04.52	JNRS	Millwall	06.70	1970-71	6	2	0	(HB)
			TR	Gillingham	07.73	1973-74	32	2	1	
COXON, Eric G.	Liverpool	31.05.46	Everton (APP)	Blackburn Rov.	12.63	1966-67	10	/	0	(FB)
COXON, John	Old Hartley	07.04.22	Hartley F.C.	Darlington	AM	1946	1		0	(FB)
COXON, William G.	Derby	28.04.33	JNRS	Derby Co.	05.50					(F)
			Ilkeston T.	Norwich C.	05.52	1952-57	98		24	
			TR	Lincoln C.	03.58	1957-58	11		6	
			TR	Bournemouth	11.58	1958-65	199	1	37	
COY, Robert A.	Birmingham	30.11.61	APP	Wolverhampton W.	12.79	1981-83	40	3	0	(D)
			L	Chester C.	03.84	1983	14	/	0	
COYLE, Anthony	Glasgow	17.01.60	Albion Rov.	Stockport Co.	12.79	1979-83	153	3	18	(M)
COYLE, Fay	Derry	01.04.24	Coleraine	Nottingham F.	03.58	1957	3		0	(CF) N.I.-4/N1.AMAT.INT.
COYLE, Robert	Belfast	31.01.48	Glentoran	Sheffield Wed.	03.72	1972-73	38	2	2	(IF) N.I.-5/
			TR	Grimsby T.	10.74	1974	24	/	1	
COYLE, William	Newcastle	24.10.26	W. Auckland	Darlington	AM	1949	16		0	
COYNE, Brian	Glasgow	13.12.59	Glasgow Celtic	Shrewsbury T.	06.79	1979	1	/	0	(M)
COYNE, Cyril	Barnsley	02.05.24		Leeds U.	+					
			Stalybridge C.	Halifax T.	06.51	1951	4		0	
COYNE, Gerard A.	Hebburn	09.08.48		York C.	08.66	1966	2	/	0	(CF)
COYNE, John D.	Liverpool	18.07.51		Tranmere Rov.	08.71	1971	12	3	3	(F)
			TR	Hartlepool U.	07.72	1972-73	47	8	9	
			Wigan Ath.	Stockport Co.	11.75	1975	3	1	0	
COYNE, Peter	Hartlepool	13.11.58	APP	Manchester U.	11.75	1975	1	1	1	(F)
			Ashton U.	Crewe Alex.	08.77	1977-80	113	21	47	
COZENS, John	London	14.05.46	Hillingdon	Notts. Co.	08.70	1970-72	41	5	13	(F)
			TR	Peterborough U.	11.72	1972-77	127	5	41	
			TR	Cambridge U.	12.77	1977-79	52	9	3	
CRABBE, S.A. John	Weymouth	20.10.54	APP	Southampton	10.72	1974-76	8	4	0	(M)
			TR	Gillingham	01.76	1976-80	181	/	12	
			TR	Carlisle U.	08.81	1981	26	/	4	
			TR	Hereford U.	08.82	1982	15	1	2	
			TR	Crewe Alex.	08.83	1983	37	/	4	
CRABTREE, Richard E.	Exeter	06.02.55	APP	Bristol Rov.	02.73	1971	7	/	0	(G)
			L	Doncaster Rov.	10.74	1974	1	/	0	
			TR	Torquay U.	N/C	1975	1	/	0	
			Dawlish	Exeter C.	N/C	1983	1	/	0	
CRADDOCK, L. Miller	Newent	21.09.26	Chelsea (AM)	Newport Co.	05.46	1946	7		0	(CF) d.1960
			Hereford U.	Aston Villa	09.48	1948-50	34		10	
CRAGGS, John E.	Flint Hill	31.10.48	APP	Newcastle U.	12.65	1966-70	50	2	1	(D)E.YTH.INT.●
			TR	Middlesbrough	08.71	1971-81	408	1	12	
			TR	Newcastle U.	08.82	1982	10	2	0	
			TR	Darlington	08.83	1983	44	/	0	
CRAIG, Ben	Leadgate	06.12.15	Huddersfield T.(*)	Newcastle U.	*	1946-49	57		0	(FB) *Eden Col./d.1982
CRAIG, David J.	Belfast	08.06.54	APP	Newcastle U.	04.62	1963-77	347	5	8	(D)NI-25/NI.U23-1/ NI.YTH.INT.
CRAIG, Derek M.	Dilston	28.07.52	JNRS	Newcastle U.	08.69					(D)
			TR	Darlington	09.75	1975-79	186	1	10	
			TR	York C.	05.80	1980-81	53	/	1	
CRAIG, Jim	Glasgow	30.04.43	Glasgow Celtic	Sheffield Wed.	12.72	1972-73	5	1	0	(FB) S-1

Players Names	Birthplace	Date	Previous Club	League Club	Date Signed	Seasons Played	Apps	Sub	Gls	
CRAIG, Joe	Alloa	14.05.54	Glasgow Celtic	Blackburn Rov.	09.78	1978-80	44	4	8	(F)S-1/S.U23-4
CRAIG, Robert	Consett	16.06.28	JNRS.	Sunderland	+	1949	1		0	(FB)
CRAIG, Robert	Airdrie	08.04.35	T.Lanark	Sheffield Wed.	11.59	1959-61	84		25	(IF)
			TR	Blackburn Rov.	04.62	1961-62	8		3	
			St. Johnstone	Oldham Ath.	03.64	1963-64	18		4	
CRAIG, Tommy B.	Glasgow	21.11.50	Aberdeen	Sheffield Wed.	05.69	1968-74	210	4	38	(M)S-1/S.U23-9/
			TR	Newcastle U.	12.74	1974-77	122	2	23	S.U21-1/S.SCH.INT.
			TR	Aston Villa	01.78	1978	27	/	2	
			TR	Swansea C.	07.78	1979-80	47	5	9	
			TR	Carlisle U.	03.82	1981-83	82	6	9	
CRAIG, William D.	Liverpool	27.12.21		Blackpool	05.46					(OR)
			TR	Southport	08.48	1948	5		2	
CRAIG, William J.	Aberdeen	11.09.29	Dundee	Millwall	08.56	1956-58	18		1	(HB)
CRAINIE, Daniel	Kilsyth	24.05.62	Glasgow Celtic	Wolverhampton W.	12.83	1983	27	1	3	(W)
CRAKER, Laurie	Aylesbury	01.03.53	Chelsea(AM)	Watford	11.72	1972-76	60	6	4	(D)
CRAM, Robert	Hetton le Hole	19.11.30	JNRS	W.B.A.	01.57	1959-66	141	/	25	(WH)Uncle of athlete Steve Cram
			Vancouver	Colchester U.	01.70	1969-71	99	1	4	
CRAMPTON, David	Durham	09.06.44	Spennymoor	Blackburn Rov.	03.68					(G)
			TR	Darlington	07.69	1969	14	/	0	
CRANFIELD, Harry R.	Chesterton	25.12.17	Cambridge T.	Fulham	*	1946	1		0	(OL) nephew of Vic Watson (pre-war international)
			TR	Bristol Rov.	06.47	1947	24		2	
CRANGLE, Jim	Glasgow	04.04.53	Campsie B.W.	York C.	08.72	1972	4	/	0	(W)
CRANSON, Ian	Easington	02.07.64	APP	Ipswich T.	07.82	1983	8	/	0	(D)
CRANSTON, William	Kilmarnock	18.01.42	Saxone YC	Blackpool	08.60	1961-64	33		0	(WH)
			TR	Preston N.E.	12.64	1964-69	80	7	1	
			TR	Oldham Ath.	07.70	1970-72	98	2	2	
CRAVEN, John R.	St. Annes	15.05.47	APP	Blackpool	01.65	1965-70	154	9	24	(F)
			TR	Crystal Palace	09.71	1971-72	56	7	14	
			TR	Coventry C.	05.73	1973-76	86	3	8	
			TR	Plymouth Arg.	01.77	1976-77	45	/	3	
CRAVEN, Mike	Birkenhead	20.11.57		Chester C.	09.75	1975-76	4	/	0	(G)
CRAVEN, Steve	Birkenhead	17.09.57	JNRS	Tranmere Rov.	03.78	1977-81	106	8	17	(D)
			TR	Crewe Alex.	08.82	1982	26	3	3	
CRAVEN, Terry	Barnsley	27.11.44	JNRS	Barnsley	06.63	1964	3		0	(HB)E.YTH.INT.
CRAWFORD, Alan P.	Rotherham	30.10.53	APP	Rotherham U.	06.72	1973-78	233	4	49	(F)
			L	Mansfield T.	01.73	1972	1	1	0	
			TR	Chesterfield	08.79	1979-81	88	6	20	
			TR	Bristol C	08.82	1982-83	75	1	22	
CRAWFORD, Andy	Filey	30.01.59	APP	Derby Co.	01.78	1977-79	16	5	4	(F)
			TR	Blackburn Rov.	10.79	1979-81	56	/	21	
			TR	Bournemouth	11.81	1981-82	31	2	10	
			TR	Cardiff C.	08.83	1983	6	/	1	
			Scarborough	Middlesbrough	10.83	1983	8	1	1	
CRAWFORD, Campbell H.R.	Alexandria	01.12.43	JNRS	W.B.A.	12.60	1963-66	10	/	0	(FB)S.SCH.INT.
			TR	Exeter C.	07.67	1967-73	224	7	3	
CRAWFORD, Graeme	Falkirk	07.08.47	E. Stirling	Sheffield U.	09.68	1969-70	2	/	0	(G)
			L	Mansfield T.	07.71	1971	2	/	0	
			TR	York C.	10.71	1971-76	235	/	0	
			TR	Scunthorpe U.	08.77	1977-79	104	/	0	
			TR	York C.	01.81	1979	17	/	0	
			TR	Rochdale	09.80	1980-82	70	/	0	
CRAWFORD, Ian	Edinburgh	14.07.34	Hearts	West Ham U.	07.61	1961-62	24		5	(OL)S.U23-1
			TR	Scunthorpe U.	02.63	1962-63	35		2	
			TR	Peterborough U.	07.64	1964-68	172		6	
CRAWFORD, J.R. Bruce	Preston	10.10.38	JNRS	Blackpool	05.56	1959-64	98		7	(WH)E.U23-1
			TR	Tranmere Rov.	09.65	1965-66	25	2	5	Son of Robert (pre-war player)
CRAWFORD, James C.	Bellshill	27.09.30	JNRS	Leicester C.	10.47	1950-53	10		2	(IF)
			TR	Plymouth Arg.	03.54	1953-55	25		4	
CRAWFORD, John C.	Falkirk	27.06.22	Ayr U.	Oldham Ath.	07.52	1952-53	24		8	(CF)
			TR	Halifax T.	07.54	1954	11		2	
CRAWFORD, Ray	Portsmouth	13.07.36	JNRS	Portsmouth	12.54	1957-58	18		9	(CF)E-2/E.F.LGE REP.●
			TR	Ipswich T.	09.58	1958-63	197		142	
			TR	Wolverhampton W.	09.63	1963-64	57		39	
			TR	W.B.A.	02.65	1964-65	14	/	6	
			TR	Ipswich T.	03.66	1965-68	123	/	61	
			TR	Charlton Ath.	03.69	1968-69	21	/	7	
			TR	Colchester U.	06.70	1970	45	/	25	
CRAWLEY, Tom	Blantyre	10.11.11	Preston N.E.(*)	Coventry C.	*	1946	13		1	(CH) *Motherwell/d.1977
CRAWSHAW, Cyril B.	York	02.03.16	Stalybridge	Hull C.	06.46	1946	2		1	(IF) +Exeter C.

Players Names	Birthplace	Date	Previous Club	League Club	Date Signed	Seasons Played	Career Record Apps	Sub	Gls	
CREAMER, Peter A.	Hartlepool	20.09.53	APP	Middlesbrough	10.70	1972-73	9	/	0	(D)E.SCH.INT.
			L	York C.	11.75	1975	4	/	0	
			TR	Doncaster Rov.	12.75	1975-76	31	1	0	
			TR	Hartlepool U.	10.76	1976-77	63	/	3	
			Gateshead	Rochdale	N/C	1978	18	2	0	
CREANE, Gerry	Lincoln	02.02.62	APP	Lincoln C.	02.80	1978-82	6	1	0	(D)
CRELLIN, Andrew	Gainsborough	11.10.54	Ashby Inst.	Doncaster Rov.	03.74	1974	4	/	0	(FB)
CRERAND, Pat T.	Glasgow	19.02.39	Glasgow Celtic	Manchester U.	02.63	1962-70	304	/	10	(WH)S-16/S.U23-1/ S.F.LGE REP.
CRESSWELL, Corbett	Sunderland	03.08.32	B.Auckland	Carlisle U.	03.58	1957-58	14		2	(CH)E.AMAT.INT./ Son of pre-war international
CRESSWELL, Peter F.	Linby	09.11.35	Heanor T.	Derby Co.	04.54	1954-56	12		2	(OR)
CRESSWELL, Philip	Hucknall	11.05.33	JNRS	Coventry C.	05.50	1954	2		0	(F)
CRIBLEY, Alex	Liverpool	01.04.57		Liverpool	06.78					(D)
			TR	Wigan Ath.	10.80	1980-83	144	2	2	
CRICHTON, George	Leslie(Fife)	11.12.25	Loughboro.Coll.	Workington	N/L	1951	4		0	(FB)
CRICKETT, Norman	Carlisle	13.10.32		Carlisle U.	11.52	1955	1		0	(FB)
CRICKMORE, Charlie	Hull	11.02.42	JNRS	Hull C.	02.59	1959-61	53		13	(OL)
			TR	Bournemouth	07.62	1962-65	128	/	17	
			TR	Gillingham	06.66	1966-67	53	/	13	
			TR	Rotherham U.	11.67	1967	7	1	1	
			TR	Norwich C.	01.68	1967-69	54	2	9	
			TR	Notts. Co.	03.70	1969-71	59	/	11	
CRICKSON, Gerry E.	Dover	21.09.34	JNRS	Q.P.R.	09.51	1952-55	5		0	(WH)E.YTH.INT./E.SCH.INT.
CRIPPS, Harry R.	Dereham	29.04.41	JNRS	West Ham U.	09.58					(FB)
			TR	Millwall	06.61	1961-74	387	10	38	
			TR	Charlton Ath.	10.74	1974-75	17	3	4	
CRIPSEY, Brian	Hull	26.06.31	Brunswick Inst.	Hull C.	11.51	1952-58	145		19	(OL)
			TR	Wrexham	09.58	1958-59	27		3	
CRISP, Ron J.	Slough	24.09.38	Dulwich H.	Watford	01.61	1960-64	89		14	(IF)
			TR	Brentford	08.65	1965-66	17	/	0	
CRISPIN, Tim	Leicester	07.06.48		Notts.Co.	07.66	1966-67	9	/	0	(FB)
			TR	Lincoln C.	07.68					
CROFT, Alex R.	Chester	17.06.37		Chester C.	08.58	1958-60	53		3	(F)
CROFT, Charles	Thornhill	26.11.18		Huddersfield T.	+					
			TR	Mansfield T.	05.47	1947-49	84		5	
CROFT, Stuart D.	Ashington	12.04.54	APP	Hull C.	04.72	1972-80	187	3	4	(D)
			TR	Portsmouth	03.81	1980	6	/	1	
			TR	York C.	08.81	1981	14	/	0	
CROKER, Edward A.	Kingston	13.02.24	Dartford	Charlton Ath.	07.48	1950	8		0	(CH) F.A. Secretary
CROKER, Peter H.	Kingston	21.12.21	Bromley	Charlton Ath.	+	1946-50	59		0	(RB)
			TR	Watford	06.52	1952	22		0	
CROMACK, David C.	Leeds	22.12.48	Hull C.(AM)	Doncaster Rov.	11.66	1966	8	/	0	(G)
			TR	Huddersfield T.	07.67					
CROMACK, Vic	Mansfield	17.03.20		Mansfield T.	+	1946	9		0	(G)
CROMBIE, Dean	Lincoln	09.08.57	Ruston Spts.	Lincoln C.	02.77	1976-77	33	/	0	(D)
			TR	Grimsby T.	08.78	1978-83	225	3	2	
CROMBIE, Tom R.	Kirkcaldy	03.06.30	Jeanfield Swifts	Blackpool	08.51					(LB)
			TR	Gillingham	07.55	1955-56	17		0	
CROMPTON, Alan	Manchester	06.03.58	APP	Sunderland	03.75					(F)
			TR	Blackburn Rov.	07.76	1976	2	2	0	
			TR	Wigan Ath.	N/L	1978-79	7	7	0	
CROMPTON, David G.	Wigan	06.03.45		Rochdale	AM	1966-67	15	2	0	(WH)
CROMPTON, Dennis	Tonge Moor	12.03.42	Wigan Ath.	Burnley	12.59					(HB)
			TR	Doncaster Rov.	06.63	1963	23		0	
CROMPTON, John	Manchester	18.12.21	Oldham Ath.(AM)	Manchester U.	+	1946-55	191		0	(G)
CROMPTON, Steve W.	Rossett	03.12.58	Wolverhampton W.(APP)	Hereford U.	02.77	1976-78	30	4	6	(F)
CRONIN, Tom P.	Richmond	17.12.32	E.Sheen.Ath.	Fulham	09.50	1953-54	2		0	(WH)
			TR	Reading	06.56	1956-57	30		4	
CROOK, Alf R.	Brewood	13.08.23	Boulton Paul	Wolverhampton W.	+	1948	1		0	(FB)
CROOK, George	Durham	30.01.35		Oldham Ath.	02.53	1953-57	57		13	(IF)
			TR	Middlesbrough	11.58					
CROOK, Ian S.	Romford	18.01.63	APP	Tottenham H.	08.80	1981-83	5	4	0	(M)
CROOK, Les R.	Manchester	26.06.49		Oxford U.	10.68	1968	1	/	0	(IF)
			TR	Hartlepool U.	07.70	1970	23	2	3	
CROOK, Walter	Chorley	28.04.13	JNRS	Blackburn Rov.	*	1946	21		0	(FB)
			TR	Bolton W.	05.47	1947	28		0	
CROOK, William C.	Wolverhampton	07.06.26	JNRS	Wolverhampton W.	+	1946-52	196		1	(WH)
			TR	Walsall	10.54	1954-55	46		2	
CROOKES, Robert E.	Retford	29.02.24	Retford T.	Notts. Co.	06.49	1949-55	177		45	(IF)

Players Names	Birthplace	Date	Previous Club	League Club	Date Signed	Seasons Played	Career Record Apps	Sub	Gls	
CROOKS, Garth A.	Stoke	10.03.58	APP	Stoke C.	03.76	1975-79	141	6	48	(F).E.U21-4
			TR	Tottenham H.	07.80	1980-83	99	4	38	
			L	Manchester U.	11.83	1983	6	1	2	
CROOKS, Sammy D.	Bearpark	16.01.08	Durham C.	Derby Co.	*	1946	3		0	(OR)E-26/E.F.LGE REP./d.1981
CROPLEY, Alex	Aldershot	16.01.51	Hibernian	Arsenal	12.74	1974-76	29	1	5	(M)S-2/S.U23-3/
			TR	Aston Villa	09.78	1976-79	65	2	7	Son of John
			L	Newcastle U.	02.80	1979	3	/	0	
			TR	Portsmouth	09.81	1981	8	2	2	
CROPLEY, John T.	Edinburgh	27.09.24	Tranent J.	Aldershot	10.46	1947-53	162		3	(WH)
CROSBIE, Robert G.	Glasgow	02.09.25		Bury	05.47	1947-48	9		5	(CF)
			TR	Bradford P.A.	05.49	1949-53	139		72	
			TR	Hull C.	10.53	1953-54	61		22	
			TR	Grimsby T.	07.55	1955-56	64		45	
CROSBY, Geoff J.	Stoke	24.08.31	Leek T.	Stockport Co.	09.52	1952-53	5		1	(F)
CROSBY, Malcolm	Sth. Shield	04.07.54	APP	Aldershot	07.72	1971-81	272	22	23	(M)
			TR	York C.	11.81	1981-83	88	4	4	
CROSBY, Phil	Leeds	09.11.62	APP	Grimsby T.	09.80	1979-82	34	5	1	(D)E.YTH INT.
			TR	Rotherham U.	08.83	1983	39	/	0	
CROSLAND, John R.	St. Annes	10.11.22	Ansdell Rov.	Blackpool	+	1946-53	68		0	(FB) E'B'-2/
			TR	Bournemouth	06.54	1954-56	106		0	
CROSS, David	Heywood	08.12.50	JNRS	Rochdale	08.69	1969-71	50	9	21	(F)
			TR	Norwich C.	10.71	1971-73	83	1	21	
			TR	Coventry C.	11.73	1973-76	90	1	29	
			TR	W.B.A.	11.76	1976-77	38	/	18	
			TR	West Ham U.	12.77	1977-81	178	1	77	
			TR	Manchester C.	08.82	1982	31	/	12	
			Vancouver W.	Oldham Ath.	10.83	1983	18	4	6	
CROSS, Graham F.	Leicester	15.11.43	APP	Leicester C.	11.60	1960-75	495	3	29	(D)●Leicester Cricketer
			L	Chesterfield	03.76	1975	12	/	0	
			TR	Brighton & H.A.	06.76	1976	46	/	3	
			TR	Preston N.E.	07.77	1977-78	45	/	1	
			Enderby	Lincoln C.	03.79	1978	19	/	0	
CROSS, Jack	Bury	05.02.27	Guildford C.	Bournemouth	06.47	1947-53	137		64	(CF)
			TR	Northampton T.	10.53	1953	10		10	
			TR	Sheffield U.	02.54	1953-55	44		16	
			TR	Reading	10.55	1955	15		7	
CROSS, Jim K.	Liverpool	03.12.26		Everton	10.50					(HB)
			TR	Swindon T.	07.53	1953-57	155		5	
CROSS, Mick J.	Little Hulton	25.04.56	Bolton W.(APP)	Stockport Co.	07.75	1975	27	/	2	(IF)
CROSS, Nicky J.R.	Birmingham	07.02.61	APP	W.B.A.	02.79	1980-83	53	28	10	(M)
CROSS, Paul	Barnsley	31.10.65	APP	Barnsley	11.83	1982	1	/	0	(D)
CROSS, Roger G.	E. Ham	20.10.48	APP	West Ham U.	07.64	1968-69	5	2	1	(F)
			L	Orient	10.68	1968	4	2	2	
			TR	Brentford	03.70	1969-71	62	/	18	
			TR	Fulham	09.71	1971-72	39	/	8	
			TR	Brentford	12.72	1972-76	141	4	52	
			TR	Millwall	01.77	1976-78	9	3	0	
CROSS, Roy	Walsall	04.12.47	JNRS	Walsall	07.66	1966-69	11	1	0	(CH)
			TR	Port Vale	07.70	1970-74	135		0	
CROSS, Steve C.	Wolverhampton	22.12.59	APP	Shrewsbury T.	12.77	1976-83	165	22	20	(M)
CROSSAN, Eddie	Londonderry	17.11.25	Derry C.	Blackburn Rov.	11.47	1947-56	287		73	(IF) NI-3
			TR	Tranmere Rov.	08.57	1957	39		6	
CROSSAN, Errol G.	Canada	06.10.30	N. Westminster R.	Manchester C.	01.54					(F)
			TR	Gillingham	07.55	1955-56	75		16	
			TR	Southend U.	08.57	1957-58	40		11	
			TR	Norwich C.	09.58	1958-60	102		28	
			TR	Orient	01.61	1960	8		1	
CROSSAN, John A.	Londonderry	29.11.38	Standard Liege	Sunderland	10.62	1962-64	82		39	(IF) NI-23
			TR	Manchester C.	01.65	1964-66	94	/	24	
			TR	Middlesbrough	08.67	1967-69	54	2	8	
CROSSLEY, John	Belfast	19.07.22	Portsmouth(+)	Reading	07.46	1946	1		0	(LB)
CROSSLEY, Paul	Rochdale	14.07.48	JNRS	Rochdale	09.65	1965-66	17	/	2	(F)
			TR	Preston N.E.	11.66	1966-67	3	/	0	
			L	Southport	09.68	1968	10	/	2	
			TR	Tranmere Rov.	06.69	1969-75	186	17	37	
			TR	Chester C.	09.75	1975-77	93	6	26	
CROSSLEY, Roy	Hebden Bridge	16.10.23		Huddersfield T.	05.46					(IF) Brother of Russell
				Halifax T.	09.48	1948-50	41		15	
CROSSLEY, Russell	Hebden Bridge	25.06.27	JNRS	Liverpool	06.47	1950-53	68		0	(G)
				Shrewsbury T.	07.54	1954-59	173		0	
CROSSLEY, Terry	Rockferry	24.02.36	Bangor Univ.	Oldham Ath.	07.58	1957	2		1	(OL)
CROSSON, David	Durham	24.11.52	JNRS	Newcastle U.	11.70	1973-74	6	/	0	(D)
			TR	Darlington	08.75	1975-79	115	13	2	

Players Names	Birthplace	Date	Previous Club	League Club	Date Signed	Seasons Played	Career Record Apps	Sub	Gls	
CROTTY, Colin	Aberfan	12.2.51	JNRS	Swansea C.	AM	1968	1	1	1	(F)
CROUCH, Nigel J.	Ardleigh	24.11.58	APP	Ipswich T.	08.78					(D)
			L	Lincoln C.	08.79	1979	7	/	0	
			TR	Colchester U.	07.80	1980	9	1	0	
CROWE, Alex A.	Motherwell	24.11.24	St.Mirren	Ipswich T.	05.53	1953-54	50		9	(IF)
CROWE, Charlie A.	Byker	30.10.24	Wallsend St.L.	Newcastle U.	+	1946-56	179		5	(WH)
			TR	Mansfield T.	02.57	1956-57	37		0	
CROWE, Chris	Newcastle	11.06.39	JNRS	Leeds U.	06.56	1956-59	95		27	(IF)E-1/E.U23-4/
			TR	Blackburn Rov.	03.60	1959-61	51		6	E.YTH.INT./S.SCH.INT.
			TR	Wolverhampton W.	02.62	1961-63	83		24	
			TR	Nottingham F.	08.64	1964-66	74	/	12	
			TR	Bristol C.	01.67	1966-68	66	1	13	
			TR	Walsall	09.69	1969	10	3	1	
CROWE, Mark A.	Southwold	21.01.65	APP	Norwich C.	01.83	1982	0	1	0	(D)
CROWE, Matt J.	Bathgate	04.07.32	Bathgate Th.	Bradford P.A.	07.49	1952	1		0	(WH)
			Partick Th.	Norwich C.	05.57	1957-61	186		14	
			TR	Brentford	07.62	1962-63	73		0	
CROWE, Mick	Ulverston	13.08.42	Ulverston Ath.	Barrow	08.60	1960-62	15		1	(IF)
CROWE, Vic H.	Abercynon	31.01.32	W.B.A.(AM)	Aston Villa	06.52	1954-63	294		10	(WH) W-16
			TR	Peterborough U.	07.64	1964-66	56	/	0	
CROWN, David I.	Enfield	16.02.58	Walthamstow	Brentford	07.80	1980-81	44	2	8	(F)
			TR	Portsmouth	10.81	1981-82	25	3	2	
			L	Exeter C.	03.83	1982	6	1	3	
			TR	Reading	08.83	1983	45	/	7	
CROWSHAW, Alan	Willenhall	12.12.32	Bloxwich Strollers	W.B.A.	05.50	1954-55	11		2	(IF)
			TR	Derby Co.	06.56	1956-57	18		6	
			TR	Millwall	05.58	1958-59	49		7	
CROWTHER, Ken	Halifax	17.12.24	Halifax T.(AM)	Burnley	+					(IF)
			TR	Bradford P.A.	07.48	1948	6		1	
			TR	Rochdale	08.50	1950	2		0	
CROWTHER, Stan	Bilston	03.09.35	Bilston	Aston Villa	08.55	1956-57	50		4	(WH) E.U23-3
			TR	Manchester U.	02.58	1957-58	13		0	
			TR	Chelsea	12.58	1958-59	51		0	
			TR	Brighton & H.A.	03.61	1960	4		0	
CROWTHER, Steve	Romiley	16.01.55		Stockport Co.	01.74	1973-74	42	2	4	(FB)
			TR	Hartlepool U.	07.75	1975	3	/	0	
CROY, John	Falkirk	23.02.25	T.Lanark	Northampton T.	07.50	1951-54	24		0	(FB)
CROZIER, Joe	Coatbridge	02.12.14	E.Fife	Brentford	*	1946-48	123		0	(G)
CRUDGINGTON, Geoff	Wolverhampton	14.02.52	Wolverhampton W.(AM)	Aston Villa	09.69	1970-71	4	/	0	(G)E.SCH.INT.
			L	Bradford C.	03.71	1970	1	/	0	
			TR	Crewe Alex.	03.72	1971-77	250	/	0	
			TR	Swansea C.	07.78	1978-79	52	/	0	
			TR	Plymouth Arg.	10.79	1979-83	219	/	0	
CRUICKSHANK, Frank J.	Falkirk	20.11.31	Nuneaton	Notts. Co.	01.50	1953-59	151		5	(FB)
CRUICKSHANK, George	Malaya	22.07.31	Q. of South	Carlisle U.	08.57	1957	14		0	
CRUICKSHANK, J. Paul	Oldham	18.01.60	APP	Blackpool	08.77					(F)
			TR	Bury	07.79	1979-82	65	17	4	
CRUMBLEHULME, Kevin	Manchester	17.06.52	APP	Oldham Ath.	07.70	1971	2	/	0	(WH)
CRUMPLIN, Ian	Lemington	12.09.54	Blue Star	Hartlepool U.	06.78	1978	25	4	5	(F)
CRUSE, Peter	London	10.01.51	Slough T.	Arsenal	04.72					(IF) E.AMAT.INT.
			TR	Luton T.	07.73	1973	3	1	0	
			L	Shrewsbury T.	02.74	1973	2	/	0	
CRUTCHLEY, W. Ron	Walsall	20.06.22		Walsall	+	1946-49	62		4	(WH)
			TR	Shrewsbury T.	09.50	1950-53	146		1	
CRYLE, George	Aberdeen	10.04.28	JNRS	Wolverhampton W.	+					(WH)
			TR	Reading	06.48	1948-50	8		3	
			Ayr U.	Swindon T.	08.52	1952	12		0	
CUBIE, Neil	S. Africa	03.11.32	Clyde S.A.	Bury	10.56					
			TR	Hull C.	07.57	1957	4		0	
CUDDIHEY, Russell	Accrington	08.09.39		Accrington St.	09.60	1960	10		0	(HB)
CUDDY, Paul	Radcliffe	21.02.59	JNRS	Rochdale	N/C	1977	0	1	0	(D)
CUFF, Pat J.	Middlesbrough	19.03.52	APP	Middlesbrough	05.69	1973-77	31	/.	0	(G)E.SCH.INT.
			L	Grimsby T.	09.71	1971	2	/	0	
			TR	Millwall	08.78	1978	42	/	0	
			TR	Darlington	06.80	1980-82	110	/.	0	
CULLEN, Mike J.	Glasgow	03.07.31	Douglasdale J.	Luton T.	08.49	1951-57	111		16	(OL)S-1/S'B'-1
			TR	Grimsby T.	04.58	1958-62	178		35	
			TR	Derby Co.	12.62	1962-64	24		5	
CULLEN, Pat J.	Mexborough	09.08.49	Mexborough	Halifax T.	AM	1967-73	1	5	0	EI.AMAT.INT.
CULLEN, S. John R.	Oxford	09.10.62	APP	Reading	10.80	1979-81	14	6	0	(D)

Players Names	Birthplace	Date	Previous Club	League Club	Date Signed	Seasons Played	Career Record Apps	Sub	Gls	
CULLERTON, Mike	Edinburgh	25.11.48		Port Vale	01.66	1965-68	95	2	22	(F)
			L	Chester C.	03.69	1968	5	2	0	
			Stafford Rgrs.	Port Vale	07.75	1975-77	67	16	28	
CULLINGFORD, Robert	Bradford	03.12.53	JNRS	Bradford C.	AM	1969-71	1	1	0	
CULLIS, Stan	Ellesmere Port	25.10.15	Ellesmere Port	Wolverhampton W.	*	1946	37		0	(CH)E-12/E.F.LGE REP.
CULLUM, Arthur R.	Colchester	28.01.31		Colchester U.	01.51	1950-53	2		1	(F)
CULLUM, Riley G.	West Ham	02.04.23	Dartford	Charlton Ath.	10.47	1949-52	32		6	(IF)
CULVERHOUSE, Ian B.	Bishops Stortford	22.09.64	APP	Tottenham H.	09.82	1983	1	1	0	(D)
CUMBES, Jim	Manchester	04.05.44	Runcorn	Tranmere Rov.	09.68	1966-69	137	/	0	(G)Worc/Lancs/Surrey/Warwicks
			TR	W.B.A.	08.69	1969-71	64	/	0	Warwicks.Cricketer
			TR	Aston Villa	10.71	1971-75	157	/	0	
			Portland Timbers	Southport	N/C	1977	19	/	0	
CUMMING, David S.	Aberdeen	06.05.10	Aberdeen	Middlesbrough	*	1946	37		0	(G) S-1
CUMMING, Gordon	Renfrew	23.01.48	Glasgow U.	Arsenal	01.65					(M)
			TR	Reading	12.69	1969-77	278	18	51	
CUMMING, Robert	Airdrie	07.12.55	Baillieston J.	Grimsby T.	03.74	1974-83	280	18	49	(M)
CUMMINGS, George	Thornbridge	05.06.13	Partick Th.	Aston Villa	*	1946-48	95		0	(FB)S-9/S.F.LGE REP.
CUMMINGS, John	Greenock	05.05.44	Aberdeen	Port Vale	08.65	1965	2	1	0	(CF)
CUMMINGS, Robert D.	Ashington	17.11.35	N.Hartley	Newcastle U.	05.54					(F)
			Aberdeen	Newcastle U.	10.63	1963-65	43	1	14	
			TR	Darlington	10.65	1965-67	72	1	43	
			TR	Hartlepool U.	02.68	1967-68	48	4	12	
CUMMINGS, Tom S.	Sunderland	12.09.28	Stanley U.	Burnley	10.47	1948-62	434		3	(CH)E'B'-3/E.F.LGE REP.●
			TR	Mansfield T.	03.63	1962-63	11		0	
CUMMINS, George P.	Dublin	12.03.31	St.Patricks	Everton	11.50	1951-52	24		0	(IF) EI-19
			TR	Luton T.	08.53	1953-60	186		21	
			Cambridge C.	Hull C.	11.62	1962-63	21		2	
CUMMINS, Jim W.H.	Hebburn	15.02.25	Horden CW	Southport	09.49	1949	9		1	(CF)
CUMMINS, Stan	Durham	06.12.58	APP	Middlesbrough	12.76	1976-79	39	5	9	(M)
			TR	Sunderland	11.79	1979-82	132	1	29	
			TR	Crystal Palace	08.83	1983	17	1	4	
CUMNER, R. Horace	Aberdare	31.03.18	Hull C.(*)	Arsenal	*					(IF)
			TR	Notts.Co.	08.46	1946-47	66		10	
			TR	Watford	07.48	1948-50	62		8	
			TR	Scunthorpe U.	09.50	1950-52	104		22	
			TR	Bradford C.	08.53					
CUNLIFFE, Arthur	Blackrod	05.02.09	Hull C.(*)	Rochdale	+	1946	23		5	(OL)*Chorley/Blackburn Rov./
										Aston Villa/Middlesbrough/
										Burnley/E-2
CUNLIFFE J. Graham	Hindley	16.06.36		Bolton W.	01.55	1957-62	25		0	(WH)
			TR	Rochdale	07.64	1964	36		0	
CUNLIFFE, Jack	Wigan	04.02.30		Port Vale	12.50	1950-59	283		51	(OL)
			TR	Stoke C.	09.59	1959	26		3	
CUNLIFFE, Jim N.	Blackrod	05.07.12	Adlington	Everton	*					(IF) Cousin of Arthur/
			TR	Rochdale	09.46	1946	2		0	E-1
CUNLIFFE, Jim W.	Adlington	04.10.41	Horwich R.M.I.	Stockport Co.	AM	1960	1		0	(CF) Nephew of Jim
CUNLIFFE, Reg	Wigan	04.12.20	Wigan Ath.	Swansea C.	06.46	1946-47	2		0	(LB)
CUNLIFFE, Robert	Manchester	17.05.45	APP	Manchester C.	08.62	1963	3		1	(F)
			TR	York C.	06.65	1965	11	1	2	
CUNLIFFE, Robert A.	Bryn	27.12.28		Manchester C.	+	1949-55	44		9	(OL)
			TR	Chesterfield	06.56	1956-57	62		18	
			TR	Southport	07.58	1958	17		2	
CUNNING, Robert R.	Dunfermline	12.02.30	Port Glasgow	Sunderland	06.50	1950	4		0	(OL)
CUNNINGHAM, Anthony E.	W. Indies	12.11.57	Stourbridge	Lincoln C.	05.79	1979-82	111	12	32	(F)
			TR	Barnsley	09.82	1982-83	40	2	11	
			TR	Sheffield Wed.	11.83	1983	26	2	5	
CUNNINGHAM, David	Kirkcaldy	10.08.53	Brechin	Southend U.	04.73	1973-76	56	4	4	(F)
			L	Hartlepool U.	03.77	1976	10	2	1	
			TR	Swindon T.	06.77	1977-78	18	5	3	
			L	Peterborough U.	11.78	1978	4	/	1	
			TR	Aston Villa	12.78					
			TR	Hereford U.	08.79	1979	28	2	2	
			TR	Newport Co.	08.80					
CUNNINGHAM, Edward	South Shields	20.03.28		Blackburn Rov.	09.49					(HB)
			TR	Chesterfield	08.52	1952-54	56		0	
CUNNINGHAM, Edwin	Jarrow	20.06.19		Bristol C.	+	1946	1		0	
CUNNINGHAM, Hugh	Kirkintilloch	05.04.47	Glasgow Celtic	Fulham	05.66	1967	0	1	0	(HB)
CUNNINGHAM, Ian	Glasgow	06.09.56	APP	Bournemouth	08.74	1974-80	180	8	4	(D)
CUNNINGHAM, Ken H.	Glasgow	26.10.41	Falkirk	Hartlepool U.	07.63	1963	2		0	(CF)

Players Names	Birthplace	Date	Previous Club	League Club	Date Signed	Seasons Played	Apps	Sub	Gls	
CUNNINGHAM, Laurie	Archway	08.03.56	APP	Orient	07.74	1974-76	72	3	15	(W)E.U21-6/E-6
			TR	W.B.A.	03.77	1976-78	81	5	21	
			Real Madrid	Manchester U.	03.83	1982	3	2	1	
CUNNINGHAM, Laurie	Consett	20.10.21	Consett U.	Barnsley	+	1946-47	52		1	(FB)
			TR	Bournemouth	06.48	1948-56	273		0	
CUNNINGHAM, Tommy	London	07.12.55	APP	Chelsea	10.73					(D)
			TR	Q.P.R.	05.75	1976-78	27	3	2	
			TR	Wimbledon	03.79	1978-81	99	/	12	
			TR	Orient	09.81	1981-83	82	/	9	
CUNNINGHAM, William C.	Fife	22.02.25	Airdrie	Preston N.E.	07.49	1949-62	440		3	(FB)S-8/Cousin of Jim C.
			TR	Southport	03.64	1964	12		0	Baxter (Preston N.E.)●
CUNNINGHAM, William E.	Mallusk	20.02.30	St.Mirren	Leicester C.	12.54	1954-59	127		4	(FB) NI-30●
CUNNINGHAM, William L.	Paisley	11.07.38	T.Lanark	Barnsley	07.64	1964	24		0	(WH)
CUNNINGTON, Shaun C.	Bourne	04.01.66	JNRS	Wrexham	01.84	1982-83	43	3	0	(D)
CURBISHLEY, L.C. (Alan)	Forest Gate	08.11.57	APP	West Ham U.	07.75	1974-78	78	7	5	(M)E.YTH.INT./
			TR	Birmingham C.	07.79	1979-82	128	2	11	E.SCH.INT./E.U21-1
			TR	Aston Villa	03.83	1982-83	31	12	1	
CURLE, Keith	Bristol	14.11.63	APP	Bristol Rov.	11.81	1981-82	21	11	4	(F)
			TR	Torquay U.	11.83	1983	16	/	5	
			TR	Bristol C.	03.84	1983	5	1	0	
CURLEY, Tom,	Glasgow	11.06.45	Glasgow Celtic	Brentford	08.65	1965-66	40	/	6	(F)
			TR	Crewe Alex.	08.67	1967-68	48	4	7	
CURLEY, William	Trimdon	20.11.45	APP	Darlington	11.63	1962-65	32	/	1	(FB)
CURRAN, E. (Terry)	Kinsley	20.03.55	JNRS	Doncaster Rov.	07.73	1973-75	67	1	11	(W)
			TR	Nottingham F.	08.75	1975-76	46	2	12	
			L	Bury	10.77	1977	2	/	0	
			TR	Derby Co.	11.77	1977	26	/	2	
			TR	Southampton	08.78	1978	25	1	0	
			TR	Sheffield Wed.	03.79	1978-81	122	3	35	
			TR	Sheffield U.	08.82	1982	31	2	3	
			L	Everton	12.82	1982	7	/	1	
			TR	Everton	09.83	1983	8	/	0	
CURRAN, Frank	Royton	31.05.17	Bristol C.(+)	Bristol Rov.	05.46	1946	11		3	(IF)*Southport/Accrington St.
			TR	Tranmere Rov.	06.47	1947	17		7	
CURRAN, Hugh	Glasgow	25.09.43	T. Lanark	Millwall	03.64	1963-65	58	/	27	(F)S-5
			TR	Norwich C.	01.66	1965-68	112	/	46	
			TR	Wolverhampton W.	01.69	1968-71	77	5	40	
			TR	Oxford U.	09.72	1972-74	69	1	26	
			TR	Bolton W.	09.74	1974-76	40	7	13	
			TR	Oxford U.	07.77	1977-78	30	5	11	
CURRAN, Jim	Macclesfield	24.09.47		Newcaslfied U.	10.64					(G)
				Oldham Ath	12.66	1966	3	/	0	
			TR	Crewe Alex.	04.67	1968	3	/	0	
CURRAN, John	Glasgow	22.06.24	E.Fife	Shrewsbury T.	08.56	1956	24		0	(G)
			TR	Watford	06.57	1957	30		0	
CURRAN, Pat J.	Sunderland	14.09.18	Ipswich T.(*)	Watford	+					(IF)
			TR	Bradford C.	06.47	1947	5		1	
CURRAN, Terry W.	Staines	29.06.40	Tottenham H.(AM)	Brentford	09.57	1960	5		0	(F)
CURRIE, Anthony W.	Edgware	01.01.50	APP	Watford	05.67	1967	17	1	9	(M)E-17/E.U23-13/
			TR	Sheffield U.	02.68	1967-75	313	/	55	E.F.LGE REP./E.YTH.INT.●
			TR	Leeds U.	06.76	1976-78	102	/	11	
			TR	Q.P.R.	08.79	1979-82	79	2	5	
			Chesham U.	Torquay U.	N/C	1983	9	/	0	
CURRIE, Charles J.	Belfast	17.04.20	Belfast Celtic	Bradford P.A.	06.49	1949-53	118		2	(CH) IRISH LGE REP.
CURRIE, David N.	Stockton	27.11.62		Middlesbrough	02.82	1981-83	39	9	15	(F)
CURRIE, Jim A.C.	Glasgow	25.04.32	Falkirk	Exeter C.	06.56	1956-57	54		19	(F)
			TR	Workington	10.57	1957-59	23		8	
CURRIE, Jim T.	Stirling	06.08.48		Scunthorpe U.	09.68	1968-69	4	2	0	(HB)
CURRIE, John	Motherwell	19.03.35	Cleland J.	Accrington St.	11.53	1953-54	16		3	(IR)
CURRIE, John E.	Liverpool	18.03.21	Stafford Rgrs.	Bournemouth	AM	1946	8		2	(OR)
			TR	Port Vale	06.47	1947	9		4	
CURRIE, John G.	Dumfries	07.04.39		Leicester C.	04.57					(WH) S.SCH.INT.
			TR	Workington	07.61	1961-62	55		2	
			TR	Chester C.	07.63	1963	2		0	
CURRIE, Malcolm	Rutherglen	05.02.32	Glencairn	Bradford C.	07.56	1956-60	136		1	(FB)
CURRY, Robert	Galeshead	02.11.18	Gainsborough	Colchester U.	N/L	1950	32		13	(IR)+Sheffield U.
CURRY, William M.	Newcastle	12.10.35		Newcastle U.	10.53	1954-58	80		34	(CF)E.U23-1●
			TR	Brighton & H.A.	07.59	1959-60	49		26	
			TR	Derby Co.	10.60	1960-64	148		63	
			TR	Mansfield T.	02.65	1964-67	103		53	
			TR	Chesterfield	01.68	1967-68	14		2	
CURTIN, Doug J.	Cardiff	15.09.47	Cardiff C.(APP)	Mansfield T.	11.65	1965	3	/	0	(OL) W.SCH.INT

Players Names	Birthplace	Date	Previous Club	League Club	Date Signed	Seasons Played	Apps	Sub	Gls	
CURTIS, Alan T.	Rhondda	16.04.54	JNRS	Swansea C.	07.72	1972-78	244	4	72	(F)W-30/W.E23-1/
			TR	Leeds U.	06.79	1979-80	28	/	5	W.U.21-1
			TR	Swansea C.	12.80	1980-83	82	8	21	
			TR	Southampton	11.83	1983	8	1	0	
CURTIS, Dermot	Dublin	26.08.32	Shelbourne	Bristol C.	09.56	1956-57	26		16	(CF)EI-17
			TR	Ipswich T.	09.58	1958-62	41		17	
			TR	Exeter C.	08.63	1963-65	98	/	23	
			TR	Torquay U.	08.66	1966	12	/	1	
			TR	Exeter C.	06.67	1967-68	64	3	10	
CURTIS, George, F.	Orsett	03.12.19	Anglo(Purfleet)	Arsenal	*	1946	11		0	(WH)
			TR	Southampton	08.47	1947-51	174		11	
CURTIS, George W.	Dover	05.05.39	Snowdown Col.	Coventry C.	05.56	1955-69	483	3	11	(CH) E.YTH.INT.●
			TR	Aston Villa	12.69	1969-71	51	/	3	
CURTIS, John	Poulton	02.09.54	APP	Blackpool	09.72	1973-76	96	6	0	(D)
			TR	Blackburn Rov.	07.77	1977-78	9	1	0	
			TR	Wigan Ath.	03.79	1978-80	32	/	0	
CURTIS, Norman W.	Dinnington	10.09.24	Gainsborough	Sheffield Wed.	01.50	1950-59	310		21	(FB)
			TR	Doncaster Rov.	08.60	1960	39		3	
CURTIS, Paul A.E.	London	01.07.63	APP	Charlton Ath.	07.81	1982-83	42	2	4	(D)
CURTIS, Robert D.	Langwith	25.01.50	APP	Charlton Ath.	02.67	1966-77	324	13	35	(D)
			TR	Mansfield T.	02.78	1977-79	69	4	7	
CURWEN, Eric	Blackpool	16.09.47	APP	Everton	05.65					(FB) E.SCH.INT.
			TR	Southport	12.66	1966-68	89	/	0	
CURZON, Terry	Winsford	26.05.36	Bolton W.(AM)	Crewe Alex.	10.53	1953-56	11		1	(OL)
CUSACK, David S.	Rotherham	06.06.56	APP	Sheffield Wed.	10.75	1957-77	92	3	1	(D)
			TR	Southend U.	09.78	1978-82	186	/	17	
			TR	Millwall	03.83	1982-83	53	/	1	
CUSH, Wilbur	Lurgan	10.06.28	Glenavon	Leeds U.	11.57	1957-59	87		9	(WH)N.I.-26/IRISH LGE REP./
										d.1981
CUSHIN, Edward	Whitehaven	27.01.27	Lowca	Workington	N/L	1951-55	119		4	(FB)
CUSHLEY, John	Blantyre	21.01.43	Glasgow Celtic	West Ham U.	07.67	1967-69	38	/	0	(CH)
CUSHLOW, Richard	Shotton	15.06.20	Murton Col.	Chesterfield	05.46	1946-47	34		0	(CH)
			TR	Sheffield U.	12.47					
			TR	Derby Co.	03.48	1948-49	2		0	
			TR	Crystal Palace	02.51	1950-51	28		0	
CUTBUSH, W. John	Malta	28.06.49	APP	Tottenham H.	09.66					(D)Son of Amat. Int.
			TR	Fulham	07.72	1972-76	132	3	3	
			TR	Sheffield U.	03.77	1976-80	126	3	1	
CUTHBERT, Ean R.	Ayr	05.02.42	Alyth U.	Blackpool	07.59					(FB)
			TR	Stockport Co.	07.63	1963-65	94	/	0	
			TR	Crewe Alex.	11.66	1966	1	/	0	
CUTHBERTSON, Jim	Sunderland	07.12.47	APP	Bradford C.	07.66	1966-67	25	3	7	(F)
CUTHBERTSON, John	Glasgow	10.03.32		Mansfield T.	10.53	1953	3		0	
CUTLER, Chris P.	Manchester	07.04.64	JNRS	Bury	08.81	1981-83	7	12	2	(F)
CUTLER, Paul	Welwyn	18.06.46	APP	Crystal Palace	04.64	1964-65	10	/	1	(F)
CUTLER, Reg V.	Birmingham	17.02.35	JNRS	W.B.A.	02.52	1951-54	5		0	(OL)
			TR	Bournemouth	06.56	1956-58	96		21	
			TR	Portsmouth	09.58	1958-61	100		13	
			TR	Stockport Co.	07.62	1962	34		0	
CUTTING, Fred C.	N. Walsham	04.12.21		Leicester C.	+					(IF)
			TR	Norwich C.	09.46					
			TR	Colchester U.	08.50	1950-51	29		12	
CUTTING, Jack A.	Fleetwood	15.04.24		Oldham Ath.	11.46	1946	4		1	
				Accrington St.	06.48	1948	23		5	
CUTTING, Stan W.	St. Friths	21.09.14	Southampton(*)	Exeter C.	+	1946-47	38		2	(RH)
CZUCZMAN, Mike	Carlisle	27.05.53	Preston N.E.(APP)	Grimsby T.	08.71	1971-75	108	6	6	(D)
			TR	Scunthorpe U.	08.76	1976-78	115	1	1	
			TR	Stockport Co.	05.79	1979	36	/	7	
			San Jose E.	Grimsby T.	09.80	1980-81	9	/	0	
			TR	York C.	11.81	1981	17	/	0	

Players Names	Birthplace	Date	Previous Club	League Club	Date Signed	Seasons Played	Apps	Sub	Gls	
DADLEY, Peter R.	Farnham	10.12.48	APP	Aldershot	12.66	1966	1	/	1	(F)
DAGG, Henry C.	Sunderland	04.03.24	Boston U.	Lincoln C.	AM	1946	1		1	(F)
DAGGER, J. Les	Preston	25.04.33	W.Auckland	Preston N.E.	05.56	1956-60	61		8	(OR)
			TR	Carlisle U.	06.61	1961-62	74		9	
			TR	Southport	07.63	1963-64	81		9	
DAILEY, Jim	Airdrie	08.09.27	T.Lanark	Sheffield Wed.	10.46	1946-48	37		24	(CF)●
			TR	Birmingham C.	02.49	1948-51	51		14	
			TR	Exeter C.	08.52	1952-53	45		14	
			TR	Workington	12.53	1953-57	176		74	
			TR	Rochdale	10.57	1957-58	53		25	
DAINES, Barry R.	Witham	30.09.51	APP	Tottenham H.	09.69	1971-80	146	/	0	(G) E.YTH.INT.
				Mansfield T.	N/C	1983	21	/	0	
DAINTY, Albert	Lancaster	04.12.23		Preston N.E.	+	1946	1		1	(CF) d.1979
			TR	Stockport Co.	04.47	1946-48	36		16	
			TR	Southport	02.49	1948-50	49		11	
DAINTY, James	Coleshill	21.01.54		Walsall	02.72	1971-72	4	1	0	(F)
DALE, Alan G.	Moorend	20.09.58	APP	Scunthorpe U.	09.76	1975-76	1	2	0	(F)
DALE, Chris	York	16.04.50	Hull C.(AM)	York C.	AM	1968	5	/	0	(OL)
DALE, Eric	Manchester	06.07.24		Shrewsbury T.	N/L	1950	1		0	(F)
DALE, Fred W.	Doncaster	26.10.25		Halifax T.	08.49	1949-51	69		16	(F)
			TR	Southport	07.52	1952-53	47		5	
			TR	Accrington St.	07.54	1954	1		0	
			TR	Crewe Alex.	10.54	1954	4		3	
DALE, Gordon	Worksop	20.05.28	Worksop T.	Chesterfield	02.48	1948-50	91		3	(OL)
			TR	Portsmouth	07.51	1951-56	115		18	
			TR	Exeter C.	10.57	1957-60	122		8	
DALE, Joe	Northwich	03.07.21	Witton A.	Manchester U.	06.47	1947	2		0	(OR)
			TR	Port Vale	04.48	1947-48	9		1	
DALE, Leo	Esh Winning	11.10.33	Durham c.	Doncaster Rov.	02.54	1954	1		0	(W)
DALE, Robert J.	Irlam	31.10.31	Altrincham	Bury	09.51	1952-53	15		2	(IF)
			TR	Colchester U.	12.53	1953-56	127		11	
DALEY, Alan J.	Mansfield	11.10.27	Pleasley BC	Mansfield T.	09.46					(OL)
			TR	Hull C.	07.47	1947	7		0	d.1975
			Worksop T.	Doncaster Rov.	03.50	1949	1		1	
			Boston U.	Scunthorpe U.	07.52	1952	35		9	
			Corby T.	Mansfield T.	11.53	1953-55	98		24	
			TR	Stockport Co.	02.56	1955-57	73		17	
			TR	Crewe Alex.	06.58	1958	14		1	
			TR	Coventry C.	11.58	1958-60	55		10	
DALEY, Steve	Barnsley	15.04.53	APP	Wolverhampton W.	06.71	1971-78	191	21	37	(M)E.YTH.INT.
			TR	Manchester C.	09.79	1979-80	47	1	4	
			Seatle Sounders	Burnley	11.83	1983	20	3	4	
DALEY, Tom E.	Grimsby	15.11.33		Grimsby T.	08.51	1951-56	14		0	(G)
			TR	Huddersfield T.	03.57	1956	1		0	
			TR	W.B.A.	08.58					
DALGLISH, Kenny	Glasgow	04.03.51	Glasgow Celtic	Liverpool	08.77	1977-83	277	/	103	(F)S-93/S.U23-4●
DALL, David G.	St. Andrews	10.10.57	Grantham	Scunthorpe U.	10.79	1979-81	77	/	2	(D)
DALLAS, William R.D.	Glasgow	06.03.31		Luton T.	09.52					(CH)
				St. Mirren	Wrexham	07.57	1957	8		0	
DALLING, Nigel A.	Swansea	20.02.59	APP	Swansea C.	02.77	1974-77	3	5	0	(F)
DALLMAN, William	Mansfield	08.08.18		Mansfield T.	03.47	1946-47	5		0	(CH)
DALRYMPLE, Malcolm O.	Bedford	08.10.51	Cambridge U.	Bristol Rov.	10.71	1971-72	7	/	0	(G) E.YTH.INT.
			TR	Watford	07.73	1973	5	/	0	
DALTON, George	Newcastle	04.09.41	JNRS	Newcastle U.	11.58	1960-66	85	/	2	(FB)
			TR	Brighton & H.A.	06.67	1967	24	/	0	
DALY, Gerry	Dublin	30.04.54	Bohemians	Manchester U.	04.73	1973-76	107	4	23	(M) EI-37/EI.U21-1
			TR	Derby Co.	03.77	1976-79	111	1	31	
			TR	Coventry C.	08.80	1980-83	82	2	15	
			L	Leicester C.	01.83	1982	17	/	1	
DALY, Maurice	Dublin	28.11.55	Home Farm	Wolverhampton W.	07.73	1975-77	28	4	0	(D) EI-2
DALY, Pat	Dublin	04.12.27	Shamrock Rov.	Aston Villa	11.49	1949	3		0	(FB)EI-1/L.O.I. REP.
DALY, Pat	Manchester	03.01.41	JNRS	Blackburn Rov.	01.58	1959-60	3		0	(F)
			TR	Southport	02.62	1961	10		0	
DALY, Ron G.	Clerkenwell	22.07.30		Watford	10.50	1950-51	6		0	(IF)
DALZIEL, Gordon	Motherwell	16.03.62	Glasgow Rangers	Manchester C.	12.83	1983	4	1	0	(F)
DALZIEL, Ian	S. Shields	24.10.62	APP	Derby Co.	10.79	1981-82	22	/	4	(M)
			TR	Hereford U.	05.83	1983	30	/	4	
DANCE, Trevor	Durham	31.07.58	APP	Port Vale	07.76	1976-80	84	/	0	(G)
DANDO, Phil	Liverpool	08.06.52	JNRS	Liverpool	09.69					(G)
			L	Barrow	10.70	1970	9	/	0	

Players Names	Birthplace	Date	Previous Club	League Club	Date Signed	Seasons Played	Apps	Sub	Gls	
DANGERFIELD, Chris	Birmingham	09.08.55	APP Portland Timbers	Wolverhampton W. Port Vale	08.73 09.76	1976	0	2	0	(F)
DANGERFIELD, David	Tetbury	27.09.51	APP TR	Swindon T. Charlton Ath.	08.69 06.73	1968-72	16	4	0	(F) E.SCH.INT.
DANIEL, Alan W.	Ashford	05.04.40	Bexleyheath	Luton T.	01.58	1958-63	50		3	(FB)
DANIEL, Mel J.	Llanelli	26.01.16	Ashford T. TR	Luton T. Aldershot	+ 06.49	1946-48 1949	53 28		20 1	(IF) Father of Alan
DANIEL, Peter A.	Ripley	22.12.46	APP	Derby Co.	12.64	1965-78	188	7	7	(D)
DANIEL, Peter W.	Hull	12.12.55	JNRS TR	Hull C. Wolverhampton W.	09.73 05.78	1974-77 1978-83	113 157	/ /	9 13	(D) E.U23-3/E.U21-7
DANIEL, Ray C.	Luton	10.12.64	APP L	Luton T. Gillingham	09.82 09.83	1982-83 1983	8 5	2 /	2 0	(F)
DANIEL, Ray W.	Swansea	02.11.28	Swansea C.(AM) TR TR TR	Arsenal Sunderland Cardiff C. Swansea C.	10.46 06.53 10.57 03.58	1948-52 1953-56 1957 1957-59	87 137 6 44		0 6 0 6	(CH) W-21
DANIEL, Tom	Middleton	14.04.23	Castleton	Bury	12.46	1947-57	276		58	(IF)
DANIELS, Bernard	Salford	24.11.50	JNRS Ashton U. TR TR	Manchester U. Manchester C. Chester C. Stockport Co.	04.69 04.73 07.75 07.76	12973-74 1975 1976-77	9 8 45	4 1 2	2 1 17	(F)
DANIELS, David G.	Farnborough	09.04.62	Cardiff Corries	Cambridge U.	11.83	1983	20	/	2	(W)
DANIELS, Doug	Manchester	21.08.24	TR TR	New Brighton Chesterfield Accrington St.	08.47 07.48 10.49	1947 1949-52	25 112		0 0	(G)
DANIELS, Harry A.G.	Kensington	25.06.20	· TR TR	Q.P.R. Brighton & H.A. York C.	+ 08.48 08.50	1946-47 1948-49 1950	14 32 5		0 0 2	(LH)
DANIELS, John F.	St.Helens	08.01.25	British Cider	Lincoln C. New Brighton	05.46 03.48	1946 1948	17 3		0 0	
DANIELS, Steve R.	Leeds	17.12.61	APP	Doncaster Rov.	10.79	1979	0	1	0	(D)
DANKS, P. Derek	Cheadle	15.02.31		Northampton T.	11.53	1954	1		0	
DANN, Terry	London	06.07.36	Penzance Sittingbourne	Plymouth Arg. Torquay U.	07.59 07.62	1959 1962	8 1		0 0	(F)
DANSKIN, Robert	Scotwood	28.05.08	Leeds U.(*)	Bradford P.A.	*	1946-47	19		2	(CH) *Wallsend
DARBY, Alan	Sheffield	03.06.42	Goole T.	Doncaster Rov.	06.59	1960	1		0	(G)
DARBY, Doug	Bolton-on-Dearne	26.12.19	Wath.W. TR	Wolverhampton W. Walsall	+ 05.46	1946	15		4	(F) d.1963
DARBYSHIRE, Harry	Leeds	22.10.31	TR TR TR	Leeds U. Halifax T. Bury Darlington	02.50 07.52 08.57 06.59	1952-56 1957-58 1959	161 29 15		32 12 2	(WH)
D'ARCY, Arnold J.	Blackburn	13.01.33	Wigan Ath.	Accrington St. Swindon T.	03.52 11.56	1951-52 1956-63	39 223		7 29	(OL)
D'ARCY, Colin	Greasby	05.08.54	TR TR	Everton Bury Wigan Ath.	04.73 01.75 01.79	1974	4	/	0	(G)
D'ARCY, Frank J.	Liverpool	08.12.46	APP TR	Everton Tranmere Rov.	08.64 07.72	1965-70 1972	8 7	7 1	0 1	(FB)
D'ARCY, Mick E.	Dublin	08.03.33	Dundalk	Oldham Ath.	09.54	1954-55	45		0	(G)
D'ARCY, Seasmus D.	Newry	14.12.21	Ballymena TR TR	Charlton Ath. Chelsea Brentford	03.48 10.51 10.52	1947-50 1951-52 1952	13 23 13		1 12 3	(IF) N.I.-5
D'ARCY, Tom M.	Edinburgh	22.06.32	Hibernian Hibernian	Bournemouth Southend U.	09.54 05.56	1956-57	3		0	(F)
DARE, Kevin	Finchley	15.11.59	APP	Crystal Palace	02.77	1980-81	6	/	0	(D)
DARE, Reg. A.	Blandford	26.11.21	Windsor & Eton TR	Southampton Exeter C.	06.49 08.50	1950	6		0	(CF) Hants Cricketer
DARE, William T.	Willesden	14.02.27	Hendon TR	Brentford West Ham U.	11.48 01.55	1948-54 1954-58	208 111		61 44	(CF)
DAREY, Jeff	London	26.02.34	Hendon	Brighton & H.A.	03.57	1956-60	10		2	(CF) E.AMAT.INT.
DARFIELD, Stuart C.	Leeds	12.04.50	Wolverhampton W.(APP)	Bradford P.A.	07.68	1968	15	2	0	(WH)
DARGIE, Ian C.	London	03.10.31	Tonbridge	Brentford	02.52	1951-62	263		2	(CH)
DARK, Trevor C.	St. Helier	29.01.61	APP	Birmingham C.	01.79	1978	2	3	1	(F)
DARKE, Peter C.	Exeter	21.12.53	APP L TR	Plymouth Arg. Exeter C. Torquay U.	12.71 10.76 07.77	1971-76 1976 1977-78	94 5 58	6 / 1	2 0 0	(D)
DARLING, H. Len	Gillingham	09.08.11	Gillingham(*)	Brighton & H.A.	*	1946-47	48		3	d.

Players Names	Birthplace	Date	Previous Club	League Club	Date Signed	Seasons Played	Career Record Apps	Sub	Gls	
DARLING, Malcolm	Arbroath	04.07.47	Luncarty J.	Blackburn Rov.	10.64	1965-69	114	13	30	(F)
			TR	Norwich C.	05.70	1970-71	16	/	5	
			TR	Rochdale	10.71	1971-73	82	4	16	
			TR	Bolton W.	09.73	1973	6	2	0	
			TR	Chesterfield	08.74	1974-76	100	4	33	
			L	Stockport Co.	03.77	1976	11	/	2	
			TR	Sheffield Wed.	08.77	1977	1	1	0	
			TR	Hartlepool U.	09.77	1977	2	2	0	
			Morecambe	Bury	N/C	1977	1	1	0	
DARMODY, Aubrey	Swansea	17.05.21	Cardiff Nomads	Norwich C.	10.46	1946	2		0	(FB)
DARRACOTT, Terry M.	Liverpool	06.12.50	APP	Everton	07.68	1967-78	138	10	0	(D)
			Tulsa	Wrexham	09.79	1979	22	/	0	
DARRELL, Mike A.	Bilston	14.01.47	APP	Birmingham C.	01.65	1965-68	10	4	2	(IF)
			L	Newport Co.	10.70	1970	8	/	0	
			L	Gillingham	12.70	1970	19	2	1	
			TR	Peterborough U.	05.71	1971-72	32	10	6	
DARVELL, Roger D.	Watford	10.02.31	Rickmansworth	Charlton Ath.	12.53					(CH)
			TR	Gillingham	07.57	1957	3		0	
			TR	Southport	07.58	1958-64	256		1	
DARWIN, George H.	Chester-le-Street	16.05.32	Kimblesworth J.	Huddersfield T.	05.50					(IF)
			TR	Mansfield T.	11.53	1953-56	98		63	
			TR	Derby Co.	05.57	1957-60	94		32	
			TR	Rotherham U.	10.60	1960	2		2	
			TR	Barrow	07.61	1961-63	92		28	
DAUBNEY, Ray	Oldham	07.12.46		Rochdale	12.66	1966-67	13	/	2	(F)
DAVENPORT, Carl	Bolton	30.05.44	APP	Preston N.E.	05.62					(F)
			TR	Stockport Co.	03.63	1962-63	16		4	
DAVENPORT, Peter	Birkenhead	24.03.61	Cammell Laird	Nottingham F.	01.82	1981-83	52	4	25	(F)
DAVEY, Fred	Crediton	13.04.24	Crediton	Exeter C.	08.47	1947-55	278		2	(WH)
DAVEY, Nigel	Garforth	20.06.46	JNRS	Leeds U.	02.64	1967-70	13	1	0	(FB)
			TR	Rotherham U.	07.74					
DAVEY, Steve R.	Plymouth	05.09.48	APP	Plymouth Arg.	07.66	1966-74	214	12	48	(D)E.YTH.INT
			TR	Hereford U.	08.75	1975-77	104	3	32	
			TR	Portsmouth	06.78	1978-80	82	10	8	
			TR	Exeter C.	08.81	1981	15	/	0	
DAVEY, Stuart	Crewe	04.01.38		Crewe Alex.	08.56	1956	1		0	(FB)
DAVIDS, Neil G.	Bingley	22.09.55	APP	Leeds U.	08.73					(D) E.YTH.INT.
			TR	Norwich C.	04.75	1975	2	/	0	
			L	Northampton T.	09.75	1975	9	/	0	
			L	Stockport Co.	01.76	1975	5	/	1	
			TR	Swansea C.	07.77	1977	9	/	0	
			TR	Wigan Ath.	07.78	1978-80	66	2	1	
DAVIDSON, Adam, R.	Invergowrie	28.11.29		Sheffield Wed.	03.48					(OR)
			TR	Colchester U.	08.51	1951	19		0	
DAVIDSON, Alex M.	Langholm	06.06.20	Hibernian	Chelsea	08.46	1946	2		0	(IF)
				Crystal Palace	08.48	1948	10		2	
DAVIDSON, Andrew	Douglas Water	13.07.32	JNRS	Hull C.	09.49	1952-67	520		18	(FB)● Brother of David C.
DAVIDSON, Angus	Dundee	02.10.48	Dundee	Grimsby T.	11.65	1965-68	46	3	1	(M)
			TR	Scunthorpe U.	07.69	1969-76	304	17	44	
DAVIDSON, Brian W.	Workington	23.08.51	JNRS	Workington	AM	1972	1	/	0	(OL)
DAVIDSON, David	Govan Hill	28.08.34	JNRS	Manchester C.	08.51	1953	1		0	(HB)
			TR	Workington	07.58	1958	3		0	
DAVIDSON, David B.L.	Lanark	25.03.20	Douglas Water Th.	Bradford P.A.	*	1946	13		0	d.1954
			TR	Orient	01.47	1946-49	83		1	
DAVIDSON, David C.	Drywater	19.03.26	Drywater Th.	Hull C.	10.46	1946-47	22		4	
DAVIDSON, Dennis	Aberdeen	18.05.37	JNRS	Portsmouth	05.54	1959	1		0	
DAVIDSON, Douglas B.	Dundee	02.12.18	E.Fife	Blackpool	10.48	1948-49	14		0	(IF) d.1968
			TR	Reading	04.50	1949-50	11		1	
DAVIDSON, Duncan	Elgin	05.07.54	Hong Kong	Manchester C.	09.83	1983	2	4	1	(F)
DAVIDSON, Ian	Goole	31.01.47	JNRS	Hull C.	02.65	1966-67	5	1	1	(WH)
			L	Scunthorpe U.	09.68	1968	32	3	0	
			TR	York C.	06.69	1969-70	82	4	4	
			TR	Bournemouth	07.71	1971	7	2	0	
			TR	Stockport Co.	05.72	1972-73	74	4	6	
DAVIDSON, Ian	Lothian	08.09.37	Kilmarnock	Preston N.E.	12.62	1962-64	67		1	(WH)
			TR	Middlesbrough	02.65	1964-66	46	/	0	
			TR	Darlington	09.67	1967	27	/	0	
DAVIDSON, John S.	Lanark	06.11.31	Alloa	Walsall	08.55	1955	5		0	(F)
DAVIDSON, Peter E.	Newcastle	31.10.56	Berwick Rgrs	Q.P.R.	07.79	1979	0	1	0	(M)
DAVIDSON, Robert T.	Lochgelly	27.04.13	Arsenal (*)	Coventry C.	*	1946-47	3		0	(IF) *St. Johnstone

Players Names	Birthplace	Date	Previous Club	League Club	Date Signed	Seasons Played	Apps	Sub	Gls	
DAVIDSON, Roger	London	27.10.48	APP	Arsenal	11.65	1967		1	0	(F) E.SCH.INT.
			TR	Portsmouth	06.69	1969	3	/	0	
			TR	Fulham	08.70	1970	1	/	0	
			TR	Lincoln C.	10.71	1971	6	/	0	
			L	Aldershot	02.72	1971	12	/	2	
DAVIDSON, Vic	Glasgow	08.11.50	Motherwell	Blackpool	07.78	1978	23	2	3	(M)
DAVIE, Alex	Dundee	10.06.45	Dundee	Luton T.	09.68	1968-69	58	/	0	(G)
			TR	Southampton	05.70	1970	1	/	0	
DAVIE, James G.	Newton	07.09.22	Kilmarnock	Preston N.E.	06.48	1948-49	28		0	(WH)
			TR	Northampton T.	07.50	1950-52	75		1	
			TR	Shrewsbury T.	07.53					
DAVIE, John	Dunfermline	19.02.13	Hibernian	Brighton & H.A.	*					(CF)
			TR	Barnsley	12.46	1946	6		0	
DAVIE, Willie C.	Paisley	07.01.25	St. Mirren	Luton T.	12.50	1950-51	42		11	(IF)
			TR	Huddersfield T.	12.51	1951-56	113		16	
			TR	Walsall	07.57	1957	7		0	
DAVIES, Alan	Manchester	05.12.61	APP	Manchester U.	12.78	1981-83	6	1	0	(M)W.U'21-3/W-4
DAVIES, Albert J.	Greenwich	19.04.35		Millwall	10.56	1957	2		0	(G)
DAVIES, Albert L.	Pontypridd	11.03.33	JNRS	Newport Co.	04.51	1950	1		0	
DAVIES, Alex M.	Dundonald	21.05.20	Sheffield W.(*)	Lincoln C.	+	1946-48	37		9	(F) d.1964
DAVIES, Brian W.	Doncaster	21.08.47	APP	Sheffield Wed.	08.64	1965	2		1	(F)
			TR	Doncaster Rov.	09.68					
DAVIES, Byron	Llanelli	05.02.32	Llanelli	Leeds U.	05.52	1953	1		0	(HB)
			TR	Newport Co.	06.56					
DAVIES, Cecil J.	Bedwellty	26.03.18	Charlton Ath.(*)	Barrow	*	1946	34		0	(WH) W.SCH.INT.
			TR	Millwall	07.47	1947-48	31		0	
DAVIES, Colin F.	Shrewsbury	12.04.36		Port Vale	06.59	1959-60	13		0	(F)
DAVIES, Cyril J.	Swansea	07.09.48	APP	Swansea C.	09.66					(IF) W-1/W,U23-4
			TR	Carlisle U.	06.68	1968	1	1	0	W.SCH.INT.
			Yeovil	Charlton Ath.	05.75	1970-72	70	6	6	
DAVIES, D. Lyn	Neath	29.09.47	APP	Cardiff C.	10.65	1965-66	16	/	0	(G) W.U23-1/W.SCH.INT.
			Llanelli	Swansea C.	07.72	1972	3	/	0	
DAVIES, Daniel D.	Aberdare	05.12.14	Aberamon	Hull C.	*	1946	18		1	(IF)
DAVIES, David I.	Bridgend	21.07.32	Harwich & P.	Orient	04.53	1953	4		0	(CF)
DAVIES, David J.	Port Talbot	21.05.52	Afan Lido	Swansea C.	07.73	1973-74	27	1	0	(CH)
DAVIES, David L.	Port Talbot	11.07.56	APP	Swansea C.	1972	0	1		0	(M)
			TR	Crewe Alex.	03.75	1974-80	196	13	26	
DAVIES, Dudley	Shoreham	27.12.24	Lancing T.	Charlton Ath.	01.48					(OR)
			TR	Orient	05.50	1950-51	17		2	
DAVIES, E. Reg	Cymmer	27.05.29	Southampton (AM)	Southend U.	07.49	1949-50	41		18	(IF) W-6
			TR	Newcastle U.	04.51	1951-58	156		52	
			TR	Swansea C.	10.58	1958-61	108		29	
			TR	Carlisle U.	06.62	1962-63	65		13	
DAVIES, Edmund	Oswestry	05.06.27	Liverpool (AM)	Arsenal	08.48					(CF)
			TR	Q.P.R.	04.50	1950	1		1	
			TR	Crewe Alex.	07.51	1951	7		0	
DAVIES, Edward				Newport Co.	10.46	1946	3		1	
DAVIES, Edward				Port Vale	+	1946	3		0	
DAVIES, Edward K.	Birkenhead	19.02.34		Tranmere Rov.	07.53	1953	1		0	
DAVIES, Eric	Manchester	20.02.43	Southport Trin.	Southport	07.63	1961-64	3		0	(CF)
DAVIES, Fred	Liverpool	22.08.39	Llandudno	Wolverhampton W.	04.57	1961-67	156	/	0	(G)
			TR	Cardiff C.	01.68	1967-69	99	/	0	
			TR	Bournemouth	07.70	1970-73	134	/	0	
DAVIES, Geoff	Ellesmere Port	01.07.47	Wigan Ath.	Chester C.	08.72	1972-73	18	14	5	(F)
			TR	Wrexham	10.73	1973-75	64	3	15	
			TR	Port Vale	08.76	1976	7	/	0	
			L	Hartlepool U.	11.76	1976	5	/	1	
			San Jose E.	Wimbledon	08.77	1977	23	/	1	
DAVIES, George	Oswestry	01.03.27	Oswestry T.	Sheffield Wed.	06.50	1950-54	98		1	(WH)
			TR	Chester C.	07.56	1956-57	55		9	
DAVIES, Glen	Swansea	30.06.50	JNRS	Swansea C.	07.70	1970-75	140	12	13	(CH)
DAVIES, Glyn	Swansea	31.05.32	JNRS	Derby Co.	07.49	1953-61	200		5	(WH)
			TR	Swansea C.	07.62	1962	18		1	
DAVIES, Gordon E.	Manchester	04.09.32	Ashton U.	Manchester C.	12.51	1951-54	13		5	(IF)
			TR	Chester C.	06.57	1957	2		0	
			TR	Southport	08.58	1958	11		1	
DAVIES, Gordon J.	Merthyr Tydfil	03.08.55	Merthyr Tydfil	Fulham	03.78	1977-83	234	2	107	(F)W-13/W.SCH.INT.
DAVIES, Graham G.	Swansea	03.10.21		Swansea C.	+	1946	22		0	(G) W.SCH.INT.
			TR	Watford	06.47	1947-48	9		0	

Players Names	Birthplace	Date	Previous Club	League Club	Date Signed	Seasons Played	Apps	Sub	Gls	
DAVIES, Grant	Barrow	13.10.59	APP	Preston N.E.	10.77	.				(D)
			TR	Newport Co.	07.78	1978-82	147	3	1	
			L	Exeter C.	02.83	1982	7	/	0	
DAVIES, Ian C.	Bristol	29.03.57	APP	Norwich C.	04.75	1973-78	29	3	2	(D)W.U21-1
			TR	Newcastle U.	06.79	1979-81	74	1	3	
			TR	Manchester C.	08.82	1982-83	7	/	0	
			L	Bury	11.82	1982	14	/	0	
			L	Brentford	11.83	1983	2	/	0	
			L	Cambridge U.	02.84	1983	5	/	0	
DAVIES, John G.	Llandyssul	18.11.59	APP	Cardiff C.	01.78	1978-79	7	/	0	(G)
			TR	Hull C.	07.80	1980-82	24	/	0	
DAVIES, John R.	Portsmouth	26.09.33	JNRS	Portsmouth	05.52	1953-54	2		0	(F)
			TR	Scunthorpe U.	07.55	1955-57	68		10	
			TR	Walsall	01.59	1958-60	65		16	
DAVIES, John W.	Denbigh	14.11.16	Cardiff C.(*)	Everton	*	1946	1		0	*Chester C.
			TR	Plymouth Arg.	02.47	1946-47	33		0	W.SCH.INT.
			TR	Bristol C.	05.48	1948	30		1	
DAVIES, Joseph	Tranmere	30.01.26		Chester C.	05.48	1947-51	55		10	(F)
DAVIES, Ken	Doncaster	20.09.23		Wolverhampton W.	+					(F)
			TR	Walsall	06.46	1946-47	28		5	
			TR	Brighton & H.A.	05.48	1948-49	36		5	
DAVIES, L. Ray	Birkenhead	03.10.31		Tranmere Rov.	10.49	1951-57	121		27	(IF)
DAVIES, Len				Southend U.	+	1946	3		0	(G)
DAVIES, Malcolm	Aberdare	26.06.31	Aberaman	Plymouth Arg.	04.49	1952-56	84		21	(OR)
DAVIES, Mike J.	Stretford	19.01.66	APP	Blackpool	01.84	1983	3	/	0	(M)
DAVIES, Paul	St. Asaph	10.10.52	APP	Arsenal	11.69	1971	0	1	0	(CF) W.SCH.INT.
			TR	Charlton Ath.	08.72	1972-74	51	6	9	
DAVIES, Paul A.	Kidderminster	09.10.60	Oldswinford	Cardiff C.	10.78	1979-80	1	1	0	(F)
DAVIES, Peter	Llanelli	08.03.36	Llanelli	Arsenal	11.57					(WH)
			TR	Swansea C.	03.59	1958-64	133		3	
			TR	Brighton & H.A.	07.65	1965	6	/	0	
DAVIES, Peter	Merthyr Tydfil	01.07.42	Merthyr Tydfil	Newport Co.	AM	1964	1		0	(IF)
DAVIES, Reg W.	Tipton	10.10.33	JNRS	W.B.A.	01.51	1953-54	4		0	(G)
			TR	Walsall	07.55	1955-56	53		0	
			TR	Millwall	05.58	1958-62	199		0	
			TR	Orient	07.63	1963	11		0	
			TR	Port Vale	07.64	1964	13		0	
			TR	Orient	03.65	1964-65	16	/	0	
DAVIES, Robert G.	Blaenau	19.10.13	Blaenau	Nottingham F.	*	1946	6		0	(CH) d.1978
DAVIES, Roger	Wolverhampton	25.10.59	Worcester C.	Derby C.	09.71	1972-75	98	16	32	(F).E.U23-1
			L	Preston N.E.	08.72	1972	2	/	0	
			Bruges	Leicester C.	12.77	1977-78	22	4	6	
			Tulsa	Derby Co.	09.79	1979	22	/	3	
			Fort Lauderdale	Darlington	11.83	1983	10	/	1	
DAVIES, Ron G.	Swansea	13.11.35	Tower U.	Swansea C.	05.58	1958	2		0	(WH)
			TR	Plymouth Arg.	06.59					
DAVIES, Ron T.	Merthyr Tydfil	21.09.32		Cardiff C.	10.52	1955-57	32		3	(FB)
			TR	Southampton	03.58	1957-63	163		0	
			TR	Aldershot	08.64	1964-66	83	1	1	
DAVIES, Ron T.	Holywell	25.05.42	JNRS	Chester C.	07.59	1959-62	94		44	(CF)W-29/W.U23-3/●
			TR	Luton T.	10.62	1962-63	32		21	Brother to Paul
			TR	Norwich C.	09.63	1963-65	113	/	58	
			TR	Southampton	08.66	1966-72	239	1	134	
			TR	Portsmouth	04.73	1973-74	59		18	
			TR	Manchester U.	11.74	1974	0	8	0	
			L	Millwall	11.75	1975	3	/	0	
DAVIES, Roy	London	25.10.53	Slough	Reading	09.77	1977	37	/	2	(M)
			TR	Torquay U.	08.78	1978-79	65	5	6	
			TR	Wimbledon	08.80	1980	6	3	0	
DAVIES, Roy A.	S. Africa	23.08.24	Clyde	Luton T.	05.51	1951-56	150		24	(CF)
DAVIES, W.D. (Dai)	Ammanford	01.04.48	Ammanford	Swansea C.	08.69	1969-70	9	/	0	(G) W-52/2.U23-3
			TR	Everton	12.70	1970-76	82	/	0	
			L	Swansea C.	02.74	1973	6	/	0	
			TR	Wrexham	09.77	1977-80	144	/	0	
			TR	Swansea C.	07.81	1981-82	71	/	0	
			TR	Tranmere Rov.	06.83	1983	42	/	0	
DAVIES, William	Troedyrhiw	24.06.10	Troedyrhiw	Watford	*	1946-49	107		26	(OL)
DAVIES, William	Middlesbrough	16.05.30	St. Mary's COB	Hull C.	04.49					(IF)
			TR	Leeds U.	08.50					
			Scarborough	Reading	12.52	1954-60	203		0	
DAVIES, William E.	Salford	15.01.24	Droylsden	Crewe Alex.	02.47	1946	11		3	(OR)

Players Names	Birthplace	Date	Previous Club	League Club	Date Signed	Seasons Played	Career Record Apps	Sub	Gls	
DAVIES, Wyn	Caernarvon	20.03.42	Caernarvon	Wrexham	07.61	1960-61	55	/	22	(F) W-34/W.U23-4●
			TR	Bolton W.	03.62	1961-66	155	/	66	
			TR	Newcastle U.	10.66	1966-70	180	/	40	
			TR	Manchester C.	08.71	1971-72	45	/	8	
			TR	Manchester U.	09.72	1972	15	1	4	
			TR	Blackpool	06.73	1973-74	34	2	5	
			L	Crystal Palace	08.73	1974	3	/	0	
			TR	Stockport Co.	08.75	1975	28	2	7	
			TR	Crewe Alex.	08.76	1976-77	50	5	13	
DAVIN, Joe	Dumbarton	13.02.42	Hibernian	Ipswich T.	07.63	1963-65	77	/	0	(FB) S.SCH.INT.
DAVIS, Cyril				Walsall	AM	1948	1		0	
DAVIS, Darren J.	Sutton-in-Ashfield	05.02.67	APP	Notts. Co.	APP	1983	1	/	0	(D)
DAVIS, Derek E.	Colwyn Bay	19.06.22		Norwich C.	+	1946-47	26		0	(G)
			TR	Torquay U.	08.48	1948-50	89		0	
DAVIS, Eric W.C.	Stonehouse	26.02.32	Tavistock	Plymouth Arg.	08.52	1952-56	63		23	(CF)
			TR	Scunthorpe U.	07.57	1957-58	40		20	
			TR	Chester C.	02.59	1958-59	32		12	
			TR	Oldham Ath.	09.60	1960	2		1	
DAVIS, Gareth	Bangor	11.07.49	JNRS	Wrexham	10.67	1967-82	482	7	9	(D)W.U23-4/W-3
DAVIS, Gordon	Newcastle	14.12.30	Everton (AM)	Gateshead	11.49	1951-56	87		0	(HB)
DAVIS, Ian	Hull	01.02.65	APP	Hull C.	02.83	1981-82	25	3	1	(M)
DAVIS, J. Fred	Walsall	23.05.29	Bloxwich Strollers	Reading	12.52	1953-54	62		1	(WH)
			TR	Wrexham	07.55	1955-60	230		12	
DAVIS, John L.	Hackney	31.05.57	Arsenal (APP)	Gillingham	07.75	1975	2	1	1	(D)
			TR	Sheffield Wed.	02.77	1976	1	/	0	
DAVIS, Joseph	Glasgow	22.05.41	Hibernian	Carlisle U.	12.69	1969-71	75	4	0	(OL)
DAVIS, Joseph T.	Bristol	24.08.38	JNRS	Bristol Rov.	03.56	1960-66	209	1	4	(CH)
			TR	Swansea C.	03.67	1966-67	38	/	0	
DAVIS, Ken E.	Romsey	06.02.33	JNRS	Bristol C.	05.52	1952	1		0	(F)
DAVIS, Len P.	Cork	31.07.31		Arsenal	11.49					(CF)
			TR	Walsall	02.54	1953-54	25		5	
DAVIS, Paul V.	London	09.12.61	APP	Arsenal	07.79	1979-83	118	8	10	(M)E.U'21-6
DAVIS, Richard D.	Birmingham	22.01.22	Morris & J.	Sunderland	*	1946-53	144		73	(CF) E.SCH.INT.
			TR	Darlington	05.54	1954-56	93		32	
DAVIS, Richard F.	Plymouth	14.11.43	APP	Plymouth Arg.	11.61	1962-63	23		0	(FB)
			TR	Southampton	07.64	1964	1		0	
			TR	Bristol C.	07.65	1967-68	7	/	0	
			TR	Barrow	03.69	1968-69	50	/	0	
DAVIS, Steve P.	Birmingham	26.07.65	Stoke C.(APP)	Crewe Alex.	08.83	1983	23	1	0	(D)
DAVISON, Alan	Sunderland	08.09.31		Norwich C.	09.49					
				Darlington	08.51	1951	1		0	
DAVISON, Arthur E.	Hackney	21.12.15	Stockport Co.(+)	Torquay U.	11.46	1946	1		0	
DAVISON, Daniel	Newcastle	11.11.47	Newcastle U.(AM)	Barrow	09.65	1966-69	7	/	0	(FB)
DAVISON, Edward	Seaham	15.04.33	Seaham J.	Hartlepool U.	08.53	1953	1		0	(CH)
DAVISON, Jim H.	Sunderland	01.11.42	JNRS	Sunderland	11.59	1959-62	62		10	(OR)
			TR	Bolton W.	11.63	1963	21		1	
DAVISON, Joe H.	Newcastle	29.07.19	Throckley Welf.	Darlington	01.47	1946-53	239		7	(RB)
DAVISON, Robert	Sth. Shields	17.07.59	Seaham CW	Huddersfield T.	07.80	1980	1	1	0	(F)
			TR	Halifax T.	08.81	1981-82	63	/	29	
			TR	Derby Co.	12.82	1982-83	63	3	22	
DAVOCK, Mike	St. Helens	27.04.35	St. Helens	Stockport Co.	01.57	1956-63	235		37	(OL)
D'AVRAY, J. Mich	S. Africa	19.02.62	APP	Ipswich T.	05.79	1979-83	44	16	11	(F)E.U'21-1
DAVY, Steve	Norwich	09.04.55	West Ham U.(N/C)	Scunthorpe U.	08.77	1977-81	126	8	1	(D)
DAWES, Derek M.	Dawley	23.06.44	APP	Shrewsbury T.	06.62	1961-62	9		0	
DAWES, Fred W.	Frimley Green	02.05.11	Northampton T.(*)	Crystal Palace	*	1946-49	111		0	(IF)
DAWES, Ian R.	Croydon	22.02.63	APP	Q.P.R.	12.80	1981-83	89	/	2	(D) E.SCH.INT.
DAWES, Les A.	Woolwich	17.03.25		Reading	10.48					(IF)
			TR	Watford	07.49	1949	1		0	
DAWES, Malcolm	Trimdon	03.03.44		Darlington	03.62					(D)
			Horden CW	Aldershot	08.65	1965-69	160	3	2	
			TR	Hartlepool U.	07.70	1970-75	193	1	12	
			TR	Workington	11.75	1975-76	49	2	1	
DAWKINS, Derek	London	29.11.59	APP	Leicester C.	11.77	1977	3	/	0	(D)
			TR	Mansfield	12.78	1978-80	73	/	0	
			TR	Bournemouth	08.81	1981-82	4	4	0	
			TR	Torquay U.	02.84	1983	14	2	0	
DAWKINS, Trevor A.	Rochford	07.10.45	APP	West Ham U.	10.62	1964-66	5	1	0	(WH)E.YTH. INT./
			TR	Crystal Palace	10.67	1967-70	24	1	3	E.SCH.INT.
			L	Brentford	09.71	1971	3	1	0	

Players Names	Birthplace	Date	Previous Club	League Club	Date Signed	Seasons Played	Apps	Sub	Gls	
DAWSON, Alex	Aberdeen	21.02.40	JNRS	Manchester U.	04.57	1956-61	80		43	(CF)●
			TR	Preston N.E.	10.61	1961-66	197		114	
			TR	Bury	03.67	1966-68	49	1	21	
			TR	Brighton & H.A.	12.68	1968-70	53	4	26	
			L	Brentford	09.70	1970	10	/	6	
DAWSON, Alex	Glasgow	23.10.33	Gourock J.	Q.P.R.	02.57	1956-58	58		5	(F)
DAWSON, Carl M.	Dovercourt	24.06.34	JNRS	Lincoln C.	AM	1950	1		0	
DAWSON, Edward	Durham	16.01.13	Manchester C.(*)	Bristol C.	*					(G)
			TR	Gateshead	08.46	1946-48	83		0	
DAWSON, George	Glasgow	13.09.30	Motherwell	Q.P.R.	05.55	1955	1		0	
DAWSON, J. Reg	Sheffield	04.10.14		Rotherham U.	*	1946	46		2	
DAWSON, Jim E.I.B.	Stoneyburn	21.12.27		Leicester C.	05.46	1946-48	5		0	(OR)
			TR	Portsmouth	06.49	1949	1		0	
			TR	Northampton T.	09.51					
				Southend U.	09.52					
DAWSON, Owen	Christchurch	07.03.43	JNRS	Portsmouth	06.60					(FB) E.YTH.INT.
			TR	Swindon T.	06.62	1962-70	196	8	4	
DAWSON, Peter	Crewe	19.01.33		Crewe Alex.	01.54	1955	2		0	
DAWSON, Richard	York	06.07.62		York C.	07.80	1981-82	45	/	0	(D)
DAWSON, Richard	Chesterfield	19.01.60	APP	Rotherham	01.78	1977-79	21	3	3	(F)
			TR	Doncaster	02.81	1980-81	39	4	14	
			TR	Chesterfield	08.82	1982	6	6	0	
DAWSON, Robert	South Shields	31.01.35	South Shields	Leeds U.	11.53	1953	1		0	(FB)
			TR	Gateshead	11.55	1955-59	118		1	
DAWSON, Robert A.	Doncaster	21.06.44		Doncaster Rov.	12.64	1965-66	28	/	0	(G)
DAWSON, Tom	Middlesbrough	06.02.15	Spennymoor	Charlton Ath.	*	1946	22		2	(IF)*Darlington
			TR	Brentford	08.47	1947	36		10	
			TR	Swindon T.	05.48	1948-49	65		15	
DAWSON, William	Glasgow	05.02.31	Ashfield J.	Northampton T.	03.55	1954-55	14		6	(CF)
DAWTRY, Kevin A.	Southampton	15.06.58	APP	Southampton	06.76	1978	0	1	0	(M)
			TR	Crystal Palace	05.80					
			TR	Bournemouth	03.81	1980-83	58	7	11	
			L	Reading	09.82	1982	4	/	0	
DAY, Albert	Camberwell	07.03.18		Brighton & H.A.	*					(F)
			TR	Ipswich T.	05.46	1946-48	63		25	
			TR	Watford	08.49	1949	4		1	
DAY, Clive A.	Orsett	27.01.61	APP	Fulham	08.78	1980-81	2	8	0	(D)
			L	Mansfield	08.82	1982	10	2	1	
			TR	Aldershot	08.83	1983	28	3	0	
DAY, Eric C.	Dartford	06.11.21		Southampton	+	1946-56	398		146	(OR)
DAY, Graham	Bristol	22.11.53		Bristol Rov.	05.73	1974-78	129	1	1	(D)
			Forest Green	Bristol Rov.	03.83					
DAY, Jack N.	Northfleet	21.01.24		Gillingham	07.50	1950	1		0	(G)
DAY, Mervyn R.	Chelmsford	26.06.55	APP	W. Ham	03.73	1973-78	194	/	0	(G)E.U23-5/E.YTH.INT.
			TR	Orient	07.79	1979-82	170	/	0	
			TR	Aston Villa	08.83	1983	14	/	0	
DAY, Roger	Romford	03.12.39	Enfield	Watford	AM	1961	1		0	(F) E.AMAT.INT.
DAY, William	Middlesbrough	27.12.36	South Bank	Middlesbrough	05.55	1955-61	116		18	(OR)
			TR	Newcastle U.	03.62	1961-62	13		1	
			TR	Peterborough U.	04.63	1962-63	18		2	
DAYKIN, Brian	Long Eaton	04.08.37	Long Eaton U.	Derby Co.	11.55	1959-61	4		1	(HB)
			TR	Notts.Co.	07.62	1962	3		0	
DE GARIS, Jim F.	Worcester	09.10.52	APP	Arsenal	06.70					(IF)
			TR	Bournemouth	09.71	1971-73	8	4	0	
			TR	Torquay U.	03.74	1973	7	2	0	
DE GOEY, Leendert	Holland	29.02.52	Sparta Rotterdam	Sheffield U.	08.79	1979	33	/	5	(M)
DE GRAFT ROSENOIR, Leroy	London	24.03.64	JNRS	Fulham	08.82	1982-83	23	1	8	(F)
DE GRUCHY, Ray P.	Guernsey	18.05.32		Nottingham F.	08.53					(FB)
			TR	Grimsby T.	05.54	1954-57	74		2	
			TR	Chesterfield	06.58	1958	1		0	
DE PLACIDO, Mike	Scarborough	09.03.54		York C.	03.72	1971-72	4	7	0	(W) E.YTH.INT.
DEACON, David B.	Broome	10.03.29	Bungay	Ipswich T.	11.50	1950-59	66		0	(FB)
DEACY, Eamonn	Galway	01.10.58	Galway Rov.	Aston Villa	03.79	1979-83	27	6	1	(D)EI-4
			L	Derby Co.	10.83	1983	5	/	0	
DEACY, Mike	Cardiff	29.11.43		Newport Co.	01.68	1966-69	47	1	2	(CH)
DEACY, Nick	Cardiff	19.07.53	Merthyr Tydfil	Hereford	09.74	1974	13	4	2	(F)W-12/W.U23-1/
			L	Workington	12.74	1974	5	/	2	W.U21-1
			Vitesse	Hull C.	02.80	1979-81	80	7	7	
				Bury	10.83	1983	30	1	0	
DEAKIN, Alan	Birmingham	27.11.41	JNRS	Aston Villa	12.58	1959-69	230	1	9	(WH) E.U23-6
			TR	Walsall	10.69	1969-71	46	4	0	

Players Names	Birthplace	Date	Previous Club	League Club	Date Signed	Seasons Played	Career Record Apps	Sub	Gls	
DEAKIN, Fred A.	Birmingham	05.02.20		Crystal Palace	09.46	1946-47	6		0	(RB) *Birmingham C.
DEAKIN, Mike R.F.	Birmingham	25.10.33	Bromsgrove	Crystal Palace	11.54	1954-59	144		56	(IF)
			TR	Northampton T.	10.59	1959-60	45		31	Brother of Alan
			TR	Aldershot	01.61	1960-61	17		5	
DEAKIN, Peter	Normanton	25.03.38	JNRS	Bolton W.	05.55	1957-63	63		13	(IF)
			TR	Peterborough U.	06.64	1964-66	74	1	34	
			TR	Bradford P.A.	09.66	1966-67	36	/	9	
			TR	Peterborough U.	09.67	1967	16	/	1	
			TR	Brentford	07.68	1968	7	1	2	
DEAKIN, Ray J.	Liverpool	19.06.59	APP	Everton	07.77					(D)
			TR	Port Vale	08.81	1981	21	2	6	
				Bolton W.	08.82	1982-83	71	/	2	
DEAKIN, William E.	Maltby	19.01.25	Sunnyside YMCA	Barnsley	05.49	1949-51	25		3	(OL)
			TR	Chester C.	07.52	1952	27		5	
DEAN, Alan J.	Aldershot	20.01.50	APP	Aldershot	01.68	1966-67	3	/	0	(FB)
DEAN, Andy G.	Salford	27.11.66	Burnley(JNR)	Rochdale	N/C	1983	1	/	0	
DEAN, Brian	Stockport	10.09.47	JNRS	Blackpool	09.64	1967	0	1	0	(HB)
			TR	Barrow	07.69	1969-70	44	2	0	
DEAN, George C.	Walsall	22.02.30	Hillery St.O.B.	Walsall	05.50	1950-53	73		13	(HB)
DEAN, Joby	Chesterfield	25.11.34		Q.P.R.	11.52	1955-56	15		0	(HB)
			Sutton T.	Bradford P.A.	12.57	1957-58	53		1	
DEAN, Joseph	Manchester	04.04.39	JNRS	Bolton W.	04.56	1955-59	17		0	(G)E.YTH.INT./E.SCH.INT.
			TR	Carlisle U.	07.62	1962-69	137	/	0	
			TR	Barrow	07.70	1970-71	41	/	0	
			TR	Stockport Co.	08.72					
DEAN, Mark C.	Northwich	18.11.64	APP	Chester	10.82	1981-82	23	2	0	(D)
DEAN, Norman	Corby	13.09.44	Corby T.	Southampton	04.63	1963-65	19	/	11	(F)
			TR	Cardiff C.	03.67	1966-68	20	1	3	
			TR	Barnsley	09.68	1968-72	58	2	19	
DEAN, Ray	Steventon	15.12.45		Reading	05.66	1966-68	50	4	0	(CH)
			TR	Aldershot	07.69	1969-74	256	/	6	
DEANS, J. (Dixie)	Linwood	30.07.46	Glasgow Celtic	Luton T.	06.76	1976	13	1	6	(F) S-2
			L	Carlisle U.	02.77	1976	4	/	2	
DEANS, Tom	Shieldhill	07.01.22	Clyde	Notts. Co.	10.49	1949-55	239		0	(FB) S.F.LGE REP.
DEAR, Brian C.	Plaistow	18.09.43	APP	West Ham U.	11.60	1962-70	63	2	33	(CF) E.SCH.INT.
			L	Brighton & H.A.	03.67	1966	7	/	5	
			TR	Fulham	02.69	1968	13	/	7	
			TR	Millwall	07.69	1969	5	1	0	
				West Ham U.	10.70	1970	4	/	0	
DEAR, Gerry	Kensington	05.01.37		Swindon T.	08.58	1956	4		0	
DEARDEN, William	Oldham	11.02.44	JNRS	Oldham Ath.	09.63	1964-66	32	2	2	(F)
			TR	Crewe Alex.	12.66	1966-67	44	3	7	
			TR	Chester	06.68	1968-69	85	/	22	
			TR	Sheffield U.	04.70	1970-75	170	5	61	
			TR	Chester	02.76	1975-76	35	1	7	
			TR	Chesterfield	08.77	1977-78	18	9	2	
DEARSON, Don J.	Ynysybwl	13.05.14	Barry T.	Birmingham C.	*	1946	25		1	(IF)W-3/W.AMAT.INT.
			TR	Coventry C.	02.47	1946-49	84		10	
			TR	Walsall	03.50	1949-50	51		13	
DEARY, John S.	Ormskirk	18.10.62	APP	Blackpool	03.80	1980-83	104	9	12	(M)
DEATH, Steve V.	Elmswell	19.09.49	APP	West Ham U.	06.67	1968	1	/	0	(G)E.SCH.INT.●
			TR	Reading	11.69	1969-81	471	/	0	
DEEHAN, John M.	Birmingham	06.08.57	APP	Aston Villa	04.75	1975-79	107	3	42	(F) E.U21-7/E.YTH.INT.
			TR	W.B.A.	09.79	1979-81	44	3	5	
			TR	Norwich C	12.81	1981-83	96	/	45	
DEELEY, Norman V.	Wednesbury	30.11.33	JNRS	Wolverhampton W.	12.50	1951-61	206		67	(OR)E-2/E.SCH.INT.
			TR	Orient	02.62	1961-63	73		9	
DEERE, Steve	Burnham	31.03.48	Norwich C. (AM)	Scunthorpe	11.67	1967-72	232	6	21	(D)
			TR	Hull C.	06.73	1973-74	65	1	2	
			L	Barnsley	10.75	1975	4	/	0	
			L	Stockport Co.	12.75	1975	6	/	0	
			Scarborough	Scunthorpe	02.78	1977-79	105	/	2	
DELANEY, James	Lanark	03.09.14	Glasgow Celtic	Manchester U.	+	1946-50	164		25	(W)S-13/S.F.LGE REP.
DELANEY, John	Slough	03.02.42	Wycombe W.	Bournemouth	08.73	1973-74	25	/	0	(HB) E.AMAT.INT.
DELANEY, Louis P.	Bothwell	28.02.21	Nunhead	Arsenal	+					(FB)
			TR	Crystal Palace	11.49	1949	3		0	
DELAPENHA, Lloyd L.	West Indies	20.05.27		Portsmouth	04.48	1948-49	8		0	(OR)
			TR	Middlesbrough	04.50	1949-57	260		90	
			TR	Mansfield T.	06.58	1958-60	115		27	
DELF, Barrie S.	Rochford	05.06.61		Southend U.	N/C	1982	1	/	0	(G)

Players Names	Birthplace	Date	Previous Club	League Club	Date Signed	Seasons Played	Apps	Sub	Gls	
DELGADO, Robert	Cardiff	29.01.49	Barry T.	Luton T.	02.70					(D)
			TR	Carlisle U.	07.71	1972-73	25	10	3	
			L	Workington	10.73	1973	7	/	0	
			TR	Rotherham U.	12.73	1973-75	69	1	5	
			TR	Chester C.	10.75	1975-78	125	3	8	
			TR	Port Vale	12.78	1978-79	41	/	0	
DELLOW, Ron W.	Crosby	13.07.14	Tranmere Rov.(*)	Carlisle U.	+	1946	16		5	(OR)Mansfield/Manchester C.
DELVE, John F.	London	27.09.53	APP	Q.P.R.	07.71	1972-73	9	6	0	(M)
			TR	Plymouth Arg.	07.74	1974-77	127	5	6	
			TR	Exeter C.	03.78	1977-82	215	/	20	
			TR	Hereford U.	06.83	1983	35	1	3	
DEMAINE, David	Cleveleys	07.05.42	JNRS	Blackpool	07.60					(F)
			TR	Tranmere Rov.	08.61	1961	2		0	
			TR	Southport	07.62	1962	5		0	
DEMPSEY, John	Cumbernauld	22.06.13	Hearts	Ipswich T.	06.48	1948	22		5	
DEMPSEY, John T.	Hampstead	15.03.46	APP	Fulham	03.64	1964-68	149	/	4	(CH) EI-19
			TR	Chelsea	01.69	1968-75	161	4	4	
DEMPSEY, John W.	Birkenhead	02.04.51	APP	Tranmere Rov.	04.69	1967-71	52	1	1	(FB)
DENHAM, Charles H.	Hartlepool	28.04.37	West.Amats.	Hartlepool U.	AM	1958	5		3	(CF)
DENHAM, John W.	Middleton	06.11.25	Yorks.Amats.	Hull C.	06.48					(LH)
			TR	Hartlepool U.	08.49	1949	1		0	
DENIAL, Geoff	Sheffield	03.01.32		Sheffield U.	01.52	1952-54	10		0	(WH)
			TR	Oxford U.	N/L	1962	6		0	
DENNEHY, Miah	Cork	29.03.50	Cork Hibs	Nottingham F.	01.73	1972-74	37	4	4	(F) EI-10
			TR	Walsall	07.75	1975-77	123	5	22	
			TR	Bristol Rov.	07.78	1978-79	47	5	6	
			TR	Cardiff C.	08.80					
DENNIS, Alan G.	Colchester	22.12.51	JNRS	Colchester U.	08.70	1969-70	2	3	0	(HB)
DENNIS, J. Anthony	Taplow	01.12.63	APP	Plymouth Arg.	12.81	1981-82	7	2	0	(F)
			TR	Exeter C.	08.83	1983	3	1	0	
DENNIS, Mark E.	Streatham	02.05.61	APP	Birmingham C.	08.78	1978-82	130	/	1	(D) E.U21-3/3.YTH.INT.
			TR	Southampton	11.83	1983	20	/	0	
DENNISON, Charles R.	Hull	12.09.32	JNRS	Hull C.	07.54	1954-57	24		1	(FB)
DENNISON, Robert S.	Ambleside	06.03.12	Fulham(*)	Northampton T.	+	1946-47	55		0	(CH)*Redcliffe W./ Newcastle U./Nottingham F.
DENNY, Paul N.	Croydon	05.09.57	APP	Southend U.	09.75	1976	8	1	2	(F)
			TR	Wimbledon	08.77	1977-80	87	16	11	
DENTON, Peter R.	Gorleston	01.03.46	APP	Coventry C.	03.64	1965-67	10	/	1	(F)
			TR	Luton T.	01.68	1967-68	4	1	0	
DENTON, Roger	Manchester	06.01.53	JNRS	Bolton W.	05.71	1971	3	1	0	(FB)
			TR	Bradford C.	07.72	1972-73	25	5	0	
			L	Rochdale	02.74	1973	2	/	0	
DENYER, Albert F.T.	Swindon	06.12.24		Swindon T.	+	1946	7		1	
			TR	Cardiff C.	05.48					
			TR	Norwich C.	08.49					
DENYER, Peter R.	Haslemere	26.11.57	APP	Portsmouth	12.75	1975-78	123	8	15	(M)
			TR	Northampton T.	07.79	1979-82	138	9	28	
DEPEAR, E. Roly	Spalding	10.12.23	Boston U.	Leeds U.	05.48	1948	4		0	(CH)
			TR	Newport Co.	06.49	1949	16		0	
			TR	Shrewsbury T.	07.50	1950-51	74		5	
DEPLEDGE, William	Bradford	12.11.24	JNRS	Bradford P.A.	+	1946-55	274		62	(OL)
DERBYSHIRE, Tom	Manchester	10.12.30		Hartlepool U.	AM	1950	1		0	
DERKO, Franco	Italy	22.12.46	APP	Mansfield T.	01.65	1966	1	/	0	(FB)
DERRETT, Steve C.	Cardiff	16.10.47	APP	Cardiff C.	10.65	1966-71	61	5	0	(D) W-4/W.U23-3/ W.SCH.INT.
			TR	Carlisle U.	04.72	1972	13	/	0	
			L	Aldershot	10.73	1973	4	/	0	
			TR	Rotherham U.	12.73	1973-75	79	2	2	
			TR	Newport Co.	06.76	1976-77	61	/	0	
DERRICK, Albert E.	Newport	08.09.08	Newport Co.(*)	Swindon T.	+	1946	1		0	d.1975
DERRICK, Edward A.	Newport	06.08.39		Newport Co.	12.60	1960	3		0	(IF) Son of Albert
			Hereford U.	Newport Co.	07.69	1969	25	2	7	
DERRICK, Jantzen S.	Bristol	10.01.43	JNRS	Bristol C.	01.60	1959-70	253	7	31	(OR) E.SCH.INT.
			L	Mansfield T.	03.71	1970	2	/	0	
DESMEULES, Rod L.	Newbury	23.09.48	APP	Swindon T.	10.66	1966-67	4	/	0	(FB)
DESMOND, Peter	Cork	23.11.26	Shelbourne	Middlesbrough	05.49	1949	2		0	(IF)EI-4/L.O.I. REP.
			TR	Southport	08.50	1950	12		2	
			TR	York C.	12.51	1951	1		0	
				Hartlepool U.	08.53	1953	1		0	
DEVANNEY, Alan	Otley	05.09.41	JNRS	Bradford C.	02.59	1959-61	12		4	(F)
DEVERALL, Harry R.	Reading	05.05.16	Maidenhead	Reading	*	1946-47	64		7	(OL) E.SCH.INT.
			TR	Orient	08.48	1948-52	114		2	

Players Names	Birthplace	Date	Previous Club	League Club	Date Signed	Seasons Played	Apps	Sub	Gls	
DEVEREUX, Anthony	Gilbraltar	06.01.40	Chelsea(AM)	Aldershot	11.58	1959-65	133	/	0	(CH)
DEVEY, Ray	Birmingham	19.12.17		Birmingham C.	*	1946	1		0	
			TR	Mansfield T.	08.47	1947-49	77		4	
DEVINE, J. Henry	Liverpool	09.07.33	Rhyl	Chester C.	07.55	1955	1		0	
DEVINE, John	Dublin	11.11.58	APP	Arsenal	10.76	1977-82	86	3	0	(D) EI-11/EI.U21-2
			TR	Norwich C.	08.83	1983	31	1	3	
DEVINE, Peter	Blackburn	25.05.60	Chorley	Bristol C.	07.81	1981	19	2	1	(F)
			TR	Blackburn Rov.	N/C	1982-83	8	/	2	
DEVINE, Steve B.	Strabane	11.12.64	APP	Wolverhampton W.	12.82					(M)
			TR	Derby Co.	03.83	1983	9	1	0	
DEVINE, Willie	Paisley	22.08.33	St.Mirren	Watford	03.58	1957-58	30		6	(IF)
			Partick Th.	Accrington St.	05.60	1960	46		6	
DEVITT, Malcolm	Bradford	26.01.37		Bradford C.	03.59	1958-62	100		13	(F)
DEVLIN, Alan	Edinburgh	10.10.53	Dundee U.	Exeter C.	11.73	1973	1	/	0	(IF)
DEVLIN, Doug K.	Glasgow	17.03.53	APP	Wolverhampton W.	06.71					(IF)
			TR	Walsall	07.72	1972	15	3	0	
DEVLIN, Ernie	Gateshead	06.03.20		Gateshead	+					(FB) d.1976
			TR	West Ham U.	06.46	1946-52	70		0	
			TR	Darlington	02.54	1953-56	115		1	
DEVLIN, John	Airdrie	11.12.17	Kilmarnock	Walsall	12.47	1947-51	159		50	(IF)
DEVLIN, Joseph	Coatbridge	12.03.31	Falkirk	Accrington St.	07.53	1953-56	114		18	(OR)
			TR	Rochdale	09.56	1956-57	38		7	
			TR	Bradford P.A.	11.57	1957-58	34		3	
			TR	Carlisle U.	07.59	1959	5		0	
DEVLIN, William	Glasgow	30.05.31	Peterborough U.	Carlisle U.	08.56	1956	28		6	
DEVONSHIRE, Alan	London	13.04.56	Southall	West Ham U.	10.76	1976-83	269	3	24	(M) E-8/Son of Les
DEVONSHIRE, Les E.	London	13.06.26	Q.P.R.(AM)	Brentford	05.48					(OL) Father of Alan
			TR	Chester C.	06.50	1950	44		4	
			TR	Crystal Palace	08.51	1951-54	82		12	
DEVRIES, Roger	Hull	25.10.50	JNRS	Hull C.	09.67	1970-79	314	4	0	(D)
			TR	Blackburn Rov.	07.80	1980	13	/	0	
				Scunthorpe U.	10.81	1981	6	/	1	
DEWICK, John A.	Rotherham	28.11.19		Notts.Co.	10.46	1946	1		0	(G)
DEWIS, George	Burbage	22.01.13	Nuneaton	Leicester C.	*	1946-49	44		20	(F)
DEWS, George	Ossett	05.06.21		Middlesbrough	+	1946-47	33		8	(IL) Worc. Cricketer
			TR	Plymouth Arg.	10.47	1947-54	257		77	
			TR	Walsall	06.55	1955	10		1	
DEWSBURY, John	Swansea	16.02.32	JNRS	Swansea C.	07.50	1952	9		0	(FB)
			TR	Newport Co.	08.55	1955	2		0	
DEWSNIP, George E.	Salford	06.05.56	Preston N.E. (APP)	Southport	06.74	1974-76	83	4	11	(F)
DEY, Geoff	Chesterfield	11.01.64	APP	Sheffield U.	01.82					(M)
			TR	Scunthorpe U.	08.83	1983	12	/	1	
DEYNA, Kazimlerz	Poland	23.10.47	Legia Warsaw	Manchester C.	11.78	1978-80	34	4	12	(F) POLISH INT.
DIBBLE, Andy	Cwmbran	08.05.65	APP	Cardiff C.	08.82	1981-83	62	/	0	(G) W.U'21-2
DIBBLE, Chris	Morden	10.10.60	APP	Millwall	11.77	1977-81	49	14	5	(M) E.SCH.INT.
			TR	Wimbledon	07.82	1982-83	7	2	0	
DIBDEN, Keith	Southampton	17.12.33	JNRS	Southampton	01.52					(F)
			TR	Gillingham	07.57	1957	1		0	
DICK, Alistair J.	Stirling	25.04.65	APP	Tottenham H.	05.82	1981-83	13	1	2	(F) S.SCH.INT./S.YTH.INT.
DICK, George W.	Torphichen	12.06.21		Blackpool	08.46	1946-47	46		13	(IF) d.1960
			TR	West Ham U.	10.48	1948	14		1	
			TR	Carlisle U.	07.49	1949-50	52		23	
			TR	Stockport Co.	10.50	1950	25		12	
			TR	Workington	10.51	1951-52	56		16	
DICK, John	Glasgow	19.03.30	Crittalls Ath.	West Ham U.	06.53	1953-62	326		153	(IF) S-1/S'B'-1●
			TR	Brentford	09.62	1962-64	72		45	
DICK, Peter W.	Glasgow	20.08.27	T.Lanark	Accrington St.	06.55	1955-58	126		37	(F)
			TR	Bradford P.A.	12.58	1958-62	155		2	
DICK, Tom W.	Glasgow	19.07.36	T.Lanark	Bradford P.A.	06.60	1960	4		0	(F)
DICKENS, Alan W.	Plaistow	03.09.64	APP	West Ham U.	08.82	1982-83	19	6	6	(M) E.YTH.INT.
DICKENS, Leo	Hemsworth	16.03.27	Frickley Col	Rotherham U.	07.50					(HB)
			TR	Chester C.	07.52	1952	7		0	
DICKENSON, Kevin J.	London	24.11.62	Tottenham H.(APP)	Charlton Ath.	08.80	1979-83	59	3	1	(D)
DICKER, Les R.	Stockwell	20.12.26	Chelmsford	Tottenham H.	06.51	1952	10		2	(OL)
			TR	Southend U.	07.53	1953-54	18		7	
DICKIE, Alan L.	Charlton	30.01.44	APP	West Ham U.	02.62	1961-65	12	/	0	(G)
			TR	Coventry C.	03.67	1967	2	/	0	
			TR	Aldershot	07.68	1968	6	/	0	

Players Names	Birthplace	Date	Previous Club	League Club	Date Signed	Seasons Played	Apps	Sub	Gls	
DICKIE, Murdoch	Dumbarton	28.12.19	Guildford C.	Chelsea	+	1946	1		0	(OR) +Port Vale
			TR	Bournemouth	02.47	1946-47	16		2	
DICKINSON, Jim A.	South Elmsall	26.09.31	Pontefract	Barrow	08.51	1951-57	67		0	(FB)
DICKINSON, Jim W.	Alton	24.04.25	JNRS	Portsmouth	+	1946-64	764		9	(WH)E-48/E'B'-3/E.F.LGE REP.●d.1982
DICKINSON, Len	South Elmsall	06.03.42	JNRS	Sheffield Wed.	02.60					(F)
			TR	Oldham Ath.	06.61	1961	5		2	
DICKINSON, Martin J.	Leeds	14.03.63	APP	Leeds U.	05.80	1979-83	71	1	0	(D)
DICKINSON, Ron A.	Coventry	29.06.30	Nuneaton	Shrewsbury T.	AM	1953	11		0	(HB)
			TR	Coventry C.	06.54					
DICKS, Alan V.	London	29.08.34	JNRS	Chelsea	09.51	1952-57	33		1	(CH) Brother of Ronnie
			TR	Southend U.	11.58	1958-61	85		2	
			TR	Coventry C.	02.62					
DICKS, Ronnie W.	London	13.04.24	Dulwich H.	Middlesbrough	+	1947-58	319		10	(WH)
DICKSON, Adam	Hamilton	04.01.29	Thorniewood	Leicester C.	06.51	1951-54	16		0	(G)
DICKSON, Joe J.	Liverpool	31.01.34	JNRS	Liverpool	06.52	1955	6		4	(F) E.YTH.INT.
DICKSON, William	Lurgan	15.04.23	Glenavon	Notts.Co.	+	1946-47	21		2	(WH)N.I.-12
			TR	Chelsea	11.47	1947-52	101		4	
			TR	Arsenal	10.53	1953-55	29		1	
			TR	Mansfield T.	07.56	1956	19		0	
DIGBY, Derek F.	Teignmouth	14.05.31	Dawlish	Exeter C.	08.49	1951-52	31		2	(OR)
			TR	Southampton	09.53	1953-54	15		2	
DIGHTON, Richard A.	Corby	26.07.51	Coventry C. (APP)	Peterborough U.	11.69	1970-71	8	/	0	(G)
			L	Stockport Co.	10.70	1970	1	/	0	
DIGNAM, Joe	Glasgow	10.01.31	Alloa	Wrexham	07.57	1957	8			
DIGWEED, Perry	London	26.10.59	APP	Fulham	09.76	1976-80	15	/	0	(G)
			TR	Brighton & H.A.	01.81	1980-83	46	/	0	
DILLON, John	Coatbridge	09.11.42	JNRS	Sunderland	11.59	1960-61	18		1	(F)
			TR	Brighton & H.A.	07.62	1962	21		3	
			TR	Crewe Alex.	07.63	1963	5		1	
DILLON, Kevin	Sunderland	18.12.59	APP	Birmingham C.	07.77	1977-82	181	5	15	(M) E.YTH. INT./E.U21-1
			TR	Portsmouth	03.83	1982-83	47	/	14	
DILLON, Mike L.	Highgate	29.09.52	APP	Tottenham H.	12.69	1972-73	21	3	1	(HB) E.YTH.INT./
			L	Millwall	12.74	1974	4	/	0	E.SCH.INT.
			L	Swindon T.	03.75	1974	7	2	0	
DILLON, Vince	Manchester	02.10.23		Bolton W.	04.48	1947-50	17		2	(CF)
			TR	Tranmere Rov.	02.51	1950-52	33		17	
DILLSWORTH, Eddie	Sierra Leone	16.04.46	Wealdstone	Lincoln C.	AM	1966	2	/	0	(WH)
DIMMER, Hyam	Scotstown	14.03.14	Ayr U.	Aldershot	08.46	1946	7		1	(IF)
DIMOND, Stuart	Chorlton	03.01.20	Manchester U.(+)	Bradford C.	+	1946	9		1	(CF)
DINE, John	Newton Stewart	03.05.40	Bulford U.	Bradford P.A.	05.64	1962-64	32		0	(G)
DINGWALL, W. Norman	Gateshead	29.07.23		Sheffield U.	+					(F)
			TR	Halifax T.	07.47	1947	9		0	
DINSDALE, Peter	Bradford	19.10.38	Yorks Amats.	Huddersfield T.	01.56	1959-66	213	1	9	(WH)
			TR	Bradford P.A.	08.67	1967	9	/	0	
DITCHBURN, Edward	Gillingham	24.10.21	JNRS	Tottenham H.	+	1946-58	418		0	(G)E-6/E'B'-2/E.F.LGE REP.●
DIVERS, John	Clydebank	06.08.11	Morton	Oldham Ath.	08.47	1947	1		0	(IF) S-1
DIVERS, John R.	Glasgow	24.11.31	Clyde	Exeter C.	05.56	1956	13		1	(OR)
DIX, Richard	South Shields	17.01.24	JNRS	Bradford P.A.	+	1946-47	18		5	(OL)
			North Shields	Bradford C.	08.52	1952	8		1	
DIX, Ronnie W.	Bristol	05.09.12	Derby Co.(*)	Tottenham H.	+	1946-47	35		5	(IF) *Blackburn Rov./Bristol Rov./
			TR	Reading	11.47	1947-48	44		13	Aston Villa E-1/E.F.LGE REP./E.SCH.INT.
DIXEY, Richard	Leicester	02.09.56	Enderby T.	Burnley	12.74	1974	3	/	0	(HB)
			L	Stockport Co.	02.76	1975	14	/	1	
DIXON, Arthur	Middleton	17.11.21	Hearts	Northampton T.	11.49	1949-51	68		23	(IF)
			TR	Leicester C.	10.51	1951-52	11		0	
DIXON, Cecil H.	Trowbridge	28.03.35	Trowbridge T.	Cardiff C.	07.54	1954-56	21		1	(IF)
			TR	Newport Co.	07.57	1957-60	107		15	
			TR	Northampton T.	08.61	1961	15		4	
DIXON, Colin	Newcastle	24.09.63	APP	Southampton	09.81					(D)
				Hartlepool U.	11.83	1983	1	/	0	
DIXON, David	Seaham	03.11.51	APP	Middlesbrough	11.68	1969	1	/	0	(FB)
DIXON, Joe	Newcastle (Staffs)	24.09.16	Audley U.	Northampton T.	+					
			TR	Port Vale	10.46	1946	1		0	
DIXON, John T.	Hebburn	10.12.23	Spennymoor	Aston Villa	+	1946-60	392		131	(IF)
DIXON, John W.	Hartlepool	12.03.34		Hartlepool U.	10.57	1958-60	35		2	(FB)

Players Names	Birthplace	Date	Previous Club	League Club	Date Signed	Seasons Played	Career Record Apps	Sub	Gls	
DIXON, Kerry M.	Luton	24.07.61	Dunstable	Reading	07.80	1980-82	110	6	51	(F)
			TR	Chelsea	08.83	1983	42	/	28	
DIXON, Kevin L.	Consett	27.07.60	Tow Law	Carlisle U.	08.83	1983	5	4	0	(F)
			L	Hartlepool U.	10.83	1983	6	/	3	
DIXON, Lee M.	Manchester	17.03.64	JNRS	Burnley	07.82	1982-83	4	/	0	(D)
			TR	Chester C.	02.84	1983	16	/	1	
DIXON, Mike	Willesden	14.03.37	Hitchin T.	Luton T.	04.57	1958-60	3		0	(F) Father of Kerry
			TR	Coventry C.	05.61	1961	18		12	
DIXON, Mike G.	Reading	12.10.43	JNRS	Reading	08.61	1962-67	112	/	0	(G) E.SCH.INT.
			TR	Aldershot	07.69	1969-70	38	/	0	
DIXON, Milton	Manchester	30.03.25		Huddersfield T.	02.48					(CF)
			TR	Stockport Co.	10.50	1950	21		2	
DIXON, Paul K.	Londonderry	22.02.60	APP	Burnley	06.78	1979-81	23	1	1	(M)
DIXON, Ray	Denaby	31.12.30	Denaby U.	Rotherham U.	06.55	1955-56	14		4	(F)
DIXON, Robert	Felling	11.01.36	Crook T.	Arsenal	08.57					(OL)
			TR	Workington	11.58	1958	28		5	
			TR	W.B.A.	05.59	1959	7		1	
DIXON, Stan	Burnley	28.08.20	Burnley(*)	Plymouth Arg.	*	1946-50	60		1	(CH)
DIXON, Tommy C.	Newcastle	08.06.29	Newcastle U.(AM)	West Ham U.	02.51	1952-54	39		21	(CF)
			TR	Reading	03.55	1954-58	123		63	
			TR	Brighton & H.A.	10.58	1958-59	35		12	
			TR	Workington	07.60	1960-61	53		17	
			TR	Barrow	10.61	1961-62	62		23	
DIXON, Wilf E.	London	20.02.50	APP	Arsenal	05.68					(D)
			TR	Reading	07.69	1969-72	150	3	0	
			TR	Colchester U.	08.73					
			TR	Swindon T.	09.73	1973-76	134	6	10	
			TR	Aldershot	07.77	1977-79	114	6	6	
DOBBIE, Harold	Bishop Auckland	20.02.23	South Bank	Middlesbrough	12.46	1946-49	23		6	(IF)
			TR	Plymouth Arg.	03.50	1949-53	27		6	
			TR	Torquay U.	10.53	1953-56	110		47	
DOBBIN, James	Dunfermline	17.09.63	Glasgow Celtic	Doncaster Rov.	03.84	1983	11	/	2	(M)
DOBBING, Robert	Sunderland	27.06.49	Coventry C.(APP)	Hartlepool U.	07.69	1969	34	/	1	(FB)
DOBBS, Eric	Forehoe	15.10.20		Coventry C.	08.46	1946-47	5		0	
			TR	Bristol Rov.	07.48					
DOBING, Brian	Sheffield	29.12.37	Knutsford	Crewe Alex.	09.59	1958	1		0	(G)
DOBING, Peter	Manchester	01.12.38	JNRS	Blackburn Rov.	12.55	1956-60	179		89	(IF) E.U23-7/E.F.LGE REP.●
			TR	Manchester C.	07.61	1961-62	82		31	
			TR	Stoke C.	08.63	1963-72	303	/	80	
DOBSON, Brian A.	Colchester	01.03.34		Colchester U.	01.56	1955-59	24		0	(F)
DOBSON, Colin	Middlesbrough	09.05.40	JNRS	Sheffield Wed.	11.57	1961-65	177	/	49	(W) E.U23-2
			TR	Huddersfield T.	08.66	1966-70	149	5	50	
			L	Brighton & H.A.	01.72	1971	2	2	0	
			TR	Bristol Rov.	07.72	1972-75	62	/	4	
DOBSON, George R.	Chiswick	24.08.49	APP	Brentford	08.67	1966-69	75	5	10	(F)
DOBSON, Ian	Hull	03.10.57	APP	Hull C.	10.75	1975-79	86	6	7	(D)
			TR	Hereford U.	06.80	1980-81	41	/	5	
DOBSON, J. Martin	Blackburn	14.02.48	JNRS	Bolton W.	07.66					(M) E-5/E.F.LGE.REP.●
			TR	Burnley	08.67	1967-74	220	4	43	
			TR	Everton	08.74	1974-78	190	/	29	
			TR	Burnley	08.79	1979-83	186	/	20	
			TR	Bury	03.84	1983	10	/	0	
DOBSON, Paul	Hartlepool	17.12.62		Hartlepool U.	11.81	1981-83	50	8	20	(F)
DOBSON, Robert P.	Frimley	13.06.25	Wisbech T.	Ipswich T.	10.49	1949-53	30		6	(F)
DOCHERTY, Bernard	Bellshill	11.08.41	Cambuslang	Notts. Co.	08.64	1964	25		2	(IF)
DOCHERTY, James	Clydebank	21.04.26	Glasgow Celtic	Northampton T.	07.50	1950	1		0	(F)
DOCHERTY, James	Clydebank	22.04.29	Airdrie	Doncaster Rov.	05.51	1951	11		4	(WH)
			Limerick	Crewe Alex.	02.57	1956	2		0	
DOCHERTY, Jim	Broxburn	08.11.56	E. Stirling	Chelsea	03.79	1978	2	1	0	(F)
DOCHERTY, John	Glasgow	29.04.40	St.Rochs	Brentford	07.59	1960	17		2	(OR)
			TR	Sheffield U.	03.61	1960-65	41	/	9	
			TR	Brentford	12.65	1965-67	97	/	31	
			TR	Reading	02.68	1967-69	45	1	8	
			TR	Brentford	03.70	1970-73	137	4	34	
			TR	Q.P.R.	07.74					
DOCHERTY, John	Glasgow	28.02.35	Hearts	Colchester U.	06.63	1963-64	77		2	(HB)
DOCHERTY, Mike	Preston	29.10.50	APP	Burnley	04.67	1968-75	149	4	0	(D)E.YTH.INT./
			TR	Manchester C.	04.76	1975-76	8	/	0	Son of Tommy
			TR	Sunderland	12.76	1976-78	72	1	6	

Players Names	Birthplace	Date	Previous Club	League Club	Date Signed	Seasons Played	Apps	Sub	Gls	
DOCHERTY, Peter	Hebburn	14.02.29		Fulham	09.49					
			TR	Darlington	09.50	1950	3		1	
DOCHERTY, Tom	Penshaw	15.04.24	Murton C.W.	Lincoln C.	07.47	1947-49	45		3	(OL)
			TR	Norwich C.	06.50	1950-52	85		4	
			TR	Reading	07.53	1953-54	53		2	
			TR	Newport Co.	06.55	1955-57	107		1	
DOCHERTY, Tommy	Glasgow	24.08.28	Glasgow Celtic	Preston N.E.	11.49	1949-57	324		5	(WH)S-25/S'B'-1
			TR	Arsenal	08.58	1958-60	84		0	
			TR	Chelsea	09.61	1961	4		0	
DOCKER, John	Coventry	25.09.47	JNRS	Coventry C.	08.65					(F)
			L	Torquay U.	07.67	1967	4	1	0	
DODD, Alan	Stoke	20.09.53	APP	Stoke C.	10.70	1972-82	349	7	3	(D) E.U23-6
			TR	Wolverhampton W.	11.82	1982-83	68	/	3	
DODD, Jim E.	Wallasey	12.12.33	Upton FC	Tranmere Rov.	05.56	1956-59	63		22	(F)
DODD, William	Bedlington	30.09.36	Whitley Bay	Burnley	02.56					(F)
			TR	Workington	09.58	1958	1		1	
			TR	Halifax T.	11.58					
DODD, William D.	Chester-le-Street	25.08.33	Derby Co.(AM)	Shrewsbury T.	08.50	1950-54	28		1	(WH) d.1982
			TR	Southport	06.57	1957-58	70		2	
DODDS, Ephraim	Grangemouth	07.09.15	Sheffield U.(*)	Blackpool	*					(CF)*Meddomsley J./
			TR	Everton	11.46	1946-48	56		36	Huddersfield T.
			TR	Lincoln C.	10.48	1948-49	60		38	
DODDS, Gerry	Sheffield	04.01.35	JNRS	Sheffield U.	02.52					(F)
			TR	Chesterfield	06.55	1955	4		0	
			South Shields	Scunthorpe U.	05.59					
DODDS, Les	Newcastle	12.10.36	JNRS	Sunderland	10.53	1954-55	6		0	(G) E.SCH.INT.
				Bristol C.	08.60					
DODDS, Robert	Gateshead	01.07.23		Darlington	02.47	1946-48	34		1	
DODDS, Tom B.	South Shields	20.12.18	North Shields	Aston Villa	*	1946	1		0	
			TR	Swansea C.	01.47	1946-47	11		2	
DODGE, William	Hackney	10.03.37	Eton Manor	Tottenham H.	10.57	1958-59	6		0	(WH)
			TR	Crystal Palace	07.62	1962	3		0	
DODGIN, Norman	Gateshead	01.11.21	Whitehall BC	Newcastle U.	+	1947-49	84		1	(WH) Brother of William
			TR	Reading	06.50	1950	13		1	(Snr) & Uncle of
			TR	Northampton T.	09.51	1951-52	19		1	William (Jnr).
			TR	Exeter C.	08.53	1953-54	33		1	
DODGIN, William	Durham	04.11.31	Southampton(AM)	Fulham	09.49	1951-52	35		0	(CH) E.U23-1
			TR	Arsenal	12.52	1952-59	191		0	
			TR	Fulham	03.61	1960-63	69		0	
DODSON, David A.	Gravesend	20.01.40	JNRS	Arsenal	11.57					(OL) E.YTH.INT.
			TR	Swansea C.	07.59	1959-61	30		12	
			TR	Portsmouth	12.61	1961-64	54		20	
			TR	Aldershot	01.65	1964-66	59	/	12	
DOHERTY, James C.	Douglas	31.01.57	Cumnock J.	Notts. Co.	07.79	1979-80	6	2	0	(F)
DOHERTY, John	Manchester	12.03.35	JNRS	Manchester U.	03.52	1952-57	25		5	(IF)
			TR	Leicester C.	10.57	1957	12		5	
DOHERTY, John M.	Stoneleigh	26.04.36	Chelsea(AM)	Fulham	09.54	1956-61	49		7	(F)
			S.Coast U.	Aldershot	01.65	1964-65	18	/	1	
DOHERTY, Mike	Liverpool	08.03.61	Basingstoke	Reading	10.82	1982	23	2	5	(M)
DOHERTY, Peter D.	Magherafelt	05.06.13	Manchester C.(*)	Derby Co.	+	1946	15		7	(IF)*Glentoran/Blackpool/
			TR	Huddersfield T.	12.46	1946-48	83		33	N.I.-16●
			TR	Doncaster Rov.	06.49	1949-52	103		55	
DOLAN, Andy	Glasgow	02.08.20	Raith Rov.	Bury	08.48	1948	10		2	
			TR	Accrington St.	09.49	1949	19		4	
DOLAN, Terry	Bradford	11.06.50	Bradford C. (AM)	Bradford P.A.	04.69	1968-69	46	2	0	(F)
			TR	Huddersfield T.	10.70	1971-75	157	5	14	
			TR	Bradford C.	08.76	1976-80	191	4	43	
			TR	Rochdale	08.81	1981	42	1	1	
DOLBY, Peter	Derby	18.05.40	Heanor T.	Shrewsbury T.	02.60	1960-75	304	22	21	(CH)
DOLDING, D. Len	Belgium	13.12.22	Wealdstone	Chelsea	+	1946-47	26		2	(W) d.1954/
			TR	Norwich C.	07.48	1948-49	12		1	Middlesex Cricketer
DOMINEY, Barry	Edmonton	21.10.55	Enfield WMC	Colchester U.	01.74	1973-76	56	15	3	(D)
DONACHIE, Willie	Glasgow	05.10.51	JNRS	Manchester C.	12.68	1969-79	347	4	2	(D)S-35/S.U23-2
			Portland Timbers	Norwich C.	09.81	1981	11	/	0	
			Portland Timbers	Burnley	11.82	1982-83	60	/	3	
DONAGHY, Barry	Consett	21.03.56	APP	W.B.A.	05.73	1973-74	4	2	1	(M) E.YTH.INT.
			TR	Workington	12.75	1975-76	40	4	3	
DONAGHY, Mal	Belfast	13.09.57	Larne	Luton T.	06.78	1978-83	246	/	14	(D)NI-31/NI.U21-1
DONALD, Alex	Edinburgh	05.06.48		Port Vale	10.65	1965-67	41	2	0	(F)
DONALD, Ian	Aberdeen	28.11.51	JNRS	Manchester U.	07.69	1972	4	/	0	(FB) S.SCH.INT.
DONALD, Warren R.	Uxbridge	07.10.64	APP	West Ham U.	10.82	1983	1	1	0	(D)

Players Names	Birthplace	Date	Previous Club	League Club	Date Signed	Seasons Played	Apps	Sub	Gls	
DONALDSON, Andy	Newcastle	22.03.25	V.Armstrong	Newcastle U.	+	1946-48	19		6	(CF)
			TR	Middlesbrough	01.49	1948-50	21		7	
			TR	Exeter C.	09.53	1953-54	39		17	
DONALDSON, Brian	Hove	03.04.36	JNRS	Chelsea	07.53					(LH)
			TR	Swindon T.	10.57	1957	1		0	
DONALDSON, Dave J.	London	12.11.54	APP	Arsenal	07.72					(D) E.SCH.INT.
			TR	Millwall	06.73	1973-79	215	1	1	
			TR	Cambridge U.	02.80	1979-83	130	2	0	
DONALDSON, David	Hounslow	28.12.41	Walton & Hersham	Wimbledon	N/L	1977-78	61	/	0	(D)
DONALDSON, Jim D.	South Shields	11.06.27		Chesterfield	09.49	1949-50	17		4	(WH)
			TR	Newport Co.	08.51	1951-52	36		1	
DONALDSON, L. Fred	Stoke	07.04.37	JNRS	Port Vale	07.54	1954-59	47		4	(FB)
			TR	Exeter C.	08.60	1960	35		6	
			TR	Chester C.	07.61	1961	21		0	
DONALDSON, Les	Glasgow	30.07.22	Rhyl	Wrexham	06.50	1950-51	30		6	(IF)
DONALDSON, Robert S.	South Shields	26.02.21		Newcastle U.	+					
				Hartlepool U.	07.47	1947-51	131		4	
DONALDSON, William	Wallaceton	20.01.20	Leith Ath.	Bradford P.A.	05.46	1946-50	45		6	(F)
			TR	Mansfield T.	10.50	1950-51	51		10	
DONAWA, B. Louie	Ipswich	24.09.64	APP	Norwich C.	09.82	1982-83	23	3	4	(F)
DONE, Cyril C.	Liverpool	21.10.20	JNRS	Liverpool	*	1946-51	95		33	(CF)
			TR	Tranmere Rov.	05.52	1952-54	87		61	
			TR	Port Vale	12.54	1954-56	52		34	
DONN, Nigel	Maidstone	02.03.62	APP	Gillingham	02.80	1980-81	2	1	0	(M)
			TR	Orient	08.82	1982	23	1	2	
DONNELLAN, Gary	London	03.07.62	APP	Chelsea	07.80					(F)
			TR	Watford	11.80					
			TR	Reading	11.81	1981-82	33	8	5	
DONNELLY, Andy	Lanark	01.05.43	Clyde	Millwall	05.63					(G)
			Weymouth	Torquay U.	08.67	1967-71	160	/	0	
DONNELLY, James	Cork	06.05.19	Sligo Rov.	Accrington St.	08.51	1951	4		1	
DONNELLY, John	Glasgow	08.03.61	Dumbarton	Leeds U.	03.83	1982-83	36	3	4	(M)
DONNELLY, John	West Lothian	17.12.36	Glasgow Celtic	Preston N.E.	04.62	1962-66	56	1	1	(FB)
DONNELLY, Peter	Hull	22.09.36	JNRS	Doncaster Rov.	03.54	1953-56	6		1	(CF)
			TR	Scunthorpe U.	07.58	1958-59	39		19	
			TR	Cardiff C.	06.60	1960-61	30		8	
			TR	Swansea C.	10.61	1961	16		3	
			TR	Brighton & H.A.	07.62	1962-64	56		13	
			TR	Bradford C.	03.65	1964-65	13	/	5	
DONNELLY, Peter J.	Chester	11.05.65		Chester C.	N/C	1983	1	/	0	
DONOVAN, Donal	Cork	23.12.29	Dalymount Rov.	Everton	05.49	1951-57	178		2	(FB) E.I-5
			TR	Grimsby T.	08.58	1958-63	236		1	
DONOVAN, Frank J.	Pembroke	21.02.19	Pembroke Bor.	Swansea C.	05.50	1950	15		2	(OR) W.AMAT.INT.
DONOVAN, Terry	Liverpool	27.02.58	Louth U.	Grimsby T.	08.76	1976-78	52	12	23	(F) EI-2/EI.U21-1
			TR	Aston Villa	09.79	1979-81	17	/	6	Son of Donal
			L	Oxford U.	02.83	1982	3	/	0	
			TR	Burnley	02.83	1982-83	13	2	6	
			TR	Rotherham U.	09.83	1983	5	1	0	
DOOLEY, Derek	Sheffield	13.12.29	JNRS	Lincoln C.	AM	1946	2		2	(CF)●
			TR	Sheffield Wed.	06.47	1949-52	61		62	
DOOLEY, George W.	Chesterfield	29.12.22	Parkhouse Col.	Chesterfield	+					
			TR	Halifax T.	12.46	1946	11		2	
			TR	Chesterfield	06.47					
DOONAN, Tom	West Calder	05.10.22	Albion Rov.	Bradford C.	06.49	1949	13		7	(CF)
			TR	Tranmere Rov.	07.50	1950	4		2	
DORAN, Robert	Carlisle	26.12.33		Carlisle U.	10.52	1953-61	107		0	(WH)
DORAN, Terry	Jarrow	02.04.40	St.Mary's BC	Gateshead	AM	1959	1		0	
DORE, Charlie	Gosport	30.09.28	Fleetlands BC	Portsmouth	05.50	1951-53	19		0	(G)
DORIGO, Anthony R.	Australia	31.12.65	APP	Aston Villa	07.83	1983	0	1	0	(D)
DORLING, George C.	Edmonton	27.07.18	JNRS	Tottenham H.	*					(FB)
				Gillingham	N/L	1950	10			
DORMAN, Dan	Birmingham	18.09.22	JNRS	Birmingham C.	05.46	1946-51	60		4	(IF)
			TR	Coventry C.	09.51	1951-54	91		29	
			TR	Walsall	10.54	1954-56	115		33	
DORNAN, Peter	Belfast	30.06.53	Linfield	Sheffield U.	12.76	1976	1	2	0	(F)
			Linfield	Swindon T.	02.79	1978	0	1	0	
DORNEY, Alan	Bermondsey	18.05.47	JNRS	Millwall	05.65	1968-76	249	3	1	(D)
DORSETT, Richard	Brownhills	03.12.19		Wolverhampton W.	*	1946	1		0	(IF)
			TR	Aston Villa	09.46	1946-52	256		33	
DOUGAL, Jack	Falkirk	07.08.34	Pegasus	Halifax T.	AM	1956	2		0	(CH) E.AMAT.INT.

Players Names	Birthplace	Date	Previous Club	League Club	Date Signed	Seasons Played	Apps	Sub	Gls	
DOUGAL, Jim	Denny	03.10.13	Falkirk	Preston N.E.	*	1946	5		1	(OR) S-1
			TR	Carlisle U.	10.46	1946-48	70		15	
			TR	Halifax T.	10.48	1948	22		2	
DOUGALL, Neil	Falkirk	07.11.21	Burnley(+)	Birmingham C.	+	1946-48	93		16	(IF) S-1/
			TR	Plymouth Arg.	03.49	1948-58	278		22	Son of famous player
DOUGAL, Tom	Wishaw	17.05.21		Coventry C.	+					
			TR	Brentford	08.47	1947	2		0	
			TR	Sunderland	11.48	1948	3		0	
DOUGAL, Willie	Falkirk	30.10.23	Glasgow Rgrs.	Preston N.E.	12.47	1947-48	22		2	(HB)
			TR	Barnsley	08.52	1952	21		0	
DOUGAN, Derek	Belfast	20.01.38	Distillery	Portsmouth	08.57	1957-58	33		9	(CF) N.I.-43/N.I.'B'-1/
			TR	Blackburn Rov.	03.59	1958-60	59		25	N.I. SCH. INT.●
			TR	Aston Villa	08.61	1961-62	51		19	
			TR	Peterborough U.	06.63	1963-64	77		38	
			TR	Leicester C.	05.65	1965-66	68	/	35	
			TR	Wolverhampton W.	03.67	1966-74	244	14	93	
DOUGAN, George	Glasgow	22.03.39	Yiewsley	Ipswich T.	03.63	1962-63	17		0	(HB)
DOUGAN, John M.	Glasgow	12.01.31	Bellshill Ath.	Brighton & H.A.	12.51					(IF)
			TR	Torquay U.	02.54	1953-54	20		3	
DOUGAN, Max	West Lothian	23.05.38	Queens Pk.	Leicester C.	09.63	1963-66	9	/	0	(CH) S.AMAT.INT.
			TR	Luton T.	12.66	1966-69	117	1	0	
DOUGHERTY, Paul	Leamington	12.05.66	APP	Wolverhampton W.	05.84	1983	5	/	0	
DOUGHERTY, Vic R.	Glasgow	17.01.55	APP	Bury	APP	1972	9	/	0	(FB)
DOUGHTY, Eric	Radstock	09.04.32	Peasdown	Arsenal	05.51					(WH)
			TR	Plymouth Arg.	07.58	1958	1		0	
DOUGLAS, Bryan	Blackburn	27.05.34	JNRS	Blackburn Rov.	04.52	1954-68	438	/	102	(OR)E-36/E.U23-5/E'B'-1/ E.F.LGE REP.●
DOUGLAS, Colin F.	Hurlford	09.09.62	Glasgow Celtic	Doncaster Rov.	11.81	1981-83	115	9	25	(F)
DOUGLAS, Jim S.	Sunderland	16.09.41	Evenwood T.	Hartlepool U.	AM	1962	13		4	(F)
DOUGLAS, John S.	West Hartlepool	01.12.17	Hartlepool U.(*)	Middlesbrough	+	1946	2		0	
			TR	Hartlepool U.	11.48	1948-49	28		1	
DOUGLAS, Pat G.	Baschurch	07.09.51	APP	Shrewsbury T.	07.69	1968	12	1	1	(IF)
DOUGLASS, Norman	Durham	14.05.30	Crook T.	Chelsea	03.52					(FB)
			TR	Exeter C.	06.53	1953-54	63		0	
DOVE, Henry W.	London	11.03.32	Essex Co.Cad.	Arsenal	08.50					(CH)
			TR	Millwall	04.58	1958	7		0	
DOVEY, Alan R.	Stepney	18.07.52	APP	Chelsea	10.69					(G)
			TR	Brighton & H.A.	03.71	1970-72	6	/	0	
DOW, David J.	Manchester	10.06.47	Avorton FC	Rochdale	AM	1966-67	7	/	0	(CH)
DOWD, Harry	Manchester	04.07.38	Blackley ICI	Manchester C.	07.60	1961-69	181	/	1	(G)
			L	Stoke C.	10.69	1969	3	/	0	
			TR	Oldham Ath.	12.70	1970-73	121	/	0	
DOWD, Hugh	Lurgan	19.05.51	Glenavon	Sheffield Wed.	07.74	1974-78	110	3	0	(D) NI-3
			TR	Doncaster Rov.	08.79	1979-82	94	/	3	
DOWEY, Walter L.	Lockton	12.06.23		Crewe Alex.	+	1947-48	15		0	(RH)
DOWIE, John	Hamilton	12.12.55	APP	Fulham	05.73	1973-76	32	5	2	(M)
			Glasgow Celtic	Doncaster Rov.	07.79	1979-80	21	/	0	
DOWKER, Tom	Liverpool	07.11.22	S.Liverpool	Oldham Ath.	07.47	1947	1		0	
DOWLER, Mike J.	Caldicot	12.10.57	Hereford U.(APP)	Newport Co.	07.76	1975-80	19	/	0	(G) W.SCH.INT.
DOWLING, Mick L.	Bodmin	03.10.52	APP	Plymouth Arg.	10.70	1969-73	26	5	0	(FB)
DOWMAN, Steve J.	Manor Park	15.04.58	APP	Colchester U.	04.76	1976-79	150	4	21	(D)
			TR	Wrexham	07.80	1980-82	87	/	2	
			TR	Charlton Ath.	08.83	1983	35	/	3	
DOWN, David F.	Bristol	07.07.48	APP	Bristol C.	09.65	1966-67	6	1	3	(CF)
			TR	Bradford P.A.	10.67	1967-68	39	/	7	
			TR	Oldham Ath.	09.68	1968	8	/	1	
			TR	Swindon T.	08.69	1969-70	1	1	0	
DOWN, William	Bristol	08.11.63	APP	Bristol C.	10.81	1981	1	/	0	(D)
DOWNES, Eric R.	Wigan	25.08.26	Chester C.(AM)	Rochdale	05.49	1950-53	55		0	(CH)
DOWNES, Robert	Bloxwich	18.08.49	JNRS	W.B.A.	08.66					(M)
			TR	Peterborough U.	09.67	1967-68	23	3	3	
			TR	Rochdale	08.69	1969-73	164	10	10	
			TR	Watford	05.74	1974-79	192	7	19	
			TR	Barnsley	03.80	1979-80	43	/	1	
			TR	Blackpool	07.82	1982-83	27	1	3	
DOWNES, Steve	Leeds	02.12.49	Leeds M.D.B.C.	Rotherham U.	04.67	1967-69	54	8	18	(CF)
			TR	Sheffield Wed.	12.69	1969-71	26	4	4	
			TR	Chesterfield	08.72	1972-73	37	4	11	
			TR	Halifax T.	07.74	1974-75	38	12	12	
			L	Blackburn Rov.	03.76	1975	6	/	0	

Players Names	Birthplace	Date	Previous Club	League Club	Date Signed	Seasons Played	Career Record Apps	Sub	Gls	
DOWNES, Wally J.	London	09.06.61	APP	Wimbledon	01.79	1978-83	171	4	14	(M) Nephew to Terry Downes (Boxer)
DOWNIE, John D.	Lanark	19.07.25	Lanark ATC	Bradford P.A.	+	1946-48	86		34	(IF)
			TR	Manchester U.	03.49	1948-52	110		35	
			TR	Luton T.	08.53	1953	26		12	
			TR	Hull C.	07.54	1954	28		5	
			Wisbech	Mansfield T.	10.58	1958	19		4	
			TR	Darlington	05.59	1959	15		2	
DOWNIE, Mitchell	Troon	09.02.23	Airdrie	Bradford P.A.	08.50	1950-53	156		0	(G)
			TR	Lincoln C.	05.54	1954-58	157		0	
			Goole T.	Bradford C.	09.59	1959-62	134		0	
			TR	Doncaster Rov.	09.63	1963	7		0	
DOWNING, Derek	Doncaster	03.11.45	Frickley C.W.	Middlesbrough	02.65	1965-71	171	11	39	(F)
			TR	Orient	05.72	1972-74	100	4	11	
			TR	York C.	07.75	1975-76	44	3	2	
			TR	Hartlepool U.	07.77	1977	40	/	4	
DOWNS, David	Glasgow	07.03.34		Plymouth Arg.	11.57					(HB)d.1978
			TR	Torquay U.	07.59	1959	3		0	
DOWNS, Greg	Carlton	13.12.58	APP	Norwich C.	12.76	1977-83	143	6	7	(D)
			L	Torquay U.	11.77	1977	1	/	1	
DOWNS, Ron H.	Southwark	27.08.32	Grove U.	Crystal Palace	12.52	1952-53	23		2	(F)
DOWNSBOROUGH, Peter	Halifax	13.09.43	JNRS	Halifax T.	09.60	1959-64	148	/	0	(G)●
			TR	Swindon T.	08.65	1965-72	274	/	0	
			L	Brighton & H.A.	08.73	1973	3	/	0	
			TR	Bradford C.	11.73	1973-78	225	/	0	
DOWSETT, Gilbert J.	Chelmsford	03.07.31	Sudbury T.	Tottenham H.	05.52	1954	1		1	(CF)
			TR	Southend U.	05.55	1955	20		4	
			TR	Southampton	07.56	1956	2		0	
			TR	Bournemouth	06.57	1957-62	169		79	
			TR	Crystal Palace	11.62	1962-64	54		22	
DOWSON, John S.	Ashington	18.09.26		Manchester C.	03.50					(OR)
			Peterborough U.	Darlington	06.52	1952-53	65		11	
DOYLE, Alistair	Limavady	25.10.49	Coleraine	Oldham Ath.	10.66	1967-68	31	2	0	(FB)
DOYLE, Ian P.	Torquay	27.02.59	Barnstaple	Bristol C.	12.78	1979-80	2	1	0	(F)
DOYLE, J. Brian	Manchester	15.07.30	Lostock Green	Stoke C.	03.51	1952	17		0	(FB)
			TR	Exeter C.	04.54	1954-56	100		0	
			TR	Bristol Rov.	08.57	1957-59	43		1	
DOYLE, John	Oxford	08.02.60	APP	Oxford U.	02.78	1977-81	66	/	0	(D)
			TR	Torquay U.	08.82	1982	40	1	3	
DOYLE, Mick	Manchester	25.11.46	APP	Manchester C.	05.64	1974-77	441	7	32	(D)E-5/E.U23-8/
			TR	Stoke C.	06.78	1978-81	115	/	5	E.F.LGE.REP.●
			TR	Bolton W.	01.82	1981-82	40	/	2	
			TR	Rochdale	08.83	1983	24	/	1	
DOYLE, Robert	Dumbarton	27.12.53	Dumbarton	Barnsley	12.72	1972-75	148	1	16	(M)
			TR	Peterborough U.	07.76	1976-78	130	/	10	
			TR	Blackpool	07.79	1979-80	47	2	2	
			TR	Portsmouth	12.80	1908-83	149	/	14	
DOYLE, Robert L.	Liverpool	28.06.27	JNRS	Everton	+					(CH)
			TR	Exeter C.	08.49	1949-54	82		0	
DOYLE, Steve C.	Neath	02.06.58	APP	Preston N.E.	06.75	1974-81	178	19	8	(M) W.U21-1
			TR	Huddersfield T.	09.82	1982-83	75	3	4	
DOZZELL, Jason A.W.	Ipswich	09.12.67	APP	Ipswich T.	APP	1983	0	5	1	(F)
DRAKE, Ken L.	Skipton	17.02.22		Halifax T.	01.47	1946-51	132		0	(WH)
DRAKE, Len	Dorchester	26.07.37	Dorchester T.	Bristol Rov.	08.57	1958-59	8		1	(F)
DRAKE, Ray B.	Stockport	24.10.34		Stockport Co.	03.55	1956-57	23		19	(CF)
DRAKE, Robert	Southgate	07.09.43	Chelsea(AM)	Fulham	12.61	1963-67	16	/	0	(FB) Son of Ted Drake
DRAKE, Steve	Goole	27.08.48	Leeds U.(AM)	Huddersfield T.	06.66					(G)
			TR	Scunthorpe U.	07.67	1967-69	23	/	0	
DRAPER, Derek	Swansea	11.05.43	JNRS	Swansea C.	05.62	1962-65	61	/	10	(F)W.U23-1
			TR	Derby Co.	04.66	1966	8	/	1	
			TR	Bradford P.A.	09.67	1967-68	60	3	9	
			TR	Chester C.	01.69	1968-76	315	7	55	
DRAPER, Richard W.	Leamington	26.09.32	Lockheed FC	Northampton T.	06.55	1955-56	49		20	(CF)
DREWERY, Mike	Snettisham	16.01.49	Snettisham	Peterborough U.	07.67	1968-73	209	/	0	(G)
DRING, Ray	Lincoln	13.02.24		Huddersfield T.	AM	1947	4		0	(G) E.SCH.INT.
DRINKELL, Kevin S.	Grimsby	18.06.60	APP	Grimsby T.	06.78	1976-83	212	23	75	(F)
DRINKWATER, Charlie J.	Willesden	25.06.14	Gillingham	Watford	+	1946	1		0	(OL)*Hendon/Aston Villa/ Charlton Ath.
DRINKWATER, Jim A.	Northwich	10.02.18	St.Mirren	Torquay U.	06.52	1952-53	67		1	(FB)

Players Names	Birthplace	Date	Previous Club	League Club	Date Signed	Seasons Played	Career Record Apps	Sub	Gls	
DRINKWATER, Ray	Jarrow	18.05.31	Guildford C.	Portsmouth	11.55	1956	8		0	(G)
			TR	Q.P.R.	02.58	1957-62	199		0	
DRIVER, Allenby	Sheffield	29.09.18		Sheffield Wed.	*					(IF)
			TR	Luton T.	10.46	1946-47	41		13	
			TR	Norwich C.	01.48	1947-49	49		19	
			TR	Ipswich T.	01.50	1949-51	86		25	
			TR	Walsall	07.52	1952	26		2	
DRIVER, Phil A.	Huddersfield	10.08.59	Bedford T.	Wimbledon	12.78	1978-80	7	9	3	(F)
				Chelsea	09.80	1980-82	25	19	4	
			TR	Wimbledon	07.83	1983	0	2	0	
DROY, Micky	Highbury	07.05.51	Slough T.	Chelsea	09.70	1970-82	262	8	13	(D)
DRUMMOND, Ian P.	Brechin	27.08.23		Portsmouth	+					(FB)
			TR	Bournemouth	06.49	1949-55	265		1	
DRUMMY, Dermot	London	16.01.61	APP	Arsenal	01.79					(M)
			L	Blackpool	03.80	1979	4	1	0	
DRURY, Charles	Darlaston	04.07.37	FH Lloyds FC	W.B.A.	02.55	1957-63	146		1	(WH) E.YTH.INT
			TR	Bristol C.	08.64	1964-66	51	/	1	
			TR	Bradford P.A.	03.68	1967-68	31	/	1	
DRURY, George B.	Hucknall	22.01.14	Sheffield Wed.(*)	Arsenal	*	1946	4		0	(IF) *Heanor T./d.1972
			TR	W.B.A.	10.46	1946-47	29		8	
			TR	Watford	07.48	1948-49	35		3	
DRURY, Jim	Cummock	29.05.24	Stirling A.	Rochdale	05.51	1951	4		1	(F)
			TR	Carlisle U.	08.52	1952-53	35		5	
			TR	Southport	07.54	1954	24		0	
DRYBURGH, Tom J.D.	Kircaldy	23.04.23	Lochgelly Albert.	Aldershot	06.47	1947	19		2	(OL)
			TR	Rochdale	07.48	1948-49	77		17	
			TR	Leicester C.	09.50	1950-53	95		29	
			TR	Hull C.	05.54	1954	23		3	
			TR	Oldham Ath.	08.57	1957	1		0	
			TR	Rochdale	11.57	1957	5		0	
DRYDEN, Jackie G.	Sunderland	16.09.19	Washington Chem.	Charlton Ath.	+					(OL)
			Hylton Col.	Swindon T.	05.47	1947	21		3	
			TR	Orient	06.48	1948-49	40		10	
DRYHURST, Carl D.	Sutton Coldfield	08.11.60	Sutton C.T.	Halifax T.	11.79	1979	4	4	0	(F)
DRYSDALE, Brian	W. Hartlepool	24.02.43	JNRS	Lincoln C.	09.60	1959-64	21	/	0	(D)
			TR	Hartlepool U.	07.65	1965-68	169	1	2	
			TR	Bristol C.	05.69	1969-76	280	2	3	
			L	Reading	02.77	1976	16	/	0	
			TR	Oxford U.	07.77	1977	15	/	0	
DUBLIN, Keith B.L.	Wycombe	29.01.66	APP	Chelsea	01.84	1983	1	/	0	(D)
DUBOIS, Joe M.	Monkstown	27.12.27	Brantwood	Doncaster Rov.	05.49	1949-51	31		5	(OR)N.I.AMAT.INT.
			TR	Grimsby T.	07.53	1953	6		1	
			TR	Halifax T.	07.54	1954-56	78		10	
DUCHART, Alex	Falkirk	03.05.33	Hibernian	Southend U.	05.56	1956	8		2	(W)
DUCK, George T.	Tottenham	22.02.52	APP	Millwall	02.70					(IF)
			TR	Southend U.	06.71	1971	3	/	0	
DUCKHOUSE, Edward	Walsall	09.04.18	Streetly Wks	Birmingham C.	*	1946-49	117		2	(CH)
			TR	Northampton T.	08.50	1950-51	68		0	
DUDDY, John M.	Manchester	08.02.56	APP	Oldham Ath.	06.75					(IF)
			TR	Stockport Co.	03.76	1975	6	/	0	
DUDLEY, Frank E.	Southend	09.05.25		Southend U.	+	1946-48	88		32	(IF)
			TR	Leeds U.	08.49	1949-50	64		23	
			TR	Southampton	02.51	1950-53	67		31	
			TR	Cardiff C.	09.53	1953	4		1	
			TR	Brentford	12.53	1953-56	72		31	
DUDLEY, Jim	Gartcosh	24.08.28	Albright YC	W.B.A.	+	1949-59	285		9	(WH) S'B'-1
			TR	Walsall	12.59	1959-63	167		3	
DUDLEY, Phil	Basildon	17.02.59	APP	Southend U.	07.77	1977-82	107	3	3	(D)
DUDLEY, Reg. A.	Hemel Hempstead	03.02.15	Apsley FC	Millwall	*	1946	12		0	(FB) E.AMAT.INT.
			TR	Q.P.R.	12.46	1946-49	57		0	
			TR	Watford	07.50	1950	1		0	
DUERDEN, Harry	Barnsley	05.03.48	APP	Barnsley	09.65	1965-66	24	1	1	(HB)
DUFF, Willie	Winchburgh	06.02.35	Hearts	Charlton Ath.	12.56	1956-61	213		0	(G) S.U23-1/S.F.LGE REP.
			TR	Peterborough U.	05.63	1963-66	118	/	0	
DUFF, William F.	Littleborough	16.12.38		Rochdale	05.56					(F)
			TR	Scunthorpe U.	10.58					
			TR	Grimsby T.	10.59	1959	3		1	
			TR	Accrington St.	10.60	1960	14		3	
DUFFETT, Edgar	Worcester	29.08.26	W.B.A.(AM)	Norwich C.	11.47					(IF)
			TR	Carlisle U.	08.50	1950-52	47		8	

Players Names	Birthplace	Date	Previous Club	League Club	Date Signed	Seasons Played	Career Record Apps	Sub	Gls	
DUFFEY, Chris P.	Liverpool	08.01.52	APP	Bolton W.	04.70	1969-71	8	/	0	(IF)
			TR	Crewe Alex.	09.72	1972-74	60	3	15	
			TR	Bury	10.74	1974	17	4	8	
			TR	Shrewsbury T.	05.75	1975	4	4	1	
			L	Rochdale	11.75	1975	2	/	0	
DUFFIELD, Martin J.	Park Royal	28.02.64	APP	Q.P.R.	01.82	1982	0	1	0	(M) E.YTH.INT.
			L	Bournemouth	09.83	1983	6	/	1	
DUFFIN, Lionel J.	Barrow	08.08.45	JNRS	Barrow	07.64	1964-67	46	/	0	(G)
DUFFY, Alan	W. Stanley	20.12.49	APP	Newcastle U.	03.67	1968-69	2	2	0	(IF) E.YTH.INT.
			TR	Brighton & H.A.	01.70	1969-71	34	15	8	
			TR	Tranmere Rov.	03.72	1971-72	29	4	2	
			TR	Darlington	08.73	1973	19	5	0	
DUFFY, Chris	East Fife	21.10.18	Leith Ath.	Charlton Ath.	+	1946-52	162		33	(OL)
DUFFY, Gerry	Middlewich	12.09.34	Middlewich	Oldham Ath.	05.56	1956-58	58		21	(F)
DUFFY, John	Glasgow	24.04.22	Clyde	Norwich C.	03.49	1949-53	78		0	(FB)
DUFFY, John	Dunfermline	06.09.43	Dunfermline	Darlington	08.63	1963	10		1	(LH)
DUFFY, John G.	Dundee	24.08.29	Glasgow Celtic	Southend U.	05.54	1954-59	113		4	(WH)
DUFFY, Mike K.	Leicester	12.06.61	JNRS	Leicester C.	07.78	1978-79	7	5	1	(M)
DUFFY, Vince	Nottingham	21.09.62	Nottingham F.(APP)	Scunthorpe	12.80	1980-81	3	5	0	(M)
DUGDALE, Alan	Liverpool	11.09.52	APP	Coventry C.	11.69	1972-77	139	3	0	(D) E. YTH.INT
			TR	Charlton Ath.	10.77	1977-78	34	/	0	
			L	Barnsley	08.79	1979	7	/	0	
DUGDALE, Gordon	Liverpool	21.02.24	JNRS	Everton	06.47	1947-49	58		0	
DUGDALE, Jim R.	Liverpool	15.01.32	Harrowby FC	W.B.A.	06.52	1952-55	63		0	(CH)E'B'-3/E.F.LGE REP./
			TR	Aston Villa	01.56	1955-61	215		3	Uncle of Alan
			TR	Q.P.R.	10.62	1962	10		0	
DUGGAN, Edward J.	London	27.07.22	JNRS	Luton T.	+	1946-48	47		20	(IF)
			TR	Q.P.R.	02.49	1948-50	47		5	
			Bedford T.	Luton T.	02.56					
DUGGAN, Jim	Droitwich	17.11.20	Droitwich OB	W.B.A.	*	1946	25		8	(IF)
DUGGINS, Eric E.	Tamworth	24.11.28	Atherstone T.	Portsmouth	08.48					(FB)Brother of John
			TR	Southend U.	07.52	1952-53	28		0	
DUGGINS, Gordon	Tamworth	08.12.32	Gresley Rov.	Barnsley	11.55	1955-57	17		6	(F)
DUGGINS, John	Tamworth	04.08.31	Atherstone T.	Portsmouth	06.50					
			TR	Walsall	08.52	1952	16		3	
DUGNOLLE, John	India	24.03.14	Brighton & H.A.(*)	Plymouth Arg.	*					d.1977
			TR	Brighton & H.A.	08.46	1946-47	58		0	
DUKE, George E.	Westhampnet	06.09.20	Southwick	Luton T.	*	1946-48	16		0	(G)
			TR	Bournemouth	05.49	1949	10		0	
DUKE, Harry P.	Portsmouth	31.03.12	Bedford T.	Norwich C.	09.46	1946	13		0	(G)*Orwell W./Ipswich T./ Norwich C.
DULIN, Mick C.	London	28.10.35	JNRS	Tottenham H.	11.52	1955-57	10		2	(OR)
DULSON, Gary	Nottingham	21.12.53	Nottingham F.(APP)	Port Vale	10.74	1974-77	108	2	3	(D)
			TR	Crewe Alex.	11.78	1978-79	33	5	0	
DUMIGHAN, Joe	Langley Park	25.09.38	JNRS	Sunderland	11.55					(F)
			TR	Darlington	07.58	1958	4		1	
DUNCAN, Colin J.	Plymouth	05.08.57	APP	Oxford U.	12.74	1974-79	188	1	6	(M)
			TR	Gillingham	01.80	1979-83	83	2	5	
			TR	Reading	09.83	1983	33	/	2	
DUNCAN, Dally	Aberdeen	14.10.09	Hull C.(*)	Derby Co.	*	1946	2		0	(W) S-14/
			TR	Luton T.	10.46	1946-47	33		4	*Aberdeen
DUNCAN, David M.	East Fife	21.11.21	Raith Rov.	Crewe Alex.	08.55	1955	22		0	S-3/S.F.LGE REP.
DUNCAN, George	Glasgow	16.01.37	Glasgow Rgrs.	Southend U.	06.60	1960	6		2	(OR)
			TR	Chesterfield	08.61	1961-64	140		13	
DUNCAN, James R.	Hull	02.04.38	JNRS	Hull C.	04.55	1955-59	26		3	(F)
			TR	Bradford C.	06.60	1960	18		5	
DUNCAN, John G.	Glasgow	10.12.26	Ayr U.	Newcastle U.	11.50	1951-52	5		3	(F)
DUNCAN, John P.	Lochee	22.02.49	Dundee	Tottenham H.	10.74	1974-78	101	2	53	(F)S.F.LGE.REP.
			TR	Derby Co.	09.78	1978-80	35	1	12	
			TR	Scunthorpe U.	06.81	1981-82	3	6	0	
DUNCAN, Joseph J.	Liverpool	24.02.50	JNRS	Wrexham	AM	1968	1	/	0	(OR)
DUNCAN, Robert	Kirkcaldy	02.11.43	JNRS	Southend U.	08.61	1961	1		0	(FB)
DUNCAN, Tom	Portsoy	15.07.36	Airdrie	Newport Co.	03.58	1957	1		0	
DUNCLIFFE, M. John	Brighton	17.09.47	APP	Brighton & H.A.	09.65	1966-67	22	/	0	(FB)
			TR	Grimsby T.	06.68	1968-69	71	1	0	
			TR	Peterborough U.	07.70	1970-72	120	/	0	
DUNDERDALE, William L.	Gainsborough	06.02.15	Leeds U.(*)	Watford	*	1946-47	44		15	(CF) *Sheffield Wed./Walsall

Players Names	Birthplace	Date	Previous Club	League Club	Date Signed	Seasons Played	Apps	Sub	Gls	
DUNGWORTH, John	Rotherham	30.03.55	APP	Huddersfield T.	07.70	1972-74	18	5	1	(F)
			L	Barnsley	10.74	1974	2	1	1	
			TR	Oldham Ath.	03.75	1975	2	2	0	
			L	Rochdale	03.77	1976	14	/	3	
			TR	Aldershot	09.77	1977-79	105	/	58	
			TR	Shrewsbury T.	11.79	1979-81	81	5	17	
			L	Hereford	10.81	1981	7	/	3	
			TR	Mansfield T.	08.82	1982-83	50	6	16	
			TR	Rotherham U.	02.84	1983	22	/	3	
DUNKLEY, Maurice E.	Kettering	19.02.14	Northampton T.(*)	Manchester C.	*	1946	32		4	(OR)
			Kettering T.	Northampton T.	07.49	1949	4		0	Northants Cricketer
DUNKLEY, Robert	Stoke	06.04.22		Stoke C.	+					(OL)
			TR	Barrow	08.46	1946	11		0	
DUNLEAVY, Chris	Liverpool	30.12.49	JNRS	Everton	03.68					(D)
			TR	Southport	07.69	1969-73	145	2	9	
			TR	Chester C.	09.73	1973-76	74	2	0	
			TR	Halifax T.	10.76	1976-80	181	/	13	
DUNLOP, Albert	Liverpool	21.04.32	JNRS	Everton	08.49	1956-62	211		0	(G)
			TR	Wrexham	11.63	1963-64	15		0	
DUNLOP, Rex. W.	Glasgow	21.09.27	Glasgow Rgrs.	Workington	11.53	1953-55	110		20	(WH)
DUNLOP, William L.	Airdrie	20.12.26	Dunfermline	Exeter C.	07.50	1950	4		0	(IF)
			Ilfracombe	Bristol Rov.	05.52					
			TR	Bradford P.A.	05.53	1953	36		12	
			TR	Darlington	10.54	1954	18		2	
DUNMORE, David G.	Whitehaven	08.02.34	Cliftonville	York C.	05.52	1951-53	48		25	(CF)
			TR	Tottenham H.	02.54	1953-59	75		23	
			TR	West Ham U.	03.60	1959-60	36		16	
			TR	Orient	03.61	1960-64	147		55	
			TR	York C.	06.65	1965-66	61	2	13	
DUNN, Barry	Harrogate	17.12.39		Doncaster Rov.	02.58					(F)
			TR	Halifax T.	09.59	1959-60	7		1	
DUNN, Barry	Sunderland	15.02.52	Blue Star	Sunderland	09.79	1979-80	16	7	2	(F)
			TR	Preston N.E.	10.81	1981	8	/	1	
			TR	Darlington	08.82	1982	16	/	4	
DUNN, Brian J.	Boston	04.10.40	JNRS	Grimsby T.	10.57					(F)
			TR	Hartlepool U.	06.58	1958-60	27		1	
DUNN, James	Rutherglen	23.10.22	Glencairn	Leeds U.	06.47	1947-58	422		1	(FB)
			TR	Darlington	07.59	1959	27		0	
DUNN, James	Edinburgh	25.11.23	Maghull Ath.	Wolverhampton W.	+	1946-52	123		33	(IF) Son of Wembley
			TR	Derby Co.	11.52	1952-54	57		20	Wizard
DUNN, John A.	Barking	21.06.44	APP	Chelsea	02.62	1962-65	13	/	0	(G)
			TR	Torquay U.	10.66	1966-67	44	/	0	
			TR	Aston Villa	01.68	1967-70	101	/	0	
			TR	Charlton Ath.	07.71	1971-74	104	/	0	
DUNN, Joseph	Springburn	20.09.25	Clyde	Preston N.E.	08.51	1951-60	223		2	(CH)
DUNN, Norman	South Shields	20.10.28	Murton C.W.	Aldershot	08.51	1952	1		0	(CH)
			TR	Darlington	07.54					
DUNN, Richard	Easington	23.12.19	Ferryhill Ath.	West Ham U.	*	1946-47	11		2	(IF)
			TR	Hartlepool U.	08.49	1949	13		2	
DUNN, William C.	Hebburn	25.03.20		Darlington	05.46	1946-55	340		0	(G)
DUNNE, Anthony P.	Dublin	24.07.41	Shelbourne	Manchester U.	08.56	1960-72	415	/	2	(D)EI-32
			TR	Bolton W.	08.73	1973-78	166	4	0	
DUNNE, Austin	Limerick	31.07.34	Limerick	Colchester U.	10.53	1954	1		0	
DUNNE, James C.	Dublin	01.12.47	Shelbourne	Millwall	02.66					(D)EI-1
			TR	Torquay U.	07.67	1967-69	125	1	13	
			TR	Fulham	07.70	1970-73	142	1	2	
			TR	Torquay U.	04.76	1975-78	119	3	6	
DUNNE, James P.	Dublin	16.03.35		Leicester C.	09.53	1954-55	4		0	(F) E1-3/L.O.I. REP.
			St. Patricks	Peterborough U.	07.60	1960-61	4		1	
DUNNE, Pat	Dublin	09.02.43	JNRS	Everton	05.60					(G) E1-5/
			Shamrock Rov.	Manchester U.	05.64	1964-65	45	/	0	Brother of Anthony
			TR	Plymouth Arg.	02.67	1966-70	152	/	0	
DUNNE, Seamus	Wicklow	13.04.30	Shelbourne	Luton T.	07.50	1951-60	300		0	(FB) E1-15
DUNNE, Thomas	Dublin	19.03.27	Shamrock Rov.	Leicester C.	11.49	1950-53	33		0	(HB)
			TR	Exeter C.	07.54	1954-55	27		1	
			TR	Shrewsbury T.	08.56	1956	3		0	
			TR	Southport	07.57	1957	21		0	
DUNNE, Thomas J.	Glasgow	22.06.46	St. Anthonys	Orient	05.64	1964	1		0	(IF)
DUNNIGAN, John Y.	Dalmuir	30.11.20	Bridgeton Wav.	Barrow	+	1946	1		0	(OR)
DUNNING, William	Bury	15.11.52	APP	Blackburn Rov.	11.70	1970-71	10	3	2	(F)
DUNNS, Len	Newcastle	28.09.16	Newcastle WE	Sunderland	*	1946-51	113		14	(OR)

Players Names	Birthplace	Date	Previous Club	League Club	Date Signed	Seasons Played	Apps	Sub	Gls	
DUNPHY, Eamon	Dublin	03.08.45	APP	Manchester U.	08.62					(M) EI-23
			TR	York C.	08.65	1965	22	/	3	
			TR	Millwall	01.66	1965-73	267	7	24	
			TR	Charlton Ath.	11.73	1973-74	39	3	3	
			TR	Reading	07.75	1975-76	74	3	3	
DUNWELL, Peter M.	Ecclesfield	22.11.38	Ecclesfield	Lincoln C.	09.58	1959-60	14		1	(OL)
DUQUEMIN, Len S.	Guernsey	17.07.24	Vauxbelets	Tottenham H.	09.46	1947-56	275		114	(CF)
DURANDT, Cliff	S. Africa	16.04.40	Marist FC	Wolverhampton W.	06.57	1958-61	43		10	(OL)
			TR	Charlton Ath.	03.63	1962-64	36		4	
DURBAN, Alan	Port Talbot	07.07.41	JNRS	Cardiff C.	09.58	1959-62	52	/	9	(M) W-27/W.U23-14●
			TR	Derby Co.	07.63	1963-72	336	10	91	
			TR	Shrewsbury T.	09.73	1973-77	150	6	33	
DURHAM, Jon S.	Rotherham	12.06.65	APP	Rotherham U.	06.83	1983	3	3	1	(F)
DURHAM, R. Dennis	East Halton	26.09.23	E. Halton	Hull C.	04.47	1946-58	267		7	(WH)
DURIE, David	Blackpool	13.08.31	Oxford Amats.	Blackpool	05.52	1952-63	301		84	(IF)
			TR	Chester C.	09.64	1964-66	87	2	4	
DURKIN, John	Hill of Beath	18.04.30	Hearts	Gillingham	08.53	1953-54	30		5	(CF)
DURKIN, William	Bradford	29.09.21		Bradford C.	01.47	1946-47	28		1	(IF)
			TR	Rotherham U.	08.48	1948	2		0	
			TR	Aldershot	08.49	1949-53	127		15	
DURRANT, Fred H.	Dover	19.06.21	Folkestone	Brentford	+	1946	4		3	(CF)
			TR	Q.P.R.	09.46	1946-48	51		27	
			TR	Exeter C.	02.49	1948-49	17		5	
DURRANT, Paul	East Howdon	21.02.43	Sunderland (AM)	Wolverhampton W.	07.61					(F)
			TR	Bury	07.62	1963-64	21		6	
			TR	Doncaster Rov.	07.65	1965-66	13	2	1	
DURRELL, Joe T.	London	15.03.53	APP	West Ham U.	10.70	1971	5	1	0	(F)
			TR	Bristol C.	07.73	1973-74	5	3	0	
			L	Cardiff C.	08.75	1975	2	/	0	
			TR	Gillingham	11.75	1975-76	43	6	9	
DUTHIE, Ian M.	Forfar	18.01.30	Forfar Celtic	Huddersfield T.	06.49	1949-52	7		0	(IF)
			TR	Bradford C.	06.54	1954-55	28		4	
DUTHIE, Jim	Trumperton	23.09.23		Grimsby T.	09.49	1948-50	39		0	(CH)
			TR	Hull C.	06.51	1951-52	17		3	
			TR	Southend U.	05.53	1953-57	160		7	
DUTHOIT, Jack	Leeds	04.11.18		York C.	05.46	1946-49	36		0	
DUTTON, Charles A.	Rugeley	10.04.34	Derby Co. (AM)	Coventry C.	10.52	1953-55	26		8	(IF)
			TR	Northampton T.	03.56	1955-56	10		2	
DUTTON, Len L.D.	Cardiff	17.01.22	JNRS	Arsenal	+					(WH) W.SCH.INT.
			TR	Norwich C.	08.46	1946-52	138		11	
DUXBURY, Mike	Accrington	01.09.59	APP	Manchester U.	10.76	1980-83	127	11	3	(D) E.U21-7/E-5
DWIGHT, Roy	Belvedere	09.01.33	JNRS	Fulham	06.50	1954-57	72		54	(OR) Uncle of singer Elton John
			TR	Nottingham F.	07.58	1958-59	44		21	
			Gravesend	Coventry C.	01.62	1961-62	31		8	
			TR	Millwall	01.64	1963-64	7		2	
DWYER, Alan	Liverpool	05.10.52	Halewood Y.C.	Wrexham	10.73	1974-80	169	11	2	(M)
				Stockport Co.	10.81	1981	4	/	0	
DWYER, Noel M.	Dublin	30.10.34	Ormeau	Wolverhampton W.	08.53	1957	5		0	(G) E1-14/E1.'B'-1
			TR	West Ham U.	12.58	1958-59	36		0	
			TR	Swansea C.	08.60	1960-64	140		0	
			TR	Plymouth Arg.	01.65	1964-65	26	/	0	
			TR	Charlton Ath.	12.65	1965	6	/	0	
DWYER, Phil	Cardiff	28.10.53	JNRS.	Cardiff C.	10.71	1972-83	435	5	38	(D) W.U23-5/W.U21-1/ W-10/W.SCH.INT.
DYAS, Gordon	Hednesford	17.05.36	Hednesford T.	Walsall	06.55	1955	12		0	(HB)
DYER, Alex C.	West Ham	14.11.65	Watford(APP)	Blackpool	10.83	1983	4	5	0	(M)
DYER, Joe A.	Crewe	13.04.13	Crewe Alex.(*)	Plymouth Arg.	*	1946	33		0	
DYER, Paul	Leicester	24.01.53		Notts. Co.	09.72	1972-73	1	6	0	(F)
			TR	Colchester U.	07.75	1975-79	124	20	4	
DYER, Peter R.F.	Devonport	12.10.37	Oak Villa	Plymouth Arg.	06.55	1955-56	8		0	(G)
DYER, Ray	Stockport	12.05.38	Bolton W.(AM)	Stockport Co.	09.56	1956	1		0	(F)
DYER, Steve P.	Chelmsford	21.03.54	APP	Southend U.	03.72	1972-76	59	8	0	(D)
DYKE, Charlie H.	Caerphilly	23.09.26	Troedyrhiw	Chelsea	11.47	1947-50	24		2	(OR)
DYKES, Don W.	Ashby	08.06.30	M & BDC FC	Lincoln C.	06.49	1949-58	95		4	(IF)
DYMOND, William H.	Kenton (Devon)	13.02.20		Bristol C.	+	1946-47	9		1	
			TR	Exeter C.	06.47	1947-48	41		7	
DYSON, Barry	Oldham	06.09.42	JNRS	Bury	09.60					(IF)
			TR	Tranmere Rov.	07.62	1962-66	174	/	99	
			TR	Crystal Palace	09.66	1966-67	33	1	9	
			TR	Watford	01.68	1967-68	38	/	19	
			TR	Orient	12.68	1968-72	154	6	28	
			TR	Colchester U.	07.73	1973-74	41	1	6	

Players Names	Birthplace	Date	Previous Club	League Club	Date Signed	Seasons Played	Career Record Apps	Sub	Gls	
DYSON, Geoff	Huddersfield	16.03.23	JNRS	Huddersfield T.	+					
			TR	Bradford C.	06.47	1947	1		0	
			TR	Accrington St.	01.48	1947-48	20		1	
DYSON, Jack	Oldham	08.07.34	JNRS	Manchester C.	05.52	1955-59	62		26	(IF) E.U23-1/
			Stirling A.	Oldham Ath.	10.62					Lancs Cricketer
DYSON, Jim	Ryhope	16.12.35		Hartlepool U.	04.55	1954-58	63		0	(G)
DYSON, Keith	Durham	10.02.50	JNRS	Newcastle U.	08.68	1968-71	74	2	21	(IF) E.U23-1
			TR	Blackpool	10.71	1971-75	91	3	30	
DYSON, Paul I.	Birmingham	27.12.59	APP	Coventry C.	06.77	1978-82	140	/	5	(D)E.U21-4
			TR	Stoke C.	07.83	1983	38	/	2	
DYSON, Terry K.	Malton	29.11.34	Scarborough	Tottenham H.	04.55	1954-64	184		42	(OL) Son of famous jockey
			TR	Fulham	06.65	1965	22	1	3	
			TR	Colchester U.	08.68	1968-69	53	3	4	
DZIADULEWICZ, Mark	London	29.01.60	APP	Southend U.	02.78					(F)
			Chelmsford	Wimbledon	02.79	1978-79	22	6	1	

IAN CALLAGHAN (Liverpool & England/Swansea C./Crewe Alex.)
Callaghan first figured in the great Liverpool sides of the 1960s and 1970s mainly as a skilful right winger, but he settled down latterly in midfield and achieved great acclaim. He appeared only four times for England, scant reward for sterling club performances, which included five First Division Championship winning medals as well as two F.A.Cup, two European Cup, UEFA Cup and Super Cup winners medals. He left the "Reds" in August 1978, immediately helping his old team mate John Toshack lift Swansea City out of the Third Division. His greatest asset was his ability to beat defenders and centre accurately. He was player of the year in 1974. After playing for Cork Hibs of the Irish League, he finished in 1981/2 with Crewe.

JOHNNY CAREY (Manchester U. & Ireland)
Starting his career in Ireland, Carey was signed by United from St. James Gate in 1938 as an inside forward. He became known to all football followers as "Gentleman John", because of his impeccable manners. He was also one of the most versatile players the game has known. Johnny appeared in every position for United except in goal, but settled down mainly at right back. He captained the great United side in the 1947/8 Cup Final, rallying the team, who were twice behind to Stan Matthews' Blackpool, to eventually win 4-2. He won League Championship medals, becoming player of the year in 1948 and captaining the rest of Europe against Great Britain in 1947 before retiring at the end of the 1952/3 season. He made his mark as a manager with Blackburn and Everton.

WILLIE CARR (Coventry C. & Scotland/Wolverhampton W./Millwall)
A brilliant little ginger haired, scheming inside forward, Carr came to the fore with Coventry City and went on to play six times for Scotland's full side as well as gaining under 23 caps. He signed for the Wolves in March 1975 and made a vain effort to help the club avert relegation the following season. His valuable contribution in 1976/7 gained him a Second Division winners medal as Wolves stormed back into the elite League along with Chelsea. In 1980 he was a member of the Football League Cup winning side that put paid to Nottingham Forest, 1-0 at Wembley, later coming down to London to play for Millwall in August 1982. He played only a handful of games for the "Lions" before joining Worcester City of the Alliance League.

RAICH CARTER (Sunderland, Derby Co. & England/Hull C.)
Silver haired Carter was a Sunderland product, winning schoolboy International honours. Amazingly he played for England only an 'unlucky' 13 games, but captained his beloved Sunderland when they won the F.A. Cup in 1937. The war came when Raich was only 26 years old and in his prime, but afterwards he again distinguished himself at the highest level, getting another Cup medal, this time with Derby County in 1946. He became player-manager in April 1948 of Hull City, steering the "Tigers" to promotion from the Third Division North in 1949. Raich also excelled in other sports playing cricket for Derbyshire and Durham.

WILF CARTER (W.B.A./Plymouth Arg./Exeter C.)
Signed for Albion as an inside forward after starring for the S.E. Staffs schools side, Carter, whilst at the Hawthorns, occasionally played in defence and, not really becoming a regular, was transferred to Plymouth Argyle in March 1957. Settling down in the "Pilgrims" forward line, Wilf became quite a prodigious goalscorer, topping the club's charts in his first five seasons, before again reverting to defensive duties. Instrumental in Argyle's promotion to the Second Division in 1958/9, Wilf became a good and valued clubman before moving on to Exeter City in 1964.

MICK CHANNON (Southampton, Manchester C. & England/Southampton/Newcastle U./Bristol Rov./Norwich C.)
A strong running, powerful striker, Channon made his debut for Southampton during Easter 1966 and really came to the fore when forming a double spearhead with the awesome heading power of Ron Davies, after Martin Chivers had moved on to Spurs. Apart from a two-year spell at Manchester City during the Malcolm Allison reign, Mick remained a Saint, playing nearly 500 games in their colours and scoring not far short of 200 League goals, before leaping into action with Newcastle, Bristol Rovers and Norwich City. The highlight of his career, not forgetting 46 full England caps, was Southampton's marvellous F.A. Cup Final with Manchester United in 1976, when against all the odds victory was achieved.

ROY CHAPMAN (Aston Villa/Lincoln C./Mansfield T./Lincoln C./Port Vale/Chester C.)
Chapman was one of the few players to play in all four Divisions of the Football League, over a period of nearly 20 seasons. This lanky, long striding inside forward surprisingly did not blossom with the Villa during the five years spent with them after arriving from Kynochs. Joining Lincoln City in November 1957, he became a regular goalscorer before moving on to Mansfield Town in 1961. He spent a further three seasons with Lincoln before going to Port Vale and Chester. He scored just over 200 goals from 400 odd games, albeit not in the First Division but still impressive.

JOHN CHARLES (Leeds U., Cardiff C. & Wales)
The famous Major Buckley enticed the young John Charles away from his native Swansea in January 1949 to sign for Leeds United. Capped by Wales just after his 18th birthday, John could play both centre back and centre forward with equal efficiency. Because of his temperament he became known at the "gentle giant". In 1953/4 he scored 42 League goals and a season later a further 30 helped the Elland Road side back into the top section. In 1956/7, after helping himself to 38 League goals, he was taken to Italy by Juventus for a record £65,000. He became an idol in that country before returning briefly to Leeds in 1962. After a few months he moved back to Italy with Roma for £70,000 before finishing his playing career with Cardiff City.

MEL CHARLES (Swansea C., Arsenal, Cardiff C. & Wales/Port Vale)
Overshadowed by his big brother, the great John, at Leeds, Mel eventually made his own way in the game signing for Swansea in May 1952.
Like his brother he was extremely versatile, but was probably most effective at wing half. The long time target of bigger clubs, Mel eventually signed for Arsenal for £42,750. Unfortunately he never settled in the big city and after three years, went home to Cardiff City in 1962 for £27,000. He showed good form before being dogged by injuries and leaving the game, although later playing a few matches for Port Vale. He played 31 times for his country, being remembered more for versatility than the undoubted skill at his disposal.

BOBBY CHARLTON (Manchester U. & England/Preston NE)
Related to the famous Milburn footballing family, Charlton was a brilliant boy prodigy before going from England schoolboys on to Old Trafford, and turning pro in October 1954. Brother Jack had already begun a career for himself at Leeds United without any fanfares. Young Bobby would soon become famous for terrific shooting ability. It was not until after Munich, where Bobby was a survivor of that horrific air crash, that he came home to prominence amongst mass hysteria. He won honours galore: 106 England appearances, two League Championship medals, an F.A. Cup winners medal, footballer of the year, and finally he was awarded the C.B.E. for services to football. He finished as player-manager at Preston.

JACKIE CHARLTON (Leeds U. & England)
Jackie Charlton could have been totally overshadowed by his younger brother Bobby, but quietly and efficiently he built a reputation for himself as a future International centre half. When John Charles moved to centre forward, Jack filled the role so efficiently for Leeds that the famous "gentle giant" stayed up front. Jack gained experience mainly in the Second Division, and it was not until 1964 when he was just short of 30, that England picked him to replace the injured Maurice Norman. Playing for England 35 times, Jackie was made player of the year the season after brother Bobby. He retired at the age of 37 to go into football management after winning F.A. Cup, League Championship, Football League Cup and Fairs Cup medals. He was known as the "giraffe" because of his height and style.

RAY CHARNLEY (Blackpool & England/Preston N.E./Wrexham/Bradford Pk. Av.)
An ideally built leader of any attack, having speed and thrust, Charnley was always among the goals. Preston North End must rue the day when they allowed the young amateur to leave. Charnley played with Morecambe in the Northern League. Blackpool were very happy to sign the youngster as a professional in May 1957. Ray almost immediately took over the reins as their leading goalscorer, going on to play for England against France in 1963. After scoring nearly 200 League goals he arrived back at Preston, staying half a season before going on to Wrexham and Bradford Park Avenue, leaving League soccer at the same time as his last club.

TREVOR CHERRY (Huddersfield T./Leeds U. & England/Bradford C.)
After leaving Huddersfield Town for Leeds United in June 1972, in a £100,000 deal, Trevor Cherry missed less than 40 League matches in nine seasons, a testament to his consistency. With the Town, he played mainly in the centre of the defence, alongside Roy Ellam, but on going to Elland Road settled down at full back. He achieved England International status 1976, in all collecting 27 caps. In his first season with Leeds he played in the 1973 F.A. Cup Final defeat by Sunderland and later picked up a League Championship medal. Steady and reliable, Trevor was the cornerstone of the defence and consistent to the utmost. He is now the player-manager of Third Division Bradford City.

CHRIS CHILTON (Hull C./Coventry C.)
Chilton is really remembered as a one club man with Hull City, for it was at Boothferry Park that the tall youngster started, eventually going on to become one of the country's most prolific goalscorers. He was not picked up in the "Tigers" youth scheme until he wrote in for a trial, after which he was promptly signed, making his debut within a month of going professional. Good on the ground as well as in the air, he occasionally played at inside forward, where he was quite as effective. He scored just under 200 League goals from 441 games. After less than a season with Coventry City injury forced the still young man out of the game for good.

MARTIN CHIVERS (Southampton/Tottenham H. & England/Norwich C./Brighton & H.A.)
A 6ft 1½in tall, strongly built forward Chivers scored well over 200 League goals in a career that started at Southampton in September 1962, before playing only a handful of games for Brighton and finally leaving the top class soccer scene 1979/80. This prolific goalscorer was allowed to leave the Dell after the arrival of Ron Davies, when signing for Spurs for a fee of £125,000. He was an outstanding success at White Hart Lane, overcoming serious knee trouble and being capped 27 times by England before leaving for Servette of Switzerland. He came back briefly with Norwich, then Brighton, and but for his injuries would have played many more times for his country.

ALAN CLARKE (Walsall/Fulham/Leicester C./Leeds U. & England/Barnsley)
One of five brothers who all played League soccer, Alan was the outstanding member of the family. He started out as a youngster with Walsall, and was still learning the trade when Fulham snapped him up in March 1966 for £33,000. In June 1968 he moved to Leicester City for £150,000 and a year later Leeds United enticed the elegant striker to Elland Road for only £165,000 after he had gained an F.A. Cup losers medal for Leicester City against Manchester City. He won a Championship medal in 1973/4 and scored the only goal against Arsenal in 1972 when collecting a F.A. Cup winners medal. An outstanding forward who played 19 times for England, he formed a brilliant double spearhead at Leeds with Mick Jones. He went on to football management with Barnsley and his old club Leeds United.

DOUG CLARKE (Bury/Hull C./Torquay U.)
Clarke made a reputation in the lower Divisions as an outside right who could score goals, getting more than 100 in a career of 15 or so seasons. Before coming into the League from Darwen, signing for Bury, he had been a Bolton Wanderers amateur. Transferred to Hull City in November 1955 he immediately made an impact, becoming a firm favourite and starring in the promotion winning side of 1958/9, going on to appear in over 350 games for the "Tigers". After making the move to Devon with Torquay United in 1965, he was instrumental in helping them to promotion to the Third Division that same season.

RONNIE CLAYTON (Blackburn Rov. & England)
Classy, totally constructive in approach, Clayton made his debut at the age of 16 in 1950/1. He showed real signs of developing into one of the great wing halves of the day, and could have had more than the 35 appearances, some as captain, made in England's colours. He captained the Rovers back into the First Division as the runners up 1957/8, and gained an F.A. Cup losers medal against the Wolves in 1959/60. He played nearly 600 League games for Blackburn before leaving to become player manager at Morecambe in 1969. Those who saw him play will always remember Ronnie Clayton for grand sportsmanship allied to great ability.

RAY CLEMENCE (Scunthorpe U./Liverpool, Tottenham H. & England)
One of the great modern goalies, Clemence's career Internationally coincided with Peter Shilton's. Ray would otherwise have gained even more than his 50 plus England caps. He played behind a highly organised defence at Liverpool, winning five Championships, one F.A. Cup and three European Cup winners medals, quite an achievement for a player who started out in the lower reaches of League soccer. He turned professional with Scunthorpe after being a Notts County amateur, and when signed by Liverpool, was for several seasons deputy to their regular choice Tommy Lawrence. Since signing for the Spurs, Ray has collected F.A. Cup winners and League Cup runners up medals.

DAVE CLEMENTS (Wolverhampton W./Coventry C., Sheffield Wed., Everton & N. Ireland)
Clements came to the Wolves from Portadown after being a member of the mini-World Cup Northern Ireland youth team. He had already won schoolboy, youth and amateur honours, but at Molineux didn't play a single League game and was transferred to Coventry City in July 1964. He had by now become a fixture at full back-cum-wing half in the Irish National side, playing nearly 50 times in all. After leaving Everton he was still being capped whilst in the U.S.A. playing for New York Cosmos.

BRIAN CLOUGH (Middlesbrough & England/Sunderland)
A goalscoring machine, Clough made his name in season 1956/7, and finished the next six seasons in the top two of the Second Division leading goalscorers charts, before injury took him from the game at the early age of 29. It has been often argued that it would have been more difficult to score as many goals in the First Division; certainly in two International appearances he did not find the net. What is undisputed is that in 274 League games he scored 251 goals, the highest post-war ratio. Since leaving the playing side, he has had startling successes as a manager and ranks as one of the greatest of all time.

GEORGE COHEN (Fulham & England)
A cool, thoughtful full back, a star of the England World Cup winning side, Cohen played over 400 League games for Fulham before injury ended his career. From nearby Kensington, he joined the club straight from school, and developed into one of the finest defenders in the country. He played for England 37 times and without injuries would have undoubtedly played more. Cohen was highly thought of as an outstanding sportsman, a model of consistency and an object lesson for any youngster to imitate. He never sought the glare of publicity.

CECIL COLDWELL (Sheffield U.)
A really consistent defender, signed from Norton Woodseats in September 1951, Coldwell made his debut that same season. He became one of the many long service United defenders of the post-war years when forming a full back partnership with International Graham Shaw, whose namesake Joe was at the heart of the defence. This consistency was mainly responsible for helping United back to the First Division in 1960/1, with Coldwell missing only one of their promotion winning games. He left the "Blades" at the end of season 1966/7, coincidently at the same time as equally long serving team mate Graham Shaw.

BOBBY COLLINS (Everton, Leeds U. & Scotland/Bury/Oldham Ath.)
One of the smallest forwards at 5ft 4in in the game, Collins first made a reputation with the crack Scottish side Glasgow Celtic before coming to Goodison in 1958 for £25,000. Clever, with a great shot, he was one of the game's superlative ball players, who could also fight for every ball. He was seen by Leeds United as the man to bring them back into the big time, and moved from Everton, again for £25,000, in March 1962. He masterminded the promotion to Division One 1963/4 and led Leeds to the losing 1964/5 F.A. Cup Final against Liverpool. He was made the player of the year. With the Leeds rebuilding behind him, he moved to Bury in 1967, helping them immediately into the Second Division, before going home to play for Morton of the Scottish League. In 1972/3 he made a few appearances with Oldham before calling it a day.

RON (SAMMY) COLLINS (Bristol C./Torquay U.)
A Bristolian born forward of only 5ft 8in, Collins became a scorer of some merit after leaving Ashton Gate, the home of Bristol City, in June 1948, bound for Torquay United of the Third Division South. Although finding the net every one game in two he never claimed a regular position until 1951/2, alternating between outside and inside left. In 1955/6 he topped the Third Division goal charts with 39 from 45 games and on two other occasions was runner up in the goal stakes. He finished his career at Plainmoor with 203 goals from 355 games, an outstanding performance considering many appearances were made from the wing position.

JOHN CONNELLY (Burnley, Manchester U. & England/Blackburn Rov./Bury)
Connelly became one of the best scoring wingmen in the game, being recognised by England on 20 occasions. Starting out at inside forward, he was signed from St. Helens by Burnley in 1956, and soon made his debut. He scored 20 goals in 34 matches when helping Burnley to the League Championship 1959/60, later playing in the losing F.A. Cup Final against Spurs in 1962. Manchester United took him to Old Trafford in 1964; he won a Championship medal in his first season. After two years with the "Red Devils" he moved to Blackburn Rovers, then Bury. He was a direct winger who could play on both flanks with skill.

JACK CONNOR (Ipswich T./Carlisle U./Rochdale/Bradford C./Stockport Co./Crewe Alex.)
Connor became known up and down the country as the man who scored three consecutive hat-tricks for Stockport County, after joining them in October 1951 from Bradford City. A sturdy bustling centre forward of the old school, he had started during the war with Ipswich Town, then on to Carlisle before making his mark with the Irish side Ards. Rochdale brought him back to England in December 1948 and Jack scored 42 goals in 81 games before joining Bradford City for a short sojourn in April 1951. With Stockport, in three consecutive seasons he was in the top two Third Division North goalscoring charts. At the age of 37 he moved on to Crewe Alexandra before finishing.

MIKE COOK (Colchester U.)
A long serving defender, Cook started out soccer life as an Orient amateur, before signing professional forms for the "U's" in July 1969. In ten seasons between 1973/4 and 1982/3, he missed only 16 games, and his sterling efforts in the back four are of great value in terms of consistency as well as of flair. He has twice helped Colchester to promotion from Division Four, both times in third place, 1973/4 and 1976/7. He was a member of the best-ever Cup squad which got through to the sixth round in 1971, which is a joint record for a Fourth Division club. He is young enough to be a first teamer for a few years to come.

MICK COOP (Coventry C./Derby Co.)
Mick Coop played over 400 League games for Coventry City in the full back position after first signing professional as a young 17-year-old, back in January 1966. A true "Sky Blue" right from word go, he became a regular in the side in 1968/9, going on to captain the club, and also specialising in spot kicks. He proved that the wealth of First Division experience picked up had not deserted him by becoming the most senior player on Coventry City's books. He left Coventry for Derby County in July 1981, to help guide the youngsters coming up through their ranks.

KEN COOTE (Brentford)
Coote became a Griffin Park regular, playing over 500 League games from 1949/50 to 1963/4, after signing from local amateur side Wembley Town. Starting out at inside forward, he was a successful wing half before conversion to full back completed the transition. Reliable and dependable, "Mr. Consistency" brought those qualities to the "Bees", who were still striving to climb back to pastures old. He finally left the only League club he knew at the age of 35.

STEVE COPPELL (Tranmere Rov./Manchester U. & England)

A positive right-sided flank player, Coppell signed for Tranmere Rovers whilst still at Liverpool University, and soon proved to be a great prospect for the future. Manchester United stepped in smartly to take Steve to Old Trafford for £60,000 in February 1975, where his ability to go in, win the ball, and then carry it deep into the oppositions' territory, endeared him to the fans. A First Division Championship medal eluded him, but an F.A. Cup winners medal, in 1977 when United beat Liverpool 2-1, somewhat compensated for the losing Finals against Southampton and Arsenal. Before injury cruelly took him from the game in 1983, Steve had played for his country 42 times and made well over 300 League appearances as a "Red Devil".

JOE CORRIGAN (Manchester C. & England/Brighton & H.A.)

A brilliant 6ft 4in tall goalkeeper Corrigan proved himself outstanding in the 1981 losing F.A. Cup Final against Spurs, where on the basis of two games he collected the 'man of the match' award. Joe turned professional for Manchester City in January 1967 and apart from being temporarily replaced by Keith MacRae in the mid 1970s, he consistently guarded the "Citizens" net. He was unlucky not to have played more than a handful of games for England due to Shilton and Clemence being in good form. He won a European Cup Winners Cup medal in 1970. After leaving Maine Road for Seattle Sounders in the U.S.A., he is now minding the Brighton goal and looks a good bet for a few years to come.

JOHN CRAGGS (Newcastle U./Middlesbrough/Newcastle U./Darlington)

A rugged, fast into the tackle, full back, Craggs first came into prominence with Newcastle United when winning youth International honours. He was later allowed to sign for fellow North-Easterners, Middlesbrough, in August 1971, for a fee of £60,000, and went on to play over 400 games for the 'Boro. He gained a Second Division winners medal in 1973/4, when playing 39 games, to help take the Yorkshire side back to the First Division after an absence of 20 years. He is now with Darlington following a second spell with the "Magpies".

RAY CRAWFORD (Portsmouth/Ipswich T. & England/Wolverhampton W./W.B.A./Ipswich T./Charlton Ath./Colchester U.)

Crawford was a goalscorer with a penchant for turning half chances into goals, an exuberant opportunist and one of the most prolific matchwinners of the day. For some reason better known to themselves, Portsmouth allowed Ipswich to sign Ray, in September, 1958. Scoring 142 goals in five seasons, he helped take the Town from the Second to First Division Titles in successive seasons. Excursions to Wolves and W.B.A. followed before he arrived back at Portman Road. He had a spell with Charlton and ended his playing career going out in glorious style by helping Colchester slay the mighty Leeds in the fifth round of the F.A. Cup, ending the season with 25 League goals.

GRAHAM CROSS (Leicester C/Brighton & H.A./Preston N.E./Lincoln C.)

A central defender who spent most of his career at Leicester City after signing from the junior ranks in November 1960, Cross was highly effective in partnership with John Sjoberg, where the pair formed a defensive barrier to opponents for many years, and was considerably unlucky to play in two F.A. Cup Finals without collecting a winners medal. As a cricketer he was an all rounder with Leicestershire, without making due progress, a problem that was highlighted by football commitments. After Leicester, where he made just under 500 appearances, Graham played for Brighton, Preston, Lincoln City, whom he joined after a short stay outside the League with Endersby.

TOMMY CUMMINGS (Burnley/Mansfield T.)

As an amateur, after gaining Durham youth honours, Cummings failed a trial with Spurs, going back home to play for Hylton Colliery Welfare before Burnley took him to Turf Moor in October 1947. He succeeded Alan Brown as the regular Burnley pivot in 1949/50, after making his debut the season before, and was commanding in the box, relying on positional skill and judgement. He played for England "B" and also represented the Football League, and probably would have gained further honours but for the brilliance of Billy Wright. Before going to Mansfield in March 1963 as player-manager, he had collected League Championship and Cup runner-up medals.

BILL CUNNINGHAM (Preston NE.& Scotland/Southport)
Cunningham was a tough right back, who surprisingly was well known for the use of his left foot. Signed from Airdrie for about £6,000 in July 1949, he went on to become a regular in the North End defence for 14 seasons. Joining the side when they had slipped into the Second Division he was one of the successes and within two seasons was a member of the promotion winning team. He became captain of Scotland's 1954 World Cup team four days after getting a losers medal from the Cup Final against W.B.A. Dark and swarthy, Bill was in distinct contrast to his cousin and team mate at Preston, Jimmy Baxter, who was a dainty elusive ball player.

WILLY CUNNINGHAM (Leicester C. & N. Ireland)
Not to be confused with his Preston namesake of the same period, also a full back, Cunningham was transferred to Leicester City from St. Mirren for a big fee in December 1954, immediately becoming a valuable member of the side. A well built blond haired constructive defender, he would rather look to play the ball out of defence than use the big boot. He made his debut for Ireland in 1951, appearing 30 times in all, including the 1957/8 World Cup. Not always a regular at Filbert Street due to injuries as well as competition, but before leaving he had won a Second Division medal.

TONY CURRIE (Watford/Sheffield U., Leeds U. & England/Q.P.R.)
Classic, well built, fair haired, scheming midfield player, Currie combined flair with a good work rate, as demanded by the modern game, and was always likely to score important goals, often from long range. Signing for Watford at 17 years of age, after briefly playing as a junior for Chelsea, he was snapped up by Sheffield United only nine months later for the bargain basement fee of £27,000. After rendering over eight years invaluable service to the "Blades" he was transferred to Leeds United, adding artistry to the club's hope of emulating past triumphs. The Londoner came home in August 1979 to Q.P.R., following 17 England appearances made whilst in Yorkshire, then he played for Chesham before making non-contract appearances for Torquay.

BILL CURRY (Newcastle U./Brighton & H.A./Derby Co./Mansfield T./Chesterfield)
Although playing for England under 23s, the young centre forward Curry did not get many chances to shine when at Newcastle United, before being transferred for £10,000 to Brighton in July 1959. Immediately he got amongst the goals, topping the "Seagull's" scoring list in his first season with them. Transferred to Derby County just over a year later, he became a valued goalscoring member of the Second Division side before going on to Mansfield Town. At Field Mill he again scored frequently and by the time he had left League football had accumulated 178 goals. Not big for a striking forward, he ran at defences using mobility and speed to create openings.

GEORGE CURTIS (Coventry C./Aston Villa)
Known in soccer circles as the "iron man", George came to Coventry from Snowdown Colliery, playing nearly 500 League games before finishing at the Villa. He appeared in five Divisions whilst at Highfield Road, starting out in the old Third Division South, winning medals in the Third and Second on route to entering the First Division for the first time in the "Sky Blues" history. He very rarely missed a game as a tough uncompromising centre half giving nothing away, and was the foundation stone of the Coventry success story. He would have probably gained International honours if his early career had been in the limelight.

JIM DAILEY (Sheffield Wed./Birmingham C./Exeter C./Workington/Rochdale)
A dynamic centre forward, Dailey joined the "Owls" from Third Lanark in October 1946 and proceeded to equal Jimmy Trotter's Sheffield Wednesday record by scoring all five goals against Barnsley in 1947/8. Not really settling at Hillsborough, he moved on to Birmingham in February 1949 and then to Exeter City before signing for Workington in December 1953. In 176 games he scored 74 goals, finding the Third Division more to his liking. He finished his League soccer career with Rochdale, bowing out in 1958/9.

KENNY DALGLISH (Liverpool & Scotland)
When Kevin Keegan left Liverpool in the summer of 1977 bound for S.V.Hamburg, many footballing experts wondered how irreplaceable he would be. However, in August 1977, the "Reds" looked no further than Kenny Dalglish, Celtic's young goalscorer with a Scottish record of a goal a match from over 200 League games. Within months the "Kopites" were charmed as the Liverpool machine rolled on regardless of change. Kenny has since gained five League Championship, four League Cup and three European Cup winners medals. He has now played nearly 100 times for Scotland, twice been player of the year and shows plenty of fire for the future.

ANDY DAVIDSON (Hull C.)
A consistently reliable defender Davidson made a reputation as a player who could overcome injuries. Joining Hull City from Scottish junior soccer in September 1949, he waited three years before making a first team debut at Boothferry Park. He was a member of the side that gained promotion in 1958/9 as runner-up, and later won a Third Division medal 1965/6. That same season Hull had a great Cup run before going out to the eventual semi-finalists Chelsea in the sixth round after a replay. Davidson amazingly made 520 appearances after suffering three broken legs in a career that would have surely surpassed the 600 total if not for those injuries.

RON DAVIES (Chester/Luton T./Norwich C., Southampton, Portsmouth & Wales/Manchester U.)
One of the great post-war goalscoring machines, Davies was devastatingly brilliant with heading chances. A well built 6ft, he came out with Chester, learning the trade for three years, then signing for Luton Town for £10,000 in October 1962. Norwich City tempted the by now much wanted striker to Carrow Road, where he gained the first of many Welsh International caps. It was really at Southampton, where he became a spectacular success, getting on the end of centres from Terry Paine and John Sydenham, after signing for £55,000. His blond head was reckoned by many to be the most valuable First Division asset. He saw out the remainder of his career with ''Pompey'' and then Tommy Docherty's Manchester United.

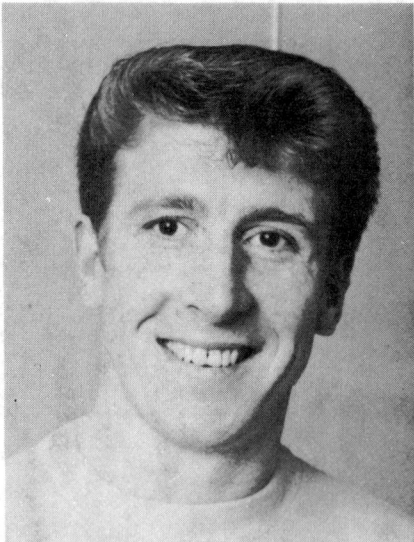

WYN DAVIES (Wrexham/Bolton W., Newcastle U., Manchester C., Manchester U., Blackpool & Wales/Stockport Co./Crewe Alex.)
Born in Caernarvon, Davies made his debut with Wrexham, developing into a most powerful centre forward who at 6ft 1½in tall became one of the most dangerous strikers in the air. Bolton spotted his potential, signing the youngster in March 1962, and his talent gained him in 1964 the first of 34 Welsh caps. With Wales, he formed a highly successful double spearhead with the equally brilliant Ron Davies. He signed for Newcastle in October 1966 for an £80,000 fee, later playing for both Manchester clubs in the space of two years. He became an ideal target man who laid on chances effectively for others, before closing his playing account with Blackpool, Stockport County and finally Crewe in 1978.

ALEX DAWSON (Manchester U./Preston NE./Bury/Brighton & HA)
A bustling old fashioned type of centre forward, Dawson signed for United after starring in the England schools side, although being born in Aberdeen. He came to the fore after Munich, when with other youngsters he was pushed into the first team prematurely. Although playing in 80 League games and scoring heavily, he was allowed to leave Old Trafford for Preston in October 1961, where he became one of the most prolific goalscorers of the day. Whilst at Preston, he helped them through to the 1963/4 F.A. Cup Final when going down 3-2 to West Ham; although Alex scored it wasn't enough. He finished his playing career with Bury and Brighton, after being on loan to Brentford in 1970/1.

STEVE DEATH (West Ham U./Reading)
Standing only 5ft 8in, one of the smallest League keepers, Steve Death gave outstanding service to Reading after joining them in November 1969 from West Ham. Highly efficient in handling, he made up for lack of inches with shrewd positional play. He was originally signed by West Ham in the summer of 1966 after starring for England schoolboys, playing just once for the ''Hammers'' before being released.

JOHN DICK (West Ham U. & Scotland/Brentford)
A tall, leggy inside forward, with a great goalscoring record, Dick made a real impact with the "Hammers" after joining them from Crittalls Athletic. He made his debut soon after signing in June 1953, and it wasn't long before Scotland picked the young man for their "B" team. He was one of the main forces behind West Ham's drive back into the First Division after an absence of over 25 years. He was capped fully by Scotland, but by 1962 was in dispute with West Ham and was transferred to Brentford for £17,000. The "Bees," who were in the Fourth Division, looked to the big man for goals and guidance in climbing out, this being accomplished that same season. In 1964/5, at the age of 35, Dick retired, just one short of 200 League goals.

JIMMY DICKINSON (Portsmouth & England)
A brilliantly consistent, no frills wing half, Dickinson was industrious, sure footed and elegant in a League career embracing 764 appearances, a total that until recently had not been beaten. He made his debut with Portsmouth in 1943 as an amateur, turning pro whilst still serving with the Royal Navy. He was an automatic choice for England for several seasons at left half, losing his place when switched to centre half by his club. He formed a brilliant half back line for "Pompey" alongside Jack Froggat and Jimmy Scoular, succeeding the last named as captain. Two League Championship medals in succession, 1948/9 and 1949/50, were won with countless other honours. He will be remembered as a gentleman both on and off the field, and he was awarded the M.B.E.

TED DITCHBURN (Tottenham H. & England)
Ditchburn nearly followed his father into professional boxing, but his huge hands were of more value keeping guard of the Spurs goal. Standing just over 6ft, lithe, daring, tremendously acrobatic, he was also known for his marvellous kicking ability which could clear the lines instantly. He played over 400 League games for Spurs, including a spell of 247 consecutive appearances. The last line of defence in the wonderful "push and run" side of the early 1950s, he was an outstanding keeper during a period renowned for them, resulting unfortunately in only six England caps coming his way. Spectacular to the end, he bowed out at the age of 37 after losing his place to the younger Ron Reynolds.

PETER DOBING (Blackburn Rov./Manchester C./Stoke C.)
Dobing enjoyed instant success on his debut with Blackburn Rovers when 17 years old, soon putting his name at the top of their Second Division goalscoring charts. Building up a great partnership with the brilliant Bryan Douglas, he helped the Rovers back into the big time in 1957/8. He gained England under 23 honours, which were followed by representing the Football League, before signing for Manchester City for £37,500 in July 1961. Although being a City fan in younger days, he never really settled, eventually signing for Stoke City in 1963. He spent ten happy seasons at the Victoria ground culminating in gaining a Football League Cup winners medal when Stoke beat Chelsea in 1971/2.

MARTIN DOBSON (Bolton W./Burnley, Everton & England/Burnley/Bury)
After coming through the Bolton ranks, Dobson was surprisingly allowed a free transfer to neighbours Burnley in August 1967. His excellent midfield qualities were soon recognised by the "Clarets" and by 1972/3 he was a regular in the side that gained promotion to the First Division in top position. Everton forked out £300,000 in August 1974 to bring this hard-working player to Goodison, where he went on to play nearly 200 League games and gain an England Cap to go with the four collected whilst at Turf Moor. Burnley were later allowed to buy him back for £100,000 in August 1979, and the investment paid off in 1981/2 when Martin was a key member in getting the side back into the Second Division as Champions. He is now with Bury.

PETER DOHERTY (Blackpool, Manchester C., Derby Co., Huddersfield T., Doncaster Rov. & N. Ireland)
A native of Magherafelt, coming to Blackpool from Glentoran, Doherty saw further service before the war with Manchester City, winning a League Championship medal and playing for his country on many occasions. He was probably the finest inside forward produced by Northern Ireland. With his flame hair, Peter Doherty combined tireless energy with tactical awareness to disrupt the most disciplined of defences. He won a Cup medal with Derby County in 1946, when partnering Raich Carter at inside forward. In 1949, at the age of 36, he became player-manager of Doncaster Rovers, driving the team on to winning promotion that season from the Third Division North.

DEREK DOOLEY (Lincoln C./Sheffield Wed.)
Swashbuckling Derek Dooley first hit the headlines in 1951/2, the season after Wednesday had been relegated from the First Division. Looking for an early return, the club examined its own staff and decided that the raw 21 year old centre forward, with just two previous appearances behind him, would be given an extended run. The result was staggering, as 6ft 2in dynamite Derek smashed 46 goals from 30 games, collecting a Second Division medal. In the First Division tragedy struck him down during the game against Preston on 14 February 1953, where after fracturing a leg, gangrene set in, resulting in eventual amputation. The football world mourned the loss of a rising star, but the indomitable youngster got down to a new career, later coming back as the Sheffield Wednesday manager.

DEREK DOUGAN (Portsmouth, Blackburn Rov., Aston Villa & N. Ireland/Peterborough U./Leicester C./Wolverhampton W. & N. Ireland)
A marvellous extrovert centre forward, Dougan had great skill on the ground and was quite capable of winning any aerial battle. One of the game's great characters who once shaved his head prior to appearing in an important match, he played for many varied clubs, only really settling when joining Wolves in March 1967 from Leicester City. Previous to that he had dropped into the Third Division with Peterborough, where for two years it was quite apparent that he was too good a player to be languishing in the lower region. He was a great favourite with most fans, always giving entertainment, and was well worth the 43 caps gained with Ireland.

BRYAN DOUGLAS (Blackburn Rov. & England)
An unorthodox, brilliant ball playing forward, Douglas, only 6ft 6in, made up for lack of inches with great vision and artistry. He began at outside right, where England eventually preferred to play him, but settled down for Blackburn at inside forward, utilising great skill and shooting ability. He was an outstanding influence in helping the Rovers back into the top flight of 1957/8, and instrumental two seasons later in getting them to Wembley, where they were beaten by the Wolves 3-0. He will always be remembered amongst the elite of great Blackburn Rovers stars, winning most of the individual honours the game had to offer, before moving on to Great Harwood in 1969.

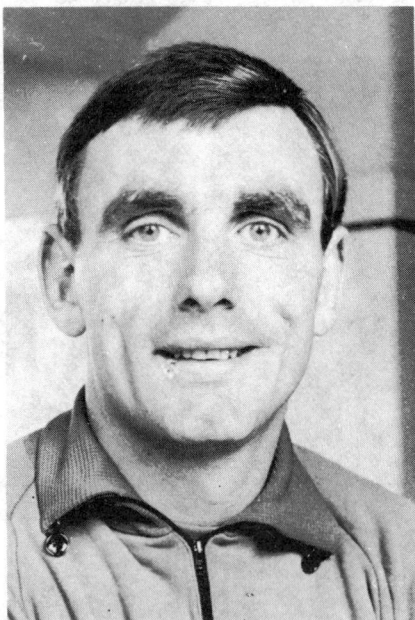

PETER DOWNSBOROUGH (Halifax T./Swindon T./Bradford C.)
Downsborough made his debut with his local side Halifax in season 1959/60, creating a great impression almost immediately although he was never to play in the First Division. He joined Swindon Town in August 1965, helping the Wiltshire side gain promotion to the Second Division in 1968/9, but his and the club's greatest moment came during that same season, when the little Third Division side reached Wembley, eventually beating mighty Arsenal in the League Cup Final 3-1 for one of the greatest upsets of modern times. Downsborough was outstanding during the famous Cup run, obviously the pinnacle of his career; he left to play for Bradford City and in all made over 650 League appearances before leaving the game.

MICK DOYLE (Manchester C. & England/Stoke C./Bolton W./Rochdale)
A Mancunian who worked his way through the Manchester City junior sides before turning professional in May 1964, some 17 years later Doyle was still going strong with Stoke City. After becoming a City regular, within a season he had made several appearances for the England under 23 side, a fore-runner of five full caps. He became a commanding midfield star, instrumental in driving the City out of the Second Division into a highly prestigious period of the club's history, when in four years he collected League Championship, F.A. Cup, League Cup and European Cup Winners Cup medals. He was allowed to join Stoke City in the summer of 1978 prior to service with Bolton Wanderers and Rochdale.

ALAN DURBAN (Cardiff C./Derby Co & Wales/Shrewsbury T.)
A skilful midfield player with precision passing, Durban made his debut with Cardiff City, signing professional in September 1958, but never became a regular with the "Bluebirds", although gaining the first of 14 Welsh under 23 caps whilst still at Ninian Park. Recruited by Derby County in July 1963, Durban immediately gained a first team place, going on to collect a Second Division winners medal in season 1968/9, to take the County back to the big time. Alan was instrumental in the club's success story and gained a Championship medal in 1971/2. He represented Wales on 27 occasions. Later he went on to play for and manage Shrewsbury Town.

Players Names	Birthplace	Date	Previous Club	League Club	Date Signed	Seasons Played	Apps	Sub	Gls	
EADES, Kevin M.	Rotherham	11.03.59	APP	Rotherham U.	03.77	1975	1	/	0	(IF)
EADES, Terry	Bambridge	05.03.44	Chelmsford	Cambridge U.	N/L	1970-76	248	/	5	(D)
			L	Watford	09.76	1976	4	/	0	
EADIE, Doug	Edinburgh	22.09.46		West Ham U.	09.66	1966	2	/	0	(OL)
			L	Orient	09.67	1967	2	/	0	
EADIE, Gordon	Glasgow	17.11.50	Glasgow U.	Bury	AM	1967	2	/	0	(F)
EADIE, Jim	Kirkintilloch	04.02.47		Cardiff C.	09.66	1969-71	43	/	0	(G)
			L	Chester C.	08.72	1972	6	/	0	
			TR	Bristol Rov.	02.73	1972-76	183	/	0	
EAGLES, Alan J.	Edgware	06.09.33	Carshalton	Orient	09.57	1957-60	76		0	(FB)
			TR	Colchester U.	01.61	1960	16		1	
			TR	Q.P.R.	08.61					
			TR	Aldershot	11.61	1961-62	14		1	
EALING, William H.	Tamworth	12.03.30		Blackburn Rov.	02.50					
			TR	Walsall	07.52	1952	1		0	
EAMES, Terry	Croydon	13.10.57	Crystal Palace (AM)	Wimbledon	N/L	1977-79	46	1	1	(D)
EAMES, William	Emsworth	20.09.57	APP	Portsmouth	09.75	1975	9	3	1	(F)
				Brentford	08.78	1978	2	/	1	
EARL, Albert T.	Gateshead	10.02.15		Stockport Co.	08.46	1946-47	42		12	(IF) *Bury/York C.
			TR	Rochdale	11.47	1947	4		1	
			TR	New Brighton	03.48	1947	9		1	
EARL, Stan W.J.	Alton	09.07.29		Portsmouth	11.49	1950-51	8		0	(FB)
			TR	Orient	07.53	1953-55	33		0	
			TR	Swindon T.	11.56	1956-57	23		0	
EARL, Steve	Scunthorpe	31.08.56	Appleby Frod.	Scunthorpe U.	11.78	1974-79	37	2	10	(F)
EARLAM, Don	Altrincham	25.06.31	Stoke C.(AM)	Southport	AM	1954	2		0	(LH)
EARLE, Robert	Stoke	27.01.65	Stoke C. (N/C)	Port Vale	07.82	1982-83	14	6	1	(F)
EARLE, Steve	Fulham	01.11.45	APP	Fulham	11.63	1963-73	285	7	97	(F)
			TR	Leicester C.	11.73	1973-77	91	8	20	
			L	Peterborough U.	11.77	1977	1	/	0	
EARLES, Pat J.	Tichfield	22.03.55	APP	Southampton	11.72	1974-76	4	8	1	(F)E.SCH.INT.
			TR	Reading	01.77	1976-82	240	7	68	
EARLS, Mike M.	Limerick	25.03.54	APP	Southampton	03.72	1973-74	8	/	0	(D)
			TR	Aldershot	06.75	1975-78	68	5	0	
EARLY, Mike	Dumbarton	04.04.28	Strathleven	Watford	06.46	1946	5		1	(OR)
EARNSHAW, Robert I.	Rotherham	15.03.43		Barnsley	06.64	1962-72	230	2	35	(F)
EASDALE, John	Dumbarton	16.01.19		Liverpool	*	1946	2		0	
			TR	Stockport Co.	09.48	1948	6		0	
EAST, Keith M.G.	Southampton	31.10.44	APP	Portsmouth	06.63					(CF)
			TR	Swindon T.	05.64	1964-66	43	1	21	
			TR	Stockport Co.	12.66	1966-67	23	2	7	
			TR	Bournemouth	11.67	1967-69	93	1	34	
			TR	Northampton T.	07.70	1970	26	3	7	
			TR	Crewe Alex.	07.71	1971	32	2	8	
EASTHAM, Brian	Bolton	26.04.37		Bury	09.58	1958-66	188	1	3	(FB)
				Rochdale	07.67	1967	13	/	0	
			Toronto Falcons							
EASTHAM, George E.	Blackpool	23.09.36	Ards	Newcastle U.	05.56	1956-59	124		29	(IF) E-19/E.U.23-6/
			TR	Arsenal	10.60	1960-65	207	/	41	E.F.LGE.REP.
			TR	Stoke C.	08.66	1966-73	184	10	4	
EASTHAM, George R.	Blackpool	13.09.14	Brentford(*)	Blackpool	*	1946	24		6	(IF) E-1/*Bolton W./
				Swansea C.	08.47	1947	15		0	Father of George E.
			TR	Rochdale	06.48	1948	2		0	
			TR	Lincoln C.	01.49	1948-49	27		1	
EASTHAM, Henry	Blackpool	30.06.17	Blackpool (AM)	Liverpool	*	1946	19		0	(OR) Brother of George R.
			TR	Tranmere Rov.	05.48	1948-52	154		13	
			TR	Accrington St.	07.53	1953	42		3	
EASTHAM, Stan	Bolton	26.11.13	Liverpool(*)	Exeter C.	+					E.AMAT.INT.
			TR	Stockport Co.	06.46	1946	14		1	
EASTHOPE, Joe D.	Liverpool	26.09.29		Everton	04.50	1952	2		0	(F)
			TR	Stockport Co.	06.54	1954	9		2	
EASTMAN, Don J.	Eastry	09.08.23	JNRS	Crystal Palace	AM	1946	1		0	(FB)
EASTOE, Peter R.	Tamworth	02.08.53	APP	Wolverhampton W.	06.71	1971-73	4	2	0	(F)E.YTH.INT.
			TR	Swindon T.	11.73	1973-75	91	/	43	
			TR	Q.P.R.	03.76	1976-78	69	3	15	
			TR	Everton	03.79	1978-81	88	7	26	
			TR	W.B.A.	08.82	1982	30	1	8	
			L	Leicester C	10.83	1983	5	/	1	
			L	Huddersfield T.	03.84	1983	8	2	0	
EASTON, Harry	Shoreham	12.09.38		Crystal Palace	11.56	1959-61	8		1	(F)
EASTWAY, Ray J.	Croydon	12.04.29		Watford	08.49	1951	12		0	(CH)
EASTWOOD, Eric	Bolton	24.03.16		Manchester C.	*	1946	9		0	(CH)
			TR	Port Vale	03.47	1946-48	28		1	

Players Names	Birthplace	Date	Previous Club	League Club	Date Signed	Seasons Played	Apps	Sub	Gls	
EASTWOOD, Ray	Manchester	01.01.13	Altrincham	Aldershot	*					(FB)
			TR	Accrington St.	07.46	1946	3		0	
EATON, Joe D.	Cuckney	16.05.31	Langwith Col.	Mansfield T.	08.51	1952-53	4		1	(IF)
EATON, Steve	Liverpool	25.12.59		Tranmere Rov.	03.79	1978	1	/	0	(D)
EAVES, Ernie	Ashton	04.01.27	Newton Y.M.C.A.	New Brighton	08.50	1948-50	14		3	(F)
EBANKS, M. Wayne A.	Birmingham	02.10.64	APP	W.B.A.	04.82	1983	6	1	0	(D)
EBDON, Richard	Ottery St. Mary	03.05.13	Ottery St. Mary	Exeter C.	*	1946-47	47		23	(IF)
			TR	Torquay U.	07.48	1948	5		1	
ECCLES, Terry S.	Leeds	02.03.52	APP	Blackburn Rov.	08.69	1969-72	33	13	6	(F)
			TR	Mansfield T.	07.73	1973-76	115	3	47	
			TR	Huddersfield T.	01.77	1976-77	41	5	6	
			Ethnikos	York C.	09.79	1979-80	64	/	18	
ECCLESHARE, Keith	Bolton	14.12.50	APP	Bury	12.68	1968-71	79	3	0	(FB) E.YTH.INT.
ECCLESTON, Stuart I.	Stoke	04.10.61	APP	Stoke C.	10.79					(D)
			TR	Hull C.	01.81	1980-81	22	1	0	
				Port Vale	10.82					
ECKERSALL, Mike W.	Bury	03.02.39	Mossley	Torquay U.	10.59	1960-62	28		2	(F)
			TR	Stockport Co.	07.63	1963-65	39	1	2	
ECKERSLEY, William	Southport	16.07.26	High Park	Blackburn Rov.	03.48	1947-60	407		21	(FB) E-17/E'B'-3/E.F.LGE REP./d.1982
ECONOMOU, Jon	Holloway	25.10.61	APP	Bristol C.	10.79	1981-83	62	3	3	(F)
EDDOLLS, John D.	Bristol	19.08.19	Peasdown	Bristol C.	+	1946	6		0	(G)
			TR	Bristol Rov.	08.48					
EDDS, Ernie F.	Plymouth	19.03.26	Portsmouth (AM)	Plymouth Arg.	10.46	1946-49	59		18	(CF)
			TR	Blackburn Rov.	12.49	1949-50	18		3	
			TR	Torquay U.	06.51	1951-53	84		34	
			TR	Plymouth Arg.	10.53	1953-54	26		4	
			TR	Swindon T.	07.55	1955	3		0	
EDDY, Keith	Barrow	03.09.44	Holker COB	Barrow	06.62	1962-65	127	1	5	(WH)
			TR	Watford	07.66	1966-71	239	1	26	
			TR	Sheffield U.	08.72	1972-75	113	1	16	
EDELSTON, Maurice	Hull	27.04.18	Brentford(AM)	Reading	07.47	1946-51	202		70	(CF) *Fulham(AM)
			TR	Northampton T.	07.52	1952-53	39		17	E.AMAT.INT. d.1976
EDEN, Alan	Sunderland	08.10.58	Lambton St.B.C.	Lincoln C.	08.77	1977-78	5	2	0	(M)
EDEN, Anthony	Birmingham	15.03.41	JNRS	Aston Villa	04.58					(HB)
			TR	Walsall	07.60	1960-62	14		0	
EDGAR, Edward	Bristol	31.10.56	APP	Newcastle U.	08.78					(G)
			TR	Hartlepool U.	07.76	1976-78	75	/		
EDGAR, John	Barnsley	09.04.36	JNRS	Barnsley	05.54	1955-57	22		6	(F)
			TR	Gillingham	06.58	1958	45		23	
			TR	York C.	06.59	1959-60	47		16	
			TR	Hartlepool U.	06.61	1961-62	72		31	
			TR	Exeter C.	07.63	1963	6		0	
EDGAR, John D.	Aldershot	01.12.30	Ferryhill Ath.	Darlington	12.54	1954-55	12		0	
EDGE, Anthony	Wirral	14.03.37	Devizes	Bristol Rov.	08.59	1959-60	13		4	(F)
EDGE, Derek	Stoke	14.02.42	Stoke C.(AM)	Port Vale	09.60	1961	2		0	(F)
			TR	Crewe Alex.	07.62					
EDGLEY, Brian K.	Shrewsbury	26.08.37	JNRS	Shrewsbury T.	02.56	1955-59	113		12	(IF)
			TR	Cardiff C.	07.60	1960	10		1	
			TR	Brentford	06.61	1961-62	31		9	
			TR	Barnsley	11.62	1962	4		0	
EDISBURY, William	Tyldesley	12.11.37	JNRS	Bolton W.	10.56	1956-57	2		0	(FB)
EDMONDS, Derek J.	Newcastle	09.10.50	APP	Leeds U.	11.67					(G) E.YTH.INT.
			TR	Watford	05.70	1970-71	15	/	0	
			S.Africa	Southport	07.74	1974	2	/	0	
EDMONDSON, D. Barry	Southport	10.02.43	Blackpool(AM)	Southport	12.61	1961	1		0	(WH)
EDMONDSON, Stan G.	Bacup	10.08.22	Bacup	Bradford C.	AM	1946	3		0	(OL) d.1977
EDMUNDS, Paul	Leicester	02.12.57	Troston W.	Leicester C.	04.79	1979-80	8	/	2	(F)
				Bournemouth	07.81	1981	13	1	2	
EDMUNDS, Redfern E.	Newport	10.01.43	JNRS	Portsmouth	06.60	1960	4		0	(F) W.SCH.INT.
			TR	Newport Co.	07.61	1961	4		0	
EDWARDS, Andy J.	Wrexham	28.03.65	JNRS	Wrexham	08.83	1982-83	27	16	7	(M)
EDWARDS, Brian A.	Portsmouth	06.10.30	JNRS	Portsmouth	10.48	1951	1		0	(FB)
EDWARDS, Bryan	Leeds	27.10.30	JNRS	Bolton W.	10.47	1950-64	483		8	(WH)
EDWARDS, Cliff	Carmarthen	04.12.28	JNRS	Swansea C.	10.51	1952	1		0	(G)
EDWARDS, Cliff I.	Cannock	08.03.21	Cannock T.	W.B.A.	+	1946-47	40		1	(HB)
			TR	Bristol C.	06.48	1948-49	33		3	
EDWARDS, David			Ipswich T.(+)	Swindon T.	06.46	1946	3		1	
EDWARDS, David A.				Wrexham	AM	1949	1		1	
EDWARDS, David J.	Treharris	10.12.34	Treharris	Fulham	05.52	1956-63	37		0	(WH)

Players Names	Birthplace	Date	Previous Club	League Club	Date Signed	Seasons Played	Career Record Apps	Sub	Gls	
EDWARDS, Dean S.	Wolverhampton	25.02.62	APP	Shrewsbury T.	02.80	1979-81	7	6	1	(F)
EDWARDS, Dennis	Slough	19.01.37	Woking	Charlton Ath.	02.59	1958-64	171		61	(CF) E.AMAT.INT.
			TR	Portsmouth	01.65	1964-67	69	4	14	
			L	Brendford	09.67	1967	11	/	2	
			TR	Aldershot	12.67	1967	11	3	1	
EDWARDS, Don	Wrexham	02.08.30	Wrexham Vic.	Norwich C.	09.47	1947	2		0	(G)
EDWARDS, Duncan	Dudley	01.10.36	JNRS	Manchester U.	10.53	1952-57	151		19	(WH)E-18/E.U23-6/E'B'-4/ E.F.LGE REP./E.YTH.INT./ E.SCH.INT./d.1958
EDWARDS, Edward	Seaham	13.02.36		Hartlepool U.	02.57	1957	1		0	(FB)
EDWARDS, George	Treherbert	02.12.20	Coventry C.(AM)	Birmingham C.	+	1946-48	82		9	(OL) *Swansea C.
			TR	Cardiff C.	12.48	1948-54	194		34	W-12/W.AMAT.INT.
EDWARDS, George R.	Great Yarmouth	01.04.18	Norwich C.(*)	Aston Villa	*	1946-50	135		35	(F)
EDWARDS, Gordon	Wrexham	14.10.35	JNRS	Bolton W.	10.52	1955-58	4		0	(HB) W.SCH.INT.
EDWARDS, Henry P.	Wigan	13.02.32		Blackpool	06.51					(IF)
			TR	Southport	08.53	1954	1		0	
EDWARDS, Howard	Tipton	02.06.19	Stourbridge	Derby Co.	01.47					(HB)
			TR	Crewe Alex.	06.52	1952	5		0	
EDWARDS, Ian	Wrexham	30.01.55	Rhyl	W.B.A.	02.73	1974-76	13	3	3	(F)W.U21-2/W-4
			TR	Chester C.	11.76	1976-79	104	/	36	
			TR	Wrexham	11.79	1979-81	71	4	20	
			TR	Crystal Palace	07.82	1982	16	2	4	
EDWARDS, J. Elfyn	Aberystwyth	04.05.60	JNRS	Wrexham	07.78					(D)
			TR	Tranmere Rov.	07.79	1979-80	62	/	1	
EDWARDS, Jack	Manchester	23.02.24	Long Eaton U.	Nottingham F.	+	1946-48	77		20	(OL) d.1978
			TR	Southampton	06.49	1949-51	82		16	
			TR	Notts. Co.	11.52	1952-53	25		3	
EDWARDS, John	Wrexham	23.05.40	Bradley Spts.	Wrexham	AM	1965	1	/	0	(G)
EDWARDS, John F.	Wath-on-Dearne	27.12.21	Manders Col.	Rotherham U.	+	1946-53	296		9	(WH)
EDWARDS, John W.	Monmouth	06.07.29	Lovells Ath.	Crystal Palace	09.49	1949-58	223		0	(FB)
			TR	Rochdale	06.59	1959-60	68		1	
EDWARDS, Keith	Stockton	16.07.57		Sheffield U.	08.75	1975-77	64	6	29	(F)
			TR	Hull C.	08.78	1978-81	130	2	57	
			TR	Sheffield U	09.81	1981-83	122	5	81	
EDWARDS, Keith B.	Chester	10.06.44		Chester C.	AM	1965-66	3	/	0	(CF)
EDWARDS, Len O.	Wrexham	30.05.30		Sheffield Wed.	01.51	1951	2		0	(WH)
			TR	Brighton & H.A.	03.54	1954	6		0	
			TR	Crewe Alex.	12.55	1955-56	40		0	
EDWARDS, Leslie R.	Guildford	12.04.24	Nailsea U.	Bristol Rov.	05.48	1950-56	46		0	(HB)
EDWARDS, M. Keith	Neath	26.09.52	APP	Leeds U.	10.69	1971	0	1	0	(HB) W.SCH.INT.
			TR	Swansea C.	07.72					
EDWARDS, Malcolm	Wrexham	25.10.39	JNRS	Bolton W.	11.56	1956-60	14		1	(HB) W.U23-2/W.SCH.INT.
			TR	Chester C.	02.61	1960-61	43		5	
			TR	Tranmere Rov.	07.62	1962-63	34		2	
			TR	Barrow	07.64	1964-68	177	/	9	
EDWARDS, Nigel	Wrexham	31.12.50	Blackburn Rov.(AM)	Chester C.	09.68	1968-77	281	9	15	(D)W.U23-3
			TR	Aldershot	07.78	1978-81	137	/	6	
			TR	Chester C.	06.82	1982	8	/	1	
EDWARDS, Patrick K.	Wolverhampton	09.12.39		Walsall	10.57	1958	1		0	(F)
			TR	Chesterfield	07.59					
EDWARDS, Paul	Crompton	07.10.47	JNRS	Manchester U.	02.65	1969-72	52	2	0	(D)E.U23-3/E.F.LGE REP.
			TR	Oldham Ath.	09.72	1972-77	108	4	7	
			L	Stockport Co.	01.77	1976	2	/	0	
			TR	Stockport Co.	08.78	1978-79	64	3	2	
EDWARDS, Reg E.	Rugeley	28.01.53	Nuneaton	Port Vale	08.72	1972-74	8	/	0	(G)
EDWARDS, Reg G.	Newton-le-Willows	24.07.19	Alloa	Luton T.	+					(FB)
			TR	Accrington St.	08.46	1946-48	65		11	
EDWARDS, Richard L.	Kingsbury	05.11.43	Admult FC	Luton T.	06.64	1964-65	15	2	1	(FB)
EDWARDS, Richard T.	Kirkby-in-Ashfield	20.11.42	JNRS	Notts. Co.	10.59	1959-66	219	/	18	(CH)
			TR	Mansfield T.	03.67	1966-67	45	/	1	
			TR	Aston Villa	03.68	1967-69	68	/	2	
			TR	Torquay U.	06.70	1970-72	99	3	5	
			TR	Mansfield T.	07.73	1973	31	2	1	
EDWARDS, Robert H.	Guildford	22.05.31	Woking	Chelsea	11.51	1952-54	13		2	(IF) Brother of Leslie
			TR	Swindon T.	07.55	1955-59	173		64	
			TR	Norwich C.	12.59	1959	1		0	
			TR	Northampton T.	03.61	1960-61	23		10	
EDWARDS, Ron	Liverpool	11.07.27	S. Liverpool	Chesterfield	07.53	1953	13		2	(IF)
EDWARDS, Roy	Sheffield	26.11.20		Lincoln C.	06.47	1947-48	6		0	
EDWARDS, Stan	West Bromwich	11.12.42	JNRS	Everton	12.59					(F)
			TR	Port Vale	05.61	1961-62	49		9	

Players Names	Birthplace	Date	Previous Club	League Club	Date Signed	Seasons Played	Apps	Sub	Gls	
EDWARDS, Stan L.	Dawdon	17.10.26	Horden CW	Chelsea	10.49					(CF)
			TR	Colchester U.	06.52	1952	16		5	
			TR	Orient	06.53	1953	2		1	
EDWARDS, Steve	Birkenhead	11.01.58	APP	Oldham Ath.	01.76	1977-82	77	3	0	(D)
			TR	Crewe Alex.	02.83	1982-83	57	1	1	
EDWARDS, Trevor	Rhondda	24.01.37	JNRS	Charlton Ath.	05.55	1956-59	64		0	(FB) W-2/W.U23-2
			TR	Cardiff C.	06.60	1960-63	73		3	
EDWARDS, Walter	Mansfield	26.06.24	Woodhouse	Mansfield T.	11.47	1947-48	25		5	
			TR	Leeds U.	03.49	1948	2			
			TR	Leicester C.	08.49					
			TR	Rochdale	09.50					
EDWARDS, Walter T.	Llanelli	13.03.23	Workington T.	Fulham	08.46	1947	2		0	
			TR	Southend U.	03.48	1947-48	11		1	
			TR	Leicester C.	12.48	1948	3		1	
			Bath C.	Walsall	05.52	1952	12		0	
EDWARDS, William	Bowburn	10.12.23	Bowburn	Middlesbrough	03.52	1952-54	16		4	
EDWARDS, William	Hackney	08.01.52	Tottenham H.(APP)	Wimbledon	N/L	1977	21	/	2	(D)
EDWARDSON, John	Manchester	09.03.44	Bethesda	Crystal Palace	11.66				–	(HB)
			L	Crewe Alex.	01.68	1967	1	/	0	
EGAN, Chris	Dublin	06.08.53	Cork Celtic	Derby Co.	10.73					(M)
			TR	Newport Co.	08.76	1976	5	2	0	
EGAN, John	Stirling	19.08.37	Stenhousemuir	Halifax T.	10.59	1959	5		0	(W)
			TR	Accrington St.	08.60	1960	1		0	
EGDELL, Ernie	Newcastle	29.05.22		Darlington	AM	1946	1		0	(CH)
EGERTON, Frank	Atherton	05.04.26		Blackburn Rov.	+					
			TR	Accrington St.	06.47	1947-48	8		0	
EGGLESTON, Pat	Penrith	17.03.27	Portsmouth (AM)	Bradford C.	AM	1948	2		0	(G)
			TR	Halifax T.	09.49	1949	20		0	
			TR	Shrewsbury T.	08.50	1950-52	109		0	
			TR	Wrexham	02.53	1952-55	84		0	
EGGLESTON, Tom	Mitcham	21.02.20		Derby Co.	*					(FB)
			TR	Leicester C.	08.46	1946-47	34		2	
			TR	Watford	02.48	1947-52	177		6	
EGLINGTON, Tom	Dublin	15.01.23	Shamrock Rov.	Everton	07.46	1946-56	394		76	(OL) E1-24/N1-6
			TR	Tranmere Rov.	06.57	1957-60	172		36	
EISENTRANGER, Albert	Germany	20.07.27	Trowbridge	Bristol C.	01.50	1949-57	228		46	(W)
EKNER, Dan H.	Sweden	05.02.27	Sweden	Portsmouth	AM	1949	4		0	d.1975
ELDER, Alex	Perth	11.09.23	Dundee U.	Hartlepool U.	08.51	1951-52	65		19	(WH)
ELDER, Alex	Glentoran	25.04.41	Glentoran	Burnley	01.59	1959-66	271	/	13	(FB) N.I.-40/N.I.U23-1/
			TR	Stoke C.	08.67	1967-72	80	3	1	N.I.SCH.INT.●
ELDER, Jim	Perth	05.03.28		Portsmouth	+	1949	1		0	(WH)
			TR	Colchester U.	07.50	1950-54	199		15	
ELEY, Kevin	Mexborough	04.03.68	JNRS	Rotherham U.	N/C	1983	0	1	0	
ELGIN, Robert	Edinburgh	23.06.49	Hearts	Stockport Co.	07.69	1969-70	30	4	3	(IF)
ELLAM, Roy	Hemsworth	13.01.43	JNRS	Bradford C.	05.61	1961-65	149	/	12	(CH)
			TR	Huddersfield T.	01.66	1966-71	207	/	8	
			TR	Leeds U.	08.72	1972-73	9	2	0	
			TR	Huddersfield T.	07.74	1974	18	/	2	
ELLAWAY, William	Crediton	12.10.32	Crediton	Exeter C.	11.54	1953-55	30		9	(IF)
			TR	Bournemouth	06.56	1956-57	4		0	
ELLERINGTON, William	Southampton	30.06.23	Fatfield Col.	Southampton	+	1946-55	225		10	(FB) E-2/E'B'-1/E.F.LGE REP./E.SCH.INT.
ELLIOTT, Andy	Ashton-U-Lyne	21.11.63	APP	Manchester C.	11.81	1981	1	/	0	(M)
			Sligo R.	Chester C.	09.83	1983	24	8	3	
ELLIOTT, Bernard H.	Beeston	03.05.25	Beeston BC	Nottingham F.	+	1947-48	10		0	(WH)
			TR	Southampton	10.49	1949-57	235		3	
ELLIOTT, Charlie S.	Bolsover	24.04.12		Coventry C.	*	1946-47	37		0	(FB) Derby Cricketer
ELLIOTT, Dave	Tantobie	10.02.45	APP	Sunderland	02.62	1963-66	30	1	0	(M)
			TR	Newcastle U.	12.66	1966-70	78	2	4	
			TR	Southend U.	02.71	1970-74	173	4	10	
			TR	Newport Co.	07.75	1975-78	21	2	0	
ELLIOTT, Edward	Carlisle	24.05.19	Carlisle U.(*)	Wolverhampton W.	*	1946-47	7		0	(G)
			TR	Chester C.	10.48	1948-50	59		0	
			TR	Halifax T.	11.50	1950-51	33		0	
ELLIOTT, Frank F.G.	Merthyr Tydfil	23.07.29	Thornton Hth	Swansea C.	09.49					(G)
			TR	Stoke C.	12.52	1952-53	22		0	
			TR	Fulham	03.54	1953-55	25		0	
			TR	Mansfield T.	07.56	1956-57	63		0	
ELLIOTT, Harvey	Middleton	21.01.22		Hull C.	12.46	1946	4		0	(F)
ELLIOTT, Ian	Barrow	16.12.53	JNRS	Barrow	AM	1969	1	/	0	(G)
ELLIOTT, John	Eden	06.05.38		Carlisle U.	08.58	1955-57	2		1	

Players Names	Birthplace	Date	Previous Club	League Club	Date Signed	Seasons Played	Apps	Sub	Gls	
ELLIOTT, John W.	Ashington	23.12.46	Ashington	Notts. Co.	08.67	1967-68	61	3	7	(F)
ELLIOTT, Kevin	Chilton	05.09.58	APP.	Hartlepool U.	09.76	1975-76	24	3	1	(F)
ELLIOTT, M. Richard	Rhondda	20.03.59	Merthyr Tydfil	Brighton & H.A.	02.77	1976	3	/	0	(M)
			TR	Cardiff C.	09.79	1979	6	1	0	
			L	Bournemouth	01.80	1979	4	/	0	
			TR	Wimbledon	N/C	1981	7	4	1	
ELLIOTT, Paul M.	London	18.03.64	APP	Charlton Ath.	03.81	1981-82	61	2	1	(D) E.YTH.INT.
			TR	Luton T.	03.83	1982-83	51	/	3	
ELLIOTT, Ray C.	Southampton	11.06.47	APP	Charlton Ath.	06.65					(F)
			TR	Exeter C.	03.66	1965-66	28	/	3	
ELLIOTT, Ray J.	Rhondda	23.03.29		Millwall	11.46	1947-48	2		0	
ELLIOTT, Shaun	Hebden Bridge	26.01.58	APP	Sunderland	01.75	1976-83	253	4	10	(D)
ELLIOTT, Stephen B.	Haltwhistle	15.09.58	APP	Nottingham F.	08.77	1978	4	/	0	(F)
			TR	Preston N.E.	03.79	1978-83	202	6	70	
ELLIOTT, William	Poole	23.10.61	APP	Plymouth Arg.	03.79					(M)
			TR	Bournemouth	05.80	1980	6	5	1	
ELLIOTT, William B.	Harrington	06.08.19	Bournemouth(*)	W.B.A.	*	1946-50	153		35	(OL)*Carlisle U./Wolverhampton W. W./Dudley/d.1966
ELLIOTT, William H.	Bradford	20.03.25	JNRS	Bradford P.A.	+	1946-50	176		21	(OL) E-5/E.F.LGE REP.
			TR	Burnley	09.51	1951-52	74		14	
			TR	Sunderland	06.53	1953-58	193		23	
ELLIS, Alan	Somercotes	17.11.51	APP	Charlton Ath.	11.69	1970-72	9	5	0	(WH)
ELLIS, Dave			Pollock	Bury	04.47					(W)
			TR	Halifax T.	01.48	1947	3	/	0	
			TR	Barrow	10.48	1948	1		0	
ELLIS, Glen D.	Dagenham	31.10.57	APP	Ipswich T.	10.75					(G) E.SCH.INT.
			L	Colchester U.	12.76	1976	2	/	0	
ELLIS, Keith D.	Sheffield	06.11.35	JNRS	Sheffield Wed.	04.55	1954-63	103		54	(CF)
			TR	Scunthorpe U.	03.64	1963	10		5	
			TR	Cardiff C.	09.64	1964	22		10	
			TR	Lincoln C.	06.65	1965	7	/	0	
ELLIS, Ken	Buckley	22.01.28	JNRS	Chester C.	AM	1946	1		0	(IR)
				Wrexham	AM	1949	5		0	
ELLIS, Ken	Sunderland	29.05.48	Scarborough	Hartlepool U.	07.71	1971	32	2	4	(F)
			Verna	Darlington	07.79	1979	21	/	0	
ELLIS, Mark E.	Bradford	06.01.62		Bradford C.	05.81	1980-83	81	3	12	(M)
ELLIS, Peter J.	Portsmouth	20.03.56	APP	Portsmouth	03.74	1973-83	226	29	1	E.U23-3
ELLIS, Sam	Ashton-under-Lyne	12.09.46		Sheffield Wed.	09.64	1965-70	155	2	1	(D)
			TR	Mansfield T.	01.72	1971-72	64	/	7	
			TR	Lincoln C.	05.73	1973-76	173	/	33	
			TR	Watford	08.77	1977-78	30	4	4	
ELLIS, Sid	Charlton	16.08.31	Crystal Palace (AM)	Charlton Ath.	05.49	1953-57	48		0	(FB) E.U23-1
			TR	Brighton & H.A.	11.57	1957-58	43		0	
ELLISON, Norman	Bebbington	02.11.29		Tranmere Rov.	10.49	1949-50	2		0	(F)
ELLISON, Peter E.	Adlem	21.08.25	Crewe R.P.	Crewe Alex.	06.49	1948-55	219		0	(G)
ELLISON, Ray	Newcastle	31.12.50	APP	Newcastle U.	10.68	1971	5	/	0	(FB)
			TR	Sunderland	03.73	1972	2	/	0	
			TR	Torquay U.	07.74	1974	11	5	0	
			TR	Workington	07.75	1975-76	57	/	3	
ELLISON, Sam W.	Leadgate	27.08.23		Sunderland	+	1946	3		0	(OR)
			Consett	Reading	06.49	1949	4		0	
				Brighton & H.A.	08.51					
ELLISON, W. Roy	Newbiggin	05.07.48	APP	Newcastle U.	06.66					(IF)
			TR	Barrow	02.68	1967-70	76	9	7	
			L	Hartlepool U.	10.70	1970	5	/	0	
ELMES, Timmy	Croydon	28.09.62	APP	Chelsea	07.80	1980	2	2	0	(M)
ELMS, Jimmy B.	Manchester	16.09.40	JNRS	Manchester U.	04.58					(F) E.YTH.INT.
			TR	Crewe Alex.	10.60	1960	1		0	
ELSBY, Ian C.	Stoke	13.09.60	JNRS	Port Vale	06.78	1978-80	32	11	1	(M)
ELSBY, Jim	Newcastle-under-Lyme	01.08.28		Port Vale	05.47	1948-53	12		0	(FB)
ELSE, Fred	Golborne	31.03.33	Wigan Ath.	Preston N.E.	08.53	1953-60	215		0	(G) E'B'-1●
			TR	Blackburn Rov.	08.61	1961-65	187	/	0	
			TR	Barrow	07.66	1966-69	148	/	0	
ELSEY, Karl W.	Swansea	20.11.58	Pembroke Bor.	Q.P.R.	01.79	1978-79	6	1	0	(M)
			TR	Newport Co.	07.80	1980-83	114	9	15	
			TR	Cardiff C.	09.83	1983	29	/	1	
ELSEY, W. John	Swansea	23.12.38	JNRS	Swansea C.	04.56	1956	1		0	(F) W.SCH.INT.
			TR	Wrexham	05.59					
ELSWORTHY, John T.	Nantyderry	26.07.31	Newport Co.(AM)	Ipswich T.	05.49	1949-64	396		44	(WH)

Players Names	Birthplace	Date	Previous Club	League Club	Date Signed	Seasons Played	Apps	Sub	Gls	
ELVY, Reg	Leeds	25.11.20		Halifax T.	+	1946	22		0	(G)
			TR	Bolton W.	03.47	1947-49	31		0	
			TR	Blackburn Rov.	11.51	1951-55	192		0	
			TR	Northampton T.	07.56	1956-58	67		0	
ELWELL, Terry	Newport	13.04.26	Barry T.	Swansea C.	08.48	1948-50	48		0	(FB)
			TR	Swindon T.	07.52	1952-53	61		0	
ELWISS, Mike	Doncaster	02.05.54	JNRS	Doncaster Rov.	07.71	1971-73	96	1	30	(F)
			TR	Preston N.E.	02.74	1973-77	191	1	60	
			TR	Crystal Palace	07.78	1978	19	1	7	
			L	Preston N.E.	03.80	1979	8	2	3	
ELWOOD, Joe	Belfast	26.10.39	Glenavon	Orient	04.58	1958-65	102	2	26	(OL) N.I.'B'-1/N.I.U23-1/ N.I.SCH.INT.
EMANUEL, Len D.	Treboreth	03.09.17		Swansea C.	*	1946	4		0	(FB) W.SCH.INT.
			TR	Newport Co.	05.46	1946-47	33		7	
EMBERRY, Ben J.	Barking	10.10.44	APP	Tottenham H.	06.62					(WH)
			TR	Exeter C.	06.66	1966-67	36	2	0	
EMBLETON, David	Newcastle	14.09.52	APP	Newcastle U.	08.71					(CH)
			TR	Bury	07.72	1972	6	1	0	
			TR	Hartlepool U.	07.73	1973-75	24	2	0	
EMERSON, Dean	Salford	27.12.62		Stockport Co.	07.82	1981-83	112	/	5	(M)
EMERSON, Mark	Cuddington	07.08.65	JNRS	Wrexham	N/C	1982	1	1	0	(M)
EMERY, Anthony J.	Lincoln	04.11.27	JNRS	Lincoln C.	08.47	1946-58	402		1	(CH)●
			TR	Mansfield T.	06.59	1959-60	26		0	
EMERY, Dennis	Sandy	04.10.33	Eynesbury	Tottenham H.	12.51					(IF)
			Eynesbury	Peterborough U.	N/L	1960-62	68		29	
EMERY, Don F.H.	Cardiff	11.06.20	Cardiff C.(*)	Swindon T.	*	1946-47	60		2	(IF) W.SCH.INT.
EMERY, Jim	Lisburn	02.03.40	Distillery	Exeter C.	08.59					(IR)
			TR	Barrow	07.60	1960	2		0	
EMERY, Steve R.	Ledbury	07.02.56	APP	Hereford U.	04.74	1973-79	203	1	10	(D)
			TR	Derby Co.	09.79	1979-80	73	2	4	
			TR	Newport Co.	03.83					
			TR	Hereford U.	10.83	1983	32	2	1	
EMERY, Terry	Bristol	08.09.36		Bristol C.	02.57	1956-57	11		0	(HB)
EMMANUEL, J. Gary	Swansea	01.02.54	APP	Birmingham C.	07.71	1974-78	61	10	6	(M)W.U23-1
			TR	Bristol Rov.	12.78	1978-80	59	6	2	
			TR	Swindon T.	07.81	1981-83	109	2	8	
EMMANUEL, John	Swansea	05.04.48	Ferndale	Bristol C.	05.71	1971-75	124	4	10	(M)W-2
			L	Swindon T.	01.75	1975	6	/	0	
			L	Gillingham	02.76	1975	4	/	0	
			TR	Newport Co.	06.76	1976-77	79	/	4	
EMMERSON, Morris	Sunniside	23.10.42	JNRS	Middlesbrough	10.59	1962	10		0	(G) E.SCH.INT.
			TR	Peterborough U.	07.63	1963	7		0	
EMMERSON, Wayne	Canada	02.11.47	JNRS	Manchester U.	09.65					(F)
			TR	Crewe Alex.	07.68	1968	6	1	1	
EMPTAGE, Albert T.	Grimsby	26.12.17	Scunthorpe	Manchester C.	*	1946-50	123		1	(WH) E.F.LGE.REP.
			TR	Stockport Co.	01.51	1950-52	36		1	
EMSON, Paul	Lincoln	22.10.58	Brigg T.	Derby Co.	09.78	1978-82	112	15	13	(F)
			TR	Grimsby T.	08.83	1983	39	/	6	
ENDEAN, Barry	Chester-le-Street	22.03.46	Pelton Fell	Watford	09.68	1968-70	72	5	28	(F)
			TR	Charlton Ath.	02.71	1970-71	27	/	1	
			TR	Blackburn Rov.	10.71	1971-74	63	12	18	
			TR	Huddersfield T.	03.75	1974-75	8	4	1	
			L	Workington	10.75	1975	8	/	2	
			TR	Hartlepool U.	03.76	1975-76	24	1	5	
ENDERSBY, Scott A.G.	Lewisham	20.02.62	APP	Ipswich T.	03.79					(G)E.YTH.INT.
			TR	Tranmere Rov.	07.81	1981-82	79	/	0	
			TR	Swindon T.	08.83	1983	37	/	0	
ENGLAND, Fred W.	Holmfirth	11.07.23	Huddersfield T.(AM)	Halifax T.	AM	1946-47	18		1	(IF)
ENGLAND, Mike	Prestatyn	02.12.41	JNRS	Blackburn Rov.	04.59	1959-65	165	/	21	(CH) W-44/W.U23-11●
			TR	Tottenham H.	08.66	1966-74	300	/	14	
			TR	Cardiff C.	08.75	1975	40	/	1	
ENGLAND, Mike	Bristol	04.01.61	APP	Bristol Rov.	01.79	1978	1	/	0	(D)
ENGLEFIELD, Graham	Eltham	21.09.31	JNRS	Charlton Ath.	01.49					(HB)
			TR	Norwich C.	04.54	1955-56	22			
ENGLISH, Jack	Durham	19.03.23		Northampton T.	10.46	1947-59	301		135	(OR)
ENGLISH, Robert	Stockport	19.04.39	JNRS	Manchester U.	03.57					(WH)
			TR	Southport	11.61	1961-62	20		0	
ENGLISH, Tom S.	Cirencester	18.10.61	APP	Coventry C.	06.79	1979-81	62	4	17	(F)E.YTH.INT.
			TR	Leicester C.	09.82	1982-83	29	15	3	
ENNIS, Mark E.	Bradford	06.01.62	Joiners Libs.	Rochdale	N/C	1983	1	/	0	(D)

Players Names	Birthplace	Date	Previous Club	League Club	Date Signed	Seasons Played	Career Record Apps	Sub	Gls	
ENTWISTLE, Robert P.	Bury	06.10.38		Rochdale	AM	1958	1		0	
			TR	Accrington St.	09.60	1960	2		0	
			Llandudno	Hartlepool U.	10.64	1964	14		3	
			TR	Chesterfield	07.65					
ENTWISTLE, Wayne P.	Bury	06.08.58	APP	Bury	08.76	1976-77	25	6	7	(F)E.YTH.INT.
			TR	Sunderland	11.77	1977-79	43	2	12	
			TR	Leeds U.	10.79	1979	7	4	2	
			TR	Blackpool	11.80	1980-81	27	5	6	
			TR	Crewe Alex.	03.82	1981	11	/	0	
			TR	Wimbledon	07.82	1982	4	5	3	
			TR	Bury	08.83	1983	35	3	11	
EPHGRAVE, George A.	Swindon	29.04.18		Southampton	09.46	1946-47	36		0	(G) *Aston Villa/Swindon T.
			TR	Norwich C.	07.48	1948-50	5		0	
			TR	Watford	08.51	1951	4		0	
ESSER, David	Bowden	20.06.57	APP	Everton	05.75					(F)
			TR	Rochdale	07.77	1977-81	169	11	24	
ETHERIDGE, Brian G.	Northampton	04.03.44	JNRS	Northampton T.	07.62	1961-64	17		1	(F) E.YTH.INT.
			TR	Brentford	02.66	1965-66	22	/	2	
ETHERIDGE, R. Keith	Ivybridge	14.05.44	St. Blazey	Plymouth Arg.	07.66	1966-67	30	1	5	(F)
ETHERIDGE, Robert	Gloucester	21.03.34	Gloucester C.	Bristol C.	09.56	1956-63	259		42	(WH) Gloucester Cricketer
EUSTACE, Peter	Stocksbridge	31.07.44	APP	Sheffield Wed.	06.62	1962-69	190	3	20	(WH)
			TR	West Ham U.	01.70	1969-71	41	2	6	
			L	Rotherham U.	03.72	1971	6	/	1	
			TR	Sheffield Wed.	08.72	1972-74	48	8	4	
			TR	Peterborough U.	07.75	1975	42	1	5	
EVANS, Allan	Dunfermline	12.10.56	Dunfermline	Aston Villa	05.77	1977-83	232	2	35	(D)S-4
EVANS, Alun J.	Penrycadery	01.12.22	Wilden FC	W.B.A.	+	1947	18		0	(IF)
EVANS, Alun W.	Bewdley	30.04.49	APP	Wolverhampton W.	10.66	1967-68	20	1	4	(F)E.U23-4/E.YTH.INT./
			TR	Liverpool	09.68	1968-71	77	2	21	E.SCH.INT./Son of Alun
			TR	Aston Villa	06.72	1972-73	53	9	11	
			TR	Walsall	12.75	1975-77	78	9	7	
EVANS, Andrew D.S.	Rhondda	03.10.57	APP	Bristol Rov.	09.75	1975-77	34	8	2	(F)W.U21-1/W.SCH.INT./
										W.YTH.INT.
EVANS, Anthony	Liverpool	11.01.54	Formby	Blackpool	06.73	1974	4	2	0	(F)
			TR	Cardiff C.	06.75	1975-78	120	4	47	
			TR	Birmingham C.	07.79	1979-82	62	4	28	
			TR	Crystal Palace	08.83	1983	19	2	7	
EVANS, Anthony W.	Colchester	30.08.58	APP	Colchester U.	03.78	1977-80	21	9	2	(F)
EVANS, Arthur	Urmston	13.05.33	JNRS	Bury	06.50	1950	2		0	(G) E.YTH.INT.
			TR	Stockport Co.	08.52					
			TR	Gillingham	09.53	1953-54	14		0	
EVANS, Bernard	Chester	04.01.37	JNRS	Wrexham	08.54	1954-60	113		49	(CF)
			TR	Q.P.R.	10.60	1960-62	77		34	
			TR	Oxford U.	12.62	1962-63	13		2	
			TR	Tranmere Rov.	10.63	1963	12		5	
			TR	Crewe Alex.	07.64					
EVANS, Bernard R.	Rotherhithe	07.10.29		Millwall	03.50					
			TR	Watford	08.51	1951	2		1	
EVANS, Brian	Swansea	02.12.42	Abergavenny	Swansea C.	07.63	1963-72	355	4	57	(OR) W-7/W.U23-2
			TR	Hereford U.	08.73	1973-74	44	4	9	
EVANS, Charlie J.	West Bromwich	04.02.23	Cordley Vic	W.B.A.	+	1946	1		0	(IF)
EVANS, Chris B.	Rhondda	13.10.62	APP	Arsenal	06.80					(D)
			TR	Stoke C.	09.81					
			TR	York C.	08.82	1982-83	62	3	0	
EVANS, Clive	Birkenhead	01.05.57	APP	Tranmere Rov.	03.77	1976-80	175	3	27	(M)
			TR	Wigan Ath.	07.81	1981	29	3	2	
			TR	Crewe Alex.	08.82	1982	26	2	7	
			TR	Stockport Co.	08.83	1983	31	/	7	
EVANS, D. Doug	Swansea	27.09.56	APP	Norwich C.	08.74	1976-79	14	4	1	(M)
			TR	Cambridge U.	03.80	1979-80	11	1	2	
EVANS, D. Ralph	Hungerford	09.10.15	Halifax T.(*)	Watford	*	1946-47	42		19	(CF) *Yeovil T.
EVANS, David	Colwyn Bay	19.06.34	Llandudno	Crewe Alex.	03.57	1956-59	50		0	(G)
EVANS, David	Chester	04.04.67	APP	Chester C.	05.84	1983	10	/	0	(D)
EVANS, David	Peterlee	06.04.59		Hartlepool U.	07.78	1978-79	2	2	0	(F)
EVANS, David G.	W. Bromwich	20.05.58	APP	Aston Villa	02.76	1978	2	/	0	(D)
			TR	Halifax T.	06.79	1979-83	218	/	9	
EVANS, Dennis	Chester	23.07.35		Wrexham	03.55	1955-57	11		0	(FB)
			TR	Tranmere Rov.	06.58	1958-59	3		0	
EVANS, Dennis J.	Ellesmere Port	18.05.30	Ellesmere Port	Arsenal	01.51	1953-59	189		10	(FB)
EVANS, Elfed	Rhondda	28.08.26	Treharris	Cardiff C.	05.49	1949-51	46		18	(IF)
			L	Torquay U.	03.51	1950	12		6	
			TR	W.B.A.	06.52	1952	17		3	
			TR	Wrexham	06.55	1955-56	34		13	
			TR	Southport	12.56	1956	13			

Players Names	Birthplace	Date	Previous Club	League Club	Date Signed	Seasons Played	Career Record Apps	Sub	Gls	
EVANS, Emrys B.	Tonypandy	16.09.30	Tottenham H.(AM)	Newport Co.	08.52	1952	18		4	(IF)
EVANS, Fred J.	Petersfield	20.05.23		Portsmouth	+	1946	9		3	(IF)
			TR	Notts. Co.	07.47	1947-50	40		14	
			TR	Crystal Palace	03.51	1950-52	52		11	
			TR	Rochdale	06.53	1953	12		0	
EVANS, George A.	Wrexham	26.07.35	Oswestry T.	Wrexham	07.57	1957-62	175		8	(WH)
			TR	Chester C.	06.63	1963-68	109	2	0	
EVANS, Gwyn	Treorchy	24.02.35	Treorchy	Crystal Palace	03.55	1958-62	80		0	(WH)
EVANS, Harry A.	Lambeth	17.04.19		Southampton	+	1946	1		0	*Woking/Fulham/
			TR	Exeter C.	04.47	1947-48	41		6	d.1962
			TR	Aldershot	03.49	1948-49	16		5	
EVANS, Hugh	Llanwonno	12.12.19	Redditch	Birmingham C.	12.47	1948-49	11		0	(IF)
			TR	Bournemouth	06.50	1950	22		8	
			TR	Walsall	08.51	1951	33		12	
			TR	Watford	08.52	1952	7		2	
EVANS, Hugh W.R.	Swansea	10.08.22		Swansea C.	+					(WH)
			Lovells Ath.	Newport Co.	04.51	1950-51	14		1	
EVANS, Ian P.	Egham	30.01.52	APP	Q.P.R.	01.70	1970-73	39	/	2	(D)W-13/W.U23-2
			TR	Crystal Palace	09.74	1974-77	137	/	14	
			TR	Barnsley	12.79	1979-82	102	/	3	
			L	Exeter C.	08.83	1983	4	/	0	
			L	Cambridge U.	10.83	1983	1	/	0	
EVANS, Ivor	Cardiff	25.10.33	Guest Keen	Portsmouth	09.56	1956	1		0	(IF)
EVANS, John	Hetton le Hole	21.10.32	JNRS	Norwich C.	10.49					(F)
			TR	Sunderland	08.54	1954	1		0	
			TR	Chesterfield	05.56					
EVANS, John	Tilbury	28.08.29	Tilbury Bata	Charlton Ath.	05.55	1950-53	90		38	(IF) E.F.LGE REP.
			TR	Liverpool	12.53	1953-57	97		49	
			TR	Colchester U.	11.57	1957-59	56		22	
EVANS, John A.	Aberystwyth	22.10.22		Millwall	+	1946-49	73		2	(FB) d.1956
			TR	Orient	06.50	1950-53	149		1	
EVANS, John C.	Torquay	24.03.47	APP	Torquay U.	04.65	1964-65	6	/	1	(F)
EVANS, John D.	Liverpool	13.03.38		Liverpool	05.58					(IF)
				Bournemouth	05.59					
			Army	Stockport Co.	10.62	1962-63	52		21	
			TR	Carlisle U.	02.64	1963-65	78	/	37	
			TR	Exeter C.	03.66	1965-66	11	/	2	
			TR	Barnsley	11.66	1966-70	165	5	54	
EVANS, John D.	Chester	24.03.41		Chester C.	08.61	1961-64	40		0	(FB)
EVANS, John J.	Coventry	11.03.26		Coventry C.	06.47	1948-50	8		1	(CF)
EVANS, John L.	Newport	04.10.37	Lovells Ath.	Gillingham	04.56	1957	7		0	(HB)
EVANS, John R.	Rhondda	28.07.32	JNRS	Swansea C.	08.50	1951	14		0	(FB)
			TR	Bristol Rov.	06.53					
EVANS, Keith	Trealaw	15.09.53	APP	Swansea C.	08.71	1970-72	14	/	0	(WH)
EVANS, Ken P.	Swansea	17.07.31	Carmarthen	Swansea C.	06.50	1954-56	13		0	(G)
			TR	Walsall	08.57	1957	2		0	
EVANS, Leslie N.	Kingswinford	13.10.29	Brierley Hill	Cardiff C.	10.50	1950-51	3		0	(OL)
			TR	Plymouth Arg.	06.52					
EVANS, Leslie T.	Rhondda	26.12.24		Cardiff C.	+					
			TR	Torquay U.	07.47	1947	24		0	
EVANS, Maurice G.	Didcot	22.09.36	JNRS	Reading	09.53	1955-66	407	/	14	(WH)
EVANS, Medwyn J.	Bryntec	08.11.64	JNRS	Wrexham	08.83	1982-83	13	4	0	(D) W.SCH.INT.
EVANS, Mike	W. Bromwich	03.08.46	Vono F.C.	Walsall	05.64	1965-72	229	3	7	(D)
			TR	Swansea C.	12.72	1972-74	92	/	7	
			TR	Crewe Alex.	07.75	1975-76	62	/	4	
EVANS, Mike G.	Llanidloes	04.06.47	APP	Wolverhampton W.	07.64					(D)W.U23-2/W.SCH.INT.
			TR	Wrexham	07.66	1966-78	368	12	19	
EVANS, Nick	Trimdon	23.11.25	Heselden	New Brighton	AM	1946	1		0	(OR)
EVANS, Oswald	Llanelli	02.09.15	Milford Haven	Fulham	+	1946	1		0	(G)
EVANS, Paul	Sheffield	24.02.49	JNRS	Sheffield Wed.	02.66					(G)
			Boston F.C.	Mansfield T.	10.75	1975	6	/	0	
EVANS, Paul A.	Brentwood	14.09.64	JNRS	Cardiff C.	09.82	1983	0	2	0	
EVANS, Phil A.	Swansea	14.05.57	JNRS	Swansea C.	08.75	1975	9	/	0	(CH)
EVANS, Ray	Mansfield	27.11.27		Coventry C.	05.48					(F)
			Stafford Rgrs	Mansfield T.	11.49	1949-52	39		12	
				Stockport Co.	07.54					
EVANS, Ray F.	Carlisle	08.10.29	Hightown YC	Crewe Alex.	10.48	1948-50	21		0	(G)
EVANS, Ray L.	Edmonton	20.09.49	APP	Tottenham H.	06.67	1968-74	132	4	2	(D)E.YTH.INT.
			TR	Millwall	01.75	1974-76	74	/	3	
			TR	Fulham	03.77	1976-78	86	/	6	
			TR	Stoke C.	08.79	1979-81	94	/	1	

Players Names	Birthplace	Date	Previous Club	League Club	Date Signed	Seasons Played	Apps	Sub	Gls	
EVANS, Ray P.	Preston	21.06.33	JNRS	Preston N.E.	05.51	1953-56	33		2	(W)
			TR	Bournemouth	06.59	1959-60	36		9	
EVANS, Reg	Consett	18.03.39	JNRS	Newcastle U.	03.56	1958	4		0	(F)
			TR	Charlton Ath.	03.59	1958-59	14		2	
EVANS, Reuben	Dublin	19.03.41	Glasgow Rgrs.	Bradford P.A.	06.63	1963	13		5	(F)
EVANS, Robert	Glasgow	16.07.27	Glasgow Celtic	Chelsea	05.60	1960	32		0	(WH)S-48/S.F.LGE REP.●
			TR	Newport Co.	06.61	1961	31		0	
EVANS, Ron	St. Helens	21.02.29	Bolton W.(AM)	Stockport Co.	07.50	1950-53	6		0	(HB)
EVANS, Roy Q.	Bootle	04.10.48	APP	Liverpool	10.65	1969-73	9	/	0	(HB) E.SCH.INT.
EVANS, Roy S.	Swansea	05.06.43	JNRS	Swansea C.	07.60	1962-67	211	2	8	(FB) W-1/W.U23-3
EVANS, Royson	Lampeter	09.02.39	Bangor	Wolverhampton W.	08.56					(F)
			TR	Wrexham	07.57					
			TR	Chester C.	10.57	1957-59	23		3	
				Halifax T.	10.60	1960	7		0	
EVANS, Stewart J.	Maltby	15.11.60	APP	Rotherham U.	11.78					(F)
			Gainsborough	Sheffield U.	11.80					
			TR	Wimbledon	03.82	1981-83	102	3	30	
EVANS, William E.	Birmingham	05.09.21	Linread	Aston Villa	09.46	1946-48	7		3	(IF) d.1960
			TR	Notts. Co.	06.49	1949-52	94		14	
			TR	Gillingham	07.53	1953-54	89		12	
			TR	Grimsby T.	06.55	1955-57	102		27	
EVANS, Wyndham E.	Llanelli	19.03.51	Stoke C. (AM)	Swansea C.	02.71	1970-82	349	5	19	(D)
			Llanelli	Swansea C.	N/C	1983	17	/	0	
EVANSON, John	Newcastle-under-Lyme	10.05.47	Towcester	Oxford U.	02.65	1966-73	145	13	10	(M)
			TR	Blackpool	02.74	1973-75	63	4	0	
			TR	Fulham	08.76	1976-78	84	11	5	
			TR	Bournemouth	07.79	1979-80	52	1	2	
EVELEIGH, Gordon E.	Lymington	26.07.22	Guildford C.	Bristol C.	05.48	1948	2		0	(OL)
EVERALL, William F.	Nantwich	18.07.28		Crewe Alex.	08.53	1953	1		0	
EVERETT, Harold P.	Worksop	09.06.22	Notts. Co.(+)	Mansfield T.	09.46	1946	2		0	(LH) Brother to Harry
EVERETT, Harry	Worksop	11.11.20	Shirebrook W.	Mansfield T.	+	1946	16		0	(LB)
EVERETT, Mike R.	Mile End	21.03.58	Crystal Palace (APP)	Orient	03.76	1975		1	0	(F)
EVERITT, Mike D.	Clacton	16.01.41	JNRS	Arsenal	02.58	1959-60	9		1	(WH)
			TR	Northampton T.	02.61	1960-66	206	1	15	
			TR	Plymouth Arg.	03.67	1966-67	29	/	0	
			TR	Brighton & H.A.	07.68	1968-69	24	3	1	
EVERITT, Richard E.	Carlisle	03.05.22	Sheffield Wed.(AM)	Darlington	+	1946	1		0	(W)
EVES, John R.	Sunderland	28.02.22		Sunderland	+					(FB)
			TR	Darlington	09.46	1946-51	177		1	
EVES, Mel J.	Wednesbury	10.09.56	JNRS	Wolverhampton W.	07.75	1977-83	169	11	44	(F)
			L	Huddersfield T.	03.84	1983	7	/	4	
EWING, Dave	Perth	10.05.29	Luncarty J.	Manchester C.	06.49	1952-61	279		1	(CH)
			TR	Crewe Alex.	07.62	1962-63	48		0	
EWING, Tommy	Swinhill	02.05.37	Partick Th.	Aston Villa	02.62	1961-63	39		4	(OR) S-2/S.F.LGE REP.
EWING, Tommy M.H.	Musselburgh	08.08.34	JNRS	Doncaster Rov.	08.51	1951-57	39		6	(HB)
EXLEY, William	Bradford	02.05.24		Bradford C.	AM	1952	2		0	
EYRE, Fred	Manchester	03.02.44	APP	Manchester C.	07.61					(WH)
			TR	Lincoln C.	07.63					
			TR	Crewe Alex.	08.64					
			Rossendale U.	Bradford P.A.	12.69	1969	1	/	0	
EYRE, Leslie E.	Ilkeston	07.01.22	Cardiff C. (AM)	Norwich C.	07.46	1946-51	185		59	(IF)
			TR	Bournemouth	11.51	1951-52	38		10	

Players Names	Birthplace	Date	Previous Club	League Club	Date Signed	Seasons Played	Career Record Apps	Sub	Gls	
FACEY, Ken. W.	Hackney	12.10.27	Leyton	Orient	06.52	1952-60	301		49	(IF)
FAGAN, Bernard	Houghton-le-Spring	29.01.49	APP	Sunderland	02.66					(F)
			TR	Northampton T.	07.69	1969	6	/	0	
FAGAN, Chris	Manchester	05.06.50		Liverpool	07.70	1970	1	/	0	(FB)
			TR	Tranmere Rov.	07.71	1971-74	77	7	2	
FAGAN, Fionan	Dublin	07.06.30	Transport	Hull C.	03.51	1951-53	25		2	(W) EI-8/EI.'B'-1
			TR	Manchester C.	12.53	1953-59	153	34		
			TR	Derby Co.	03.60	1959-60	24		6	
FAGAN, George	Dundee	27.09.34	Dundee St.J.	Leeds U.	11.53					(FB)
			TR	Halifax T.	06.58	1958-61	67		3	
FAGAN, Joe F.	Liverpool	12.03.21	Earlestown	Manchester C.	*	1946-50	148		2	(CH)
				Bradford P.A.	08.53	1953	3		0	
FAGAN, Mike J.	Newcastle	22.02.60	Carlisle U.(N/C)	Hartlepool U.	08.79	1979-82	36	1	1	(D)
FAGAN, Willie	Mussleburgh	20.02.17	Preston N.E.(*)	Liverpool	*	1946-51	88		25	(IF) *Glasgow Celtic
FAHY, John J.	Paisley	13.05.43	Bedford T.	Oxford U.	01.64	1963-65	23	/	14	(F)
FAIRBROTHER, Barry	Hackney	30.12.50	APP	Orient	01.69	1969-74	171	18	41	(F)
			TR	Millwall	06.74	1975-76	12	3	1	
FAIRBROTHER, Jack	Burton	16.08.17	Burton A.	Preston N.E.	*	1946	41		0	(G)
			TR	Newcastle U.	07.47	1947-51	133			
FAIRBROTHER, John	Cricklewood	12.02.41	Bennetts End	Watford	08.59	1960-62	40		19	(F)
			Worcester C.	Peterborough U.	05.65	1965-67	69	3	37	
			TR	Northampton T.	02.68	1967-71	135	5	56	
			TR	Mansfield T.	09.71	1971-72	83	2	35	
			TR	Torquay U.	06.73	1973	15	/	3	
FAIRCHILD, Mike P.	Northampton	24.11.42	Lowestoft	Luton T.	11.60	1960-63	21		1	(F)
			TR	Reading	07.64	1964-65	24	/	6	
FAIRCLOUGH, Chris H.	Nottingham	12.04.64	APP	Nottingham F.	10.81	1982-83	43	3	0	(D)
FAIRCLOUGH, Cyril	Manchester	21.04.23	Urmston	Bury	+	1946-57	191		2	(FB)
FAIRCLOUGH, David	Liverpool	05.01.57	APP	Liverpool	01.74	1975-82	64	34	34	(F)E.U21-1
FAIRCLOUGH, Mick	Drogheda	21.10.52	Drogheda	Huddersfield T.	08.71	1971-74	25	10	2	(CF)
FAIRFAX, Ray	Smethwick	13.11.41	JNRS	W.B.A.	08.59	1962-67	79	2	0	(FB)
			TR	Northampton T.	06.68	1968-70	116	/	2	
FAIRHURST, John	Bentley	15.03.44	APP	Doncaster Rov.	07.61	1961-65	21	/	0	(HB)
FAIRLEY, Tom	Durham	12.10.32		Sunderland	10.51	1952	2		0	(G)
			TR	Carlisle U.	05.56	1955-58	56		0	
FAIRWEATHER, John	Dornoch	12.08.24		Blackburn Rov.	+					
				Carlisle U.	11.48	1949	1		0	
FALCO, Mark P.	Hackney	22.10.60	APP	Tottenham H.	07.78	1978-83	75	11	27	(F)E.YTH.INT.
			L	Chelsea	11.82	1982	3	/	0	
FALCONER, Andy G.	S. Africa	27.06.25	S. Africa	Blackpool	09.49	1949	4		0	
FALCONER, Henry	Newcastle	22.12.54	Burnley(APP)	Bournemouth	07.74	1974	4	3	0	(FB)
FALDER, Dave E.J.	Liverpool	21.10.22	Wigan Ath.	Everton	+	1949-50	25	0	0	(CH)
FALLON, Harry	Paisley	28.04.42	St. Johnstone	York C.	09.65	1965-67	67	1	0	(G)
FALLON, Kevin B.	Maltby	03.12.48	APP	Rotherham U.	12.65					(CH)
			Sligo	Southend U.	07.70	1970	4	/	0	
FALLON, Peter D.	Dublin	19.10.22		Exeter C.	06.47	1947-52	110		7	(IR) Brother of William
			TR	Q.P.R.	08.53	1953	1		0	
FALLON, Steve	Whittlesey	03.08.56	Kettering	Cambridge U.	12.79	1974-83	366	5	25	(D)
FALLON, William J.	Dublin	14.01.12	Notts. Co.(*)	Sheffield Wed.	*					(OL) *Dolphin/
			TR	Notts.Co.	06.46	1946	16		3	EI-9
			TR	Exeter C.	06.47	1947	8		2	
FANTHAM, John	Sheffield	06.02.39	JNRS	Sheffield Wed.	10.56	1957-69	383	7	147	(IF)E-1/E.U23-1/
			TR	Rotherham U.	10.69	1969-70	46	5	8	E.F.LGE REP.
FAREY, John A.	Darlington	22.07.22		Carlisle U.	11.47	1947	2		0	+Sunderland/d.1962
FARLEY, Alex J.	Finchley	11.05.25	Cromwell Ath.	Orient	+	1946-47	15		0	(OL) Cousin of Tom Barnett
			TR	Bournemouth	06.48					
FARLEY, Brian	Ross	01.01.27	Chelmsford	Tottenham H.	07.49	1951	1		0	(WH) d.1962
FARLEY, John	Middlesbrough	21.09.51	Stockton	Watford	07.69	1970-73	96	8	8	(F)
			L	Halifax T.	09.71	1971	6	/	3	
			TR	Wolverhampton W.	05.74	1974-77	35	5	0	
			L	Blackpool	10.76	1976	1	/	0	
			TR	Hull C.	05.78	1978-79	59	1	5	
			TR	Bury	08.80	1980	17	1	2	
FARM, George N.	Slateford	13.07.24	Hibernian	Blackpool	09.48	1948-59	462		3	(G) S-10●
FARMER, F. Brian W.	Wordsley	29.07.33	Stourbridge	Birmingham C.	07.54	1956-61	117		0	(FB)
			TR	Bournemouth	01.62	1961-64	132		0	
FARMER, James E.	Rowley Regis	21.01.40	JNRS	Wolverhampton W.	08.57	1960-63	57		44	(CF) E.U23-2

Players Names	Birthplace	Date	Previous Club	League Club	Date Signed	Seasons Played	Apps	Sub	Gls	
FARMER, John	Biddulph	31.08.47	JNRS	Stoke C.	01.65	1965-74	163	/	0	(G) E.U23-1
			L	Leicester C.	12.74	1974	2	/	0	
FARMER, Kevin J.	Ramsgate	24.01.60	APP	Leicester C.	11.77	1977	1	/	0	(F)
			TR	Northampton T.	08.79	1979-81	70	7	12	
FARMER, Mike C.	Leicester	22.11.44	APP	Birmingham C.	04.62	1963	1		1	(WH)
			TR	Lincoln C.	05.65	1965	21	1	0	
FARMER, Ron	Guernsey	06.03.36	JNRS	Nottingham F.	05.53	1957	9		1	(WH) Brother of William
			TR	Coventry C.	11.58	1958-67	281	3	46	
			TR	Notts. Co.	10.67	1967-68	69	/	5	
FARMER, Terry	Rotherham	11.05.31	Gainsborough	Rotherham U.	07.52	1952-57	61		25	(CF)
			TR	York C.	01.58	1957-59	66		28	
FARMER, William A.	Guernsey	24.11.27	St. Martins	Nottingham F.	05.51	1953-56	52		0	(G)
			TR	Oldham Ath.	07.57	1957	5		0	
FARNEN, Les	St.Helens	17.01.19		Watford	05.46	1946-48	77		0	(CH)
			TR	Bradford C.	05.49	1949	8		0	
FARNSWORTH, Peter A.	Barnsley	17.05.46	APP	Barnsley	09.63	1964	1		0	(HB)
FARNWORTH, Simon	Chorley	28.10.63	APP	Bolton W.	09.81	1983	36	/	0	(G)
FARQUHAR, Doug	Methil	11.06.21	St.Andrews U.	Arsenal	+					(WH)
			TR	Reading	09.50	1950-51	9		1	
FARR, Brian S.	Swindon	19.10.30		Swindon T.	08.51	1950-51	11		0	(WH)
FARR, Ian	Swindon	13.02.59	APP	Swindon T.	APP	1975	0	1	0	(F)
FARR, Tom F.	Bathgate	19.02.14	Broxburn Ath.	Bradford P.A.	*	1946-49	132		0	(G) d.1980
FARRALL, Alec	Liverpool	03.03.36	JNRS	Everton	03.53	1952-56	5		0	(WH) E.SCH.INT.
			TR	Preston N.E.	05.57	1957-59	27		9	
			TR	Gillingham	07.60	1960-64	202		21	
			TR	Lincoln C.	06.65	1965	20	/	2	
			TR	Watford	07.66	1966-67	47	1	9	
FARRAR, John N.	St. Helens	06.05.28		Manchester C.	03.48					
			TR	Crewe Alex.	01.51	1950	2		0	
FARRELL, Andy J.	Colchester	07.10.65	APP	Colchester U.	09.83	1983	15	/	0	(D)
FARRELL, Arthur	Huddersfield	01.11.20		Bradford P.A.	+	1946-50	156		4	(FB)
			TR	Barnsley	05.51	1951	18		0	
FARRELL, Gerrard W.	Liverpool	19.03.52	APP	Wolverhampton W.	05.70					(FB)
			TR	Blackburn Rov.	10.71	1971-72	21	1	1	
FARRELL, Greg J.P.	Motherwell	19.03.44	APP	Birmingham C.	03.61	1962-63	4		0	(OR)
			TR	Cardiff C.	03.64	1963-66	93	1	8	
			TR	Bury	03.67	1966-69	83	/	15	
FARRELL, John	Perth	22.06.33	Perth Celtic	Accrington St.	08.54	1954	2		0	
FARRELL, K. Mike	Ilkley	13.03.59	APP	Scunthorpe U.	07.77	1975-77	5	4	1	(F)
FARRELL, Paul A.	Liverpool	01.11.58	APP	Southport	APP	1975	0	2	0	(F)
FARRELL, Peter	Liverpool	10.01.57		Bury	09.75	1975-78	49	5	9	(M)
			TR	Port Vale	11.78	1978-81	85	4	10	
			TR	Rochdale	08.82	1982-83	67	1	17	
FARRELL, Peter B.	Dublin	16.08.22	Shamrock Rov.	Everton	08.46	1946-56	421		14	(WH)E1-28/N1-7●
			TR	Tranmere Rov.	10.57	1957-59	114		1	
FARRELL, Ray	Cardiff	31.05.33	Treharris	Crystal Palace	05.57	1957-58	5		0	(F)
FARRELLY, Mike J.	Manchester	01.01.62	Manchester Avarians	Preston N.E.	06.81	1981-83	38	5	2	(D)E.SCH.INT.
FARRIMOND, Syd	Hindley	17.07.40	JNRS	Bolton W.	01.58	1958-70	363	1	1	(FB) E.YTH.INT.
			TR	Tranmere Rov.	02.71	1970-73	132	2	0	
			TR	Halifax T.	11.74					
FARRINGTON, John R.	Lynemouth	19.06.47	APP	Wolverhampton W.	06.65	1964-69	33	3	2	(F)
			TR	Leicester C.	10.69	1969-73	115	3	18	
			TR	Cardiff C.	11.73	1973-74	23	/	6	
			TR	Northampton T.	10.74	1974-79	224	8	29	
FARRINGTON, Mark A.	Liverpool	15.06.65	Everton(APP)	Norwich C.	05.83	1983	1	1	0	(F)
FARRINGTON, Roy A.	Tonbridge	06.06.25		Crystal Palace	11.47	1947-48	3		0	
FARROW, Des A.	Peterborough	11.02.26	Leicester C.(AM)	Q.P.R.	+	1948-52	119		8	(IF)
			TR	Stoke C.	10.52	1952-53	8		0	
FARROW, George H.	Whitburn	04.10.13	Bournemouth (*)	Blackpool	*	1946-47	42		4	(WH)*Stockport Co./
			TR	Sheffield U.	01.48	1947	1		0	Wolverhampton W.
FASCIONE, Joe	Coatbridge	05.02.45	Kirkintilloch	Chelsea	10.62	1965-68	22	7	1	(W)
FASHANU, John	Kensington	18.09.62	Cambridge U.(Jnrs)	Norwich C.	10.79	1981-82	6	1	1	(F)Brother of Justin
			L	Crystal Palace	08.83	1983	1	/	0	
			TR	Lincoln C.	09.83	1983	22	4	7	
FASHANU, Justin	Hackney	19.02.61	APP	Norwich C.	12.78	1978-80	84	6	34	(F)E.U21-11/E.YTH.INT.
			TR	Nottingham F.	08.81	1981	31	1	3	
			L	Southampton	08.82	1982	9	/	3	
			TR	Notts. Co.	12.82	1982-83	32	/	11	

Players Names	Birthplace	Date	Previous Club	League Club	Date Signed	Seasons Played	Career Record Apps	Sub	Gls	
FAULKES, Brian	Abingdon	10.04.45	JNRS	Reading	09.63	1963-66	23	2	0	(FB)
			TR	Northampton T.	07.67	1967-68	51	1	2	
			TR	Torquay U.	07.69	1969	6	/	0	
FAULKNER, John G.	Orpington	10.03.48	Sutton U.	Leeds U.	07.70	1969	2	/	0	(D)
			TR	Luton T.	03.72	1972-77	209	/	6	
FAULKNER, Ken G.	Smethwick	10.09.23		Birmingham C.	+	1946	2		0	E.SCH.INT.
FAULKNER, Mike	Conisborough	03.01.50	APP	Sheffield U.	12.67					(HB)
			TR	Oldham Ath.	07.69	1969	1	/	0	
FAULKNER, Ray A.	Horncastle	26.05.34	JNRS	Grimsby T.	10.54	1954	5		1	(OR)
FAULKNER, Roy V.	Manchester	28.06.35	JNRS	Manchester C.	12.52	1955	7		4	(F)
			TR	Walsall	03.58	1957-60	102		46	
FAULKNER, Steve A.	Sheffield	18.12.54	APP	Sheffield U.	02.72	1972-76	14	1	0	(D)
			L	Stockport Co.	03.78	1977	3	1	0	
			TR	York C.	05.78	1978-80	90	/	7	
FAWCETT, Brian	Bentley	14.02.32	Bentley Col.	Scunthorpe U.	02.55	1954	1		0	(OR)
			TR	Bradford P.A.	07.56					
FAWCETT, Roy	Leeds	20.01.38	JNRS	Blackpool	03.55	1955-59	3		0	(F)
FAWELL, Derek S.	Hartlepool	22.03.44	Spennymoor	Notts. Co.	10.64	1964	1		0	(IF)
			TR	Lincoln C.	09.65	1965	4	/	0	
FAWLEY, Ron	Ashton	22.04.27	Ashton U.	Oldham Ath.	06.51	1950-57	93		10	(F)
FAZACKERLEY, Derek	Preston	05.11.51	APP	Blackburn Rov.	01.71	1970-83	511	2	18	(D)
FAZACKERLEY, Mick	Manchester	08.04.32		Bradford P.A.	08.55	1955	2		0	
FEAR, Keith	Bristol	08.05.52	JNRS	Bristol C.	06.69	1970-76	126	25	33	(F)Brother of Viv
			L	Hereford U.	09.77	1977	6	/	0	
			L	Blackburn Rov.	12.77	1977	5	/	2	
			TR	Plymouth Arg.	02.78	1977-79	40	5	9	
			L	Brentford	11.79	1979	7	1	2	
			TR	Chester C.	01.80	1979-80	41	3	3	
FEAR, Vivien J.	Bristol	24.10.55	Bristol C.(APP)	Hereford U.	07.47	1974	2	1	0	(F) Brother of Keith
FEARNLEY, Gordon	Bradford	25.01.50		Sheffield Wed.	07.68					(F)
			TR	Bristol Rov.	07.70	1970-76	95	27	21	
FEARNLEY, Harry	Penistone	16.06.35	JNRS	Huddersfield T.	12.52	1955-62	90		0	(G)
			TR	Oxford U.	10.63	1963-65	90	/	0	
			TR	Doncaster Rov.	02.66	1965-66	32	/	0	
FEARNLEY, Harry L.	Morley	27.05.23	Bradford P.A.(AM)	Leeds U.	+	1946-48	28		0	(G)
			TR	Halifax T.	01.49	1948	3		0	
			TR	Newport Co.	07.49	1949-52	103		0	
			TR	Rochdale	07.55	1955	1		0	
FEARON, Ron T.	Romford	19.11.60	Q.P.R. (APP)	Reading	02.80	1980-82	61	/	0	(G)
FEASEY, Paul C.	Hull	04.05.33	JNRS	Hull C.	05.50	1952-64	271		0	(CH)
FEATHERSTONE, Keith	Bradford	30.08.35	Wyke Celtic	Bradford P.A.	AM	1955	1		0	(G)
FEE, Gregory P.	Halifax	24.06.64		Bradford C.	05.83	1982-83	6	1	0	(D)
FEEHAN, Ignatius	Dublin	17.09.26	Waterford	Manchester U.	11.48	1949	12		0	(G)
			TR	Northampton T.	08.50	1950-51	39		0	
			TR	Brentford	08.54	1954-58	30		0	
FEELEY, Andy J.	Hereford	30.09.61	APP	Hereford U.	08.79	1978-79	50	1	3	(M)
			Trowbridge	Leicester C.	02.84	1983	2	1	0	
FEELY, Peter	London	03.01.50	Enfield T.	Chelsea	05.70	1970-72	4	1	2	(F)E.AMAT.INT./
			TR	Bournemouth	02.73	1972-73	8	1	2	E.YTH.INT.
			TR	Fulham	07.74					
			TR	Gillingham	10.74	1974-75	41	/	22	
			TR	Sheffield W.	02.76	1975-76	17	2	2	
			L	Stockport Co.	01.77	1976	2	/	0	
FEENEY, James M.	Belfast	23.06.21	Linfield	Swansea C.	12.46	1946-49	88		0	(FB)NI-2
			TR	Ipswich T.	03.50	1949-55	214		0	
FEENEY, Joe	Glasgow	21.07.26	St.Theresa's	Sunderland	07.47					(IL)
				Chester C.	09.51	1951	5		0	
FELGATE, David	Blaenau Ffestiniog	04.03.60	JNRS	Bolton W.	08.78					(G)W.SCH.INT/W-1
			L	Rochdale	10.78	1978-79	47	/	0	
			L	Crewe Alex.	09.79	1979	14	/	0	
			TR	Lincoln C.	09.80	1980-83	177	/	0	
FELIX, Gary	Manchester	31.10.57	APP	Leeds U.	11.75					(M)
			TR	Chester C.	01.79	1978	8	/	0	
FELL, Geoff M.	Carlisle	08.05.60	JNRS	Carlisle U.	06.77	1977-79	0	3	0	(F)
FELL, Gerry	Newark	01.03.51	Long Eaton	Brighton & N.E.	11.74	1974-77	65	14	19	(F)
			TR	Southend U.	11.77	1977-79	43	2	10	
			TR	Torquay U.	07.80	1980-81	50	/	12	
				York C.	03.82	1981	2	3	0	
FELL, Jimmy	Grimsby	04.01.36	Waltham FC	Grimsby T.	04.54	1956-60	166		35	(OL)
			TR	Everton	03.61	1960-61	27		4	
			TR	Newcastle U.	03.62	1961-62	49		16	
			TR	Walsall	07.63	1963	21		4	
			TR	Lincoln C.	01.64	1963-65	63	/	10	

Players Names	Birthplace	Date	Previous Club	League Club	Date Signed	Seasons Played	Apps	Sub	Gls	
FELL, Les J.	London	16.12.20	Gravesend	Charlton Ath.	+	1946-51	13		2	(OR)
			TR	Crystal Palace	10.52	1952-53	65		6	
FELLOWES, William J.	Bradford	15.03.10	Luton T.(*)	Exeter C.	*	1946	14		0	(CH) *Orient
FELLOWS, Geoff A.	West Bromwich	26.07.44	APP	Aston Villa	10.61					(FB)
			TR	Shrewsbury T.	06.65	1965-72	277	4	2	
FELLOWS, Greg F.A.	Dudley	10.10.53	APP	Aston Villa	09.71					(CF)
			L	Crewe Alex.	02.73	1972	3	/	1	
			TR	Manchester U.	08.73					
FELLOWS, Stewart	Stockton	09.10.48	APP	Newcastle U.	03.66					(HB)
			TR	York C.	06.67	1967	0	2	0	
FELTON, Graham	Cambridge	01.03.49	Cambridge U.	Northampton T.	09.66	1966-75	243	13	25	(F)E.YTH.INT.
			TR	Barnsley	02.76	1975-76	36	/	5	
FELTON, Ken C.	Blackhall	18.02.49		Darlington	04.67	1967-69	50	2	8	(HB)
FELTON, Robert F.F.	Gateshead	12.08.18		Port Vale	*					
			TR	Crystal Palace	09.46	1946	1		0	
FELTON, Vivien E.	Southgate	13.08.29		Crystal Palace	08.54	1954-55	2		0	
FENCOTT, Ken S.	Walsall	27.12.43	APP	Aston Villa	01.61	1961-63	3		0	(F)
			TR	Lincoln C.	06.64	1964-66	67	6	13	
FENNEY, Stan	Barry	21.06.23	Stranraer	Barrow	+	1946	26		0	
FENOUGHTY, Tom	Rotherham	07.06.41	Sheffield FC	Sheffield U.	09.64	1963-68	47	2	4	(IF)
			TR	Chesterfield	07.69	1969-71	99	3	15	
FENTON, Benny R.V.	West Ham	28.10.18	West Ham U.(*)	Millwall	*	1946	18		7	(WH)
			TR	Charlton Ath.	01.47	1946-54	264		22	
			TR	Colchester U.	02.55	1954-57	103		16	
FENTON, Ewan	Dundee	17.11.29	Dundee NE	Blackpool	11.46	1948-58	203		20	(WH)
			TR	Wrexham	05.59	1959	24		0	
FENTON, Mick	Stockton	30.10.13	South Bank	Middlesbrough	*	1946-48	105		58	(CF) E-1
FENTON, Ron	South Shields	02.09.40	JNRS	Burnley	09.57	1960-61	11		1	(IF)
			TR	W.B.A.	11.62	1962-64	59		16	
			TR	Birmingham C.	01.65	1964-67	28	6	7	
			TR	Brentford	01.68	1967-69	87	4	19	
			TR	Notts Co.	07.70					
FENTON, Steve J.	Hartlepool	25.02.51	JNRS	Middlesbrough	08.69					(FB) E.YTH.INT.
			TR	Bradford C.	06.72	1972	9	1	1	
FENTON, William H.	Hartlepool	23.06.26	Horden CW	Blackburn Rov.	12.48	1948-50	33		7	(OL) +Barnsley/d.1973
			TR	York C.	05.51	1951-57	258		118	
FENWICK, Terry	Durham	17.11.59	APP	Crystal Palace	12.76	1977-80	62	8	0	(M)E.YTH.INT./E.U21-11/E-3
			TR	Q.P.R.	12.80	1980-83	135	/	20	
FEREBEE, Steward R.	Carshalton	06.09.60	Harrogate T.	York C.	07.79	1979-80	7	6	0	(F)
FEREDAY, Wayne	Warley	16.06.63	APP	Q.P.R.	09.80	1980-83	18	14	6	(M)
FERGUSON, Alex	Glasgow	04.08.04	Newport Co.(*)	Bristol C.	05.46	1946	32		0	(G) *Wigan Ath./Gillingham/
			TR	Swindon T.	09.47	1947	7		0	Swansea C./Bury
FERGUSON, Archie	Lochore	09.12.18	Raith Rov.	Doncaster Rov.	+	1946-47	61		0	(G)
			TR	Wrexham	07.48	1948-52	126		0	
FERGUSON, Brian J.	Irvine	14.12.60	Mansfield T.(APP)	Newcastle U.	01.79	1979	4	1	1	(M)
			TR	Hull C.	12.80	1980-81	24	4	2	
			Goole T.	Southend U.	10.83	1983	28	1	5	
FERGUSON, Charlie	Glasgow	22.04.30	Hamilton	Accrington St.	05.54	1954	1		0	(FB)
			TR	Rochdale	09.55	1955-58	150		4	
			TR	Oldham Ath.	07.59	1959-60	57		0	
FERGUSON, David	Bonnybridge	11.03.29	Alloa	Coventry C.	10.56	1956	4		0	
FERGUSON, Eddie	Dumbarton	10.09.49	Dumbarton	Rotherham U.	02.71	1970-73	64	3	5	(WH)
			L	Grimsby T.	11.71	1971	1	1	0	
FERGUSON, Hugh	Belfast	23.05.26	Ballymena	Bradford C.	07.48	1948-52	133		0	(FB)
			TR	Halifax T.	09.54	1954-57	95		0	
FERGUSON, James C.M.	Glasgow	20.02.35	Falkirk	Oldham Ath.	05.59	1959	36		0	(G)
			TR	Crewe Alex.	08.60	1960-61	26		0	
			TR	Darlington	07.62	1962	32		0	
FERGUSON, John	Maybole	29.08.39	Airdrie	Southend U.	06.67	1967	13	1	2	(F)
FERGUSON, John T.	Edinburgh	14.06.39	St. Andrews U.	Oldham Ath.	11.56	1956	1		0	(F)
FERGUSON, Mark	Liverpool	06.11.60		Tranmere Rov.	08.82	1981-83	57	12	12	(F)
FERGUSON, Martin	Glasgow	21.12.42	Partick Th.	Barnsley	08.65	1965	40	/	17	(F)
			TR	Doncaster Rov.	07.66	1966	3	/	0	
FERGUSON, Mike J.	Newcastle	03.10.54	APP	Coventry C.	12.71	1974-80	121	6	51	(F)
			TR	Everton	08.81	1981	7	1	4	
			TR	Birmingham C.	11.82	1982	20	/	8	
			L	Coventry C.	03.84	1983	7	/	3	

Players Names	Birthplace	Date	Previous Club	League Club	Date Signed	Seasons Played	Apps	Sub	Gls	
FERGUSON, Mike K.	Burnley	09.03.43	Plymouth Arg.(AM)	Accrington St.	07.60	1960	23	/	1	(M)
			TR	Blackburn Rov.	03.62	1962-67	220	/	29	
			TR	Aston Villa	05.68	1968-69	38	/	2	
			TR	Q.P.R.	11.69	1969-72	68	1	2	
			TR	Cambridge U.	07.73	1973	39	/	4	
			TR	Rochdale	07.74	1974-75	68	1	5	
			IA. Akranes	Halifax T.	12.76	1976	2	/	0	
FERGUSON, Robert	Ardrossan	01.03.45	Kilmarnock	West Ham U.	06.67	1967-79	240	/	0	(G)S-7/S.U23-1/
			L	Sheffield Wed.	02.74	1973	5	/	0	S.F.LGE REP.
FERGUSON, Robert	Darlington	27.07.17	Middlesbrough(*)	York C.	+	1946	26		0	(G)
FERGUSON, Robert B.	Dudley	08.01.38	JNRS	Newcastle U.	05.55	1955-62	11		0	(FB)
			TR	Derby Co.	10.62	1962-65	121	/	0	
			TR	Cardiff C.	12.65	1965-68	87	1	0	
			Barry T.	Newport Co.	07.69	1969-70	71	/	2	
FERGUSON, Ron C.	Accrington	09.02.57	APP	Sheffield W.	02.75	1974	10	1	1	(F)
			L	Scunthorpe U.	12.75	1975	3	/	0	
			TR	Darlington	02.76	1975-79	101	13	18	
FERN, Rod	Burton	13.12.48	Measham Imps.	Leicester C.	12.66	1967-71	133	18	32	(F)
			TR	Luton T.	06.72	1972-74	34	5	5	
			TR	Chesterfield	06.75	1975-78	150	2	54	
			TR	Rotherham U.	06.79	1979-82	98	7	34	
FERNIE, Jim	Kirkcaldy	31.10.36	Arbroath	Doncaster Rov.	10.58	1958-60	89		30	(F)
FERNIE, Willie	East Fife	22.11.28	Glasgow Celtic	Middlesbrough	12.58	1958-60	66		3	(IF) S-12/S'B'-1/S.F.LGE REP.
FERNS, Phil	Liverpool	14.11.37		Liverpool	09.57	1962-64	27		1	(FB)
			TR	Bournemouth	08.65	1965	46	/	0	
			TR	Mansfield T.	08.66	1966-67	55	1	1	
FERNS, Phil D.	Liverpool	12.09.61	APP	Bournemouth	02.79	1978-80	94	1	6	(D) Son of Phil (SNR)
			TR	Charlton Ath.	08.81	1981-82	45	3	1	
			L	Wimbledon	12.82	1982	7	/	0	
			TR	Blackpool	08.83	1983	37	1	0	
FERRIDAY, Les	Manchester	03.06.29	Buxton	Walsall	05.54	1954	32		1	(WH)
FERRIER, Harry	Ratho	20.05.20	Barnsley(*)	Portsmouth	+	1946-53	241		8	(FB)
FERRIER, John	Edinburgh	06.10.27		Brighton & H.A.	10.46	1946	1		1	(LB)
			Clyde	Exeter C.	05.56	1956	31		0	
FERRIER, Ron J.	Cleethorpes	26.04.14	Manchester U.(*)	Oldham Ath.	*	1946	2		0	(IF) *Grimsby T.
			TR	Lincoln C.	08.47					
FERRIS, John	Bristol	04.09.39		Torquay U.	09.58	1958	3		0	(G)
FERRIS, Paul J.	Lisburn	10.07.65	APP	Newcastle U.	03.83	1981-82	1	6	0	(M)
FERRIS, Ray	Newry	22.09.20	Brentford(+)	Crewe Alex.	+	1946-48	101		23	(WH) +Cambridge U./
			TR	Birmingham C.	03.49	1948-52	90		3	NI-3/Son of pre-war player
FERRIS, Sam	Motherwell	14.03.51	Albion Rov.	Chesterfield	03.72	1971-73	25	6	3	(IF)
			L	Workington	02.74	1973	2	1	0	
FERRY, Gordon	Sunderland	22.12.43	APP	Arsenal	01.61	1964	11		0	(CH)
			TR	Orient	05.65	1965	42	/	0	
FEWINGS, Pat. J.H.	Barnstaple	21.01.31	Barnstaple	Torquay U.	11.53	1953-54	8		0	(OR)
FIDLER, Dennis J.	Stockport	22.06.38	Manchester U.(AM)	Manchester C.	01.57	1957-58	5		1	(IF)
			TR	Port Vale	06.60	1960-61	38		12	
			TR	Grimsby T.	10.61	1961	9		0	
			TR	Halifax T.	04.63	1962-66	142	1	40	
			TR	Darlington	10.66	1966-67	32	2	3	
FIDLER, Frank	Middleton	16.08.24	JNRS	Manchester U.	+					(CF)
			Witton A.	Wrexham	05.50	1950-51	36		15	
			TR	Leeds U.	10.51	1951-52	22		8	
			TR	Bournemouth	12.52	1952-54	61		32	
FIDLER, Tom G.	Hounslow	04.09.33	Hounslow	Q.P.R.	05.54	1954	12		2	
FIELD, Anthony	Halifax	06.07.46	JNRS	Halifax T.	07.63	1963-65	21	/	3	(CF)
			TR	Barrow	08.66	1966-67	36	2	16	
			TR	Southport	03.68	1967-71	127	6	41	
			TR	Blackburn Rov.	10.71	1971-73	104	2	46	
			TR	Sheffield U.	03.74	1973-75	63	3	13	
FIELD, Anthony F.	Chester	23.05.42		Chester C.	08.61	1960	2		0	
			TR	Southport	07.62					
FIELDER, Colin M.R.	Winchester	05.01.64	APP	Aldershot	01.82	1981-83	5	5	0	(D)
FIELDING, John A.	Liverpool	02.09.39	Wigan Ath.	Southport	03.61	1960-62	76		21	(IF)
			TR	Brentford	03.63	1962-65	82	/	18	
			TR	Grimsby T.	12.65	1965	25	/	7	
FIELDING, Mark J.	Bury	10.11.56	APP	Preston N.E.	11.74	1974	9	/	0	(FB)
FIELDING, Paul A.	Rochdale	04.12.55	APP	Rochdale	12.73	1972-75	65	7	5	(WH)
FIELDING, Wally A.	London	26.11.19	Walthamstow	Everton	+	1946-58	381		50	(IF)
			TR	Southport	01.59	1958-59	20		1	
FIELDING, William J.	Broadbottom	17.06.15	Cardiff C.(*)	Bolton W.	+					(G)
			TR	Manchester U.	01.47	1946	6		0	

Players Names	Birthplace	Date	Previous Club	League Club	Date Signed	Seasons Played	Career Record Apps	Sub	Gls	
FIELDS, Alf G.	London	15.11.18	Margate	Arsenal	*	1946-50	16		0	(CH)
FIELDS, Mike J.	Chester	12.08.35		Chester C.	05.56	1955-57	22		1	(F)
FIELDS, Norman	Durham	27.08.27		Portsmouth	+					(HB)
			TR	Mansfield T.	06.50	1951-52	18		0	
FIFIELD, David	Plymouth	10.12.66	JNRS	Torquay U.	N/C	1983	0	1	0	
FIGGINS, Phil	Portsmouth	20.08.55	Waterlooville	Portsmouth	07.73	1974-77	35	/	0	(G)
FILBY, Ian F.	East Ham	09.10.54	APP	Orient	08.73					(F)
			L	Brentford	09.74	1974	1	2	0	
FILLERY, Mike	Mitcham	17.09.60	APP	Chelsea	08.78	1978-82	156	5	32	(M)E.SCH.INT./
			TR	Q.P.R.	08.83	1983	29	1	1	E.YTH.INT.
FINAN, Robert J.	Kilpatrick	13.01.12	Yoker Ath.	Blackpool	*					(CF)
			TR	Crewe Alex.	09.47	1947-48	59		14	
FINCH, A. Roy	Barry	07.04.22	Swansea C.(+)	W.B.A.	+	1946-48	15		1	(OL) +Barians FC
			TR	Lincoln C.	02.49	1948-58	275		57	
FINCH, Derek	Arley	29.07.40	JNRS	W.B.A.	08.57					(FB)
			TR	Aldershot	06.60	1960	3		0	
FINCH, Des	Worksop	26.02.50		Mansfield T.	03.69	1968-70	4	/	0	(G)
FINCH, Mike	Stockton	20.06.65		Hartlepool U.	N/C	1983	1	/	0	
FINCH, Robert J.	London	24.08.48	APP	Q.P.R.	08.66	1967-69	6	1	0	(FB) d.1978
FINCHAM, Gordon R.	Peterborough	08.01.35	Fletton	Leicester C.	11.52	1952-57	50		0	(CH)
			TR	Plymouth Arg.	07.58	1958-62	136		4	
			TR	Luton T.	07.63	1963-64	64		0	
FINDLAY, Jake W.	Blairgowrie	13.07.54	APP	Aston Villa	06.72	1973-76	14	/	0	(G)
			TR	Luton T.	11.78	1978-82	164	/	0	
			L	Barnsley	09.83	1983	6	/	0	
			L	Derby Co.	01.84	1983	1	/	0	
FINDLAY, Ken	Pegswood	24.03.26	Aberdeen	Aldershot	08.50	1950	7		0	
FINLAY, Alan	Edinburgh	09.01.39	Hearts	Newport Co.	07.61	1961	20		1	(IF) S.SCH.INT
FINLAY, John	Glasgow	01.07.25		New Brighton	03.51	1950	15		2	(OR)
			TR	Leeds U.	06.51	1951	1		0	
			TR	Walsall	08.53	1953	11		0	
FINLAY, John	Birtley	16.02.19	Grimsby T.(*)	Sunderland	+	1946	1		0	(IF)
FINLAY, Pat	Birkenhead	18.03.38		Tranmere Rov.	08.59	1961	3		0	(FB)
FINLAYSON, Malcolm	Dumbarton	14.06.30	Renfrew J.	Millwall	02.48	1947-55	229		0	(G)
			TR	Wolverhampton W.	08.56	1956-63	179		0	
FINLEY, Tom	Frizington	06.10.33	Northside J.	Workington	01.56	1955-59	94		2	(FB)
			TR	Southport	02.60	1959	6		0	
FINN, Mike G.	Liverpool	01.05.54	APP	Burnley	12.71	1973-74	4	/	0	(G)
FINNEY, Alan	Langwith	31.10.53	JNRS	Sheffield Wed.	11.50	1950-65	455	/	83	(OR) E.U23-3/E'B'-1●
			TR	Doncaster Rov.	01.66	1965-66	30	/	3	
FINNEY, C. William	Stoke	05.09.31	Crewe Alex.(AM)	Stoke C.	05.49	1952-54	57		14	(IF)
			TR	Birmingham C.	11.55	1955-56	14		0	
			TR	Q.P.R.	05.57	1957	10		1	
			TR	Crewe Alex.	07.58	1958	1		0	
			TR	Rochdale	09.58	1958	31		1	
FINNEY, R. Ken	St.Helens	10.03.29		Stockport Co.	12.47	1947-57	192		32	(F)
			TR	Tranmere Rov.	03.58	1957-62	180		26	
FINNEY, Richard	Rotherham	14.03.56	JNRS	Rotherham U.	07.74	1973-80	236	/	67	(F)E.YTH.INT.
FINNEY, Tom	Preston	05.04.22	JNRS	Preston N.E.	+	1946-59	433		187	(F) E-76/E.F.LGE REP.●
FINNEY, Tom	Belfast	6.11.54	Crusaders	Luton T.	08.73	1973	13	1	5	(F)NI-14
			TR	Sunderland	07.74	1974-75	8	7	1	
			TR	Cambridge U.	08.76	1976-83	259	9	56	
			TR	Brentford	02.84	1983	14	1	2	
FINNIESTON, Steve	Edinburgh	30.11.54	APP	Chelsea	12.71	1974-77	78	2	34	(F)S.YTH.INT.
			L	Cardiff C.	10.74	1974	9	/	2	
			TR	Sheffield U.	06.78	1978	23	/	4	
FINNIGAN, Dennis	Sheffield	23.03.40		Sheffield U.	04.59	1959-66	14	/	0	(HB)
			TR	Chesterfield	09.68	1968-69	26	/	0	
FINNIGAN, John	Glasgow	03.07.43	Clyde	Millwall	06.63	1963	6		0	(FB)
FINNIGAN, Ray W.	Wallsend	22.01.47	APP	Newcastle U.	01.65					(F)
			TR	Darlington	07.66	1966-67	8	4	0	
FINNIGAN, Trevor	Bedlington	14.10.52		Everton	05.71					(D)
			Runcorn	Blackpool	03.77	1976-77	13	4	3	
			TR	Bournemouth	01.78	1977-78	23	2	5	
FINNIS, Harold A.	Liverpool	21.11.20		Everton	06.46	1946	1		0	
FIOCCA, Paul	Italy	13.01.55	APP	Swindon T.	01.73	1973	1	/	0	(IF)
FIRM, Neil J.	Bradford	23.01.58	APP	Leeds U.	01.76	1979-81	11	1	0	(D)
			L	Oldham Ath.	03.82	1981	9	/	0	
			TR	Peterborough U.	08.82	1982-83	63	1	2	

Players Names	Birthplace	Date	Previous Club	League Club	Date Signed	Seasons Played	Apps	Sub	Gls	
FIRMAN, Ken	Felling	05.02.41	Jarrow Mercantile	Gateshead	AM	1958	1		0	(IL)
FIRMANI, Eddie R.	S.Africa	07.08.33	Clyde SA	Charlton Ath.	02.50	1951-54	99		50	(IF)
			Sampdoria	Charlton Ath.	10.63	1963-64	55		32	
			TR	Southend U.	06.65	1965-66	55	/	24	
			TR	Charlton Ath.	03.67	1966-67	10	/	6	
FIRMANI, Peter W.	S. Africa	14.02.36	Clyde SA	Charlton Ath.	09.53	1955-58	31		2	(FB) Brother of Eddie
FIRTH, Frank M.	Dewsbury	27.05.56	APP	Huddersfield T.	11.73	1973-76	26	1	4	(M)
			TR	Halifax T.	02.78	1977-81	157	11	19	
			TR	Bury	08.82	1982	33	/	4	
FISHENDEN, Paul	Hillingdon	02.08.63	APP	Wimbledon	10.81	1981-83	21	16	13	(F)
FISHER, Bernard	York	23.02.34		Hull C.	11.55	1955-62	126		0	(G)
			TR	Bradford C.	07.63	1963-64	60		0	
FISHER, Charlie K.	Pontypridd	04.01.15	Lovells Ath.	Swansea C.	+	1946-47	65		0	
FISHER, Fred	Hetton-le-Hole	28.11.24	Slough T.	Reading	+	1946-51	139		23	(OR)
			TR	Shrewsbury T.	07.52	1952-53	64		9	
			TR	Orient	07.54	1954	2		1	
FISHER, Fred T.	Wednesbury	14.01.20	Fallings Heath	Grimsby T.	*	1946-50	165		0	(FB)
			TR	Rochdale	06.51	1951	1		0	
FISHER, George S.	Bermondsey	19.06.25		Millwall	+	1946-54	286		3	(FB)
			TR	Fulham	11.54	1954	8		0	
			TR	Colchester U.	09.55	1955-59	163		6	
FISHER, Hugh	Glasgow	09.01.44		Blackpool	08.62	1963-66	51	3	1	(M)
			TR	Southampton	03.67	1966-76	297	5	7	
			TR	Southport	03.77	1976-77	60	/	1	
FISHER, James	Barrow	12.06.34	Holker COB	Barrow	10.55	1952-57	10		1	(IF)
FISHER, John A.	Bermondsey	19.06.25		Millwall	05.46	1947-48	3		0	(FB) Brother of George
			TR	Bournemouth	06.49	1949-52	52		0	
FISHER, Ken D.	Westwood	30.09.21		Southampton	09.46					(FB)
			TR	Watford	08.47	1947-50	106		2	
FISHER, Les	Southampton	08.01.48		Blackpool	12.67	1968	1	/	0	(FB)
FISHER, Paul	Mansfield	19.01.51		Huddersfield T.	02.69					(FB)
			TR	Darlington	06.70	1970	2	1	0	
FISHER, Peter M.	Edinburgh	17.02.20		Northampton T.	09.47	1947	8		0	(FB)
			TR	Shrewsbury T.	08.50	1950-51	39		0	
			TR	Wrexham	10.51	1951-53	85		0	
FISHER, Phil J.	Carmarthen	10.01.58	Bridgend.	Exeter C.	02.81	1980-81	9	2	1	(F)
FISHER, Robert P.	Wembley	03.08.56	APP	Orient	08.73	1973-82	308	6	4	(D)
			TR	Cambridge U.	11.82	1982-83	42	/	0	
			TR	Brentford	02.84	1983	17	/	0	
FISHER, Ron	Sheffield	09.03.23		Halifax T.	08.50	1950	6		0	(RB)
FISHER, Stan	Barnsley	29.09.24	Rockingham Col.	Barnsley	+	1946	1		0	(IF)
			TR	Halifax T.	01.47	1946-47	26		7	
FITCH, Barry E.	Brighton	19.11.43		Brighton & H.A.	11.61	1963	1		0	(FB)
FITTON, John	Oldham	12.01.51	JNRS	Oldham Ath.	10.68	1969	3	/	0	(G)
FITZGERALD, Alf	Conisbrough	25.01.11	Q.P.R.(*)	Aldershot	+	1946-47	59		1	(IF) *Denaby U./Reading/ d. 1981
FITZGERALD, Peter	Waterford	17.06.37	Sparta Rotterdam	Leeds U.	08.60	1960	8		1	(F)
			TR	Chester C.	07.61	1961-63	80		12	EI-5/L.O.I. REP.
FITZPATRICK, Anthony C.	Glasgow	03.03.56	St. Mirren	Bristol C.	08.79	1979-80	75	/	1	(M)S.U21-5
FITZPATRICK, John	Aberdeen	18.08.46	JNRS	Manchester U.	09.63	1964-72	111	6	8	(WH)
FITZPATRICK, Peter	Bebbington	27.04.29		New Brighton	AM	1949	1		0	
FITZSIMMONS, Arthur	Dublin	16.12.29	Shelbourne	Middlesbrough	05.49	1949-58	223		54	(IF) EI-26/L.O.I. REP.
			TR	Lincoln C.	03.59	1958	7		0	
			TR	Mansfield T.	08.59	1959-60	61		23	
FITZSIMMONS, Eric J.	Oldham	23.10.48		Bradford P.A.	AM	1969	1	/	0	(IR) Oldham Rugby Lge
FLACK, Doug W.	Staines	24.10.20	JNRS	Fulham	*	1948-52	54		0	(G)
			TR	Walsall	08.53	1953	11		0	
FLACK, W. Len	Cambridge	01.06.16	Cambridge T.	Norwich C.	*	1946	25		0	(FB) E.SCH.INT.
FLANAGAN, Daniel C.	Dublin	24.11.24	Dundalk	Notts.Co.	AM	1946	2		2	(CF)
			Shelbourne	Manchester C.	02.47					
			TR	Bradford C.	12.47	1947	13		5	
FLANAGAN, Mike A.	Ilford	09.11.52	Tottenham H.(AM)	Charlton Ath.	08.71	1971-78	241	13	85	(F)E.YTH.INT.
			TR	Crystal Palace	08.79	1979-80	56	/	8	
			TR	Q.P.R.	12.80	1980-83	71	7	20	
			TR	Charlton Ath.	01.84	01.84	1983	18	/	2
FLANAGAN, Shaun	Doncaster	25.12.60	APP	Doncaster Rov.	01.79	1978-80	41	9	3	(D)
FLANNIGAN, Ray	London	15.03.49	Margate	Reading	04.70	1970-71	36	4	0	(FB)
FLATLEY, Albert	Bradford	05.09.19		Bury	12.46					(IF)*York C./
			Alessandria	Workington	11.51	1951	8		0	+Bradford P.A.

Players Names	Birthplace	Date	Previous Club	League Club	Date Signed	Seasons Played	Apps	Sub	Gls	
FLATT, Colin	Blyth	30.01.40	Wisbech	Orient	05.65	1965	32	1	8	(F)
			TR	Southend U.	06.66	1966	20	2	8	
FLAVELL, John A.	Stourbridge	15.05.29	Lye T.	W.B.A.	05.47					(FB)Worcester/England
			TR	Walsall	09.53	1953	22		0	Cricketer
FLAVELL, Robert W.	Berwick	07.03.56	APP	Burnley	03.73					(D)
			TR	Halifax T.	02.76	1975-77	91	/	7	
			TR	Chesterfield	08.78	1978	27	2	2	
			TR	Barnsley	07.79	1979	25	/	0	
			TR	Halifax T.	N/C	1980	1	/	0	
FLAY, Steve	Poole	02.10.54	APP	Oxford U.	08.71	1973-74	3	/	0	(FB)
FLEET, Steve	Salford	02.07.37	JNRS	Manchester C.	02.55	1957-60	5		0	(G)
			TR	Wrexham	06.63	1963-65	79	/	0	
			TR	Stockport Co.	01.66	1965-67	36	/	0	
FLEETING, Jim	Glasgow	08.04.55	Kilbirnie Ladeside	Norwich C.	04.75	1976	0	1	0	(D)
FLEMING, Bernard	Middlesbrough	08.01.37	RAF Binbrook	Grimsby T.	04.57	1957-60	22		0	(FB)
			TR	Workington	07.61	1961	19		0	
			TR	Chester C.	05.62	1962-63	64		0	
FLEMING, Charlie	Blairhall	12.07.27	E.Fife	Sunderland	01.55	1954-57	107		62	(CF) S-1
FLEMING, Frank	South Shields	21.12.45		Darlington	07.64	1964	2		0	(G)
FLEMING, George K.	Gourock	25.02.35	Morton	Watford	06.58	1958-59	27		10	(F)
			TR	Carlisle U.	06.60	1960	7		0	
			TR	Barrow	09.60	1960	17		3	
FLEMING, Ian J.H.	Maybole	15.01.53	Aberdeen	Sheffield Wed.	02.79	1978-79	13	/	1	(F)
FLEMING, James	Tannochside	04.11.52	Manchester U.(APP)	Carlisle U.	07.71					(IF)
			L	Barrow	01.72	1971	1	1	0	
FLEMING, James F.	Glasgow	07.01.29	Stirling A.	Workington	05.54	1954-57	89		1	(FB)
FLEMING, James P.	Alloa	07.01.42	Partick Th.	Luton T.	11.60	1960-62	66		9	(W)
FLEMING, John J.	Nottingham	01.07.53	JNRS	Oxford U.	09.70	1971-74	67	8	2	(M)
			TR	Lincoln C.	07.75	1975-78	109	12	17	
			TR	Port Vale	03.80	1979	3	/	0	
FLEMING, Mike A.	Rochdale	23.02.28		Tranmere Rov.	09.53	1953-57	115		8	(IF)
FLEMING, Neil	Felixstowe	09.01.50	Swiss Cottage	Lincoln C.	AM	1973	1	/	0	(CH)
FLETCHER, Alan F.	Pendleton	28.10.17	Bournemouth(*)	Bristol Rov.	+					(IF) *Blackpool
				Crewe Alex.	09.47	1947	1		0	
FLETCHER, Chris	Buncrana	14.06.33	Cheltenham	Brentford	12.57	1957	3		0	(F)
FLETCHER, Doug	Sheffield	17.09.30		Sheffield Wed.	01.48	1948-49	4		0	(IF)
			TR	Bury	05.51	1951-55	67		17	
			TR	Scunthorpe U.	07.56	1956-57	64		26	
			TR	Darlington	07.58	1958	43		13	
			TR	Halifax T.	06.59	1959	20		4	
FLETCHER, Gavin	Bellshill	30.10.41	T.Lanark	Bradford C.	07.63	1963	8		1	(IF)
FLETCHER, Hugh M.	Lochgilphead	08.04.33	Glasgow Celtic	Carlisle U.	05.56	1956-60	124		18	(FB)
FLETCHER, J. Rod	Preston	23.09.45		Leeds U.	12.62					(F)
				Crewe Alex.	03.67	1966	1	/	0	
			TR	Lincoln C.	08.67	1967-70	86	4	29	
			TR	Scunthorpe U.	06.71	1971-73	97	1	30	
			TR	Grimsby T.	11.73	1973-74	9	3	1	
FLETCHER, James	Houghton-le-Spring	06.11.34	Appleton CW	Doncaster Rov.	01.58	1957-59	45		15	(F)
			TR	Stockport Co.	01.60	1959-60	61		19	
FLETCHER, James A.	Wouldham	10.11.31	Maidstone	Gillingham	07.57	1957	23		8	(IF) E.AMAT.INT.
			TR	Southend U.	07.58					
FLETCHER, James R.	Brewood	23.12.26	Bilston U.	Birmingham C.	06.50					
			TR	Chester C.	07.51	1951	23		9	
FLETCHER, John	Sheffield	22.02.43		Doncaster Rov.	06.61	1961	1		0	(FB)
FLETCHER, Joseph	Manchester	25.09.46	Manchester C.(AM)	Rochdale	01.67	1966-68	55	2	21	(IF)
			TR	Grimsby T.	07.69	1969	11	/	1	
			TR	Barrow	10.69	1969	7	1	1	
FLETCHER, Ken	Liverpool	31.12.31	JNRS	Everton	08.49					(FB)
			TR	Chester C.	07.53	1953-55	34		0	
FLETCHER, Len G.G.	Hammersmith	28.04.29		Ipswich T.	11.49	1949-54	20		0	(WH)
FLETCHER, Mark R.J.	Barnsley	01.04.65	APP	Barnsley	04.83	1983	1	/	0	(D)
FLETCHER, Paul J.	Bolton	13.01.51	APP	Bolton W.	11.68	1968-70	33	3	5	(F)E.U23-4
			TR	Burnley	03.71	1970-79	291	2	71	
			TR	Blackpool	02.80	1979-81	19	1	8	
FLETCHER, Peter	Manchester	02.12.53	APP	Manchester U.	12.70	1972-73	2	5	0	(F)
			TR	Hull C.	05.74	1974-75	26	10	5	
			TR	Stockport Co.	05.76	1976-77	43	8	13	
			TR	Huddersfield T.	07.78	1978-81	83	16	37	
FLEWIN, Reg	Portsmouth	28.11.20	Ryde	Portsmouth	*	1946-52	151		0	(CH)

Players Names	Birthplace	Date	Previous Club	League Club	Date Signed	Seasons Played	Career Record Apps	Sub	Gls	
FLINT, Ken	Kirkby	12.11.23	Bedford T.	Tottenham H.	07.47	1947	5		1	(OL)
			TR	Aldershot	07.50	1950-57	324		70	
			TR	Orient	06.58	1958	4		0	
FLOCKETT, Tommy	Ferryhill	17.07.27	Spennymoor	Chesterfield	04.49	1949-56	200		1	(FB)
			TR	Bradford C.	06.57	1957-62	227		1	
FLOOD, Edward	Liverpool	19.11.52	APP	Liverpool	11.69					(D)
			TR	Tranmere Rov.	07.72	1972-80	313	2	6	
			TR	York C.	08.81	1981	13	2	0	
FLOOD, John E.	Southampton	21.10.32	JNRS	Southampton	11.49	1952-57	122		28	(OR) E.SCH.INT.
			TR	Bournemouth	06.58	1958	17		3	
FLOOD, John G.	Glasgow	25.12.60	APP	Sheffield U.	10.78	1978-80	16	3	1	(F)
FLOOD, Paul	Dublin	29.06.48	Bohemians	Brighton & H.A.	06.67	1967-70	32	3	7	(OR)
FLOUNDERS, Andy J.	Hull	13.12.63	APP	Hull C.	12.81	1980-83	54	12	27	(F)
FLOWER, Anthony	Carlton	02.01.45	JNRS	Notts.Co.	01.62	1961-66	127	2	17	(W)
			TR	Halifax T.	07.67	1967-69	78	1	6	
FLOWERS, John E.	Doncaster	26.08.44	APP	Stoke C.	09.61	1963-65	8	/	0	(WH) Brother of Ron
			TR	Doncaster Rov.	08.66	1966-70	162	2	4	
			TR	Port Vale	08.71	1971	34	/	0	
FLOWERS, Malcolm	Mansfield	09.08.38		Mansfield T.	08.56	1956	4		0	(HB)
FLOWERS, Ron	Edlington	28.07.34	JNRS	Wolverhampton W.	08.51	1952-66	467	/	32	(WH) E-49/E.U23-2/
			TR	Northampton T.	09.67	1967-68	61	/	4	E.F.LGE REP.●
FLOYD, Ron C.	Coventry	17.08.32	JNRS	W.B.A.	11.49					(G)
			TR	Crewe Alex.	07.53	1953-54	39		0	
FLYNN, Brian	Port Talbot	12.10.55	APP	Burnley	10.72	1973-77	115	5	8	(M)W-64/W.U23-2/
			TR	Leeds U.	11.77	1977-82	152	2	11	W.SCH.INT.●
			L	Burnley	03.82	1981	2	/	0	
			TR	Burnley	11.82	1982-83	71	/	10	
FLYNN, John E.	Workington	20.03.48	JNRS	Workington	09.67	1966-68	35	3	0	(D)
			TR	Sheffield U.	07.69	1969-77	185	5	8	
			TR	Rotherham U.	07.78	1978-79	30	1	1	
FLYNN, Peter	Glasgow	11.10.36	JNRS	Leeds U.	10.53	1953	1		0	(F)
			TR	Bradford P.A.	06.57	1958-65	130	1	9	
FLYNN, William	Kirkmalden	02.01.27	Maybold J.	Rotherham U.	07.49	1949	6		0	
FOAN, Albert T.	Rotherhithe	30.10.23	D.A.O.R.	Norwich C.	04.47	1947-49	18		3	(IF)
			TR	West Ham U.	07.50	1950-56	53		6	
FOGARTY, Ambrose	Dublin	11.09.33	Glentoran	Sunderland	10.57	1957-63	152		37	(W) EI-11
			TR	Hartlepool U.	11.63	1963-66	127	1	22	
FOGARTY, Ken A.	Manchester	25.01.55	APP	Stockport Co.	11.72	1971-79	265	4	6	(M)
FOGARTY, William F.	London	27.06.57	APP	Gillingham	07.75	1975-76	25	3	0	(M)
			TR	Charlton Ath.	12.79					
FOGG, Dave	Liverpool	28.05.51		Wrexham	02.72	1970-75	159	2	0	(D)
			TR	Oxford U.	07.76	1976-83	287	4	16	
FOGG, Ron W.J.	Tilbury	03.06.38		Southend U.	AM	1959	2		0	(F)
			Weymouth	Aldershot	07.63	1963-64	64		29	
FOGGO, Ken	Perth	07.11.43	JNRS	W.B.A.	11.60	1962-67	128	1	30	(IF) S.SCH.INT.
			TR	Norwich C.	10.67	1967-72	183	4	54	
			TR	Portsmouth	01.73	1972-74	47	13	3	
			TR	Southend U.	09.75	1975	30	/	6	
FOGGON, Alan	Chester-le-Street	23.02.50	APP	Newcastle U.	11.67	1967-70	54	6	13	(F)E.YTH.INT.
			TR	Cardiff C.	08.71	1971-72	14	3	1	
			TR	Middlesbrough	10.72	1972-75	105	10	45	
			TR	Manchester U.	07.76	1976	0	3	0	
			TR	Sunderland	09.76	1976	7	1	0	
			TR	Southend U.	06.77	1977	22	/	0	
			L	Hartlepool U.	02.78	1977	18	/	2	
FOITHERINGHAM, Jim G.	Hamilton	19.12.33	JNRS	Arsenal	03.51	1954-58	72		0	(CH) d.1977
			Hearts	Northampton T.	08.59	1959	11		0	
FOLDS, Robert J.	Bedford	18.04.49	APP	Gillingham	11.67	1968-70	38	6	1	(F)
			TR	Northampton T.	08.71	1971	29	/	0	
FOLEY, Charles	Salford	07.01.52	APP	Stockport Co.	01.70	1969-70	6	1	0	(WH)
FOLEY, Peter	Glasgow	28.06.44		Workington	02.65	1964-66	74	/	14	(F)
			TR	Scunthorpe U.	07.67	1967-68	15	2	3	
			TR	Chesterfield	08.69	1969	2	/	0	
FOLEY, Peter J.	Bicester	10.09.56	APP	Oxford U.	09.74	1974-82	262	15	70	(F)EI.YTH INT.
			L	Gillingham	02.83	1982	5	/	0	
FOLEY, Steve	Liverpool	04.10.62	APP	Liverpool	09.80					(F)
			L	Fulham	12.83	1983	2	1	0	
FOLEY, Steve P.	Clacton	21.06.53	APP	Colchester U.	09.71	1971-81	273	10	54	(F)
FOLEY, Terry	Portsmouth	08.02.38	Ryde	Portsmouth	05.59	1959	7		0	(F)
			TR	Chesterfield	07.60	1960	28		11	

Players Names	Birthplace	Date	Previous Club	League Club	Date Signed	Seasons Played	Career Record Apps	Sub	Gls	
FOLEY, Theo C.	Dublin	02.04.37	Home Farm	Exeter C.	03.55	1955-60	154		1	(FB) EI-9
			TR	Northampton T.	05.61	1961-66	205	/	8	
			TR	Charlton Ath.	08.67	1967	6	/	0	
FOLLAN, Eddie	Greenock	03.10.29	Prescot Cables	Aston Villa	06.52	1954-55	34		6	(IF)
FOLLAND, Robert	West Hartlepool	03.12.40		Hartlepool U.	05.59	1959-62	58		24	(F)
FOOTE, Chris R.T.	Bournemouth	19.11.50	APP	Bournemouth	08.68	1968-69	44	1	2	(IF)
			TR	Cambridge U.	03.71	1970-73	76	10	6	
FOOTITT, Don	Grantham	24.05.29	St. Johns	Lincoln C.	01.47	1946	24		0	(G)
			TR	Crewe Alex.	07.49	1949	1		0	
FORBES, Alex R.	Dundee	21.01.25	Dundee NE	Sheffield U.	+	1946-47	61		6	(WH) S-14
			TR	Arsenal	02.48	1947-55	217		21	
			TR	Orient	08.56	1956	8		0	
			TR	Fulham	11.57	1957	4		0	
FORBES, Duncan	Edinburgh	19.06.41	Musselburgh	Colchester U.	09.61	1961-68	270	/	2	(D)●
			TR	Norwich C.	09.68	1968-80	287	6	11	
			L	Torquay U.	10.76	1976	7	/	0	
FORBES, Dudley D.	S. Africa	19.04.26	Marist Bros	Charlton Ath.	12.47	1948-50	57		1	(WH)
FORBES, George P.	Cheadle	21.07.14		Blackburn Rov.	*					(WH)
			TR	Barrow	06.46	1946-50	177		3	
FORBES, Richard J.	Ashford	12.03.55	Woking	Exeter C.	07.79	1977-80	55	4	5	(M)
			Bideford	Plymouth Arg.	08.83	1983	3	/	0	
FORBES, Willie	Glasgow	25.05.22	Dunfermline	Wolverhampton W.	09.46	1946-49	71		23	(WH)
			TR	Preston N.E.	12.49	1949-55	192		7	
			TR	Carlisle U.	07.56	1956-57	25		0	
FORD, Alan L.	Ferndale	28.10.25		Workington	AM	1951-53	39		0	(G) d.1963
FORD, Andy	Minehead	04.05.54	Minehead	Bournemouth	07.72					(D)
			TR	Southend U.	05.73	1973-76	135	3	3	
			TR	Swindon T.	08.77	1977-79	92	6	0	
			TR	Gillingham	07.80	1980-81	62	/	3	
FORD, Anthony	Grimsby	14.05.59	APP	Grimsby T.	05.77	1975-83	247	31	45	(F)
FORD, Anthony M.	Thornbury	26.11.44	APP	Bristol C.	11.61	1961-69	170	1	10	(FB) E.YTH.INT.
			TR	Bristol Rov.	12.69	1969-70	28	/	1	
FORD, Clive	West Bromwich	10.04.45	APP	Wolverhampton W.	10.62	1964	2		0	(F)
			TR	Walsall	12.64	1964-66	11	3	0	
			TR	Lincoln C.	02.67	1966-67	48	1	16	
FORD, Colin	Lewisham	18.09.60	APP	Gillingham	09.78	1979	1	/	0	(M)
FORD, Dave	Sheffield	02.03.45	APP	Sheffield Wed.	01.63	1965-69	118	5	31	(IF) E.U23-2
			TR	Newcastle U.	12.69	1969-70	24	2	3	
			TR	Sheffield U.	01.71	1970-72	21	6	2	
			TR	Halifax T.	08.73	1973-75	83	2	6	
FORD, Fred G.L.	Dartford	10.02.16	Charlton Ath.(*)	Millwall	+	1946	9		0	*Erith & B
			TR	Carlisle U.	07.47	1947	28		0	
FORD, Gary	York	08.02.61	APP	York C.	02.79	1978-83	230	7	41	(M)
FORD, Ken	Sheffield	01.12.40	JNRS	Sheffield Wed.	03.60					(F)
			TR	Oldham Ath.	06.61	1961	5		1	
FORD, Peter	Stoke	10.08.33	W.B.A.(AM)	Stoke C.	05.53	1956-58	14		0	(HB)
			TR	Port Vale	09.59	1959-62	104		5	
FORD, Robert	Rutherglen	13.08.34	Vale of Clyde	Aldershot	07.57	1957	2		0	(IF)
FORD, Steve D.	Shoreham	17.02.59	Lewes	Stoke C.	07.81	1981	1	1	0	(F)
FORD, Trevor	Swansea	01.10.23	JNRS	Swansea C.	+	1946	16		9	(CF) W-38●
			TR	Aston Villa	01.47	1946-50	121		59	
			TR	Sunderland	10.50	1950-53	108		67	
			TR	Cardiff C.	12.53	1953-56	96		39	
			PSV Eindhoven	Newport Co.	07.60	1960	8		3	
FORDE, Clevere	London	14.11.58	Hounslow	Plymouth Arg.	12.78	1978	4	1	0	(F)
FORDE, Steve	Pontefract	29.08.14	Rotherham U.(*)	West Ham U.	*	1946-51	163		1	(FB)
FOREMAN, Alec G.	West Ham	01.03.14	West Ham U.(*)	Tottenham H.	+	1946	37		15	(CF) Walthamstow/ E.AMAT.INT./d.1969
FOREMAN, Dennis J.	S. Africa	01.02.33	Hibs(S.Africa)	Brighton & H.A.	03.52	1952-60	212		62	(OL) Sussex Cricketer
FOREMAN, William	Havant	03.02.58	Bournemouth (APP)	Bristol Rov.	05.76	1976-77	0	2	0	(M)
FORGAN, Tommy C.	Middlesbrough	12.10.29	Sutton Est.	Hull C.	05.49	1952-53	11		0	(G)
			TR	York C.	06.54	1954-65	388	/	0	
FORREST, Ernie	Sunderland	19.02.19	Usworth Col	Bolton W.	*	1946-47	64		1	
			TR	Grimsby T.	05.48	1948	33		1	
			TR	Millwall	06.49	1949	37		4	
FORREST, Gerry	Stockton	21.01.57	South Bank	Rotherham U.	02.77	1977-83	296	/	7	(D)
FORREST, J. Robert	Rossington	13.05.31	Retford T.	Leeds U.	12.52	1952-58	119		36	(IF)
			TR	Notts Co.	02.59	1958-61	117		37	
FORREST, James	Glasgow	22.09.44	Glasgow Rgrs.	Preston N.E.	03.67	1966-67	24	2	3	(CF)S-5/S-'U'23-2/ S.SCH.INT.

Players Names	Birthplace	Date	Previous Club	League Club	Date Signed	Seasons Played	Apps	Sub	Gls	
FORREST, James	Dalkeith	14.11.29	Musselborough	Leeds U.	12.50					(F)
			TR	Accrington St.	11.51	1951	5		3	
FORREST, John	Bury	09.10.47	JNRS	Bury	03.66	1967-80	430	/	0	(G)
FORREST, Keith	Hartlepool	18.02.51		Hartlepool U.	AM	1969-70	4	2	0	(IF)
FORREST, William	Bo'Ness	19.01.45	Hearts	Carlisle U.	07.62	1962-63	10		0	(HB)
			TR	Brighton & H.A.	07.64					
FORRESTER, Anthony	Parkstone	14.01.40	JNRS	W.B.A.	03.57	1958	6		3	(OR)
			TR	Southend U.	04.59	1959	10		1	
FORRESTER, George H.	Glasgow	28.08.34		Sunderland	03.53					(FB)
			Eyemouth	Accrington St.	02.60	1959-60	54		0	
FORRESTER, George L.	Cannock	08.06.27		Gillingham	N/L	1950-54	100		3	(HB) d.1982
			TR	Reading	07.55	1955	6		2	
FORSTER, Derek	Newcastle	19.02.49	APP	Sunderland	02.66	1964-71	18	/	0	(G) E.SCH.INT.
			TR	Charlton Ath.	07.73	1973	9	/	0	
			TR	Brighton & H.A.	07.74	1974	3	/	0	
FORSTER, Geoff P.	Middlesbrough	03.08.54	Winnybanks	Rochdale	N/C	1978	0	1	0	(F)
			Whitby T.	Hartlepool U.	05.80	1980	10	4	4	
FORSTER, Leslie J.	Newcastle	22.07.15	JNRS	Blackpool	*					(OR)
			TR	York C.	09.46	1946	10		2	
			TR	Gateshead	02.47	1946-47	15		3	
FORSTER, Mark E.	Middlesbrough	01.11.64	Guisborough	Leicester C.	06.83					(F)
			L	Darlington	03.84	1983	10	2	4	
FORSTER, Martyn G.	Kettering	01.02.63	Kettering	Northampton T.	10.83	1983	41	1	0	(D)
FORSTER, Ron	Norton	19.08.35	Shotton Col.	Darlington	05.56	1956-59	57		4	(F)
FORSTER, Stan	Aylesham	01.11.43	Margate	Crystal Palace	11.61	1962	2		0	(F)
FORSYTH, Alex	Swinton	05.02.52	Partick Thistle	Manchester U.	12.72	1972-77	99	2	4	(D)S-10/S.U23-1/S.F.LGE REP.
FORSYTH, Alex S.	Falkirk	29.09.28	Falkirk	Darlington	08.52	1952	26		7	(OL)
FORSYTH, Campbell	Plean	05.05.34	Kilmarnock	Southampton	12.65	1965-67	48	/	0	(G) S-4/S.F.LGE REP.
FORSYTH, Dave	Falkirk	05.05.45	Kirkintilloch	Orient	05.64	1965-66	32	/	0	(FB)
FORSYTH, John	Dumbarton	20.12.18	Luton T.(+)	New Brighton	07.46	1946-47	64		4	
			TR	Chester C.	07.48	1948	32		1	
FORSYTH, Mike E.	Liverpool	20.03.66	APP	W.B.A.	11.83	1983	8	/	0	(D)
FORSYTH, Robert	Belfast	27.02.25	Ballymoney	Bradford C.	07.48	1948	1		0	(OR)
FORSYTH, William A.	Glasgow	29.03.32		Blackburn Rov.	08.49					(FB)
			TR	Southport	07.52	1952-56	55		5	
FORT, Sam M.	Bentley	27.04.29	Retford T.	Walsall	02.54	1953-54	28		0	(FB) d.1976
FOSS, Sid R.	Barking	28.11.12	Southall	Chelsea	*	1946-47	15		0	(IF)
FOSTER, Alan	South Shields	20.11.34	Northwich Vic.	Crewe Alex.	07.60	1959-60	19		7	(F)
FOSTER, Anthony J.	Dublin	13.02.49	JNRS	Arsenal	02.66					(HB)
			TR	Oldham Ath.	09.66	1966-67	8	1	0	
FOSTER, Barry	Worksop	21.09.51	JNRS	Mansfield T.	07.70	1971-81	282	5	0	(D)E.YTH.INT.
FOSTER, Cliff	Wigan	14.01.31		Southport	AM	1951-52	10		2	
FOSTER, Colin	Nottingham	26.12.52	APP	Mansfield T.	12.70	1971-78	195	10	17	(D)Brother of Barry
			TR	Peterborough U.	06.79	1979-80	71	/	5	
FOSTER, Colin J.	Chislehurst	16.07.64	APP	Orient	02.82	1981-83	76	1	5	(D)
FOSTER, Emanuel	Woolstanton	04.12.21		Stoke C.	+	1946	1		0	(G)
FOSTER, George W.	Plymouth	26.09.56	APP	Plymouth Arg.	09.74	1973-81	201	11	6	(D)
			L	Torquay U.	10.76	1976	6	/	3	
			L	Exeter C.	12.81	1981	28	/	0	
			TR	Derby Co.	06.82	1982	30	/	0	
			TR	Mansfield T.	08.83	1983	42	/	0	
FOSTER, Karl A.	Birmingham	15.09.65	APP	Shrewsbury T.	09.83	1982	1	1	0	(F)
FOSTER, Mike	Leicester	03.02.39		Leicester C.	08.59					(F)
			TR	Colchester U.	05.61	1961	36		8	
			TR	Norwich C.	09.62					
			TR	Millwall	07.63	1963	13		2	
FOSTER, Robert J.	Sheffield	19.07.29	JNRS	Chesterfield	09.47	1948-50	4		0	(IF) E'B'-1
			TR	Preston N.E.	07.51	1951-56	99		40	
			TR	Rotherham U.	05.58	1958	1		0	
FOSTER, Ron E.	Islington	22.11.38	Clapton	Orient	03.57	1959-62	72		18	(IF)
			TR	Grimsby T.	12.62	1962-66	134	1	25	
			TR	Reading	07.66	1966-67	45	/	5	
			Dallas	Brentford	03.69	1968	3	1	0	
FOSTER, Steve B.	Portsmouth	24.09.57	APP	Portsmouth	10.75	1975-78	101	8	6	(D)E.U21-1/E-3
			TR	Brighton & H.A.	07.79	1979-83	171	1	6	
			TR	Aston Villa	03.84	1983	7	/	1	
FOSTER, Trevor	Walsall	11.01.41	JNRS	Walsall	07.59	1959-64	62		12	(IF)
FOSTER, Wayne P.	Leigh	11.09.63	APP	Bolton W.	08.81	1981-83	68	9	9	(F) E.YTH.INT.

Players Names	Birthplace	Date	Previous Club	League Club	Date Signed	Seasons Played	Career Record Apps	Sub	Gls	
FOSTER, Winston A.	Birmingham	01.11.41	JNRS	Birmingham C.	11.58	1960-68	152	1	2	(CH)
			L	Crewe Alex.	03.69	1968	13	/	0	
			TR	Plymouth Arg.	06.69	1969-70	33	/	0	
FOULDS, Albert	Salford	08.08.19	Yeovil T.	Chester C.	08.48	1948	31		14	(IF)
			TR	Rochdale	09.50	1950-52	62		24	
			TR	Crystal Palace	07.53	1953	17		4	
			TR	Crewe Alex.	01.54	1953	14		2	
FOULKES, Reg. E.	Shrewsbury	23.02.23		Walsall	+	1946-49	160		6	(CH) E.SCH.INT.
			TR	Norwich C.	05.50	1950-55	216		8	
FOULKES, William A.	St.Helens	05.01.32	Whiston BC	Manchester U.	08.51	1952-69	563	4	6	(FB) E-1/E.U23-2/E.F.LGE REP.●
FOULKES, William I.	Merthyr Tydfil	29.05.26		Cardiff C.	+					(IF) W-11
			Winsford	Chester C.	05.48	1948-51	118		14	
			TR	Newcastle U.	10.51	1951-53	58		8	
			TR	Southampton	08.54	1954	23		1	
			TR	Chester C.	07.56	1956-60	178		22	
FOUNTAIN, Jack	Leeds	27.05.32	Ashley Rd. F.C.	Sheffield U.	11.49	1950-55	31		0	(WH)
			TR	Swindon T.	01.57	1956-59	81		2	
			TR	York C.	08.60	1960-63	130		3	
FOWLER, Derek W.	Torquay	28.11.61		Torquay U.	03.84	1983	7	1	0	(M)
FOWLER, H. Norman	Stockton	03.09.19	South Bank	Middlesbrough	*					(FB) E.SCH.INT.
			TR	Hull C.	09.46	1946-49	52		0	
			TR	Gateshead	11.49	1949-51	64		0	
FOWLER, Jack	Rotherham	13.04.35		Sheffield U.	07.54					(F)
			TR	Halifax T.	06.56	1956-58	19		3	
FOWLER, John	Leith	17.10.33	Bonnyrigg	Colchester U.	06.55	1955-67	415	/	5	(FB)
FOWLER, Martin	York	17.01.57	APP	Huddersfield T.	01.74	1973-77	62	11	2	(M)
			TR	Blackburn Rov.	07.78	1978-79	36	2	0	
			L	Hartlepool U.	03.80	1979	6	/	0	
			TR	Stockport Co.	08.80	1980-81	74	1	6	
			TR	Scunthorpe U.	09.82	1982	15	3	0	
FOWLER, Tom	Prescot	16.12.24	Everton(AM)	Northampton T.	+	1946-61	521		82	(OL)●
			TR	Aldershot	61.12	1961-62	14		0	
FOX, Alan	Holywell	- 10.07.36		Wrexham	04.54	1953-63	350		3	(CH) W.U23-1
			TR	Hartlepool U.	06.64	1964-65	58	/	0	
			TR	Bradford C.	10.65	1965	33	/	0	
FOX, Geoff R.	Bristol	19.01.25	M.C.W.	Ipswich T.	+	1946	11		1	(FB)
			TR	Bristol Rov.	06.47	1947-54	306		2	
			TR	Swindon T.	10.55	1955-56	48		0	
FOX, Kevin	Sheffield	22.09.60	JNRS	Lincoln C.	03.78	1979	4	/	0	(G)
FOX, Oscar	Clowne	01.01.21		Sheffield Wed.	+	1946-49	44		3	(IF)
			TR	Mansfield T.	06.50.	1950-56	247		30	
FOX, Peter D.	Scunthorpe	05.07.57	APP	Sheffield W.	06.75	1972-76	49	/	0	(G)
			L	Barnsley	12.77	1977	1	/	0	
			TR	Stoke C.	03.78	1978-83	181	/	0	
FOX, Ray	Didsbury	13.12.34		Oldham Ath.	AM	1957	1		0	(OL)
FOX, Ray V.	Bristol	28.01.21	St. Aldheims	Bristol C.	10.46	1946-48	23		0	(FB)
FOX, Reg	Edmonton	16.10.29		Fulham	12.49					(FB)
			TR	Brighton & H.A.	10.52	1952-55	20		0	
FOX, Steve D.	Tamworth	17.02.58	APP	Birmingham C.	08.76	1976-78	26	3	1	(M)
			TR	Wrexham	12.78	1978-82	136	6	10	
			TR	Port Vale	10.82	1982-83	71	3	6	
FOX, Walter	Bolsover	10.04.21	Creswell Col.	Mansfield T.	05.46	1946-49	60		0	(FB)
FOXON, D. Neil	Nottingham	02.10.47	APP	Scunthorpe U.	08.65	1966-67	20	2	1	(W)
FOXTON, D. Graham	Harrogate	10.07.48	JNRS	Scunthorpe U.	10.67	1967-72	148	4	2	(FB)
FOXTON, Jack D.	Salford	17.06.21		Portsmouth	+	1946	1		0	
			TR	Swindon T.	09.48	1948-50	49		0	
FOY, John	Liverpool	28.05.50	Ormskirk	Southport	AM	1974	1	/	0	(OL)
FOYLE, Martin J.	Salisbury	02.05.63	APP	Southampton	08.80	1982-3	6	6	1	(F)
FRAIN, Peter A.	Birmingham	18.03.65	APP	W.B.A.	03.82	1983				(F)
			L	Mansfield T.	01.84	1983	1	1	0	
FRAME, William	Carluke	07.05.12	Shawfield J.	Leicester C.	*	1946-49	89		0	(FB)
FRAME, William J.	Castleford	01.08.39		Workington	11.58	1958	9		0	(G)
FRANCE, Anthony	Huddersfield	11.04.39	JNRS	Huddersfield T.	04.56	1957-59	9		2	(IF)
			TR	Darlington	12.61	1961-62	47		9	
			TR	Stockport Co.	07.63	1963	30		8	
FRANCE, Gary	Whitwell	18.06.55	APP	Sheffield U.	06.73	1973-74	1	1	0	(IF)
FRANCE, Gary L.	Stalybridge	05.05.46	Stalybridge	Burnley	04.66	1966-67	1	2	0	(F)
			TR	Bury	07.68	1968	0	1	0	
FRANCE, Jack	Stalybridge	30.11.13	Bath C.	Halifax T.	+	1946-47	50		1	(HB) *Swindon T.

Players Names	Birthplace	Date	Previous Club	League Club	Date Signed	Seasons Played	Apps	Sub	Gls	
FRANCE, Peter	Huddersfield	27.03.36		Huddersfield T.	09.56					(G)
			TR	Bradford P.A.	05.57	1957	16		0	
FRANCIS, Carl E.	West Ham	21.08.62	APP	Birmingham C.	08.80	1982	2	3	0	(F)
			L	Hereford U.	12.83	1983	5	/	0	
FRANCIS, George E.	Acton	04.02.34	JNRS	Brentford	01.53	1954-61	228		109	(CF)
			TR	Q.P.R.	05.61	1961	2		1	
			TR	Brentford	10.61	1961	32		14	
			TR	Gillingham	08.62	1962-63	51		19	
FRANCIS, Gerald	S. Africa	06.12.33	Johannesburg	Leeds U.	07.57	1957-61	48		9	(F)
			TR	York C.	10.61	1961	16		4	
FRANCIS, Gerry C.J.	Chiswick	06.12.51	APP	Q.P.R.	06.69	1969-78	289	4	53	(M)E-12/E.U23-6
			TR	Crystal Palace	07.79	1979-80	59	/	7	
			TR	Q.P.R.	02.80	1980-81	17	/	4	
			TR	Coventry C.	02.82	1981-82	50	/	2	
			TR	Exeter C.	08.83	1983	28	/	3	
FRANCIS, Keith R.	Yeovil	22.07.29	Yeovil T.	Orient	06.50	1950	3		0	(HB)
FRANCIS, Steve S.	Billericay	29.05.64	APP	Chelsea	04.82	1981-82	66	/	0	(G) E.YTH.INT.
FRANCIS, Terry	Hartlepool	18.06.43		Hartlepool U.	12.63	1963-64	18		4	(F)
FRANCIS, Thomas G.	Bermondsey	30.10.20	Cheltenham	Millwall	05.46	1946	1		0	
FRANCIS, Trevor J.	Plymouth	19.04.54	APP	Birmingham C.	05.71	1970-78	278	2	118	(F)E-43/E.U23-5/●
			TR	Nottingham F.	02.79	1978-81	69	1	28	E.YTH.INT.
			TR	Manchester C.	09.81	1981	26	/	12	
FRANCOMBE, Peter	Cardiff	04.08.63	Crystal Palace (APP)	Cardiff C.	09.81	1981	2	1	0	(D)
FRANKLIN, C. Neil	Stoke	24.01.22	JNRS	Stoke C.	*	1946-49	142		0	(CH) E-27/E.F.LGE REP.
			TR	Hull C.	02.51	1950-55	95		0	
			TR	Crewe Alex.	02.56	1955-57	66		4	
			TR	Stockport Co.	10.57	1957	20		0	
FRANKLIN, Graham N.	Bicester	25.01.57	Lowestoft	Southend U.	12.77	1977-78	1	5	1	(F)
FRANKLIN, John L.	Stockton	27.11.24	Bath C.	Darlington	08.47	1947	8		3	(OL) +Middlesbrough
FRANKLIN, Paul L.	Ilford	05.10.63	APP	Watford	08.81	1982-83	25	/	0	(D)
FRANKLIN, Stan T.	Shrewsbury	16.09.19	Kenwood J.	Blackpool	*					(FB)
			TR	Crewe Alex.	04.46	1946-47	28		0	
FRANKLIN, William	Tiverton	03.03.55	APP	Charlton Ath.	03.73	1972-74	13	/	0	(G)
FRANKS, Albert	Boldon	13.04.36	Boldon C.W.	Newcastle U.	12.53	1956-59	72		4	(WH)
			Glasgow Rgrs.	Lincoln C.	11.61	1961-62	58		5	
FRANKS, Colin	Wembley	16.04.51	JNRS	Watford	07.69	1969-72	99	14	8	(D)
			TR	Sheffield U.	07.73	1973-78	139	11	7	
FRANKS, Ken	Motherwell	24.04.44		Brighton & H.A.	06.62	1962	1		0	(OL)
FRASER, Andy	Newton Grange	29.08.40	Hearts	Hartlepool U.	10.61	1961-63	82		2	(CH)
FRASER, Cammie	Blackford	24.05.41	Dunfermline	Aston Villa	10.62	1962-63	17		1	(FB) S.U23-2
			TR	Birmingham C.	02.65	1964-65	38	1	0	
FRASER, David M.	Newton Grange	06.06.37	JNRS	Hull C.	07.54	1955-57	11		7	(F)
			TR	Mansfield T.	07.58	1958	6		1	
FRASER, Doug. M.	Aberdeen	08.12.41	Aberdeen	W.B.A.	09.63	1963-70	255	2	8	(FB) S-2
			TR	Nottingham F.	01.71	1970-72	85	/	3	
			TR	Walsall	07.73	1973	26	1	0	
FRASER, Gordon	Elgin	27.11.43	Forres	Cardiff C.	01.61	1962	4		0	(F)
			TR	Millwall	09.63	1963	5		0	
			Barry T.	Newport Co.	08.66	1966	11	2	2	
FRASER, James	Coatbridge	17.11.32	Bellshill Ath.	Barrow	03.58	1957-58	32		0	(FB)
FRASER, John	London	12.07.53	APP	Fulham	06.71	1971-75	54	1	1	(D)
			TR	Brentford	07.76	1976-79	121	2	6	
FRASER, John W.	Belfast	15.09.38	Glentoran	Sunderland	03.59	1958-59	22		1	(IF)
			TR	Portsmouth	06.60	1960	1		0	
			Margate	Watford	07.62	1962-63	24		3	
FRASER, Ronnie	Glasgow	23.01.17	Hibernian	Newcastle U.	01.47	1946-48	26		0	(CH)
FRASER, William	Edinburgh	12.08.45	JNRS	Huddersfield T.	04.63	1963-64	8		2	(F)
FRASER, Willie A.	Australia	24.02.29	Airdrie	Sunderland	03.54	1953-58	127		0	(G) S-2
			TR	Nottingham F.	12.58	1958	2		0	
FREAR, Brian	Cleckheaton	08.07.33	JNRS	Huddersfield T.	09.50	1951-56	37		10	(IF)
			TR	Chesterfield	02.57	1956-63	281		85	
			TR	Halifax T.	07.64	1964	35		5	
FREEBURN, William	Dunfermline	07.04.30	E.Stirling	Grimsby T.	08.51	1951-54	34		0	(FB)
FREEMAN, Alf	Bethnal Green	02.01.20		Southampton	+	1946	7		2	
			TR	Crystal Palace	08.48	1948	1		0	
FREEMAN, Anthony	Melton Mowbray	29.08.28	Melton T.	Notts.Co.	+	1946-49	43		2	(OR)

Players Names	Birthplace	Date	Previous Club	League Club	Date Signed	Seasons Played	Career Record Apps	Sub	Gls	
FREEMAN, Don R.	Dartford	29.08.21	Dartford T.	Charlton Ath.	+					(HB)
			TR	Bristol C.	05.49	1949	8		0	
			TR	Watford	11.50					
			TR	Gillingham	06.51					
FREEMAN, Henry G.	Woodstock	04.11.18	Woodstock T.	Fulham	*	1946-51	178		6	(FB)
				Walsall	10.52	1952	20		1	
FREEMAN, Neil	Northampton	16.02.55	JNRS	Arsenal	06.72					(G)
			TR	Grimsby T.	03.74	1973-75	33	/	0	
			TR	Southend U.	07.76	1976-77	69	/	0	
			TR	Birmingham C.	07.78	1978-79	31	/	0	
			L	Walsall	08.80	1980	8	/	0	
			L	Huddersfield T.	01.81	1980	18	/	0	
			TR	Peterborough U.	09.81	1981	41	/	0	
			TR	Northampton T.	N/C	1982	22	/	0	
FREEMAN, Neville F.	Briseworth	25.01.25		Northampton T.	10.49	1950	1		0	(G)
FREEMAN, Percy	Redditch	04.07.45	Stourbridge	W.B.A.	04.68	1969	2	1	0	(F)
			TR	Lincoln C.	06.70	1970-72	76	4	30	
			TR	Reading	01.73	1972-74	53	7	13	
			TR	Lincoln C.	01.75	1974-76	62	10	34	
FREESTONE, Trevor	Market Bosworth	16.02.54	JNRS	Peterborough U.	01.73	1972	2	1	1	(IF)
FRENCH, George N.	Colchester	10.11.26		Colchester U.	AM	1952-53	3		0	
FRENCH, Graham E.	Wolverhampton	06.04.45	APP	Shrewsbury T.	11.62	1961-62	27		1	(OR) E.YTH.INT.
			TR	Swindon T.	08.63	1963	5		0	
			TR	Watford	08.64	1964	4		0	
			Wellington	Luton T.	10.65	1965-72	179	2	22	
			L	Reading	11.73	1973	3	/	0	
				Southport	03.76	1975	2	/	0	
FRENCH, Jim R.	Stockton	27.01.26		Middlesbrough	+					(IF)
				Northampton T.	08.51	1951	1		0	
			TR	Darlington	08.53	1953-54	52		8	
FRENCH, John W.	Stockton	19.01.25		Middlesbrough	+					(WH) Brother of Jim R.
			TR	Southend U.	02.47	1946-52	182		20	
			TR	Nottingham F.	11.52	1952-55	80		8	
			TR	Southend U.	07.56	1956	5		0	
FRENCH, Mick J.	Eastbourne	07.05.55	APP	Q.P.R.	08.74					(F)E.YTH.INT.
			TR	Brentford	02.75	1974-76	56	9	16	
			TR	Swindon T.	02.77	1976-77	5	5	1	
			TR	Doncaster Rov.	07.78	1978	36	/	5	
			TR	Aldershot	05.79	1979-81	70	4	16	
			TR	Rochdale	08.82	1982	35	1	11	
FRENCH, Ray	Wigton	16.12.46	Wigton	Workington	AM	1973	2	/	0	(CH)
FRETWELL, Dave	Normanton	18.02.52	JNRS	Bradford C.	11.72	1970-77	247	6	5	(D)
			TR	Wigan Ath.	10.78	1978-80	111	1	0	
FRIAR, J. Paul	Glasgow	06.06.63	APP	Leicester C.	08.80	1980-82	56	2	0	(D)
			TR	Rotherham U.	02.83	1982-83	20		0	
FRIDAY, Robin	London	27.07.52	Hayes	Reading	02.74	1973-76	121	0	46	(F)
			TR	Cardiff C.	12.76	1976-77	20	1	6	
FRIDAY, Terry J.	Sittingbourne	01.05.36		Gillingham	AM	1960	2		0	(G)
FRIEDMANIS, Edward	Latvia	22.02.20	Peterborough	Northampton T.	06.49	1948-49	19		4	(CF) LATVIAN INT.
FRIEL, Bernard	Glasgow	16.09.41	Dumbarton	Southend U.	06.63	1963-64	17		8	(F)
FRIEL, John P.	Glasgow	01.09.23	T.Lanark	New Brighton	06.50	1950	3		0	
			Q. of South	Torquay U.	10.52					
FRIEL, Peter	Wishaw	27.08.39	Cambuslang Rgrs.	Workington	08.61	1961	4		0	(W)
FRIEND, Barry	London	13.10.51	Leatherhead	Fulham	10.73	1973	2	1	0	(IF) E.AMAT.INT.
FRITH, David W.M.	Liverpool	17.03.29	JNRS	Blackpool	05.49	1952-56	32		0	(FB)
			TR	Tranmere Rov.	08.58	1958-62	177		0	
FRITH, William	Sheffield	09.06.12	Chesterfield(*)	Coventry C.	*	1946	7		0	(WH)*Worksop/Mansfield T.
FRIZZELL, Jimmy L.	Greenock	16.02.37	Morton	Oldham Ath.	05.60	1960-69	309	9	57	(WH)
FROGGATT, John L.	Stanton Hill	13.12.45	E. Kirkby M.W.	Notts. Co.	06.64	1963-64	4		0	(F)
			Boston U.	Colchester U.	07.74	1974-77	155	0	29	
			TR	Port Vale	02.78	1977-78	12	2	3	
			TR	Northampton T.	09.78	1978	42	0	13	
FROGGATT, Jack	Sheffield	17.11.22		Portsmouth	+	1946-53	279		65	(WH) E-1/E.F.LGE REP./
			TR	Leicester C.	03.54	1953-57	143		18	Cousin of Redfern
FROGGATT, Redfern	Sheffield	23.08.24	Sheffield YMCA	Sheffield Wed.	+	1946-59	434		138	(IF) E-4/E'B'-/E.F.LGE REP./●Son of famous player
FROST, Brian P.	Sheffield	05.06.38	Oswestry T.	Chesterfield	05.59	1959-64	102		15	(F)
FROST, Des	Congleton	03.08.26	Congleton T.	Leeds U.	04.49	1949-50	10		2	(CF)
			TR	Halifax T.	01.51	1950-53	117		55	
			TR	Rochdale	11.53	1953-54	16		6	
			TR	Crewe Alex.	09.54	1954-55	42		12	

Players Names	Birthplace	Date	Previous Club	League Club	Date Signed	Seasons Played	Apps	Sub	Gls	
FROST, John	Wallsend	13.02.20	North Shields	Grimsby T.	+					(G)
			TR	York C.	07.48	1948-51	45		0	
FROST, Lee A.	Woking	04.12.57	APP	Chelsea	07.76	1977-79	11	3	5	(F)
			L	Brentford	10.78	1978	5	1	0	
			TR	Brentford	12.80	1980	15	/	3	
FROST, Ron A.	Hazel Grove	16.01.47	APP	Manchester C.	05.64	1963	2		1	(F)
FROST, Stan. D.	Northampton	19.10.22	Northampton T.(+)	Leicester C.	+					(OR)
			TR	Northampton T.	01.47	1946	6		1	
FROWEN, John	Trelewis	11.10.31	Tredomen	Cardiff C.	05.51	1952-57	35		0	(CH)
			TR	Bristol Rov.	08.58	1958-62	84		0	
			TR	Newport Co.	03.63	1962-65	67	1	0	
FRUDE, Roger G.	Plymouth	19.11.46	APP	Bristol Rov.	12.64	1963-67	38	3	8	(F)
			TR	Mansfield T.	09.67	1967-68	15	1	0	
			TR	Brentford	07.69	1969	1	1	0	
FRY, Barry F.	Bedford	07.04.45	APP	Manchester U.	04.62					(IF) E.SCH.INT.
			TR	Bolton W.	05.64	1964	3		1	
			TR	Luton T.	07.65	1965	6	/	0	
			Gravesend	Orient	12.66	1966	2	1	0	
			Bedford T.	Orient	06.67	1967	5	4	0	
FRY, David	Bournemouth	05.01.60	APP	Crystal Palace	01.77	1977-82	40	/	0	(G)
			TR	Gillingham	07.83	1983	38	/	0	
FRY, Keith F.	Cardiff	11.04.41	JNRS	Newport Co.	10.58	1958-61	58		2	(OR) W.SCH.INT.
			TR	Notts.Co.	02.62	1961-63	73		9	
			Merthyr Tydfil	Chesterfield	01.66	1965	2	/	0	
FRY, Robert P.	Pontypridd	29.06.35		Crystal Palace	04.56	1955	6		0	(G)
			Bath C.	Q.P.R.	08.57	1957	1		0	
FRY, Roger	Southampton	18.08.48		Southampton	10.67	1970-71	23	/	0	(D)
			TR	Walsall	07.73	1973-76	120	/	1	
FRYATT, Jim E.	Southampton	02.09.40	JNRS	Charlton Ath.	10.57	1959	5		3	(CF)●
			TR	Southend U.	06.60	1960-62	61		24	
			TR	Bradford P.A.	06.63	1963-65	101	/	38	
			TR	Southport	03.66	1965-66	39	/	15	
			TR	Torquay U.	03.67	1966-67	27	/	11	
			TR	Stockport Co.	10.67	1967-68	44	/	28	
			TR	Blackburn Rov.	10.68	1968-69	29	8	5	
			TR	Oldham Ath.	02.70	1969-71	76	/	40	
			TR	Southport	11.71	1971-73	102	6	24	
			TR	Stockport Co.	09.74	1974	1	/	1	
			TR	Torquay U.	12.74	1973-74	4	/	0	
FRYE, John	Ardrossan	27.07.33	St.Mirren	Sheffield Wed.	01.61					(F)
			TR	Tranmere Rov.	10.61	1961	21		6	
FRYER, John H.	Manchester	24.06.24	Goslings FC	Oldham Ath.	04.47	1947	9		3	(CF)
FUCCILLO, Pasquale	Bedford	02.05.56	APP	Luton T.	07.74	1974-82	153	7	24	(M)
			Tulsa R.	Southend U.	12.83	1983	19	4	2	
FUDGE, Mick H.	Bristol	05.12.45	APP	W.B.A.	12.63	1963-64	13		5	(IF)
			TR	Exeter C.	06.67	1967	32	4	6	
FULLAM, John	Dublin	22.03.40	Home Farm	Preston N.E.	10.58	1959-60	49		6	(WH) EI-11/EI'B'-1
FULLBROOK, John F.	London	15.07.18	Plymouth Arg.(+)	Orient	+	1946-47	36		1	
FULLER, William	Brixton	06.04.44	JNRS	Crystal Palace	01.63	1962-64	3		0	(FB)
FULLERTON, George	Ballymena	14.06.39	Glentoran	Leeds U.	05.58					(G)
			Distillery	Barrow	07.60	1960	12		0	
FULTON, Bryce	Prestwick	07.08.35		Manchester U.	03.53					(FB)
			TR	Plymouth Arg.	08.57	1957-63	176		0	
			TR	Exeter C.	07.64	1964-65	37	/	0	
				Stockport Co.	01.67					
FULTON, Ray H.	Hendon	24.09.53	West Ham U.(APP)	Orient	08.72	1972	1	/	0	(FB)
FUNNELL, Anthony	Eastbourne	20.08.57	Eastbourne	Southampton	01.77	1977-78	13	4	8	(F)
			TR	Gillingham	03.79	1978-79	27	6	10	
			TR	Brentford	03.80	1979-80	29	3	8	
			TR	Bournemouth	09.81	1981-82	59	5	22	
FURIE, John P.C.	Hammersmith	13.05.48	APP	Watford	05.66	1966	0	1	0	(FB)
			TR	Gillingham	07.67	1967	17	/	0	
FURNELL, Jim	Clitheroe	23.11.37	JNRS	Burnley	11.54	1959-60	2		0	(G)
			TR	Liverpool	02.62	1961-63	28		0	
			TR	Arsenal	11.63	1963-67	141	/	0	
			TR	Rotherham U.	09.68	1968-69	76	/	0	
			TR	Plymouth Arg.	12.70	1970-75	183	/	0	
FURNESS, William I.	Washington	08.06.09	Leeds U.(*)	Norwich C.	*	1946	12		3	(IF) *E-1/Unsworth Col./ d.1980
FURNISS, Fred	Sheffield	10.07.22	Hallam T.	Sheffield U.	+	1946-54	279		14	(FB)
			TR	Chesterfield	08.55					

Players Names	Birthplace	Date	Previous Club	League Club	Date Signed	Seasons Played	Career Record Apps	Sub	Gls	
FURPHY, Ken	Stockton	28.05.31		Everton	11.50					(WH)●
			Runcorn	Darlington	08.53	1953-61	316		5	
			TR	Workington	07.62	1962-64	105		3	
			TR	Watford	11.64	1964-67	95	6	1	
FURSDON, Alan	Grantham	16.10.47		Swindon T.	09.65					(FB)
				Oxford U.	05.67	1968	0	1	0	
FURY, Paul	Swansea	16.03.55	APP	Swansea C.	APP	1971-72	11	/	0	(FB) W.SCH.INT.
FUSCHILLO, Paul	London	20.10.48	Wycombe W.	Blackpool	07.71	1971-73	8	3	0	(FB) E.AMAT.INT.
			TR	Brighton & H.A.	02.74	1973-74	17	/	1	
FUTCHER, Graham	Chester	15.06.53		Chester C.	08.71	1971-72	5	5	0	(CF) Brother of Ron/Paul
FUTCHER, Paul	Chester	25.09.56	APP	Chester C.	01.74	1972-73	20	/	0	(D)E.U21-11
			TR	Luton T.	06.74	1974-77	131	/	1	
			TR	Manchester C.	06.78	1978-79	36	/	0	
			TR	Oldham Ath.	08.80	1980-82	98	/	1	
			TR	Derby Co.	01.83	1982-83	35	/	0	
			TR	Barnsley	03.84	1983	10	/	0	
FUTCHER, Ron	Chester	25.09.56	APP	Chester C.	01.74	1973	4	/	0	(F) Twin of Paul/
			TR	Luton T.	07.74	1974-77	116	4	40	Brother of Graham
			TR	Manchester C.	08.78	1978	10	7	7	

ALEX ELDER (Burnley, Stoke C. & N. Ireland)
A terrific full back acquisition from Glentoran when only 18, Elder signed for Burnley after making rapid progress in the Irish League. He gained a Championship medal in his first playing season, 1959/60, followed by a runner-up medal from the losing F.A. Cup Final against the mighty Spurs in 1962. He was very unfortunate in later breaking an ankle which hindered his first team prospects with the "Clarets." Eventually he moved on to Stoke City in August 1967, playing on an irregular first team basis as a valued member of the squad. He was picked 40 times for Northern Ireland, for whom he displayed great powers of recovery allied to first class tackling ability.

FRED ELSE (Preston NE./Blackburn Rov./Barrow)
A consistently sound custodian, only 5ft 8in tall, Else epitomised the art of positional play and kept the North End net intact for long periods. Apart from representing England "B", he was never rewarded by further International recognition during a career spent mainly in the First Division until leaving Blackburn Rovers for Barrow in July 1966. He played nearly 150 games for the Third Division side before relegation sent them down, coinciding with Fred Else's last League appearance. On reflection he rates amongst the best keepers of that period.

TONY EMERY (Lincoln C./Mansfield T.)
A clubman who graduated from school right through the ranks, being the nephew of Fred Emery, a well known manager of the day. He did not need much help from the family, settling into the hub of the defence at centre half. Well built, over 6ft tall, Emery was watched consistently in his early days by a posse of scouts, but for some obscure reason did not end up in the First Division. In 1947/8 was a member of the side that gained promotion to the Second Division, and just as quickly returned, but in 1951/2 he gained a Third Division North medal. He left Sincil Bank in June 1958 for Mansfield Town.

MIKE ENGLAND (Blackburn Rov., Tottenham H. & Wales/Cardiff C.)
A tall defender, England developed with Blackburn Rovers junior sides, not establishing himself as a regular until 1963/4 despite having being capped at under 23 level previously. He became a tremendous centre half of quality – cool, calm and collected – with great skill for one of giant stature. Spurs reckoned the young man to be one of the key players to rebuild their once famous side, signing him for £95,000 in August 1966. Within a year, he had picked up an F.A. Cup Final winners medal against Chelsea. After playing 300 League games for Tottenham, he decided to finish his career back in his native Wales with Cardiff City.

BOBBY EVANS (Chelsea & Scotland/Newport Co.)
Wherever the fray was at its thickest red haired Bobby Evans, although only 5½ ft high, would be found deep in the heart of battle. He made his name long before coming to England near the end of a brilliant career. He played for Scotland in 48 full International appearances, starting in 1949 against the "old enemy" England. Although his best position was wing half for Celtic, in 1957, when George Young retired, the National side converted Bobby to the centre of the defence. Coming to Chelsea in 1960 was not very successful and after a season he moved on as player manager to Newport County.

GEORGE FARM (Blackpool & Scotland)
An unorthdox but effective black vested goalkeeper, Farm became custodian of the Blackpool net after signing from Hibernian in September 1948 for a moderate fee. With diligent practice he was finally capped by his country four years later, appearing ten times in all in 1951. He was on the losing side in the Cup Final, when on the receiving end of Jackie Milburn's vicious shooting for Newcastle, but was back in 1953/4 for the greatest Final of them all against Bolton. Within seconds he had been beaten by a soft shot from Nat Lofthouse, but the team recovered, winning eventually 4-3. He is one of the few goalies to score goals against the opposition – three in all.

PETER FARRELL (Everton & Eire/Tranmere Rov.)
Farrell was signed by Everton from Shamrock Rovers as a wing half for the future, although it was as an inside right when playing for the Republic at Goodison Park that he scored a goal which beat England. He was a tireless worker, cajoling the team wherever needed, fully justifying the captaincy. He played for his country 28 times before following Tommy Egglington once again, this time to Tranmere Rovers, to spend the "evensong" of his career. He spent three seasons and played well over 100 games as captain, as energetically as ever, before retiring.

ALAN FINNEY (Sheffield Wed./Doncaster Rov.)
No relative to the immortal Tom, Alan was a brilliant Hillsboro wing product in his own right, going on to play over 450 games for Wednesday before finishing his League career with Doncaster in 1966/7. Really elusive and tricky in his prime, with an adroit turn of pace which bewildered the best of defences, Alan became well known for his partnership with the "golden boy" Albert Quixall. He wasn't far removed from the International scene, but settled for England "B" and under 23 honours as well as two Second Division medals.

TOM FINNEY (Preston NE. & England)
Arguably the greatest England wing forward of all time, Finney played in the shadow of the also great Stan Matthews, and was still able to exercise his own brilliance to loud acclaim. Joining Prestron in 1937, he turned pro in 1940 after being an apprentice plumber and was thereafter known as the "Preston Plumber". In a long career the only honours won with his home club were in the form of runners-up medals. He made up for that by playing over 75 times for England in full internationals, scoring 30 goals. Preston experimented by using Tom at centre forward, and he scored 26 goals in 1957/8. He will be remembered for his all round performances, being two footed and a scintillating dribbler. Twice in 1954 and 1958 Tom was player of the year.

RON FLOWERS (Wolverhampton W. & England/Northampton T.)
A fair haired young Wolves prodigy who developed in that famous nursery Wath Wanderers, Flowers made his debut in 1951/2 only two months after signing on the dotted line. Well-built, strong, remarkably consistent, he was first picked for England in 1955, not playing again until 1958, then going on to collect 49 caps. An automatic member of the great Wolves side of the 1950s which gained prestige at the expense of the foreigners, he was seen by the media as a carbon copy of Billy Wright. Later in his career he helped the once great Wolves weather the storm when their glory days had ended, before joining Northampton Town in September 1967.

BRIAN FLYNN (Burnley, Leeds U., Burnley & Wales)
Small, only 5ft 3in tall, but stocky and durable, Flynn has developed into an outstanding midfielder and is well on the way to collecting 70 Welsh International caps. He was produced by the famous Burnley nursery, following a long line of highly individualistic midfield artists, and signed professional in October 1972 after starring in the Welsh schoolboy side. In November 1977 he was allowed to leave Turf Moor for Leeds United, who were looking to replace their long standing midfield partnership. After a period on loan was allowed to rejoin Burnley in November 1982, where he is still going strong.

TREVOR FORD (Swansea C., Aston Villa, Sunderland, Cardiff C. & Wales/Newport Co.)
A fiery and explosive centre forward, Ford was always involved in action packed goalmouth scenes. Signing for the "Swans" during the war, he was quickly snapped up by Aston Villa in 1947 and then created a major sensation by being the first £30,000 transfer in a 1950 move to Sunderland. Playing nearly 40 games for Wales, he was seen to great effect in their red shirt. At League level many goalies got the full impact of his well proportioned shoulders in the days of the old fashioned shoulder barge, whilst two footed shooting efforts on sight of the target made sure that no one could relax. After joining Cardiff he later moved on to Eindhoven of Holland, returning to finish his career with lowly Newport in 1960.

BILL FOULKES (Manchester U. & England)
Tall and long legged, Foulkes rendered valuable service at Old Trafford; whether at full back or centre half in playing over 550 League games. He came to the fore after being spotted playing for a boys club and became a regular in 1953/4, going on quickly to win his only England cap. He was one of the survivors of the horrific Munich air disaster, and on returning to England captained United in the gallant attempt to win the F.A. Cup against Bolton, after being runners up the year previously. He finally gained a winners medal in 1963 to go with four League Championship medals. He was a member of United's European Cup winning side that defeated Benfica of Portugal in 1968.

TOM FOWLER (Northampton T./Aldershot)
An outside left, Fowler was on the books of Everton during the war, before turning pro with the "Cobblers". A fast running, direct player, he became a great favourite with the locals, playing consistently for 15 seasons, and notching up a club record of 521 appearances before leaving for Aldershot. In four consecutive seasons, he was ever present, always seemingly able to conjure up important goals, and was a vital member of the 1949/50 side that got to the fifth round, being beaten by their First Division opponents.

TREVOR FRANCIS (Birmingham C., Nottingham F., Manchester C. & England)
Nottingham Forest splashed out £1,000,000 for the highly skilled forward Trevor Francis in February 1979, when recruiting him from Birmingham City to assist in the winning of further club honours. Three months later he scored the only goal which decided the European Cup Final against Malmo of Sweden and the following year was a member of the Forest side that achieved success once again in winning the European Cup for the second year running. A regular member of the England side, injuries permitting, he did not gain his first cap until 1977, an indictment on the state of English soccer. He was transfered to Sampdoria for a large fee in the summer of 1982.

REDFERN FROGGATT (Sheffield Wed. & England)
A cousin of the ebullient Jack Froggatt, Redfern also had a father who was a pre-war Sheffield Wednesday star. Tall, blond, with great constructive ability, specialising in the crossfield pass, he was the driving force behind the "Owls" for over 15 seasons. As a regular member of the side, he must have felt like a yo-yo, being either promoted or relegated from First to Second Division seven times in all after the war. In that period he won three Second Division medals. The first of his four England caps came in 1952/3. He also played for England "B" as well as representing the Football League. He scored 138 League goals in a career during which he played mainly in a midfield role.

JIM FRYATT (Charlton Ath./Southend U./Bradford Pk. Av./Southport/Torquay U./Stockport Co./Blackburn Rov./Oldham Ath./Southport/Stockport Co./Torquay U.)
A well built leader of the attack, Fryatt created the fastest scoring record in history when netting after only four seconds for Bradford against Tranmere Rovers on 25 April 1964, the time being confirmed by the referee. He might also be amongst the record holders for the number of clubs for which he appeared. He scored nearly 200 goals during his playing career, although whilst with Southend he played at full back. He started out at the Valley, waiting two years to make his debut in 1959/60. He was very popular amongst players and fans alike on his wanderings.

KEN FURPHY
(Everton/Darlington/Workington/Watford)
Furphy never made the grade with Everton, going into the Cheshire League with Runcorn. Darlington spotted his potential and signed him in August 1953; Furphy went on to play more than 300 games, mainly as a wing half. One of the great highlights of his career was in helping the "Quakers" defeat Chelsea in the fourth round of the F.A. Cup following a replay in 1957/8. He became one of the youngest player managers when signing for Workington in 1962, eventually transferring himself to Watford in a similar capacity, later going on to become a fully fledged manager on finishing his playing career.

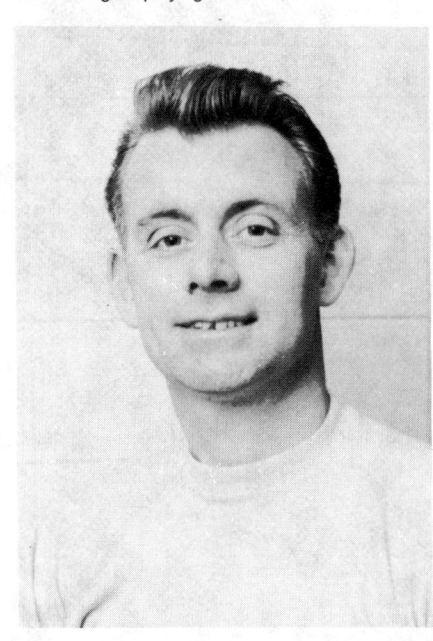

Players Names	Birthplace	Date	Previous Club	League Club	Date Signed	Seasons Played	Career Record Apps	Sub	Gls	
GABRIEL, Jimmy	Dundee	16.10.40	Dundee	Everton	03.60	1959-66	255	1	33	(WH)S-2/S.U23-6/
			TR	Southampton	07.67	1967-71	190	1	26	S.SCH.INT.●
			TR	Bournemouth	07.72	1972-73	53	/	4	
			L	Swindon T.	10.73	1973	6	/	0	
			TR	Brentford	03.74	1973	9	/	0	
GADDES, Robert	Byfleet	27.09.41	JNRS	Portsmouth	06.60	1959	1		0	(G) E.YTH.INT.
GADSBY, Ken J.	Chesterfield	03.07.16	Scarborough	Leeds U.	*	1946-47	40		0	
GADSBY, Mick	Oswestry	01.08.47	Ashbourne	Notts. Co.	01.68	1967	11	/	0	(G)
			TR	York C.	07.69	1969	13	/	0	
			L	Grimsby T.	09.70	1970	2	/	0	
			L	Bradford C.	12.70	1970	6	/	0	
			TR	Hartlepool U.	07.71	1971	21	/	0	
GADSTON, Joe E.	London	13.09.45	West Ham U.(AM)	Brentford	08.64					(CF)
			Cheltenham T.	Bristol Rov.	06.68	1968	9	1	5	
			TR	Exeter C.	11.69	1969-71	85	/	30	
			TR	Aldershot	07.72	1972	2	2	0	
			L	Hartlepool U.	02.73	1972	1	/	0	
GAFFNEY, Terry	Hartlepool	15.02.52	Billingham	Hartlepool U.	07.77	1977	10	3	1	(F)
GAGE, Albert	London	20.09.22	Fulham(+)	Aldershot	07.46	1946-47	39		0	(G) +Walthamstow
			Canada	Fulham	08.48	1948	3		0	
			TR	Gillingham	06.50	1950	40		0	
GAGE, Kevin W.	London	21.04.64	APP	Wimbledon	01.82	1980-83	48	20	9	(M)E.YTH.INT.
GAGE, Wakeley A.J.	Northampton	05.05.58	Desborough	Northampton T.	10.79	1979-83	173	2	13	(CH)
GAGER, Horace E.	London	25.01.17	Vauxhall M.	Luton T.	*	1946-47	59		2	(CH)
			TR	Nottingham F.	02.48	1947-54	258		11	
GAILLARD, Marcel J.	Belgium	15.01.27	Tonbridge	Crystal Palace	02.48	1947-49	22		3	(W)
			TR	Portsmouth	02.51	1950-52	58		7	
GALBRAITH, Walter	Glasgow	26.05.18	Clyde	New Brighton	09.48	1948-50	109		1	
			TR	Grimsby T.	08.51	1951-52	77		0	
			TR	Accrington St.	06.53	1953	21		0	
GALE, Anthony	London	19.11.59	APP	Fulham	08.77	1977-83	277	/	19	(D)E.U'21-1
GALE, Colin M.	Pontypridd	31.08.32	JNRS	Cardiff C.	07.50	1953-55	12		0	(WH)
			TR	Northampton T.	03.56	1955-60	212		1	
GALE, Darren	Port Talbot	25.10.63	APP	Swansea C.	10.80	1981-83	26	10	6	(F)
GALE, Ian J.	Slough	03.03.61	APP	Millwall	03.78	1978	4	1	0	(D)
GALE, Tom	Durham	04.01.20	Gateshead(AM)	Sheffield Wed.	+	1946	6		0	(CH)
			TR	York C.	08.47	1947-48	76		0	
GALL, Norman	Wallsend	30.09.42	Gateshead	Brighton & H.A.	03.62	1962-73	427	12	5	(CH)
GALLACHER, Connor	Derry	25.04.22	Lochee Harp.	Middlesbrough	01.47	1946	1		0	(IF)
			TR	Hull C.	05.47	1947	18		3	
			TR	Rochdale	03.48	1947	6		1	
GALLACHER, Pat	Glasgow	09.01.13	Blackburn Rov.(*)	Bournemouth	*	1946-47	21		2	(IF) d.1983
GALLAGHER, Barry P.	Bradford	07.04.61	APP	Bradford C.	04.79	1977-82	66	5	22	(F)
			L	Mansfield T.	01.83	1982	2	1	0	
			TR	Halifax T.	03.83	1982-83	42	3	14	
GALLAGHER, Brian	Oldham	22.07.38	Ashton U.	Bury	10.56	1957-64	130		1	(FB)
			TR	Carlisle U.	05.65	1965-66	42	2	1	
			TR	Stockport Co.	07.67	1967	13	/	0	
GALLAGHER, Jack C.	Wisbech	06.04.58	March T.	Lincoln C.	02.76	1976	1	/	0	(F)
			Wisbech	Peterborough U.	08.80	1979-80	11	2	1	
			Hong Kong	Torquay U.	N/C	1982	38	4	7	
GALLAGHER, James	Bury	02.09.11	Notts Co.(coach)	Exeter C.	09.48	1948	1		0	(CH) *Bury/Notts.Co.
GALLAGHER, Joe	Liverpool	11.01.55	APP	Birmingham Co.	01.72	1973-80	281	5	17	(D)
			TR	Wolverhampton W.	08.81	1981-82	31	/	0	
			TR	West Ham U.	12.82	1982	8	1	0	
			TR	Burnley	08.83	1983	1	/	0	
			L	Halifax T.	10.83	1983	4	/	0	
GALLAGHER, Mike	Cambuslang	16.01.32	Benburb FC	Bolton W.	01.52					(OL) d.1975
			TR	W.B.A.	12.52	1952	1		0	
GALLANT, David	Middlesbrough	12.10.49	JNRS	Leeds U.	12.66					(F)
			L	Darlington	01.68	1967	1	/	0	
GALLEGO, Antonio	Spain	02.06.24	Abbey U.	Norwich C.	03.47	1946	1		0	(G)
GALLEGO, Jose	Spain	08.04.23	Abbey U.	Brentford	01.47	1946-47	6		0	(OL) Brother to Antonio
			TR	Southampton	05.48	1948	1		0	
			TR	Colchester U.	N/L	1950	4		0	
GALLEY, Gordon W.	Worksop	04.02.30	JNRS	Sheffield Wed.	06.47					
			TR	Darlington	10.48	1948-51	60		12	
GALLEY, John	Clowne	07.05.44	JNRS	Wolverhampton W.	05.61	1962-64	5	/	2	(F)
			TR	Rotherham U.	12.64	1974-67	112	/	48	
			TR	Bristol C.	12.67	1967-72	174	/	82	
			TR	Nottingham F.	12.72	1972-74	31	6	6	
			L	Peterborough U.	10.74	1974	7	/	1	
			TR	Hereford T.	12.74	1974-76	77	3	10	

Players Names	Birthplace	Date	Previous Club	League Club	Date Signed	Seasons Played	Apps	Sub	Gls	
GALLEY, Keith	Worksop	17.10.55	Morecambe	Southport	12.75	1975-76	50	10	11	(F)
GALLEY, Maurice	Clowne	10.08.34	JNRS	Chesterfield	07.52	1954-58	55		5	(WH)
GALLEY, Tom	Hednesford	04.08.15	Cannock T.	Wolverhampton W.	*	1946-47	41		5	(IF)E-2/E.F.LGE REP.
			TR	Grimsby T.	11.47	1947-48	33		2	
GALLIER, William H.	Cannock	24.04.32	Beaudesert Spts.	W.B.A.	07.53					(LH)
			TR	Walsall	06.55	1955	10		0	
GALLIERS, Steve	Fulwood	21.08.57	Chorley	Wimbledon	08.77	1977-81	148	7	10	(M)
			TR	Crystal Palace	10.81	1981	8	5	0	
			TR	Wimbledon	08.82	1982-83	69	1	3	
GALLIMORE, Len	Winnington	14.09.13	Preston N.E.(*)	Watford	*	1946	8		0	(FB) *Liverpool/d.1978
GALLOGLY, Charlie	Banbridge	16.06.25	Glenavon	Huddersfield T.	12.49	1949-51	76		0	(FB) N1-2
			TR	Watford	08.52	1952-53	47		0	
			TR	Bournemouth	07.54					
GALLON, John W.	Newcastle,	12.02.14	Swansea C.(+)	Gateshead	+	1946	20		2	(IF)*Bradford C./ Bradford P.A.
GALLOWAY, John	Bo'ness	29.10.18	Glasgow Rgrs.	Chelsea	08.46	1946-47	4		0	(IF)
GALLOWAY, Mike	Oswestry	30.05.65		Mansfield T.	09.83	1983	12	5	0	(D)
GALVIN, Anthony	Huddersfield	12.07.56	Goole T.	Tottenham H.	01.78	1978-83	113	3	12	(F)EI-3
GALVIN, Chris	Huddersfield	24.11.51	APP	Leeds U.	11.68	1969-72	7	1	0	(M) E.YTH.INT/
			TR	Hull C.	08.73	1973-78	132	11	11	Brother of Tony
			L	York C.	12.76	1976	22	/	6	
			TR	Stockport Co.	04.79	1978-80	67	1	3	
GALVIN, Dave	Denaby	05.10.46	JNRS	Wolverhampton W.	05.65	1968	5	/	0	(D)
			TR	Gillingham	10.69	1969-76	239	6	17	
			TR	Wimbledon	08.77	1977-78	73	/	7	
GAMBLE, Francis	Liverpool	21.08.61	Burscough	Derby Co.	05.81	1981-82	5	1	2	(M)
GAMBLIN, Derek	Havant	07.04.43	Sutton U.	Portsmouth	AM	1965	1	/	0	(FB) E.AMAT.INT.
GAMBRILL, Brian	Whitstable	23.12.43		Millwall	12.65	1965	1	/	0	(G)
GAMMON, Steve	Swansea	24.09.39		Cardiff C.	04.58	1958-64	67		1	(WH) W.U23-2
GANE, Alan	Chiswick	11.06.50	Slough T.	Brentford	08.73					(F)
			TR	Hereford U.	09.73	1973	6	3	1	
GANNON, Eddie	Dublin	03.01.21	Shelbourne	Notts Co.	08.46	1946-48	106		2	(IF) EI-14
			TR	Sheffield Wed.	03.49	1948-54	204		4	
GANNON, Mick	Liverpool	02.02.43	JNRS	Everton	02.60	1961	3		0	(FB)
			TR	Scunthorpe U.	05.62	1962-63	15		0	
			TR	Crewe Alex.	10.64	1964-69	206	4	2	
GARBETT, Terry G.	Murton	09.09.45	Pelton Fell	Middlesbrough	08.63	1965	7	/	1	(IF)
			TR	Watford	08.66	1966-71	196	4	47	
			TR	Blackburn Rov.	09.71	1971-73	90	/	6	
			TR	Sheffield U.	02.74	1973-75	26	5	0	
GARBETT, W. Eddie	Dawley	14.09.49	APP	Shrewsbury T.	09.67	1967-68	7	5	2	(W)
			TR	Barrow	07.69	1969-71	119	/	27	
			TR	Stockport Co.	07.72	1972-73	63	7	11	
GARBUTT, John E.	Scarborough	27.03.20	Billingham	Newcastle U.	*	1946-49	51		0	(G)
GARBUTT, Peter	Corbridge	28.12.39	Crook T.	Carlisle U.	08.64	1964-70	134	2	13	(HB) E.AMAT.INT.
GARBUTT, Ray H.	Middlesbrough	09.05.25	Sth Bank E.E.	Manchester C.	09.47					(CF)
			Spennymoor	Watford	05.50	1950	22		8	
			TR	Brighton & H.A.	03.51	1950-51	32		18	
			TR	Workington	10.52	1952	8		2	
GARDINER, Doug	Douglas	29.03.17	Auchinleck T.	Luton T.	*	1946-50	121		1	(WH)
GARDINER, John	Chester-le-Street	05.11.14	Holfords FC	Southend U.	AM	1946	1		0	(IF)
GARDINER, Mark C.	Cirencester	25.12.66	APP	Swindon T.	APP	1983	1	/	0	(F)
GARDINER, Willie S.	Glasgow	15.08.29	Glasgow Rgrs.	Leicester C.	08.55	1955-57	69		48	(CF) S'B'-1
			TR	Reading	11.58	1958-59	8		2	
GARDNER, Charlie C.	Dundee	17.03.25	St. Mirren	Aldershot	08.50	1950	5		0	
GARDNER, Don	Jamaica	30.08.55	APP	Wolverhampton W.	08.73	1974	1	2	0	(IF)
GARDNER, Fred C.	Coventry	04.06.22	Birmingham C.(+)	Coventry C.	05.46	1946-48	13		3	(F) Warwicks. Cricketer/
			TR	Newport Co.	05.49	1949	4		2	d.Jan.1979
GARDNER, Paul A.	Southport	22.09.57	APP	Blackpool	09.75	1976-81	149	3	1	(D)
			TR	Bury	08.82	1982-83	90	/	0	
GARDNER, Steve	Hemsworth	07.10.58	APP	Ipswich T.	10.75					(M)E.SCH.INT
			TR	Oldham Ath.	12.77	1977-80	41	12	2	
GARDNER, Tom	Huyton	28.05.10	Burnley(*)	Wrexham	+	1946	33		4	(WH)*Liverpool/Grimsby T./ Hull C./Aston Villa/E-2/d.1970
GARDNER, Tom	Liverpool	17.03.23	Sth. Liverpool	Liverpool	10.46					(OR)
			TR	Everton	06.47	1947	1			
GARGAN, John	York	06.06.28	Cliftonville	York C.	+	1946	1		0	(CH)
GARIANI, Moshe	Israel	18.06.57	Macabbi Netanya	Brighton & H.A.	06.80	1980	0	1	0	(M) ISRAEL INT.

Players Names	Birthplace	Date	Previous Club	League Club	Date Signed	Seasons Played	Apps	Sub	Gls	
GARLAND, Chris S.	Bristol	24.04.49	APP	Bristol C.	05.66	1966-71	141	1	32	(F) E.U23-1
			TR	Chelsea	09.71	1971-74	89	3	22	
			TR	Leicester C.	02.75	1974-76	52	3	15	
			TR	Bristol C.	12.76	1976-82	53	11	11	
GARLAND, Dave	Grimsby	18.06.48	JNRS	Grimsby T.	07.65	1965	2	/	0	(F)
			TR	Scunthorpe U.	07.67					
GARLAND, Ron	Middlesbrough	28.07.31		Oldham Ath.	12.51	1954-55	9		3	(F)
GARNER, Alan	Lambeth	02.02.51	APP	Millwall	02.69	1970	2	/	0	(D)
			TR	Luton T.	07.71	1971-74	88	/	3	
			TR	Watford	02.75	1974-79	200	/	15	
			TR	Portsmouth	02.80	1979-81	36	/	2	
GARNER, Andy	Chesterfield	08.03.66	APP	Derby Co.	12.83	1983	13	/	5	(F)
GARNER, Paul	Doncaster	01.12.55	APP	Huddersfield T.	12.72	1972-75	96	/	2	(D) E.YTH.INT
			TR	Sheffield U.	11.75	1975-83	248	3	7	
			L	Gillingham	09.83	1983	5	/	0	
GARNER, Simon	Boston	23.11.59	APP	Blackburn Rov.	07.78	1978-83	194	11	76	(F)
GARNER, William	Leicester	14.12.47		Notts. Co.	07.66	1966	2	/	0	(F)
			Bedford T.	Southend U.	11.69	1969-72	101	1	41	
			TR	Chelsea	09.72	1972-78	94	11	31	
			TR	Cambridge U.	11.78	1978-79	17	7	3	
GARNER, William D.			Glasgow Celtic	Rochdale	10.82	1982	4	/	0	(D)
				Brentford	N/C	1983	2	1	1	
GARNETT, Malcolm	Rotherham	08.09.43	JNRS	Doncaster Rov.	07.61	1961	1		0	(HB)
GARNEYS, Tom T.	Leyton	25.08.23	Leytonstone	Notts.Co.	08.48					(CF)
			Chingford T.	Brentford	12.49	1949-50	12		2	
			TR	Ipswich T.	05.51	1951-58	248		126	
GARNHAM, Stuart E.	Selby	30.11.55	APP	Wolverhampton W.	12.73					(G)
			L	Northampton T.	09.74	1974	1	/	0	
			TR	Peterborough U.	03.77	1976	2	/	0	
			L	Northampton T.	08.77	1977	11	/	0	
GARRATT, Geoff	Whitehaven	02.02.30	Barrow Social	Barrow	09.51	1952	2		0	(OL)
			TR	Workington	08.53	1953	2		0	
GARRETT, Archie E.	Lesmahagow	17.06.19	Hearts	Northampton T.	09.46	1946-47	51		35	(CF)*Preston N.E.
			TR	Birmingham C.	12.47	1947-48	18		6	
			TR	Northampton T.	12.48	1948-50	43		16	
GARRETT, Jim	Dumfries	15.03.39	Q.of South	Carlisle U.	08.63	1963	1		0	(W)
GARRETT, Len	Hackney	14.05.36	Eton Manor	Arsenal	05.54					(FB) E.YTH.INT.
			TR	Ipswich T.	05.58	1958	1		0	
GARRETT, Tom	Durham	28.02.26	Horden CW	Blackpool	+	1946-60	308		3	(FB) E-3/E.F.LGE REP.
			TR	Millwall	05.61	1961	12		0	
GARRITY, Ken	Blackburn	06.08.35		Accrington St.	02.56	1958-59	37		5	(F)
GARROW, Herbert A.	Elgin	24.01.42	Fochabers	Newcastle U.	02.60	1960-62	4		0	(G)
GARTH, Jimmy	Bridgeton	01.05.22	Morton	Preston N.E.	11.46	1946-47	23		7	(F) d.1968
GARTLAND, Paul E.	Shipley	08.02.59	APP	Huddersfield T.	02.77	1976-78	8	/	0	(D)
GARVEY, Brian	Hull	03.07.37	JNRS	Hull C.	01.58	1957-64	232		3	(WH)
			TR	Watford	07.65	1965-69	179	1	2	
			TR	Colchester U.	06.70	1970-71	75	2	1	
GARVEY, Jim	Holytown	04.06.19	Northampton T.(+)	Leicester C.	06.46	1946-48	15		0	
GARVIE, John	Bellshill	16.10.27	Hibernian	Preston N.E.	08.49	1949	5		0	(CF)
			TR	Lincoln C.	08.50	1950-55	183		73	
			TR	Carlisle U.	05.56	1956	25		6	
GARWOOD, Colin	Measham	29.06.49	JNRS	Peterborough U.	07.67	1967-70	58	8	30	(F) E.YTH.INT
			TR	Oldham Ath.	07.71	1971-74	83	9	36	
			TR	Huddersfield T.	12.74	1974-75	22	6	8	
			TR	Colchester U.	02.76	1975-77	83	4	25	
			TR	Portsmouth	03.78	1977-79	62	9	34	
			TR	Aldershot	02.80	1979-81	79	2	25	
GARWOOD, Len F.	India	28.07.23	Hitchin T.	Tottenham H.	05.46	1948	2		0	(WH)d.1979
GASKELL, Alex	Leigh	30.07.32	Manchester U.(AM)	Southport	11.52	1951-53	44		18	(CF)
			TR	Newcastle U.	10.53	1953	1		0	
			TR	Mansfield T.	06.54	1954-55	41		16	
			TR	Tranmere Rov.	06.57	1957	6		6	
GASKELL, Dave	Wigan	05.10.40	JNRS	Manchester U.	10.57	1957-66	95		0	(G) E.YTH.INT./E.SCH.INT.
			Wigan Ath.	Wrexham	06.69	1969-71	95	/	0	
GASKELL, Edward	Bedbury	19.12.16	Leicester C.(*)	Brentford	*	1947-51	34		0	(G)
GASKELL, Ron	Worsley	01.3.26	Walkden Hill	Southport	09.50	1949-50	2		0	(WH)
GASTON, Ray	Belfast	22.12.46	Coleraine	Wolverhampton W.	05.65					(F) NI-1/NI.U23-1/
			Coleraine	Oxford U.	09.68	1968	12	/	2	
			L	Lincoln C.	02.70	1969	4	/	1	
GATE, B. Ken	W.Hartlepool	26.10.48	St. Josephs	Hartlepool U.	AM	1968	1	/	0	(FB)

Players Names	Birthplace	Date	Previous Club	League Club	Date Signed	Seasons Played	Career Record Apps	Sub	Gls	
GATER, Roy	Chesterton	22.06.40	JNRS	Port Vale	04.60	1960-61	5	/	0	(CH)
			TR	Bournemouth	07.62	1962-68	216	/	3	
			TR	Crewe Alex	01.69	1968-72	156	/	5	
GATES, Eric L.	Ferryhill	28.06.55	APP	Ipswich T.	10.72	1973-83	246	29	60	(F) E-2/Brother of William
GATES, William	Ferryhill	08.05.44	JNRS	Middlesbrough	10.61	1961-73	279	6	12	(CH) E.YTH.INT.
GATTING, Steve P.	Willesden	29.05.59	APP	Arsenal	03.77	1978-80	50	8	5	(D) Brother of Mike
			TR	Brighton & H.A.	09.81	1981-83	114	/	11	(Eng. Cricketer).
GAUDEN, Alan	Ashington	20.11.44	JNRS	Sunderland	03.62	1965-67	40	4	6	(IF)
			TR	Darlington	10.68	1968-71	125	3	39	
			TR	Grimsby T.	02.72	1971-72	54	1	12	
			TR	Hartlepool U.	08.73	1973-74	63	/	15	
			TR	Gillingham	12.74	1974-75	41	/	3	
GAULD, Jimmy	Aberdeen	09.05.31	Waterford	Charlton Ath.	05.55	1955-56	47		21	(IF)
			TR	Everton	10.56	1956	23		7	
			TR	Plymouth Arg.	10.57	1957-58	64		25	
			TR	Swindon T.	08.59	1959	41		14	
			St.Johnstone	Mansfield T.	11.60	1960	4		3	
GAVAN, John	Walsall	08.12.39	Walsall Wood	Aston Villa	11.62	1962-65	9	/	0	(G)
			TR	Doncaster Rov.	07.67	1967-68	21	/	0	
GAVIN, John	Limerick	20.04.28	Limerick	Norwich C.	08.48	1948-54	203		76	(OR) EI-7
			TR	Tottenham H.	10.54	1954-55	32		15	
			TR	Norwich C.	11.55	1955-57	110		46	
			TR	Watford	07.58	1958	43		12	
			TR	Crystal Palace	05.59	1959-60	66		15	
GAVIN, Mark W.	Baillieston	10.12.63	APP	Leeds U.	12.81	1982-83	13	6	2	(M)
GAVIN, Pat J.O.	Drogheda	06.06.29	Dundalk	Doncaster Rov.	06.53	1953-59	145		6	(FB) EI'B'-1/L.O.I.REP.
GAWLER, Ron N.	Canterbury	10.07.24	Canterbury C.	Southend U.	06.49	1949-50	8		0	(HB)
GAY, Geoff	Romford	04.02.57	APP	Bolton W.	01.75					(D)
			L	Exeter C.	03.77	1976	5	1	0	
			TR	Southport	08.77	1977	40	/	5	
			TR	Wigan Ath.	07.78	1978	1	/	0	
GAYLE, Howard	Liverpool	18.05.58		Liverpool	11.77	1980	3	1	1	(F) E.U'21-3
			L	Fulham	01.80	1979	14	/	0	
			L	Newcastle U.	11.82	1982	8	/	2	
			TR	Birmingham C.	01.83	1982-83	45	1	9	
GAYNER, Len A.	Ollerton	22.09.25	Eastwood	Hull C.	04.48	1950	2		0	(IF)
			TR	Bournemouth	06.51	1951-53	51		12	
			TR	Southampton	03.54	1953	12		1	
			TR	Aldershot	02.55	1954-56	62		9	
			TR	Oldham Ath.	07.57	1957	5		0	
GAYNOR, Jimmy	Dublin	22.08.28	Shamrock Rov.	Ipswich T.	03.52	1951-52	47		3	(OR) L.O.I. REP.
			TR	Aldershot	09.53	1953-57	165		37	
GAZZARD, Gerry	Westbury	15.03.25	Penzance	West Ham U.	05.49	1949-53	119		29	(IF)
			TR	Brentford	01.54	1953	13		6	
GEARD, Len	Hammersmith	12.02.34	JNRS	Fulham	05.51					
			TR	Brentford	03.53	1954-55	4		0	
GEBBIE, Bert	Cambuslang	18.11.34	Q.of South	Bradford P.A.	07.60	1960-63	112		0	(G)
GEDDES, Andy	Craigbank	06.09.22	Kilmarnock	Bradford C.	06.49	1949-50	30		4	(HB) d.1957
			TR	Mansfield T.	08.51	1951	11		2	
			TR	Halifax T.	07.52	1952-54	50		4	
GEDDES, Jim	Burntisland	25.05.42	T.Lanark	Bradford P.A.	08.65	1965	1	/	0	(WH)
GEDDES, Paul	Paisley	19.04.61	Kilbirnie Ladeside	Leicester C.	04.79					(M)
			Hibernian	Wimbledon	N/C	1981	2	/	0	
GEDDIS, David	Carlisle	12.03.58	APP	Ipswich T.	08.75	1976-68	26	17	5	(F) E.YTH.INT
			L	Luton T.	02.77	1976	9	4	4	
			TR	Aston Villa	09.79	1979-82	43	4	12	
			L	Luton T.	12.82	1982	4	/	0	
			TR	Barnsley	09.83	1983	31	/	14	
GEDNEY, Chris	Boston	01.09.45	JNRS	Lincoln C.	AM	1962-65	9	/	1	(WH)
GEE, Alan A.	Chesterfield	16.03.32		Rotherham U.	AM	1952	2		0	
GEE, James P.	Plymouth	06.06.32	Launceston T.	Plymouth Arg.	AM	1956	1		0	(G)
GEIDMINTIS, Anthony	Workington	30.07.49	APP	Workington	08.66	1964-75	323	5	37	(D)
			TR	Watford	07.76	1976-77	48	1	0	
			TR	Northampton T.	02.78	1977-78	63	/	1	
			TR	Halifax T.	07.79	1979	10	2	0	
GELDARD, Albert	Bradford	11.04.14	Everton(*)	Bolton W.	*	1946	9		0	(OR)*Bradford P.A./E-4/ E.F.LGE REP./E.SCH.INT.
GELSON, Peter W.J.	London	18.10.41	JNRS	Brentford	03.60	1961-74	468	3	17	(WH)●
GEMMELL, Andy	Greenock	27.07.45	Morton	Bradford C.	01.67	1966	3	/	0	(W)
GEMMELL, Eric	Manchester	07.04.21	Manchester U.(AM)	Manchester C.	+					(CF)
			TR	Oldham Ath.	06.47	1947-53	194		110	
			TR	Crewe Alex.	02.54	1953-54	15		5	
			TR	Rochdale	09.54	1954-55	64		32	

Players Names	Birthplace	Date	Previous Club	League Club	Date Signed	Seasons Played	Apps	Sub	Gls	
GEMMELL, Jim	Sunderland	17.11.11	Bury(*)	Southport	+	1946	25		0	(FB) *W.Stanley
GEMMELL, Matt	Glasgow	10.03.31	Shawfield	Portsmouth	09.51	1953-54	3		0	(F)
			TR	Swindon T.	10.54	1954	8		2	
GEMMELL, Tommy	Glasgow	16.10.43	Glasgow Celtic	Nottingham F.	12.71	1971-72	39	/	6	(FB) S-18/S.F.LGE REP.
GEMMILL, Archie	Paisley	24.03.47	St. Mirren	Preston N.E.	06.67	1967-70	93	6	13	(M) S-43/S.U23-1●
			TR	Derby Co.	09.70	1970-77	261	/	18	
			TR	Nottingham F.	09.77	1977-78	56	2	4	
			TR	Birmingham C.	08.79	1979-81	97	/	12	
			Jacksonville	Wigan Ath.	N/C	1982	11	/	0	
			TR	Derby Co.	11.82	1982-83	63	/	8	
GENDALL, Richard M.	Wrexham	25.09.60	APP	Chester C.	10.78	1980	4	1	0	(M)
GENNOE, Terry	Shrewsbury	16.03.53	Bricklayers Spts.	Bury	06.73	1972-73	3	/	0	(G)
			TR	Halifax T.	05.75	1975-77	78	/	0	
			TR	Southampton	02.78	1978-79	36	/	0	
			L	Crystal Palace	01.81	1980	3	/	0	
			TR	Blackburn Rov.	08.81	1981-83	98	/	0	
GEORGE, Charlie F.	Islington	10.10.50	APP	Arsenal	03.68	1969-74	113	20	31	(F)E.U23-5/E-1
			TR	Derby Co.	07.75	1975-78	106	/	34	
			TR	Southampton	12.78	1978-79	22	/	3	
			L	Nottingham F.	01.80	1979-80	24	/	8	
			Bulova, H.K.	Bournemouth	03.82	1981	2	/	0	
			TR	Derby Co.	03.82	1981	11	/	2	
GEORGE, Frank R.	Stepney	20.11.33	Carshalton	Orient	07.54	1956-62	119		0	(G)
			TR	Watford	07.63	1964	10		0	
GEORGE, Rickie	Barnet	28.06.46	APP	Tottenham H.	10.63					(F)
			TR	Watford	08.64	1964	4		0	
			TR	Bournemouth	05.65	1965	2	1	0	
			TR	Oxford U.	07.66	1966	6	/	0	
GEORGE, Ron A.	Bristol	14.08.22	Bristol Aero	Crystal Palace	02.47	1948-53	122		2	(FB)
			TR	Colchester U.	07.54	1954	5		0	
GEORGESON, Rod	Edinburgh	31.07.48		Port Vale	01.66	1965-66	26	1	6	(F)
GERHARDI, Hugh	S. Africa	05.05.33	Thistle F.C.	Liverpool	08.52	1952	6		0	(HB)
GERNON, F.A. Irvin	Birmingham	30.12.62	APP	Ipswich T.	01.80	1981-83	49	/	0	(D) E.SCH.INT./E.U'21-1
GERRIE, Sid	Aberdeen	14.06.27	Dundee	Hull C.	11.50	1950-56	146		60	(IF)
GERULA, Stan E.	Poland	21.02.14	Carpathians	Orient	AM	1948-49	30		0	(G) POLISH AMAT.INT./d.1979
GIBB, J. Barry	Workington	21.05.40		Workington	07.60	1959-60	6		0	(WH)
GIBB, Tommy	W. Lothian	13.12.44	Partick Thistle	Newcastle U.	08.68	1968-74	190	9	12	(M) S.U23-1
			TR	Sunderland	06.75	1975-76	7	3	1	
			TR	Hartlepool T.	07.77	1977	40	/	4	
GIBBINS, Eddie	Shoreditch	24.03.26	JNRS	Tottenham H.	09.46	1952	1		0	(F) Father to Roger
GIBBINS, Roger G.	Enfield	06.09.55	APP	Tottenham H.	12.72					(M) Son of Eddie/E.SCH.INT.
			TR	Oxford U.	08.75	1975	16	3	2	
			TR	Norwich C.	06.76	1976-77	47	1	12	
			N. England Teamen	Cambridge U.	09.79	1979-81	97	3	12	
			TR	Cardiff C.	08.82	1982-83	88	/	12	
GIBBON, Malcolm	Newcastle	24.10.50	APP	Port Vale	APP	1966-67	4	1	0	(HB)
GIBBONS, Albert H.	Fulham	10.04.14	Tottenham H.(AM)	Bradford P.A.	05.46	1946	42		21	(CF)*Brentford(AM)/
			TR	Brentford	08.47	1947-48	56		16	E.AMAT.INT.
GIBBONS, Arthur T.	Durham	24.05.37		Hartlepool U.	09.58	1958	13		0	(HB)
GIBBONS, Dave	Belfast	04.11.52	APP	Manchester C.	08.70					(FB)
			L	Stockport Co.	02.72	1971	1	/	0	
GIBBONS, John R.	Charlton	08.04.25	Dartford	Q.P.R.	12.47	1948	8		2	(CF)
			TR	Ipswich T.	05.49	1948-49	12		3	
			TR	Tottenham H.	03.50					
GIBBONS, Len	Wirral	22.11.30	JNRS	Wolverhampton W.	02.48	1951-53	25		0	(FB)
GIBBS, Alan M.	Orpington	07.02.34		Cardiff C.	10.54					(F)
			TR	Swindon T.	05.56	1956	16		5	
GIBBS, Brian R.	Gillingham	06.10.36	Gosport Bor.	Bournemouth	10.57	1957-62	58		15	(IF)
			TR	Gillingham	10.62	1962-68	259	/	101	
			TR	Colchester U.	09.68	1968-71	153	4	37	
GIBBS, Derek W.	Fulham	22.12.34	JNRS	Chelsea	04.55	1956-60	23		5	(IF)
			TR	Orient	11.60	1960-62	33		5	
			TR	Q.P.R.	08.63	1963-64	27		0	
GIBBS, Nigel J.	St. Albans	20.11.65	APP	Watford	11.83	1983	2	1	0	(D)
GIBBS, Peter	Rhodesia	24.08.56	Tring T.	Watford	07.75	1975-76	4	/	0	(G)
GIBLIN, John	Stoke	29.06.23		Stoke C.	+	1947	1		0	(HB)
GIBSON, Aidan M.	Clayton	17.05.63	APP	Derby Co.	05.81	1980-81	0	2	0	(M)
			TR	Exeter C.	07.82	1982	17	1	1	
GIBSON, Alex	Glasgow	25.01.25	Clyde	Hull C.	03.50	1949-50	21		0	
GIBSON, Alex P.S.	Kirkconnel	28.11.39	Auchinleck Talbot	Notts.Co.	04.59	1959-68	344	3	10	(CH)

Players Names	Birthplace	Date	Previous Club	League Club	Date Signed	Seasons Played	Career Record Apps	Sub	Gls	
GIBSON, Alf	Wakefield	09.09.19		Rotherham U.	+	1946-53	152		0	(CH)
			TR	Chesterfield	07.54					
GIBSON, Archie	Girvan	30.12.33	Coylston J.	Leeds U.	05.51	1954-59	169		5	(WH)
			TR	Scunthorpe U.	07.60	1960-63	138		5	
			TR	Barnsley	09.64					
GIBSON, Brian	Huddersfield	22.02.28	Paddock Ath.	Huddersfield T.	05.51	1951-60	157		1	(FB)
GIBSON, Charles	Dumbarton	12.06.61	St. Anthony's	Shrewsbury T.	03.81	1981	2	4	0	(F)
GIBSON, Colin	Bridport	06.04.60	APP	Aston Villa	04.78	1978-83	134	4	7	(D)E.U'21-1/E.SCH.INT.
GIBSON, Colin H.	Normanby	16.09.23	Penarth.Pont.	Cardiff C.	+	1946-47	71		16	(OR) E 'B'-1/E.F.LGE REP.
			TR	Newcastle U.	07.48	1948	23		5	
			TR	Aston Villa	02.49	1948-55	157		24	
			TR	Lincoln C.	01.56	1955-56	36		12	
GIBSON, Dave	Seaham	14.02.58	APP	Hull C.	12.75	1975-77	19	5	0	(M)
			TR	Scunthorpe U.	07.78	1978-79	16	6	1	
GIBSON, Dave J.	Runcorn	18.03.31	Aberdeen	Everton	08.50	1950-51	3		0	(F)
			TR	Swindon T.	11.54	1954-56	70		6	
GIBSON, Dave W.	Winchburgh	23.09.38	Hibernian	Leicester C.	01.62	1961-69	274	6	41	(IF) S-7
			TR	Aston Villa	09.70	1970-71	16	3	1	
			TR	Exeter C.	01.72	1971-73	69	2	3	
GIBSON, Frank A.	Croxley Green	07.06.14	Rickmansworth	Watford	AM	1946	1		0	
GIBSON, Henry	Newcastle	17.04.30	Spennymoor	Fulham	11.52	1954	1		0	(HB)
			TR	Aldershot	08.56	1956	3		0	
GIBSON, Ian S.	Newton Stewart	30.03.43	JNRS	Accrington St.	AM	1958	9		3	(IF)S.U23-2/S.SCH.INT.
			TR	Bradford P.A.	05.61	1959-61	88		18	
			TR	Middlebrough	03.62	1961-65	168		44	
			TR	Coventry C.	07.66	1966-69	90	3	13	
			TR	Cardiff C.	07.70	1970-72	89	1	11	
			TR	Bournemouth	10.72	1972-73	17	3	0	
GIBSON, J. Steve	Huddersfield	02.05.49	Huddersfield T.(AM)	Bradford P.A.	12.67	1967-68	28	4	0	(HB)
GIBSON, Jim	Belfast	04.09.40	Linfield	Newcastle U.	01.59	1958-60	2		1	(F)
			Cambridge U.	Luton T.	02.65	1964-65	31	1	0	
GIBSON, Mike J.	Derby	15.07.39	Nuneaton	Shrewsbury T.	03.60	1960-62	76		0	(G) E.YTH.INT.
			TR	Bristol C.	04.63	1962-71	331	/	0	
			TR	Gillingham	07.72	1972-73	80	/	0	
GIBSON, Reg	Tideswell	15.05.19	Manchester U.(*)	Plymouth Arg.	+	1946	6		0	(IF)
			TR	Exeter C.	06.47	1947-48	39		0	
GIBSON, Robert	Washington	29.12.16		Southend U.	+	1946	2		0	(IF)
GIBSON, Robert H.	Ashington	05.08.27	Aberdeen	Hull C.	10.49	1949	12		5	(CF)
			TR	Lincoln C.	05.51	1951-54	41		20	
			Peterborough U.	Gateshead	03.57	1956-58	49		27	
GIBSON, Simon J.	Nottingham	10.12.64	APP	Chelsea	12.82					(D)
			TR	Swindon T.	11.83	1983	29	/	3	
GIBSON, T.R. Don	Manchester	12.05.29	JNRS	Manchester U.	08.47	1950-54	108		0	(WH)
			TR	Sheffield Wed.	06.55	1955-59	80		2	
			TR	Orient	06.60	1960	8		0	
GIBSON, Terry B.	Walthamstow	23.12.62	APP	Tottenham H.	01.80	1979-82	16	2	4	(F)E.SCH.INT./E.YTH.INT.
			TR	Coventry C.	08.83	1983	35	1	17	
GIBSON, William	Lanark	24.06.59		Leicester C.	07.79	1980-81	28	/	0	(D)
GIBSON, William	Glasgow	17.09.26	Arsenal(AM)	Brentford	01.47					(FB)
			TR	Tranmere Rov.	06.51	1951-53	72		1	
GIDMAN, John	Liverpool	10.01.54	Liverpool(AM)	Aston Villa	08.71	1972-79	196	1	9	(D)E-1/E.U23-4/
			TR	Everton	10.79	1979-80	64	/	2	E.YTH.INT.
			TR	Manchester U.	08.81	1981-83	43	1	1	
GILBERG, Harry	Tottenham	27.06.23	JNRS	Tottenham H.	+	1946-47	2		0	(IF)
			TR	Q.P.R.	08.51	1951-52	66		12	
			TR	Brighton & H.A.	12.52	1952-55	67		3	
GILBERT, Carl G.	Folkestone	20.03.48		Gillingham	10.65	1967-69	28	2	11	(F)
			TR	Bristol Rov.	12.69	1969-70	39	6	15	
			TR	Rotherham U.	03.71	1970-73	78	16	37	
GILBERT, David G.	Smethwick	05.08.40	Redditch	Chesterfield	05.60	1960	22		2	(OR)
GILBERT, David J.	Lincoln	22.06.63	APP	Lincoln C.	06.81	1980-81	15	15	1	(F)
			TR	Scunthorpe U.	08.82	1982	1	/	0	
GILBERT, Noel	Nth.Walsham	25.12.31	Nth.Walsham	Norwich C.	08.55	1955-56	2		0	(OR)
GILBERT, Philip	Margate	11.09.44	Ramsgate	Brighton & H.A.	01.62	1961-63	7		3	(F)
GILBERT, Tim H.	Sth. Shields	28.08.58	APP	Sunderland	08.76	1976-79	34	2	3	(D)
			TR	Cardiff C.	02.81	1980-81	33	/	1	
			TR	Darlington	08.82	1982-83	62	3	3	
GILBERT, William	Lewisham	10.11.59	APP	Crystal Palace	12.76	1977-83	235	2	3	(D) E.U21-11/E.SCH.INT./ E.YTH.INT.
GILBERT, William A.	Newcastle	07.11.25	Murton C.W.	Coventry C.	09.48	1951-52	14		0	(G)
			Snowdown Col.	Stockport Co.	07.54	1954	33		0	

Players Names	Birthplace	Date	Previous Club	League Club	Date Signed	Seasons Played	Apps	Sub	Gls	
GILCHRIST, Alex	Holytown	28.09.23		Cardiff C.	05.48	1948	1		0	
GILCHRIST, John	Wishaw	05.09.39	Airdrie	Millwall	03.61	1960-68	280	/	10	(FB) S.SCH.INT.
			TR	Fulham	07.69	1969	20	3	1	
			TR	Colchester U.	07.70	1970-71	41	/	2	
GILCHRIST, Paul A.	Dartford	05.01.51	APP	Charlton Ath.	03.68	1969	5	2	0	(F)
			TR	Doncaster Rov.	07.71	1971	22	/	8	
			TR	Southampton	03.72	1971-76	96	11	17	
			TR	Portsmouth	03.77	1976-77	38	1	3	
			TR	Swindon T.	08.78	1978-79	10	7	6	
			TR	Hereford U.	03.80	1979	11	/	1	
GILCHRIST, Robert	Bellshill	17.08.32	Dumfermline	Aldershot	06.52	1952-56	48		0	(FB)
GILDER, Carlton	Newport	25.07.57		Cambridge U.	01.75	1974-75	0	2	0	(F)
GILES, Albert	Swansea	04.05.24	JNRS	Bristol Rov.	+	1946	1		0	
GILES, Chris	Dublin	17.07.28	Drumcondra	Doncaster Rov.	06.50	1950-51	27		4	(OR) EI-1
			TR	Aldershot	08.53					
GILES, David C.	Cardiff	21.09.56	APP	Cardiff C.	09.74	1974-78	51	8	3	(F)W.U21-3/W-12/
			TR	Wrexham	12.78	1978-79	38	/	2	W.SCH.INT.
			TR	Swansea C.	11.79	1979-80	49	5	13	
			L	Orient	11.81	1981	3	/	2	
			TR	Crystal Palace	03.82	1981-83	83	5	6	
GILES, Jimmy	Kidlington	21.04.46	Kidlington	Swindon T.	03.65	1965-67	12	1	0	(D)
			TR	Aldershot	10.68	1968-70	80	1	3	
			TR	Exeter C.	03.71	1970-74	183	/	6	
			TR	Charlton Ath.	06.75	1975-77	92	1	6	
			TR	Exeter C.	12.77	1977-80	130	/	5	
GILES, John	Walsall	04.06.33	Hednesford T.	Walsall	12.50	1952	1		0	(IF)
GILES, John E.	Bristol	07.11.47	APP	Bristol C.	06.65	1966	3	/	1	(F) Nephew of Albert
			L	Bradford P.A.	03.68	1967	9	/	0	
			TR	Exeter C.	05.69	1969-71	54	4	3	
GILES, John M.	Dublin	06.01.40	Home Farm	Manchester U.	11.57	1959-62	98		10	(M) EI-50●
			TR	Leeds U.	08.63	1963-74	380	3	86	
			TR	W.B.A.	06.75	1975-76	74	1	3	
GILES, Paul A.	Cardiff	21.02.61	JNRS	Cardiff C.	06.79	1980-82	17	7	1	(M) Brother of David/W.U'21-3
			TR	Exeter C.	03.82	1981	9	/	1	
GILES, Philip R.	Walsall	08.10.29	JNRS	Walsall	05.48	1948-52	67		14	(OL) E.YTH.INT.
GILES, Terry	Halifax	25.03.43		Halifax T.	AM	1961-62	2	1		(F)
GILFILLAN, Robert	Cowdenbeath	29.06.38	Cowdenbeath	Newcastle U.	10.59	1959-60	7		2	(F)
			Raith Rov.	Southend U.	06.63	1963-65	67	1	33	
			TR	Doncaster Rov.	11.65	1965-70	178	8	33	
GILFILLAN, Robert	Dunfermline	14.03.26	Jeanfield Swifts	Blackpool	07.47					(IF)
			Cowdenbeath	Rochdale	06.51	1951-53	63		11	
GILL, Colin J.	Swindon	20.01.33		Swindon T.	10.55	1955	1		0	(G)
GILL, Eric N.	London	03.11.30	Broomfields FC	Charlton Ath.	04.48	1951	1		0	(G)
			TR	Brighton & H.A.	06.52	1952-59	280		0	
GILL, Frank	Manchester	05.12.48	APP	Manchester U.	12.65					(W)
			TR	Tranmere Rov.	07.68	1968-70	70	4	8	
GILL, Gary	Middlesbrough	28.11.64	APP	Middlesbrough	12.82	1983	4	2	0	(M)
			L	Hull C.	12.83	1983	0	1	0	
GILL, John	Wednesbury	03.02.41	JNRS	Nottingham F.	03.58					(CH)
			TR	Mansfield T.	07.61	1961-65	139	1	0	
			TR	Hartlepool U.	02.66	1965-70	202	3	1	
GILL, Joseph	Sunderland	10.11.45	Ashington	Hartlepool U.	AM	1968	4	/	0	(G)
GILL, Mervyn J.	Exeter	13.04.31		Portsmouth	AM	1953	6		0	(G)
			Woking	Southampton	04.56	1955	1		0	
			TR	Torquay U.	09.56	1956-61	159		0	
GILL, Ray	Manchester	08.12.24		Manchester C.	09.47	1948-49	8		0	(WH)
			TR	Chester C.	06.51	1951-61	408		2	
GILLARD, Ian T.	Hammersmith	09.10.50	APP	Q.P.R.	10.68	1968-81	403	5	9	(D) E-3/E.U23-5●
			TR	Aldershot	07.82	1982-83	65	/	2	
GILLESPIE, Gary	Stirling	05.07.60	Falkirk	Coventry C.	03.78	1978-82	171	1	6	(D) S.U21-8
			TR	Liverpool	07.83					
GILLESPIE, Ian C.	Plymouth	06.05.13	Crystal Palace(*)	Ipswich T.	+	1946	6		1	
GILLESPIE, Norman	Edinburgh	20.04.40	Falkirk	Wrexham	12.63	1963	3		0	(IF)
GILLESPIE, Pat	Bellshill	05.07.28	Partick Th.	Watford	+	1946	6		0	(WH) 7 apps. in goal
				Northampton T.	08.47	1947	1		0	for Doncaster Rov.
			TR	Doncaster Rov.	11.47	1947-48	8		1	
GILLETT, David	Edinburgh	02.04.51	Hibernian	Crewe Alex.	08.72	1972.74	64	5	2	(WH)
GILLIAM, Reg	Farnham	19.02.31	Farnham T.	Aldershot	02.56	1956	1		0	(G)
GILLIBRAND, Ian V.	Blackburn	24.11.48	APP	Arsenal	12.65					(D)
			TR	Wigan Ath.	N/L	1978	7	/	0	

Players Names	Birthplace	Date	Previous Club	League Club	Date Signed	Seasons Played	Career Record Apps	Sub	Gls	
GILLIES, Don	Glencoe	20.06.51	Morton	Bristol C.	03.73	1972-79	183	17	26	(D)S.U23-1
			TR	Bristol Rov.	06.80	1980-81	56	3	0	
GILLIES, John C.	Glasgow	22.10.18	St.Mirren	Brentford	05.46	1946	5		0	
GILLIES, Matt M.	Loganlea	12.08.21	R.A.F. Weaton	Bolton W.	+	1946-51	145		1	(CH)
			TR	Leicester C.	01.52	1951-54	102		0	
GILLIGAN, Augustus	Abingdon	19.08.59	APP	Swindon T.	08.77	1977	3	1	0	(F)Brother of John
			L	Doncaster Rov.	09.78	1978	1	/	0	
GILLIGAN, James M.	Hammersmith	24.01.64	APP	Watford	08.81	1981-83	13	4	6	(F) E.YTH.INT.
			L	Lincoln C.	10.82	1982	0	3	0	
GILLIGAN, John	Abingdon	02.05.57	APP	Swindon T.	10.75	1975-76	2	4	0	(F)
			L	Huddersfield T.	09.76	1976	0	1	0	
			L	Northampton T.	01.77	1976	5	/	1	
GILLIGAN, Malcolm	Cardiff	11.10.42		Swansea C.	05.62	1962	2		0	(F)
GILLIVER, Alan	Shefffield	03.08.44	JNRS	Huddersfield T.	08.61	1962-65	46	/	22	(F)
			TR	Blackburn Rov.	06.66	1966-67	32	2	9	
			TR	Rotherham U.	05.68	1968	23	3	2	
			TR	Brighton & H.A.	07.69	1969-70	54	3	19	
			TR	Lincoln C.	02.71	1970-71	33	4	8	
			TR	Bradford C.	06.72	1972-73	68	2	30	
			TR	Stockport Co.	06.74	1974	22	3	5	
			Boston U.	Bradford C.	N/C	1978	1	1	0	
GILLOTT, Peter	Barnsley	20.07.35	JNRS	Barnsley	05.53	1955-58	5		0	(FB) E.YTH.INT.
GILMOUR, George R.	Barrhead	07.05.19		Halifax T.	09.48	1948-49	37		2	
GILMOUR, Ron	Workington	28.02.35	JNRS	Workington	12.52	1953	2		0	(HB)
GILPIN, Jim	Edinburgh	12.06.45	Raith Rov.	Bradford P.A.	08.65	1965	10	1	1	(OL)
GILROY, Joe	Glasgow	19.10.41	Clyde	Fulham	10.67	1967-68	23	1	7	(F)
GILZEAN, Alan	Perth	22.10.38	Dundee	Tottenham H.	12.64	1964-73	335	8	93	(CF)S-22/S.U23-3/ S.F.LGE.REP.
GIRLING, Howard M.	Birmingham	24.05.22		Crystal Palace	+	1946	26		6	(OL)
			TR	Brentford	02.47	1946-49	86		8	
			TR	Bournemouth	07.51	1951	4		0	
GISBOURNE, Charles J.	Bury	07.10.52	APP	Bury	10.72	1972-74	13	3	1	(FB)
			TR	Crewe Alex.	10.74	1974	5	1	0	
GISSING, John W.	Stapleford	24.11.38	Stapleford BC.	Notts.Co.	07.56	1957-60	22		1	(OR)
			TR	Chesterfield	07.61	1961	2		0	
GITSHAM, Jim W.	London	12.05.42	JNRS	Brentford	07.59	1960-62	54		0	(FB)
GIVENS, Don J.	Limerick	09.08.49	APP	Manchester U.	12.66	1969	4	4	1	(F) EI-56
			TR	Luton T.	04.70	1970-71	80	3	19	
			TR	Q.P.R.	07.72	1972-77	242	/	76	
			TR	Birmingham C.	08.78	1978-80	49	10	10	
			L	Bournemouth	03.80	1979	5	/	4	
			TR	Sheffield U.	03.81	1980	11	/	3	
GLADWIN, Robin	Harlow	12.08.40	Chelmsford	Norwich C.	01.66	1965-67	17	/	0	(FB)
				Oxford U.	07.68	1968-69	44	/	0	
GLAISTER, George	Bywell	18.05.18	Nth Shields	Blackburn Rov.	*	1946	8		1	(OL)
			TR	Stockport Co.	04.47	1946-49	92		21	
			TR	Halifax T.	08.50	1950	34		7	
			TR	Accrington St.	09.51	1951	24		1	
GLASBY, Herbert	Bradford	21.09.19	Aldershot(AM)	Bradford P.A.	05.46	1946-48	11		1	
GLAVIN, Ronald M.	Glasgow	27.03.51	Glasgow Celtic	Barnsley	06.79	1979-83	171	5	73	(M) S-1
GLAZIER, William	Nottingham	02.08.43		Crystal Palace	10.61	1961-64	106		0	(G)E.F.LGE REP./ E.U23-3
			TR	Coventry C.	10.64	1964-74	346	/	0	
			TR	Brentford	06.75	1975	9	/	0	
GLAZZARD, Jim	Normanton	23.04.23	Altofts	Huddersfield T.	+	1946-55	299		139	(CF)
			TR	Everton	09.56	1956	3		0	
			TR	Mansfield T.	12.56	1956-57	21		10	
GLAZZARD, Malcolm	Eastham	01.07.31	JNRS	Liverpool	05.49					
			TR	Accrington St.	08.51	1951	1		0	
GLEADALL, Dennis	Sheffield	15.02.34		Bury	08.54					(HB)
			TR	Bradford P.A.	07.56	1956-57	34			
GLEADALL, Eddie	Sheffield	21.08.31		Bury	01.52	1951-56	74		17	(OR) Brother of Dennis
			TR	Scunthorpe U.	03.57	1956-57	6		2	
GLEASURE, Peter	Luton	08.10.60	APP	Millwall	08.78	1980-82	55	/	0	(G)
			TR	Northampton T.	03.83	1982-83	57	/	0	
GLEAVE, Colin	Stockport	06.04.19		Stockport Co.	*	1946-47	57		1	
GLEDHILL, Sam	Castleford	07.07.13		York C.	*	1946-48	64		1	(WH)
GLEDSTONE, Peter	Bournemouth	04.05.34	Bournemouth GW	Bournemouth	11.55	1957-63	131		2	(WH)
GLEESON, Percy	Acton	18.07.21	Hounslow	Brentford	03.47	1947	9		1	(IF)
GLENDINNING, Brian	Newcastle	26.12.34	Felham B.C.	Darlington	05.55	1955	12		2	(CF)
GLENDINNING, Kevin	Corbridge	23.01.62		Darlington	08.80	1980	4	/	0	(D)

Players Names	Birthplace	Date	Previous Club	League Club	Date Signed	Seasons Played	Apps	Sub	Gls	
GLENDON, Kevin W.	Manchester	21.06.61	APP	Manchester C.	07.79					(F)
			TR	Crewe Alex.	08.80	1980	3	1	0	
			Hyde U.	Burnley	12.83	1983	4	/	0	
GLENN, David A.	Wigan	30.11.62	APP	Wigan Ath.	11.80	1980-82	68	4	4	(D)
			TR	Blackburn Rov.	11.83	1983	21	1	0	
GLENNON, Chris D.	Manchester	29.10.49	APP	Manchester C.	11.67	1968-69	3	1	0	(F)
			L	Tranmere Rov.	01.71	1970	2	/	0	
GLIDDEN, Gilbert S.	Sunderland	15.12.15	Port Vale(*)	Reading	*	1946-49	78		18	(WH)*Sunderland/
			TR	Orient	11.50	1950	1		0	E.SCH.INT.
GLOSSOP, Terry	Sheffield	10.05.40		Chesterfield	05.59	1959	8		1	(OR)
GLOVER, Alan R.	Windsor	21.10.50	APP	Q.P.R.	03.68	1968	5	1	0	(M)
			TR	W.B.A.	06.69	1969-76	84	8	9	
			L	Southend U.	01.76	1975	0	1	0	
			L	Brentford	10.76	1976	6	/	0	
			TR	Orient	03.77	1976-77	37	/	5	
			TR	Brentford	11.78	1978-79	21	2	2	
GLOVER, Alex	Glasgow	28.02.22	Partick Th.	Bradford P.A.	03.48	1947-49	48		5	(OR)
			TR	Luton T.	09.49	1949-50	56		6	
			TR	Blackburn Rov.	09.51	1951-53	65		4	
			TR	Barrow	08.54	1954-57	86		7	
GLOVER, Arthur	Barnsley	27.03.18	JNRS	Barnsley	*	1946-52	183		5	(HB)
GLOVER, Benny D.	Birmingham	30.11.46		Coventry C.	10.66	1966	0	1	0	(HB)
GLOVER, Bev. A.	Manchester	25.03.26	Cheadle	Stockport Co.	01.48	1947-53	137		1	(CH)
			TR	Rochdale	03.54	1953-58	169		1	
GLOVER, Gerry J.	Liverpool	27.09.46	APP	Everton	08.64	1964-65	2	1	0	(IF)E.YTH.INT./E.SCH.INT.
			TR	Mansfield T.	09.67	1967	18	/	0	
GLOVER, John J.	Workington	06.02.35	Marsh BC	Workington	10.54	1954	2		0	(F)
GLOVER, Len	Kennington	31.01.44	JNRS	Charlton Ath.	05.62	1962-67	178	/	20	(OL)
			TR	Leicester C.	11.67	1967-75	245	7	38	
GLOVER, Peter	Bradford	16.10.36		Bradford C.	11.57	1957	1		0	
GLOZIER, Robert	E. Ham	20.11.48	APP	West Ham U.	05.66					(FB) E.SCH.INT.
			TR	Torquay U.	08.69	1969-71	57		1	
GLYNN, Terry R.	Hackney	17.12.58	APP	Orient	12.76	1976	1	1	0	(F)
GOAD, Alan	Exeter	08.08.48	JNRS	Exeter C.	12.65					(D)
			TR	Hartlepool U.	07.67	1967-77	366	9	11	
GOALEN, Harry K.	Hindley	24.05.33	JNRS	Stockport Co.	04.53	1950-55	18		2	(F)
GOBLE, Steve R.	Erpingham	05.09.60	APP	Norwich C.	09.78	1979-80	30	/	2	(F)
GODBOLD, Daryl M.	Ipswich	05.09.64	APP	Norwich C.	09.82	1983	0	2	0	(D)
GODBOLD, Harry	Gateshead	31.01.39	Unsworth Col.	Sunderland	05.56	1957-59	12		1	(W)
			TR	Hartlepool U.	01.61	1960-62	66		8	
			Boston U.	Lincoln C.	03.66	1965-66	22	/	3	
GODDARD, Howard J.	Over Wallop	10.05.57	APP	Bournemouth	07.74	1972-75	62	2	18	(F)
			TR	Swindon T.	06.76	1976	10	3	0	
			TR	Newport Co.	08.77	1977-81	101	4	42	
			L	Blackpool	09.81	1981	4	/	2	
			TR	Bournemouth	12.81	1981	6	3	2	
			TR	Aldershot	08.82	1982	26	2	9	
GODDARD, Paul	Harlington	12.10.59	APP	Q.P.R.	07.77	1977-79	63	7	23	(F)E.U21-8/E-1
			TR	West Ham U.	08.80	1980-83	117	3	43	
GODDARD, Ray	Birmingham	17.10.20	Red Rov.	Wolverhampton W.	*					(CH)d.1974
			TR	Chelsea	09.46	1946-47	14		1	
			TR	Plymouth Arg.	07.48	1948-49	43		1	
			TR	Exeter C.	12.49	1949-53	130		2	
GODDARD, Ray	Fulham	13.02.49	Fulham (APP)	Orient	02.67	1966-73	279	/	0	(G)
			TR	Millwall	11.74	1975-77	80	/	0	
			TR	Wimbledon	02.78	1977-80	119	/	1	
GODDEN, Anthony	Gillingham	02.08.55	Ashford T.	W.B.A.	08.75	1976-82	205	/	0	(G)
			L	Luton T.	03.83	1982	12	/	0	
			TR	Walsall	10.83	1983	19	/	0	
GODDERIDGE, Alan E.	Amington	23.05.28	Tamworth	Swansea C.	10.50	1951	1		0	(HB)
			TR	Walsall	07.52	1952	3		0	
GODDING, Earl G.	Wrexham	06.01.34		Wrexham	04.54	1952-58	21		0	(G)
			TR	Workington	08.59	1959	10		0	
GODFREY, Brian C.	Flint	01.05.40	Flint Alex	Everton	05.58	1959	1		0	(IF) W-3/W.U23-1●
			TR	Scunthorpe U.	06.60	1960-63	87		24	
			TR	Preston N.E.	10.63	1963-67	121	1	52	
			TR	Aston Villa	09.67	1967-70	139	4	22	
			TR	Bristol Rov.	05.71	1971-72	79	2	16	
			TR	Newport Co.	06.73	1973-75	117	1	14	
GODFREY, Kevin	Kennington	24.02.60	APP	Orient	03.77	1977-83	144	15	31	(F)

Players Names	Birthplace	Date	Previous Club	League Club	Date Signed	Seasons Played	Apps	Sub	Gls	
GODFREY, Peter R.	Woolwich	15.03.38	JNRS	Charlton Ath.	11.55	1960	1		0	(OR)
			TR	Gillingham	07.61	1961-64	66	/	9	
			TR	Chesterfield	07.65	1965	28	/	2	
			TR	Exeter C.	06.66	1966	42	/	4	
GODFREY, Tony	Newbury	30.04.39	Basingstoke	Southampton	04.58	1958-65	140	/	0	(G)
			TR	Aldershot	12.65	1965-69	172	/	0	
			TR	Rochdale	07.70	1970-71	71	/	0	
			TR	Aldershot	07.72	1972-75	68	/	0	
GODMUNDSSON, Albert S.	Iceland	05.10.23	Iceland	Arsenal	AM	1946	2		0	(IR)
GODSELL, John D.	Fife	13.09.24		Huddersfield T.	06.46					
			TR	Bradford C.	09.48	1949	9		0	
			TR	Southport	08.51	1951	3		0	
GODWIN, Don	Bargoed	05.07.32	Bargoed	Cardiff C.	12.53	1956	2		0	
GODWIN, Robert G.	Wootton	03.02.28		Swindon T.	09.51	1951	2		0	
GODWIN, Tom F.	Dublin	20.08.27	Shamrock Rov.	Leicester C.	10.49	1949-51	45		0	(G)EI-13/L.O.I. REP.
			TR	Bournemouth	06.52	1952-61	357		0	
GODWIN, Verdi	Blackburn	11.02.26		Blackburn Rov.	+	1946-47	27		6	(CF)
			TR	Manchester C.	06.48	1948	8		3	
			TR	Stoke C.	06.49	1949	22		2	
			TR	Mansfield T.	01.50	1949-50	31		9	
			TR	Middlesbrough	11.51					
			TR	Grimsby T.	01.52	1951	1		0	
			TR	Brentford	03.52	1951-52	7		0	
			TR	Southport	07.54	1954	17		0	
			TR	Barrow	08.55	1955	16		3	
			TR	Tranmere Row.	08.56	1956	14		2	
GOFFIN, William C.	Tamworth	12.12.20	JNRS	Aston Villa	*	1946-53	158		36	(IF)
			TR	Walsall	08.54	1954	8		1	
GOLAC, Ivan	Yugoslavia	15.06.50	Partizan Belgrade	Southmpton	11.78	1978-81	143	1	4	(D) YUGOSLAV. INT.
			TR	Bournemouth	11.82	1982	9	/	0	
			TR	Manchester C.	03.83	1982	2	/	0	
				Southampton	N/C	1983	11	/	0	
GOLDBERG, Les	Leeds	03.01.18	JNRS	Leeds U.	*	1946	12		0	(FB) E.SCH.INT.
			TR	Reading	03.47	1946-49	71		0	
GOLDER, Jim	Manchester	28.03.55	APP	Stockport Co.	APP	1971	0	1	0	
GOLDIE, Jim	Denny	29.06.40	Kilsyth Rgrs.	Luton T.	04.62	1962	7		2	(F)
			TR	York C.	06.63	1963	22		7	
GOLDIE, Peter	Dumbarton	07.06.34	Glasgow Celtic	Aldershot	06.58	1958	5		0	(FB)
GOLDING, Norman J.	London	32.01.37	Tonbridge	Q.P.R.	08.59	1959-60	31		6	(F)
GOLDSMITH, Martin S.	Carmarthen	25.05.62	Carmarthen	Cambridge U.	04.80	1980-83	28	7	5	(F)
			TR	Cardiff C.	01.84	1983	3	6	2	
GOLDTHORPE, Robert	Osterley	06.12.50	JNRS	Crystal Palace	07.68	1971	1	/	0	(D)
			TR	Charlton Ath.	12.72	1972-75	70	9	6	
			L	Aldershot	02.76	1975	16	/	0	
			TR	Brentford	07.76	1976	19	/	2	
GOLDTHORPE, Wayne	Staincross	19.09.57	APP	Huddersfield T.	09.75	1975-77	19	7	7	(F)
			L	Hartlepool U.	12.76	1976	6	1	1	
			TR	Hartlepool U.	08.78	1978-79	43	4	8	
			TR	Crewe Alex.	10.79	1979	0	1	0	
GOMERSALL, Vic	Manchester	17.06.42	JNRS	Manchester C.	07.60	1961-65	39	/	0	(FB)
			TR	Swansea C.	08.66	1966-70	179	1	6	
GOOCH, Jim A.G.	Ilford	11.07.21	Becontree	Preston N.E.	+	1946-51	135		0	(G)
			TR	Bradford C.	07.53	1953	22		0	
			TR	Watford	07.54	1955-56	43		0	
GOOD, John R.	Portsmouth	29.01.33		Nottingham F.	06.53					
			TR	Bury	06.54					
			Buxton	Tranmere Rov.	07.55	1955	5		0	
GOODALL, Bernard	Slough	04.10.37		Reading	07.59	1959-61	98		0	(FB)
			TR	Carlisle U.	07.63	1963	1		0	
			TR	Halifax T.	11.64	1964	23		0	
GOODALL, David G.	Madeley	18.05.43	JNRS	Shrewsbury T.	05.61	1961	1		0	(HB)
GOODCHILD, Gary D.	Chelmsford	27.01.58	APP	Arsenal	01.75					(F) E.SCH.INT.
			TR	Hereford U.	06.76	1976	1	3	0	
			TR	Reading	09.77	1977	0	1	0	
			Kramfors	Crystal Palace	12.79	1979-80	0	2	0	
GOODCHILD, John	Gateshead	02.01.39	Ludworth J.	Sunderland	09.56	1957-60	44		21	(OL)
			TR	Brighton & H.A.	05.61	1961-65	162	1	45	
			TR	York C.	06.66	1966	29	/	7	
			TR	Darlington	07.67	1967	2	/	0	
GOODE, Terry J.	London	29.10.61	APP	Birmingham C.	09.79	1980	0	2	0	(F)
GOODEVE, Ken G.A.	Manchester	03.09.50	APP	Manchester U.	09.67					(HB)
			TR	Luton T.	04.70	1970-72	9	6	0	
			TR	Brighton & H.A.	12.73	1973	5	1	0	
			TR	Watford	06.74	1974-75	67	/	4	

Players Names	Birthplace	Date	Previous Club	League Club	Date Signed	Seasons Played	Apps	Sub	Gls	
GOODFELLOW, Derek O.	Shilbottle	26.06.17	Gateshead(*)	Sheffield Wed.	*	1946	7		0	(G)
			TR	Middlesbrough	06.47	1947	36		0	
GOODFELLOW, Jim	B. Auckland	16.09.43	B. Auckland	Port Vale	06.66	1966-68	77	8	11	(F)
			TR	Workington	07.69	1969-73	199	/	15	
			TR	Rotherham U.	01.74	1973-77	192	/	8	
			TR	Stockport Co.	08.78	1978	2	1	0	
GOODFELLOW, Jim B.	Edinburgh	30.07.38	T. Lanark	Leicester C.	05.63	1963-67	96	2	26	(CF)
			TR	Mansfield T.	03.68	1967-70	95	6	14	
GOODFELLOW, Sid	Woolstanton	06.07.15	Rochdale(*)	Chesterfield	*	1946-47	80		0	(WH) *Port Vale
			TR	Doncaster Rov.	05.48	1948-49	65		2	
			TR	Oldham Ath.	09.50	1950-51	72		2	
			TR	Accrington St.	06.52	1952	28		2	
GOODGAME, Anthony A.	Hammersmith	19.02.46	APP	Fulham	02.64					(HB)
			TR	Orient	08.66	1966	7	/	0	
GOODING, Mike C.	Newcastle	12.04.59	B. Auckland	Rotherham U.	07.79	1979-82	90	15	9	(M)
			TR	Chesterfield	12.82	1982	12	/	0	
			TR	Rotherham U.	09.83	1983	24	2	7	
GOODING, Ray	Hartlepool	16.02.59	APP	Coventry C.	06.76	1976-81	46	3	5	(M)
			L	Bristol C.	03.82	1981	3	/	0	
			TR	Plymouth Arg.	08.82	1982	7	/	1	
GOODISON, C. Wayne	Wakefield	23.09.64	APP	Barnsley	09.82	1982	3	/	0	(D)
GOODLASS, Ron	Liverpool	06.09.53	APP	Everton	07.71	1975-77	31	4	2	(M) E.SCH.INT.
			Den Haag	Fulham	09.80	1980	21	1	1	
			TR	Scunthorpe U.	04.82	1981	9	/	0	
			Hong Kong	Tranmere Rov.	12.83	1983	18	2	0	
GOODMAN, Donald R.	Leeds	09.05.66	JNRS	Bradford C.	N/C	1983	0	2	0	
GOODMAN, John	Kings Lynn	08.09.35		Crewe Alex.	10.58	1958	1		0	(G)
GOODMAN, Malcolm J.	Solihull	06.05.61	Bromsgrove	Halifax T.	09.79	1979-82	70	16	1	(D)
GOODWIN, Dave	Nantwich	15.10.54	APP	Stoke C.	06.72	1973-77	22	4	3	(F)
			L	Workington	10.76	1976	7	/	0	
			TR	Mansfield T.	11.77	12977-79	42	4	5	
			TR	Bury	09.80	1980	2	2	0	
			TR	Rochdale	08.81	1981	34	5	6	
			TR	Crewe Alex.	08.82	1982	4	3	0	
GOODWIN, Eric	Chesterfield	06.03.29		Mansfield T.	09.53	1953-54	9		0	
GOODWIN, Fred	Heywood	28.06.33		Manchester U.	10.53	1954-59	95		6	(WH) Lancs. Cricketer
			TR	Leeds U.	03.60	1959-63	107		2	
			TR	Scunthorpe U.	12.64	1965	5	1	1	
GOODWIN, Fred J.	Stockport	04.01.44	JNRS	Wolverhampton W.	01.61	1961-65	44	1	0	(WH)
			TR	Stockport Co.	01.66	1965-69	171	5	20	
			TR	Blackburn Rov.	03.70	1969-71	63	1	4	
			TR	Southport	10.71	1971	10	2	0	
			TR	Port Vale	08.72	1972	27	/	2	
			Macclesfield	Stockport Co.	08.74	1974	29	/	1	
GOODWIN, Ian D.	Irlam	14.11.50		Coventry C.	08.70	1970	4	/	0	(WH)
			TR	Brighton & H.A.	10.70	1970-73	52	4	0	
GOODWIN, John W.	Worcester	29.09.20	Worcester C.	Birmingham C.	05.46	1946-48	32		8	(OR)
			TR	Brentford	04.49	1949-53	131		23	
GOODWIN, Les	Manchester	30.04.24		Oldham Ath.	+	1946	7		0	(W)
			TR	Southport	07.47	1947-48	16		2	
GOODWIN, Mark	Sheffield	23.02.60	APP	Leicester C.	11.77	1977-80	69	22	8	(M)
			TR	Notts. Co.	03.81	1980-83	103	8	10	
GOODWIN, Sam	Tarbolton	14.03.43	Airdrie	Crystal Palace	09.71	1971	18	7		(HB)
GOODWIN, Steve A.	Chadderton	23.02.54	APP	Norwich C.	02.72	1970-74	2	1	0	(M)
			L	Scunthorpe U.	09.73	1973	2	/	0	
			TR	Southend U.	06.75	1975-78	68	7	10	
GOODYEAR, Clive	Lincoln	15.01.61	Lincoln C. (N/C)	Luton T.	10.78	1979-83	85	5	4	(D)
GOODYEAR, George W.	Luton	05.07.16	Hitchin T.	Luton T.	*	1946	10		0	(WH)
			TR	Southend U.	07.47	1947-48	59		1	
			TR	Crystal Palace	06.49						
GORAM, Andy L.	Bury	13.04.64	W.B.A.(APP)	Oldham Ath.	08.81	1981-83	63	/	0	(G)
GORAM, Lewis A.	Edinburgh	02.07.26	T. Lanark	Bury	06.50	1950-56	111		0	(G)
GORDINE, Barry	London	01.09.48		Sheffield U.	06.68					(G)
			TR	Oldham Ath.	12.68	1968-70	83	/	0	
			TR	Southend U.	08.71						
				Brentford	10.74						
GORDON, Andy	Bathgate	06.07.44	W.Auckland	Darlington	AM	1969	1	2	0	(CF)
GORDON, Dennis W.	Wolverhampton	07.06.24	Oxford C.	W.B.A.	09.47	1947-51	27		2	(OR)
			TR	Brighton & H.A.	07.52	1952-60	276		63	
GORDON, Henry	Glasgow	10.12.31	Petershill	Bury	06.51	1951-56	24		0	(HB)
GORDON, Henry A.	Livingstone	25.07.40	Dundee U.	Bradford P.A.	08.65	1965-66	61	/	2	(HB)

Players Names	Birthplace	Date	Previous Club	League Club	Date Signed	Seasons Played	Apps	Sub	Gls	
GORDON, James S.	Stretford	03.09.55	Blackpool (APP)	Luton T.	09.73			/		(G) E.SCH.INT
			TR	Lincoln C.	07.74	1976-77	4	/	0	
			TR	Reading	08.78					
			TR	Scunthorpe U.	09.78	1979-80	34	/	0	
GORDON, Jim	Fauldhouse	23.10.15	Newcastle U.(*)	Middlesbrough	+	1946-53	231		3	(WH) *Wishaw J.
GORDON, John D.S.	Portsmouth	11.09.31	JNRS	Portsmouth	01.49	1951-58	211		70	(IF)●
			TR	Birmingham C.	09.58	1958-60	96		32	
			TR	Portsmouth	03.61	1960-66	234	/	36	
GORDON, Peter J.	Northampton	21.05.32	Northants Amats.	Norwich C.	12.49	1953-57	159		35	(HB)
			TR	Watford	07.58	1958-59	43		13	
			TR	Exeter C.	07.60	1960-61	67		11	
			TR	Newport Co.	07.62	1962	8		1	
GORDON, Robert B.				Millwall	+	1946-47	6		0	
GORDON, William J.W.	Carlisle	22.11.26		Carlisle U.	08.48	1948	15		4	(CF)●
			TR	Barrow	07.50	1949-57	301		145	
			TR	Workington	03.58	1957-58	33		7	
			TR	Barrow	10.59					
GORE, Tommy	Liverpool	26.11.53	Tranmere Rov.(N/C)	Wigan Ath.	N/L	1978-80	102	/	14	(M)
			TR	Bury	10.80	1980-82	118	1	15	
			TR	Port Vale	07.83	1983	33	3	2	
GORIN, Edward R.	Cardiff	02.06.24	Grange A.	Cardiff C.	10.48	1948-49	6		2	(CF)
			TR	Scunthorpe U.	07.50	1950	26		12	
			TR	Shrewsbury T.	01.51	1950-51	18		3	
GORING, Peter	Bishops Cleve	02.01.27	Cheltenham	Arsenal	01.48	1949-58	220		50	(CF)
GORMAN, John	Winchburgh	16.08.49	Glasgow Celtic	Carlisle U.	09.70	1970-76	228	1	5	(D)
			TR	Tottenham H.	01.76	1976-78	30	/	0	
GORMAN, Paul A.	Dublin	06.08.63	APP	Arsenal	10.80	1981-83	5	1	0	(M)
GORMAN, William C.	Sligo	13.07.11	Bury(*)	Brentford	*	1946-49	101		1	(FB) EI-13/NI-4/d.1978
GORMLEY, Phil	Greenock	13.10.24	Glasgow Celtic	Aldershot	08.50	1950-52	65		9	(CF)
GORNALL, John	Preston	28.03.41	JNRS	Preston N.E.	07.60	1961-62	4		0	(HB)
GORRIE, David	Liverpool	21.01.43	JNRS	Everton	05.60					(HB)
			TR	Stockport Co.	07.62	1962	18		0	
GORRY, Martin C.	Derby	29.12.54	APP	Barnsley	11.73	1975-76	34	/	3	(D)
			TR	Newcastle U.	10.76	1977	0	1	0	
			TR	Hartlepool U.	07.78	1978-79	59	/	0	
GOSLIN, Richard W.	Bovey Tracey	31.10.56	Nottingham F.(APP)	Torquay U.	07.74	1974-75	13	5	2	(F)
GOSNEY, Andy R.	Southampton	08.11.63	APP	Portsmouth	11.81	1981	1	/	0	(G) E.YTH.INT.
GOSS, Jeremy	Cyprus	11.05.65		Norwich C.	03.83	1983	0	1	0	(M)
GOTTS, Jim	Seaton Delavel	17.01.17	Ashington	Brentford	+					
			TR	Brighton & H.A.	07.46	1946	2		0	
GOUGH, Charles	Glasgow	21.05.39	Alton T.	Charlton Ath.	06.63	1964	4		0	(HB)
GOUGH, Keith	Willenhall	04.02.53	APP	Walsall	02.71	1969-71	11	4	0	(W) E.SCH.INT.
			TR	Oxford U.	07.72	1972-74	32	7	5	
GOUGH, Mike	Beeston	29.12.35		Aldershot	05.56	1956-58	20		1	(HB)
GOUGH, Ray	Belfast	08.02.38	Linfield	Exeter C.	10.63					(HB)
			TR	Millwall	10.64	1964	13		0	
GOUGH, Robert G.	Birmingham	20.07.49	APP	Walsall	07.67	1966	1	/	0	(F)
			TR	Port Vale	07.68	1968-73	189	21	33	
			L	Stockport Co.	02.73	1973	6	/	0	
			TR	Southport	07.74	1974-75	61	/	16	
			TR	Colchester U.	01.76	1975-80	195	1	65	
GOUGH, Tony	Bath	18.03.40	Bath C.	Bristol Rov.	05.58	1958	1		0	(IF)
			Bath C.	Swindon T.	07.70	1970	24	1	2	
			Hereford	Torquay U.	07.72	1972	2	/	0	
GOULD, Geoff	Blackburn	07.01.45	APP	Bradford P.A.	01.62	1962-68	129	2	18	(F)
			L	Lincoln C.	02.68	1967	1	/	0	
			TR	Notts.Co.	07.69	1969	1	/	0	
GOULD, Harry	Birkenhead	05.01.25		Tranmere Rov.	09.46	1946-48	5		2	(IF)
			Northwich Vic.	Southport	09.50	1950	16		2	
			TR	Tranmere Rov.	07.51					
GOULD, J. Barry	Ammanford	18.01.44	APP	Arsenal	11.61					(WH)
			TR	Chelsea	02.64					
			TR	Peterborough U.	07.65	1965	18	/	3	
GOULD, Robert A.	Coventry	12.06.46	APP	Coventry C.	06.64	1963-67	78	3	40	(F)
			TR	Arsenal	02.68	1967-69	57	8	16	
			TR	Wolverhampton W.	06.70	1970-71	39	1	18	
			TR	W.B.A.	09.71	1971-72	52	/	18	
			TR	Bristol C.	12.72	1972-73	35	/	15	
			TR	West Ham U.	11.73	1973-75	46	5	15	
			TR	Wolverhampton W.	12.75	1975-76	24	10	13	
			TR	Bristol C.	10.77	1977-78	35	1	12	
			TR	Hereford U.	09.78	1978-79	42	3	13	

Players Names	Birthplace	Date	Previous Club	League Club	Date Signed	Seasons Played	Career Record Apps	Sub	Gls	
GOULD, Trevor	Coventry	05.03.50	JNRS	Coventry C.	07.67	1969	9	/	0	(IF) E.SCH.INT./
			TR	Northampton T.	10.70	1970-72	102	3	6	Brother of Robert
GOULD, Walter	Rotherham	25.09.38	Rawmarsh	Sheffield U.	03.58	1958	5		1	(OR)
			TR	York C.	02.61	1960-63	120		26	
			TR	Brighton & H.A.	01.64	1963-67	166	2	44	
GOULDEN, Albert	Salford	05.02.45	JNRS	Bolton W.	02.62	1962	1		0	(FB)
GOULDEN, Len A.	W. Ham	16.07.12	West Ham U.(*)	Chelsea	+	1946-49	99		17	(IF) E-14/E.F.LGE REP./ E.SCH.INT.
GOULDEN, Roy L.	London	22.09.37	JNRS	Arsenal	09.54	1958	1		0	(IF) E.SCH.INT./
			TR	Southend U.	05.61	1961	9		2	Son of Len
			TR	Ipswich T.	07.62					
GOULDING, Eric	Winsford	22.11.24	Everton(+)	Crewe Alex.	10.46	1946	1		0	(RB) +Over A.
GOULDING, Steve	Mexborough	21.01.54	APP	Sheffield U.	05.71	1971-75	28	/	0	(FB)
GOUNDRY, William	Middlesbrough	28.03.34	Huddersfield T.(AM)	Brentford	05.55	1955-60	141		12	(F)
GOVAN, Alex	Glasgow	16.06.29	JNRS	Plymouth Arg.	09.46	1946-52	110		0	(OL)
			TR	Birmingham C.	06.53	1953-57	165		53	
			TR	Portsmouth	03.58	1957-58	11		2	
			TR	Plymouth Arg.	09.58	1958-59	32		8	
GOVAN, Charles	Belfast	12.01.43	JNRS	Burnley	01.60					(F) N.I.SCH.INT.
			TR	Mansfield T.	06.63	1963-64	10		0	
GOVIER, Steve	Watford	06.04.52	APP	Norwich C.	07.69	1970-73	22	/	1	(D)
			TR	Brighton & H.A.	04.74	1974	12	/	1	
			TR	Grimsby T.	12.74	1974-76	23	1	0	
GOW, Gerry	Glasgow	29.05.52	JNRS	Bristol C.	06.69	1969-80	368	/	47	(M) S.U23-1
			TR	Manchester C.	10.80	1980-81	26	/	5	
			TR	Rotherham U.	01.82	1981-82	58	/	4	
			TR	Burnley	08.83	1983	8	1	0	
GOWANS, Peter T.	Dundee	25.05.44	Glasgow Celtic	Crewe Alex.	07.63	1963-66	141	/	43	(IF)
			TR	Aldershot	07.67	1967-69	111	2	27	
			TR	Rochdale	07.70	1970-73	135	8	21	
			TR	Southport	07.74	1974	3	1	0	
GOWLING, Alan E.	Stockport	16.03.48	Manchester Univ.	Manchester U.	09.68	1967-71	64	7	18	(F) E.U23-1/E.AMAT.INT.
			TR	Huddersfield T.	06.72	1972-74	128	/	58	
			TR	Newcastle U.	08.75	1975-77	91	1	30	
			TR	Bolton W.	03.78	1977-81	147	2	28	
			TR	Preston N.E.	09.82	1982	37	3	5	
GOY, Peter	Beverley	08.06.38	JNRS	Arsenal	06.55	1958	2		0	(G)
			TR	Southend U.	10.60	1960-63	118		0	
			TR	Watford	07.64	1964	27		0	
			TR	Huddersfield T.	07.65	1966	4	/	0	
GRACE, Derek G.	Chiswick	29.12.44	Q.P.R.(APP)	Exeter C.	05.62	1962-64	40		4	(IF)
			TR	Gillingham	07.65	1965	4	/	1	
GRAFTON, Stan T.	Heathton	02.04.23		Aldershot	08.47	1947-48	2		0	(HB) d.1953
GRAHAM, Alan W.	Ryhope	23.10.37	Silksworth J.	Sunderland	05.55	1957	3		0	(FB)
GRAHAM, Arthur	Glasgow	26.10.52	Aberdeen	Leeds U.	07.77	1977-82	222	1	37	(F) S-10/S.U23-3
			TR	Manchester U.	08.83	1983	33	4	5	
GRAHAM, Donald	Oldham	02.04.53	Hyde U	Bury	10.79	1979-80	3	4	0	(M)
GRAHAM, Doug	Morpeth	15.07.21	Barrington U.	Newcastle U.	+	1946-50	71		0	(FB)
			TR	Preston N.E.	11.50					
			TR	Lincoln C.	12.51	1951-56	182		0	
GRAHAM, George	Bargeddie	30.11.44	APP	Aston Villa	12.61	1962-63	8		2	(F)S12/S.U23-2/
			TR	Chelsea	07.64	1974-66	72	/	35	S.SCH.INT.
			TR	Arsenal	09.66	1966-72	219	8	60	
			TR	Manchester U.	12.72	1972-74	41	2	2	
			TR	Portsmouth	11.74	1974-76	61	/	5	
			TR	Crystal Palace	11.76	1976-77	43	1	2	
GRAHAM, Gerry W.	Aspatria	31.01.41		Blackpool	08.59					(WH)
			TR	Peterborough U.	07.60	1960-63	17		1	
			TR	Mansfield T.	06.64	1964	18		3	
			Hereford U.	Workington	07.68	1968	6	/	0	
GRAHAM, Jackie	Glasgow	16.07.46	Guildford C.	Brentford	07.70	1970-79	371	3	38	(M)
GRAHAM, John	Leyland	26.04.26		Aston Villa	11.46	1946-48	10		3	
			TR	Wrexham	06.49	1949-51	45		7	
			TR	Rochdale	01.53	1952	10		1	
			TR	Bradford C.	07.53	1953	18		1	
GRAHAM, Les	Manchester	14.05.24	Flixton	Blackburn Rov.	04.47	1947-52	151		42	(IF)
			TR	Newport Co.	02.53	1952-54	96		40	
			TR	Watford	07.55	1955-57	90		26	
			TR	Newport Co.	09.57	1957-58	65		15	
GRAHAM, Malcolm	Hall Green	26.01.34	Crigglestone	Barnsley	04.53	1954-58	109		35	(IF)
			TR	Bristol C.	05.59	1959	14		8	
			TR	Orient	06.60	1960-62	75		30	
			TR	Q.P.R.	07.63	1963	21		7	
			TR	Barnsley	07.64	1964	20		6	

Players Names	Birthplace	Date	Previous Club	League Club	Date Signed	Seasons Played	Apps	Sub	Gls	
GRAHAM, Mike	Lancaster	24.02.59	APP	Bolton W.	03.77	1977-80	43	3	0	(D)
			TR	Swindon T.	07.81	1981-83	112	/	1	
GRAHAM, Milton M.	Hackney	02.11.62		Bournemouth	05.81	1981-83	41	14	9	(M)
GRAHAM, Peter	Barnsley	19.04.47	Worsboro Br.	Barnsley	01.67	1966-69	16	3	1	(M)
			L	Halifax T.	03.70	1969	6	/	0	
			TR	Darlington	06.70	1970-73	118	1	43	
			TR	Lincoln C.	09.73	1973-77	142	16	47	
			TR	Cambridge U.	06.78	1978-79	35	3	0	
GRAHAM, Ralph C.	Durham	29.12.29	Broadway Ath.	Doncaster Rov.	05.47	1948-49	15		0	(W)
			TR	Southport	07.50	1950-51	30		9	
GRAHAM, Richard D.	Corby	06.05.22	Leicester C.(*)	Crystal Palace	+	1946-50	155		0	(G) *Northampton T.
GRAHAM, Robert	Motherwell	22.11.44	APP	Liverpool	11.61	1964-71	96	7	31	(CF)
			TR	Coventry C.	03.72	1971-72	19	/	3	
			L	Tranmere Rov.	01.73	1972	10	/	3	
GRAHAM, Tommy	Glasgow	31.03.58	Arthurlie	Aston Villa	04.78					(F)
			TR	Barnsley	12.78	1968-79	36	2	13	
			TR	Halifax T.	10.80	1980-81	68	3	17	
			TR	Doncaster Rov.	N/C	1982	9	2	2	
			TR	Scunthorpe U.	08.83	1982-83	37	3	7	
GRAHAM, William G.L.	Belfast	17.10.25	Brantwood	Doncaster Rov.	10.49	1950-58	303		3	(FB) NI-14
			TR	Torquay U.	11.58	1958	20		0	
GRAHAM, William R.	Carlisle	08.05.29		Workington	07.51					(FB)
			Consett	Carlisle U.	01.54	1953-60	35		2	
GRAHAM, William V.	Armagh	14.02.59	Northampton T.(APP)	Brentford	08.77	1977-80	42	6	3	(M)
GRAINGER, Colin	Wakefield	10.06.33	Sth. Elmsall	Wrexham	10.50	1950-52	5		0	(OL) E-7/E.F.LGE REP./
			TR	Sheffield U.	07.53	1953-56	88		26	Brother of Jack
			TR	Sunderland	02.57	1956-59	120		14	(Rotherham)/
			TR	Leeds U.	08.60	1960	33		7	Cousin of Dennis/Jack
			TR	Port Vale	10.61	1961-63	39		6	(Southport)
			TR	Doncaster Rov.	08.64	1964-65	40	/	4	
GRAINGER, Dennis	Barnsley	05.03.20	Southport(*)	Leeds U.	+	1946-47	37		5	Cousin of Colin
			TR	Wrexham	12.47	1947-50	98		11	Brother of Jack
			TR	Oldham Ath.	06.51	1951	3		0	(Southport)
GRAINGER, Jack	Sth. Elmsall	17.07.12	Barnsley(*)	Southport	*	1946	8		0	(FB) d.1976
GRAINGER, Jack	Havercroft	03.04.24		Rotherham U.	+	1947-56	352		110	(OR) E'B'-1/d.1983/
			TR	Lincoln C.	06.57	1957-58	42		14	Brother to Colin
GRANGER, Mike	Leeds	07.10.31	Cliftonville	York C.	12.51	1954-61	71		0	(G)
			TR	Hull C.	07.62	1962	2		0	
			TR	Halifax T.	07.63	1963-64	2		0	
GRANT, Alan	Havant	06.01.35	Gosport Bor.	Brighton & H.A.	04.56	1956	1		0	(HB)
			TR	Exeter C.	06.60	1960	4		0	
GRANT, Alick F.	Camerton	11.08.16		Leicester C.	*	1946	2		0	(G)
			TR	Derby Co.	11.46	1946-47	12		0	
			TR	Newport Co.	11.48	1948	20		0	
			TR	Leeds U.	08.49					
			TR	York C.	03.50	1949	3		0	
GRANT, Bernard	Airdrie	23.05.20	T. Lanark	Exeter C.	07.47	1948	4		0	(IF)
GRANT, Brian	Coatbridge	10.05.43	JNRS	Nottingham F.	05.60	1960-64	18		0	(FB)
			TR	Hartlepool U.	01.66	1965-66	35	/	0	
			TR	Bradford C.	08.67					
				Cambridge U.	N/L	1970	14	/	0	
GRANT, Cyril	Wath	10.07.20	Mexborough	Lincoln C.	+					(CF)
			TR	Arsenal	07.46	1946	2		0	
			TR	Fulham	12.46	1946-47	15		4	
			TR	Southend U.	03.48	1947-54	174		62	
GRANT, David	Sheffield	02.06.60	APP	Sheffield Wed.	02.78	1977-81	132	1	4	(D)
			TR	Oxford U.	07.82	1982-83	24	/	1	
			L	Chesterfield	09.83	1983	7	/	0	
			TR	Cardiff C.	03.84	1983	12	/	0	
GRANT, David B.	Edinburgh	31.07.43	T.Lanark	Reading	05.63	1963-64	17		3	(F)
GRANT, David J.	Liverpool	18.12.47	APP	Everton	12.65					(HB) E.SCH.INT.
			TR	Wrexham	09.66	1966	5	5	0	
GRANT, Edward A.	Greenock	01.10.28	Weymouth	Sheffield U.	05.50	1950	4		0	(HB)
			TR	Grimsby T.	07.52	1952-53	15		5	
GRANT, Jim				Brighton & H.A.	AM	1946	1		0	
GRANT, Jim	Chapelhall	10.06.40	Larkhall Th.	Scunthorpe U.	11.58	1958	1		0	
GRANT, John A.	High Spen	08.09.24	High Spen Ath.	Everton	+	1946-54	122		10	(WH)
			TR	Rochdale	05.56	1956-58	102		3	
			TR	Southport	01.59	1958-59	40		0	
GRANT, Ken	High Spen	13.11.38	Crook T.	Gateshead	AM	1958	5		0	(CF)
GRANT, Robert	Edinburgh	25.09.40	St.Johnstone	Carlisle U.	07.62	1962	2	1	(CF)	

Players Names	Birthplace	Date	Previous Club	League Club	Date Signed	Seasons Played	Apps	Sub	Gls	
GRANT, Wilf	Ashington	03.08.20		Manchester C.	+					(CF) E'B'-1
			TR	Southampton	10.46	1946-49	61		11	
			TR	Cardiff C.	03.50	1949-54	155		65	
			TR	Ipswich T.	10.54	1954-56	75		22	
GRANT, William	Perth	07.10.33	Brechin	Gillingham	08.56	1956	1		0	(HB)
GRANVILLE, Norman T.	Newport	25.11.19	Cliftonville	Newport Co.	+	1946	1		0	
			TR	Exeter C.	10.46	1946-47	20		1	
GRANVILLE, Ralph	Glasgow	23.04.31	Clyde	Gateshead	10.57	1957	2		0	
GRANYCOMBE, Neil	Middlesbrough	23.10.58	South Bank	Hartlepool	N/C	1980	1	/	0	(F)
GRAPES, Steve P.	Norwich	25.02.53	APP	Norwich C.	07.70	1970-76	34	7	3	(M)
			L	Bournemouth	03.76	1975	7	/	1	
			TR	Cardiff C.	10.76	1976-81	138	9	6	
			TR	Torquay U.	08.82	1982	31	/	0	
GRATRIX, Roy	Salford	09.02.32	Taylor Bros.	Blackpool	03.53	1953-64	400		0	(CH) E'B'-1/E.F.LGE REP.●
			TR	Manchester C.	09.64	1964	15		0	
GRATTAN, Jimmy	Belfast	30.11.58	APP	Sunderland	10.76					(F)
			L	Mansfield T.	11.78	1978	1	/	0	
GRATTON, Dennis	Rotherham	21.04.34	Worksop T.	Sheffield U.	10.52	1955-58	6		0	(HB)
			TR	Lincoln C.	09.59	1959-60	45		0	
GRAVER, Andy M.	Craghead	12.09.27	Annfield Plain	Newcastle U.	09.47	1949	1		0	(CF)●
			TR	Lincoln C.	09.50	1950-54	172		107	
			TR	Leicester C.	12.54	1954	11		3	
			TR	Lincoln C.	07.55	1955	15		4	
			TR	Stoke C.	11.55	1955-56	37		12	
			Boston U.	Lincoln C.	10.58	1958-60	89		33	
GRAVES, Mark	Isleworth	14.12.60	APP	Plymouth Arg.	09.78	1977-80	24	9	3	(F)
GRAVES, Robert E.	London	07.11.42	Kirton F.C.	Lincoln C.	04.60	1959-64	77		0	(G)
GRAY, Alex D.	Arbroath	07.11.36	Dundee Violet	Burnley	06.54					(FB)
			Arbroath	Cardiff C.	03.57	1958	1		0	
GRAY, Andy M.	Glasgow	30.11.55	Dundee U.	Aston Villa	10.75	1975-78	112	1	54	(F) S-19/S.U23-4
			TR	Wolverhampton W.	09.79	1979-83	131	3	38	
			TR	Everton	11.83	1983	23	/	5	
GRAY, Dave	Dundee	08.02.22	Glasgow Rgrs.	Preston N.E.	05.47	1947	36		0	(FB)
			TR	Blackburn Rov.	08.48	1948-52	107		5	
GRAY, David D.	Clydebank	13.04.23	Queensbury	Bradford C.	09.48	1948-55	242		13	(WH)
GRAY, Eddie	Glasgow	17.01.48	JNRS	Leeds U.	01.65	1965-83	439	13	52	(M) S-12/S.U23-2/S./S.SCH.INT.● Brother of Frank
GRAY, Edward	Glasgow	19.10.34	Yeovil T.	Barrow	12.57	1957-58	17		4	(F) S.SCH.INT.
			TR	Accrington St.	07.59	1959	6		0	
GRAY, Frank T.	Glasgow	27.10.54	APP	Leeds U.	11.71	1972-78	188	5	17	(D)S-32/S.U23-5/ S.SCH.INT.
			TR	Nottingham F.	08.79	1979-80	81	/	5	
			TR	Leeds U.	05.81	1981-83	102	1	9	
GRAY, George	Glasgow	06.10.29	Sligo	Scunthorpe U.	08.51	1951	9		3	(F)
GRAY, George			Vale of Clyde	Carlisle U.	11.47	1947	1		1	(F)
GRAY, George J.P.	Sunderland	07.07.25		Grimsby T.	01.47	1950	3		0	
			TR	Swindon T.	07.51	1951-52	45		0	
			TR	Darlington	07.53	1953	6		0	
GRAY, George W.	Canning Town	30.11.22	West Ham U.(AM)	Aldershot	02.47	1946-47	9		0	
GRAY, Harry	Hemsworth	26.10.18	Ardsley Rec.	Barnsley	*	1946	9		1	
			TR	Bournemouth	12.46	1946-47	30		7	
			TR	Southend U.	06.48	1948-49	19		0	
GRAY, Irvine	Barnsley	27.02.33		Barnsley	09.52					
			TR	Gillingham	08.56	1956	9		0	
GRAY, Mark	Pembroke	24.11.59	APP	Swansea C.	09.77	1977	1	1	0	(F)
			TR	Fulham	01.78					
			TR	Orient	02.79	1978	1	1	0	
GRAY, Matt	Renfrew	11.07.36	T. Lanark	Manchester C.	03.63	1962-66	87	4	21	(IF)
GRAY, Mike			Glenavon	Aldershot	09.46	1946	7		1	(IF)
			TR	Watford	06.47	1947	10		3	
GRAY, Nigel R.	Fulham	02.11.56	APP	Orient	07.74	1974-82	233	/	2	(D)
			L	Charlton Ath.	12.82	1982	3	/	0	
			TR	Swindon T.	07.83	1983	15	/	0	
			L	Brentford	03.84	1983	16	/	1	
GRAY, Robert	Cambuslang	18.06.27	Wishaw J.	Lincoln C.	10.49	1949	2		0	
GRAY, Robert	Glasgow	08.06.53	Nottingham F.(APP)	Workington	08.72	1972	0	1	0	(IF) S.SCH.INT.
GRAY, Robert	Newcastle	14.12.23	Newcastle U.(AM)	Gateshead	+	1947-58	432		0	(G)
GRAY, Robert H.W.	Aberdeen	21.01.51	Inverurie Loco.	Torquay U.	AM	1969	2	/	0	(G)
GRAY, (Ron) Roland	Nth.Shields	25.06.20	Sheffield U.(+)	Watford	+	1946	16		0	(LH)
GRAY, Stewart A.	Leeds	16.10.50	APP	Doncaster Rov.	09.68	1967-70	53	5	0	(D)
			TR	Grimsby T.	09.70	1970-76	263	1	2	
			TR	Doncaster Rov.	03.78	1977	6	/	0	

Players Names	Birthplace	Date	Previous Club	League Club	Date Signed	Seasons Played	Career Record Apps	Sub	Gls	
GRAY, Stuart	Withernsea	19.04.60	Withernsea Y.C.	Nottingham F.	12.80	1980-82	48	1	3	(M)
			L	Bolton W.	03.83	1982	10	/	0	
			TR	Barnsley	08.83	1983	16	1	8	
GRAY, Terry I.	Bradford	03.06.54	Ashley Rd.	Huddersfield T.	08.72	1972-78	146	17	36	(F)E.YTH.INT.
			TR	Southend U.	07.79	1979-81	106	4	28	
			TR	Bradford C.	08.82	1982-83	65	4	15	
GRAY, William M.	Binley	03.12.31	JNRS	Coventry C.	12.48	1951	2		0	(IF)
GRAY, William P.	Durham	24.05.27	Dinnington Col.	Orient	05.47	1947-48	19		1	(W) E'B'-1●
			TR	Chelsea	03.49	1948-52	146		12	
			TR	Burnley	08.53	1953-56	119		30	
			TR	Nottingham F.	06.57	1957-62	201		35	
			TR	Millwall	12.63	1963-64	20		1	
GRAYDON, Ray J.	Bristol	21.07.47	APP	Bristol Rov.	09.65	1965-70	132	2	27	(F) E.YTH.INT.
			TR	Aston Villa	06.71	1971-76	189	4	67	
			TR	Coventry C.	07.77	1977	17	3	5	
			Washington Dips	Oxford U.	11.78	1978-80	36	6	10	
GRAYSON, Barry J.	Manchester	12.10.44	APP	Manchester U.	11.61					(F)
			TR	Bury	01.65	1964	1		0	
GREALISH, Anthony P.	Paddington	21.09.56	APP	Orient	07.74	1974-78	169	2	10	(M) EI-37
			TR	Luton T.	08.79	1979-80	78	/	2	
			TR	Brighton & H.A.	07.81	1981-83	95	5	6	
			TR	W.B.A.	03.84	1983	11	/	0	
GREATREX, Edward	Nuneaton	18.11.36	JNRS	Norwich C.	06.54	1957	1		0	(G)
GREAVES, Danny T.	Upminster	31.01.63	Tottenham H.(N/C)	Southend U.	01.81	1981-83	30	19	14	(F)
GREAVES, Ian D.	Oldham	26.05.32	Buxton	Manchester U.	05.53	1954-59	67		0	(FB)
			TR	Lincoln C.	12.60	1960	11		0	
			TR	Oldham Ath.	05.61	1961-62	22		0	
GREAVES, Jimmy P.	East Ham	20.02.40	JNRS	Chelsea	05.57	1957-60	157		124	(IF) E-57/E.U23-12/
			Milan	Tottenham H.	12.61	1961-68	321	/	220	E.YTH.INT./E.F.LGE REP.●
				West Ham U.	03.70	1969-70	36	2	13	
GREAVES, Roy	Farnworth	04.04.47	JNRS	Bolton W.	01.65	1965-79	487	7	66	(M)
			Seatle Sounders	Rochdale	11.82	1982	19	2	0	
GREEN, Adrian	Leicester	22.10.57	APP	Leicester C.	06.76					(D)
			L	Rochdale	12.77	1977	7	/	0	
			TR	Aldershot	07.78	1978-79	7	14	0	
GREEN, Alan	Darfield	14.12.39	Dodworth Col.	Barnsley	01.59	1960-61	19		0	(FB)
			TR	York C.	07.62					
GREEN, Alan P.	Worcester	01.01.54	APP	Coventry C	01.71	1971-78	98	19	30	(F)E.YTH.INT.
GREEN, Alan P.C.	Fordingbridge	19.04.51	JNRS	Bournemouth	07.69					(F)
			TR	Mansfield T.	07.72	1972	1	/	0	
GREEN, Anthony	Glasgow	13.10.46	Albion Rov.	Blackpool	05.67	1966-71	123	/	13	(IF) S-6
			TR	Newcastle U.	10.71	1971-72	33	/	3	
GREEN, Arthur	Liverpool	28.04.28	Burscough	Huddersfield T.	02.51	1951	3		0	(FB)
GREEN, Brian G.	Droylsden	05.06.35	Haggate Lads	Rochdale	08.55	1954-58	48		8	(CF)
			TR	Southport	03.59	1958-59	20		7	
			TR	Barrow	09.60	1960	3		0	
			Altrincham	Exeter C.	08.62	1962	9		1	
			TR	Chesterfield	02.63	1962	2		0	
GREEN, Clive	Portsmouth	06.12.59	JNRS	Portsmouth	07.76	1976-77	34	6	4	(F)
GREEN, Colin R.	Wrexham	10.02.42	JNRS	Everton	02.59	1960-61	15		1	(FB) W-15/W.U23-7
			TR	Birmingham C.	12.62	1962-70	185	/	1	
			L	Wrexham	01.71	1970	3	/	0	
GREEN, Don	Blackburn	13.05.32		Accrington St.	AM	1952	12		0	
GREEN, Don	Needham Market	30.11.24		Ipswich T.	03.47	1946-51	52		0	(CH)
GREEN, Fred Z.	Sheffield	09.09.16	Torquay U.(*)	Brighton & H.A.	*	1946-47	24		0	(FB)
GREEN, George F.	Halifax	22.12.14	Yeovil T.	Huddersfield T.	+	1946-47	9		1	(WH)
			TR	Reading	10.47	1947-48	44		6	
GREEN, H. Rodney	Halifax	24.06.39		Halifax T.	08.60	1960-61	9		2	(CF)
			TR	Bradford P.A.	06.62	1962	19		6	
			TR	Bradford C.	01.63	1962-63	66		39	
			TR	Gillingham	07.64	1964	33		17	
			TR	Grimsby T.	08.65	1965-66	65	/	20	
			TR	Charlton Ath.	02.67	1966	3	1	1	
			TR	Luton T.	08.67	1967	9	2	3	
			TR	Watford	08.68	1968-69	19	11	8	
GREEN, Horace	Barnsley	23.04.18	Worsboro Br.	Halifax T.	*	1946-48	84		3	(FB)
			TR	Lincoln C.	02.49	1948-54	193		14	
GREEN, Ivan D.	Bexhill	29.07.33		Millwall	09.53	1954	1		0	
GREEN, John	Warrington	22.05.39	Stockton Hth	Tranmere Rov.	02.58	1958	17		5	(IF)
			TR	Blackpool	03.59	1959-66	135	/	9	
			TR	Port Vale	09.67	1967-70	92	2	7	
GREEN, John R.	Rotherham	07.08.58	APP	Rotherham U.	03.76	1975-83	247	1	8	(D)
			TR	Scunthorpe U.	09.83	1983	45	/	2	

Players Names	Birthplace	Date	Previous Club	League Club	Date Signed	Seasons Played	Apps	Sub	Gls	
GREEN, Ken	West Ham	27.04.24	Millwall (AM)	Birmingham C.	+	1947-58	402		2	(FB) E'B'-2/E.F.LGE.REP.●
GREEN, Ken	Hull	20.11.29	Selby T.	Grimsby T.	04.51	1951	1		0	(RH)
GREEN, Len H.	Darlington	02.10.36		Darlington	10.55	1955-60	48		0	(FB)
GREEN, Les	Atherstone	17.10.41	Atherstone	Hull C.	08.60	1961	4	/	0	(G)
			Burton A.	Hartlepool U.	07.65	1965-66	34	/	0	
			TR	Rochdale	04.67	1967	44	/	0	
			TR	Derby Co.	05.68	1968-70	107	/	0	
GREEN, Mel	Hull	20.10.51	APP	Hull C.	07.70	1971-72	10	/	0	(CH)
			TR	Cambridge U.	07.74	1974	3	/	0	
GREEN, Mike C.	Carlisle	08.09.46	APP	Carlisle U.	09.64	1965	2	/	0	(D)
			TR	Gillingham	07.68	1968-70	131	1	24	
			TR	Bristol Rov.	07.71	1971-73	74	3	2	
			TR	Plymouth Arg.	07.74	1974-76	108	/	8	
			TR	Torquay U.	03.77	1976-78	88	/	7	
GREEN, Mike J.	London	20.11.57	APP	Exeter C.	11.75	1976	0	1	0	(D)
GREEN, N. Russell	Donnington	13.08.33	Quadring FC	Lincoln C.	08.51	1951-63	145		8	(HB)
GREEN, Philip	Cardiff	30.10.57		Newport Co.	N/C	1983	8	1	2	(F)
GREEN, Rick	Scunthorpe	23.11.52	Appleby Frod.	Scunthorpe U.	09.75	1975-76	66	/	19	(F)
			TR	Chesterfield	02.77	1976-77	45	3	13	
			TR	Notts Co.	06.78	1978	6	3	0	
			TR	Scunthorpe U.	08.79	1979-81	66	5	19	
GREEN, Roger	Cardiff	20.09.44	Barry T.	Newport Co.	01.72	1971	1	/	0	(WH)
GREEN, Ron	Birmingham	03.10.56	Alvechurch	Walsall	06.77	1977-83	163	/	0	(G)
GREEN, Roy	Loughborough	08.06.31	Bloxwich Strollers	Reading	12.52	1955-56	14		3	(IF)
GREEN, Stan	W. Bromwich	06.09.28	Accles & P.	Bristol Rov.	08.52	1951	1		0	(CH)
GREEN, Tom			W.Lancs ATC	Southport	05.46	1946	4		0	(RH)
GREEN, William	Newcastle	22.12.50		Hartlepool U.	06.69	1969-72	128	3	9	(D)
			TR	Carlisle U.	07.73	1973-75	119	/	4	
			TR	West Ham U.	06.76	1976-77	35	/	1	
			TR	Peterborough U.	07.78	1978	30	/	0	
			TR	Chesterfield	06.79	1979-82	160	/	5	
			TR	Doncaster Rov.	06.83	1983	10	1	1	
GREEN, William C.	Hull	09.10.27	JNRS	Wolverhampton W.						(WH) 1 app. in goal
			TR	Walsall	09.49	1949-53	182		8	for Walsall
			TR	Wrexham	06.54	1954-55	60		2	
GREENALL, George E.	Liverpool	05.11.37	JNRS	Manchester C.	11.58					(HB)
			TR	Oldham Ath.	09.60	1960	25		0	
GREENALL, Colin A.	Billinge	30.12.63	APP	Blackpool	01.81	1980-83	89	4	5	(D)
GREENAWAY, Arthur R.	Swindon	05.04.28		Plymouth Arg.	08.47					(F)
			TR	Exeter C.	05.50	1950	1		0	
			TR	Swansea C.	10.51					
GREENAWAY, Brian	London	26.09.57	APP	Fulham	06.75	1976-80	68	17	8	(F)
GREENER, Ron	Easington	31.01.34	Easington Col.	Newcastle U.	05.51	1953	3		0	(CH)
			TR	Darlington	08.55	1955-66	442		5	
GREENHALGH, Brian A.	Southport	20.02.47	APP	Preston N.E.	02.65	1965-67	19	/	9	(IF)
			TR	Aston Villa	09.67	1967-68	37	3	12	
			TR	Leicester C.	02.69	1968	2	2	0	
			TR	Huddersfield T.	06.69	1969-70	15	/	0	
			TR	Cambridge U.	07.71	1971-73	116	/	47	
			TR	Bournemouth	02.74	1973-74	23	1	7	
			L	Torquay U.	06.74	1974	9	/	1	
			TR	Watford	03.75	1974-75	17	1	1	
GREENHALGH, Jim R.	Manchester	25.08.23	Newton Heath	Hull C.	08.46	1946-50	148		5	(WH)
			TR	Bury	12.50	1950-54	122		1	
			TR	Gillingham	07.56	1956	16		0	
GREENHALGH, Norman	Bolton	10.08.14	Bolton W.(*)	Everton	*	1946-48	52		0	*New Brighton/E.F.LGE REP.
GREENHOFF, Brian	Barnsley	28.04.53	APP	Manchester U.	06.70	1973-78	218	3	13	(D) E-18/E.U23-4/
			TR	Leeds U.	08.79	1979-81	68	4	1	Brother of Jim
			TR	Rochdale	12.83	1982-83	15	1	0	
GREENHOFF, Frank	Barnsley	03.03.24	Manchester C.(AM)	Barnsley	09.47					(OL)
			TR	Bradford C.	10.48	1948-51	81		11	
GREENHOFF, Jim	Barnsley	19.06.46	APP	Leeds U.	08.63	1962-68	90	6	19	(F)E.U23-5/E.F.LGE.REP●
			TR	Birmingham C.	08.68	1968	31	/	14	
			TR	Stoke C.	08.69	1969-76	274	/	76	
			TR	Manchester U.	11.76	1976-80	94	3	26	
			TR	Crewe Alex.	12.80	1980	11	/	4	
			Toronto	Port Vale	08.81	1981-82	44	4	5	
			TR	Rochdale	08.83	1982-83	16	/	0	
GREENSMITH, Ron	Sheffield	22.01.33		Sheffield Wed.	01.54	1954-57	5		0	(F)
			TR	York C.	01.58	1957-59	42		2	
GREENWAY, Mark	Halifax	19.04.66	APP	Halifax T.	04.84	1983	10	1	1	(D)
GREENWELL, Don	Chester-le-Street	04.01.24		York C.	12.46	1946	1		0	(CH)

Players Names	Birthplace	Date	Previous Club	League Club	Date Signed	Seasons Played	Apps	Sub	Gls	
GREENWOOD, Alex J.	Fulham	17.06.33	Ferryhill Ath.	Chelsea	09.53					
			TR	Crystal Palace	05.54	1954	1		0	
			TR	Darlington	06.55	1955	8		0	
GREENWOOD, John J.	Manchester	22.01.21		Manchester C.	09.46	1948	1		0	(WH)
			TR	Exeter C.	06.49	1949	31		2	
			TR	Aldershot	03.51	1950	12		0	
			TR	Halifax T.	11.51					
GREENWOOD, Paddy	Hull	17.10.46	JNRS	Hull C.	11.64	1965-71	137	12	3	(WH)
			TR	Barnsley	11.71	1971-73	110	1	6	
			TR	Nottingham F.	10.74	1974	15	/	0	
GREENWOOD, Peter	Todmorden	11.09.24		Burnley	10.46					Lancs.Cricketer
			TR	Chester C.	07.48	1948-51	62		3	
GREENWOOD, Peter	Rawtenstall	03.04.38	Bolton W.(AM)	Bury	10.56	1956	1		0	(F)
GREENWOOD, Ron	Burnley	11.11.21	Chelsea(+)	Bradford P.A.	+	1946-47	59		0	(CH)E'B'-1
			TR	Brentford	03.49	1948-52	142		1	
			TR	Chelsea	10.52	1952-54	65		0	
			TR	Fulham	02.55	1954-55	42		0	
GREENWOOD, Roy T.	Croydon	22.05.31	Beckenham	Crystal Palace	11.54	1954-58	111		0	(FB)
GREENWOOD, Roy T.	Leeds	26.09.52	APP	Hull C.	10.70	1971-75	118	6	24	(F)
			TR	Sunderland	01.76	1975-78	45	11	9	
			TR	Derby Co.	01.79	1978-79	26	5	1	
			TR	Swindon T.	02.80	1979-80	49	4	7	
			TR	Huddersfield T.	08.82	1982-83	5	3	0	
			L	Tranmere Rov.	11.83	1983	3	/	0	
GREETHAM, Harold	Grimsby	07.03.30	JNRS	Grimsby T.	06.50	1950	4		0	
GREGG, Frank	Stourbridge	09.10.42	JNRS	Walsall	10.59	1960-72	389	6	3	(FB)
GREGG, Harry	Derry	25.10.32	Coleraine	Doncaster Rov.	10.52	1952-57	93		0	(G)NI-24/IRISH LGE REP./
			TR	Manchester U.	12.57	1957-66	211	/	0	NI.AMAT.INT./
			TR	Stoke C.	12.66.	1966	2	/	0	NI.SCH.INT.
GREGOIRE, Roly B.	Liverpool	23.11.58	JNRS	Halifax T.	08.76	1977	5	/	0	(F)
			TR	Sunderland	11.77	1977-78	6	3	1	
GREGORY, Anthony	Luton	16.05.37	Vauxhall M.	Luton T.	05.55	1955-59	59		17	(OL) E.YTH.INT.
			TR	Watford	03.60	1959-63	107		14	
GREGORY, Anthony T.	Dawley	10.03.47	APP	Shrewsbury T.	03.65	1964-75	285	8	0	(FB)
GREGORY, Brian C.	Gravesend	11.01.55		Gillingham	08.74	1974	1	1	0	(IF)
			Margate	Luton T.	06.76					
GREGORY, David H.	Peterborough	06.10.51	Chatteris	Peterborough U.	08.73	1973-76	125	17	32	(F)
			TR	Stoke C.	06.77	1977	22	1	3	
			L	Blackburn Rov.	07.78	1978	5	/	3	
			TR	Bury	09.78	1978-79	50	2	13	
			TR	Portsmouth	12.79	1979-81	64	10	18	
			TR	Wrexham	08.82	1982-83	83	2	24	
GREGORY, David P.	London	19.02.60	Crystal Palace (N/C)	Millwall	08.78	1978-80	52	/	2	(D)
GREGORY, Ernie	London	10.11.21	Leytonstone	West Ham U.	+	1946-59	382		0	(G) E'B'-1
GREGORY, Fred C.	Doncaster	24.10.11	Reading(*)	Crystal Palace	*					(FB) *Doncaster Rov./
			TR	Hartlepool U.	06.46	1946	21		0	Manchester C.
			TR	Rotherham U.	02.47	1946	1		0	
GREGORY, Gordon (Harry)	Hackney	24.10.43	JNRS	Orient	10.61	1962-65	79	/	11	(IF) E.YTH.INT.
			TR	Charlton Ath.	08.66	1966-70	146	3	24	
			TR	Aston Villa	10.70	1970-71	18	6	2	
			TR	Hereford U.	08.72	1972-74	71	2	6	
GREGORY, John C.	Scunthorpe	11.05.54	APP	Northampton T.	01.73	1972-76	187	/	8	(M) E-6
			TR	Aston Villa	06.77	1977-78	59	6	10	
			TR	Brighton & H.A.	07.79	1979-80	72	/	7	
			TR	Q.P.R.	06.81	1981-83	113	/	31	
GREGORY, John E.	London	24.09.26	Bromley	West Ham U.	06.51	1951-52	24		6	(IF) Father of John C.
			TR	Scunthorpe U.	06.53	1953-56	147		64	
			TR	Aldershot	06.57	1957	6		2	
GREGORY, John L.	Southampton	25.01.25	JNRS	Southampton	+	1946-54	66		0	(FB)
			TR	Orient	07.55	1955-58	90		0	
			TR	Bournemouth	07.59	1959	17		0	
GREGORY, Paul G.	Sheffield	26.07.61	APP	Chesterfield	08.79	1980-83	23	/	0	(G)
			TR	Doncaster Rov.	03.84					
GREGSON, Colin	Newcastle	19.01.58	APP	W.B.A.	01.76					(F)
			TR	Sheffield Wed.	07.77	1977	1	1	0	
GREGSON, John	Skelmersdale	17.05.39	Skelmersdale	Blackpool	05.57	1957-58	3		1	(W)
			TR	Chester C.	05.62	1962	32		5	
			TR	Shrewsbury T.	03.63	1962-64	56		6	
			TR	Mansfield T.	11.64	1964-66	74	2	5	
			TR	Lincoln C.	06.67	1967	31	5	3	
			TR	Cambridge U.	N/L	1970	32	/	0	
GREGSON, Peter G.	Blackpool	12.05.53	Blackpool(APP)	Southport	07.71	1971-72	35	/	0	(G)
GREIG, Robert	Sunderland	13.09.49	APP	Leicester C.	01.67					(F)
			TR	Workington	02.68	1967	4	1	0	

Players Names	Birthplace	Date	Previous Club	League Club	Date Signed	Seasons Played	Career Record Apps	Sub	Gls	
GRESTY, Phil	Tarporley	02.06.53		Crewe Alex.	AM	1974	3	1	0	(OL)
GREW, Mark	Bilston	15.02.58	JNRS	W.B.A.	06.76	1981-82	33	/	0	(G)
			L	Wigan Ath.	12.78	1978	4	/	0	
			TR	Leicester C.	07.83	1983	5	/	0	
			L	Oldham Ath.	10.83	1983	5	/	0	
			TR	Ipswich T.	03.84					
GREWCOCK, Neil	Leicester	26.04.62	APP	Leicester C.	07.79	1978-80	7	1	1	(F)
			TR	Gillingham	03.82	1981-82	30	4	4	
GREY, W. Brian	Swansea	07.09.48	APP	Swansea C.	09.66	1967-69	28	3	9	(F)
GREYGOOSE, Dean	Torquay	18.12.64	APP	Cambridge U.	11.82	1983	16	/	0	(G)
GRIBBIN, Brian T.	Newcastle	02.06.54		Hartlepool U.	07.73	1972	1	/	0	(FB)
GRICE, Mike J.	Woking	03.11.31	Lowestoft	Colchester U.	06.52	1952-55	107		16	(OL)
			TR	West Ham U.	03.56	1955-60	142		18	
			TR	Coventry C.	08.61	1961	37		6	
			TR	Colchester U.	06.62	1962-65	139	1	13	
GRIEVE, David	Selkirk	15.02.29	Dalry Th.	Reading	02.52	1951-53	19		1	(W)
			TR	Crystal Palace	04.54	1954	22		3	
GRIEVE, Richard M.	Aberdeen	29.06.24		Rochdale	05.50					
			TR	Wrexham	09.50	1950	1		0	
GRIEVES, Ken J.	Australia	27.08.25	Wigan Ath.	Bury	04.47	1947-49	59		0	(G) Lancs.Cricketer
			TR	Bolton W.	12.51	1951-55	49		0	
			TR	Stockport Co.	07.57	1957	39		0	
GRIEVSON, Henry	Easington	10.04.41	JNRS	Sunderland	04.58					(HB)
			TR	Southend U.	07.61	1961	24		1	
GRIFFIN, Colin R.	Dudley	08.01.56	APP	Derby Co.	08.75					(D)
			TR	Shrewsbury T.	01.76	1975-83	322	2	6	
GRIFFIN, Frank A.	Pendlebury	28.03.28	St. Augustines	Shrewsbury T.	N/L	1950	37		5	(OR)
			TR	W.B.A.	04.51	1950-58	240		47	
			TR	Northampton T.	07.59	1959	18		0	
GRIFFIN, Kevin R.	Plymouth	05.10.53	APP	Bristol C.	09.71	1971-74	5	3	0	(IF)
			L	Mansfield T.	03.75	1974	4	/	2	
			L	Cambridge U.	09.75	1975	7	1	1	
GRIFFIN, William	Bircotes	24.09.40	JNRS	Sheffield Wed.	09.57	1958-62	34		20	(F)
			TR	Bury	12.62	1962-65	84	4	22	
			TR	Workington	02.66	1965-68	82	/	16	
			TR	Rotherham U.	01.69	1968-69	14	3	1	
GRIFFITHS, Arfon T.	Wrexham	23.08.41	JNRS	Wrexham	05.59	1959-60	42		8	(M) W-17/W.U23-3●
			TR	Arsenal	02.61	1960-61	15		2	
			TR	Wrexham	09.62	1962-78	544	6	115	
GRIFFITHS, Ashley R.	Barry	05.01.61	APP	Bristol Rov.	01.79	1979-80	6	1	0	(M) W.SCH.INT./W.YTH.INT.
			TR	Torquay U.	08.81					
GRIFFITHS, Barry	Manchester	21.11.40		Blackburn Rov.	07.62	1959-62	2		0	(G)
GRIFFITHS, Brian	Penycae	21.11.33		Wrexham	05.52	1952-57	22		8	(F)
			TR	Chester C.	07.58	1958	2		1	
GRIFFITHS, Bryan	Liverpool	21.11.39	JNRS	Everton	03.56	1958	2		0	(FB)
			TR	Southport	06.60	1960-62	118		1	
GRIFFITHS, Clive L.	Pontypridd	22.01.55	APP	Manchester U.	01.72	1973	7	/	0	(M)W.U23-2/W.SCH.INT
			L	Plymouth Arg.	07.74	1974	10	1	0	
			TR	Tranmere Rov.	11.75	1975-76	59	/	0	
GRIFFITHS, David	Woking	13.12.37		Portsmouth	03.56					(F)
			TR	Aldershot	08.57	1958-59	5		0	
GRIFFITHS, David B.	Liverpool	25.05.51	JNRS	Tranmere Rov.	02.70	1969	6	/	0	(FB)
GRIFFITHS, Dennis	Ruabon	12.08.35	JNRS	Wrexham	08.52	1953-57	67		6	(HB)
GRIFFITHS, Doug J.	Birmingham	23.10.48	APP	Wolverhampton W.	10.66					(HB)
			TR	Stockport Co.	07.68	1968-69	20	1	0	
GRIFFITHS, Estyn	Mold	22.07.27		Wrexham	04.50	1950-51	11		0	(CH) W.AMAT.INT.
GRIFFITHS, Evan G.	Aylesham	19.04.43	JNRS	Gillingham	07.61	1960	1		0	(F)
GRIFFITHS, George	Earlestown	23.06.24	Newton Pk	Bury	+	1946-53	241		7	(FB) Brother of William
			TR	Halifax T.	06.54	1954-57	166		14	
GRIFFITHS, George K.	Chester	30.12.27	Rhyl	Chester C.	07.55	1955-58	54		0	(G)
GRIFFITHS, Gerry	Swansea	15.12.34	JNRS	Swansea C.	06.52					(HB) W.SCH.INT.
			TR	Crewe Alex.	06.56	1956	21		3	
GRIFFITHS, Harry J.	Swansea	04.01.31		Swansea C.	06.49	1949-63	424		71	(OR) W-1/d.1978●
GRIFFITHS, Harry S.	Liverpool	17.11.12	Everton(*)	Port Vale	*	1946	8		0	d.1981
GRIFFITHS, Ian J.	Birkenhead	17.04.60	JNRS	Tranmere Rov.	02.79	1978-82	110	6	5	(M)
			TR	Rochdale	08.83	1983	39	2	5	
GRIFFITHS, Ivor	Port Talbot	19.06.18	Tottenham H.(AM)	Chester C.	09.46	1946	1		0	(IF)
GRIFFITHS, J. Steve	Barnsley	23.02.14	Halifax(*)	Portsmouth	+					(IF) *Chesterfield
			TR	Aldershot	06.46	1946	42		9	
			TR	Barnsley	07.47	1947-50	65		29	
			TR	York C.	06.51	1951-52	74		12	

Players Names	Birthplace	Date	Previous Club	League Club	Date Signed	Seasons Played	Apps	Sub	Gls	
GRIFFITHS, James	Gowerton	05.10.41		Stockport Co.	03.63	1962	3		0	(CF)
GRIFFITHS, Jeff	Swansea	19.03.57		Swansea C.	N/C	1975-77	6	7	1	(F)
GRIFFITHS, John	Oldbury	16.06.51	APP	Aston Villa	11.68	1968-69	1	2	0	(IF)
			TR	Stockport Co.	05.70	1970-74	167	16	31	
GRIFFITHS, Ken G.	Cardiff	11.11.25	JNRS	Cardiff C.	+					
			L	Torquay U.	01.48	1947-48	11		1	
			TR	Newport Co.	09.49	1949	14		6	
GRIFFITHS, Ken J.	Stoke	02.04.30		Port Vale	03.50	1949-57	179		52	(IF)
			TR	Mansfield T.	01.58	1957-58	42		7	
GRIFFITHS, Mal W.	Merthyr	08.03.19	Arsenal(*)	Leicester C.	*	1946-55	340		61	(W) *Merthyr/W-1/d.1960
GRIFFITHS, Neil	Stoke	12.10.51		Chester C.	11.70	1970-73	89	1	4	(D)
			TR	Port Vale	12.73	1973-80	214	4	13	
			TR	Crewe Alex.	08.81	1981	32	2	1	
GRIFFITHS, Peter J.	Barnstaple	14.08.57	Bideford	Stoke C.	11.80	1980-83	46	14	5	(M)
			L	Bradford C.	03.84	1983	2	/	0	
GRIFFITHS, Ray	Llanelli	26.09.31		Chester C.	05.56	1955-59	18		0	(HB)
GRIFFITHS, Richard D.	Earls Colne	21.03.42	JNRS	Colchester U.	06.61	1961-64	48		0	(FB)
GRIFFITHS, Robert	Birmingham	15.09.42	Rhyl	Stoke C.	09.60					(HB)
			TR	Chester C.	07.62	1962	2		0	
GRIFFITHS, Roger	Hereford	20.02.45	Worcester C.	Hereford U.	N/L	1972	7	2	0	(FB)
GRIFFITHS, Steve	Billingham	28.11.57	APP	Hartlepool U.	APP	1974	0	1	0	(F)
GRIFFITHS, Vernon	Birmingham	14.06.36		Coventry C.	02.57	1957-58	15		1	(HB)
GRIFFITHS, William	Earlestown	13.01.21	Earlestown	Bury	+	1946-51	191		11	(CH) Brother of George/d.1964
GRIFFITHS, William E.	Warrington	23.05.44	APP	Torquay U.	05.62	1962	1		0	(F)
GRIFFITHS, William R.	Blaengwynfi	17.10.19	Derby Co.(AM)	Cardiff C.	AM	1947	1		0	(G)
				Newport Co.	AM	1951	3		0	
GRIGGS, Robert J.	Petersfield	12.12.52	APP	Aldershot	07.70	1968-69	3	1	0	(HB)
GRIMES, Ashley	Dublin	02.08.57	Bohemians	Manchester U.	03.77	1977-82	62	28	10	(M)EI-16/EI.U21-2
			TR	Coventry C.	08.83	1983	29	3	1	
GRIMES, Vince	Scunthorpe	13.05.54	APP	Hull C.	05.72	1973-77	84	5	9	(F)
			L	Bradford C.	12.77	1977	7	/	1	
			TR	Scunthorpe U.	01.78	1977-81	143	/	12	
GRIMLEY, Tom W.	Dinnington	01.11.20	Swallownest FC	W.B.A.	*	1946-47	30		0	(G) d.1976
			TR	New Brighton	08.48	1948-50	94		0	
GRIMSDITCH, S. Walker	Farnworth	08.10.20	Rossendale U.	Southport	+	1946	10		0	(G) +Bolton W.
GRIMSHAW, Anthony	Manchester	08.12.57	APP	Manchester U.	12.74	1975	0	1	0	(HB)
GRIMSHAW, Chris A.	Accrington	01.10.65	APP	Burnley	10.83					(M)
			TR	Crewe Alex.	03.84	1983	1	2	0	
GRIMSHAW, Colin G.	Betchworth	16.09.25	Redhill FC	Arsenal	06.48					(IF)
			TR	Crystal Palace	10.52	1952	32		3	
GRINNEY, Ian	Crediton	08.03.36		Exeter C.	09.54	1955	2		0	(F)
GRIPTON, Ernie W.	Tipton	02.07.20	Brownhills Ath.	W.B.A.	*	1946-47	7		0	(CH)
			TR	Luton T.	06.48	1948	3		0	
			TR	Bournemouth	07.50	1950-51	79		0	
GRITT, Steve J.	Bournemouth	31.10.57	APP	Bournemouth	07.76	1976	4	2	3	(M)
			TR	Charlton Ath.	07.77	1977-83	219	19	18	
GROBBELAAR, Bruce D.	South Africa	06.10.57	Vancouver	Crewe Alex.	N/C	1979	24	/	1	(G)
			Vancouver	Liverpool	03.81	1981-83	126	/	0	
GROGAN, John	Paisley	30.10.15	Shawfield J.	Leicester C.	*	1946	17		0	(CH)
			TR	Mansfield T.	09.47	1947-51	202		1	
GROOMBRIDGE, Dave	Norbury	13.04.30	Hayes	Orient	06.51	1951-59	133		0	(G)
GROOME, Pat B.	Nottingham	16.03.34	JNRS	Notts.Co.	11.51	1952-54	29		0	(FB)
GROTIER, Peter D.	Stratford	18.10.50	APP	West Ham U.	03.68	1968-72	50	/	0	(G)
			L	Cardiff C.	11.73	1973	2	/	0	
			TR	Lincoln C.	08.74	1974-79	233	/	0	
			TR	Cardiff C.	12.79	1979-81	38	/	0	
			TR	Grimsby T.	03.82	1982	4	/	0	
GROVES, Alan	Southport	24.10.48		Southport	12.68	1968-69	10	4	2	(F) d. 1978
			TR	Chester C.	07.70	1970	21	/	3	
			TR	Shrewsbury T.	02.71	1970-72	76	/	11	
			TR	Bournemouth	10.72	1972-73	31	5	4	
			TR	Oldham Ath.	02.74	1973-77	136	4	12	
			TR	Blackpool	11.77	1977	11	4	1	
GROVES, Edward G.	Merthyr Tydfil	24.07.30	Troedyrhiw	Swansea C.	06.52	1952-53	27		0	(G) W.AMAT.INT.
GROVES, John	Derby	16.09.33	JNRS	Luton T.	10.50	1953-62	218		16	(WH)Son of pre-war player
			TR	Bournemouth	09.63	1963-64	54		0	
GROVES, Ken E.L.	Eton	09.10.21	Windsor & E.	Preston N.E.	*					(G)
			TR	Reading	08.46	1946	4		0	
GRQVES, Perry	London	19.04.65	APP	Colchester U.	06.82	1981-83	55	13	4	(M)

Players Names	Birthplace	Date	Previous Club	League Club	Date Signed	Seasons Played	Career Record Apps Sub Gls		
GROVES, Vic G.	Stepney	05.11.32	Leytonstone	Tottenham H.	AM	1952-53	4		3	(IF) E.U23-1/E'B'-1/
			Leytonstone	Orient	10.54	1954-55	42		24	E.AMAT.INT./E.YTH.INT.
			TR	Arsenal	11.55	1955-63	184		31	
GROZIER, William	Cumnock	24.08.56	APP	Mansfield T.	APP	1973	1	/	0	(FB)
GRUBB, Alan J.	Leven	05.02.28	E.Fife	Tottenham H.	03.52	1952	2		0	(W)
			TR	Walsall	08.53	1953	15		0	
GRUMMETT, Jim (Snr)	Barnsley	31.07.21	Ruston Spts.	Lincoln C.	+	1946-51	165		12	(WH)
			TR	Accrington St.	09.52	1952	40		1	
GRUMMETT, Jim (Jnr)	Barnsley	11.07.45	JNRS	Lincoln C.	06.63	1963-70	246	4	19	(WH) E.YTH.INT.
			TR	Aldershot	07.71	1971-72	81	/	6	
			TR	Chester C.	06.73	1973	15	1	0	
			TR	Rochdale	12.73	1973-74	32	2	2	
GRUMMITT, Peter M.	Bourne	19.08.42	Bourne T.	Nottingham F.	05.60	1960-69	313	/	0	(G)E.U23-3/E.F.LGE.REP.●
			TR	Sheffield Wed.	01.70	1969-72	121	/	0	
			TR	Brighton & H.A.	12.73	1973-76	136	/	0	
GRUNDY, Brian	Atherton	09.05.45	Wigan Ath.	Bury	11.67	1967-70	94	6	10	(F)
GRYBA, Ray	Liverpool	19.08.35	JNRS	Liverpool	08.52					(IF)
			TR	Blackpool	08.53					
				Southport	10.55	1955-57	72		14	
GUARD, Anthony F.	Swansea	19.04.64	APP	Swansea C.	04.82	1983	1	/	0	(M)
GUBBINS, Ralph G.	Ellesmere Port	31.01.32	Shell Mex	Bolton W.	10.52	1952-59	97		15	(IF)
			TR	Hull C.	10.59	1959-60	45		10	
			TR	Tranmere Rov.	03.61	1960-63	107		37	
GUEST, Brendan J.	Nottingham	19.12.58	APP	Lincoln C.	12.76	1976-79	99	5	2	E.YTH.INT.
			TR	Swindon T.	07.80					
GUEST, Gladstone	Rotherham	26.06.17	Rawmarsh	Rotherham U.	+	1946-55	356		130	(IF)
GUEST, William	Birmingham	08.02.13	West Ham U.(*)	Blackburn Rov.	*	1946	22		3	(OL) *Birmingham C.
			TR	Walsall	08.47	1947	5		0	
GUILD, Alan	Forfar	27.03.47	E.Fife	Luton T.	07.69	1970	1	/	0	(WH) S.AMAT.INT.
			TR	Cambridge U.	05.71	1971-73	117	10	1	
GUILD, Jim	Glasgow	10.12.28	Dunoon Ath.	New Brighton	09.50	1950	2		0	
GULLAN, Stan K.	Edinburgh	26.01.26	Clyde	Q.P.R.	07.49	1950-54	49		0	(G)
GULLIVER, Joffre	Troedyrhiw	02.08.15	Leeds U.(*)	Reading	*	1946-50	161		0	(FB) *Southend U.
			TR	Swindon T.	08.51	1951	11		0	
GULLIVER, Terry	Salisbury	30.09.44	Weymouth	Bournemouth	08.66	1966-71	162	1	2	(FB)
GUNBY, Peter	Leeds	20.11.34		Leeds U.	09.55					
			TR	Bradford C.	07.56	1956	3		0	
GUNN, Alf H.	W. Germany	11.07.24		Nottingham F.	02.47	1946	2		0	(F) d.1982
GUNN, Allistair	Dundee	02.11.24	Dundee	Huddersfield T.	01.51	1950-53	83		11	(OR)
			TR	Bournemouth	06.54	1954	27		2	
GUNN, Bryn C.	Kettering	21.08.58	APP	Nottingham F.	08.75	1975-83	112	2	1	(D)
GUNNING, Harry	Leigh	08.02.32	Gravesend	West Ham U.	06.52	1952	1		0	(OL)
			TR	Crystal Palace	05.54	1954-56	62		4	
			TR	Reading	05.57	1957	12		1	
GUNNING, James M.	Glasgow	25.06.29	Hibernian	Manchester C.	11.50	1950-52	13		0	
			TR	Barrow	07.54	1954	10		1	
			TR	Stockport Co.	09.55					
GUNTER, David R.	Portsmouth	04.03.33		Southampton	05.55	1955	7		0	Brother of Phil
GUNTER, Phil E.	Portsmouth	06.01.32	JNRS	Portsmouth	08.49	1951-63	320		2	(FB) E.U23-1/E'B'-1
			TR	Aldershot	07.64	1964-65	78	/	8	
GUNTHORPE, Ken	Sheffield	04.11.38		Rotherham U.	05.58	1958	2		0	(HB)
GURR, Gerry	Brighton	20.10.46	Guildford C.	Southampton	03.64	1966-69	42	/	0	(G)
			TR	Aldershot	03.71	1970-71	55	/	0	
GUSCOTT, Ray M.	Newport	18.11.57	APP	Bristol Rov.	11.75	1976	1	/	0	(M)W.SCH.INT.
			TR	Newport Co.	10.77	1977	12	5	1	
GUTHRIE, Chris W.	Dilston	07.09.53	APP	Newcastle U.	01.71	1971	3	/	0	(F) E.SCH.INT.
			TR	Southend U.	11.72	1972-74	107	1	35	Brother of Ron
			TR	Sheffield U.	05.75	1975-76	58	2	15	
			TR	Swindon T.	07.77	1977-78	44	1	12	
			TR	Fulham	09.78	1978-79	49	1	15	
			TR	Millwall	03.80	1979	7	/	1	
GUTHRIE, Jimmy A.T.	Luncarty	06.06.12	Dundee	Portsmouth	*					(IR) d.1981
			TR	Crystal Palace	10.46	1946	5		0	
GUTHRIE, Ralph	W.Hartlepool	13.09.32	Tow Law	Arsenal	05.53	1954	2		0	(G)
			TR	Hartlepool U.	07.56	1956-57	78		0	
GUTHRIE, Ron G.	Burradon	19.04.44	JNRS	Newcastle U.	07.63	1966-72	52	4	1	(FB)
			TR	Sunderland	01.73	1972-74	66	/	1	
GUTTRIDGE, Ron	Widnes	28.04.16	Prescot Cables	Aston Villa	*	1946-47	15		0	(LB)
			TR	Brighton & H.A.	06.48	1948-49	17		0	
GUTTRIDGE, William	Darlaston	04.03.31	Metroshaft Wks.	Wolverhampton W.	03.48	1951-53	6		0	(FB)
			TR	Walsall	11.54	1954-61	197		0	

Players Names	Birthplace	Date	Previous Club	League Club	Date Signed	Seasons Played	Career Record Apps	Sub	Gls	
GUY, Alan	Jarrow	08.09.57	APP	Newcastle U.	09.75	1976-78	3	1	0	(F)
			TR	Peterborough U.	03.79	1978-80	42	11	4	
GUY, Eddie F.	W. Hartlepool	06.02.56	APP	Hartlepool U.	03.74	1974	1	/	0	(G)
GUY, Harry G.	Wolverhampton	01.01.32	JNRS	W.B.A.	03.50	1950	1		0	(FB)
GUY, Ivor	Bristol	27.02.26	Hambrook Villa	Bristol C.	+	1945-56	404		2	(FB)
GUY, Keith	Seaham	19.05.59	APP	Newcastle U.	06.77					(M)
			TR	Hartlepool U.	06.78	1978	7	3	0	
GUY, Mike	Limavady	04.02.53	Coleraine	Sheffield U.	03.78	1977-78	12	6	2	(M)
			TR	Crewe Alex.	09.79	1979-80	54	1	7	
GUY, R. James	Swansea	29.01.21	RAF St. Athan	Norwich C.	08.46	1946-47	12		1	(IF)
GUY, Richard	Greenwich	06.01.49	Tooting & Mitcham	Wimbledon	N/L	1977	13	/	0	(G)
GUY, Ron	Salford	25.04.36		Stockport Co.	09.58	1958-59	9		2	(F)
GWATKIN, P. Arthur	Harrow	05.08.29		Wrexham	10.52	1953-55	56		8	(OR)
			TR	Tranmere Rov.	06.56	1956	21		6	
GWINNETT, Mel L.	Worcester	14.05.63	Stourbridge	Peterborough U.	05.81					(G)
			TR	Hereford U.	N/C	1982	1	/	1	
GWYTHER, Dave G.	Birmingham	06.12.48	JNRS	Swansea C.	01.67	1966-72	212	5	59	(F) W.U23-2
			TR	Halifax T.	08.73	1973-75	104	/	26	
			TR	Rotherham U.	02.76	1975-79	162	/	45	
			TR	Newport Co.	12.79	1979-82	84	21	29	
			L	Crewe Alex.	01.82	1981	7	/	1	
GWYTHER, John D.	St. Davids	03.11.46		Nottingham F.	08.65					(G) Brother of Dave
			TR	Swansea C.	03.66	1965	1	/	0	
GYMER, John P.	Romford	11.11.66	APP	Southend U.	APP	1983	2	3	1	(F)
GYNN, Mike	Peterborough	19.08.61	APP	Peterborough U.	04.79	1978-82	152	4	33	(M)
			TR	Coventry C.	08.83	1983	20	3	2	

Players Names	Birthplace	Date	Previous Club	League Club	Date Signed	Seasons Played	Apps	Sub	Gls	
HAASZ, John	Hungary	07.07.37		Swansea C.	09.60	1960	1		0	(F)
			TR	Workington	07.61	1961-62	50		13	
HABBIN, Richard	Cambridge	06.01.49	Cambridge U.	Reading	03.69	1968-74	204	14	42	(F)
			TR	Rotherham U.	01.75	1974-77	79	5	19	
			TR	Doncaster Rov.	09.77	1977-78	57	3	12	
HACKETT, Bernard	Ramsbottom	07.09.33		Aston Villa	11.53					
			TR	Chester C.	07.55	1955-56	22		3	
HACKETT, Gary S.	Stourbridge	11.10.62	Bromsgrove	Shrewsbury T.	07.83	1983	29	2	3	(F)
HACKING, John	Blackpool	24.08.25		Accrington St.	+	1946	8		0	(G)
			TR	Stockport Co.	11.46	1946-49	4		0	
HACKING, Robert	Blackburn	30.03.18		Luton T.	+	1946	1		0	(WH)
			TR	Brighton & H.A.	08.47	1947	17		2	
			TR	Southport	08.48	1948-53	180		6	
HADDINGTON, Harry	Scarborough	07.08.31		Bradford P.A.	02.49	1952	2		0	(FB)
			TR	W.B.A.	05.53					
			TR	Walsall	07.55	1955-60	226		0	
HADDINGTON, Jack	Quarry Bank	16.08.33	Cradley Heath	Walsall	02.54	1953	1		0	(OL)
HADDINGTON, Ray W.	Scarborough	18.11.23	Bradford P.A.(+)	Bradford C.	09.46					(IF)
			TR	Oldham Ath.	08.47	1947-50	117		62	
			TR	Manchester C.	11.50	1950	6		4	
			TR	Stockport Co.	12.51	1951	11		4	
			TR	Bournemouth	07.52	1952	2		0	
			TR	Rochdale	10.52	1952-53	38		11	
			TR	Halifax T.	11.53	1953	8		0	
HADDOCK, Andrew	Edinburgh	05.05.46	JNRS	Chester C.	08.63	1963	12		0	(F)
			TR	Crewe Alex.	08.64	1964	4		0	
			Falkirk	Rotherham U.	12.66	1966	4	/	0	
			TR	Bradford P.A.	12.67	1967	5	/	0	
			TR	Chester C.	03.68	1967	10	/	1	
HADDOCK, Peter M.	Newcastle	09.12.61	APP	Newcastle U.	12.79	1981-83	46	4	0	(D)
HADDON, Harry L.	Cardiff	08.04.23		Cardiff C.	+					
			Bangor C.	Newport Co.	02.47	1946-48	10		1	
			TR	Bristol Rov.	11.48	1948	2		0	
HADDRICK, Robert	W. Ham	01.05.50	APP	Southend U.	APP	1966	1	/	0	(CH)
HADLEY, Anthony	Rochford	05.07.55	Basildon U.	Southend U.	07.74	1974-82	243	22	16	(D)
			TR	Colchester U.	08.83	1983	44	1	0	
HADZIABDIC, Dzemal	Yugoslavia	25.07.53	Velez Mostar	Swansea C.	08.80	1980-82	87	2	2	(D) YUGOSLAV INT.
HAFFEY, Frank	Glasgow	28.11.38	Glasgow Celtic	Swindon T.	10.64	1964	4		0	(G) S-2
HAGAN, Jim	Monkstown	10.08.56	Larne	Coventry C.	11.77	1978	12	1	0	(D)
			L	Torquay U.	09.79	1979	7	/	0	
			Seiko	Coventry C.	07.81	1981	3	/	0	
			TR	Birmingham C.	05.82	1982-83	60	5	0	
HAGAN, Jimmy	Unsworth	21.01.18	Derby Co.(*)	Sheffield U.	*	1946-57	333		106	(IF) *Liverpool, Son of Alf (pre-war star) E-1/E.F.LGE REP./ E.SCH.INT.
HAGUE, Keith	Hull	25.05.46		York C.	10.65	1965	0	1	0	(WH)
HAGUE, Neil	Thurcroft	01.12.49	APP	Rotherham U.	12.66	1967-71	135	11	23	(M)E.YTH.INT.
			TR	Plymouth Arg.	11.71	1971-73	98	/	15	
			TR	Bournemouth	07.74	1974-75	89	/	7	
			TR	Huddersfield T.	06.76	1976	25	/	2	
			TR	Darlington	05.77	1977-78	80	/	4	
HAIGH, Gordon	Barnsley	18.08.21	Ransons FC	Burnley	+	1946-49	18		3	(IF)
			TR	Bournemouth	04.50	1949-50	17		3	
			TR	Watford	08.51	1951	29		5	
HAIGH, Graham	Huddersfield	16.09.46	APP	Halifax T.	APP	1964	1		0	(WH)
HAIGH, Jack	Rotherham	10.09.28	Gainsborough	Liverpool	10.49	1950-51	11		3	(IF)
			TR	Scunthorpe U.	08.52	1952-59	329		65	
			TR	Doncaster Rov.	07.60	1960-61	72		6	
HAIGH, Paul	Scarborough	04.05.58	APP	Hull C.	06.75	1974-80	179	1	8	(D)E.U21-1
			TR	Carlisle U.	11.80	1980-83	121	4	1	
HAILS, William	Nettlesworth	19.02.35	JNRS	Lincoln C.	03.53	1953-54	9		0	(W)
			TR	Peterborough U.	N/L	1960-62	94		28	
			TR	Northampton T.	11.62	1962-63	59		13	
			TR	Luton T.	06.64	1964	3		0	
HAILWOOD, David J.	Nottingham	17.10.54		Mansfield T.	07.74	1974	1	/	0	(F)
HAINES, Don N.	Llanwonno	23.09.25		Bournemouth	10.48					(FB)
			Yeovil T.	Newport C.	12.50	1950-53	92		2	
HAINES, John T.W.	Wickhamford	24.04.20	Liverpool(*)	Swansea C.	+	1946	28		7	(IF) *Cheltenham E-1/
			TR	Leicester C.	06.47	1947	12		3	
			TR	W.B.A.	03.48	1947-49	59		24	
			TR	Bradford P.A.	12.49	1949-53	135		36	
			TR	Rochdale	10.53	1953-54	60		16	
			TR	Chester C.	07.55	1955-56	46		8	

Players Names	Birthplace	Date	Previous Club	League Club	Date Signed	Seasons Played	Apps	Sub	Gls	
HAINES, Keith H.	Wigston	19.12.37	Matlock	Leeds U.	05.59					(CH) E.YTH.INT.
			TR	Lincoln C.	07.60	1960-62	13		0	
HAINSWORTH, Len	Rotherham	25.01.18		Rotherham U.	*	1946-47	31		6	(FB)
			TR	Doncaster Rov.	07.48	1948-50	65		0	
			TR	Workington	07.51	1951-52	75		0	
HAIR, George	Ryton	28.04.25	Spen & Black	Newcastle U.	+	1946-48	23		7	(OL)
			TR	Grimsby T.	02.49	1948-50	68		9	
HAIR, K. Grenville A.	Burton	16.11.31	JNRS	Leeds U.	11.48	1950-63	443		1	(FB) d.1968●
HAIRE, Garry	Sedgefield	24.07.63	APP	Oxford U.	07.81					(F)
			Whitley Bay	Bradford C.	06.83	1983	39	4	13	
HALE, Alfie	Waterford	28.08.39	Waterford	Aston Villa	06.60	1960-61	5		1	(IF) EI-13/EI.AMAT.INT.
			TR	Doncaster Rov.	07.62	1962-64	119		42	
			TR	Newport Co.	08.65	1965	34		21	
HALE, Denzil	Clevedon	09.04.28	Clevedon	Bristol Rov.	02.52	1953-58	118		11	(CH)
HALE, Ken	Blyth	18.09.39	JNRS	Newcastle U.	10.56	1957-62	30		15	(IF)
			TR	Coventry C.	12.62	1962-65	98	1	26	
			TR	Oxford U.	03.66	1965-67	64	/	13	
			TR	Darlington	05.68	1968-71	173	/	25	
			TR	Halifax T.	01.73	1972-73	52	/	4	
HALE, Richard J.	Waterford	29.05.35	Waterford	Swansea C.	10.59	1959-60	34		3	(WH) Brother of Alfie
			TR	Barrow	07.61	1961-63	118		16	
			TR	Workington	08.64	1964-66	131	/	10	
			TR	Watford	07.67	1967-69	95	3	7	
HALES, Derek	Lower Halstow	15.12.51	Dartford	Luton T.	03.72	1972	5	2	1	(F)
			TR	Charlton Ath.	10.73	1973-76	126	3	73	
			TR	Derby Co.	12.76	1976-77	22	1	4	
			TR	W. Ham	09.77	1977	23	1	10	
			TR	Charlton Ath.	07.78	1978-83	174	3	69	
HALES, John	Glasgow	15.05.40	St.Rochs	Brentford	09.58	1958-63	61		7	(W)
HALES, Kevin P.	Dartford	13.01.61	APP	Chelsea	01.79	1979-82	18	2	2	(M)
			TR	Orient	08.83	1983	43	/	2	
HALES, Richard	Gillingham	24.08.25	Break Row	Gillingham	AM	1951	5		0	(RB) Father of Derek
HALES, William H.	Gillingham	06.01.20	Break Row	Gillingham	AM	1950-51	15		8	(CF) Brother of Richard
HALEY, John	Sunderland	24.04.32		Gateshead	09.53	1953-56	38		2	(WH) d.1956
HALFORD, Carl	Oldham	27.11.58	Manchester C. (APP)	Stockport Co.	07.77	1977-78	65	9	5	(D)
			TR	Bury	08.79	1979-80	31	/	2	
HALL, Alan S.	Manchester	26.05.38	Manchester U.(AM)	Oldham Ath	11.57	1957-60	74		5	(HB) E.YTH.INT.
HALL, Albert E.	Barry	03.09.18	JNRS	Tottenham H.	*	1946	8		0	(IF) W.SCH.INT.
			TR	Plymouth Arg.	07.47	1947	9		0	
HALL, Alec F.	Grimsby	17.09.09	Cleethorpes	Grimsby T.	*	1946-47	21		0	(WH)
HALL, Almerick G.	Hove	12.11.12	Bradford C.(+)	West Ham U.	+	1946-48	50		11	(IF) *Tottenham H./Southend
HALL, Arthur	Sheffield	23.11.25	Gainsborough	Chesterfield	07.47	1947-48	23		4	(F)
			Goole T.	Scunthorpe U.	08.51	1951	15		3	
HALL, Arthur B.	Witney	24.03.37	Witney T.	Bristol Rov.	07.59	1960-61	2		0	(F)
HALL, Bernard	Bath	08.07.42	JNRS	Bristol Rov.	09.59	1961-66	163	/	0	(G)
HALL, Brian S.	Burbage	09.03.39	Belper T.	Mansfield T.	04.59	1958-64	74		18	(W)
			TR	Colchester U.	03.65	1964-72	324	4	29	
HALL, Brian W.	Glasgow	22.01.46	Manchester Univ.	Liverpool	07.68	1968-75	140	14	15	(M)
			TR	Plymouth Arg.	07.76	1976-77	49	2	16	
			TR	Burnley	11.77	1977-79	39	4	3	
HALL, Colin	Wolverhampton	02.02.48	JNRS	Nottingham F.	03.66	1967-69	27	8	2	(W) E.YTH.INT.
			TR	Bradford C.	06.70	1970-71	65	1	7	
			TR	Bristol C.	07.72	1972	0	1	0	
			L	Hereford U.	09.72	1972	5	/	0	
HALL, David A.	Doncaster	26.09.60	APP	Scunthorpe U.	09.78	1978-79	16	1	0	(M)
HALL, David H.	Sheffield	16.03.54	APP	Sheffield Wed.	03.72					(M)
			TR	Bradford C.	07.75	1975-76	51	3	3	
HALL, Dennis D.	Southwell	24.12.30	JNRS	Portsmouth	09.48	1952-53	10		0	(FB)
			TR	Reading	08.54	1954	13		0	
			TR	Bournemouth	07.55					
HALL, Derek R.	Ashton-U-Lyne	05.01.65	APP	Coventry C.	10.82	1982	1	/	0	(M)
			L	Torquay U.	03.84	1983	10	/	2	
HALL, Fred	Drayton	20.10.14	Hellesden Heath	Norwich C.	*	1946	3		0	(G)
HALL, Fred	Worksop	24.11.24	Whitwell OB	Birmingham C.	03.47	1946-48	5		2	(CF)
HALL, Fred W.	Chester-le-Street	18.11.17		Blackburn Rov.	*					(CH)
			TR	Sunderland	08.46	1946-54	215		1	
			TR	Barrow	09.55	1955	16		1	
HALL, Ian	Whitehaven	28.11.50	JNRS	Workington	07.27	1971-73	25	11	1	(HB)
			TR	Southport	07.74	1974	0	1	0	
HALL, Ian W.	Chesterfield	27.12.39	Wolverhampton W.(AM)	Derby Co.	09.59	1959-61	44		13	(IF) Derby Cricketer
			TR	Mansfield T.	09.62	1962-67	144	/	11	E.YTH.INT./E.SCH.INT./

Players Names	Birthplace	Date	Previous Club	League Club	Date Signed	Seasons Played	Apps	Sub	Gls	
HALL, James	Bootle	05.10.59	APP	Blackpool	10.77	1978	1	/	0	(M)
			TR	Blackburn	07.80					
HALL, James F.	Manchester	07.05.45		Oldham Ath.	07.66	1965	1	/	0	(FB)
HALL, James L.	Northampton	02.03.45	JNRS	Northampton T.	07.63	1963-67	54	2	7	(F)E.YTH.INT.
			TR	Peterborough U.	12.67	1967-74	298	4	122	
			TR	Northampton T.	01.75	1974-77	69	/	28	
			L	Cambridge U.	12.76	1976	24	/	15	
HALL, Jeff J.	Scunthorpe	07.09.29	Bradford P.A.(AM)	Birmingham C.	05.50	1950-58	227		1	(FB) E-17/E'B'-1/E.F.LGE. REP./d.1959
HALL, John	Doncaster	19.11.31		Doncaster Rov.	08.51	1951	2		0	(F)
HALL, John F.	Bramley	18.04.44	JNRS	Bradford C.	05.62	1962-73	417	13	63	(F)
HALL, Joseph E.	Durham	10.04.34	JNRS	Fulham	10.51	1955	1		0	(HB)
HALL, Lance	Darlington	23.01.15	Luton(*)	Barrow	*	1946-48	67		0	(CH)
HALL, Les F.	St. Albans	01.10.21	St. Albans	Luton T.	+	1947-54	79		0	(CH)
HALL, Peter	Stoke	29.09.39	Stoke C.(AM)	Port Vale	05.58	1958-60	16		4	(F)
			TR	Bournemouth	07.61					
			Bedford T.	Gillingham	11.67	1967	9		1	
HALL, Richard	Weymouth	03.07.45	Weymouth	Bournemouth	06.67	1967	8	3	0	(WH)
HALL, Ron	Dudley	08.02.33	Cradley Heath	Walsall	06.54	1954-55	2		0	(CF)
HALL, Stan A.	Southgate	18.02.17	Finchley	Orient	*	1946	8		0	(G)
HALL, Wilf	Haydock	14.10.34	Earlestown	Stoke C.	10.53	1954-59	45		0	(G)
			TR	Ipswich T.	06.60	1960-62	16		0	
HALL, William	Gosport	24.08.30		Gillingham	09.52	1952	9		0	(F)
HALL, William F.	Walton	06.02.26	JNRS	Preston N.E.	02.48	1947	7		0	(G)
			TR	Blackpool	07.49	1952	3		0	
			TR	Reading	07.53	1953	16		0	
HALL, William W.	Liverpool	03.06.17		Liverpool	+					
			TR	Southport	06.46	1946	16		1	
HALLAM, Anthony K.	Chesterfield	09.10.46	APP	Chesterfield	10.64	1965-66	4	1	0	(FB)
HALLAM, Norman	Stoke	23.10.20		Port Vale	05.46	1946-52	61		3	
			TR	Halifax T.	10.53	1953	3		0	
HALLARD, William	St. Helens	28.08.13	Bury(*)	Bradford P.A.	*					(WH) d.1979
			TR	Rochdale	06.46	1946	17		2	
			TR	Accrington St.	03.47	1946	3		0	
HALLAS, Geoff	Springhead	08.12.30	Warminster	West Ham U.	03.54	1954	3		0	(FB)
HALLETT, Tom R.	Glyn-Neath	10.0.4.39	JNRS	Leeds U.	04.56					(HB) W.SCH.INT.
			TR	Swindon T.	07.63	1963-65	26	/	0	
			TR	Bradford C.	06.66	1966-70	177	2	2	
HALLIDAY, Brian	Farnworth	19.01.38	Bolton W.(AM)	Stockport Co.	10.58	1958	1		0	
HALLIDAY, Brian J.	Liverpool	30.12.44	JNRS	Liverpool	05.63					(F)
			TR	Tranmere Rov.	07.65					
			TR	Crewe Alex.	10.65	1965	1	/	0	
HALLIDAY, Bruce	Sunderland	03.01.61	APP	Newcastle U.	01.79	1980-81	32	/	1	(D)
			L	Darlington	09.82	1982	7	/	0	
			TR	Bury	11.82	1982	29	/	0	
			TR	Bristol C.	08.83	1983	41	/	0	
HALLIDAY, Gary	Bradford	09.05.51	JNRS	Bradfield P.A.	08.68	1968	0	1	0	
HALLIDAY, Tom	Ayr	18.04.40	Dumbarton	Cardiff C.	10.63	1963-64	16		2	(IF)
HALLOWS, Paul C.R.	Chester	22.06.50	APP	Bolton W.	10.67	1968-73	44	2	0	(D)
			TR	Rochdale	05.74	1974-79	197	/	2	
HALLYBONE, Jim M.	Leytonstone	15.05.62	APP	Orient	05.80	1981	5	3	0	(M)
			TR	Halifax T.	07.82	1982	11	5	0	
HALOM, Vic L.	Burton	03.10.48	APP.	Charlton Ath.	01.66	1965-67	9	3	0	(F)
			TR	Orient	08.67	1967-68	53	/	12	
			TR	Fulham	11.68	1968-71	66	5	22	
			TR	Luton T.	09.71	1971-72	57	2	17	
			TR	Sunderland	02.73	1972-75	110	3	35	
			TR	Oldham Ath.	07.76	1976-79	121	2	43	
			TR	Rotherham U.	02.80	1979-80	19	1	2	
HALPIN, John T.	Manchester	05.06.27		Bury	11.48	1948	2		0	
			TR	Shrewsbury T.	08.51	1951-52	42		0	
HALSALL, Alan	Menai Bridge	17.11.40	Skelmersdale	Blackpool	05.62	1961	2		0	(G)
			TR	Oldham Ath.	07.63	1963	2		0	
HALSALL, Mike	Bootle	21.07.61	APP.	Liverpool	05.79					(M)
			TR	Birmingham C.	03.83	1982-83	33	/	3	
HALSEY, Mark A.	Romford	01.12.59	APP.	Norwich C.	04.78	1977-79	3	/	0	(D)
HALSTEAD, Roy	Whitworth	26.07.31	JNRS	Burnley	06.53					
			TR	Chester C.	06.54	1954	21		4	
HALTON, Reg. L.	Buxton	11.07.16	Notts.Co.(*)	Bury	*	1946-48	95		15	(WH) *Manchester U.
			TR	Chesterfield	12.48	1948-50	60		10	
			TR	Leicester C.	09.50	1950-51	64		3	

Players Names	Birthplace	Date	Previous Club	League Club	Date Signed	Seasons Played	Career Record Apps	Sub	Gls	
HAM, Mike T.	Plymouth	06.12.63	APP.	Plymouth Arg.	12.81	1981-83	10	1	0	(D)
HAM, Robert	Bradford	29.03.42	JNRS	Bradford P.A.	10.61	1961-62	25		6	(IF)
			Gainsborough	Grimsby T.	02.64	1963	2		1	
			TR	Bradford P.A.	08.64	1964-67	134	/	47	
			TR	Bradford C.	02.68	1967-70	115	/	40	
			TR	Preston N.E.	10.70	1970-71	43	/	14	
			TR	Rotherham U.	10.71	1971-72	67	1	24	
			TR	Bradford C.	07.73	1973-74	72	1	24	
HAMER, John A.	Bradford	05.04.44		Bradford C.	AM	1964	1		0	(LH)
HAMILL, Stewart	Glasgow	22.01.60	Pollok	Leicester C.	09.80	1980-81	10	/	2	(M)
			L	Scunthorpe U.	03.82	1981	4	/	0	
HAMILTON, Alex M.	Stranraer	21.11.37	Drummore J.	Accrington St.	08.57	1958-60	83		0	(HB)
			TR	York C.	03.62	1961	11		0	
HAMILTON, Bryan	Belfast	21.12.46	Linfield	Ipswich T.	08.71	1971-75	142	11	43	(M)NI-50/NI.U23-2
			TR	Everton	11.75	1975-76	38	3	5	
			TR	Millwall	07.77	1977-78	48	1	6	
			TR	Swindon T.	11.78	1978-80	19	5	1	
			TR	Tranmere Rov.	10.80	1980-83	95	13	6	
HAMILTON, Charles M.	Glasgow	16.06.33	JNRS	Plymouth Arg.	07.50					(F)
			TR	Stockport Co.	11.55	1955	27		1	
HAMILTON, Dave S.	Carlisle	08.02.19	Shawfield J.	Newcastle U.	+					(OR)
			TR	Southend U.	05.46	1946	4		0	
HAMILTON, David	Sth. Sheilds	07.11.60	APP.	Sunderland	09.78					(D)
			TR	Blackburn Rov.	01.81	1980-83	70	8	4	
HAMILTON, Eddie	Glasgow	17.01.27	Dundalk	Barnsley	04.49	1949	1		0	(IL)
HAMILTON, Gary J.	Glasgow	27.12.65	APP.	Middlesbrough	06.83	1982-83	34	6	5	(D)S.YTH.INT.
HAMILTON, Hugh	Glasgow	16.06.42	Falkirk	Hartlepool U.	07.63	1963-65	36	1	7	(F)
HAMILTON, Ian	Bristol	12.09.40	JNRS	Bristol Rov.	01.58	1958-67	148	/	60	(IF)
			L	Exeter C.	10.67	1967	4	/	1	
			TR	Newport Co.	07.68	1968	13	2	2	
HAMILTON, Ian M.	Streatham	31.10.50	APP.	Chelsea	01.68	1966	3	2	2	(F)E.YTH.INT.
			TR	Southend U.	09.68	1968	35	2	11	
			TR	Aston Villa	06.69	1969-75	189	17	39	
			TR	Sheffield U.	07.76	1976-77	55	5	13	
HAMILTON, Ian W.	Sth. Shields	21.07.56	Boldon C.W.	Darlington	11.79	1979-81	99	4	19	(F) Brother of David
HAMILTON, James	Uddingston	14.06.55	APP.	Sunderland	06.72	1971-73	9	8	2	(M)
			TR	Plymouth Arg.	11.75	1976	6	2	0	
			TR	Bristol Rov.	12.76	1976-77	16	4	1	
			TR	Carlisle U.	09.77	1977-81	150	4	12	
			TR	Hartlepool U.	11.82	1982	2	1	0	
HAMILTON, John	Larkhall	22.01.35	Hearts	Watford	05.67	1967	7	1	2	(F)S.U23-2/S.F.LGE REP.
HAMILTON, John T.	Glasgow	10.07.49	Glasgow Rgrs.	Millwall	06.78	1978	1	1	0	
HAMILTON, Neville	Leicester	19.04.60	APP.	Leicester C.	11.77	1977	4	/	0	(M)
			TR	Mansfield T.	01.79	1978-80	84	5	4	
			TR	Rochdale	08.81	1981-83	72	2	5	
HAMILTON, Robert M.	Edinburgh	25.04.24	Hearts	Chester C.	+	1946-47	68		10	(W)
HAMILTON, William	Airdrie	16.02.38	Drumpelier	Sheffield U.	02.56	1956-60	79		21	(IF)S-1/S.F.LGE REP./
			TR	Middlesbrough	02.61	1960-61	10		1	d.
			Hibernian	Aston Villa	08.65	1965-66	49	/	9	
HAMILTON, William	Hamilton	01.09.18	Blantyre	Preston N.E.	*	1946	37		0	(WH)
HAMILTON, William R.	Belfast	09.05.57	Linfield	Q.P.R.	04.78	1978-79	9	3	2	(F)NI-25/NI.U21-1
			TR	Burnley	11.79	1979-82	200	/	58	
HAMLETT, Tom L.	Stoke	21.01.17	Congleton T.	Bolton W.	*	1946-48	72		4	(FB)
			TR	Port Vale	05.49	1949-51	109		0	
HAMMILL, John	Irvine	08.01.24	Arbroath	Newport Co.	04.47	1946-47	12		0	(RH)
HAMMOND, Albert W.A.	Islington	05.02.24	Q.P.R.(AM)	Brentford	+					
			TR	Exeter C.	06.46	1946	2		0	
HAMMOND, Cyril S.	Woolwich	10.10.27	Erith & B.	Charlton Ath.	+	1950-57	201		2	(WH)
			TR	Colchester U.	07.58	1958-60	95		5	
HAMMOND, Geoff	Sudbury	24.03.50	JNRS	Ipswich T.	07.68	1970-73	53	3	2	(D)
			TR	Manchester C.	09.74	1974-75	33	1	2	
			TR	Charlton Ath.	07.76	1976	15	1	0	
HAMMOND, Paul A.	Nottingham	26.07.53	APP.	Crystal Palace	09.71	1972-76	117	/	0	(G)
HAMPSHIRE, Paul	Guildford	10.10.61	JNRS	Aldershot	06.79	1980-81	4	1	2	(F)
HAMPSON, Alan	Prescot	31.12.27		Everton	08.49	1950	1		0	(OR)
			TR	Halifax T.	11.52	1952-55	121		32	
			TR	Bradford C.	07.56	1956	6		4	
HAMPSON, Eric.	Norton	11.11.21	Stafford Rgrs.	Stoke C.	+	1948-51	8		0	(HB)
HAMPSON, Ray G.	Manchester	27.07.32	JNRS	Manchester U.	04.51					(F)
			TR	Reading	04.53					
			TR	Aldershot	07.55	1955-56	20		2	
			TR	Bournemouth	07.57	1957-58	15		2	

Players Names	Birthplace	Date	Previous Club	League Club	Date Signed	Seasons Played	Apps	Sub	Gls	
HAMPTON, Derek	Saltburn	25.04.52	Whitby T.	Hartlepool U.	11.79	1979-81	66	8	18	(F)
HAMPTON, Ivan K.	Heanor	15.10.42	Rotherham U.(AM)	Notts.Co.	03.61	1960-66	139	2	1	(FB)
			TR	Halifax T.	07.67	1967-68	57	2	1	
			TR	Peterborough U.	07.69	1969	3	1	0	
HAMPTON, Peter	Oldham	12.09.54	APP.	Leeds U.	09.71	1972-79	63	5	2	(D)E.YTH.INT.
			TR	Stoke C.	08.80	1980-83	134	4	4	
HAMSON, Gary	Nottingham	24.08.59	APP.	Sheffield U.	11.76	1976-78	107	1	8	(M)
			TR	Leeds U.	07.79	1979-83	65	8	3	
HAMSTEAD, George W.	Rotherham	24.01.46		York C.	09.64	1964-65	32	3	1	(W)
			TR	Barnsley	07.66	1966-70	147	2	22	
			TR	Bury	07.71	1971-78	189	7	29	
			L	Rochdale	01.77	1976	3	1	0	
HANCOCK, Barry J.	Stoke	30.12.38		Port Vale	07.57	1960-63	21		1	(F)
			TR	Crewe Alex.	08.64	1964	3		0	
HANCOCK, Charles	Stoke	16.02.25		Port Vale	05.48	1948-55	50		0	(G)
HANCOCK, David J.	Exeter	24.07.38	JNRS	Plymouth Arg.	09.55	1956	2		0	(WH)
			TR	Torquay U.	01.59	1958-63	177		12	
			TR	Exeter C.	03.64	1963-64	40		3	
HANCOCK, Ken P.	Milton	25.11.37	Stoke C. (AM)	Port Vale	12.58	1958-64	240		0	(G)
			TR	Ipswich T.	12.64	1964-68	163	/	0	
			TR	Tottenham H.	03.69	1969-70	3	/	0	
			TR	Bury	07.71	1971-72	35	/	0	
HANCOCK, Mike	Newport	17.02.54	JNRS	Newport Co.	08.73	1971-75	51	9	1	(CH) W.SCH.INT.
HANCOCKS, Johnny	Oakengates	30.04.19	Oakengates	Walsall	*					(OR) E-3/E.F.LGE REP.●
			TR	Wolverhampton W.	05.46	1946-55	343		158	
HANCOX, David T.	Conisborough	02.10.47	APP	Sheffield U.	09.65					(F)
			TR	Chester C.	07.67	1967	17	2	4	
HANCOX, Ray	Mansfield	01.05.29	Sutton U.	Crystal Palace	08.50	1950-52	20		2	(F)
			TR	Southend U.	06.53					
HAND, Eoin	Dublin	30.03.46	Drumcondra	Swindon T.	06.64					(D)EI-19
			Drumcondra	Portsmouth	10.68	1968-75	259	1	12	
			S. Africa	Portsmouth	12.77	1977-78	15	2	2	
HANDFORD, Philip M.	Chatham	18.07.64	APP	Gillingham	07.82	1982-83	29	3	1	(M)
HANDLEY, Brian	Wakefield	21.06.36	Goole T.	Aston Villa	09.57	1959	3		0	(CF) d.1982
			TR	Torquay U.	09.60	1960-63	80		33	
			Bridgwater	Rochdale	02.66	1965	3	/	0	
HANDSCOMBE, Mal	Normanton	29.06.34		Chester C.	AM	1957	4		0	(CH)
HANDYSIDES, Ian	Jarrow	14.12.62	APP	Birmingham C.	01.80	1980-83	44	18	2	(M)
			TR	Walsall	01.84	1983	17	1	4	
HANFORD, Harry	Blaengwynfi	09.10.07	Sheffield Wed.(*)	Exeter C.	05.46	1946	37		0	(CH) *Swansea C./W-7/ W.SCH.INT.
HANKEY, Albert A.	Stoke	24.05.14		Southend U.	*	1946-49	104		0	(G)
HANKIN, Ray	Wallsend	02.02.56	APP	Burnley	02.73	1972-76	110	2	37	(F)E.U23-3/E.YTH.INT.
			TR	Leeds U.	09.76	1976-79	82	1	32	
			Vancouver	Middlesbrough	09.82	1982	19	2	1	
			TR	Peterborough U.	09.83	1983	25	2	7	
HANKINSON, Jim	Preston	01.07.28		Preston N.E.	09.47					(F)
			TR	Chester C.	06.50	1950	15		1	
HANLON, John	Manchester	12.10.17	JNRS	Manchester U.	*	1946-48	36		8	(CF)
			TR	Bury	10.48	1948-49	31		1	
HANLON, Steve H.	Chester	18.07.63	APP	Crewe Alex.	08.81	1980-82	23	4	0	(M)
HANLON, Walter	Glasgow	23.09.19	Clyde	Brighton & H.A.	08.46	1946-47	72		4	(OL)
			TR	Bournemouth	05.48	1948	19		3	
			TR	Crystal Palace	07.49	1949-54	125		8	
HANN, Ralph	Whitburn	04.07.11	Newcastle U.(*)	Derby Co.	*					(CH)
				Crystal Palace	04.47	1946	1		0	
HANNABY, Cyril	Doncaster	11.10.23	Wath W.	Wolverhampton W.	+					(G)
			TR	Hull C.	08.46	1946-47	17		0	
			TR	Halifax T.	02.48	1947	2		0	
HANNAH, George	Liverpool	11.12.28	Linfield	Newcastle U.	09.49	1949-56	167		41	(IF) N1.F.LGE REP.
			TR	Lincoln C.	09.57	1957-58	38		4	
			TR	Manchester C.	09.58	1958-63	114		15	
			TR	Notts. Co.	07.64	1964-65	25	/	1	
			TR	Bradford C.	10.65	1965	29	1	2	
HANNAH, John	Wakefield	25.10.62	Fryston C.W.	Darlington	N/C	1983	9	4	3	(F)
HANNAH, William K.	Shotts	06.08.21	Albion Rov.	Preston N.E.	12.47	1947-49	15		4	(IF)
			TR	Barrow	02.51	1950-53	106		16	
HANNAM, Dave	Islington	10.05.44	JNRS	Brighton & H.A.	06.61	1962	5		2	(F)
HANNAWAY, Jack	Bootle	22.10.27	Seaforth Fellows	Manchester C.	04.50	1951-56	64		0	(FB)
			TR	Gillingham	06.57	1957-59	126		4	
			TR	Southport	06.60	1960-61	73		2	
HANNIGAN, Brendan	Dublin	03.09.43	Shelbourne	Wrexham	12.65	1965	7	/	2	(F)

Players Names	Birthplace	Date	Previous Club	League Club	Date Signed	Seasons Played	Apps	Sub	Gls	
HANNIGAN, Ernie	Glasgow	23.01.43	Q. of South	Preston N.E.	08.64	1964-67	97	/	29	(W)
			TR	Coventry C.	11.67	1967-69	43	4	6	
			L	Torquay U.	12.69	1969	2	/	0	
HANNIGAN, John L.	Glasgow	17.02.33	Morton	Sunderland	07.55	1955-57	33		8	(W)
			TR	Derby Co.	05.58	1958-60	72		19	
			TR	Bradford P.A.	06.61	1961-63	96		26	
HANSBURY, Roger	Barnsley	26.01.55	APP	Norwich C.	01.73	1974-80	78	/	0	(G)
			L	Cambridge U.	11.77	1977	11	/	0	
			Hong Kong	Burnley	08.83	1983	46	/	0	
HANSELL, Ron A.	Norwich	03.10.30	Norwich St. B.	Norwich C.	06.50	1953-55	29		7	(IF)
			TR	Chester C.	06.56	1956	36		9	
HANSEN, Alan	Alloa	13.06.55	Partick Thistle	Liverpool	04.77	1977-83	247	/	7	(D)S-21/S.U23-3
HANSEN, Karl A.	Denmark	04.07.21	Denmark	Huddersfield T.	AM	1948	15		2	(IF)
HANSON, Edwin	Denmark		Denmark	Grimsby T.	AM	1946	1		0	(OL)
HANSON, Fred	Sheffield	23.05.15	Crystal Palace(*)	Rotherham U.	*	1946	9		0	(OL) d.1967
HANSON, John	Bradford	03.12.62	APP	Bradford C.	12.80	1980	1	/	0	(F)
HANSON, Neil	Blackburn	16.06.64	APP	Preston N.E.	09.81					(F)
			TR	Halifax T.	08.83	1983	0	1	0	
HANSON, Stan	Bootle	27.12.15	Liverpool(*)	Bolton W.	*	1946-55	336		0	(G) Brother of Adolph (pre-war player)
HANVEY, Keith	Manchester	18.01.52		Manchester C.	08.71					(D)
			TR	Swansea C.	07.72	1972	11	/	0	
			TR	Rochdale	07.73	1973-76	121	/	10	
			TR	Grimsby T.	02.77	1976-77	54	/	2	
			TR	Huddersfield T.	07.78	1978-83	205	/	14	
HAPGOOD, Edris A.	Kettering	13.06.30		Burnley	03.48	1951	7		2	(F) Son of Eddie
			TR	Watford	07.53	1953	1		0	(pre-war international)
HARBER, William H.	Hitchin	03.12.44	APP	Swindon T.	12.61	1962	2		0	(HB)
			TR	Luton T.	09.64	1964-65	28	/	2	
HARBERTSON, Ron	Redcar	23.12.29	Nth. Shields	Newcastle U.	01.49					(CF)
			TR	Bradford C.	08.50	1950	16		1	
			TR	Brighton & H.A.	10.51					
			TR	Bradford C.	05.52	1953	13		3	
			TR	Grimsby T.	07.54	1954	26		6	
			Ashington	Darlington	01.57	1956-57	49		21	
			TR	Lincoln C.	03.58	1957-59	57		22	
			TR	Wrexham	03.60	1959-60	28		13	
			TR	Darlington	01.61	1960	14		2	
			TR	Lincoln C.	07.61	1961	29		3	
HARBEY, Graham K.	Chesterfield	29.08.64	APP	Derby Co.	08.82	1983	19	/	0	(M)
HARBURN, Peter A.	Finsbury Park	18.06.31	Portsmouth(AM)	Brighton & H.A.	02.56	1954-57	126		64	(F)
			TR	Everton	08.58	1958	4		1	
			TR	Scunthorpe U.	01.59	1958-59	20		8	
			TR	Workington	10.59	1959-60	67		23	
HARBURN William M.	Stockton	19.11.23		Darlington	AM	1947	1		0	
HARBY, Mick	Nottingham	07.11.48	JNRS	Nottingham F.	07.66	1967	3	/	0	(G)
HARDCASTLE, Cyril	Halifax	22.11.19		Bradford C.	AM	1948	4		1	(CF)
HARDCASTLE, Peter	Leeds	27.01.49	Skelmersdale	Blackpool	07.71	1971-73	29	7	0	(D)E.AMAT.INT.
			TR	Plymouth Arg.	07.74	1974-75	12	2	1	
			TR	Brad. C.	07.76	1976-77	62	/	1	
HARDEN, Les J.	W. Hartlepool	07.05.23		Hartlepool U.	05.46	1946-55	170		47	(OL)
HARDIE, John C.	Edinburgh	07.02.38	Falkirk	Oldham Ath.	07.60	1960	17		0	(G)
			TR	Chester C.	07.61	1961-62	84		0	
			TR	Bradford P.A.	12.63	1963-69	265	/	0	
			TR	Crystal Palace	08.70					
HARDING, Alan	Sunderland	14.05.48	Spennymoor	Darlington	01.70	1969-72	125	4	38	(F)
			TR	Lincoln C.	03.73	1972-78	203	6	38	
			TR	Hartlepool U.	03.79	1978-82	79	5	8	
HARDING, David	Liverpool	14.08.46		Wrexham	09.65	1965	9	1	0	(W)
HARDING, Edward	Croydon	05.04.25	Coalville	Crystal Palace	+	1946–52	151		0	(FB)
HARDING, Kevin R.F.	Isleworth	19.03.57	APP	Brentford	APP	1973–74	8	/	0	(FB)
HARDING, Steve J.	Bristol	23.07.56	APP	Bristol C.	12.74	1975	2	/	0	(D)
			L	Southend U.	01.76	1975	2	/	0	
			L	Grimsby T.	09.76	1976	8	/	0	
			TR	Bristol Rov.	06.77	1977-79	37	1	1	
			L	Brentford	01.80	1979	3	1	0	
HARDISTY, J. Robert E.	Chester–le–Street	01.02.21	B. Auckland	Darlington	AM	1946-48	6		0	(WH)E.AMAT.INT.
HARDMAN, Colin	Altrincham	13.11.55		Stockport Co.	03.76	1975-76	6	3	1	(W)
HARDMAN, John	Bury	17.12.40		Rochdale	08.60	1960–66	40	/	2	(HB)
HARDS, Neil A.	Portsmouth	28.01.62	APP	Plymouth Arg.	01.80	1979-82	6	/	0	(G)
HARDSTAFF, Cecil	Crewe	14.11.31	Wolverhampton W.(AM)	Crewe Alex.	06.49	1949	1		0	

Players Names	Birthplace	Date	Previous Club	League Club	Date Signed	Seasons Played	Career Record Apps Sub Gls			
HARDWICK, George F. M.	Saltburn	02.02.20	South Bank	Middlesbrough	*	1946–50	135		5	(FB)E–13/E.F.LGE REP.
			TR	Oldham Ath.	11.50	1950–55	190		15	
HARDWICK, Ken	W. Auckland	06.01.24	Rossington Col.	Doncaster Rov.	+	1947–56	308		0	(G)
			TR	Scunthorpe U.	04.57	1956–59	96		0	
			TR	Barrow	12.59	1959	12		0	
HARDWICK, Steve	Mansfield	06.09.56	JNRS	Chesterfield	07.74	1974-76	38	/	0	(G)E.YTH.INT.
			TR	Newcastle U.	12.76	1977-82	92	/	0	
			TR	Oxford U.	02.83	1982-83	64	/	0	
HARDY, Edwin	Chesterfield	16.10.53	JNRS	Chesterfield	08.71	1972	6	/	0	(G)
HARDY, Gordon D.	Kingston	23.05.23	Charlton Rov.	Millwall	+	1946	3		0	(CH)
			TR	Southport	07.48	1948–49	16		0	
			TR	Bournemouth	06.50	1951–53	76		0	
HARDY, Herbert	Barrow	06.12.29		Barrow	05.52	1951	2		1	(IF)
HARDY, John H.	Chesterfield	15.06.10	Hull C.(*)	Lincoln C.	+	1946	18		0	(CH)*Chesterfield/d.1978
HARDY, Robin	Worksop	18.01.41	JNRS	Sheffield Wed.	02.58	1961–63	30		1	(WH)
			TR	Rotherham U.	02.65	1964–65	41	/	2	
			TR	Cambridge U.	N/L	1970	15	1	0	
HARDY, William	Whitehaven	23.08.29	Q. of South	Workington	10.51	1951–53	55		2	(HB)
HARDYMAN, Paul G.	Manchester	15.09.65	Fareham T.	Portsmouth	05.84	1983	2	1	0	(M)
HARE, Tom	Motherwell	01.04.44	Fauldhouse	Southampton	04.63	1965	13	/	0	(FB)
			TR	Luton T.	07.67	1967	12	/	0	
HAREIDE, Age F.	Norway	23.09.53	Molde F.K.	Manchester C.	10.81	1981-82	17	7	0	(D) NORWAY INT.
			TR	Norwich C.	11.82	1982-83	38	2	2	
HARFIELD, Les P.	Southampton	22.11.52	APP	Southampton	11.69	1970	2	/	1	(IF)E.YTH.INT./E.SCH.INT
				Luton T.	09.72	1972	0	/	0	
HARFORD, Mick G.	Sunderland	12.02.59	Lambton St.B.C.	Lincoln C.	07.77	1977-80	109	6	41	(F)
			TR	Newcastle U.	12.80	1980	18	/	4	
			TR	Bristol C.	08.81	1981	30	/	11	
			TR	Birmingham C.	03.82	1981-83	80	/	23	
HARFORD, Ray	Halifax	01.06.45	JNRS	Charlton Ath.	05.64	1965	3	/	0	(HB)
			TR	Exeter C.	01.66	1965–66	55	/	1	
			TR	Lincoln C.	07.67	1967–70	161	/	10	
			TR	Mansfield T.	06.71	1971	7	/	0	
			TR	Port Vale	12.71	1971–72	20	/	1	
			TR	Colchester U.	01.73	1972–74	107	1	4	
HARGREAVES, Alan	Dewsbury	29.03.31		Bradford C.	07.54	1954–55	3		1	
HARGREAVES, David	Accrington	27.08.54	Accrington	Blackburn Rov.	12.77	1977	2	/	0	(F)
HARGREAVES, John	Rotherham	01.05.15	Leeds U.(*)	Bristol C.	+	1946	26		9	(OL)d.1978
			TR	Reading	04.47	1946–47	15		1	
HARGREAVES, Joseph	Accrington	30.10.15	Rossendale	Rochdale	+	1946–47	33		24	(CF)
HARGREAVES, Tom	Blackburn	29.10.17		Blackburn Rov.	*					(CF)
			TR	Rochdale	05.46	1946	9		0	
HARGREAVES, Wilf O.	Rawmarsh	15.12.21	Rawmarsh	Rotherham U.	+	1946–47	3		0	(RH)
HARKER, Chris	Shiremoor	29.06.37	JNRS	Newcastle U.	03.55	1957	1		0	(G)
			Aberdeen	Bury	12.61	1961–66	178	/	0	
			TR	Grimsby T.	06.67	1967	10	/	0	
			TR	Rochdale	07.68	1968–69	92	/	0	
HARKIN, Jim	Brinsworth	08.08.13	Rotherham U.(*)	Mansfield T.	*	1946	4		1	(CH)*Doncaster Rov.
HARKIN, Terry	Londonderry	14.09.41	Coleraine	Port Vale	09.62	1962–63	27		11	(CF)NI–5/NI.U23–1
			TR	Crewe Alex.	06.64	1964	42		34	
			TR	Cardiff C.	08.65	1965	19	2	10	
			TR	Notts. Co.	09.66	1966	27	1	10	
			TR	Southport	07.67	1967–68	63	1	31	
			TR	Shrewsbury T.	03.69	1968–70	79	/	30	
HARKNESS, Jim	Edinburgh	19.05.40	Hamilton Ac.	Carlisle U.	08.61	1961–62	17		0	(G)
HARKNESS, William J.	Glasgow	21.07.18		Carlisle U.	10.47					(IF)
				Workington	N/L	1951	7		1	
HARKOUK, Rachid	Chelsea	19.05.56	Feltham	Crystal Palace	06.76	1976-77	51	3	21	(M)
			TR	Q.P.R.	06.78	1978-79	15	5	3	
			TR	Notts. Co.	06.80	1980-83	70	19	17	
HARLAND, Stan	Liverpool	19.06.40	New Brighton	Everton	12.59					(WH)
			TR	Bradford C.	07.61	1961–63	120		20	
			TR	Carlisle V.	06.64	1964–65	77	/	7	
			TR	Swindon T.	08.66	1966–71	237	/	6	
			TR	Birmingham C.	12.71	1971–72	37	1	0	
HARLE, David	Denaby	15.08.63	APP	Doncaster Rov.	11.80	1979-81	48	13	3	(M)
			TR	Exeter C.	07.82	1982-83	42	1	2	
			TR	Doncaster Rov.	09.83	1983	28	1	6	
HARLEY, Albert G.	Chester	17.04.40	JNRS	Shrewsbury T.	04.57	1956–64	219		14	(WH)Brother of Les
			TR	Swansea C.	09.64	1964–65	26	1	0	
			TR	Crewe Alex.	07.66	1966	22	/	4	
			TR	Stockport Co.	02.67	1966–68	78	3	11	
			TR	Chester C.	06.69	1969	3	/	1	

Players Names	Birthplace	Date	Previous Club	League Club	Date Signed	Seasons Played	Apps	Sub	Gls	
HARLEY, Alex	Glasgow	20.04.36	T.Lanark	Manchester C.	08.62	1962	40		23	(CF)d.1969
			TR	Birmingham C.	08.63	1963–64	28		9	
			Dundee	Leicester C.	05.65					
HARLEY, James	Methil	21.02.17	Hill of Beath	Liverpool	*	1946–47	37		0	(FB)
HARLEY, John	Peterborough	22.04.49	Stevenage	Reading	09.69	1969-72	64	10	6	(F)
			TR	Aldershot	07.73	1973-74	16	12	0	
			Wokingham	Hartlepool U.	09.76	1976	4	/	1	
HARLEY, Les	Chester	26.09.46	JNRS	Chester C.	09.64	1964–66	22	3	3	(F)
			TR	Blackpool	07.67					
			L	Rochdale	02.68	1967	5	/	0	
HARLOCK, Des S.	Blaenau Ffestiniog	20.12.22		Tranmere Rov.	+	1946–53	151		17	(OR)d.1981
HARMAN, Peter R.	Guildford	11.10.50	APP	Bournemouth	08.68	1969	1	/	0	(CF)
			TR	Reading	08.71	1971–72	34	2	9	
HARMER, Tommy C.	Hackney	02.02.28	Finchley	Tottenham H.	08.48	1951–59	205	/	47	(IF)E"B"–1
			TR	Watford	10.60	1960–61	63		6	
			TR	Chelsea	09.62	1962–63	8		1	
HARMSTON, Mick J.	Sheffield	07.04.50	APP	Sheffield U.	05.67	1968	5	/	0	(FB)
			L	Southend U.	12.70	1970	1	/	0	
HARNBY, Don R.	Durham	20.07.23		Newcastle U.	+					(FB)
				York C.	08.47	1947	1		0	
			Spennymoor	Grimsby T.	09.49	1949–51	34		0	
HARNEY, Dave	Jarrow	02.03.47		Grimsby T.	11.64					(F)
			TR	Scunthorpe U.	07.67	1967–68	20	5	1	
			TR	Brentford	10.69	1969	0	1	0	
HARNEY, Steve G.	Bradford	18.02.51	Drum Rov.	Bradford C.	AM	1968–70	13	1	0	(RB)
HARPER, Alan	Liverpool	01.11.60	APP	Liverpool	04.78					(D)
			TR	Everton	06.83	1983	26	3	1	
HARPER, Anthony F.	Oxford	26.05.25	Headington	Brentford	04.48	1948–54	173		6	(WH)
HARPER, Colin	Ipswich	25.07.46		Ipswich T.	08.64	1965–74	143	4	5	(D)
			L	Grimsby T.	12.76	1976	3	/	0	
			L	Cambridge U.	02.77	1976	15	/	0	
			TR	Port Vale	08.77	1977	4	/	0	
HARPER, David	Peckham	29.09.38	JNRS	Millwall	05.57	1957–64	165		4	(WH)E.YTH.INT.
			TR	Ipswich T.	03.65	1964–66	70	2	2	
			TR	Swindon T.	07.67	1967	4	/	0	
			TR	Orient	10.67	1967–70	82	3	4	
HARPER, Dennis	Wednesbury	12.10.36		Birmingham C.	08.56	1956	1		0	(F)
HARPER, Don	Mansfield	26.10.21	Chesterfield(+)	Mansfield T.	07.46	1946	21		1	(OR)
HARPER, Ian	Scunthorpe	23.11.44	JNRS	Scunthorpe U.	07.62	1963–64	21		0	(FB)
HARPER, Ivor R.	Watford	23.06.33	Aylesbury U.	Watford	AM	1951	5		0	(IF)
HARPER, Joe J.	Southampton	12.01.20	Twechar U.	Watford	*	1946–51	157		1	(FB)
HARPER, Joe M.	Greenock	11.01.48	Morton	Huddersfield T.	03.67	1966–67	25	2	3	(CF)S–3/S.U23–2/
			Aberdeen	Everton	12.72	1972–73	40	3	12	S.F.LGE REP.
HARPER, Ken	Barnsley	15.04.17	Walsall(*)	Bradford C.	+	1946–48	50		0	(FB)
HARPER, Ken	Farnworth	27.04.24		Blackpool	+					(CH)
				Rochdale	12.47					
				Shrewsbury T.	08.50	1950	1		0	
HARPER, Robert	Glasgow	06.06.20		Huddersfield T.	06.46					(OL)
			TR	Newport Co.	11.46	1946–49	114		12	
			TR	Southend U.	07.50	1950	6		0	
HARRIGAN, Duncan	Paisley	26.06.21	St. Mirren(AM)	Crewe Alex.	08.46	1946–47	55		24	(CF)
			TR	Aston Villa	04.48					
			TR	Chester C.	10.48	1948	20		4	
HARRINGTON, Alan C.	Cardiff	17.11.33	Cardiff Nomads	Cardiff C.	10.51	1952–65	349	/	6	(FB)W–11
HARRINGTON, Colin	Bicester	03.04.43	Wolverhampton W.(AM)	Oxford U.	10.62	1962–70	231	2	30	(IF)
			TR	Mansfield T.	06.71	1971	7	6	0	
HARRINGTON, Paul	Hartlepool	26.09.64		Hartlepool U.	04.83	1983	0	2	0	(M)
HARRINGTON, Phil	Bangor	20.11.63	APP	Chester C.	11.81	1981-83	70	/	0	(G)W.YTH.INT.
HARRIS, Alan J.	Hackney	28.12.42	JNRS	Chelsea	06.60	1960–64	70		0	(FB)E.YTH.INT./
			TR	Coventry C.	11.64	1964–65	60	/	/	E.SCH.INT./Brother of Ron
			TR	Chelsea	05.66	1966	12	2	0	
			TR	Q.P.R.	07.67	1967–70	90	3	0	
			TR	Plymouth Arg.	03.71	1970–72	64	/	0	
			TR	Cambridge U.	07.73	1973	6	/	0	
HARRIS, Albert E.	Bootle	21.11.31		Everton	01.55	1955	5		0	(G)
			TR	Tranmere Rov.	05.57	1957–59	33		0	
			TR	Southport	07.60	1960–64	159		0	
HARRIS, Alex	Hong Kong	22.10.34	JNRS	Blackpool	11.51	1952–57	21		4	(F)
HARRIS, Anthony T.	Berrington	20.12.45	APP	Shrewsbury T.	07.63	1963–66	54	1	4	(HB)
			TR	Bradford P.A.	07.68	1968	10	/	0	
HARRIS, Arthur	Foleshill	28.07.14	Coventry Col	Southend U.	*	1946	41		0	(RH)d.1973

Players Names	Birthplace	Date	Previous Club	League Club	Date Signed	Seasons Played	Apps	Sub	Gls	
HARRIS, Brian	Bebington	16.05.35	Port Sunlight	Everton	01.54	1955–66	310	/	23	(WH)E.YTH.INT.●
			TR	Cardiff C.	10.66	1966–70	147	2	0	
			TR	Newport Co.	07.71	1971–73	85	/	0	
HARRIS, Carl S.	Neath	03.11.56	APP	Leeds U.	11.73	1974-81	124	30	26	(F)W-24/W.U23-1/
			TR	Charlton Ath.	07.82	1982-83	66	/	7	W.SCH.INT.
HARRIS, Chris	Hastings	23.01.57	Bexhill U.	Millwall	10.76	1976	3	/	0	(F)
HARRIS, David	Stoke	19.11.53		Port Vale	08.73	1973-78	175	1	8	(D)
			TR	Halifax T.	07.79	1979-80	69	2	3	
HARRIS, Derek H.	Undy	02.11.33	Undy U.	Newport Co.	09.54	1954–57	156		56	(IF)●
			TR	Portsmouth	07.58	1958–70	377	2	48	
			L	Newport Co.	10.70	1970	17	/	2	
HARRIS, Fred	Birmingham	02.07.12	Osborne A.	Birmingham C.	*	1946–49	117		2	(IF)E.F.LGE REP.
HARRIS, Gary W.	Birmingham	31.05.59	APP	Cardiff C.	08.78	1978-79	4	/	0	(D)
HARRIS, Geoff	Manchester	01.02.56	Oldham Ath. (APP)	Halifax T.	07.75	1975-76	10	5	1	(F)
HARRIS, George	Durham	24.08.36		Preston N.E.	08.57					(F)
			TR	Southport	07.59	1959	1		0	
HARRIS, George A.	London	10.06.40	Woking	Newport Co.	07.61	1961	31		7	(W)
			TR	Watford	04.62	1961–65	162	1	56	
			TR	Reading	07.66	1966–69	134	2	56	
			TR	Cambridge U.	07.70	1970–71	33	2	11	
HARRIS, Gerry	Claverley	08.10.35	Bebington FC	Wolverhampton W.	01.54	1956–65	234		2	(FB)E.U23–4
			TR	Walsall	04.66	1965–67	14	2	1	
HARRIS, Gordon	Worksop	02.06.40	Firbeck Col.	Burnley	01.58	1958–67	258	/	69	(OL)E–1/E.U23–2/
			TR	Sunderland	01.68	1967–71	124	1	16	E.F.LGE REP.
HARRIS, Gordon W.	Perth	19.02.43	Forfar	Cardiff C.	03.65	1964	5		0	(FB)
HARRIS, James	Birkenhead	18.08.33	JNRS	Everton	09.51	1955–60	191		66	(CF)E.U23–1/E.F.LGE
			TR	Birmingham C.	12.60	1960–63	93		37	REP.
			TR	Oldham Ath.	07.64	1964–65	28	1	9	
			TR	Tranmere Rov.	08.66					
HARRIS, Jeff	London	11.06.42	Enfield	Orient	05.64	1964	14		0	(WH)E.AMAT.INT.
HARRIS, John	Glasgow	30.06.17	Wolves(+)	Chelsea	+	1946–55	326		14	(FB)Son of Neil(pre–war)
			TR	Chester C.	07.56	1956	26		1	*Swansea C./Tottenham H.
HARRIS, John D.	Gornal	03.04.39	JNRS	Wolverhampton W.	05.58	1961–62	3		0	(FB)
			TR	Walsall	01.65	1964–68	73	5	2	
HARRIS, John P.	Bermondsey	20.12.31		Millwall	AM	1956	1		0	(IF)
HARRIS, Joseph	Belfast	08.04.29	Distillery	Blackburn Rov.	01.51	1950–51	35		14	(CF)
			TR	Oldham Ath.	03.53	1952–53	27		4	
HARRIS, Joseph A.	Liverpool	20.09.26		Everton	07.50	1950–52	14		4	(F)
HARRIS, Kevin	Dublin	20.02.18		Notts. Co	+					(WH)
				Brentford	08.48	1948	4		0	
HARRIS, Len	Nuneaton	29.05.49	JNRS	Nottingham F.	06.66	1968–69	2	/	0	(FB)
			L	Doncaster Rov.	09.70	1970	4	/	0	
HARRIS, Les	Llanfair	01.11.41	Aberystwyth Univ.	Swansea C.	08.63	1963–64	4		0	(FB)
HARRIS, Les H.	Sheffield	29.05.55	JNRS	Barnsley	09.75	1975–76	11	15	2	(F)
HARRIS, Martin	Doncaster	22.12.55	Grimsby T. (APP)	Workington	07.74	1974–76	97	9	13	(F)
				Hartlepool U.	12.77	1977	0	1	0	
HARRIS, Neil	Glasgow	09.02.20	Swansea C.(+)	Q.P.R.	09.46	1946	1		1	(CF)Brother of John
HARRIS, Paul E.	Hackney	19.05.53	APP	Orient	07.70	1970-74	96	/	4	(D)
			TR	Swansea C.	07.75	1975-76	47	2	2	
HARRIS, Peter	Neath	09.08.53	APP	Newport Co.	08.71	1970–72	20	11	1	(F)
HARRIS, Peter P.	Portsmouth	19.12.25	Gosport Bor.	Portsmouth	+	1946–59	479		194	(OR)E–2/E.F.LGE REP●
HARRIS, Phil J.	Swindon	18.12.58	APP	Swindon T.	APP	1976	0	1	0	(M)
HARRIS, Ron E.	Hackney	13.11.44	APP	Chelsea	11.61	1961-79	646	9	13	(D)E.U23-4/E.YTH.INT./
			TR	Brentford	05.80	1980-83	60	1	0	E.SCH.INT.●
HARRIS, Tom A.	Chelsea	08.11.24		Fulham	09.47					(IF)
			TR	Orient	09.51	1951–52	31		11	
			TR	Colchester U.	06.53	1953	3			
HARRIS, Tom J.G.	Ogmore	15.02.16	Ameraman	Plymouth Arg.	05.48	1948	3		0	(G)+Charlton Ath.
HARRIS, Tom J.	Swansea	18.05.34		Leeds U.	11.51					(CH)
			TR	Halifax T.	10.55	1955–56	9			
HARRIS, Trevor J.	Colchester	06.02.36		Colchester U.	07.54	1954–62	100		6	(WH)
HARRIS, William	Dudley	01.12.18	Whiteheath	W.B.A.	*					(G)
			TR	Oldham Ath.	06.46	1946	32		0	
			TR	Accrington St.	08.47	1947–49	99		0	
HARRIS, William C.	Swansea	31.10.28	Llanelli	Hull C.	03.50	1949–53	131		6	(WH)W–6
			TR	Middlesbrough	03.54	1953–64	359		64	
			TR	Bradford C.	03.65	1964–65	9	/	1	
HARRIS, William T.	Bedwellty	30.06.13		Watford	*	1946–48	91		6	(FB)

Players Names	Birthplace	Date	Previous Club	League Club	Date Signed	Seasons Played	Apps	Sub	Gls	
HARRISON, Anthony	Gateshead	09.01.54	Whitley Bay	Southport	02.77	1976-77	48	/	0	(G)
			TR	Carlisle U.	06.78	1980	8		0	
HARRISON, Bernard R.S.	Worcester	28.09.34	Portsmouth(AM)	Crystal Palace	10.55	1955-58	92		13	(F)Hants Cricketer
			TR	Southampton	08.59	1959	3	/	0	
			TR	Exeter C.	07.60	1960	18		4	
HARRISON, Chris C.	Launceston	17.10.56	APP	Plymouth Arg.	10.74	1975-83	287	4	6	(D)
HARRISON, Colin	Pelsall	18.03.46	JNRS	Walsall	11.63	1964-81	452	15	33	(D)
HARRISON, Derek	Leicester	09.02.50	APP	Leicester C.	02.67					(HB)
			TR	Torquay U.	01.71	1970-74	124	3	4	
			TR	Colchester U.	06.75	1975	5	2	0	
HARRISON, Eric G.	Halifax	05.02.38	Mytholmroyd	Halifax T.	07.57	1957-63	199		10	(WH)●
			TR	Hartlepool U.	08.64	1964-65	81	/	4	
			TR	Barrow	07.66	1966-68	127	3	1	
			TR	Southport	06.69	1969-70	75	/	0	
			TR	Barrow	07.71	1971	31	1	1	
HARRISON, Frank J.	Gateshead	12.11.31	JNRS	Hull C.	05.49	1952-59	199		0	(FB)E.YTH.INT.
HARRISON, Harry	Sunderland	26.06.17	Chesterfield(*)	Southport	+	1946-50	135		1	(FB)
HARRISON, Herbert K.G.	Burnley	23.01.16	Morecambe	Accrington St.	AM	1947	3		0	(OR)
HARRISON, James C.	Leicester	12.02.21	JNRS	Leicester C.	+	1946-48	81		1	(FB)
			TR	Aston Villa	07.49	1949	8		1	
			TR	Coventry C.	07.51	1951-52	20		2	
HARRISON, James H.	Hammersmith	31.07.28		Q.P.R.	02.52	1952	5		1	(F)
HARRISON, John	Swansea	30.09.32		Crewe Alex.	08.56	1956	2		0	(G)
HARRISON, John G.	Worksop	18.05.46	Worksop T.	Sheffield U.	01.67					(F)
			TR	Lincoln C.	07.68	1968	4	/	0	
HARRISON, John J.	York	07.06.61	APP	York C.	06.79	1979	8	/	0	(M)
HARRISON, John M.	London	16.01.58	APP	Charlton Ath.	01.76	1975	5	/	2	(F)
HARRISON, John W.	Leicester	27.09.27		Aston Villa	08.48					(FB)
			TR	Colchester U.	07.50	1950-56	237		1	
HARRISON, Ken	Stockton	20.01.26	Billingham	Hull C.	04.47	1946-54	237		47	(OR)
			TR	Derby Co.	07.54	1954-55	13		3	
HARRISON, Mark S.	Spondon	11.12.60	APP	Southampton	12.78					(G)
			TR	Port Vale	02.80	1980-81	70	/	0	
			TR	Stoke C.	08.82	1982	7	/	0	
HARRISON, Mike	Leicester	21.02.52	APP	Birmingham C.	10.70	1970-71	3	/	0	(WH)
			TR	Southend U.	07.72	1972	16	/	0	
HARRISON, Mike J.	Ilford	18.04.40	JNRS	Chelsea	04.57	1956-62	61		8	(OL)E.U23-3/E.SCH.INT.
			TR	Blackburn Rov.	09.62	1962-67	160	/	40	
			TR	Plymouth Arg.	09.67	1967	18	/	3	
			TR	Luton T.	06.68	1968-69	29	3	6	
HARRISON, Peter	Sleaford	25.10.27	Peterborough U.	Leeds U.	01.49	1949-51	63		9	(OR)
			TR	Bournemouth	08.52	1952-56	172		34	
			TR	Reading	06.57	1957-58	40		5	
			TR	Southport	07.59	1959-61	126		22	
HARRISON, Ralph	Clayton-le-Moor	18.12.26		Leeds U.	01.49	1949	2		0	
HARRISON, Ray W.	Boston	21.06.21	Boston U.	Burnley	+	1946-49	62		20	(CF)
			TR	Doncaster Rov.	01.50	1949-53	126		47	
			TR	Grimsby T.	07.54	1954	38		7	
HARRISON, Reg F.	Derby	22.05.23	JNRS	Derby Co.	+	1946-54	256		51	(OR)
HARRISON, Robert A.	Chatham	25.12.47		Gillingham	06.67	1966	1	/	0	(F)
HARRISON, Robert J.	Manchester	23.12.30		Carlisle U.	02.53	1952-54	66		16	(OR)
			TR	Stockport Co.	07.56					
HARRISON, Ron	Hebburn	15.05.23	Gateshead(+)	Darlington	+	1946	8		3	(F)
				Gateshead	07.47	1947	6		1	
HARRISON, Steve J.	Blackpool	26.12.52	APP	Blackpool	12.70	1971-77	141	7	0	(D)
			Vancouver	Watford	09.78	1978-80	82	1	0	
			TR	Charlton Ath.	07.81	1981	3	/	0	
HARRISON, Terry	Thornaby	12.09.50	Stockton	Newcastle U.	11.67					(F)
			TR	Barrow	07.70	1970	4	/	0	
HARRISON, Walter E.	Coalville	16.01.23	JNRS	Leicester C.	+	1946-50	125		3	(WH)E'B'-2
			TR	Chesterfield	12.50	1950-52	75		13	
HARRISON, Wayne M.	Whitehaven	16.10.57	Everton (AM)	Workington	N/C	1975	1	3	0	(M)
			Sheffield Wed.(N/C)	Blackpool	09.79	1979-81	81	5	6	
HARRITY, Mike D.	Sheffield	05.10.46		Rotherham U.	10.65	1965-68	36	3	0	(FB)
			TR	Doncaster Rov.	09.68	1968	2	1	0	
HARROLD, Mark	Halifax	29.01.57		Halifax T.	08.74	1974-75	8	5	1	(IF)
HARROLD, Mike L.	Stockport	22.09.43	Manchester C.(AM)	Stockport Co.	08.65	1964	4		0	(FB)
HARROP, Jack	Manchester	25.06.29		Swansea C.	08.52	1952-53	10		0	(FB)
			TR	Watford	07.56	1956-59	111		0	

Players Names	Birthplace	Date	Previous Club	League Club	Date Signed	Seasons Played	Apps	Sub	Gls	
HARROP, Robert	Manchester	25.08.36	Benchill Y.C.	Manchester U.	05.54	1957–58	9		0	(CH)
			TR	Tranmere Rov.	11.59	1959–60	41		2	
HARROW, Andy	Kirkcaldy	06.11.56	Raith Rov.	Luton T.	09.80	1980	3	1	0	(F)
HARROWER, James	Alva	18.08.35	Hibernian	Liverpool	01.58	1957–60	96		21	(IF)S.U23–1
			TR	Newcastle U.	03.61	1960–61	5		0	
HARROWER, James S.	Dunfermline	19.06.24	T. Lanark	Accrington St.	12.54	1954–60	246		2	(FB)
HARROWER, Steve G.	Exeter	09.10.61	Dawlish	Exeter C.	01.84	1983	10	3	1	(F)
HARROWER, William	Dunfermline	13.04.22	T. Lanark	Torquay U.	05.46	1946–47	16		3	Brother of James S.
			TR	Exeter C.	07.48	1948–51	86		10	
HARSTON, John C.	Barnsley	07.10.20	Wolverhampton W.(*)	Barnsley	*	1946–48	19		0	
			TR	Bradford C.	06.49	1949	24		1	
HART, Alan M.	London	21.02.56	APP	Charlton Ath.	09.74	1974	3	/	2	(IF)
			TR	Millwall	06.75	1975	13	3	0	
HART, Andy	Yarmouth	14.01.63	APP	Norwich C.	01.81	1981	0	1	0	(M)
HART, Brian P.	Farnworth	14.07.59	Bolton W.(APP)	Rochdale	03.78	1977–79	73	5	0	(D)Brother of Paul
HART, Harry	Sheffield	29.09.26		Rotherham U.	+	1949	10		3	(IF)
			TR	Coventry C.	06.50	1950–51	10		1	
			TR	Grimsby T.	12.52	1952	13		3	
HART, John L.	Ashton	28.02.17	Ashton	Bury	*	1946–53	256		1	(CH)
HART, John P.	Golborne	08.06.28	JNRS	Manchester C.	+	1947–60	169		67	(IF)Father of Paul
HART, Marvin S.	Derby	15.01.41	Long Eaton U.	Exeter C.	08.67	1967	20	2	1	(OR)
HART, Nigel	Golborne	01.10.58		Wigan Ath.	08.78	1979	1	/	0	(D) Brother of Paul
				Leicester C.	10.79					
			TR	Blackpool	08.81	1981-82	36	1	0	
			TR	Crewe Alex.	11.82	1982-83	64	1	3	
HART, Paul	Manchester	04.05.53	JNRS	Stockport Co.	09.70	1970-72	88	/	5	(D)Son of Johnny
			TR	Blackpool	06.73	1973-77	143	/	17	
			TR	Leeds U.	03.78	1977-82	191	/	16	
			TR	Nottingham F.	05.83	1983	36	/	0	
HART, Peter A.	Wickersley	06.09.49	Rotherham U.(APP)	Bradford P.A.	AM	1967	3	/	0	(FB)
HART, Peter O.	Mexborough	14.08.57	APP	Huddersfield	08.74	1973-79	208	2	7	(D)
			TR	Walsall	08.80	1980-83	180	/	9	
HART, Roy E.	Acton	30.05.33	JNRS	Brentford	06.50	1954	2		0	(HB)E.SCH.INT.
HART, William R.	Newcastle	01.04.23	Nth. Shields	Chesterfield	+	1946	1		0	(RH)
			TR	Bradford C.	05.47	1946-48	25		0	
HARTBURN, John	Durham	20.12.20	Yeovil T.	Q.P.R.	03.47	1947-48	58		10	(OR)
			TR	Watford	09.49	1949-50	66		18	
			TR	Millwall	03.51	1950-53	104		29	
			TR	Orient	06.54	1954-57	112		36	
HARTERY, John	Waterford	25.11.20	Limerick	Plymouth Arg.	06.48	1949	1		0	L.O.I.REP.
HARTFORD, Asa	Clydebank	24.10.50	JNRS	W.B.A.	11.67	1967-73	206	7	18	(M)S-50/S.U23-5/●
			TR	Manchester C.	08.74	1974-78	184	1	22	S.U21-1
			TR	Nottingham F.	07.79	1979	3	/	0	
			TR	Everton	08.79	1979-81	81	/	6	
			TR	Manchester C.	10.81	1981-83	75	/	7	
HARTLAND, Mick	Birmingham	07.01.44	Nuneaton	Oxford U.	06.63	1963-64	18		6	(HB)
			TR	Barrow	07.65	1965-70	169	7	20	
			TR	Crewe Alex.	12.70	1970	3	/	2	
			TR	Southport	07.71	1971-72	32	5	4	
HARTLE, Barry	Salford	08.08.39	JNRS	Watford	08.56	1958-59	39		7	(OL)
			TR	Sheffield U.	06.60	1960-65	101	/	16	
			TR	Carlisle U.	07.66	1966-67	28	1	1	
			TR	Stockport Co.	09.67	1967-69	87	/	1	
			TR	Oldham Ath.	06.70	1970	8	1	2	
			TR	Southport	01.71	1971	37	4	6	
HARTLE, L. Roy	Bromsgrove	04.10.31	Bromsgrove	Bolton W.	02.52	1952-65	446	1	11	(FB)E.F.LGE REP.●
HARTLEY, Edmund	Burnley	05.05.32	JNRS	Burnley	11.50					(F)
			Rossendale U.	Oldham Ath.	07.56	1956	1		0	
HARTLEY, Tom W.	Gateshead	07.05.17		Chesterfield	+					(IF)*Birtley BC/
			TR	Leicester C.	01.48					Gateshead
			TR	Watford	02.48	1947	6		1	
HARTLEY, Trevor	Doncaster	16.03.47	JNRS	West Ham U.	07.64	1966-68	4	1	0	(IF)
			TR	Bournemouth	07.69	1969-70	35	7	2	
HARTNETT, James B.	Dublin	21.03.27	Dundalk	Middlesbrough	06.48	1948-54	48		8	EI-2/L.O.I.REP.
			Barry T.	Hartlepool U.	09.57	1957	7		1	
			TR	York C.	08.58	1958	2		1	
HARVEY, Alex	Ayr	28.09.28	Saltcoats Vic.	Chesterfield	11.50	1950-52	27		9	(IF)
HARVEY, Alex	Kirkconnel	25.08.25	Q. of South	Carlisle U.	08.46	1946	1		0	(LH)
HARVEY, Brian	Liverpool	12.01.47	Sheffield Wed.(APP)	Chester C.	09.64	1964-65	2	/	0	(HB)
HARVEY, Bryan R.	Stepney	26.08.38	Wisbech	Newcastle U.	09.58	1958-60	86		0	(G)
			Cambridge C.	Blackpool	02.62	1961-63	11		0	
			TR	Northampton T.	10.63	1963-67	165	/	0	

Players Names	Birthplace	Date	Previous Club	League Club	Date Signed	Seasons Played	Career Record Apps	Sub	Gls	
HARVEY, David	Hetton-le-Hole	15.02.54	APP	Hartlepool U.	APP	1970	3	2	0	(HB)
HARVEY, David	Leeds	07.02.48	JNRS	Leeds U.	02.65	1965-79	276	/	0	(G)S-16
			Vancouver	Leeds U.	12.80	1982-83	53	/	0	
HARVEY, Gary	Colchester	19.11.61	APP	Colchester U.	11.79	1979-80	6	2	0	(F)
HARVEY, J.Colin	Liverpool	16.11.44	APP	Everton	10.62	1963-74	317	4	18	(WH)E-1/E.U23-5/
			TR	Sheffield Wed.	09.74	1974-75	45	/	2	E.F.LGE.REP.
HARVEY, James	Lurgan	02.05.58	Glenavon	Arsenal	08.77	1977-78	2	1	0	(M)
			TR	Hereford U.	03.80	1979-83	166	2	19	
HARVEY, Joseph	Doncaster	11.06.18	Bradford C.(*)	Newcastle U.	+	1946-52	224		12	(WH)*Wolverhampton W./Bradford P.A./Bournemouth
HARVEY, Keith W.	Crediton	25.12.34	Crediton	Exeter C.	08.52	1952-68	483		28	(CH)●
HARVEY, Lee D.	Harlow	21.12.66	APP	Orient	APP	1983	0	4	0	
HARVEY, Leighton	Neath	27.08.59	APP	Swansea C.	APP	1975-76	1	1	0	(W)
HARVEY, Lol	Heanor	25.07.34	JNRS	Coventry C.	07.51	1951-60	140		1	(HB)
HARVEY, Martin	Belfast	19.09.41	JNRS	Sunderland	09.58	1959-71	310	4	6	(WH)NI-33/NI U.23-3/ NI'B'-1/NI SCH.INT.●
HARVEY, William D.	Doncaster	30.09.34	JNRS	Doncaster Rov.	11.51	1952	2		0	(FB)
			Rossington Col	Aldershot	04.56					
HARVEY, William J.	Clydebank	23.11.29	Dunfermline	Bradford P.A.	01.59	1958-59	26		1	(F)
HARWOOD, Lee	Southall	04.10.60	APP	Southampton	10.78					(D)
			TR	Wimbledon	01.79	1978	1	/	0	
			Leatherhead	Port Vale	02.80	1979-80	19	/	1	
HARWOOD, Richard A.	Sheffield	13.09.60	APP	Sheffield U.	07.78	1978	2	1	0	(M)
HASELDEN, John	Doncaster	03.08.43	Denaby U.	Rotherham U.	02.62	1961-68	100	2	0	(HB)
			TR	Doncaster Rov.	09.68	1968-73	168	4	20	
			L	Mansfield T.	02.72	1971	4	/	0	
HASKINS, Anthony	Northampton	26.07.35		Northampton T.	01.59	1959-61	8		0	(FB)
HASLAM, Graham	Doncaster	29.04.56	APP	Rotherham U.	11.74	1975	2	/	0	(G)
HASLAM, Harry	Manchester	30.07.21	Manchester U.(+)	Oldham Ath.	05.46	1946	2		0	(FB)
				Brighton & H.A.	09.47					
			TR	Orient	07.48	1948	7		0	
HASLEGRAVE, Sean	Stoke	07.06.51	JNRS	Stoke C.	11.68	1970-75	106	7	5	(M)
			TR	Nottingham F.	07.76	1976	5	2	1	
			TR	Preston N.E.	09.77	1977-80	111	2	2	
			TR	Crewe Alex.	08.81	1981-82	78	4	1	
			TR	York C.	07.83	1983	24	2	0	
HASPELL, Alan	Northwich	23.01.43	JNRS	Burnley	01.60					(HB)
			TR	Doncaster Rov.	07.63	1963	1			
HASSALL, Harold W.	Astley	04.03.29	Astley F.C.	Huddersfield T.	09.46	1948-51	74		26	(IF)E-5/E.F.LGE REP.
			TR	Bolton W.	01.52	1951-54	102		34	
HASSALL, Wilf	Manchester	23.09.23	R.M. Alsager	Hull C.	09.46	1946-52	142		3	(FB)
HASSELL, Rick	Coatbridge	12.01.51	JNRS	Carlisle U.	01.69	1968-69	3	1	0	(HB)
HASSELL, Tom W.	Stonham	05.04.19		Southampton	+					(F)
			TR	Aldershot	05.46	1946-49	113		16	
			TR	Brighton & H.A.	08.50	1950	11		3	
HASTIE, John K.G.	S.Africa		Clyde Ath.S.A.	Leeds U.	08.52	1952	4		2	(IF)
HASTY, Paddy J.	Belfast	17.03.32	Tooting & M	Orient	AM	1958	2		2	(CF)NI.AMAT.INT.
			TR	Q.P.R.	AM	1959	1		0	
			Tooting & M	Aldershot	03.61	1960-62	35		14	
HATCH, Peter D.	Wargrave	22.10.49	APP	Oxford U.	10.66	1967-72	15	4	2	(M)
			TR	Exeter C.	12.73	1973-81	343	3	18	
HATCHER, Cliff H.	Currie Dando	27.06.25		Reading	06.46	1947-48	2		0	(G)
HATCHER, Doug T.	Carshalton	06.03.62	APP	Fulham	03.80					(G)
			Wokingham	Aldershot	08.83	1983	1	/	0	
HATELEY, Anthony	Derby	13.06.41	JNRS	Notts. Co	06.58	1958-62	131		77	(CF)●Father of Mark
			TR	Aston Villa	08.63	1963-66	127	/	68	
			TR	Chelsea	10.66	1966	26	1	6	
			TR	Liverpool	07.67	1967-68	42	/	17	
			TR	Coventry C.	09.68	1968	17	/	4	
			TR	Birmingham C.	08.69	1969-70	28	/	6	
			TR	Notts. Co.	11.70	1970-71	57	/	32	
			TR	Oldham Ath.	07.72	1973	1	4	1	
HATELEY, Mark W.	Liverpool	07.11.61	APP	Coventry C.	12.78	1978-82	86	7	25	(F)E.YTH.INT./E.U'21-10/E7/
			TR	Portsmouth	06.83	1983	38	/	21	Son of Tony
HATSELL, Dennis	Preston	09.06.30	JNRS	Preston N.E.	06.48	1953-59	115		54	(CF)
HATTER, Steve	London	21.10.58	APP	Fulham	05.76	1977-80	25	1	1	(D)
			L	Exeter C.	09.82	1982	11	1	1	
			TR	Wimbledon	11.82	1982-83	67	1	3	
HATTON, Cyril	Grantham	14.09.18	Notts. Co.(*)	Q.P.R.	+	1946-52	164		63	(IF)
			TR	Chesterfield	06.53	1953	36		10	

Players Names	Birthplace	Date	Previous Club	League Club	Date Signed	Seasons Played	Career Record Apps	Sub	Gls	
HATTON, Dave	Farnsworth	30.10.43	JNRS	Bolton W.	11.60	1961-69	231	/	7	(WH)
			TR	Blackpool	09.69	1969-75	249	1	6	
			TR	Bury	08.76	1976-78	96	1	2	
HATTON, Robert J.	Hull	10.04.47	JNRS	Wolverhampton W.	11.64	1966	10	/	7	(F)●
			TR	Bolton W.	03.67	1966-67	27	1	2	
			TR	Northampton T.	10.68	1968	29	4	8	
			TR	Carlisle U.	07.69	1969-71	93	/	38	
			TR	Birmingham C.	10.71	1971-75	170	5	58	
			TR	Blackpool	07.76	1976-77	75	/	32	
			TR	Luton T.	07.78	1978-79	81	1	29	
			TR	Sheffield U.	07.80	1980-82	92	3	34	
			TR	Cardiff C.	12.82	1982	29	1	9	
HAUGHEY, Fred	Conisborough	12.05.21	Halifax T.(AM)	Bradford C.	AM	1946	3		0	(LB)
HAUGHEY, Willie	Glasgow	20.12.32	Larkhall Th.	Everton	06.56	1956-57	4		1	(F)
HAUSER, Peter	S. Africa	20.04.34	S. Africa	Blackpool	11.55	1957-61	83		10	(HB)
			Cheltenham	Chester C.	08.63	1963-66	117	4	3	
HAVENGA, Willie S.	S. Africa	06.11.24	Bremner OB	Birmingham C.	07.48	1949	1		0	(IF)
			TR	Luton T.	05.50	1950-51	18		6	
			TR	Ipswich T.	01.52	1951-52	18		3	
HAVENHAND, Keith	Dronfield	11.09.37	JNRS	Chesterfield	09.54	1953-61	174		57	(F)E.YTH.INT.
			TR	Derby Co.	10.61	1961	26		14	
			TR	Oxford U.	12.63	1963-64	12		3	
HAVERSON, Paul T.	Chigwell	19.02.59	APP	Q.P.R.	08.76					(D)E.SCH.INT.
			TR	Wimbledon	10.78	1978-79	27	1	2	
HAVERTY, Joe	Dublin	17.02.36	St. Patricks	Arsenal	07.54	1954-60	115		25	(OL)EI-32
			TR	Blackburn Rov.	08.61	1961-62	27		1	
			TR	Millwall	09.62	1962-63	68		8	
			TR	Bristol Rov.	102.64	1964	13		1	
HAWDEN, Ken	Huddersfield	16.09.31		Derby Co.	04.53	1953	2		0	(F)
HAWKER, David	Hull	29.11.58	APP	Hull C.	08.76	1977-79	33	2	2	(M)
			TR	Darlington	03.80	1979-82	84	4	2	
HAWKER, Phil N.	Solihull	07.12.62	APP	Birmingham C.	06.80	1980-82	34	1	1	(D)
			TR	Walsall	12.82	1982-83	16	/	0	
HAWKES, Barry	Durham	21.03.38	Shotton Col.	Luton T.	11.55	1958-59	8		0	(F)Brother of Ken
			TR	Darlington	06.60	1960	13		3	
			TR	Hartlepool U.	07.61	1961	9		0	
HAWKES, Ken	Durham	06.05.33	Shotton Col.	Luton T.	10.51	1957-60	90		1	(FB)
			TR	Peterborough U.	06.61	1961	1		0	
HAWKINGS, Barry	Birmingham	07.11.31	JNRS	Coventry C.	01.49	1953-55	34		11	(IF)
			TR	Lincoln C.	03.56	1955-56	15		6	
			TR	Northampton T.	06.57	1957-58	64		25	
HAWKINS, Bertram	Bristol	29.09.23	De Veys	Bristol Rov.	08.47					(CF)
			TR	Bristol C.	05.49	1949	8		4	
			Bath C.	West Ham U.	09.51	1951-52	34		16	
			TR	Q.P.R.	06.53	1953	8		3	
HAWKINS, David J.	Kingston	11.08.31	Sheppey U.	Gillingham	AM	1955	14		8	(CF)
HAWKINS, Dennis R.	Swansea	22.10.47	APP	Leeds U.	10.64	1966-67	2	/	0	(CF)W.U23-6/W.SCH.INT.
			TR	Shrewsbury T.	10.68	1968-69	55	7	9	
			L	Chester C.	09.70	1970	6	2	1	
			L	Workington	03.72	1971	6	/	1	
			TR	Newport Co.	05.72	1972	9	/	1	
HAWKINS, Graham N.	Darlaston	05.03.46	APP	Wolverhampton W.	06.63	1964-67	28	6	0	(D)
			TR	Preston N.E.	01.68	1967-73	241	4	3	
			TR	Blackburn Rov.	06.74	1974-77	108	1	4	
			TR	Port Vale	01.78	1977-79	61	1	3	
HAWKINS, Harry	Middlesbrough	24.11.15	Watford(*)	Southport	*	1946	37		16	(CF)*South Bank/Middlesbrough
			TR	Gateshead	06.47	1947	27		12	
			TR	Hartlepool U.	03.48	1947-48	30		4	
HAWKINS, Herbert	Lembert	15.07.23	Gravesend	Orient	06.51	1951-52	5		0	(CF)
HAWKINS, Peter M.	Swansea	18.12.51	APP	Northampton T.	12.68	1968-73	49	10	10	(F)W.SCH.INT.
HAWKSBY, John F.	York	12.06.42	JNRS	Leeds U.	06.59	1960-62	36		2	(IF)E.YTH.INT.
			TR	Lincoln C.	08.64	1964-65	64	1	4	
			TR	York C.	03.66	1965-67	72	2	7	
HAWKSFORD, Eddie	Liverpool	07.11.31		Mansfield T.	03.52	1952	1		0	(OR)
HAWKSWORTH, Anthony	Sheffield	15.01.38	JNRS	Manchester U.	04.55	1956	1		0	(G)E.YTH.INT/E.SCH.INT.
HAWKSWORTH, Derek	Bradford	16.07.27	Huddersfield T.(AM)	Bradford C.	10.48	1948-50	75		20	(OL)E'B'-1
			TR	Sheffield U.	12.50	1950-57	255		88	
			TR	Huddersfield T.	05.58	1958-59	55		14	
			TR	Lincoln C.	02.60	1959-60	36		14	
			TR	Bradford C.	01.61	1960-61	44		8	
HAWLEY, Alan J.	Woking	07.06.46	APP	Brentford	06.63	1962-73	316	2	5	(FB)

Players Names	Birthplace	Date	Previous Club	League Club	Date Signed	Seasons Played	Career Record Apps	Sub	Gls	
HAWLEY, John	Whithernsea	08.05.54	JNRS	Hull C.	07.76	1972-77	101	13	22	(F)
			TR	Leeds U.	04.76	1978-79	30	3	16	
			TR	Sunderland	10.79	1979-80	25	/	11	
			TR	Arsenal	09.81	1981-82	14	6	3	
			L	Orient	10.82	1982	4	/	1	
			L	Hull C.	12.82	1982	3	/	1	
			TR	Bradford C.	09.83	1983	43	/	22	
HAWORTH, Herbert	Accrington	05.05.20	Woodcock Amats.	Accrington St.	AM	1946	2		0	(IF)
HAWSON, Alex	Auchincairn	23.10.23	Aberdeen	Rochdale	12.48	1948	1		0	(RH)
HAY, Allan B.	Dunfermline	28.11.58	Dundee	Bristol C.	07.78	1979-81	72	2	1	(D)
			TR	York C.	08.82	1982-83	84	/	2	
HAY, David	Paisley	29.01.48	Glasgow Celtic	Chelsea	08.74	1974-78	107	1	2	(D)S-27/S.U23-3/ S.F.LGE REP.
HAYCOCK, Fred J.	Liverpool	19.04.12	Aston Villa(*)	Wrexham	+	1946	6		1	(IL)*Prescot Cables
HAYDOCK, Frank	Eccles	29.11.40		Manchester U.	12.58	1960-62	6		0	(CH)Brother of William
			TR	Charlton Ath.	08.63	1963-65	84	/	4	
			TR	Portsmouth	12.65	1965-68	72	/	1	
			TR	Southend U.	01.69	1968-69	29	4	4	
HAYDOCK, William E.	Salford	19.01.36	Buxton	Manchester C.	03.59	1959-60	3		1	(FB)
			TR	Crewe Alex.	03.61	1960-64	142		30	
			TR	Grimsby T.	11.64	1964	21		4	
			TR	Stockport Co.	08.65	1965-70	257	4	4	
			S. Africa	Southport	11.71	1971	7	/	0	
HAYES, Arthur E.T.	Birmingham	23.05.24		Aston Villa	+	1946	4		0	
			TR	Walsall	05.48	1948	2		0	
HAYES, Austin W.P.	London	15.07.58	APP	Southampton	07.76	1976-79	22	9	5	(F)EI-1/EI.U21-1
			TR	Millwall	02.81	1980-82	40	7	5	
			TR	Northampton T.	08.83	1983	40	3	8	
HAYES, Hugh	Bangor	23.06.25	Bangor	Ipswich T.	06.46	1946-49	9		0	
			Bangor	Ipswich T.	05.51	1951	1		0	
HAYES, Joe	Kearsley	20.01.36		Manchester C.	08.53	1953-64	331		142	(IF)E.U23-2
			TR	Barnsley	07.65	1965	25	/	3	
HAYES, Mike	Newport	11.09.54		Newport Co.	N/C	1975	4	/	0	(IF)
HAYES, Mike C.	Aberdare	24.04.44	JNRS	Swansea C.	06.61	1962-64	5		0	(HB)W.SCH.INT.
HAYES, Phil H.	Chiswick	23.102.35	Slough T.	Millwall	12.56	1956-58	16		1	(F)
HAYES, Sam	Accrington	21.06.20	Blackburn Rov.(AM)	Accrington St.	AM	1946	13		0	(G)d.1959
HAYES, Steve C.	Smethwick	28.01.52	Warley	Shrewsbury T.	02.74	1974-79	69	3	0	(M)
			L	Torquay U.	09.75	1975	1	/	0	
			TR	Torquay U.	07.80	1980	25	/	0	
HAYES, William	Runcorn	08.06.19	Halton J.	Oldham Ath.	*	1946-50	106		3	(IF)
HAYES, William	Newcastle–under–Lyne	02.03.18	ROF.Radway G'n	Crewe Alex.	09.46	1946	29		0	(CH)
HAYES, William E.	Cork	07.11.15	JNRS	Huddersfield T.	*	1946-49	112		0	(FB)EI-2/NI-4
			TR	Burnley	02.50	1949-50	12		0	
HAYES, William J.	Limerick	30.03.28	Limerick	Wrexham	07.50	1950	14		0	(G)EI-1/L.O.I.REP.
			Ellesmere Port	Torquay U.	08.52	1952-55	54		0	EI.AMAT.INT.
HAYHURST, Stan	Leyland	13.05.25		Blackburn Rov.	+	1946-48	27		0	(G)
			TR	Tottenham H.	10.48					
			TR	Barrow	06.50	1950	26		0	
			TR	Grimsby T.	01.51	1950-52	62		0	
HAYLOCK, Paul	Lowestoft	24.03.63	APP	Norwich C.	01.81	1981-83	101	1	1	(D)
HAYMAN, Jim	Ramsbottom	19.02.28	Radcliffe	Bury	11.50	1950	5		0	(FB)
HAYNES, Eric	Sheffield	18.06.36	Thorncliffe	Rotherham U.	04.56	1955	1		0	(F)
HAYNES, Johnny N.	Edmonton	17.10.34	JNRS	Fulham	05.52	1952-69	594		145	(IF)E–56/E'B'–5/E.U23–8/● E.F.LGE REP./E.YTH.INT./ E.SCH.INT.
HAYS, C.Jack	Ashington	12.12.18	Bradford P.A.(*)	Burnley	+	1946-50	146		12	(OR)d.1983
			TR	Bury	09.51	1951-52	27		2	
HAYTON, Eric	Carlisle	14.01.22		Carlisle U.	+	1946-50	49		5	(HB)
			TR	Rochdale	05.51	1951	12		0	
			TR	Workington	10.52	1952	19		0	
HAYWARD, C.Basil	Leek	07.04.28	Northwood H.	Port Vale	05.46	1946-57	349		32	(CH)Brother of Doug/Eric
			TR	Portsmouth	07.58	1958-59	44		4	
HAYWARD, Doug S.	Wellington	23.08.20		Bristol Rov.	09.46	1946	1		0	(FB) +Huddersfield T.
			TR	Newport Co.	11.46	1946-55	258		11	
HAYWARD, Keith W.	Hove	21.11.51	APP	Charlton Ath.	APP	1968	1	/	0	(G)
HAYWARD, L.Eric	Woolstanton	02.08.17	Port Vale(*)	Blackpool	*	1946-51	205		0	(CH)d.1976
HAYWOOD, Clive	Ramsgate	01.11.60	APP	Coventry C.	08.78	1980	1	/	0	(F)
HAYWOOD, Ray	Dudley	12.01.49	Stourbridge	Shrewsbury T.	05.74	1974-76	75	12	27	(F)
			TR	Northampton T.	03.77	1976-77	14	2	2	
HAZARD, Mike	Sunderland	05.02.60	APP	Tottenham H.	02.78	1979-83	55	9	8	(M)

Players Names	Birthplace	Date	Previous Club	League Club	Date Signed	Seasons Played	Apps	Sub	Gls	
HAZELDEN, Walter	Ashton-in-Makerfield	13.02.42	JNRS	Aston Villa	02.58	1957–58	17		5	(IF)E.YTH.INT.
HAZELL, Anthony	High Wycombe	19.09.47	JNRS	Q.P.R.	10.64	1964-74	362	7	4	(D)E.YTH.INT.●
			TR	Millwall	12.74	1974-78	153	/	6	
			TR	Crystal Palace	11.78	1978	5	/	0	
			TR	Charlton Ath.	09.79	1979-80	37	/	0	
HAZELL, Cliff	Woolwich	14.09.37	Hastings U.	Gillingham	07.55	1957	2		0	(F)
			TR	Millwall	07.58					
HAZELL, Robert	Jamaica	14.06.59	APP	Wolverhampton W.	05.77	1977-78	32	1	1	(D)E.U21-1/EYTH.INT.
			TR	Q.P.R.	09.79	1979-83	100	6	8	
			TR	Leicester C.	09.83	1983	27	/	2	
HAZLEDINE, Albert V.	Royton	28.07.18	West Ham U.(AM)	Halifax T.	+	1946	10		2	(LH)
HAZLEDINE, Don	Derby	10.07.29	Notts Regent	Derby Co.	08.51	1952–53	26		6	(IF)Brother of Geoff
			TR	Northampton T.	06.54	1954	22		4	
HAZLEDINE, Geoff	Derby	27.02.32	Notts Regent	Derby Co.	07.52	1953	1		0	(F)
			Boston U.	Southport	07.57	1957	29		5	
HAZLETT, George	Glasgow	10.03.23	Belfast Celtic	Bury	08.49	1949–51	101		9	(OR)
			TR	Cardiff C.	08.52	1952	7		1	
			TR	Millwall	05.53	1053 57	120		10	
HAZZLETON, Jim	Bolton	29.09.30	Atherton Col.	Bury	05.50					
			TR	Rochdale	08.51	1951	11		1	
			TR	Accrington St.	07.52	1952	4		0	
HEAD, Bert J.	Midsomer Norton	08.06.16	Midsomer N.	Torquay U.	*	1946–50	151		3	(CH)
			TR	Bury	02.52	1951–52	22		0	
HEAD, David G.	Midsomer Norton	11.08.40	JNRS	Swindon T.	08.58					(F)Son of Bert
			TR	Arsenal	03.59					
			TR	Reading	07.60	1960	12		0	
			TR	Bristol Rov.	07.61					
HEAD, Mike	Hull	13.04.33	Bridlington	Hull C.	12.53	1954	3		0	(OL)
HEALE, Gary J.	Canvey Island	15.07.58	Canvey	Luton T.	08.77	1977	7	/	1	(F)
			L	Exeter C.	12.77	1977	3	1	0	
			TR	Reading	08.79	1979-81	68	8	20	
HEALER, Ernie	Birtley	13.11.41		Darlington	08.61					(IF)
			Berwick Rgrs	Brighton & H.A.	10.63	1963	3		1	
HEALEY, Daniel K.	Manchester	02.12.53	APP	Manchester U.	01.71					(W)
			TR	Bolton W.	05.73					
			TR	Workington	07.74	1974	13	4	2	
HEALEY, Ron	Manchester	30.08.52	APP	Manchester C.	10.69	1970-73	30	/	0	(G)EI-2
			L	Coventry C.	12.71	1971	3	/	0	
			L	Preston N.E.	12.73	1973	6	/	0	
			TR	Cardiff C.	03.74	1973-81	216	/	0	
HEALEY, William R.	Liverpool	22.05.26	Chorley	Arsenal	05.49					(FB)
			TR	Fulham	12.52	1952	1		0	
			TR	Hartlepool U.	08.55	1955	6		0	
HEALY, Felix P.J.	Londonderry	27.09.55	Finn Harps	Port Vale	10.78	1978-79	40	1	2	(M)
HEANEY, Anthony	Plymouth	09.05.40	JNRS	Southampton	06.58	1960	1		0	(FB)E.YTH.INT.
HEARD, T. Pat	Hull	17.03.60	APP	Everton	03.78	1978-79	10	1	0	(M)E.YTH.INT.
			TR	Aston Villa	10.79	1979-82	20	4	2	
			TR	Sheffield Wed.	01.83	1982-83	21	3	3	
HEARN, Frank G.	St. Pancras	05.11.29		Torquay U.	08.50					(F)
			TR	Northampton T.	10.51					
			TR	Crystal Palace	06.54	1954	8		1	
HEASLEGRAVE, Sam E.	Smethwick	01.10.16	W.B.A.(*)	Northampton T.	+	1946–47	42		4	(IR)*Brierley H./d.1975
HEATH, Adrian P.	Stoke	11.01.61	APP	Stoke C.	01.79	1978-81	94	1	16	(F)E.U21-8
			TR	Everton	01.82	1981-83	95	1	28	
HEATH, Dennis J.	Chiswick	28.09.34	JNRS	Brentford	09.52	1954–60	125		20	(OR)
HEATH, Don	Stockton	28.9.44	APP	Middlesbrough	12.62					(W)
			TR	Norwich C.	07.64	1964–67	79	3	15	
			TR	Swindon T.	09.67	1967–69	82	6	2	
			TR	Oldham Ath.	07.70	1970–71	43	2	2	
			TR	Peterborough U.	07.72	1972	43	1	4	
			TR	Hartlepool U.	07.73	1973–74	36	1	2	
HEATH, Duncan N.	Stoke	23.10.61	APP	Aston Villa	07.79					(D)
			TR	Crewe Alex.	11.80	1981	17	6	0	
HEATH, John	Heywood	05.06.36	Blackburn Rov.(AM)	Bury	09.56	1956–61	8		0	(G)
			TR	Tranmere Rov	01.62	1961–63	58		0	
			Wigan Ath.	Rochdale	02.66	1965	6	/	0	
HEATH, Mick F.	Hillingdon	09.01.53	Walton & H	Brentford	AM	1970	1	/	0	(IF)
HEATH, Norman H.	Wolverhampton	31.01.24	Meadows FC	W.B.A.	+	1947–53	121		0	(G)d.1983
HEATH, Philip A.	Stoke	24.11.64	APP	Stoke C.	10.82	1982-83	3	2	1	(F)
HEATH, R. Terry	Leicester	17.11.43	APP	Leicester C.	11.61	1962–63	8		2	(F)
			TR	Hull C.	05.64	1964–67	27	6	1	
			TR	Scunthorpe U.	03.68	1967–72	174	3	50	
			TR	Lincoln C.	02.73	1972–73	17	/	1	

Players Names	Birthplace	Date	Previous Club	League Club	Date Signed	Seasons Played	Apps	Sub	Gls	
HEATH, Seamus M.J.P.	Belfast	06.12.61	JNRS	Luton T.	04.79					(M)
			L	Lincoln C.	08.82	1982	6	1	0	
			TR	Wrexham	08.83	1983	32	/	1	
HEATH, William	Bournemouth	15.04.34	JNRS	Bournemouth	12.51	1956–57	34		0	(G)
			TR	Lincoln C.	11.58	1958–61	84		0	
HEATH, William J.	Stepney	26.06.20		Q.P.R.	+	1946–52	93		3	(FB)
HEATHCOTE, Peter G.S.	Leicester	13.11.32	JNRS	Southend U.	11.51	1951	2		0	(G)
HEATHCOTE, Wilf	Hemsworth	29.06.11		Q.P.R.	+	1946	5		1	(CF)
			TR	Millwall	12.46	1946	8		2	
HEATHER, John L.	Winchcomb	25.04.33	Belper T.	Mansfield T.	08.52	1953	1		0	(F)
HEATON, J. Mick	Sheffield	15.01.47	APP	Sheffield U.	11.64	1966–70	31	2	0	(FB)
			TR	Blackburn Rov.	10.71	1971–75	169	2	1	
HEATON, Paul	Hyde	24.01.61	APP	Oldham Ath.	01.79	1977–83	124	12	28	(M)
			L	Rochdale	03.84	1983	2	3	0	
HEATON, William H.	Leeds	26.08.18		Leeds U.	*	1946–48	59		5	(OL)
			TR	Southampton	02.49	1948	15		0	
			TR	Rochdale	11.50	1950	4		0	
HEAVISIDE, John	Buryhill	07.10.43	Bishops Middleham	Darlington	AM	1963	2		0	(LB)
HEBBERD, Trever N.	Winchester	19.06.58	APP	Southampton	07.76	1976–81	69	28	7	(M)
			L	Bolton W.	09.81	1981	6	/	0	
			L	Leicester C.	11.81	1981	4	/	1	
			TR	Oxford U.	03.82	1981–83	100	/	23	
HEBDITCH, Alan F.	Wigan	11.10.61		Bradford C.	11.81	1980	2	/	0	(D)
HECKMAN, Ron E.	Peckham	23.11.29	Bromley	Orient	07.55	1955–57	87		38	(W)E.AMAT.INT.
			TR	Millwall	11.57	1957–59	90		21	
			TR	Crystal Palace	07.60	1960–62	84		25	
HECTOR, Kevin	Leeds	02.11.44	JNRS	Bradford P.A.	07.62	1962–66	176	/	113	(F)E-2/E.F.LGE REP.●
			TR	Derby Co.	09.66	1966–77	426	4	146	
			Vancouver	Derby Co.	10.80	1980–81	52	4	8	
HEDLEY, Graeme	Easington	01.03.57	APP	Middlesbrough	03.75	1976–81	36	14	6	(F)
			L	Sheffield Wed.	02.78	1977	6	/	1	
			L	Darlington	03.79	1978	14	/	1	
			L	York C.	10.81	1981	5	/	1	
HEDLEY, Jack R.	Wellington Quay	11.12.23	Nth. Shields	Everton	+	1947–49	54		0	(FB)
			TR	Sunderland	08.50	1950–58	269		0	
			TR	Gateshead	07.59	1959	11		0	
HEDMAN, Rudi	London	16.11.64		Colchester U.	N/C	1983	3	1	0	(D)
HEDWORTH, Chris	Wallsend	05.01.64	APP	Newcastle U.	01.82	1982	3	1	0	(D)
HEELEY, D. Mark	Peterborough	08.09.59	APP	Peterborough U.	11.76	1975–76	12	5	3	(F)
			TR	Arsenal	09.77	1977–78	9	6	1	
			TR	Northampton T.	03.80	1979–82	84	8	3	
HEENAN, Tom	Glasgow	16.06.32	Stirling A.	Bradford P.A.	05.58	1958	5		1	(F)
HEFFER, Paul	W. Ham	21.12.47	JNRS	West Ham U.	08.65	1966–71	11	4	0	(CH)
HEFFER, Robert W.	Eriswell	09.11.35	RAF H.St Faiths	Norwich C.	04.56	1956	2		1	(W)
HEFFERNAN, Tom P.	Dublin	30.04.55	Dunleary Co.	Tottenham H.	10.77					(D)
			TR	Bournemouth	05.79	1979–82	152	2	21	
			TR	Sheffield U.	08.83	1983	42	/	2	
HEFFRON, Charles	Belfast	13.08.27	Short & Harland	Bradford P.A.	06.49	1951–52	25		0	(G)
HEGAN, Danny	Coatbridge	14.06.43	Albion Rov.	Sunderland	09.61					(IF) NI–7
			TR	Ipswich T.	07.63	1963–68	207	/	34	
			TR	W.B.A.	05.69	1969	13	1	2	
			TR	Wolveshampton W.	05.70	1970–73	50	3	6	
			TR	Sunderland	07.73	1973	3	3	0	
HEGARTY, Kevin	Edinburgh	30.07.50	Hearts	Carlisle U.	09.71	1971	1	6	0	(F)
HEGGIE, William C.	Scone	07.06.27	Jeanfield Swifts	New Brighton	02.51	1950	10		5	(F)
			TR	Leeds U.	06.51					
			TR	Wrexham	08.52	1952–54	33		13	
			Winsford	Accrington St.	02.55	1954	1		0	
HEGGINBOTTOM, Brian	Hyde	03.10.37	JNRS	Stockport Co.	10.54	1958–59	11		0	(HB)
HEIGHWAY, Steve	Dublin	25.11.47	Skelmersdale	Liverpool	05.70	1970–80	312	19	50	(W)EI-33
HELLAWELL, John	Keighley	20.12.43	Salts	Bradford C.	06.63	1962–64	48		13	(IF)Brother of Mike
			TR	Rotherham U.	01.65	1964–65	5	1	2	
			TR	Darlington	07.66	1966	6	3	1	
				Bradford P.A.	10.68	1968	1	/	0	
HELLAWELL, Mike S.	Keighley	30.06.38	Salts	Q.P.R.	08.55	1955–56	45		7	(W)E–2/
			TR	Birmingham C.	05.57	1957–64	178		30	Warwicks Cricketer
			TR	Sunderland	01.65	1964–66	43	1	3	
			TR	Huddersfield T.	09.66	1966–71	46	1	1	
			TR	Peterborough U.	12.68	1968	9	/	0	
HELLEWELL, Keith	Barnsley	01.04.44	JNRS	Doncaster Rov.	05.61	1962–63	12		0	(G)
HELLIN, Anthony	Merthyr Tydfil	26.09.44	APP	Swindon T.	06.62					(HB)W.SCH.INT.
			TR	Torquay U.	07.64	1964–65	29	/	1	

Players Names	Birthplace	Date	Previous Club	League Club	Date Signed	Seasons Played	Career Record Apps	Sub	Gls	
HELLINGS, Dennis	Lincoln	09.12.23		Lincoln C.	+	1946	3		0	
HELLIWELL, Dave	Blackburn	28.03.48	APP	Blackburn Rov.	05.66	1966-68	15	/	1	(W)
			TR	Lincoln C.	05.69	1969	11	2	1	
			TR	Workington	07.70	1970-75	184	13	20	
			TR	Rochdale	07.76	1976	20	11	3	
HEMMERMAN, Jeff L.	Hull	25.02.55	APP	Hull C.	03.73	1973-76	45	14	10	(F)
			L	Scunthorpe U.	09.75	1975	4	1	1	
			TR	Port Vale	06.77	1977	13	2	5	
			TR	Portsmouth	07.78	1978-81	114	9	39	
			TR	Cardiff C.	07.82	1982-83	54	1	22	
HEMMING, Chris A.J.	Stoke	13.04.66	JNRS	Stoke C.	N/C	1983	1	/	0	(D)
HEMSLEY, Edward J.	Stoke	01.09.43	JNRS	Shrewsbury T.	07.61	1960-68	234	1	21	(D)Worc. Cricketer
			TR	Sheffield U.	08.68	1968-76	247	/	8	
			TR	Doncaster Rov.	07.77	1977-78	32	/	1	
HEMSTEAD, Derek W.	Scunthorpe	22.05.43	JNRS	Scunthorpe U.	05.60	1960-68	249	/	2	(FB)
			TR	Carlisle U.	07.69	1969-72	97	1	1	
HEMSTOCK, Brian	Goldthorpe	09.02.49		Barnsley	12.66	1966	1	/	0	(F)
			TR	Bradford P.A.	07.68	1968	4	/	0	
HENCHER, Ken E.	Romford	02.02.28		Millwall	12.49	1949-55	50		0	(CH)
HENDERSON, Anthony	Newcastle	14.01.54	APP	Rotherham U.	07.72	1973	5	1	0	(CH)
HENDERSON, Brian	Allandale	12.06.30		Carlisle U.	05.50					(FB)
			TR	Darlington	07.52	1952-63	422		3	
HENDERSON, George	Hartlepool	07.03.46	B. Auckland	Hartlepool U.	AM	1970	1	/	0	(CF)
HENDERSON, John	Johnshaven	22.09.41	Montrose Vic.	Charlton Ath.	06.59	1962	3		1	(IF)
			TR	Exeter C.	11.62	1962-63	46		14	
			TR	Doncaster Rov.	07.64	1964	10		0	
			TR	Chesterfield	07.65	1965	28	/	3	
HENDERSON, John G.	Glasgow	17.01.32	JNRS	Portsmouth	01.49	1951-57	214		70	(CF)S-7/S'B'-2
			TR	Wolverhampton W.	03.58	1957-58	9		3	
			TR	Arsenal	10.58	1958-61	103		29	
			TR	Fulham	01.62	1961-63	45		7	
HENDERSON, John S.P.	Glasgow	13.10.23	T. Lanark	Rotherham U.	11.53	1953-54	47		7	(IF)
			TR	Leeds U.	03.55	1954-55	15		4	
HENDERSON, Joseph	Cleland	21.12.24	Albion Rov.	Northampton T.	05.49					(G)
			Stenhousemuir	Accrington St.	07.53	1953	14		0	
HENDERSON, Mike R.	Gosforth	31.03.56	APP	Sunderland	04.74	1975-78	81	3	2	(D)
			TR	Watford	11.79	1979-81	50	1	0	
			TR	Cardiff C.	03.82	1981	11	/	0	
			TR	Sheffield U.	08.82	1982-83	52	2	0	
HENDERSON, Peter	Berwick	29.09.52	Witton A.	Chester C.	12.78	1978-79	59	5	10	(F)
			TR	Gillingham	07.80	1980	6	1	3	
			L	Crewe Alex.	09.81	1981	6	1	0	
			TR	Chester C.	12.81	1981	28	/	5	
HENDERSON, Ray	Wallsend	31.03.37	Ashington	Middlesbrough	05.57	1957-60	10		5	(IF)
			TR	Hull C.	06.61	1961-67	226	3	54	
			TR	Reading	10.68	1968	5	/	0	
HENDERSON, Stan	Barrow	15.10.25	Holker COB	Barrow	06.46	1946-47	25		3	(OR)d.1980
HENDERSON, Stewart	Bridge of Allan	05.06.47	JNRS	Chelsea	07.64					(D)S.SCH.INT.
			TR	Brighton & H.A.	07.65	1965-72	198	/	1	
			TR	Reading	06.73	1973-82	159	7	6	
HENDERSON, Tom	Consett	06.04.49	Tow Law	Bradford P.A.	02.69	1968-69	22	/	3	(W)
			TR	York C.	10.70	1970-71	63	1	7	
HENDERSON, Tom	Burnley	01.10.27	JNRS	Burnley	+	1948	2		0	(OR)
HENDERSON, Tom W.	Glasgow	25.07.43	St. Mirren	Leeds U.	11.62	1962-64	24		2	(W)
			TR	Bury	06.65	1965	7	/	1	
			TR	Swindon T.	01.66	1965	11	/	3	
			TR	Stockport Co.	07.66	1966	17	2	4	
HENDERSON, W. Martin	Kirkcaldy	03.05.56	Glasgow Rgrs.	Leicester C.	10.78	1978-80	79	12	12	(F)
			TR	Chesterfield	09.81	1981-83	87	/	23	
			TR	Port Vale	10.83	1983	27	/	7	
HENDERSON, William	Baillieston	24.01.44	Glasgow Rgrs.	Sheffield Wed.	07.72	1972-73	42	6	5	(W)S-29/S.U23-2/S.F.LGE REP./S.SCH.INT.
HENDERSON, William J.			Q. of South	Rochdale	07.46	1946	17		0	(G)
			TR	Southport	06.47	1947	20		0	
HENDRIE, John G.	Lennoxtown	24.10.63	APP	Coventry C.	05.81	1981-83	15	6	2	(F)
			L	Hereford U.	01.84	1983	6	/	0	
HENDRIE, Paul	Glasgow	27.03.54	Rob Roy	Birmingham C.	03.72	1972-75	19	4	1	(M)S.SCH.INT.
			Portland Timbers	Bristol Rov.	09.77	1977-78	17	13	1	
			TR	Halifax T.	07.79	1979-83	187	/	12	
HENDRY, Ian	Glasgow	19.10.59	APP	Aston Villa	09.77					(M)
			TR	Hereford U.	02.79	1978-79	21	/	0	
			TR	Cambridge U.	11.80					

Players Names	Birthplace	Date	Previous Club	League Club	Date Signed	Seasons Played	Career Record Apps	Sub	Gls	
HENLEY, Les	Lambeth	26.09.22		Arsenal	+					(IF)E.SCH.INT.
			TR	Reading	12.46	1946–52	181		29	
HENNESSEY, W.Terry	Llay	01.09.42	JNRS	Birmingham C.	09.59	1960–65	178	/	3	(WH)W–39/W.U23–6/●
			TR	Nottingham F.	11.65	1965–69	160	/	5	W.SCH.INT.
			TR	Derby Co.	02.70	1969–72	62	1	4	
HENNIGAN, Mike	Thrybergh	20.12.42	Rotherham U.(AM)	Sheffield Wed.	03.61					(F)
			TR	Southampton	06.62	1963	3		0	
			TR	Brighton & H.A.	07.64	1964	4		0	
HENNIN, Derek	Prescot	28.12.31	Prescot Cables	Bolton W.	06.49	1953–60	164		8	(WH)E.YTH.INT.
			TR	Chester C.	02.61	1960–61	54		4	
HENNINGS, Roberts I.	Glyncorrwg	30.12.31		Swansea C.	10.49	1955–1956	10		1	(F)
HENRY, Anthony	Newcastle	26.11.57	APP	Manchester C.	12.74	1976-81	68	11	6	(M)
			TR	Bolton W.	09.81	1981-82	70	/	22	
			TR	Oldham Ath.	03.83	1982-83	50	3	5	
HENRY, Charles A.	Acton	13.02.62	APP	Swindon T.	02.80	1980-83	120	2	3	(D)
HENRY, Gerry R.	Barnsley	05.10.20		Leeds U.	*	1946–47	42		4	(IF)
			TR	Bradford P.A.	11.47	1947–49	79		30	
			TR	Sheffield Wed.	02.50	1949–51	40		3	
			TR	Halifax T.	12.51	1951–52	24		3	
HENRY, Gordon	Troon	09.10.30	St. Mirren	Aldershot	06.56	1956–63	176		15	(CH)
HENRY, Ron P.	Shoreditch	17.08.34	Redbourne	Tottenham H,	03.52	1954–65	247	/	1	(FB)E–1
HENSHAW, Gary	Leeds	18.02.65	APP	Grimsby T.	02.83	1983	3	1	0	(M)
HENSON, Anthony H.	Dronfield	15.10.60	Alfreton T.	Chesterfield	11.81	1981-82	26	2	0	(M)
HENSON, Len	Hull	06.08.21		Gillingham	05.50	1950	8		0	(HB)
HENSON, Philip M.	Manchester	30.03.53	APP	Manchester C.	07.70	1971-74	12	5	0	(M)
			L	Swansea C.	07.72	1972	1	/	0	
			TR	Sheffield Wed.	02.75	1974-76	65	7	9	
			TR	Stockport Co.	09.78	1978-79	65	2	13	
			TR	Rotherham U.	02.80	1979-83	87	5	7	
HENWOOD, Rod C.	Portsmouth	27.11.31		Portsmouth	05.50	1953	1		0	(OL)
HEPBURN, John	Paisley	10.03.21	Morton	Workington	08.51	1951	1		0	(OR)
HEPPELL, George B.	W. Hartlepool	02.09.16	Wolverhampton W.(*)	Port Vale	*	1946–51	165		0	(G)
HEPPLE, Gordon	Sunderland	16.09.25	N. Sands.	Middlesbrough	+	1946–53	41		0	(FB)
			TR	Norwich C.	06.54	1954	5		0	
HEPPLEWHITE, George	Edmondsley	05.09.19	Horden CW	Huddersfield T.	+	1946–50	156		3	(CH)
			TR	Preston N.E.	03.51					
			TR	Bradford C.	07.53	1953–54	57		2	
HEPPLEWHITE, Wilson	Washington	11.06.46	Crook T.	Carlisle U.	03.65	1965	3	/	0	(FB)
			TR	Hartlepool U.	07.67	1967–68	50	2	2	
HEPPOLETTE, Ricky	India	08.04.49	APP	Preston N.E.	09.64	1967-72	149	5	13	(M)
			TR	Orient	12.72	1972-76	113	/	10	
			TR	Crystal Palace	10.76	1976	13	2	0	
			TR	Chesterfield	02.77	1976-78	46	1	3	
			TR	Peterborough U.	08.79	1979	5	/	0	
HEPTON, Stan	Leeds	03.12.32	Ashley Rd.FC	Blackpool	03.50	1952–56	7		3	(CF)
			TR	Huddersfield T.	08.57	1957–58	6		1	
			TR	Bury	06.59	1959	14		3	
			TR	Rochdale	07.60	1960–63	149		21	
			TR	Southport	07.64	1964	22		2	
HEPWORTH, Maurice	Dilston	06.09.53	APP	Sunderland	09.70	1970	2	/	0	(FB)
			L	Darlington	01.75	1974	4	/	0	
HEPWORTH, Ron	Barnsley	25.01.19	Chesterfield(*)	Bradford P.A.	+	1946–50	101		0	(FB)
HERBERT, David R.	Sheffield	23.01.56	APP	Sheffield Wed.	01.74	1974–75	12	6	3	(F)
			TR	Chesterfield	07.76					
HERBERT, Frank	Sheffield	29.06.16	Sheffield Wed.(+)	Bury	+					(RH)d.1972
			TR	Oldham Ath.	06.46	1946	4		0	
HERBERT, Robert	Glasgow	21.11.25	Blantyre Vic.	Doncaster Rov.	06.50	1950–55	108		15	(WH)
HERBERT, Stan	Whitehaven	29.08.46	JNRS	Workington	AM	1966	1	/	0	(IF)
HERBERT, Trevor E.	Reading	03.06.29		Orient	08.49					(CF)
			TR	Crystal Palace	07.50	1950	8		2	
HERD, Alec	Bowhill	08.11.11	Hamilton	Manchester C.	*	1946–47	32		12	(IF)S.F.LGE REP./
			TR	Stockport Co.	03.48	1947–51	110		35	Father of David/d.1982
HERD, David G.	Hamilton	15.04.34	JNRS	Stockport Co.	04.51	1950–53	16		6	(CF)S–5●
			TR	Arsenal	08.54	1954–60	166		97	
			TR	Manchester U.	07.61	1961–67	201	1	114	
			TR	Stoke C.	07.68	1968–69	39	5	11	
HERD, George	Lanark	06.05.36	Clyde	Sunderland	04.61	1960–68	274	3	47	(IF)S–5/S.U23–2/S.F.LGE REP. 00
			TR	Hartlepool U.	06.70	1970	9	4	0	
HERNON, Jim	Cleland	06.12.24	Mossvale YMCA	Leicester C.	+	1946–47	31		7	(IF)
			TR	Bolton W.	09.48	1948–50	43		2	
			TR	Grimsby T.	08.51	1951–53	91		24	
			TR	Watford	07.54	1954–55	43		10	

Players Names	Birthplace	Date	Previous Club	League Club	Date Signed	Seasons Played	Apps	Sub	Gls	
HEROD, Dennis J.	Stoke	27.10.23	JNRS	Stoke C.	+	1946–52	191		1	(G)
			TR	Stockport Co.	07.53	1953	33		0	
HERON, Brian	Dumbarton	19.06.48	Dumbarton	Oxford U.	07.74	1974–76	40	3	8	(F)
			TR	Scunthorpe U.	07.77	1977	20	5	1	
HERON, William B.	Washington	29.03.32		Gateshead	02.55	1954–56	21		1	(IF)
HERRING, Harry	Hartlepool	04.01.39		Hartlepool U.	08.58	1958	2		0	(F)
HERRINGTON, Eric	Rotherham	30.10.43	JNRS	Doncaster Rov.	01.61	1961	1		0	(HB)
HERRIOT, James	Chapelhall	20.12.39	Dunfermline	Birmingham C.	05.65	1965–69	181	/	0	(G)S–8/S.F.LGE REP.
			L	Mansfield T.	11.70	1970	5	/	0	
HERRITTY, Alan M.	Newport	24.10.41	JNRS	Newport Co.	12.58	1959–61	29		0	(FB)W.SCH.INT.
HERRITTY, William R.	Newport	02.09.38	JNRS	Newport Co.	05.57	1956–62	61		12	(IR)Brother of Alan
HERRON, Alan	Washington	06.10.32	Newcastle U.(AM)	Blackburn Rov.	08.50	1955–56	4		0	(HB)
HERRON, John	Widdrington	02.03.38		Leeds U.	10.56					(F)
			TR	Gateshead	06.57	1957–58	8		0	
HERRON, Tom	Irvine	31.03.36	Portadown	Manchester U.	03.58	1957–60	3		0	(OL)
			TR	York C.	05.61	1961–65	192	/	6	
HESELTINE, George V.	Wolverhampton	25.03.26	Hednesford	Walsall	02.49	1948–49	8		0	(IF)
HESFORD, Iain	Kenya	04.03.60	APP	Blackpool	08.77	1977–82	202	/	0	(G)E.YTH,INT./
			TR	Sheffield Wed.	08.83					E.U21–7
HESFORD, Robert T.	Bolton	13.04.16	Blackpool(*)	Huddersfield T.	*	1946–49	71		0	(G)*Sth.Shore/d.1982/
										Father of Iain
HESLOP, Brian	Carlisle	04.08.47	APP	Carlisle U.	08.65	1965–66	5	/	0	(HB)
			TR	Sunderland	05.67	1967–70	58	1	0	
			TR	Northampton T.	03.71	1970–71	49	1	0	
			TR	Workington	09.72	1972–75	139	1	5	
HESLOP, George	Wallsend	01.07.40	Dudley Welf.	Newcastle U.	02.59	1959–61	27		0	(CH)
			TR	Everton	03.62	1962–65	10	/	0	
			TR	Manchester C.	09.65	1965–71	159	3	1	
			TR	Bury	08.72	1972	37		0	
HESLOP, Norman	Bolton	01.08.20	Bolton W.(AM)	Southport	10.46	1946–47	30		4	(IF)
HETHERINGTON, Tom B.	Walker	22.01.11	Barnsley(*)	Gateshead	10.46	1946	1		0	(G)*Walker Col./Burnley
HETHERINGTON, Harry	Chester-le-Street	07.11.28	Silksworth J.	Sunderland	05.46	1947	2		0	
			TR	Gateshead	01.49	1948	2		1	
HETZKE, Steve E.R.	Marlborough	03.06.55	APP	Reading	06.73	1971–81	254	7	23	(D)
			TR	Blackpool	07.82	1982–83	87	/	9	
HEWARD, Brian	Lincoln	17.07.35	JNRS	Scunthorpe U.	03.54	1953–60	135		0	(WH)
			TR	Lincoln C.	07.61	1961–65	97	/	1	
HEWARD, Graham K.	Newcastle	13.10.65	APP	Cambridge U.	10.83	1983	1	/	0	(F)
HEWIE, John D.	S. Africa	13.12.27	Pretoria	Charlton Ath.		1951–65	495		37	(FB) S–19/S.U23–1/S'B'–1●
										4 apps in goal
HEWITT, Gerry	Sheffield	28.01.35	JNRS	Sheffield U.	07.54	1955–56	3		0	(WH)
			TR	Workington	06.58					
HEWITT, Harry	Chesterfield	24.09.16		Mansfield T.	+	1946	1		0	(OR)
HEWITT, Len	Wrexham	20.03.20		Wrexham	05.46	1946	5		2	(F) d.1979
HEWITT, Richard	Moorthorpe	25.05.43	Moorthorpe BC	Huddersfield T.	05.61					(F)
			TR	Bradford C.	07.64	1964	20		7	
			TR	Barnsley	07.65	1965–68	95	2	20	
			TR	York C.	03.69	1968–71	87	5	7	
HEWITT, Ron	Chesterfield	25.01.24	Sheffield U.(+)	Lincoln C.	08.46	1948	3		0	(G)
HEWITT, Ron	Flint	21.06.28		Wolverhampton W.	07.48					(IF) W–5
			TR	Walsall	10.49	1949	8		2	
			TR	Darlington	06.50	1950	36		3	
			TR	Wrexham	07.51	1951–56	204		84	
			TR	Cardiff C.	06.57	1957–58	64		27	
			TR	Wrexham	07.59	1959	27		11	
			TR	Coventry C.	03.60	1959–61	59		22	
			TR	Chester C.	03.62	1961–62	29		6	
HEWKINS, Ken	S. Africa	30.10.29	Clyde S.A.	Fulham	11.55	1955–61	38		0	(G)
HEWSON, Pat G.	Gateshead	02.06.26	Crook T.	W.B.A.	11.50					(FB)
			TR	Gateshead	07.53	1953–57	130		0	
HEYDON, Cecil	Birkenhead	24.05.19	Derby Co.(+)	Doncaster Rov.	+	1946–47	6			*New Brighton
			TR	Rochdale	07.48	1948	1		0	
HEYDON, Joe	Birkenhead	19.10.28	Everton (AM)	Liverpool	01.49	1950–52	63		0	(WH)
			TR	Millwall	05.53	1953–55	72		1	
			TR	Tranmere Rov.	07.56	1956–60	76		1	
HEYES, George	Bolton	16.11.37	JNRS	Rochdale	04.56	1958–59	24		0	(G)
			TR	Leicester C.	07.60	1960–65	25	/	0	
			TR	Swansea C.	09.65	1965–68	98	/	0	
			TR	Barrow	07.69	1969	26	/	0	
HEYES, Ken	Haydock	04.01.36	JNRS	Everton	02.53					(FB)E.YTH.INT./
			TR	Preston N.E.	05.57	1959	3		0	E.SCH.INT

Players Names	Birthplace	Date	Previous Club	League Club	Date Signed	Seasons Played	Career Record Apps	Sub	Gls	
HEYS, Mike	Preston	23.06.38	JNRS	Preston N.E.	05.57					(G)
			TR	Barrow	03.59	1958–61	70		0	
			TR	Workington	08.62					
				Halifax T.	11.63	1963	1		0	
HEYWOOD, Albert E.	Hartlepool	12.05.13	Sunderland(*)	Hartlepool U.	+	1946	39		0	(G)
HIBBERD, Stuart	Sheffield	11.10.61	APP	Lincoln C.	10.79	1980-82	36	6	3	(F)
HIBBITT, Ken	Bradford	03.01.51	APP	Bradford P.A.	11.68	1967-68	13	2	0	(M)E.U23-1●
			TR	Wolverhampton W.	11.68	1968-82	446	19	88	
HIBBITT, Terry	Bradford	01.12.47	JNRS	Leeds U.	12.64	1965-70	32	15	9	(M)Brother of Ken
			TR	Newcastle U.	08.71	1971-75	138	/	7	
			TR	Birmingham C.	08.75	1975-77	110	/	11	
			TR	Newcastle U.	05.78	1978-80	89	1	5	
HIBBS, Garry T.	Hammersmith	26.01.57	APP	Orient	07.74	1975	1	/	0	(F)
			TR	Aldershot	02.77	1976	4	2	0	
HICK, Les D.	Acomb	23.04.27		Bradford C.	05.49	1948	1		0	
HICKIE, George				Barnsley	+					
			TR	Carlisle U.	09.46	1946	1		0	
HICKLIN, A. William	Dudley	20.09.24	W.B.A.(AM)	Birmingham C.	+					(HB)
			TR	Watford	06.47	1947	21		5	
			TR	W.B.A.	05.48					
HICKMAN, Geoff B.	W.Bromwich	07.01.50	APP	W.B.A.	01.68					(G)
			TR	Bradford P.A.	06.69	1969	9	/	0	
HICKMAN, Mike F.T.	Elstead	02.10.46	JNRS	Brighton & H.A.	06.65	1965-67	12	3	0	(F)
			TR	Grimsby T.	06.68	1968-74	247	6	48	
			TR	Blackburn Rov.	02.75	1974-75	23	3	8	
			TR	Torquay U.	10.75	1975-76	17	/	1	
HICKS, Anthony J.	Swindon	20.08.45	APP	Swindon T.	10.62	1964–66	51		0	(G)
HICKS, James M.	Ipswich	16.09.60	Soham	Exeter C.	N/C	1983	3	/	0	(D)
HICKS, Keith	Oldham	09.08.54	APP	Oldham Ath.	08.72	1971-79	240	2	11	(D)E.YTH.INT.
			TR	Hereford U.	09.80	1980-83	163	/	1	
HICKS, Martin	Stratford-on-Avon	27.02.57	Stratford T.	Charlton Ath.	02.77					(D)
			TR	Reading	02.78	1977-83	214	1	10	
HICKSON, Dave	Ellesmere Port	30.10.29	Ellesmere Port	Everton	05.48	1951–55	139		62	(CF)●
			TR	Aston Villa	09.55	1955	12		1	
			TR	Huddersfield T.	11.55	1955–56	56		19	
			TR	Everton	08.57	1957–59	86		32	
			TR	Liverpool	11.59	1959–60	61		36	
			TR	Bury	01.62	1961	8		0	
			TR	Tranmere Rov.	08.62	1962–63	45		21	
HICKSON, Geoff G.	Crewe	26.09.39	Blackburn Rov.(AM)	Stoke C.	08.57	1959–60	11		0	(G)
			TR	Crewe Alex	07.62	1962–66	105	/	0	
			L	Port Vale	08.68	1968	17	/	0	
			TR	Southport	12.68	1968	3	/	0	
HICKTON, John	Birmingham	24.09.44	JNRS	Sheffield Wed.	01.62	1963-65	51	1	21	(F)
			TR	Middlesbrough	09.66	1966-77	395	20	159	
			L	Hull C.	01.77	1976	6	/	1	
HICKTON, Roy	Chesterfield	19.09.48	APP	Chesterfield	11.65	1968-70	48	2	1	(FB)
HIGGINBOTTOM, Andy J.	Chesterfield	22.10.64	APP	Chesterfield	10.82	1982-83	5	3	0	(M)
			TR	Everton	07.83					
HIGGINS, Andy	Bolsover	12.02.60	APP	Chesterfield	02.78	1978	1	/	0	(D)Brother of Robert
			TR	Port Vale	02.81	1980-81	11	3	0	
			TR	Hartlepool U.	09.82	1982	3	1	1	
			Kings Lynn	Rochdale	08.83	1982-83	31	2	6	
HIGGINS, August	Dublin	19.01.31	Shamrock Rov.	Aston Villa	11.49					(F)Brother of James
			TR	Ipswich T.	07.52	1952	2		0	
HIGGINS, Charles			Arbroath	Chester C.	08.46	1946	11		0	
HIGGINS, David A.	Liverpool	19.08.61		Tranmere Rov.	08.83	1983	20	/	0	(D)
HIGGINS, Fred T.	Hackney	21.01.30	Wood Green	Crystal Palace	03.52	1952–53	11		0	(F)
HIGGINS, George	Batley	12.09.32	JNRS	Huddersfield T.	12.49					(HB)
			TR	Halifax T.	07.57	1957	5		0	
HIGGINS, George	Dundee	16.06.25	Lochee Harp	Blackburn Rov.	10.46	1946–50	53		0	(FB)●
			TR	Bolton W.	07.51	1951–53	69		0	
			TR	Grimsby T.	05.54	1954–56	47		0	
HIGGINS, James	Dublin	03.02.26	Dundalk	Birmingham C.	11.49	1949–52	48		12	(CF)EI-1
HIGGINS, John O.	Bakewell	15.11.32	Buxton	Bolton W.	10.50	1952-60	183		0	(CH)Father of Mark
HIGGINS, John W.	Kilmarnock	27.01.33	St. Mirren	Swindon T.	05.59	1959–60	28		0	(FB)
HIGGINS, Mark N.	Buxton	29.09.58	APP	Everton	08.76	1976-83	150	2	6	(D)E.YTH.INT./E.SCH.INT.
HIGGINS, Mick	Rossendale	05.09.56	APP	Blackburn Rov.	12.73					(M)
			TR	Workington	07.76	1976	11	4	1	

Players Names	Birthplace	Date	Previous Club	League Club	Date Signed	Seasons Played	Career Record Apps Sub Gls		
HIGGINS, Peter	Mansfield	01.08.44		Oxford U.	07.62	1962–68	35	5	0 (CH)
			TR	Crewe Alex	06.69	1969–71	56	3	0
HIGGINS, Peter C.	Cardiff	12.11.50	APP	Bristol Rov.	02.69	1968–72	36	1	5 (W)
			TR	Doncaster Rov.	07.73	1973–75	63	5	10
			L	Torquay U.	03.76	1975	3	1	1
HIGGINS, Robert	Bolsover	23.12.58	APP	Burnley	07.76	1977	3	/	0 (D)
			L	Hartlepool U.	11.79	1979	2	/	0
			TR	Rochdale	10.80	1980	4	1	0
HIGGINS, Ron V.	Silvertown	14.02.23		Orient	AM	1949	2		0 (F)
			Tonbridge	Brighton & H.A.	01.52	1951–52	9		0
			TR	Q.P.R.	01.53	1952	3		1
HIGGINS, Williams C.	Tranmere	26.02.24	Tranmere Rov.(AM)	Everton	+	1946–49	48		8
HIGGINSON, Tom	Newton Grange	06.01.37	Kilmarnock	Brentford	06.59	1959–69	383	3	15 (WH)
HIGH, David	Reading	22.02.41	JNRS	Reading	02.58	1959–63	73		2 (FB)E.YTH.INT.
HIGH, Sid W.	Waterbeach	30.09.22	Cambridge U.	Luton T.	10.46				(OR)
			TR	Watford	08.48	1948	7		3
HIGHAM, John P.	Liverpool	22.11.54	APP	Liverpool	05.74				(D)
			TR	Southport	01.76	1975-77	96	/	0
HIGHAM, Peter	Wigan	08.11.30		Portsmouth	AM	1949	1		0 (CF)
			TR	Bolton W.	11.50				
			TR	Preston N.E.	05.52	1953–54	15		10
			TR	Nottingham F.	08.55	1955–57	61		20
			TR	Doncaster Rov.	03.58	1957–58	22		6
HIGNETT, Alan J.	Liverpool	01.11.46	APP	Liverpool	11.63	1964	1		0 (FB)E.SCH.INT.
			TR	Chester C.	08.66	1966	6	/	0
HILAIRE, Vince	Forest Gate	10.10.59	APP	Crystal Palace	10.76	1976-83	239	16	29 (F)E.YTH.INT./E.U21-9
HILDERSLEY, Ron	Kirkcaldy	06.04.65	APP	Manchester C.	04.83	1982	1	/	0 (F)
			L	Chester C.	01.84	1983	9	/	0
HILDITCH, Mark	Royton	20.08.60	JNRS	Rochdale	11.78	1977-82	184	13	40 (F)
			TR	Tranmere Rov.	08.83	1983	39	/	8
HILL, Alan	Barnsley	03.11.43	JNRS	Barnsley	04.61	1960–65	131	/	0 (G)
			TR	Rotherham U.	06.66	1966–68	82	/	0
			TR	Nottingham F.	03.69	1968–69	41	/	0
HILL, Alan G.	Chester	22.06.55	JNRS	Wrexham	07.73	1974-82	173	26	7 (D)
HILL, Alistair	Glasgow	25.04.34	Dundee	Bristol C.	11.59	1959	3		0 (OR)
HILL, Andy R.	Ilkeston	10.11.60	Kimberley	Derby Co.	06.81	1981-83	19	3	2 (F)
			TR	Carlisle U.	09.83	1983	26	/	3
HILL, Arthur	Chesterfield	12.11.21		Chesterfield	09.46	1947	1		0 (HB)
HILL, Bert	London	08.03.30	JNRS	Chelsea	05.50				(WH)
			TR	Colchester U.	10.52	1952–57	104		3
HILL, Brian	Sheffield	06.10.37	JNRS	Sheffield Wed.	04.55	1956–65	115	1	1 (FB)d.1968
HILL, Brian	Mansfield	15.12.42	Ollerton Col.	Grimsby T.	08.60	1960–66	180	/	25 (OL)
			TR	Huddersfield T.	11.66	1966–68	84	/	6
			TR	Blackburn Rov.	09.69	1969–70	34	3	4
			TR	Torquay U.	07.71	1971	6	1	1
HILL, Brian W.	Bedworth	31.07.41	JNRS	Coventry C.	08.58	1957–70	240	4	7 (WH)
			L	Bristol C.	03.71	1970	7	/	0
			TR	Torquay U.	10.71	1971–72	49	/	1
HILL, Charles J.	Cardiff	06.09.18		Cardiff C.	*	1946	5		1 (IF)
			TR	Torquay U.	07.47	1947–48	63		15
			TR	Q.P.R.	03.49	1948–49	20		1
			TR	Swindon T.	09.50	1950	4		0
HILL, Colin F.	Uxbridge	12.11.63	APP	Arsenal	08.81	1982-83	44	/	1 (D)
HILL, Dave R.	Kettering	28.09.53	APP	Northampton T.	APP	1970	1	/	0 (G)
HILL, David	Bradford	25.05.65	JNRS	Bradford C.	N/C	1982-83	2	3	1 (F)
HILL, David M.	Nottingham	06.06.66	JNRS	Scunthorpe U.	N/C	1983	1	1	0
HILL, Dennis	Willenhall	16.08.29	Darlaston	Birmingham C.	06.51	1953–55	4		0 (F)
HILL, Dilwyn	Porth	01.04.37	Pontypridd	Exeter C.	06.55	1957–59	14		3 (F)d.1963
HILL, E.Alan	Bromborough	01.07.33	Bebington	Tranmere Rov.	AM	1956	6		1 (OL)
HILL, Frank R.	Forfar	21.05.06	Wrexham(+)	Crewe Alex.	+	1946–47	20		0 (WH)S–3/*Aberdeen/ Arsenal/Blackpool/ Southampton
HILL, Fred	Sheffield	17.01.40	JNRS	Bolton W.	03.57	1957–68	373	1	74 (IF)
			TR	Halifax T.	07.69	1969	25	/	3 E–2/
			TR	Manchester C.	05.70	1970–72	28	7	3 E.U23–10/E.F.LGE REP./
			TR	Peterborough U.	08.73	1973–74	73	2	7 (Cousin of Brian–Sheffield W.)
HILL, Geoff R.	Carlisle	31.08.29		Carlisle U.	10.49	1949–57	188		0 (FB)
HILL, Gordon	Sunbury	01.04.54	Southall	Millwall	01.73	1972-75	79	7	20 (W)E-6/E.U23-1
			TR	Manchester U.	11.75	1975-77	100	1	39
			TR	Derby Co.	04.78	1977-79	22	2	5
			TR	Q.P.R.	11.79	1979-80	10	4	1

Players Names	Birthplace	Date	Previous Club	League Club	Date Signed	Seasons Played	Apps	Sub	Gls	
HILL, Henry A.	Lambeth	19.09.47	Canada	Ipswich T.	03.69					(M)
			S. Africa	Gillingham	07.71	1971	0	1	0	
				Hereford U.	N/C	1978	0	1	0	
HILL, James	Wilshaw	19.08.31	JNRS	Coventry C.	08.48	1949–55	68		8	(OL)
			TR	Millwall	07.56	1956	1		0	
			TR	Shrewsbury T.	07.57	1957	8		0	
HILL, James W.T.	Balham	22.07.28	Reading(AM)	Brentford	05.49	1949–51	83		10	(IF)
			TR	Fulham	03.52	1951–60	277		41	
HILL, James M.	Carrickfergus	31.10.35	Linfield	Newcastle U.	07.57	1957	11		2	(IF)NI–7/NI'B'–2/
			TR	Norwich C.	07.58	1958–62	161		55	NI.AMAT.INT
			TR	Everton	08.63	1963	7	1		
			TR	Port Vale	10.65	1965–67	63	/	8	
HILL, John E.	Yeovil	29.11.48	APP	Bournemouth	08.66	1967	3	1	0	(HB)
HILL, Ken	Walsall	28.04.38		Walsall	11.56	1958–62	115		1	(WH)
			TR	Norwich C.	07.63	1963–65	44	/	0	
			TR	Walsall	10.66	1966	15	/	0	
HILL, Ken G.	Canterbury	07.03.53	APP	Gillingham	03.71	1971–76	120	5	7	(D)
			L	Lincoln C.	12.74	1974	1	/	0	
HILL, Len	Caerleon	14.04.42	Lovells Ath.	Newport Co.	11.62	1962–69	264	2	48	(WH)Glamorgan Cricketer
			TR	Swansea C.	07.70	1970	12	/	1	
			TR	Newport Co.	01.72	1971–73	93	4	13	
HILL, (Mandy)Steve	Blackpool	15.02.40	JNRS	Blackpool	05.59	1959–63	71		1	(W)E.U23–4
			TR	Tranmere Rov.	09.64	1964–67	130	/	10	
HILL, Mark S.	Perivale	21.01.61	APP	Q.P.R.	07.79					(D)
			TR	Brentford	07.80	1980-81	54	2	3	
HILL, Maurice	Halifax	02.05.20		Everton	+					(FB) d.1966
			TR	New Brighton	07.46	1946–47	75		0	
HILL, Mick	Hereford	03.12.47	Bethesda Ath.	Sheffield U.	09.65	1966–69	35	2	9	(CF)W–2
			TR	Ipswich T.	10.69	1969–72	63	2	18	
			TR	Crystal Palace	12.73	1973–75	43	2	6	
HILL, Peter	Heanor	08.08.31	JNRS	Coventry C.	08.48	1948–61	284		74	(IF)
HILL, Ray	Stourbridge	15.02.36	Redditch	Coventry C.	11.57	1957–58	14		5	(F)
HILL, Ricky A.	London	05.03.59	APP	Luton T.	05.76	1975-83	273	6	42	(M)E.YTH.INT./E.-2
HILL, Robert	Edinburgh	09.06.38	JNRS	Colchester U.	06.55	1955–64	238		20	(IF)
HILL, William	Sheffield	06.01.36	Rawmarsh	York C.	02.54	1956–59	29		3	(F)
HILL, William H.	Skegby	15.03.20	Skegby MW.	Mansfield T.	11.47	1947	2		0	(IF)
HILL, William L.	Uxbridge	09.06.30	Uxbridge T.	Q.P.R.	04.51	1951	10		1	(F)
HILLARD, Doug	Bristol	10.08.35	Bristol M.H.	Bristol Rov.	05.57	1958–67	312	5	13	(FB)
HILLARD, John G.	Aberdeen	03.09.16		Torquay U.	09.46	1946	6		0	
HILLEY, Dave	Glasgow	20.12.38	T.Lanark	Newcastle U.	08.62	1962–67	194	/	32	(IF)S.U23–1/S.F.LGE REP.
			TR	Nottingham F.	12.67	1967–70	71	16	14	
HILLIER, Barry G.	Redcar	08.04.36	JNRS	Southampton	04.53	1957–58	9		0	(FB)
HILLIER, John	Halsall	10.09.33	Llanwrst	Chester C.	AM	1954	5		0	(G)
HILLMAN, Dennis V.	Southend	27.11.18		Brighton & H.A.	+					(OR)
			TR	Colchester U.	N/L	1950	4		0	
			TR	Gillingham	08.51	1951	21		0	
HILLS, John	Northfleet	24.02.34	Gravesend	Tottenham H.	08.53	1957–59	29		0	(FB)
			TR	Bristol Rov.	07.61	1961	7		0	
HILLYARD, Ron	Rotherham	31.03.52	JNRS	York C.	12.69	1969–73	61	/	0	(G)
			L	Hartlepool U.	01.72	1971	23	/	0	
			TR	Gillingham	07.74	1974-83	382	/	0	
HILTON, Gary	Manchester	04.03.61		Bury	N/C	1983	1	/	0	(G)
HILTON, Jack	Rochdale	20.02.25	Hyde U.	Wrexham	07.50	1950	3		0	(CF)
HILTON, Joe	Bromborough	20.07.31	JNRS	Leeds U.	09.48	1949	1		0	(F)
			TR	Chester C.	08.50	1950–53	61		9	
HILTON, Mark	Middleton	15.01.60	APP	Oldham Ath.	01.78	1977-80	48	2	2	(M)
			TR	Bury	08.81	1981-82	29	3	3	
HILTON, Pat J.	Canterbury	01.05.54	Canterbury	Brighton & H.A.	02.73	1972-73	18	2	1	(W)
			TR	Blackburn Rov.	05.74	1974	16	/	2	
			TR	Gillingham	09.75	1975-76	16	10	1	
			L	Aldershot	03.77	1976	12	1	0	
			TR	Southport	07.77	1977	22	5	5	
HILTON, Paul	Oldham	08.10.59	JNRS	Bury	07.78	1978-83	136	12	39	(F)E.SCH.INT.
			TR	West Ham U.	02.84	1983	7	1	2	
HILTON, Peter B.	Tamworth	20.03.29	Tamworth FC	W.B.A.	07.49					(FB)d.1965
			TR	Swindon T.	07.53	1953–55	48		0	
HINCE, Paul	Manchester	02.03.45		Manchester C.	10.66	1966–67	7	/	4	(W)
			TR	Charlton Ath.	02.68	1967–68	23	/	2	
			TR	Bury	12.68	1968–69	38	/	3	
			TR	Crewe Alex.	07.70	1970	23	3	2	

Players Names	Birthplace	Date	Previous Club	League Club	Date Signed	Seasons Played	Career Record Apps Sub Gls			
HINCH, Jim	Sheffield	08.11.47	Portmadoc	**Tranmere Rov.**	03.70	1969-70	36	3	10	(F)
			TR	**Plymouth Arg.**	02.71	1970-73	102	5	28	
			TR	**Hereford U.**	10.73	1973	22	5	7	
			TR	**York C.**	07.74	1974-76	56	12	12	
			L	**Southport**	03.75	1974	7	/	2	
			TR	**Sheffield Wed.**	10.77	1977	0	1	0	
			TR	**Barnsley**	12.77	1977	9	3	4	
HINCHCLIFFE, Alan A.	Chesterfield	08.12.36	JNRS	**Sheffield Wed.**	12.53	1956	2		0	(G)
			TR	**Chesterfield**	07.59					
HINCHCLIFFE, Tom	Denaby	06.12.13	Derby Co.(*)	**Nottingham F.**	05.46	1946	1		0	*Grimsby T./Huddersfield T./ d.1978
HINCHLIFFE, John	Tillicoultry	04.06.38		**Aston Villa**	09.56	1957	2		0	(WH)S.SCH.INT.
			TR	**Workington**	06.58	1958-61	116		4	
			TR	**Hartlepool U.**	10.61	1961-63	88		8	
HINDLE, Frank J.	Blackburn	22.06.25		**Blackburn Rov.**	+					(FB)
			TR	**Chester C.**	06.49	1949-50	81		0	
			TR	**Bradford P.A.**	04.51	1950-56	204		0	
			TR	**Barrow**	09.57					
HINDLE, Jack R.	Preston	10.11.21		**Preston N.E.**	11.46	1947	1		0	(G)
			TR	**Barrow**	05.48	1948-49	84		0	
			TR	**Aston Villa**	06.50	1950	15		0	
			TR	**Barrow**	08.51	1951-55	182		0	
HINDLE, Tom	Keighley	22.02.21	Keighley T.	**Leeds U.**	+	1946-48	42		2	(IF)
			TR	**York C.**	02.49	1948-49	19		3	
			TR	**Halifax T.**	09.49	1949-51	85		17	
			TR	**Rochdale**	03.52	1951	6		1	
HINDLEY, Frank C.	Worksop	02.11.15	Nottingham F.(*)	**Brighton & H.A.**	+	1946	10		4	(F)
HINDLEY, Peter	Worksop	19.05.44	JNRS	**Nottingham F.**	06.61	1962-73	368	/	10	(D)E.U23-1
			TR	**Coventry C.**	01.74	1973-75	33	/	0	Son of Frank
			TR	**Peterborough U.**	07.76	1976-78	112	/	1	
HINDMARCH, Robert	Stannington	27.04.61	APP	**Sunderland**	04.78	1977-83	114	1	2	(D)E.YTH.INT.
			L	**Portsmouth**	12.83	1983	2	/	0	
HINDMARSH, Eddie	Castletown	07.09.21	Sunderland(+)	**Carlisle U.**	+	1946	15		0	(HB)
HINDMARSH, J. Wally	Crook	26.12.19	Willington	**Portsmouth**	+	1946-50	55		0	(FB)
			TR	**Swindon T.**	07.51	1951	11		0	
HINDSON, Gordon	Flint Hill	08.01.50	JNRS	**Newcastle U.**	08.68	1968-71	7	/	1	(F)
			TR	**Luton T.**	10.71	1971-74	62	6	3	
			L	**Carlisle U.**	09.75	1975	1	2	0	
			TR	**Blackburn Rov.**	10.75	1975	10	/	0	
HINES, Derek J.	Moira	08.02.31	JNRS	**Leicester C.**	03.48	1947-60	299		116	(CF)E.YTH.INT.
			TR	**Shrewsbury T.**	11.61	1961-62	16		5	
HINNIGAN, Joe	Liverpool	03.12.55	Sth. Liverpool	**Wigan Ath.**	N/L	1978-79	66	/	10	(D)
			TR	**Sunderland**	02.80	1979-82	63	/	4	
			TR	**Preston N.E.**	12.82	1982-83	51	1	8	
HINSHELWOOD, Martin	Reading	16.06.53	APP	**Crystal Palace**	08.70	1972-77	66	3	4	(M)
HINSHELWOOD, Paul	Bristol	14.08.56	APP	**Crystal Palace**	08.73	1973-82	271	5	23	(D)E.U21-2
			TR	**Oxford U.**	08.83	1983	43	/	0	
HINSHELWOOD, Wally	London	27.10.29	JNRS	**Fulham**	10.46	1946-50	18		1	(OR)Father of Martin/Paul
			TR	**Chelsea**	01.51	1950	12		1	
			TR	**Fulham**	05.51	1951	2		0	
			TR	**Reading**	12.52	1952-55	135		30	
			TR	**Bristol C.**	02.56	1955-59	148		16	
			TR	**Millwall**	06.60	1960	19		1	
			Canada	**Newport Co.**	11.61	1961	3		0	
HINSHELWOOD, Willie	Chapelhall	11.05.35	Airdrie	**Hartlepool U.**	07.63	1963	17		3	(WH)
HINSLEY, George	Sheffield	19.07.14	Barnsley(*)	**Bradford C.**	*	1946-48	87		8	
			TR	**Halifax T.**	07.49	1949	32		0	
HINTON, Alan	Wednesbury	06.10.42	JNRS	**Wolverhampton W.**	10.59	1961-63	75		29	(OL)E-3/E.U23-7/
			TR	**Nottingham F.**	01.64	1963-67	108	4	24	E.YTH.INT.
			TR	**Derby Co.**	09.67	1967-75	240	13	63	
HINTON, Edward	Belfast	20.05.22	Distillery	**Fulham**	08.46	1946-48	82		0	(G)NI-7
			TR	**Millwall**	07.49	1949-51	91		0	
HINTON, Marvin	Norwood	02.02.40	JNRS	**Charlton Ath.**	04.57	1957-63	131		2	(CH)E.U23-3
			TR	**Chelsea**	08.63	1963-74	257	8	3	
HINTON, Ron	Sutton-in-Craven	27.11.43	APP	**Doncaster Rov.**	07.61					(CH)
			TR	**Chesterfield**	07.63	1963	1		0	
HIPKIN, Reg W.	Syderstone	31.12.21		**Wolverhampton W.**	+					(RH)
			TR	**Charlton Ath.**	09.46	1947	2		0	
			TR	**Brighton & H.A.**	02.48	1947-48	15		1	
HIRD, Kevin	Colne	11.02.55	APP	**Blackburn Rov.**	02.73	1973-78	129	3	20	(M)
			TR	**Leeds U.**	03.79	1978-83	165	16	19	
HIRD, R. Keith	Annfield Plain	25.11.39	Annfield Plain	**Sunderland**	09.57	1960	1		0	(G)
			TR	**Darlington**	07.63	1963	17		0	
HIRON, Ray	Gosport	22.07.43	Fareham T.	**Portsmouth**	05.64	1964-74	324	7	110	(F)
			TR	**Reading**	07.75	1975-77	88	4	14	

Players Names	Birthplace	Date	Previous Club	League Club	Date Signed	Seasons Played	Apps	Sub	Gls	
HIRST, Keith R.H.	Bradford	15.10.32	Lowmoor Celtic	Bradford P.A.	AM	1953	1		0	(OR)
HIRST, Mal W.	Cudworth	28.12.37	Darfield Col.	Barnsley	05.56	1956	1		0	(F)
HIRST, Martyn P.	York	26.10.61	Bath Univ.	Bristol C.	10.83	1983	22	2	1	(M)
HITCH, George A.	Hammersmith	15.03.30		Q.P.R.	12.50	1951	1		0	(FB)
HITCHCOCK, Alan P.	Easthampstead	05.10.49	APP	Reading	10.67	1968–69	4	/	0	(HB)
HITCHCOCK, Kevin	Custom House	05.10.62	Barking	Nottingham F.	08.83					(G)
			L	Mansfield T.	02.84	1983	14	/	0	
HITCHEN, Harry	Liverpool	22.10.22		New Brighton	09.46	1946–47	70		2	(WH)
			TR	Sheffield U.	05.48	1948–52	154		15	
			TR	Bury	05.53	1953	2		0	
HITCHEN, Trevor	Sowerby Bridge	25.09.26	Halifax T.(AM)	Notts. Co.	+					(WH)
			Wellington	Southport	01.49	1948–55	241		34	
			TR	Oldham Ath.	08.56	1956	3		0	
			Wigan Ath.	Southport	08.58	1958	5		0	
HITCHENS, Gerry A.	Rawnsley	08.10.34	Kidderminster	Cardiff C.	01.55	1954–57	95		40	(CF)E–7/E.U23–1/
			TR	Aston Villa	12.57	1957–60	132		78	E.F.LGE REP./d.1983
HITCHON, John	Carlisle	30.08.19		Carlisle U.	10.48	1946–49	5		0	(G)
HOADLEY, Phil F.W.	Battersea	06.01.52	APP	Crystal Palace	01.69	1967-71	62	11	1	(D)E.YTH.INT.
			TR	Orient	10.71	1971-77	255	/	9	
			TR	Norwich C.	08.78	1978-81	74	3	0	
HOBBINS, Sid G.	Plumstead	06.05.16	Bromley	Charlton Ath.	*	1946	1		0	(G)d.1984
			TR	Millwall	05.48	1948	16		0	
			TR	Orient	12.49	1949	11		0	
HOBBIS, Harold	Dartford	09.03.13	Bromley	Charlton Ath.	*	1946–47	9		1	(OL)E–2
HOBBS John E.	Swanage	17.04.30	Swanage	Bournemouth	10.52	1953–54	6		1	(CF)
HOBBS, Ron G.	Aldershot	23.08.21	Woking	Aldershot	+	1946–53	170		15	(F)
HOBSON, Albert	Manchester	07.04.25	Glossop	Blackpool	+	1947–53	62		3	(OR)
			TR	Huddersfield T.	07.54	1954–55	9		0	
			TR	York C.	03.56	1955–56	22		1	
HOBSON, Gordon	Sheffield	27.11.57	Sheffield Rgrs.	Lincoln C.	12.77	1977-83	224	10	66	(F)
HOBSON, John	Barnsley	01.06.46	JNRS	Blackpool	09.63					(F)
			TR	Barnsley	07.65	1965–68	30	6	7	
			TR	Notts. Co.	05.69	1969–70	46	3	6	
HOBSON, Norman	Harlescott	22.08.33	Oswestry	Shrewsbury T.	10.54	1955–60	212		5	(FB)
HOBSON, Wilf	Consett	26.01.32	W.Stanley	Oldham Ath.	01.53	1954–58	171		1	(HB)
			TR	Gateshead	06.59	1959	31		1	
HOCKADAY, David	Billingham	09.11.57	JNRS	Blackpool	06.75	1976-82	131	16	23	(F)
			TR	Swindon T.	08.83	1983	32	4	3	
HOCKEY, Trevor	Keighley	01.05.43	JNRS	Bradford C.	05.60	1959–61	53		5	(M)W–9
			TR	Nottingham F.	11.61	1961–63	73		6	
			TR	Newcastle U.	11.63	1963–65	52	/	3	
			TR	Birmingham C.	11.65	1965–70	195	/	8	
			TR	Sheffield U.	01.71	1970–72	68	/	4	
			TR	Norwich C.	02.73	1972	13	/	0	
			TR	Aston Villa	06.73	1973	24	/	1	
			TR	Bradford C.	06.74	1974–75	43	1	1	
HODDER, Ken	Stockport	20.08.30		Stockport Co.	03.49	1951–63	238		0	(CH)
HODDLE, Glenn	Hayes	27.10.57	APP	Tottenham H.	04.75	1975-83	279	4	70	(M)E.U21-12/
										E.YTH.INT./E-19
HODGE, Eric	Edmonton	01.06.28		Tottenham H.	08.48					(G)d.1963
			TR	Newport Co.	08.49	1949	7		0	
HODGE, Eric R.	S.Africa	03.04.33	S.Africa	Brighton & H.A.	10.56	1957	3		0	(HB)
			TR	Aldershot	07.59	1959	17		0	
HODGE, Jim O.	Perth	23.10.26	York C.(AM)	Newport Co.	08.46	1946	1		0	(LB)
HODGE, Martin	Southport	04.02.59	APP	Plymouth Arg.	02.77	1977-78	43	/	0	(G)
			TR	Everton	07.79	1979-80	25	/	0	
			L	Preston N.E.	12.81	1981	28	/	0	
			L	Oldham Ath.	07.82	1982	4	/	0	
			L	Gillingham	01.83	1982	4	/	0	
			L	Preston N.E.	02.82	1982	16	/	0	
			TR	Sheffield Wed.	08.83	1983	42	/	0	
HODGE, Robert	Exeter	30.04.54		Exeter C.	07.74	1974-78	120	8	18	(M)
			TR	Colchester U.	09.78	1978-80	87	5	14	
			TR	Torquay U.	08.81	1981	3	1	1	
HODGE, Steve B.	Nottingham	25.10.62	APP	Nottingham F.	10.80	1981-83	78	1	18	(F)E.U'21-6
HODGES, Cyril L.	Hackney	18.09.19		Arsenal	+	1946	2		0	(W)
			TR	Brighton & H.A.	10.46	1946	9		3	
HODGES, Glyn P.	Streatham	30.04.63	APP	Wimbledon	02.81	1980-83	129	14	32	(M)W.U'21-3
HODGES, Kevin	Bridport	12.06.60	APP	Plymouth Arg.	03.78	1978-83	224	8	36	(M)

Players Names	Birthplace	Date	Previous Club	League Club	Date Signed	Seasons Played	Career Record Apps Sub Gls		
HODGES, Len H.	Bristol	17.02.20	Soundwell	Bristol Rov.	08.46	1946–49	87		20 (IR)
			TR	Swansea C.	08.50	1950	2		0
			TR	Reading	08.51	1951–52	6		2
HODGETTS, Frank	Dudley	30.09.24	JNRS	W.B.A.	+	1946–48	67		11 (OL)
			TR	Millwall	08.49	1949–52	34		6
HODGKINS, Jeff	Portsmouth	08.10.42	JNRS	Portsmouth	06.60	1960	3		0 (F)
HODGKINSON, Alan	Sheffield	16.08.36	Worksop	Sheffield U.	08.53	1954–70	576		0 (G)E–5/E.U23–7/E.F.LGE REP.●
HODGKINSON, Derek	Margate	30.04.44	Margate	Manchester C.	08.61	1963	1		1 (F)
			TR	Stockport Co.	06.46	1964–65	46	/	9
HODGKINSON, Edwin	Ilkeston	27.11.20		Leeds U.	12.46	1946–47	3		0
			TR	Halifax T.	07.48	1948–49	12		2
HODGKISS, Robert	Farnworth	22.03.18	Walkden Heath	Southport	*				(FB)
			TR	Everton	08.46				
			TR	Southport	07.47	1947–48	21		0
HODGKISSON, Ken	W.Bromwich	12.03.33	JNRS	W.B.A.	04.50	1952–55	21		4 (IF)
				Walsall	01.56	1955–65	333	1	54
HODGSON, Brian G.	Cleethorpes	29.01.36	Askern WMC	Grimsby T.	09.56	1956	7		1 (F) Son of John V.
				Workington	10.59	1959	1		0
HODGSON, David J.	Gateshead	01.11.60	JNRS	Middlesbrough	08.78	1978-80	116	9	16 (F)E.U21-6
			TR	Liverpool	08.82	1982-83	21	7	4
HODGSON, Don	Liversedge	22.12.22	Bradford U.	Bradford P.A.	04.48	1948–51	41		7 (F)
			TR	York C.	08.52				
HODGSON, Gordon	Newcastle	13.10.52	JNRS	Newcastle U.	06.71	1971-73	8	1	0 (M)E.YTH.INT.
			TR	Mansfield T.	05.74	1974-78	184	/	23
			TR	Oxford U.	09.78	1978-79	66	1	3
			TR	Peterborough U.	08.80	1980-81	82	1	5
HODGSON, John P.	Dawdon	10.05.22	Murton CW	Leeds U.	+	1946–47	19		0 (G)
			TR	Middlesbrough	03.48	1947–54	13		0
HODGSON, John V.	Seaham	30.09.13	Seaham Col.	Grimsby T.	*	1946–47	34		0 (FB)d.1970
			TR	Doncaster Rov.	01.48	1947–51	96		2
HODGSON, Ken	Newcastle	19.01.42	JNRS	Newcastle U.	05.59	1960	6		0 (F)
			TR	Scunthorpe U.	12.61	1961–63	88		30
			TR	Bournemouth	06.64	1964–65	77	1	24
			TR	Colchester U.	07.66	1966–68	56	1	19
HODGSON, Laurie	Tranmere	19.01.17		Tranmere Rov.	*	1946–50	78		0 (FB)
HODGSON, Mike	Newcastle	06.07.45	Billingham	Hartlepool U.	AM	1964	1		0 (OR)
HODGSON, Noel	Workington	25.12.38	JNRS	Workington	08.57	1957–62	51		12 (F)
HODGSON, Ron	Birkenhead	02.11.22		Manchester C.	+	1946	1		0
			TR	Southport	06.47	1947–48	41		1
			TR	Crewe Alex.	02.49	1948–49	31		0
HODGSON, Sam	Dawdon	21.01.19	Seaham Col.	Grimsby T.	*	1946–47	23		0 Brother of John V.
			TR	Mansfield T.	07.48	1948	2		0
HODGSON, William	Glasgow	09.07.35	St. Johnstone	Sheffield U.	05.57	1957–63	152		32 (IF)
			TR	Leicester C.	09.63	1963–64	46		10
			TR	Derby Co.	06.65	1965–67	79	/	17
			TR	Rotherham U.	09.67	1967	9	/	0
			TR	York C.	12.67	1967–69	98	/	3
HODKINSON, Andy J.	Ashton-U-Lyne	04.11.65	Bolton W.(APP)	Oldham Ath.	08.83	1983	3	1	1 (F)
HODKINSON, David	Lancaster	18.01.45	APP	Oldham Ath.	02.63	1961	2		0 (OL)
HODSON, Simeon P.	Lincoln	05.03.66	APP	Notts Co.	03.84	1983	13	/	0 (D)
HODSON, Stuart	Peterborough	05.11.50	Chatteris T.	Peterborough U.	11.74	1974-76	24	10	0 (M)
HOGAN, Charles	Bury	23.04.26		Bury	06.48	1947	1		0 (OR)
			TR	Accrington St.	08.49	1949–50	56		4
			TR	Southport	08.51	1951	9		1
			TR	Rochdale	08.52	1952	3		0
HOGAN, Roy	Hartlepool	24.09.60	APP	Hartlepool U.	09.78	1977-83	150	10	17 (M)
HOGAN, Terry	W.Hartlepool	03.06.33		Hartlepool U.	08.57	1957	9		1
HOGAN, William J.	Salford	09.01.24		Manchester C.	+	1948	3		0 (OR)
			TR	Carlisle U.	09.49	1949–55	191		27
HOGARTH, Gordon	Sunderland	18.11.36	Throckley Welf.	Gateshead	08.58	1957–58	12		0
HOGG, A. Ray	Lowick	11.12.29	Berwick	Aston Villa	03.55	1954–56	21		0 (WH)
			TR	Mansfield T.	07.58	1958–59	11		0
			TR	Peterborough U.	08.60	1960	2		0
HOGG, Adam	Airdrie	26.04.34	Airdrie	Swindon T.	06.56	1956	1		0
HOGG, Derek	Stockton	04.11.30	Chorley	Leicester C.	10.52	1952–57	161		26 (OL)E.F.LGE REP.
			TR	W.B.A.	04.58	1958–60	81		11
			TR	Cardiff C.	10.60	1960–61	41		7
HOGG, Fred	B.Auckland	24.04.18		Mansfield T.	+	1946–47	50		9
			TR	Halifax T.	10.47	1947–49	49		3
HOGG, Graeme J.	Aberdeen	17.06.64	APP	Manchester U.	06.82	1983	16	/	1 (D)

Players Names	Birthplace	Date	Previous Club	League Club	Date Signed	Seasons Played	Apps	Sub	Gls	
HOGG, Graham S.	Neath	15.01.22	Cardiff Corries	Cardiff C.	06.48	1948	1		0	(F)W.AMAT.INT.
			TR	Scunthorpe U.	N/L					
HOGG, John	Blyth	07.10.31		Sunderland	12.49					(F)
				West Ham U.	11.53					
				Portsmouth	12.54					
			Blyth Spartans							
			Peterborough U.	Gateshead	07.57	1957–59	80		21	
HOGG, Matt	Wideopen	14.04.41		Newcastle U.	05.59					(HB)
			TR	Darlington	07.61	1961	1		0	
HOGGAN, David M.	Falkirk	10.08.61	APP	Bolton W.	08.79	1979-82	83	10	11	(F)
HOGGART, Dennis J.	Glasgow	02.01.39	Ferndale Ath.	Leeds U.	02.57					(W)
			TR	York C.	08.60	1960–63	45		11	
			TR	Stockport Co.	08.64	1964–65	30	/	6	
HOLAH, Eric T.	Hull	03.08.37		Hull C.	AM	1960	1		1	(CF)
			TR	Bradford C.	08.61	1961	4		2	
HOLBROOK, Ian	Warrington	24.11.55		Bolton W.	07.74					(G)
			TR	Stockport Co.	07.76	1976	37	/	0	
HOLBROOK, Steve	Richmond	16.09.52	APP	Hull C.	09.70	1970-71	2	1	0	(W)E.SCH.INT.
			TR	Darlington	06.72	1972-76	104	12	12	
HOLBUTT, Barry L.	Birmingham	11.02.43	JNRS	Aston Villa	10.60					(CF)
			Nuneaton	Walsall	03.65	1965	0	1	0	
HOLD, John D.	Southampton	28.03.48	APP	Bournemouth	11.64	1965–70	80	5	25	(CF)
			L	Crewe Alex.	01.69	1968	0	2	0	
			TR	Northampton T.	08.71	1971–72	42	2	11	
HOLD, Oscar	Barnsley	19.10.18	Barnsley(*)	Aldershot	*	1946	14		4	(IF)
			TR	Norwich C.	03.47	1946–48	44		18	
			TR	Notts. Co.	10.48	1948	19		9	
			TR	Everton	02.50	1949–50	22		5	
			TR	Q.P.R.	02.52	1951–52	4		1	
HOLDEN, Alan	Haslingden	12.10.41		Blackburn Rov.	01.62	1963	1		0	(HB)
			TR	Stockport Co.	07.66	1966	1	/	0	
HOLDEN, Andy I.	Flint	14.09.62	Rhyl	Chester C.	08.83	1983	44	/	7	(M)
HOLDEN, Doug A.	Manchester	28.09.30	JNRS	Bolton W.	01.50	1951–62	419		40	(OR)E–5/E.F.LGE REP./●
			TR	Preston N.E.	11.62	1962–64	89		13	E.YTH.INT.
HOLDEN, J. Stuart	Huddersfield	21.04.42	JNRS	Huddersfield T.	04.59	1960–64	28		2	(HB)
			TR	Oldham Ath.	07.65	1965–66	40	3	5	
			TR	Rochdale	01.67	1966	21	/	0	
HOLDEN, Mel G.	Dundee	25.08.54	APP	Preston N.E.	09.72	1972-74	69	3	22	(F)d.1981
			TR	Sunderland	05.75	1975-77	66	7	23	
			TR	Blackpool	07.78	1978	2	1	0	
HOLDEN, Robert	Sunderland	28.10.65	Sunderland (APP)	Scunthorpe U.	09.83	1983	6	1	1	(F)
HOLDEN, William	Bolton	01.04.28	Everton(AM)	Burnley	11.49	1950–55	187		75	(CF)E'B'–1/d.
			TR	Sunderland	12.55	1955	19		5	
			TR	Stockport Co.	10.56	1956–58	87		38	
			TR	Bury	03.59	1958–61	101		33	
			TR	Halifax T.	06.62	1962	37		11	
HOLDER, Alan M.	Oxford	10.12.31		Nottingham F.	04.52	1954	3		0	(F)
			TR	Lincoln C.	07.55	1955	1		0	
			TR	Tranmere Rov.	12.56	1956	13		1	
HOLDER, Colin W.	Cheltenham	06.01.44	APP	Coventry C.	05.61	1960–61	9		5	(F)
HOLDER, David J.	Cheltenham	15.12.43	Cardiff C.(AM)	Notts. Co.	10.62	1963	8		0	(CH)
			TR	Barrow	07.64	1964	29		0	
HOLDER, Phil	Kilburn	19.01.52	APP	Tottenham H.	02.69	1971-73	9	4	1	(M)E.YTH.INT.
			TR	Crystal Palace	02.75	1974-77	93	2	5	
			TR	Bournemouth	03.79	1978-79	58	/	4	
HOLDER, Steve W.	Nottingham	21.04.52	APP	Notts. Co.	04.70	1969	0	1	0	(OR)
HOLDING, Edward J.	Wolverhampton	15.10.30		Walsall	01.49	1950–53	39		6	(FB)
			TR	Derby Co.	07.52					
			TR	Barrow	07.54	1954	5		5	
			TR	Northampton T.	10.54					
HOLE, Alan V.	Swansea	26.12.30		Swansea C.	07.53	1953	20		0	(CH)
HOLE, Barry	Swansea	16.09.42	JNRS	Cardiff C.	09.59	1959–65	211	/	16	(WH)W–30/W.U23–5/●
			TR	Blackburn Rov.	07.66	1966–68	79	/	13	W.SCH.INT./Son of famous
			TR	Aston Villa	09.68	1968–69	47	/	6	pre–war player
			TR	Swansea C.	07.70	1970–71	78	/	3	Brother to Alan/Colin
HOLE, Colin D.	Swansea	01.09.32	JNRS	Swansea C.	03.50	1953	1		0	W.SCH.INT.
HOLLAND, David W.	Chorley	06.03.35	Horwich RMI	Stockport Co.	06.59	1959–60	25		4	(HB)
HOLLAND, Eric R.	Sutton–in–Ashfield	23.01.40	JNRS	Manchester U.	05.57					(FB)E.YTH.INT./E.SCH.INT.
			TR	Wrexham	03.60	1959–65	118	/	0	
			TR	Chester C.	03.66	1965–66	5	1	0	
HOLLAND, Ken A.	Bentley	18.04.22	Wolverhampton W.(AM)	Bury	+					
			TR	Bournemouth	09.48	1948	3		0	

Players Names	Birthplace	Date	Previous Club	League Club	Date Signed	Seasons Played	Apps	Sub	Gls	
HOLLAND, Pat	Poplar	13.09.50	APP	West Ham U.	04.69	1968-80	227	18	23	(M)
			L	Bournemouth	03.71	1970	10	/	0	
			TR	Orient	09.83					
HOLLETT, Ivan R.	Pinxton	22.04.40	Sutton T.	Mansfield T.	08.58	1958-64	99		40	(F)
			TR	Chesterfield	12.64	1964-68	157	/	65	
			TR	Crewe Alex.	11.68	1968-70	55	4	19	
			TR	Cambridge U.	11.70	1970-71	37	1	13	
			TR	Hereford U.	07.72	1972	11	/	2	
HOLLEY, Tom	Wolverhampton	15.11.13	Barnsley(*)	Leeds U.	*	1946-48	94		1	(CH)
HOLLIDAY, Edwin	Barnsley	07.06.39	JNRS	Middlesbrough	08.56	1957-61	134	17		(OL)E-3/E.U23-5/
			TR	Sheffield Wed.	03.62	1961-63	55		12	E.F.LGE REP.
			TR	Middlesbrough	06.65	1965	23	/	4	
			Hereford U.	Workington	02.68	1967-68	56	/	4	
			TR	Peterborough U.	07.69	1969	12	4	1	
HOLLIDAY, Ken J.	Darwen	19.08.25	Darwen	Blackburn Rov.	10.46	1947-51	29		0	(CH)
			TR	Accrington St.	07.62	1952-54	96		5	
			TR	Barrow	09.55	1955	5		0	
HOLLIFIELD, Mike	Middlesbrough	02.05.61	APP	Wolverhampton W.	04.79	1980-81	21	/	0	(D)
			TR	Hull C.	08.83	1983	33	/	1	
HOLLINS, David M.	Bangor	04.02.38	Merrow	Brighton & H.A.	11.55	1957-60	66		0	(G)W-11/W.U23-2/
			TR	Newcastle U.	03.61	1960-66	112	/	0	Brother of John
			TR	Mansfield T.	02.67	1966-69	109	/	0	
			L	Nottingham F.	03.70	1969	9	/	0	
			TR	Aldershot	07.70	1970	16	/	0	
HOLLINS, John W.	Guildford	16.07.46	APP	Chelsea	07.63	1963-74	436	/	47	(M)E-1/E.U23-12/
			TR	Q.P.R.	06.75	1975-78	148	3	5	E.F.LGE REP./E.YTH.INT./
			TR	Arsenal	07.79	1979-82	123	4	9	Brother of Dave●
			TR	Chelsea	06.83	1983	29	/	1	
HOLLINSHEAD, Shaun	Sandbach	21.02.61	APP	Crewe Alex.	APP	1977	2	3	0	(M)
HOLLIS, Harry	Shotton	12.12.13	Connahs Quay	Wrexham	08.46	1946	1		0	(FB)+Chester C.
HOLLIS, K. Mike	Loughborough	14.11.49	APP	Leicester C.	11.66					(W)
			TR	Barrow	07.69	1969-71	88	3	13	
			TR	Chester C.	07.72	1972	34	3	8	
			TR	Stockport Co.	07.73	1973-75	106	6	33	
			TR	Reading	03.76	1975-76	18	7	6	
HOLLIS, Roy W.	Yarmouth	24.12.25	Gt. Yarmouth	Norwich C.	05.47	1947-51	96		53	(CF)●
			TR	Tottenham H.	12.52	1952	3		1	
			TR	Southend U.	02.54	1953-59	240		122	
HOLLOW, Mick	Nazeing	05.09.43	B.Stortford	Orient	08.62	1963-64	34		0	(FB)
			TR	Peterborough U.	07.65	1965	14	/	1	
HOLLOWAY, Ian S.	Kingswood	12.03.63	APP	Bristol Rov.	03.81	1980-83	63	6	8	(M)
HOLLOWBREAD, John	Enfield	02.01.34	Enfield	Tottenham H.	01.52	1958-63	67		0	(G)
			TR	Southampton	05.64	1964-65	36	/	0	
HOLLYMAN, Ken C.	Cardiff	18.11.22	Cardiff Nom.	Cardiff C.	+	1946-53	188		8	(WH)
			TR	Newport Co.	11.53	1953-59	233		4	
HOLLYWOOD, Dennis	Govan	03.11.44	APP	Southampton	12.61	1962-71	233		4	(FB)S.U23-1
			TR	Blackpool	07.72					
HOLMAN, Harry W.	Exeter	25.05.20	Buddle Est.	Exeter C.	12.47	1946	5		2	(CF)d.1977
HOLMAN, Harry (Jnr)	Exeter	16.11.57	Chelsea (APP)	Exeter C.	07.76	1976-78	47	5	9	(F)E.SCH.INT.
			TR	Peterborough u.	12.78	1978	9	/	1	
HOLME, Phil C.	Briton Ferry	21.06.47	Bridgend Th.	Swansea C.	06.71	1970-71	18	4	4	(IF)
			TR	Hull C.	07.72	1972-73	29	9	11	
HOLMES, Albert	Ecclesfield	14.02.42	E.M.Gas Bd.	Chesterfield	06.61	1961-75	467	3	9	(FB)●
HOLMES, Barry	Bradford	04.10.42	Ossett A.	Halifax T.	09.69	1966-72	82	8	8	(IF)
HOLMES, Bert H.	Norwich	27.09.24	Gothic	Norwich C.	08.47	1948-54	58		1	(CH)
HOLMES, Colin	Winchester	28.03.39	JNRS	Southampton	02.57	1959	1		0	(HB)E.YTH.INT.
HOLMES, Ian	Wombwell	08.12.50	JNRS	Sheffield U.	01.68	1971-72	4	2	0	(M)
			TR	York C.	07.73	1973-77	152	7	30	
			TR	Huddersfield T.	10.77	1977-79	65	8	21	
HOLMES, James	Dublin	11.11.53	APP	Coventry C.	11.70	1971-76	122	6	7	(D)EI-30
			TR	Tottenham H.	03.77	1976-78	81	/	2	
			Vancouver	Leicester C.	10.82	1982	2	/	0	
			TR	Brentford	N/C	1982	4	/	0	
			TR	Torquay U.	N/C	1982-83	25	/	3	
			TR	Peterborough U.	11.83	1983	20	1	2	
HOLMES, Joseph	Clay Cross	10.02.26	Parkhouse Col.	Chesterfield	09.46	1947-51	26		3	(WH)
HOLMES, Kyle	Abergavenny	25.09.59	APP	Hereford H.	10.77	1977-79	25	3	3	(M)
HOLMES, Lee J.	Aveley	28.09.55	Harringey	Brentford	06.79	1979	26	2	6	(F)
HOLMES, Nick C.	Southampton	11.11.54	APP	Southampton	11.72	1973-83	375	6	53	(M)
HOLMES, Roger W.	Scunthorpe	09.09.42	JNRS	Lincoln C.	09.59	1959-71	276	2	37	(IF)
HOLMES, Stan	Easington	27.11.20		Hartlepool U.	07.47	1949	1		0	

Players Names	Birthplace	Date	Previous Club	League Club	Date Signed	Seasons Played	Apps	Sub	Gls	
HOLMES, Tom	Hemsworth	14.12.34		Barnsley	03.53	1954–58	35		7	(F)
			TR	Halifax T.	07.59	1959–60	50		15	
			TR	Chesterfield	07.61	1961	19		4	
HOLMES, William	Hunslet	29.10.26		Doncaster Rov.	AM	1950	2		0	(CF)E.AMAT.INT.
				Blackburn Rov.	AM	1951–52	21		16	
			TR	Bradford C.	09.53	1953	22		5	
			TR	Southport	07.54	1954–55	57		9	
HOLMES, William	Balham	04.02.51	Woking	Millwall	07.70	1970	0	1	0	(M)
			TR	Luton T.	07.73	1973	0	1	0	
			Barnet	Wimbledon	N/L	1977	15	/	5	
			TR	Hereford U.	11.77	1977-78	21	10	5	
			TR	Brentford	08.79	1979	8	7	2	
HOLSGROVE, John W.	Southwark	27.09.45	Tottenham H.(AM)	Crystal Palace	02.64	1964	18		2	(WH)E.YTH.INT.
			TR	Wolverhampton W.	05.65	1965–70	178	2	7	
			TR	Sheffield Wed.	06.71	1971–74	103	1	5	
			TR	Stockport Co.	08.75	1975	9	/	0	
HOLT, David	Durham	07.01.45	JNRS	Blackburn Rov.	04.63	1965–66	10	/	0	(HB)
HOLT, David	Padiham	26.02.52	APP	Bury	10.69	1969-74	174	4	9	(D)
			TR	Oldham Ath.	12.74	1974-79	141	1	1	
			TR	Burnley	07.80	1980-82	84	/	1	
HOLT, George	Halifax	28.02.27		Halifax T.	07.52	1947–53	57		11	(IF)
HOLT, Ray	Thorne	29.10.39		Huddersfield T.	08.58	1961–63	14		0	(HB)
			TR	Oldham Ath.	07.65	1965	14	1	0	
			TR	Halifax T.	07.66	1966–67	86	/	0	
			TR	Scunthorpe U.	07.68	1968–69	50	/	0	
HOLT, William K.	Boldon	31.03.26	Boldon C.W.	Blackburn Rov.	01.49	1948–52	78		0	(CH)
			Weymouth	Barrow	06.54	1954–56	72		0	
HOLTHAM, Dean M.	Pontypridd	30.09.63	APP	Cardiff C.	10.81					(D)
			TR	Swansea C.	08.82	1983	6	/	0	
HOLTON, Cliff	Oxford	29.04.29	Oxford C.	Arsenal	11.47	1950–58	198		82	(CF)●
			TR	Watford	10.58	1958–61	120		84	
			TR	Northampton T.	09.61	1961–62	62		50	
			TR	Crystal Palace	12.62	1962–64	101		40	
			TR	Watford	05.65	1965	24	/	12	
			TR	Charlton Ath.	02.66	1965	18	/	7	
			TR	Orient	07.66	1966–67	47	/	17	
HOLTON, Jim	Lesmahagow	11.04.51	JNRS	W.B.A.	04.68					(D)S-15/S.U23-1
			TR	Shrewsbury T.	06.71	1971-72	67	/	4	
			TR	Manchester U.	01.73	1972-74	63	/	5	
			TR	Sunderland	09.76	1976	15	/	0	
			TR	Coventry C.	03.77	1976-79	91	/	0	
			TR	Sheffield Wed.	08.81						
HOLTON, Pat	Hamilton	23.12.35	Motherwell	Chelsea	03.59	1958	1		0	(FB)
			TR	Southend U.	08.60	1960	11		0	
HOLYOAK, Philip	Sunderland	22.05.59	APP	Tottenham H.	05.77					(D)
			L	Scunthorpe U.	02.78	1977	1	/	0	
HONEYWOOD, Brian R.	Gt. Waltham	08.05.49	APP	Ipswich T.	05.67					(HB)
			TR	Colchester U.	06.68	1968	12	5	0	
HONOUR, Brian	Horden	16.02.64	APP	Darlington	08.82	1981-83	59	15	4	(M)
HONOUR, John	Horden	01.11.53	APP	W.B.A.	05.71					(M)
			TR	Hartlepool U.	07.72	1972-75	107	5	6	
			TR	Workington	03.76	1975-76	38	1	1	
HOOD, Derek	Washington	17.12.58	APP	W.B.A.	12.76					(M)
			TR	Hull C.	10.77	1977-79	20	4	0	
			TR	York C.	02.80	1979-83	183	1	20	
HOOD, George W.	Houghton–le–Spring	27.11.20		Gateshead	10.47	1947–48	30		0	
HOOD, Glyn	Pentwyn	12.03.25	Nuffield FC	W.B.A.	+	1946–49	69		0	(WH)
HOOD, Harry	Glasgow	3.10.44	Clyde	Sunderland	11.64	1964–66	31	/	9	(IF)S.U23-1
HOOD, Jack	Glasgow	08.01.38	Shettleston	Everton	10.56					(F)
			TR	Tranmere Rov.	12.59	1959	3		2	
HOOD, Mel	Reading	05.10.39	JNRS	Reading	10.56	1956–57	9		0	(F)
HOOD, Ron G.	Cowdenbeath	18.11.22	Hamilton A.	Aldershot	08.47	1947	14		6	(IF)
			TR	Rochdale	11.48	1948	9		1	
HOOKER, Alan	Exeter	23.06.56		Exeter C.	07.74	1974-76	46	4	0	(D)
HOOKER, Keith W.	Winchfield	31.01.50	APP	Brentford	02.68	1966-68	24	8	2	(WH)
HOOKS, Paul	Wallsend	30.05.59	APP	Notts. Co.	06.77	1976-82	144	29	30	(M)
			TR	Derby Co.	03.83	1982-83	25	/	3	
HOOKS, Vic. R.	Belfast	04.07.55	Manchester U.(APP)	Grimsby T.	10.72	1972	0	1	0	(IF)
HOOLEY, Joe W.	Barnsley	26.12.38	JNRS	Barnsley	04.56	1956	1		0	(F)
			TR	Sheffield U.	12.57						
			TR	Workington	06.58	1958	6		2	
			Holbeach U.	Bradford P.A.	11.59	1959–60	13		4	
			Bedford T.	Accrington St.	10.61						

Players Names	Birthplace	Date	Previous Club	League Club	Date Signed	Seasons Played	Career Record Apps	Sub	Gls	
HOOLICKIN, Gary J.	Middleton	29.10.57	APP	Oldham Ath.	07.75	1976-83	128	2	2	(D)
HOOLICKIN, Steve J.	Manchester	13.12.51	APP	Oldham Ath.	12.69	1969-72	8	/	0	(D) Brother of Gary
			TR	Bury	08.73	1973-76	140	/	5	
			TR	Carlisle U.	10.76	1976-80	143	/	2	
			TR	Hull C.	12.80	1980-81	31	/	0	
HOOPER, Harry (Snr)	Burnley	16.12.10	Nelson	Sheffield U.	*					(FB)d.1970
			TR	Hartlepool U.	07.47	1947–49	67		4	
HOOPER, Harry(Jnr)	Durham	14.06.33	Hylton Col.	West Ham U.	11.50	1950–55	119		39	(OR) E'B'–6/E.F.LGE REP./
			TR	Wolverhampton W.	03.56	1956	39		19	E.U23-2
			TR	Birmingham C.	12.57	1957–60	105		34	
			TR	Sunderland	09.60	1960–62	65		16	
HOOPER, Percy G.W.	Walthamstow	17.12.14	Islington Corries	Tottenham H.	*					(G)
			TR	Swansea C.	03.47	1946–47	12		0	
HOOPER, Peter J.	Teignmouth	02.02.33	Dawlish	Bristol Rov.	05.53	1953–61	295		102	(OL)E.F.LGE REP.
			TR	Cardiff C.	07.62	1962	40		22	
			TR	Bristol C.	07.63	1963–65	54	/	14	
HOOPER, Wynne	Port Talbot	05 06 52	APP	Newport Co.	08.70	1968-76	166	14	21	(M)
			TR	Swindon T.	12.76	1976	4	2	0	
			TR	Aldershot	07.77	1977-78	21	19	1	
HOPE, Alex J.H.	Inveresk	22 06 24	Morton	Swindon T.	06.54	1954	11		1	(OL)
HOPE, Eric	Oakengates	02.12.27		Manchester C.	+					(IF)
			TR	Shrewsbury T.	08.50	1950–51	27		3	
			TR	Wrexham	10.51	1951–53	36		9	
HOPE, George	Haltwhistle	04.04.54	APP	Newcastle U.	04.72	1973	6	/	1	(F)
			TR	Charlton Ath.	06.75	1975-76	13	/	2	
			TR	York C.	11.76	1976-77	34	8	8	
HOPE, James G.	E.Wemyss	04.10.19		Manchester C.	*	1946	7		0	(HB)
			Q. of South	New Brighton	08.47	1947–49	43		0	
HOPE, John W.M.	Shildon	30.03.49	APP	Darlington	05.67	1964–68	14	/	0	(G)
			TR	Newcastle U.	03.69	1968	1	/	0	
			TR	Sheffield U.	01.71	1970–73	63	/	0	
			TR	Hartlepool U.	07.75	1975	23	/	0	
HOPE, Robert	Bridge of Allan	28.09.43	JNRS	W.B.A.	09.60	1959-71	331	/	37	(M)S-2/S.U23-1/
			TR	Birmingham C.	06.72	1972-75	33	1	5	S.SCH.INT.
			TR	Sheffield Wed.	09.76	1976-77	39	3	7	
HOPGOOD, Ron	London	24.11.34	Spicers Ath.	Crystal Palace	05.57	1957–59	14		0	(G)
HOPKIN, Gareth G.	Swansea	12.04.23		Swansea C.	11.46	1947	2		0	(W)
HOPKINS, Brian	Derby	15.03.33	Keele Univ.	Port Vale	AM	1957	2		0	(OR)
HOPKINS, Idris	Merthyr Tydfil	11.10.07	Crystal Palace(*)	Brentford	*	1946	39		4	(OR)W–12/*Merthyr T./
			TR	Bristol C.	05.47	1947	24		1	Sheffield Wed./Dartford
HOPKINS, Jeff	Swansea	14.04.64	APP	Fulham	09.81	1980-83	104	6	1	(D)W-9/W.U'21-2
HOPKINS, Kelvin R.	Perivale	26.07.53	APP	Aldershot	07.71	1970–71	2	/	0	(G)
HOPKINS, Mel	Ystrad	07.11.34	JNRS	Tottenham H.	05.52	1952–63	219		0	(FB)W–34/W.U23–1●
			TR	Brighton & H.A.	10.64	1964–66	57	1	2	
			Ballymena	Bradford P.A.	01.69	1968–69	29	1	0	
HOPKINS, Ollie T.	Sth. Kirkby	15.11.35	Burtonwood	Barnsley	03.54	1957–60	50		10	(CH)
			TR	Peterborough U.	07.61	1961–64	104		0	
HOPKINS, Robert	Birmingham	25.10.61	APP	Aston Villa	07.79	1979-82	1	2	1	(M)
			TR	Birmingham C.	03.83	1982-83	43	/	7	
HOPKINSON, Alan	Chapeltown	15.04.53	APP	Barnsley	04.71	1970–73	24	3	5	(IF)
HOPKINSON, Eddie	Royton	29.10.35	JNRS	Oldham Ath.	AM	1951	3		0	(G)E–14/E.U23–6/●
			TR	Bolton W.	11.52	1956–69	519	/	0	E.F.LGE REP.
HOPKINSON, Gordon	Sheffield	19.06.33	Beighton	Doncaster Rov.	06.57	1957	10		0	(FB)
			TR	Bristol C.	07.58	1958–60	67		1	
HOPKINSON, Ian J.	Newcastle	19.10.50	Newcastle U.(APP)	Barrow	01.69	1968–70	17	5	1	(CF)
			TR	Workington	07.71	1971	13	6	7	
			TR	Darlington	12.72	1972	7	2	1	
HOPKINSON, Mick	Ambergate	24.02.42	JNRS	Derby Co.	07.59	1960–67	110	3	4	(WH)
			TR	Mansfield T.	07.68	1968–69	47	/	1	
			TR	Port Vale	07.70	1970	12	1	0	
HOPKINSON, Paul E.	Royton	17.01.58	Manchester C.(APP)	Stockport Co.	10.75	1975-76	39	/	0	(G) Son of Eddie
HOPKINSON, Stan	Piverton Park	15.03.22	Hemel H.T.	Watford	AM	1946	1		0	(G)
HOPPER, Alan	Newcastle	17.07.37		Newcastle U.	10.59					(FB)
			Sth. Shields	Barnsley	03.61	1961–64	135		4	
			TR	Bradford C.	07.65	1965	8	/	0	
HOPPER, William	B. Auckland	20.02.38	W. Auckland	Halifax T.	12.61	1961–62	35		9	(CF)
			TR	Workington	07.63	1963–64	46		14	
			TR	Darlington	07.65	1965	6	/	0	
HORE, K. John	St. Austell	10.02.47	APP	Plymouth Arg.	12.64	1964-75	393	5	17	(D)
			TR	Exeter C.	03.76	1975-79	193	/	0	
HORMANTSCHUK, Peter A.	Coventry	11.09.62	APP	Coventry C.	09.80	1981-83	18	6	1	(D)

Players Names	Birthplace	Date	Previous Club	League Club	Date Signed	Seasons Played	Apps	Sub	Gls	
HORN, Graham R.	Westminster	23.08.54	APP	Arsenal	04.72					(G)
			L	Portsmouth	06.72	1972	22	/	0	
			TR	Luton T.	02.73	1972-74	58	/	0	
			L	Brentford	11.75	1975	3	/	0	
			L. Angeles Aztecs	Charlton Ath.	12.76					
			Kettering	Southend U.	12.77	1977-78	9	/	0	
			TR	Aldershot	01.80	1979-81	9	/	0	
			TR	Torquay U.	08.82	1982-83	47	/	0	
HORN, Robert I.	Westminster	15.12.61	APP	Crystal Palace	04.79					(G)E.Yth.Int.
			TR	Barnsley	11.80	1981-83	67	/	0	
			L	Cambridge U.	11.83	1983	8	/	0	
HORN, William	Glasgow	13.05.38	Kilmarnock	Brentford	10.58	1958	1	/		(F)
HORNBY, Eric V.	Tranmere	31.03.23	JNRS	Tranmere Rov.	+	1947–48	32		0	
			TR	Crewe Alex.	08.49	1949–50	4		0	
HORNBY, Ron	Rochdale	13.04.14	Stalybridge	Burnley	*	1946–47	5		1	(OL)
HORNE, Alf.T.	Brixworth	06.09.26		Northampton T.	+	1948	1		0	(WH)
HORNE, Des T.	S. Africa	12.12.39	JNRS	Wolverhampton W.	12.56	1958–60	40		16	(OL)
			TR	Blackpool	03.61	1960–65	117	1	17	
HORNE, George	Glasgow	23.11.33	Maryhill J.	Carlisle U.	08.57	1957	4		2	(OL)
HORNE, John R.	Netherton	04.11.61	APP	Walsall	11.79	1979-81	10	6	1	(D)
HORNE, Ken W.	Burton	25.06.26	Wolverhampton W.(AM)	Blackpool	06.49					(FB)
			TR	Brentford	05.50	1950–59	223		1	
HORNE, Les H.	Netherton	02.05.23	Netherton W.	W.B.A.	04.48	1949–51	13		0	(CH)
			TR	Plymouth Arg.	07.52					
			TR	Walsall	11.52	1952–53	52		1	
HORNE, Stan F.	Clanfield	17.12.44	APP	Aston Villa	12.61	1963	6		0	(WH)
			TR	Manchester C.	09.65	1965–67	48	2	0	
			TR	Fulham	02.69	1968–72	73	6	0	
			TR	Chester C.	08.73	1973	17	1	0	
			TR	Rochdale	12.73	1973–74	48	/	5	
HORNER, William	Cassop	07.09.42	JNRS	Middlesbrough	09.59	1960–68	183	3	9	(WH)
			TR	Darlington	06.69	1969–74	211	7	5	
HORNSBY, Brian G.	Peterborough	10.09.54	APP	Arsenal	07.72	1972-75	23	3	5	(M)E.YTH.INT./
			TR	Shrewsbury T.	06.76	1976-77	75	/	16	E.SCH.INT.
			TR	Sheffield Wed.	03.78	1977-81	102	4	25	
			L	Chester C.	11.81	1981	4	/	0	
			Edmonton Drillers	Carlisle U.	08.82	1982-83	9	1	1	
			L	Chesterfield	12.83	1983	1	/	0	
HORNSBY, John	Ferryhill	03.08.45	Evenwood T.	Colchester U.	10.64	1965	11	/	1	(F)
HOROBIN, Roy	Brownhills	10.03.35	JNRS	W.B.A.	10.52	1955–57	54		6	(IF)
			TR	Notts. Co.	11.58	1958–61	123		37	
			TR	Peterborough U.	06.62	1962–63	80		20	
			TR	Crystal Palace	07.64	1964	4		0	
HORREY, Rowland G.	B. Auckland	09.03.43	Ferryhill Ath.	Blackburn Rov.	12.63	1964–65	3	/	0	(F)
			TR	York C.	07.66	1966–67	74	/	9	
			TR	Cambridge U.	N/L	1970–71	37	1	4	
HORRIDGE, Peter	Manchester	31.05.34		Manchester C.	11.52	1958	3		0	(FB)
			TR	Crewe Alex.	06.59					
HORRIGAN, Ken P.	Gravesend	07.12.19	Imp.Paper Mill	Carlisle U.	08.46	1946	16		1	(WH)
HORRIX, Dean V.	Taplow	21.11.61	APP	Millwall	04.79	1980-82	65	7	19	(F)
			TR	Gillingham	03.83	1982	7	7	0	
			TR	Reading	08.83	1983	43	/	8	
HORROBIN, Tom	Doncaster	08.08.43	JNRS	Sheffield Wed.	08.60	1962	3		0	(FB)
HORSBURGH, John	Edinburgh	17.11.36	Dundee	Oldham Ath.	08.61	1961	1		0	(G)
HORSFALL, George F.	Australia	19.09.24		Southampton	05.47	1946	2		0	
			TR	Southend U.	07.49	1949	1		0	
				Southampton	09.55	1955	2		0	
HORSFALL, Tom	Hamilton	07.01.51	Dover	Southend U.	11.72	1972-73	11	5	1	(F)
			L	Bury	11.73	1973	0	1	0	
			L	Scunthorpe U.	11.73	1973	5	/	2	
			TR	Cambridge U.	12.74	1974-76	79	4	28	
			TR	Halifax T.	07.77	1977	15	1	3	
HORSFIELD, Arthur	Newcastle	05.07.46	APP	Middlesbrough	07.63	1963-68	107	4	51	(F)E.YTH.INT.
			TR	Newcastle U.	01.69	1968	7	2	3	
			TR	Swindon T.	06.69	1969-71	107	1	41	
			TR	Charlton Ath.	06.72	1972-75	139	/	53	
			TR	Watford	09.75	1975-76	78	/	16	
HORSFIELD, Alec.	Selby	04.08.21	Selby T.	Arsenal	11.46					(IF)
			TR	Bradford P.A.	12.50	1950	4		2	
HORSMAN, Les	Burnley	26.05.20	Guiseley	Bradford P.A.	+	1946–52	239		18	(CH)
			TR	Halifax T.	08.53	1953–56	120		8	
HORSTEAD, Barry	Brigg	08.05.35	JNRS	Scunthorpe U.	05.56	1956–67	319	2	3	(FB)

Players Names	Birthplace	Date	Previous Club	League Club	Date Signed	Seasons Played	Apps	Sub	Gls	
HORSWILL Mick	Annfield Plain	06.03.53	APP	Sunderland	03.70	1971-73	68	1	3	(M)
			TR	Manchester C.	03.74	1973-74	11	3	0	
			TR	Plymouth Arg.	06.75	1975-77	98	4	3	
			TR	Hull C.	07.78	1978-81	82	2	6	
			TR	Carlisle U.	08.83	1983	1	/	0	
HORTON, Brian	Hednesford	04.02.49	Hednesford	Port Vale	07.70	1970-75	232	4	33	(M)●
			TR	Brighton & H.A.	02.76	1975-80	217	1	33	
			TR	Luton T.	08.81	1981-83	118	/	8	
HORTON, Henry	Malvern	18.04.23	Worcester C.	Blackburn Rov.	01.47	1946-50	92		5	(WH)Worc/Hants Cricketer
			TR	Southampton	06.51	1951-53	75		11	
			TR	Bradford P.A.	05.54	1954	27		0	
HORTON, Ken J.	Preston	26.08.22	JNRS	Preston N.E.	+	1946-52	166		36	(IF)
			TR	Hull C.	10.52	1952-54	76		15	
			TR	Barrow	08.55	1955	22		4	
HORTON, Len				Walsall	06.47	1946	1		0	
HORTON, Les	Salford	12.07.21	Rochdale(+)	Oldham Ath.	+	1946-47	79		2	(HB)
			TR	Carlisle U.	08.48	1948-49	66		0	
			TR	Rochdale	04.50					
			TR	York. C.	07.50	1950	21		0	
			TR	Halifax T.	03.51	1950-51	34		1	
HORTON, William	Aldershot	27.08.42	JNRS	Aldershot	11.61	1962-64	9		2	(F)
HOSIE, Jim	Aberdeen	03.04.40	Aberdeen	Barnsley	07.62	1962	37		0	(F)
HOSKER, Robert C.	Harrogate	27.02.55	APP	Middlesbrough	03.72					(M)
				York C.	03.74	1975-76	16	9	1	
HOSKIN, Mike A.	Accrington	27.03.68	JNRS	Chesterfield	N/C	1983	0	1	0	
HOSKINS, John F.	Southampton	10.05.31	Winchester	Southampton	07.52	1952-58	221		64	(OL)
			TR	Swindon T.	07.59	1959	10		3	
HOTTE, Tim A.	Bradford	04.10.63	Arsenal (APP)	Huddersfield T.	09.81	1981-82	14	2	4	(F)
HOUCHEN, Keith M.	Middlesbrough	25.07.60	Chesterfield (N/C)	Hartlepool U.	02.78	1977-80	162	10	65	(F)
			TR	Orient	03.82	1981-83	74	2	20	
			TR	York C.	03.84	1983	1	6	1	
HOUGH, David J.	Crewe	20.02.66	APP	Swansea C.	02.84	1983	1	1	0	
HOUGH, Fred	Stoke	23.12.35		Port Vale	06.55	1957	4		0	(F)
HOUGH, Harry	Chapeltown	26.09.24	Thorncliffe W.	Barnsley	09.47	1947-58	345		0	(G)
			TR	Bradford P.A.	06.59	1959-60	57		0	
HOUGH, John	Halifax	09.06.54	Irish Dems.	Halifax T.	N/C	1979	1	/	0	(G)
HOUGH, Tom	Preston	17.01.22	JNRS	Preston N.E.	+					(IF)
			TR	Barrow	10.46	1946	3		0	
HOUGHTON, Frank C.	Preston	15.02.26	Ballymena	Newcastle U.	12.47	1947-50	54		10	(WH)
			TR	Exeter C.	08.54	1954-56	28		11	
HOUGHTON, H. Brian	India	01.09.36	St. Wrefords Y.C.	Bradford P.A.	10.55	1955-57	28		7	(IF)
			TR	Birmingham C.	10.57	1957-58	4		1	
			TR	Southend U.	10.58	1958-60	67		32	
			TR	Oxford U.	N/L	1962-63	53		16	
			TR	Lincoln C.	10.63	1963-64	54		22	
HOUGHTON, Ken	Rotherham	18.10.39	Silverwood Col.	Rotherham U.	05.60	1960-64	148		56	(IF)
			TR	Hull C.	01.65	1964-72	253	11	79	
			TR	Scunthorpe U.	06.73	1973	33	/	5	
HOUGHTON, Keith	Backworth	10.03.54	Blyth Spartans	Carlisle U.	01.80	1979-82	82	5	2	(M)
			TR	Lincoln C.	08.83	1983	26	/	0	
HOUGHTON, Peter	Liverpool	30.11.54	Sth. Liverpool	Wigan Ath.	N/L	1978-83	169	16	62	(F)
			TR	Preston N.E.	10.83	1983	30	2	10	
HOUGHTON, Ray J.	Glasgow	09.01.62		West Ham U.	07.79	1981	0	1	0	(M)
			TR	Fulham	07.82	1982-83	82	/	8	
HOUGHTON, W. Eric	Billingborough	29.06.10	Billingboro. T.	Aston Villa	*	1946	4		0	(OL)E-7/E.F.LGE REP./
			TR	Notts. Co.	12.46	1946-48	51		7	Warwicks Cricketer
HOUGHTON, William	Hemsworth	20.02.39	JNRS	Barnsley	08.57	1957-63	206		10	(WH)E.YTH.INT.●
			TR	Watford	07.64	1964-65	48	/	2	
			TR	Ipswich T.	06.66	1966-68	107	/	3	
			TR	Leicester C.	07.69	1969	6	1	0	
			TR	Rotherham U.	01.70	1969-73	139	/	1	
HOULAHAN, Harry	Coundon	14.02.30	Durham C.	Newcastle U.	02.51					(IL)
			TR	Oldham Ath.	05.52	1952-53	6		2	
			TR	Darlington	01.54	1953-54	23		8	
HOULT, Alan J.	Burbage	07.10.57	JNRS	Leicester C.	09.75					(F)E.SCH.INT.
			L	Hull C.	01.78	1977	3	/	1	
			L	Lincoln C.	03.78	1977	2	2	1	
			TR	Bristol Rov.	07.78					
HOUNSLEA, William	Liverpool	15.08.26		New Brighton	12.47	1947	16		0	
			TR	Chester C.	08.48	1948	1		0	
HOUSAM, Arthur	Sunderland	01.10.17		Sunderland	*	1946-47	35		0	(OL)d.1975
HOUSDEN, Dennis	London	15.03.53	APP	Gillingham	08.71	1971-72	12	4	1	(CF)

Players Names	Birthplace	Date	Previous Club	League Club	Date Signed	Seasons Played	Career Record Apps	Sub	Gls	
HOUSEMAN, Peter	Battersea	24.12.45	APP	Chelsea	12.62	1963-74	252	17	20	(M)d.1977
			TR	Oxford U.	05.75	1975-76	65	/	2	
HOUSLEY, Stewart	Doncaster	15.09.48	APP	Grimsby T.	07.66	1966-68	34	/	3	(F)
HOUSTON, David	Glasgow	07.07.48	JNRS	Cardiff C.	07.65	1965-66	17	1	0	(HB)
			TR	Crystal Palace	01.67					
HOUSTON, Graham R.	Gibraltar	24.02.60	JNRS	Preston N.E.	03.78	1979-83	64	33	6	(F)
HOUSTON, Joe	Wilshaw	27.12.26	Dunfermline	Aldershot	07.51	1951-52	46		0	(G)
HOUSTON, Stewart M.	Dunoon	20.08.49	Port Glasgow	Chelsea	08.67	1967-69	6	3	0	(D)S-1/S.U23-2
			TR	Brentford	03.72	1971-73	77	/	9	
			TR	Manchester U.	12.73	1973-79	204	1	13	
			TR	Sheffield U.	07.80	1980-82	93	1	1	
			TR	Colchester U.	08.83	1983	42	/	4	
HOW, Trevor A.	Amersham	08.08.57	APP	Watford	03.75	1974-79	90	1	2	(D) Son of former Speedway Star Ronnie How
HOWARD, Barry P.	Ashton	19.02.50	Runcorn	Stockport Co.	02.78	1977	12	1	1	(F)
HOWARD, David F.	Hartlepool	03.06.62	JNRS	Newcastle U.	07.79					(F)
			TR	Hartlepool U.	07.81	1980-81	6	3	4	
HOWARD, Frank H.	S. Africa	30.01.31	Guildford C.	Brighton & H.A.	05.50	1950-58	198		26	(OL)
HOWARD, Pat	Dodworth	07.10.47	JNRS	Barnsley	10.65	1965-71	177	1	6	(D)
			TR	Newcastle U.	09.71	1971-76	182	2	7	
			TR	Arsenal	09.76	1976	15	1	0	
			TR	Birmingham C.	08.77	1977-78	40	/	0	
			TR	Bury	07.79	1979-81	117	1	5	
HOWARD, Richard	Birkenhead	10.06.43		Chester C.	09.65	1965	1	/	0	(G)
HOWARD, Stan	Chorley	01.07.34	Chorley	Huddersfield T.	07.52	1957-59	62		13	(W)
			TR	Bradford C.	06.60	1960	18		6	
			TR	Barrow	01.61	1960-63	86		22	
			TR	Halifax T.	07.64	1964	21		1	
HOWARD, Trevor E.	Kings Lynn	02.06.49	APP	Norwich C.	07.67	1967-73	81	43	13	(M)
			TR	Bournemouth	08.74	1974-75	86	/	11	
			TR	Cambridge U.	07.76	1976-78	105	/	5	
HOWARTH, Frank	Ammanford	19.11.64	APP	Exeter C.	11.82	1981-83	10	8	0	(D)
HOWARTH, Jack	Crook	27.02.45	Stanley U.	Chelsea	10.63					(F)
			TR	Swindon T.	10.64	1964	2		0	
			TR	Aldershot	07.65	1965-71	258	1	113	
			TR	Rochdale	01.72	1971-72	40	/	12	
			TR	Aldershot	11.72	1972-76	163	/	58	
			TR	Bournemouth	01.77	1976-77	39	3	6	
			TR	Southport	N/C	1977	9	/	1	
HOWARTH, Syd	Newport	28.06.23	Merthyr Tydfil	Aston Villa	06.48	1948-49	8		2	(CF)Son of Tommy
			TR	Swansea C.	09.50	1950-51	39		7	(pre-war)
			TR	Walsall	09.52	1952	6		0	
HOWAT, Ian S.	Wrexham	29.07.58	APP	Chester C.	07.76	1976-81	48	9	10	(F)
			TR	Crewe Alex.	02.82	1981	16	1	1	
HOWCROFT, Brian	Farnworth	20.06.38	JNRS	Bury	09.56	1957-58	20		0	(FB)
HOWDON, Steve	Prudhoe	01.02.22	Newcastle U.(+)	Gateshead	+	1946	2		1	(F)+Hexham Hearts
HOWE, Albert R.	Charlton	16.11.38	Faversham	Crystal Palace	12.58	1958-66	192	1	0	(WH)
			TR	Orient	01.67	1966-68	91	/	0	
			TR	Colchester U.	07.69	1969	29	/	1	
HOWE, Anthony V.	Colchester	14.02.39	Colchester Cas.	Colchester U.	03.63	1960	10		2	(OL)
			Haverhill	Southend U.	07.64	1964	2		0	
HOWE, Dennis C.	London	14.09.28		West Ham U.	05.49					(CH)
			TR	Darlington	08.51	1951-53	89		1	
			TR	Southend U.	08.54	1954-57	101		0	
			TR	Aldershot	07.58	1958	33		0	
HOWE, Don	Outwood	26.11.17	Whitehall Print	Bolton W.	*	1946-51	186		17	(WH)
HOWE, Don	Wolverhampton	12.10.35	JNRS	W.B.A.	11.52	1955-63	342		17	(FB)E-23/E.U23-6/
			TR	Arsenal	04.64	1964-66	70	/	1	E'B'-1/E.F.LGE REP.
HOWE, Ernie	Chiswick	15.02.53	Hounslow	Fulham	10.73	1973-77	68	2	10	(D)
			TR	Q.P.R.	12.77	1977-81	89	/	3	
			TR	Portsmouth	08.82	1982-83	35	/	4	
HOWE, Fred	Bredbury	24.09.12	Grimsby T.(*)	Oldham Ath.	07.46	1946	30		21	(OL)*Wilmslow/Stockport/ Co./Liverpool/Manchester C.
HOWE, George	Wakefield	10.01.24	Carlton U.	Huddersfield T.	+	1946-53	40		0	(FB)
			TR	York C.	06.54	1954-60	308		0	
HOWE, Herbert	Rugby	01.04.16	Leicester Nomads	Leicester C.	*	1946	27		0	
			TR	Notts. Co.	07.47	1947-48	52		0	
HOWE, Jack R.	W. Hartlepool	07.10.15	Hartlepool U.(*)	Derby Co.	*	1946-49	122		2	(FB)
			TR	Huddersfield T.	10.49	1949-50	29		1	E-13
HOWE, Robert J.	Chadwell Heath	22.12.45	APP	West Ham U.	01.63	1966-71	68	7	4	(WH)
			TR	Bournemouth	01.72	1971-73	100	/	6	

Players Names	Birthplace	Date	Previous Club	League Club	Date Signed	Seasons Played	Apps	Sub	Gls	
HOWELL, Graham F.	Manchester	18.02.51	APP	Manchester C.	10.68					(FB)
			TR	Bradford C.	06.71	1971–72	45	/	0	
			TR	Brighton & H.A.	08.72	1972–73	40	4	0	
			TR	Cambridge U.	07.74	1974–75	68	3	3	
HOWELL, Reg W.	Wolverhampton	12.08.38		Plymouth Arg.	11.56	1956	1		0	(G)
			TR	Aston Villa	02.58					
HOWELL, Ron R.	Tottenham	22.05.49	APP	Millwall	03.67	1966–69	7	7	0	(WH)
			TR	Cambridge U.	09.70	1970	10	2	1	
			Kettering	Swindon T.	07.72	1972	22	3	1	
			TR	Brighton & H.A.	07.73	1973	26	1	9	
HOWELLS, Jeff D.	Shoreham	26.09.40	Fulham(AM)	Millwall	10.57	1958–60	56		3	(F)
HOWELLS, Peter	Middlesbrough	23.09.32		Sheffield Wed.	10.53	1954–55	3		1	(W)
			TR	Hartlepool U.	11.56	1956	1		0	
HOWELLS, Ray G.	Rhondda	27.06.26		Crystal Palace	06.47	1946–49	26		5	(F)
			TR	Exeter C.	07.51	1951–52	14		3	
HOWELLS, Roger W.	Swansea	18.09.31	Llanelli	Swansea C.	03.50					(FB)
			TR	Darlington	02.53	1952–53	2		0	
			TR	Swansea C.	07.54					
HOWELLS, Ron	Rhondda	03.08.35	Nuneaton	Wolverhampton W.	11.52	1955–57	9		0	(WH)
			TR	Portsmouth	03.59	1958–60	64		2	
			TR	Scunthorpe U.	06.61	1961–62	69		4	
			TR	Walsall	07.63	1963	13		0	
HOWELLS, Ron G.	Swansea	12.01.27		Swansea C.	04.48	1947	9		0	(G)W–2
			Barry T.	Cardiff C.	07.50	1951–56	154		0	
			Worcester C.	Chester C.	09.58	1958–59	80		0	
HOWELLS, William	Grimsby	20.03.43	JNRS	Grimsby T.	10.61	1963	6		0	(HB)
HOWEY, Peter	Kinsley	23.01.58	APP	Huddersfield T.	01.76	1976-78	20	2	3	(F)
			TR	Leeds	07.79					
			TR	Newport Co.	11.79					
HOWFIELD, Robert M.	Manchester	03.12.36	Bushey U.	Watford	09.57	1957–58	47		9	(OL)
			TR	Crewe Alex.	07.59	1959	5		0	
			TR	Aldershot	10.59	1959–61	76		44	
			TR	Watford	07.62	1962–63	45		13	
			TR	Fulham	11.63	1963–64	26		9	
			TR	Aldershot	08.65	1965–66	33	1	10	
HOWITT, Dave J.	Birmingham	04.08.52	APP	Birmingham C.	03.71	1972	2	/	0	(D)
			TR	Bury	08.73	1973	11	9	4	
			TR	Workington	07.74	1974	30	5	1	
			TR	Aldershot	06.75	1975–79	126	11	2	
HOWITT, Robert	Glasgow	15.07.29	Partick Th.	Sheffield U.	07.55	1955–57	88		30	(IF)S.F.LGE REP.
			TR	Stoke C.	04.58	1958–62	133		14	
HOWLETT, Gary P.	Dublin	02.04.63	Home Farm	Coventry C.	11.80					(M)EI.YTH.INT.
			TR	Brighton & H.A.	08.82	1982-83	24	2	1	
HOWLETT, Robert	Basildon	12.12.48	APP	Chelsea	12.65					(FB)
			TR	Southend U.	09.67	1967–68	4	2	0	
			TR	Colchester U.	07.69	1969	10	6	0	
HOWSAM, Alf D.	Sheffield	21.10.22		Sheffield Wed.	+					
			TR	Chesterfield	03.47	1946–47	12		4	
			TR	Halifax T.	06.48	1948	19		4	
HOWSHALL, Gerry T.	Stoke	27.10.44	APP	W.B.A.	05.62	1963–67	43	2	3	(WH)
			TR	Norwich C.	11.67	1967–70	36	3	0	
HOY, Robert	Halifax	10.01.50	APP	Huddersfield T.	11.67	1966-74	140	4	20	(M)
			TR	Blackburn Rov.	03.75	1974-75	13	6	0	
			TR	Halifax T.	06.76	1976	30	/	7	
			TR	York C.	08.77	1977	10	4	1	
			TR	Rochdale	12.77	1977-80	61	5	12	
HOY, Roger E.	London	06.12.46		Tottenham H.	05.64	1965–67	10	/	0	(HB)
			TR	Crystal Palace	09.68	1968–69	53	/	6	
			TR	Luton T.	06.70	1970	32	/	0	
			TR	Cardiff C.	08.71	1971–72	14	2	0	
HOYLAND, Jamie W.	Sheffield	23.01.66	APP	Manchester C.	11.83	1983	1	/	0	(M)
HOYLAND, Tom	Sheffield	14.06.32	JNRS	Sheffield U.	10.49	1949–60	181		18	(IF)
			TR	Bradford C.	10.61	1961–62	27		6	
HOYLE, Herbert	Baildon	22.04.20		Wolverhampton W.	05.46					(G)
			TR	Exeter C.	08.46	1946–49	82		0	
			TR	Bristol Rov.	05.50	1950–52	105		0	
HUBBARD, John	Wath	24.03.25		Notts. Co.	+	1946	18		2	(WH)
			Scarborough	Scunthorpe U.	08.50	1950–59	359		12	
HUBBARD, John G.	S. Africa	16.12.30	Glasgow Rgrs.	Bury	04.59	1959–61	109		29	(IF)S.F.LGE REP.
HUBBARD, Phil J.	Lincoln	25.01.49	APP	Lincoln C.	07.66	1965-71	150	1	41	(M)
			TR	Norwich	12.71	1971-72	6	4	1	
			TR	Grimsby T.	10.72	1972-75	144	2	37	
			TR	Lincoln C.	08.76	1976-79	100	9	11	
HUBBARD, Terry J.	Sebastapol	06.11.50	APP	Swindon T.	11.68	1970-75	81	1	3	(IF)W.U23–2/W.SCH.INT.

Players Names	Birthplace	Date	Previous Club	League Club	Date Signed	Seasons Played	Career Record Apps	Sub	Gls	
HUBBICK, David	South Shields	16.03.60	APP	Ipswich T.	01.78					(F)
			TR	Wimbledon	09.80	1980-81	22	4	6	
			Dagenham	Colchester U.	N/C	1983	3	7	0	
HUBBICK, Henry	Jarrow	12.11.10	Burnley(*)	Bolton W.	*	1946	34		0	(FB)*Blyth Spartans
			TR	Port Vale	10.47	1947–48	50		1	
			TR	Rochdale	01.49	1948–50	90		0	
HUCKER, Peter I.	London	28.10.59	APP	Q.P.R.	07.77	1980-83	107	/	0	(G)E.U'21-2
HUDD, Dave	Bristol	09.07.44	JNRS	Bristol Rov.	07.63	1964	5		1	(F)
HUDDART, Dave	Maryport	18.11.37		Aldershot	06.61					(G)
			TR	Gillingham	07.62	1962–64	10		0	
HUDDLESTONE, Edward	Nottingham	29.09.35	Blackpool(AM)	Nottingham F.	12.56	1956	1		0	
HUDGELL, Arthur J.	Hackney	28.12.20	Eton Manor	Crystal Palace	*	1946	25		1	(FB)
			TR	Sunderland	01.47	1946–56	260		0	
HUDSON, Alan A.	London	21.06.51	APP	Chelsea	06.68	1968-73	144	1	10	(M)E.U23-10/E-2
			TR	Stoke C.	01.74	1973-76	105	/	9	
			TR	Arsenal	12.76	1976-77	36	/	0	
			Seattle Sounders	Chelsea	08.83					
			TR	Stoke C.	01.84	1983	16	/	0	
HUDSON, Albert G.	Swansea	17.06.20	Caerau	Fulham	*	1946	1		0	(IL)W.SCH.INT.
HUDSON, C. John	Middleton	25.11.64	Manchester C. (JNRS)	Oldham Ath.	09.82	1982-83	16	4	0	(D)
HUDSON, Charles A.	Bytham	03.04.20	Guiseley	Accrington St.	AM	1946	11		4	(CF)
HUDSON, Chris B.	Rotherham	13.03.51	APP	Rotherham U.	03.68	1968–71	53	9	1	(FB)
HUDSON, Colin A.R.	Undy	05.10.35	Undy U.	Newport Co.	04.54	1953–56	81		21	(OR)
			TR	Cardiff C.	07.57	1957–60	61		9	
			TR	Brighton & H.A.	06.61	1961	1		0	
			TR	Newport Co.	02.62	1962	30		2	
HUDSON, Gary	W. Auckland	01.11.55		Preston N.E.	AM	1973	1		0	(G)
HUDSON, Gary P.	Bradford	25.02.51	JNRS	Bradford P.A.	07.68	1967–69	38	1	0	(FB)
HUDSON, Geoff A.	Leeds	14.10.31		Bradford P.A.	12.49	1950–56	94		0	(FB)
			TR	Bradford C.	02.57	1956–58	34		0	
			TR	Halifax T.	08.59	1959–60	52		0	
			TR	Exeter C.	07.61	1961	41		0	
			TR	Crewe Alex.	07.62	1962	1		0	
			TR	Gillingham	07.63	1963–64	81		1	
			TR	Lincoln C.	05.65	1965	33	/	0	
			TR	Rotherham U.	06.66					
HUDSON, George A.	Manchester	14.03.37		Blackburn Rov.	01.58	1958	4		1	(CF)●
			TR	Accrington St.	07.60	1960	44		35	
			TR	Peterborough U.	10.61	1961–62	65		39	
			TR	Coventry C.	04.63	1962–65	113	/	63	
			TR	Northampton T.	03.66	1965–66	18	/	6	
			TR	Tranmere Rov.	01.67	1966–68	53	1	20	
HUDSON, George W.	Havant	26.10.23		Portsmouth	+	1947	1		0	(CH)
			TR	Swindon T.	09.48	1948–59	402		11	
HUDSON, John	Blaydon	05.10.21	W.Stanley	Chesterfield	10.46	1946–51	169		31	(OR)
			TR	Shrewsbury T.	09.53	1953–54	48		20	
HUDSON, Maurice	Barnsley	12.09.30	JNRS	Barnsley	01.49	1950–53	35		0	(FB)
			TR	Bradford C.	07.55	1955	4		0	
HUDSON, Ray J.	Slough	21.11.37	JNRS	Reading	11.54	1955–58	10		0	(FB)
HUDSON, Ray W.	Gateshead	24.03.55	APP	Newcastle U.	03.73	1973-77	16	4	1	(M)
HUDSON, Stan R.	Fulham	10.02.23		Q.P.R.	09.48	1948–49	23		8	(F) d.1951
HUDSON, William A.	Swansea	10.03.28	Pembroke Bor.	Leeds U.	05.51	1951	4		0	(OR)W.AMAT.INT.
			TR	Sheffield U.	05.52	1953	1		0	
			TR	Mansfield T.	05.54	1954	8		1	
HUFFER, Phil	Bedworth	23.01.32	Bedworth T.	Derby Co.	10.53					
			TR	Northampton T.	05.54	1954	1		0	
HUGGINS, Joe E.	India	24.02.30	Alton T.	Aldershot	12.55	1955	6		5	(IF)
HUGHES, Alan	Wallasey	05.10.48		Liverpool	09.66					(F)
			L	Chester C.	11.67	1967	9	/	2	
HUGHES, Alan L.	Swansea	11.03.51	APP	Swansea C.	04.69	1968	2	/	0	(FB)
HUGHES, Arthur	Lothian	23.11.27	Ashfield J.	Notts. Co.	07.49					(WH)
			TR	Nottingham F.	05.51					
			Canterbury	Grimsby T.	06.54	1954	25		11	
			TR	Gillingham	07.55	1955	12		1	
HUGHES, B. Wayne	Port Talbot	08.03.58	APP	W.B.A.	03.76	1976-77	3	3	2	(M)W.U21-3/W.SCH.INT.
			Tulsa R.	Cardiff C.	10.79	1979-81	42	4	1	
HUGHES, Brian	Swansea	22.11.37	JNRS	Swansea C.	07.56	1958–68	231		6	(WH)W.U23–2/W.SCH.INT.
HUGHES, Brian D.	Ludgershall	20.08.62	APP	Swindon T.	07.80	1980-82	77	3	5	(M)
			TR	Torquay U.	08.83	1983	33	5	6	
HUGHES, Charles	Manchester	17.09.27	JNRS	Manchester U.	09.46					(F)
			TR	Leeds U.	09.50	1950–51	23		1	

Players Names	Birthplace	Date	Previous Club	League Club	Date Signed	Seasons Played	Apps	Sub	Gls	
HUGHES, Charles J.	Blackpool	07.09.39		Wrexham	10.58	1959–60	35		0	(G)
HUGHES, Darren J.	Prescot	06.10.65	APP	Everton	10.83	1983	1	/	0	(D)
HUGHES, David J.	Liverpool	23.09.51		Wrexham	AM	1970	1	/	0	(OR)
HUGHES, David J.	Connah's Quay	27.04.43	JNRS	Wrexham	05.61	1961	1		0	(F)
			TR	Tranmere Rov.	07.62	1962	2		0	
HUGHES, David R.	Blackburn	07.09.48	JNRS	Preston N.E.	09.65	1966-71	22	9	0	(F)
			TR	Southport	07.72	1972	40	/	1	
			TR	Bury	08.73	1973	12	/	3	
			TR	Southport	11.73	1973-76	109	4	4	
			TR	Crewe Alex.	N/C	1978	12	1	0	
HUGHES, David T.	Birmingham	19.03.58	APP	Aston Villa	02.76	1976	3	1	1	(D)
			TR	Lincoln C.	04.77	1977-80	61	1	1	
			TR	Scunthorpe U.	06.81	1981	17	4	0	
			TR	Lincoln C.	03.82					
HUGHES, Dennis	Stoke	09.04.31	JNRS	Stoke C.	09.48	1950	1		0	(F)
HUGHES, Emlyn	Barrow	28.08.47	JNRS	Blackpool	09.64	1965-66	27	1	0	(D)E-62/E.U23-8/●
			TR	Liverpool	03.67	1966-78	474	/	35	E.F.LGE REP.
			TR	Wolverhampton W.	08.79	1979-80	56	2	2	
			TR	Rotherham U.	09.81	1981-82	55	1	6	
			TR	Hull C.	03.83	1982	9	/	0	
			Mansfield T. (N/C)	Swansea C.	09.83	1983	7	/	0	
HUGHES, Glyn	Wrexham	29.11.31		Sheffield Wed.	01.51					(F)
			TR	Wrexham	08.52	1952–54	92		20	
			TR	Newport Co.	07.55	1955	4		0	
HUGHES, Gordon	Washington	19.06.36	Tow Law	Newcastle U.	08.56	1956–62	133		18	(W)
			TR	Derby Co.	08.63	1963–67	184	/	23	
			TR	Lincoln C.	03.68	1967–70	117	/	8	
HUGHES, Harry A.	Thurcroft	12.08.37		Rotherham U.	06.59	1959	1		0	(FB)
HUGHES, Harry J.	Nuneaton	08.10.29	Symington	Southport	08.50					(CH)
			TR	Chelsea	02.51	1951	1		0	
			TR	Bournemouth	06.52	1952–57	77		2	
			TR	Gillingham	07.58	1958–62	202		14	
HUGHES, Ian J.	Sunderland	24.08.61	APP	Sunderland	08.79	1979	1	/	0	(M)
			TR	Barnsley	08.81					
HUGHES, Iowerth	Llanddulas	26.05.25	Llandudno	Luton T.	04.49	1949–50	36		0	(G)W–4/W.AMAT.INT.
			TR	Cardiff C.	08.51	1951	26		0	
			TR	Newport Co.	08.53	1953–57	106		0	
HUGHES, James A.	Leeds	28.08.18		Fulham	09.46	1946	1		0	
HUGHES, John	Coatbridge	03.04.43	Glasgow Celtic	Crystal Palace	10.71	1971–72	20	/	4	(CF)S–8/S.U23–4/S.F.LGE REP.
			TR	Sunderland	01.73	1972	1	/	0	
HUGHES, John	W. Bromwich	13.09.29	Golden Lion FC	Walsall	05.50	1950–52	44		10	(IF)
HUGHES, John G.	Prestatyn	18.02.42	Rhyl	Chester C.	07.62	1962	2		0	(CF)
HUGHES, John I.	Bangor	04.05.51	JNRS	Blackpool	07.69	1969–70	5	3	0	(W)
			L	Southport	03.71	1970	7	1	1	
			Altrincham	Stockport Co.	01.76	1975	11	1	3	
HUGHES, John M.	Manchester	29.11.62		Bury	11.80	1981-82	1	1	0	(D)
HUGHES, John N.	Tamworth	10.07.21		Birmingham C.	06.47	1947–48	7		0	
HUGHES, L. Mark	Wrexham	01.11.63	APP	Manchester U.	11.80	1983	7	4	4	(F)W.SCH.INT./W.U'21-3/ W-2
HUGHES, Laurie	Liverpool	02.03.24	Tranmere Rov.(AM)	Liverpool	+	1946–57	303		1	(CH)E–3/E'B'–1
HUGHES, Lyndon J.	Smethwick	16.09.50	APP	W.B.A.	01.68	1968-74	89	9	3	(M)E.YTH.INT./ E.SCH.INT.
			TR	Peterborough U.	07.75	1975-77	75	2	5	
HUGHES, Mark	Port Talbot	03.02.62	APP	Bristol Rov.	02.80	1979-83	73	1	3	(D) Brother of Wayne/ W.YTH.INT.
			L	Torquay U.	12.82	1982	9	/	1	
HUGHES, Mark C.	Swindon	17.07.67	APP	Swindon T.	APP	1983	0	1	0	
HUGHES, Michael R.	Swansea	19.08.64	APP	Swansea C.	08.82	1983	21	/	0	(G)
HUGHES, Mike	Llanidloes	03.09.40	JNRS	Cardiff C.	12.58	1958	1		0	(WH)
			TR	Exeter C.	07.61	1961–62	36		0	
			TR	Chesterfield	07.63	1963–68	209	2	8	
HUGHES, Pat J.	Coatbridge	28.02.45	St. Mirren	Darlington	08.65	1965	3	/	0	(OL)
HUGHES, Philip A.	Belfast	19.11.64	Manchester U. (APP)	Leeds U.	01.83	1983	2	/	0	(G)
HUGHES, Richard M.	Barrow	27.12.50	JNRS	Barrow	AM	1971	0	2	0	(IF)
HUGHES, Robert	Cefn Mawr	17.03.46	Oswestry T.	Wrexham	02.66	1965	9	/	3	(F)
			TR	Bradford P.A.	07.67	1967	13	/	0	
HUGHES, Ron	Mold	01.07.30	Mold U.	Chester C.	09.50	1951–61	399		21	(WH)
HUGHES, Ron H.	Workington	17.08.55	R.N.A.D.	Workington	12.75	1975	15	/	0	(G)
HUGHES, Roy	Manchester	13.08.49	APP	Bury	09.66	1967–71	45	3	1	(WH)
HUGHES, Steve J.	Warrington	04.01.58	Manchester C.(APP)	Crewe Alex.	N/C	1975	0	2	0	(F)

Players Names	Birthplace	Date	Previous Club	League Club	Date Signed	Seasons Played	Apps	Sub	Gls	
HUGHES, Steve J.	Folkestone	29.07.60	JNRS	Gillingham	07.77	1975-80	110	16	8	(M)
			TR	Crystal Palace	07.81	1981	3	4	0	
			TR	Wimbledon	N/C	1981	2	/	0	
HUGHES, T. Gwyn	Blaenau	07.05.22	Blaenau	Northampton T.	+	1946-55	224		15	(IF)
HUGHES, Terry P.	Llanidloes	10.3.53	APP	Shrewsbury T.	03.71	1970-73	62	5	21	(F)
HUGHES, Tommy	Dalmuir	11.07.47	Clydebank	Chelsea	07.65	1966-69	11	/	0	(G)S.U23-2
			TR	Aston Villa	06.71	1971	16	/	0	
			L	Brighton & H.A.	02.73	1972	3	/	0	
			TR	Hereford U.	08.73	1973-81	240	/	0	
HUGHES, Walter C.J.	Liverpool	15.03.34		Liverpool	10.54					(F)
			TR	Stockport Co.	07.55					
			Winsford U.	Sheffield U.	01.56	1955	2		0	
			Wisbech	Bradford P.A.	04.57	1956-57	20		0	
			TR	Southport	02.58	1957	11		0	
HUGHES, William	Glasgow	03.03.29	Newcastle U.(AM)	York C.	05.51	1951-61	349		55	(OR)
HUGHES, William	Ballymena	09.05.29	Larne	Bolton W.	08.48	1948-52	47		2	(OR)NI-1
			TR	Bournemouth	06.53	1953	16		1	
HUGHES, William	Coatbridge	30.12.48	JNRS	Sunderland	02.66	1966-76	266	23	74	(F)S-1/Brother of John
			TR	Derby Co.	08.77	1977	17	2	8	
			TR	Leicester C.	12.77	1977-78	36	1	5	
			L	Carlisle U.	09.79	1979	5	/	0	
HUGHES, William A.	Colwyn Bay	02.02.19	Huddersfield T.(+)	Tottenham H.	+	1946-47	2		0	(G)+Newry T./
			TR	Blackburn Rov.	10.48	1948-49	27		0	W-5
			TR	Rochdale	09.50	1950	9		0	
			TR	Crystal Palace	02.51	1950-51	18		0	
HUGHES, William H.	Cardiff	02.10.20		Hartlepool U.	05.46	1946-49	123		2	W.SCH.INT.
HUGHES, William M.	Llanelli	06.03.18	Watchers Celtic	Birmingham C.	*	1946	28		0	(FB)W-10/d.1981
			TR	Luton T.	07.47	1947	31		0	
			TR	Chelsea	03.48	1947-50	93		0	
HUGHTON, Chris W.G.	Forest Gate	11.12.58	JNRS	Tottenham H.	06.77	1979-83	182	/	10	(D)EI-19/EI.U21-1/ Brother of Henry
HUGHTON, Henry T.	Stratford	18.11.59	APP	Orient	12.76	1978-81	104	7	2	(D)
			TR	Crystal Palace	07.82	1982-83	75	/	1	
HUGO, Roger V.	Woking	06.09.42	JNRS	West Ham U.	10.60	1963	3		2	(F)
			TR	Watford	05.65	1965	24	1	5	
HUKIN, Arthur	Sheffield	22.10.37	JNRS	Sheffield Wed.	10.54	1954	6		3	(F) d.1983
HULL, Gary	Sheffield	21.06.56	APP	Sheffield Wed.	06.74	1975	6	2	0	(FB)
HULL, Jeff	Rochford	25.08.60	APP	Southend U.	08.78	1978-80	10	5	1	(M)
			Basildon U	Colchester U.	07.83	1982-83	60	/	5	
HULLETT, William A.	Liverpool	19.11.15	Plymouth Arg.(*)	Manchester U.	*					(CF)*New Brighton/d.1982
			Merthyr Tydfil	Cardiff C.	02.48	1947-48	27		15	
			TR	Nottingham F.	11.48	1948	14		2	
HULLIGAN, Mick J.	Liverpool	28.02.23		Liverpool	+					(OR)
			TR	Port Vale	07.48	1948-54	197		22	
HULME, Eric	Houghton-le-Spring	14.01.49	Spennymoor	Nottingham F.	03.70	1971	5	/	0	(G)
			TR	Lincoln C.	09.72	1972-73	23	/	0	
HULME, John	Mobberley	06.02.45	JNRS	Bolton W.	02.62	1962-71	186	2	7	(CH)
			L	Notts. Co.	03.72	1971	8	/	0	
			TR	Reading	07.72	1972-73	86	1	0	
			TR	Bury	07.74	1974-75	86	/	5	
HULMES, Gary	Manchester	28.02.57		Rochdale	12.74	1974-75	4	6	1	(F)
HULSE, Robert	Crewe	05.11.48	Nantwich T.	Stoke C.	04.67	1967	2	/	0	(F)E.YTH.INT.
HULSE, Robert J.	Low Fell	05.01.57	Stade Quimperoise	Darlington	N/C	1983	3	1	0	(M)
HUMBLE, Doug	Weardale	16.02.20	B. Auckland	Sunderland	+					(CF)
			TR	Southport	06.47	1947	11		4	
HUMBLE, J. Wilf	Ashington	10.05.36	Ashington	Mansfield T.	05.59	1959-65	198	/	1	(FB)
HUME, Robert	Kirkintilloch	18.03.41	Glasgow Rgrs.	Middlesbrough	09.62	1962	19		5	(OL)
HUME, William	Armadale	18.12.35	Dunfermline	Birmingham C.	02.58	1958-59	10		1	(F)
HUMES, Jim	Carlisle	06.08.42	JNRS	Preston N.E.	09.59	1959-61	18		1	(W)
			TR	Bristol Rov.	06.62	1962	2		0	
			TR	Chester C.	07.63	1963-66	125	/	31	
			TR	Barnsley	07.67	1967	7	/	1	
HUMPHREY, John	Paddington	31.01.61	APP	Wolverhampton W.	02.79	1979-83	107	/	3	(D)
HUMPHREY, Tommy	Durham	27.10.37		Aldershot	07.59	1958-60	22		3	(F)
HUMPHREYS, Alan	Chester	18.10.39	JNRS	Shrewsbury T.	10.56	1956-59	32		0	(G)
			TR	Leeds U.	02.60	1959-61	40		0	
			TR	Mansfield T.	01.64	1964-67	60	/	0	
			TR	Chesterfield	07.68	1968-69	51	/	0	
HUMPHREYS, Derek J.B.	Belfast	05.10.49	JNRS	Arsenal	10.66					(G)
			Crusaders	Sunderland	11.67					
			L	Hartlepool U.	10.69	1969	4	/	0	

Players Names	Birthplace	Date	Previous Club	League Club	Date Signed	Seasons Played	Apps	Sub	Gls	
HUMPHREYS, Gerry	Llandudno	14.01.46	APP	Everton	09.63	1965-69	12	/	2	(F)W.U.23-5/W.SCH.INT.
			TR	Crystal Palace	06.70	1970	4	7	0	Son of John V.
			TR	Crewe Alex.	01.72	1971-76	184	9	30	
HUMPHREYS, John S.	Farnworth	18.07.64	APP	Oldham Ath.	07.82	1982-83	7	6	0	(F)
			L	Rochdale	03.84	1983	6	/	0	
HUMPHREYS, John V.	Llandudno	13.01.20	Llandudno	Everton	+	1946–50	53		0	(CH)W–1/d.
HUMPHREYS, Percy R.	Bradford	28.10.24	Boothtown	Halifax T.	+	1946	3		1	(OR)
HUMPHREYS, Ron H.	Tonypandy	04.04.25	Snowdown Col.	Southend U.	+	1946	3		0	(FB)
HUMPHRIES, Charles	Birmingham	19.03.22	Paget Rgrs.	Walsall	09.46	1947	6		0	(FB)
HUMPHRIES, Dave W.	Wolverhampton	10.08.39		Shrewsbury T.	03.60	1960	3		0	(HB)
HUMPHRIES, Glenn	Hull	11.08.64	APP	Doncaster Rov.	08.82	1980-83	94	5	7	(D)E.YTH.INT.
HUMPHRIES, Robert	Hindhead	04.07.33		Sheffield U.	12.55					(HB)
			TR	Brighton & H.A.	11.56	1956	10		2	
			TR	Millwall	08.57	1957–59	48		4	
HUMPHRIES, Steve R.	Hull	29.05.61	APP	Leicester C.	09.78					(G)
			TR	Doncaster Rov.	06.81	1981	13	/	0	
			TR	Cardiff C.	08.82	1982	1	/	0	
			TR	Wrexham	09.82	1982	2	/	0	
			TR	Oldham Ath.	10.82					
			TR	Leicester C.	01.83					
HUMPHRIES, William	Belfast	08.06.36	Ards	Leeds U.	09.58	1958–59	25		2	(OR)NI–14
			Ards	Coventry C.	04.62	1961–64	109		25	
			TR	Swansea C.	03.65	1964–67	141	/	22	
HUMPSTON, Ron	Derby	14.12.23		Portsmouth	+	1947–50	9		0	(G)
			TR	Huddersfield T.	11.51	1951	5		0	
HUNT–BROWN, Peter	Halifax	19.02.37	Elland U.	Halifax T.	AM	1958	1		0	(CF)
HUNT, David	Leicester	17.04.59	APP	Derby Co.	05.77	1977	5	/	0	(M)
			TR	Notts. Co.	03.78	1977-83	230	5	15	
HUNT, Dennis P.	Portsmouth	08.09.37		Gillingham	09.58	1958–67	319	2	6	(FB)Brother of Ralph
			TR	Brentford	06.68	1968	12	/	0	
HUNT, Doug A.	Salisbury	19.05.14	Sheffield Wed.(*)	Orient	+	1946–47	61		16	(CF) *Northfleet/ Tottenham H./Barnsley
HUNT, Roger P. (Ernie)	Swindon	17.03.43	JNRS	Swindon T.	03.60	1959–65	214	/	81	(IF)E.U23-3●
			TR	Wolveshampton W.	09.65	1965–67	74	/	32	
			TR	Everton	09.67	1967	12	2	3	
			TR	Coventry C.	03.68	1967–73	140	4	45	
			L	Doncaster Rov.	01.73	1972	9	/	1	
			TR	Bristol C.	12.73	1973–74	9	3	2	
HUNT, George H.	Bethnal Green	05.03.17	Regent St. Cong.	Barnsley	*					
			TR	Watford	06.46	1947–49	35		0	
HUNT, George R.	Swindon	27.02.22		Swindon T.	01.47	1948–57	305		0	(FB)
HUNT, George S.	Barnsley	22.02.10	Arsenal(*)	Bolton W.	*	1946	3		0	(CF)E–3/*Chesterfield/
			TR	Sheffield Wed.	11.46	1946–47	32		8	Tottenham H.
HUNT, Morgan M.	Bridgend	05.03.31	Askern Welf	Doncaster Rov.	02.52	1953–57	50		2	(HB)
			TR	Norwich C.	07.58	1958	8		0	
			TR	Port Vale	08.59	1959	2		0	
HUNT, Paul L.	Hereford	07.03.59	Coventry C.(APP)	Hereford U.	06.78	1978-80	41	10	4	(D)
HUNT, Peter J.	London	02.07.52	APP	Southend U.	09.69	1968-71	49	8	1	(M)E.YTH.INT.
			TR	Charlton Ath.	12.72	1972-76	138	20	6	
			TR	Gillingham	08.77	1977	23	/	0	
HUNT, Ralph A.	Portsmouth	14.08.33	JNRS	Portsmouth	08.50	1952–53	5		0	(CF)d.1964●
			TR	Bournemouth	02.54	1953–54	33		7	
			TR	Norwich C.	07.55	1955–57	124		67	
			TR	Derby Co.	08.58	1958	24		10	
			TR	Grimsby T.	08.59	1959–60	53		39	
			TR	Swindon T.	07.61	1961	21		15	
			TR	Port Vale	12.61	1961	14		6	
			TR	Newport Co.	07.62	1962–63	83		37	
			TR	Chesterfield	07.64	1964	17		5	
HUNT, Robert	Liverpool	04.09.34		Wrexham	07.56					(HB)
			TR	Chester C.	05.58	1958–60	83		3	
HUNT, Robert R.	Colchester	01.10.42	JNRS	Colchester U.	11.59	1959–63	148		80	(CF)Brother of Ron M./
			TR	Northampton T.	03.64	1963–65	40		10	William E.
			TR	Millwall	09.66	1966–67	43	/	13	
			TR	Ipswich T.	11.67	1967–70	16	8	4	
			TR	Charlton Ath.	09.70	1970–72	34	2	11	
			L	Northampton T.	11.72	1972	5	/	3	
			TR	Reading	01.73	1972–73	15	1	3	
HUNT, Roger	Golborne	20.07.38	Stockton Heath	Liverpool	05.59	1959–69	401	2	245	(IF)E–34/E.F.LGE REP.●
			TR	Bolton W.	12.69	1969–71	72	4	24	
HUNT, Ron G.	Paddington	19.12.45	APP	Q.P.R.	03.63	1964–72	214	5	1	(HB)
HUNT, Ron M.	Colchester	26.09.33	JNRS	Colchester U.	10.51	1951–63	177		3	(WH)
HUNT, Simon	Chester	17.11.62	JNRS	Wrexham	08.81	1981-83	102	6	18	(M)

Players Names	Birthplace	Date	Previous Club	League Club	Date Signed	Seasons Played	Apps	Sub	Gls	
HUNT, Steve	Birmingham	04.08.56	APP	Aston Villa	01.74	1974-76	4	3	1	(F)E-2
			N. York Cosmos	Coventry C.	08.78	1978-83	178	7	26	
			TR	W.B.A.	03.84	1983	12	/	2	
HUNT, William E.	Colchester	25.11.34	JNRS	Colchester U.	08.53	1953	1		0	(WH)
HUNT, William S.	Halesowen	19.11.34	JNRS	Aston Villa	01.52	1952	1		0	(FB)
HUNTER, Alan	Sion Mills	30.06.46	Coleraine	Oldham Ath.	01.67	1966-68	83	/	1	(D)NI-53/NI.U23-1/
			TR	Blackburn Rov.	06.69	1969-71	84	/	1	NI.AMAT.INT.
			TR	Ipswich T.	09.71	1971-80	280	/	8	
			TR	Colchester U.	05.82	1981-82	18	1	0	
HUNTER, Chris P.	Hong Kong	18.01.64	APP	Preston N.E.	09.81	1982	0	1	0	(F)
HUNTER, Don	Thorne	10.03.27	JNRS	Huddersfield T.	+	1948-50	26		1	(WH)
			TR	Halifax T.	08.51	1951	11		0	
			TR	Southport	08.52	1952-56	174		1	
HUNTER, Eddie	Tillicoultry	07.03.28	Falkirk	Accrington St.	08.54	1954-58	169		4	(WH)
HUNTER, Geoff	Hull	27.10.59	APP	Manchester U.	11.76					(M)
			TR	Crewe Alex.	08.79	1979-80	86	1	8	
			TR	Port Vale	08.81	1981-83	127	2	8	
HUNTER, George I.	Troon	29.08.30	Glasgow Celtic	Derby Co.	06.54	1954	19		0	(G)
			TR	Exeter C.	08.55	1955-58	147		0	
			Yiewsley	Darlington	06.61	1961	20		0	
			Burton A.	Lincoln C.	09.65	1965	1	/	0	
HUNTER, Gordon G.	Lyneham	08.11.54	Shrewsbury T.(AM)	York C.	07.73	1973-77	70	7	1	(D)
HUNTER, John D.	Backworth	20.09.34		Gateshead	08.54	1955	4		0	(G)
HUNTER, John S.	Lanark	26.05.34	Coltness U.	Rotherham U.	06.56	1956	5		1	(F)
			TR	Carlisle U.	07.57	1957	1		0	
			Kings Lynn	Barrow	07.59	1959-60	24		0	
HUNTER, Les	Middlesbrough	15.01.58	APP	Chesterfield	08.75	1975-81	156	9	8	(D)
			TR	Scunthorpe U.	07.82	1982-83	61	/	7	
			TR	Chesterfield	01.84	1983	21	/	2	
HUNTER, Mick	Hexham	27.05.48		Blackpool	01.66					(F)
			TR	Darlington	07.67	1967	2	1	0	
HUNTER, Norman	Middlesbrough	29.10.43	JNRS	Leeds U.	04.61	1962-76	541	/	18	(D)E-28/E.U23-3/●
			TR	Bristol C.	10.76	1976-78	108	/	4	
			TR	Barnsley	06.79	1979-82	28	3	0	
HUNTER, Philip	Hartlepool	28.09.50	JNRS	Hartlepool U.	AM	1969	1	/	0	(OR)
HUNTER, Reg J.	Colwyn Bay	25.10.38	Colwyn Bay	Manchester U.	11.56	1958	1		0	(F)
			TR	Wrexham	02.60	1959-61	34		3	
HUNTER, Robert	Gateshead	25.03.51		Hartlepool U.	02.71	1970	1	/	0	(W)
HUNTER, Robert R.	Lanark	12.03.31	Motherwell	Swindon T.	08.54	1954	16		3	(F)
HUNTER, William	Cambuslang	07.04.42	Glasgow Rgrs.	Bradford P.A.	07.64	1964	14		0	(IF)
HUNTLEY, Keith S.M.	Swansea	12.02.31		Swansea C.	08.51	1950	2		0	(OL)W.AMAT.INT.
HUNTLEY, Richard	Sunderland	05.01.49		Sunderland	08.67	1968	1	/	0	(HB)
HURFORD, Dave G.	Bristol	17.01.45	APP	Bristol Rov.	01.63	1962-64	6		0	(F)
HURLEY, Charlie	Cork	04.10.36	JNRS	Millwall	10.53	1953-57	105		2	(CH)EI-40●
			TR	Sunderland	09.57	1957-68	356	1	23	
			TR	Bolton W.	06.69	1969-70	41	1	3	
HURLEY, Chris	Cork	20.11.43	Rainham T.	Millwall	03.64	1963-64	4		2	(HB)Brother of Charlie
HURLEY, William H.	Leytonstone	11.12.59	APP	Orient	01.77	1976	1	1	0	(F)E.SCH.INT.
HURLOCK, Terry A.	Hackney	22.09.58	Leytonstone	Brentford	08.80	1980-83	153	/	13	(M)
HURRELL, William P.	Dundee	28.01.20	Raith Rov.	Millwall	+	1946-52	123		32	(CF)
			TR	Q.P.R.	07.53	1953	6		1	
HURRELL, William T.	Newcastle	15.09.55	APP	Northampton T.	APP	1972	5	/	0	(CH)
HURST, Charles	Denton	25.01.19	Bristol Rov.(*)	Oldham Ath.	+					(IF) Father of Geoff
			TR	Rochdale	06.46	1946	4		1	
HURST, Geoff C.	Ashton	08.12.41	JNRS	West Ham U.	04.59	1959-71	410	1	180	(CF)E-49/E.U23-4/●
			TR	Stoke C.	08.72	1972-74	103	5	30	E.F.LGE REP./E.YTH.INT./
			TR	W.B.A.	08.75	1975	10	/	2	Essex Cricketer
HURST, Gordon	Oldham	09.10.24	Oldham Ath.(AM)	Charlton Ath.	05.46	1946-57	369		75	(W)E.F.LGE REP.
HURST, John	Laver Bridge	27.10.14	Laver Br.FC	Bolton W.	*	1946	3		0	(CH)
			TR	Oldham Ath.	02.47	1946-50	98		2	
HURST, John W.	Blackpool	06.02.47	APP	Everton	10.64	1965-75	336	13	29	(D)E.U23-9/E.SCH.INT.●
			TR	Oldham Ath.	06.76	1976-80	169	1	2	
HURST, William R.	Brierfield	04.03.21	Burnley(*)	Plymouth Arg.	+	1946	4		0	
			Nelson	Bury	09.47	1947	1		0	
			TR	Accrington St.	10.48	1948	1		0	
HUSBAND, Jim	Newcastle	15.10.47	APP	Everton	10.64	1964-73	158	7	44	(F)E.U23-5/E.YTH.INT./
			TR	Luton T.	11.73	1973-77	138	5	44	E.SCH.INT.
HUSSEY, Malcolm F.	Darfield	11.09.33	JNRS	Rotherham U.	04.52	1952-55	24		0	(HB)
			TR	Scunthorpe U.	08.56	1956-57	23		0	
			TR	Rochdale	03.59	1958	1		0	

Players Names	Birthplace	Date	Previous Club	League Club	Date Signed	Seasons Played	Apps	Sub	Gls	
HUTCHINGS, Chris	Winchester	05.07.57	Harrow Bor.	Chelsea	07.80	1980-83	83	4	3	(D)
			TR	Brighton & H.A.	11.83	1983	26	/	1	
HUTCHINS, Dennis	Axminster	01.12.24	Axminster.	Exeter C.	04.47	1946–51	83		13	(OR)
HUTCHINS, Don	Middlesbrough	08.05.48	Stockton	Leicester C.	02.66	1967-68	4	/	0	(F)
			TR	Plymouth Arg.	07.69	1969-71	94	2	23	
			TR	Blackburn Rov.	07.72	1972-73	38	3	6	
			TR	Bradford C.	06.74	1974-80	252	4	44	
HUTCHINSON, Colin	Durham	20.10.36	JNRS	Stoke C.	11.53	1954-57	9		0	(IF)
HUTCHINSON, David N.	Grimsby	25.09.41		Crystal Palace	07.60					(CF)
			Brigg T.	Scunthorpe U.	07.71	1971	5	4	0	
HUTCHINSON, Doug	Gateshead	03.05.22	Stirling A.	Gateshead	08.46	1946	3		0	(CF)
HUTCHINSON, George H.	Castleford	31.10.29	JNRS	Huddersfield T.	01.47	1947	1		0	(F)
			TR	Sheffield U.	03.48	1948-52	73		10	
			TR	Tottenham H.	06.53	1953	5		1	
			TR	Leeds U.	08.55	1955	11		5	
			TR	Halifax T.	07.56	1956-57	44		12	
HUTCHINSON, Ian	Derby	04.08.48	Cambridge U.	Chelsea	07.68	1968-75	112	7	43	(CF)E.U23–2
HUTCHINSON, J.Barry	Sheffield	27.01.36	Bolton W.(AM)	Chesterfield	04.53	1954-59	155		15	(IF)
			TR	Derby Co.	07.60	1960-63	107		51	
			Weymouth	Lincoln C.	07.65	1965	24	/	18	
			TR	Darlington	02.66	1965-66	24	2	14	
			TR	Halifax T.	11.66	1966	25	/	14	
			TR	Rochdale	07.67	1967	27	/	3	
HUTCHINSON, Jim A.	Sheffield	28.12.15		Sheffield U.	*					(F)
			TR	Bournemouth	06.46	1946	8		3	
			TR	Lincoln C.	11.46	1946-48	85		54	
			TR	Oldham Ath.	02.49	1948-49	14		3	
HUTCHINSON, John	Codnor	01.06.21		Nottingham F.	+	1946-58	241		0	(FB)
HUTCHINSON, Keith	Sth. Shields	07.09.20		Darlington	05.46	1946-48	31		0	
HUTCHINSON, Paul	Eaglescliffe	20.02.53	JNRS	Darlington	09.71	1971-72	8	2	0	(FB)
HUTCHINSON, Robert	Glasgow	19.06.53	Hibernian	Wigan Ath.	07.80	1980	34	1	3	(F)
			TR	Tranmere Rov.	08.81	1981-82	32	3	6	
			TR	Mansfield T.	10.82	1982	10	/	3	
			TR	Tranmere Rov.	01.84	1983	21	/	4	
HUTCHINSON, Robert	Bolton	09.05.55	Radcliffe	Rochdale	12.74	1974	2	/	1	(CF)
HUTCHISON, Tom	Cardenden	22.09.47	Alloa	Blackpool	02.68	1967-72	163	2	10	(M)S-17●
			TR	Coventry C.	10.72	1972-80	312	2	24	
			TR	Manchester C.	10.80	1980-81	44	2	4	
			Hong Kong	Burnley	08.83	1983	46	/	4	
HUTT, Geoff	Hazelwood	28.09.49	APP	Huddersfield T.	09.67	1968-75	245	/	4	(D)
			L	Blackburn Rov.	09.75	1975	10	/	1	
			Haarlem	York C.	02.77	1976-77	63	/	1	
			TR	Halifax T.	04.78	1978-79	75	1	0	
HUTTON, Alec	Edinburgh	10.10.41		Southend U.	08.63	1964	1		0	(FB)
HUTTON, Jack	Bellshill	23.04.44	Hamilton Ac.	Scunthorpe U.	06.63	1963-65	53	1	7	(F)
HUTTON, Joe	Dundee	18.11.27	Albion Rov.	Reading	10.50	1949-50	8		0	(IF)
			Ayr U.	Stoke C.	12.53	1953-56	34		7	
			TR	Gillingham	08.57	1957	37		6	
			TR	Millwall	08.58	1958-59	24		9	
HUTTON, Tom O.	Gateshead	10.09.22		Accrington St.	+	1946	18		0	
			TR	Carlisle U.	08.47	1947-48	44		0	
			TR	Rochdale	08.49					
			TR	Tranmere Rov.	08.50					
HUXFORD, Cliff	Stroud	08.06.37	JNRS	Chelsea	02.55	1958	6		0	(WH)
			TR	Southampton	05.59	1959-66	275	2	4	
			TR	Exeter C.	06.67	1967	40	1	1	
HUXFORD, Colin J.	London	26.05.44	APP	Chelsea	10.61					(FB)E.YTH.INT./
			TR	Swindon T.	11.62	1962	1		0	Brother of Cliff
HYDE, Frank L.	Wath	11.01.27	Wath W.	Bradford C.	12.48	1948-51	34		0	(G)
HYDE, Steve	High Wycombe	18.12.43		Oxford U.	01.65	1964-65	9	/	0	(F)
HYDES, Arthur J.E.	Barnsley	24.11.10	Newport Co.(*)	Exeter C.	+	1946	5		0	(CF)*Ardsley Rec./Leeds U.
HYMERS, Tom	Thorne	29.04.35	Frickley Col.	Doncaster Rov.	11.58	1959-60	23		0	(FB)
HYND, Roger	Falkirk	02.02.42	Glasgow Rgrs.	Crystal Palace	07.69	1969	30	1	0	(D)
			TR	Birmingham C.	07.70	1970-75	162	9	4	
			L	Oxford U.	10.75	1975	5	/	0	
			TR	Walsall	12.75	1975-77	89	/	1	
HYNON, John C.	Bath	19.01.34		Crystal Palace	08.54	1954	1		0	

JIMMY GABRIEL (Everton & Scotland/Southampton/Bournemouth/Brentford)
One of the best strong tackling wing halves of the day, Gabriel took some time to settle after Everton had paid Dundee £25,000 in March 1960 for his signature. He was then only 19 but rapidly came to the fore with consistent cultured play which belied his years. At Goodison Park he won a League Championship medal which was followed by an F.A. Cup winners medal from the game against Sheffield Wednesday, 1966. A season later he was allowed to join Southampton, giving them sterling service, using his defensive qualities to the full, before going on to Bournemouth and then Brentford. Surprisingly he won only two Scottish caps.

PETER GELSON (Brentford)
Another of the long service specialists, Gelson started out with the juniors, and progressed as a tall, well-made wing half, who was more than competent and could push the ball about. Making his debut in 1961/2 he played 29 games in Brentford's promotion team from the Fourth Division. Following relegation he again helped to win promotion back to the Third Division 1971/2 as the third placed club, missing only one full game in which, incidentally, he appeared as a substitute. A grand clubman, he did not play again after September 1974 for his beloved "Bees."

ARCHIE GEMMILL (Preston N.E./Derby Co., Nottingham F., Birmingham C. & Scotland/Derby Co.)
An ebullient, aggressive, midfield dynamo only 5ft 5in tall, Gemmill made up for a lack of inches with inspired generalship and determination. He came to the fore when Derby County obtained his services for a fee of £60,000 in September 1970 from Preston, who had brought him into English soccer from St. Mirren three years earlier. He collected two Championship medals in a magical spell at the Baseball Ground and later played for Nottingham Forest from September 1977, again under Brian Clough, and again winning a Championship medal immediately, this time followed by a European Cup winners medal. Surprisingly, he was allowed to leave the City ground for Second Division Birmingham City in August 1979, where he was instrumental in promotion being achieved in third place. He has played many times for Scotland. He is now back at Derby, after serving Wigan Athletic in a non-contract capacity.

JOHNNY GILES (Manchester U., Leeds U., W.B.A. & Eire)
A product of Home Farm, Giles signed for Manchester United in November 1957 as a right winger, but later settled down in midfield as an old fashioned inside forward. After winning an F.A. Cup medal for United in 1963, he was almost immediately transferred to Leeds United to act as their playing supremo under the reins of Don Revie. He became recognised as a great player in his own right at Elland Road, when taking over from Bobby Collins, collecting two Championship medals and an F.A. Cup winners medal from the match against Arsenal in 1972. He later moved on to W.B.A. to play out the autumn of a highly meritorious career before going on to International management.

IAN GILLARD (Q.P.R. & England/Aldershot)
A tall, long striding full back, Gillard made an excellent impression, when first drafted into the Rangers side in 1968/9. He was a member of the squad that gained promotion to Division One as runners-up in 1972/3 and in 1975/6 played 41 times as Q.P.R. finished in their highest ever position – second in the First Division. He picked up three England caps, missing only 22 games in the First Division prior to leaving Loftus Road and he was a member of the 1982 F.A. Cup Final side that lost 1-0 to the Spurs following a replay.

BRIAN GODFREY (Everton/Scunthorpe U./Preston NE. & Wales/Aston Villa/Bristol Rov./Newport Co.)
An inside forward who started with Everton, Godfrey made only one appearance before joining Scunthorpe in June 1960, and winning Welsh under 23 honours whilst playing at the Old Show Ground. Preston fancied the skilful well-built schemer and he certainly impressed the Welsh selectors after joing the famous Lillywhites, gaining three caps. Everton apart, all of this player's clubs were outside of the First Division. His biggest disappointment was on signing for Preston and not being in the side that made its way to Wembley, when losing the F.A. Cup Final to West Ham.

BILLY GORDON (Carlisle U./Barrow/Workington/Barrow)
Gordon started out at centre forward with his local side Carlisle United, but after playing over a dozen games in 1948/9, did not find a place again, and was transferred to Barrow, also of the Third Division North. In nine seasons he played regularly, scoring quite prolifically, and before leaving for Workington in March 1958 had accumulated 145 goals from 301 appearances. Not very tall but stockily built, Billy was ideal for the conditions that prevailed in the lower reaches.

JOHNNY GORDON (Portsmouth/Birmingham C./Portsmouth)
A little terrier-like inside forward, Gordon signed for his local team Portsmouth making his debut in season 1951/2 and becoming a regular two years later. A 90 minute player, he showed great dash and determination and was one of Fratton Park's favourite sons. Not much to the liking of the fans, he was transferred to Birmingham City in September 1958. In March 1961 the call from his old club proved too much. During his time at Birmingham, the once great Pompey had lost their First Division status, dropping very quickly down to the Third, but when he gained a Third Division medal 1961/2 he at least had the satisfaction of again proving his value to that once great club.

ROY GRATRIX (Blackpool/Manchester C.)
One of the most consistent of centre halves to play post-war soccer, Gratrix signed for Blackpool from a local works side. Originally he joined the club as a full back, but when Harry Johnstone was injured, he deputised extremely effectively, going on to play for England "B" that same season. He never looked back. His cool constructive play helped the club to their highest ever placing in the First Division in season 1955/6. He moved to Manchester City, finishing at the age of 32 in 1964. Considered by many experts to have been worthy of higher honours, he might have been luckier with a more fashionable club.

ANDY GRAVER (Newcastle U./Lincoln C./Leicester C./Lincoln C./Stoke C./Lincoln C.)
One of soccer's regular travellers, Graver is always associated with Lincoln City, whom he joined and rejoined three times in all. Starting life with Newcastle, Andy went to Sincil Bank after spending three years with the "Magpies" and playing only one game. With Lincoln, he developed into a free scoring centre forward over four seasons, winning a Third Division North medal before moving to Leicester City for £30,000. He did not settle, and soon moved back home, but within four months was transferred to Stoke City for £15,000. He then went outside the League, but again re-signed for Lincoln from Boston United in 1958.

BILLY GRAY (Orient/Chelsea/Burnley/Nottingham F./Millwall)
A thrusting little winger, Gray joined Chelsea from Orient in March 1949 and within a year had represented England "B". He played in all the forward positions during a career where he excelled predominantly on the right wing, before settling down eventually as a full back. Chelsea surprised the football world when allowing the then very promising player to leave for Burnley in 1953. After gaining the respect of the Turf Moor regulars, he moved on to Nottingham Forest in June 1957, where he achieved what must have been his most notable performance when appearing at Wembley for Forest, who beat Luton Town in the 1958/9 Cup Final. He finished at Millwall, going on to become manager.

EDDIE GRAY (Leeds U. & Scotland)
A skilful, gliding left-sided flank player, Gray made a great reputation taking the top defences to "the cleaners" when in his prime, prior to converting to League management at Elland Road. He won all the individual honours that Scotland could offer and at the same time was able to watch brother Frank do likewise. He turned professional for Leeds in January 1965 and went on to gain two Championship medals in 1968/9 and 1973/4, apart from being a member of the side that were First Division runners-up on four different occasions. Other honours include an F.A. Cup winners medal from the 1-0 victory over Arsenal in 1972 which followed a Football League Cup winners medal from another 1-0 defeat of Arsenal in 1967/8. The European Fairs Cup was also won in 1968, but in the main Leeds became famous during this period for being consistent runners-up from European Cup down to Championship Titles.

JIMMY GREAVES (Chelsea, Tottenham H. & England/West Ham U.)
Recognised as the greatest goalscorer of modern times, Greaves netted more First Division goals than any other marksman. He made a sensational debut for Chelsea, scoring against Spurs, and going on to top the First Division goal scoring charts six times. At the age of 21 he left the "Blues" for A.C. Milan, not staying very long before being snapped up by Tottenham the season after the fabulous "double." He helped to win the F.A. Cup in his first season. Under Alf Ramsey, Greaves' England prospects began to falter, although he still managed to play 57 times. A European Cup Winners Cup medal in 1963 and a further F.A. Cup winners medal against old mates Chelsea were added to an illustrious record. The cockney genius of an inside forward was likely to go on to score from anywhere on the field, but found the modern game unpalatable, finishing down the road with the "Hammers."

KEN GREEN (Birmingham C.)
A Londoner, Green actually signed professional forms for the "Blues" whilst in the Aston Villa dressing room after writing for a trial. He made his League debut in September 1947, on return from serving in India, and went on to play over 400 games by 1959. He was nicknamed "Slasher" due to his not rushing into tackles, being more intent on drawing the winger into traps. With great poise and positional sense, he was an integral part of Birmingham's "iron curtain." He won a Division Two medal in 1955/6 and played at Wembley in the famous losing F.A. Cup Final against Manchester City that same season. He represented the Football League and also gained England "B" honours.

JIMMY GREENHOFF (Leeds U./Birmingham C./Stoke C./Manchester U./Crewe Alex./Port Vale/Rochdale)
Before becoming manager at Rochdale, Greenhoff had an illustrious career, both making and taking goalscoring chances with great flair. He turned professional with Leeds United in 1963, playing mainly in an understudy role, but later gained Football League Cup and European Fairs Cup winners medals in 1967/8. He joined Birmingham City for £75,000 in August 1968, but a season later moved to Stoke City for a £100,000 fee and collected a Football League Cup winners medal from the great victory over Chelsea in 1972. Manchester United then beckoned and Jimmy joined his brother at Old Trafford in November 1976, immediately picking up a F.A. Cup winners medal against Liverpool when he scored the winner. In December 1980, Jimmy moved on to Crewe and then Port Vale before the Rochdale opportunity arose.

ARFON GRIFFITHS (Wrexham/Arsenal/Wrexham & Wales)
A really tricky ball player, Griffiths, after coming out with Wrexham, was soon transferred to Arsenal for £14,000 in February 1961. He never settled at Highbury and, after making few First Division appearances, was sold back for a club record fee of £12,000. International recognition came rather late in life at the age of 30, but the crop haired schemer made up for lost time in going on to collect a further 16 caps.
He masterminded Wrexham's promotion from the Fourth Division in 1969/70 and was the key player in winning a Third Division medal 1977/8. He won an M.B.E. for services to soccer before becoming the manager of his beloved "Reds."

HARRY GRIFFITHS (Swansea C. & Wales)
A big hearted player, Griffiths started out in the game as a winger, signing for the "Swans" in June 1949. He became synonomous with the Vetch Field, becoming a regular in 1952/3 and rarely missing a game in the next 11 seasons before bowing out. The possessor of a great shot, he was, in the early part of his career, more at home on the left wing partnering the great Ivor Allchurch and it was there that Wales capped him versus Ireland, his only International appearance, which came in his first full season. Eventually, his fighting qualities being better suited to the defence, he was converted to full back.

PETER GRUMMITT (Nottingham F./Sheffield Wed./Brighton & H.A.).
Not tall for a keeper, Peter Grummitt came to the fore as a teenager with his agility and handling ability. He soon came in line for International honours, which ultimately passed·him by. Forest signed the youngster from Bourne Town, his place of birth, and he went on to play over 300 League games before signing for Sheffield Wednesday in January 1970, where again he displayed all the attributes of a top class keeper. He finished his career helping Brighton out of the Third Division before retiring from the game, being honoured at England under 23 level and gaining Football League representation.

GRENVILLE HAIR (Leeds U.)
A great servant to the Elland Road side, Hair was signed by the famous Major Buckley as a teenager in October 1948, making his debut two years later as a full back of the future. He had great powers of recovery, and an outstanding positional sense which came to his rescue when needed. Starting out in the Second Division, he was a member of the Title winning side of 1955/6. Unfortunately success was short lived and the club was relegated in 1959/60. Grenville Hair was an important member of that mainly young side which was preparing itself for future glories under Don Revie.

JOHNNIE HANCOCKS (Walsall/Wolverhampton W. & England)
Known as the "Mighty Atom", Hancocks with his 5ft 4in frame and size two boots, contained awesome bullet-like shooting power. He was in marvellous contrast to his Wolves opposite wing mate Jimmy Mullen. He went to Molineux in May 1946 from Walsall for just £4,000, later being capped by England on both wings. Before retiring he had scored 158 League goals in the cause of Wolves. During 1953/4 he collected 25, and followed with 26 the next season. Honours included three International caps, a League Championship medal and an F.A. Cup winners medal from the game against Leicester City in 1949. Extremely dapper, one of the little "big men" of the game he will long time be remembered for that amazing shooting ability.

BRIAN HARRIS (Everton/Cardiff C./Newport Co.)
Harris started as a highly promising outside left, being signed by Everton from Port Sunlight as a part timer, combining football with an engineering apprenticeship. He began to claim a regular spot in 1957/8, when settling down at wing half, and kept his place for many seasons, gaining a League Championship medal to go with the F.A. Cup winners medal from the game against Sheffield Wednesday at Wembley 1966. He developed into a constructive defender, who was unlucky not to be capped, and although losing his Goodison place temporarily to Tony Kay, was soon recalled when that player left the game over the bribes scandal. He later played for Cardiff City and then Newport County, whom he eventually managed.

HARRY HARRIS (Newport Co./Portsmouth)
A wing half-cum-inside forward, very lively up front, Harris was signed by Portsmouth in July 1958 after playing over 150 games in four seasons at Newport County. He was converted to wing half after winning a Third Division medal in 1961/2 with Pompey, who accumulated 65 points, a club record. He played out the rest of his footballing life in the Second Division, as an efficient constructive team member, before being loaned to his old club, Newport, and completing a rewarding, if not distinguished, playing career.

PETER HARRIS (Portsmouth & England)
Harris was born yards from Fratton Park, so Pompey didn't have to look very far for a future star. A quick thrustful outside right, always looking for the goal, Peter had clever ball control and could shoot well whilst on the move. First capped by England against Eire in 1949, he had to wait a further four years for a recall, this time in Budapest on the end of the massacre handed out by the great Hungarians. Winning two Championship medals, he was the most prolific goalscorer in Portsmouth's history, claiming nearly 200 League goals. The fact that he was a recognised wingman makes this achievement all the more outstanding.

RON HARRIS (Chelsea/Brentford)
An uncompromising, tough tackling half back, Ron Harris was affectionately known as "Chopper," although to be fair to his opponents, they did not appreciate his talent as did the Chelsea "shed". After captaining England schools, Ron turned professional for the "Blues" in November 1961, later leading England youth to its first winning World Cup Final. He became a key member of Tommy Docherty's rebuilding plans at Chelsea, which eventually culminated under Dave Sexton in the winning of the 1970 F.A. Cup, against Leeds United, followed by a European Cup Winners Cup Final win against the mighty Real Madrid a year later. He was a great Chelsea clubman who played 646 games before going to Brentford as a player-coach.

ERIC HARRISON (Halifax T./Hartlepool U./Barrow/Southport/Barrow)
A tall, well-built wing half who played his soccer in the bottom two Divisions, Harrison had finally accumulated over 600 appearances when finishing his career with Barrow the season they lost their League status. He attained promotion with Barrow in 1966/7, the club going up in third position. In his first season with them Eric played 39 games – not including three substitute appearances.

ASA HARTFORD (W.B.A., Manchester C. & Scotland/Nottingham F./Everton, Manchester C. & Scotland)
A midfield dynamo, Hartford made the headlines when dramatically turned down by Leeds United after virtually signing from W.B.A., when it was discovered that the player had a heart ailment. Asa was not too disheartened and, quickly recapturing his form, went on to complete five years with Manchester City before spending a few weeks in the 1979 close season at Nottingham Forest. In August 1979 the chunky Scot signed for Everton and became a key factor in Gordon Lee's side's resurgence towards recapturing former glories. He had been capped many times by Scotland before once again signing for the City in October 1981.

ROY HARTLE (Bolton W.)
A tall, well-made full back Hartle came up to Burnden Park from Bromsgrove of the Birmingham Combination, signing professional in February 1952. He first played in the League side in 1952/3, making 17 appearances and playing in every round of the F.A. Cup, but being left out upon reaching Wembley, where Bolton were beaten in the never to be forgotten "Matthews Final". He did not play another match for two seasons, but came back as a regular in 1955/6 and for the next ten years missed only twenty games. He made up for the 1953 disappointment by winning an F.A. Cup winners medal in 1958, against the post Munich, Manchester United side.

KEITH HARVEY (Exeter C.)
Signing from Crediton in August 1952, Harvey made his debut for Exeter that season at centre half, not becoming a regular until 1954/5. A strong upstanding type with good defensive qualities, he went on to play nearly 500 times for the club and would have broken their appearance record had it not been for injuries, of which the worst was a broken leg. Even that did not stop this tough player from missing only 24 games, before getting back to fitness and finishing the season with a flourish. He spent nearly 18 seasons with the "Grecians".

MARTIN HARVEY (Sunderland & N. Ireland)
A great all round player, Harvey worked way through the Sunderland junior side, making his debut in 1959/60, basically as understudy to Stan Anderson at wing half. He became a regular in 1963/4 when Anderson left the club to join Newcastle United, also taking over from the great Danny Blanchflower in the Irish side and going on to play 33 times in all. He gave Sunderland great service, playing over 300 games as one of the top wing halves seen at Roker, ranking along with the best – stylish, constructive and a good tackler.

TONY HATELEY (Notts. Co./Aston Villa/Chelsea/Liverpool/Coventry C./Birmingham C./Notts Co./Oldham Ath.)
A powerfully built leader, clumsy, but effective on the ground and with dynamic aerial strength Hateley made his debut with Notts County in 1958, becoming a target of the bigger clubs very quickly. Aston Villa, in assessing goal scoring prowess rather than awkward gait, signed him in August 1963, and big Tony responded with 68 goals from 127 games. Tommy Docherty saw him as the short term replacement for Peter Osgood, paying £100,000 to bring the marksman to the Bridge. Although scoring only six goals that season, Tony, got the one that mattered in taking the "Blues" through to the losing F.A. Cup Final on 1967 against Spurs. He moved on relentlessly to club after club, who handed over tremendous transfer fees still looking for the "goalden" touch. He ended his days at Oldham.

BOB HATTON (Wolverhampton W./Bolton W./Northampton T./Carlisle U./Birmingham C./Blackpool/Luton T./Sheffield U./Cardiff C.)
A regular goalscoring centre forward Hatton has played for nine sides in all, with more than £300,000 changing hands in transfer fees and he has claimed over 200 League goals in return for the investment made. He was purchased by Birmingham in October 1971 from Carlisle and went on to score 15 invaluable goals that same season to help get the club into the big time as Second Division runners-up. Following services with Blackpool and Luton Town, he signed for Sheffield United in July 1980, gaining a Fourth Division winners medal in 1981/2. He made the move to Cardiff City in December 1982, just in time to help the club back into the Second Division.

JOHNNY HAYNES (Fulham & England)
The outstanding English post-war inside forward, immaculate in appearance, brilliant in ability, Haynes was most famous for his long through ball passing. He was a schoolboy prodigy, signing for Fulham after being coveted by all the big clubs following England schoolboy International displays. He made his debut at 17 years of age in 1952/3, before leaving in 1970 for Durban City after playing 594 League games. He played 56 times for England, following International appearances at every level other than amateur. Superlative skill coupled with strategy and leadership were qualities he regularly brought to bear in his long career. He was famous for being the first £100 per week English footballer, a move that ensured that the foreigners kept their hands off. A serious car injury in 1962 put paid to the International side of his playing career.

TONY HAZELL (Q.P.R./Millwall/Crystal Palace/Charlton Ath.)
Hazell was one of the unsung heroes of the lower Divisions, albeit some of his soccer was played out in the First Division and early in his career he was tipped for future stardom. He turned professional with Q.P.R. after graduating through their junior ranks, gaining England Youth honours as a sound defensive destroyer. He played a great part in Rangers' rise to glory in the mid 1960s, when in 1966/7 he collected a Third Division medal to go with a great winning Football League Cup Final against W.B.A. The following season he assisted the club into the First Division, remaining a regular member of the side until moving on to Millwall in December 1975. Latterly with Crystal Palace, and currently with Charlton he has made over 550 League appearances.

KEVIN HECTOR (Bradford P.A./Derby Co. & England)
Hector started out as a teenager with Bradford Park Avenue, signing professional in July 1962, and scoring over 100 goals in four seasons before he came to Derby for a fee of £40,000 as an all round forward player of the future. Although only 5ft 8in tall, he broke the Bradford goalscoring record with 44 League goals the season prior to joining the "Rams", and his small stature proved not to be a problem in the higher Divisions as the Brian Clough machine rolled forward in quest of the game's major honours. Playing twice for England was some return for his goalscoring endeavour, along with two Championship medals with Derby. After a period in the States, Kevin made a successful return to the Baseball Ground, showing that he could still find the net on occasion.

TERRY HENNESSEY (Birmingham C., Nottingham F., Derby Co. & Wales)
A tall, long-striding cultured wing half Hennessey looked older than he really was, mainly due to a receding hairline. He was a Birmingham City discovery, after representing the Welsh schools, making his debut in 1960/1 and going on to play 178 League games before being transferred to Forest in November 1965 for a fee of £70,000. He became a hard driving skipper who was brilliant in breaking from deep defence, always prompting the forwards when needed. In February 1970 Derby took Terry to the Baseball Ground for a fee of £100,000 where, unfortunately, injuries ruled him out of competitive football after a short period. He played for his country on 39 occasions and won a League Championship medal with Derby County in 1971/2.

DAVID HERD (Stockport Co./Arsenal & Scotland/Manchester U./Stoke C.)
Herd made his name playing alongside father Alex, who was then player-manager of Stockport County. He was obviously better suited to a higher grade of soccer and Arsenal signed him for £8,000 in August 1954 while he was still doing National Service. He became a regular two seasons later, beginning to score quite prolifically at centre forward, and in all collecting 97 goals from 166 League games. Transferred to Manchester United July 1961 to put bite into their attack, he did just that in scoring 114 goals in seven years before moving to Stoke City. He was awarded five Scottish caps whilst at Arsenal to go with two Championship medals and an F.A. Cup winners medal achieved when assisting United.

JOHN HEWIE (Charlton Ath. & Scotland)
A highly versatile 6ft 1½in defender, Hewie was discovered by the Charlton manager, Jimmy Seed, playing for Arcadia F.C. in the Transvaal League, South Africa. Signing for Charlton in October 1949, he went on eventually to play just five short of 500 League appearances for his only club. Recognised by the "Robins" to be at best as a full back, he played for them in nine of the 11 positions, including goal. Because his father had been born near Selkirk, John was made available for Scotland and played 19 times, as well as getting honours at other levels. A top class skilful player, extra cool, who never seemed to have a bad game, he was one of many South Africans at the Valley.

KEN HIBBITT (Bradford P.A./Wolverhampton W.)
An elegant midfield, bother to Terry, Ken Hibbitt was transferred to the Wolves for £10,000, only four days after signing professional for Bradford. He served the Park Avenue side whilst still an apprentice, showing tremendous promise for the future, and has now played well over 400 games at Molineux. One Young England appearance seems scant personal return, but at club level he has a Second Division winners medal, 1967/7, plus two Football League Cup winners medals in 1973/4 and 1979/80, scoring himself in the win over Manchester City. He helped Wolves back into the First Division as Second Division runners-up in 1982/3.

DAVE HICKSON (Everton/Aston Villa/ Huddersfield T./Everton/Liverpool/Bury/ Tranmere Rov.)
A powerfully built, fair haired centre forward using a robust approach and worrying tactics, Hickson forced opponents' defences into mistakes. Everton found the raw youngster at Ellesmere Port, a hotbed of local talent. After three years in the reserves he made his debut in the 1951/2 season, knocking in 14 goals. His courageous style played a large part in getting the "Toffees" back to Division One in 1953/4. Leaving Everton in September 1955, he became a traveller getting amongst the goals where needed and always trying one hundred percent. He scored over 170 League goals in a career which stretched over 12 playing seasons.

ALAN HODGKINSON (Sheffield U. & England)
A brilliant keeper, only 5ft 9½in, Hodgkinson set the trend at International level for others to follow. Painstakingly meticulous with careful handling he was brave and above all remarkably consistent. He was signed from Worksop by United making his debut in 1954/5, eventually displacing the excellent Ted Burgin and going on to play for England in 1956/7, after picking up under 23 honours. He only missed a single game in 1960/1 when the "Blades" won promotion back to the First Division, and was still in the Bramall Lane goal at the beginning of 1970/1 when they once again won promotion.

DOUG HOLDEN (Bolton W. & England/Preston N.E.)
A fast and tricky wingman playing with the Manchester Y.M.C.A., Holden was spotted by a Bolton official, turning professional in April 1949. At home on either flank, he was a regular for over ten years, gaining England honours to go with the F.A. Cup winners medal from the game against Manchester United in 1958. This made up for being on the losing side in the "Stanley Matthews Final". Transferred to Preston in November 1962, he again weaved his spell down the touchlines, again going to Wembley in 1964 – this time coming away with a losing medal from the game against West Ham, where the still effective winger scored for Preston. He emigrated to Australia in 1965.

BARRY HOLE (Cardiff C., Blackburn Rov., Aston Villa, Swansea C. and Wales)
A tall cultured wing half-cum-inside forward, Hole is the son of a famous father who pre-war had represented Wales, also having two elder brothers who both played for Swansea, their only League club. He signed professional for Cardiff City in September 1959, went on to emulate his dad, Billy, by playing for Wales and ended with 30 appearances. He played over 200 League games for Cardiff before moving to former giants Blackburn Rovers and Aston Villa, striving to regain former glories. He finished with Swansea, the club that at one time or another housed the "Hole" family. He spent only two seasons in the First Division, but was good enough to have played at that level throughout.

JOHN HOLLINS (Chelsea & England/Q.P.R./Arsenal/Chelsea)
A quicksilver midfield player, who still delights in going forward and being able to use a rocket-like shot whever the chance arises, Hollins made his debut in League football with Chelsea as another of the endless stream of brilliant juniors coming off the Stamford Bridge assembly line. He gained an England cap against Spain in 1967, which was unusual because brother Dave was already a Welsh International goalie. With Chelsea he gained an F.A. Cup winners medal from the game against Leeds United in 1969/70 and a year later he picked up another winners medal from the European Cup Winners Cup Final against the legendary Real Madrid. After leaving Stamford Bridge in June 1975, he had four years with Q.P.R. before going to Highbury and finally back to Chelsea as player-coach where First Division status was immediately attained.

ROY HOLLIS (Norwich C./Tottenham H./Southend U.)
A tall, clever centre forward Hollis made his name with Norwich City after joining them from local Great Yarmouth in 1947. Regularly getting amongst the goals at Carrow Road, he made the transition to Spurs in December 1952, staying just over a year, scoring only one goal in three outings. Southend United saw Roy putting punch into their attack and signed him in February 1954. Once again he went back to the Third Division which obviously suited his style, and scored at the rate of one in every two matches before bowing out in 1959/60.

ALBERT HOLMES (Chesterfield)
A long service clubman who joined the "Spireites" in June 1961 from local junior soccer, Holmes eventually took over at right back from the then long-term Gerry Clarke in 1962/3 when that player moved to wing half. Rather on the short side for a defender, he made up for lacking inches with sound positional play and steadfast tackling ability. Having started out with Chesterfield he achieved a milestone when collecting a Fourth Division medal in 1969/70 after playing maximum games that season.

CLIFF HOLTON (Arsenal/Watford/Northampton T./Crystal Palace/Watford/Charlton Ath./Orient)
A centre forward who probably had the hottest shot of any post-war player, Holton was signed originally as a full back by Arsenal from Ishmian League's Oxford City in November 1947. He was converted to leader of the reserve attack, soon making his first team debut 1950/1, and going on to gain a losing F.A. Cup Final medal from the memorable 1952 game against Newcastle United. Somehow whilst at Highbury, even though scoring over 80 goals, he was never able to command the respect he deserved and he was allowed to sign for Watford in 1958. At Vicarage Road he scored 42 goals from 45 League games, breaking the club record in 1959/60, and then for £7,000 went to Northampton Town, where he broke their previous record by getting 36 goals in 41 appearances.

MEL HOPKINS (Tottenham H. & Wales/Brighton & H.A./Bradford Pk.Av.)
Hopkins was prominent for long legs and leading upfield sallies from left back. He made his debut for Spurs in 1952/3 but didn't secure a regular place until two seasons later. Displaced by Ron Henry in 1959/60 after breaking his nose, he played only 30 odd games over the next four years, culminating in a transfer to Brighton. He was unfortunate in not being a first teamer during the Spurs glory years, which included the "double". After originally joining the club following the "push and run" side, he had to settle for being a member of neither of the Spurs' two great post-war sides.

EDDIE HOPKINSON (Bolton W. & England)
Only 5ft 9in Hopkinson actually made his debut in League football as an amateur on the books of Oldham Athletic 1951/2, before turning professional with Bolton November 1952. Remarkably consistent, with brilliant daring making up for a distinct lack of inches, he was selected to play for England only a season after making his debut at Burnden Park. He won an F.A. Cup winners medal from the game against Manchester United in 1957/8 to add to 14 full England caps, under 23s, and Football League representative honours. He played over 500 League games for Bolton before retiring to join their coaching staff. Son Paul has played in goal for Stockport County.

BRIAN HORTON (Port Vale/Brighton & H.A./Luton T.)

Horton has had great success in his role as a midfield organiser since leaving Hednesford Town for Port Vale in July 1970. He proved his consistency whilst at Vale Park, hardly missing a game and later he signed for Brighton for a fee of around £30,000 in February 1976. In 1976/7 he was most influential in getting the Albion promotion to the Second Division, and in 1978/9 he helped the club into the First Division for the only time in their history. He missed only two games during the next couple of seasons, before signing for Luton Town in a £100,000 deal and immediately helped the Town become Second Division Champions as club captain.

BILLY HOUGHTON (Barnsley/Watford/Ipswich T./Leicester C./Rotherham U.)

A fine attacking wing half Houghton was a schoolboy prodigy with local Barnsley, turned pro, then picked up England youth International caps in quick succession. Very consistent at Oakwell, he appeared in over 200 games before leaving for Watford in July 1964. He stayed a couple of years at Vicarage Road prior to signing for Ipswich Town, where he played 41 games during the promotion campaign of 1967/8, collecting a Second Division medal into the bargain. He had a short spell with Leicester City, spending the remaining four years of a long career with Rotherham United, back in his native Yorkshire.

GEORGE HUDSON (Blackburn Rov./Accrington St./Peterborough U./Coventry C./Northampton T./Tranmere Rov.)

A tall, strong centre forward, Hudson made tremendous progress after being given a free transfer by Blackburn Rovers. Landing at Accrington Stanley, the young man equalled their seasonal scoring record of 35 goals in 44 matches, but unfortunately the club were forced, due to financial difficulties, to sell their best asset for £5,000 to Peterborough United. In April 1963 when still in the Third Division promotion battle the "Posh" sold Hudson to one of their leading rivals, Coventry City, which created rather a stir at the time. In three years at Highfield Road the busy striker scored 63 goals, collecting a Third Division medal in 1963/4 where his 25 goals that season were instrumental to the success.

EMLYN HUGHES (Blackpool/Liverpool, Wolverhampton W. & England/Rotherham U./Hull Co./Swansea C.)

The son of a Welsh rugby league star, Hughes turned professional for Blackpool in September 1964 and was transferred to Liverpool for £65,000 in March 1967, eventually going on to play 62 times for England mainly as a defender. Nicknamed "Crazy Horse" for his many forays deep from defence into enemy territory, he became captain of Liverpool and England, winning just about every honour the game had to offer, including four Championship medals. On signing for Wolves in August 1979, the only trophy he was still looking to attain was the Football League Cup, which remarkably was won against Nottingham Forest that season. A really tough tackling, no-holds-barred defender, who could also play in midfield when required, Emlyn was selected as player of the year, an honour shared with Kenny Burns, in 1977. In 1982/3 he helped Hull City gain promotion from the Fourth Division when playing in nine of their last ten matches.

RALPH HUNT (Portsmouth/Bournemouth/Norwich C./Derby Co./Grimsby T./Swindon T./Port Vale/Newport Co./Chesterfield)

One of the most travelled of players, with nine clubs in all, Hunt was in demand where the need for goals existed. Starting out with Pompey in August 1950, he played five games but, on not finding the net, was allowed to join Bournemouth down the road, still not creating any goalscoring headlines. When joining Norwich City, however, he came to life as a bustling centre forward who the opposition just could not keep out. Six clubs later, having then scored a total of 186 League goals, he died tragically young.

ROGER HUNT (Liverpool & England/Bolton W.)

Hunt made a reputation for himself as a marksman when shooting Liverpool back into the First Division 1961/2 and topping the Football League scoring list with 41 goals. Ideally suited to the modern Liverpool inside forward requirements, he was direct and resourceful and a thoroughly reliable 90 minute player. He became known as an Alf Ramsey man, collecting 34 England caps, mainly at the expense of the legendary Jimmy Greaves whose style did not suit the England team manager. Club honours included two Championship medals and an F.A. Cup winners medal from the game against Leeds United 1965; he also played in the European Cup Winners Cup Final 1966, Liverpool losing to Borussia Dortmund.

ROGER (ERNIE) HUNT (Swindon T./Wolverhampton W./Everton/Coventry C./Bristol C.)
Real name Roger, highly popular under the hat of "Ernie", Hunt, one of Swindon's many youngsters unearthed in the late 1950s, made rapid progress, going on to top the club's goalscoring lists. He helped the Town to promotion from the Third Division in 1962/3 as a hustling well built inside forward, who could really play the ball about if required. Capped by England at under 23 level; he was hotly pursued by the big clubs, eventually going to Wolves in September 1965, but on Wolves regaining First Division status moved on to Everton. After a few months and not having settled, he was transferred for £60,000 to Coventry City, where he finally displayed his true form.

NORMAN HUNTER (Leeds U. & England/Bristol C./Barnsley)
A tall, stylish, left-footed player, Hunter developed with Leeds United into a fierce competitor in the Wilf Copping mould, nicknamed "bite yer legs" by the Elland Road locals because of his tackling ability. Norman came to the fore in the early 1960s under Don Revie, when United were malingering in the Second Division, and became an integral part of their great successes, which culminated in the winning of First and Second Division medals to go with F.A. Cup, League Cup, Fairs Cup winners medals. He appeared 28 times for England before transferring to Bristol City in October 1976, and then playing the occasional match as player-manager of Barnsley.

CHARLIE HURLEY (Millwall, Sunderland, Bolton W. & Eire)
Discovered by the "Lions" playing for a Rainham youth club, Hurley made an impressive debut for them in 1954 at the age of 17. The ideal centre back was snapped up by Sunderland in September 1957 for £20,000. By the early 1960s Charlie was reckoned to be the best in Britain by many scribes. Not to be compared with the normal stopper, he had developed a style which was decidedly different, with forays into opponents' territory. Playing 40 times for his country he had been the cornerstone around whom Sunderland rebuilt for their return to the First Division. This great player ended his playing days with Bolton Wanderers.

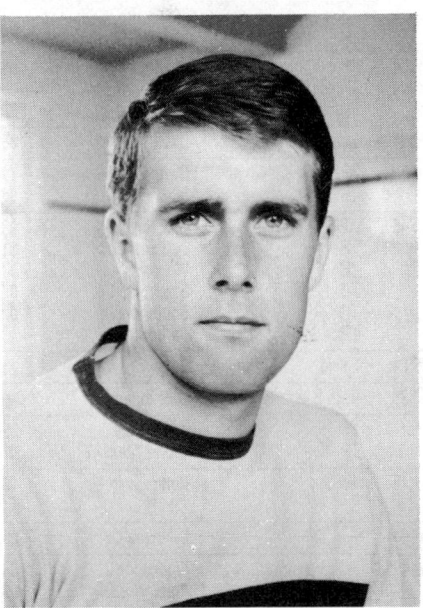

GEOFF HURST (West Ham U. & England/Stoke C./W.B.A.)
A tall, well-made striker, Hurst became famous for scoring the "hat trick" at Wembley in the World Cup Final against West Germany when England lifted the trophy in 1966. Unselfish, he was a wonderful target man for both club and country. Although starting out originally as a wing half, he soon found a niche with the "Hammers", playing up front in the winning 1964 F.A. Cup Final against Preston during which he scored. Son of a footballing dad, who appeared for Oldham, Geoff also was an accomplished cricketer, playing for Essex in the first class game. On leaving West Ham he signed for Stoke and then W.B.A., where he rendered valuable service, before going into soccer management.

JOHN HURST (Everton/Oldham Ath.)
A sturdy central defender, Hurst for many years helped bolster the Everton rearguard, firstly playing alongside Brian Labone and then Mick Lyons, creating a solid resistance to any First Division attack. He was an ever present in 1969/70 when gaining a Championship medal and in 1968, wearing the number eight shirt, was a member of the F.A. Cup Final side that lost to W.B.A. After nearly 350 League games for the "Toffees" and over ten years sterling service he was transferred to Oldham Athletic in the 1976 close season. He played out the remainder of a 16-year career at Boundary Park in the Second Division.

TOM HUTCHISON (Blackpool/Coventry C. & Scotland/Manchester C./Burnley)
Brilliantly effective on his day, especially on the flanks, with adept touches on and off the ball, Hutchison makes many chances for others. He came from the Scottish League with Alloa to sign for Blackpool in February 1968. He missed only one game in 1969/70, when promotion was achieved to the Second Division as runners-up, and with the "Seasiders" nicely consolidated he was transferred to Coventry City in October 1972. Tom went on to play 17 times for Scotland during his stay at Highfield Road, but later he joined Manchester City in time to help them to the F.A. Cup Final in 1981, where they lost to the Spurs following a replay. Early in 1982 he left the Football League bound for Hong Kong, but came back, to sign for Burnley, where his skilful play is appreciated to the full.

Players Names	Birthplace	Date	Previous Club	League Club	Date Signed	Seasons Played	Apps	Sub	Gls	
IANSON, Paul	Shipley	03.05.46	APP	Bradford P.A.	06.64	1963–67	49	3	2	(HB)
IBBOTSON, Dennis	Rotherham	04.12.20	Rotherham YMCA	Rotherham U.	AM	1946	4		0	(FB)E.SCH.INT.
IBBOTSON, Wilf	Sheffield	01.10.26	JNRS	Sheffield Wed.	+	1947	1		0	
			TR	Mansfield T.	08.48	1948	3		0	
ICETON, O. Lloyd	Workington	30.03.20		Preston N.E.	*					(F)
			TR	Carlisle U.	10.46	1946–49	77		19	
			TR	Tranmere Rov.	06.50	1950–54	140		18	
ICKE, David V.	Leicester	29.05.52	APP	Coventry C.	09.69					(G)T.V.Sportscaster.
			TR	Hereford U.	N/L	1972	37	/	0	
IDDON, Harry	Preston	20.02.21	JNRS	Preston N.E.	+					
			TR	Barrow	10.46	1946	25		6	
			TR	Southport	06.47	1947–48	42		3	
IGGLEDEN, Ray	Hull	17.03.25	JNRS	Leicester C.	+	1946–47	11		2	(IF)
			TR	Leeds U.	01.49	1948–54	169		47	
			TR	Exeter C.	07.55	1955	27		8	
IKIN, David	Stoke	18.02.46		Port Vale	08.65	1965	2	/	0	(G)
ILES, Robert J.	Leicester	02.09.55	Weymouth	Chelsea	06.78	1978-82	14	/	0	(G)
ILEY, Jim	Sth. Kirkby	15.12.35	JNRS	Sheffield U.	06.53	1954–57	99		7	(WH)E.U23–1/E.F.LGE REP.●
			TR	Tottenham H.	08.57	1957–58	53		1	
			TR	Nottingham F.	07.59	1959–62	92		3	
			TR	Newcastle U.	09.62	1962–68	227	5	15	
			TR	Peterborough U.	01.69	1968–72	64	4	4	
IMLACH, J.J. Stuart	Lossiemouth	06.01.32	Lossiemouth	Bury	10.52	1952–53	71		14	(OL)S–4
			TR	Derby Co.	05.54	1954	36		2	
			TR	Nottingham F.	07.55	1955–59	184		43	
			TR	Luton T.	06.60	1960	8		0	
			TR	Coventry C.	10.60	1960–61	73		12	
			TR	Crystal Palace	07.62	1962–66	51	/	3	
IMLACH, Mike T.	Croydon	19.09.62	Everton (APP)	Preston N.E.	08.80					(D)
			TR	Leeds U.	11.81					
			TR	Peterborough U.	08.82	1982-83	37	5	1	
IMPEY, John E.	Exeter	11.08.54	APP	Cardiff C.	08.72	1972-74	13	8	0	(D) E.YTH.INT./E.SCH.INT.
			TR	Bournemouth	07.75	1975-82	280	4	7	
			TR	Torquay U.	08.83	1983	41	/	0	
IMRIE, Adam	Dumfries	01.10.33	Kilmarnock	Carlisle U.	05.57	1957	10		5	(IF)
INGER, Jim	Nottingham	10.08.53	Long Eaton U.	Walsall	AM	1972	2	/	0	(G)
INGHAM, Anthony	Harrogate	18.02.25		Leeds U.	04.47	1947–49	3		0	(FB)●
			TR	Q.P.R.	06.50	1950–62	514		3	
INGHAM, Fred R.	Manchester	03.04.54	APP	Stockport	04.72	1971-72	12	5	0	(F)
			TR	Blackburn Rov.	08.73					
			Falmouth	Exeter C.	03.78	1977-78	4	4	1	
INGHAM, R. John	Hebburn	18.10.24	Newburn	Gateshead	08.47	1947–57	431		109	(OR)
INGHAM, Willie C.	Stakeford	22.10.52	APP	Burnley	11.69	1971–79	181	31	22	(M)
			TR	Bradford C.	08.80	1980-81	78	/	4	
INGLE, Steve P.	Bradford	22.10.46	APP	Bradford C.	08.64	1964–66	89	1	15	(FB)
			TR	Southend U.	01.67	1966	14	1	3	
			TR	Wrexham	07.67	1967–71	145	4	5	
			TR	Stockport Co.	07.72	1972	29	/	0	
			TR	Southport	07.73	1973	2	/	0	
			TR	Darlington	10.73	1973	8	/	0	
INGLIS, James M.	Glasgow	14.02.24	Falkirk	Bury	05.50	1950	2		0	
INGLIS, John	Gateshead	05.08.33	Blyth Spartans	Gateshead	AM	1957	2		0	(G)
INGLIS, John F.	Leven	19.05.47		Aston Villa	09.65	1967	1	1	0	(F)
			TR	Crewe Alex.	07.68	1968–69	46	1	10	
INGRAM, Alex.	Edinburgh	02.01.45	Ayr U.	Nottingham F.	12.69	1969–70	28	/	3	(IF)S.F.LGE REP./ S.AMAT.INT.
INGRAM, Gary	Merthyr Tydfil	28.01.51		Swansea C.	08.70	1970–72	36	2	1	(IF)W.SCH.INT.
INGRAM, Gerry	Hull	19.08.47	Hull Brunswick	Blackpool	03.67	1966-67	33	1	18	(F)
			TR	Preston N.E.	09.68	1968-71	107	3	40	
			TR	Bradford C.	03.72	1971-76	171	3	60	
INGRAM, Godfrey P.	Luton	25.10.59	APP	Luton T.	10.77	1977-81	22	5	6	(F) E.SCH.INT./E.YTH.INT.
			L	Northampton T.	03.80	1979	10	/	4	
			TR	Cardiff C.	09.82	1982	7	4	2	
INSKIP, Fred C.	Cheadle	20.10.24		Nottingham F.	+					
			TR	Crewe Alex.	04.48	1947–48	26		4	
INWOOD, Gordon F.	Kislingbury	18.06.28	Rushden T.	W.B.A.	01.49	1949	10		0	(OL)
				Hull C.	05.50	1950	3		0	
IPPOLITO, Mario	Peterborough	16.04.64	JNRS	Peterborough U.	04.83	1982	8	/	3	(F)
IRELAND, Geoff	London	01.12.35	Finchley	Tottenham H.	11.57	1957–58	3		0	(OR)
			TR	Shrewsbury T.	06.59	1959	38		4	
IRELAND, Gerry	Chester	14.09.38		Chester C.	09.57	1957–61	40		8	(WH)
IRELAND, Roy P.	Exeter	03.02.61	APP	Exeter C.	02.79	1978-80	17	4	0	(D)

Players Names	Birthplace	Date	Previous Club	League Club	Date Signed	Seasons Played	Career Record			
							Apps	Sub	Gls	
IRONSIDE, Roy	Sheffield	28.05.35	JNRS	Rotherham U.	07.54	1956–64	220		0	(G)
			TR	Barnsley	07.65	1965–68	113	/	0	
IRVIN, Derek V.	Stockton	23.08.43		Middlesbrough	09.61					(W)
			Brechin C.	Watford	06.67	1967	0	1	0	
IRVINE, Archie	Coatbridge	25.06.46	Airdrie	Sheffield Wed.	09.68	1968–69	25	3	1	(IF)
			TR	Doncaster Rov.	12.69	1969–74	220	8	16	
			TR	Scunthorpe U.	07.75	1975	22	1	1	
IRVINE, J. Allan	Glasgow	12.07.58	Queen's Park	Everton	05.81	1981-83	51	9	4	(W)
IRVINE, James	Whitburn	17.08.40	Dundee U.	Middlesbrough	05.64	1964–66	90	1	37	(CF)S.SCH.INT.
			Hearts	Barrow	07.70	1970–71	67	/	17	
IRVINE, Robert	Carrickfergus	17.01.42	Linfield	Stoke C.	06.63	1963–65	25	/	0	(G)NI–8/NI.U23–1/ NI.SCH.INT.
IRVINE, Sam	Glasgow	07.01.56	APP	Shrewsbury T.	01.74	1972-77	198	9	18	(M)
			TR	Stoke C.	06.78	1978-79	67	/	11	
IRVINE, Willie	Carrickfergus	18.06.43	JNRS	Burnley	06.60	1962–67	123	2	78	(CF)NI–23/NI.U23–3/
			TR	Preston N.E.	03.68	1967–70	77	4	27	NI.SCH.INT./
			TR	Brighton & H.A.	03.71	1970–72	66	3	27	Brother of Robert
			TR	Halifax T.	12.72	1972	9	1	1	
IRVING, Dave	Workington	10.09.51	JNRS	Workington	05.70	1970-72	57	8	16	(F)
			TR	Everton	01.73	1973-75	4	2	0	
			TR	Sheffield U.	09.75	1975	0	2	0	
			TR	Oldham Ath.	06.76	1976-77	18	3	7	
IRVING, Gerry	Maryport	19.09.37		Workington	08.56	1956	1		0	(W)
IRWIN, Cecil	Ellington	08.04.42	JNRS	Sunderland	04.59	1958–71	311	3	1	(FB)E.YTH.INT.
IRWIN, Colin T.	Liverpool	09.02.57	JNRS	Liverpool	12.74	1979-80	26	3	3	(D)
			TR	Swansea C.	08.81	1981-83	48	/	0	
IRWIN, Dennis J.	Cork	31.10.65	APP	Leeds U.	11.83	1983	12	/	0	(D)
IRWIN, William	Newtonards	23.07.51	Bangor C.	Cardiff C.	10.71	1971-77	180	/	0	(G)
ISAAC, James	Cramlington	23.10.16	Huddersfield T.(*)	Bradford C.	+	1946	24		3	(IF)*Cramlington
			TR	Hartlepool U.	07.47	1947–48	56		9	
ISAAC, William H.	Pontypridd	16.05.35		Stoke C.	03.53					(G)
			Barry T.	Northampton T.	07.58	1959	8		0	
ISHERWOOD, Dennis	Brierley Hill	20.01.47	APP	Birmingham C.	01.64	1966	5	/	1	(FB)
ISHERWOOD, Dennis	Northwich	09.01.24	Wrexham(+)	Chester C.	+	1946	3		0	(F) d.1974
ISHERWOOD, Roy	Blackburn	24.01.34	Nelson	Blackburn Rov.	10.58	1957–61	49		9	(OR)
ITHELL, William J.	Hawarden	07.02.16		Bolton W.	*					
			TR	Swindon T.	05.46	1946–49	107		1	
IVERSON, Robert T.	Folkstone	17.10.10	Wolverhampton W.(*)	Aston Villa	*	1946–47	32		3	(IF)*Folkestone/Lincoln C. Tottenham H./ d.1953
IVEY, George H.	W.Stanley	29.10.23	Stanley U.	York C.	06.48	1948–50	79		13	(W)
IVEY, Paul H.W.	Westminster	01.04.61	APP	Birmingham C.	01.79	1978-80	4	3	0	(F)
			Karlskrona	Chesterfield	N/C	1982	0	6	0	

Players Names	Birthplace	Date	Previous Club	League Club	Date Signed	Seasons Played	Apps	Sub	Gls	
JACK, Andrew M.	Glasgow	30.06.23	Wishaw	Tranmere Rov.	06.48	1948	3		3	(F)
JACK, J. Ross	Inverness	21.03.59	APP	Everton	02.77	1978	1	/	1	(F)
			TR	Norwich C.	12.79	1980-82	31	25	10	
			TR	Lincoln C.	08.83	1983	34	2	9	
JACK, Vince	Glasgow	06.08.33		Bury	04.54	1955-56	10		0	(HB)
			TR	Swindon T.	10.56	1956-58	26		0	
			TR	Accrington St.	07.59	1959	22		0	
JACKETT, Frank	Pontardawe	05.07.27		Watford	11.49	1949-52	14		0	(RH)Father of Ken
			TR	Orient	07.53	1953	4		0	
JACKETT, Ken F.	Watford	05.01.62	APP	Watford	01.80	1979-83	133	1	10	(M)W-10/W.U21-2/Son of Frank
JACKMAN, Clive E.	Farnborough	21.02.36	JNRS	Aldershot	05.53	1952-56	38		0	(G)
			TR	W.B.A.	06.57	1957-58	21		0	
JACKMAN, Derek C.	Colchester	20.08.27	Chelmsford	Crystal Palace	+					(WH)
			TR	West Ham U.	08.48	1948-50	8		0	
JACKS, George C.	London	14.03.46	APP	Q.P.R.	01.64	1964	1		0	(IF)
			TR	Millwall	07.65	1965-70	143	7	5	
			TR	Gillingham	07.72	1972-75	158	/	20	
JACKSON, Alan	Newhall	22.08.38	JNRS	Wolverhampton W.	08.55	1957-58	4		1	(IF)
			TR	Bury	06.59	1959-62	124		43	
			TR	Brighton & H.A.	11.62	1962-63	21		5	
JACKSON, Alan E.	Scunthorpe	14.02.38	Brigg T.	Lincoln C.	11.58	1958-60	5		0	(F)
JACKSON, Albert	Manchester	12.09.43		Oldham Ath.	12.62	1963-65	22	/	4	(FB)
JACKSON, Alec	Tipton	29.05.37	JNRS	W.B.A.	09.54	1954-63	192		50	(IF)E.F.LGE REP.
			TR	Birmingham C.	06.64	1964-66	78	/	10	
			TR	Walsall	02.67	1966-67	35	2	7	
JACKSON, Alex J.	Glasgow	28.11.35	Shettleston	Birmingham C.	04.58	1958	6		6	(CF)
			TR	Plymouth Arg.	03.60	1959-63	69		22	
JACKSON, Alex W.	Lesmahagow	02.10.21		York C.	09.46	1946-49	50		5	
JACKSON, Anthony	Tarleton	16.08.42	Preston N.E.(AM)	Southport	08.62	1962-64	12		0	(FB)
JACKSON, Arnold	Blackley	10.11.25		Shrewsbury T.	N/L	1950-53	144		40	(IF)
			TR	Stockport Co.	06.54	1954-58	153		46	
JACKSON, Brian	Maltby	02.02.36		Rotherham U.	09.54	1955-64	131		4	(WH)
			TR	Barnsley	07.65	1965	29	/	0	
JACKSON, Brian H.	Walton-on-Thames	01.04.33	Arsenal(AM)	Orient	10.50	1950-51	38		2	(OR)E.SCH.INT.
			TR	Liverpool	11.51	1951-57	126		12	
			TR	Port Vale	07.58	1958-61	159		29	
			TR	Peterborough U.	07.62	1962-63	47		4	
			TR	Lincoln C.	05.64	1964	10		1	
JACKSON, C. Barry	York	02.02.38	Cliftonville	York C.	12.56	1958-69	481	/	9	(CH)
JACKSON, Cliff	Swindon	03.09.41	JNRS	Swindon T.	09.58	1958-62	91		28	(IF)E.SCH.INT.
			TR	Plymouth Arg.	06.63	1963-66	69	/	19	
			TR	Crystal Palace	09.66	1966-69	100	6	26	
			TR	Torquay U.	08.70	1970-73	114	13	13	
JACKSON, David	Stoke	23.01.37	JNRS	Wrexham	AM	1954	7		1	(IF)Twin brother of Peter
			TR	Bradford C.	07.57	1954-60	250		61	
			TR	Tranmere Rov.	07.61	1961-62	38		5	
			TR	Halifax T.	07.63	1963-64	66		2	
JACKSON, David P.	Bradford	16.09.58	APP	Manchester U.	09.75					(F)
			TR	Bradford C.	09.78	1978	9	3	3	
JACKSON, Dennis L.	Birmingham	08.03.32	Hednesford	Aston Villa	10.54	1956-58	8		0	(FB)
			TR	Millwall	05.59	1959-60	78		0	
JACKSON, Ernie	Sheffield	11.06.14	Atlas.F.C.	Sheffield U.	*	1946-48	88		7	(WH)
JACKSON, Gary	Swinton	30.09.64	JNRS	Manchester C.	10.81	1981	6	2	0	(M)
JACKSON, George	Liverpool	14.01.11	Walton FC	Everton	*	1946-47	17		0	(FB)
JACKSON, George	Stretford	10.02.52	APP	Stoke C.	07.69	1971	8	/	0	(F)
JACKSON, Harry	Halifax	20.07.17	Sutherley WE	Halifax T.	*	1946	6		0	(FB)
			TR	Stockport Co.	08.47	1947	2		0	
JACKSON, Harry	Blackburn	30.12.18	Darwen	Burnley	+					(CF)
			TR	Manchester C.	06.46	1946-47	8		2	
			TR	Preston N.E.	12.47	1947-48	18		5	
			TR	Blackburn Rov.	12.48	1948	1		0	
			TR	Chester C.	07.49	1949	21		10	
JACKSON, Harry	Crompton	12.05.34	JNRS	Oldham Ath.	06.51	1951-55	10		3	(F)
			TR	Rochdale	10.55	1955	1		1	
JACKSON, James	Glasgow	26.03.32	Mapperley Celtic	Notts. Co.	03.49	1948-57	113		47	(CF)
JACKSON, James	Glasgow	01.01.21		Bolton W.	+	1947-49	13		1	(IF)
			TR	Carlisle U.	07.50	1950-54	100		22	
JACKSON, James P.	Glasgow	04.08.24	T.Lanark	Bury	05.50	1950	1		0	
JACKSON, James W.	Ashington	30.12.33	JNRS	Newcastle U.	01.51					(FB)E.SCH.INT.
			TR	Aldershot	07.55	1955-60	195		19	
JACKSON, Joe G.	Wolverhampton	22.04.66	JNRS	Wolverhampton W.	08.83	1983	1	/	0	(F)

Players Names	Birthplace	Date	Previous Club	League Club	Date Signed	Seasons Played	Apps	Sub	Gls	
JACKSON, John	Newcastle	07.01.23		Stoke C.	+	1946–47	4		3	(F)
JACKSON, John K.	Hammersmith	05.09.42	JNRS	Crystal Palace	03.62	1964-73	346	/	0	(G) E.F.LGE
			TR	Orient	10.73	1973-78	226	/	0	REP./E.YTH.INT.●
			TR	Millwall	08.79	1979-80	79	/	0	
			TR	Ipswich T.	08.81	1981	1	/	0	
			TR	Hereford U.	08.82	1982	4	/	0	
JACKSON, Len			Manchester C.(+)	Rochdale	+	1946–47	61		0	
JACKSON, Len W.	Birmingham	06.09.22		Birmingham C.	09.46					
			TR	Northampton T.	07.48	1948	2		0	
JACKSON, Maurice	Barnsley	06.11.28	Carlton U.	Barnsley	09.49	1952–55	31		0	(WH)
			TR	Barrow	08.56	1956–58	74		0	
JACKSON, Nigel A.	Pudsey	27.06.50	APP	Scunthorpe U.	07.68	1968–72	112	3	5	(FB)
JACKSON, Norman E.	Bradford	06.07.25		Sheffield Wed.	10.48	1949–52	31		0	(FB)
			TR	Bristol C.	06.54	1954–55	8		0	
			TR	Oldham Ath.	07.56	1956	2		0	
JACKSON, Peter	Stoke	23.01.37	JNRS	Wrexham	AM	1954	7		0	(WH)
			TR	Bradford C.	07.57	1954–60	199		15	
			TR	Tranmere Rov.	07.61	1961–64	81		3	
JACKSON, Peter A.	Bradford	06.04.61	APP	Bradford C.	04.79	1978-83	170	11	16	(D)
JACKSON, Philip J.	Manchester	08.09.58	Manchester C. (APP)	Stockport Co.	08.76	1976-77	15	3	1	(F)
JACKSON, Richard G.	Rotherham	13.12.32	JNRS	Rotherham U.	07.51					(G)
			TR	York C.	08.54					
				Rotherham U.	07.56	1956	1		0	
JACKSON, Robert	Middleton	05.06.34	JNRS	Oldham Ath.	08.51	1951–54	30		0	(CH)
			TR	Lincoln C.	03.55	1955–63	233		0	
JACKSON, Robert G.	Cornsay	12.05.15	Stanley U.	Southend U.	*	1946–47	64		0	(WH)
JACKSON, Ron	Crook	15.10.19		Wrexham	+	1946–49	108		0	(FB)
			TR	Leicester C.	12.49	1949–54	161		0	
JACKSON, Roy L.	Swindon	22.10.31		Swindon T.	11.53	·1954	2		0	(WH)
JACKSON, Tommy	Belfast	03.11.46	Glentoran	Everton	02.68	1967-70	30	2	0	(M) NI-35/NI.U23-1
			TR	Nottingham F.	10.70	1970-74	73	8	6	
			TR	Manchester U.	07.75	1975-76	18	1	0	
JACKSON, William	Liverpool	08.12.24		Swindon T.	10.47	1948–49	4		1	(HB)
			TR	Tranmere Rov.	04.51	1951–53	14		1	
JACOBS, Frank	Bristol	22.04.40		Bristol C.	05.58	1959–60	5		0	(HB)
JACOBS, Steve D.	W. Ham	05.07.61	APP	Coventry C.	11.78	1979-83	94	7	0	(D)
JACOBS, Trevor F.	Bristol	28.11.46	APP	Bristol C.	07.65	1966–72	130	1	2	(FB)
			L	Plymoutn Arg.	09.72	1972	4	/	0	
			TR	Bristol Rov.	05.73	1973–75	82	/	3	
JACOBSEN, Viggo L.	Denmark	11.08.53	Kastrup	Charlton Ath.	11.79	1979	9	/	0	(M)
JACQUES, Anthony	Oddington	10.10.42	JNRS	Oxford U.	N/L	1962	7		0	(HB)
JACQUES, Joe	Consett	12.09.44	JNRS	Preston N.E.	09.61					(WH)
			TR	Lincoln C.	05.64	1964	22		0	
			TR	Darlington	07.65	1965–69	150	3	5	
			TR	Southend U.	10.69	1969–72	85	2	0	
			TR	Gillingham	11.72	1972–74	73	/	1	
			TR	Hartlepool U.	01.76	1975	5	/	0	
JAGGER, George N.	Gt.Houghton	30.09.41	Houghton M.C.W.	Barnsley	06.60	1960–62	46		2	(F)
JAGO, Gordon H.	Poplar	22.10.32	Dulwich H.	Charlton Ath.	05.51	1954–61	137		1	(CH) E.YTH.INT./ E.SCH.INT.
JAKEMAN, Les	Nuneaton	14.03.30	Atherstone	Derby Co.	06.47					(F)
			Hinckley	Leicester C.	05.51	1954	1		0	
JAKUB, Yanek	Falkirk	07.12.56	APP	Burnley	12.73	1975-79	42	/	0	(M)
			TR	Bury	10.80	1980-83	169	2	17	
JALES, Richard A.	Chiswick	03.04.22		Bradford C.	+					(FB)
			TR	Aldershot	05.46	1946–50	77		1	
JAMES, Anthony	Swansea	24.02.60	APP	Swansea C.	12.77	1977-79	6	5	1	(M)
JAMES, David	Swansea	29.09.17	Mossley	Chelsea	*					(CF) d 1981
			TR	Swansea C.	06.47	1947	12		7	
JAMES, David	Camberley	02.12.42	Blantyre Vic.	Brighton & H.A.	05.62	1962	5		0	(OR)
JAMES, David J.	Southend	11.03.48	APP	West Ham U.	03.65					(HB)
			TR	Torquay U.	05.67	1967	8	/	0	
JAMES, Glyn	Llangollen	17.12.41	JNRS	Blackpool	05.59	1960–74	393	6	22	(CH) W-9/W.U23-2
JAMES, John B.	Stoke	24.10.48	JNRS	Port Vale	04.66	1965-72	202	7	40	(F)
			TR	Chester C.	02.73	1972-75	97	1	40	
			TR	Tranmere Rov.	09.75	1975-77	59	14	22	
JAMES, John E.	Birmingham	19.02.34	JNRS	Birmingham C.	03.51	1952–53	5		2	(IF)
			TR	Torquay U.	06.55	1955–60	123		11	
JAMES, John S.	Sth. Shields	12.09.23	Sth. Shields	Bradford P.A.	+	1949–50	13		1	(FB)

Players Names	Birthplace	Date	Previous Club	League Club	Date Signed	Seasons Played	Apps	Sub	Gls	
JAMES, Joseph	Bootle	09.09.54	JNRS	Liverpool	01.74					(CH)
			TR	Southport	07.75	1975	11	2	0	
JAMES, Keith A.	Hillingdon	18.08.61	APP	Portsmouth	07.79	1978-79	5	1	0	(D)E.YTH.INT.
JAMES, Leighton	Loughor	16.02.53	APP	Burnley	02.70	1970-75	180	1	44	(W)W-54/W.U23-7/
			TR	Derby Co.	10.75	1975-77	67	1	15	W.SCH.INT.●
			TR	Q.P.R.	10.77	1977-78	27	1	4	
			TR	Burnley	09.78	1978-79	76	/	9	
			TR	Swansea C.	05.80	1979-82	88	10	27	
			TR	Sunderland	01.83	1982-83	50	2	4	
JAMES, Leslie				Darlington	AM	1953	4		0	
JAMES, Martin	Langley	18.02.53		Reading	08.71	1971	21	/	0	(CH)
JAMES, Percy G.B.	Rhondda	09.03.17	Oxford C.	Luton T.	08.49	1949	2		1	W.AMAT.INT
JAMES, Robert M.	Swansea	23.03.57	APP	Swansea C.	04.74	1972-82	386	8	99	(F) W.U21-3/W-25
			TR	Stoke C.	07.83	1983	40	/	6	
JAMES, Ron	Birmingham	16.03.22		Birmingham C.	10.47					(WH)
			L	Northampton T.	07.48	1948	4		1	
JAMES, Roy W.	Bristol	19.02.41		Bristol Rov.	07.60	1960	· 1		0	(F)
JAMES, Steve R	Coseley	29.11.49	APP	Manchester U.	12.66	1968-74	129	/	4	(D) E.YTH.INT.
			TR	York Co.	01.76	1975-79	105	/	1	
JAMES, T. Anthony G.	Llanwonno	16.09.19	Folkestone	Brighton & H.A.	+	1946–48	70		19	(F)
			TR	Bristol Rov.	06.49	1949–50	22		5	
JAMES, Tyrone	Paddington	19.09.56	JNRS	Fulham	09.74	1975-77	18	2	0	(D)
			TR	Plymouth Arg.	03.78	1977-81	77	4	0	
			L	Torquay U.	03.83	1982	13	/	1	
JAMES, Walter G.	Swansea	15.06.24		Swansea C.	+	1949	4		0	(F)
			TR	Newport Co.	07.50	1950–51	13		5	
JAMES, William J.	Cardiff	18.10.21	Cardiff Corries	Cardiff C.	+	1946	6		2	(CF) d. 1980
JAMESON, John	Belfast	11.03.58	Bangor	Huddersfield T.	03.77	1977	1	/	0	(F)
JAMIESON, Ian	Edinburgh	22.10.34	T.Lanark	Crewe Alex.	08.56	1956	4		2	(F)
			TR	Birmingham C.	07.57					
JAMIESON, John	Dumbarton	14.10.28	Aberdeen	Coventry C.	01.49	1948–57	181		6	(WH)
JANKOVIC, Bozo	Yugoslavia	22.05.51	Zeljeznicar	Middlesbrough	02.79	1978-80	42	8	16	(F) YUGOSLAV INT.
JANTUNEN, Pertti K.	Finland	25.06.52	Eskilstuna	Bristol C.	03.79	1978-79	7	1	1	(M) FINLAND INT.
JARDINE, Alec	Motherwell	12.04.26	Dundee U.	Millwall	08.50	1950–57	302		25	(FB) d 1978
JARDINE, Fred	Edinburgh	27.09.41	Dundee U.	Luton T.	05.61	1961–69	218	2	9	(OL)
			TR	Torquay U.	02.71	1970–71	11	/	0	
JARMAN, Harold	Bristol	04.05.39	Clifton St. Vincents	Bristol Rov.	08.59	1959–72	441	12	130	(OR) Glouc. Cricketer
			TR	Newport Co.	05.73	1973	34	6	8	
JARMAN, John E.	Rhymney	04.02.31	Lowhill YC	Wolverhampton W.	07.49					(WH)
			TR	Barnsley	10.50	1951–55	45		1	
			TR	Walsall	06.56	1956–57	37		2	
JARMAN, William B.	Pontypridd	18.07.20	Llandrach	Bury	10.46	1946	10		1	(CF)
JARRIE, Fred	Hartlepool	02.08.22		Hartlepool U.	AM	1947	1		0	(G)
JARVIS, Alan	Wrexham	04.08.43	JNRS	Everton	07.61					(WH) W–3
			TR	Hull C.	06.64	1965–70	148	11	12	
			TR	Mansfield T.	03.71	1970–72	76	6	0	
JARVIS, Harry	Maltby	08.10.28	Worksop T.	Notts Co.	05.51	1952–54	29		0	(WH)
JARVIS, Brian	Wrexham	26.08.33		Wrexham	07.52	1953–58	64		3	(HB)
			TR	Oldham Ath.	07.59	1959–62	88		3	
JARVIS, Joseph	Farnworth	27.06.29		Stockport Co.	09.53	1954–56	43		0	(FB)
JARVIS, Mervyn J.	Bristol	20.10.24		Bristol C.	05.48	1948	4		0	
JARVIS, Nick C.	Mansfield	19.09.55	Grantham	Scunthorpe U.	07.80	1980	21	/	0	(D)
JASPER, Brian	Plymouth	25.11.33	Astor Inst.	Plymouth Arg.	07.54	1956	2		0	(FB)
JASPER, Dale W.	Croydon	14.01.64	APP	Chelsea	01.82	1983	3	/	0	(D)
JAYES, Alf G.	Leicester	26.09.23	Leic. C.(+)	Notts. Co.	10.46	1946–47	27		7	(IF)E.SCH.INT.
JAYES, Brian	Leicester	13.12.32		Leicester C.	07.54	1955	3		0	(HB)
			TR	Mansfield T.	07.56	1956–59	115		1	
JAYES, Carl	Leicester	15.03.54	JNRS	Leicester C.	06.71	1974	5	/	0	(G) E.SCH.INT.
			TR	Northampton T.	11.77	1977-79	68	/	0	
JEAVONS, Pat	Deptford	05.07.46	Gravesend	Lincoln C.	02.66	1965	1	/	0	(G)
JEFFELS, Simon	Darton	18.01.66	APP	Barnsley	01.84	1983	3	/	0	(D)
JEFFERIES, Alf J.	Oxford	09.02.22	Oxford C.	Brentford	09.47	1949–56	116		0	(G)
				Torquay U.	06.54	1954	45		0	
JEFFERSON, Arthur	Goldthorpe	14.12.16	Peterborough U.	Q.P.R.	*	1946–49	124		1	(FB)
			TR	Aldershot	03.50	1949–54	170		0	

Players Names	Birthplace	Date	Previous Club	League Club	Date Signed	Seasons Played	Apps	Sub	Gls	
JEFFERSON, Derek	Morpeth	05.09.48	APP	Ipswich T.	02.66	1966-72	163	2	1	(D)
			TR	Wolverhampton W.	10.72	1972-75	41	1	0	
			L	Sheffield Wed.	10.76	1976	5	/	0	
			TR	Hereford U.	11.76	1976-77	39	/	0	
JEFFERSON, Stan	Doncaster	26.06.31	Dearne Ath.	Aldershot	08.52	1952-57	82		0	(FB)
			TR	Southend U.	07.58					
JEFFREY, Alick J.	Rawmarsh	29.01.39	JNRS	Doncaster Rov.	02.56	1954-56	71		34	(IF)
			Skegness	Doncaster Rov.	12.63	1963-68	190	1	95	E.U23-2/E.AMAT.INT./
			TR	Lincoln C.	01.69	1968-69	14	3	3	E.YTH.INT./E.SCH.INT.
JEFFREY, Robert	Aberdeen	24.05.20		Derby Co.	+					(WH)
			Aberdeen	Exeter C.	10.47	1947	7		0	
JEFFREY, William G.	Clydebank	25.10.56	APP	Oxford U.	10.73	1973-81	311	3	24	(M)
			TR	Blackpool	06.82	1982	12	2	1	
			TR	Northampton T.	03.83	1982-83	53	1	6	
JEFFRIES, Derek	Manchester	22.03.51	APP	Manchester C.	08.68	1969-72	64	9	0	(D)
			TR	Crystal Palace	09.73	1973-75	107	/	1	
			L	Peterborough U.	10.76	1976	7	/	0	
			TR	Millwall	03.77	1976	10	1	0	
			TR	Chester C.	07.77	1977-80	116	5	2	
JEFFRIES, Ron J.	Birmingham	24.03.30	Moor Green	Aston Villa	12.50	1950	2		0	(IF)
			TR	Walsall	11.53	1953	3		0	
JEFFRIES, William R.	Acton	11.03.21		Mansfield T.	+	1946	3		0	(CH) d.1981
			TR	Hull C.	01.47					
JELLY, Horace E.	Leicester	28.08.21		Leicester C.	05.46	1946-50	56		1	(FB)
			TR	Plymouth Arg.	08.51	1952-53	11		0	
JENKIN, Ken	Grimsby	27.11.31		Grimsby T.	07.50	1950-53	23		6	(F)
JENKINS, Brian	Treherbert	01.08.35	Cwmparc	Cardiff C.	04.57	1956-60	30		7	(F)
			TR	Exeter C.	06.61	1961-62	72		12	
			TR	Bristol Rov.	07.63	1963	7		0	
JENKINS, David J.	Bristol	02.09.46	APP	Arsenal	10.63	1967-68	16	1	3	(F)
			TR	Tottenham H.	10.68	1968-69	11	3	2	
			TR	Brentford	07.72	1972	13	5	1	
			TR	Hereford U.	03.73	1972-73	18	4	3	
			L	Newport Co.	03.74	1973	6	/	1	
			TR	Shrewsbury T.	08.74	1974	2	/	1	
			S. Africa	Workington	10.75	1975	6	/	0	
JENKINS, Iori	Neath	11.12.59	APP	Chelsea	08.78					(D) W.SCH.INT.
			TR	Brentford	11.79	1979-80	12	3	1	
JENKINS, Lee R.	W. Bromwich	17.03.61	APP	Aston Villa	01.79	1978-79	0	3	0	(F) E.YTH.INT.
			TR	Port Vale	11.80	1980	1	/	0	
JENKINS, Lindley	W. Bromwich	06.04.54	APP	Birmingham C.	07.71	1973	2	/	0	(WH)
			TR	Walsall	07.74	1974	3	/	0	
JENKINS, Peter L.	London	07.02.47	Chelsea(APP)	Charlton Ath.	03.65	1965	2	/	0	(FB)
JENKINS, Randolph J.	Sligo	05.09.23		Northampton T.	06.46	1946-47	18		6	(IF)+Walsall
			TR	Fulham	05.48					
			TR	Gillingham	06.50	1950	2		0	
JENKINS, Reg	Millbrook	07.10.38	Truro	Plymouth Arg.	10.57	1958-59	16		3	(IF)
			TR	Exeter C.	12.60	1960	20		6	
			TR	Torquay U.	07.61	1961-63	88		23	
			TR	Rochdale	06.64	1964-72	294	11	119	
JENKINS, Ross A.	Kensington	04.11.51	APP	Crystal Palace	11.69	1971-72	15	/	2	(F)
			TR	Watford	11.72	1972-82	312	27	118	
JENKINS, Tom F.	Stockton	05.12.25	Q. of South	Chelsea	07.49	1949	5		0	(IF)
			Kettering	Leicester C.	07.54					
JENKINS, Tom J.	London	02.12.47		Orient	01.66	1965	1	/	0	(OL)
				West Ham U.	12.67					
			Margate	Reading	07.69	1969	21	/	5	
			TR	Southampton	12.69	1969-72	84	/	4	
			TR	Swindon T.	11.72	1972-75	89	11	4	
JENNINGS, Dennis B.	Birmingham	20.07.10	Grimsby T.(*)	Birmingham C.	*	1946-49	100		0	(OR) * Kidderminster/ Huddersfield T.
JENNINGS, H. William	Norwich	07.01.20		Northampton T.	*	1946	1		0	(CF)
			TR	Ipswich T.	05.47	1947-50	102		41	
			TR	Rochdale	06.51	1951	3		1	
			TR	Crystal Palace	09.51					
JENNINGS, Nick	Wellington	18.01.46	Wellington	Plymouth Arg.	08.63	1963-66	99	/	10	(F)
			TR	Portsmouth	01.67	1966-73	198	8	43	
			L	Aldershot	11.73	1973	4	/	1	
			TR	Exeter C.	05.74	1974-77	119	5	15	
JENNINGS, Pat	Newry	12.06.45	Newry T.	Watford	05.63	1962-63	48		0	(G) NI-105/NI.U23-1/
			TR	Tottenham H.	06.64	1964-76	472	/	0	NI.YTH.INT.●
			TR	Arsenal	08.77	1977-83	226	/	0	
JENNINGS, Roy T.E.	Swindon	31.12.31	Southampton(AM)	Brighton & H.A.	05.52	1952-63	277		22	(FB)E.YTH.INT.

Players Names	Birthplace	Date	Previous Club	League Club	Date Signed	Seasons Played	Apps	Sub	Gls	
JENNINGS, William	Hackney	20.02.52	JNRS	Watford	04.70	1970-74	80	12	33	(F) E.YTH.INT.
			TR	West Ham U.	09.74	1974–78	89	10	34	
			TR	Orient	08.79	1979–81	67	3	21	
			TR	Luton T.	03.82	1981	0	2	1	
JENSEN, Vigo	Denmark	29.03.21	Esbjerg	Hull C.	12.50	1948–56	308		50	(FB)DANISH INT.
JEPPSON, Hans O.	Sweden	10.05.25	Sweden	Charlton Ath.	AM	1950	11		9	(CF)SWEDISH INT.
JEPSON, Arthur	Basford	12.07.15	Mansfield T.(*)	Port Vale	*					(G)
			TR	Stoke C.	09.46	1946–47	28		0	Notts.Cricketer
			TR	Lincoln C.	12.48	1948–49	58		0	
JEPSON, C. Barry	Alfreton	29.12.29	Ilkeston T.	Mansfield T.	03.54	1953–56	57		36	(CF)
			TR	Chester C.	01.57	1956–59	89		35	
			TR	Southport	11.59	1959	24		7	
JERVIS, William	Liverpool	22.01.42	JNRS	Blackburn Rov.	01.59					(F)
			TR	Gillingham	07.61	1961	1		0	
JESSOP, Stan T.	Liverpool	05.08.32	Kidderminster	Southport	08.53	1953	11		1	(IF)
JESSOP, William	Preston	02.04.22	JNRS	Preston N.E.	+	1946	4		0	
			TR	Stockport Co.	04.47	1946–47	17		4	
			TR	Oldham Ath.	02.48	1947–50	94		16	
			TR	Wrexham	06.51	1951	14		2	
JEST, Syd	Ramsgate	04.06.43	Ramsgate	Brighton & H.A.	12.61	1961–62	12		0	(FB)
JEWELL, Ron P.	Plymouth	06.12.20	Plymouth Arg.(AM)	Torquay U.	09.46	1946	1		0	(OL)
JEZZARD, Bedford	Clerkenwell	19.10.27	Croxley B.C.	Fulham	10.48	1948–55	292		154	(CF)E–2/E'B'–3/E.F. LGE REP.●
JINKS, James J.	Camberwell	19.08.16	Downham Com	Millwall	*	1946–47	44		17	(CF)d.1981
			TR	Fulham	08.48	1948–49	11		3	
			TR	Luton T.	03.50	1949–50	9		2	
			TR	Aldershot	09.51	1951	5		1	
JOBLING, Keith	Grimsby	26.03.34	JNRS	Grimsby T.	07.53	1953–68	448	/	5	(WH)
JOBSON, Richard I.	Holderness	09.05.63	Burton A.	Watford	11.82	1982-83	24	2	3	(M)
JOEL, Steve P.	Liverpool	13.10.54	Portmadoc	Southport	N/C	1977	0	1	0	(M)
JOHANNESON, Albert	S. Africa	12.03.40	Germiston C.	Leeds U.	04.61	1960–69	167	2	48	(OL)
			TR	York C.	07.70	1970–71	26	/	3	
JOHN, Dennis C.	Swansea	27.01.35	JNRS	Plymouth Arg.	02.52	1955–56	3		0	(FB)
			TR	Swansea C.	08.58	1958	4		0	
			TR	Scunthorpe U.	08.59	1959–61	88		0	
			TR	Millwall	06.62	1962–65	101	5	6	
JOHN, Dilwyn	Cardiff	03.06.44	JNRS	Cardiff C.	06.61	1961–66	88	/	0	(G)W.U23–1
			TR	Swansea C.	03.67	1966–69	80	/	0	
JOHN, Malcolm	Bridgend	09.12.50	Swansea C.(AM)	Bristol Rov.	09.71	1971–73	4	1	2	(CF)
			TR	Northampton T.	03.74	1973–74	34	7	9	
JOHN, Ray C.	Swansea	22.11.32		Barnsley	05.53					(CF)
			TR	Exeter C.	07.54	1954–58	143		18	
			TR	Oldham Ath.	12.58	1958–59	32		5	
JOHNS, F. Stan	Liverpool	28.06.24	Sth. Liverpool	West Ham U.	08.50	1950	6		2	(IF)
JOHNS, Nick P.	Bristol	08.06.57	Minehead	Millwall	02.76	1976-77	50	/	0	(G)
			Tampa Bay	Sheffield U.	09.78	1978	1	/	0	
			TR	Charlton Ath.	12.78	1978-83	199	/	0	
JOHNSON, Alan	Stoke	13.03.47	JNRS	Port Vale	09.64	1965	2	/	1	(HB)
JOHNSON, Albert	Morpeth	07.09.23	Ashington	Bradford C.	05.47	1946–49	35		0	
JOHNSON, Albert	Weaverham	15.07.20		Everton	+	1946–47	9		0	
			TR	Chesterfield	09.48	1948	20		1	
JOHNSON, Arthur	Liverpool	23.01.33	JNRS	Blackburn Rov.	01.50	1951	1		0	(G)
			TR	Halifax T.	03.55	1954–59	216		0	
			TR	Wrexham	06.60	1960–61	52		0	
			L	Chester C.	08.62	1962	3		0	
JOHNSON, Brian	Gateshead	20.03.36		Millwall	10.57	1957	7		2	(OR)
JOHNSON, Brian	Newcastle	12.11.48	APP	Sunderland	11.65					(F)
			TR	Luton T.	07.66	1966–67	9	1	0	
			TR	Darlington	07.68					
JOHNSON, Brian A.	Rudheath	28.05.30		Wrexham	04.50	1950–51	14		2	(F)
JOHNSON, Brian F.	Isleworth	21.10.55	APP	Plymouth Arg.	08.73	1973-80	186	11	40	(F)
			L	Torquay U.	01.79	1978	5	/	2	
			L	Torquay U.	09.81	1981	2	/	0	
JOHNSON, Brian J.	Liverpool	29.10.48	JNRS	Tranmere Rov.	11.66	1968	0	1	0	(HB)
JOHNSON, David	Blackburn	17.04.51	Atherstone	Tranmere Rov.	07.74	1974–75	3	/	0	(G)
			L	Southport	01.76	1975	6	/	0	
JOHNSON, David	Sth. Shields	19.11.55	Doncaster Rov.(AM)	Bristol C.	05.74					(IF)E.YTH.INT.
			TR	Hartlepool U.	02.75	1974	1	/	0	

Players Names	Birthplace	Date	Previous Club	League Club	Date Signed	Seasons Played	Apps	Sub	Gls	
JOHNSON, David E.	Liverpool	23.10.51	APP	Everton	04.69	1970-72	47	3	11	(F) E-8/E.U23-9
			TR	Ipswich T.	11.72	1972-75	134	3	35	
			TR	Liverpool	08.76	1976-81	128	21	55	
			TR	Everton	08.82	1982-83	32	8	4	
			L	Barnsley	02.84	1983	4	/	1	
			TR	Manchester C.	03.84	1983	4	2	1	
JOHNSON, David N.	Gloucester	26.12.63	Redhill	Watford	03.82	1981-83	4	3	0	(F)
JOHNSON, Dennis	Seaham	20.05.34		Hartlepool U.	02.54	1957	2	/	0	(F)
JOHNSON, Eric	Moulton	25.05.27	Winsford U.	Coventry C.	09.52	1952–56	90		7	(IF)
			TR	Torquay U.	07.57	1957–58	48		1	
JOHNSON, Eric	Birkenhead	16.12.44	Everton (AM)	Wrexham	06.63	1963–65	28	/	0	(HB)
JOHNSON, Gary J.	Peckham	14.09.49	APP	Chelsea	08.78	1978-80	16	3	9	(F)
			TR	Brentford	12.80	1980-82	55	5	13	
JOHNSON, George	Manchester	27.04.36		Rochdale	12.54	1954–55	2		0	(IF)
			Ashton U.	Southport	01.63	1962	6		0	
JOHNSON, George J.	Esh	06.10.32		Lincoln C.	09.51	1951	3		1	(OL)
JOHNSON, Glen W.	Barrow	07.03.52	Arsenal(APP)	Doncaster Rov.	06.70	1970-72	95	/	0	(G) E.YTH.INT.
			L	Walsall	12.72	1972	3	/	0	
			TR	Aldershot	07.73	1973-82	424	/	0	
JOHNSON, Herbert	Stockton	04.06.16	Spennymoor	Charlton Ath.	*	1946–52	142		1	(WH)
JOHNSON, Howard	Sheffield	17.07.25	Norton Woodseats	Sheffield U.	03.51	1950–56	92		0	(CH)
			TR	York C.	08.57	1957	28		0	
JOHNSON, James	Stockton	26.02.23		Grimsby T.	+	1946–49	4		0	(CF)
			TR	Carlisle U.	03.51	1950	8		1	
JOHNSON, Jeff	Manchester	29.10.50	Hyde U.	Stockport Co.	09.76	1976	6	2	0	(M)
JOHNSON, Jeff D.	Cardiff	26.11.53	APP	Manchester C.	12.70	1970-71	4	2	0	(M) W.SCH.INT.
			L	Swansea C.	07.72	1972	37	2	4	
			TR	Crystal Palace	12.73	1973-75	82	5	4	
			TR	Sheffield Wed.	07.76	1976-80	177	5	6	
			TR	Newport Co.	08.81	1981-82	67	/	3	
			TR	Gillingham	09.82	1982-83	61	2	4	
JOHNSON, John	Hazel Grove	11.12.21	Stockport Co.(+)	Millwall	+	1946–56	310		38	(CF)
JOHNSON, John E.	Sth. Shields	04.02.29		Manchester C.	05.49					(F)
			Nth. Shields	Gateshead	01.51	1950–54	73		13	
JOHNSON, John W.	Newcastle	12.02.19	Huddersfield T.(*)	Grimsby T.	*	1946–47	44		3	d.1975
JOHNSON, Joseph	Sth. Kirkby	16.05.16	Folkestone	Southport	12.46	1946	5		0	(RH)*Doncaster Rov/ Yorks Cricketer
JOHNSON, Joseph R.	Greenock	13.09.20	Glasgow Rgrs.	Lincoln C.	11.52	1952	11		2	
			TR	Workington	07.53	1953	38		5	
JOHNSON, Ken	W. Hartlepool	15.02.31	Seaton H.T.	Hartlepool U.	07.52	1949–63	384		98	(IF)
JOHNSON, Kevin P.	Doncaster	29.08.52	APP	Sheffield Wed.	07.70	1970	0	1	0	(M)
			TR	Southend U.	09.72	1972-73	13	4	1	
			L	Gillingham	02.74	1973	1	/	0	
			TR	Workington	07.74	1974	15	/	1	
			TR	Hartlepool U.	02.75	1974-76	60	1	9	
			TR	Huddersfield T.	09.76	1976-77	80	1	23	
			TR	Halifax T.	08.78	1978-80	51	6	10	
			TR	Hartlepool U.	01.81	1980-83	74	13	3	
JOHNSON, Lloyd	Canada	22.04.51	Vancouver	W.B.A.	10.69	1971	2	1	0	(IF)
JOHNSON, Mike	York	04.10.33	JNRS	Newcastle U.	04.51					(F)
				Brighton & H.A.	12.55	1956	2		0	
			Gloucester C.	Fulham	08.58	1958–61	23		6	
			TR	Doncaster Rov.	07.62	1962	15		2	
			TR	Barrow	03.63	1962	12		1	
JOHNSON, Mike	Oxford	24.02.28		Preston N.E.	09.50					
			TR	Accrington St.	06.51	1951	3		0	
JOHNSON, Mike G.	Swansea	13.10.41	JNRS	Swansea C.	10.58	1959–65	167		1	(CH)W-1/W.U23-2
JOHNSON, Neil J.	Grimsby	03.12.46	APP	Tottenham H.	06.64	1965–70	27	7	5	(OL)
			L	Charlton Ath.	02.71	1970	1	/	0	
			TR	Torquay U.	07.71	1971	5	1	1	
JOHNSON, Nigel M.	Rotherham	23.06.64	APP	Rotherham U.	08.82	1982-83	54	/	1	(D)
JOHNSON, Owen E.	Grimsby	13.11.19		Derby Co.	*					(OL)Brother of Joe (post war int.)
			TR	Bradford C.	10.46	1946	10		1	
JOHNSON, Paul	Stoke	25.05.59	APP	Stoke C.	07.77	1978-80	33	1	0	(D)
			TR	Shrewsbury T.	05.81	1981-83	91	1	2	
JOHNSON, Paul	Scunthorpe	10.05.63	APP	Scunthorpe U.	05.81	1981	2	/	0	(G)
JOHNSON, Paul A.	Stoke	19.09.55	APP	Stoke C.	06.73	1976-81	51	5	0	(M)
			TR	Chester C.	08.82	1982	18	1	0	
JOHNSON, Peter	Rotherham	31.07.31	Rawmarsh	Rotherham U.	03.53	1953–57	153		23	(FB)
			TR	Sheffield Wed.	12.57	1957–64	181		6	
			TR	Peterborough U.	07.65	1965–66	42	/	1	

Players Names	Birthplace	Date	Previous Club	League Club	Date Signed	Seasons Played	Apps	Sub	Gls	
JOHNSON, Peter	Hackney	18.02.54	Tottenham H. (AM)	Orient	04.72	1971-72	1	2	0	(F)
			TR	Crystal Palace	01.75	1974-75	5	2	0	
			TR	Bournemouth	06.76	1976-78	99	8	11	
JOHNSON, Peter E.	Harrogate	05.10.58	APP	Middlesbrough	10.76	1977-79	42	1	0	(D)
			TR	Newcastle U.	10.80	1980	16	/	0	
			L	Bristol C.	09.82	1982	20	/	0	
			TR	Doncaster Rov.	03.83	1982	12	/	0	
			TR	Darlington	08.83	1983	44	/	1	
JOHNSON, Richard R.	Liverpool	20.02.53	JNRS	Tranmere Rov.	08.72	1971-81	355	/	0	(G)
JOHNSON, Robert	Fencehouses	25.10.11	Blackpool(*)	Burnley	*	1947–48	9		0	(CF)*Blackburn Rov./d.1982
JOHNSON, Robert N.	London	30.03.62	APP	Arsenal	02.80					(D)
			TR	Brentford	03.81	1980-81	2	/	0	
JOHNSON, Robert S.	Bedford	22.02.62	APP	Luton T.	08.79	1983	2	/	0	(D)
			L	Lincoln C.	08.83	1983	4	/	0	
JOHNSON, Rod	Leeds	08.01.45	JNRS	Leeds U.	03.62	1962-67	19	3	4	(M) E.YTH.INT.
			TR	Doncaster Rov.	03.68	1967-70	106	1	23	
			TR	Rotherham U.	12.70	1970-73	108	2	8	
			TR	Bradford C.	12.73	1972-78	190	2	16	
JOHNSON, Roy	Swindon	18.05.33		Swindon T.	04.52	1952–55	32		4	(F)
JOHNSON, Sam	Barnton	10.02.19	Northwich Vic.	Hull C.	04.47	1946–47	10		0	(RB)
JOHNSON, Steve	Netherfield	23.03.61	APP	Mansfield T.	08.79	1980	1	/	0	(D)
JOHNSON, Steve A.	Liverpool	23.06.57	Altrincham	Bury	11.77	1977-82	139	15	52	(F)
			TR	Rochdale	08.83	1983	17	2	7	
			TR	Wigan Ath.	02.84	1983	21	/	7	
JOHNSON, Terry	Newcastle	30.08.49	Longbenton J.	Newcastle U.	05.67					(F)
			L	Darlington	11.69	1969	4	/	1	
			TR	Southend U.	01.71	1970-74	155	2	34	
			TR	Brentford	11.74	1974-76	98	3	27	
JOHNSON, Tom	Gateshead	21.09.21		Gateshead	+	1946–47	52		19	(IF)
			TR	Nottingham F.	08.48	1948–51	68		27	
JOHNSON, Tom	Stockton	05.03.26		Middlesbrough	+					(LH)
			TR	Darlington	08.47	1947	6		1	
				Bradford P.A.	08.52	1952	1		0	
JOHNSON, Tom	Ecclesfield	04.05.11	Sheffield U.(*)	Lincoln C.	+	1946–48	75		0	(FB)*Ecclesfield
JOHNSON, V. Ralph	Hethersett	15.04.22	Chesterfield(AM)	Norwich C.	+	1946	19		8	(CF)
			TR	Orient	04.47	1947–48	7		2	
JOHNSTON, Alan	Workington	23.09.44	JNRS	Blackpool	10.61					(FB)
			TR	Workington	07.62	1962–64	65		0	
JOHNSTON, Clem	Lothian	03.09.33	Haddington	Walsall	08.56	1956	7		2	
JOHNSTON, Craig	S. Africa	08.12.60	APP	Middlesbrough	02.78	1977-80	61	3	16	(F) E.U21-2
			TR	Liverpool	04.81	1981-83	71	9	15	
JOHNSTON, David	Scothern	17.09.41	B. Auckland	Leicester C.	02.60					(FB)Son of pre-war
			TR	Exeter C.	05.62	1962	10		0	Sunderland player
			TR	Stockport Co.	07.63	1963	26		0	
			TR	Tranmere Rov.	05.64					
JOHNSTON, George	Glasgow	21.03.47	JNRS	Cardiff C.	05.64	1964–66	57	3	21	(IF)
			TR	Arsenal	03.67	1967–68	17	3	3	
			TR	Birmingham C.	05.69	1969	6	3	1	
			L	Walsall	09.70	1970	5	/	1	
			TR	Fulham	10.70	1970–71	33	6	12	
			TR	Hereford U.	08.72	1972	15	3	5	
			TR	Newport Co.	09.73	1973	2	1	0	
JOHNSTON, Harry	Manchester	26.09.19	Droylsden	Blackpool	*	1946–54	331		10	(CH)E-10/E.F.LGE REP./● d.1973
JOHNSTON, Ian	Workington	19.09.57	JNRS	Workington	08.75	1974-76	46	2	0	(D)
JOHNSTON, James	Aberdeen	12.04.23	Aberdeen	Leicester C.	04.47	1948–49	35		0	(WH)
			TR	Reading	05.50	1950–52	120		0	
			TR	Swindon T.	03.53	1952–54	74		0	
JOHNSTON, John	Belfast	02.05.47	Glentoran	Blackpool	11.68	1968-71	19	5	2	(M) NI.U23-1
			L	Halifax T.	10.71	1971	3	1	1	
			TR	Bradford C.	07.72	1972-73	55	4	4	
			TR	Southport	07.74	1974-75	82	/	6	
			TR	Halifax T.	07.76	1976-78	67	6	7	
JOHNSTON, Les H.	Glasgow	16.08.20	Glasgow Celtic	Stoke C.	10.49	1949–52	88		21	(IF)S–2
			TR	Shrewsbury T.	07.53	1953	16		6	
JOHNSTON, Maurice	Glasgow	30.03.63	Partick Thistle	Watford	11.83	1983	28	1	20	(F)S.U21-3/S-3
JOHNSTON, Pat	Dublin	16.07.24	Shelbourne	Middlesbrough	12.47	1947–48	3		0	(WH)L.O.I.REP.
			TR	Grimsby T.	02.49	1948–56	250		16	
JOHNSTON, Robert	Carlisle	28.01.33		Carlisle U.	11.51	1951–59	122		1	(WH)
JOHNSTON, Ron	Glasgow	03.04.21	Glasgow Perthshire	Rochdale	11.47	1947	17		7	(F)
			TR	Exeter C.	06.48	1948	10		2	
			TR	Brighton & H.A.	11.50	1950	1		0	

Players Names	Birthplace	Date	Previous Club	League Club	Date Signed	Seasons Played	Apps	Sub	Gls	
JOHNSTON, Stan	Wallsend	23.02.34	JNRS	Fulham	08.51					(F)
			Durham C.	Gateshead	09.54	1954	10		1	
JOHNSTON, Tom B.	Midlothian	18.08.27	Kilmarnock	Darlington	04.51	1951	27		9	(CF)●
			TR	Oldham Ath.	03.52	1951	4		3	
			TR	Norwich C.	06.52	1952–54	61		28	
			TR	Newport Co.	10.54	1954–55	63		46	
			TR	Orient	02.56	1955–58	102		79	
			TR	Blackburn Rov.	03.58	1957–58	36		22	
			TR	Orient	02.59	1959–60	79		40	
			TR	Gillingham	09.61	1961	35		10	
JOHNSTON, Tom D.	Berwick	30.12.18	Peterborough U.	Nottingham F.	+	1946–47	64		26	(OL)
			TR	Notts. C.	08.48	1948–56	268		86	
JOHNSTON, William	Glasgow	19.12.46	Glasgow Rgrs.	W.B.A.	12.72	1972-78	203	4	18	(F)S-22/S.U23-2/
			U.S.A.	Birmingham C.	10.79	1979	15	/	1	S.F.LGE.REP.
JOHNSTON, William			Morton	Barrow	04.47	1946	1		0	
JOHNSTON, William C.	Tyrone	21.05.42	Glenavon	Oldham Ath.	06.66	1966–68	28	1	6	(F)NI–2
JOHNSTON, William J.	Sunderland	03.09.48		Northampton T.	07.67	1967	0	1	0	(F)
JOHNSTONE, Cyril	Hamilton	21.12.20	Hamilton	Exeter C.	07.47	1947–50	134		0	(FB)
JOHNSTONE, Derek J.	Dundee	04.11.53	Glasgow Rangers	Chelsea	09.83	1983	0	2	0	(F)S-14/S.U'23-6
JOHNSTONE, Eric	Newcastle	22.03.43	Tow Law	Carlisle U.	06.63	1963–64	15		3	(F)
			TR	Darlington	07.65	1965–66	27	1	10	
JOHNSTONE, Ian	Galashiels	02.03.39	Ormiston Prim.	Colchester U.	06.58	1958–59	2		0	(F)
JOHNSTONE, Jimmy	Glasgow	30.09.44	Glasgow Celtic	Sheffield U.	11.75	1975-76	11	/	2	(F)S-23/S.U23-2/S.F.LGE REP.
JOHNSTONE, Robert	Selkirk	07.09.29	Hibernian	Manchester C.	03.55	1954–59	124		41	(IF)S–17/S.F.LGE REP.
			TR	Oldham Ath.	10.60	1960–64	143		35	
JOHNSTONE, Robert	Cleland	13.09.18	Raith Rov.	Tranmere Rov.	09.46	1946–47	40		0	
JOHNSTONE, Robert G.	Edinburgh	19.11.34	Ormiston Prim	West Ham U.	04.53	1956	2		0	(HB)
			TR	Ipswich T.	07.57	1957–58	35		4	
JOHNSTONE, Stan	Shiremoor	28.10.40	Durham C.	Gateshead	12.58	1958	5		1	
JOICEY, Brian	Winlaton	19.12.45	Nth. Shields	Coventry C.	06.69	1969-71	31	8	9	(F)
			TR	Sheffield Wed.	08.71	1971-75	144	1	48	
			TR	Barnsley	07.76	1976-78	77	15	43	
JOL, Martin	Holland	16.01.56	Twente	W.B.A.	10.81	1981-83	63	1	4	(M)
JOLLEY, Charlie	Liverpool	03.03.36	Liverpool(AM)	Tranmere Rov.	07.53	1953–54	6		2	(CF)E.YTH.INT.
			TR	Chester C.	05.55	1955	7		3	
JOLLEY, Terry A.	London	13.04.59	JNRS	Gillingham	11.76	1976-79	14	7	5	(F)
JONES, Alan	Abermodda	13.01.44		Wrexham	07.64	1964	2		0	(OR)
JONES, Alan	Grimethorpe	21.01.51	APP	Huddersfield T.	12.68	1970-72	30	2	0	(D)
			TR	Halifax T.	08.73	1973-76	109	/	6	
			TR	Chesterfield	09.76	1976-77	39	/	6	
			TR	Lincoln C.	11.77	1977-78	24	2	4	
			TR	Bradford C.	09.79	1979	16	3	1	
			TR	Rochdale	08.80	1980	40	4	5	
JONES, Alan H.	Wrexham	22.09.49	APP	Shrewsbury T.	05.67	1968	3	/	0	(HB)W.SCH.INT.
JONES, Alan M.	Swansea	06.10.45	APP	Swansea C.	10.63	1964–67	59	/	6	(WH)
			TR	Hereford U.	N/L	1972–73	52	1	2	
			TR	Southport	08.74	1974–75	49	/	2	
JONES, Alan P.	Flint	06.01.40	JNRS	Liverpool	05.57	1959–62	5		0	(FB)W.SCH.INT.
			TR	Brentford	08.63	1963–69	244	5	2	
JONES, Alan R.	Winshill	03.11.41	JNRS	Aston Villa	11.58	1961	1		0	(F)
JONES, Alan W.	Paddington	19.09.40		Fulham	04.58	1959	7		3	(F)
JONES, Alex	Blackburn	27.11.64	APP	Oldham Ath.	12.82	1982-83	4	/	0	(D)
JONES, Alf	Liverpool	02.03.37	Marine Crosby	Leeds U.	04.60	1960–61	25		0	(FB)
			TR	Lincoln C.	06.62	1962–66	177	1	3	
JONES, Anthony P.	Birmingham	12.11.37	Birmingham C.(AM)	Oxford U.	N/L	1962–67	226		41	(WH)
			TR	Newport Co.	11.67	1967–68	53	/	6	
JONES, Arthur			Goslings FC	Rochdale	+	1946	1		0	(OR)
JONES, Barrie	Barnsley	31.10.38		Notts. Co.	09.61	1961–63	42		15	(CF)
JONES, Barrie S.	Swansea	10.10.41	JNRS	Swansea C.	04.59	1959–64	166		23	(W)W–15/W.U23–8
			TR	Plymouth Arg.	09.64	1964–66	98	1	9	
			TR	Cardiff C.	03.67	1966–69	107	/	18	
JONES, Ben J.	Rhondda	16.11.19	Slough T.	Watford	09.47	1947–53	158		0	(FB)W.AMAT.INT.
JONES, Bernard	Coventry	10.04.34		Northampton T.	10.52	1953–55	43		16	(IF)
			TR	Cardiff C.	03.56	1955–56	9		0	
			TR	Shrewsbury T.	07.57	1957–58	43		4	
JONES, Bernard	Stoke	27.09.24		Port Vale	10.48	1948	6		0	
JONES, Brian	Barnsley	15.09.38		Barnsley	05.57	1957–58	15		0	(FB)
			TR	York C.	05.59	1959	1		0	

Players Names	Birthplace	Date	Previous Club	League Club	Date Signed	Seasons Played	Apps	Sub	Gls	
JONES, Brian	Doncaster	05.09.33		Walsall	11.53	1953	2		0	
JONES, Bryn	Merthyr Tydfil	14.02.12	Wolverhampton W.(*)	Arsenal	*	1946–48	41		3	(IF)W–17/
			TR	Norwich C.	06.49	1949	23		1	*Aberaman
JONES, Bryn	St. Asaph	16.05.59	APP	Chester C.	05.77	1976-81	149	13	17	(F)
JONES, Bryn E.	Bagillt	26.05.39	Holywell	Watford	01.63	1962	2		0	(FB)
			TR	Chester C.	08.64	1964–66	30	/	0	
JONES, Bryn H.	Llandrindd Wells	08.02.48	APP	Cardiff C.	02.66	1966–67	1	2	0	(IF)W.U23–1/W.SCH.INT.
			L	Newport Co.	02.69	1968	13	/	1	
			TR	Bristol Rov.	06.69	1969–74	84	6	6	
JONES, Bryn R.	Swansea	20.05.31		Swansea C.	09.51	1952–57	121		4	(IF)Brother of Cliff
			TR	Newport Co.	06.58	1958–59	71		11	Nephew of Bryn (Arsenal)
			TR	Bournemouth	02.60	1959–63	118		5	Son of Ivor(pre–war)
			TR	Northampton T.	10.63	1963	7		0	
			TR	Watford	11.63	1963–66	90	1	1	
JONES, Charles W.	Wrexham	29.04.14	Wrexham(*)	Birmingham C.	*	1946	9		4	(CF) W-2
			TR	Nottingham F.	09.47	1947	5		5	
JONES, Chris H.	Jersey	18.04.56	APP	Tottenham H.	05.73	1974-81	149	15	37	(F) E.U21-1
			TR	Manchester C.	09.82	1982	3	/	0	
			TR	Crystal Palace	11.82	1982	18	/	3	
			TR	Charlton Ath.	09.83	1983	17	6	2	
JONES, Chris M.	Altrincham	19.11.45	JNRS	Manchester C.	05.64	1966-67	6	1	2	(F)
			TR	Swindon T.	07.68	1968-71	49	19	18	
			L	Oldham Ath.	01.72	1971	3	/	1	
			TR	Walsall	02.72	1971-72	54	5	14	
			TR	York C.	06.73	1973-75	94	1	33	
			TR	Huddersfield T.	08.76	1976	9	5	2	
			TR	Doncaster Rov.	07.77	1977-78	14	6	4	
			L	Darlington	01.78	1977	14	2	3	
			TR	Rochdale	12.78	1978-79	51	5	19	
JONES, Cliff W.	Swansea	07.02.35	JNRS	Swansea C.	05.52	1952–57	168		46	(W)W–59/W.U23–1/●
			TR	Tottenham H.	02.58	1957–68	314	4	134	E.F.LGE REP.
			TR	Fulham	10.68	1968–69	23	2	2	
JONES, Cyril	Ponciau	17.07.20	Johnstown	Wrexham	+	1946	29		0	(RB)
JONES, David	Blaenau Ffestiniog	08.09.14	Stoke C(*)	Carlisle U.	+	1946–47	66		0	(G)
			TR	Rochdale	12.48					
JONES, David	Whitwell	09.04.14	Worksop T.	Bury	*	1946–49	70		5	(WH)
JONES, David	Swansea	03.03.35		Swansea C.	12.55	1956–57	3		0	(G)
JONES, David	Aberdare	07.01.32	Dover	Brentford	12.51					(G)
			TR	Reading	07.53	1953–60	215		0	
			TR	Aldershot	07.61	1961–65	187	/	0	
JONES, David A.B.	Neath	31.03.41	Ton Pentre	Millwall	03.64	1963–64	13		3	(F)
			TR	Newport Co.	07.65	1965–67	81	/	25	
			TR	Mansfield T.	11.67	1967–71	116	14	32	
			TR	Newport Co.	11.71	1971–73	43	4	12	
JONES, David E.	Chester	05.03.36		Wrexham	04.55	1956–58	70		11	(F)
			TR	Crewe Alex.	07.59	1959	1		1	
JONES, David E.	Gosport	11.02.52	APP	Bournemouth	01.70	1970-74	128	6	5	(D) W-8/W.U23-4
			TR	Nottingham F.	08.74	1974	36	/	1	
			TR	Norwich C.	09.75	1975-79	120	3	4	
JONES, David F.	Brixham	18.05.50	APP	Arsenal	02.68					(F)
			TR	Oxford U.	10.68	1968–70	17	4	0	
			TR	Torquay U.	07.72	1972	0	1	0	
JONES, David H.	Tetbury	04.08.37	Gloucester C.	Leeds U.	12.54					(HB)
			TR	Crewe Alex.	05.60	1960–61	15		0	
JONES, David J.	Ruabon	16.09.52	Telford U.	Hereford U.	05.78	1978-79	44	3	11	(F)
JONES, David M.	Bradford	29.12.50		Wolverhampton W.	08.68					(W)
			TR	York C.	08.70	1970	3	/	0	
JONES, David O.	Cardiff	28.10.10	Orient(*)	Leicester C.	*	1946	33		1	(FB) * Ebbw V./
			TR	Mansfield T.	10.47	1947–48	74		0	Millwall/W–7
JONES, David R.	Onllwyn	18.01.46		Derby Co.	07.65					(G)
			Burton A.	Newport Co.	05.68	1967–68	3		0	
JONES, David R.	Liverpool	17.08.56	APP	Everton	05.74	1975-78	79	7	1	(D) E.U21-1/E.YTH.INT.
			TR	Coventry C.	06.79	1979-80	8	3	0	
			Hong Kong	Preston N.E.	08.83	1983	37	/	1	
JONES, David W.L.	Kingsley	09.04.40	JNRS	Crewe Alex.	AM	1956–57	26		4	(IF)E.YTH.INT.
			TR	Birmingham C.	04.57	1957–58	9		0	
			TR	Millwall	12.59	1959–63	164		71	
JONES, Dennis J.	Aberdare	19.10.30	JNRS	Norwich C.	04.51	1951–52	5		2	(F)
JONES, Desmond	Gelligaer	15.03.30	JNRS	Swansea C.	01.48					(F)
			TR	Bristol Rov.	06.52	1952	6		0	
			TR	Workington	07.54	1954–59	210		23	
JONES, E. Peter	Manchester	30.11.37	JNRS	Manchester U.	04.55	1957	1		0	(FB)E.YTH.INT.
			TR	Wrexham	03.60	1959–66	226	1	7	
			TR	Stockport Co.	07.66	1966–67	51	3	1	

Players Names	Birthplace	Date	Previous Club	League Club	Date Signed	Seasons Played	Career Record Apps Sub Gls		
JONES, Edward M.	Abercynon	20.03.14	BoltonW.(*)	Swindon T.	*	1946	21		2	(OR)W.SCH.INT.
JONES, Edward W.	Finchley	17.09.52	JNRS	Tottenham H.	10.70					(FB)W.SCH.INT.
			TR	Millwall	07.73	1973–75	58	1	0	
JONES, Eric	Ulverston	23.06.31		Preston N.E.	01.52	1953–54	13		0	(OR)
			TR	Nottingham F.	09.55	1955–57	18		3	
			TR	Donchester Rov.	03.58	1957–58	15		2	
			TR	Accrington St.	07.59	1959	18		0	
			TR	Southport	07.60	1960–61	76		18	
JONES, Eric J.	Dover	05.03.38	Snowdown Col.	Coventry C.	05.55	1955–60	15		0	(WH)
JONES, Eric N.	Birmingham	05.02.15	W.B.A.(+)	Brentford	+					(W) * Kidderminster/
			TR	Crewe Alex.	07.46	1946–47	53		14	Wolverhampton W./Portsmouth
JONES, Ernie	Ruabon	09.12.19		Chester C.	08.49	1949–50	6		1	(F)
JONES, Ernie J.	Bristol	12.05.19	JNRS	Bristol C.	+	1946–47	27		1	(OL)
JONES, F.W. Derek	Little Sutton	24.04.29	Ellesmere Port	Tranmere Rov.	07.53	1953–60	155		19	(FB)
JONES, Frank	Llandudno	32.10.60	JNRS	Wrexham	07.79	1978-80	8	/	0	(D)W.U21-1
JONES, Fred A.	Stoke	21.10.22	Sth. Liverpool	Port Vale	06.46	1946	12		1	
JONES, Fred G.	Caerphilly	11.01.38	Hereford U.	Arsenal	01.58					(OL)W.U23–2
			TR	Brighton & H.A.	09.58	1958–60	69		14	
			TR	Swindon T.	12.60	1960	18		1	
			TR	Grimsby T.	07.61	1961–62	58		9	
			TR	Reading	07.63	1963	30		7	
JONES, G. Colin	Chester	08.09.40	JNRS	Chester C.	06.60	1959	3		0	(HB)
			TR	Wrexham	08.62					
JONES, Gary A.	Cardiff	18.06.52		Torquay U.	10.72	1972–73	11	5	0	(F)
			TR	Bournemouth	03.74	1973–74	1	3	0	
JONES, Gary E.	Manchester	11.12.50	APP	Bolton W.	01.68	1968-78	195	8	42	(F)
			L	Sheffield U.	02.75	1974	3	/	1	
			TR	Blackpool	11.78	1978-79	18	9	5	
			TR	Hereford U.	08.80	1980	21	4	4	
JONES, Gary K.	Liverpool	05.01.51		Everton	10.68	1970–75	76	6	12	(F)
			TR	Birmingham C.	07.76	1976–77	33	2	1	
JONES, George	Wrexham	19.07.30		Wrexham	08.50	1950–53	113		5	(HB)
JONES, George A.	Radcliffe	21.04.45	APP	Bury	06.62	1961–73	63	/	14	(F) E.YTH.INT.
			TR	Blackburn Rov.	03.64	1963-66	36	3	14	
			TR	Bury	11.66	1966-72	249	7	100	
			TR	Oldham Ath.	03.73	1972–75	63	8	19	
			TR	Halifax T.	02.76	1975-76	18	1	4	
			TR	Southport	01.77	1976–77	54	1	11	
JONES, George H.	Sheffield	27.11.18	Woodburn	Sheffield U.	*	1946–50	101		27	(OL)
			TR	Barnsley	02.51	1950–51	23		6	
JONES, Gerry	Middleport	30.12.45	APP	Stoke C.	06.63	1964–66	7	/	0	(F)
JONES, Gerry K.	Newport	21.04.50	Barry T.	Luton T.	07.72					(W)
			L	Crewe Alex.	02.73	1972	6	1	1	
JONES, Glanville	Merthyr Tydfil	27.02.21	Merthyr Tydfil	Hull C.	06.46	1946	7		0	(OL)
			TR	Bournemouth	05.47	1948	9		3	
			TR	Crewe Alex.	03.49					
JONES, Glyn	Rotherham	08.04.36	Rotherham U.(AM)	Sheffield U.	06.54	1955–57	29		4	(F)E.YTH.INT.
			TR	Rotherham U.	12.57	1957–58	22		6	
			TR	Mansfield T.	07.59	1959–60	45		18	
JONES, Glyn A.	Newport	29.03.59	APP	Bristol Rov.	09.77	1977–79	9	/	0	(G)
			TR	Shrewsbury T.	07.80					
			Yeovil T.	Newport Co.	N/C	1983	3	/	0	
JONES, Gordon E.	Sedgefield	06.03.43	JNRS	Middlesbrough	03.60	1960–72	457	5	4	(FB) E.U23–9/E.YTH.INT.●
			TR	Darlington	02.73	1972–74	80	5	5	
JONES, Gordon R.	Llanrwst	25.06.32	Holyhead	W.B.A.	09.53					(HB)
				Holyhead	Crewe Alex.	01.57	1956–59	75		0	
JONES, Graham	Worsley	02.06.59	APP	Luton T.	06.76	1975–79	31	8	0	(D)
			TR	Torquay U.	01.80	1979–82	214	/	6	
			TR	Stockport Co.	07.83	1983	32	3	2	
JONES, Graham	Bradford	05.10.57		Bradford C.	N/C	1975-77	1	3	0	(D)
JONES, Graham O.	Wrexham	16.09.49	JNRS	Wrexham	10.67	1967	3	/	0	(CH)
JONES, Grenville	Nuneaton	23.11.32	JNRS	W.B.A.	12.49	1953	2		0	(OR)E.YTH.INT./
			TR	Wrexham	06.55	1955–60	241		36	E.SCH.INT.
JONES, Gwyn	Llandwrog	20.03.35	Caernarvon	Wolverhampton W.	09.55	1955–61	22		0	(FB)
			TR	Bristol Rov.	08.62	1962–65	153	/	0	
JONES, Gwyn	Newport	20.11.32	Llanelli	Leeds U.	08.50					(F)
			TR	York C.	09.53					
			TR	Walsall	11.53	1953	11		0	
JONES, Harold	Liverpool	22.05.33	JNRS	Liverpool	02.52	1953	1		0	(HB)
JONES, Harvey C.	Rhos	16.08.36	Liverpool(AM)	Wrexham	AM	1959	13		0	(HB)
			TR	Chester C.	08.60	1960	19		0	

Players Names	Birthplace	Date	Previous Club	League Club	Date Signed	Seasons Played	Apps	Sub	Gls	
JONES, Haydn	Caernarvon	08.05.46	Caernarvon	Wrexham	06.64	1964–65	15	1	0	(FB)
JONES, Henry	W. Hartlepool	28.09.18		Hartlepool U.	09.46	1946–48	75		1	
JONES, Herbert N.	Mold	20.01.29	Colwyn Bay	Wrexham	07.51	1951	1		0	(IF)
JONES, Idwal G.	Ton Pentre	03.08.24	Ton Pentre	Swansea C.	10.46	1946	4		0	(OR)
JONES, Islwyn	Merthyr Tydfil	08.04.35		Cardiff C.	11.52	1954–55	26		0	(CH)
JONES, Ivor J.	Rhondda	01.04.25		Crystal Palace Reading	+ 02.50	1946	1		1	(IF)
JONES, J. Gwillym	Cardigan	03.04.25	Abergwynf	Torquay U.	09.47	1947	6		1	(CF)
JONES, James A.	Birkenhead	03.08.27		Everton	+					(G)
			TR	New Brighton	08.50	1950	32		0	
			TR	Lincoln C.	08.51	1951–53	76		0	
			TR	Accrington St.	02.54	1953–54	46		0	
			TR	Rochdale	09.55	1955–60	177		0	
JONES, James M.				Hull C.	AM	1946	1		0	
JONES, John	Gourock		T. Lanark	Bradford C.	09.46	1946	2		1	(IL)
JONES, John	Wrexham	09.04.21		Wrexham	06.47	1946–47	20		1	
			TR	Doncaster Rov.	07.48	1948	6		0	
			TR	New Brighton	08.49	1949–50	78		11	
JONES, John A.	Wrexham	12.09.39	Druids	Cardiff C.	05.58	1957	1		0	(G)
			TR	Exeter C.	07.59	1959–61	90		0	
			TR	Norwich C.	07.62	1962	9		0	
			TR	Wrexham	08.63	1963	18		0	
JONES, John E.	Bromborough	03.07.13	Everton(*)	Sunderland	+	1946	24		0	(FB) * Ellesmere Port
JONES, John M.	Llanelli	31.10.24		Fulham	01.47	1947	1		0	(CF)
			TR	Millwall	03.50	1949–50	28		7	
JONES, John T.	Holywell	25.11.16	Port Vale(*)	Northampton T.	*	1946–47	56		0	(G)
			TR	Oldham Ath.	08.48	1948	22		0	
JONES, Joseph P.	Llandudno	04.03.55	JNRS	Wrexham	01.73	1972-74	98	/	2	(D) W-60/W.U'23-4
			TR	Liverpool	07.75	1975-77	72	/	3	
			TR	Wrexham	10.78	1978-82	145	1	6	
			TR	Chelsea	10.82	1982-83	62	/	2	
JONES, Keith	Nantyglo	23.10.28	Kidderminster	Aston Villa	05.46	1947–56	185		0	(G) W–1
			TR	Port Vale	07.57	1957–58	66		0	
			TR	Crewe Alex.	04.59	1958–59	46		0	
			TR	Southport	07.60					
JONES, Keith A.	Dulwich	14.10.65	APP	Chelsea	08.83	1982	0	2	0	(F)
JONES, Ken	Easington	01.10.36	JNRS	Sunderland	10.53	1959	10		0	(FB)E.SCH.INT.
			TR	Hartlepool U.	01.61	1960–61	33		0	
JONES, Ken	Aberdare	02.01.36	JNRS	Cardiff C.	05.53	1957–58	24		0	(G) W.U23–1
			TR	Scunthorpe U.	12.58	1958–63	168		0	
			TR	Charlton Ath,	09.64	1964–65	25	/	0	
			TR	Exeter C.	06.66	1966	17	/	0	
JONES, Ken	Havercroft	26.06.44	Monkton Col.	Bradford P.A.	09.61	1962–64	100		3	(FB)
			TR	Southampton	06.65	1965–69	79	/	0	
			TR	Cardiff C.	07.71	1971	6	/	0	
JONES, Ken B.	Rhos	11.05.37	JNRS	Wrexham	05.54	1957–59	31		0	(FB)
			TR	Crystal Palace	06.60	1960	4		0	
			TR	Swindon T.	03.61	1960–61	35		0	
JONES, Ken B.	Keighley	09.02.41		Southend U.	10.60	1960–63	86		35	(IF)
			TR	Millwall	09.64	1964–69	170	3	12	
			TR	Colchester U.	11.69	1969–71	72	5	23	
JONES, Len	Barnsley	09.06.13	Chelmsford	Plymouth Arg.	+	1946–48	39		2	(OR) * Barnsley
			TR	Southend U.	08.49	1949	29		0	
			TR	Colchester U.	07.50	1950–52	71		3	
			TR	Ipswich T.	07.53					
JONES, Les	Llanwonno	08.12.22		Millwall	12.47	1948–51	8		1	(HB)
JONES, Les A.	Wrexham	09.11.40	JNRS	Bolton W.	11.57					(IF) W.SCH.INT.
			TR	Tranmere Rov.	07.62	1962–64	68		29	
			TR	Chester C.	04.65	1965–68	132	3	35	
JONES, Les C.	Mountain Ash	01.01.30	Craig Ath.	Luton T.	10.50	1950–57	99		1	(FB)
			TR	Aston Villa	01.58	1957	5		0	
JONES, Les J.	Aberdare	01.07.11	Coventry C.(*)	Arsenal	*					(IF) W–11
			TR	Swansea C.	06.46	1946	2		0	*Aberdare/Cardiff C.
			Barry T.	Brighton & H.A.	08.48	1948	3		0	
JONES, Linden	Tredegar	05.03.61	APP	Cardiff C.	03.79	1978-83	142	3	2	(D)W.U21-3
			TR	Newport Co.	09.83	1983	32	/	0	
JONES, Mark	Barnsley	15.06.33	JNRS	Manchester U.	07.50	1950–57	104		1	(CH) E.SCH.INT./d.1958
JONES, Mark	Berinsfield	26.09.61	APP	Oxford U.	09.79	1979-83	87	18	7	(M)
JONES, Mark A.W.	Warley	22.10.61	APP	Aston Villa	07.79	1981-83	24	/	0	(D)
			TR	Brighton & H.A.	03.84	1983	6	/	0	
JONES, Mark D.	Doncaster	02.10.58	APP	Doncaster Rov.	11.75	1975-77	10	3	0	(F)

Players Names	Birthplace	Date	Previous Club	League Club	Date Signed	Seasons Played	Career Record Apps Sub Gls		
JONES, Mark G.	Bristol	02.12.65	APP	Bristol C.	APP	1982	0	1	0
JONES, Mark R.	Mansfield	21.12.65	APP	Notts Co.	12.83	1983	0	2	0 (M)
JONES, Mark T.	Liverpool	16.09.60		Preston N.E.	02.84	1983	4	/	0 (D)
JONES, Mervyn J.	Bangor	30.04.31	Bangor C.	Liverpool	12.51	1951–52	4		0 (W)
			TR	Scunthorpe U.	08.53	1953–58	240		29
			TR	Crewe Alex.	06.59	1959–60	84		14
			TR	Chester C.	08.61	1961–62	63		10
			TR	Lincoln C.	10.63	1963	1		0
JONES, Mick	Sunderland	24.03.47	JNRS	Derby Co.	11.64				(HB)
			TR	Notts. Co.	07.69	1969–72	82	20	1
			TR	Peterborough U.	08.73	1973–75	82	6	4
JONES, Mick A.	Sutton–in–Ashfield	04.12.42	Mansfield Co–op	Mansfield T.	10.60	1962–65	91	1	0 (FB)
JONES, Mick D.	Worksop	24.04.45	APP	Sheffield U.	11.62	1962–67	149	/	63 (CF) E–3/E.U23–9
			TR	Leeds U.	09.67	1967–73	215	4	76
JONES, Mick H.	Llangurig	25.08.38		Shrewsbury T.	07.59	1958–61	22		1 (F)
JONES, Mick K.	Berkhamstead	08.01.45	APP	Fulham	01.63				(FB)
			TR	Chelsea	12.64				
			TR	Orient	02.66	1965–71	223	4	16
			TR	Charlton Ath.	12.71	1971–73	58	1	0
JONES, Norman G.	Rhoystyllen	15.11.23	JNRS	Wrexham	+	1946	1		0 (G)W.SCH.INT.
JONES, P. Wayne	Treorchy	20.10.48	JNRS	Bristol Rov.	10.66	1966–72	217	6	29 (F) W–1/W.U23–6
JONES, Pat J.	Plymouth	07.09.20	Astor Inst.	Plymouth Arg.	03.47	1946–57	425		2 (FB)●
JONES, Paul A.	Walsall	06.09.65	APP	Walsall	09.83	1982-83	3	3	0 (M)
JONES, Paul B.	Ellesmere Port	13.05.53	APP	Bolton W.	06.70	1970-82	440	4	37 (D)
			TR	Huddersfield T.	07.83	1983	36	/	7
JONES, Paul S.	Stockport	10.09.53	APP	Manchester U.	12.70				(HB)
			TR	Mansfield T.	06.73	1973	15	5	1
			TR	Chesterfield	08.74				
JONES, Peter A.	Ellesmere Port	25.11.49	APP	Burnley	05.67	1968–69	2	/	0 (FB)
			TR	Swansea C.	01.71	1971–73	80	/	1 E.YTH.INT./E.SCH.INT.
JONES, Phil H.	Mansfield	12.09.61	APP	Sheffield U.	06.79	1978-80	25	3	1 (D)
JONES, Ralph	Maesteg	19.05.21	Leic. C.(+)	Newport Co.	05.46	1946–47	19		0
			TR	Bristol Rov.	12.47	1947–49	12		1
JONES, Ray M.	Chester	04.06.44	JNRS	Chester C.	10.62	1962–68	169	1	0 (FB)
JONES, Richard K.	Llanelli	16.04.26	Llanelli	Coventry C.	11.49	1951–55	83		0 (FB)
JONES, Robert	Coventry	17.11.64	Manchester C. (APP)	Leicester C.	09.82	1982-83	8	2	3 (F)W.YTH.INT.
JONES, Robert S.	Bristol	28.10.38	Soundwell	Bristol Rov.	05.65	1957–66	251	/	64 (OL)
			TR	Northampton T.	09.66	1966	18	/	1
			TR	Swindon T.	02.67	1966	11	/	0
			TR	Bristol Rov.	08.67	1967–72	160	9	37
JONES, Robert W.	Liverpool	28.03.33		Southport	07.51	1951–52	21		0 (G)
			TR	Chester C.	08.53	1953–57	166		0
			TR	Blackburn Rov.	03.58	1958–65	49	/	0
JONES, Rod	Rhiwderyn	14.06.46	Lovells Ath.	Newport Co.	08.71	1969–78	271	17	68 (F)
JONES, Rod E.	Ashton	23.09.45	Ashton U.	Rotherham U.	09.65	1965–66	35	/	0 (G)
			TR	Burnley	03.67	1967–68	9	/	0
			TR	Rochdale	06.71	1971–73	19	/	0
JONES, Roger	Upton	08.11.46	APP	Portsmouth	11.64				(G) E.U23-1
			TR	Bournemouth	05.65	1965-69	160	/	0
			TR	Blackburn Rov.	01.70	1969-75	242	/	0
			TR	Newcastle U.	03.76	1975	5	/	0
			TR	Stoke C.	02.77	1976-79	101	/	0
			TR	Derby Co.	07.80	1980-81	59	/	0
			L	Birmingham C.	02.82	1981	4	/	0
			TR	York C.	08.82	1982-83	83	/	0
JONES, Ron	Crewe	09.04.18	Heslington V.	Crewe Alex.	+	1946	1		1 (OL)
JONES, Ron J.	Rhondda	27.02.26		Swansea C.	07.49				
			TR	Scunthorpe U.	08.50	1950	3		0
JONES, Roy	Stoke	29.08.24		Stoke C.	+	1947–49	7		0 (CH)
JONES, Roy J.	Clacton	26.07.42		Swindon T.	10.67	1967–71	34	/	0 (G)
JONES, Sam	Lurgan	14.09.11	Distillery	Blackpool	*	1946	1		0 (WH) NI–2
JONES, Selwyn T.	Rhos	03.04.29		Everton	07.49				
				Sheffield Wed.	08.51				
			TR	Orient	07.52	1952	6		0
JONES, Sid	Wrexham	10.10.21	Bolton W.(*)	Norwich C.	+	1946–47	39		10 (OL)
JONES, Simon	Nettleham	16.05.45	Gainsborough	Rochdale	06.63	1963–66	47	/	0 (G)
			Bangor C.	Chester C.	10.67	1967	3	/	0
JONES, Stan G.	Highley	16.11.38	Kidderminster	Walsall	05.56	1957–59	30		0 (CH)
			TR	W.B.A.	05.60	1960–66	239	/	2
			TR	Walsall	03.68	1967–72	204	1	7

Players Names	Birthplace	Date	Previous Club	League Club	Date Signed	Seasons Played	Apps	Sub	Gls	
JONES, Stan J.				Crewe Alex.	08.47	1947–48	14		1	
JONES, Steve A.	Wrexham	28.11.62	JNRS	Wrexham	08.81	1980-81	3	2	0	(F)
			TR	Crewe Alex.	08.82	1982	6	4	1	
JONES, Steve F.	Liverpool	18.10.60	APP	Manchester U.	10.77					(M)
			TR	Port Vale	05.79	1979-80	24	1	3	
JONES, Steve R.	Eastbourne	12.11.58	APP	Q.P.R.	10.74					(D)
			TR	Walsall	01.79	1978	15	/	0	
			TR	Wimbledon	07.79	1979-82	77	2	0	
JONES, Steve T.	Harrogate	06.09.55	APP	Bradford C.	09.73	1972	2	/	0	(G)
JONES, Steve W.	Wrexham	23.10.64	JNRS	Wrexham	08.83	1982-83	9	1	1	(D)
JONES, Syd	Rothwell	15.02.21	Kippax J.	Arsenal	+					(FB)
			TR	Walsall	07.48	1948–51	146		1	
JONES, T. Benny	Frodsham	23.03.20		Tranmere Rov.	+	1946–47	54		19	(W) d.1973
			TR	Chelsea	11.47	1947–51	55		11	
			TR	Accrington St.	07.53	1953	14		0	
JONES, Tecwyn	Holywell	03.01.30		Brentford	03.50	1951–52	5		0	(FB)
			TR	Wrexham	07.53	1953	4		0	
JONES, Tecwyn L.	Ruabon	27.01.41	JNRS	Wrexham	05.59	1961–64	57		2	(WH) W.U23–1
			TR	Colchester U.	10.64	1964–65	28	/	0	
			TR	Crewe Alex.	10.65	1965	8	/	0	
JONES, Tom E.	Liverpool	11.04.30	JNRS	Everton	01.48	1950–61	384		14	(CH) E.YTH.INT.
JONES, Tom G.	Connahs Quay	12.10.17	Wrexham(*)	Everton	*	1946–49	97		4	(CH) W–17/W.SCH.INT.
JONES, Tom W.	Oakengates	23.03.07	Blackpool(*)	Grimsby T.	*	1946	8		3	(IF) * Oakengates/Burnley/
				Accrington St.	06.48					d.1980
JONES, Trevor	Aberdare	27.01.23		Plymouth Arg.	05.48					
			TR	Watford	08.49	1949–50	15		2	
JONES, Vaughan	Tonyrefail	02.09.59	APP	Bristol Rov.	09.77	1976-81	93	8	3	(D) W.U21-2/W.YTH.INT.
			TR	Newport Co.	08.82	1982-83	67	1	4	
JONES, W. Ernie A.	Swansea	12.11.20		Swansea C.	+	1946	37		3	(W) W–4
			TR	Tottenham H.	06.47	1946–48	55		14	
			TR	Southampton	05.49	1949–51	44		4	
			TR	Bristol C.	11.51	1951–53	50		7	
JONES, Walter	Lurgan	04.04.25	Linfield	Blackpool	12.47					(HB)
			TR	Doncaster Rov.	06.50	1950–52	69		2	
			TR	Grimsby T.	09.54					
			TR	York C.	11.54	1954	1		0	
			TR	Halifax T.	08.55					
JONES, Walter S.	Rochdale	09.01.25	St. Chads	Rochdale	11.46	1946	2		2	(CF) Played Rugby League
JONES, William H.	Whalley	13.05.21	Hayfield St.M.	Liverpool	*	1946–53	256		17	(WH) E–2/E'B'–1/E.F.LGE REP.
JONES, William J.	Bedwellty	05.05.25	Bargoed	Ipswich T.	04.49	1949–54	33		1	(HB)
JONES, William J.B.	Liverpool	06.06.24		Manchester C.	05.48	1948–49	3		0	
			TR	Chester C.	06.51	1951	30		5	
JONES, William M.	Liverpool	30.11.19	Sth. Liverpool	Port Vale	06.46	1946–47	53		26	(IF)
			TR	Swindon T.	11.47	1947–49	94		48	
			TR	Crystal Palace	05.50	1950	17		3	
			TR	Watford	03.51	1950–51	27		7	
			TR	Orient	03.52					
JOPLING, Joe	Sth. Shields	21.04.51	Horton Westhoe	Aldershot	08.69	1969-70	35	/	2	(D)
			TR	Leicester C.	09.70	1970-73	2	1	0	
			L	Torquay U.	01.74	1973	6	/	0	
			TR	Aldershot	03.74	1973-83	321	11	11	
JORDAN, Brian A.	Doncaster	31.01.32		Derby Co.	10.51					(CH)
			Denaby U.	Rotherham U.	07.53	1953–58	38		0	
			TR	Middlesbrough	11.58	1958	5		0	
			TR	York C.	07.60	1960	8		0	
JORDAN, Clarrie	Sth. Kirkby	20.06.22	Sth. Kirkby Col.	Doncaster Rov.	+	1946–47	60		47	(CF)
			TR	Sheffield Wed.	02.48	1947–54	92		36	
JORDAN, Colin	Hemsworth	02.06.34		Bradford P.A.	04.52	1953–56	27		0	(FB)
				York C.	11.59					
JORDAN, Gerry	Seaham	04.04.49	JNRS	Northampton T.	06.66	1966	1	/	0	(FB)
JORDAN, Joe	Carluke	15.12.51	Morton	Leeds U.	10.70	1971-77	139	30	35	(F)S-52/S.U'23-1●
			TR	Manchester U.	01.78	1977-80	109	/	37	
JORDAN, John	Glasgow	25.02.44	Glasgow Celtic	Reading	10.48	1948	3		0	(OR)
			TR	Brentford	10.49					
JORDAN, John W.	Bromley	08.11.21	Grays Ath.	Tottenham H.	08.47	1847	24		10	(IF) Cousin of Clarrie
			Juventus	Birmingham C.	03.49	1948–49	25		3	
			TR	Sheffield Wed.	09.50	1950	10		2	
JORDAN, Mick	Exeter	08.01.56		Exeter C.	07.75	1975-76	15	3	3	(F)
JORDAN, Tim E.	Littleborough	12.04.60	JNRS	Oldham Ath.	06.78	1968-79	2	3	0	(F)
JOSEPH, Francis	London	06.03.60	Hillingdon Bor.	Wimbledon	11.80	1980-81	42	9	14	(F)
			TR	Brentford	07.82	1982-83	85	1	41	

Players Names	Birthplace	Date	Previous Club	League Club	Date Signed	Seasons Played	Apps	Sub	Gls	
JOSEPH, Leon	London	26.02.20	Leytonstone	Tottenham H.	AM	1946	1		0	(OL) E.AMAT.INT./d.1983
JOSLIN, Phil J.	Kingsteignton	01.09.16		Torquay U.	*	1946–47	66		0	(G)
			TR	Cardiff C.	05.48	1948–50	108		0	
JOSLYN, Roger D. W.	Colchester	07.05.50	JNRS	Colchester U.	05.68	1967-70	91	7	4	(M)
			TR	Aldershot	10.70	1970-74	186	/	17	
			TR	Watford	11.74	1974-79	178	4	17	
			TR	Reading	11.79	1979-81	67	1	1	
JOVANOVIC, Nikola	Yugoslavia	18.09.52	Red Star	Manchester U.	01.80	1979-80	20	1	4	(D)YUGOSLAV.INT.
JOWETT, Albert W.				Halifax T.	AM	1946	7		0	
JOWETT, Harry O.	Halifax	15.11.23		Halifax T.	09.50	1950	9		1	
JOWETT, Ken S.	Bradford	09.03.27	Fryston Col.	Halifax T.	02.47	1946–48	22		2	
JOWETT, S. Jim	Shiregreen	27.01.26	Sheffield U.(AM)	York C.	AM	1946	1		0	
JOY, Bernard	Fulham	29.10.11	Corinthian Cas.	Arsenal	AM	1946	13		0	(CH) * Southend U./Fulham/ E-1/E.AMAT.INT.
JOY, Brian	Reading	26.02.51	Blackburn Rov.(AM)	Torquay U.	08.69	1969	26	1	0	(D)
			TR	Tranmere Rov.	06.70	1970	21	/	1	
			TR	Doncaster Rov.	07.72	1972	28	6	1	
			TR	Exeter C.	07.73	1973-75	89	1	2	
			TR	York C.	09.76	1976	18	/	0	
JOY, David	Barnard Castle	23.09.43	Evenwood T.	Huddersfield T.	07.62	1965	1	/	0	(WH) E.YTH.INT.
			TR	York C.	06.67	1967	13	1	0	
JOY, Harold	Cardiff	08.01.21	Lovells Ath.	Norwich C.	02.47	1946	8		4	(FB)
			TR	Newport Co.	01.48	1947	2		0	
JOYCE, Chris	Dumbarton	19.04.33	Vale of Leven	Nottingham F.	09.56	1957	10		0	(F)
			TR	Notts. Co.	07.59	1959–61	62		19	
JOYCE, Eric	Durham	03.07.24		Bradford C.	+	1946	5		0	d.1977
JOYCE, John	Easington	06.01.49	Peterlee J.	Hartlepool U.	AM	1966–68	4	/	0	(OR)
JOYCE, Joseph	Consett	18.03.61		Barnsley	09.80	1979-83	131	2	2	(D)
JOYCE, Nick	Leeds	27.07.47	Ashley Rd.FC	Bradford C.	AM	1971	5	/	1	(W)
JOYCE, Walter	Oldham	10.09.37	JNRS	Burnley	10.54	1960–63	70		3	(WH)
			TR	Blackburn Rov.	02.64	1963–67	119	1	4	
			TR	Oldham Ath.	09.67	1967–69	68	3	2	
JOYCE, Warren G.	Oldham	20.01.65	JNRS	Bolton W.	06.82	1982-83	50	3	3	(M)
JUDD, Mike D.	Southampton	18.06.48	APP	Southampton	08.65	1967–69	14	2	3	(F)
JUDD, Walter J.	Salisbury	25.10.26		Southampton	08.49	1950–52	33		13	(F)
JUDGE, Alan G.	Kingsbury	14.05.60	JNRS	Luton T.	01.78	1979-82	11	/	0	(G)
			TR	Reading	09.82	1982-83	74	/	0	
JUDGES, Barry J.	Rainham	23.09.40	JNRS	Gillingham	12.57	1957–58	3		0	(HB)
JUKES, Norman G.	Leeds	14.10.32		Huddersfield T.	07.51					
			TR	York C.	10.53	1953	1		0	
JULIANS, Len B.	Tottenham	19.06.33	Walthamstow	Orient	06.55	1955–58	67		35	(CF)
			TR	Arsenal	12.58	1958–59	18		7	
			TR	Nottingham F.	06.60	1960–63	59		24	
			TR	Millwall	01.64	1963–66	125	/	58	
JULIUSSEN, Albert L.	Blyth	20.02.20	Dundee	Portsmouth	03.48	1947	7		4	
			TR	Everton	09.48	1948	10		1	
JUMP, Stewart P.	Crumpsall	27.01.52	APP	Stoke C.	07.69	1970-73	36	8	1	(D)
			TR	Crystal Palace	12.73	1973-77	79	2	2	
			L	Fulham	01.77	1976	3	/	0	
JURYEFF, Ian M.	Gosport	24.11.62	APP	Southampton	11.80	1983	0	2	0	(F)
			L	Mansfield T.	03.84	1983	12	/	5	

Players Names	Birthplace	Date	Previous Club	League Club	Date Signed	Seasons Played	Apps	Sub	Gls	
KABIA, Jim P.	Mansfield	11.11.54	APP	Chesterfield	11.72	1972–73	10	1	1	(IF)
KAILE, Gordon W.	Pimperne	07.12.24	R.E.P.	Nottingham F.	+	1947–49	65		8	(F)
			TR	Preston N.E.	07.51	1951–53	7		1	
			TR	Exeter C.	08.54	1954	6		1	
KAISER, Rudi	Holland	26.12.60	Antwerp	Coventry C.	08.81	1981	11	5	3	(F)
KAMARA, Alan	Sheffield	15.07.58	Kiveton Pk.	York C.	07.79	1979	10	/	0	(D)
			TR	Darlington	06.80	1980-82	134	/	1	
KAMARA, Chris	Middlesbrough	25.12.57	APP	Portsmouth	01.76	1975-76	56	7	7	(M)
			TR	Swindon T.	08.77	1977-80	133	14	21	
			TR	Portsmouth	08.81	1981	11	/	0	
			TR	Brentford	10.81	1981-83	112	1	22	
KANE, Alan	Falkirk	20.01.57	Hibernian	Portsmouth	03.75	1974–75	6	1	0	(IF)
KANE, John P.	Hackney	15.12.60	APP	Orient	12.78	1978	0	1	0	(D)
KANE, Len R.	Belfast	27.01.26	Glentoran	Preston N.E.	05.47	1948–49	5		0	
			TR	Plymouth Arg.	01.50					
KANE, Peter	Petershill	04.04.39	Queens Pk	Northampton T.	10.59	1959	28		16	(IF)
			TR	Arsenal	07.60	1960	4		1	
			TR	Northampton T.	09.63	1963	18		8	
			TR	Crewe Alex.	03.64	1963–66	82	1	31	
KANE, Robert	Cambuslang		St.Rochs	Leeds U.	*	1946	1		0	(CH)
KAPENGWE, Emment	Zambia	27.03.43	Atlanta (USA)	Aston Villa	09.69	1969	3	/	0	(OR)
KAPLER, Konrad	Poland	25.02.25	Glasgow Celtic	Rochdale	05.49	1949	4		0	(OL)
KATALINIC, Ivan	Yugoslavia	17.05.51	Red Star	Southampton	02.80	1979-81	48	/	0	(G) YUGOSLAV. INT.
KAVANAGH, Eamon	Manchester	05.01.54	JNRS	Manchester C.	06.71					(M)
			TR	Rochdale	10.73	1973	2	2	0	
			TR	Workington	03.74	1973-76	123	6	11	
			TR	Scunthorpe U.	08.77	1977-79	68	8	3	
KAVANAGH, Edward	Glasgow	20.07.41	Cambuslang	Notts. Co.	05.64	1964	25		4	(OR)
KAVANAGH, Mike	Dublin	27.12.27		Brighton & H.A.	02.48	1948–49	26		7	
KAVANAGH, Peter J.	Romford	03.11.38	Dagenham	Fulham	10.56					(OL)
				Romford						
				Everton	02.61	1960	6		0	
KAY, Anthony H.	Sheffield	13.05.37	JNRS	Sheffield Wed.	05.54	1954–62	180		10	(WH) E–1/E.U23–7/
			TR	Everton	12.62	1962–63	50		4	E.F.LGE REP.
KAY, Jim	Preston	03.05.32	Leyland M.	Stockport Co.	05.53	1954–55	9		3	(F)
			TR	Crewe Alex.	12.56	1956	4		0	
KAY, John	Sunderland	29.01.64	APP	Arsenal	08.81	1982-83	13	1	0	(D)
KAY, Ken	Newark	09.03.20	Ransome & M	Mansfield T.	06.47	1947	1		0	(OL)
KAY, Robert	Edinburgh	24.10.49	Hearts	York C.	07.78	1978-81	160	/	8	(D)
KAYE, Arthur	Barnsley	09.05.33	JNRS	Barnsley	05.50	1950–58	265		55	(OR) E.U23–1/E.F.LGE
			TR	Blackpool	05.59	1959–60	38		9	REP./E.SCH.INT.●
			TR	Middlesbrough	11.60	1960–64	165		38	
			TR	Colchester U.	06.65	1965–66	48	1	3	
KAYE, George H.	Liverpool	19.04.19		Liverpool	+	1946	1		0	(WH)
			TR	Swindon T.	05.47	1947–52	169		5	
KAYE, John	Goole	03.03.40	Goole T.	Scunthorpe U.	09.60	1960–62	77		25	(CF) E.F.LGE REP.
			TR	W.B.A.	06.63	1963–71	281	2	44	
			TR	Hull C.	11.71	1971–73	71	1	9	
KEANE, Tom R.	Limerick	31.08.22	Limerick	Swansea C.	06.47	1947–54	164		0	(FB) EI–4/NI–1
KEAR, Mike	Coleford	27.05.43	Cinderford T.	Newport Co.	08.63	1963	6		0	(WH)
			TR	Nottingham F.	12.63	1963–66	26	/	5	
			TR	Middlesbrough	09.67	1967–69	56	2	6	
			L	Barnsley	08.70	1970	6	/	1	
KEARNEY, Mark J.	Ormskirk	12.06.62	Marine	Everton	10.81					(D)
			TR	Mansfield T.	04.83	1982-83	28	/	3	
KEARNEY, Mike J.	Glasgow	18.02.53	Petershill	Shrewsbury T.	12.72	1972-76	143	6	41	(F)
			TR	Chester C.	03.77	1976-77	37	1	5	
			TR	Reading	01.78	1977-79	78	9	24	
			TR	Chester C.	07.80	1980	9	/	0	
			TR	Reading	10.80	1980-82	57	1	12	
KEARNEY, Noel M.	Ipswich	07.10.42	JNRS	Ipswich T.	10.60					(F)
			TR	Colchester U.	09.64	1964	3		0	
KEARNEY, Sid F.	Liverpool	28.03.17	Tranmere Rov.(*)	Accrington St.	*	1946	13		5	d.1983
			TR	Bristol C.	01.47	1946–49	66		5	
KEARNS, Fred T.	Cork	08.11.27	Shamrock Rov.	West Ham U.	05.48	1949–53	43		14	(CF) EI–1
			TR	Norwich C.	06.54	1954–55	28		10	
KEARNS, Mike D.	Nuneaton	10.03.38	Stockingford	Coventry C.	09.55	1957–67	343	/	14	(FB)

Players Names	Birthplace	Date	Previous Club	League Club	Date Signed	Seasons Played	Apps	Sub	Gls	
KEARNS, Mike	Banbury	25.11.50	APP	Oxford U.	07.68	1969-71	67	/	0	(G) EI-18.
			L	Plymouth Arg.	10.72	1972	1	/	0	Brother of Oliver
			L	Charlton Ath.	02.73	1972	4	/	0	
			TR	Walsall	07.73	1973-78	249	/	0	
			TR	Wolverhampton W.	07.79	1979-80	9	/	0	
			TR	Walsall	08.82	1982-83	21	/	0	
KEARNS, Oliver A.	Banbury	12.06.56	Banbury T.	Reading	07.77	1976-79	75	11	40	(F)
			TR	Oxford U.	08.81	1981	9	9	4	
			TR	Walsall	08.82	1982	31	7	11	
			TR	Hereford U.	06.83	1983	39	2	10	
KEARNS, Peter V.	Wellingborough	26.03.37	Wellingboro T.	Plymouth Arg.	04.56	1956–59	65		8	(IF)
			Corby T.	Aldershot	12.62	1962–67	184	1	64	
			TR	Lincoln C.	03.68	1967–68	45	1	11	
KEATING, Brian A.	Lewisham	19.03.35	Barry T.	Crewe Alex.	AM	1956–57	7		1	(F)
KEATING, Dennis	Cork	18.10.40		Chester C.	06.62	1962	1		0	(OL)
KEATING, Pat J.	Cork	17.09.30	Cork	Sheffield U.	02.50	1950	3		0	(OL)
			Wisbech	Bradford P.A.	09.53	1953	2		0	
			TR	Chesterfield	10.53	1953–56	95		21	
KEATING, Robert	Oldham	24.06.17	Oldham Ath.(+)	Accrington St.	12.46	1946	5		0	
KEAY, John	Glasgow	14.06.60	Glasgow Celtic	Shrewsbury T.	07.77	1977-81	152	3	20	(D)
			TR	Wrexham	09.82	1982-83	75	/	5	
KEE, Paul J.	Derry	21.02.67	JNRS	Mansfield T.	N/C	1983	0	1	0	
KEEBLE, Brian	Holbeach	11.07.38	Holbeach	Grimsby T.	05.59	1959-64	172		1	(FB)
			TR	Darlington	07.65	1965–68	154	/	2	
KEEBLE, Fred W.	Coventry	30.08.19	Albion Rov.	Grimsby T.	09.46	1946	7		1	(IF)
			TR	Notts. Co.	07.47	1947	4		1	
KEEBLE, Vic A.W.	Colchester	25.06.30	King George YC	Colchester U.	N/L	1950–51	46		23	(CF)
			TR	Newcastle U.	02.52	1951–57	104		56	
			TR	West Ham U.	10.57	1957–59	76		45	
KEEFE, David E.	Dagenham	23.06.57	APP	Southend U.	07.75	1974-75	4	2	1	(F)
			TR	Torquay U.	08.77	1977	2	/	0	
KEEGAN, Gerard A.	Manchester	03.10.55	APP	Manchester C.	03.73	1974-78	32	5	2	(M) E.U21-1
			TR	Oldham Ath.	02.79	1978-82	139	5	5	
				Mansfield T.	10.83	1983	18	/	1	
KEEGAN, J. Kevin	Doncaster	14.02.51	APP	Scunthorpe U.	12.68	1968-70	120	4	18	(F) E-63/E.U23-5●
			TR	Liverpool	05.71	1971-76	230	/	68	
			S.V. Hamburg	Southampton	07.80	1980-81	68	/	37	
			TR	Newcastle U.	08.82	1982-83	78	/	48	
KEELAN, Kevin D.	India	05.01.41	JNRS	Aston Villa	07.58	1959-60	5		0	(G)●
			TR	Stockport Co.	04.61	1960	3		0	
			Kidderminster	Wrexham	11.61	1961-62	68		0	
			TR	Norwich C.	07.63	1963-69	571	/	0	
KEELEY, Andy J.	Basildon	16.09.56	APP	Tottenham H.	01.74	1976	5	1	0	(D) E.YTH.INT.
			TR	Sheffield U.	12.77	1977-80	28	/	0	Brother of Glen
			TR	Scunthorpe U.	07.81	1981-82	75	2	1	
KEELEY, Damian	Salford	14.02.63		Torquay U.	N/C	1981	1	2	0	(F)
KEELEY, Glen M.	Basildon	01.09.54	APP	Ipswich T.	08.72	1972-73	4	/	0	(D) E.YTH.INT.
			TR	Newcastle U.	08.72	1972-73	43	1	2	
			TR	Blackburn Rov.	08.76	1976-83	258	5	16	
			L	Everton	10.82	1982	1	/	0	
KEELEY, Jack J.	Liverpool	18.10.36	JNRS	Everton	05.54	1957	4		1	(IF) E.YTH.INT./
			TR	Accrington St.	07.59	1959	10		1	E.SCH.INT.
			TR	Southport	12.59	1959	4		0	
KEELEY, John H.	Plaistow	27.07.61	APP	Southend U.	08.79	1979-83	54	/	0	(G)
KEELEY, Nolan	E. Barsham	24.05.51	Gt. Yarmouth	Scunthorpe U.	07.73	1972-79	255	4	37	(M)
			TR	Lincoln C.	01.80	1979-80	52	/	3	
KEELEY, Ray	London	25.12.46	APP	Charlton Ath.	12.64	1964	1		0	(F)
			TR	Exeter C.	03.66	1965-66	45	1	10	
			Crawley T.	Mansfield T.	06.68	1968-69	48	4	5	
KEELEY, Walter	Manchester	01.04.21	Chesterfield(+)	Accrington St.	+	1946–47	48		19	(IF)
			TR	Bury	10.47	1947	7		0	
			TR	Port Vale	01.48	1947–48	18		3	
			TR	Accrington St.	09.48	1948–51	100		35	
			TR	Rochdale	10.51	1951	4		0	
KEEN, Alan	Barrow	29.05.30	Barrow Social	Barrow	05.49	1949-53	95		14	(IF)
			TR	Chesterfield	07.54	1954–55	54		12	
			Cheltenham	Bradford P.A.	02.57	1956	11		1	
			Cheltenham	Carlisle U.	09.58	1958–59	8		0	
KEEN, Herbert	Barrow	09.09.26	Netherfield	Barrow	07.53	1953	8		0	(OL)
KEEN, John	Barrow	26.01.29	W.B.A.(AM)	Barrow	01.48	1947–58	273		19	(WH)
			TR	Workington	07.59	1959	19		0	Brother to Herbert/Alan
KEEN, Mike	Wycombe	19.03.40		Q.P.R.	06.58	1959-68	393	/	41	(WH)●
			TR	Luton T.	01.69	1968-71	144	1	11	
			TR	Watford	07.72	1972-74	124	2	5	

Players Names	Birthplace	Date	Previous Club	League Club	Date Signed	Seasons Played	Career Record Apps	Sub	Gls	
KEENAN, Gerry P.	Liverpool	25.07.54		Bury	08.75	1974–78	69	2	3	(D)
			TR	Port Vale	09.78	1978–81	105	1	7	
			TR	Rochdale	11.82	1982–83	35	/	1	
KEENAN, William G.	Llanelli	29.12.18	Hereford U.	Everton	*					(OL)
			TR	Newport Co.	06.46	1946	4		1	
KEENE, Doug C.	London	30.08.28	JNRS	Brentford	09.47	1948–49	13		1	(OL)
			TR	Brighton & H.A.	06.50	1950–52	61		10	
			TR	Colchester U.	07.53	1953	22		1	
KEERS, Jim	Graghead	10.12.32	Evenwood	Darlington	03.52	1951–55	73		15	(OR)
KEERY, Stan	Derby	09.09.31	Blackburn Rov.(AM)	Shrewsbury T.	08.52	1952	15		2	(WH)
			TR	Newcastle U.	11.52	1952–56	19		1	
			TR	Mansfield T.	05.57	1957–58	53		18	
			TR	Crewe Alex.	10.58	1958–64	254		23	
KEETCH, Robert	Tottenham	25.10.41	West Ham U.(AM)	Fulham	04.59	1962–65	106	/	2	(CH)
			TR	Q.P.R.	11.66	1966-68	48	3	0	
KEETLEY, Albert E.	Radford	22.02.30		Bury	03.50	1950	4		0	(FB)
			TR	Bournemouth	07.52	1953–57	86		0	
KEETON, Albert	Chesterfield	15.01.18	Brad C.(*)	Torquay U.	*	1946–47	51		0	(RB)
KEIGHLEY, John P.	Ribchester	15.02.61	APP	Bolton W.	02.79					(F)
			TR	Crewe Alex.	08.81	1981	25	4	0	
KEIR, Colin	Bournemouth	14.01.38	JNRS	Portsmouth	05.55					(F)
			TR	Workington	06.59	1959	4		0	
KEIRS, John	Irvine	14.08.47	Annbank	Charlton Ath.	06.65	1965–70	73	5	1	(HB)
KEITH, Adrian J.	Colchester	16.12.62	APP	West Ham U.	12.80					(D)
				Colchester U.	N/C	1982	4	/	0	
KEITH, Richard M.	Belfast	15.05.33	Linfield	Newcastle U.	09.56	1956–63	208		2	(FB)NI–3/NI'B'–1
			TR	Bournemouth	02.64	1963–65	47	/	0	d.1967
KELL, G. Allan	Spennymoor	09.04.49		Darlington	AM	1967	0	2	0	
KELL, Len W.	Stockton	27.05.32	JNRS	Chelsea	02.52	1953	3		0	(IF)
			TR	Norwich C.	06.54	1954	2		0	
KELLARD, Robert S.W.	Edmonton	01.03.43	JNRS	Southend U.	05.60	1959–62	106		15	(M)E.YTH.INT.●
			TR	Crystal Palace	09.63	1963–65	76	/	6	
			TR	Ipswich T.	11.65	1965	13	/	3	
			TR	Portsmouth	03.66	1965–67	91	/	8	
			TR	Bristol C.	07.68	1968–69	77	/	6	
			TR	Leicester C.	08.70	1970–71	48	/	8	
			TR	Crystal Palace	09.71	1971–72	44	2	4	
			TR	Portsmouth	12.72	1972–74	62	1	6	
			L	Hereford U.	01.75	1974	3	/	1	
			Sth. Africa	Torquay U.	09.75	1975	2	/	0	
KELLEY, Alan W.	Liverpool	24.12.52	APP	Southport	12.70	1970–71	17	6	2	(FB)
			TR	Crewe Alex.	08.72	1972–75	105	2	0	
KELLEY, Stan R.	Foleshill	14.06.20	JNRS	Coventry C.	+	1946	4		0	(FB)
KELLOCK, William	Glasgow	07.02.54	Aston Villa (APP)	Cardiff C.	02.72	1972-72	33	2	2	(M) S.SCH.INT.
			TR	Norwich C.	06.73	1973	1	2	0	
			TR	Millwall	07.74					
			Kettering	Peterborough U.	08.79	1979–81	134	/	43	
			TR	Luton T.	07.82	1982	2	5	0	
			TR	Wolverhampton W.	03.83	1982-83	12	3	0	
			TR	Southend U.	09.83	1983	40	/	6	
KELLOW, Anthony	Buddock Water	01.05.52	Falmouth	Exeter C.	07.76	1976–78	107	/	40	(F)
			TR	Blackpool	11.78	1978–79	57	7	23	
			TR	Exeter C.	03.80	1979–83	140	3	61	
			TR	Plymouth Arg.	11.83	1984	8	2	2	
KELLY, Alan J.	Dublin	05.07.36	Drumcondra	Preston N.E.	04.58	1960–73	447	/	0	(G)EI–47●
KELLY, Anthony G.	Prescot	01.10.64	APP	Liverpool	09.82					(D)
				Wigan Ath.	01.84	1983	27	2	2	
KELLY, Arthur	Belfast	12.03.14	Belfast Celtic	Barrow	09.46	1946	8		2	(F) d.1973
KELLY, Bernard	N.Stevenston	21.10.32	Raith Rov.	Leicester C.	07.58	1958	24		13	(IF)S'B'–1/
			TR	Nottingham F.	04.59	1958	2		0	S.F.LGE REP.
KELLY, Bernard A.	Kensington	21.08.28	Bath C.	Brentford	08.50	1950	1		1	
KELLY, Brian L.	Bradford	22.05.43	JNRS	Bradford C.	05.60	1961–64	83		2	(FB)
			TR	Doncaster Rov.	01.65	1964–67	130	1	3	
			TR	York C.	07.68	1968–69	32	1	0	
			TR	Halifax T.	07.70					
KELLY, Chris	Epsom	14.10.48	Leatherhead	Millwall	01.75	1974	9	2	0	(CF)E.AMAT.INT.
KELLY, David T.	Birmingham	25.11.65		Walsall	12.83	1983	5	1	3	(F)
KELLY, Des	Limerick	01.11.50	Limerick	Norwich C.	07.70					(G)
			TR	Colchester U.	06.72	1972	1	/	0	
KELLY, Don J.	Mkt. Harborough	02.07.22	Coventry C.(AM)	Torquay U.	07.47	1946–47	5		3	(CF)
KELLY, Doug C.	Worsborough	30.05.34	JNRS	Barnsley	08.51	1952–54	18		7	(F)
			TR	Bradford C.	06.55	1955–56	43		14	
			TR	Chesterfield	06.57	1957	1		1	

Players Names	Birthplace	Date	Previous Club	League Club	Date Signed	Seasons Played	Apps	Sub	Gls	
KELLY, Eddie	Glasgow	07.02.51	JNRS	Arsenal	02.68	1969-75	168	7	13	(M) S.U23-3
			TR	Q.P.R.	09.76	1976	28	/	1	
			TR	Leicester C.	07.77	1977-79	85	/	3	
			TR	Notts. Co.	07.80	1980	26	1	1	
			TR	Bournemouth	08.81	1981	13	/	0	
			TR	Leicester C.	12.81	1981-82	34	/	0	
KELLY, Errington E.	St. Vincent	08.04.58	Ledbury T.	Bristol Rov.	09.81	1981-82	12	6	3	(F)
			TR	Lincoln C.	N/C	1982	0	2	0	
			TR	Bristol C.	03.83	1982	4	1	1	
			TR	Coventry C.	08.83					
			L	Peterborough U.	03.84	1983	11	/	7	
KELLY, Fred C.	Wednesbury	11.02.21		Walsall	+	1946-47	16		6	
KELLY, George L.	Aberdeen	29.06.33	Aberdeen	Stoke C.	02.56	1955-57	67		35	(IF)
			TR	Cardiff C.	05.58	1958	8		4	
			TR	Stockport Co.	07.59	1959	34		4	
KELLY, Hugh	Valleyfield	23.07.23	Jeanfield Swifts	Blackpool	+	1946-59	429		5	(WH)S-1/S'B'-1●
KELLY, Hugh R.	Belfast	17.08.19	Belfast Celtic	Fulham	03.49	1949	25		0	(G)NI-4/
			TR	Southampton	08.50	1950	28		0	IRISH LGE REP.
			TR	Exeter C.	06.52	1952-55	99		0	
KELLY, James	Bellshill	04.06.33	Peterborough U.	Preston N.E.	05.55					(F)
			TR	Swindon T.	02.58	1957-58	30		14	
			TR	Walsall	02.59	1958	8		1	
KELLY, James	Bradford	01.07.38	Queensbury U.	Halifax T.	10.62	1963	3		0	(F)
KELLY, James	Morpeth	11.08.31	Blyth Spartans	Watford	03.49	1950-54	120		4	(WH)
			TR	Blackpool	10.54	1954-60	198		9	
KELLY, James	Aldergrove	06.02.54	Cliftonville	Wolverhampton W.	12.71	1973-77	20	2	0	(F)
			L	Wrexham	09.75	1975	4	/	0	
			TR	Walsall	08.78	1978-79	19	7	3	
KELLY, James	Drogheda	16.02.25	Glenavon	Tottenham H.	07.49					(F)
			TR	Carlisle U.	02.50	1949-51	43		6	
KELLY, James E.	Seaham	29.12.07	York C(*)	Barrow	*	1946	1		0	(FB)*Southport/Barrow/
										Grimsby T./Bradford P.A.
KELLY, James J.				Barrow	+	1946	1		0	(CF)
KELLY, James L.	Holborn	14.07.26	Dartford	Gillingham	05.51	1951	3		0	
KELLY, James P.	Seaham	22.11.51		Hartlepool U.	08.70	1971	5	/	0	(FB)
KELLY, James W.	Carlisle	02.05.57	APP	Manchester U.	05.74	1975	0	1	0	(WH)
KELLY, John	Bebington	20.10.60	Cammell Laird	Tranmere Rov.	09.79	1979-81	55	9	9	(F)
			TR	Preston N.E.	10.81	1981-83	85	8	20	
KELLY, John C.	Paisley	21.02.21	Morton	Barnsley	+	1946-52	218		25	(IF)S-2
			Morton	Halifax T.	07.56	1956-57	38		2	
KELLY, John G.	Glasgow	14.12.35	T. Lanark	Crewe Alex.	08.59	1959	20		1	(WH)S.SCH.INT.
			Morton	Barnsley	09.63					
KELLY, Laurie	Wolverhampton	28.04.25	JNRS	Wolveshampton W.	+	1947-49	60		0	(FB)
			TR	Huddersfield T.	10.50	1950-56	223		2	
KELLY, Mike	London	18.10.42	Wimbledon	Q.P.R.	03.66	1967-69	54	/	0	(G)E.AMAT.INT.
			TR	Birmingham C.	08.70	1970-74	62	/	0	
KELLY, Mike J.			Wolverhampton W.(+)	Crewe Alex.	+	1946	15		2	(OL)
KELLY, Mike L.	Belvedere	22.10.54	APP	Millwall	10.72	1972-74	16	2	2	(IF)
			TR	Charlton Ath.	12.74	1974	10	/	3	
KELLY, Noel	Dublin	28.12.21	Glentoran	Arsenal	10.47	1949	1		0	(IF)EI-1/
			TR	Crystal Palace	03.50	1949-50	42		6	L.O.I. REP.
			TR	Nottingham F.	08.51	1951-54	48		11	
			TR	Tranmere Rov.	07.55	1955-56	52		6	
KELLY, Nyrere	Coventry	14.02.66	JNRS	Bristol C.	N/C	1982	2	4	1	(F)
KELLY, Pat	S. Africa	09.04.18	Aberdeen	Barnsley	10.46	1946-50	145		0	(G)NI-1
			TR	Crewe Alex.	02.52	1951-52	38		0	
KELLY, Peter A.	Lothian	06.12.56	APP	Newcastle U.	07.74	1975-80	31	2	0	(D)
KELLY, Phil	Dublin	10.07.39	Sheldon T.	Wolverhampton W.	09.57	1958-61	16		0	(FB)EI-5
			TR	Norwich C.	08.62	1962-66	115	1	2	
KELLY, Robert	Dysart	16.11.19	Raith Rov.	Millwall	06.46	1946-47	53		1	(WH)
			TR	Bury	05.48	1948	9		0	
KELLY, Robert A.	Birmingham	21.12.64	APP	Leicester C.	12.82	1983	1	/	0	(M)
KELLY, Terry J.	Gateshead	14.05.42	JNRS	Newcastle U.	05.60					(HB)
			TR	Lincoln C.	07.62	1962	8		3	
KELLY, Terry W.J.	Luton	16.01.32	Vauxhall Mot.	Luton T.	04.50	1954-62	136		1	(CH)
KELLY, Thomas W.	Darlington	22.11.19		Darlington	*	1946-50	149		3	(FB)
			TR	York C.	08.51					
KELLY, Walter M.	Hill of Beath	15.04.29	Raith Rov.	Bury	08.52	1952-56	160		76	(CF)Brother of William M.
			TR	Doncaster Rov.	06.57	1957	29		6	
			TR	Stockport Co.	03.58	1957-59	48		12	
			TR	Chester C.	08.59	1959-60	56		24	

Players Names	Birthplace	Date	Previous Club	League Club	Date Signed	Seasons Played	Apps	Sub	Gls	
KELLY, William B.	Isleworth	25.09.37		Q.P.R.	11.58	1958	6		0	
KELLY, William M.	Hill of Beath	14.08.22	Airdrie	Blackburn Rov.	09.51	1951–56	186		1	(CH)
			TR	Accrington St.	09.57	1957	24		0	
KELSALL, Charles	Hawarden	15.04.21		Wrexham	+	1946–51	39		0	(HB)
KELSEY, A. Jack	Llansamlet	19.11.29	Winch Wen	Arsenal	08.49	1950–61	327		0	(G)W–41/E.F.LGE REP.●
KEMBER, Steve D.	Croydon	08.12.48	APP	Crystal Palace	12.65	1965-71	216	2	34	(M) E.U23-3
			TR	Chelsea	09.71	1972-74	125	5	13	
			TR	Leicester C.	07.75	1975-78	115	2	6	
			TR	Crystal Palace	10.78	1978-79	39	3	1	
KEMP, David M.	Harrow	20.02.53	Slough T.	Crystal Palace	04.l75	1974-76	32	3	10	(F)
			TR	Portsmouth	11.76	1976-77	63	1	30	
			TR	Carlisle U.	03.78	1977-79	60	1	22	
			TR	Plymouth Arg.	09.79	1979-81	82	3	39	
			L	Gillingham	12.81	1981	9	/	2	
			L	Brentford	03.82	1981	3	/	1	
KEMP, Fred	Italy	27.02.46	APP	Wolverhampton W.	06.63	1964	3		0	(WH)
			TR	Southampton	06.65	1965–69	58	4	9	
			TR	Blackpool	11.70	1970–71	20	2	1	
			TR	Halifax T.	12.71	1971–73	106	5	10	
			TR	Hereford U.	07.74	1974	12	1	2	
KEMP, John J.	Clydebank	11.04.34	Clyde	Leeds U.	12.57	1958	1		0	(OL)
			TR	Barrow	03.59	1958–63	170		46	
			TR	Crewe Alex.	12.63	1963–65	47		7	
KEMP, Ray W.	Bristol	18.01.22	Grays Ath.	Reading	AM	1949	3		0	(G)
KEMP, Robert	Falkirk	15.08.41	Falkirk	Carlisle U.	11.60	1960	1		0	(OL)
KEMP, Sam	Stockton	29.08.32	Whitby T.	Sunderland	03.52	1952–56	17		2	(F)
			TR	Sheffield U.	02.57	1956–57	16		1	
			TR	Mansfield T.	05.58	1958	3		1	
			TR	Gateshead	10.58	1958	7		1	
KEMP, Steve D.	Shrewsbury	02.05.55	APP	Shrewsbury T.	07.73	1972–73	7	1	0	(WH)
KENDAL, Steve J.	Birtley	04.08.61	APP	Nottingham F.	07.81	1981	1	/	0	(M)
			TR	Chesterfield	12.82	1982-83	65	/	9	
KENDALL, Arnold	Siddall	06.04.25	Ossett T.	Bradford C.	02.49	1948–52	113		13	(F)
			TR	Rochdale	09.53	1953–56	110		25	
			TR	Bradford P.A.	09.56	1956–58	90		12	
KENDALL, Howard	Ryton-on-Tyne	22.05.46	APP	Preston N.E.	05.63	1962-66	104	/	13	(M) E.U23-6/E.F.LGE.REP./
			TR	Everton	03.67	1966-73	227	3	21	E.YTH.INT./E.SCH.INT.●
			TR	Birmingham C.	02.74	1973-76	115	/	16	
			TR	Stoke C.	08.77	1977-78	82	/	9	
			TR	Blackburn Rov.	07.79	1979-80	79	/	6	
			TR	Everton	N/C	1981	4	/	0	
KENDALL, Ian	Blackburn	11.12.47	APP	Blackburn Rov.	12.65					(F)
			TR	Southport	08.67	1967	1	1	0	
KENDALL, Jim B.	Birtley	04.10.22		Barrow	05.47	1946–48	44		16	(CF)
			TR	Gateshead	11.48	1948–51	57		21	
			TR	Barrow	10.51	1951–52	22		6	
			TR	Accrington St.	09.52	1952	26		8	
KENDALL, Mark	Blackwood	20.09.58	APP	Tottenham H.	07.76	1978-80	29	/	0	(G) W.U21-1/W.SCH.INT.
			L	Chesterfield	11.79	1979	9	/	0	
			TR	Newport Co.	09.80	1980-83	161	/	0	
KENDALL, Mark I.	Nuneaton	10.12.61	APP	Aston Villa	11.79					(G) E.YTH.INT.
			TR	Northampton T.	06.82	1982	11	/	0	
			TR	Birmingham C.	02.84	1983	1	/	0	
KENDALL, Paul S.	Halifax	19.10.64	APP	Halifax T.	11.82	1981-83	50	12	2	(D)
KENNEDY, Alan P.	Sunderland	31.08.54	APP	Newcastle U.	09.72	1972-77	155	3	9	(D) E.U23-6/E-2
			TR	Liverpool	08.78	1978-83	209	2	14	
KENNEDY, David	Sunderland	30.11.50		Leeds U.	05.68	1969	2	/	1	(WH)
			TR	Lincoln C.	07.71	1971	6	2	1	
KENNEDY, David	Birkenhead	14.02.49	JNRS	Tranmere Rov.	05.67	1967-69	16	1	0	(W)
			TR	Chester C.	05.70	1970-73	79	9	9	
			TR	Torquay U.	09.73	1973-76	144	7	7	
KENNEDY, Gordon	Dundee	15.04.24		Blackpool	+	1946–49	8		0	(FB)
			TR	Bolton W.	09.50	1950	17		0	
			TR	Stockport Co.	08.53	1953	20		1	
KENNEDY, Joe P.	Cleator Moor	15.11.25	Altrincham	W.B.A.	12.48	1948–60	364		3	(CH)E'B'–3
			TR	Chester C.	06.61	1961	35		0	
KENNEDY, John	Newtonards	04.09.39	Glasgow Celtic	Lincoln C.	07.67	1967–73	251	/	0	(G)
KENNEDY, John	Kilwinning	26.02.41	Saltcoats Vic.	Charlton Ath.	03.62	1961–64	46		8	(F)
			TR	Exeter C.	11.65	1965–66	40	1	6	
KENNEDY, Keith V.	Sunderland	05.03.52	APP	Newcastle U.	07.70	1971	1	/	0	(D) Brother of Alan
			TR	Bury	10.72	1972-81	405	/	4	
			TR	Mansfield T.	08.82	1982	32	2	0	
KENNEDY, Malcolm S.J.	Swansea	13.10.39	JNRS	Swansea C.	05.57	1957–60	19		0	(HB)
			TR	Carlisle U.	06.61					

Players Names	Birthplace	Date	Previous Club	League Club	Date Signed	Seasons Played	Apps	Sub	Gls	
KENNEDY, Mick F.	Salford	09.04.61	APP	Halifax T.	01.79	19788-79	74	2	4	(M)
			TR	Huddersfield T.	08.80	1980-81	80	1	9	
			TR	Middlesbrough	08.82	1982-83	68	/	5	
KENNEDY, Pat A.	Dublin	09.10.34	JNRS	Manchester U.	02.53	1954	1		0	(FB)
			TR	Blackburn Rov.	08.56	1957	3		0	
			TR	Southampton	07.59	1959	2		0	
			TR	Oldham Ath.	07.60					
KENNEDY, Ray	Seaton Delavel	28.07.51	APP	Arsenal	11.68	1969-73	156	2	53	(M) E-17/E.U23-6
			TR	Liverpool	07.74	1974-81	265	3	51	
			TR	Swansea C.	01.82	1981-83	42	/	2	
			TR	Hartlepool U.	11.83	1983	18	5	3	
KENNEDY, Robert	Motherwell	23.06.37	Kilmarnock	Manchester C.	07.61	1961–68	216	3	9	(FB)S.U23–1
			TR	Grimsby T.	03.69	1968–70	84	/	1	
KENNEDY, Steve	Audenshaw	22.07.65	APP	Burnley	07.83	1983	7	/	0	(D)
KENNERLEY, Kevin R.	Chester	26.04.54	Arsenal (APP)	Burnley	05.72	1975	6	/	1	(M)
			TR	Port Vale	05.76	1976-77	16	8	1	
			L	Swansea C.	02.78	1977	2	/	0	
KENNING, Mike J.	Birmingham	18.08.40		Aston Villa	10.59	1960	3		0	(W)
			TR	Shrewsbury T.	05.61	1961 62	62		17	
			TR	Charlton Ath.	11.62	1962–66	152	1	43	
			TR	Norwich C.	12.66	1966–67	44	/	9	
			TR	Wolverhampton W.	01.68	1967–68	35	6	5	
			TR	Charlton Ath.	03.69	1968–71	60	7	12	
			TR	Watford	12.71	1971–72	35	6	2	
KENNON, Neil S.(Sandy)	S. Africa	28.11.33	Bulawayo	Huddersfield T.	08.56	1956–58	78		0	(G)
			TR	Norwich C.	02.59	1958–64	213		0	
			TR	Colchester U.	03.65	1964–66	77	/	0	
KENNY, Fred	Manchester	14.01.23		Stockport Co.	12.47	1948–56	204		0	(FB)
KENNY, Vince	Sheffield	29.12.24		Sheffield Wed.	+	1946–54	144		0	(FB)
			TR	Carlisle U.	07.55	1955–57	103		3	
KENNY, William	Liverpool	23.10.51	APP	Everton	07.69	1970-73	10	3	0	(M)
			TR	Tranmere Rov.	03.75	1974-76	36	18	6	
KENT, Kevin J.	Stoke	19.03.65	APP	W.B.A.	12.82	1983	1	1	0	(F)
KENT, Mike J.	Rotherham	12.01.51	Wath W.	Wolverhampton W.	08.68	1971	0	1	0	(F)
			L	Gillingham	03.71	1970	11	/	0	
			TR	Sheffield Wed.	09.73	1973	4	/	0	
KENT, Paul	Rotherham	23.02.54	APP	Norwich C.	02.72	1973	1	2	0	(D)
			TR	Halifax T.	08.76	1976	12	/	0	
KENT, Terry	London	21.10.39		Southend U.	05.58	1958	1		0	(HB)Essex Cricketer
			TR	Millwall	08.60					
KENWORTHY, Anthony	Leeds	30.10.58	APP	Sheffield U.	07.76	1975-83	250	4	34	(D) E.YTH.INT.
KENWORTHY, Steve	Wrexham	06.11.59	JNRS	Wrexham	11.77	1977-80	19	1	0	(D)
			TR	Bury	08.81	1982	14	/	0	
KENYON, Fred	Carlisle	14.01.22		Carlisle U.	+	1947–48	4		0	(WH)
KENYON, John	Blackburn	02.12.53	Gt. Harwood	Blackburn Rov.	12.72	1972–75	31	15	7	(F)
KENYON, Roger N.	Blackpool	04.01.49	APP	Everton	09.66	1967-78	254	14	6	(D)
			Vancouver W.	Bristol C.	10.79	1979	4	/	0	
KENYON, Roy	Manchester	10.03.33	Bolton W.(AM)	Leeds U.	12.50					(F)
			TR	Southport	09.54	1954	1		0	
KERFOOT, Eric	Ashton–u–Lyne	31.07.24	Stalybridge	Leeds U.	12.49	1949–58	336		9	(WH)
			TR	Chesterfield	07.59	1959	8		0	
KERNAN, Anthony P.	Letterkenny	31.08.63	APP	Wolverhampton W.	01.81	1981	1	/	0	(M)EI.YTH.INT.
KERNICK, Dudley	Camelford	29.08.21	Tintagel	Torquay U.	*	1946–47	38		7	(F)
			TR	Northampton T.	08.48					
			TR	Birmingham C.	12.48					
KERR, Albert W.	Lanchester	11.08.17		Aston Villa	*	1946	1		0	d.1979
KERR, Andy	Ayr	29.06.31	Partick Th.	Manchester C.	06.59	1959	10		0	(CF)S–2/S'B'–1/
			Kilmarnock	Sunderland	04.63	1962–63	18		5	S.F.LGE REP.
KERR, Archie	Motherwell	30.08.35	Motherwell	Shrewsbury T.	01.57	1956	13		0	(F)
KERR, Charles	Glasgow	10.12.33	Morton	Carlisle U.	08.56	1956–57	9		3	
				Barrow	07.59	1959	20		3	
KERR, David	Glasgow	04.12.36		Liverpool	04.56					(F)
			TR	Southport	07.58	1958	32		4	
KERR, George A.M.	Alexandria	09.01.43	Vale of Leven	Barnsley	05.60	1961–65	170	/	39	(IF)
			TR	Bury	03.66	1965–66	15	/	2	
			TR	Oxford U.	09.66	1966–67	40	1	6	
			TR	Scunthorpe U.	02.68	1967–72	151	6	32	
KERR, Jim	Newcastle	03.03.32	Blyth Spartans	Lincoln C.	11.52	1952–53	15		1	(OL)
			TR	Oldham Ath.	06.54	1954–55	34		4	
KERR, Jim P.	Glasgow	02.09.49	JNRS	Bury	08.66	1965–69	150	2	37	(WH)S.SCH.INT.
			TR	Blackburn Rov.	05.70	1970	11	/	0	

Players Names	Birthplace	Date	Previous Club	League Club	Date Signed	Seasons Played	Apps	Sub	Gls	
KERR, John	Birkenhead	23.11.59	APP	Tranmere Rov.	11.77	1978-82	126	9	38	(F)
			TR	Bristol C.	08.83	1983	13	1	4	
			TR	Stockport Co.	01.84	1983	21	/	6	
KERR, Paul A.	Portsmouth	09.06.64	APP	Aston Villa	05.82	1983	1	1	0	(F)
KERR, Peter	Paisley	25.09.43	T. Lanark	Reading	05.63	1963–64	41		7	(F)
KERR, Peter	Glasgow	03.01.28	Maryhill Hearts	Hartlepool U.	09.49	1949	2		0	(IR)
KERR, Robert	Alexandria	16.11.47	JNRS	Sunderland	11.64	1966-78	355	13	57	(M)
			TR	Blackpool	03.79	1978-79	18	4	2	
			TR	Hartlepool U.	07.80	1980-81	48	1	2	
KERR, Robert	W. Lothian	10.07.42	Arbroath	Millwall	08.62	1962	1		0	(CF)
KERR, Robert J.	Coatbridge	29.11.29	T. Lanark	Darlington	10.52	1952	10		2	
KERRAY, Jim R.	Stirling	02.12.35	Dunfermline	Huddersfield T.	08.60	1960–61	54		13	(IF)
			TR	Newcastle U.	02.62	1961–62	38		10	
KERRIGAN, Don	Seamill	07.05.41	Dunfermline	Fulham	02.68	1967–68	4	2	1	(OR)
			L	Lincoln C.	03.69	1968	12	/	0	
KERRINS, Pat M.	Fulham	13.09.36	JNRS	Q.P.R.	12.53	1953–59	145		30	(OL)
			TR	Crystal Palace	06.60	1960	5		0	
			TR	Southend U.	07.61	1961	11		0	
KERRY, Brian P.	Maltby	18.12.48	APP	Grimsby T.	01.66	1965	0	1	0	(F)
			TR	Huddersfield T.	04.67					
KERRY, David	Derby	06.02.37	Derby Co.(AM)	Preston N.E.	05.55					(F)E.YTH.INT.
			TR	Chesterfield	07.61	1961–62	55		21	
			TR	Rochdale	07.63	1963	12		4	
KERSHAW, Alan D.	Southport	23.04.54	APP	Preston N.E.	09.72					(FB)
			TR	Southport	07.74	1974	19	5	0	
KERSLAKE, Mike	London	27.02.58	APP	Fulham	10.75	1975-77	1	2	0	(D) E.YTH.INT.
			TR	Brighton & H.A.	06.78					
KETTERIDGE, Steve J.	Stevenage	07.11.59	Derby Co.(APP)	Wimbledon	04.78	1978-83	201	7	28	(M)
KETTLE, Albert H.	Colchester	03.06.22	Arkwright Spts.	Colchester U.	N/L	1950–54	23		0	(RB)
KETTLE, Brian	Prescot	22.04.56	APP	Liverpool	05.73	1975-76	3	/	0	(D) E.YTH. INT.
			TR	Wigan Ath.	08.80	1980	14	/	1	
KETTLEBOROUGH, Keith	Rotherham	29.06.35	Rotherham YMCA	Rotherham U.	12.55	1955–60	119		20	(IF)
			TR	Sheffield U.	12.60	1960–65	154	/	17	
			TR	Newcastle U.	12.65	1965–66	30	/	0	
			TR	Doncaster Rov.	12.66	1966–67	35	1	0	
			TR	Chesterfield	11.67	1967–68	66	/	3	
KETTLEY, Spencer C.	Rhondda	22.05.21	Newbury T.	Luton T.	+	1946	1		0	(WH)
KEVAN, Derek T.	Ripon	06.03.35	Ripon YMCA	Bradford P.A.	10.52	1952	15		8	(IF)E-14/E.U23-4/●
			TR	W.B.A.	07.53	1955–62	262		157	E.F.LGE REP.
			TR	Chelsea	03.63	1962	7		1	
			TR	Manchester C.	08.63	1963–64	67		48	
			TR	Crystal Palace	07.65	1965	21	/	5	
			TR	Peterborough U.	03.66	1965–66	16	1	2	
			TR	Luton T.	12.66	1966	10	/	4	
			TR	Stockport Co.	03.67	1966–67	38	2	10	
KEWLEY, Kevin	Liverpool	02.03.55	APP	Liverpool	03.72	1977	0	1	0	(F)
KEY, John	Chelsea	05.11.37	JNRS	Fulham	05.56	1958–65	163		29	(W)
			TR	Coventry C.	05.66	1966–67	27	/	7	
			TR	Orient	03.68	1967–68	9	1	0	
KEY, Richard	Market Harborough	13.04.56	Coventry C.(AM)	Exeter C.	07.75	1975-77	109	/	0	(G)
			TR	Cambridge U.	08.78	1978-82	52	/	0	
			L	Northampton T.	11.82	1982	2	/	0	
			TR	Orient	08.83	1983	42	/	0	
KEYES, Anthony J.	Salford	29.10.53	Manchester U.(AM)	Stockport Co.	02.73	1971–73	7	1	0	(IF)
KEYS, Paul	Ipswich	04.09.62		Luton T.	07.81					(M)
			L	Halifax T.	03.82	1981	1	1	0	
KEYWORTH, Ken	Rotherham	24.02.34		Rotherham U.	01.52	1955–57	85		7	(WH)
			TR	Leicester C.	05.58	1958–64	177		63	
			TR	Coventry C.	12.64	1964	7		3	
			TR	Swindon T.	08.65	1965	5	/	0	
KICHENBRAND, Don	S. Africa	13.08.33	Glasgow Rgrs.	Sunderland	03.58	1957–59	53		28	(CF)
KIDD, Brian	Manchester	29.05.49	APP	Manchester U.	06.66	1967-73	195	8	53	(F)E-2/E.U23-10/
			TR	Arsenal	08.74	1974-75	77	/	30	E.F.LGE.REP./E.YTH.INT.
			TR	Manchester C.	07.76	1976-78	97	1	44	
			TR	Everton	03.79	1978-79	40	/	11	
			TR	Bolton W.	05.80	1980-81	40	3	14	
KIDD, John O.	Birkenhead	15.01.36	Everton(AM)	Tranmere Rov.	08.55	1955–58	34		4	(F)
KIDD, William E.	Pegswood	31.10.07	Pegswood	Chesterfield	*	1946–47	44		0	(FB)d.1978
KIERAN, Len V.	Birkenhead	25.07.26	JNRS	Tranmere Rov.	+	1947–56	346		6	(WH)
KIERNAN, Fred W.	Dublin	07.07.19	Shamrock Rov.	Southampton	10.51	1951–55	132		0	(G)EI–5/d.1981
KIERNAN, Joe	Coatbridge	22.10.42	JNRS	Sunderland	11.59	1962	1		0	(WH)
			TR	Northampton T.	07.63	1963–71	303	3	13	

Players Names	Birthplace	Date	Previous Club	League Club	Date Signed	Seasons Played	Apps	Sub	Gls	
KIERNAN, Tom	Coatbridge	20.10.18	Glasgow Celtic	Stoke C.	09.47	1947–48	28		6	(IF)S.F.LGE REP.
			TR	Luton T.	11.48	1948–50	55		10	
KIERNAN, William E.	Croydon	22.05.25	Hong Kong	Charlton Ath.	07.49	1949–60	378		89	(OL)E'B'–1
KILCLINE, Brian	Nottingham	07.05.62	APP	Notts. Co.	05.80	1979-83	156	2	9	(D)E.U21-2
KILEY, Tom J.	Swansea	15.06.24		Swansea C.	06.47	1949–56	130		2	(CH)
KILFORD, John	Derby	08.11.38	Derby Corries	Notts. Co.	07.57	1958	26		0	(FB)
			TR	Leeds U.	02.59	1958–61	21		0	
KILGALLON, Mark C.	Glasgow	20.12.62	Ipswich T.(APP)	Hull C.	08.80	1980	0	1	0	(D)
KILGANNON, John	Stenhousemuir	26.06.36	Stenhousemuir	Luton T.	04.59	1958–59	13		1	(F)d.1967
KILKELLY, Tom F.	Galway	22.08.55	APP	Leicester C.	07.73					(HB)
			L	Northampton T.	09.74	1974	2	2	0	
KILKENNY, Jim	Stanley	21.11.34	Annfield Plain	Doncaster Rov.	05.52	1955–60	131		1	(WH)
KILLARNEY, Arthur	Huddersfield	26.02.21		Halifax T.	05.46	1946	2		0	(IR)
KILLIN, Harry R.	Canada	18.07.29		Manchester U.	04.49					(FB)
			TR	Lincoln C.	08.52	1953	7		0	
KILMORE, Kevin	Scunthrope	11.11.59	JNRS	Scunthorpe U.	01.77	1976-79	93	9	28	(F)E.YTH.INT.
			TR	Grimsby T.	09.79	1979-82	70	32	27	
			TR	Rotherham U.	08.83	1983	45	/	13	
KILNER, John I.	Bolton	03.10.59	APP	Preston N.E.	10.77					(G)
			TR	Halifax T.	02.79	1978-80	114	/	0	
			Bangor C.	Wigan Ath.	N/C	1983	4	/	0	
KILSHAW, Eddie A.	Prescot	25.12.19	Prescot Cables	Bury	*	1946–48	85		10	(OR)
			TR	Sheffield Wed.	12.48	1948	17		1	
KILSHAW, Fred	Wrexham	24.08.16		New Brighton	07.46	1946	8		1	(IR)+Leicester C.
KIMBERLEY, S. Ken	Walsall	07.08.20	Cannock C.Col	Walsall	05.46	1946	1		0	(G)
KINDON, Steve M.	Warrington	17.12.50	APP	Burnley	12.67	1968-71	102	7	28	(F) E.YTH.INT.
			TR	Wolverhampton W.	07.72	1972-77	111	27	28	
			TR	Burnley	11.77	1977-79	73	3	18	
			TR	Huddersfield T.	12.79	1979-81	69	4	35	
KING, Alan	Gateshead	25.11.47	Horden C.W.	Hartlepool U.	AM	1967	0	1	0	(OL)
KING, Alan	Birkenhead	18.01.45	JNRS	Tranmere Rov.	07.62	1962–71	342	/	33	(WH)
KING, Andy E.	Luton	14.08.56	APP	Luton T.	07.74	1974-75	30	3	9	(M)E.U21-2
			TR	Everton	04.76	1975-79	150	1	38	
			TR	Q.P.R.	09.80	1980-81	28	2	9	
			TR	W.B.A.	09.81	1981	21	4	4	
			TR	Everton	07.82	1982-83	43	1	11	
KING, Barry	Chesterfield	30.03.35	Norton Woodseats	Chelsea	11.57					(OR)
			TR	Reading	02.58	1957	3		0	
KING, Dave J.	Hull	24.10.40	JNRS	Hull C.	10.58	1959–62	65		24	(IF)
KING, David M.	Colchester	18.09.62	APP	Derby Co.	09.80					(M)
			Gresley Rovers	York C.	N/C	1982	0	1	0	
KING, Dennis	Bearpark	16.09.32		Bradford P.A.	09.50					(OR)
			Spennymoor	Oldham Ath.	05.54	1954–55	22		7	
KING, Derek A.	London	15.08.29	JNRS	Tottenham H.	08.50	1951–54	19		0	(CH)
			TR	Swansea C.	08.56	1956	5		0	
KING, Fred A.B.	Northampton	19.09.19	Northampton T.(*)	Wolverhampton W.	+	1946	6		3	(OR)
			TR	Northampton T.	12.47	1947–49	56		17	
KING, George	Warkworth	05.01.23		Newcastle U.	08.46	1946	2		0	(CF)Brother of Ray
			TR	Hull C.	03.48	1947–48	3		0	
			TR	Port Vale	04.49	1948–49	10		5	
			TR	Barrow	02.50	1949–51	86		35	
			TR	Bradford C.	01.52	1951–52	23		9	
			TR	Gillingham	10.52	1952	19		5	
KING, Gerry H.	Cardiff	09.04.47	JNRS	Cardiff C.	06.64	1964	6		0	(F)W.SCH.INT.
			TR	Torquay U.	06.65	1965	17	/	2	
			TR	Luton T.	06.66	1966	22	1	4	
			TR	Newport Co.	07.67	1967–68	49	3	9	
KING, Ian A.	Glasgow	27.05.37	Arniston Rovers	Leicester C.	06.57	1957–65	244	/	6	(CH)S.SCH.INT.
			TR	Charlton Ath.	03.66	1965–67	63	/	0	
KING, Jeff	Fauldhouse	09.11.53	Albion Rov.	Derby Co.	04.74	1975-77	13	2	0	(M)
			L	Notts. Co.	01.76	1975	3	/	0	
			L	Portsmouth	03.76	1975	4	/	0	
			TR	Walsall	11.77	1977-78	50	1	4	
			TR	Sheffield Wed.	08.79	1979-81	54	3	5	
			TR	Sheffield U.	01.82	1981-82	35	2	5	
			TR	Chesterfield	10.83	1983	1	/	0	
KING, John	Glasgow	29.01.55	APP	Shrewsbury T.	03.73	1972-81	304	2	20	(D)
			TR	Wrexham	08.82	1982-83	77	1	5	
KING, John	Ferndale	29.11.33	JNRS	Swansea C.	02.51	1950-63	368		0	(G)W-1/W.SCH.INT

Players Names	Birthplace	Date	Previous Club	League Club	Date Signed	Seasons Played	Apps	Sub	Gls	
KING, John A.	Liverpool	15.04.38	JNRS	Everton	03.56	1957–59	48		1	(WH)
			TR	Bournemouth	07.60	1960	21		1	
			TR	Tranmere Rov.	02.61	1960–67	239	2	4	
			TR	Port Vale	07.68	1968–70	99	2	0	
KING, John C.	Gt. Gidding	05.11.26	Peterborough U.	Leicester C.	+	1946–54	197		5	(WH)
KING, John W.	Wrenbury	09.08.32	JNRS	Crewe Alex.	10.49	1950–53	48		17	(CF)●
			TR	Stoke C.	09.53	1953–60	284		105	
			TR	Cardiff C.	08.61	1961	33		6	
			TR	Crewe Alex.	06.62	1962–66	178	/	43	
KING, M. Brian	Bishop Stortford	18.05.47	Chelmsford	Millwall	06.67	1967–74	302	/	0	(G)
			TR	Coventry C.	08.75	1975	23	/	0	
KING, Martyn	Birmingham	23.08.37	Pegasus	Colchester U.	09.58	1956–64	212		131	(CF)
			TR	Wrexham	10.64	1964–65	45	/	15	
KING, Peter	Liverpool	05.07.64	APP	Liverpool	07.82					(M)
			TR	Crewe Alex.	08.83	1983	38	4	4	
KING, Peter C.	Worcester	03.04.43	Worcester C.	Cardiff C.	09.60	1961–73	352	5	66	(CF)
KING, Ray	Warkworth	15.08.24		Newcastle U.	+					(G)E'B'–1
			TR	Orient	10.46	1946	1		0	
			Ashington	Port Vale	05.49	1949–56	252		0	
KING, Robert	Edinburgh	07.09.41	Glasgow Rgrs.	Southend U.	08.63	1963–65	77	2	2	(FB)
KING, Tom	Edinburgh	18.07.33	Ormiston Primrose	Watford	03.54	1955	20		0	(G)
KING, Tom F.	Barrow	02.04.34	Holker COB	Barrow	07.53	1952–59	73		1	(WH)
KINGSHOTT, Fred,J.	St. Pancras	20.06.29		Doncaster Rov.	02.53	1952	2		0	(G)
			TR	Gillingham	11.55	1955–56	45		0	
KINGSNORTH, Tom	Milton	16.04.17		Gillingham	N/L	1950	29		0	(HB)
KINGSTON, Andy K.	Oxford	21.02.59	APP	Oxford U.	10.76	1976–81	44	6	0	(D) E.YTH.INT.E.SCH.INT.
KINLOCH, Tom S.	Glasgow	22.02.27	Falkirk	Carlisle U.	05.50	1950–55	182		15	(HB)
			TR	Workington	07.56	1956–57	70		12	
			TR	Southport	02.58	1957–58	53		0	
KINNEAR, Joe P.	Dublin	27.12.46	St. Albans	Tottenham H.	02.65	1965–75	189	7	2	(FB)EI–25
			TR	Brighton & H.A.	08.75	1975	15	1	1	
KINNELL, George	Cowdenbeath	22.12.37	Aberdeen	Stoke C.	11.63	1963–65	89	2	6	(CH)
			TR	Oldham Ath.	08.66	1966	12	/	8	
			TR	Sunderland	10.66	1966–68	67	2	3	
			TR	Middlesbrough	10.68	1968	12	1	1	
KINSELL, T. Harry	Cannock	03.05.21	JNRS	W.B.A.	*	1946–48	83		0	(FB)
			TR	Bolton W.	06.49	1949	17		0	
			TR	Reading	05.50	1950	12		0	
			TR	West Ham U.	01.51	1950–54	101		2	
KINSELLA, Anthony S.	Orsett	30.10.61	APP	Millwall	11.78	1978–80	55	6	1	(M) EI.U21-2
			Tampa Bay	Ipswich T.	04.82	1982–83	7	2	0	
KINSELLA, Len	Alexandria	14.05.46	APP	Burnley	05.63	1965–69	7	5	0	(WH)
			TR	Carlisle U.	09.70	1970–71	10	4	0	
			TR	Rochdale	09.71	1971–73	82	3	4	
KINSELLA, Pat G.	Liverpool	08.11.43	JNRS	Liverpool	11.60					(F)
			Bangor C.	Tranmere Rov.	08.66	1966	1	/	0	
			TR	Wrexham	07.67					
			Rhyl	Stockport Co.	10.68	1968	12	1	0	
KINSEY, Albert	Liverpool	19.09.45	APP	Manchester U.	10.62					(IF)E.SCH.INT.
			TR	Wrexham	03.66	1965–72	245	8	80	
			TR	Crewe Alex.	03.73	1972–74	30	2	1	
KINSEY, Brian R.	Charlton	04.03.38	Bromley	Charlton Ath.	10.56	1956–70	371	1	24	(FB)
KINSEY, Noel	Treorchy	24.12.25	JNRS	Cardiff C.	+					(IF)W–7
			TR	Norwich C.	05.47	1947–52	222		56	
			TR	Birmingham C.	05.53	1953–57	149		46	
			TR	Port Vale	02.58	1957–60	72		6	
KINSEY, Steve	Manchester	02.01.63	APP	Manchester C.	01.80	1980–83	42	11	8	(M)
			L	Chester C.	09.82	1982	3	/	1	
			L	Chesterfield	11.82	1982	3	/	0	
KIPPAX, Dennis H.	Sheffield	07.08.26	Stocksbridge Wks.	Sheffield Wed.	+	1946	1		0	(OR)d.1970
KIPPAX, F. Peter	Burnley	17.07.22	JNRS	Burnley	AM	1946–47	32		6	(OL)E.AMAT.INT./ 00
			TR	Liverpool	AM	1948	1		0	E.F.LGE REP.
KIRBY, Alan	Barrow	19.12.26	Notts.Co.(+)	Barrow	09.47	1950–51	21		0	(G)
KIRBY, Dennis	Holbeck	08.11.24		Leeds U.	+	1947	8		0	
				Halifax T.	08.50					
KIRBY, Eric	Sheffield	12.10.26		Sheffield Wed.	12.49	1950	1		0	(WH)
			TR	York C.	08.52	1952	1		0	

Players Names	Birthplace	Date	Previous Club	League Club	Date Signed	Seasons Played	Career Record Apps	Sub	Gls	
KIRBY, George	Liverpool	20.12.33	JNRS	Everton	06.52	1955–57	26		9	(CF)
			TR	Sheffield Wed.	03.59	1959	3		0	
			TR	Plymouth Arg.	01.60	1959–62	93		38	
			TR	Southampton	09.62	1962–63	64		28	
			TR	Coventry C.	03.64	1963–64	18		10	
			TR	Swansea C.	10.64	1964	26		9	
			TR	Walsal	05.65	1965–66	74	1	25	
			New York C.	Brentford	10.68	1968	5	/	1	
KIRK, Harry	Saltcoats	25.08.44	Ardeer Rec.	Middlesbrough	05.63	1963	1		0	(W)
			Dumbarton	Darlington	06.67	1967–69	59	3	7	
			TR	Hartlepool U.	10.69	1969–70	42	3	5	
			TR	Scunthorpe U.	11.70	1970–72	112	/	16	
			TR	Stockport Co.	09.73	1973–74	60	8	7	
KIRK, James	Tarbolton	12.11.25	St. Mirren	Bury	08.51	1951–53	79		0	(G)
			TR	Colchester U.	06.54	1954	32		0	
			TR	Torquay U.	08.55	1955	39		0	
			TR	Aldershot	07.56	1956	5		0	
KIRK, John F.	Leicester	07.02.22		Nottingham F.	08.48					
			TR	Darlington	08.51	1951	31		4	
KIRK, John M.	Canada	13.03.30		Portsmouth	01.51					(F)
			TR	Accrington St.	02.53	1952–53	14		1	
KIRK, Roy	Bolsover	11.06.29	Bolsover Col.	Leeds U.	10.48	1950–51	34		1	(WH)
			TR	Coventry C.	03.52	1951–59	329		6	
KIRK, Steve	Kirkcaldy	03.01.63	E. Fife	Stoke C.	05.80	1981	12	/	0	(D)
KIRKALDIE, Jack	Coventry	02.08.17	West Ham U.(*)	Doncaster Rov.	*	1946–47	51		16	(OR)*Southend U.
KIRKBY, John	U.S.A.	29.11.29	JNRS	Stoke C.	12.46	1948	1		0	(FB)d.1953 during
			TR	Wrexham	08.51	1951–52	5		0	Reserve Match
KIRKHAM, John	Ellesmere Port	16.06.18	Wolverhampton W.(*)	Bournemouth	*	1946	23		12	(F)*Ellesmere Port
KIRKHAM, John K.	Wednesbury	13.05.41	JNRS	Wolverhampton W.	05.58	1959–64	100		12	(WH)E.U23–2/E.YTH.INT.
			TR	Peterborough U.	11.65	1965–67	46	/	2	
			TR	Exeter C.	07.68	1968	31	2	5	
KIRKHAM, Ray	Thorne	16.12.34	Thorne T.	Mansfield T.	12.57	1957–59	41		0	(G)
KIRKHAM, Reg	Ormskirk	08.05.19	Ormskirk FC	Wolverhampton W.	+					(FB)
			TR	Burnley	03.47	1948–50	13		1	
KIRKHAM, Royce	Ollerton	17.10.37	Ollerton Col.	Notts. Co.	05.55	1956	1		0	(FB)
KIRKLAND, James	Bedford	30.10.46	Aberdeen	Grimsby T.	07.70	1970	12	/	0	(FB)
KIRKMAN, Alan J.	Bolton	21.06.36	Bacup	Manschester C.	02.56	1956–58	7		7	(IF)
			TR	Rotherham U.	03.59	1958–63	143		58	
			TR	Newcastle U.	09.63	1963	5		1	
			TR	Scunthorpe U.	12.63	1963–64	32		5	
			TR	Torquay U.	07.65	1965–66	59	/	8	
			TR	Workington	01.67	1966–67	55	/	3	
KIRKMAN, Ken R.	Bolton	20.03.31		Bournemouth	07.51					
			TR	Southport	08.53	1953	1		0	
KIRKMAN, Norman	Bolton	06.06.20		Burnley	+					(FB)
			TR	Rochdale	09.46	1946–47	53		0	
			TR	Chesterfield	12.47	1947–48	40		0	
			TR	Leicester C.	08.49	1949	12		0	
			TR	Southampton	07.50	1950–51	20		0	
			TR	Exeter C.	03.52	1951–52	11		1	
KIRKPATRICK, John	Annan	03.03.19	JNRS	Carlisle U.	*	1946	35		2	
KIRKPATRICK, Roger	Chester	29.05.23		Chester C.	08.47	1947–52	111		26	(WH)
KIRKUP, Brian A.	Slough	16.04.32	Bedford T.	Reading	08.55	1955–57	55		18	(CF)
			TR	Northampton T.	07.58	1958–59	26		7	
			TR	Aldershot	11.59	1959–61	59		14	
KIRKUP, Frank W.	Spennymoor	12.01.39	Spennymoor	Blackburn Rov.	02.57					(OL)
			TR	Workington	06.59	1959–62	140		31	
			TR	Carlisle U.	12.62	1962–64	76		15	
			TR	Notts. Co.	06.65	1965	29	/	0	
			TR	Workington	11.66	1966	9	/	0	
KIRKUP, Graeme S.	Cramlington	31.05.65	APP	Exeter C.	06.83	1981-83	59	2	1	(D)
KIRKUP, Joe R.	Hexham	17.12.39	JNRS	West Ham U.	05.57	1958–65	165	/	6	(FB)E.U23–3/
			TR	Chelsea	03.66	1965–67	48	5	2	E.YTH.INT.
			TR	Southampton	02.68	1967–73	169	/	3	
KIRKWOOD, Ian	Edinburgh	29.11.32	Wokingham T.	Reading	02.53	1952–54	5		1	(IR)
KIRKWOOD, John F.	Falkirk	27.02.32	Blairhall Col.	Reading	12.49	1952–53	31		0	(G)
KIRMAN, Harry	Hull	03.12.30	F. Askew YC	Hull C.	12.50					(FB)
			TR	Gillingham	07.52	1953	8		0	
			TR	Hull C.	05.55	1955	2		0	
KIRSTEN, Ken	S. Africa	28.10.22	Park Villa	Charlton Ath.	03.48					(W)
			TR	Aldershot	08.51	1951	5		0	
KIRTLEY, J. Harry	Washington	23.05.30	Fatfield J.	Sunderland	05.48	1948–54	95		18	(IF)
			TR	Cardiff C.	05.55	1955	38		4	
			TR	Gateshead	03.57	1956–59	96		14	

Players Names	Birthplace	Date	Previous Club	League Club	Date Signed	Seasons Played	Apps	Sub	Gls	
KIRTON, John	Aberdeen	04.03.16	Banks o'Dee	Stoke C.	*	1946–52	162		2	(WH)
			TR	Bradford C.	07.53	1953	8		0	
KISBY, Chris N.	Pudsey	07.11.52	APP	Scunthorpe U.	10.70	1970-72	30	9	2	(D)
			TR	Workington	08.73	1973-76	162	2	2	
			TR	Southport	08.77	1977	42	/	1	
KITCHEN, John	Whitehaven	28.02.25	Ketts. Ath.	Barnsley	+	1946–51	54		0	(CH)
KITCHEN, Peter	Mexborough	16.02.52	JNRS	Doncaster Rov.	07.70	1970-76	221	7	89	(F)
			TR	Orient	07.77	1977-78	64	1	28	
			TR	Fulham	02.79	1978-79	21	3	6	
			TR	Cardiff C.	08.80	1980-81	64	3	21	
			Happy Valley H.K.	Orient	12.82	1982-83	46	3	21	
KITCHENER, Barry R.	Dagenham	11.12.47	APP	Millwall	08.65	1966-81	518	5	24	(D)●
KITCHENER, Ray A.	Letchworth	31.10.30	Hitchin T.	Chelsea	07.54	1955	1		0	(OL)
			TR	Norwich C.	09.56	1956	18		0	
KITCHENER, William H.	Arlesey	03.11.46	APP	West Ham C.	11.63	1966-67	11	/	0	(FB)
			L	Torquay U.	09.66	1966	25	/	3	
			TR	Torquay U.	12.67	1967-70	142	/	5	
			TR	Bournemouth	07.71	1971	36	/	2	
KITE, Phil D.	Bristol	26.10.62	APP	Bristol Rov.	10.80	1980-83	96	/	0	(G) E.YTH.INT.
KLETZENBAUER, C. Frank	Coventry	21.07.36	Coventry M.S.C.	Coventry C.	03.56	1956–63	122		3	(FB)
			TR	Walsall	03.64	1963–64	12		0	
KLONER, Hymie	S. Africa		S. Africa	Birmingham C.	11.50	1950	1		0	
KLUG, Bryan P.	Coventry	08.10.60	APP	Ipswich T.	11.77					(M)E.YTH.INT.
			L	Wimbledon	03.80	1979	10	1	0	
			TR	Chesterfield	08.83	1983	27	7	2	
KNAPP, Anthony	Newstead	13.10.36	JNRS	Leicester C.	12.53	1955–60	86		0	(CH)E.F.LGE REP.
			TR	Southampton	08.61	1961–66	233	/	2	
			TR	Coventry C.	08.67	1967	12	/	0	
			Los Angeles	Bristol C.	03.69					
			Los Angeles	Tranmere Rov.	10.69	1969–70	36	/	1	
KNIGHT, Alan E.	Balham	03.07.61	APP	Portsmouth	03.79	1977-83	143	/	0	(G) E.YTH.INT./E.U'21-2
KNIGHT, Anthony	Romford	06.03.59	APP	Luton T.	05.76	1976-77	6	/	0	(G)
			Dover	Brighton & H.A.	08.79					
KNIGHT, Arnold W.	Guisborough	30.05.19		Leeds U.	*					
			TR	Plymouth Arg.	07.47	1947	7		0	
			TR	Bradford C.	02.48	1947–48	7		0	
KNIGHT, Brian M.	Dundee	28.03.49	Dundee	Huddersfield T.	07.69					(FB)
			TR	Northampton T.	10.69	1969	9	3	0	
KNIGHT, Brian T.	High Wycombe	14.11.46	APP	Reading	11.64	1965	1	/	0	(F)
KNIGHT, Frank	Hucknall	26.10.21		Nottingham F.	+	1946–49	48		1	
KNIGHT, George R.	Bolton	12.05.21	Holdens Temp.	Burnley	*	1946	1		0	(IR)
KNIGHT, Graham J.	Rochester	05.01.52	APP	Gillingham	01.70	1970-78	230	17	9	(D)
KNIGHT, Jeff W.	Sudbury	10.12.26		Derby Co.	05.46					(F)
			TR	Walsall	08.52	1952	4		0	
KNIGHT, John	Bolton	12.09.22	JNRS	Burnley	+	1946–48	26		5	(IL)Brother of Geo. R.
			TR	Preston N.E.	12.48	1948–49	39		7	
			TR	Chesterfield	07.51	1951	35		6	
			TR	Exeter C.	08.52	1952–53	56		6	
KNIGHT, Lyndon A.	Lydbrook	03.02.61	APP	Hereford U.	02.79	1978	2	/	0	(G)
KNIGHT, Peter R.	Brighton	12.11.39	Lewes	Brighton & H.A.	01.64	1963–65	9	1	1	(W)
KNIGHT, Peter R.	Ilford	26.12.37		Southend U.	06.58					(W)
			TR	Nottingham F.	08.59	1959	4		0	
			TR	Oxford U.	N/L	1962–64	95		12	
			TR	Reading	11.64	1964–65	29	/	4	
KNIGHT, Terry G.	London	01.02.32	Alton T.	Aldershot	AM	1958	4		0	(G)
KNIGHTON, Ken	Barnsley	20.02.44	APP	Wolverhampton W.	02.61	1964–66	13	3	0	(WH)
			TR	Oldham Ath.	11.66	1966–67	45	/	5	
			TR	Preston N.E.	11.67	1967–68	62	/	3	
			TR	Blackburn Rov.	06.69	1069–70	70	/	11	
			TR	Hull C.	03.71	1970–72	79	1	9	
			TR	Sheffield Wed.	08.73	1973–75	71	5	2	
KNIGHTS, Anthony F.	Grimsby	13.03.40	JNRS	Grimsby T.	06.58	1959–63	75		1	(LH)
			TR	Luton T.	08.64	1964	2		0	
			TR	Aldershot	07.65	1965	20	/	0	
KNOTT, Herbert	Goole	05.12.14	Brierley Hill	Hull C.	+	1946	6		1	(CF)*Walsall
KNOTT, William F.	Leeds	16.03.34	JNRS	Leeds U.	05.51					E.YTH.INT.
			TR	Walsall	02.55	1954	1		0	
			TR	Bradford C.	09.55					
KNOWLES, Cyril B.	Ponterfract	13.07.44	Monkton Col.	Middlesbrough	10.62	1962–63	37		0	(FB)E-4/E.U23-6/●
			TR	Tottenham H.	05.64	1964–75	400	1	15	E.F.LGE REP.
KNOWLES, Harry F.	Hednesford	06.09.32	Excelsior	Walsall	09.50	1950	10		1	(OL)
			Worcester C.	Cardiff C.	02.59	1958–59	8		0	

Players Names	Birthplace	Date	Previous Club	League Club	Date Signed	Seasons Played	Career Record Apps	Sub	Gls	
KNOWLES, J. David	Halifax	11.04.41	JNRS	Halifax T.	12.58	1958–62	72		0	(G)
			TR	Bury	07.63	1964	1		0	
			TR	Bradford C.	08.66	1966	21	/	0	
KNOWLES, Jim	Preston	31.07.34	JNRS	Preston N.E.	10.57	1957	2		0	(G)
			TR	Barrow	08.58	1958–59	11		0	
KNOWLES, Peter R.	Frickley	30.09.45	APP	Wolverhampton W.	10.62	1963–69	171	3	62	(IF)E.U23–4/E.YTH.INT./ Brother of Cyril
KNOWLES, Ray	London	30.09.52	Southall	Wimbledon	07.78	1978-79	31	8	6	(F)
KNOX, Jim	Brechin	26.11.35	Raith Rov.	Coventry C.	05.57	1957	2		0	(F)
KNOX, Robert P.	Ulverston	26.02.46	JNRS	Barrow	07.65	1964–71	94	12	19	(CF)2 apps in goal
KNOX, Tom	Glasgow	05.09.39	E. Stirling	Chelsea	06.62	1962–64	20		0	(OL)
			TR	Newcastle U.	02.65	1964–66	24	1	1	
			TR	Mansfield T.	03.67	1966–67	35	/	5	
			TR	Northampton T.	11.67	1967–68	28	2	0	
KNOX, William J.	Kilmarnock	09.09.37	T. Lanark	Barrow	07.59	1959	1		0	S.SCH.INT.
			TR	Rotherham U.	11.59					
KOENEN, Fransiscus	Holland	04.11.58	Nijmegen	Newcastle U.	08.80	1980	11	1	1	(M) DUTCH U21 INT.
KOFFMAN, S. Jack	Prestwich	03.08.20	Manchester U.(+)	HUll C.	06.46	1946	4		0	(OL)d.1977
				Oldham Ath.	06.47	1947	3		0	
KOPEL, Frank	Falkirk	28.03.49	JNRS	Manchester U.	04.66	1967–68	8	2	0	(FB)S.SCH.INT.
			TR	Blackburn Rov.	03.69	1968–71	23	2	0	
KOSMINA, A. John	Australia	17.08.56	Polonia	Arsenal	03.78	1978	0	1	0	(F)
KOWALSKI, Andy	Mansfield	26.02.53	Worksop T.	Chesterfield	02.73	1972-82	354	11	30	(M)
			TR	Doncaster Rov.	07.83	1983	32	/	1	
KOWENICKI, Ryszard	Poland	22.12.48	Widzew Lodz	Oldham Ath.	12.79	1979-80	40	2	5	(M)
KRAAY, Hans	Utrecht	22.12.59		Brighton & H.A.	02.84	1983	2	3	0	(D)
KRUSE, Pat K.	Biggleswade	30.11.53	APP	Leicester C.	02.72	1973	2	/	0	(D)
			L	Mansfield T.	09.74	1974	6	/	1	
			TR	Torquay U.	03.75	1974-76	79	/	4	
			TR	Brentford	03.77	1976-81	186	/	12	
			L	Northampton T.	02.82	1981	18	/	0	
KRZYWICKI, Richard	Penley	02.02.47	APP	W.B.A.	02.65	1964–69	51	6	9	(W)W–8/W.U23–3
			TR	Huddersfield T.	03.70	1969–72	39	8	7	
			L	Scunthorpe U.	02.73	1972	2	/	0	
			L	Northampton T.	11.73	1973	8	/	3	
			TR	Lincoln C.	07.74	1974–75	55	13	11	
KUBICKI, Eryk	Poland		Polish Army	York C.	AM	1946	5		0	
KUHL, Martin	Frimley	10.01.65	APP	Birmingham C.	01.83	1982-83	22	2	1	(M)
KURILA, John	Glasgow	10.04.41	Glasgow Celtic	Northampton T.	08.62	1962	40		1	(WH)
			TR	Bristol C.	08.63	1963	6		0	
			TR	Northampton T.	11.63	1963–67	106	2	3	
			TR	Southend U.	07.68	1968–69	87	1	1	
			TR	Colchester U.	05.70	1970–71	53	/	4	
			TR	Lincoln C.	12.71	1971	23	1	0	
KURZ, Fred J.	Grimsby	03.09.18	Grimsby T.(*)	Crystal Palace	+	1946–50	148		50	(CF)
KWIATSKOWSKI, Rick	Peterborough	07.04.48	JNRS	Peterborough U.	07.67	1967–71	49	11	0	(FB)
KYDD, David R.	Penge	22.12.45	APP	Brighton & H.A.	09.63	1965	2	/	0	(HB)
KYLE, Maurice	Darlington	08.11.37	JNRS	Wolverhampton W.	09.55					(CH)
			TR	Oxford U.	N/L	1962–69	275	/	2	
			L	Southend U.	03.70	1969	8	/	0	
KYNMAN, David J.	Hull	20.05.62	APP	Hull C.	05.80	1980-81	11	/	0	(M)

Players Names	Birthplace	Date	Previous Club	League Club	Date Signed	Seasons Played	Apps	Sub	Gls	
LABONE, Brian L.	Liverpool	23.01.40	JNRS	Everton	07.57	1957–71	451	/	2	(CH)E–26/E.U23–7/E.F. LGE REP.●
LACEY, Anthony	Leek	18.03.44		Stoke C.	10.65	1967-68	2	2	0	(D)
			TR	Port Vale	02.70	1969-74	193	7	9	
			TR	Rochdale	07.75	1975-76	83	/	0	
LACEY, Desmond P.	Dublin	03.08.25		Chester C.	AM	1946	1		0	d. 1974
LACEY, William	Tynemouth	17.11.31		Middlesbrough	05.52					(IF)
			TR	Aldershot	02.53	1952–58	211		59	
			TR	Reading	07.59	1959–62	90		40	
LACK, Harry	Bolsover	29.11.30		Leeds U.	07.51					
			TR	Blackburn Rov.	08.52					
			TR	Chesterfield	08.53	1953	1		0	
LACKENBY, George	Newcastle	22.05.31		Newcastle U.	10.50	1951–56	19		0	(FB)
			TR	Exeter C.	12.56	1956	24		5	
			TR	Carlisle U.	07.57	1957–58	46		0	
			TR	Gateshead	07.59	1959	43		2	
			TR	Hartlepool U.	08.60	1960–62	86		1	
LACY, John	Liverpool	14.08.51	Kingstonians	Fulham	06.72	1972-77	164	4	7	(D)
				Tottenham H.	07.78	1978-82	99	5	2	
			TR	Crystal Palace	08.83	1983	24	3	0	
LADD, Ian M.	Peterborough	22.11.58		Notts Co.	09.77	1977	1	/	0	(D)
			TR	Cambridge U.	08.78					
LAHTINEN, Aki A.	Finland	31.10.58	OPS Oulu	Notts. Co.	09.81	1981-83	23	8	2	(M) FINLAND INT.
LAIDLAW, John	Aldershot	05.07.36	Easthouses	Colchester U.	06.57	1959–60	41		1	(HB)
LAIDLAW, John R.	Windermere	05.01.19	Netherfield	Carlisle U.	06.46	1946	27		3	(OL) *Barrow
LAIDLAW, Joseph D.	Wallsend	12.07.50	APP	Middlesbrough	08.67	1967-71	104	7	20	(M)
			TR	Carlisle U.	07.72	1972-75	146	5	44	
			TR	Doncaster Rov.	06.76	1976-78	127	1	27	
			TR	Portsmouth	06.79	1979-80	60	/	19	
			TR	Hereford U.	12.80	1980-81	61	1	8	
			TR	Mansfield T.	07.82	1982	4	/	0	
LAIDMAN, Fred	Durham	20.06.13	Stockton	Darlington	07.48	1949	2		0	*Everton/Bristol C.
LAING, David	Strathmiglo	20.02.25	Hibernian	Gillingham	08.57	1957–58	81		5	(HB) S.F. LGE. REP
LAING, Fred J.	Glasgow	25.02.20	Ashfield J.	Luton T.	*					(IF)
			TR	Middlesbrough	07.47					
			TR	Bristol Rov.	07.48	1948	2		0	
LAING, Robert S.	Glasgow	01.02.25	Falkirk	Birmingham C.	+	1947–49	19		2	(W)
			TR	Watford	06.50	1950–51	60		8	
LAIRD, Alex	Newmains	02.06.26	Stirling A.	Chelsea	11.51					(OR)
			TR	Notts Co.	07.53	1953	1		0	
LAIRD, Alex W.	Edinbrugh	23.10.28	Dunfermline	Barrow	11.57	1957	22		0	(FB)
			TR	Scunthorpe U.	08.58					
LAIRD, David S.	Rutherglen	11.02.36	St. Mirren	Aldershot	07.57					(IF)
			St. Mirren	Northampton T.	06.60	1960	12		1	
LAIRD, David W.	Clackmannan	09.05.26	Alloa Ath.	Aldershot	05.48	1948–53	126		22	(WH)
LAISBY, John	Ulverston	27.03.57	APP	Liverpool	04.75					(G)
			TR	Rochdale	03.76					
			Barrow	Workington	N/C	1976	2	/	0	
LAITT, David	Colchester	01.11.46	Colchester Cas.	Colchester U.	08.65	1965	0	1	0	(FB)
LAKE, Huw G.T.	Swansea	20.08.63	APP	Swansea C.	08.81	1982-84	14	5	2	(M)W.SCH.INT.
LAKE, Leslie E.	Luton	29.01.23	Holly Rgrs	Luton T.	+	1946–50	59		0	(FB) d.
LAKING, George E.	Harthill	17.03.13	Wolverhampton W.(*)	Middlesbrough	*	1946	1		0	(FB) *Dinnington
LALLY, Pat A.	Paddington	11.01.52	APP	Millwall	01.70	1969	1	/	0	(M)
			TR	York C.	07.71	1971-72	64	8	5	
			TR	Swansea C.	08.73	1973-78	152	8	10	
			L	Aldershot	10.75	1975	3	/	0	
			TR	Doncaster Rov.	09.78	1978-81	118	4	0	
LAMB, Alan	Falkirk	03.07.52	APP	Preston N.E.	05.70	1972-76	76	4	2	(M) S.U23-1
			TR	Port Vale	03.77	1976-77	54	/	3	
LAMB, Harry E.	Bebington	03.06.25	JNRS	Tranmere Rov.	+	1947–52	88		12	(F)
LAMB, Harry T.	Stourbridge	20.04.28	Wordsley FC	Aston Villa	10.49					(FB) d. 1982
			TR	Scunthorpe U.	06.54	1954–55	36		0	
LAMB, Steve P.	Southend	02.10.55	APP	Southend U.	10.73	1974–75	6	1	0	(IF)
LAMBDEN, Vic D.	Bristol	24.10.25	Oldland	Bristol Rov.	+	1946–54	271		116	(CF)
LAMBERT, Anton J.	Nottingham	29.11.59	Long Eaton	Scunthorpe U.	07.80	1980-81	35	4	3	(M)
LAMBERT, Brian	Sutton-in-Ashfield	10.07.36	Sutton T.	Mansfield T.	10.54	1954–59	23		0	(FB)
LAMBERT, David	Ruabon	07.07.39		Cardiff C.	03.59					(HB)
			TR	Wrexham	07.63	1963	5		0	
LAMBERT, Eric V.	Derby	04.08.20	Nottingham F.(AM)	Derby Co.	+					
			TR	Hartlepool U.	06.46	1946	16		0	

Players Names	Birthplace	Date	Previous Club	League Club	Date Signed	Seasons Played	Career Record Apps	Sub	Gls	
LAMBERT, Gilbert J.	Preston	16.03.37	JNRS	Preston N.E.	03.55	1958–60	22		6	(F)
LAMBERT, Ken	Sheffield	07.06.28	Ecclesfield	Barnsley	01.50	1950–51	11		2	(F)
			TR	Gillingham	07.52	1952–554	37		10	
			TR	Swindon T.	07.53	1953–54	30		6	
			TR	Bradford C.	11.54	1954	19		4	
LAMBERT, Martin C.	Southampton	24.09.65	APP	Brighton & H.A.	08.83	1983	2	1	0	(F)
LAMBERT, Mick A.	Balsham	20.05.50	Newmarket	Ipswich T.	11.67	1968–78	181	30	39	(M)
			TR	Peterborough U.	07.79	1979-80	15	6	2	
LAMBERT, Ray	Bagillt	18.07.22	JNRS	Liverpool	+	1946–55	309		2	(FB) W–5/W.SCH.INT
LAMBERT, Roy	Sheffield	16.07.33	Thorncliffe Col.	Rotherham U.	07.54	1956–64	306		6	(WH)
			TR	Barnsley	11.65	1965	3	/	0	
LAMBLE, John	Reading	10.11.48	APP	Reading	05.67	1967	3	2	0	(F)
LAMBOURNE, Dennis J.	Swansea	07.10.45	Llanelli	Wrexham	07.64	1964–65	15	/	4	(F)
LAMBTON, Colin	Newcastle	21.02.42	Chester Moor	Newcastle U.	02.60					(FB)
			TR	Doncaster Rov.	07.63	1963	6		0	
LAMBTON, William E.	Nottingham	02.12.14	Nottingham F.(*)	Exeter C.	+					(G) d. 1976
			TR	Doncaster Rov.	10.46	1946	3		0	
LAMIE, Robert	Newarthill	28.12.28	Stonehouse Violet	Cardiff C.	10.49	1949–50	6		1	(IF)
			TR	Swansea C.	03.51	1951	2		0	
			TR	Lincoln C.	10.52					
LAMONT, David	Glasgow	02.04.49	APP	Colchester U.	04.67	1967	0	1	0	(HB)
LAMONT, Wiliam T.	Glasgow	25.12.26	Kilmarnock	New Brighton	07.50	1950	27		0	(FB)
			TR	Tranmere Rov.	09.51	1951–55	143		3	
LAMPARD, Frank R.G.	West Ham	20.09.48	APP	West Ham U.	09.65	1967-83	545	5	18	(D) E-2/E.U23-4/ E.YTH.INT.●
LAMPE, Derek	Edmonton	20.05.37	JNRS	Fulham	05.54	1956–62	88		0	(CH) E.YTH.INT.
LAMPKIN, Steve C.A.	Keighley	15.10.64		Bradford C.	03.83	1982-83	5	2	1	(F)
LANCASTER, Brian	Bradford	08.05.39		Torquay U.	07.60	1961	18		0	(HB)
LANCASTER, Des C.	Burnley	16.07.37	JNRS	Burnley	08.54	1956	1		0	(F)
			TR	Darlington	03.58	1957–58	31		18	
			TR	Tranmere Rov.	06.59	1959	1		0	
LANCASTER, Joe G.	Stockport	28.04.26	Heaton MOB	Manchester U.	02.50	1949	2		0	(G)
			TR	Accrington St.	11.50	1950	1		0	
LANCASTER, Ray	Rotherham	17.08.41	JNRS	Rotherham U.	11.58	1960–64	66		2	(WH)
			TR	Grimsby T.	12.64	1964–66	16	2	0	
			TR	Lincoln C.	01.67	1966–67	24	/	0	
LANCELOTTE, Eric C.	India	26.02.17	Romford	Charlton Ath.	*	1946–47	28		6	(IF)
			TR	Brighton & H.A.	02.48	1947–49	60		15	
LANDSBOROUGH, Murray	Thornhill	30.12.15	Kilmarnock	Carlisle U.	08.47	1947	1		0	(LB)
LANE, Frank	Wallasey	20.07.48		Tranmere Rov.	08.68	1969–71	76	/	0	(G)
			TR	Liverpool	09.71	1972	1	/	0	
			TR	Notts. Co.	07.75	1975	2	/	0	
LANE, Henry	Hednesford	21.03.09	Plymouth Arg.(*)	Southend U.	05.46	1946–48	65		13	(IF) *Hednesford/ Birmingham C./Southend U.
LANE, John G.	Birmingham	10.11.31	Boldmere St. M.	Birmingham C.	09.49	1952–55	47		14	(CF)
			TR	Notts. Co.	07.56	1956–58	57		19	
LANE, Kevin J.	Wolverhampton	11.05.57	Walsall (APP)	Torquay U.	08.75	1975-76	17	13	5	(F)
LANE, Martin J.	Altrincham	12.04.61	JNRS	Manchester U.	05.79					(D)
			TR	Chester C.	08.82	1982-83	79	/	2	
LANE, Mike E.	Wellington	06.12.66	APP	Exeter C.	APP	1983	1	/	0	(D)
LANE, Sean B.	Bristol	16.01.64	APP	Hereford U.	03.81	1980-82	39	11	3	(M)E.SCH.INT.
			TR	Derby Co.	05.83	1983	1	/	0	
LANG, Gavan	Lanark	21.03.26	Hereford U.	Chester C.	08.56	1956	3		0	
LANG, Gavin T.	Hereford	10.11.51	Newcastle U.(APP)	Crewe Alex.	09.70	1970	3	/	0	(W)
LANG, Malcolm C.	Barnsley	14.01.41	Bridlington	York C.	08.63	1963	12		2	(W)
LANG, Tom	Larkhall	03.04.06	Q. of South	Ipswich T.	10.46	1946	5		1	(OL) *Larkhall Th./ Newcastle U./Huddersfield T. Manchester U./Swansea C.
LANGAN, David	Dublin	15.02.57	APP	Derby Co.	06.76	1976-79	143	/	1	(D) EI-13
			TR	Birmingham C.	07.80	1980-82	92	/	3	
LANGE, Anthony S.	London	10.12.64	APP	Charlton Ath.	12.82	1983	6	/	0	(G)
LANGFORD, John W.	E. Kirby	04.08.37	Leicester C. (AM)	Nottingham F.	08.55	1955	4		0	(F)
			TR	Notts. Co.	08.58	1958	16		0	
LANGLAND, John R.	Easington	09.11.29		Sunderland	06.48					(F)
			Consett	Chesterfield	01.51	1952–53	7		0	
			Blyth Spartans	Hartlepool U.	07.58	1958–59	38		11	

Players Names	Birthplace	Date	Previous Club	League Club	Date Signed	Seasons Played	Career Record Apps	Sub	Gls	
LANGLEY, E. Jim	Kilburn	07.02.29	Guildford C.	Leeds U.	06.52	1952	9		3	(FB) E–3/E'B'3/●
			TR	Brighton & H.A.	07.53	1953–56	166		14	E.F.LGE.REP.
			TR	Fulham	02.57	1956–64	323		31	
			TR	Q.P.R.	07.65	1965–66	86	1	9	
LANGLEY, Geoff R.	Gateshead	31.03.62	APP	Bolton W.	03.80	1981	3	3	0	(F)
LANGLEY, Kevin J.	St. Helens	24.05.64	APP	Wigan Ath.	05.82	1981-83	71	3	3	(M)
LANGLEY, Tom W.	Lambeth	08.02.58	APP	Chelsea	04.75	1974–79	129	13	40	(F) E.YTHG.INT./E.SCH.INT.
			TR	Q.P.R.	08.80	1980	24	1	8	E.U21-1
			TR	Crystal Palace	03.81	1980-82	54	5	9	
			AEK Athens	Coventry C.	03.84	1983	2	/	0	
LANGMAN, H. Neil	Bere Alston	21.02.32	Tavistock	Plymouth Arg.	09.53	1953–57	97		49	(F) Brother of Peter
				Colchester U.	11.57	1957–60	128		50	
LANGMAN, Peter J.H.	Bere Alston	01.04.28	Tavistock	Plymouth Arg.	06.51	1954–57	89		0	(CH)
LANGRIDGE, John	Newcastle	14.11.57	Easington C.W.	Hartlepool U.	N/C	1982	5	1	0	(F)
LANGSTRETH, Horace	Blackburn	19.07.31		Accrington St.	07.53	1953	3		0	(FB)
				Netherfield	Torquay U.	08.56	1956	1		0	
LANGTON, Robert	Burscough	08.09.18	Burscough	Blackburn Rov.	*	1946–47	70		10	(OL) E–11/E'B'–3/
			TR	Preston N.E.	08.48	1948–49	55		14	E.F.LGE.REP
			TR	Bolton W.	11.49	1949–52	118		16	
			TR	Blackburn Rov.	09.53	1953–55	105		33	
LANSDOWNE, William	Shoreditch	09.11.35	Woodford T.	West Ham U.	02.56	1955–62	57		5	(WH) Father of William
LANSDOWNE, William	Epping	28.04.59	JNRS	West Ham U.	06.78	1978-79	5	4	1	(F)
			TR	Charlton Ath.	07.81	1981-82	28	4	4	
			TR	Gillingham	01.83	1982	6	/	2	
LAPOT, Stan	Edinburgh	20.01.44	Smeaton BC	Preston N.E.	06.62	1962–66	16	3	2	(HB)
LARAMAN, Peter K.	Rochester	24.10.40	JNRS	Charlton Ath.	02.58	1958–59	2		1	(F) E.YTH.INT.
			TR	Torquay U.	07.61	1961	9		5	
LARGE, Frank	Leeds	26.01.40		Halifax T.	06.59	1958–61	133		50	(CF)●
			TR	Q.P.R.	06.62	1962	18		5	
			TR	Northampton T.	03.63	1962–63	47		30	
			TR	Swindon T.	03.64	1963–64	17		4	
			TR	Carlisle U.	09.64	1964–65	51	/	18	
			TR	Oldham Ath.	12.65	1965–66	35	/	19	
			TR	Northampton T.	12.66	1966–67	37	/	15	
			TR	Leicester C.	11.67	1967	26	/	8	
			TR	Fulham	06.68	1968–69	20	4	3	
			TR	Northampton T.	08.69	1969–72	133	2	42	
			TR	Chesterfield	11.72	1972–73	46	/	15	
LARKIN, Anthony G.	Wrexham	12.01.56	JNRS	Wrexham	07.75					(D)
			TR	Shrewsbury T.	07.78	1978-80	54	1	0	
			TR	Carlisle U.	07.81	1981-82	47	2	2	
			TR	Hereford U.	03.83	1982-83	20	1	1	
LARKIN, Bernard (Bunny)	Birmingham	11.01.36	JNRS	Birmingham C.	07.54	1956–59	79		23	(WH)
			TR	Norwich C.	03.60	1959–61	41		12	
			TR	Doncaster Rov.	09.61	1961	25		12	
			TR	Watford	06.62	1962–64	49		3	
			TR	Lincoln C.	11.64	1964–65	25	2	3	
LARKIN, G. Tony	W. Hartlepool	12.10.58		Hartlepool U.	07.78	1977-79	5	9	1	(M)
LARMOUR, Albert A.	Belfast	27.05.51	Linfield	Cardiff C.	07.72	1972-78	152	2	0	(D)
			TR	Torquay U.	06.79	1979-81	46	4	4	
LARNACH, Ian J.	Ferryhill	10.07.51	APP	Darlington	07.69	1969	1	1	1	(F)
LARNACH, Mike	Caithness	09.11.52	Clydebank	Newcastle U.	12.77	1977	12	2	0	(F)
LARONDE, Everald	West Ham	12.11.61	APP	West Ham U.	01.81	1981	6	1	0	(D)
			TR	Bournemouth	09.83	1983	18	/	0	
LARYEA, Benny M.	Ghana	20.03.62	Maidenhead	Torquay U.	N/C	1983	1	/	0	(F)
LASKEY, Russell	Norwich	17.03.37	Gothic	Norwich C.	01.56	1956	4		2	(F)
LATCHAM, Les A.	Stanley	22.12.42	JNRS	Burnley	01.60	1964–70	149	5	10	(FB)
			TR	Plymouth Arg.	07.71	1971–72	83	/	13	
			TR	Bradford C.	07.73	1973	15	/	2	
LATCHFORD, Dave B.	Birmingham	09.04.49	APP	Birmingham C.	07.66	1968-77	206	/	0	(G) Brother of Peter/Robert
				Motherwell	Bury	03.79	1978	2	/	0	
LATCHFORD, Peter W.	Birmingham	27.09.52	APP	W.B.A.	10.69	1972–74	81	/	0	(G) E.U23–2
LATCHFORD, Robert	Birmingham	18.01.51	APP	Birmingham C.	08.68	1968-73	158	2	68	(F) E.U23-6/E-12/
			TR	Everton	02.74	1973-80	235	1	106	E.F.LGE.REP./E.YTH.INT.●
			TR	Swansea C.	07.81	1981-83	87	/	35	
LATHAM, David C.	Manchester	17.10.43	APP	Manchester U.	10.61					
			TR	Southport	07.63	1963	22		0	
LATHAM, Harry	Sheffield	09.01.21	JNRS	Sheffield U.	*	1946–52	190		1	(CH) d. 1983
LATHAM, Les	Foleshill	31.12.17		Aston Villa	*					E.SCH.INT
			TR	Coventry C.	10.46	1946	1		0	

Players Names	Birthplace	Date	Previous Club	League Club	Date Signed	Seasons Played	Apps	Sub	Gls	
LATHAN, John G.	Sunderland	12.04.52	APP	Sunderland	04.69	1969-73	41	12	14	(M)
			TR	Mansfield T.	02.74	1973-75	72	2	14	
			TR	Carlisle U.	02.76	1975-77	55	6	8	
			L	Barnsley	02.77	1976	6	1	0	
			TR	Portsmouth	03.78	1977-79	56	2	4	
			TR	Mansfield T.	08.79	1979	29	/	1	
LATTIMER, Frank J.	Durham	03.10.23	Snowdown Col.	Brentford	+	1946–55	171		3	(WH)
LAUGHTON, Dennis,	Dingwall	22.01.48	Morton	Newcastle U.	10.73	1973–74	7	/	0	(HB)
LAUREL, John A.	Dartford	11.06.35	JNRS	Tottenham H.	07.52					(WH) E. YTH. INT.
			TR	Ipswich T.	06.59	1960–62	4		0	
LAVERICK, Mick G.	Trimdon	13.03.54	JNRS	Mansfield T.	05.72	1972-75	73	16	13	(M)
			TR	Southend U.	10.76	1976-78	108	2	18	
			TR	Huddersfield T.	07.79	1979-82	74	/	9	
			TR	York C.	01.82	1981-82	38	3	6	
			L	Huddersfield T.	01.83	1982	2	/	0	
LAVERICK, Peter	Grimsby	29.01.39	JNRS	Grimsby T.	03.56	1957–60	4		0	(F)
				Bristol C.	08.61					
LAVERICK, Robert	Trimdon	11.06.38	JNRS	Chelsea	06.55	1956–57	7		1	(OL) E. YTH. INT
			TR	Everton	02.59	1958–59	22		6	
			TR	Brighton & H.A.	06.60	1960–61	63		20	
			TR	Coventry C.	07.62	1962	4		0	
LAVERTY, Pat J.	Gorseinon	24.05.34	Wellington	Sheffield U.	05.56	1956–59	7		0	(F)
			TR	Southend U.	07.60	1960	21		6	
LAVERY, James	Glasgow	13 12.48		Scunthorpe U.	08.66	1967	15	/	0	(G)
			TR	Halifax T.	07.69					
			TR	Barnsley	08.69					
			Brigg T.	Scunthorpe U.	08.74	1974	11	/	0	
LAVERY, John	Belfast	24.11.19	Linfield	Bradford C.	08.48	1948	5		0	(OL) I.SCH.INT
			TR	Halifax T.	09.48	1948	3		1	
LAW, Cecil R.	Rhodesia	10.03.30	S. Africa	Derby Co.	08.51	1952–53	33		2	(OL)
			TR	Bury	05.54	1954–55	44		5	
LAW, Denis	Aberdeen	24.02.40	JNRS	Huddersfield T.	02.57	1956–59	81		16	(IF) S–55/S.U23–3/●
			TR	Manchester C.	03.60	1959–60	44		21	E.F.LGE.REP.
			TR	Manchester U.	08.62	1962–72	305	4	171	
			TR	Manchester C.	07.73	1973	22	2	9	
LAW, Nicky	London	08.09.61	APP	Arsenal	07.79					(D) E.SCH.INT.
			TR	Barnsley	08.81	1981-83	77	1	1	
LAWLER, Chris	Liverpool	20.10.43	JNRS	Liverpool	10.60	1962-74	406	/	41	(D) E-4/E.U23-4/
			TR	Portsmouth	10.75	1975-76	35	1	0	E.YTH.INT./E.F.LGE.REP.●
			TR	Stockport Co.	08.77	1977	33	3	3	
LAWLER, James H.	Dublin	20.11.23	Glentoran	Portsmouth	10.47					(WH) Brother of Robin
			TR	Southend U.	01.49	1948–56	269		18	
LAWLER, Joseph (Robin)	Dublin	28.08.25	Belfst Celtic	Fulham	03.49	1949–61	281		0	(WH) EI–8/L.O.I. REP.
LAWLESS, Arthur T.	Retford	23.03.32	Worcester C.	Plymouth Arg.	07.55	1955	8		0	(FB)
			TR	Oldham Ath.	07.56	1956	9		0	
			TR	Aldershot	07.57	1957	2		0	
			TR	Southport	07.58	1958	15		0	
LAWLOR, James J.	Dublin	10.05.33	Drumcondra	Doncaster Rov.	08.52	1954	9		0	(CH) Brother of John C.
			TR	Bradford C.	03.57	1956–61	153		5	
LAWLOR, John B.	Glasgow	30.01.37	Kilmarnock	Aldershot	05.59	1959–60	57		17	(F) S.SCH.INT
LAWLOR, John C.	Dublin	03.12.22	Drumcondra	Doncaster Rov.	06.50	1950–54	128	·	46	(F)
LAWRENCE, Cyril	Salford	12.06.20	JNRS	Blackpool	*					(OR)
			TR	Rochdale	04.47	1946–49	46		5	
			TR	Wrexham	09.50	1950–51	50		9	
LAWRENCE, Dave	Swansea	18.01.47	Merthyr Tydfil	Swansea C.	05.67	1967–70	94	2	2	(FB) W.AMAT.INT
LAWRENCE, Dave	Poole	12.05.33	Poole T.	Bristol Rov.	06.55	1956	5		0	(FB)
				Reading	06.57	1957–58	23		0	
LAWRENCE, George R.	London	14.09.62	APP	Southampton	09.80	1981-82	7	3	1	(F)
			L	Oxford U.	03.82	1981	15	/	4	
			TR	Oxford U.	11.82	1982-83	56	/	18	
LAWRENCE, Keith D.	St. Pauls Cray	25.03.54	APP	Chelsea	07.73					(CH)
			TR	Brentford	05.74	1974–75	78	/	1	
LAWRENCE, Les	Wolverhampton	18.05.57	Stourbridge	Shrewsbury T.	02.75	1975-76	10	4	2	(F)
			Telford U.	Torquay U.	07.77	1977-81	170	19	45	
			Weymouth	Port Vale	08.82	1982	5	3	0	
			TR	Aldershot	07.83	1983	39	/	22	
LAWRENCE, Mark	Middlesbrough	04.12.58		Hartlepool U.	07.78	1977-83	155	13	24	(M)
			L	Port Vale	03.83	1982	10	1	0	
LAWRENCE, Tom	Dailly	14.05.40	JNRS	Liverpool	10.57	1962-70	306	/	0	(G) S–3/S.U23–1
			TR	Tranmere Rov.	09.71	1971–73	80	/	0	
LAWRENSON, Mark	Preston	02.06.57	JNRS	Preston N.E.	08.74	1974-76	73	/	2	(D) EI-25
			TR	Brighton & H.A.	07.77	1977-80	152	/	5	Son of Tom
			TR	Liverpool	08.81	1981-83	119	2	7	

Players Names	Birthplace	Date	Previous Club	League Club	Date Signed	Seasons Played	Career Record Apps	Sub	Gls	
LAWRENSON, Tom	Preston	24.05.29		Preston N.E.	04.49	1954	1		0	(F) Father of Mark
			TR	Southport	07.55	1955–56	37		0	
LAWRIE, Sam	Glasgow	15.12.34	JNRS	Middlesbrough	02.52	1951–56	35		5	(OL)
			TR	Charlton Ath.	11.56	1956–62	193		70	
			TR	Bradford P.A.	10.62	1962–65	72	1	16	
LAWS, Brian	Wallsend	14.10.61	APP	Burnley	10.79	1979-82	125	/	12	(D)
			TR	Huddersfield T.	08.83	1983	31	/	0	
LAWS, Jonathan	Peterborough	01.09.64	APP	Wolverhampton W.	09.82					(M)
			TR	Mansfield T.	03.83	1982	0	1	0	
LAWSON, Alan	Lennoxtown	13.09.41	Glasgow Celtic	Oldham Ath.	06.64	1964–69	127	10	1	(HB)
LAWSON, David	Wallsend	22.12.47	JNRS	Newcastle U.	04.66					(G)
			TR	Shrewsbury T.	08.67					
			TR	Bradford P.A.	10.67	1967-68	13	/	0	
			TR	Huddersfield T.	05.69	1969-71	51	/	0	
			TR	Everton	06.72	1972-76	124	/	0	
			TR	Luton T.	10.78	1978	5	/	0	
			TR	Stockport Co.	03.79	1978-80	106	/	0	
LAWSON, Ian	Onslow	24.03.39	JNRS	Burnley	03.56	1956–60	23		7	(CF) E.YTH.INT.
			TR	Leeds U.	03.62	1961–64	44		16	
			TR	Crystal Palace	06.65	1965	15	2	6	
			TR	Port Vale	08.66	1966	7	1	0	
			TR	Barnsley	08.67					
LAWSON, James	Middlesbrough	11.12.47	JNRS	Middlesbrough	12.64	1965-67	25	6	3	(M)
			TR	Huddersfield T.	08.68	1968-75	234	10	42	
			TR	Halifax T.	06.76	1976-78	93	/	9	
LAWSON, John R.	York	03.02.25	Dringhouses	York C.	+	1946	1		0	
LAWSON, Norman	Durham	06.04.35	Hednesford	Bury	09.55	1955–57	56		8	(OL)
			TR	Swansea C.	07.58	1958–59	24		3	
			TR	Watford	07.60					
LAWSON, William	Dundee	28.11.47	Brechin	Sheffield Wed.	10.69	1969–70	9	1	0	(W)
LAWTHER, Ian	Belfast	20.10.39	Crusaders	Sunderland	03.58	1959–60	75		41	(CF) NI–4/NI'B'–1●
			TR	Blackburn Rov.	07.61	1961–62	59		21	
			TR	Scunthorpe U.	07.63	1963–64	60		21	
			TR	Brentford	11.64	1964–67	138	1	43	
				Halifax T.	08.68	1968–70	87	14	23	
			TR	Stockport Co.	07.71	1971–75	158	6	29	
LAWTON, H. Malcolm	Leeds	07.11.35	JNRS	Leeds U.	11.52					(FB)
			TR	Bradford P.A.	06.57	1957–62	113		0	
LAWTON, James M	Middlesbrough	06.07.42	Middlesbrough (AM)	Darlington	10.61	1961–65	120	/	60	(CF)
			TR	Swindon T.	09.65	1965–66	10	/	3	
			TR	Watford	03.67	1966–67	10	3	1	
			TR	Darlington	03.68	1967–68	22	/	3	
LAWTON, John K.	Woore	06.07.36	JNRS	Stoke C.	06.54	1955	9		3	(F)
LAWTON, Norbert	Manchester	25.03.40	JNRS	Manchester U.	04.58	1959–62	36		6	(WH)
			TR	Preston N.E.	03.63	1962–67	143	/	22	
			TR	Brighton & H.A.	09.67	1967–70	112	/	14	
			TR	Lincoln C.	02.71	1970–71	20	/	0	
LAWTON, Peter	Barnsley	25.02.44	JNRS	Barnsley	05.62	1962–63	2		0	(FB)
LAWTON, Tommy	Bolton	06.10.19	Everton(*)	Chelsea	+	1946–47	42		30	(CF) E–23/E.F.LGE.REP./●
			TR	Notts. Co.	11.47	1947–51	151		90	*Burnley
			TR	Brentford	03.52	1951–53	50		17	
			TR	Arsenal	09.53	1953–55	35		13	
LAWTON, William	Ashton-u-Lyne	04.06.20		Oldham Ath.	+	1946–48	10		0	
			TR	Chester C.	10.49					
LAY, Peter J.	Stratford	04.12.31		Nottingham F.	04.53	1954	1		0	(FB)
			TR	Q.P.R.	07.56	1956	1		0	
LAYBOURNE, Keith E.	Sunderland	27.01.59	Lambton St B.C.	Lincoln C.	07.77	1977-78	18	/	1	(D)
LAYNE, David R.	Sheffield	29.07.39		Rotherham U.	07.57	1957–58	11		4	(CF)
			TR	Swindon T.	06.59	1959–60	41		28	
			TR	Bradford C.	12.60	1960–61	65		44	
			TR	Sheffield Wed.	02.62	1962–63	74		52	
			L	Hereford U.	12.72	1972	4	/	0	
LAYTON, Alan	Bury	27.11.28		Bolton W.	04.49					(OR)
			TR	Barrow	10.50	1950–55	142		19	
LAYTON, John	Hereford	29.06.51	Gloucester C.	Hereford U.	09.74	1974–79	198	2	13	(M)
			Trowbridge T.	Newport Co.	N/C	1983	1	/	0	
LAYTON, William R.	Shipley	13.01.15	Shipley T.	Reading	*	1946	12		4	(IF)
			TR	Bradford P.A.	01.47	1946–48	47		5	
			TR	Colchester U.	08.50	1950	7		0	

Players Names	Birthplace	Date	Previous Club	League Club	Date Signed	Seasons Played	Career Record Apps	Sub	Gls	
LAZARUS, Mark	Stepney	05.12.38	Barking	Orient	11.57	1958–60	20		4	(W) Brother of famous
			TR	Q.P.R.	09.60	1960–61	37		19	Lazar Boxers
			TR	Wolverhampton W.	09.61	1961	9		3	Harry/Lew
			TR	Q.P.R.	02.62	1961–63	81		29	
			TR	Brentford	01.64	1963–65	62	/	21	
			TR	Q.P.R.	11.65	1965–67	86	2	29	
			TR	Crystal Palace	11.67	1967–69	63	/	17	
			TR	Orient	10.69	1969–71	83	1	14	
LAZARUS, Paul	London	04.09.62	JNRS	Charlton Ath.	08.80	1980	2	/	1	(F)
				Wimbledon	10.81	1981	17	1	6	
LE CORNU, Craig D.	Birkenhead	17.09.60	APP	Liverpool	09.78					(M)
			TR	Tranmere Rov.	12.80	1980	3	3	0	
LEA, Cyril	Moss	05.08.34	Bradley Rgrs	Orient	07.57	1957–64	205		0	(WH) W–2/W.AMAT.INT
			TR	Ipswich T.	11.64	1964–68	103	4	2	
LEA, Harold	Wigan	14.09.31	Horwich RMI	Stockport Co.	05.58	1958–63	117		1	(G)
LEA, Leslie	Manchester	05.10.42	JNRS	Blackpool	10.59	1960–67	159	1	13	(W)
			TR	Cardiff C.	11.67	1967–69	75	1	7	
			TR	Barnsley	08.70	1970–75	198	7	32	
LEACH, Albert	Bolton	10.07.31		Shrewsbury T.	11.51	1951	2		0	(G)
			Astley Br.	Bury	03.53					
LEACH, Brian E.	Reading	20.07.32		Reading	11.50	1952–56	108		1	(WH)
LEACH, John N	Whitehaven	17.01.19	Barrow Celtic	Barrow	09.47	1947–49	74		10	(OL)
LEACH, Mick J.C.	London	16.01.47	APP	Q.P.R.	02.64	1964–77	291	22	61	(F) E.YTH.INT.
			Detroit Express	Cambridge U.	09.78	1978	18	1	1	
LEADBEATER, Albert	Newton le Willows	17.08.21	Earlestown	Accrington St.	AM	1946	4		0	
LEADBEATER, Jim H.	Edinburgh	15.07.28	Edinburgh Th.	Chelsea	07.49	1951	3		0	(OL)
			TR	Brighton & H.A.	08.52	1952–54	107		29	
			TR	Ipswich T.	06.55	1955–64	344		41	
LEADBITTER, John	Sunderland	07.05.53	APP	Sunderland	05.70					(HB)
			TR	Darlington	08.72	1972	15	4	0	
LEAF, Andy K.	York	18.01.62	APP	York C.	01.80	1979	1	/	0	(D)
LEAHY, Steve D.	Battersea	23.09.59	APP	Crystal Palace	10.76	1980-81	3	1	0	(F) E.SCH.INT.
LEAKE, Albert G.	Stoke	07.04.30	Stoke C.(AM)	Port Vale	02.50	1950–59	269		34	(IF) E.YTH.INT.,
LEAMON, Fred W.	Jersey	11.05.19		Newport Co.	+	1946	4		2	(CF)
			TR	Bristol Rov.	10.46	1946–47	43		24	
			TR	Brighton & H.A.	07.49	1949	11		4	
LEAN, David	Plymouth	28.08.45	Embankment FC	Plymouth Arg.	08.69	1969–70	44	1	0	(HB)
LEAR, Graham J.	Exeter	18.12.30	Exmouth T.	Exeter C.	AM	1950–51	20		0	(G)
LEARY, Stuart, E.	S. Africa	30.04.33	Clyde S.A.	Charlton Ath.	02.50	1951–61	376		153	(CF) E.U23–1/
			TR	Q.P.R.	12.62	1962–65	94	/	28	Kent Cricketer
LEATH, Terry	Liverpool	06.11.34		Southport	07.59	1958–59	17		0	(FB)
			TR	Crewe Alex.	08.61					
LEATHER, Maurice P.	Eastleigh	09.11.29		Portsmouth	01.50	1950–52	18		0	(G) E.YTH.INT
LEAVER, Derek	Blackburn	13.11.30		Blackburn Rov.	05.49	1950–54	14		5	(F)
			TR	Bournemouth	07.55	1955	29		5	
			TR	Crewe Alex.	03.56	1955–56	28		6	
LEAVY, Steve	Longford	18.06.25	Sligo	Swansea C.	07.50	1950–57	36		1	(FB) L.O.I. REP
LECK, Derek A.	Northbourne	08.02.37	Leyton Y.C.	Millwall	05.55	1955–57	8		2	(IF)
			TR	Northampton T.	06.58	1958–65	247	/	46	
			TR	Brighton & H.A.	11.65	1965–66	29	1	0	
LEDGARD, Ian	Stockport	09.02.48	Leeds U. (AM)	Blackburn Rov.	07.67					(HB)
			TR	Stockport Co.	10.67	1967–68	4	4	0	
LEDGER, Robert	Craghead	05.10.37	JNRS	Huddersfield T.	10.54	1955–61	58		7	(OR)
			TR	Oldham Ath.	05.62	1962–67	222	1	37	
			TR	Mansfield T.	11.67	1967–69	51	6	15	
			TR	Barrow	10.69	1969	21	1	2	
LEDGER, Roy	Barnsley	09.12.30	JNRS	Barnsley	04.48	1950	1		0	
			TR	Rotherham U.	10.51					
			TR	Bradford C.	12.51					
LEDGERTON, Terry	Liverpool	07.10.30		Brentford	05.50	1951–53	40		8	(OL)
			TR	Millwall	05.54	1954	6		2	
LEE, Alan R.	W. Germany	19.06.60	Philadelphia	Leicester C.	02.79	1978-79	6	/	0	(F)
LEE, Alf	Farnworth	11.06.27		Bolton W.	10.48					
			TR	Oldham Ath.	07.50	1950	3		1	
LEE, Anthony	Manchester	04.06.37	Cheadle Rov.	Southport	AM	1957–58	10		1	(OL)
LEE, Colin	Torquay	12.06.56	APP	Bristol C.	07.74					(F)
			L	Hereford U.	11.74	1974	7	2	0	
			TR	Torquay U.	01.77	1976-77	35	/	14	
			TR	Tottenham H.	10.77	1977–79	57	5	18	
			TR	Chelsea	01.80	1979–83	134	14	35	
LEE, Eric G.	Chester	18.10.22		Chester C.	08.50	1946–56	363		10	(CH) E.AMAT.INT.

Players Names	Birthplace	Date	Previous Club	League Club	Date Signed	Seasons Played	Career Record Apps	Sub	Gls	
LEE, F. Stuart	Manchester	11.02.53	APP	Bolton W.	10.71	1971-74	77	8	20	(M)
			TR	Wrexham	11.75	1975-77	46	8	12	
			TR	Stockport Co.	08.78	1978-79	49	/	21	
			TR	Manchester C.	09.79	1979	6	1	2	
LEE, Francis H.	Westhoughton	29.04.44	JNRS	Bolton W.	05.61	1960-67	189	/	92	(W) E-27/E.F.LGE REP./●
			TR	Manchester C.	10.67	1967-73	248	1	112	E.YTH.INT
			TR	Derby Co.	08.74	1974-75	62	/	25	
LEE, Frank	Chorley	17.02.44	JNRS	Preston N.E.	11.61	1962-70	144	9	22	(W)
			TR	Southport	11.70	1970-73	115	/	21	
			TR	Stockport Co.	07.74	1974	13	/	1	
LEE, Garth	Sheffield	30.09.43	JNRS	Sheffield U.	05.61					(F) E.YTH.INT
			TR	Chester C.	09.63	1963-64	29		7	
LEE, George	York	04.06.19	Scarborough	York C.	*	1946	1		0	(OL)
			TR	Nottingham F.	08.47	1947-48	76		20	
			TR	W.B.A.	07.49	1949-57	271		59	
LEE, Gordon	Hednesford	13.07.34	Hednesford	Aston Villa	10.55	1958-64	118		2	(FB)
			TR	Shrewsbury T.	07.66	1966	2	/	0	
LEE, Harry	Mexborough	13.01.33	Thomas Hill YC	Derby Co.	10.50	1952	8		0	(F)
				Doncaster Rov.	07.55					
			TR	Mansfield T.	08.55	1955	3		2	
LEE, J. Anthony	Middlesbrough	26.11.47		Leicester C.	10.65					(F)
			TR	Bradford C.	07.67	1967	6	2	3	
			Stockton	Darlington	05.68	1968	10	4	0	
LEE, Jackie	Sileby	04.11.20	Quorn	Leicester C.	+	1946-49	123		74	(CF) E-1/
			TR	Derby Co.	07.50	1950-53	85		54	Leicester Cricketer
			TR	Coventry C.	11.54	1954	16		8	
LEE, James	Rotherham	26.01.26	Wath W.	Wolverhampton W.	+					(FB)
			TR	Hull C.	10.48	1949	3		1	
			TR	Halifax T.	12.51	1950-51	26		0	
			TR	Chelsea	10.51					
			TR	Orient	07.54	1954-55	67		1	
			TR	Swindon T.	11.56	1956-58	35		0	
LEE, Jeff	Countesthorpe	03.10.45	Huddersfield T.(AM)	Halifax T.	01.65	1964-72	231	9	2	(D)
			TR	Peterborough U.	08.73	1973-77	170	2	12	
LEE, Mike	Mold Junction	27.06.38	Saltney J.	W.B.A.	08.56	1956	1		0	(OL) W.SCH.INT
			TR	Crewe Alex.	06.58	1958	1		0	
LEE, Norman T.	Trealaw	29.05.39	JNRS	Tottenham H.	11.57					(HB)
			TR	Bournemouth	09.61					
			TR	Southend U.	02.62	1961-62	22		1	
LEE, Paul	Oxford	30.05.52	Oxford C.	Hereford U.	09.72	1973-74	21	7	5	(F)
LEE, Richard	Sheffield	11.09.44	JNRS	Rotherham U.	05.63					(HB)
			TR	Notts. Co.	06.64					
			TR	Mansfield T.	08.65	1965	3	1	0	
			TR	Halifax T.	07.66	1966-67	16	/	0	
LEE, Robert	Newcastle	23.12.57	APP	Doncaster Rov.	APP	1974	1	/	0	(M)
			TR	Scunthorpe U.	07.76	1976-77	17	2	0	
LEE, Robert G.	Melton Mowbray	02.02.53	Blaby B.C.	Leicester C.	02.72	1971-76	55	8	17	(F)
			L	Doncaster Rov.	08.74	1974	14	/	4	
			TR	Sunderland	09.76	1976-79	101	8	32	
			TR	Bristol Rov.	08.80	1980	19	4	2	
			TR	Carlisle U.	08.81	1981-82	47	8	12	
			TR	Southampton	03.83					
			TR	Darlington	08.83	1983	5	/	0	
LEE, Robert M.	West Ham	01.02.66	APP	Charlton Ath.	07.83	1983	10	1	4	(F)
LEE, Sammy	Liverpool	07.02.59	APP	Liverpool	04.76	1977-83	161	4	13	(M) E-13/E.U21-6/E.YTH.INT.
LEE, Terry W.G.	Stepney	20.09.52	JNRS	Tottenham H.	05.70	1973	1	/	0	(G)
			TR	Torquay U.	07.75	1975-77	106	/	0	
			TR	Newport Co.	11.78	1978	1	/	0	
LEE, Thomas	Horden	19.12.49		Hartlepool U.	11.68	1969	6	/	0	(F)
LEE, Trevor	London	03.07.54	Epsom & Ewell	Millwall	10.75	1975-78	99	9	23	(F)
			TR	Colchester U.	11.78	1978-80	95	1	35	
			TR	Gillingham	01.81	1980-82	43	4	14	
			L	Orient	10.82	1982	5	/	0	
			TR	Bournemouth	11.82	1982-83	28	6	9	
			TR	Cardiff C.	12.83	1983	21	/	5	
LEE, William R.	Darwen	24.10.19		Blackburn Rov.	*					(WH)
			TR	Barrow	05.47	1946-52	158		1	
LEECH, Fred	Stalybridge	05.12.23	Hurst FC	Bradford C.	+	1946	7		2	(F)
LEECH, Vincent	Rochdale	06.12.40	Burnley (AM)	Blackburn Rov.	04.59					(HB)
			TR	Bury	07.61	1961-67	108	3	0	
			TR	Rochdale	07.68	1968-70	59	/	1	
LEEDER, Fred	Seaton Delavel	15.09.36		Everton	03.55	1957	1		0	(FB)
			TR	Darlington	07.58	1958-59	21		0	
			TR	Southport	07.60	1960-61	63		0	

Players Names	Birthplace	Date	Previous Club	League Club	Date Signed	Seasons Played	Career Record Apps Sub Gls		
LEEDHAM, John R.	Morden	08.11.42	Barking	Millwall	10.62	1962–63	9		0 (HB)
			TR	Walsall	05.64	1964	13		0
			TR	Orient	08.65				
LEEK, Ken	Ynysybwl	26.07.35	Pontypridd	Northampton T.	08.52	1955–57	71		26 (CF) W–13/W.U23–1
			TR	Leicester C.	05.58	1958–60	93		34
			TR	Newcastle U.	06.61	1961	13		6
			TR	Birmingham C.	11.61	1961–64	104		51
			TR	Northampton T.	12.64	1964–65	15		4
			TR	Bradford C.	11.65	1965–67	99	/	25
LEEMING, Cliff	Turton	02.02.20	Bolton W. (AM)	Bury	10.46	1946	1		0 (IF)
			TR	Tranmere Rov.	07.47	1947	13		2
LEES, Alf	Worsley	28.07.23		Bolton W.	05.47	1947	2		0 (CH)
			TR	New Brighton	08.49	1949–50	72		0
			TR	Crewe Alex.	09.51	1951–55	185		5
LEES, Geoff	Rotherham	01.10.33	JNRS	Barnsley	03.51				(HB)
			TR	Bradford C.	07.55	1955	3		0
LEES, Norman	Newcastle	18.11.48	APP	Hull C.	11.66	1966-70	4	1	0 (D)
			L	Hartlepool U.	12.70	1970	20	/	1
			TR	Darlington	07.71	1971–76	108	12	5
LEES, Terry	Stoke	30.06.52	APP	Stoke C.	07.69	1970-73	17	7	0 (D)
			L	Crewe Alex.	03.75	1974	6	/	0
			TR	Port Vale	08.75	1975	40	1	2
			Roda	Birmingham C.	07.79	1979-80	11	1	0
			TR	Newport Co.	08.81	1981	25	/	0
LEES, Walter	Glasgow	02.02.47	Kilsyth Rgrs.	Watford	06.68	1968–75	220	6	10 (FB)
LEESE, William	Stoke	10.03.61	APP	Port Vale	03.79	1979	1	/	0 (D)
LEESON, Don	Doncaster	25.08.35	Askern BC	Barnsley	05.54	1956–60	98		0 (G)
LEET, Norman D.	Leicester	13.03.62	JNRS	Leicester C.	06.80	1980-82	19	/	0 (D)
LE FLEM, Richard P.	Bradford-on-Avon	12.07.42	JNRS	Nottingham F.	05.60	1960–63	132		18 (OL) E.U23–1
			TR	Wolverhampton W.	01.64	1963–64	19		5
			TR	Middlesbrough	02.65	1964–65	9	/	1
			TR	Orient	03.66	1965–66	11	/	2
LEGATE, Roland	Arlesey	04.05.39	JNRS	Luton T.	05.56	1956–61	15		8 (F)
LEGG, Richard	Chippenham	23.04.52	Chippenham	Swindon T.	08.71	1971–73	13	7	3 (IF)
LEGG, William C.	Bradford	17.04.48	APP	Huddersfield T.	05.65	1964–68	53	2	4 (F)
LEGGAT, Graham	Aberdeen	20.06.34	Aberdeen	Fulham	08.58	1958–66	252	3	127 (F) S–18/S.F.LGE.REP./
			TR	Birmingham C.	01.67	1966–67	13	3	3 S.U23–1
			TR	Rotherham U.	07.68	1968	13	3	7
LEGGETT, Peter R.	Newton-le-Willows	16.12.43	Weymouth	Swindon T.	05.62	1963–64	15		2 (F)
			TR	Brighton & H.A.	07.65	1965	2	1	0
			Chelmsford C.	Lincoln C.	01.70				
			TR	Cambridge U.	08.70	1970	21	/	0
LEIGH, Dennis	Barnsley	26.02.49	APP	Doncaster Rov.	03.67	1966-67	34	2	1 (D)
			TR	Rotherham U.	02.68	1967-72	154	5	10
			TR	Lincoln C.	02.73	1972-78	201	5	3
LEIGH, Ian R.	Ilfracombe	11.06.62	Swaythling	Bournemouth	10.79	1981-83	105	/	0 (G)
LEIGH, Mark B.	Manchester	04.10.61	Manchester C. (APP)	Stockport Co.	N/C	1980-83	6	5	1 (F)
LEIGH, Peter	Altrincham	04.03.39		Manchester C.	08.57	1959	2	/	0 (FB)
			TR	Crewe Alex.	06.61	1961–71	430	/	3
LEIGHTON, Anthony	Leeds	27.11.39	Ashley Rd. FC.	Leeds. U.	12.56				(CF)●
			TR	Doncaster Rov.	06.59	1959–61	83		45
			TR	Barnsley	05.62	1962–64	106		59
			TR	Huddersfield T.	01.65	1964–67	90	1	40
			TR	Bradford C.	03.68	1967–69	84	4	23
LEIPER, John	Aberdeen	26.06.38	Aberdeen EE	Plymouth Arg.	04.58	1960–66	75	/	0 (G)
LEISHMAN, Tom	Stenhousemuir	03.09.37	St. Mirren	Liverpool	11.59	1959–62	107		6 (WH)
LEITCH, Andy	Bristol	27.03.50		Swansea C.	07.75	1975	15	2	6 (CF)
LEIVERS, William E.	Bolsover	29.01.32	JNRS	Chesterfield	02.50	1951–52	27		0 (FB)
			TR	Manchester C.	11.53	1954–63	250		4
			TR	Doncaster Rov.	07.64	1964–65	24	/	1
LELLO, Cyril F.	Ludlow	24.02.20		Lincoln C.	+				(WH)
			Shrewsbury T.	Everton	09.47	1947–56	236		9
			TR	Rochdale	11.56	1956	11		0
LEMAN, Dennis	Newcastle	01.12.54	APP	Manchester C.	12.71	1973-75	10	7	1 (M) E.SCH.INT.
			TR	Sheffield Wed.	12.76	1976-81	89	15	9
			L	Wrexham	02.82	1981	17	/	1
			TR	Scunthorpe U.	08.82	1982-83	38	/	3
LEMON, Arthur	Neath	25.01.31		Nottingham F.	02.51	1952–54	23		1 (CF)
LENG, Mike	Rotherham	14.06.52	APP	Rotherham U.	07.71	1971-75	94	7	2 (D)
			TR	Workington	07.76	1976	43	/	2
LENIHAN, Mike	Swansea	15.10.46	Swansea GPO	Swansea C.	08.72	1972–73	9	4	0 (CF)

Players Names	Birthplace	Date	Previous Club	League Club	Date Signed	Seasons Played	Career Record Apps	Sub	Gls	
LENNARD, David	Manchester	31.12.44	JNRS	Bolton W.	12.61	1962-68	114	5	3	(M)
			TR	Halifax T.	07.69	1969-71	97	/	16	
			TR	Blackpool	10.71	1971-72	42	3	9	
			TR	Cambridge U.	08.73	1973-74	39	1	6	
			TR	Chester C.	09.74	1974-75	73	2	11	
			TR	Stockport Co.	07.76	1976	39	/	4	
			TR	Bournemouth	09.77	1977-78	56	3	4	
LENNARDUZZI, Robert	Canada	01.05.55	APP	Reading	05.73	1971-75	63	4	2	(WH)
LENNON, Alex V.	Glasgow	23.10.25		Q.P.R.	01.47	1948	1		0	+ Rotherham U.
			TR	Mansfield T.	02.49	1948	3		0	
LENNOX, Steve J.M.	Aberdeen	14.11.64	APP	Stoke C.	12.81	1982	1	1	0	(M)
			L	Torquay U.	12.83	1983	11	/	0	
LEONARD, Carleton C.	Oswestry	03.02.58	JNRS	Shrewsbury T.	09.75	1975-82	224	3	1	(D)
			TR	Hereford U.	06.83	1983	24	1	0	
LEONARD, Chris	Jarrow	11.07.27	Sth. Shields	Darlington	03.52	1951-53	26		0	(CH)
LEONARD, Gary E.	Northampton	23.03.62	APP	Northampton T.	03.80	1979-80	2	/	0	(M)
LEONARD, Henry	Jarrow	19.05.24		Bradford P.A.	+	1947	1		0	Brother of Chris
			TR	Hartlepool U.	11.48	1948	2		0	
LEONARD, Keith	Birmingham	10.11.50	Highgate U.	Aston Villa	04.72	1972-75	36	2	11	(CF)
			L	Port Vale	11.73	1973	12	1	1	
LEONARD, Mark A.	St. Helens	27.09.62	Witton A.	Everton	02.82					(F)
			L	Tranmere Rov.	03.83	1982	6	1	0	
			TR	Crewe Alex.	06.83	1983	36	2	10	
LEONARD, Mike C.	Carshalton	09.05.59	Epsom & Ewell	Halifax T.	07.76	1976-79	69	/	0	(G)
			TR	Notts. Co.	09.79	1979-83	37	/	0	
LEONARD, Pat D.	Dublin	25.07.29	Bath C.	Bristol Rov.	07.52	1952-53	14		2	(IF)
			TR	Southend U.	07.53					
			TR	Colchester U.	07.54	1954	34		5	
LEONARD, Stan	Hawarden	08.10.25		Chester C.	AM	1946	1		0	(OR) Capt. RN (OBE)
LE ROUX, Daniel	S. Africa	25.11.33	Q.Pk. Durban	Arsenal	02.57	1957	5		0	(CF) S.A.AMAT.INT
LESLIE, John A.	London	25.10.55	Dulwich Hamlet	Wimbledon	N/L	1977-82	242	11	85	(F)
			TR	Gillingham	08.83	1973	44	1	9	
LESLIE, Ken	W. Ham	04.01.23		Ipswich T.	08.47					(OR)
				Watford	07.48	1948	7		1	
LESLIE, Lawrie	Edinburgh	17.03.35	Airdrie	West Ham U.	06.61	1961-62	57		0	(G) S-5/S.F.LGE.REP.
			TR	Stoke C.	10.63	1963-65	78	/	0	
			TR	Millwall	07.66	1966-67	67	/	0	
			TR	Southend U.	07.68	1968	13	/	0	
LESLIE, Maurice H.	India	19.08.23		Swindon T.	06.47	1946	1		0	(CH)
LESLIE, Steve	Brentwood	04.09.52	JNRS	Colchester U.	05.71	1970-83	411	21	40	(M) E.YTH.INT.
LESTER, Abe B.	Sheffield	10.02.20	Selby T.	Hull Co.	09.46	1946-47	27		18	(CF)
			TR	Lincoln C.	01.48	1947-48	37		10	
			TR	Stockport Co.	08.49	1949	8		2	
LESTER, Leslie J.	Cardiff	17.11.23	Cardiff Corries	Cardiff C.	+					(RH)
			TR	Torquay U.	08.48	1948-49	31		1	
			TR	Newport Co.	09.50	1950	2		0	
LESTER, Mike J.	Manchester	04.08.54	APP	Oldham Ath.	12.72	1972-73	26	1	1	(M)
			TR	Manchester C.	11.73	1973-76	1	1	0	
			L	Stockport Co.	08.75	1975	8	1	1	
			Washington Dips	Grimsby T.	11.77	1977-79	45	3	10	
			TR	Barnsley	10.79	1979-80	64	/	11	
			TR	Exeter C.	08.81	1981	18	1	6	
			TR	Bradford C.	02.82	1981-82	46	3	2	
			TR	Scunthorpe U.	03.83	1982-83	44	/	6	
LETHERAN, Glan	Llanelli	01.05.56	APP	Leeds U.	05.73	1974	1	/	0	(G) W.U23-1/W.U21-2
			L	Scunthorpe U.	08.76	1976	27	/	0	
			TR	Chesterfield	12.77	1977-79	63	/	0	
			TR	Swansea C.	09.79	1979	21	/	0	
LEUTY, Leon H.	Shrewsbury	23.10.20	Notts. Co. (AM)	Derby Co.	+	1946-49	131		1	(CF) E.F. LGE. REP./E'B'-3/
			TR	Bradford P.A.	03.50	1949-50	19		0	d. 1955
			TR	Notts. Co.	09.50	1950-55	187		3	
LEVER, Arthur R.	Cardiff	25.03.20	JNRS	Cardiff C.	+	1946-50	156		9	(FB) W-1
			TR	Leicester C.	09.50	1950-53	119		0	
			TR	Newport Co.	07.54	1954-56	72		0	
LEVERTON, Ron	Whitewell	08.05.26		Nottingham F.	+	1946-53	104		36	(IF)
			TR	Notts.Co.	10.53	1953-55	45		6	
			TR	Walsall	07.56	1956	17		3	
LEVY, Anthony S.	Edmonton	20.10.59	APP	Plymouth Arg.	08.78	1978	0	1	0	(F)
			TR	Torquay U.	07.79	1979	8	5	1	
LEVY, Len	London	24.12.26		Aldershot	10.50	1950	2		0	(G)
LEWIN, D. Ron	Edmonton	21.06.20		Bradford C.	+					(FB)
			TR	Fulham	06.46	1946-48	41		0	
			TR	Gillingham	06.50	1950-54	191		0	

Players Names	Birthplace	Date	Previous Club	League Club	Date Signed	Seasons Played	Apps	Sub	Gls	
LEWIN, Derek J.	Manchester	18.05.30	St. Annes Ath.	Oldham Ath.	AM	1953–54	10		1	(IF) E.AMAT.INT.
			B. Auckland	Accrington St.	AM	1957	1		0	
LEWINGTON, Ray	Lambeth	07.09.56	APP	Chelsea	02.74	1975-78	80	5	4	(M)
			Vancouver	Wimbledon	09.79	1979	23	/	0	
			TR	Fulham	03.80	1979-83	134	2	15	
LEWIS, Alan T.	Oxford	19.08.54	APP	Derby Co.	05.72	1972	2	/	0	(D) E.YTH.INT.
			TR	Peterborough U.	03.74	1973	10	/	1	
			TR	Brighton & H.A.	01.75	1974	3	/	0	
			TR	Reading	07.77	1977-81	145	4	5	
LEWIS, Bernard	Merthyr Tydfil	12.03.45	JNRS	Cardiff C.	04.64	1963–67	87	1	7	(OL) W. U23–5
			TR	Watford	11.67	1967–69	42	9	9	
			TR	Southend U.	09.70	1970–71	55	3	5	
LEWIS, Brian	Woking	26.01.43	JNRS	Crystal Palace	04.60	1960–62	32		4	(F)
			TR	Portsmouth	07.63	1963–66	134	/	23	
			TR	Coventry C.	01.67	1966–67	33	2	2	
			TR	Luton T.	07.68	1968–69	45	4	22	
			TR	Oxford U.	01.70	1969–70	12	2	4	
			TR	Colchester U.	12.70	1970–71	46	/	17	
			TR	Portsmouth	04.72	1971–74	44	16	8	
LEWIS, Charles	Liverpool	11.05.21	Sth. Liverpool	Halifax T.	10.47	1947–48	24		4	
LEWIS, David S.	Swansea	12.02.36		Swansea C.	12.57	1957–58	19		1	(F)
			TR	Torquay U.	07.60	1960	16		2	
LEWIS, Dennis G.	Treherbert	21.04.25		Swansea C.	08.46					(WH)
			TR	Torquay U.	08.47	1947–58	443		30	
LEWIS, Derek I.E.	Edmonton	10.06.29	Fulham (AM)	Gillingham	05.50	1950–51	48		31	(IF) d. 1953
			TR	Preston N.E.	02.52	1951–52	37		14	
LEWIS, Dudley K.	Swansea	17.11.62	APP	Swansea C.	11.79	1980-83	71	/	1	(D) W.SCH.INT./W.U'21-4/ W-1
LEWIS, Edward	Manchester	03.01.35	JNRS	Manchester U.	01.52	1952–55	20		9	(FB)
			TR	Preston N.E.	12.55	1955–56	12		2	
			TR	West Ham U.	11.56	1956–57	31		12	
			TR	Orient	06.58	1958–63	142		4	
LEWIS, Edward	Yardley	.19	W.B.A.(+)	Orient	+	1946	5		0	(G)
LEWIS, Fred A.	Broughton	27.07.23	Aylesbury	Chelsea	+	1946–52	23		0	(FB)
			TR	Colchester U.	07.53	1953–54	85		0	
LEWIS, Glyn	Abertillery	03.07.21		Crystal Palace	+	1946–47	60		4	
			TR	Bristol C.	07.48	1948	18		0	
LEWIS, Gwyn	Bangor	22.04.31	JNRS	Everton	05.48	1951–55	10		6	(CF) W.YTH.INT.
			TR	Rochdale	06.56	1956	27		10	
			TR	Chesterfield	02.57	1956–60	123		59	
LEWIS, Idris	Tonypandy	26.08.15	Swansea C.(+)	Bristol Rov.	07.46	1946	13		2	(OR) *Swansea C./
			TR	Newport Co.	10.46	1946–47	27		4	Sheffield Wed.
LEWIS, Jack F.	Long Eaton	22.03.48	Long Eaton	Lincoln C.	03.67	1966-69	47	15	9	(F) W.U23-1
			TR	Grimsby T.	01.70	1969–76	231	27	74	
			TR	Blackburn Rov.	08.77	1977	24	4	6	
			TR	Doncaster Rov.	08.78	1978–79	48	16	10	
LEWIS, James L.	Hackney	26.06.27	Walthamstow	Orient	AM	1950	4		0	(CF) E.AMAT.INT.
			Walthamstow	Chelsea	AM	1952–57	90		38	
LEWIS, John	Tredegar	15.10.55	Pontllanfraith	Cardiff C.	08.78	1978-83	135	10	4	(M)
			TR	Newport Co.	09.83	1983	25	/	1	
LEWIS, John	Tamworth	01.05.20	Boldmere St. M.	Walsall	+	1946–52	271		0	(G)
LEWIS, John	Walsall	26.08.19	W.B.A.(*)	Crystal Palace	*	1946–49	123		4	(WH)
			TR	Bournemouth	11.49	1949–50	25		1	
			TR	Reading	07.51	1951–52	74		17	
LEWIS, John	Birmingham	06.10.23	JNRS	W.B.A	+					(WH)
			TR	Mansfield T.	08.48	1948–52	164		10	
LEWIS, John G.	Hackney	09.05.54	Tottenham H.(AM)	Orient	07.72	1972	0	2	0	(F) E.YTH.INT
LEWIS, Ken	Cardiff	07.11.24		Torquay U.	01.50	1950–52	27		0	(FB)
LEWIS, Ken	Bangor	12.10.29	Bangor C.	Walsall	03.54	1953–54	18		1	(IF)
			Bangor C.	Scunthorpe U.	08.56	1956	1		0	
LEWIS, Kevin	Ellesmere Port	19.09.40		Sheffield U.	10.57	1957–59	62		23	(W) E.YTH.INT
			TR	Liverpool	06.60	1960–62	72		39	
			TR	Huddersfield T.	08.63	1963–64	47		13	
LEWIS, Kevin W.	Hull	25.09.52	APP	Manchester U.	09.69					(D)E.SCH.INT.
			TR	Stoke C.	07.72	1972-75	15	/	0	
			TR	Crewe Alex.	06.79	1979-81	117	5	2	
LEWIS, Mike	Birmingham	15.02.65	APP	W.B.A.	02.82	1981-83	21	2	0	(M) E.YTH.INT.
LEWIS, Mike	Ollerton	26.08.50	APP	Rotherham U.	12.67	1967	0	1	0	(F)
LEWIS, Morgan R.	Bournemouth	08.09.65	JNRS	Bournemouth	N/C	1983	1	/	0	(M)
LEWIS, Norman	Shifnal	28.05.27	Oakengates	Shrewsbury T.	08.50	1950–52	62		0	(LB)
			Gravesend	Newport Co.	06.54	1954	15		0	
LEWIS, Paul S.	Rhondda	27.09.56	APP	Bristol Rov.	10.74	1975	1	/	0	(G) W.YTH.INT.

Players Names	Birthplace	Date	Previous Club	League Club	Date Signed	Seasons Played	Career Record Apps	Sub	Gls	
LEWIS, Reg	Bilston	07.03.20	Margate	Arsenal	*	1946–51	134		94	(CF)E'B'–2
LEWIS, Roland	Sandbach	21.09.25		Port Vale	03.50	1950–53	7		0	(F)
LEWIS, Ron	Belfast	10.02.32	Glentoran	Burnley	06.49					(IF)
			TR	Barrow	05.54	1954	5		1	
LEWIS, Russell	Neath	15.09.56	Everwarm	Swindon T.	10.76	1976-82	175	6	7	(D)
			TR	Northampton T.	08.83	1983	45	/	4	
LEWIS, Terry J.	Newport	22.10.50	APP	Cardiff C.	10.68	1968–69	2	/	0	(HB) W.SCH.INT.
LEWIS, Thomas G.	Merthyr Tydfil	20.10.13	Troedyrhiw	Watford	*					(FB)
			TR	Southampton	07.46	1946–47	43		12	
			TR	Brighton & H.A.	06.48	1948	24		8	
LEWIS, Trevor	Bedwellty	06.01.21	Redditch	Coventry C.	02.48	1947–52	11		0	(W)
			TR	Gillingham	02.52	1952	27		4	
LEWIS, William	Cardiff	04.07.23		Cardiff C.	+	1946–47	9		0	(OR)
			TR	Newport Co.	10.47	1947–49	49		12	
LEWIS, William A.	London	23.11.21	West Ham U.(AM)	Blackpool	+	1946–49	30		0	(FB) E.SCH.INT.
			TR	Norwich C.	11.49	1949–55	232		1	
LEWORTHY, David J.	Portsmouth	22.10.62	APP	Portsmouth	09.80	1981	0	1	0	(M)
LEY, George O.A.	Exminster	07.04.46	JNRS	Exeter C.	09.63	1963–66	91	/	7	(FB)
			TR	Portsmouth	05.67	1966–72	183	1	10	
			TR	Brighton & H.A.	09.72	1972–73	47	/	1	
			TR	Gillingham	08.74	1974–75	87	/	2	
LEYFIELD, John G.	Chester	05.08.23		Wrexham	07.46	1946–49	34		1	
			TR	Southport	08.50	1950	26		0	
LEYLAND, Harry K.	Liverpool	12.05.30	JNRS	Everton	08.50	1951–55	36		0	(G)
			TR	Blackburn Rov.	08.56	1956–60	166		0	
			TR	Tranmere Rov.	03.61	1960–65	180	/	0	
LIDDELL, Gary	Bannockburn	27.08.54	APP	Leeds U.	09.71	1972-74	2	1	0	(F)
			TR	Grimsby T.	03.77	1976-80	90	15	24	
			Hearts	Doncaster Rov.	03.82	1981-82	25	12	4	
LIDDELL, John				Bolton W.	09.46					+ Orient
				Brighton & H.A.	03.47	1946	4		1	
LIDDELL, John C.	Stirling	13.12.33	St Johnstone	Oldham Ath.	09.60	1960–61	23		10	(F)
LIDDELL, William B.	Dunfermline	10.01.22	Lochgelly Viol.	Liverpool	*	1946-60	492		216	(OL) S–28●
LIDDLE, Daniel	Bo'ness	19.02.12	Leicester C.(*)	Mansfield T.	07.46	1946	1		0	(OL) S–3/*E.Fife/d.1982
LIDDLE, David N.	Bedford	21.05.57	APP	Northampton T.	05.75	1977-78	28	3	3	(D)
LIDDLE, Gavin	Houghton-le-Spring	09.05.63	Hartlepool U.(APP)	Darlington	08.82	1981-82	33	/	4	(D)
LIDDLE, Ken	Gateshead	06.10.28		Sunderland	12.49					(F)
			TR	Darlington	06.50	1950	1		0	
LIDDLE, Tom B.	Middleton	22.04.21		Bournemouth	02.47	1947	1		0	
LIEVESLEY, Dennis	Chesterfield	19.09.19		Aldershot	08.46	1946–48	8		0	(CH) Son of pre–war player
LIGGITT, Norman	Thornaby	21.07.41	JNRS	Middlesbrough	08.59					(HB)
			TR	Southend U.	07.62	1962	1		0	
LIGHT, Daniel	Chiswick	10.07.48	APP	Crystal Palace	12.65	1966–67	18	1	5	(F)
			TR	Colchester U.	08.68	1968–69	65	2	17	
LIGHT, James P.	Oxford	13.01.54	APP	Oxford U.	07.72	1972–75	64	/	1	(FB)
LIGHTBOWN, Trevor J.	Blackburn	21.11.39	Burnley (AM)	Accrington St.	AM	1959	8		0	(CF)
			TR	Bradford P.A.	AM	1960	2		0	
LIGHTENING, Arthur	S. Africa	01.08.36	S. Africa	Nottingham F.	12.56	1957–58	6		0	(G)
			TR	Coventry C.	11.58	1958–62	150		0	
			TR	Middlesbrough	08.62	1962	15		0	
LIGHTLY, Brian	Portsmouth	12.05.36	Portsmouth (AM)	Exeter C.	06.57	1957	4		0	(IF)
LIGHTOWLER, Gerald	Bradford	05.09.40	St Bede's	Bradford P.A.	12.58	1958–67	206	2	1	(FB)
			L. Angeles Wolves	Bradford C.	10.68	1968	11	/	1	
LILL, David A.	Aldbrough	17.02.47	JNRS	Hull C.	03.65	1966–69	16	2	2	(CF)
			TR	Rotherham U.	10.69	1967–70	33	7	5	
			TR	Cambridge U.	07.71	1971–75	166	6	22	
LILL, James A.	Wentworth	04.06.33	Weatworth F.C.	Mansfield T.	03.54	1953–56	4		0	(OL)
LILL, Micky J.	Romford	03.08.36	Storey Ath.	Wolverhampton W.	06.54	1957–59	30		15	(OL) E.YTH.INT.
			TR	Everton	02.60	1959–61	31		11	
			TR	Plymouth Arg.	06.62	1962	21		7	
			TR	Portsmouth	03.63	1962–64	39		5	
LILLEY, Henry J.G.	Bristol	19.08.18	Dockland Sett	Bristol Rov.	10.46	1946–49	27		0	(G)
LILLIS, Mark A.	Manchester	17.01.60		Huddersfield T.	07.78	1978-83	164	7	42	(F)
LILYGREEN, Chris L.	Newport	09.06.65	JNRS	Newport Co.	N/C	1983	15	7	4	(F)
LINACRE, John	Middlesbrough	13.12.55	Whitby T.	Hartlepool U.	07.77	1977-83	207	4	12	(M) Son of William
LINACRE, Phil	Middlesbrough	17.05.62	Coventry C.(APP)	Hartlepool U.	08.80	1980-83	78	4	17	(F) Brother of John

Players Names	Birthplace	Date	Previous Club	League Club	Date Signed	Seasons Played	Apps	Sub	Gls	
LINACRE, William	Chesterfield	10.08.24	JNRS	Chesterfield	+	1946–47	22		3	(OR)
			TR	Manchester C.	10.47	1947–49	75		6	
			TR	Middlesbrough	09.49	1949–51	31		2	
			TR	Hartlepool U.	08.53	1953–55	89		10	
			TR	Mansfield T.	10.55	1955	13		0	
LINAKER, John E.	Southport	14.01.27	Everton (AM)	Manchester C.	+					(OL)
			TR	Southport	11.46	1946	15		0	
			TR	Nottingham F.	09.47	1948–49	15		2	
			TR	York C.	06.50	1950–51	59		15	
			TR	Hull C.	10.51	1951–52	26		3	
			TR	York C.	05.53	1953–55	39		3	
			Scarborough	Crewe Alex.	07.57	1957	34		3	
LINDLEY, Edwin	Epworth	22.04.31	Scunthorpe U.	Nottingham F.	10.49	1949	1		0	d. 1951
			TR	Scunthorpe U.	08.51					
LINDLEY, W. Maurice	Keighley	05.12.15	Keighley T.	Everton	*	1947–51	51		0	(CH)
LINDORES, William	Newcastleton	03.05.33	Hearts of Liddleston	Barrow	07.59	1959	5		0	(FB) S.SCH.INT.
LINDSAY, Alec	Bury	27.02.48	APP	Bury	03.65	1964-68	126	/	14	(D) E-4/E.YTH.INT.
			TR	Liverpool	03.69	1969-76	168	2	12	
			TR	Stoke C.	08.77	1977	20	/	3	
LINDSAY, David	Alexandria	23.09.19	St. Mirren	Luton T.	05.48	1948	7		0	(CH)
			TR	Barnsley	11.48	1948–51	78		3	
LINDSAY, David	Cambuslang	29.06.26	Blantyre Vic.	Sunderland	08.46	1946	1		0	(FB)
			TR	Southend U.	05.48	1948–50	52		1	
LINDSAY, David J.	Havering	17.05.66	APP	Crystal Palace	05.84	1983	1	/	0	(M)
LINDSAY, Hugh M.	Ickenham	23.08.38	Kingstonian	Southampton	AM	1960	2		0	(IF) E.AMAT.INT.
LINDSAY, Ian	Canonbie	10.02.44	Hearts of Lidd.	Workington	11.64	1964–65	10	/	0	(G)
				Carlisle U.	11.66					
LINDSAY, Jimmy	Hamilton	12.07.49	JNRS	West Ham U.	08.66	1968-70	36	3	2	(M)
			TR	Watford	08.71	1971-73	64	1	12	
			TR	Colchester U.	07.74	1974	45	/	6	
			TR	Hereford U.	08.75	1975-76	79	/	6	
			TR	Shrewsbury T.	08.77	1977-80	80	6	0	
LINDSAY, John M.	Cambuslang	11.12.21	Morton	Sheffield Wed.	+	1946	1		1	(CF)
			TR	Bury	10.46	1946	11		7	
			TR	Carlisle U.	08.47	1947–50	103		46	
			TR	Southport	03.51	1950–51	50		20	
			Wigan Ath.	Carlisle U.	01.55	1954	13		2	
LINDSAY, John S.	Auchinleck	08.08.24	Glasgow Rgrs.	Everton	03.51	1950–53	105		2	(FB)
			TR	Bury	05.56	1956	7		0	
LINDSAY, Lawrie	Alexandria	07.10.21	Hibernian	Crewe Alex.	01.48	1947–48	40		0	(CH)
LINDSAY, Mal	Ashington	26.09.40	Kings Lynn	Cambridge U.	N/L	1970	6	/	0	(CF)
LINDSAY, Mark E.	Lambeth	06.03.55	APP	Crystal Palace	08.73	1973–74	27	3	0	(WH)
LINDSEY, Barry	Scunthorpe	17.04.44	APP	Scunthorpe U.	05.61	1961–70	209	6	14	(WH)
LINDSEY, Keith	Scunthorpe	25.11.46	APP	Scunthorpe U.	12.64	1965	16	/	0	(FB) Brother of Barry
			TR	Doncaster Rov.	07.66	1966	16	2	0	
			Cambridge U.	Southend U.	01.69	1968–71	88	3	4	
			TR	Port Vale	12.71	1971–72	24	/	0	
			TR	Gillingham	12.72	1972–74	73	/	5	
LINEKER, Gary W.	Leicester	30.11.60	APP	Leicester C.	12.78	1978-83	146	7	71	(F)E-1
LINES, Barry	Bletchley	16.05.42	Bletchley T.	Northampton T.	09.60	1960–69	259	7	49	(OR)
LINEY, Pat	Paisley	14.07.36	St Mirren	Bradford P.A.	06.66	1966	11	/	0	(G)
			TR	Bradford C.	09.67	1967–71	147	/	0	
LINFORD, John	Norwich	06.02.57	Gorleston	Ipswich T.	08.81					(F)
			L	Colchester U.	01.83	1982	7	/	0	
			L	Southend U.	03.83	1982	6	/	3	
LING, Martin	London	15.07.66	APP	Exeter C.	01.84	1982-83	23	7	0	
LINIGHAN, Andy	Hartlepool	18.06.62	Smiths B.C.	Hartlepool U.	09.80	1980-83	110	/	5	(M)Brother of David
			TR	Leeds U.	05.84					
LINIGHAN, Brian	W. Hartlepool	17.03.36		Lincoln C.	12.53					(HB)
			L	Darlington	10.58	1958	1		1	
LINIGHAN, David	Hartlepool	09.01.65	JNRS	Hartlepool U.	09.81	1981-83	31	4	1	(M)
LINK, Tom H.	Halifax	15.12.18		Bradford C.	05.48	1947–48	6		0	
LINNECOR, Albert	Birmingham	30.11.33	JNRS	Birmingham C.	05.52	1955–56	17		0	(WH)
			TR	Lincoln C.	04.57	1956–63	264		52	
LINNELL, John L.	Northampton	02.01.44	JNRS	Northampton T.	09.63					(WH)
			TR	Peterborough U.	07.67	1967	24	2	1	
LINNEY, W. David	Birmingham	05.09.61	APP	Birmingham C.	09.79	1981	0	1	0	(M)
			TR	Oxford U.	08.82	1982	26	/	0	
LINSTREM, Ken R.	Salford	12.10.28		Crewe Alex.	06.50	1950–51	13		1	(HB)
			TR	Bournemouth	08.52					
LINTERN, Mel	Newcastle	17.05.50	JNRS	Port Vale	03.68	1966	0	1	0	(CH)

Players Names	Birthplace	Date	Previous Club	League Club	Date Signed	Seasons Played	Apps	Sub	Gls	
LINTON, Ivor	W. Bromwich	20.11.59	APP	Aston Villa	09.77	1976-81	16	11	0	(F)
			TR	Peterborough U.	08.82	1982-83	24	3	3	
			TR	Birmingham C.	12.83	1983	3	1	0	
LINTON, James A.	Glasgow	02.12.30	Kirkintilloch	Notts. Co.	11.52	1952-58	112		0	(G)
			TR	Watford	07.59	1959-62	72		0	
LINTON, Malcolm W.	Southend	13.02.52	Southend U.(AM)	Orient	12.72	1972-74	14	5	0	(HB) Son of Tom
LINTON, Tom G.N.	Falkirk	15.10.20		Southend U.	+	1946-48	68		0	
LINWOOD, Alex B.	Drumsmudden	13.03.20	St Mirren	Middlesbrough	06.46	1946	14		3	(IF) S-1/S.F.LGE REP.
LIPTROTT, Dave A.	Stockport	26.02.65	JNRS	Stockport Co.	N/C	1982	0	1	0	
LISHMAN, Doug J.	Birmingham	14.09.23	Paget Rgrs.	Walsall	08.46	1946-47	59		26	(IF)E'B–1/E.F. LGE REP.●
			TR	Arsenal	07.48	1948-55	227		127	
			TR	Nottingham F.	03.56	1955-56	38		22	
LISTER, Alex O.	Glasgow	20.01.24	Alloa Ath.	Rochdale	05.52	1952	2		0	(IF)
LISTER, Eric	Willenhall	13.08.33	Wolverhampton W. (AM)	Notts Co.	09.51	1954-56	8		0	(OL)
LISTER, Herbert F.	Manchester	04.10.39		Manchester C.	11.57	1958	2		0	(CF)
			TR	Oldham Ath.	10.60	1960-64	135		77	
			TR	Rochdale	01.65	1964-66	56		16	
			TR	Stockport Co.	01.67	1966	16	/	11	
LISTER, Steve H.	Doncaster	18.11.61	APP	Doncaster Rov.	07.78	1978-83	193	8	28	(D)
LITCHFIELD Peter	Manchester	27.07.56	Droylsden	Preston N.E.	01.79	1980-83	89	/	0	(G)
LITHGO, Gordon	W. Hartlepool	14.08.42	JNRS	Hartlepool U.	08.59	1960-63	37		8	(F)
LITT, Steve E.	Carlisle	21.05.54	Blackpool(APP)	Luton T.	06.72	1973-75	15	/	0	(D)
			Minnesota Kicks	Northampton T.	09.77	1977	19	1	0	
LITTLE, Alan	Newcastle	05.02.55	APP	Aston Villa	01.73	1974	2	1	0	(M) Brother of Brian
			TR	Southend U.	12.74	1974-76	102	1	12	
			TR	Barnsley	08.77	1977-79	91	/	14	
			TR	Doncaster Rov.	12.79	1979-82	84	1	11	
			TR	Torquay U.	10.82	1982-83	51	/	4	
			TR	Halifax T.	11.83	1983	27	/	3	
LITTLE, Barry	Greenwich	25.08.64	APP	Charlton Ath.	07.82	1982	2	/	1	(M) E.YTH.INT.
LITTLE, Brian	Durham	25.11.53	APP	Aston Villa	03.71	1971-79	242	5	60	(F) E-1
LITTLE, George	Newcastle	30.06.15	Throckley Welf.	Doncaster Rov.	*	1947	1		0	(W)
			TR	York Co.	12.47	1947	15		2	
LITTLE, John A.	Gateshead	17.05.12	Needham Mkt.	Ipswich T.	*	1946-49	115		14	
LITTLE, Ron	Carlisle	1934		Carlisle U.	AM	1955	5		0	(OR)
LITTLE, Roy,	Manchester	01.06.31	Greenwood Vic	Manchester C.	08.49	1952-58	168		2	(FB)
			TR	Brighton & H.A.	10.58	1958-60	83		0	
			TR	Crystal Palace	05.61	1961-62	38		1	
LITTLEJOHN, Roy D.	Bournemouth	02.06.33	JNRS	Bournemouth	AM	1952-55	22		2	(CF) E.AMAT.INT.
LITTLER, Joe	St. Helens	14.04.29	Stubshaw Cross	Leicester C.	05.51	1951-54	5		2	(CF)
			TR	Lincoln C.	12.54	1954	6		2	
			TR	Wrexham	06.55	1955	12		1	
			TR	Crewe Alex.	12.55	1955	10		2	
LITTLER, Tom	Stockport	06.03.36		Stockport Co.	04.55	1955	1		0	(F)
LIVERMORE, Doug	Liverpool	27.12.47	JNRS	Liverpool	11.65	1967-70	13	3	0	(M)
			TR	Norwich C.	11.70	1970-74	113	1	4	
			L	Bournemouth	03.75	1974	10	/	0	
			TR	Cardiff C.	08.75	1975-77	84	4	5	
			TR	Chester C.	10.77	1977-78	71	/	6	
LIVERSIDGE, Ron	Huddersfield	12.09.34	Ossett T.	Bradford C.	10.56	1956-58	48		27	(F)
LIVESEY, Charles E.	London	06.02.38	Wolverhampton W.(AM)	Southampton	03.56	1958	25		14	(CF)
			TR	Chelsea	05.59	1959-60	39		17	
			TR	Gillingham	08.61	1961-62	47		17	
			TR	Watford	10.62	1962-64	64		26	
			TR	Northampton T.	08.64	1964-65	28	/	4	
			TR	Brighton & H.A.	09.65	1965-68	124	1	30	
LIVESEY, John	Preston	08.03.24	Preston N.E.(+)	Bury	05.46	1946	7		1	(IF)
			TR	Doncaster Rov.	01.47	1947	3		0	
			TR	Rochdale	04.48	1947-50	113		36	
			TR	Southport	07.51	1951	31		9	
LIVIE, Gordon	Billingham	10.06.32		Leicester C.	12.49					(FB)
			TR	Mansfield T.	07.52	1952-53	53		25	
LIVINGSTONE, Archie	Pencaithland	15.11.15	Newcastle U.(*)	Bury	*					(IF) *Ormiston Prim./
			TR	Everton	05.46	1946	4		2	d.1961
			TR	Southport	06.47	1947	23		1	
LIVINGSTONE, Joe	Middlesbrough	18.06.42	JNRS	Middlesbrough	01.60	1960-62	20		7	(IF)
			TR	Carlisle U.	11.62	1962-65	79	1	40	
			TR	Hartlepool U.	05.66	1965-66	15	/	5	
LIVINGSTONE, Wilf	Barrow	22.10.19	Holker COB	Barrow	09.47	1947-48	4		0	(CF)
LIVINGSTONE, William	Greenock	08.02.29	Ardeer Rec.	Reading	04.49	1949-54	49		1	(CH)
			TR	Chelsea	06.55	1956-57	20		0	
			TR	Brentford	07.59	1959	19		0	

Players Names	Birthplace	Date	Previous Club	League Club	Date Signed	Seasons Played	Apps	Sub	Gls	
LIVINGSTONE, William	Coventry	13.08.64	APP	Wolverhampton W.	08.82	1982-83	21	3	4	(F)S.YTH.INT.
LIVSEY, Gordon	Keighley	24.01.47	Kettering	Wrexham	01.67	1967-70	79	/	0	(G)
			TR	Chester C.	08.71	1971	44	/	0	
			Kettering	Hartlepool U.	12.77	1977	6	/	0	
LLEWELLYN, Andy D.	Bristol	26.02.66	APP	Bristol C.	03.84	1982	5	2	0	(D)
LLEWELLYN, David	Cardiff	09.08.49	JNRS	West Ham U.	08.66	1969-71	2	4	0	(F) W.U23-1
			TR	Peterborough U.	08.73	1973-74	11	2	3	
			L	Mansfield T.	08.74	1974	6	2	0	
LLEWELLYN, Herbert	Golborne	05.02.39	JNRS	Everton	05.56	1956-57	11		2	(CF) E.YTH.INT
			TR	Crewe Alex.	07.58	1958-60	96		51	
			TR	Port Vale	11.60	1960-62	88		42	
			TR	Northampton T.	02.63	1962	1		0	
			TR	Walsall	02.64	1963-64	17	*	6	
LLOYD, Barry D.	Hillingdon	19.02.49	APP	Chelsea	02.66	1966-68	8	2	0	(M) E.YTH.INT.
			TR	Fulham	12.68	1968-75	249	6	28	
			TR	Hereford U.	10.76	1976	12	2	0	
			TR	Brentford	06.77	1977	26	5	4	
LLOYD, Brian	St. Asaph	18.03.48	Rhyl	Stockport Co.	03.67	1967-68	32	/	0	(G)W-3/W.U23-2
			TR	Southend U.	09.69	1969-70	48	/	0	
			TR	Wrexham	08.71	1971-77	266	/	0	
			TR	Chester C.	09.77	1977-79	94	/	0	
			L	Port Vale	02.81	1980	16	/	0	
			TR	Stockport Co.	08.81	1981-82	91	/	1	
LLOYD, Cliff	Brymbo	14.11.16	Wrexham (+)	Fulham	+	1946	2		0	(OR) * Liverpool
			TR	Bristol Rov.	05.50					
LLOYD, David	Gateshead	01.06.28		Sheffield U.	09.49					
			TR	York C.	03.51	1950	1		0	
			TR	Swindon T.	08.51					
LLOYD, Frank	Maplewell	16.01.28		Bradford C.	07.51	1951-53	24		0	(HB)
LLOYD, Geoff	Wrexham	18.08.42		Wrexham	10.66	1966	13	1	5	(F)
			TR	Bradford P.A.	07.67	1967	32	/	10	
LLOYD, Graham	Liverpool	10.01.51	APP	Liverpool	01.68					(G)
			Motherwell	Portsmouth	07.75	1975-76	74	/	0	
LLOYD, Harold	Flint	12.03.20	Flint T.	Tranmere Rov.	+	1946-56	189		0	(G)
LLOYD, John D.	Hitchin	10.12.44	APP	Swindon T.	01.62					(FB)
			TR	Oxford U.	10.64	1965-68	68	4	0	
			TR	Aldershot	02.69	1968-69	11	2	0	
LLOYD, John W.	Rossett	15.02.48	JNRS	Wrexham	AM	1965-66	2	/	0	(OR)
LLOYD, Joseph M.	Shotton	30.09.10	Swansea C. (*)	Wrexham	07.46	1946	20		0	(WH)
LLOYD, Kevin J.J.	Wolverhampton	12.06.58	Darlaston	Cardiff C.	05.79	1979	0	1	0	(F)
			TR	Gillingham	07.80	1980	0	1	0	
LLOYD, Larry	Bristol	06.10.48	JNRS	Bristol Rov.	07.67	1968	43	/	1	(D) E-4/E.U23-8/
			TR	Liverpool	04.69	1969-73	150	/	4	E.YTH.INT.
			TR	Coventry C.	08.74	1974-76	50	/	5	
			TR	Nottingham F.	10.76	1976-80	148	/	6	
			TR	Wigan Ath.	03.81	1980-82	52	/	2	
LLOYD, Norman P.	Skewen	08.03.30		Cardiff C.	03.48					(WH)
			TR	Torquay U.	08.49	1952-56	29		1	
LLOYD, Norman W.	Torrance	06.09.49	JNRS	Preston N.E.	09.66	1968-70	18	2	6	(IF)
			L	Stockport Co.	01.71	1970	10	/	0	
			TR	Southport	07.71	1971-73	93	9	13	
			TR	Stockport Co.	07.74	1974	36	2	2	
LLOYD, Peter J.	Pattingham	26.04.33	Pattingham	Walsall	03.51	1953	5		0	(OL)
LLOYD, Philip R.	Hemsworth	26.12.64	APP	Middlesbrough	01.83					(D)
			Barnsley (N/C)	Darlington	N/C	1983	14	/	0	
LLOYD, R. Clive	Merthyr Tydfil	04.09.45	APP	Norwich C.	09.62					(F)
			TR	Cardiff C.	08.64	1964	2		0	
			TR	Swindon T.	08.65					
LLOYD, Ray	W. Seaham	06.12.30	Seaham Col.	Lincoln C.	01.50	1950	1		0	
LLOYD, William F.	Poplar	10.07.34	Bromley	Millwall	08.56	1956-57	72		0	(G)
LLOYD, William L.	Rhondda	22.05.15		Swindon T.	+	1946-50	107		2	
LLOYD William S.	W. Auckland	01.10.24	JNRS	Sunderland	+	1946-47	24		5	(F) E.SCH.INT.
			TR	Grimsby T.	08.48	1948-52	148		23	
			Worksop T.	Scunthorpe U.	07.54	1954	1		0	
LOADWICK, Derek	Middlesbrough	04.10.56	APP	Leeds U.	10.73					(D)
			TR	Stockport Co.	07.76	1976-78	84	/	0	
			TR	Hartlepool U.	10.78	1978-79	49	2	1	
LOASBY, Alan A.	Wellingborough	19.03.37	JNRS	Luton T.	04.54					(IF)
			TR	Northampton T.	07.58	1958	2		0	
LOBBETT, John	Exeter	08.01.38	Barnstaple	Exeter Co.	03.56	1958-60	44		0	(G)
LOCHERTY, Joe	Dundee	05.09.25		Sheffield Wed.	09.47	1948-49	10		0	
			TR	Colchester U.	07.50	1950	10		1	

Players Names	Birthplace	Date	Previous Club	League Club	Date Signed	Seasons Played	Career Record Apps Sub Gls			
LOCHHEAD, Andy L.	Milngavie	09.03.41	Renfrew J.	Burnley	12.58	1960–68	225	1	102	(CF) S.U23–1
			TR	Leicester C.	10.68	1968–69	40	4	12	
			TR	Aston Villa	02.70	1969–72	127	4	34	
			TR	Oldham Ath.	08.73	1973–74	44	1	10	
LOCK, Frank W.	London	12.03.22	Finchley	Charlton Ath.	+	1946–53	221		8	(FB)
			TR	Liverpool	12.53	1953–54	41		0	
			TR	Watford	06.55	1955–56	42		1	
LOCK, Kevin J.	Plaistow	27.12.53	APP	West Ham U.	12.71	1972-77	122	10	2	(D) E.U23-4/E.YTH.INT.
			TR	Fulham	05.78	1978-83	180	1	22	
LOCKE, Gary R.	Kingsbury	12.07.54	APP	Chelsea	07.71	1972-82	270	2	3	(D)ENG.YTH.INT.
			TR	Crystal Palace	01.83	1982-83	49	/	1	
LOCKE, Leslie	Perth	24.01.34	Bromley	Q.P.R.	05.58	1956–59	77		22	(IF) S.AMAT.INT.
LOCKHART, Crichton	Perth	06.03.30	Chertsey	Southend U.	08.50	1950–56	45		11	(F)
			TR	Rochdale	06.57	1957–58	42		11	
LOCKHART, Keith S.	Wallsend	19.07.64	APP	Cambridge U.	07.82	1981-83	28	2	5	(F)
LOCKHART, Norman	Belfast	04.03.24	Linfield	Swansea C.	10.46	1946–47	47		13	(OL)N1–8
			TR	Coventry C.	10.47	1947–52	182		41	
			TR	Aston Villa	09.52	1952–55	73		10	
			TR	Bury	11.56	1956–57	41		6	
LOCKIE, Alex J.	Sth. Shields	11.04.15	Sth. Shields	Sunderland	*					(CH)
			TR	Notts. Co.	09.46	1946	23		0	
LOCKIER, Maurice R.	Bristol	27.11.24		Bristol Rov.	07.47	1949	2		0	(OL)
LOCKWOOD, Edward	Barmborough	04.08.25	Denaby	Scunthorpe U.	06.51	1951–53	11		0	(FB)
LOCKWOOD, Roy	Barnsley	20.06.33	JNRS	Sheffield Wed.	04.51					(FB) E.YTH.INT.
			TR	Norwich C.	09.55	1955–57	36		0	
LODGE, Frank	Oldham Ath.	28.11.19	Ward St. O.B.	Stockport Co.	AM	1946	1		0	(CF) d.1973
LODGE, George	Wallsend	27.01.43		Workington	12.61					(OL)
			TR	Newcastle U.	07.62					
			TR	Barrow	07.63	1963	6		0	
LODGE, Paul	Liverpool	13.02.61	APP	Everton	02.79	1980-81	20	4	0	(M)E.SCH.INT.
			L	Wigan Ath.	08.82	1982	5	/	1	
			L	Rotherham U.	01.83	1982	4	/	0	
			TR	Preston N.E.	02.83	1982-83	36	2	0	
LODGE, Robert W.	Retford	01.07.41		Sheffield Wed.	09.59	1960	3		2	(OR)
			TR	Doncaster Rov.	05.61	1961	23		4	
LODGE, Tom J.	Huddersfield	16.04.21	JNRS	Huddersfield T.	+	1947	2		0	(LH) Yorks.Cricketer
LOFTHOUSE, Nat	Bolton	27.08.25	JNRS	Bolton W.	+	1946–60	452		255	(CF) E–33/E'B'–1/E.F. LGE. REP.●
LOFTUS, Robert	Liverpool	15.12.31	Llanelli	Bradford P.A.	12.55	1955	3		0	
LOFTY, Jim K.	Farnham	05.12.45	JNRS	Reading	05.63	1963	2		0	(F)
			TR	Birmingham C.	07.64					
LOGAN, Doug	Aberdeen	30.08.33		Southampton	01.54	1955–57	21		0	(HB)
LOGAN, Gordon	Edinburgh	03.10.49		Port Vale	03.67	1966–69	34	2	1	(FB)
LOGAN, John W.	Horden	16.08.12	Darlington (*)	Barnsley	*	1946	12		0	(WH) * Charlton Ath./
			TR	Sheffield Wed.	01.47	1946	4		0	d.
LOGGIE, David M.	Newbiggin	31.05.57	APP	Burnley	06.74	1975-77	6	1	0	(F)
			TR	York C.	06.78	1978-79	47	3	11	
LOGIE, Jimmy T.	Edinburgh	23.11.19	Lochore Welf.	Arsenal	+	1946–54	296		68	(IF)S–1/d.1984
LOGUE, Sam W.	Glasgow	09.04.34	Clyde	Accrington St.	06.60	1960	2		0	(F)
LOHMAN, Jan H.P.	Holland	18.02.59	Lokeren	Watford	10.81	1981-83	46	6	5	(W) HOLLAND U'21.
LOMAS, Albert	Tyldesley	14.10.24		Leeds U.	09.48	1948	1		0	(G)
				Rochdale	05.50	1950	9		0	
			TR	Chesterfield	07.51	1951	29		0	
LOMAS, Clive I.	Ealing	18.01.47	APP	Watford	01.65	1965	6	1	0	(HB)
LOMAS, Peter	Manchester	09.05.33		Southport	12.52	1951–56	18		0	(FB)
LOMAX, Geoff W.	Droylsden	06.07.64	JNRS	Manchester C.	07.81	1982-83	17	1	1	(D)
LONG, Chris	Hatfield	07.02.48	Hatfield T.	Luton T.	02.66	1965	1	/	0	(F)
LONG, John W.	Southampton	08.05.21	Chester (AM)	Exeter C.	+	1946	1		0	(FB)
LONG, Nigel S.	Doncaster	31.03.55		Doncaster Rov.	N/C	1974	1	/	0	(WH)
LONG, Ray	Stickney	04.10.36	Louth U.	Lincoln C.	12.58	1959	1		0	(CH)
LONG, Terry A.	Beaconsfield	17.11.34	Wycombe W.	Crystal Palace	05.55	1955–68	432	10	16	(WH)
LONG, Trevor G.	Smethwick	01.07.31	Mitchell & B	Wolverhampton W.	12.50					(WH)
			TR	Gillingham	07.52	1952	61		15	
			TR	Reading	07.55	1955	12		5	
LONG, Wilfred R.	Wallasey	28.12.22	Everton (AM)	New Brighton	AM	1946	2		0	(OL)

Players Names	Birthplace	Date	Previous Club	League Club	Date Signed	Seasons Played	Apps	Sub	Gls	
LONGBOTTOM, Arthur (Langley)	Leeds	30.01.33	Methley U.	Q.P.R.	03.54	1954–60	201		62	(IF)
			TR	Port Vale	05.61	1961–62	62		15	
			TR	Millwall	01.63	1962	10		1	
			TR	Oxford U.	08.63	1963–64	34		14	
			TR	Colchester U.	10.64	1964	33		12	
LONGDEN, Colin	Rotherham	21.07.33	JNRS	Rotherham U.	08.50	1952	3		0	(F) E.SCH.INT.
				York C.	08.55	1957	2		0	
LONGDEN, D. Paul	Wakefield	28.09.62	APP	Barnsley	08.81	1981-82	5	/	0	(D)
			TR	Scunthorpe U.	08.83	1983	43	/	0	
LONGDON, Charles W.	Mansfield	06.05.17	Brighton & H.A.(+)	Bournemouth	05.46	1946	9		1	(WH)
			TR	Rochdale	07.47	1947	2		0	
LONGHORN, Dennis	Southampton	12.09.50	APP	Bournemouth	08.68	1967-71	23	7	1	(M)
			TR	Mansfield T.	12.71	1971-73	93	3	5	
			TR	Sunderland	02.74	1973-76	35	5	3	
			TR	Sheffield U.	10.76	1976-77	34	2	1	
			TR	Aldershot	02.78	1977-79	46	7	3	
			TR	Colchester U.	05.80	1980-82	62	9	0	
LONGLAND, John	Southampton	24.09.32		Brighton & H.A.	04.54	1954	3		0	(HB)
LONGLEY, Nick	Mexborough	21.05.61		Crewe Alex.	12.83	1901	3	/	0	(G)
LONGRIDGE, George	Glasgow	23.08.31	Dennistoun FC	Orient	07.50					(G)
			TR	Darlington	09.51	1951	2		0	
LONSDALE, J. Stan	Washington	13.04.31	Seaham J.	Huddersfield T.	12.48					(HB)
			TR	Halifax T.	03.55	1954–59	202		21	
			TR	Hartlepool U.	11.60	1960	9		0	
LORD, Albert	Farnworth	10.09.44	JNRS	Bolton W.	01.63					(G)
			TR	Southport	03.66	1965	16	/	0	
LORD, Barry	Goole	17.11.37	Goole Buch'n	Hull C.	04.56	1958–60	5		0	(G)
LORD, Frank	Chadderton	13.03.36	JNRS	Rochdale	10.53	1953–60	120		54	(CF)●
			TR	Crewe Alex.	07.61	1961–63	108		68	
			TR	Plymouth Arg.	11.63	1963–65	69	1	23	
			TR	Stockport Co	02.66	1965–66	27	/	18	
			TR	Blackburn Rov.	12.66	1966	10	/	1	
			TR	Chesterfield	08.67	1967	12	/	6	
			TR	Plymouth Arg.	10.67	1968	6	/	2	
LORD, Malcolm	Driffield	25.10.46	APP	Hull C.	08.65	1966-78	271	32	24	(M)
LORD, W. Graham	Rawtenstall	09.07.36		Accrington St.	07.57	1958–60	67		0	(F)
LORD, Walter	Grimsby	01.11.33	JNRS	Grimsby T.	08.51	1952–53	7		1	(F)
			TR	Lincoln C.	05.56	1956	1		0	
LORENSON, Roy V.	Liverpool	08.04.32	St Elizabeths	Halifax T.	02.52	1951–60	216		7	(HB)
			TR	Tranmere Rov.	10.60	1960–61	14		0	
LORIMER, Peter	Dundee	14.12.46	JNRS	Leeds U.	12.63	1962-78	430	21	151	(F) S-21/S.U23-2/
			Toronto	York C.	09.79	1979	29	/	8	S.SCH.INT.●
			Vancouver W.	Leeds U.	03.84	1983	20	2	4	
LORNIE, John	Aberdeen	02.03.39	Banks o'Dee	Leicester C.	03.58	1958–60	8		3	(IF) S.SCH.INT.
			TR	Luton T.	06.61	1961–62	19		6	
			TR	Carlisle U.	06.63	1963	4		0	
			TR	Tranmere Rov.	06.64	1964–65	33	2	7	
LOSKA, Anthony S.	Chesterton	11.02.50	APP	Shrewsbury T.	03.68	1968-70	12	/	0	(D)
			TR	Port Vale	07.71	1971-73	74	6	5	
			TR	Chester C.	12.73	1973-76	103	7	5	
			TR	Halifax T.	10.76	1976-78	101	1	0	
LOUGH, John D.	Gateshead	31.10.22		Gateshead	AM	1946	1		0	
LOUGHLAN, John	Coatbridge	12.06.43		Leicester C.	08.61					(FB)
			Morton	Crystal Palace	09.68	1968–71	58	2	0	
			L	Wrexham	03.72	1971	5	/	0	
LOUGHNANE, J. Brian	Manchester	16.08.30		Leeds U.	08.52					(F)
			TR	Shrewsbury T.	07.53	1953–55	42		7	
			TR	Bournemouth	07.56	1956–58	43		6	
LOUGHNANE, Peter	Bournemouth	18.03.58	APP	Manchester U.	03.75					(F) Son of Brian
			TR	Shrewsbury T.	02.77	1976-78	24	7	4	
LOUGHRAN, Joe	Consett	12.08.15	Luton T.(*)	Burnley	+	1946–49	65		0	(FB) *Birmingham C.
			TR	Southend U.	09.49	1949–52	147		1	
LOUGHTON, Mike G.	Colchester	08.12.42	JNRS	Colchester U.	08.61	1964–67	121	1	6	(CH)
LOUKES, Gordon	Sheffield	15.06.28		Sheffield U.	04.49	1950	1		0	
			TR	Southend U.	07.51	1951	2		0	
LOVATT, Jack	Burton	23.08.41	JNRS	W.B.A.	12.58	1960–62	18		5	(CF)
LOVATT, John	Middlesbrough	21.01.62	APP	Derby Co.	01.80	1981	2	2	0	(D)
LOVE, Alistair	Edinburgh	09.05.55	Melbourne Th.	W.B.A.	03.73					(IF)
			TR	Southend U.	05.74	1974	6	5	0	
			TR	Newport Co.	07.75	1975	41	1	2	
LOVE, John	Oxford	11.03.37	Wolverhampton W.(AM)	Oxford U.	N/L	1962–63	30		5	(OL)
LOVE, John E.	Hillingdon	22.04.51	Staines	Crystal Palace	01.75	1974	1	/	0	(HB)

Players Names	Birthplace	Date	Previous Club	League Club	Date Signed	Seasons Played	Career Record Apps	Sub	Gls	
LOVE, John T.	Edinburgh	18.03.24	Albion Rov.	Nottingham F.	02.49	1948–51	59		21	(IF)
			Llanelli	Walsall	03.55	1954–55	39		11	
LOVELL, Alan J.	Swansea	17.05.40	JNRS	Swansea C.	06.57					(F)
			TR	Stockport Co.	07.60	1960	1		0	
LOVELL, Fred W.	Crewe Alex.e	18.06.29	Loughboro Coll	Notts. Co.	AM	1952–53	7		2	(IF)
LOVELL, Mark A.	London	20.01.61	APP	Fulham	08.78	1977-78	4	1	0	(F)
LOVELL, Mike G.	Doncaster	28.10.46	APP	Doncaster Rov.	10.64	1965	2	/	0	(FB)
LOVELL, Steve J.	Swansea	16.07.60	APP	Crystal Palace	08.77	1980-82	68	6	3	(M)W.SCH.INT./
			L	Stockport Co.	10.79	1979	12	/	0	W-1
			TR	Millwall	03.83	1982-83	63	/	8	
LOVELL, Trevor	Halifax	19.01.40	JNRS	Halifax T.	AM	1960–62	9		0	(W)
LOVEMAN, Robert	Greenock	30.09.21	Bailleston J.	Newport Co	03.48	1947–48	20		0	(G)
			TR	Aldershot	08.50					
LOVERIDGE, James C.	Swansea	19.10.62	APP	Swansea C.	11.79	1979-83	34	5	3	(M) W.SCH.INT.
LOVERIDGE, John	Wolverhampton	28.02.59	APP	W.B.A.	03.77					(M)
			TR	Walsall	08.81	1981	23	3	2	
LOVERING, John	Nuneaton	10.12.22		Coventry Co.	06.46	1946–47	6		0	
LOVESAY, William	London	08.12.22	Wolverhampton W.(+)	Swindon T.	+	1946	4		0	(LH) + Q.P.R.
LOVETT, Eric	Radcliffe	20.08.25		Accrington St.	11.49	1949–50	41		1	(CH)
LOVETT, Graham J.	Sheldon	05.08.47	APP	W.B.A.	11.64	1964–70	106	8	8	(WH)
			L	Southampton	11.71	1971	3	/	0	
LOVETT, John	Portsmouth	31.10.40		Portsmouth	09.58					(F)
			TR	Milwall	03.60	1959	6		2	
LOVETT, Percy R.	Bayston	01.08.21	Kenwood J.	Everton	*					(G)
			TR	Wrexham	02.47	1946	13		0	
LOVIE, Jim T.H.	Peterhead	19.09.32	Peterhead	Bury	01.57	1957–59	51		10	(WH)
			TR	Bournemouth	07.60	1960	9		0	
			TR	Chesterfield	07.61	1961–63	95		8	
LOW, Gordon A.	Aberdeen	11.07.40	JNRS	Huddersfield T.	07.57	1957–60	67		6	(WH)
			TR	Bristol C.	03.61	1960–67	203	2	12	
			TR	Stockport Co.	07.68	1968–69	63	1	8	
			TR	Crewe Alex.	08.70	1970	5	/	0	
LOW, Norman H.	Newcastle	23.03.14	Liverpool (*)	Newport Co.	*	1946	4		0	(CH)
			TR	Norwich C.	10.46	1946–49	.150		0	
LOW, Roy	Watford	08.07.44	JNRS	Tottenham H.	07.61	1964–66	6	2	1	(F) E.SCH.INT
			TR	Watford	02.67	1966–68	25	1	4	
LOWDEN, George	Isleworth	02.03.33	JNRS	Brentford	05.51	1953–56	29		0	(HB)
LOWDER, Tom W.	Worksop	17.10.24	Crystal Palace (AM)	Rotherham U.	08.47	1948	8		5	(OL)
			TR	Southampton	10.49	1949–52	39		2	
			TR	Southend U.	05.53	1953	21		3	
LOWE, David A.	Liverpool	30.08.65	APP	Wigan Ath.	06.83	1982-83	62	6	14	(F)
LOWE, Eddie	Halesowen	11.07.25	Finchley	Aston Villa	+	1946–49	104		3	(WH) E-3●
			TR	Fulham	05.50	1950–62	474		8	
			TR	Notts. Co.	09.63	1963–64	9		0	
LOWE, Gary W.	Manchester	25.09.59	APP	Crystal Palace	10.76					(F)
			TR	Manchester C.	12.79					
			TR	Hereford U.	06.80	1980	9	/	0	
LOWE, Ken	Sedgefield	06.11.61	APP	Hartlepool U.	11.78	1981-83	50	4	3	(M)
LOWE, Nick P.	Oxford	28.10.52	APP	Oxford U.	07.70	1972-76	71	/	3	(D)
			L	Halifax T.	08.74	1974	9	/	0	
LOWE, Reg	Halesowen	15.12.26	Finchley	Aston Villa	+					(WH) Brother of Eddie
			TR	Fulham	05.50	1950–52	66		0	
LOWE, Simon J.	London	26.12.62	Ossett A.	Barnsley	12.83	1980	2	/	0	(F)
LOWE, Terry J.	Stoke	27.05.43	Stoke C. (AM)	Port Vale	06.60	1961–65	55	/	0	(FB)
LOWELL, Eric J.	Cheadle	08.03.35	JNRS	Derby Co.	03.52	1953	1		1	(IF)
			TR	Stoke C.	05.55	1955	7		3	
LOWERY, Anthony W.	Wallsend	06.07.61	Ashington	W.B.A.	03.81	1981	1	/	0	(M)
			L	Walsall	02.82	1981	4	2	1	
			TR	Mansfield T.	04.83	1982-83	46	/	6	
LOWERY, Harry	Moor Row	26.02.18	W.B.A. (*)	Northampton T.	+	1946–48	76		2	(WH) *Cleator Moor
LOWERY, Jerry	Newcastle	19.10.24	C.A. Parsons (Eng)	Newcastle U.	06.47	1949–51	6		0	(G)
			TR	Lincoln C.	03.52	1952–53	51		0	
			Peterborough U.	Barrow	06.56	1956–57	86		0	
			TR	Crewe Alex.	07.58	1958	4		0	
LOWERY, Stuart	Thornaby	21.02.51	B. Auckland	Watford	01.70					(F)
			L	Walsall	11.70	1970	0	1	0	
LOWES, Arnold R.	Sunderland	27.02.19	Washington Chem.	Sheffield Wed.	*	1946–47	36		6	(IF)
			TR	Doncaster Rov.	02.48	1947–50	72		3	

Players Names	Birthplace	Date	Previous Club	League Club	Date Signed	Seasons Played	Apps	Sub	Gls	
LOWES, Barry T.	Barrow	16.03.39	Holker COB	Barrow	01.60	1959–61	55		15	(OR)
			TR	Blackpool	11.61			/		
			TR	Workington	08.62	1962–65	121	/	34	
			TR	Bury	02.66	1965–66	33	/	6	
			TR	Coventry C	03.67	1966	3	/	0	
			TR	Swindon T.	08.67	1967	2	/	0	
LOWEY, John A.	Manchester	07.03.58	APP	Manchester U.	03.75					(M)
			Chicago Stings	Blackburn Rov.	07.77					
			TR	Port Vale	12.77					
			California	Sheffield Wed.	10.78	1978-79	35	7	4	
			TR	Blackburn Rov.	11.80	1980-83	95	2	8	
LOWIS, Paul	Shap.	17.10.37	B.A.B.C.	Blackpool	05.57					(WH)
			TR	Stockport Co.	06.59	1959	9		0	
LOWNDES, Steve R.	Cwmbran	17.06.60	JNRS	Newport Co.	10.77	1977-82	200	8	39	(F)W.U21-2/W-2
			TR	Millwall	08.83	1983	20	/	3	
LOWNDS, Mark	Sunderland	28.11.40	Ryhope Col.	Luton T.	01.60	1961–64	59		3	(WH)
LOWREY, Pat	Newcastle	11.10.50	Newcastle U.(APP)	Sunderland	11.67	1968-71	13	2	2	(M) E.SCH.INT.
			Royal Union	Darlington	08.75	1975	14	6	2	
			TR	Workington	07.76	1976	15	/	3	
LOWRIE, George	Rhondda	19.12.19	Preston N.E.(*)	Coventry C.	+	1946–47	56		44	(IF) W–4/
			TR	Newcastle U.	03.48	1947–49	12		5	*Swansea C.
			TR	Bristol C.	09.49	1949–51	48		21	
			TR	Coventry C.	02.52	1951–52	26		12	
LOWRIE, Tom	Glasgow	14.01.28	Troon Ath.	Manchester U.	08.47	1947–49	13		0	(HB)
			Aberdeen	Oldham Ath.	08.52	1952–54	79		5	
LOWRY, Brian	Manchester	12.12.36	Manchester U. (AM)	Grimsby T.	08.54	1954–55	12		1	(F)
			TR	Aldershot	07.56					
LOWRY, Tom	Liverpool	26.08.45	APP	Liverpool	04.63	1964	1	/	0	(D)
			TR	Crewe Alex.	07.66	1966-77	435	1	2	
LOXLEY, Anthony D.	Nottingham	14.12.59	APP	Lincoln C.	12.77	1978	1	/	0	(D)
LOXLEY, Herbert	Bonsall	03.02.34	JNRS	Notts. Co.	03.52	1954–63	245		9	(WH)Father of Tony
			TR	Mansfield T.	07.64					
			Leamington	Lincoln C.	10.66	1966	7	/	0	
LOYDEN, Eddie	Liverpool	22.12.45	JNRS	Blackpool	12.63	1964	2		0	(CF)
			TR	Carlisle U.	06.66					
			TR	Chester C.	07.67	1967	37	/	22	
			TR	Shrewsbury T.	05.68	1968	11	1	2	
			TR	Barnsley	12.68	1968–70	65	/	23	
			TR	Chester C.	11.70	1970–71	62	/	26	
			TR	Tranmere Rov.	06.72	1972–73	61	/	22	
LUCAS, Alec L.	Bradley	01.12.45	JNRS	Wrexham	08.65	1965–66	51	4	0	(FB) W.U23-1
LUCAS, Brian A.	Farnborough	31.01.61	JNRS	Aldershot	07.78	1979-83	112	13	19	(M)
LUCAS, Fred C.	Slade Green	29.09.33	JNRS	Charlton Ath.	01.52	1955–63	185		29	(IF) Kent Cricketer
			TR	Crystal Palace	10.63	1963–64	16		0	
LUCAS, Mal	Wrexham	07.10.38	Bradley Rgrs.	Orient	09.58	1958–64	157		6	(WH) W–4/W.U23–1
			TR	Norwich C	09.64	1964–69	179	3	8	
			TR	Torquay U.	03.70	1969–73	118	4	3	
LUCAS, Oliver	Paisley	14.01.23	St. Mirren	Orient	07.48	1948–49	2		0	
LUCAS, Paul	Coseley	27.04.36	JNRS	Aston Villa	04.54					(F)
			TR	Gillingham	08.56	1956–57	45		8	
LUCAS, Richard J.	Witney	22.01.48	JNRS	Oxford U.	07.65	1967–74	190	1	2	(FB)
LUCAS, Robert W.	Bethnal Green	06.01.25	Hendon	Crystal Palace	+	1946	4		0	(G)
LUCAS, William	Newport	15.01.18	Wolverhampton W. (*)	Swindon T.	*	1946–47	70		17	(IF) W–7
			TR	Swansea C.	03.48	1947–53	203		35	
			TR	Newport Co.	12.53	1953–57	93		5	
LUCKETT, Paul	Coventry	12.01.57	Coventry C.(APP)	Halifax T.	08.71	1974-75	26	1	0	(D)
			TR	Hartlepool U.	03.76	1975-76	19	/	0	
LUDFORD, George	Barnet	22.03.15	JNRS	Tottenham H.	*	1946–49	63		2	(CF)
LUDLAM, Steve J.	Chesterfield	18.10.55	APP	Sheffield U.	01.73	1975-76	26	1	1	(M)
			TR	Carlisle U.	05.77	1977-79	90	6	11	
			TR	Chester C.	07.80	1980-82	100	2	12	
LUGG, Ray	Jarrow	18.07.48	JNRS	Middlesbrough	07.65	1966-68	34	3	3	(M)
			TR	Watford	11.69	1969-71	51	8	3	
			TR	Plymouth Arg.	07.72	1972	22	2	1	
			TR	Crewe Alex.	07.73	1973-77	183	2	10	
			TR	Bury	07.78	1978-79	68	3	2	
LUKE, George	Hetton-le-Hole	09.11.48	APP	Newcastle U.	03.66					(WH) E.SCH.INT/d.1968
			TR	Chelsea	03.67	1966	1	/	0	
LUKE, George B.	Lanchester	20.10.32		Sheffield U.	01.52	1953–54	7		0	(F)
			TR	Scunthorpe U.	05.56	1956	18		6	
LUKE, George T.	Newcastle	17.12.33	JNRS	Newcastle U.	12.50					(OL)
			TR	Hartlepool U.	10.53	1953–59	186		61	
			TR	Newcastle U.	10.59	1959–60	27		4	
			TR	Darlington	01.61	1960–62	68		10	

Players Names	Birthplace	Date	Previous Club	League Club	Date Signed	Seasons Played	Apps	Sub	Gls	
LUKE, Noel E.	Birmingham	28.12.64	APP	W.B.A.	04.82	1982-83	8	1	1	(M)
LUKE, William	Aberdeen	19.04.32	E. Fife	Crewe Alex.	10.55	1955	1		0	(IL)
LUKIC, Jovan	Chesterfield	11.12.60	APP	Leeds U.	12.78	1979-82	146	/	0	(G)E.U21-7/E.YTH.INT.
			TR	Arsenal	07.83	1983	4	/	0	
LUMBY, Jim A.	Grimsby	02.10.54		Grimsby T.	03.74	1973-74	28	3	12	(F)Son of pre-war
			Brigg T.	Scunthorpe U.	03.77	1976-77	55	/	28	Grimsby T. player
			TR	Carlisle U.	04.78	1977-78	24	3	7	
			TR	Tranmere Rov.	07.79	1979-80	43	3	21	
			TR	Mansfield T.	01.81	1980-81	49	2	18	
LUMLEY, I. Tommy	Leadgate	09.12.24	Consett	Charlton Ath.	12.48	1948-51	37		10	(IF)
			TR	Barnsley	03.52	1951-55	145		36	
			TR	Darlington	08.56	1956	15		3	
LUMLEY, Robert	Leadgate	06.01.33	JNRS	Charlton Ath.	01.50	1953-54	6		0	(IF) Brother of Tom
			TR	Hartlepool U.	02.55	1954-57	106		20	
			TR	Chesterfield	12.57	1957-58	25		2	
			TR	Gateshead	06.59	1959	40		5	
			TR	Hartlepool U.	07.60	1960	38		6	
LUMSDEN, Alex	Fife	24.05.46	Camelon J.	Southend U.	02.66	1965-66	2	/	0	(F)
LUMSDEN, Jim	Glasgow	07.11.47	JNRS	Leeds U.	11.66	1966-69	3	/	0	(IF)
			TR	Southend U.	09.70	1970	12	1	0	
LUMSDEN, John D.	Stoke	30.07.56	APP	Stoke C.	08.73	1975-77	26	2	0	(D)
			L	Port Vale	03.78	1977	5	/	0	
LUMSDEN, John I.	Smalley	01.07.42	JNRS	Aston Villa	07.59					(FB)
			TR	Workington	02.62	1961-67	249	2	7	
			TR	Chesterfield	03.68	1967-70	94	/	0	
LUMSDEN, John W.	Edinburgh	15.12.60	E. Fife	Stoke C.	02.80	1979-81	2	4	0	(M)
LUND, Gary J.	Grimsby	13.09.64	JNRS	Grimsby T.	07.83	1983	4	3	4	(F)
LUNDSTRUM, Colin	Colchester	09.10.38	West Ham U.(AM)	Ipswich T.	11.56	1957-59	13		1	(F)
			TR	Colchester U.	08.61	1961	1		0	
LUNN, Dennis	Barnsley	20.11.38	Wombwell	Doncaster Rov.	10.58	1959-61	85		0	(HB)
LUNN, George	Bolton–On–Dearne	28.06.15	Frickley Col	Aston Villa	*					(CH)
			TR	Birmingham C.	09.46					
			TR	Watford	10.47	1947	5		0	
LUNN, Henry	Lurgan	20.03.25	Lurgan	Notts. Co.	07.46	1946	24		5	(OR)
			TR	Portsmouth	07.47	1947	1		0	
			TR	Swindon T.	05.48	1948-53	196		29	
LUNN, Jack	Barnsley	14.10.37	JNRS	Barnsley	05.56	1956-60	56		19	(F)
			TR	Chesterfield	07.61	1961	41		12	
LUNN, William J.	Lurgan	08.05.23	Glenavon	W.B.A.	+	1946-47	10		5	(IF) NI.SCH.INT.
			TR	Bournemouth	02.48	1947-49	47		19	
			TR	Newport Co.	07.50	1950-51	6		1	
LUNNISS, Roy E.	London	04.11.39	Carshalton	Crystal Palace	04.60	1959-62	25		1	(FB)
			TR	Portsmouth	06.63	1963-65	69	1	1	
			TR	Luton T.	12.66	1966	1	/	0	
LUSTED, Leslie R.	Reading	20.09.31	Harwich & P	Orient	12.52	1952-53	53		6	(IF)
			TR	Aldershot	07.54	1954-55	9		1	
LUTTON, Robert J.	Banbridge	13.07.50	JNRS	Wolverhampton W.	09.67	1968-70	16	5	1	(W) N1–6
			TR	Brighton & H.A.	09.71	1971–72	18	11	4	
			TR	West Ham U.	01.73	1972–73	8	4	1	
LYALL, George	Wick	04.05.47	Raith Rov.	Preston N.E.	03.66	1965-71	90	15	16	(M)
			TR	Nottingham F.	05.72	1972-75	108	8	23	
			TR	Hull C.	12.75	1975-76	42	/	5	
LYALL, John A.	Ilford	24.02.40	JNRS	West Ham U.	05.57	1959-62	31		0	(FB) E.YTH.INT
LYDON, George M.	Sunderland	25.11.33	JNRS	Sunderland	12.50					(OL) E.SCH.INT
			TR	Leeds U.	06.54	1954	4		1	
			TR	Gateshead	11.55	1955-58	106		24	
LYMAN, Colin C.	Northampton	09.03.14	Northampton T.(*)	Tottenham H.	*					(OL) *Southend U.
			TR	Port Vale	05.46	1946	11		1	
			TR	Nottingham F.	10.46	1946	23		9	
			TR	Notts. Co.	08.47	1947	21		5	
LYNCH, Anthony J.	Paddington	20.01.66		Brentford	01.84	1983	2	/	0	(F)
LYNCH, Barrie	Birmingham	08.06.51	APP	Aston Villa	01.69	1968-69	2	/	0	(D)
			TR	Grimsby T.	09.72	1972	10	5	0	
			TR	Scunthorpe U.	07.73	1973-74	62	2	0	
			U.S.A.	Torquay U.	09.75	1975-76	67	3	2	
LYNCH, John	Uddingston	22.09.17	St. Mirren	Workington	10.52	1952	2		0	(G)
LYNCH, Pat	Belfast	22.01.50	Cliftonville	Middlesbrough	06.70	1971	0	1	0	(F)
LYNCH, Terry J.	Newport	17.05.52	JNRS	Newport Co.	11.69	1969-71	56	/	0	(G)
LYNEX, Steve C.	W. Bromwich	23.01.58	APP	W.B.A	01.76					(F)
			Shamrock Rov.	Birmingham C.	04.79	1978-80	28	18	9	
			TR	Leicester C.	02.81	1980-83	123	8	36	
LYNN, Frank	Consett	29.05.29	Blackhall C.W.	Grimsby T.	12.47	1948	2		0	

Players Names	Birthplace	Date	Previous Club	League Club	Date Signed	Seasons Played	Career Record Apps	Sub	Gls	
LYNN, Joe	Cramlington	31.01.25	Cramlington	Huddersfield T.	05.47	1949	5		0	(IF)
			TR	Exeter C.	06.50	1950	28		2	
			TR	Rochdale	07.51	1951–55	193		23	
LYNN, Sam	St Helens	25.12.20	JNRS	Manchester U.	*	1947–49	13		0	(CH)
			TR	Bradford P.A.	02.51	1950–52	73		0	
LYNN, Stan	Bolton	18.06.28	Whitworths F.C.	Accrington St.	07.47	1946–49	25		2	(FB)
			TR	Aston Villa	03.50	1950–61	281		36	
			TR	Birmingham C.	10.61	1961–65	130	/	26	
LYNN, William	Newcastle	20.01.47		Huddersfield T.	07.65	1956–66	4	/	0	(F)
			TR	Rotherham U.	04.67					
LYNNE, Mike G.A.	Kettering	20.03.38	JNRS	Preston N.E.	03.56	1958	2		0	(G)
			TR	Bournemouth	06.59	1959–60	17		0	
			TR	Brighton & H.A.	07.61					
LYON, David E.	Oldham	21.01.48	APP	Bolton W.	11.66					(M)
			TR	Bury	08.67					
			Wigan Ath.	Southport	09.76	1976	11	2	1	
LYON, David G.	Northwich	18.01.51	APP	Bury	01.69	1968-71	65	6	0	(D)
			TR	Huddersfield T.	09.71	1971-73	24	1	0	
			L	Mansfield T.	11.73	1973	2	/	0	
			TR	Cambridge U.	07.74	1974-76	84	1	11	
			TR	Northampton T.	10.77	1977	6	/	0	
LYON, Tom K.	Clydebank	17.03.25	Blackpool (*)	Chesterfield	*	1947	5		0	(CF) *Albion Rov.
			TR	New Brighton	07.48	1948	36		7	
LYONS, Albert E.	Rochdale	20.05.20		Bury	+	1947–48	2		0	(FB) Brother of George
			TR	Millwall	03.50	1949–51	6		0	
			TR	Crewe Alex.	07.52	1952–53	23		0	
			TR	Rochdale	12.53	1953–54	19		1	
LYONS, Barry	Shirebrook	14.03.45		Rotherham U.	09.62	1963-66	125	/	24	(W)
			TR	Nottingham F.	11.66	1966-72	201	2	28	
			TR	York C.	09.73	1973-75	80	5	11	
			TR	Darlington	07.76	1976-78	97	/	10	
LYONS, Brian	Darfield	03.12.48	Houghton MCW	Bradford P.A.	AM	1967	3	/	0	(CH)
LYONS, George W.	Rochdale	01.05.35		Rochdale	12.53	1953–56	29		4	(OR)
LYONS, John P.	Buckley	08.11.56	JNRS	Wrexham	06.75	1974-78	63	23	23	(F) d. 1982
			TR	Millwall	07.79	1979-80	55	/	20	
			TR	Cambridge U.	10.80	1980-81	20	1	6	
			TR	Colchester U.	02.82	1981-82	31	2	9	
LYONS, Mick	Liverpool	08.12.51	APP	Everton	07.69	1970-81	364	26	48	(D)) E.U23-5
			TR	Sheffield Wed.	08.82	1982-83	81	/	8	
LYONS, Mike C.	Bristol	31.01.32	JNRS	Bristol C.	06.50	1950–51	2		0	(FB)
			TR	Bristol Rov.	07.53	1953	2		0	
			TR	Bournemouth	07.56	1956–58	105		0	
			TR	Swindon T.	11.59	1959	2		0	
LYONS, Terry	Bradford	14.04.29		Burnley	10.49	1950	12		3	(OL)
			TR	Bradford P.A.	09.51	1951–52	38		6	
LYSKE, James	Lurgan	07.10.32	Glenavon	Sunderland	11.57					(FB)
			TR	Darlington	02.58	1957–58	16		0	
LYTHGOE, Arnold	Bolton	07.03.22	Ashton Nat	Accrington St.	+	1946	10		0	
LYTHGOE, Derek	Bolton	05.05.33	JNRS	Blackpool	05.50	1955–57	4		1	(F) Father of Phil
			TR	Norwich C.	03.58	1957–61	62		22	
			TR	Bristol C.	08.62	1962–63	13		1	
LYTHGOE, Phil	Norwich	18.12.59	APP	Norwich C.	12.77	1977-79	9	3	1	(F) Son of Derek
			L	Bristol Rov.	09.78	1978	6	/	0	
			TR	Oxford U.	08.80	1980-81	23	5	3	

JIM ILEY (Sheffield U./Tottenham H./Nottingham F./Newcastle U./Peterborough U.)
A well-built classy wing half, Iley was still down the pits when signing for Sheffield United; not until being recognised by the Football League in 1956 did the youngster become a full-timer. In August 1957 he came to the metropolis when signing for Spurs at a fee of £16,000, but he never settled at White Hart Lane, moving on to Forest two years later, a similar sum changing hands. Joining Newcastle United in September 1962 the now balding Jim showed his true ability in collecting a Second Division medal in 1964/5, before moving on to the "Posh." He was a clever constructive player who played the ball out of defence in the best of traditions.

TONY INGHAM (Leeds U./Q.P.R.)
A Leeds United discovery Ingham made only three appearances whilst at Elland Road, being allowed to move in June 1950 to Q.P.R. He soon made up for the lack of League experience when settling down at full back in the Rangers' colours, appearing 514 times before leaving Loftus Road in 1962/3. Whilst making the clubs's record appearance total he scored only three goals, one of them being from well inside his own half during a Third Division South fixture against Gillingham. Constructive, sound and a good tackler, he epitomised the modern full back.

JOHN JACKSON (Crystal Palace/Orient/Millwall/Ipswich T./Hereford U.)
Jackson was a first-class custodian for three London clubs after coming into League soccer with Palace in March 1962, on leaving Westminster School. He replaced Bill Glazier as the regular Palace keeper in 1964/5, and in the following eight seasons missed only 12 matches, a remarkable testament to his consistency, which was rewarded by Football League representative honours. Joining Orient in October 1973, this sterling player carried on once again where he had left off, not missing a game before signing for Millwall in August 1979. He played over 650 League matches in a career spanning nearly 20 years.

LEIGHTON JAMES (Burnley, Derby Co., Q.P.R., Burnley, Swansea C., Sunderland & Wales)
One of the most brilliant of outside lefts, James is quite capable of scoring invaluable goals as well as setting up chances for others. One of the Burnley discoveries, he signed for the club following Welsh schoolboy International honours, which have since been supplemented by more than 50 full caps. He was allowed to leave Turf Moor for Derby County in October 1975, helping the "Clarets" balance their books once again by selling rather than buying. He never really settled, moving to Q.P.R. and again to Burnley, before going home to Wales with Swansea City, where he was a major influence in helping John Toshack's side to the First Division for the first time in the club's history, before he signed for Sunderland on a free transfer in January, 1983.

PAT JENNINGS (Watford, Tottenham H., Arsenal & N. Ireland)
A brilliant 6ft tall custodian of the Arsenal goal, with the largest hands in soccer, Jennings surprised the football world when in August 1977 he was allowed to join the "Gunners" from fellow neighbours Spurs. Holder of the Irish appearance record, Pat has gone on whilst at Highbury to collect another F.A. Cup Winners medal from the sensational 1979 game against Manchester United, which was won in the dying seconds. Starting out with Newry Town, he joined Watford in 1963, but within a year had been transferred to Tottenham, where he collected an F.A. Cup winners medal in 1967 when Spurs defeated Chelsea. Rated as one of the outstanding keepers in the world, he was honoured as player of the year 1973.

BEDFORD JEZZARD (Fulham & England)
Jezzard was accepted as just about the fastest centre forward of the day, certainly in heavy conditions. Discovered by Fulham playing for a boys' club near Watford after being evacuated, he was first signed as an amateur. He really developed as a leader of the attack, scoring regularly, with England awarding him a cap against Hungary in Budapest 1954. This was followed by another, as well as playing for England "B" and the Football League. He struck up a brilliant partnership with Johnny Haynes and Bobby Robson, so much so that Newcastle United offered Fulham a fabulous figure which was turned down flat. Unfortunately Beddy's football career was halted at the age of 28 by injury.

HARRY JOHNSTON (Blackpool & England)
Elegant and calm in his approach to the game, Johnston was rarely ruffled throughout a long career. Although being born next to the Maine Road ground of Manchester City, Harry joined Blackpool at the age of 15 in 1934, going on to become one of the most outstanding players of his generation. This was reflected in 1951 when he became footballer of the year. After starting out at wing half, he had been recognised by England on ten occasions, and also skippered the "Seasiders" through to great successes, mainly in the F.A. Cup, culminating with the brilliant 1952/3 winning Final against Bolton after two previous losing appearances.

TOM JOHNSTON (Darlington/Oldham Ath./Norwich C./Newport Co./Orient/Blackburn Rov./Orient/Gillingham)
A hustling centre forward Johnston played virtually all his soccer in the lower Divisions, although with Blackburn Rovers he finally achieved First Division status during his short stay with them. He gained notoriety with Norwich City in 1953/4 when scoring the two goals at Highbury which knocked the mighty Arsenal out of the F.A. Cup fourth round. This moment of success gave the craggy Scot quite an uplift, with many clubs beckoning for his services. It was later with Orient that his goalscoring prowess made the Divisional charts. He was a very direct, old fashioned type of player.

CLIFF JONES (Swansea C., Tottenham H., Fulham & Wales)
A terrific left winger with an amazing turn of speed who joined Spurs from his native Swansea for £35,000 in February 1958, Jones belonged to a famous family: father Ivor was a Welsh International of the 1920s; uncle Bryn, the famous Wolves, Arsenal and Welsh star, and brother Bryn played for five League sides. Breaking a leg soon after joining Tottenham it did not affect his form, and he came right back in tremendous fashion in the great "double" winning side, picking up an abundance of honours. Capped by Wales on 59 occasions, he was recognised during the peak of his career as just about the finest left winger in the World. He moved down the road to Fulham before fading from the soccer scene.

GORDON JONES (Middlesbrough/Darlington)
Jones was only 17 when making his debut for the 'Boro' in January 1961. He subsequently made great progress and won England under 23 honours. Rather on the small side for a full back, he made up for any suspected deficiencies with an ability to recover quickly. Positionally sound, his constructive placements from defence made sure the "Teesiders" did not miss Cyril Knowles' departure to Spurs. He played out the whole of his career outside of the First Division, ending with Darlington before leaving the game for good.

PAT JONES (Plymouth Arg.)
A local discovery with Astor Institute, Jones developed into a fine consistent full back. He turned professional in the first post-war season, playing in the League side almost immediately and going on to make 279 consecutive League appearances from April 1947 to November 1953, when he was forced out of the side owing to an injured ankle. During this period he gained a Third Division South medal in 1951/2 and the following season he helped the club climb to its highest ever position in Division Two, also to reach the fifth round of the F.A. Cup that same year.

JOE JORDAN (Leeds U., Manchester U. & Scotland)
A tough centre forward, Jordan was used primarily as a target man to provide others with chances, his personal scoring rate being around a goal every four matches played. A then record fee for Manchester United of £350,000 obtained his purchase from Leeds United in January 1978. He was originally brought to Elland Road from Morton of the Scottish League in 1970, at the age of 20, but he had to sit in the shadow of Mick Jones for quite some time before establishing a regular place in the side. With the "Reds," he collected a losers F.A. Cup Final medal, from the game against Arsenal in 1979, and has now gained over 50 Scottish International caps. A whole-hearted battler over any 90 minute period, he is often engulfed in the white hot element of the game. He was transferred to A.C. Milan of the Italian League in the 1981/2 close season.

ARTHUR KAYE
(Barnsley/Blackpool/Middlesborough/Colchester U.)
A local schoolboy International wizard, Kaye joined Barnsley straight from school, going on to become a brilliant right winger for his home club. Amazingly he stayed at Oakwell for nine years before being tempted by First Division club Blackpool. Then it was only the chance of replacing the most famous of all players, Stan Matthews, in the tangerine colours that persuaded this outstanding 26 year old to leave his beloved Barnsley. Even more surprising was the fact that he could not totally displace the much older man, and he moved on to Middlesbrough in November 1960. He finished at Colchester, on the way having collected an England under 23 cap to go with a Football League representative award.

KEVIN KEEGAN (Scunthorpe U./Liverpool, Southampton & England/Newcastle U.)
One of the great favourites of the modern game, Keegan, now a soccer millionaire, set an example to all aspiring youngsters who need to work at the business of football. Plucked by Bill Shankley's Liverpool from Scunthorpe for a fee of £35,000 in May 1971, he became an immediate success, making a rapid rise to full England International status. With Liverpool he won two League Championships, and F.A. Cup and European Cup winners medals. He left Liverpool during the summer of 1977 for S.V. Hamburg, Germany, becoming European footballer of the year two years in succession. He returned to England with Southampton in July 1980, before signing for Newcastle in August 1982 to help the promotion charge from the Second Division, which was duly accomplished in 1983/4, after which he announced his retirement.

KEVIN KEELAN (Aston Villa/Stockport Co./Wrexham/Norwich C.)
A 6ft tall goalkeeper born in India, where his father served as an Army Warrant Officer, Keelan moved back to England at an early age, signing for Aston Villa in July 1958, after being a junior. Because of the lack of opportunity at Villa Park where Nigel Sims was a regular, Kevin was allowed to move on to Stockport. In July 1963 he was snapped up from Wrexham by Norwich City for £7,000 after showing great form for the Welsh side. He won a Second Division medal in 1971/2 and later collected two Football League Cup runners-up medals before leaving the Norfolk side, having made nearly 600 appearances in their colours.

MIKE KEEN (Q.P.R./Luton T./Watford)
A tall, imposing, powerful wing half Keen performed highly consistently during a League career which was a credit to the game. He made his debut with Q.P.R. in 1959/60 and led them from the Third Division in 1966/7, which was even more remarkable for the fact that in the same season the club did "their double" by winning the Football League Cup, beating W.B.A. 3-2 at Wembley in front of 98,000 spectators. He joined Luton Town in January 1969, becoming a member of the side that gained promotion to the Second Division 1969/70, before moving on to Watford, where he later became manager.

BOBBY KELLARD (Southend U./Crystal Palace/Ipswich T./Portsmouth/Bristol C./Leicester C./Crystal Palace/Portsmouth/Torquay U.)
Kellard made his debut for Southend United when only 16 years of age, later gaining England Youth International honours. A wing half-cum-inside forward, he was in great demand as a stylish, constructive, busy type, especially in going forward, and it came as no surprise when he was transferred to Crystal Palace in September 1963 for around £9000. With the Palace the youngster achieved Second Division status when the club was promoted as runners-up 1963/4, but it was not until several clubs later that he reached the First Division with Leicester City. He collected a Second Division Championship medal in 1970/1 after playing 39 games for Leicester City that season. He rejoined Crystal Palace for £55,000 in September 1971.

ALAN KELLY (Preston NE. & Eire)
A first class keeper, tall and commanding, Kelly shined with Drumcondra in the League of Ireland, being capped for the Republic three times during 1957 and winning an Irish Cup winners medal. Preston moved in fast, signing the youngster in April 1958, and he was able to make two appearances before the season finished, taking over the net minding duties from Fred Else. During service at Deepdale, he collected a losing F.A. Cup Final medal from the game against West Ham 1964 and in 1970/1 achieved Second Division status with the club once again going up as Champions. A highly reliable keeper he made a record 47 appearances for his country.

HUGH KELLY (Blackpool & Scotland)
A hard tackling, clever, constructive wing half Kelly went to Blackpool from the Scottish junior side, Jeanfield Swifts, in 1943. Unfortunate in missing the "Matthews Final", he had played in the two losing F.A. Cup Finals of 1948 and 1951, also playing one solitary game for Scotland versus the U.S.A. in 1952. Consistent over a period of 14 years in which he averaged over 30 games per season, he called it a day in 1959.

JACK KELSEY (Arsenal & Wales)
Kelsey was the village blacksmith at Llansalet when Arsenal signed him from the local side Winch Wen to understudy the ageing Swindon in the "Gunners" goal. This was later seen as a very shrewd move by Tom Whittaker, the then Arsenal manager, when the young goalkeeper, after making his debut versus Charlton early in 1951, went on to become a great goalie at club and International levels. Displaying marvellous agility on his goal line, Jack had quickly gained a League Championship medal by 1953 and won the first of many Welsh caps in 1954. The climax of his career was in 1958 when little Wales fought their way through to the World Cup quarter finals, eventually losing 1-0 to the future champions – Brazil.

HOWARD KENDALL (Preston N.E./Everton/Birmingham C./Stoke C./Blackburn Rov.)
A brilliant midfielder Kendall became an overnight sensation when becoming the youngest player at the time to appear in a Wembley Cup Final, where his side Preston lost to West Ham in 1963/4. He was unlucky not to be capped, although collecting Football League representative honours and England under 23 awards. He was transferred to Everton for £80,000 in March 1967, and became part of a great midfield trio with Colin Harvey and Alan Ball, winning a Championship medal in 1969/70 to follow a losing F.A. Cup Final against W.B.A. two years earlier. He later became player-manager of the very successful Blackburn Rovers, seemingly having a new lease of life, before entering full management with Everton.

DEREK KEVAN (Bradford Pk Av./W.B.A. & England/Chelsea/Manchester C./Crystal Palace/Peterborough U./Luton T./Stockport Co.)
A big blond striker, tremendously powerful, Kevan made a terrific reputation with W.B.A. where, teaming up with the great Ronnie Allen, he scored over 150 League goals. After signing for Albion from Bradford in July 1953, he had to wait over two years before displacing Johnny Nicholls, but on gaining a first team place he never looked back eventually being capped. His rugged bustling tactics were sometimes frowned upon, but there was no doubting the positive effect they had upon the opposition's defence. After Albion, he went on a merry-go-round of clubs before retiring; although scoring fairly well during a short stay with Manchester City, Derek never set the other sides alight, but overall his goalscoring record speaks for itself.

JOHNNY W. KING (Crewe Alex./Stoke C./Cardiff C./Crewe Alex.)
A chunky inside-cum-centre forward, King made an early reputation at Gresty Road in forming a brilliant partnership with the equally young Frank Blunstone, who later went on to play for Chelsea and England. He was himself transferred to Stoke City in September 1953, scoring over 100 League goals prior to signing for Cardiff City and having a season in Wales, before going back to Crewe Alexandra. The wanderer had finally returned home, playing out the next five seasons with his first club, in all making nearly 500 League appearances.

BARRY KITCHENER (Millwall)
A long serving Millwall defender, Kitchener signed professional in August 1965, after being an apprentice, and played over 500 League matches. Nearly 6ft tall, weighing in near the 15 stone mark, he was a formidable barrier to opposing forwards for many years, and in 12 seasons after becoming a regular in the side, he missed only 24 games. He was a leading member of the side that nearly gained promotion to Division One in 1971/2, failing by only two points, the highest haul in the "Lions" history. When first making the side, he played a part in the club's longest unbeaten home run from August 1964 to January 1967.

CYRIL KNOWLES (Middlesbrough/Tottenham H. & England)
Over 6ft tall, Knowles was a well-made full back; great in upfield surges, especially on overlaps, and highly competent in defensive duties. He made a reputation with the 'Boro' before coming to White Hart Lane, after being a professional for under two years. He picked up under 23 honours on his way to four England caps and collected an F.A. Cup winners medal from the 1967 game against Chelsea. His brilliant brother Peter created a stir when leaving the game because it clashed with his religious beliefs. Cyril left Spurs on making his 400th League appearance in their colours.

BRIAN LABONE (Everton & England)
Everton had some difficulty in persuading the young local to sign for them as he was going to university, but Labone had second thoughts and turned professional July 1957. Neither regretted the change of heart, and after taking over from Tommy Jones the tall young centre half went on to play over 450 League games before retiring. Calm and reliable, resolute, down to earth, with good heading ability, he brought a steadying influence to bear in the heart of the "Toffees" defence over many years. Before leaving Goodison he had collected two Championship medals to go with an F.A. Cup winners medal from the game against Sheffield Wednesday in 1966; he was also capped 26 times by England.

FRANK LAMPARD (West Ham U. & England)
One of the long serving West Ham academy, the highly dependable full back Frank Lampard ventures on many forays well into the opponents' half, searching for a shot on target or at the least an accurate cross. He started out in the apprentice ranks, turned professional in 1965, and went on to collect many honours, including two full England caps. The proud holder of two F.A. Cup winners medals, he was probably more satisfied with the 1980 win against Arsenal, when it was his semi-final goal against Everton which decided that the "Hammers" future lay at Wembley.

JIMMY LANGLEY (Leeds U./Brighton & HA./Fulham & England/Q.P.R.)
A great wholehearted player, who was plucked from the obscurity of the Third Division South by Fulham for £12,000 in February 1957, Langley went on to play three times for England. At Craven Cottage, as a tough tackling left full back, he always enjoyed the licence to roam, given that his recovery powers were highly effective. In 1959, he achieved his ambition to play in the First Division, Fulham finally gaining promotion as runners-up. Langley started with Leeds as a winger, going on to Guildford City before Brighton converted him to full back. Before completing his career at Shepherds Bush, he struck up a great partnership at Fulham with young George Cohen, who also went on to represent his country.

FRANK LARGE (Halifax T./Q.P.R./Northampton T./Swindon T./Carlisle U./Oldham Ath./Northampton T./Leicester C./Fulham/Northampton T./Chesterfield)
Discovered by Halifax Town playing local junior soccer, Large was persuaded to turn professional in June 1959 and topped the "Shaymen's" scoring list the three years he spent with them. For £7,500 he moved to Q.P.R., but on the arrival of Stuart Leary was transferred to Northampton Town, there scoring 30 goals from 47 games. He reached the First Division finally with Leicester City, only staying a season. In a League career with eleven clubs he scored 210 goals from 563 games.

BOB LATCHFORD (Birmingham C./Everton & England/Swansea C.)
A strong bustling centre forward, who technically has more skill than often credited, Latchford first came to the fore with Birmingham City after turning professional in August 1968. He played for the England under 23 side whilst at St. Andrews, but it was not until he joined Everton in February 1974 that full England recognition was finally achieved. From a footballing family, with brothers Dave and Peter all playing First Division soccer, Bob has one of the highest goal scoring ratios among modern forwards. He signed for Swansea in July 1981 for £125,000 and put in nearly three seasons of excellent service before moving out of the League.

DENIS LAW (Huddersfield T., Manchester C., Manchester U., Manchester C. & Scotland)
Law was signed by the great Bill Shankly as a skinny bespectacled youngster for Huddersfield, along with his great friend from Aberdeen, Gordon Low. He developed into one of the most dangerous forwards of the modern game with terrific reflexes, snapping up half chances and climbing steeple high to head balls home. In a Cup game against Luton Town in 1961, the magical Denis had already scored six goals when the game was abandoned. Amazingly enough, the "Hatters" won the replay. He moved from City to Torino in Italy for a season before joining United, helping them to win two Championships and one F.A. Cup Final against Leicester City in 1963. He also represented the Rest of Europe against Scandinavia in 1964. He returned to Maine Road to end his illustrious career; one of soccer's great personalities.

CHRIS LAWLER (Liverpool & England/Portsmouth/Stockport Co.)
Liverpool right full back for some 15 years after signing in October 1960, Lawler was noted for overlaps down the "Reds" flank, which resulted in him scoring over 40 League goals. Tall and commanding, he was very quick, being highly effective at the heart of the defence, where playing over 400 games under Bill Shankly, the legendary manager. He played for England on four occasions, adding to Football League and Cup medals, before travelling to Portsmouth where he played under the managership of his former team mate Ian St. John. He finished his soccer career with Stockport County at the age of 35.

IAN LAWTHER (Sunderland, Blackburn Rov. & N. Ireland/Scunthorpe U./Brentford/Halifax T./Stockport Co.)
A sharp shooter from the Belfast Crusaders, Lawther turned professional with Sunderland in March 1958, going on to make his debut and topping their scoring list the next season. Although netting 24 goals from 37 games the next term, he was transferred to Blackburn Rovers for £20,000, when Brian Clough was brought to Roker from nearby Middlesbrough. After fairly consistent goalscoring, he settled down to a role alongside the main strike force without losing too much efficiency. On retiring he had played nearly 600 League games and been capped four times by Northern Ireland.

TOMMY LAWTON (Burnley/Everton, Chelsea, Notts Co. & England/Brentford/Arsenal)
Signed on his 17th birthday as a pro by Burnley, Lawton scored a hat trick a few days later against Spurs. Tommy had the ideal build for a centre forward, was great in the air and with a powerful shot was one of the most prolific natural scorers of all time. He quickly replaced the immortal Dixie Dean for £6,500 at Everton and moved on to Chelsea in 1945, playing in the memorable friendly against the Moscow Dynamos. He became the first £20,000 transfer when Notts County bought him in November 1947. He was still a threat to the best of defences, continuing to play for England. By 1952 his peak had passed him by, which resulted in Brentford bringing him back to the Capital. At the end of his footballing days Arsenal took Tommy from Brentford to help bring their younger players along before he moved on to Kettering. In the best tradition of International centre forwards, he won 23 England caps.

FRANCIS LEE (Bolton W./Manchester C. & England/Derby Co.)
An effective probing, bustling, sturdy little forward, Lee could find a way through the best of organised defences. He made his debut with Bolton where, on winning England youth honours he settled down in a striking role, eventually dropping into the Second Division. He was seen by Manchester City as an important cog in their machinery, signing in October 1967 for a large fee and finally realising his talent at the highest level. With City he won Football League Championship, F.A. Cup, Football League Cup and European Cup Winners Cup medals. He finished with Derby County before going fully into business. He still holds the penalty record of 13 goals in a season in 1971/2 and played for England on 27 occasions.

TONY LEIGHTON (Leeds U./Doncaster Rov./Barnsley/Huddersfield T./Bradford C.)
Leighton started out with Leeds United, but after nearly three years without a first team appearance was give a free transfer to Doncaster Rovers in the summer of 1959. He made a mark in the Fourth Division, topping the Rovers' scoring lists in two out of three seasons, before being surprisingly given another free transfer, this time being snapped up by Barnsley. Not tall for a centre forward, but effective and adept in putting away half chances, he was very nippy across the ground in collecting goals, albeit not in the First Division. Huddersfield and then Bradford City also recognised his scoring talent before the striker left League football.

BILLY LIDDELL (Liverpool and Scotland)
A powerful, extremely direct old fashioned outside left, the idol of the "Spion Kop" fanatics, Billy came to Anfield from Lochgelly Violet the Scottish junior side. From the end of the war until 1960 he was a regular, playing nearly 500 games and scoring in a high proportion of them. He was commissioned · during the war whilst serving in the R.A.F. Remembered as one of the great Liverpool favourites of all time, he played for the "Reds" in the 1950 losing Cup Final against the Arsenal, also representing Great Britain against Europe in 1947. Billy later qualified as an accountant.

DOUG LISHMAN (Walsall/Arsenal/Nottingham F.)
A great opportunist, both on the ground and in the air, Lishman relished any challenge on the opposition's goal. He played mainly at inside left when joining Walsall, after starting as a central defender. He was transferred to Arsenal for about £11,000 in May 1948, winning a Championship and F.A. Cup medal, before moving on to Forest in 1956. The memory of his overhead kick shaving the Newcastle crossbar in the 1951/2 losing Cup Final must still be fresh in the mind of any attending Arsenal supporter who remembers their side's ten men epic struggle. Lishman included amongst his honours an England "B" cap as well as representing the Football League.

NAT LOFTHOUSE (Bolton W. & England)
Lofthouse was depicted by journalists as the "Lion of Vienna" after the "never-say-die" approach which led to this dashing centre forward scoring a dramatic goal against Austria. A native of Bolton, Nat virtually followed Tommy Lawton into the local school side, finally capturing the great man's England place and gaining his first cap against Yugoslavia in 1951. Footballer of the year 1953, he will also be remembered shoulder barging the Manchester United keeper into the net on the way to winning an F.A. Cup medal in 1958. He made a great comeback to England's attack at the age of 35 in 1959 against Wales and the U.S.S.R.

FRANK LORD (Rochdale/Crewe Alex./Plymouth Arg./Stockport Co./Blackburn Rov./Chesterfield/Plymouth Arg.)
A Third Division North centre forward discovery with Rochdale in his teens, Lord was a steady goalscorer at Spotland without too much recognition until joining Crewe Alexandra in July 1961. Immediately he broke the old club goalscoring record when netting 31 goals at Gresty Road. The Argyle, also looking for the goal touch, paid five figures to stave off relegation before letting him go to pastures new. This big, strong bustling forward never played in the top League, but would have been ideally suited as a target man in today's soccer.

PETER LORIMER (Leeds U. & Scotland/York C./Leeds U.)
Lorimer was famous for scoring rocket-like goals, mainly from set pieces outside the penalty area for Leeds United, where, rather more often than not, he was the club's leading scorer. He signed professional for United in December 1963 after being one of the youngest players to play League soccer, following up Scottish schoolboy International honours. Two League Championships and one F.A. Cup winners medal were amongst the dark-haired winger's pickings. He was associated with one of the amazing episodes of F.A. Cup drama when he smashed a free kick into the Chelsea net during a semi-final, only to be told that it would have to be retaken due to the whistle not having been blown – a match, needless to say, which Leeds lost. He recently returned from the U.S.A. to rejoin Leeds and assist the youngsters.

EDDIE LOWE (Aston Villa & England/Fulham/Notts. Co.)
A tall blond post-war left half, very strong in the tackle, highly constructive with good ball skill, Lowe made his way into League football with Aston Villa and soon gained three England caps. He was a wartime amateur with the strong Athenian Leaguers, Finchley, where many admirers watched both Eddie and brother Reg perform before they jointly went to Villa Park. He seemingly lost his way with Villa before Fulham came for the brothers in May 1950, but soon found form again at the "Cottage," going on to achieve First Division status in 1959, eventually being one of the oldest men playing in that League. He finished with Notts County just short of 40, and then became their manager.

Players Names	Birthplace	Date	Previous Club	League Club	Date Signed	Seasons Played	Career Record Apps Sub Gls		
MABBUTT, Gary V.	Bristol	23.08.61	APP	Bristol Rov.	01.79	1978-81	122	9	10 (M)E.YTH.INT./E.U'21-4/E-9
			TR	Tottenham H.	08.82	1982-83	59	/	12
MABBUTT, Kevin R.	Bristol	05.12.58	APP	Bristol C.	01.76	1977-81	112	17	28 (F)E.SCH.INT./E.YTH.INT.
			TR	Crystal Palace	10.81	1981-83	64	3	21
MABBUTT, Ray W.	Aylesbury	13.03.36	Oxford C.	Bristol Rov.	08.56	1957-68	393	3	18 (WH)Father of Gary/Kevin
			TR	Newport Co.	09.69	1969-70	38	6	14
MABEE, Gary L.	Oxford	01.02.55	APP	Tottenham H.	02.72				(CF)
			TR	Northampton T.	08.74	1974-75	29	4	13
MACARI, Lou	Aberdeen	04.06.49	Glasgow Celtic	Manchester U.	01.73	1972-83	311	18	78 (F)S-24/S.U23-2
MACAULEY, Archie R.	Falkirk	30.07.15	Glasgow Rgrs.	West Ham U.	*	1946	8		3 (WH) S-7
			TR	Brentford	10.46	1946	26		2
			TR	Arsenal	07.47	1947-49	103		1
			TR	Fulham	06.50	1950-52	49		4
MACAULEY, James A.R.	Edinburgh	19.10.22	Edinburgh Th.	Chelsea	10.46	1946-49	86		5 (WH)
			TR	Aldershot	08.51	1951	31		3
McADAM, David	Hereford	03.04.23	Stapenhill W.	Leeds U.	05.48	1948-49	24		0 (FB)
			TR	Wrexham	05.50	1950	10		0
McADAM, Neil B.	E. Kilbride	30.07.57	Northwich Vic.	Port Vale	08.82	1982	2	/	0 (G)
McADAM, Steve	Portadown	02.04.60	Portadown	Burnley	05.78	1979	5	/	0 (D)
			TR	Oldham	08.80				
			Barnsley(N/C)	Wigan Ath.	11.80	1980-81	26	/	0
McADAMS, William J.	Belfast	20.01.34	Distillery	Manchester C.	12.53	1953-59	127		62 (CF) NI-15
			TR	Bolton W.	09.60	1960-61	44		26
			TR	Leeds U.	12.61	1961	11		3
			TR	Brentford	07.62	1962-64	75		36
			TR	Q.P.R.	09.64	1964-65	33	/	13
			TR	Barrow	07.66	1966-67	53	/	9
McALEA, Robert J.	Belfast	13.09.20	Ballymoney	Bradford C.	07.48	1948	4		0 (IF)
McALEER, Frank	Glasgow	16.10.45	Morton	Shrewsbury T.	03.70				(IF)
			TR	Barrow	08.70	1970	9	1	0
McALINDEN, James	Belfast	31.12.17	Belfast Celtic	Portsmouth	*	1946-47	33		5 (CF) EI-3/NI-4/
			TR	Stoke C.	09.47	1947-48	33		2 IRISH LGE REP.
			TR	Southend U.	10.48	1948-53	218		12
McALINDEN, John	Carlisle	25.12.30.	Glasgow Celtic	Shrewsbury T.	05.57	1957	12		3 (F)
McALINDEN, Robert J.	Salford	22.05.46	Aston Villa(APP)	Manchester C.	05.64	1963	1		0 (F)
			TR	Port Vale	09.65				
			Glentoran	Stockport Co.	10.66				
			L. Angeles Aztecs	Bournemouth	09.76	1976	1	/	0
McALISTER, Tom G.	Clydebank	10.12.52	APP	Sheffield U.	05.70	1971-75	63	/	0 (G)
			TR	Rotherham U.	01.76	1975-78	159	/	0
			TR	Blackpool	07.79	1979	16	/	0
			TR	Swindon T.	05.80	1980	1	/	0
			L	Bristol Rov.	02.81	1980	13	/	0
			TR	West Ham U.	05.81	1981	3	/	0
McALLE, John E.	Liverpool	31.01.50	APP	Wolverhampton W.	02.67	1967-80	394	13	0 (D)
			TR	Sheffield U.	08.81	1981	18	/	0
			TR	Derby Co.	04.82	1981-83	51	7	1
McALLISTER, Don	Radcliff	26.05.53	APP	Bolton W.	06.70	1969-74	155	1	2 (D)
			TR	Tottenham H.	02.75	1974-80	168	4	9
			TR	Charlton Ath.	08.81	1981-82	55	/	6
McALLISTER, James	Barrhead	30.10.31	Neilston	Millwall	06.54	1954-55	20		6 (IF)
			Morton	Bradford P.A.	05.59	1959-60	43		14
McALONE, Robert	Whitehaven	16.02.28		Workington	N/L	1951-53	68		3 (CH)
McALOON, Gerry	Glasgow	13.09.16	Wolverhampton W.(*)	Brentford	+	1946	7		3 (IF) *St. Francis/Brentford
McANDREW, Anthony	Lanark	11.04.56	APP	Middlesbrough	08.73	1973-81	245	2	13 (D)
			TR	Chelsea	09.82	1982-83	20	/	4
MacANDREW, Robert	Derby	06.04.43	JNRS	Derby Co.	06.61	1963	1		0 (HB)
McANEARNEY, James	Dundee	20.03.35	JNRS	Sheffield Wed.	03.52	1953-59	38		9 (IF) Brother of Tom
			TR	Plymouth Arg.	01.60	1959-63	135		33
			TR	Watford	11.63	1963-66	84	1	19
			TR	Bradford C.	09.66	1966-67	41	4	5
McANEARNEY, Tom	Dundee	06.01.33	Dundee St. S	Sheffield Wed.	10.51	1952-64	352		20 (WH)
			TR	Peterborough U.	11.65	1965	12	/	0
			TR	Aldershot	03.66	1965-68	106	/	5
McARTHUR, Barry	Nottingham	06.05.47	JNRS	Nottingham F.	05.65	1965	7	1	4 (F)
			TR	Barrow	07.69	1969	5	2	0
			TR	York.C.	12.69	1969	0	1	0
McARTHUR, Tom	Neilston	23.04.25	Neilston Vic	Leicester C.	01.47	1946-53	97		0 (CH)
			TR	Plymouth Arg.	01.54	1953	2		0
McARTHUR, Walter J.	Denaby	21.03.12	Goldthorpe Col.	Bristol Rov.	*	1946-49	113		4 (WH) d.1980
MacATEER, Andy W.	Preston	24.04.61	APP	Preston N.E.	04.79	1979-83	158	2	5 (D)
McAUGHTRIE, Dave	Cumnock	30.01.63	APP	Stoke C.	01.81	1980-83	48	3	2 (D)

Players Names	Birthplace	Date	Previous Club	League Club	Date Signed	Seasons Played	Career Record Apps	Sub	Gls	
McAULEY, Hugh A.	Bootle	08.01.53	APP	Liverpool	01.70					(W)
			L	Tranmere Rov.	08.73	1973	13	/	1	
			TR	Plymouth Arg.	10.74	1974-76	76	1	7	
			TR	Charlton Ath.	12.76	1976-77	55	/	9	
			TR	Tranmere Rov.	08.78	1978	41	2	0	
			TR	Carlisle U.	07.79	1979-80	14	3	1	
McAULEY, Pat J.	Arthurlie	31.07.21	Glasgow Celtic	Luton T.	12.50	1950	8		1	(WH) S.F.LGE REP.
McAVOY, Alan J.	Wigton	04.10.63		Blackpool	02.81	1981	6	/	0	(F)
McAVOY, Doug H.	Kilmarnock	29.11.18	Kilmarnock	Liverpool	12.47	1947–48	2		0	(IF)
McBAIN, Alan	Aberdeen	10.02.40	Aberdeen E.E.	Swansea C.	01.59					(FB)
			TR	Carlisle U.	06.60	1960–62	70		0	
			TR	Luton T.	06.63	1963–64	60		0	
McBAIN, Gordon	Glasgow	04.12.34	Kilmarnock	Rochdale	05.58	1958	10		1	(F)
McBAIN, Neil	Campbeltown	15.11.1895	(Team Mgr)	New Brighton	03.47	1946	1		0	(WH) S–3/*Ayr U./ Manchester U./Everton/ St. Johnstone/Liverpool Watford/d.1974
MacBENNETT, Seamus	Newcastle N.I.	16.11.25		Cardiff C.	09.47	1947	4		2	
			TR	Tranmere Rov.	11.48	1948–49	12		1	
McBETH, George	Belfast	04.09.54	APP	Manchester C.	10.71					(M)
			TR	Stockport Co.	07.76	1976-77	51	5	3	
McBLAIN, Andy	W.Lothian	11.08.26	Grange Rov.	Newport Co.	02.47	1946–48	36		1	(LH)
McBRIDE, Andy D.	Kenya	15.03.54	APP	Crystal Palace	10.71	1973	1	/	0	(CH)
McBRIDE, John	Kilsyth	31.12.23	T.Lanark	Reading	03.48	1947–52	100		0	(G)
			TR	Shrewsbury T.	12.52	1952–55	78		0	
McBRIDE, Joseph	Kilmarnock	10.06.38	Kilmarnock	Wolverhampton W.	12.59					(CF) S–2/S.F.LGE REP.
			TR	Luton T.	02.60	1959–60	25		9	Father of Joe (Jnr)
McBRIDE, Joe	Glasgow	17.08.60	APP	Everton	08.78	1979-81	51	6	9	(W)S.U21-1/S.SCH.INT./
			TR	Rotherham U.	08.82	1982-83	45	/	12	Son of Joe
			TR	Oldham Ath.	09.83	1983	19	6	4	
MacBRIDE, Peter P.	Motherwell	22.12.46	JNRS	Manchester U.	12.63					(HB)
			TR	Southport	07.66	1966	1	2	0	
			TR	Bradford P.A.	07.67	1967	5	2	0	
McBRIDE, Vince	Manchester	21.01.34	Ashton U.	Walsall	05.54	1954	11		0	(G)
			TR	Aston Villa	03.56					
			TR	Mansfield T.	07.58	1958	10		0	
McBRIDE, William	Newtown	08.11.13		Carlisle U.	+	1946	15		0	(IF)
McBURNEY, Mike L.	Wrexham	12.09.53	JNRS	Wrexham	07.71	1970–72	20	4	4	(F) W.SCH.INT.
			TR	Bolton W.	05.73	1973	1	/	0	
			L	Hartlepool U.	11.74	1974	5	1	1	
			L	Tranmere Rov.	03.75	1974	4	1	0	
MacCABE, Andy B.	Glasgow	22.02.35	Corby T.	Chesterfield	11.55	1955–58	53		7	(F)
McCABE, James J.	Derry	17.09.18	South Bank	Middlesbrough	*	1946–47	34		0	(WH) NI–6
			TR	Leeds U.	03.48	1947–53	151		0	
McCAFFERTY, James	Motherwell	10.07.57	Bristol C. (APP)	Hereford U.	04.75	1975	0	3	0	(F)
McCAFFREY, Aiden	Newcastle	30.08.57	APP	Newcastle U.	01.75	1974-77	57	2	4	(D)E.YTH.INT.
			TR	Derby Co.	08.78	1978-79	31	6	4	
			TR	Bristol Rov .	08.80	1980-83	156	1	11	
			L	Bristol C.	02.82	1981	6	/	1	
McCAFFREY, James	Luton	12.10.51	APP	Nottingham F.	03.69	1969	2	6	1	(F)E.YTH.INT.
			TR	Mansfield T.	07.72	1972-76	170	8	21	
			TR	Huddersfield T.	01.77	1976-77	23	4	0	
			TR	Portsmouth	02.78	1977-78	11	1	1	
			TR	Northampton T.	12.78	1978-79	56	1	6	
McCAIG, Robert A.M.	Dumfries	15.08.23		Carlisle U.	08.48	1948	5		0	(F)
			TR	Blackburn Rov.	12.48	1948–50	30		2	
			TR	Stockport Co.	08.51	1951	15		2	
			TR	Halifax T.	01.52	1951	17		2	
			TR	Crewe Alex.	08.52	1952–53	19		1	
McCALL, Alex H.	Annan	26.03.39		Carlisle U.	09.58	1959	1		0	(HB)
McCALL, Andy	Hamilton	15.03.25	Blantyre Vic.	Blackpool	07.47	1947–50	84		15	(IF)
			TR	W.B.A.	01.51	1950–51	31		3	
			TR	Leeds U.	08.52	1952–54	62		8	
			TR	Halifax T.	07.56	1956–59	139		15	
McCALL, Anthony E.	Bucklebury	15.01.36	JNRS	Reading	05.53	1955–56	8		1	(F)
McCALL, David	Carlisle	24.01.48	JNRS	Workington	01.66	1966	1	/	0	(OR)
McCALL, John	Glasgow	29.09.18	Workington	Bradford P.A.	*	1946–47	10		1	(WH)
McCALL, Peter	W.Ham	11.09.36	Kings Lynn	Bristol C.	04.55	1957–61	79		1	(WH)
			TR	Oldham Ath.	05.62	1962–64	108		5	
McCALL, Robert H.	Worksop	29.12.15		Nottingham F.	*	1946–51	120		0	(FB)
McCALL, Steve H.	Carlisle	15.10.60	APP	Ipswich T.	10.78	1979-83	159	8	7	(M)E.YTH.INT./E.U21-6
McCALL, Stuart M.	Leeds	10.06.64	APP	Bradford C.	06.82	1982-83	71	3	9	(M) E.YTH.INT.

Players Names	Birthplace	Date	Previous Club	League Club	Date Signed	Seasons Played	Apps	Sub	Gls	
McCALL, William	Glasgow	14.11.20	Aberdeen	Newcastle U.	01.48	1947–48	16		4	(OL)
McCALLIOG, Jim	Glasgow	23.09.46	Leeds U.(AM)	Chelsea	09.63	1964–65	7	/	2	(M)S–5/S.U23–2/S.SCH.INT.
			TR	Sheffield Wed.	10.65	1965–68	150	/	19	
			TR	Wolverhampton W.	08.69	1969–73	158	5	34	
			TR	Manchester U.	03.74	1973–74	31	/	7	
			TR	Southampton	02.75	1974–76	70	2	8	
			Chicago Sting	Lincoln C.	09.78	1978	9	/	0	
MacCALLUM, Stewart	Dumbarton	09.05.27	Rhyl	Wrexham	06.50	1950–52	67		0	(HB)
			Kettering	Workington	06.54	1954–55	10		1	
			TR	Coventry C.	02.56					
			TR	Hartlepool U.	07.56	1956	2		0	
			TR	Southport	08.57	1957	9		0	
McCALMAN, Don S.	Greenock	18.10.35	Hibernian	Bradford P.A.	06.59	1959–65	296	/	5	(CH)
			TR	Barrow	07.66	1966	13	/	0	
McCAMBRIDGE, David T.	Larne	26.07.21	Larne	Barrow	09.46	1946–49	15		1	(WH)
McCANN, Albert	Maidenhead	01.11.41	JNRS	Luton T.	04.59	1959–60	6		0	(IF)
			TR	Coventry C.	08.61	1961	22		3	
			TR	Portsmouth	08.62	1962–73	331	8	84	
McCANN, James	Dundee	20.05.54	APP	Nottingham F.	07.73	1974–75	2	4	1	(F)
			L	Stockport Co.	10.75	1975	4	1	0	
			L	Halifax T.	10.76	1976	2	/	1	
McCANN, John	Govan	23.07.34	Bridgeton B.C.	Barnsley	12.55	1955–58	118		17	(OL) S'B'–1
			TR	Bristol C.	05.59	1959–60	30		0	
			TR	Huddersfield T.	10.60	1960–62	20		1	
			TR	Derby Co.	09.62	1962–63	56		2	
			TR	Darlington	08.64	1964	4		0	
			TR	Chesterfield	10.64	1964–65	40	/	9	
McCARRICK, Mark B.	Liverpool	04.02.62	Witton A.	Birmingham C.	05.83	1983	12	3	0	(D)
McCARRON, Frank P.	Glasgow	01.10.43	Glasgow Celtic	Carlisle U.	07.67	1967	7	2	1	(HB)
McCARTER, James J.	Glasgow	19.03.23	Vale of Clyde	Sheffield Wed.	+	1946	6		0	(OL)
			TR	Mansfield T.	08.48	1948–49	67		10	
McCARTHY, Danny J.	Abergavenny	26.09.42	Abergavenny	Cardiff C.	07.60	1961	7		0	(F)
McCARTHY, Gerard	Limerick	30.03.34	Limerick	Charlton Ath.	07.56	1956	4		0	(HB)
McCARTHY, Ian	Porth	04.09.60	Coventry C.(APP)	Swansea C.	03.78	1977	0	1	0	(F)
McCARTHY, John F.	Cork	22.01.22	Cork	Bristol C.	07.49	1949	3		0	
McCARTHY, Kevin J.	London	24.12.57	APP	Watford	01.76	1975–77	35	1	1	(M)
McCARTHY, Mike	Barnsley	07.02.59	APP	Barnsley	07.77	1977–83	272	/	7	(D)EI-1
			TR	Manchester C.	12.83	1983	24	/	1	
McCARTHY, Philip	Liverpool	19.02.44	Skelmersdale	Oldham Ath.	07.65	1965	2	1	0	(WH)
			TR	Halifax T.	01.66	1965–70	180	1	14	
McCARTHY, Robert Z.	Overton	02.11.48	APP	Southampton	11.65	1967–74	112	/	2	(FB)
McCARTHY, Roy S.	Barnsley	17.01.45	JNRS	Barnsley	05.62	1961–62	3		0	(W)
			TR	Barrow	07.64	1964–68	188	/	41	
			TR	Southport	06.69	1969	33	1	4	
McCARTHY, William E.	Bootle	25.11.41	JNRS	Liverpool	12.58					(FB)E.SCH.INT.
			TR	Southport	10.60	1960–62	27		1	
McCARTNEY, Mike	Edinburgh	28.09.54	APP	W.B.A.	12.71					(D)S.SCH.INT.
			TR	Carlisle U.	05.73	1973–79	148	8	17	
			TR	Southampton	07.80	1980	22	/	1	
			TR	Plymouth Arg.	08.81	1981–82	49	/	5	
			TR	Carlisle U.	03.83	1982–83	30	/	0	
McCARTNEY, William R.	Newcraighall	01.08.47		Port Vale	06.66	1966	14	1	1	(F)
McCAVANA, William T.	Belfast	24.01.21	Coleraine	Notts. Co.	AM	1948	3		0	(CH)NI–2/IRISH LGE REP./ NI AMAT.INT.
McCLAREN, Steve	Fulford	03.05.61	APP	Hull C.	04.79	1979–83	131	7	12	(M)
McCLATCHEY, Derek H.	Whiston	29.04.56	APP	Liverpool	05.73					(IF)
			L	Southport	02.76	1975	2	1	0	
McCLELLAN, Alistair A.	Glasgow	16.04.22		New Brighton	08.46	1946–47	34		7	
			TR	Tranmere Rov.	05.48	1948	2		0	
MacCLELLAN, Sid B.	Dagenham	11.06.25	Chelmsford	Tottenham H.	08.49	1950–55	68		29	(OR)
			TR	Portsmouth	11.56	1956–57	36		9	
			TR	Orient	07.58	1958	12		4	
McCLELLAND, Charles	Manchester	08.01.24	Hyde U.	Blackburn Rov.	12.46	1946–48	13		2	(IF) Son of pre–war player
			TR	Exeter C.	07.49	1949–54	183		58	
McCLELLAND, David	Newcastle	25.12.41	B. Auckland	Port Vale	08.67	1967	2	2	0	(W)
McCLELLAND, John	Belfast	07.12.55	Portadown	Cardiff C.	02.74	1974	1	3	1	(D)NI-8
			Bangor C.	Mansfield T.	05.78	1978–80	122	3	8	
McCLELLAND, John B.	Bradford	05.03.35		Manchester C.	03.53	1956–58	8		2	(OR) Son of James(pre–war player)
			TR	Lincoln C.	09.58	1958–61	121		32	
			TR	Q.P.R.	09.61	1961–62	71		23	
			TR	Portsmouth	05.63	1962–67	135	1	36	
			TR	Newport Co.	07.68	1968	36	/	11	

Players Names	Birthplace	Date	Previous Club	League Club	Date Signed	Seasons Played	Apps	Sub	Gls	
McCLELLAND, John T.	Lurgan	19.05.40	Glenavon	Arsenal	10.60	1960–63	46		0	(G) NI–6/
			TR	Fulham	12.64	1965–68	51	/	0	d.1976
			L	Lincoln C.	12.68	1968	12	/	0	
McCLELLAND, John W.	Colchester	11.08.30		Colchester U.	09.51					(F)
			TR	Stoke C.	06.52	1952	4		0	
			TR	Swindon T.	06.54	1954	14		1	
			TR	Rochdale	06.55	1955	26		5	
McCLELLAND, Joseph	Edinburgh	12.10.35	Hibernian	Wrexham	06.64	1964	32		0	(FB)
McCLENAGHAN, Albert	Hamilton	07.07.54	Larne	Watford	12.77	1977	2	/	0	(D)
McCLURE, William	Shotts	16.05.21	Albion Rov.	Preston N.E.	12.47	1947	12		2	(OL)
			TR	New Brighton	07.48	1948–49	45		7	
			TR	Carlisle U.	10.49	1949	8		1	
			TR	Hartlepool U.	08.50	1950–52	119		24	
McCLUSKEY, Andy	Manchester	29.03.51		Hartlepool U.	09.69	1969	4	2	0	(WH)
McCLUSKEY, George M.	Hamilton	19.09.57	Glasgow Celtic	Leeds U.	08.83	1983	24	8	8	(F)
McCLUSKEY, Ron	Johnstone	03.11.36	East Fife	Accrington St.	11.60	1960	4		0	(G)
McCLUSKIE, James A.	Rossendale	29.09.66	JNRS	Rochdale	N/C	1983	4	1	0	
McCOIST, Ally	Glasgow	04.08.63	St. Johnstone	Sunderland	08.81	1981–82	38	18	8	(F)
McCOLE, John	Glasgow	18.09.36	Falkirk	Bradford C.	09.58	1958–59	42		32	(CF)
			TR	Leeds U.	09.59	1959–61	78		46	
			TR	Bradford C.	10.61	1961–62	46		15	
			TR	Rotherham U.	12.62	1962	14		5	
			Shelbourne	Newport Co.	10.64	1964	6		2	
McCOLL, Duncan	Glasgow	28.12.45	Partick Th.	Barnsley	01.66	1965	5	/	0	(IF)
McCOLL, Tom G.	Glasgow	19.09.45	Dennistoun	Colchester U.	06.63	1963–64	11		2	(IF)
			TR	Chelsea	12.64					
McCONNELL, Peter	Reddish	03.03.37	JNRS	Leeds U.	03.54	1958–61	48		4	(WH)
			TR	Carlisle U.	08.62	1962–68	272	1	27	
			TR	Bradford C.	07.69	1969–70	76	3	0	
McCONVILLE, Ian J.	Doncaster	01.05.59	APP	Doncaster Rov.	04.77	1975-77	9	2	1	(F)
McCORKINDALE, John	Argyll	10.08.34	Tonbridge	Gillingham	10.57	1957	7		0	
McCORMACK, Cecil J.	Newcastle	15.02.22		Gateshead	+	1946	27		19	(CF)
			TR	Middlesbrough	04.47	1946–48	37		15	
			TR	Barnsley	07.50	1950–51	50		42	
			TR	Notts.Co.	11.51	1951–55	82		35	
McCORMACK, Frank A.	Glasgow	25.09.24	Clyde	Oldham Ath.	11.49	1949	14		0	
McCORMACK, Murdoch	Glasgow	07.10.20	Glasgow Rgrs.	Manchester C.	04.47	1946	1		0	(OL) d.1951
			TR	Blackpool	07.47	1947	12		3	
			TR	Crewe Alex.	07.48	1948	31		3	
McCORMICK, David	Halifax	03.11.20		Halifax T.	10.47	1947–54	117		0	(G)41 apps on field
McCORMICK, David J.	London	29.12.51	Biggleswade	Peterborough U.	N/C	1975	1	/	0	(CF)
McCORMICK, Harry	Coleraine	10.01.24	Coleraine	Derby Co	10.46	1946–47	7		0	IRISH LGE.REP.
			TR	Everton	07.48	1948	4		0	
McCORMICK, James	Rotherham	26.09.12	Tottenham H. (*)	Fulham	+	1946	9		2	d.1968
			TR	Lincoln C.	08.47	1947–48	64		6	
			TR	Crystal Palace	02.49	1948	13		2	
McCORMICK, James	Rotherham	01.04.37		Sheffield U.	10.56	1956	1		0	
			TR	Rotherham U.	07.57					
McCORMICK, John	Glasgow	18.07.36	Aberdeen	Crystal Palace	05.66	1966–72	194		6	(CH)
McCORMICK, Joseph M.	Holywell	15.07.16	Bolton W.(*)	Rochdale	05.46	1946–47	67		0	(RH)
			Boton U.	Scunthorpe U.	N/L	1950	7?		0	
McCOURT, Frank J.	Portadown	09.12.25	Shamrock Rov.	Bristol Rov.	+					(WH) NI–6
			Shamrock Rov.	Bristol Rov.	03.49	1949	32		2	
			TR	Manchester C.	12.50	1950–53	61		4	
			TR	Colchester U.	06.54	1954	12		0	
McCOY, Mick	Sunderland	29.01.34		Burnley	10.53	1954	1		0	(F)
			TR	Southport	07.57	1957	5		1	
McCOY, Peter J.	Wingate	31.07.23	Shotton J.	Newcastle U.	09.46					
			TR	Norwich C.	02.49	1948	6		0	
McCOY, Wilf	Birmingham	04.03.21		Portsmouth	08.46	1946–47	18		0	(CH)
			TR	Northampton T.	12.48	1948–49	61		0	
			TR	Brighton & H.A.	01.51	1950–53	112		0	
McCRAE, Alex	Stoneyburn	02.01.20	Hearts	Charlton Ath.	05.47	1947–48	43		8	(CF)
			TR	Middlesbrough	11.48	1948–52	122		47	
McCRAE, Ian	London	01.10.35		Accrington St.	07.57	1959–60	14		0	(HB)
McCREADIE, Eddie	Glasgow	15.04.40	E. Stirling	Chelsea	04.62	1962–73	327	4	4	(FB) S–23
McCREADIE, Eddie				Walsall	09.53	1953	4		0	
McCREADIE, Tom S.	Port Glasgow	28.09.23		Hartlepool U.	08.49	1949	34		3	
			TR	Lincoln C.	08.50	1950	11		1	

Players Names	Birthplace	Date	Previous Club	League Club	Date Signed	Seasons Played	Career Record Apps	Sub	Gls	
McCREADIE, W. Harvey	Glenluce	01.10.42	JNRS	Accrington St.	10.59	1958–59	28		10	(CF)
			TR	Luton T.	01.60	1959	1		0	
			TR	Wrexham	11.60	1960	10		2	
McCREADY, Bernard	Dumbarton	23.04.37	Glasgow Celtic	Rochdale	05.57	1957–58	29		0	(G)
			TR	Oldham Ath.	03.59	1958	7		0	
McCREADY, Tom	Jonhstone	19.10.43	Hibernian	Watford	07.63	1963	1		0	(FB) S.SCH.INT.
McCREDIE, Norman J.	Glasgow	17.05.28	Partick Th.	Accrington St.	05.55	1955–56	51		3	(FB) 1 app in goal
			TR	Southport	08.57	1957	33		2	for Barrow
			TR	Barrow	08.58	1958	23		0	
McCREERY, David	Belfast	16.09.57	APP	Manchester U.	10.74	1974-78	48	39	7	(M)NI-46/NI.U21-1/
			TR	Q.P.R.	08.79	1979–80	54	1	4	NI.SCH.INT.
			Tulsa R.	Newcastle U.	10.82	1982-83	63	3	0	
McCREESH, Andy	Billingham	08.09.62	APP	Middlesbrough	09.80	1981	2	/	0	(M)
McCRINDLE, William	Hurlford	28.07.23	Pollock J.	Newport Co.	12.48	1948	2		0	(IF) d.1982
McCROHAN, Roy	Reading	22.09.30	JNRS	Reading	01.49	1949–50	4		1	(WH)
			TR	Norwich C.	08.51	1951–61	384		20	
			TR	Colchester U.	09.62	1962–63	62		5	
			TR	Bristol Rov.	08.64	1964	10		1	
McCRORY, Sam	Beltast	11.10.24	Linfield	Swansea C.	10.46	1946–49	103		46	(CF) NI–1/NI'B'–1
			TR	Ipswich T.	03.50	1949–51	98		38	
			TR	Plymouth Arg.	08.52	1952–54	50		11	
			TR	Southend U.	06.55	1955–59	205		90	
McCRYSTAL, Dennis	Welwyn Garden C.	13.01.32	Kingsway Y.C.	Watford	03.50	1950	1		0	(G)
McCUBBIN, Robert	Kilmarnock	13.02.43	Ayr U.	Hartlepool U.	06.63	1963	2		0	(OR)
McCUE, Alex B.	Greenock	25.11.27	Falkirk	Carlisle U.	10.50	1950	32		11	(OL)
			TR	Grimsby T.	07.51	1951–52	37		20	
			TR	Shrewsbury T.	05.53	1953–55	91		28	
McCUE, John W.	Stoke	22.08.22	JNRS	Stoke C.	+	1946–59	502		2	(FB)
			TR	Oldham Ath.	09.60	1960–61	56		0	
McCULLOCH, Adam B.	Crossford	04.06.20	T.Lanark	Northampton T.	06.49	1949–51	89		38	(CF)
			TR	Shrewsbury T.	01.52	1951–52	46		17	
			TR	Aldershot	02.53	1952–54	78		33	
McCULLOCH, Andy	Northampton	03.01.50	Walton & Hersham	Q.P.R.	10.70	1970-72	30	12	10	(F)S.U23-1/
			TR	Cardiff C.	10.72	1972-73	58	/	24	Son of Adam
			TR	Oxford U.	07.74	1974-75	41	/	9	
			TR	Brentford	03.76	1975-78	115	2	48	
			TR	Sheffield Wed.	06.79	1979-82	122	3	43	
			TR	Crystal Palace	08.83	1983	25	/	3	
McCULLOCH, David	Hamilton	05.10.11	Brentford(*)	Derby C.	*					(CF) *Hearts
			TR	Leicester C.	08.46	1946	4		2	S–7/S.F.LGE.REP.
McCULLOCH, Ian	Kilmarnock	28.12.54	Kilmarnock	Notts. Co.	04.78	1978-83	218	3	51	(F)S.U'21-2
McCULLOCH, Tom	Glasgow	25.12.21	Q.of South	Northampton T.	12.49	1949	2		0	(OR)
			TR	Bradford C.	01.51	1950–53	109		9	
			TR	Crewe Alex.	07.54	1954	28		5	
McCULLOCH, William D.	Edinburgh	25.06.22		Stockport Co.	+	1946–53	309		4	(FB) d.1961
			TR	Rochdale	07.54	1954–57	139		2	
McCULLOUGH, Paul J.	Birmingham	26.10.59	Brixham	Reading	09.78					(G)
			Dawlish	Brentford	07.80	1980	7	/	0	
McCULLOUGH, William	Woodburn	27.07.35	Portadown	Arsenal	09.58	1958–65	253	/	4	(FB) NI–10
			TR	Millwall	08.66	1966	17	2	0	
McCUNNELL, Barry	Hull	20.09.48	Endike J.	Hull C.	10.66	1969	0	1	0	(F)
McCURDY, Colin C.	Belfast	18.07.54	Larne	Fulham	11.77	1977	1	/	0	(F)
McCURLEY, Kevin	Consett	02.04.26		Brighton & H.A.	09.48	1948–50	21		9	(CF)
			TR	Liverpool	06.51					
			TR	Colchester U.	03.52	1951–59	224		91	
			TR	Oldham Ath.	06.60	1960	1		0	
McCUSKER, Jim	Maghera	27.12.39	JNRS	Bradford C.	02.57	1958	7		0	(G)
			TR	Stockport Co.	08.59	1959	2		0	
McDERMENT, William S.	Paisley	05.01.43	Johnstone Burgh	Leicester C.	05.61	1962–66	20	3	1	(WH)
			TR	Luton T.	07.67	1967–68	28	12	1	
			TR	Notts.Co.	05.69	1969	2	1	0	
McDERMOTT, Brian J.	Slough	08.04.61	APP	Arsenal	02.79	1978-83	38	23	12	(F)E.YTH.INT.
			L	Fulham	03.83	1982	0	3	0	
McDERMOTT, Jim	Earlestown	05.05.32	Crompton Rec.	Southport	07.55	1955–58	157		30	(F)
McDERMOTT, John C.	Manchester	14.10.59	APP	Manchester U.	10.76					(M)
			Wigan Ath.	Rochdale	09.79	1979	5	3	1	
McDERMOTT, Maurice P.	Pelton Fell	21.02.23	Consett	Sunderland	+					(RB)
			Consett	York C.	07.47	1947	7		0	
McDERMOTT, Steve	Gateshead	30.12.64	Sunderland (APP)	Darlington	02.83	1982	0	2	0	(F)

Players Names	Birthplace	Date	Previous Club	League Club	Date Signed	Seasons Played	Career Record Apps	Sub	Gls	
McDERMOTT, Terry	Kirkby	08.12.51	APP	Bury	10.69	1969-72	83	7	8	(M)E.U23-1/E-25●
			TR	Newcastle U.	02.73	1972-74	55	1	6	
			TR	Liverpool	11.74	1974-82	221	11	54	
			TR	Newcastle U.	09.82	1982-83	74	/	12	
McDEVITT, Ken	Liverpool	04.03.29.		Tranmere Rov.	01.50	1951-59	237		39	(IF)
McDONAGH, Jim M.	Rotherham	06.10.52	APP	Rotherham U.	12.70	1970-75	121	/	0	(G)EI-16/E.YTH.INT.
			TR	Bolton W.	08.76	1976-79	161	/	0	
			TR	Everton	07.80	1980	40	/	0	
			TR	Bolton W.	08.81	1981-82	81	/	1	
			TR	Notts Co.	07.83	1983	24	/	0	
McDONALD, Alan	Belfast	12.10.63	APP	Q.P.R.	08.81	1983	5	/	0	(D)
			L	Charlton Ath.	03.83	1982	9	/	0	
McDONALD, Colin A.	Tottington	15.10.30	Hankshaw ST.H.	Burnley	10.48	1953–58	186		0	(G) E–8/E.F.LGE. REP.
McDONALD, Colin B.	Norwich	15.05.50	APP	Norwich C.	07.67	1967	7	/	0	(IF)
			TR	Scunthorpe U.	07.70	1970–72	78	8	11	
MacDONALD, Dave A.	Dundee	09.05.31	Dundee Violet	Crystal Palace	03.51	1952–54	30		0	(G)
MacDONALD, Gary	Middlesbrough	26.03.62	APP	Middlesbrough	03.80	1980-83	40	13	5	(F)
McDONALD, Gerrard	Milnthorpe	03.12.52	APP	Blackburn Rov.	08.71	1971	19	2	2	(W)
			TR	Halifax T.	08.73	1973	10	3	0	
McDONALD, Gordon	Hampstead	07.02.32		Crystal Palace	12.54	1954–56	13		0	(FB)
			TR	Swindon T.	07.57	1957	10		0	
McDONALD, Harry	Salford	11.09.26	Ashton U.	Crystal Palace	09.50	1950–54	140		1	(FB)
McDONALD, Ian	Inverness	05.02.51	JNRS	Wolverhampton W.	08.68					(F)
			TR	Darlington	09.70	1970	21	4	3	
McDONALD, Ian C.	Barrow	10.05.53	APP	Barrow	05.71	1970-71	30	5	2	(M)
			TR	Workington	02.73	1972-73	42	/	4	
			TR	Liverpool	01.74					
			L	Colchester U.	02.75	1974	5	/	2	
			TR	Mansfield T.	07.75	1975-76	47	9	4	
			TR	York. C.	11.77	1977-81	175	/	29	
			TR	Aldershot	11.81	1981-83	123	/	20	
MacDONALD, Ian C.A.	W. Germany	30.08.53	St. Johnstone	Carlisle U.	05.76	1976-80	186	1	7	(D)
McDONALD, James	Renfrew	18.04.32		Gillingham	08.52	1956	2		0	
MacDONALD, John	Liverpool	01.09.21		Liverpool	+					(FB)
			TR	Tranmere Rov.	06.49	1949–51	89		0	
McDONALD, John C.	Maltby	27.08.21	Wolverhampton W.(*)	Bournemouth	+	1946–47	80		35	(OL)
			TR	Fulham	06.48	1948–51	75		19	
			TR	Southampton	08.52	1952	16		4	
			TR	Southend U.	05.53	1953–54	28		6	
MacDONALD, John S.	Edinburgh	23.09.22	Carshalton Ath.	Notts.Co.	08.48	1948	1		0	
			TR	Q.P.R.	03.49					
McDONALD, Joseph	Blantyre	10.02.29	Falkirk	Sunderland	03.54	1953–57	137		1	(FB) S–2
			TR	Nottingham F.	07.58	1958–60	109		0	
MacDONALD, Kevin D.	Inverness	22.12.60	Inverness Caley	Leicester C.	05.80	1980-83	120	5	8	(M)
MacDONALD, Les	Newcastle	02.04.34	JNRS	Portsmouth	05.55					(FB)
			TR	Exeter C.	06.57	1957–65	294	/	0	
MacDONALD, Malcolm	Fulham	07.01.50	Tonbridge	Fulham	08.68	1968	10	3	5	(F)E-14/E.U23-4/
			TR	Luton T.	07.69	1969-70	88	/	49	E.F.LGE REP.●
			TR	Newcastle U.	05.71	1971-75	187	/	95	
			TR	Arsenal	08.76	1976-78	84	/	42	
McDONALD, Malcolm	Glasgow	26.10.13	Kilmarnock	Brentford	10.46	1946–48	86		1	(HB)
MacDONALD, Martin	Ballymena	05.09.31	JNRS	Portsmouth	11.48					(FB)
			TR	Bournemouth	11.51	1952–55	51		1	
McDONALD, Mike F.	Glasgow	08.11.50	Clydebank	Stoke C.	10.72	1972–73	5	/	0	(G)
McDONALD, Neil J.	Barrow	27.05.54	Barrow	Workington	N/C	1976	5	1	0	(F)
McDONALD, Neil R.	Wallsend	02.11.65	APP	Newcastle U.	02.83	1982-83	32	4	4	(M)
McDONALD, Richard	Paisley	18.12.33	Saltcoats	Barnsley	12.57	1958	1		0	(F)
MacDONALD, Robert	Kilpatrick	26.10.35	Vale of Leven	Manchester C.	09.56	1961	5		0	(FB)
			TR	Bournemouth	09.63	1963	1		0	
McDONALD, Robert R.	Hull	22.01.59	APP	Hull C.	01.77	1976-79	17	8	2	(D)
McDONALD, Robert W.	Aberdeen	13.04.55	APP	Aston Villa	09.72	1972-75	33	6	3	(D)
			TR	Coventry C.	08.76	1976-80	161	/	14	
			TR	Manchester C.	10.80	1980-82	96	/	11	
			TR	Oxford U.	09.83	1983	39	/	4	
McDONALD, Roger	Glasgow	02.02.33	St. Mirren	Mansfield T.	03.55	1954–55	14		0	(FB)
			Cheltenham	Crystal Palace	01.58					
McDONALD, Terry	Belfast	05.02.47	JNRS	Middlesbrough	02.64					(FB)
			TR	Southport	07.65	1965–66	33	/	1	
			TR	Barrow	07.67	1967–68	35	1	0	
			TR	York C.	07.69					

Players Names	Birthplace	Date	Previous Club	League Club	Date Signed	Seasons Played	Career Record Apps Sub Gls		
McDONALD, Terry J.	London	12.11.38	JNRS	West Ham U.	04.56				(W) E.YTH INT.
			TR	Orient	07.59	1959–64	151		21
			TR	Reading	05.65	1965	13	/	2
McDONALD, Tommy	Glasgow	24.05.30	Hibernian	Wolverhampton W.	04.54	1954–55	5		1	(OR) S'B'–1
			TR	Leicester C.	07.56	1956–59	113		27
McDONALD, William L.	Longriggend	30.08.18	Airdrie	Carlisle U.	08.46	1946	3		0	(WH)
McDONNELL, Charles	Birkenhead	15.07.36		Tranmere Rov.	09.57	1957–60	67		25	(IF)
			TR	Stockport Co.	06.61	1961–63	85		32
			TR	Tranmere Rov.	10.63	1963–64	45		25
			TR	Southport	07.65	1965	10	/	1
McDONNELL, Martin	Newton–le–Willows	27.04.24		Everton	+					(CH)
			TR	Southport	08.46	1946	38		0
			TR	Birmingham C.	05.47	1947–49	32		0
			TR	Coventry C.	10.49	1949–54	232		0
			TR	Derby Co.	07.55	1955–57	93		0
			TR	Crewe Alex.	07.58	1958	17		0
McDONNELL, Peter A.	Kendall	11.06.53	Netherfield	Bury	03.74	1973	1	/	0	(G)
			TR	Liverpool	08.74				
			TR	Oldham Ath.	08.78	1978-81	137	/	0
McDONOUGH, Darren	Belgium	07.11.62	APP	Oldham Ath.	01.80	1980-83	122	5	14	(M)
McDONOUGH, Roy	Solihull	16.10.58	APP	Birmingham C.	10.76	1976	2	/	1	(F)
			TR	Walsal	09.78	1978-80	76	6	15
			TR	Chelsea	10.80				
			TR	Colchester U.	02.81	1980-82	89	4	24
			TR	Southend U.	08.83	1983	22	/	4
			TR	Exeter C.	01.84	1983	15	1	0
MacDOUGALL, Edward J.	Inverness	08.01.47	ICI Recs (Widnes)	Liverpool	01.66					(F)S-7●
			TR	York C.	07.67	1967-68	84	/	34
			TR	Bournemouth	07.69	1969-72	146	/	103
			TR	Manchester U.	09.72	1972	18	/	5
			TR	West Ham U.	03.73	1972-73	24	/	5
			TR	Norwich C.	12.73	1973-76	112	/	51
			TR	Southampton	09.76	1976-78	86	/	42
			TR	Bournemouth	11.78	1978-79	51	1	16
			TR	Blackpool	03.80	1979-80	11	2	0
McDOUGALL, Laybourne	Tynemouth	12.05.17	Preston N.E.(*)	Blackpool	*					(LB)
			TR	Gateshead	10.46	1946–48	60		0
McDOWALL, Daniel	Kirkintilloch	22.05.29		Middlesbrough	02.47					(WH)
			Kilmarnock	Workington	08.51	1951–52	82		23
			TR	Lincoln C.	07.53	1953	17		4
			TR	Millwall	06.54	1954–55	10		1
McDOWALL, James C.	Glasgow	25.10.40	Baillieston	Notts.Co.	09.59					(G)
			Boston U.	Scunthorpe U.	12.61	1961	1		0
McDOWALL, Ken F.	Manchester	06.05.38	Rhyl	Manchester U.	09.59					(F)
			TR	Rochdale	10.60	1960	6		0
McDOWALL, Les J.	India	25.10.12	Sunderland(*)	Manchester C.	*	1946–48	67		3	(WH)
			TR	Wrexham	11.49	1949	3		0
McDOWELL, Duncan J.	Paddington	18.12.63	APP	Birmingham C.	08.81	1981	2	/	0	(M)
McDOWELL, John A.	E. Ham	07.09.51	APP	West Ham U.	06.70	1970-78	243	6	8	(D)E.U23-13/E.YTH.INT.
			TR	Norwich C.	08.79	1979-80	40	1	1
			TR	Bristol R.	05.82				
MACEDO, Anthony	Gibraltar	22.02.38	JNRS	Fulham	10.55	1957–67	346	/	0	(G) E.U23–10
			TR	Colchester U.	09.68	1968	38	/	0
McELHINNEY, Gerry A.	Londonderry	19.09.56	Distillery	Bolton W.	09.80	1980-83	94	1	2	(D)NI-5
			L	Rochdale	11.82	1982	20	/	1
McELVANEY, David A.	Chesterfield	03.11.54		Chesterfield	10.75	1975	4	/	1	(IF)
McEVOY, Andy M.	Dublin	15.07.38	Bray W.	Blackburn Rov.	10.56	1958–66	183	/	89	(IF) EI-17
McEVOY, Don W.	Golcar	03.12.28	Bradley Rgrs.	Huddersfield T.	09.47	1949–54	148		3	(CH)
			TR	Sheffield Wed.	12.54	1954–57	105		1
			TR	Lincoln C.	01.59	1958–59	23		0
			TR	Barrow	07.60	1960–61	74		1
			TR	Halifax	08.63				
McEWAN, James	Dundee	22.03.29	Raith Rov.	Aston Villa	07.59	1959–65	143	/	29	(W)
			TR	Walsall	08.66	1966	10	/	1
McEWAN, Peter M.	S. Africa	23.05.33	Pretoria	Luton T.	02.54	1953–55	27		15	(CF)
McEWAN, Stan	Cambusrethan	08.06.57	APP	Blackpool	07.74	1974-81	204	10	24	(D)
			TR	Exeter C.	07.82	1982-83	65	/	15
			TR	Hull C.	03.84	1983	16	/	1
McEWAN, Steve	Bowhill	28.03.30		Liverpool	07.50					
			TR	Accrington St.	08.51	1951	2		1
McEWAN, William	Glasgow	29.08.14		Q.P.R.	*	1946–49	83		15	(IF)
			TR	Orient	02.50	1949–50	21		3

Players Names	Birthplace	Date	Previous Club	League Club	Date Signed	Seasons Played	Career Record		
							Apps	Sub	Gls
McEWAN, William J.M.	Cleland	20.06.51	Hibernian	Blackpool	05.73	1973	4	/	0	(M)
			TR	Brighton & H.A.	02.74	1973-74	27	/	3
			TR	Chesterfield	11.74	1974-76	79	1	7
			TR	Mansfield T.	01.77	1976-77	32	/	3
			TR	Peterborough U.	11.77	1977-78	62	1	3
			TR	Rotherham U.	07.79	1079-83	86	9	10
McEWEN, Frank K.	Dublin	15.02.48	APP	Manchester U.	05.65					(F)
			TR	Rochdale	11.66	1966-67	17	/	3
MACEY, John R.T.	Bristol	13.11.47	APP	Bristol C.	05.65					(G) E.SCH.INT.
			TR	Grimsby T.	07.68	1968-69	36	1	0
			TR	Newport Co.	07.70	1970-75	194	/	0
McFADDEN, Anthony	Hexham	18.05.57	Reyrolles	Darlington	08.81	1981-82	44	3	10	(F)
McFADZEAN, Clive S.	Kilmarnock	11.03.58	APP	Bradford C.	03.76	1975-76	3	1	2	(F)
McFADZEAN, John P.	Sheffield	02.04.66	APP	Rotherham U.	APP	1983	0	1	0
McFALL, Dave	Ballymena	14.03.35	Sittingbourne	Aldershot	10.58	1958	3		0	(IF)
McFARLAND, Roy	Liverpool	05.04.48	JNRS	Tranmere Rov.	07.66	1966-67	35	/	0	(D)E-28/E.U23-5/
			TR	Derby Co.	08.67	1967-80	434	/	44	E.F.LGE REP.●
			TR	Bradford C.	06.81	1981-82	40	/	1
			TR	Derby Co.	N/C	1983	3	5	0
McFARLANE, Ian	Lanark	26.01.33	Aberdeen	Chelsea	08.56	1956-57	40	/	0	(FB)
			TR	Leicester C.	05.58	1958	1		0
McFARLANE, Noel W.	Bray	20.12.34	JNRS	Manchester U.	04.52	1953	1		0	(F)
McFARLANE, Robert R.	Bo'ness	12.10.13	Arsenal(*)	Doncaster Rov.	*	1946-47	55		0	(WH) d.1971
McFAUL, William	Coleraine	01.10.43	Linfield	Newcastle U.	11.66	1966-74	290	/	0	(G) NI-6/AMAT.INT.
McFEAT, Archie	Kincardine	23.01.24	Morton	Torquay U.	05.48	1948	9		0	(G)
McGAIRY, Tom	Glasgow	25.11.27	Dumbarton	Walsall	08.54	1954	7		1
McGANN, William T.A.	Wilmslow	12.07.23		Stockport Co.	05.48	1949-50	14		0	(FB)
			TR	Bournemouth	07.51				
McGARRIGLE, Dennis	Luton	04.11.36	Gourock J.	Bristol C.	02.60					(G)
			TR	Crewe Alex.	06.60	1960-61	12		0
			TR	Chester	11.62				
MacGARRITY, Tom W.	Scotstoun	24.11.22	Morton	Southampton	11.52	1952	5		1
McGARRY, Ron	Cockermouth	25.10.38		Workington	07.60	1960	2		0
McGARRY, Ron J.	Whitehaven	05.12.37	Whitehaven	Workington	10.60	1958-61	92		25	(CF)
			TR	Bolton W.	02.62	1961-62	27		7
			TR	Newcastle U.	12.62	1962-66	118	3	41
			TR	Barrow	03.67	1966-67	30	/	4
			Australia	Barrow	09.70	1970	14	3	4
McGARRY, William H.	Stoke	10.06.27	Northwood Mission	Port Vale	+	1946-50	146		5	(WH) E-4/●
			TR	Huddersfield T.	03.51	1950-60	363		25	E'B'-1/
			TR	Bournemouth	03.61	1960-62	78		2	E.F.LGE REP.
McGARVEY, Scott	Glasgow	22.04.63	APP	Manchester U.	04.80	1980-82	13	12	3	(F)S.U'21-2
			L	Wolverhampton W.	03.84	1983	13	/	2
McGEACHIE, George	Falkirk	09.09.39	Dundee	Darlington	01.64	1963-66	119	/	9	(OL)
McGEACHIE, George	Calder	26.10.16	St. Johnstone	New Brighton	07.46	1946-47	63		3	(WH)
			TR	Orient	07.48				
			TR	Rochdale	12.48	1948-50	90		6
			TR	Crystal Palace	06.51	1951	46		5
McGEACHY, Joe	Glasgow	21.04.20	T.Lanark	Orient	05.48	1948-50	75		5
			Hereford U.	Workington	09.52	1952	2		1
McGEADY, John	Glasgow	17.04.58	T. Lanark	Sheffield U.	01.76	1975-76	13	3	0	(F)
			TR	Newport Co.	10.78	1978	2	/	0
McGEE, Paul G.	Dublin	19.06.54	Sligo Rov.	Hereford U.	08.73					(F)EI-16/EI.U21-2
			Toronto	Q.P.R.	11.77	1977-78	31	8	7
			TR	Preston N.E.	10.79	1979-81	62	4	13
			TR	Burnley	11.81	1981-82	33	1	9
McGEORGE, Jim L.	Sunderland	08.06.45	Spennymoor	Orient	03.64	1964-65	16	/	0	(F)
			TR	Mansfield T.	07.66	1966	5	6	0
McGEOUGH, Jim	Waterford	14.07.46	Waterford	Lincoln C.	06.72	1972-74	61	4	0	(IF)
			L	Hartlepool U.	03.73	1972	1	1	0
McGETTIGAN, John A.	Motherwell	28.11.45		Workington	03.68	1967-68	13	1	0	(F)
McGETTIGAN, Laurie	Hackney	25.12.52	APP	Watford	11.70	1971-74	40	10	3	(W)
			TR	Barnsley	07.75				
McGHEE, Jim W.	Motherwell	21.08.30	Kilmarnock	Darlington	07.52	1952	15		4	(CF)
			Barry T.	Newport Co.	05.54	1954	10		1
McGHEE, Mark	Glasgow	20.05.57	Morton	Newcastle U.	12.77	1977-78	21	7	5	(F)S-2
McGHEE, Tommy E.	Manchester	10.05.29	Wealdstone	Portsmouth	05.54	1954-58	135		0	(FB) E'B'-1/
			TR	Reading	07.59	1959	8		0	E.AMAT.INT.
McGHIE, William L.	Lanark	19.01.58	APP	Leeds U.	01.76	1976	2	/	1	(M)
			TR	York C.	12.79	1979-81	39	4	1

Players Names	Birthplace	Date	Previous Club	League Club	Date Signed	Seasons Played	Apps	Sub	Gls	
McGIBBON, Doug	Southampton	24.02.19		Southampton	*	1946	12		9	(CF)
			TR	Fulham	01.47	1946–47	43		18	
			TR	Bournemouth	09.48	1948–50	103		65	
McGIFFORD, Graham L.	Carshalton	01.05.55	APP	Huddersfield T.	07.72	1972-75	41	1	0	(D)
			TR	Hull C.	05.76	1976	1	/	0	
			TR	Port Vale	06.77	1977	20	/	0	
McGILL, Andrew	Glasgow	11.07.24	Clyde	Bradford C.	11.47	1947–51	165		24	(WH)
			TR	Scunthorpe U.	07.52	1952–56	182		15	
McGILL, Austin M.	Dumfries	29.01.35	Q.of South	Carlisle U.	08.59	1959	30		12	(F)
McGILL, James	Kilsyth	10.03.26		Bury	+	1946	1		0	
			TR	Derby Co.	03.47	1946–47	8		0	
McGILL, James H.	Bellshill	02.10.39	Partick Th.	Oldham Ath.	05.59	1959	39		2	(FB)
			TR	Crewe Alex.	08.60	1960–62	81		2	
			TR	Chester C.	10.62	1962–63	32		0	
			TR	Wrexham	10.63	1963	17		1	
			Macclesfield	Bournemouth	10.64					
McGILL, James M.	Glasgow	27.11.46	Possilpark J.	Arsenal	07.65	1965-66	6	4	0	(M)
			TR	Huddersfield T.	09.67	1967-71	161	3	8	
			TR	Hull C.	10.71	1971-75	141	6	2	
			TR	Halifax T.	02.76	1975-76	31	1	0	
McGILLIVRAY, Findlay	Newton Grange	19.03.40	Glasgow Rgrs.	Bradford P.A.	05.66	1966	38	1	0	(FB)
McGINLEY, John	Rowlands Gill	11.06.59	Gateshead	Sunderland	01.82	1981	3	/	0	(M)
McGINLEY, William D.	Dumfries	12.11.54	APP	Leeds U.	01.72	1972	0	1	0	(M)S.SCH.INT.
			TR	Huddersfield T.	09.74	1974	11	4	1	
			TR	Bradford C.	06.75	1975-76	52	8	11	
			TR	Crewe Alex.	08.77	1977	36	2	2	
McGINN, Frank	Cambuslang	02.03.19		Wrexham	04.47	1946	2		0	
			TR	Ipswich T.	08.48	1948	7		2	
McGINN, William	Ardrossan	02.02.43	Ardrossan	Oldham Ath.	11.63	1963–65	37	1	0	(FB)
McGIVEN, Mick	Newcastle	07.02.51	JNRS	Sunderland	07.68	1969-73	107	6	9	(M)
			TR	West Ham U.	11.73	1973-77	46	2	0	
McGLEISH, John J.	Lanark	09.11.51	JNRS	Northampton T.	11.68	1970–72	7	1	0	(IF)
McGLENN, William	Bedlington	27.04.21	Blyth Spartans	Manchester U.	05.46	1946–51	110		2	(WH)
			TR	Lincoln C.	07.52	1952	13		0	
			TR	Oldham Ath.	02.53	1952–55	68		3	
McGLENNON, Tom	Whitehaven	20.10.33	JNRS	Blackpool	11.50					(HB)
			TR	Rochdale	05.57	1957–58	60		2	
			Burton A.	Barrow	11.59	1959–60	60		6	
McGOLDRICK, John	Coatbridge	23.09.63	Glasgow Celtic	Leeds U.	06.83	1983	7	/	0	
McGOLDRICK, Tom J.	Doncaster	20.09.29	Maltby	Rotherham U.	11.49	1951	5		2	(IF)
			TR	Chesterfield	05.53	1953–54	36		16	
McGONIGAL, Robert	Cookstown	02.05.42	Glentoran	Brighton & H.A.	02.62	1962–65	57	/	0	(G) NI SCH.INT.
McGORRIGHAN, Frank C.	Easington	20.11.21	Carlisle U.(+)	Hull C.	08.46	1946	20		2	(IF) + Middlesbrough
			TR	Blackburn Rov.	02.47	1946–47	5		0	
			TR	Hull C.	09.47	1947	6		0	
			TR	Southport	08.48	1948	4		0	
McGOVERN, John P.	Montrose	28.10.49	APP	Hartlepool U.	05.67	1965-68	68	3	5	(M)S.U23-2●
			TR	Derby Co.	09.68	1968-73	186	4	16	
			TR	Leeds U.	08.74	1974	4	/	0	
			TR	Nottingham F.	02.75	1974-81	249	4	6	
			TR	Bolton W.	06.82	1982-83	16	/	0	
McGOVERN, Mick J.	Hayes	15.02.51	APP	Q.P.R.	11.68	1967-71	10	2	0	(WH)
			L	Watford	08.72	1972	4	/	0	
			TR	Swindon T.	02.73	1972-74	28	4	2	
			L	Aldershot	03.75	1974	6	/	1	
McGOVERN, Patrick M.	Edinburgh	14.05.48		Notts.Co.	07.67	1967	1	2	0	(F)
McGOVERN, Simon	Bradford	25.02.65	JNRS	Bradford C.	N/C	1982	1	/	0	(M)
McGOWAN, Aloysius	Whiterigg	22.01.30	St. Johnstone	Wrexham	05.53	1953–64	408		2	(FB)
McGOWAN, Andy	Corby	17.05.56	Corby T.	Northampton T.	06.75	1975-77	93	12	15	(M)E.YTH.INT.
McGOWAN, Daniel	Dublin	08.11.24	Shelbourne	West Ham U.	05.48	1948–53	82		8	(WH) EI–3/L.O.I. REP.
McGOWAN, George	Carluke	30.11.43	Wishaw	Preston N.E.	08.62					(F)
			TR	Chester C.	03.63	1962–63	18		3	
			TR	Stockport Co.	09.64	1964	5		0	
McGOWAN, Gerry	Kilwinning	04.08.44	Arder Rec.	Oldham Ath.	11.63	1965	5	/	1	(F)
McGOWAN, Jim	Cambuslang	12.01.24	Dumbarton	Grimsby T.	07.46	1946–48	34		4	(HB)
			TR	Southampton	03.50	1949–57	79		9	
McGOWAN, Jim	Glasgow	31.07.39	St. Johnstone	Mansfield T.	06.61	1961	3		0	(OR)
McGOWAN, Ken J.	Wolverhampton	13.05.20		Walsall	10.47	1947–48	11		4	
McGRATH, James A.	Belfast	15.11.21		Barrow	+	1946	3		0	(WH)
McGRATH, John	Tidworth	21.05.32		Notts.Co.	08.53	1955–57	54		5	(F)
			TR	Darlington	05.58	1958	25		6	

Players Names	Birthplace	Date	Previous Club	League Club	Date Signed	Seasons Played	Apps	Sub	Gls	
McGRATH, John T.	Manchester	23.08.38	Bolton W.(AM)	Bury	10.55	1956–60	148		2	(CH) E.U23–1/
			TR	Newcastle U.	02.61	1960–67	169	1	2	E.F.LGE REP.
			TR	Southampton	02.68	1967–73	167	1	1	
			L	Brighton & H.A.	12.72	1972	3	/	0	
McGRATH, Lloyd A.	Birmingham	24.02.65	APP	Coventry C.	12.82	1983	1	/	0	
McGRATH, Martin	London	15.10.60	APP	Southampton	10.78	1979	0	1	0	(M)E.SCH.INT.
			TR	Bournemouth	06.80	1980	17	5	0	
McGRATH, Mick	Dublin	07.04.36	Home Farm	Blackburn Rov.	08.54	1955–65	269	/	8	(WH) EI–22/EI'B'–1
				Bradford P.A.	03.66	1965–66	50	/	1	
McGRATH, Paul	Ealing	04.12.59	St. Patricks	Manchester U.	04.82	1982-83	23	/	4	(D)
McGRATH, R. Chris	Belfast	29.11.54	APP	Tottenham H.	01.72	1973-75	30	8	5	(M)NI-21
			L	Millwall	02.76	1975	15	/	3	
			TR	Manchester U.	10.76	1976-80	12	16	1	
McGRAW, Ian	Glasgow	30.08.26	Arbroath	Leicester C.	12.48	1948–50	13		0	(G)
McGREEVEY, Brian E.	Prestwich	29.09.35	Preston N.E.(AM)	Arsenal	03.54					(F)
			TR	Stockport Co.	03.57	1956	1		0	
McGREGOR, Alex	Glasgow	12.11.50	Hibernian	Shrewsbury T.	01.75	1974-75	46	3	7	(F)
			TR	Aldershot	09.76	1976-81	168	9	17	
MacGREGOR, Colin	Bradford	13.11.40	Bradford C.(AM)	Bradford P.A.	03.58	1958–59	3		0	(F)
MacGREGOR, Jim P.	W. Hartlepool	22.12.31		Hartlepool U.	02.50	1952–56	5		0	(HB)
			TR	Darlington	07.58					
MacGREGOR, Terry J.	W. Hartlepool	24.05.38		Hartlepool U.	12.56	1956–62	47		2	(F)
McGREGOR, William	Paisley	01.12.23	Mossdale Y.M.C.A.	Leicester C.	04.47	1947–51	9		0	(FB)
			TR	Mansfield T.	09.53	1953–55	118		0	
McGRELLIS, Frank	Falkirk	05.10.58	APP	Coventry C.	10.76					(F)
			L	Huddersfield T.	08.78	1978	4	1	0	
			TR	Hereford U.	03.79	1978-81	80	5	24	
McGROARTY, Jim	Londonderry	30.08.57	Finn Harps	Stoke C.	09.77	1977-78	6	1	2	(F)
McGROGAN, Hugh	Dumbarton	01.03.57	APP	Oxford U.	03.75	1974-79	101	25	13	(F)
			TR	Carlisle U.	05.80	1980	1	1	0	
McGROTTY, Wiliam	Glasgow	12.08.52	Yoker Ath.	Blackpool	06.70	1970–72	2	2	1	(F)
McGUCKIN, George	Dundee	11.08.38	Dundee Shamrock	Cardiff C.	12.55	1957	4		0	(HB)
McGUFFIE, Alwyn S.	Stranraer	13.04.37	Q.of South	Luton T.	09.54	1955–63	79		10	(WH)
McGUGAN, John H.	Airdrie	12.06.39	St. Mirren	Leeds U.	08.60	1960	1		0	(HB)
			TR	Tranmere Rov.	02.61	1960–61	35		0	
McGUIGAN, James	Glasgow	01.03.24	Hamilton	Sunderland	06.47	1947–48	3		1	(WH)
			TR	Stockport Co.	06.49	1949–50	43		9	
			TR	Crewe Alex.	08.50	1950–55	207		32	
			TR	Rochdale	08.56	1956–58	72		2	
McGUIGAN, John J.	Motherwell	29.10.32	St. Mirren	Southend U.	05.55	1955–57	126		35	(IF)
			TR	Newcastle U.	07.58	1958–61	50		15	
			TR	Scunthorpe U.	01.62	1961–62	57		17	
			TR	Southampton	08.63	1963–64	34		8	
			TR	Swansea C.	03.65	1964–65	27	/	5	
McGUIGAN, Tom	Whiterigg	22.11.22	Ayr U.	Hartlepool U.	08.50	1950–57	324		76	(IF)
McGUINESS, Henry	Saltcoats	17.02.28		Torquay U.	03.48	1949–54	81		0	(CH)
McGUINNESS, Wilf	Manchester	25.10.37	JNRS	Manchester U.	11.54	1955–59	81		2	(WH)E–2/E.U23–4/
										E.YTH.INT./E.F.LGE REP./
										E.SCH.INT.
McGUINNESS, Robert F.	Motherwell	29.01.54	Motherwell	Portsmouth	07.75	1975-76	27	4	3	(F)
McGUIRE, Bernard P.	Liverpool	23.11.32		Shrewsbury T.	07.53	1953	2		0	
McGUIRE, Gary J.	York	30.09.38	Hakoah (N.S.W.)	Torquay U.	02.66	1965–66	32	/	0	(G)
McGUIRE, Mick	Blackpool	04.09.52	JNRS	Coventry C.	11.69	1971-74	60	12	1	(M)E.YTH.INT.
			TR	Norwich C.	01.75	1974-82	172	10	10	
			TR	Barnsley	03.83	1982-83	43	/	6	
McGUIRE, Reg A.	Birkenhead	24.08.59		Tranmere Rov.	N/C	1982	0	4	0	
MacHALE, John	Odiham	07.05.54	Alton T.	Reading	AM	1974	1	/	0	(CH)
McHALE, Kevin J.	Darfield	01.10.39	JNRS	Huddersfield T.	10.56	1956-67	345	/	60	(OR)E.YTH. INT./●
			TR	Crewe Alex.	01.68	1967-70	116	/	22	E.SCH.INT.
			TR	Chester C.	10.70	1970-71	61	3	5	
McHALE, Ray	Sheffield	12.08.50		Chesterfield	09.71	1971-74	123	1	27	(M)
			TR	Halifax T.	10.74	1974-76	86	/	21	
			TR	Swindon T.	09.76	1976-79	171	2	33	
			TR	Brighton & H.A.	05.80	1980	9	2	0	
			TR	Barnsley	03.81	1980-81	52	1	1	
			TR	Sheffield U.	08.82	1982-83	54	/	1	
			L	Bury	02.83	1982	6	/	0	
McHALE, Tom A.	Liverpool	03.09.51	Prescot Cables	Bradford C.	09.71	1971–72	34	2	0	(FB)
McHALE, William	E. Fife	09.08.29		Carlisle U.	08.53	1953	1		0	
				Halifax T.	03.55	1954	3		0	

Players Names	Birthplace	Date	Previous Club	League Club	Date Signed	Seasons Played	Career Record Apps	Sub	Gls	
McHARD, Archie	Dumbarton	10.06.34	Clyde	Bradford P.A.	05.59	1959–60	27		3	(F)
MACHENT, Stan C.	Chesterfield	23.03.21		Sheffield U.	*	1946–47	22		2	
			TR	Chesterfield	11.47	1947–48	21		7	
MACHIN, Alec H.	Hampstead	06.07.20	Hampshire Reg't	Chelsea	+	1946–47	53		8	(WH)
			TR	Plymouth Arg.	06.48	1948–50	26		1	
MACHIN, Ernie	Little Hulton	26.04.44	Nelson	Coventry C.	03.62	1962–72	254	2	32	(IF)
			TR	Plymouth Arg.	12.72	1972–73	57	/	6	
			TR	Brighton & H.A.	08.74	1974–75	64	/	2	
MACHIN, Mel	Stoke	16.04.45	JNRS	Port Vale	07.62	1962-65	29	1	6	(M)
			TR	Gillingham	07.66	1966–70	155	1	11	
			TR	Bournemouth	12.70	1970–73	110		7	
			TR	Norwich C.	12.73	1973-77	93	3	4	
McILHATTON, John	Ardrossan	03.01.21	Albion Rov.	Everton	+	1946–48	55		1	d.1954
McILMOYLE, Hugh	Cambuslang	29.01.40	Port Glasgow	Leicester C.	08.59	1960–61	20		5	(CF)
			TR	Rotherham U.	07.62	1962	12		4	
			TR	Carlisle U.	03.63	1962–64	77		44	
			TR	Wolverhampton W.	10.64	1964–66	90	/	35	
			TR	Bristol C.	03.67	1966–67	20	/	4	
			TR	Carlisle U.	09.67	1967–69	79	/	30	
			TR	Middlesbrough	09.69	1969–70	69	1	19	
			TR	Preston N.E.	07.71	1971–72	59	1	10	
			Morton	Carlisle U.	07.74	1974	15	3	2	
McILROY, Jimmy	Lambeg	25.10.31	Glentoran	Burnley	03.50	1950–62	437		114	(IF) NI–55/E.F.LGE REP.●
			TR	Stoke C.	03.63	1962–65	96	2	16	
			TR	Oldham Ath.	03.66	1965–67	35	1	1	
McILROY, Sam B.	Belfast	02.08.54	APP	Manchester U.	08.71	1971-81	320	22	57	(M)NI-75●
			TR	Stoke C.	02.82	1981-83	98	1	12	
McILVENNY, Edward	Glasgow	21.10.24		Wrexham	03.47	1946–47	7		1	(WH) U.S.A. INT.
			Philadelphia Nats	Manchester U.	08.50	1950	2		0	
McILVENNY, Harry J.	Bradfdord	05.10.22	Yorks Amats.	Bradford P.A.	AM	1946–49	43		16	(F) E.AMAT.INT.
McILVENNY, John A.	Hinckley	02.03.30	Hinckley U.	W.B.A.	10.49					(OR)
			TR	Bristol Rov.	07.52	1952–58	79		11	
			TR	Reading	06.59	1959–60	77		4	
McILVENNY, Pat D.	Belfast	11.09.24	Merthyr Tydfil	Cardiff C.	05.50					(WH)
			TR	Brighton & H.A.	07.51	1951–54	61		5	
			TR	Aldershot	12.55	1955–56	17		0	
McILVENNY, Robert	Belfast	07.07.26	Merthyr Tydfil	Oldham Ath.	03.50	1949–53	139		31	(IF)Brother of Pat
			TR	Bury	08.54	1954	12		1	
			TR	Southport	08.55	1955–56	77		16	
			TR	Barrow	07.57	1957–58	43		11	
McILWAIN, Matt	Glasgow	20.09.20		Reading	09.50					(HB)
			Ayr	Bolton W.	08.51	1952	2		0	
McILWRAITH, Jim M.	Troon	17.04.54	Motherwell	Bury	09.75	1975-77	80	9	21	(M)
			TR	Portsmouth	07.79	1978	16	3	0	
			TR	Bury	07.79	1979	28	1	3	
			TR	Halifax T.	10.80	1980-81	33	3	6	
McINALLY, Charles	Glasgow	01.02.39	St. Rochs	Brentford	09.58	1959	1		0	(HB)
McINALLY, John S.	Gatehouse of Fleet	29.06.51	JNRS	Manchester U.	03.69					(G) S.SCH.INT
			TR	Lincoln C.	08.70	1970–71	22	/	0	
			TR	Colchester U.	11.72	1972	27	/	0	
McINCH, Jim	Glasgow	27.06.53	JNRS	Cardiff C.	08.70	1972–74	11	2	0	(IF)
McINDEWAR, Archie	Glasgow	26.07.21	Glasgow Rgrs.	Workington	08.51	1951	20		0	(G)
McINNES, Graham J.	Aberdeen	07.04.38	Aberdeen	Bury	06.59	1960	1		0	(F)
McINNES, Ian	Hamilton	22.03.67	APP	Rotherham U.	APP	1983	1	1	0	(W)
McINNES, John	Ayr	29.03.23	Partick Th.	Bradford C.	05.49	1949–50	21		6	(F)
McINNES, John S.	Glasgow	11.08.27	Morton	Chelsea	05.47	1946–49	37		5	(IF)
McINNES, Joseph C.	Glasgow	09.12.32	Partick Th.	Accrington St.	03.56	1955	14		2	
McINNES, William	Lesmahagow	20.05.31	Alloa Ath.	Accrington St.	10.55	1955–60	177		0	(G)
			TR	Southport	07.61	1961–62	26		0	
McINTOSH, Alan	Llandudno	29.07.39	Llandudno	Cardiff C.	06.62	1961–63	64		11	(W) W.AMAT.INT.
McINTOSH, Albert	Dundee	06.04.30		Swansea C.	03.54	1953–56	14		3	(CF)
McINTOSH, Alex	Dunfermline	14.04.16	Folkestone	Wolverhampton W.	*	1946	3		0	(IF)
			TR	Birmingham C.	01.47	1946–47	23		4	
			TR	Coventry C.	02.48	1947–48	20		3	
McINTOSH, Alex J.	Aberdeen	19.10.23	Dundee	Barrow	04.47	1946–49	89		1	(FB)
			TR	Carlisle U.	10.49	1949–54	228		4	
McINTOSH, Dave	Girvan	04.05.25	Girvan Ath.	Sheffield Wed.	10.47	1947–57	294		0	(G)
			TR	Doncaster Rov.	01.58	1957–58	15		0	
McINTOSH, James M.	Dumfries	05.04.18	Blackpool(*)	Preston N.E.	*					(CF)
			TR	Blackpool	05.46	1946–48	69		25	
			TR	Everton	03.49	1948–50	58		19	

Players Names	Birthplace	Date	Previous Club	League Club	Date Signed	Seasons Played	Apps	Sub	Gls	
McINTOSH, James W.	Forfar	19.08.50	Montrose	Nottingham F.	10.70	1970-75	45	8	2	(W)
			L	Chesterfield	01.76	1975	3	/	0	
			TR	Hull C.	03.76	1975-76	20	/	1	
McINTOSH, Malcolm	Oxford	06.07.59	APP	Oxford U.	07.77	1978-80	53	3	0	(D)
			Kettering	Oxford U.	N/C	1982	2	/	0	
McINTOSH, McGregor J.	Glasgow	14.09.33	Partick Th.	Bury	12.57	1957–58	29		13	(F)
McINTOSH, William D.	Glasgow	07.12.19	St. Johnstone	Preston N.E.	05.46	1946–48	91		46	(CF)
			TR	Blackpool	01.49	1948–51	51		12	
			TR	Stoke C.	09.51	1951–52	26		6	
			TR	Walsall	11.52	1952	22		9	
McINTYRE, James	Motherwell	22.03.33	Albion Rov.	Accrington St.	03.57	1956	4		0	(G)
McINTYRE, Patrick F.	Canterbury	14.03.43	JNRS	Gillingham	07.61	1960–62	11		0	(FB)
McIVOR, Ron W.	Edinburgh	23.03.51	E. Fife	Wigan Ath.	10.79	1979	3	/	1	(D)
McIVORY, Fred	Birtley	14.02.52	APP	Sunderland	04.69	1971	1	/	0	(WH)
			Racing Jet.	Sheffield Wed.	07.74	1974–75	34	3	0	
McJANNET, W. Les	Cumnock	02.08.61		Mansfield T.	08.79	1979–81	73	1	0	(D)
McJARROW, Hugh	Motherwell	29.01.28	Mary Hill	Chesterfield	+	1946–49	33		9	(CF)
			TR	Sheffield Wed.	03.50	1949–51	46		21	
			TR	Luton T.	02.52	1951–53	15		10	
			TR	Plymouth Arg.	12.53	1953–55	30		3	
MACKAY, Angus M.	Glasgow	24.04.25	Hamilton	Ipswich T.	05.46	1946	5		0	(OL)
			TR	Exeter C.	09.47	1947–54	257		79	
			TR	Millwall	06.55	1955	17		4	
MACKAY, Dave C.	Edinburgh	14.11.34	Hearts	Tottenham H.	03.59	1958–67	268	/	42	(WH) S–22/S.U23–4/●
			TR	Derby Co.	07.68	1968–70	122	1	5	S.F.LGE REP./
			TR	Swindon T.	05.71	1971	25	1	1	S.SCH.INT.
McKAY, Derek	Banff	13.12.49	Aberdeen	Barrow	09.71	1971	18	/	0	(W)
MACKAY, Donald S.	Partick	19.03.40	Dundee U.	Southend U.	07.72	1972–73	13	/	0	(G)
McKAY, James	Stirling	11.06.18		Tranmere Rov.	08.49	1949	12		1	
McKAY, Joffre	Conan Bridge	21.01.37	Ross Co.	Bury	12.58					(G)
			TR	Rochdale	07.60	1960	9		0	
McKAY, John	Port Glasgow	27.06.27	Irvine	Q.P.R.	03.49	1949–51	16		1	(OL)
McKAY, Peter W.	Newburgh	23.02.25	Dundee U.	Burnley	05.54	1954–56	60		35	(CF)
MACKAY, Robert	Harthill	06.05.48	Harthill	Leicester C.	05.65	1968	6	1	1	(HB)
McKAY, William	Rothesay	10.03.27	Deal T.	Q.P.R.	07.55	1955	6		0	
McKECHNIE, Ian H.	Lenzie	04.10.41	JNRS	Arsenal	05.59	1961–63	23		0	(G)
			TR	Southend U.	05.64	1964–65	62	/	0	
			TR	Hull C.	08.66	1966–73	255	/	0	
McKECHNIE, Tom S.	Milngavie	09.02.40	Kirkintilloch	Luton T.	05.61	1961–65	129	2	31	(F)
			TR	Bournemouth	07.66	1966	14	/	2	
			TR	Colchester U.	09.67	1967	23	1	5	
McKEE, Frank	Cowdenbeath	25.01.23	Dundee U.	Birmingham C.	02.48	1948–50	23		0	(WH)
			TR	Gillingham	07.52	1952–54	53		0	
McKEE, Ray	Plaistow	16.06.26	Finchley	Northampton T.	AM	1946	5		0	(G)
McKEE, Steve	Belfast	15.04.56	Linfield	Sheffield U.	12.76	1976	4	3	0	(M)
McKEE, William A.	Warrington	06.06.28		Blackburn Rov.	11.49	1950	1		0	
			TR	Newport Co.	07.53					
McKEENAN, A. Peter	Kilbirnie	08.01.23	Port Glasgow	Orient	06.46	1946	1		0	
McKELLAR, David N.	Irvine	22.05.56	APP	Ipswich T.	03.74					(G)
			Ardrossan	Derby Co.	04.78	1978–79	41	/	0	
			TR	Brentford	09.80	1980-81	84	/	0	
			TR	Carlisle U.	08.83	1983	42	/	0	
MACKEN, Anthony	Dublin	30.07.50	Waterford	Derby Co.	08.74	1975-77	20	3	1	(D)EI-1
			L	Portsmouth	11.75	1975	10	/	1	
			TR	Walsall	10.77	1977-81	190	/	1	
McKENNA, Alan M.	Edinburgh	04.08.61	APP	Millwall	10.78	1978-81	23	7	4	(F)
McKENNA, Frank	Blaydon	08.01.33	B. Auckland	Leeds U.	07.56	1956	6		4	(W) E.AMAT.INT
			TR	Carlisle U.	02.58	1957–58	45		12	
			TR	Hartlepool U.	07.59	1959	32		5	
McKENNA, John	Belfast	06.06.26	Linfield	Huddersfield T.	09.48	1948–52	134		10	(OR) N1–7/d.1980
			TR	Blackpool	07.54	1954–56	25		2	
			TR	Southport	07.57	1957	15		1	
McKENNA, Ken	Birkenhead	02.07.60		Tranmere Rov.	N/C	1982	2	2	0	(M)
McKENNA, Mike			Bromsgrove	Northampton T.	07.46	1946	4		0	
McKENNA, Patrick	Glasgow	26.04.20	Aberdeen	Plymouth Arg.	08.52	1952	1		0	
McKENNA, Tom	Paisley	11.11.19	St. Mirren	Reading	06.46	1946–47	28		1	
			TR	Grimsby T.	06.48	1948–49	50		2	

Players Names	Birthplace	Date	Previous Club	League Club	Date Signed	Seasons Played	Career Record Apps	Sub	Gls	
McKENNAN, Peter S.	Airdrie	16.07.18	Partick Th.	W.B.A.	10.47	1947	11		4	(IF) S.F.LGE.REP
			TR	Leicester C.	03.48	1947–48	18		7	
			TR	Brentford	09.48	1948	24		6	
			TR	Middlesbrough	05.49	1949–50	40		18	
			TR	Oldham Ath.	07.51	1951–53	78		28	
MacKENZIE, Aiden	Athlone	15.07.59	Galway Rov.	Lincoln C.	12.78	1979	4	2	0	(F)
MacKENZIE, Don A.	Liverpool	30.01.42		Everton	01.63					(F)
			TR	Rochdale	10.63	1963–64	41		7	
McKENZIE, Don C.	Glasgow	09.06.27	Glasgow Rgrs.	Grimsby T.	08.51	1951	4		0	(IF)
McKENZIE, Duncan	Grimsby	10.06.50	JNRS	Nottingham F.	07.68	1969–73	105	6	41	(F)
			L	Mansfield T.	03.70	1969	7	3	3	
			L	Mansfield T.	02.73	1972	6	/	7	
			TR	Leeds U.	08.74	1974–75	64	2	27	
			Anderlecht	Everton	12.76	1976–77	48	/	14	
			TR	Chelsea	09.78	1978	15	/	4	
			TR	Blackburn Rov.	03.79	1978–80	74	/	16	
MacKENZIE, Hamish J.T.	Denny	11.03.45	APP	Liverpool	03.62					(FB)
			Dunfermline	Brentford	08.64	1965–66	19	/	0	
MacKENZIE, Ian S.	Rotherham	27.09.50	JNRS	Sheffield U.	06.68	1969–73	43	2	1	(D)
			L	Southend U.	03.75	1974	5	1	0	
			TR	Mansfield T.	07.75	1975–77	69	1	1	
McKENZIE, John A.	Glasgow	04.09.25	Partick Th.	Bournemouth	08.47	1947	38		9	(W) S–9/S.F.LGE.REP
McKENZIE, Malcolm J.	Edinburgh	01.05.50	JNRS	Port Vale	05.67	1965–67	7	1	0	(F)
McKENZIE, Matt L.	Kilpatrick	07.07.24		Sheffield Wed.	+	1946–47	6		0	(IF)
			TR	Grimsby T.	07.49	1949–51	58		11	
MacKENZIE, Steve	Romford	23.11.61	APP	Crystal Palace	07.79					(M)E.YTH.INT./E.U'21-3
			TR	Manchester C.	07.79	1979–80	56	2	8	
			TR	W.B.A.	08.81	1981–83	56	1	9	
McKEOWN, I. Lindsay	Belfast	11.07.57	APP	Manchester U.	07.74					(F)
			TR	Sheffield Wed.	07.76	1976–77	6	5	0	
McKEOWN, Joe	Bannockburn	09.04.24	Stirling A.	Hartlepool U.	08.50	1950	46		7	(IF)
McKEOWN, Tom	Cleland	02.10.30	Q. of South	Accrington St.	05.54	1954	11		2	(OR)
MACKIE, Tom F.	Burntisland	30.03.18	St. Johnstone	New Brighton	05.47	1947	2		0	
			TR	Chester C.	08.48	1948	5		0	
McKIM, John	Greenock	22.01.26	Port Glasgow	Chelsea	06.47					(IF)
			TR	Colchester U.	08.50	1950–54	129		42	
MACKIN, John	Glasgow	18.11.43		Northampton T.	11.63	1965–68	95	9	11	(FB)
			TR	Lincoln C.	07.69	1969	3	/	0	
			TR	York C.	09.69	1969–72	157	3	7	
			TR	Darlington	03.73	1972	2	/	0	
McKINLAY, Ian J.	Liverpool	21.06.49	Wrexham (AM)	Southport	09.66	1966–67	11	1	1	(OR)
McKINLAY, Robert	E. Fife	10.10.32	Bowhill Rov.	Nottingham F.	10.49	1951–69	611	3	9	(CH)●
McKINNEY, William	Newcastle	20.07.36	Wallsend St. L.	Newcastle U.	05.56	1957–64	85		6	(FB)
			TR	Bournemouth	08.65	1965	17	/	0	
			TR	Mansfield T.	07.66	1966–67	51	1	2	
McKINVEN, John J.	Campbeltown	01.05.41	Raith Rov.	Southend U.	05.60	1960–69	284	2	62	(OL)
			TR	Cambridge U.	N/L	1970	18		2	
MACKLEWORTH, Colin	Bow	24.03.47	APP	West Ham U.	04.64	1966	3	/	0	(G)
			TR	Leicester C.	11.67	1967–70	6	/	0	
McKNIGHT, George	Belfast	17.11.23	Linfield	Blackpool	06.46	1946–53	41		9	(CF)
			TR	Chesterfield	07.55	1955	5		1	
			TR	Southport	09.57	1957	1		0	
McKNIGHT, Phil	Kamladrie	15.06.24	Alloa Ath.	Chelsea	01.47	1947–53	33		1	(WH)
			TR	Orient	07.54	1954–58	162		1	
MACKRETH, Steve	Wrexham	01.07.50	JNRS	Wrexham	10.67	1968	1	1	0	(FB)
McLACHLAN, Dougald	Falkirk	10.09.53	APP	Preston N.E.	11.71					(F)
			L	Halifax T.	10.72	1972	1	1	0	
			TR	Peterborough U.	07.73	1973	1	/	0	
McLACHLAN, Steve	Kirkcudbright	19.09.18	Dalbeattie	Derby Co.	*	1946–52	60		1	(WH)
McLAFFERTY, Maurice	Lanark	07.08.22		Sheffield U.	08.51	1951	18		0	
			TR	Brighton & H.A.	07.52	1952	21		0	
McLAIN, Tom	Linton	19.01.22	Ashington	Sunderland	08.46	1946–51	67		1	(WH)
			TR	Northampton T.	07.52	1952–55	96		10	
McLAREN, Andy	Larkhall	24.01.22	JNRS	Preston N.E.	*	1946–48	69		29	(IF) S–4
			TR	Burnley	12.48	1948	3		1	
			TR	Sheffield U.	03.49	1948–50	31		4	
			TR	Barrow	02.51	1950–54	155		52	
			TR	Bradford P.A.	10.54	1954	18		7	
			TR	Southport	06.55	1955	4		1	
			TR	Rochdale	11.55	1955–56	42		12	

Players Names	Birthplace	Date	Previous Club	League Club	Date Signed	Seasons Played	Career Record Apps	Sub	Gls	
MacLAREN, Dave	Auchterarder	12.06.34	Dundee	Leicester C.	01.57	1956–59	85		0	(G)
			TR	Plymouth Arg.	06.60	1960–64	131		0	
			TR	Wolverhampton W.	01.65	1964–66	44	/	0	
			TR	Southampton	09.66	1966	24	/	0	
McLAREN, Eddie	Dundee	08.09.29	Dunkeld J.	Blackpool	06.48					(WH)
			TR	Reading	10.52	1953–58	185		2	
McLAREN, Hugh	Hamilton	24.06.26	Kilmarnock	Derby Co.	10.49	1949–53	118		52	(OL)
			TR	Nottingham F.	01.54	1953–54	33		15	
			TR	Walsall	07.55	1955	31		8	
McLAREN, James D.	Birkenhead	29.07.36	Wigan Ath.	Chesterfield	06.58	1959	11		1	(F)
McLAREN, Robert	Chryston	05.08.29		Cardiff C.	02.50	1949	1		0	
			TR	Scunthorpe U.	08.51	1951	6		0	
McLAREN, Ross	Edinburgh	14.04.62	Glasgow Rgrs.	Shrewsbury T.	08.80	1980-83	116	3	12	(M)
McLAREN, Roy J.J.	Auchterarder	12.02.30	St Johnstone	Bury	12.55	1955–58	86		0	(G)
			TR	Sheffield Wed.	10.58	1958–63	31		0	
MacLAREN, Scott J.	Crieff	26.11.21	Berwick Rgrs.	Chester C.	01.47	1946–48	30		0	(G)
			TR	Carlisle U.	12.48	1948–54	261		0	
McLAREN, Tom	Livingston	01.06.49		Port Vale	11.67	1967-76	301	32	28	(M) d.1978
McLARTY, Jesse J.	Ayr.	03.03.20	Chester C. (+)	Wrexham	+	1946–47	24		9	(IF)
McLAUGHLAN, Alex D.	Kinwinning	17.07.36	Kilmarnock	Sunderland	09.64	1964–65	43	/	0	(G) S.F. LGE.REP
McLAUGHLAN, John I.	Stirling	03.01.48	Falkirk	Everton	10.71	1971–75	59	2	1	(FB)
McLAUGHLIN, Anthony	Liverpool	24.09.46	JNRS	Everton	02.64					(F)
			TR	Wrexham	07.66	1966–67	27	2	9	
			TR	Chester C.	10.67	1967	2	2	0	
McLAUGHLIN, Hugh	Glasgow	02.09.43	St. Rochs	Brentford	09.61	1963–65	4	1	0	(WH)
McLAUGHLIN, James	Paisley	11.02.26	Glasgow Celtic	Walsall	06.48	1948–49	15		0	(CH)
McLAUGHLIN, James	Stirling	10.12.26		Hartlepool U.	07.53	1953	13		2	
McLAUGHLIN, James C.	Londonderry	22.12.40	Derry C.	Birmingham C.	06.58					(W) N1–12/N1.U23–2
			TR	Shrewsbury T.	07.60	1960–62	124		56	
			TR	Swansea C.	05.63	1963–66	120	3	45	
			TR	Peterborough U.	03.67	1966	8	/	2	
			TR	Shrewsbury T.	09.67	1967–72	159	14	21	
			TR	Swansea C.	11.72	1972–73	20	8	2	
McLAUGHLIN, John	Lennoxtown	13.11.36	Morton	Millwall	07.63	1963	21		5	(CF)
McLAUGHLIN, John	Edmonton	29.10.54	APP	Colchester U.	05.72	1971-73	66	/	2	(D)E.YTH.INT.
			TR	Swindon T.	12.73	1973-78	199	3	8	
			TR	Portsmouth	07.79	1979-83	172	/	1	
McLAUGHLIN, John M.L.	Clarkston	12.04.36	Third Lanark	Shrewsbury T.	09.63	1963	5		0	(G)
McLAUGHLIN, John T.	Liverpool	25.02.52	APP	Liverpool	02.69	1969–73	38	2	2	(IF)
			L	Portsmouth	10.75	1975	5	/	0	
McLAUGHLIN, Joe	Greenock	02.06.60	Morton	Chelsea	06.83	1983	41	/	0	(D)
McLAUGHLIN, Mike A.	Newport	05.01.43		Newport Co.	11.61					(D)
			Lovells Ath.	Newport Co.	08.68	1968-69	90	/	2	
			TR	Hereford U.	N/L	1972-74	84	/	1	
			Cheltenham	Newport Co.	N/C	1977	7	/	0	(M)
McLAUGHLIN, Robert	Belfast	06.12.25	Distillery	Wrexham	01.50	1949	17		0	(WH) IRISH LGE.REP.
			TR	Cardiff C.	04.50	1950–53	48		3	
			TR	Southampton	10.53	1953–58	168		5	
McLAUGHLIN, William J.	U.S.A.	31.01.18		Crewe Alex.	10.46	1946	1		0	d. 1972
McLEAN, Angus	Queensferry	20.09.25	Aberwystwyth	Wolverhampton W.	+	1946–50	144		1	(CH) d. 1979
			Bromsgrove	Bury	05.53	1953	12		0	
			TR	Crewe Alex.	06.54	1954	39		11	
McLEAN, Colin	Stirling	16.05.28	Forfar Ath.	Southport	06.52	1952–53	59		18	(IF)
			TR	Crewe Alex.	07.54	1954	14		0	
McLEAN, David J.	Newcastle	24.11.57	APP	Newcastle U.	11.75	1975-77	7	2	0	(M)E.SCH.INT.
			TR	Carlisle U.	03.78	1977-78	9	6	0	
			TR	Darlington	08.79	1979-83	208	4	27	
McLEAN, Derek J.	Brotton	21.12.32		Middlesbrough	10.52	1955–61	119		30	(OR)
			TR	Hartlepool U.	10.61	1961–63	89		17	
McLEAN, George R.	Paisley	16.09.37	Glasgow Rgrs.	Norwich C.	03.62					(CF)
			TR	Grimsby T.	09.62	1962–64	92		41	
			TR	Exeter C.	06.65	1965–66	47	/	12	
			TR	Workington	01.67	1966–67	53	/	16	
			TR	Barrow	06.68	1968	26	1	9	
McLEAN, Hugh	Larkhall	20.01.52	JNRS	W.B.A.	02.69	1971–72	4	2	0	(IF)
			TR	Swindon T.	07.74	1974	17	2	0	
McLEAN, Jim	Alloa	03.04.34	Alva Rgrs.	Port Vale	03.58	1957	3		0	(F)Brother of Colin
McLEAN, Peter Y.	E. Fife	27.11.23	Bo'ness U.	Reading	01.49	1949–52	70		6	(WH)
			TR	Exeter C	08.53	1953	15		0	
McLEAN, Stewart D.	Barrhead	30.08.23	Partick Th.	Rotherham U.	05.46	1946–47	35		18	(IL)
McLEAN, William	Liverpool	14.08.31	Burscough	Blackburn Rov.	02.53	1953	12		0	(OR)

Players Names	Birthplace	Date	Previous Club	League Club	Date Signed	Seasons Played	Career Record Apps	Sub	Gls	
McLEAN, William			Q. of South	New Brighton	06.47	1947	12		1	
McLEAN, William G.	Dumbarton	14.10.33		Walsall	02.54	1953	2		0	
McLEARY, Alan T.	London	06.10.64	APP	Millwall	10.81	1982-83	25	8	1	(M)E.YTH.INT.
McLEISH, Hugh	Shotts	10.06.48		Sunderland	08.67					(CF)
			TR	Luton T.	11.67	1967	1	/	0	
McLEOD, Alex H. M.	Glasgow	01.01.51	St. Mirren	Southampton	05.73	1973	2	1	0	(IF)
			L	Huddersfield T.	10.74	1974	3	1	1	
McLEOD, Ally	Glasgow	26.02.31	St Mirren	Blackburn Rov.	06.56	1956-60	193		47	(OL)
McLEOD, George J.	Inverness	30.11.32	Inverness	Luton T.	01.55	1955-58	51		6	(OL)
			TR	Brentford	10.58	1958-63	207		20	
			TR	Q.P.R	01.64	1963-64	41		4	
MacLEOD, John M.	Edinbrugh	23.11.28	Hibernian	Arsenal	07.61	1961-64	101		23	(OR) S-4/S.U23-1/
			TR	Aston Villa	09.64	1964-67	123	3	16	S.F.LGE.REP
McLEOD, Norman	Manchester	29.07.30	Hyde U.	Crewe Alex.	08.57	1957-58	25		1	(F)
McLEOD, Robert	Inverness	24.02.47		Hartlepool U.	11.65	1965-68	24	5	0	(HB)
McLEOD, Robert B.				Brighton & H.A.	11.47	1947	1		0	
McLEOD, Sam M.	Glasgow	04.01.34	Easthouses	Colchester U.	06.55	1955-62	156		23	(F)
McLEOD, Tom	Musselburgh	26.12.20		Liverpool	+	1946-48	7		0	(F)
			TR	Chesterfield	07.51	1951	25		3	
McLINTOCK, Frank	Glasgow	28.12.39	Shawfield J.	Leicester C.	01.57	1959-64	168		25	(D)S-9/S.U23-1●
			TR	Arsenal	10.64	1964-72	313	2	26	
			TR	Q.P.R.	06.73	1973-76	126	1	5	
MacLUCKIE, George R.	Falkirk	19.09.31	Lochore Welf	Blackburn Rov.	08.52	1952	20		2	(OL)
			TR	Ipswich T.	05.53	1953-57	141		24	
			TR	Reading	06.58	1958-60	84		8	
McLUCKIE, Robert J.	Doncaster	05.10.55	APP	Doncaster Rov.	10.73	1972-73	2	2	0	(CF)
McMAHON, Des	Reading	22.03.56	Hungerford T.	Reading	N/C	1982	0	2	0	(F)
McMAHON, Francis G.	Belfast	04.01.50	Distillery	Coventry C.	10.69					(IF)
			Waterford	Lincoln C.	07.71	1971-72	54	1	2	
			TR	Darlington	03.73	1972-73	19	4	1	
			L	Hartlepool U.	10.73	1973	7	/	0	
McMAHON, Hugh	Grangetown	24.09.09	Sunderland (*)	Hartlepool U.	+	1946-47	28		7	(OL)*Mexborough/
			TR	Rotherham U.	09.47	1947-48	59		8	Sheffield Wed./Southend/ Reading/Q.P.R.
McMAHON, Ian	Wells	07.10.64	APP	Oldham Ath.	10.82	1982	2	/	0	(D)
			TR	Rochdale	01.84	1983	21	/	1	
McMAHON, John J.	Manchester	07.12.49	APP	Preston N.E.	12.67	1970-78	256	1	7	(D)
			L	Southend U.	09.70	1970	3	/	0	
			L	Chesterfield	09.79	1979	1	/	0	
			TR	Crewe Alex.	10.79	1979-80	67	/	2	
			TR	Wigan Ath.	08.81	1981-82	71	/	5	
			TR	Tranmere Rov.	08.83	1983	39	1	0	
McMAHON, Kevin	Tantobie	01.03.46	Consett	Newcastle U.	08.67					(IF)
			TR	York C.	05.69	1969-71	85	6	31	
			L	Bolton W.	03.72	1971	4	2	1	
			TR	Barnsley	07.72	1972	4	1	0	
			TR	Hartlepool U.	07.73	1973-75	104	3	28	
McMAHON, Patrick	Kilsyth	19.09.45	Glasgow Celtic	Aston Villa	06.69	1969-74	121	8	25	(W)
McMAHON, Peter J.	Marylebone	30.04.34	Chertsey	Orient	05.51	1951-57	64		1	(WH)
			TR	Aldershot	10.58	1958-59	39		0	
McMAHON, Steve	Liverpool	20.08.61	APP	Everton	08.79	1980-82	109	1	11	(M)E.U21-6
			TR	Aston Villa	05.83	1983	37	/	5	
McMANUS, Brendan	Kilkeel	02.12.23	Newry T.	Huddersfield T.	+	1946	1		0	(G)
			TR	Oldham Ath.	07.47	1947	35		0	
			TR	Bradford C.	10.48	1948-52	125		0	
McMANUS, Eddie, J.	Ramsgate	08.08.37	Dover	Bournemouth	08.54	1958-59	4		0	(F)
			TR	Gillingham	08.60	1960	3		0	
McMANUS, Eric C.	Limavady	14.11.50	Coleraine	Coventry C.	08.68	1969-71	6	/	0	(G)NI.AMAT.INT.
			TR	Notts. Co.	05.72	1972-78	229	/	0	
			TR	Stoke C.	10.79	1981	4	/	0	
			L	Lincoln C.	12.79	1979	21	/	0	
			TR	Bradford C.	08.82	1982-83	73	/	0	
McMANUS, Stan	Carlisle	31.10.32		Bury	01.56					
			TR	Southport	07.57	1957	5		0	
McMASTER, Chris	Darlington	16.06.59	APP	Hartlepool U.	07.77	1976-77	3	1	0	(F)
McMICHAEL, Alf	Belfast	01.10.27	Linfield	Newcastle U.	09.49	1949-62	403		1	(FB) NI-40/IRISH LGE REP.●
MacMILLAN, Duncan	Glasgow	18.01.22	Glasgow Celtic	Grimsby T.	03.49	1948-54	188		2	(CH)
McMILLAN, Eric	Beverley	02.11.36		Chelsea	04.58	1959	5		0	(WH)
			TR	Hull C.	07.60	1960-63	150		3	
			TR	Halifax T.	07.65	1965-66	49	1	8	
McMILLAN, George S.	Motherwell	15.03.30	Aberdeen	Wrexham	05.52	1952	1		0	(F)

Players Names	Birthplace	Date	Previous Club	League Club	Date Signed	Seasons Played	Apps	Sub	Gls	
McMILLAN, George S.	Stonehouse	10.08.29	Newarthill J.	Ipswich T.	02.53	1954–57	53		0	(G)
McMILLAN, John S.	Dumbarton	14.04.37	Dumbarton	Cardiff C.	02.58	960	2		0	(F)
			TR	Exeter C.	10.61	1961–62	20		1	
McMILLAN, Paul A.	Lennoxtown	13.07.50	JNRS	Chelsea	08.67	1967	1	/	0	(WH)
McMILLAN, Sam	Belfast	29.09.41	Boyland Y.C.	Manchester U.	11.59	1961–62	15		6	(IF)N1–2/N1.U23·1
			TR	Wrexham	12.63	1963–67	149		52	
			TR	Southend U.	09.67	1967–69	76	1	5	
			TR	Chester C.	12.69	1969	16	2	0	
			TR	Stockport Co.	07.70	1970–71	74	/	29	
McMILLAN, Tom	Glasgow	12.02.31	Glasgow Celtic	Norwich C.	07.54	1954	19		2	(OL)
			TR	Workington	09.55	1955	2		0	
McMILLAN, Tom P.	Auchinleck	16.01.36	Ayr U.	Watford	09.56	1956–57	33		13	(F)
			TR	Carlisle U.	07.58	1958–60	89		7	
McMILLEN, Walter S.	Belfast	24.11.13	Chesterfield(*)	Millwall	+	1946–49	92		0	(WH)*Cliftonville/ Manchester U./N1–7
McMINN, Robert W.	Doncaster	09.10.46	APP	Doncaster Rov.	10.64	1963–65	4	1	0	(FB)
McMORDIE, (Eric) A. A.	Belfast	12.08.46	Dundela	Middlesbrough	09.64	1965–73	231	10	23	(M)NI–21/NI.U23·1
			L	Sheffield Wed.	10.74	1974	9	/	6	
			TR	York C.	05.75	1975-76	42	/	2	
			TR	Hartlepool U.	12.76	1976-77	46	1	2	
McMORRAN, Edward J.	Larne	02.09.23	Belfast Celtic	Manchester C.	08.47	1947–48	33		12	(IF)NI–15/IRISH LGE.REP./ NI SCH INT/d.1984
			TR	Leeds U.	01.49	1948–49	39		6	
			TR	Barnsley	07.50	1950–52	102		32	
			TR	Doncaster Rov.	02.53	1952–57	126		32	
			TR	Crewe Alex.	11.57	1957	24		6	
McMORRAN, James W.	Muirkirk	29.10.42	JNRS	Aston Villa	10.59	1960–61	11		1	(IF)S.SCH.INT.
			T.Lanark	Walsall	11.64	1964–67	95	2	10	
			TR	Swansea C.	06.68	1968	14	/	2	
			TR	Walsall	11.68	1968	9		1	
			TR	Notts Co.	07.69	1969	6	/	0	
			TR	Halifax T.	09.69					
McMORRAN, John	Forth	11.05.34		Bradford C.	12.54	1954	1		0	
McMORRAN, Robert	Forth	12.03.26	Glasgow Rgrs.	Manchester U.	02.47					
			TR	Walsall	02.50	1949–50	10		1	
McMULLEN, David	Denny	13.06.60	Cumbernauld U.	Wigan Ath.	02.80	1979-80	20	7	1	(M)
McMULLEN, David	Harrington	06.01.36		Workington	08.59	1959	1		0	(WH)
McMURRAY, John	Billingham	05.10.31	Billingham	Middlesbrough	05.49	1953–54	3		0	(HB)
McNAB, Alex	Birmingham	06.04.32		Shrewsbury T.	12.54	1954–55	4		0	(WH)S.SCH.INT.
McNAB, Alex	Glasgow	27.12.11	W.B.A.(*)	Newport Co.	+	1946	3		0	(WH)S–2/d.1962/ *Pollock/Sunderland
McNAB, Jim	Denny	13.04.40	JNRS	Sunderland	06.57	1958–66	284	1	12	(WH)S.SCH.INT.●
			TR	Preston N.E.	03.67	1966–73	222	2	6	
			TR	Stockport Co.	07.74	1974–75	30	/	1	
McNAB, Neil	Greenock	04.06.57	Morton	Tottenham H.	02.74	1973-78	63	9	3	(M)S.SCH.INT./S.U21-1
			TR	Bolton W.	11.78	1978-79	33	2	4	
			TR	Brighton & H.A.	02.80	1979-82	100	3	4	
			L	Leeds U.	12.82	1982	5	/	0	
			TR	Manchester C.	07.83	1983	33	/	1	
McNAB, Robert	Huddersfield	20.07.43	Moldgreen Y.C.	Huddersfield T.	04.62	1963–66	68	/	0	(FB)E–4/E.F. LGE.REP
			TR	Arsenal	10.66	1966–74	277	1	4	
			TR	Wolverhampton W.	07.75	1975	13	/	0	
McNAB, Sam	Glasgow	20.10.26	Dalry Th.	Sheffield U.	01.52	1952–53	11		4	
			TR	York C.	05.54	1954	19		3	
McNAB, Tom C.	Glasgow	15.07.33		Nottingham F.	03.54					(HB)
			Partick Th.	Wrexham	03.57	1956–58	43		5	
			TR	Barrow	03.59	1958–60	44		4	
McNALLY, Bernard A.	Shrewsbury	17.02.63	APP	Shrewsbury T.	02.81	1980-83	98	2	6	(M)
McNALLY, Brendan J.	Dublin	22.01.35	Shelbourne	Luton T.	05.56	1956–62	134		2	(FB)E1–3/E1'B'–1
McNALLY, Errol	Lurgan	27.08.43	Portadown	Chelsea	12.61	1961–63	9		0	(G)
McNALLY, Paul A.	Consett	19.12.49	Newcastle U.(AM)	Bradford C.	07.67	1968	1	2	0	(F)
McNAMARA, Anthony	Liverpool	03.10.29		Everton	05.50	1951–57	111		21	(OR)
			TR	Liverpool	12.57	1957	9		3	
			TR	Crewe Alex.	07.58	1958	9		2	
			TR	Bury	09.58	1958	14		0	
McNAMARA, Dennis A.	Liverpool	08.03.35		Tranmere Rov.	11.54	1954	1		0	
McNAMEE, Gerard	Consett	16.08.60		Hartlepool	11.79	1979-82	2	2	1	(F)
McNAMEE, John	Coatbridge	11.06.41	Hibernian	Newcastle U.	12.66	1966–71	115	2	8	(CH)
			TR	Blackburn Rov.	11.71	1971–72	56	/	9	
			Morton	Hartlepool U.	12.73	1973	2	/	0	
			Lancaster C.	Workington	N/C	1975	2	/	0	
McNAMEE, John J.	Edinburgh	31.07.42	Montrose	Reading	12.64					(F)
			Raith Rov.	Tranmere Rov.	08.67	1967–69	67	5	11	

Players Names	Birthplace	Date	Previous Club	League Club	Date Signed	Seasons Played	Apps	Sub	Gls	
McNAMEE, Peter	Glasgow	20.03.35	Lanark A.	Peterborough U.	N/L	1960–65	192	/	60	(OR)
			Kings Lynn	Notts.Co.	01.66	1965	3		0	
McNAUGHT, Ken	Kirkcaldy	11.01.55	APP	Everton	05.72	1974-76	64	2	3	(D)Son of Scot. Int.
			TR	Aston Villa	08.77	1977-82	207	/	8	
			TR	W.B.A.	08.83	1983	42	/	1	
McNEE, Terry A.	Birkenhead	05.06.25	Park Villa	Wrexham	01.57	1946	11		0	(G)
McNEICE, Vince	Cricklewood	02.10.38	JNRS	Watford	03.57	1957–63	231		0	(CH)
McNEIL, David	Chester	14.05.21	Chester Rov.	Chester C.	+	1946–50	114		0	
McNEIL, Hamish	Alva	16.11.34	Bonnyrigg Rose	Colchester U.	08.57	1957	2		1	(F)
McNEIL, Mark S.	Bethnal Green	03.12.62	APP	Orient	12.79	1981-83	72	9	13	(M)
McNEIL, Mick	Middlesbrough	07.02.40	JNRS	Middlesbrough	06.57	1958–63	178		4	(FB)E–9/E.U23–9/
			TR	Ipswich T.	07.64	1964–71	141	5	4	E.F.LGE.REP.
McNEIL, Richard (Dixie)	Melton Mowbray	16.01.47	Holwell Wks.	Leicester C.	11.64					(CF)●
			TR	Exeter C.	06.66	1966	31	/	11	
			Corby T.	Northampton T.	05.69	1969-71	85	1	33	
			TR	Lincoln C.	01.72	1971-73	96	1	53	
			TR	Hereford U.	08.74	1974-77	128	1	85	
			TR	Wrexham	09.77	1977-82	166	1	54	
			TR	Hereford U.	10.82	1982	12	/	3	
McNEIL, Robert M.	Bellshill	01.11.62	APP	Hull C.	11.80	1980-83	111	3	3	(D)
McNEILL, Alan A.	Belfast	16.08.45	Crusaders	Middlesbrough	08.67	1967-68	3	/	0	(M)NI.AMAT.INT.
			TR	Huddersfield T.	11.68	1968	1	1	0	
			TR	Oldham Ath.	10.69	1969-74	154	14	19	
			TR	Stockport Co.	07.75	1975-76	69	2	1	
McNEILL, Brian	Newcastle	01.04.56	APP	Bristol C.	10.74	1975-76	0	3	0	(D)
			TR	Plymouth Arg.	12.78	1978-80	47	/	0	
McNEILL, Edward V.	Warrenpoint	26.03.29	Portadown	Sunderland	12.51	1953	7		0	(G)
McNEILL, Ian M.	Glasgow	24.02.32	Aberdeen	Leicester C.	03.56	1955–58	72		26	(IF)
			TR	Brighton & H.A.	03.59	1958–61	116		12	
			TR	Southend U.	07.62	1962–63	41		3	
McNEILL, Matt A.	Glasgow	28.07.27	Hibernian	Newcastle U.	12.49	1950	9		0	(CH)
			TR	Barnsley	08.51	1951–52	69		1	
			TR	Brighton & H.A.	07.53	1953–55	53		0	
			TR	Norwich C.	03.56	1955–56	44		2	
McNEISH, Sam	Bo'ness	04.08.30	Linlithgow R.	Leeds U.	02.51	1950	1		0	(F)
McNICHOL, Alex	Baillieston	10.10.19	Dunfermline	Aldershot	08.47	1947–50	109		20	(IF)
			TR	Rochdale	01.51	1950	18		3	
McNICHOL, James A.	Glasgow	09.06.58	Ipswich T. (APP)	Luton T.	07.76	1976-78	13	2	0	(D)S.U21-7
			TR	Brentford	10.78	1978-83	·151	4	22	
McNICHOL, John	Kilmarnock	20.08.25	Hurlford J.	Newcastle U.	08.46					(IF)●
			TR	Brighton & H.A.	08.48	1948–51	158		36	
			TR	Chelsea	08.52	1952–57	181		60	
			TR	Crystal Palace	03.58	1957–62	189		15	
McNICOL, Robert H.	Bonhill	13.02.33	E. Stirling	Accrington St.	05.56	1956–58	134		5	(FB)1 app in goal for
			TR	Brighton & H.A.	06.59	1959–61	93		0	Accrington St.
			Gravesend	Carlisle U.	10.63	1963	1		0	
McNIVEN, David S.	Stonehouse	09.09.55	APP	Leeds U.	09.72	1975-77	15	7	6	(F)S.U23-3/S.SCH.INT.
			TR	Bradford C.	02.78	1977-82	202	10	64	
			TR	Blackpool	02.83	1982-83	45	4	11	
McNULTY, Joe	Dundalk	17.07.23	Ards.	Burnley	05.49	1950–51	8		0	(G)
			TR	Sheffield U.	06.52					
McNULTY, Tom	Salford	30.12.20	JNRS	Manchester U.	06.47	1949–53	57		0	(FB)
			TR	Liverpool	02.54	1953–57	36		0	
McNULTY, William G.	Edinburgh	09.02.49	JNRS	Port Vale	04.66	1966	1	/	0	(G)
			TR	Chesterfield	07.68	1968	6	/	0	
McPARLAND, Ian J.	Edinburgh	04.10.61	Ormiston Prim.	Notts. Co.	12.80	1980-83	26	20	3	(F)
MacPARLAND, Peter J.	Newry	25.04.34	Dundalk	Aston Villa	09.52	1952–61	293		98	(OL) NI–34/E.F. LGE.REP.●
			TR	Wolverhampton W.	01.62	1961–62	21		10	
			TR	Plymouth Arg.	01.63	1962–63	38		15	
McPARTLAND, Des	Middlesbrough	05.10.47	APP	Middlesbrough	10.64	1965–67	35	/	0	(G) E.YTH.INT
			TR	Carlisle U.	12.67	1967	5	/	0	
			TR	Northampton T.	07.69	1969	6	/	0	
			TR	Hartlepool U.	03.70	1969–70	56	/	0	
McPEAKE, Matt	Ballymena	19.06.19	Ballymena	Everton	07.46					
			TR	Grimsby T.	06.47					
			TR	New Brighton	07.48	1948–49	53		2	
McPHAIL, John	Dundee	07.12.55	Dundee	Sheffield U.	01.79	1978-82	135	/	7	(D)
			TR	York C.	02.83	1982-83	57	1	12	
McPHEAT, Willie	Caldercruix	04.09.42	JNRS	Sunderland	09.59	1960–62	58		19	(F)
			TR	Hartlepool U.	09.65	1965	13	2	2	
McPHEE, John	Motherwell	21.11.37	Motherwell	Blackpool	07.62	1962–69	249	10	15	(WH)
			TR	Barnsley	06.70	1970	26	/	3	
			TR	Southport	07.71	1971–72	85	/	1	

Players Names	Birthplace	Date	Previous Club	League Club	Date Signed	Seasons Played	Apps	Sub	Gls	
McPHEE, Magnus G.	Edinburgh	30.04.14	Coventry C.(*)	Reading	*	1946–48	90		63	(CF)*Belfast Celtic/ Workington/Bradford P.A.
McPHERSON, Albert	Salford	08.07.27		Bury	06.49					(HB)
			Stalybridge	Walsall	05.45	1954–63	351		8	
McPHERSON, Ian B.	Glasgow	26.07.20	Glasgow Rgrs.	Notts.Co.	+	1946–50	153		19	(W) d.1983
			TR	Arsenal	08.46	1946–50	153		19	
			TR	Notts. Co.	08.51	1951–52	52		17	
			TR	Brentford	07.53	1953	4		0	
McPHERSON, Ken	W. Hartlepool	25.03.27		Notts. Co.	08.50	1950–52	24		0	(CF)
			TR	Middlesbrough	08.53	1953–55	33		15	
			TR	Coventry C.	11.55	1955–57	89		36	
			TR	Newport Co.	06.58	1958–60	128		52	
			TR	Swindon T.	08.61	1961–64	107		3	
McQUADE, Jim	Renfrew	14.10.33	Dumbarton	Halifax T.	08.57	1957	9		2	(F)
McQUADE, Terry J.	Woodberry Down	24.02.41	Enfield	Millwall	10.61	1961–62	34		7	(W)
			TR	Q.P.R.	07.63	1963	20		2	
			Dover T.	Orient	08.65					
			TR	Millwall	11.65	1965	3	/	1	
McQUAID, Tom A.	Dublin	01.02.36		Bradford C.	11.57	1958–59	23		2	(HB)
McQUARRIE, Andy	Glasgow	02.10.39	Albion Rov.	Chesterfield	11.62	1962–63	38		12	(IF)
			TR	Brighton & H.A.	07.64	1964	2	/	1	
McQUEEN, Gordon	Kilbirnie	26.06.52	St. Mirren	Leeds U.	09.72	1972-77	140	/	15	(D)S-30
			TR	Manchester U.	02.78	1977-83	172	/	19	
McQUEEN, Ian	Manchester	04.02.46		Rochdale	01.66	1965–66	13	2	4	(F)
McQUEEN, Tom	Calder	21.02.29	Q.of South	Accrington St.	06.54	1954–56	57		0	(G) Father of Gordon
McQUILLAN, Dennis	Derby	16.03.34	JNRS	Derby Co.	03.51	1952–55	20		1	(OR)
			TR	Aldershot	07.56					
			TR	Luton T.	03.57					
MacQUILLAN, Pat G.	Belfast	27.06.61	Pembroke Bor.	Swansea C.	08.79	1983	19	/	0	(D)
MacRAE, Keith	Glasgow	05.02.51	Motherwell	Manchester C.	10.73	1973-80	56	/	0	(G)S.U23-2/S.F.LGE REP.
			Portland Timbers	Leeds U.	03.82					
McREADY, Brian L.	Leicester	25.03.42	Willerby B.C.	W.B.A.	02.60	1960–63	14		1	(W)
			TR	Mansfield T.	07.64	1964–65	49	1	11	
MACROW, Geoff C.	E. Harling	26.09.32	Thetford T.	Ipswich T.	08.55	1955–56	2		0	
McSEVENEY, John H.	Shotts	08.02.31	Hamilton	Sunderland	10.51	1951–54	35		3	(OL)
			TR	Cardiff C.	05.55	1955–56	75		18	
			TR	Newport Co.	07.57	1957–60	172		51	
			TR	Hull C.	07.61	1961–64	161		60	
McSHANE, Anthony	Belfast	28.02.27	Brantwood	Plymouth Arg.	12.48	1949–54	85		2	(WH)
			TR	Swindon T.	06.55	1955–56	41		0	
McSHANE, Harry	Holytown	08.04.20		Blackburn Rov.	*					(OR) Father of Ian (Famous actor)
			TR	Huddersfield T.	09.46	1946	15		1	
			TR	Bolton W.	07.47	1947–50	93		6	
			TR	Manchester U.	09.50	1950–53	56		8	
			TR	Oldham Ath.	02.54	1953–54	41		5	
McSTAY, Jim G.	Newry	04.08.22	Dundalk	Grimsby T.	08.48	1948–50	61		2	(W) L.O.I. REP
McTAFF, Steve	Tanfield	11.03.22		Bradford P.A.	+	1946–47	29		0	
			TR	New Brighton	07.48	1948–50	100		3	
			TR	York C.	10.51					
McTAVISH, John R.	Glasgow	02.02.32.	Dalry T.	Manchester C.	06.52	1953–59	93		0	(CH)
McTURK, John	Lugar	11.07.36	St Mirren	Wrexham	07.57	1957	2		0	(FB)
McVAY, David R.	Workington	05.03.55	JNRS	Notts. Co.	07.73	1973-78	101	12	2	(D)
			L	Torquay U.	09.77	1977	8	/	0	
			TR	Peterborough U.	07.79	1979-80	47	2	1	
			TR	Lincoln C.	08.81	1981	13	/	0	
McVEIGH, Jim	Bamford	02.07.49		Wolverhampton W.	05.68	1968	2	/	0	(FB)
			TR	Gillingham	10.70	1970–71	48	/	1	
MacVINISH, Tom	Inverness	01.01.21	Hamilton	Preston N.E.	08.48					
				Darlington	08.50	1950	1		0	
McVITIE, George J.	Carlisle	07.09.48	APP	Carlisle U.	12.65	1965-70	124	4	21	(W)E.SCH.INT.
			TR	W.B.A.	08.70	1970-71	42	/	5	
			TR	Oldham Ath.	08.72	1972-75	108	5	19	
			TR	Carlisle U.	12.75	1975-80	191	7	20	
McWHINNIE, Archie	Glasgow	17.07.26	Rutherglen	Wrexham	05.51	1951	2		0	(WH)
MADDEN, Craig	Manchester	25.09.58	Northern Nomads	Bury	03.78	1977-83	198	19	92	(F)
MADDEN, David J.	London	06.01.63	APP	Southampton	01.81					(M)
			L	Bournemouth	01.83	1982	5	/	0	
			TR	Arsenal	08.83	1983	2	/	0	

Players Names	Birthplace	Date	Previous Club	League Club	Date Signed	Seasons Played	Career Record Apps	Sub	Gls	
MADDEN, Lawrie D.	London	28.09.55	Arsenal (AM)	Mansfield T.	N/C	1974-75	9	1	0	(D)
			Manchester Univ.	Charlton Ath.	03.78	1977-81	109	4	7	
			TR	Millwall	03.82	1981-82	44	3	1	
			TR	Sheffield Wed.	08.83	1983	38	/	1	
MADDEN, Neil	Luton	06.02.62	APP	Luton T.	12.79	1979	1	/	0	(M)
MADDEN, Peter	Bradford	31.10.34	Thornton F.C.	Rotherham U.	10.55	1955–65	308	2	7	(CH)
			TR	Bradford P.A.	07.66	1966	25	3	1	
			TR	Aldershot	07.67	1967	26	1	1	
MADDISON, Don	Washington	13.02.27	Sunderland (AM)	Bradford P.A.	06.46					(G)
			TR	Blackpool	02.48					
			TR	Darlington	08.50	1950	1		0	
MADDISON, Frank	Worksop	06.05.34		Notts. Co.	08.53	1956–57	15		0	(FB)
MADDISON, George	Sculcoates	06.10.30		Aldershot	08.48	1948	2		0	(G) Son of George (pre-war)
			TR	York C.	09.52	1953	11		0	
MADDISON, James	Sth. Shields	09.11.24		Middlesbrough	+	1946	1		0	(OL)
			TR	Darlington	08.49	1949	41		7	
			TR	Grimsby T.	06.50	1950–58	272		39	
			TR	Chesterfield	03.59	1958–60	98		16	
MADDISON, John A.	Barrow	01.10.40	Holker C.O.B.	Barrow	09.63	1961–64	88		18	(W)
MADDISON, Ralph	Bentley	28.08.18	Bentley Col	Doncaster Rov.	+	1946–47	61		19	(W)
			TR	Stockport Co	05.48	1948	5		0	
			TR	Southport	02.49	1948–49	34		4	
MADDISON, William H.	Sunderland	06.04.54		Hartlepool U.	AM	1973–74	3	1	0	(OR)
MADDOCK, Cyril	Sandbach	14.06.33	JNRS	Crewe Alex.	05.51	1951	1		0	
MADDREN, Willie D.	Billingham	11.01.51	APP	Middlesbrough	06.68	1968-77	293	2	19	(D).E.U23-5
MADDY, Paul M.	Cwmcarn	17.08.62	APP	Cardiff C.	08.80	1980-82	35	8	3	(M)W.U'21-1
			L	Hereford U.	03.83	1982	9	/	1	
			TR	Swansea C.	08.83	1983	18	2	3	
			TR	Hereford U.	03.84	1983	10	/	1	
MADELEY, Paul	Leeds	20.09.44	Farsley Celtic	Leeds U.	05.62	1963-80	526	8	24	(D)E-24/E.F.LGE● REP./E.YTH.INT.
MAFFEY, Dennis	Sunderland	22.02.22	Walton U.	Ipswich T.	07.47	1947	5		1	(CF)
MAGEE, Eric	Lurgan	24.08.47	Glenavon	Oldham Ath.	06.67	1967–68	42	4	9	(F) N1.AMAT.INT.
			TR	Port Vale	07.69	1969	11	7	1	
MAGGIORE, Anthony	Sunderland	28.10.57	Sunderland (APP)	Hartlepool U.	11.75	1975-76	24	4	0	(D)
MAGILL, Eddie	Carrickfergus	17.05.39	Portadown	Arsenal	05.59	1959–64	116		0	(FB)N1–26/N1 U.23–1
			TR	Brighton & H.A.	10.65	1965–67	50	/	1	
MAGUIRE, James E.	Meadowfield	23.07.17	Willington	Wolverhampton W.	*					(OR)
			TR	Swindon T.	05.47	1947	28		4	
			TR	Halifax T.	10.48	1948–49	55		8	
MAGUIRE, James S.	Eaglesham	03.02.32	Q. of South	Rochdale	08.58	1958	16		0	(OL)
MAGUIRE, Leslie	Bethnal Green	31.1.29		Gillingham	N/L	1950–51	6		2	
MAGUIRE, Paul B.	Glasgow	21.08.56	Kilbirnie Ladeside	Shrewsbury T.	08.76	1976-79	143	8	35	(F)
			TR	Stoke C.	09.80	1980-83	93	14	24	
MAGUIRE, Tom	Dublin	22.7.55	APP	Liverpool	11.72					(IF)
			TR	Crewe Alex.	02.74	1973–75	23	4	1	
MAHER, Aiden	Liverpool	01.12.46	APP	Everton	12.64	1967	1	/	0	(W).E.SCH.INT
			TR	Plymouth Arg.	10.68	1968–70	64	/	3	
			TR	Tranmere Rov.	06.71	1971	2	5	1	
MAHER, John	Manchester	06.11.33	Manchester C. (AM)	Walsall	05.54	1954	1		0	(F)
			TR	Gillingham	07.55	1955	2		1	
MAHON, Mike J.	Manchester	17.09.44	N. Shields	Port Vale	04.67	1966–68	91	1	22	(W) E. AMAT.INT
			TR	York C.	07.69	1969	27	2	10	
			TR	Colchester U.	05.70	1970–73	131	5	26	
MAHONEY, Brian	Tantobie	12.05.52	APP	Huddersfield T.	11.69	1970–71	18	2	2	(IF)
			TR	Barnsley	03.72	1971–74	82	8	15	
MAHONEY, John F.	Cardiff	20.09.46	Ashton U.	Crewe Alex.	03.66	1965-66	16	2	5	(M)W-51/W.U23-3●
			TR	Stoke C.	03.67	1966-76	272	12	25	
			TR	Middlesbrough	08.77	1977-78	77	/	1	
			TR	Swansea C.	07.79	1979-82	106	4	1	
MAHONEY, Mike J.	Bristol	25.10.50	APP	Bristol C.	08.68	1967-69	4	/	0	(G)
			TR	Torquay U.	08.70	1970-74	157	/	0	
			TR	Newcastle U.	03.75	1974-78	108	/	0	
MAHONEY, Tony	Barking	29.09.59	APP	Fulham	08.77	1976-80	53	6	10	(F)
			L	Northampton T.	10.81	1981	6	/	0	
			TR	Brentford	07.82	1982-83	33	8	11	
MAHY, Barry	Doncaster	21.01.42	North.Ath	Scunthorpe U.	05.63	1963–66	21	1	2	(F)
MAIDMENT, Ian M.	Newbury	09.08.47	APP	Reading	08.65	1965	7	/	0	(F)
MAIL, David	Bristol	12.09.62	APP	Aston Villa	07.80					(D)
			TR	Blackburn Rov.	01.82	1982-83	42	3	1	
MAILER, Ron G.	Auchterarder	18.05.32	Dunfermline	Darlington	03.54	1954	11		2	

Players Names	Birthplace	Date	Previous Club	League Club	Date Signed	Seasons Played	Career Record Apps	Sub	Gls	
MAILEY, William	Duntochter	13.06.43	JNRS	Everton	06.60					(G) S.SCH.INT
			TR	Crewe Alex.	03.63	1963–69	215	/	0	
MAIN, Ian	Swindon	31.10.59	Gloucester C.	Exeter C.	08.79	1978-81	78	/	0	(G)
MAIR, Gordon	Coatbridge	18.12.58	APP	Notts. Co.	12.76	1976-83	123	8	18	(M)S.SCH.INT.
MAITLAND, Lloyd C.	Coleshill	21.03.57	APP	Huddersfield T.	03.74	1974-76	31	8	2	(W)
			TR	Darlington	03.77	1976-78	58	13	6	
MAJOR, Jack L.	Islington	12.03.29	Hull Amats	Hull C.	AM	1946	3		0	(W) E.AMAT.INT
			B. Auckland	Hull C.	06.55	1955–56	10		0	
MAJOR, Leslie D.	Yeovil	25.01.26		Leicester C.	+	1947–48	26		0	(G)
			TR	Plymouth Arg.	05.49	1949–55	75		0	
MAKEPEACE, Brian	Rossington	06.10.31	Rossington Col	Doncaster Rov.	03.49	1950–60	353		0	(FB)
MAKIN, Joe	Manchester	21.09.50	APP	Oldham Ath.	10.67	1966–67	6	/	0	(F)
MAKIN, Sam H.	Radcliffe	14.11.25	Moss Rov.	Rochdale	+	1946	5		1	(W) d. 1981
MALAM, Albert	Liverpool	20.01.13	Doncaster Rov.(*)	Wrexham	+	1946	6		1	(IF)*Colwyn Bay/ Chesterfield/Huddersfield T.
MALAN, Norman F.	S. Africa	23.11.23	S. Africa	Middlesbrough	+	1946	2		0	(G)
			TR	Darlington	08.48					
			TR	Scunthorpe U.	06.50	1950–55	136		0	
			TR	Bradford P.A.	07.57	1956	24		0	
MALCOLM, Alex M.	Alloa	15.12.21	Alloa Ath.	Barnsley	06.46	1946–47	5		0	
MALCOLM, Alex A.	Hamilton	13.02.56	APP	Luton T.	07.73					(D)
			TR	Northampton T.	08.76	1976	2	/	0	
MALCOLM, Andy	West Ham U.	04.05.33	JNRS	West Ham U.	07.50	1953–61	283		4	(WH)E.F.LGE.REP./ E.YTH.INT./E.SCH.INT
			TR	Chelsea	11.61	1961	27		1	
			TR	Q.P.R.	10.62	1962–64	84		4	
MALCOLM, Grant W.	Musselburgh	25.10.40	Dalkeith Th.	Newcastle U.	11.57	1959	1		0	(F)S.SCH.INT
MALCOLM, John M.	Clackmannan	20.05.17		Accrington St.	+	1946	25		0	
			TR	Tranmere Rov.	07.47	1947	22		0	
MALCOLM, Ken C.	Aberdeen	25.07.26	Arbroath	Ipswich T.	05.54	1954–62	274		2	(FB) + St.Clements/ Wolverhampton W.
MALE, Charles G.	W. Ham	08.05.10	Clapton	Arsenal	*	1946–47	23		0	(FB) E–19/E.F.LGE.REP.
MALE, Norman A.	W. Bromwich	27.05.17	W.B.A.(*)	Walsall	*	1946–48	36		2	(FB)*Bush Rov
MALKIN, John	Stoke	09.11.25		Stoke C.	07.47	1947–55	175		23	(IF)
MALLALIEU, Anthony P.	Prestatyn	03.10.46	Rhyl	Manchester U.	06.64					(F)
				Stockport Co.	03.70	1969	0	1	0	
MALLENDER, Gary	Barnsley	12.03.59	APP	Barnsley	03.77	1976-78	0	2	0	(D)
MALLENDER, Ken	Thrybergh	10.12.43	APP	Sheffield U.	02.61	1961–68	142	2	2	(FB)
			TR	Norwich C.	10.68	1968–70	46	/	1	
			TR	Hereford U.	N/L	1972–73	71	1	1	
MALLETT, Joe	Gateshead	08.01.16	Charlton Ath.(*)	Q.P.R.	*	1946	27		7	(WH)
			TR	Southampton	02.47	1946–52	215		3	
			TR	Orient	07.53	1953–54	27		1	
MALLEY, Phil	Felling	01.11.65	Sunderland (APP)	Hartlepool U.	11.83	1983	0	1	0	
			TR	Burnley	02.84	1983	1	1	0	
MALLINSON, David J.	Sheffield	07.07.46	JNRS	Mansfield T.	09.65	1965	10	1	0	(HB)
MALLINSON, Trevor	Huddersfield	25.04.45	Huddersfield T.(AM)	Halifax T.	AM	1964	3		0	(FB)
MALLON, Jim G.	Glasgow	28.08.38	Partick Th.	Oldham Ath.	03.59	1958–59	31		8	(FB)
			Morton	Barrow	10.65	1965–68	149	1	3	
MALLORY, Richard J.L.	Paget	10.08.42	Bermuda	Cardiff C.	05.63	1963	3		0	(F)
MALLOY, Danny	Dennyloan	06.11.30	Dundee	Cardiff C.	10.53	1955–60	225		1	(CH)S'B'–2/S.F.LGE.REP
			TR	Doncaster Rov.	08.61	1961	42		0	
MALONE, Richard	Carfin	22.08.47	Ayr U.	Sunderland	10.70	1970-76	235	1	2	(D)S.U23-1
			TR	Hartlepool U.	07.77	1977-78	36	/	1	
			TR	Blackpool	11.78	1978-79	48	/	1	
MALONEY, Derek T.	Newton	27.03.36		Crewe Alex.	02.58	1957	15		0	
MALONEY, Joe J.	Liverpool	26.01.34	JNRS	Liverpool	01.51	1952–53	12		0	(CH)
			TR	Shrewsbury T.	07.54	1954–59	237		0	
			TR	Port Vale	07.61	1961	1		0	
			TR	Crewe Alex.	08.61	1961–62	26		0	
MALONEY, Paul J.	Edlington	13.01.52	APP	Huddersfield T.	11.69					(IF)
			TR	York C.	02.70	1969–71	2	5	0	
MALONEY, Sean	Hyde	04.10.62	JNRS	Stockport Co.	N/C	1979	0	1	0	(F)
MALOY, Ken F.	London	16.09.40	Ilford	Plymouth Arg.	09.59	1960–63	62		11	(OL)
			TR	Peterborough U.	07.64	1964	6		1	
			TR	Aldershot	07.65	1965–66	51	1	12	
MALPASS, Frank L.	Consett	16.10.32	JNRS	Gateshead	10.49	1949	3		0	(G)
MALPASS, Sam T.	Consett	12.09.18	Huddersfield T.(*)	Fulham	+	1946	2		0	(FB)
			TR	Watford	01.47	1946–48	41		0	

Players Names	Birthplace	Date	Previous Club	League Club	Date Signed	Seasons Played	Apps	Sub	Gls	
MALT, Robert	Ryehope	04.11.51	APP	Leeds U.	11.68					(CF)
			TR	Darlington	06.70	1970	2	2	0	
MALTBY, John	Leadgate	31.07.39	JNRS	Sunderland	08.57	1956–60	22		4	(OL)
			TR	Darlington	06.61	1961–64	115		32	
			TR	Bury	07.65	1965–66	56	1	8	
MANCINI, Mike L.	London	08.06.56		Orient	N/C	1983	2	/	0	(F)
MANCINI, Terry J.	Camden Town	04.10.42	JNRS	Watford	07.61	1961-65	66	/	0	(D)EI-5/
			Port Elizabeth	Orient	11.67	1967–71	167	/	16	From famous boxing family
			TR	Q.P.R.	10.71	1971–74	94	/	3	
			TR	Arsenal	10.74	1974-75	52	/	1	
			TR	Aldershot	09.76	1976	21	/	0	
MANDERS, Ron E.	Shrewsbury	13.11.31	JNRS	Shrewsbury T.	12.54	1954–55	6		0	(HB)
MANKELOW, Jamie A.	Clapton	04.09.64	APP	Orient	09.82	1982	1	1	0	(F)
MANKTELOW, Brian	Farnham	29.03.51	APP	Aldershot	APP	1968	1	/	0	(CF)
MANLEY, Malcolm R.	Johnstone	01.12.49	Johnstone Burgh	Leicester C.	01.67	1967–72	109	11	5	(HB)S.SCH.INT
			TR	Portsmouth	12.73	1973–74	11	/	0	
MANLEY, Tommy	Northwich	07.10.12	Manchester U.(*)	Brentford	+	1946–50	116		6	(OL)*Northwich Vic
MANN, Adrian G.	Northampton	12.07.67	JNRS	Northampton T.	N/C	1983	2	/	0	(F)
MANN, Arthur F.	Burntisland	23.01.48	Hearts	Manchester C.	11.68	1968-70	32	3	0	(M)
			L	Blackpool	11.71	1971	3	/	0	
			TR	Notts. Co.	07.72	1972-78	243	10	21	
			TR	Shrewsbury T.	06.79	1979	8	/	1	
			TR	Mansfield T.	10.79	1979-81	114	2	3	
MANN, James A.	Goole	15.12.52	APP	Leeds U.	12.69	1971-72	2	/	0	(M)
			TR	Bristol C.	05.74	1974-81	205	26	31	
			TR	Barnsley	02.82	1981-82	14	1	0	
			TR	Scunthorpe U.	N/C	1982	2	/	0	
			TR	Doncaster Rov.	02.83	1982	13	/	0	
MANN, Ron H.	Doncaster	08.10.32		Notts. Co.	12.50	1950	1		0	(FB)
			TR	Aldershot	07.56	1956–57	26		4	
MANNERS, Peter J.	Sunderland	31.07.59	APP	Newcastle U.	07.77	1978	2	/	0	(F)
MANNERS, Wingrove	W. Indies	07.03.55	APP	Bradford C.	APP	1971	1	/	0	(IF)
MANNING, John J.	Liverpool	11.12.40	Liverpool (AM)	Tranmere Rov.	05.62	1962–66	130	/	70	(CF)
			TR	Shrewsbury T.	10.66	1966–67	39	/	18	
			TR	Norwich C.	09.67	1967–68	57	/	21	
			TR	Bolton W.	03.69	1968–70	27	2	7	
			TR	Walsall	07.71	1971	13	1	6	
			TR	Tranmere Rov.	03.72	1971	5	/	1	
			TR	Crewe Alex.	08.72	1972	37	1	6	
			TR	Barnsley	09.73	1973–74	41	4	7	
			TR	Crewe Alex.	11.75	1975	7	/	5	
MANNION, Gerry	Burtonwood	21.12.39	JNRS	Wolverhampton W.	11.57	1959–60	17	/	0	(OR)E.U23–2/E.YTH.INT
			TR	Norwich C.	09.61	1961–67	99	/	17	
			TR	Chester C.	01.68	1967	6	/	0	
MANNION, Wilf J.	South Bank	16.05.18	South Bank	Middlesbrough	*	1946–53	279		81	(IF)E.26/E'B'-2/●
			TR	Hull C.	12.54	1954	16		1	E.F.LGE.REP.
MANNS, Paul	Gt. Haywood	15.04.61	Cardiff C.(N/C)	Notts. Co.	08.79	1979-80	5	2	1	(F)
			TR	Chester C.	03.83	1982-83	28	/	3	
MANSELL, Barry R.	Petersfield	08.03.32	JNRS	Portsmouth	08.49	1951–53	16		0	(FB)
			TR	Reading	02.54	1953–55	84		0	
			TR	Bournemouth	06.57					
MANSELL, George W.	Doncaster	19.01.43		Doncaster Rov.	09.62	1962	1		0	(F)
MANSELL, Jack	Manchester	22.08.27	Manchester U.(AM)	Brighton & H.A.	03.49	1948–52	116		11	(FB)E'B'–2/E.F.LGE.REP
			TR	Cardiff C.	10.52	1952–53	24		0	
			TR	Portsmouth	11.53	1953–57	134		7	
MANSFIELD, Fred C.A.	Cambridge	09.03.15	Cambridge C.	Brentford	*					(RB)
			TR	Norwich C.	02.47	1946–47	34		0	
MANSFIELD, John V.	Colchester	13.09.46	JNRS	Colchester U.	08.64	1964–68	28	6	3	(F)
MANSFIELD Ron W.	Romford	31.12.23	Ilford	Millwall	+	1946–52	95		25	(OL)
			TR	Southend U.	11.52	1952	7		3	
MANSLEY, Alan	Liverpool	31.08.46	Skelmersdale	Blackpool	06.67					(W)
			TR	Brentford	01.68	1967–70	94	1	24	
			TR	Fulham	12.70	1970	1	/	0	
			L	Notts. Co.	03.71	1971	11	/	2	
			L	Lincoln C.	12.71	1971	3	/	0	
MANSLEY, Cliff V.	Skipton	05.04.21	Preston N.E.(+)	Barnsley	+	1946–47	31		0	
			TR	Chester C.	06.48	1948	22		0	
			Yeovil T.	Orient	07.52	1952	10		0	
MAPSON, John	Birkenhead	02.05.17	Reading*)	Sunderland	*	1946–52	225		0	(G)*Guildford C.
MARANGONI, Claudio O.	Argentine	17.11.54	San Lorenzo	Sunderland	12.79	1979-80	19	1	3	(M)ARGENTINE INT.
MARCH, John E.	Norwich	12.05.40	JNRS	Norwich C.	05.57					(HB)
			TR	Bradford P.A.	06.61	1961–62	62		1	
MARCH, Stan	Manchester	26.12.38	Altrincham	Port Vale	08.59	1959	1		0	(F)

Players Names	Birthplace	Date	Previous Club	League Club	Date Signed	Seasons Played	Apps	Sub	Gls	
MARCH, William	Chester–le–Street	28.02.25	Ferryhill Ath.	Barnsley	11.47	1951	2		0	(FB)
			TR	Gateshead	07.52	1952–56	134		0	
MARCHANT, Marwood	Milford	19.06.22	Milford Haven	Cardiff C.	01.51	1950	12		3	(F)
			TR	Torquay U.	11.51	1951–52	40		19	
MARCHI, Anthony	Edmonton	21.01.33	JNRS	Tottenham H.	06.50	1949–56	131		2	(WH) E'B'–1/E.YTH
			Juventus	Tottenham H.	07.59	1959–64	101		5	INT,'/E.SCH.INT.
										Nephew of G. Dorling
MARDEN, Reuben J.	Fulham	10.02.27	Chelmsford	Arsenal	02.50	1950–54	42		11	(W)
			TR	Watford	06.55	1955–56	41		11	
MARDENBOROUGH, Steve A.	Birmingham	11.09.64	APP	Coventry C.	08.82					(F)
			TR	Wolverhampton W.	09.83	1983	9	/	1	
			L	Cambridge U.	02.84	1983	6	/	0	
MARGERRISON, John W.	Bushey	20.10.55	APP	Tottenham H.	12.72					(M)
			TR	Fulham	07.75	1975-78	68	8	9	
			TR	Orient	07.79	1979-81	77	3	6	
MARINELLO, Peter	Edinburgh	20.02.50	Hibernian	Arsenal	01.70	1969-72	32	5	3	(W)S.U23-2
			TR	Portsmouth	07.73	1973-75	92	3	7	
			Motherwell	Fulham	12.78	1978-79	25	2	1	
MARINER, Paul	Bolton	22.05.53	Chorley	Plymouth Arg.	07.73	1973-76	134	1	56	(F)E-33●
			TR	Ipswich T.	09.76	1976-83	260	/	97	
			TR	Arsenal	02.84	1983	15	/	7	
MARKER, Nick R.T.	Budleigh Salterton	03.05.65	APP	Exeter C.	05.83	1981-83	57	6	2	(D)
MARKHAM, Colin	Clowne	02.03.16		Torquay U.	*	1946	17		1	(FB) d. 1967
MARKHAM, Leo	Aylesbury	22.03.53	Marlow	Watford	08.72	1972-74	22	11	3	(HB)S.SCH.INT
MARKHAM, Peter	Scunthorpe	18.03.54	APP	Scunthorpe U.	03.72	1971-76	121	1	1	(D)
MARKIE, John	Bo'ness	16.12.44	APP	Newcastle U.	04.62	1963	2	/		(HB)S.SCH.INT
MARKLEW, Roger K.	Sheffield	30.01.40	Sheffield U.(AM)	Sheffield Wed.	05.58					(W)
			TR	Accrington St.	05.59					
			TR	Grimsby T.	08.50	1960	6		1	
MARKS, Charles A.	Eccles	21.12.19		Gillingham	N/L	1950-56	277		8	(FB)
MARKS, George W.	Figheldean	09.04.15	Sailsbury C.	Arsenal	*					(G)
			TR	Blackburn Rov.	08.46	1946-47	67		0	
			TR	Bristol C.	08.48	1948	9		0	
			TR	Reading	10.48	1948-52	128		0	
MARLEY, Alan	Durham	29.02.56	APP	Grimsby T.	11.73	1974-75	39	1	2	(FB)
MARLEY, George	Gateshead	22.04.21		Gateshead	09.47	1947-49	22		2	
MARLOW, Fred	Sheffield	09.11.28	Hillsboro B.C.	Arsenal	09.47					(IF)
			TR	Sheffield Wed.	09.50					
			Buxton	Grimsby T.	08.51	1951	12		6	
			Boston U.	York C.	10.53	1953-54	23		0	
MARLOW, Geoff A.	Worksop	13.12.14	Dinnington	Lincoln C.	+	1946-48	64		21	(OL) d.1978
MARLOWE, Richard	Edinburgh	10.08.50		Derby Co.	07.73					(CF)
			TR	Shrewsbury T.	12.73	1973	31	/	4	
			TR	Brighton & H.A.	07.74	1974	24	1	5	
			L	Aldershot	01.76	1975	2	/	0	
MARMON, Neale	Bournemouth	21.04.61		Torquay U.	N/C	1979	4	/	0	(F)
MARRIOTT, Ernest	Sutton-in-Ashfield	25.01.13	Sutton T.	Brighton & H.A.	*	1946-47	72		0	(FB)
MARRIOTT, John	Sheffield	16.07.15	Normanton Spts	Doncaster Rov.	+	1946-47	6		0	(CF)
			TR	Southport	12.47	1947-48	23		6	
MARRIOTT, John L.	Scunthorpe	01.04.28	Scunthorpe U.	Sheffield Wed.	02.47	1946-54	153		18	(OR)
			TR	Huddersfield T.	07.55	1955-56	38		4	
			TR	Scunthorpe U.	06.57	1957-63	212		26	
MARRIOTT, Stan	Rochdale	21.07.29	Leeds U. (AM)	Rochdale	AM	1952	6		2	(CF
MARRON, Chris	Jarrow	07.02.25	Sth.Shields	Chesterfield	10.47	1947-51	107		44	(CF)
			TR	Mansfield T.	07.52	1952-53	53		25	
			TR	Bradford P.A.	07.54	1954	2		1	
MARSDEN, Anthony J.	Bolton	11.09.48	APP	Blackpool	07.66	1967-68	4	1	0	(CF)
			TR	Doncaster Rov.	07.69	1969-70	14	3	2	
			L	Grimsby T.	11.69	1969	2	/	0	
MARSDEN, Eric	Bolsover	03.01.30	Winchester C.	Crystal Palace	04.50	1950-52	34		12	(CF)
			TR	Southend U.	10.52	1952	14		6	
			TR	Shrewsbury T.	03.53	1952-53	11		0	
MARSDEN, Fred	Blackburn	06.09.11	Wolverhampton W.(*)	Bournemouth	*	1946-48	85		0	(FB)*Accrington St.
MARSDEN, James	Rotherham	10.04.28	Parkgate W.	Rotherham U.	08.52	1952-54	12		2	(F)
MARSDEN, John	Leeds	17.12.31	Osmondthorpe	Leeds U.	08.50	1952-58	71		0	(CH)
			TR	Barrow	03.59	1958-59	47		0	
			TR	Carlisle U.	09.60	1960-63	88		0	
			TR	Doncaster Rov.	07.64	1964	2		0	
MARSDEN, Keith	Darley Dale	10.04.34	Youlgreave B.C.	Chesterfield	06.52	1953-54	22		15	(IF)
			TR	Manchester C.	07.55	1955-57	14		1	
			TR	Accrington St.	08.59					

Players Names	Birthplace	Date	Previous Club	League Club	Date Signed	Seasons Played	Apps	Sub	Gls	
MARSDEN, Liddell	Fatfield	13.05.36	Sth.Shields	Workington	11.56	1956	2		0	(HB)
MARSH, Arthur	Dudley	04.05.47	Brierley Hill	Bolton W.	07.64	1966–70	73	2	0	(FB)
			TR	Rochdale	12.71	1971–73	89	1	0	
			TR	Darlington	07.74	1974	23	/	1	
MARSH, Cliff	Atherton	29.12.20	Winsford U.	Leeds U.	09.48	1948	4		1	(IF)
			TR	Bournemouth	05.49	1949–51	39		2	
MARSH, Edward W.	London	14.12.27	Erith & B.	Charlton Ath.	+	1950–56	26		0	(G)
			TR	Luton T.	06.57	1957–58	2		0	
			TR	Torquay U.	07.59	1959–61	61		0	
MARSH, Frank K.	Bolton	07.06.16		Chester C.	+	1946–47	69		2	*Bolton W.
MARSH, John H.	Stoke	31.05.48	APP	Stoke C.	06.65	1967-78	344	8	2	(D)
MARSH, John K.	Mansfield	08.10.22		Notts.Co.	+	1946–48	42		18	(IF)
			TR	Coventry C.	09.48	1948–49	20		6	
			TR	Leicester C.	03.50	1949–50	14		4	
			TR	Chesterfield	09.50	1950	27		4	
MARSH, John S.	Bolton	31.08.40	JNRS	Oldham Ath.	10.57	1959	2		0	(F)
MARSH, John W.	Leeds	17.12.47		Bradford C.	05.66	1966–67	12	/	0	(G)
MARSH, Kevin W.	Liverpool	27.03.49	APP	Liverpool	03.66					(CF)
			TR	Southport	05.70	1970	35	2	8	
MARSH, Rod	Hatfield	11.10.44	APP	Fulham	10.62	1962-65	63	/	22	(F)E-9/E.U23-2
			TR	Q.P.R.	03.66	1965-71	211	/	106	
			TR	Manchester C.	03.72	1971-75	116	2	37	
			Tampa Bay	Fulham	08.76	1976	16	/	5	
MARSHALL, Alex S.	Alloa	27.11.35	Stirling A.	Accrington St.	10.60	1960	8		2	(IF)
MARSHALL, Alf G.	Dagenham	21.05.33	Dagenham	Colchester U.	10.57	1958–60	29		0	(FB)
MARSHALL, Brian	Doncaster	20.09.54	APP	Huddersfield T.	12.71	1972–74	30	2	0	(HB)
			L	Scunthorpe U.	10.74	1974	3	/	0	
MARSHALL, Cliff	Liverpool	04.11.55	APP	Everton	11.73	1974-75	6	1	0	(F)E.SCH.INT.
			TR	Southport	09.76	1976	11	2	0	
MARSHALL, David H.	Manchester	12.11.55	Headley Col.	Workington	N/C	1976	2	/	0	(D)
MARSHALL, Ernie	Dinnington	23.05.18	Sheffield U.(*)	Cardiff C.	+	1946	1		0	(WH) d.1983
MARSHALL, Frank	Sheffield	26.01.29	Scarborough	Rotherham U.	05.51	1951–56	118		5	(IF)
			TR	Scunthorpe U.	07.57	1957–58	80		0	
			TR	Doncaster Rov.	10.59	1959–61	35		0	
MARSHALL, Gary	Bristol	20.04.64	Shepton Mallet	Bristol C.	N/C	1983	0	1	0	
MARSHALL, Gordon	Farnham	02.07.39	Hearts	Newcastle U.	06.63	1963–67	177	/	0	(G) E.U23–1
			TR	Nottingham F.	10.68	1968	7	/	0	
MARSHALL, John	Accrington	01.11.38		Accrington St.	05.57	1957–58	7		0	(G)
MARSHALL, John G.	Bolton	29.05.17	JNRS	Burnley	*	1946	1		0	(FB)
MARSHALL, John J.	Glasgow	12.02.49		Preston N.E.	02.67					(W)
			Ross Co.	Rotherham U.	09.68	1968	4	/	0	
			TR	Barnsley	04.69					
MARSHALL, John P.	Epsom	18.08.64	APP	Fulham	08.82	1983	21	4	0	(D)
MARSHALL, Julian P.	Swansea	06.07.57	Merthyr Tydfil	Hereford U.	08.75	1976-79	91	1	4	(D)
			TR	Bristol C.	08.80	1980-81	29	/	0	
			TR	Walsall	08.82	1982	10	/	0	
MARSHALL, Peter	Barrow	02.10.47	Holker C.O.B.	Barrow	01.66	1965–66	4	/	1	(OR)
MARSHALL, Peter W.	Worksop	05.12.34	Worksop T.	Scunthorpe U.	09.54	1954–56	64		0	(G)
MARSHALL, Ralph	Airdrie	30.01.44	Glasgow Rgrs	Crewe Alex.	09.64	1964–66	72	1	0	(FB)
MARSHALL, Richard	Leicester	23.11.45	APP	Leicester C.	08.63					(F)
			TR	Southport	07.65	1965–66	29	2	7	
MARSHALL, Roy C.	Fulham	22.05.32	JNRS	Brighton & H.A.	06.50					(G)
			TR	Aldershot	08.57	1957–60	34		0	
MARSHALL, Stan K.	Goole	20.04.46	Goole T.	Middlesbrough	08.63	1965	2	/	0	(F)
			TR	Notts.Co.	06.66	1966–67	43	6	17	
MARSHALL, Terry W.J.	Whitechapel	26.12.35	Wisbech T.	Newcastle U.	12.58	1958–60	5		1	(OR)
MARSHALL, William	Belfast	11.07.36	Distillery	Burnley	10.53	1959–60	6		0	(FB) N1'B'–2
			TR	Oldham Ath.	08.62	1962–63	57		0	
			TR	Hartlepool U.	08.64	1964–65	57	/	0	
MARSHALL, William F.	Rutherglen	09.05.33	Glencairn	Bradford C.	01.57	1956–58	33		16	(F)
			TR	Swindon T.	02.59	1958–59	29		12	
			TR	Chesterfield	07.61					
MARSLAND, Gordon	Blackpool	20.03.45	APP	Blackpool	05.62					(WH)
			TR	Carlisle U.	06.65	1965–68	63	1	4	
			TR	Bristol Rov.	06.69	1969	16	1	1	
			L	Crewe Alex.	09.70	1970	5	/	0	
			L	Oldham Ath.	03.71	1970	1	3	0	
MARSTON, Joe	Australia	07.01.26	Leichardt F.C.	Preston N.E.	02.50	1950–54	185		0	(CH) E.F.LGE.REP.
MARSTON, Maurice	Trimdon	24.03.29	JNRS	Sunderland	06.49	1951–52	9		0	(FB)
			TR	Northampton T.	07.53	1953–56	149		2	

Players Names	Birthplace	Date	Previous Club	League Club	Date Signed	Seasons Played	Apps	Sub	Gls	
MARTIN, Alan J.	Stoke	23.11.23		Port Vale	+	1946–51	169		28	(WH)
			TR	Stoke C.	09.51	1951–54	104		6	
			Bangor	Port Vale	07.57	1957–58	19		0	
MARTIN, Alvin E.	Bootle	29.07.58	APP	West Ham U.	07.76	1977–83	203	2	15	(D)E-12/E.YTH.INT.
MARTIN, Barrie	Birmingham	29.09.35	JNRS	Blackpool	12.53	1957–63	189		1	(FB)
			TR	Oldham Ath.	08.64	1964	42		4	
			TR	Tranmere Rov.	06.65	1965–67	99	3	0	
MARTIN, Con J.	Dublin	20.03.23	Glentoran	Leeds U.	01.47	1946–48	47		1	(CH) E1–30/N1–6/26 apps
			TR	Aston Villa	10.48	1948–55	194		1	in goal for Aston Villa
MARTIN, David	E. Ham	25.04.63	APP	Millwall	05.80	1979–83	129	9	6	(M)E.YTH.INT.
MARTIN, Dennis V.	Southampton	08.11.28	JNRS	Bournemouth	08.47	1948–53	23		0	(HB)
MARTIN, Dennis W.	Edinburgh	27.10.47	Kettering	W.B.A.	07.67	1967–69	14	2	1	(W)
			TR	Carlisle U.	07.70	1970–77	271	4	48	
			TR	Newcastle U.	10.77	1977	9	2	2	
			TR	Mansfield T.	03.78	1977–78	46	/	3	
MARTIN, Don	Corby	15.02.44	JNRS	Northampton T.	07.62	1962–67	135	/	52	(F)E.YTH.INT.
			TR	Blackburn Rov.	02.68	1967–75	218	4	57	
			TR	Northampton T.	11.75	1975–77	77	15	17	
MARTIN, Eddie	Baillieston	31.03.21	Alloa Ath.	Accrington St.	08.50	1950	2		0	(F)
MARTIN, Eric	Perth	31.03.46	Dunfermline	Southampton	03.67	1966–74	246	/	0	(G)
MARTIN, Fred A.	Nottingham	13.12.25		Nottingham F.	+	1947–48	5		0	
MARTIN, Fred J.	Nottingham	14.04.25		Ipswich T.	01.49					
				Blackburn Rov.	12.49					
			TR	Accrington St.	07.50	1950–51	64		0	
MARTIN, Geoff	Chesterfield	09.03.40	Parkhouse Col.	Chesterfield	10.58	1958	2		0	(OL)
			TR	Leeds U.	05.60					
			TR	Darlington	07.61	1961	20		6	
			TR	Carlisle U.	05.62	1961–62	15		2	
			TR	Workington	12.62	1962–66	144	/	24	
			TR	Grimsby T.	11.66	1966–67	71	/	5	
			TR	Chesterfield	07.68	1968–69	44	/	5	
MARTIN, Harold J.	Blackburn	15.03.55	APP	Bolton W.	11.73					(CH)
			TR	Rochdale	07.74	1974	11	2	0	
MARTIN, James C.	Dundee	27.05.38		Blackpool	12.61					(F)
			TR	Reading	06.62	1962–63	22		6	
MARTIN, James P.	Glasgow	03.03.37	Baillieston	Nottingham F.	06.58	1958	1		0	(F)
MARTIN, John	Ashington	04.12.46	APP	Aston Villa	07.64	1964	1		0	(W)
			TR	Colchester U.	05.66	1966–68	76	1	11	
			TR	Workington	07.69	1969–73	206	1	32	
			TR	Southport	08.74	1974–75	54	9	7	
			TR	Torquay U.	07.67					
MARTIN, John G.	Dundee	20.08.35	Dundee St. S.	Sheffield Wed.	02.54	1954–60	63		0	(FB)
			TR	Rochdale	06.62	1962–63	24		1	
MARTIN, John R.	Birmingham	05.08.14	Hednesford T.	Aston Villa	*	1946–48	57		13	
MARTIN, Lionel J.	Ludlow	15.05.47	APP	Aston Villa	07.64	1966–70	36	12	6	(F)
			L	Doncaster Rov.	03.71	1970	2	/	0	
MARTIN, Mick P.	Dublin	09.07.51	Bohemians	Manchester U.	01.73	1972–74	33	7	2	(M)EI-52/EI.AMAT.INT./
			TR	W.B.A.	10.75	1975–78	85	4	11	Son of Con.
			TR	Newcastle U.	12.78	1978–82	139	8	5	
MARTIN, Neil	Tranent	20.10.40	Hibernian	Sunderland	10.65	1965–67	86	/	38	(CF) S–3/S.U23–1/
			TR	Coventry C.	02.68	1967–70	106	/	40	S.F.LGE.REP
			TR	Nottingham F.	02.71	1970–74	116	3	28	
			TR	Brighton & H.A.	07.75	1975	13	4	8	
			TR	Crystal Palace	03.76	1975	8	1	1	
MARTIN, Peter	Sth. Shields	29.12.50	Chilton B.C.	Middlesbrough	06.69					(W)
			TR	Darlington	07.71	1971	3	/	0	
			TR	Barnsley	10.71	1971–72	18	8	6	
MARTIN, Ray B.	Wolverhampton	23.01.45	Aston Villa (APP)	Birmingham C.	05.62	1963–75	323	8	1	(FB)
MARTIN, Roy	Kilwinning	16.05.29	Kilwinning	Birmingham C.	03.50	1950–55	69		0	(FB)
			TR	Derby Co.	03.56	1955–59	81		0	
			TR	Chesterfield	07.60					
MARTIN, Tom	Glasgow	21.12.24	Stirling A.	Doncaster Rov.	07.50	1950–52	71		9	(IF)
			TR	Nottingham F.	11.52	1952–54	48		4	
			TR	Hull C.	06.55	1955–56	32		2	
MARTIN, Wayne L.	Basildon	16.12.65	APP	Crystal Palace	APP	1983	1	/	0	
MARTINDALE, Len	Bolton	30.06.20	JNRS	Burnley	*	1948–50	21		0	(WH)
			TR	Accrington St.	12.51	1951	16		0	
MARTINEZ, Eugene	Chelmsford	06.07.57		Bradford C.	07.77	1977–79	38	14	5	(M)
			TR	Rochdale	07.80	1980–82	110	6	16	
			TR	Newport Co.	08.83	1983	18	2	1	
			L	Northampton T.	02.84	1983	12	/	2	
MARUSTIK, Chris	Swansea	10.08.61	APP	Swansea C.	08.78	1978–83	94	8	5	(D)W.SCH.INT./W–6/W.U'21-5
MARVIN, Walter	Derby	06.07.20		Accrington St.	10.47	1946–47	9		3	

Players Names	Birthplace	Date	Previous Club	League Club	Date Signed	Seasons Played	Career Record Apps	Sub	Gls	
MARWOOD, Brian	Easington	05.02.60	APP	Hull C.	02.78	1979-83	154	4	51	(W)
MASEFIELD, Keith L.	Birmingham	26.02.57	APP	Aston Villa	10.74	1974-76	1	3	0	(D)
MASIELLO, Luciano	Italy	02.01.51	APP	Charlton Ath.	01.69	1969-70	6	/	0	(W)
MASKELL, Dennis	Mountain Ash	16.04.31		Watford	09.51	1951	5		0	
MASKELL, Mick	Eynsham	25.01.52	APP	Chelsea	02.69					(FB)
			TR	Brentford	07.70	1970	1	/	0	
MASKERY, Chris P.	Stoke	25.09.64	APP	Stoke C.	09.82	1982-83	19	7	0	(M)
MASON, Cliff E.	York	27.11.29		Sunderland	01.50					(FB)
			TR	Darlington	07.52	1952–54	107		0	
			TR	Sheffield U.	08.55	1955–61	97		2	
			TR	Leeds U.	03.62	1961–62	31		0	
			TR	Scunthorpe U.	02.64	1963	12		1	
			TR	Chesterfield	07.64	1964	5		0	
MASON, James	Glasgow	17.04.33	Dundee	Accrington St.	06.55	1955–56	14		1	(HB)
			TR	Chester C.	06.57	1957–58	64		7	
			Chelmsford	Crystal Palace	05.60					
MASON, John F.	Coventry	23.01.43	Alvechurch	Peterborough U.	05.66	1966–67	37	/	18	(CF) E.AMAT.INT
MASON, Keith M.	Leicester	19.07.58		Huddersfield T.	07.82	1982-83	20	/	0	(G)
MASON, Maurice	Sedgfield	25.06.27		Huddersfield T.	01.48					(IF)
			Blackhall C.W.	Darlington	07.52	1952	3		0	
MASON, Mike B.	Bloxwich	20.10.44	APP	Walsall	09.62	1963	4		0	(F)
			TR	W.B.A.	07.64					
MASON, Richard J.	Arley	02.04.18	Nuneaton	Coventry C.	05.46	1946–53	250		2	(FB)
MASON, Robert H.	Tipton	22.03.36	JNRS	Wolverhampton W.	05.53	1955–61	146		44	(IF)
			Chelmsford C.	Orient	03.63	1962–63	23		0	
MASON, Stuart J.	Whitchurch	02.06.48	JNRS	Wrexham	07.66	1965-66	28	/	0	(M)E.YTH.INT.
			TR	Liverpool	10.66					
			L	Doncaster Rov.	11.67	1967	1	/	0	
			TR	Wrexham	06.68	1968-72	144	13	3	
			TR	Chester C.	06.73	1973-77	132	5	7	
			L	Rochdale	12.76	1976	2	/	0	
			L	Crewe Alex.	10.77	1977	4	/	1	
MASON, Tom H.A.	Buxton	20.02.53	APP	Derby Co.	07.72					(WH)
			TR	Brighton & H.A.	09.74	1974	23	2	2	
MASON, Tom J.R.	Fulham	19.06.60	APP	Fulham	01.78	1977-79	6	/	0	(D)
			TR	Brighton & H.A.	06.81					
MASON, Tom W.M.	Hartlepool	21.4.25	Railway Ath.	Hartlepool U.	05.46	1946	4		0	(CH)
MASON George W.	Birmingham	05.09.13		Coventry C.	*	1946–51	135		1	(CH)E.SCH.INT
MASSART, Dave L.	Birmingham	02.11.19		Birmingham C.	*	1946	3		0	(CF)
			TR	Walsall	06.47	1947	27		23	
			TR	Bury	03.48	1947–50	85		45	
			TR	Chesterfield	02.51	1950	11		5	
MASSEY, Andy T.	London	20.10.61	JNRS	Millwall	03.79	1980-83	73	15	8	(M)E.YTH.INT.
			L	Port Vale	03.84	1983	4	/	1	
MASSEY, Bernard W.	Ripley	05.11.20	Peterborough U.	Halifax T.	*	1946–50	81		6	
MASSEY, Eric	Derby	11.09.23	Arsenal(AM)	Bury	09.46	1946–56	202		6	(WH)
MASSEY, Kevin J.	Gainsborough	30.11.65	APP	Cambridge U.	12.83	1983	1	/	0	(F)
MASSEY, Robert W.	Bournemouth	06.04.40		Bournemouth	05.58	1959–60	5		0	(FB)
MASSEY, Roy	Mexborough	10.09.43		Rotherham U.	05.65	1964–66	15	1	6	(CF)E. YTH.INT
			TR	Orient	09.67	1967–68	59	5	13	
			TR	Colchester U.	07.69	1969–70	30	4	11	
MASSEY, Steve	Denton	28.03.58	APP	Stockport Co.	07.75	1974-77	87	14	20	(F)
			TR	Bournemouth	07.78	1978-80	85	12	19	
			TR	Peterborough U.	08.81	1981	13	5	2	
			TR	Northampton T.	02.82	1981-82	60	/	25	
			TR	Hull C.	07.83	1983	11	2	4	
MASSIE, Les	Aberdeen	20.07.35	Banks O'Dee	Huddersfield T.	08.53	1956–66	334	1	98	(IF)●
			TR	Darlington	10.66	1966	20	/	2	
			TR	Halifax T.	06.67	1967–68	89	/	41	
			TR	Bradford P.A.	08.69	1969	14	/	2	
			TR	Workington	12.69	1969–70	62	/	15	
MASSON, Don S.	Banchory	26.08.46	JNRS	Middlesbrough	09.63	1964-67	51	3	6	(M)S-17●
			TR	Notts. Co.	09.68	1968-74	273	/	81	
			TR	Q.P.R.	12.74	1974-77	116	/	18	
			TR	Derby Co.	10.77	1977	23	/	1	
			TR	Notts. Co.	08.78	1978-81	129	/	11	
MASTERS, Graham J.	Bristol	13.08.31	JNRS	Bristol C.	08.48	1951	9		1	(F)
MATHER, Harry	Bolton	24.01.21	JNRS	Burnley	*	1946–54	300		0	(FB)
			Limerick	Hull C.	06.56					
MATHER, Shaun L.	Hereford	09.09.65		Newport Co.	N/C	1983	0	1	0	
MATHIAS, Ray	Liverpool	13.12.46	APP	Tranmere Rov.	12.64	1967-83	555	10	6	(D)

Players Names	Birthplace	Date	Previous Club	League Club	Date Signed	Seasons Played	Apps	Sub	Gls	
MATHIAS, Terry	Wrexham	10.11.49	APP	Shrewsbury T.	05.67	1965–73	96	3	0	(WH)W.SCH.INT
MATHIE, David	Motherwell	15.08.19	Kilmarnock	Workington	10.53	1953	2		0	(CF) d. 1954
MATIER, Gerry	Lisburn	01.12.12	Blackburn Rov.(*)	Bradford C.	+					(G)*Coleraine
			TR	Plymouth Arg.	09.46					
			TR	Torquay U.	11.46	1946	17		0	
MATTHEWS, Barry J.	Sheffield	18.01.26	Sheffield U.(AM)	Lincoln C.	AM	1949	2		0	
MATTHEWS, David I.	Rhondda	24.09.21		Cardiff C.	09.47					(G)
			TR	Newport Co.	04.48	1948–49	9		0	
MATTHEWS, Frank J.	London	07.01.48	APP	Southend U.	01.66	1965–67	21	6	0	(FB)
			TR	Torquay U.	06.68	1968	6	1	0	
			TR	Reading	06.69					
MATTHEWS, Graham	Stoke	02.11.42	JNRS	Stoke C.	11.59	1960–62	16		3	(F)
			TR	Walsall	08.63	1963–64	67		21	
			TR	Crewe Alex.	08.65	1965–66	55	1	19	
MATTHEWS, John M.	London	01.11.55	APP	Arsenal	08.73	1974-77	38	7	2	(M)
			TR	Sheffield U.	08.78	1978–81	98	5	14	
			TR	Mansfield T.	08.82	1982-83	70	2	6	
MATTHEWS, Keith J.	Wrexham	07.03.34		Wrexham	12.52	1952–54	9		0	(F)
MATTHEWS, Mark	Reading	17.09.61		Reading	N/C	1981-83	5	3	1	(M)
MATTHEWS, Mike	Hull	25.09.60	APP	Wolverhampton W.	10.78	1980-83	72	4	7	(M)
			TR	Scunthorpe U.	02.84	1983	25	/	1	
MATTHEWS, Paul W.	Leicester	30.09.46	APP	Leicester C.	08.64	1964-70	56	5	5	(M)
			L	Southend U.	09.72	1972	1	/	0	
			TR	Mansfield T.	12.72	1972-77	121	3	6	
			TR	Rotherham U.	10.77	1977	8	/	0	
			L	Northampton T.	03.79	1978	13	/	0	
MATTHEWS, Reg D.	Coventry	20.12.33	JNRS	Coventry C.	05.50	1952–56	111		0	(G)E–5/E.U23–4/E'B'–3/
			TR	Chelsea	11.56	1956–60	135		/	E.F.LGE.REP.
			TR	Derby Co.	10.61	1961–67	225	/	0	
MATTHEWS, Roy	Slough	29.03.40	Arbroath Vic	Charlton Ath.	04.57	1959–66	160	/	46	(IF)
MATTHEWS, Stanley	Hanley	01.02.15	JNRS	Stoke C.	*	1946	23		4	(OR)E–54/E.F.LGE.REP./●
			TR	Blackpool	05.47	1947–61	379		17	E.SCH.INT./
			TR	Stoke C.	10.61	1961–64	59		3	Son of Famous Boxer
MATTHEWS, Terry G.	Leyton	25.02.36	JNRS	West Ham U.	02.53	1955	9		1	(F)
			TR	Aldershot	07.57	1957–61	62		22	
			TR	Gillingham	08.62	1962	9		1	
MATTHEWS, Wayne J.	Cardiff	11.09.64	JNRS	Cardiff C.	01.83	1983	4	10	0	(M)
MATTHEWSON, Reg	Sheffield	06.08.39		Sheffield U.	06.58	1961–67	145	3	3	(CH)
			TR	Fulham	02.68	1967–72	156	2	1	
			TR	Chester C.	01.73	1972–75	86	1	1	
MATTHEWSON, Robert	Newcastle	13.04.30	Byker Y.C.	Bolton W.	03.48	1950–52	3		0	(CH) (Became Referee)
			TR	Lincoln C.	06.53					
MATTHEWSON, Trevor	Sheffield	12.02.63	APP	Sheffield Wed.	02.81	1980-82	3	/	0	(D)
			TR	Newport Co.	10.83	1983	30	2	0	
MATTISON, Harry	Ireby	20.07.25		Middlesbrough	+	1946	3		0	(CH)
			TR	Preston N.E.	03.49	1948–58	124		0	
MAUGHAN, Wesley	Southampton	17.02.39	Cowes I.O.W.*	Southampton	05.57	1958–61	6		1	(F)
			TR	Reading	03.62	1961–62	16		3	
MAUND, John H.	Hednesford	05.01.16	Aston Villa(*)	Nottingham F.	+					(OR)*Hednesford T.
			TR	Walsall	10.46	1946–47	30		7	
MAW, John	Scunthorpe	22.12.34		Scunthorpe U.	06.57	1957	1		0	(HB)
MAWER, Shaun K.	Ulceby	06.08.59	APP	Grimsby T.	08.77	1977-79	57	3	1	(D)
MAWSON, Joe	Workington	07.01.34		Workington	AM	1955	1		0	
MAWSON, Ron	B. Auckland	16.09.14	R.A.F. Tern Hill	Crewe Alex.	+	1946–47	23		0	(G)
			TR	Wrexham	09.48	1948	6		0	
MAXFIELD, John	Carlisle	17.06.19		Carlisle U.	01.47	1946–50	25		4	(F)
			TR	Workington	07.51	1951	13		4	
MAXWELL, Hugh	Rigghead	14.05.38	E. Stirling	Bradford P.A.	04.62	1961–62	12		5	(IF)
MAXWELL, Ken	Glasgow	11.02.28	Kilmarnock	Northampton T.	06.49	1950	2		0	(HB)
			Canada	Bradford P.A.	11.57	1957	2		0	
MAXWELL, Pat	Ayr	10.01.29	Saltcoats Vic.	Chesterfield	08.51	1951–52	19		3	(IF)
MAY, Andy M.	Bury	26.01.64	APP	Manchester C.	02.82	1980-83	49	8	5	(M)
MAY, Don I.	Broseley	31.05.31		Bury	03.51	1951–61	133		11	(WH)
MAY, Eddie	Epping	19.05.43	Dagenham	Southend U.	01.65	1964-67	107	4	3	(D)●
			TR	Wrexham	06.68	1968-75	330	4	34	
			TR	Swansea C.	08.76	1976-77	90	/	8	
MAY, Harry	Glasgow	15.10.28	Thorniewood U.	Cardiff C.	08.48	1949	1		0	(FB)
			TR	Swindon T.	06.50	1950–51	78		1	
			TR	Barnsley	05.52	1952–54	108		0	
			TR	Southend U.	09.55	1955	19		1	

Players Names	Birthplace	Date	Previous Club	League Club	Date Signed	Seasons Played	Career Record Apps	Sub	Gls	
MAY, John	Crosby	28.01.60	APP	Blackpool	11.78	1978	4	/	0	(D)E.SCH.INT.
			TR	Exeter C.	08.80					
MAY, Larry C.	Sutton Coldfield	26.12.58	APP	Leicester C.	01.77	1976-82	180	7	12	(D)
			TR	Barnsley	09.83	1983	41	/	1	
MAY, Warren D.	Rochford	31.12.64	APP	Southend U.	01.83	1982-83	27	9	3	(M)
MAYBANK, Edward	Lambeth	11.10.56	APP	Chelsea	02.74	1974-76	28	/	6	(F)
			TR	Fulham	11.76	1976-77	27	/	14	
			TR	Brighton & H.A.	11.77	1977-79	62	2	16	
			TR	Fulham	12.79	1979	19	/	3	
MAYERS, Alan	Chester	20.04.37	JNRS	Chester C.	05.55	1955	1		0	(OR)
MAYERS, Derek	Liverpool	24.01.35	JNRS	Everton	08.52	1952-56	18		7	(OR)
			TR	Preston N.E.	05.57	1957-60	118		25	
			TR	Leeds U.	06.61	1961	20		5	
			TR	Bury	07.62	1962-63	32		6	
			TR	Wrexham	10.63	1963	21		2	
MAYES, Alan K.	London	11.12.53	APP	Q.P.R.	07.71					(F)
			TR	Watford	11.74	1974-78	110	23	31	
			L	Northampton T.	01.76	1975	10	/	4	
			TR	Swindon T.	02.79	1978-80	89	/	38	
			TR	Chelsea	12.80	1980-82	61	5	18	
			TR	Swindon T.	07.83	1983	34	5	17	
MAYFIELD, Les	Mansfield	19.01.26		Mansfield T.	09.48	1949-52	33		0	(FB)
MAYLE, Robert J.	Llandyssil	18.12.38	Sentinel J.	Shrewsbury T.	05.57	1957	8		0	(F)
			TR	Walsall	08.59					
MAYMAN, Paul F.	Crewe	29.05.58	JNRS	Crewe Alex.	07.76	1975-76	42	1	3	(M)
MAYNARD, Mike C.	B.Guiana	07.01.47	Hounslow T.	Crystal Palace	03.66					(HB)
			TR	Peterborough U.	07.67	1967	2	1	0	
MAYO, Joe	Tipton	25.05.51	Dudley T.	Walsall	09.72	1972	2	5	1	(F)
			TR	W.B.A.	02.73	1973-76	68	5	16	
			TR	Orient	03.77	1976-81	150	5	35	
			TR	Cambridge U.	09.81	1981-82	35	1	14	
			L	Blackpool	10.82	1982	5	/	1	
MAYS, Albert E.	Rhondda	18.04.29	JNRS	Derby Co.	05.46	1949-59	272		20	(WH) Son of pre-war player/
			TR	Chesterfield	07.60	1960	37		5	d. 1973
MAZZON, Giorgio	Cheshunt	04.09.60	Hertford T.	Tottenham H.	04.79	1980-82	3	1	0	(D)
			TR	Aldershot	08.83	1983	45	/	3	
MEACHIN, Paul	Bebington	17.07.56	Ashville	Southport	AM	1974	3	/	0	(CF)
MEAD, Peter S.	Luton	09.09.56	APP	Luton T.	07.74					(D)
			TR	Northampton T.	08.77	1977-78	75	2	4	
MEADE, Raphael J.	London	22.11.62	APP	Arsenal	06.80	1981-83	19	14	11	(F)
MEADOWS, Frank	Maltby	27.06.33		Rotherham U.	04.52	1953-55	8		0	(F)
			TR	Coventry C.	06.56	1956	8		0	
MEADOWS, James	Bolton	21.07.31	Bolton Y.M.C.A.	Southport	03.49	1948-50	60		7	(FB)E-1/E.F.LGE.REP
			TR	Manchester C.	03.51	1950-54	130		30	
MEADOWS, John A.	Hoxton	13.11.30	Kingsbury	Watford	06.51	1951-59	222		43	(WH)
MEADOWS, John R.	Lancaster	04.12.20		Burnley	09.46					(G)
			TR	Bournemouth	04.50	1950-51	16		0	
			TR	Accrington St.	07.52	1952	18		0	
MEADOWS, Robert	Melton Mowbray	25.04.38	JNRS	Stoke C.	05.55					(FB)
			Northwich V.	Doncaster Rov.	12.62	1962-63	43		0	
MEAGAN, Mick K.	Dublin	29.05.34	Johnville	Everton	09.52	1957-63	165		1	(WH)E1-17/E1'B'-1/
			TR	Huddersfield T.	07.64	1964-67	118	3	1	E1.SCH.INT
			TR	Halifax T.	07.68	1968	23	/	0	
MEAGAN, Tom P.	Liverpool	14.11.59	APP	Doncaster Rov.	11.77	1977-78	32	5	1	(M)
				Doncaster Rov.	N/C	1982	2	/	0	
MEAGON, John G.	Shap.	11.11.35	JNRS	Workington	12.52	1952-54	3		0	(FB)
MEAKIN, Harry	Stoke	08.09.19		Stoke C.	+	1946-49	35		0	(FB)
MEALAND, Barry	Carshalton	24.01.43	JNRS	Fulham	10.61	1961-67	28	1	0	(FB)
			TR	Rotherham U.	08.68	1968-69	44	1	0	
MEANEY, John F.	Stoke	19.11.19	Ravensdale	Crewe Alex.	03.47	1946-53	288		31	(IF)
MEANEY, Terry	Ravensdale	25.05.22		Bury	+	1946	4		2	(F) Brother to John F.
			TR	Crewe Alex.	07.47	1947	3		2	
MEASURES, George A.	Walthamstow	17.12.58		Cambridge U.	N/C	1983	4	/	0	(F)
MEATH, Trevor J.	Wednesbury	20.03.44	Darlaston	Walsall	05.64	1964-69	59	8	11	(HB)
			TR	Lincoln C.	10.69	1969-71	42	1	5	
MEDD, Gordon E.	Birmingham	17.08.25		Birmingham C.	10.46					
				Walsall	06.49	1949	22		2	
			TR	Rochdale	07.50	1950	5		1	
			TR	York C.	01.51	1950	1		0	
MEDHURST, Harry E.	Byfleet	05.02.16	Woking	West Ham U.	*	1946	3		0	(G)d.1984
			TR	Chelsea	01.47	1946-51	143		0	
			TR	Brighton & H.A.	11.52	1952	12		0	

Players Names	Birthplace	Date	Previous Club	League Club	Date Signed	Seasons Played	Apps	Sub	Gls	
MEDLEY, Les D.	Edmonton	03.09.20	JNRS	Tottenham H.	*	1946–52	150		45	(OL)E–6/E.F.LGE.REP/ E.SCH.INT
MEDLOCK, Owen	Peterborough	08.03.38	JNRS	Chelsea	05.55					(G)
			TR	Swindon T.	02.59	1959	3		0	
			TR	Oxford U.	N/L	1962	19		0	
MEDWIN, Terry C.	Swansea	25.09.32	JNRS	Swansea C.	11.49	1951–55	148		59	(W) W–30/W.SCH.INT.●
			TR	Tottenham H.	04.56	1956–62	197		65	
MEE, George E.	Blackpool	20.05.23	Aston Villa+	Nottingham F.	+	1946	9		1	(IF) Son of G.W. Mee –
			TR	Blackpool	10.47					Nephew of Bertie/d.1974
MEECHAM, David A.	Loganlea	10.11.43	Burnley (AM)	Sheffield Wed.	12.60					(F)
			TR	Scunthorpe U.	06.61					
			TR	York C.	06.63	1963	6		0	
MEEK, George	Glasgow	15.02.34	Hamilton	Leeds U.	08.52	1952–59	196		19	(W)
			L	Walsall	01.54	1953–54	44		6	
			TR	Leicester C.	08.60	1960	13		0	
			TR	Walsall	07.61	1961–64	129		22	
MEENS, Harold	Doncaster	05.10.19	Shepherds Rd.J.	Hull C.	*	1946–51	131		0	(CH)
MEESON, David J.	Oxford	06.07.34	Oxford C.	Wolverhampton W.	02.52					(G)
			TR	Reading	08.54	1954–62	156		0	
			TR	Coventry C.	09.62	1962–64	24		0	
MEGSON, Don H.	Sale	12.06.36	JNRS	Sheffield Wed.	05.53	1959–69	386	/	7	(FB)E.F.LGE.REP/
			TR	Bristol Rov.	03.70	1969–70	31	/	1	Father of Gary
MEGSON, Gary J.	Manchester	02.05.59	APP	Plymouth Arg.	05.77	1977–79	78	/	10	(M) Son of Don
			TR	Everton	12.79	1979–80	20	2	2	
			TR	Sheffield Wed.	08.81	1981–83	123		14	
MEHMET, David	London	02.12.60	APP	Millwall	12.77	1976–80	97	17	15	(M)
			Tampa Bay	Charlton Ath.	01.82	1981–82	29	/	3	
			TR	Gillingham	03.83	1982–83	55	1	19	
MEIJER, Geert	Holland	15.03.51	Ajax	Bristol C.	03.79	1978–79	12	3	2	(F) DUTCH INT.
MELDRUM, Colin	Glasgow	26.11.41	JNRS	Arsenal	12.58					(FB)
			TR	Watford	12.60	1960–62	32		0	
			TR	Reading	04.63	1962–69	265	/	8	
			TR	Cambridge U.	N/L	1970	37	1	0	
			TR	Workington	12.74	1974	0	2	0	
MELIA, Jimmy	Liverpool	01.11.37	JNRS	Liverpool	11.54	1955–63	268		79	(IF)E–2/E.F.LGE.REP./●
			TR	Wolverhampton W.	03.64	1963–64	24		4	E.SCH.INT./E.YTH.INT
			TR	Southampton	11.64	1964–68	139	/	11	
			TR	Aldershot	11.68	1968–71	135	/	14	
			TR	Crewe Alex.	02.72	1971	2	2	0	
MELL, Stewart A.	Doncaster	15.10.57	Appleby Frod.	Doncaster Rov.	02.80	1979–82	62	14	14	(F)
			TR	Halifax T.	07.83	1983	22	8	8	
MELLEDEW, Steve	Rochdale	28.11.45	Whipp & Bourne	Rochdale	12.66	1966–69	89	8	23	(F)
			TR	Everton	09.69					
			TR	Aldershot	07.71	1971–73	90	2	27	
			TR	Bury	11.73	1973–74	14	6	2	
			TR	Crewe Alex.	10.74	1974–75	49	7	2	
			TR	Rochdale	07.76	1976–77	76	2	12	
MELLING, Terry	Haverton Hill	24.01.40	Tow Law	Newcastle U.	12.65					(IF)
			TR	Watford	05.66	1965–66	23	1	5	
			TR	Newport Co.	02.67	1966–67	34	/	14	
			TR	Mansfield T.	11.67	1967–68	31	/	7	
			TR	Rochdale	09.68	1968	20	/	8	
			TR	Darlington	03.67	1968–69	21	/	6	
MELLOR, Ian	Sale	19.02.50	Wythenshawe	Manchester C.	12.69	1970–72	36	4	7	(F)
			TR	Norwich C.	03.73	1972–73	28	1	2	
			TR	Brighton & H.A.	04.74	1974–77	116	6	31	
			TR	Chester C.	02.78	1977–78	38	2	11	
			TR	Sheffield Wed.	06.79	1979–81	54	16	11	
			TR	Bradford C	06.82	1982–83	27	9	4	
MELLOR, John A.	Manchester	16.10.21	Ashton U.	Hull C.	05.47	1947–51	104		5	(WH)
MELLOR, Ken E.	Leicester	22.08.34		Leicester C.	07.55					(HB)
			TR	Mansfield T.	07.57	1957–58	65		0	
			TR	Swindon T.	07.59	1959–60	32		4	
MELLOR, Peter J.	Prestbury	20.11.47	Witton A.	Burnley	04.69	1969–71	69	/	0	(G)E.YTH.INT.
			L	Chesterfield	01.72	1971	4	/	0	
			TR	Fulham	02.72	1971–76	189	/	0	
			TR	Hereford U.	09.77	1977	32	/	0	
			TR	Portsmouth	07.78	1978–80	129	/	0	
MELLOR, R. Brett	Huddersfield	04.02.60	APP	Huddersfield T.	02.78	1977	1	/	0	(D)
			TR	Barnsley	11.80					
MELLOR, William	Manchester	29.06.25	Droylsden	Accrington St.	06.50	1950–53	138		1	(FB)
MELLOWS, Mick	London	14.11.47	Sutton U.	Reading	AM	1970	14	2	2	(M)E.AMAT.INT./
			Winchester	Portsmouth	09.73	1973–77	174	8	16	E.YTH.INT.
MELROSE, Jim M.	Glasgow	07.10.58	Partick Th.	Leicester C.	07.80	1980–82	57	15	21	(F)S.U21–8/S.F.LGE REP./
			TR	Coventry C	09.82	1982	21	3	8	S.SCH.INT.

Players Names	Birthplace	Date	Previous Club	League Club	Date Signed	Seasons Played	Apps	Sub	Gls	
MELVILLE, Alan A.	Hartlepool	13.03.41		Hartlepool U.	09.60	1960–61	5		0	(HB)
MELVILLE, Les	Ormskirk	29.11.30	JNRS	Everton	04.50					(HB)E.YTH.INT
			TR	Bournemouth	07.56	1956–57	25		0	
			TR	Oldham Ath.	03.58	1957	2		0	
MENDHAM, Peter S.	Kings Lynn	09.04.60	APP	Norwich C.	04.78	1978-83	126	11	11	(M)
MENMUIR, William F.	Glasgow	03.02.52		Bristol C.	06.69	1969–70	1	1	0	(WH)
MENZIES, Norman	Washington	20.06.26	Hexham Hearts	Barnsley	10.49					(IF)
			TR	Aldershot	05.50	1950–57	221		95	
MENZIES, Ross	Glasgow	31.10.34	Glasgow Rgrs.	Cardiff C.	08.57	1957	1		0	(HB)S.SCH.INT
MERCER, Arthur D.	Sculcoates	14.02.18		Torquay U.	+	1946–48	66		8	
MERCER, James R.	Dunfermline	17.03.35	Rosyth Rgrs.	Bury	06.57	1957–58	18		1	(F)
			TR	Crewe Alex.	06.59	1959	3		0	
MERCER, Joe	Ellesmere Port	09.08.14	Ellesmere Port	Everton	*	1946	12		0	(WH)E–5/E.F.LGE.REP.●
			TR	Arsenal	12.46	1946–53	246		2	Son of pre-war player
MERCER, Keith	Lewisham	14.10.56	APP	Watford	09.74	1972-78	109	25	46	(F)
			TR	Southend U.	02.80	1979-82	132	/	35	
			TR	Blackpool	08.83	1983	31	/	9	
MERCER, Stan	Tranmere	11.09.19		Leicester C.	+	1946	1		0	(F)
			TR	Accrington St.	01.47	1946–48	68		36	
			TR	Mansfield T.	10.48	1948	12		6	
MERCER, Steve J.	Barking	01.05.65	Cambridge U. (N/C)	Peterborough U.	09.82	1982	3	/	0	(D)
MEREDITH, John F.	Doncaster	23.09.40	JNRS	Doncaster Rov.	01.58	1958–60	58		8	(W)
			TR	Sheffield Wed.	02.61	1960	1		0	
			TR	Chesterfield	07.62	1962–63	81		6	
			TR	Gillingham	03.64	1963–68	227	1	7	
			TR	Bournemouth	08.69	1969–70	51	/	1	
MEREDITH, Robert G.	Swansea	03.09.17		Carlisle U.	01.47	1946	1		0	(OR)W.SCH.INT
MEREDITH, Trevor G.	Bridgnorth	25.12.36	Kidderminster	Burnley	11.57	1959–63	36		9	(OR)
			TR	Shrewsbury T.	04.64	1964–71	229	6	42	
MERRICK, Alan R.	Birmingham	20.06.50	APP	W.B.A.	08.67	1968–75	131	8	5	(FB) E.YTH.INT.
			L	Peterborough U.	09.75	1975	5	/	0	
MERRICK, Geoff	Bristol	29.04.51	APP	Bristol C.	08.68	1967-81	361	6	10	(D)E.SCH.INT.
MERRICK, Gil	Birmingham	26.01.22	Solihull T.	Birmingham C.	+	1946–59	485		0	(G) E–23/E.F.LGE.REP.●
MERRICK, Neil G.	Birmingham	06.04.52	Worcester C.	Bournemouth	09.74	1974	13	2	0	(CH)Son of Gil
MERRIFIELD, Roy G.	Mile End	11.10.31	Rainham T.	Chelsea	02.54					(W)
			TR	Millwall	06.56	1956	2		0	
MERRINGTON, Dave R.	Newcastle	26.01.45	APP	Burnley	02.62	1964–70	96	2	1	(CH)
			TR	Bristol C.	07.71					
MERRITT, Harry G.	Ormskirk	22.09.20	JNRS	Everton	*					(OL)
			TR	Orient	09.46	1946	1		0	
METCALF, Colin C.A.	Norwich	03.03.39	Norman O.B.	Norwich C.	07.60	1962–63	12		1	(CH)
			TR	Southend U.	09.64	1964	3		0	
METCALF, Mark P.	Norwich	25.09.65	APP	Norwich C.	09.83	1982	0	1	0	
METCALF, Mike	Liverpool	24.05.39	Everton(AM)	Wrexham	05.57	1957–63	120		58	(IF)
			TR	Chester C.	12.63	1963–68	221	/	68	
METCALFE, John	Birmingham	02.06.35	JNRS	Birmingham C.	10.52	1952	2		0	(W)
			TR	York C.	06.57	1957	3		2	
			TR	Walsall	07.58	1958	2		0	
METCALFE, Ron	Sth. Shields	08.12.47	JNRS	Derby Co.	01.65	1966	1	/	0	(F)
METCALFE, Stuart M.	Blackburn	06.10.50	APP	Blackburn Rov.	01.68	1967-79	376	11	21	(M)E.YTH.INT.
			TR	Carlisle U.	07.80	1980	23	2	3	
			Carolina Lights	Blackburn Rov.	N/C	1982	1	/	0	
			TR	Crewe Alex.	01.83	1982	3	/	0	
METCALFE, Vic	Barrow	03.02.22	Ravensthorpe	Huddersfield T.	+	1946–57	434		87	(OL)E–2/E.F.LGE.REP.●
			TR	Hull C.	06.58	1958–59	6		2	
METCHICK, Dave J.	Derby	14.08.43	JNRS	Fulham	08.61	1961–64	47		9	(IF)E.YTH.INT.
			TR	Orient	12.64	1964–66	75	/	15	
			TR	Peterborough U.	03.67	1966–67	38	/	6	
			TR	Q.P.R.	03.68	1968–69	0	3	1	
			TR	Arsenal	09.70					
			Atlanta (USA)	Brentford	09.73	1973–74	57	4	4	
METHLEY, Irvin	Barnsley	22.09.25	Wolverhampton W. (+)	Walsall	+	1946–50	112		0	(FB)
METHVEN, Colin J.	India	10.12.55	E. Fife	Wigan Ath.	10.79	1979-83	209	1	14	(D)
MEYER, Barry J.	Bournemouth	21.08.32	JNRS	Bristol Rov.	11.49	1950–57	141		55	(IF)Glouc. Cricketer
			TR	Plymouth Arg.	08.58	1958	8		5	
			TR	Newport Co.	02.59	1958–60	70		28	
			TR	Bristol C.	09.61	1961–62	11		7	
MICALLEF, Constantine	Cardiff	24.01.61	APP	Cardiff C.	01.79	1978-82	67	14	11	(F)W.SCH.INT./W.U'21-2
			TR	Newport Co.	09.83	1983	22	2	2	
MICKLEWHITE, Gary	London	21.03.61	APP	Manchester U.	03.78					(M)
			TR	Q.P.R.	07.79	1980-83	84	7	10	

Players Names	Birthplace	Date	Previous Club	League Club	Date Signed	Seasons Played	Apps	Sub	Gls	
MICKLEWRIGHT, Andy	Birmingham	31.01.31	Smethwick H.	Bristol Rov.	01.52	1951–52	7		1	(IF)
			TR	Bristol C.	05.53	1953–54	39		16	
			TR	Swindon T.	09.58	1955–58	115		31	
			TR	Exeter C.	07.59	1959	38		10	
MICKLEWRIGHT, Les J.	Stoke	13.10.15	Stafford Rgrs.	Crewe Alex.	09.46	1946–49	71		0	(LH)
MIDDLEBROUGH, Alan	Rochdale	04.12.25		Bolton W.	07.46	1946–47	5		1	(CF)
			TR	Bradford C.	08.48	1948	4		0	
			TR	Rochdale	10.48	1948–51	47		25	
MIDDLEMASS, Clive	Wortley	25.08.44	JNRS	Leeds U.	08.62					(D)
			TR	Workington	11.63	1963–69	168	1	6	
MIDDLEMASS, Ernie	Newcastle	30.8.20	Sth. Shields	Lincoln C.	06.48	1948	2		0	(CF)
MIDDLETON, Derek	Ashby	30.05.34	Burton A.	York C.	11.58	1958	1		0	
MIDDLETON, Fred T.	W. Hartlepool	02.08.30	JNRS	Newcastle U.	04.48					(WH)
			TR	Lincoln C.	05.54	1954–62	300		16	
MIDDLETON, Harry	Birmingham	18.03.37	JNRS	Wolverhampton W.	08.54	1955	1		0	(CF)E.YTH.INT
			TR	Scunthorpe U.	09.59	1959–60	29		11	
			TR	Portsmouth	06.61	1961	17		5	
			TR	Shrewsbury T.	02.62	1961–64	85		37	
			TR	Mansfield T.	11.64	1964–65	44	1	24	
			TR	Walsall	03.66	1965–67	55	2	26	
MIDDLETON, James	Blackridge	25.04.22		Bradford C.	05.49	1949	8		0	
MIDDLETON, John	Rawmarsh	11.07.55	APP	Bradford C.	07.73	1972-78	188	4	5	(D)
MIDDLETON, John	Lincoln	24.12.56	APP	Nottingham F.	11.74	1974-77	90	/	0	(G)E.U21-3/E.YTH.INT.
			TR	Derby Co.	09.77	1977-79	73	/	0	
MIDDLETON, Matt Y.	Jarrow	24.10 07	Sunderland(*)	Plymouth Arg.	+					(G)*Boldon C.W./Southport/
			TR	Bradford C.	08.46	1946–48	94		0	d. 1979/Brother of Ray
			TR	York C.	02.49	1948–49	55		0	
MIDDLETON, Peter W.	Rawmarsh	13.09.48	APP	Sheffield Wed.	09.65					(IF) d. 1977
			TR	Bradford C.	06.68	1968–72	127	4	25	
			TR	Plymouth Arg.	09.72	1972	1	/	1	
MIDDLETON, Ray	Boldon	06.09.19	Nth. Shields	Chesterfield	*	1946–50	210		0	(G)E'B'–4
			TR	Derby Co.	06.51	1951–53	115		0	Justice of Peace
MIDDLETON, Robert R.	Retford	08.12.33	Bulford U.	Southend U.	11.57	1957	5		1	(F)
			TR	Luton T.	07.58					
			TR	Workington	10.58	1958	2		2	
			TR	Swindon T.	12.58	1958	5		0	
			TR	Aldershot	07.59	1959	5		0	
MIDDLETON, Steve R.	Portsmouth	28.03.53	APP	Southampton	07.70	1973-76	24	/	0	(G)
			L	Torquay U.	03.75	1974	10	/	0	
			TR	Portsmouth	07.77	1977	26	/	0	
MIELCZAREK, Ray	Caernarvon	10.02.46	JNRS	Wrexham	05.64	1964–67	76	/	0	(CH) W–1/W.U23–2
			TR	Huddersfield T.	09.67	1967–70	25	1	1	
			TR	Rotherham U.	01.71	1970–73	114	1	7	
MIHALY, Ron R.	Chesterfield	14.10.52	JNRS	Chesterfield	08.71	1971	4	/	0	(HB)
MILBURN, George W.	Ashington	24.06.10	Leeds U.(*)	Chesterfield	*	1946–47	26		9	(FB) d. 1980
MILBURN, James	Ashington	21.09.19	Ashington	Leeds U.	*	1946–51	206		15	(FB) Brother of John,Stan,
			TR	Bradford P.A.	06.52	1952–54	90		10	Geo.,Cousin of John E.T.
MILBURN, John	Ashington	18.03.08	Leeds U.(*)	Norwich C.	*					(FB)Spen Black/
			TR	Bradford C.	10.46	1946	14		3	d. 1979
MILBURN, John E.T.(Jackie)	Ashington	11.05.24	Ashington ATC	Newcastle U.	+	1946–56	354		173	(CF)E–13/E.F.LGE.REP.●
MILBURN, Stan	Ashington	27.10.26	Ashington	Chesterfield	01.47	1946–51	179		0	(FB)E'B'–1/E.F.LGE.REP.●
			TR	Leicester C.	03.52	1951–57	173		1	
			TR	Rochdale	01.59	1958–64	237		26	
MILBURN, William R.	Sunnyside	25.01.32		Gateshead	04.55	1956	2		0	(HB)
MILES, Dennis	Normanton	06.08.36	JNRS	Bradford P.A.	09.53	1953–54	24		1	
			TR	Southport	06.55	1955–56	51		12	
MILES, Jeff M.	Caldicot	17.01.49	JNRS	Newport Co.	AM	1967–68	4	/	0	(G)
MILES, Sid	Bournemouth	16.05.34		Bournemouth	12.56	1957	1		0	(HB)
MILES, Terry	Stoke	07.05.37	Milton Y.C.	Port Vale	06.55	1956–67	358	7	17	(WH)
MILKINS, John	Dagenham	03.01.44	JNRS	Portsmouth	05.61	1960-73	344	/	0	(G)E.YTH.INT.
			TR	Oxford U.	08.74	1974-78	53	/	0	
MILLAR, Alistair	Glasgow	15.01.52	Benburb	Barnsley	02.71	1970-79	273	16	17	(M)
			TR	York C.	07.80	1980	11	1	0	
MILLAR, James	Dunfermline	21.12.27	Deal	Crewe Alex.	08.58	1958–59	56		1	(FB)
MILLAR, John R.	W. Lothian	25.10.23		Bradford C.	06.49	1949	3		1	
MILLAR, John W.	Auchterderran	31.12.27	Q.of South	Bradford C.	10.48	1949–51	44		7	(F)
			TR	Grimsby T.	05.52	1952	5		3	
MILLAR, Tommy T.	Edinburgh	03.12.38	Bo'ness	Colchester U.	06.59	1959–61	46		4	(FB)
MILLAR, William	Irvine	24.07.24	E. Stirling	Swindon T.	08.50	1950–52	75		17	(IF)
			TR	Gillingham	07.53	1953–55	91		34	
			TR	Accrington St.	07.56	1956	26		11	

Players Names	Birthplace	Date	Previous Club	League Club	Date Signed	Seasons Played	Apps	Sub	Gls	
MILLAR, William	Mansfield	07.02.52	Folkhouse O.B.	Doncaster Rov.	AM	1974	1	/	0	(G)
MILLARD, Lance J.	Bristol	24.06.38		Aldershot	03.62	1960	12		0	(G)
			TR	Barrow	07.64	1964–65	52	/	0	
MILLARD, Len	Coseley	07.03.19	Sunbeam F.C.	W.B.A.	+	1946–57	436		7	(FB)●
MILLARD, Robert	Sth.Shields	02.06.27		Middlesbrough	+					(IF)
			Blyth Spartans	Reading	06.49	1949	2		0	
			TR	Walsall	06.50	1950	7		1	
				Crystal Palace	08.55					
MILLBANK, Joe H.	Edmonton	30.09.19		Crystal Palace	+	1946–47	38		1	
			TR	Q.P.R.	07.48	1948	1		0	
MILLER, Alf G.	Portsmouth	05.03.17	Southport(*)	Plymouth Arg.	+	1946–47	9		0	(CF)*Bristol Rov./Portsmouth
MILLER, Alistair W.	Glasgow	24.01.36	St Mirren	Brighton & H.A.	04.62	1961	1		0	(OL)
			TR	Norwich C.	05.62	1962–63	23		2	
MILLER, Anthony W.	Colchester	26.10.37	JNRS	Colchester U.	05.58	1959–63	6		0	(F)
MILLER, Archie	Larkhall	05.09.13	Hearts	Blackburn Rov.	11.47	1947	6		0	(WH) S–1
			Kilmarnock	Carlisle U.	09.50	1950	1		0	
			Hearts	Workington	02.52					
MILLER, Brian G.	Burnley	19.01.37	JNRS	Burnley	02.54	1955–66	379		30	(WH)E–1/E.U23–3/ E.F. LGE.REP.
MILLER, David	Middlesbrough	21.01.21.	Middlesbrough(*)	Wolverhampton W.	+	1946	2		0	(WH)
			TR	Derby Co.	04.47					
			TR	Doncaster Rov.	01.48	1947–52	140		3	
			TR	Aldershot	03.54	1953	11		0	
MILLER, David B.	Burnley	08.01.64	APP	Burnley	01.82	1982-83	15	3	2	(D)
			L	Crewe Alex.	03.83	1982	3	/	0	
MILLER, Edward	Ulveston	21.06.20	Ulveston	Barrow	05.46	1946–50	124		32	(IF)
MILLER, Ernie G.	S. Africa	17.10.27	Arcadia F.C.	Leeds U.	11.50	1950–51	14		1	(F)
			TR	Workington	03.52	1951	11		0	
MILLER, George	Larkhall	20.05.39	Dunfermline	Wolverhampton W.	10.64	1964–65	37	/	3	(WH)S.F.LGE.REP
MILLER, Graham J.P.	S. Africa	25.08.27		Workington	12.52	1952	8		1	
			TR	Aldershot	07.53					
MILLER, Ian	Perth	13.05.55		Bury	08.73	1973	9	6	0	(W)
			TR	Nottingham F.	03.75					
			TR	Doncaster Rov.	08.75	1975-77	124	/	14	
			TR	Swindon T.	07.78	1978-80	123	4	9	
			TR	Blackburn Rov.	08.81	1981-83	108	2	10	
MILLER, J. Paul	Wolverhampton	09.12.40	St.Nicks B.C.	Shrewsbury T.	07.59	1959–62	77		0	(G) d. 1963
MILLER, John T.	Ipswich	21.09.50	JNRS	Ipswich T.	07.68	1968-73	37	13	2	(F)
			TR	Norwich C.	10.74	1974-75	22	1	3	
			TR	Mansfield T.	07.76	1976-79	109	4	14	
			TR	Port Vale	N/C	1980	22	4	4	
MILLER, Joseph Mc.	Glasgow	02.10.34	Hamilton	Swindon T.	06.56	1956	12		0	
MILLER, Keith R.	Lewisham	26.01.48	Walthamstow	West Ham U.	09.65	1968-69	1	2	0	(M)
			TR	Bournemouth	07.70	1970-79	381	2	19	
MILLER, Lumley R.	Blaydon	03.08.38		Sheffield U.	07.62					(W)
			TR	Hartlepool U.	11.62	1962	9		2	
MILLER, Mark J.	Newcastle	22.09.62	Whitley Bay	Gillingham	10.81	1981-82	5	4	1	(W)
			Whitley Bay	Doncaster Rov.	08.83	1983	21	9	4	
MILLER, Paul R.	Stepney	11.10.59	APP	Tottenham H.	05.77	1978-83	136	2	5	(D)
MILLER, Peter D.	Hoyland	04.12.29		Bradford C.	08.52	1952–55	18		2	(HB)
MILLER, Ralph E.	Slough	22.06.41	Slough T.	Charlton Ath.	09.63	1964	8		0	(CH)
			TR	Gillingham	05.65	1965–67	103	/	4	
			TR	Bournemouth	07.68	1968–70	71	1	1	
MILLER, Roger L.	Moulton	18.08.38	JNRS	Northampton T.	11.56	1956–58	4	1	0	(F)
MILLER, Walter	Cornforth	11.08.30		Hartlepool U.	09.48	1949	1		0	(WH)
			Spennymoor	Luton T.	02.52					
MILLIGAN, Charles	Ardrossan	26.07.30	Ardrossan	Colchester U.	05.56	1956–60	186		3	(HB)
MILLIGAN, Dudley	S. Africa	07.11.16	Clyde	Chesterfield	*	1946	19		6	NI–1
			TR	Bournemouth	08.47	1947–48	45		26	
			TR	Walsall	10.48	1948	5		1	
MILLIGAN, Laurie C.	Liverpool	20.04.58	APP	Blackpool	04.76	1976-78	19	/	0	(D)
			L	Portsmouth	03.79	1978	7	/	0	
			Aldershot(N/C)	Rochdale	10.79	1979	8	1	0	
MILLIN, Alf	Rotherham	18.12.33	JNRS	Derby Co.	08.51	1955	1		0	(FB)
MILLINGTON, Anthony	Hawarden	05.06.43	JNRS	W.B.A.	07.60	1961–62	40		0	(G) W–21/W.U23–4/
			TR	Crystal Palace	10.64	1964–65	16	/	0	Brother of Gren
			TR	Peterborough U.	03.66	1966–68	118	/	0	
			TR	Swansea C.	07.69	1969–73	178	/	0	

Players Names	Birthplace	Date	Previous Club	League Club	Date Signed	Seasons Played	Career Record Apps	Sub	Gls	
MILLINGTON, Grenville	Queensferry	10.12.51	Rhyl	Chester C.	AM	1968	1	/	0	(G)W.AMAT.INT./
			Witton A.	Brighton & H.A.	08.73					Brother of Tony
			TR	Chester C.	09.73	1973-82	289	/	0	
			TR	Wrexham	N/C	1983	13	/	0	
MILLINGTON, John H.	Coseley	21.02.30	JNRS	Aston Villa	09.48					(HB)
			TR	Walsall	07.51	1951–52	23		0	
MILLINGTON, Ralph V.	Neston	18.06.30	Neston F.C.	Tranmere Rov.	01.50	1950–60	357		3	(WH)
MILLION, Esmond	Ashington	15.03.38	Amble J.	Middlesbrough	05.56	1956–61	52		0	(G)
			TR	Bristol Rov.	06.62	1962	38		0	
MILLS, David J.	Whitby	06.12.51	APP	Middlesbrough	12.68	1968-78	278	17	76	(F)E.U23-8
			TR	W.B.A.	01.79	1978-82	44	15	6	
			L	Newcastle U.	01.82	1981	23	/	4	
			TR	Sheffield Wed.	01.83	1982	15	/	3	
			TR	Newcastle U.	08.83	1983	10	6	5	
MILLS, Don	Rotherham	17.08.26		Q.P.R.	08.46	1946–48	43		6	(IF)
			TR	Torquay U.	03.49	1948–49	34		13	
			TR	Q.P.R.	01.50	1949–50	30		3	
			TR	Cardiff C.	02.51	1950	1		0	
			TR	Leeds U.	09.51	1951–52	34		9	
			TR	Torquay U.	12.52	1952–61	310		68	
MILLS, Gary R.	Northampton	11.11.61	APP	Nottingham F.	07.78	1978-81	50	8	8	(M)E.U21-2/E.SCH.INT./
			Seatle Sounders	Derby Co.	10.82	1982	18	/	1	E.YTH.INT./Son of Roly
			Seatle Sounders	Nottingham F.	12.83	1983	5	2	0	
MILLS, Henry	B. Auckland	23.07.22		Sheffield U.	06.46	1946	3		2	(IF)
			TR	Rotherham U.	03.48	1947	7		5	
			TR	Rochdale	04.51	1950	1		0	
			TR	Halifax T.	08.52					
MILLS, Henry O.	Blyth	23.08.22	Blyth Spartans	Huddersfield T.	03.48	1947–55	157		0	(G)
			TR	Halifax T.	12.55	1955–56	26		0	
MILLS, James	Dalton	30.09.15	Dinnington Col.	Rotherham U.	*					(WH)
			TR	Hull C.	10.46	1946–47	42		1	
			TR	Halifax T.	12.47	1947	19		0	
MILLS, John	Bagillt	19.12.20		Chester C.	05.46	1946	3		0	(RH)
MILLS, Keith D.	Egham	29.12.42	JNRS	Grimsby T.	01.60	1960	2		0	(HB)
MILLS, Mick D.	Godalming	4.1.49	Portsmouth(APP)	Ipswich T.	02.66	1965-82	588	3	22	(D)E-42/E.U23-5/●
			TR	Southampton	11.82	1982-83	61	/	3	E.YTH.INT./E.F.LGE REP.
MILLS, Robert B.	London	16.03.55	APP	Colchester U.	12.72	1971–73	20	6	0	(IF)
MILLS, Roly W.G.	Daventry	22.6.33	JNRS	Northampton T.	05.51	1954–63	305		30	(OR) E.YTH.INT
MILLS, Simon A.	Sheffield	16.08.64	APP	Sheffield Wed.	08.82	1982-83	1	2	0	(M) E.YTH.INT.
MILLS, Steve J.	Portsmouth	09.12.53	APP	Southampton	07.71	1972-76	57	4	0	(D)E.U23-1
MILLWARD, Horace D.	Sheffield	10.07.31	Doncaster Rov. (AM)	Southampton	02.52					(F)
			TR	Ipswich T.	07.55	1955–62	143		35	
MILNE, Alex	Dundee	04.06.37	Arbroath	Cardiff C.	03.57	1957–64	172		1	(FB) S.U23–1
MILNE, Gordon	Preston	29.03.37	Morecambe	Preston N.E.	01.56	1956–60	81		3	(WH) E–14/E.F.LGE.REP.
			TR	Liverpool	09.60	1960–66	234	2	17	
			TR	Blackpool	05.67	1967–69	60	4	4	
MILNE, John B.	Aberdeen	27.04.11		Barrow	08.46	1946	33		0	(FB) *Plymouth Arg./Southend
			TR	Oldham Ath.	08.47	1947	13		0	
MILNE, Maurice	Dundee	21.10.32	Dundee U.	Norwich C.	05.57	1957	5		0	(IF)
MILNE, Mike	Aberdeen	17.08.59	APP	Sunderland	05.77					(D)
				Rochdale	02.79	1978	1	1	0	
MILNER, Alf J.G.	Harrogate	06.02.19		Aldershot	08.46	1946	7		1	(OR)
				Darlington	03.48	1947–48	28		4	
			Stockton	Hartlepool U.	11.51					
MILNER, James E.	Newcastle	03.02.33	Blyth Spartans	Burnley	12.52	1953	1		0	(F)
			TR	Darlington	12.57	1957–60	148		27	
			TR	Accrington St.	09.61					
			TR	Tranmere Rov.	06.62	1962	16	/	3	
MILNER, John	Huddersfield	14.05.42	JNRS	Huddersfield T.	05.59	1960–62	17		0	(WH)
			TR	Lincoln C.	10.63	1963–66	109	/	6	
			TR	Bradford P.A.	02.67	1966	6	2	0	
MILNER, Mike	Hull	21.09.39	JNRS	Hull C.	07.57	1958–67	160	/	0	(HB)
			TR	Stockport Co.	07.68	1968	41	/	0	
			TR	Barrow	09.69	1969	11	/	0	
			TR	Bradford C.	12.69	1969	0	1	0	
MILTON, C. Arthur	Bristol	10.03.28	JNRS	Arsenal	07.46	1950–54	75		18	(OR)E–1/Glouc.& England
			TR	Bristol C.	02.55	1954	14		3	cricketer.
MILTON, Roy	Brixham	27.11.34	JNRS	Bury	10.52					(G)
			TR	Torquay U.	08.56	1956	1		0	
MIMMS, Robert A.	York	12.10.63	APP	Halifax T.	08.81					(G)
			TR	Rotherham U.	11.81	1981-83	37	/	0	
MINNOCK, John J.	Tullamore	12.11.49	St Patricks	Charlton Ath.	02.69	1969	0	1	0	(W)

Players Names	Birthplace	Date	Previous Club	League Club	Date Signed	Seasons Played	Apps	Sub	Gls	
MINSHULL, Ray	Bolton	15.07.20	High Park	Liverpool	09.46	1946–49	28		0	(G)
			TR	Southport	07.51	1951–57	218		0	
			TR	Bradford P.A.	12.57	1957–58	28		0	
MINTON, Albert	Walsall	22.09.37	Derby Co. (AM)	Blackpool	10.54					(CF) E.YTH.INT
			TR	Scunthorpe U.	07.57	1957–58	5		0	
			TR	Doncaster Rov.	12.58	1958	11		2	
MINTON, Roger C.	Birmingham	04.06.51	APP	W.B.A.	06.69	1970–74	24	2	1	(FB)
MIROCEVIC, Anton	Yugoslavia	06.08.52	FC Budocnost	Sheffield Wed.	10.80	1980-82	58	3	6	(M)YUGOSLAV INT.
MITCHELL, Albert J.	Stoke	22.01.22	JNRS	Stoke C.	+	1946–47	10		2	(OL)E'B'–1
			TR	Blackburn Rov.	02.48	1947	3		0	
			TR	Northampton T.	05.49	1949–50	81		19	
			TR	Luton T.	07.51	1951–54	106		41	
			TR	Middlesbrough	09.54	1954–56	50		5	
			TR	Southport	08.56	1956	16		3	
MITCHELL, Alex R.	Greenock	24.05.18	Bute	Ipswich T.	08.46	1947–49	42		2	(FB)
MITCHELL, Anthony J.	London	07.09.59	Leatherhead	Exeter C.	07.79	1978-81	60	/	0	(M)
MITCHELL, Arnold	Rotherham	01.12.29		Derby Co.	02.48					(HB)●
			TR	Nottingham F.	03.50					
			TR	Notts. Co.	05.51	1951	1		0	
			TR	Exeter C.	07.52	1952–65	495	/	44	
MITCHELL, Barrie	Aberdeen	15.03.47	Aberdeen	Tranmere Rov.	02.74	1973-75	77	6	10	(F)
			TR	Preston N.E.	07.76	1976	7	4	2	
			TR	York C.	09.77	1977	1	2	0	
MITCHELL, David J.	Stoke	24.08.45	JNRS	Port Vale	03.64	1964–65	21	/	4	(F)
			TR	Ipswich T.	08.66	1966	0	2	0	
MITCHELL, Frank R.	Australia	03.06.22	Coventry C. (AM)	Birmingham C.	+	1946-48	93		6	(WH)Warwicks Cricketer/
			TR	Chelsea	01.49	1948–51	75		1	d.1984
			TR	Watford	08.52	1952–56	193		0	
MITCHELL, Ian J.	Falkirk	09.05.46	Dundee U.	Newcastle U.	07.70	1970	2	1	0	(F) S.U23–2/S.SCH.INT
MITCHELL, James	Ilkeston	01.07.37	Ilkeston T.	Derby Co.	10.58	1958–59	6		0	(G)
MITCHELL, John	London	12.03.52	St. Albans	Fulham	02.72	1972-77	158	11	56	(F)
			TR	Millwall	06.78	1978-80	78	3	18	
MITCHELL, John D.	Titchfield	19.01.28		Southampton	03.49	1950	7		0	
MITCHELL, John G.				Hartlepool U.	11.46	1946	3		2	(CF)
MITCHELL, Ken	Sunderland	26.05.57	APP	Newcastle U.	04.75	1976-80	61	5	2	(D)
			TR	Darlington	08.81	1981	12	1	1	
MITCHELL, Ken S.	Wearhead	26.12.33	Whitby Rov.	Plymouth Arg.	06.56	1956	6		2	(F)
			Bridgwater	Hartlepool U.	08.59					
			TR	Darlington	09.59					
MITCHELL, Norman	Sunderland	07.11.31	W. Stanley	Chesterfield	10.51	1951–52	66		7	(F)
			TR	Workington	11.53	1953–57	138		23	
			TR	Hartlepool U.	03.58	1957–58	23		6	
MITCHELL, Reg	Plymouth	25.09.36	JNRS	Plymouth Arg.	02.55	1955	2		2	
MITCHELL, Robert	Sth. Shields	04.01.55	APP	Sunderland	01.72	1973-75	1	2	0	(M)
			TR	Blackburn Rov.	07.76	1976-77	17	12	6	
			TR	Grimsby T.	06.78	1978-81	142	/	6	
			TR	Carlisle U.	08.82	1982	2	/	0	
			TR	Rotherham U.	03.83	1982-83	46	7	2	
MITCHELL, Robert	Petersfield	17.12.48	Alton T.	Aldershot	09.69	1969–70	5	7	1	(CF)
MITCHELL, Robert	Glasgow	16.08.24	T. Lanark	Newcastle U.	02.49	1948–60	367		95	(OL) S–2/S.F.LGE.REP
MITCHELL, Ron G.	Morecambe	13.02.35	Morecambe	Leeds U.	11.58	1958	4		0	(FB)
MITCHELL, Ron J.	Renfrew	27.05.25	Glasgow Celtic	Exeter C.	08.49	1949–51	6		0	(OR)
MITCHELL, Stewart A.	Glasgow	03.03.33	Benburb	Newcastle U.	09.53	1954–62	45		0	(G)
MITCHELSON, Ken G.	Edmonton	16.05.28	Tottenham H.(AM)	Charlton Ath.	09.47					(FB)
			TR	Bristol C.	05.49	1949–52	18		0	
MITCHESON, Frank J.	Stalybridge	10.03.24	Droylsden	Doncaster Rov.	+	1946–48	22		5	(IF)
			TR	Crewe Alex.	11.48	1948–53	181		34	
			TR	Rochdale	06.54	1954–55	50		8	
MITCHINSON, Tom W.	Sunderland	24.02.43	JNRS	Sunderland	12.60	1962–65	16	1	2	(IF)
			TR	Mansfield T.	01.66	1965–67	76	/	15	
			TR	Aston Villa	08.67	1967–68	49	/	9	
			TR	Torquay U.	05.69	1968–71	108	/	9	
			TR	Bournemouth	12.71	1971–72	31	1	1	
MITTEN, Charles	Rangoon	17.01.21	JNRS	Manchester U.	*	1946–49	142		50	(OL) Father of John
			TR	Fulham	01.52	1951–55	156		32	and Charles E.
			TR	Mansfield T.	02.56	1955–57	97		24	
MITTEN, Charles E.	Altrincham	14.12.43	Newcastle U. (APP)	Manchester U.	11.61					(F)
			TR	Bury	09.64					
			Altrincham	Halifax T.	10.65	1965	1	/	0	
			Yeovil T.	Plymouth Arg.	07.67					

Players Names	Birthplace	Date	Previous Club	League Club	Date Signed	Seasons Played	Apps	Sub	Gls	
MITTEN, John	Manchester	30.03.41	JNRS	Mansfield T.	AM	1957	3		0	(W) E.YTH.INT./
			TR	Newcastle U.	09.60	1957–60	9		3	E.SCH.INT/
			TR	Leicester C.	09.61	1961	12		0	Leic. Cricketer
			TR	Manchester U.	04.63					
			TR	Coventry C.	08.63	1963–66	35	2	6	
			TR	Plymouth Arg.	01.67	1966–67	43	/	8	
			TR	Exeter C.	07.68	1968–70	96	4	17	
MITTON, Gilbert K.	Leyland	30.12.28	Leyland Mot.	Preston N.E.	05.50	1953	2		0	(G)
			TR	Carlisle U.	06.54	1954–56	48		0	
MOBLEY, David L.	Oxford	24.08.48	JNRS	Sheffield Wed.	09.65					(HB) Brother of Vic
			TR	Grimsby T.	07.69	1969	26	2	0	
MOBLEY, Vic J.	Oxford	11.10.43	Oxford C.	Sheffield Wed.	09.61	1963–69	187	/	8	(CH) E.U23–13/
			TR	Q.P.R.	10.69	1969–70	24	1	0	E.F.LGE.REP
MOCHAN, Dennis	Falkirk	12.12.35	Raith Rov.	Nottingham F.	06.62	1962–65	107	/	1	(FB)
			TR	Colchester U.	09.66	1966–69	114	3	2	
MOCHAN, Neil	Larbert	06.04.27	Morton	Middlesbrough	05.51	1951–52	38		14	(CF) S–3/S'B'–1
MOFFAT, Adam	Dunfermline	01.04.41	E. Fife	Newport Co.	10.61	1961	17		5	(F)
MOFFAT, Robert W.	Portsmouth	07.10.45	APP	Portsmouth	10.63					(HB)
			TR	Gillingham	05.65	1965–67	23	1	1	
MOFFATT, Gregory T.	Liverpool	08.01.64	APP	Chester C.	01.82	1982	6	1	0	(D)
MOFFATT, John B.	Greenock	22.12.29	Bellshill Ath.	Brighton & H.A.	12.51	1952	2		0	
MOFFATT, Norman	Bootle	18.11.20		Workington	08.51	1951	1		0	(IF)
MOFFITT, Ken	Newcastle	02.02.33	Berwick Rgrs.	Brentford	08.53					(FB)
			Berwick Rgrs.	Gateshead	09.57	1957–59	76		2	
MOGFORD, Reg W.G.	Newport	12.06.19	JNRS	Newport Co.	*	1946–47	19		9	(OL)
MOIR, Ian	Aberdeen	30.06.43	JNRS	Manchester U.	07.60	1960–64	46		5	(W)
			TR	Blackpool	02.65	1964–66	61	/	12	
			TR	Chester C.	05.67	1967	25	/	3	
			TR	Wrexham	01.68	1967–71	144	6	20	
			TR	Shrewsbury T.	03.72	1971–72	22	3	2	
			TR	Wrexham ·	07.73	1973–74	11	4	0	
MOIR, James	Newcastle	23.03.18	Accrington St.(*)	Carlisle U.	08.46	1946–47	42		20	(CF) *Newcastle W.E.
MOIR, Richard J.	Glasgow	22.10.45	Cumnock	Shrewsbury T.	03.69	1969–73	159	7	30	(IF)
			TR	Halifax T.	07.74	1974	16	3	5	
MOIR, Willie	Bucksbourne	19.04.22	R.A.F. Kirkham	Bolton W.	+	1946–55	325		113	(IF) S·1/S'B'–1
			TR	Stockport Co.	09.55	1955–57	69		26	
MOKONE, Steve	S. Africa	23.03.32	Pretoria	Coventry C.	10.56	1956	4		1	(F)
			Holland	Cardiff C.	06.59	1959	3		1	
			TR	Barnsley	08.61					
MOLLATT, Ron V.	Edwinstowe	24.02.32	JNRS	Leeds U.	02.50	1951–54	17		0	(WH)
			TR	York C.	07.55	1955–59	124		1	
			TR	Bradford C.	07.60	1960–62	88		0	
MOLLER, Jan B.	Sweden	17.09.53	Malmo	Bristol C.	12.80	1980–81	48	/	0	(G)SWEDISH INT.
MOLLOY, Gerry	Rochdale	13.03.36	JNRS	Rochdale	11.53	1955–56	6		0	(OL)
MOLLOY, Peter	Rossendale		Distillery	Notts. Co.	04.48	1947	1		0	(WH) NI.F.LGE.REP/
										*Q.P.R./Cardiff C./Carlisle U./
										Bradford C.
MOLLOY, William G.	Coventry	28.08.29		Southampton	10.49	1949	1		0	(RH)
				Newport Co.	11.50	1950	3		0	
			Lockheed A.P.	Millwall	03.52					
			TR							
MOLYNEUX, Bernard	Prescot	17.09.33	JNRS	Everton	12.51					
			TR	Tranmere Rov.	05.56	1956	12		3	
MOLYNEUX, Fred G.	Wallasey	25.07.44	JNRS	Liverpool	06.62					(HB)
			TR	Southport	08.65	1965–68	123	/	1	
			TR	Plymouth Arg.	08.68	1968–70	79	/	5	
			TR	Exeter C.	02.71	1970	2	/	0	
			TR	Tranmere Rov.	02.71	1970–72	71	1	0	
			TR	Southport	07.73	1973	32	1	1	
MOLYNEUX, Geoff B.	Warrington	23.01.43	Rylands Y.C.	Chester C.	AM	1962	1		0	(OR)
MOLYNEUX, John A.	Warrington	03.02.31		Chester C.	02.49	1949–54	178		1	(FB) E.YTH.INT/
			TR	Liverpool	06.55	1955–61	228		2	Brother of Geoff B.
			TR	Chester C.	08.62	1962–64	67		0	
MOLYNEUX, Ray	Kearsley	13.06.30		Bradford C.	02.46	1948	2		1	
			TR	Bournemouth	02.53					
MOLYNEUX, William S.	Liverpool	10.01.44		Liverpool	11.63	1964	1		0	(G)
			TR	Oldham Ath.	06.67	1968	8	/	0	
MONAGHAN, Derek J.	Bromsgrove	20.01.59	APP	W.B.A.	01.77	1979–83	14	5	2	(F)E.YTH.INT.
MONCREIFF, James C.	Todmorden	14.06.22		Halifax T.	AM	1946–54	42		13	(CF) d. 1975
MONCUR, Robert	Perth	19.01.45	APP	Newcastle U.	04.62	1962–73	293	3	3	(D)S–16/S.U23–1/
			TR	Sunderland	06.74	1974–76	86	/	2	S.SCH.INT.
			TR	Carlisle U.	11.76	1976	11	/	0	

Players Names	Birthplace	Date	Previous Club	League Club	Date Signed	Seasons Played	Apps	Sub	Gls	
MONEY, Richard	Lowestoft	13.10.55	Lowestoft T.	Scunthorpe U.	07.73	1973-77	165	8	4	(D)
			TR	Fulham	12.77	1977-79	106	/	3	
			TR	Liverpool	04.80	1980	12	2	0	
			L	Derby Co.	12.81	1981	5	/	0	
			TR	Luton T.	04.82	1981-82	44	/	1	
			TR	Portsmouth	08.83	1983	16	/	0	
MONK, Brian	Leeds	15.05.37	JNRS	Leeds U.	02.55					(F)
			TR	Crewe Alex.	05.58	1958	5		0	
			TR	Halifax T.	01.59					
MONK, Fred J.	Brighton	09.10.20	Guildford C.	Brentford	03.48	1947–53	205		48	(FB)E.SCH.INT.
			TR	Aldershot	07.54	1954–55	48		0	
MONKHOUSE, Alan W.	Stockton	23.10.30	Thornaby	Millwall	08.50	1949–53	65		20	(CF)
			TR	Newcastle U.	10.53	1953–55	21		9	
			TR	York C.	06.56	1956	12		1	
MONKHOUSE, Graham	Carlisle	26.04.54	Penrith	Workington	08.76	1976	4	/	0	(G)
MONKS, John	Stockport	03.06.21		Stockport Co.	04.47	1946–52	91		1	(WH)
MONOGHAN, William	Glasgow	02.09.19	Alloa	Bury	08.46					
				Carlisle U.	08.47	1947–49	19		0	
MONTGOMERY, Alec W.	Tamworth	16.09.26	Baddesley F.C.	Walsall	08.49	1951–52	29		0	(CF)
MONTGOMERY, Derek	Houghton	05.05.50	APP	Leeds U.	12.67					(F)
			TR	Bradford C.	08.68	1968	4	/	0	
MONTGOMERY, Jim	Sunderland	09.10.43	JNRS	Sunderland	10.60	1961-76	537	/	0	(G)E.U23-6/E.YTH.INT.●
			L	Southampton	10.76	1976	5	/	0	
			TR	Birmingham C.	02.77	1976-78	66	/	0	
			TR	Nottingham F.	08.79					
			TR	Sunderland	08.80					
MONTGOMERY, Stan W.J.	W. Ham	07.07.20	Romford	Hull C.	+	1946	5		0	(CH)Glamorgan cricketer/
			TR	Southend U.	09.46	1946–48	96		6	Brother-in-law of
			TR	Cardiff C.	12.48	1948–54	231		4	J.A. Nelson
			TR	Newport Co.	11.55	1955	9		0	
MOODY, Alan	Middlesbrough	18.01.51	APP	Middlesbrough	01.68	1968-72	44	2	0	(D)E.SCH.INT.●
			TR	Southend U.	10.79	1972-83	444	2	41	
MOODY, Ken G.	Grimsby	12.11.24	JNRS	Grimsby T.	+	1947–50	114		0	(FB)
MOODY, V. Roy	Worksop	12.03.23		Lincoln C.	11.46	1946	1		0	(OR)
MOONEY, Dean F.	Paddington	24.07.56	APP	Orient	07.47	1974-75	16	6	3	(F)
			Gais	Bournemouth	12.80	1980-81	27	/	10	
MOONEY, Frank	Fauldhouse	01.01.32	Bathgate St.M.	Manchester U.	05.49					(OR)
			TR	Blackburn Rov.	02.54	1953–55	58		19	
			TR	Carlisle U.	05.56	1956–59	124		23	
MOONEY, John	Fauldhouse	21.02.26	Hamilton	Doncaster Rov.	05.53	1953–58	170		32	(OR)
MOONEY, Kevin W.	Liverpool	23.08.59	Bangor C.	Bury	03.80	1980	1	/	0	(D)
			Telford	Tranmere Rov.	08.82	1982	21	1	0	
MOOR, Anthony J.	York	18.01.40	Scarborough	York C.	05.62	1962–64	57		0	(G)
			TR	Darlington	07.65	1965–71	239	/	0	
MOORCROFT, David S.	Liverpool	16.03.47	Skelmersdale	Tranmere Rov.	12.68	1968–71	107	1	1	(WH)
MOORCROFT, Maurice	Chesterfield	04.11.29	JNRS	Sheffield U.	07.48					(G) E.YTH.INT
			TR	Gillingham	07.52	1952	8		0	
MOORE, Alan	Hebburn	07.03.27		Sunderland	05.46					(OR)
			Spennymoor	Chesterfield	12.48	1948–50	66		3	
			TR	Hull C.	07.51	1951	14		4	
			TR	Nottingham F.	01.52	1951–54	101		39	
			TR	Coventry C.	12.54	1954–56	57		11	
			TR	Swindon T.	07.57	1957–58	19		3	
			TR	Rochdale	11.58	1958	11		2	
MOORE, Andy D.	Wantage	02.10.64	APP	Reading	APP	1981	0	1	0	(M)
MOORE, Andy R.	Cleethorpes	14.11.65	APP	Grimsby T.	11.83	1983	8	1	0	(D)
MOORE, Anthony P.	York	07.02.43	Heworth	York C.	AM	1962	2		0	(CF)
MOORE, Anthony P.	Scarborough	04.09.47	APP	Chesterfield	01.65	1964–70	147	8	13	(IF)
			L	Grimsby T.	03.71	1970	2	1	0	
			TR	Chester C.	08.71	1971	9	4	3	
MOORE, Anthony P.	Wolverhampton	19.09.57	Burton A.	Sheffield U.	07.79	1979-81	29	/	0	(D)
			TR	Crewe Alex.	08.82	1982	17	/	2	
MOORE, Bernard J.	Brighton	18.12.23	JNRS	Brighton & H.A.	+	1947	8		2	(CF)
			Hastings U.	Luton T.	01.51	1950–53	73		31	
			TR	Brighton & H.A.	03.54	1953–54	29		10	
MOORE, Brian	Hamsworth	24.12.38	Loughboro Coll.	Mansfield T.	AM	1960	4		0	(OR)
			TR	Notts Co.	12.61	1961–62	27		3	
			TR	Doncaster Rov.	07.63	1963	1		0	
MOORE, Brian M.	Belfast	29.12.33	Distillery	West Ham U.	02.55	1954–55	9		1	
MOORE, David	Grimsby	17.12.59	APP	Grimsby T.	12.77	1978-82	136	/	2	(D)
			TR	Carlisle U.	08.83	1983	13	/	1	
			TR	Blackpool	12.83	1983	28	/	1	

Players Names	Birthplace	Date	Previous Club	League Club	Date Signed	Seasons Played	Apps	Sub	Gls	
MOORE, Eric	St Helens	16.07.26		Everton	02.49	1949–56	171		0	(FB)
			TR	Chesterfield	01.57	1956	6		0	
			TR	Tranmere Rov.	07.57	1957	36		0	
MOORE, Gary	Sunderland	04.11.45	JNRS	Sunderland	11.62	1964-66	13	/	2	(F)
			TR	Grimsby T.	02.67	1966-68	52	/	15	
			TR	Southend U.	11.68	1968-73	156	6	46	
			L	Colchester U.	03.74	1973	11	/	7	
			TR	Chester C.	08.74	1974-75	29	14	4	
			TR	Swansea C.	07.76	1976-77	30	4	8	
MOORE, Graham	Hengoed	07.03.41	JNRS	Cardiff C.	05.58	1958–61	85		23	(CF) W–21/W.U23–9/
			TR	Chelsea	12.61	1961–63	68		13	E.F. LGE. REP.
			TR	Manchester U.	11.63	1963	18		4	
			TR	Northampton T.	12.65	1965–66	54	/	10	
			TR	Charlton Ath.	06.67	1967–70	110	/	8	
			TR	Doncaster Rov.	09.71	1971–73	67	2	3	
MOORE, Howard	Harbledown	05.03.47	Ashford T.	Coventry C.	03.67					(F)
			TR	Gillingham	07.67	1967	17	/	0	
			TR	Southend U.	01.68	1967–68	6	2	0	
			TR	Port Vale	07.69					
MOORE, John	Liverpool	09.09.45	Everton (APP)	Stoke C.	07.63	1967	12	1	0	(WH)
			TR	Shrewsbury T.	08.68	1968–72	144	/	3	
			TR	Swansea C.	01.73	1972–73	31	/	0	
MOORE, John	Harthill	21.12.43	Motherwell	Luton T.	05.65	1965–72	263	9	13	(WH)
			TR	Brighton & H.A.	10.72	1972	5	/	0	
				Northampton T.	08.74	1974	14	/	0	
MOORE, John F.B.	Cardiff	25.12.19	Bangor C.	Cardiff C.	+	1947–48	6		4	(OL)
			Bangor C.	Newport Co.	07.50	1950–52	121		46	
MOORE, John M.	Carlton	01.02.43	Arnold St.M.	Lincoln C.	11.61	1961–64	30		5	(W)
MOORE, John W.	Chiswich	25.09.23		Brentford	09.46	1946–47	5		0	
			TR	Colchester U.	07.50	1951	2		0	
MOORE, Jon	Cardiff	17.11.55	APP	Bristol Rov.	11.73					(D)W.SCH.INT./W.YTH.INT.
			TR	Millwall	12.74	1974-78	119	/	5	
			TR	Bournemouth	05.79	1979-80	36	/	2	
MOORE, Keith	Arnold	14.01.34		Nottingham F.	08.52	1952	1		0	
MOORE, Ken	Bradford	13.09.21		Halifax T.	11.47	1947–49	31		2	
MOORE, Kevin	Loughborough	20.10.57	APP	Shrewsbury T.	10.75	1974-77	15	3	1	(M)
MOORE, Kevin J.	Blackpool	30.01.56	APP	Blackpool	10.73	1974-76	33	5	3	(W)
			L	Bury	12.76	1976	4	/	0	
			TR	Swansea C.	07.77	1977-78	51	4	6	
			TR	Newport Co.	02.79	1978-82	140	8	13	
			L	Swindon T.	03.83	1982	1	/	0	
MOORE, Kevin T.	Grimsby	29.04.58	JNRS	Grimsby T.	07.76	1976-83	311	2	16	(D)E.SCH.INT.
MOORE, Les J.	Sheffield	07.07.33	Worksop T.	Derby Co.	11.57	1957–63	144		3	(CH)
			Boston U.	Lincoln C.	10.65	1965–66	59	/	0	
MOORE, Malcolm	Silksworth	18.12.48	APP	Sunderland	12.65	1967-68	10	2	3	(F)
			L	Crewe Alex.	03.70	1969	8	/	0	
			TR	Tranmere Rov.	07.70	1970-72	83	8	21	
			TR	Hartlepool U.	08.73	1973-75	127	2	34	
			TR	Workington	08.76	1976	22	/	2	
MOORE, Mick	Chorley	20.07.52		Preston N.E.	06.70					(F)
			TR	Southport	07.71	1971-73	62	21	10	
			Wigan Ath.	Port Vale	03.78	1977	13	/	0	
			TR	Wigan Ath.	08.78	1978-79	57	7	12	
MOORE, Norman W.	Grimsby	15.10.19	JNRS	Grimsby T.	*	1946	7		1	(CF) Father of Kevin/
			TR	Hull C.	04.47	1946–49	81		46	David/Brother of Tom R.
			TR	Blackburn Rov.	03.50	1949–50	7		1	
			TR	Bury	08.51	1951	2		0	
MOORE, Ray	Workington	02.11.56	Sekers F.C.	Workington	N/C	1975	3	/	0	(W)
MOORE, Robert	Campsall	14.12.32	Worksop T.	Rotherham U.	05.55	1955–56	19		2	(F)
			TR	Chesterfield	10.56	1956–58	19		3	
MOORE, Robert F.	Barking	12.04.41	JNRS	West Ham U.	06.58	1958-73	543	1	24	(D)E-108/E.U23-8/●
			TR	Fulham	03.74	1973-76	124	/	1	E.F.LGE REP./E.YTH.INT.
MOORE, Ron D.	Liverpool	29.01.53	JNRS	Tranmere Rov.	08.73	1971-78	248	1	72	(F)
			TR	Cardiff C.	02.79	1978-79	54	2	6	
			TR	Rotherham U.	08.80	1980-83	124	1	51	
			TR	Charlton Ath.	09.83	1983	27	1	8	
MOORE, Sam	Birmingham	06.09.34		Wolverhampton W.	11.54					(F)
			TR	Walsall	05.55	1955–57	64		12	
			TR	Gillingham	06.58	1958–59	33		8	
MOORE, Tom L.	Trimdon	25.07.36	Trimdon	Darlington	AM	1956	1		0	(G)
MOORE, Tom R.	Grimsby	18.12.23		Grimsby T.	06.47	1948–49	3	/	0	
MOORE, Watty	W. Hartlepool	30.08.25		Hartlepool U.	05.48	1948–59	448		1	(CH)

Players Names	Birthplace	Date	Previous Club	League Club	Date Signed	Seasons Played	Career Record Apps	Sub	Gls	
MOORES, Ian R.	Chesterton	05.10.54	APP	Stoke C.	06.72	1973-75	40	10	14	(F)E.U23-2
			TR	Tottenham H.	08.76	1976-78	25	4	6	
			TR	Orient	10.78	1978-81	110	7	26	
			TR	Bolton W.	07.82	1982	23	3	3	
			L	Barnsley	02.83	1982	3	/	0	
MOORES, J. Craig	Macclesfield	01.02.61	APP	Bolton W.	02.79	1980	0	1	0	(F)
			TR	Swindon T.	07.81	1981	1	1	0	
MOORHOUSE, Alan	Wardle	12.10.25	Blackburn Rov.(AM)	Rochdale	03.47	1946–47	17		3	
MORAN, Brian J.	Hemsworth	03.06.47		Barnsley	01.67	1966	1	/	0	(OR)
MORAN, Doug W.	Musselburgh	29.07.34	Falkirk	Ipswich T.	07.61	1961–63	104		35	(IF)
MORAN, Edward	Cleland	20.07.30		Leicester C.	09.47	1948–50	8		1	(IF)
			TR	Stockport Co.	10.51	1951–56	110		42	
			TR	Rochdale	02.57	1956–58	42		13	
			TR	Crewe Alex.	09.58	1958	22		8	
MORAN, James	Wishaw	06.03.35	Wishaw J.	Leicester C.	12.55	1956	3		1	(IF)
			TR	Norwich C.	11.57	1957–59	37		17	
			TR	Northampton T.	01.61	1960–61	24		5	
			TR	Darlington	08.62	1962	27		6	
			TR	Workington	07.63	1963–65	100	/	22	
MORAN, John	Cleland	09.03.33	Coltness U.	Derby Co.	11.54	1954	2		0	
MORAN, Kevin B.	Dublin	29.04.56	Pegasus(Gaelic)	Manchester U.	02.78	1978-83	139	/	17	(D)EI-17
MORAN, Lister F.	Clara Vale	24.06.30	Wearmouth Col.	Gateshead	10.50	1951–56	22		0	(WH)
MORAN, Mike E.	Leek	26.12.35		Port Vale	07.54					
			TR	Crewe Alex.	07.57	1957	14		3	
MORAN, Ron	Liverpool	28.02.34	JNRS	Liverpool	01.52	1952–64	342		15	(FB)E.F.LGE.REP
MORAN, Steve J.	Croydon	10.01.61	JNRS	Southampton	08.79	1979-83	117	3	59	(F)E.U'21-2
MORAN, Tom	Glasgow	31.05.24	Alloa Ath.	Accrington St.	08.53	1953	7		0	
MORAN, Tom	Edinburgh	05.02.30	Cowdenbeath	Carlisle U.	05.54	1954–55	36		5	(OL)
			TR	Darlington	05.56	1956–57	66		13	
MORDUE, James	Seaton Delaval	18.02.24		Bradford P.A.	09.46	1948	2		0	
MORDUE, William	Durham	23.2.37	Bentley Col.	Doncaster Rov.	09.58	1957–60	78		0	(HB)
MOREFIELD, John W.	Barnwood	26.10.22		Halifax T.	05.46	1946–48	66	*	0	(FB)
MORELAND, Vic.	Belfast	15.06.57	Glentoran	Derby Co.	09.78	1978–79	38	4	1	(D)NI-6/NI.U21-1
MORELINE, David J.	Stepney	02.12.50	APP	Fulham	01.68	1968–73	63	7	0	(D)
			TR	Reading	06.74	1974–80	166	/	0	
MOREMONT, Ralph	Sheffield	24.09.24		Sheffield U.	09.46	1949	2		0	(WH)
			TR	Chester C.	05.50	1950–52	121		19	
MORGAN, Alan	Swansea	02.01.36		Leeds U.	01.54					
			TR	Crewe Alex.	09.56	1956–57	6		0	
MORGAN, Arthur R.	Ogmore	13.09.30		Swansea C.	12.48	1950–52	13		0	(FB)
			TR	Plymouth Arg.	11.53	1953–56	36		4	
MORGAN, Cliff I.	Bristol	26.09.13		Bristol C.	*	1946–48	66		4	(WH)
MORGAN, Denley J.	Llanelli	13.02.51		Swansea C.	02.71	1968–71	14	1	0	(FB)
MORGAN, Dennis	Seven Sisters	22.09.25	Cardiff C. (+)	Norwich C.	10.46	1946–55	225		3	(FB) + Britton Ferry
MORGAN, Don	Huddersfield	08.06.25	Huddersfield T.(AM)	Accrington St.	06.47	1946–47	8		1	d. 1976
			TR	Tranmere Rov.	05.48					
			TR	Halifax T.	10.48					
MORGAN, Ernest	Barnsley	13.01.27	Royston Y.C.	Lincoln C.	09.49	1952	3		0	(CF)
			TR	Gillingham	08.53	1953–56	155		73	
MORGAN, George W.	Cardiff	28.03.23	Cardiff C.(AM)	Norwich C.	01.47	1946–49	65		15	(IF)
			TR	Newport Co.	06.50					
MORGAN, Gerry	Llanidloes	23.02.50		Walsall	AM	1973	1	/	0	(G)
MORGAN, Huw	Neath	20.08.64	APP	Swansea C.	08.82	1983	5	2	0	(M)
MORGAN, Ian A.	Walthamstow	14.11.46	APP	Q.P.R.	09.64	1964–72	161	11	26	(W) Twin brother of Roger
			TR	Watford	10.73	1973	15	1	1	
MORGAN, Keith	Trowbridge	19.02.40	Westbury	Swindon T.	08.58	1958–66	326	/	6	(WH)
MORGAN, Ken S.	Swansea	28.07.32		Fulham	09.50					
			TR	Watford	09.52					
				Northampton T.	09.54					
			TR	Brentford	08.55					
			TR	Crystal Palace	10.55	1955	2		0	
MORGAN, Laurie	Rotherham	05.05.31	Sheffield U.(AM)	Huddersfield T.	03.49	1949–50	7		0	(FB)
			TR	Rotherham U.	08.54	1954–63	290		0	
			TR	Darlington	07.64	1964–65	29	1	0	
MORGAN, Lewis	Cowdenbeath	30.04.11	Portsmouth(*)	Watford	07.46	1946–47	50		0	(FB)
MORGAN, Nick	E. Ham	30.10.59	APP	West Ham U.	11.77	1978-82	14	7	2	(F)
			TR	Portsmouth	03.83	1982-83	19	12	10	

Players Names	Birthplace	Date	Previous Club	League Club	Date Signed	Seasons Played	Apps	Sub	Gls	
MORGAN, Peter W.	Cardiff	28.10.51	JNRS	Cardiff C.	11.69	1972	16	/	0	(D)
			TR	Hereford U.	08.74	1974	16	/	0	
			TR	Newport Co.	03.76	1975-76	22	2	1	
MORGAN, Ritchie	Cardiff	03.10.46	Cardiff Corries	Cardiff C.	02.66	1967–76	69	/	0	(HB) W.U23–1/ W. SCH. INT.
MORGAN, Roger E.	Walthamstow	14.11.46	APP	Q.P.R.	09.64	1964–68	180	/	39	(W) E.U23–1/E. YTH. INT
			TR	Tottenham H.	02.69	1968–71	66	2	8	
MORGAN, Ron	Twynrodeyn	06.09.15	Doncaster Rov. (*)	Accrington St.	+	1946	4		0	(F)
MORGAN, Sam J.	Belfast	03.12.46	Gorleston	Port Vale	07.70	1969-72	109	4	24	(F)NI-18
			TR	Aston Villa	08.73	1973-75	35	5	9	
			TR	Brighton & H.A.	12.75	1975-76	19	16	9	
			TR	Cambridge U.	08.77	1977	34	3	4	
MORGAN, Stan A.	Abergwynfi	10.10.20	Gwynfl. W.	Arsenal	+	1946	2		0	(IF)
			TR	Walsall	06.48	1948	10		1	
			TR	Millwall	12.48	1948–52	156		40	
			TR	Orient	05.53	1953–55	96		26	
MORGAN, Stuart E.	Swansea	23.09.49	JNRS	West Ham U.	03.67					(D)
			L	Torquay U.	02.69	1968	14	/	0	
			TR	Reading	11.69	1969-71	42	4	1	
			TR	Colchester U.	08.72	1972-74	79	2	10	
			TR	Bournemouth	03.75	1974-76	80	1	5	
MORGAN, Sydney S.	Bristol	01.08.26	A.G. Farmers	Bristol C.	12.47	1948–53	71		0	(G)
			TR	Millwall	03.58	1957–58	16		0	
MORGAN, Trevor J.	Forest Gate	30.09.56	Leytonstone	Bournemouth	09.80	1980-81	53	/	13	(F)
			TR	Mansfield T.	11.81	1981	12	/	6	
			TR	Bournemouth	03.82	1981-83	88	/	33	
			TR	Bristol C.	03.84	1983	15	/	5	
MORGAN, W. James	Bristol	19.06.22		Bristol Rov.	+	1946–51	104		24	(IF)
MORGAN, Wendell	Gorseinon	22.04.35	JNRS	Cardiff C.	05.52					(F)
			TR	Brentford	06.54	1955–57	47		6	
			TR	Gillingham	09.57	1957	35		3	
			TR	Swansea C.	07.58	1958	7		0	
			TR	Newport Co.	06.59	1959	26		3	
			TR	Carlisle U.	06.60	1960	35		2	
MORGAN, William	Glasgow	02.10.44	JNRS	Burnley	10.61	1962-67	183	/	19	(W)S-21/S.U23-1●
			TR	Manchester U.	08.68	1968-74	236	2	24	
			TR	Burnley	06.75	1975	12	1	0	
			TR	Bolton W.	03.76	1975-79	154	1	10	
			Vancouver W.	Blackpool	09.80	1980-81	41	1	4	
MORGAN, William A.	Rotherham	26.09.26	Wolverhampton W.(+)	Sheffield U.	09.46					(WH)
			TR	Halifax T.	08.48	1948–52	109		3	
			TR	Rochdale	07.53	1953–54	29		0	
MORGAN, Wyn	Abergwynfi	07.08.25		Bristol Rov.	AM	1946	2		0	
MORGANS, Jeff	Farnborough	12.08.42	JNRS	Crewe Alex.	09.59	1960–61	9		2	(F)
MORGANS, Ken G.	Swansea	16.03.39	JNRS	Manchester U.	04.56	1957–60	17		0	(W) W. U23–2
			TR	Swansea C.	03.61	1960–63	55		8	
			TR	Newport Co.	06.64	1964–66	125	/	46	
MORGANS, Morgan G.	Blaenau Ffestiniog	20.04.32		Northampton T.	08.55					(HB)
			TR	Wrexham	07.56	1956–57	29		2	
			TR	Southport	07.58	1958	14		0	
MORLEY, Anthony W.	Ormskirk	26.08.54	APP	Preston N.E.	09.72	1972-75	78	6	15	(W)E-6/E.U23-1/E.YTH.INT.
			TR	Burnley	02.76	1975-78	78	13	5	
			TR	Aston Villa	06.79	1979-83	128	9	25	
			TR	W.B.A.	12.83	1983	26	/	4	
MORLEY, Brian J.	Fleetwood	04.10.60	APP	Blackburn Rov.	10.78	1978-79	20	/	0	(D)
			TR	Tranmere Rov.	08.81	1981	10	6	2	
MORLEY, William	Nottingham	30.07.25	Grove Celtic	Nottingham F.	+	1946–58	282		10	(WH) d. 1981
MORONEY, Tommy	Cork	10.11.23	Cork	West Ham U.	08.47	1947–52	148		8	(WH) E1–12/L.O.I. REP./ d. 1981
MORRAD, Frank G.	London	28.02.20		Notts. Co.	+	1946	1		0	(CF)
			TR	Orient	11.46	1946	25		11	
			TR	Fulham	08.47					
			TR	Brighton & H.A.	02.48	1947–50	43		3	
			TR	Brentford	08.51	1951–52	7		2	
MORRALL, Alf D.	Duddeston	01.07.16		Northampton T.	+	1946–47	34		1	(CF)
			TR	Newport Co.	07.48	1948	28		0	
MORRALL, Steve A.	Torquay	25.09.52	JNRS	Torquay U.	08.72	1972-76	133	31	12	(W)
MORRALL, Terry S.	Smethwick	24.11.38	JNRS	Aston Villa	11.55	1959–60	8		0	(CH)
			TR	Shrewsbury T.	05.61	1960–62	31		0	
			TR	Wrexham	07.63	1963–64	42		0	
			TR	Southport	07.65	1965	1		0	
MORRELL, Paul D.	Poole	23.03.61	Weymouth	Bournemouth	06.83	1983	19	3	2	(M)
MORRELL, Robert I.	Heselden	04.06.44		Hartlepool U.	07.64	1963–64	34		0	(WH)
MORREY, Bernard J.	Liverpool	08.04.27	Llandudno	Newport Co.	10.52	1952–53	24		2	(OR) + Tranmere Rov.
			TR	Chester C.	12.53	1953–54	29		6	

Players Names	Birthplace	Date	Previous Club	League Club	Date Signed	Seasons Played	Apps	Sub	Gls	
MORRIN, Anthony J.	Manchester	21.07.46	APP	Bury	10.63	1963-64	3		0	(M)
			TR	Burnley	07.65					
			TR	Doncaster Rov.	08.66					
			TR	Stockport Co.	10.66	1966-68	27	5	2	
			TR	Barrow	03.69	1968-70	97	3	6	
			TR	Exeter C.	07.71	1971-76	180	2	15	
			TR	Stockport Co.	03.77	1976	13	/	1	
			TR	Rochdale	08.77	1977-78	29	1	0	
MORRIS, Alan	Swansea	06.04.41	JNRS	Swansea C.	06.58	1957-62	12		1	(W)
			TR	Reading	08.63	1963	12		0	
MORRIS, Alf	Manchester			Accrington St.	+	1946-47	15		0	
MORRIS, Chris B.	Newquay	24.12.63		Sheffield Wed.	10.82	1983	8	5	1	(F)
MORRIS, Chris J.	Spilsby	12.10.39		Hull C.	10.57	1958-60	17		4	(F)
			TR	York C.	06.61					
MORRIS, Colin	Blyth	22.08.53	APP	Burnley	09.71	1974-75	9	1	0	(W)
			TR	Southend U.	01.77	1976-79	133	/	25	
			TR	Blackpool	12.79	1979-81	87	/	27	
			TR	Sheffield U.	02.82	1981-83	108	/	38	
MORRIS, David M.	Swansea	20.09.57	APP	Manchester U.	10.74					(F)
			L	York C.	03.77	1976	1	6	0	
MORRIS, Doug	Durham	29.07.25		Hartlepool U.	+	1946-50	19		3	
MORRIS, Edward E.	Mold	15.04.40		Chester C.	06.60	1960	1		0	(FB)
MORRIS, Edwin C.	Pontypool	06.05.21	Bewdley	Cardiff C.	05.48	1948-50	8		0	(G)
MORRIS, Elfed	Colwyn Bay	09.06.42		Wrexham	05.60	1960-61	11		6	(F)
			TR	Chester C.	06.62	1962-67	164	/	69	
			TR	Halifax T.	03.68	1967-68	9	/	2	
MORRIS, Ernest	Stocksbridge	11.05.21		Nottingham F.	08.47	1947	6		1	
			TR	York C.	06.48					
			Grantham	Halifax T.	11.50	1950	1		0	
MORRIS, Frank	Penge	28.03.32		Crystal Palace	03.56	1956	8		0	A.B.A. Rep. Boxer
MORRIS, Fred A.	Sheffield	11.03.20		Barnsley	09.46	1946-48	23		9	d.
			TR	Southend U.	01.49	1948-49	34		16	
MORRIS, Fred W.	Oswestry	15.06.29	Oswestry T.	Walsall	05.50	1950-56	210		43	(OR)
			TR	Mansfield T.	03.57	1956-57	56		17	
			TR	Liverpool	05.58	1958-59	47		14	
			TR	Crewe Alex.	06.60	1960	8		1	
			TR	Gillingham	01.61	1960	10		1	
			TR	Chester C.	07.61	1961	29		3	
MORRIS, Geoff	Birmingham	08.02.49	APP	Walsall	02.66	1965-72	172	5	35	(W)
			TR	Shrewsbury T.	01.73	1972-74	71	4	9	
			TR	Port Vale	08.75	1975	10	5	1	
MORRIS, George E.	Birkenhead	22.11.29	Crewe Cadets	Crewe Alex.	08.48	1948-54	30		0	(FB)
MORRIS, Gordon J.	Wrottesley	27.06.26	E. Park F.C.	W.B.A.	+					(OL)
			TR	Walsall	07.49	1949-50	9		2	
MORRIS, Ian G.	Manchester	10.06.48		Stockport Co.	03.68	1967	1	1	0	(F)
MORRIS, James	St. Helens	16.11.15		Stockport Co.	+	1946-48	61		3	
MORRIS, John	Radcliffe	27.09.24	JNRS	Manchester U.	+	1946-48	83		32	(IF) E-3/E'B'-1/
			TR	Derby Co.	03.49	1948-52	130		44	E.F.LGE. REP.
			TR	Leicester C.	10.52	1952-57	206		33	
MORRIS, John E.	Crewe	27.11.37	JNRS	Crewe Alex.	12.54	1954	3		0	
MORRIS, John R.	Canning Town	13.04.34		Crewe Alex.	08.54	1954	1		0	
MORRIS, Kevin G.	Much Wenlock	22.09.53	APP	Shrewsbury T.	07.71	1970-71	9	/	0	(W)
MORRIS, Maldwyn	Swansea	03.08.32	Pembroke Bor.	Swansea C.	10.56	1956-57	15		5	(F)
MORRIS, Mark J.	Morden	26.09.62	APP	Wimbledon	10.81	1981-83	98	/	7	(D)
MORRIS, Mike J.	Plaistow	20.01.43	Faversham	Oxford U..	07.64	1964-66	89	1	15	(W)
			TR	Port Vale	08.67	1967-71	176	7	25	
MORRIS, Paul W.	Glassryn	08.01.57	Llanelli	Hereford U.	02.80	1979-80	2	2	1	(F)
MORRIS, Peter A.	Farnworth	23.11.58	APP	Preston N.E.	10.76					(F)
			TR	Blackburn Rov.	07.78	1978	2	2	0	
MORRIS, Peter J.	Nth. Houghton	08.11.43	JNRS	Mansfield T.	11.60	1960-67	285	1	50	(M)●
			TR	Ipswich T.	03.68	1967-73	213	7	13	
			TR	Norwich C.	06.74	1974-75	66	/	1	
			TR	Mansfield T.	07.76	1976-77	41	/	3	
			TR	Peterborough U.	N/C	1979	1	/	0	
MORRIS, Sam	Warrington	12.02.30	Stockton Heath	Chester C.	12.51	1951-56	92		0	(WH)
MORRIS, Steve A.	Bristol	06.07.49	APP	Bristol C.	06.67					(WH)
			TR	Exeter C.	06.69	1969-71	61	11	2	
MORRIS, Steve G.	Swansea	08.10.58	APP	Swansea C.	06.76	1975-78	33	6	1	(D)
			TR	Plymouth Arg.	01.80					

Players Names	Birthplace	Date	Previous Club	League Club	Date Signed	Seasons Played	Apps	Sub	Gls	
MORRIS, William	Radcliffe	01.04.31	JNRS	Bury	05.48					Brother of John (Manchester U.)
			TR	Derby Co.	10.51					
			TR	Rochdale	11.52	1952	4		1	
MORRIS, William	Colwyn Bay	30.07.18	Llandudno	Burnley	*	1946–52	200		46	(IF) W–5
MORRIS, William H.	Swansea	28.09.20		Swansea C.	05.46	1947–48	16		1	
			TR	Brighton & H.A.	09.49	1949–50	27		4	
MORRIS, William W.	Handsworth	26.03.13	Halesowen	Wolverhampton W.	*	1946	10		0	(FB) E–3
MORRISON, Angus C.	Dingwall	26.04.24	Inverness Caley	Derby Co.	+	1946–47	52		21	(OL) S'B'–1
			TR	Preston N.E.	11.48	1948–56	262		70	
			TR	Millwall	10.57	1957	15		4	
MORRISON, Charles	Newton Aycliffe	12.01.53	Chelsea (APP)	Doncaster Rov.	07.72	1972	5	1	0	(WH)
MORRISON, George C.	Ayr	27.11.24	St. Johnstone	Hartlepool U.	08.51	1951	2		0	
MORRISON, John	Greenock	04.08.29	Morton	Torquay U.	07.51	1951	2		0	
MORRISON, Murdoch	Glasgow	09.10.24	Bell Haven Star	Luton T.	+	1946	1		0	(G) d. 1974
			TR	Orient	08.47	1947	10		0	
MORRISON, Robert C.	Glasgow	16.02.33	Glasgow Rgrs.	Nottingham F.	07.58	1958	1		0	(F)
			TR	Workington	07.59	1959–60	53		20	
MORRISON, Tom	Croy	06.03.43	Aberdeen	Port Vale	08.65	1965	5	1	0	(IF)
MORRISON, William	Edinburgh	31.03.34	Merchiston T.	Sunderland	05.51	1954–56	19		0	(WH)
			TR	Southend U.	01.58	1957–59	60		4	
MORRISON, William	Croy	10.10.39	Croy Guild	Portsmouth	05.58	1958	3		0	(FB)
MORRISSEY, John	Liverpool	18.04.40	JNRS	Liverpool	05.57	1957–60	36		6	(W) E.F.LGE.REP./
			TR	Everton	09.62	1962–71	257	1	43	E.SCH. INT
			TR	Oldham Ath.	05.72	1972	6	/	1	
MORRISSEY, Pat J.	Enniscorthy	23.2.48		Coventry C.	07.65	1966-67	6	4	0	(F)
			TR	Torquay U.	07.68	1968	19	2	0	
			TR	Crewe Alex.	07.69	1969-71	95	1	28	
			TR	Chester C.	10.71	1971	9	/	1	
			TR	Watford	12.71	1971-74	101	6	27	
			TR	Aldershot	11.74	1974-76	109	/	27	
			L	Swansea C.	10.77	1977	3	1	0	
MORRITT, Gordon R.	Rotherham	08.02.42	S.P.& T.	Rotherham U.	06.61	1961–65	77	/	0	(G)
			Durban City	Doncaster Rov.	09.67	1967–68	40	/	0	
			TR	Northampton T.	08.68	1968–69	42	/	0	
			TR	York C.	10.69	1969–71	41	/	0	
			TR	Rochdale	08.72	1972	31	/	0	
			TR	Darlington	08.73	1973	34	/	0	
MORROW, Hugh J.E.	Larne	09.07.30	JNRS	W.B.A.	08.47	1948	5		2	(OR)
			Lockheed A.P.	Northampton T.	06.56	1956	30		3	
MORSE, Richard A.	Newport	17.12.66	JNRS	Newport Co.	N/C	1983	0	1	0	
MORTENSEN, Stan H.	Sth. Shields	26.05.21	JNRS	Blackpool	*	1946–55	317		197	(IF) E–25/E.F.LGE.REP.●
			TR	Hull C.	11.55	1955–56	42		18	
			TR	Southport	02.57	1956–57	36		10	
MORTIMER, Dennis	Liverpool	05.04.52	APP	Coventry C.	09.69	1969-75	175	14	10	(M)E.U'23-6/E.YTH.INT./E'B'
			TR	Aston Villa	12.75	1975-83	311	/	31	
MORTIMER, John M.	Birkenhead	05.12.23		Wrexham	01.47	1946–48	23		0	
			TR	New Brighton	10.49	1949–50	5		0	
MORTIMORE, Charlie F.	Gosport	12.04.28	Woking	Aldershot	AM	1949–52	67		27	(CF) E.AMAT.INT/
			Woking	Portsmouth	AM	1953	1		0	Brother of John A.
			Woking	Aldershot	AM	1955	2		0	
MORTIMORE, John H.	Farnborough	23.09.34	Woking	Chelsea	08.57	1955–64	249		8	(CH) E.AMAT.INT./
			TR	Q.P.R.	09.65	1965	10	/	0	E.YTH.INT.
MORTON, Alan	Peterborough	06.03.42.	Peterborough U.	Arsenal	04.59					(F)
			TR	Peterborough U.	10.61	1961–62	7		2	
			Wisbech T.	Lincoln C.	07.63	1963–64	58		20	
			TR	Chesterfield	07.65	1965	28	1	6	
MORTON, Alan	Erith	13.04.50	Woking	Crystal Palace	11.67					(F)
			L	Stockport Co.	08.69	1969	10	2	1	
			Nuneaton	Fulham	08.70	1970	1	/	1	
MORTON, Albert	Newcastle	27.07.19		Sheffield Wed.	*	1947–50	40		0	(G)
			TR	Rochdale	07.53	1953–56	89		0	
MORTON, Geoff D.	Acton	27.07.24	Chelmsford	Watford	10.48	1948–51	107		0	(G) Midd'x cricketer
			TR	Southend U.	02.52	1951–52	25		0	
				Exeter C.	09.54	1954	6		0	
MORTON, George E.	Liverpool	30.09.43	JNRS	Everton	10.60					(IF)
			TR	Rochdale	07.62	1962–65	147	1	50	
MORTON, Gerry W.	Newcastle	17.03.44	Nth. Shields	Newcastle U.	08.62					(HB)
			TR	Workington	04.63	1962–63	3		0	
MORTON, Keith	Ferryhill	11.08.34		Crystal Palace	AM	1953	5		3	(CF)
				Sunderland	07.54					
			TR	Darlington	05.55	1955–60	175		50	

Players Names	Birthplace	Date	Previous Club	League Club	Date Signed	Seasons Played	Career Record Apps Sub Gls		
MORTON, Ken	Corley	19.05.47	APP	Manchester U.	05.64				E.SCH.INT
			TR	York C.	05.65	1965	9	1	2
			TR	Blackpool	08.66				
			Fleetwood	Darlington	07.68	1968	3	1	0
MORTON, Norman	Barnsley	22.05.25	Woolley Col.	Leeds U.	+	1947	1		0 (CF) + Sunderland/d.1977
MORTON, Robert H.	Aston Clinton	25.09.27	Eaton Bray	Luton T.	+	1948–63	494		49 (WH) E'B–1●
MORTON, Roy S.	Birmingham	29.10.55	APP	Manchester U.	11.72				(IF) E.YTH.INT.
			TR	Birmingham C.	09.73	1974	3	/	0
MORTON, William	Grangemouth	02.04.28		Millwall	+	1946–50	9		0 (CH)
MOSBY, Harold	Kippax	25.06.26	Huddersfield T.(AM)	Rotherham U.	01.47	1947–49	25		9 (F)
			TR	Scunthorpe U.	07.50	1950–54	147		22
			Worksop	Crewe Alex.	08.56	1956	38		4
MOSELEY, Graham	Manchester	16.11.53	APP	Blackburn Rov.	09.71				(G)E.YTH.INT.
			TR	Derby Co.	09.71	1972-76	32	/	0
			L	Aston Villa	08.74	1974	3	/	0
			L	Walsall	10.77	1977	3	/	0
			TR	Brighton & H.A.	11.77	1977-83	138	/	0
MOSES, George	High Spen	11.09.20	Newcastle U. (+)	Hartlepool U.	08.46	1946	19		4 (IR) d
MOSES, Remi M.	Manchester	14.11.60	APP	W.B.A.	11.78	1979-81	63	/	5 (M)E.U21-8
			TR	Manchester U.	09.81	1981-83	80	5	2
MOSS, Amos	Birmingham	28.08.21	JNRS	Aston Villa	+	1946–55	109		5 (WH) Brother of Frank
MOSS, Craig A.	Birmingham	11.03.61	APP	Wolverhampton W.	03.79	1978-81	4	/	0 (F)
MOSS, David J.	Witney	18.03.52	Witney T.	Swindon T.	07.69	1971-77	217	13	60 (F)
			TR	Luton T.	05.78	1978-83	201	9	81
MOSS, Don R.	Tamworth	27.06.25	Boldmere St. M.	Cardiff C.	05.51				(WH)
			TR	Crystal Palace	05.53	1953–56	56		2
MOSS, Edward	Skelmersdale	27.10.39	Skelmersdale	Liverpool	10.58				(F)
			TR	Southport	07.59	1959–60	51		15
MOSS, Ernie	Chesterfield	19.10.49	Chesterfield Tube	Chesterfield	10.68	1968-75	271	/	94 (F)●
			TR	Peterborough U.	01.76	1975-76	34	1	9
			TR	Mansfield T.	12.76	1976-78	56	1	21
			TR	Chesterfield	01.79	1978-80	105	2	33
			TR	Port Vale	06.81	1981-82	74	/	23
			TR	Lincoln C	03.83	1982	10	1	2
			TR	Doncaster Rov.	06.83	1983	41	3	15
MOSS, Frank	Birmingham	16.09.17	Wolverhampton W. (*)	Aston Villa	*	1946–54	288		3 (CH) *Sheffield Wed./ Son of Frank Moss (Snr)
MOSS, Jack	Blackrod	01.09.23		Bury	+	1946	7		2 (IF)
			TR	Rochdale	01.47	1946–48	58		17
			TR	Leeds U.	01.49	1948–50	23		2
			TR	Halifax T.	01.51	1950–53	124		10
MOSS, Paul M.	Birmingham	02.08.57		Wolverhampton W.	07.76				(M) Brother of Craig
			TR	Hull C.	09.79	1979-80	53	1	7
			TR	Scunthorpe U.	09.81	1981	42	/	7
MOSS, Robert	Chigwell	13.02.52	APP	Orient	02.70	1970	2	3	1 (IF)
			TR	Colchester U.	05.72	1972	16	1	3
MOSS, Robert S.	Kenton	15.02.49	APP	Fulham	02.66	1967	8	1	3 (W)
			TR	Peterborough U.	07.69	1969–72	86	18	17
MOSS, Roy G.	Malden	5.9.41	JNRS	Tottenham H.	01.60				(F) E.SCH.INT.
			TR	Gillingham	09.62	1962–63	14		3
MOSS, Terry J.	Bristol	02.01.32		Swindon T.	AM	1955	7		0 (OL)
MOSSOP, Graham	Wellington	11.01.58	Liverpool(APP)	Workington	11.75	1975	1	/	0 (M)
				Carlisle U.	07.79	1980	2	/	0
MOSTYN, Roger	Wrexham	31.08.53		Wrexham	11.71	1971–73	16	3	4 (IF)
MOTTERSHEAD, Brian L.	Rochdale	13.07.35	JNRS	Notts. Co.	09.52				
			TR	Rochdale	08.53	1953	1		0
MOTTERSHEAD, Keith A.	Stafford	12.12.44	Stafford Rgrs.	Doncaster Rov.	10.66	1966–67	34	5	0 (W)
MOUGHTON, Colin E.	London	30.12.47	APP	Q.P.R.	12.65	1965–66	6	/	0 (WH)
			TR	Colchester U.	07.68	1968	4	/	0
MOULD, William	Stoke	06.10.19	Summerbank	Stoke C.	*	1946–51	145		1 (FB)
			TR	Crewe Alex.	07.52	1952–53	66		1
MOULDEN, Anthony	Farnworth	28.08.42	Blackburn Rov.(AM)	Bury	05.60	1960–61	4		0 (W)
			TR	Rochdale	06.62	1962	5		1
			TR	Peterborough U.	11.62	1962–64	62		9
			TR	Notts. Co.	05.65	1965	23	/	1
			TR	Rochdale	09.66	1966	1	1	0
MOULSEN, George B.	Clogheen	06.08.14		Grimsby T.	*	1946	1		0 (G)E1–3
			TR	Lincoln C.	06.47	1947–48	60		0
MOUNCER, Frank E.	Grimsby	22.11.20	Humber U.	Grimsby T.	*	1946–48	22		0 E.SCH.INT
MOUNTAIN, Robert B.	Wombwell	11.09.56	APP	Huddersfield T.	11.73	1973	1	/	0 (F)
			TR	Bolton W.	07.75				

Players Names	Birthplace	Date	Previous Club	League Club	Date Signed	Seasons Played	Apps	Sub	Gls	
MOUNTFIELD, Derek N.	Liverpool	02.11.62	APP	Tranmere Rov.	11.80	1980-81	26	/	1	(D)
			TR	Everton	06.82	1982-83	32	/	3	
MOUNTFORD, David	Hanley	09.01.31	JNRS	Crewe Alex.	11.48	1948–51	33		5	(F)
			TR	W.B.A.	12.51	1952	4		0	
			TR	Crewe Alex.	10.53	1953–56	27		7	
MOUNTFORD, Derek	Stoke	24.03.34	JNRS	Port Vale	05.51	1954–56	26		0	(HB)
			TR	Crewe Alex.	07.57	1957	13		0	
MOUNTFORD, Frank	Stoke	30.03.23	JNRS	Stoke C.	+	1946–57	392		21	(CH)
MOUNTFORD, George F.	Stoke	30.03.21	JNRS	Stoke C.	*	1946–52	147		27	(IF) Brother of Frank/
			TR	Q.P.R.	10.52	1952–53	34		2	d.
MOUNTFORD, Peter	Stoke	13.09.60	APP	Norwich C.	10.78	1981-82	1	3	0	(M)
			TR	Charlton Ath.	09.83	1983	10	1	1	
MOUNTFORD, Ray	Mexborough	28.04.58	APP	Manchester U.	04.75					(G)
			TR	Rotherham U.	07.78	1978-82	123	/	0	
			L	Bury	11.83	1983	4	/	0	
MOUNTFORD, Robert W.	Stoke	23.02.52	APP	Port Vale	07.70	1968-74	64	13	9	(F)
			L	Scunthorpe U.	10.74	1974	1	2	0	
			L	Crewe Alex.	12.74	1974	5	/	0	
			TR	Rochdale	01.75	1974-77	97	1	37	
			TR	Huddersfield T.	10.77	1977	12	2	4	
			TR	Halifax T.	03.78	1977-79	56	6	11	
			TR	Crewe Alex.	08.80	1980	3	/	0	
			TR	Stockport Co.	11.80	1980	6	1	3	
MOWBRAY, Anthony M.	Saltburn	22.11.63	APP	Middlesbrough	11.81	1982-83	58	3	1	(D)
MOWBRAY, Henry	Hamilton	01.05.47	Cowdenbeath	Blackpool	05.67	1967–70	88	3	0	(FB)
			TR	Bolton W.	06.71	1971–72	31	/	0	
MOWER, Ken M.	Walsall	01.12.60	APP	Walsall	11.78	1978-83	200	1	5	(D)
MOWL, William J.	Bulwell	23.06.22		Notts. Co.	+	1948	3		0	(G)
			TR	Mansfield T.	07.49					
MOXHAM, Graham	Exeter	03.01.49	Preston N.E. (APP)	Bournemouth	07.66					(IF)
			Bideford T.	Exeter C.	07.75	1975	4	2	0	
MOXHAM, Robert	Barrow	05.07.22	Holker C.O.B.	Barrow	09.48	1948	5		1	(CF)
MOYES, David W.	Blythswood	25.04.63	Glasgow Celtic	Cambridge U.	10.83	1983	30	/	0	(D)
MOYES, John K.	Heage	17.07.51	APP	Chesterfield	08.69	1968–71	13	/	0	(FB)
MOYSE, Alec R.	Mitcham	05.08.35	Chatham	Crystal Palace	02.56	1955–56	4		1	(F)
				Swindon T.	08.58	1958	4		0	
			TR	Millwall	09.58	1958–59	22		3	
MOYSE, Ron	Portsmouth	02.04.20	Portsmouth (AM)	Reading	10.46	1946–52	189		0	(FB)
MOYSES, Chris R.	Lincoln	01.11.65	APP	Lincoln C.	N/C	1983	2	2	0	(M)
MOZLEY, Bert	Derby	23.09.23	Shelton U.	Derby Co.	06.46	1946–54	297		2	(FB)E–3/E.F.LGE.REP.
MUDIE, Jackie K.	Dundee	10.04.30	JNRS	Blackpool	05.47	1949–60	320		143	(IF) S–17
			TR	Stoke C.	03.61	1960–63	89		32	
			TR	Port Vale	11.63	1963–66	54	/	9	
MUHREN, Arnold J.H.	Holland	02.06.51	F.C. Twente	Ipswich T.	08.78	1978-81	161	/	21	(M)DUTCH INT.
			TR	Manchester U.	08.82	1982-83	58	/	13	
MUIR, Alex J.	Inverkeithing	10.12.23		Liverpool	07.47	1947	4		0	
MUIR, Ian	Coventry	05.05.63	APP	Q.P.R.	09.80	1980	2	/	2	(F)E.SCH.INT.
			L	Burnley	11.82	1982	1	1	1	
			TR	Birmingham C.	08.83	1983	1	/	0	
			TR	Brighton & H.A.	02.84	1983	2	/	0	
MUIR, Ian B.	Motherwell	16.06.29	Motherwell	Bristol Rov.	05.53	1953–56	26		0	(HB) Son of pre-war
			TR	Oldham Ath.	06.57	1957	35		0	Bristol Rovers Star
MUIR, Maurice	Wimbledon	19.03.63	APP	Northampton	N/C	1979-83	15	13	0	(M)E.SCH.INT.
MUIR, William M.	Ayr	27.08.25	Irvine	Q.P.R.	02.49	1948–52	18		4	(F)
			TR	Torquay U.	10.52	1952	9		0	
MUIR, William N.	Port Glasgow	14.08.34	St. Mirren	Aldershot	05.56	1956	7		4	(F)
MULDOON, John P.	Clatterbridge	21.11.64	JNRS	Wrexham	12.82	1982-83	48	9	7	(M)
MULDOON, Terry	Ashington	10.08.51		Scunthorpe U.	AM	1970	1	/	0	(W) d.1971
MULGREW, Tommy	Motherwell	13.04.29	Morton	Northampton T.	07.49	1950–52	8		1	(IF)
			TR	Newcastle U.	10.52	1952–53	14		1	
			TR	Southampton	07.54	1954–61	293		91	
			TR	Aldershot	08.62	1962–64	112		2	
MULGROVE, Keith A.	Haltwhistle	21.08.59	APP	Newcastle U.	07.77	1978	0	1	0	(D)
MULHALL, George	Falkirk	08.05.36	Aberdeen	Sunderland	09.62	1962–68	250	4	55	(OL) S–3/S.F.LGE.REP.
MULHEARN, Ken J.	Liverpool	16.10.45	APP	Everton	07.63					(G)●
			TR	Stockport Co.	08.64	1964-67	100	/	0	
			TR	Manchester U.	09.67	1967-69	50	/	0	
			TR	Shrewsbury T.	03.71	1970-79	370	/	0	
			TR	Crewe Alex.	08.80	1980-81	88	/	0	
MULHEREN, Peter	Glasgow	21.06.21		Crystal Palace	10.48	1948–49	38		2	

Players Names	Birthplace	Date	Previous Club	League Club	Date Signed	Seasons Played	Apps	Sub	Gls	
MULHOLLAND, Frank G.	Belfast	28.10.27	Glentoran	Middlesbrough	10.51	1951–57	46		0	(WH) IRISH LGE. REP.
MULHOLLAND, George R.	Ayr	04.08.28		Stoke C.	07.50	1950	3		0	(FB)
			TR	Bradford C.	07.53	1953–59	277		0	
			TR	Darlington	07.60	1960–62	106		0	
MULHOLLAND, James	Knightswood	10.04.38	E. Stirling	Chelsea	10.62	1962–63	11		2	(IF)
			Morton	Barrow	08.65	1965–68	132	2	47	
			TR	Stockport Co.	10.68	1968–69	29	4	5	
			TR	Crewe Alex.	08.70	1970	0	1	0	
MULHOLLAND, John A.	Dumbarton	20.01.32	Condorat Th.	Southampton	12.51					(F)
			TR	Chester C.	07.56	1956	8		1	
			TR	Halifax T.	06.57	1957	8		1	
MULHOLLAND, John R.	Jamestown	07.12.28	Renton Boys Guild	Plymouth Arg.	10.46					
			TR	Grimsby T.	08.49	1949–50	2		0	
			TR	Scunthorpe U.	10.50	1950	6		1	
MULKERRIN, James	Dumbarton	25.12.31	Hibernian	Accrington St.	03.57	1956–58	70		35	(F) S'B'–1
			TR	Tranmere Rov.	08.59	1959–60	38		8	
MULLAN, Brendan G.	Coleraine	02.01.50	Coleraine	Fulham	02.68	1967–68	2	1	0	(CF) N1.U23–1
			TR	Millwall	07.69					
MULLARD, Albert T.	Walsall	22.11.20		Walsall	+	1946–48	63		12	(CF)
			TR	Crewe Alex.	06.49	1949–50	44		14	
			TR	Stoke C.	08.50	1950–51	21		3	
			TR	Port Vale	09.51	1951–55	164		22	
MULLEN, Andy	Newcastle	28.07.28		Aston Villa	07.48					(OL) Brother to James
			TR	Brighton & H.A.	08.49					(Wolverhampton W.)
			Annfield Plain	Workington	08.51	1951–52	66		5	
			Sth. Shields	Scunthorpe U.	08.55	1955–56	10		1	
MULLEN, James	Newcastle	06.01.23	JNRS	Wolverhampton W.	+	1946–58	437		99	(OL) E–12/E'B'–3/● E.F.LGE.REP./E.SCH.INT
MULLEN, James	Jarrow	08.11.52	APP	Sheffield Wed.	10.70	1970-79	222	7	10	(D)
			TR	Rotherham U.	08.80	1980-81	49	/	1	
			L	Preston N.E.	11.81	1981	1	/	0	
			TR	Cardiff C.	03.82	1981-83	59	4	2	
MULLEN, James	Oxford	16.03.47	Oxford C.	Reading	11.66	1966-67	7	/	1	(W)
			TR	Charlton Ath.	11.67	1967-68	7	/	0	
			TR	Rotherham U.	02.69	1968-73	173	3	24	
			TR	Blackburn Rov.	08.74	1974-75	6	4	0	
			TR	Bury	06.76	1976	2	2	0	
			L	Rochdale	03.77	1976	6	2	1	
MULLEN, James W.	Larne	10.01.21	Belfast Celtic	Barrow	+	1946–47	55		8	(OL)
			TR	Crystal Palace	07.48	1948	10		0	
			TR	Bristol C.	02.49	1948–49	17		2	
			TR	Barrow	09.50	1950	9		0	
MULLEN, Roger C.	Cowbridge	2.03.66	APP	Swansea C.	03.84	1983	0	1	0	
MULLEN, Steve A.	Glasgow	08.09.59	Darwen	Bury	02.79	1978-81	76	17	5	(W)
MULLERY, Alan P.	Notting Hill	23.11.41	JNRS	Fulham	12.58	1958–63	199		13	(WH) E–35/E.U23–3/● E.F.LGE.REP.
			TR	Tottenham H.	03.64	1963–71	312	/	25	
			TR	Fulham	03.72	1971–75	164	1	24	
MULLETT, Joe	Birmingham	02.10.36	Malt Mill U.	Birmingham C.	02.55	1957	3		0	(FB)
			TR	Norwich C.	02.59	1958–67	211	2	2	
MULLIGAN, Pat	Dublin	17.03.45	Shamrock Rov.	Chelsea	10.69	1969-72	55	3	2	(D)EI-51
			TR	Crystal Palace	09.72	1972-74	57	/	2	
			TR	W.B.A.	09.75	1975-77	109	/	1	
MULLIGAN, Peter G.	Barnsley	17.07.42	JNRS	Barnsley	07.63	1959–63	9		0	(IF)
MULLINGTON, Phil T.	Oldham	25.09.56	APP	Oldham Ath.	07.75					(M)
			TR	Rochdale	01.76	1975-76	59	7	6	
			Northwich Vic.	Crewe Alex.	N/C	1977	1	/	0	
			Winsford U.	Rochdale	08.78	1978	8	1	0	
MULRANEY, Ambrose	Wishaw	18.05.16	Ipswich T. (*)	Birmingham C.	+	1946	28		9	
			TR	Aston Villa	09.48	1948	12		2	
MULVANEY, James	Sunderland	13.05.41	Whitby T.	Hartlepool U.	08.65	1965–67	67	2	32	(IF)
			TR	Barrow	11.67	1967–69	71	8	34	
			TR	Stockport Co.	07.70	1970–71	38	2	8	
MULVANEY, James	Airdrie	27.04.21	Dumbarton	Luton T.	06.48	1948–49	8		2	(FB)
			TR	Brighton & H.A.	08.50	1950	8		0	
			TR	Bradford C.	10.51	1951	16		0	
			TR	Halifax T.	11.52	1952	1		0	
MULVANEY, Richard	Sunderland	05.08.42	Billingham Syn.	Blackburn Rov.	02.64	1964-70	135	6	4	(D)
			TR	Oldham Ath.	08.71	1971-74	88	4	2	
			TR	Rochdale	10.74	1974-76	72	1	4	
MULVEY, Edward P.	Dublin	29.12.34	Glentoran	Stockport Co.	11.57	1957–59	26		5	(F)
MULVOY, Terry	Manchester	02.12.38		Rochdale	02.56	1956	2		0	(F)
MUMFORD, Wayne E.	Rhymney	03.11.64	Manchester C.(APP)	Birmingham C.	09.82	1982-83	5	2	0	(D)
MUNCIE, William	Carluke	28.08.11	Southend U.(*)	Crewe Alex.	10.46	1946	2		0	(CF) *Shettleston/Leicester C.

Players Names	Birthplace	Date	Previous Club	League Club	Date Signed	Seasons Played	Career Record Apps	Sub	Gls	
MUNDEE, Brian G.	London	12.01.64	Hungerford T.	Bournemouth	01.82	1982	3	1	0	(M)
			TR	Northampton T.	10.83	1983	33	3	1	
MUNDY, Albert E.	Gosport	12.05.26	Gosport Bor.	Portsmouth	01.51	1950–53	50		12	(IF)
			TR	Brighton & H.A.	11.53	1953–57	166		86	
			TR	Aldershot	02.58	1957–60	130		11	
MUNDY, H. James	Manchester	02.09.48		Manchester C.	01.68	1968–69	2	1	0	(IF)
			L	Oldham Ath.	09.70	1970	3	5	2	
MUNGALL, Steve H.	Bellshill	22.05.58	Motherwell	Tranmere Rov.	07.79	1979–83	154	9	5	(D)
MUNKS, David	Sheffield	29.04.47	APP	Sheffield U.	08.64	1965–68	108	4	1	(WH) E.YTH.INT
			TR	Portsmouth	05.69	1969–73	132	5	2	
			TR	Swindon T.	12.73	1973–74	21	/	0	
			TR	Exeter C.	12.74	1974–75	20	/	0	
MUNRO, A. Iain F.	Uddingston	24.08.51	St. Mirren	Stoke C.	10.80	1980	32	/	1	(D)S–7
			TR	Sunderland	08.81	1981–83	80	/	0	
MUNRO, Alex	Glasgow	03.10.44	Drumchapel	Bristol Rov.	10.62	1962–70	157	10	11	(WH)
MUNRO, Alex D.	Corridon	06.04.12	Hearts	Blackpool	*	1946–48	60		6	(OR) S–3
MUNRO, Frank M.	Dundee	25.10.47	Aberdeen	Wolves	01.68	1967–76	290	6	14	(D)S–9/S.U23–4
MUNRO, James F.	Garmouth	25.03.26	Waterford	Manchester C.	11.47	1947–49	25		4	(OR)
			TR	Oldham Ath.	03.50	1949–52	119		21	
			TR	Lincoln C.	02.53	1952–57	161		24	
			TR	Bury	01.58	1957–58	41		8	
MUNRO, Malcolm G.	Leicester	21.05.53	APP	Leicester C.	05.70	1971–74	69	1	1	(CH) E.YTH.INT./ E.SCH.INT
MUNRO, Rod A.	Inverness	27.07.20		Brentford	05.46	1946–52	199		0	(FB)
MUNRO, Wiliam D.	Glasgow	21.06.34	Kilmarnock	Barrow	06.59	1959–60	15		2	(F)
MUNROE, William J.	Dublin	28.11.33	Ards	Bristol C.	12.57	1957	1		0	
			TR	Scunthorpe U.	07.58					
MURCHISON, Ron A.	Hurlford	12.02.27	Auchterarder Prin.	Ipswich T.	06.50	1950–54	42		2	(HB)
MURCOTT, Steve	Streetly	17.01.61	APP	Coventry C.	11.78	1979	1	/	0	(G)
MURDOCH, Robert W.	Rothwell	17.08.44	Glasgow Celtic	Middlesbrough	09.73	1973–75	93	2	6	(WH) S–12/S.U23–1/ S.F. LGE. REP.
MURDOCH, William R.	Liverpool	25.01.36		Liverpool	05.57	1957–58	17		5	(F)
			TR	Barrow	09.59	1959	42		17	
			TR	Stockport Co.	08.60	1960–61	58		18	
			TR	Carlisle U.	01.62	1961	10		1	
			TR	Southport	07.62	1962	33		10	
MURPHY, Andy C.	Preston	18.10.66	JNRS	Preston N.E.	N/C	1983	4	1	0	(M)
MURPHY, Barry	Consett	10.02.40	Sth. Shields	Barnsley	07.62	1962–77	510	2	3	(D)●
MURPHY, Bernard A.P.	Dublin	19.11.47	APP	Torquay U.	11.65	1964–66	6	/	0	(HB)
MURPHY, Daniel	Burtonwood	10.05.22	Burtonwood Ath.	Bolton W.	+	1946–50	66		1	(WH)
			TR	Crewe Alex.	01.52	1951–53	106		1	
			TR	Rochdale	07.54	1954–56	109		0	
MURPHY, Donal P.	Dublin	23.02.55	APP	Coventry C.	08.72	1975–77	33	10	10	(F)
			L	Millwall	10.77	1977	3	/	0	
			TR	Torquay U.	05.78	1978–79	81	4	20	
			TR	Plymouth Arg.	06.80	1980–81	44	4	9	
			L	Torquay U.	12.81	1981	2	1	0	
			TR	Blackburn Rov.	02.82	1981	1	2	0	
MURPHY, Edward	Glasgow	01.06.34	Clyde	Oldham Ath.	05.56	1956–68	71		0	(HB)
MURPHY, Edward	Hamilton	13.05.24	Morton	Northampton T.	06.49	1949–50	71		14	(IF)
			TR	Barnsley	03.51	1950–51	18		2	
			TR	Exeter C.	06.52	1952–55	94		13	
MURPHY, Frank J.	Edinburgh	16.08.39	Edwina J.	Notts. Co.	08.67	1967–68	17	2	2	(HB) d.
MURPHY, George	Newport	22.07.15	Cwmfelinfach	Bradford C.	*	1946–47	46		21	(F)d.1983
			TR	Hull C.	12.47	1947	15		9	
MURPHY, James B.	Glasgow	29.11.42	Raith Rov.	Notts. Co.	02.68	1967–68	33	/	7	(F)
MURPHY, Jerry M.	Stepney	23.09.59	APP	Crystal Palace	10.76	1976–83	179	14	17	(M)E.SCH.INT./EI–3
MURPHY, John W.	Birstal	21.11.21	Liverpool (AM)	Bradford C.	09.46	1946–51	146		9	(WH)
MURPHY, Joseph P.	Waterford	30.03.24		Brighton & H.A.	02.48					(FB)
				Crystal Palace	02.49	1948–50	37		0	
MURPHY, Marcus M.	Tavistock	16.11.14	Plymouth U.	Plymouth Arg.	08.46	1946–47	15		1	(IF)
MURPHY, Mike	Reading	15.04.39	Thorneycroft A.	Reading	AM	1957	1		0	(G)
MURPHY, Nick M.	W. Bromwich	25.12.46	JNRS	Manchester U.	02.66					(CH)
			TR	Reading	07.70	1970	2	1	0	
MURPHY, Patrick	Merthyr	19.12.47	APP	Cardiff C.	12.65	1965	0	1	0	(HB)
MURPHY, Paul	Ashington	16.03.54	Ashington U.	Rotherham U.	02.72	1973	1	/	0	(CF)
			L	Workington	08.73	1973	10	2	1	
MURPHY, Peter	W. Hartlepool	07.03.22	Birmingham C. (AM)	Coventry C.	05.46	1946–49	116		37	(IF) d.1975
			TR	Tottenham H.	06.50	1950–512	38		14	
			TR	Birmingham C.	01.52	1951–59	245		107	

Players Names	Birthplace	Date	Previous Club	League Club	Date Signed	Seasons Played	Career Record Apps	Sub	Gls	
MURPHY, Terry	Liverpool	14.01.40		Crewe Alex.	09.61	1961	1		0	(WH)
MURPHY, Tom E.	South Bank	25.03.21	South Bank	Middlesbrough	*	1946–47	9		1	(IF)
			TR	Blackburn Rov.	12.47	1947–48	31		6	
			TR	Halifax T.	03.49	1948–53	217		30	
MURPHY, William R.	Barrhead	22.03.28	E. Stirling	Exeter C.	11.49	1949	1		0	(W)
			TR	Bristol Rov.	07.50	1950	3		0	
MURRAY, A. James	Thornton	04.02.45		Southport	07.65	1964	3		0	(W)
MURRAY, Alan	Newcastle	05.12.49	JNRS	Middlesbrough	09.67	1969-70	6	4	1	(M)
			L	York C.	01.72	1971	4	/	0	
			TR	Brentford	06.72	1972	42	3	7	
			TR	Doncaster Rov.	07.73	1973-76	133	13	21	
MURRAY, Albert G.	Hoxton	22.09.42	JNRS	Chelsea	05.61	1961–65	156	4	39	(OR) E.U23–6/E.YTH.INT./●
			TR	Birmingham C.	08.66	1966–70	127	11	22	E.SCH.INT
			TR	Brighton & H.A.	02.71	1970–73	99	3	25	
			TR	Peterborough U.	09.73	1973–75	123	/	10	
MURRAY, Alistair	Longtown	22.12.43	JNRS	Sunderland	01.61					(IF)
			TR	Barnsley	07.63	1963	21		1	
			TR	Carlisle U.	07.64					
			TR	Hartlepool U.	08.65					
MURRAY, David	Otterburn	11.07.49		Workington	03.74	1973–75	79	3	22	(CF)
MURRAY, Dennis P.	Stoke	11.06.32	JNRS	Crewe Alex.	10.50	1951	2		0	(G)
MURRAY, Don J.	Duffus	18.01.46	JNRS	Cardiff C.	01.63	1962-74	406	/	6	(D)S.U23-1
			L	Swansea C.	10.74	1974	5	/	0	
			Hearts	Newport Co.	10.76	1976	16	2	0	
MURRAY, Hugh	Drybridge	03.08.36	Dalry Ath.	Manchester C.	04.55	1955	1		0	(F)
MURRAY, Ivan	Ballymoney	29.05.44	Coleraine	Fulham	02.68	1967–68	4	2	0	(HB)
MURRAY, James	Motherwell	13.07.22	Shawfield J.	Exeter C.	+	1946	1		0	(FB)
MURRAY, James	Edinburgh	04.02.33	Hearts	Reading	02.54	1953–54	7		3	(F)
MURRAY, James G.	Glasgow	27.12.58	Rivet Spts.	Cambridge	09.76	1976-83	213	16	3	(D)
			L	Sunderland	03.84	1983	0	1	0	
MURRAY, James R.	Dover	11.10.35	JNRS	Wolverhampton W.	11.53	1955–63	276		155	(CF) E.U23–2/●
			TR	Manchester C.	11.63	1963–66	70	/	43	E.F.LGE REP.
			TR	Walsall	05.67	1966–68	54	4	13	
MURRAY, James W.	Lambeth	16.03.35		Crystal Palace	07.55	1955–57	37		13	(F)
			TR	Walsall	06.58	1957–58	14		2	
MURRAY, John	Newcastle	02.03.48	JNRS	Burnley	03.65	1966-69	20	2	6	(F)
			TR	Blackpool	03.70	1969-70	5	3	1	
			TR	Bury	02.71	1970-73	117	9	37	
			TR	Reading	08.74	1974-77	123	8	43	
			TR	Brentford	02.78	1977	2	3	1	
MURRAY, John	Glasgow	09.03.45	Stirling A.	Lincoln C.	11.66	1966	4	/	0	(LB)
MURRAY, John A.	Saltcoats	05.02.49	Morton	Cambridge U.	07.71	1971	3	/	0	(FB)
MURRAY, John G.	Lambeth	15.07.27		Orient	08.49					(FB)
			Sittingbourne	Gillingham	06.51	1951	4		0	
MURRAY, Ken	Darlington	02.04.28	B. Auckland	Darlington	07.50	1950–52	70		19	(F)
			TR	Mansfield T.	07.53	1954–56	138		60	
			TR	Oldham Ath.	03.57	1956–57	35		14	
			TR	Wrexham	02.58	1957–58	32		12	
			TR	Gateshead	08.59	1959	18		7	
MURRAY, Leslie	E. Fife	29.09.28	Raith Rov.	Rochdale	05.52	1952	16		3	
MURRAY, Matt	Paisley	25.12.29	St. Mirren	Barrow	08.58	1958	33		2	(OL)
			TR	Carlisle U.	07.59	1959	28		4	
MURRAY, Max	Falkirk	07.11.35	Glasgow Rgrs	W.B.A.	11.62	1962	3		0	(CF) S.U23–2/S.AMAT.INT
MURRAY, Robert L.	Kemnay	24.04.32	Inverurie Loco	Stockport Co.	11.51	1952–62	465		31	(FB)●
MURRAY, Terry	Dublin	22.05.28	Dundalk	Hull C.	10.51	1951–53	32		6	EI-1/EI.F.LGE.REP
			TR	Bournemouth	03.54	1953–54	13		1	
MURRAY, Thomas	Bellshill	14.01.33	Q. of South	Leeds U.	08.60	1960	7		2	(F)
			TR	Tranmere Rov.	03.61	1960–61	10		1	
MURRAY, Thomas	Airdrie	05.02.33	Headington	Darlington	06.56	1956	3		0	(IF)
MURRAY, Thomas	Caldercruix	01.06.43	Airdrie	Carlisle C.	03.67	1966–70	122	11	37	(F)
MURRAY, Thomas A.	Barrow	16.10.44	JNRS	Barrow	07.64	1963–64	8		0	(FB)
MURRAY, William	Burnley	26.01.22	Arbroath	Manchester C.	01.47	1946–49	20		1	
MURTY, Joe	Glasgow	06.11.57	APP	Rochdale	11.75	1974-75	15	5	2	(F)
			TR	Bury	11.77	1977	0	1	0	
MUSGRAVE, David	Sth. Shields	20.04.28	Johannesburg	Manchester U.	12.47					(OL)
			Fleetwood	Brighton & H.A.	08.50	1950	35		2	
			TR	Preston N.E.	08.51					
			TR	Southport	10.51	1951–52	52		7	
			TR	Accrington St.	09.53	1953	30		7	

Players Names	Birthplace	Date	Previous Club	League Club	Date Signed	Seasons Played	Apps	Sub	Gls	
MUSGROVE, Malcolm	Lynemouth	08.07.33	Lynemouth Col.	West Ham U.	12.53	1953–62	283		84	(OL)
			TR	Orient	12.62	1962–65	83	/	14	
MUSGROVE, Martin	Wanstead	21.11.61	Heavitree	Torquay U.	N/C	1981	1	1	0	(M)
MUSIAL, Adam	Poland	18.12.48	Arkagydnia	Hereford U.	08.80	1980-82	44	2	0	(M)POLISH INT.
MUSKER, Russell	Plymouth	10.07.62	APP	Bristol C.	08.79	1980-83	44	2	1	(M)
			L	Exeter C.	10.83	1983	6	/	0	
			TR	Gillingham	11.83	1983	23	4	5	
MUSSON, Ian S.	Lincoln	13.12.53	APP	Sheffield Wed.	02.71					(W)
			TR	Lincoln C.	07.73	1973	11	/	0	
MUSSON, Walter U.	Belper	08.10.20	Holbrook St. M.	Derby Co.	*	1946–53	246		0	(WH) E.F. LGE. REP./d.1975
MUSTARD, William	Sth Shields	28.11.20	Bath C.	Exeter C.	05.46	1946	14		0	(CF) d. 1976
MUTCH, George	Aberdeen	21.09.12	Manchester U.(*)	Preston N.E.	*	1946	6		3	(IF)*Arbroath
			TR	Bury	10.46	1946	21		8	S–1/S.SCH.INT
			TR	Southport	10.47	1947	14		2	
MUTRIE, Les A.	Newcastle	01.04.52	Gateshead	Carlisle U.	06.77	1977	4	1	0	(F)
			Blyth Spartans	Hull C.	12.80	1980-83	114	1	49	
			L	Doncaster Rov.	12.83	1983	6	/	1	
			TR	Colchester U.	01.83	1983	10	4	2	
MUXWORTHY, Graham	Bristol	11.10.38	Exeter U.	Crystal Palace	09.57	1957	2		0	(F)
			Chippenham	Bristol Rov.	06.60	1962	8		0	
MUZINIC, Drazen	Yugoslavia	25.01.53	Hadjuk Split	Norwich C.	09.80	1980-81	15	4	0	(D)YUGOSLAV INT.
MWILA, Fred	Zambia	06.07.46	Atlanta	Aston Villa	09.69	1969	1	/	0	(IF)
MYCOCK, Albert	Manchester	31.01.23	Manchester U. (+)	Crystal Palace	06.46	1946–47	58		9	
			TR	Barrow	07.48	1948–49	42		4	
MYCOCK, David	Sunderland	30.08.21		Halifax T.	05.46	1946–51	170		17	(CH)
MYCOCK, Jack	Manchester	11.02.36	Congleton T.	Shrewsbury T.	AM	1958	6		1	(OR)
MYCOCK, Tom	Ryhope	22.08.23	Swansea C. (AM)	Southport	10.46	1946	19		3	(IF) IRISH LGE. REP.
			TR	Aldershot	04.47	1946–47	16		4	Brother of David
			Distillery	Brentford	12.50					
			TR	Tranmere Rov.	05.52	1952–53	46		2	
			TR	Bradford C.	02.54	1953–54	21		3	
MYERS, Cliff W.	London	23.09.46	APP	Charlton Ath.	09.64	1965–66	16	2	2	(M)
			TR	Brentford	06.67	1967	7	3	0	
			Yeovil T.	Torquay U.	07.73	1973–75	80	6	11	
MYERS, Rod J.	Sheffield	16.02.39	Scarborough	Doncaster Rov.	01.63	1963	19		0	(FB)
MYERSCOUGH, William	Bolton	22.06.30	Ashfield	Walsall	06.54	1954	26		6	(CF) d.1977
			TR	Aston Villa	07.55	1956–58	64		15	
			TR	Rotherham U.	07.59	1959	39		11	
			TR	Coventry C.	07.60	1960–61	58		16	
			TR	Chester C.	03.62	1961–62	36		11	
			TR	Wrexham	07.63	1963	35		5	
MYLES, Neil T.	Falkirk	17.06.27	T.Lanark	Ipswich T.	08.49	1949–59	224		22	(WH)
MYNARD, Les D.	Bewdley	19.12.25	Bewdley F.C.	Wolverhampton W.	+	1947	3		0	(OL)
			TR	Derby Co.	07.49	1949–50	15		2	
			TR	Scunthorpe U.	08.52	1952	18		3	
MYTON, Brian	Strensall	26.09.50	APP	Middlesbrough	09.67	1968–70	10	/	0	(HB)
			L	Southend U.	11.71	1971	0	1	0	

Players Names	Birthplace	Date	Previous Club	League Club	Date Signed	Seasons Played	Apps	Sub	Gls	
NAGY, Miklos	Hungary	01.05.29		Scunthorpe U.	01.51					
			TR	Swindon T.	08.51	1951	3		0	
NAIL, Desmond R.	St. Columb	28.12.24	St. Blazey	Plymouth Arg.	10.47	1947	1		0	
NAINBY, John	Seaton	02.01.40		Sheffield Wed.	02.58					(F)
			TR	Darlington	07.59	1959	3		1	
NAPIER, Alex S.	Kirkcaldy	08.08.35	Raith Rov.	Darlington	05.55	1955	1		0	(IF)
NAPIER, C. (Kit) R.A.	Dunblane	26.09.43	JNRS	Blackpool	11.60	1962	2		0	(F)NI SCH. INT.
			TR	Preston N.E.	06.63	1963	1		0	
			TR	Workington	07.64	1964–65	58	/	25	
			TR	Newcastle U.	11.65	1965	8	/	0	
			TR	Brighton & H.A.	09.66	1966–72	249	7	84	
			TR	Blackburn Rov.	08.72	1972–73	53	1	10	
NAPIER, Robert	Lurgan	23.09.46	JNRS	Bolton W.	09.63	1964-66	69	/	2	(D) NI-1/NI.U23-2
			TR	Brighton & H.A.	08.67	1967-72	218	1	5	
			TR	Bradford C.	10.72	1972-76	106	1	3	
NARDIELLO, Donato	Cardigan	09.01.57	APP	Coventry C.	04.74	1977-79	32	1	1	(F) W-2/W.U21-1
NARDIELLO, Gerardo	Warley	05.05.66	APP	Shrewsbury T.	05.84	1982-83	11	1	5	(F)
NASH, Frank C.	South Bank	30.06.19	South Bank	Middlesbrough	*	1946–47	3		0	(G)
			TR	Southend U.	12.47	1947–50	57		0	
NASH Robert G.	London	08.02.46	JNRS	Q.P.R.	02.64	1964	17		0	(FB)
			TR	Exeter C.	06.66	1966	1	/	0	
NASTRI, Carlo	Finchley	22.10.35	Kingstonian	Crystal Palace	07.58	1958	2		0	(W)
NATTRASS, Irving	Fishburn	12.12.52	APP	Newcastle U.	07.70	1970-78	226	12	16	(D) E.U23-1
			TR	Middlesbrough	08.79	1979-83	137	5	2	
NATTRESS, Clive	Durham	24.05.51	Consett	Blackpool	08.70					(D)
			TR	Darlington	08.72	1972-79	297	5	15	
			TR	Halifax T.	06.80	1980	37	/	5	
NAUGHTON, William B.S.	Catrine	20.03.62	APP	Preston N.E.	03.80	1979-83	117	12	9	(M)
NAYLOR, Edward A.	Bradford	24.12.21		Bradford P.A.	+					
			TR	Halifax T.	09.48	1948	7		0	
NAYLOR, Geoff	Goole	28.09.49	APP	Scunthorpe U.	09.67	1967	9	1	0	(HB)
NAYLOR, Harry F.	Leeds	06.06.28		Oldham Ath.	AM	1950	1		0	(CF)
NAYLOR, Stuart W.	Leeds	06.12.62	JNRS	Lincoln C.	06.80	1981-82	4	/	0	(G) E.YTH.INT.
			L	Peterborough U.	02.83	1982	8	/	0	
			L	Crewe Alex.	10.83	1983	38	/	0	
NAYLOR, Terry	Islington	05.12.48		Tottenham H.	07.69	1969-79	237	6	0	(D)
			TR	Charlton Ath.	11.80	1980-83	69	4	0	
NAYLOR, Tom V.	Blackburn	01.04.46	APP	Bournemouth	10.63	1964-70	139	3	3	(FB)
			TR	Hereford U.	08.72	1972-74	73	2	4	
NAYLOR, Tom W.	Leeds	07.12.24		Huddersfield T.	+					(FB) Brother of Harry
			TR	Oldham Ath.	03.48	1947–58	225		0	
NAYLOR, William H. (formerly Barke)	Sheffield	23.11.19	Hampton Spts.	Crystal Palace	*	1946	18		8	(IF)
			TR	Brentford	02.47	1946	11		2	
			TR	Orient	06.47	1947–49	65		12	
NEAL, Chris	Kirby in Ashfield	27.06.47	Crook T.	Darlington	AM	1967	5	/	0	(W)
NEAL, Dean J.	Edmonton	05.01.61	APP	Q.P.R.	08.79	1979-80	20	3	8	(F)
			Tulsa R.	Millwall	10.81	1981-83	84	12	35	
NEAL, George	Wellingborough	29.12.19	Kettering	Northampton T.	+	1946	3		0	(RH)
NEAL, John	Silksworth	03.04.32	Silksworth J.	Hull C.	08.49	1949-55	60		1	(FB)
			TR	Swindon T.	07.57	1957-58	91		2	
			TR	Aston Villa	07.59	1959-62	112		0	
			TR	Southend U.	11.62	1962-65	101	/	1	
NEAL, John J.	London	11.03.66	APP	Millwall	03.83	1983	3	3	1	(F)
NEAL, Philip G.	Irchester	29.02.51	APP	Northampton T.	12.68	1968-74	182	4	29	(D) E-52●
			TR	Liverpool	10.74	1974-83	400	/	36	
NEAL, Richard M.	Dinnington	01.10.33	JNRS	Wolverhampton W.	03.51					(WH) E.U23–4
			TR	Lincoln C.	07.54	1954–56	115		11	
			TR	Birmingham C.	04.57	1956–61	164		15	
			TR	Middlesbrough	10.61	1961–62	33		4	
			TR	Lincoln C.	08.63	1963–64	41		4	
NEALE, Duncan F.	Worthing	01.10.39	Ilford	Newcastle U.	06.59	1960–62	88		8	(WH)
			TR	Plymouth Arg.	08.63	1963–69	142	3	8	
NEALE, John	Barnstaple	15.01.49	Barnstaple	Exeter C.	03.72	1971–74	51	14	5	(F)
NEALE, Keith I.	Birmingham	19.01.35	JNRS	Birmingham C.	02.54	1956–57	6		1	(WH)
			TR	Lincoln C.	11.57	1957–58	8		1	
NEALE, Peter	Chesterfield	09.04.34		Oldham Ath.	01.53	1955–58	117		28	(HB)
			TR	Scunthorpe U.	10.58	1958–66	221	5	7	
			TR	Chesterfield	10.66	1966–67	69	/	3	
NEALE, Philip A.	Scunthorpe	05.04.54	Scunthorpe U.(AM)	Lincoln C	07.75	1974-83	300	7	22	(D) Worc. cricketer
NEALE, William	Wallsend	20.05.33	JNRS	Sunderland	06.50					(HB)
			Nth. Shields	Darlington	05.57	1957	15		0	

Players Names	Birthplace	Date	Previous Club	League Club	Date Signed	Seasons Played	Apps	Sub	Gls	
NEARY, H. Frank	Aldershot	06.03.21	Finchley	Q.P.R.	+	1946	9		4	(CF)
			TR	West Ham U.	01.47	1946–47	17		15	
			TR	Orient	11.47	1947–49	78		44	
			TR	Q.P.R.	10.49	1949	18		5	
			TR	Millwall	08.50	1950–53	123		50	
NEATE, Derek G.	London	01.10.27	Hayes	Brighton & H.A.	04.56	1955–56	24		6	(OL)
NEATE, Gordon	Reading	14.03.41	JNRS	Reading	03.58	1958–65	98	/	2	(FB)
NEAVE, I.J. Gordon	Glasgow	10.10.24	Pollock	Portsmouth	03.47					(HB)
			TR	Bournemouth	06.49	1950–53	85		0	
			TR	Aldershot	07.55	1955–57	79		1	
			TR	Portsmouth	09.58					
NEBBELING, Gavin M.	S. Africa	15.05.63	Arcadia Shepherds	Crystal Palace	08.81	1981-83	40	5	1	(D)
NEEDHAM, Andy P.	Oldham	13.09.55	APP	Birmingham C.	08.73	1975	2	1	1	(F)
			TR	Blackburn Rov.	07.76	1976	4	.1	0	
			TR	Aldershot	03.77	1976-79	92	3	29	
NEEDHAM, Anthony	Scunthorpe	04.01.41		Scunthorpe U.	07.59	1959–64	33		0	(FB)
NEEDHAM, Dave W.	Leicester	21.05.49	APP	Notts. Co.	07.66	1965–76	428	1	32	(D)●
			TR	Q.P.R.	06.77	1977	18	/	3	
			TR	Nottingham F.	12.77	1977-81	81	5	9	
NEEDHAM, Paul A.	Buxton	15.06.61	APP	Chester C.	06.79	1980-82	55	2	1	(D)
NEENAN, Joe P.	Manchester	17.03.59	APP	York C.	03.77	1976-79	56	/	0	(G)
			TR	Scunthorpe U.	01.80	1979-83	177	/	0	
NEIGHBOUR, Jim E.	Chingford	15.11.50	APP	Tottenham H.	11.68	1970-76	104	15	8	(W)
			TR	Norwich C.	09.76	1976-79	104	2	5	
			TR	West Ham U.	09.79	1979-82	66	7	5	
			L	Bournemouth	01.83	1982	6	/	0	
NEIL, Hugh	Lugar	02.10.36	St. Johnstone	Carlisle U.	06.61	1961–68	246	1	2	(FB) S.SCH.INT/d.
NEIL, Pat	Portsmouth	24.10.37	JNRS	Portsmouth	AM	1955	9		3	(OL) E.AMAT.INT
			TR	Wolverhampton W.	AM	1956	4		1	
			Pegasus	Portsmouth	05.62	1962	1		0	
NEIL, William W.	Roslin	10.11.44	Bonnyrigg Rose	Millwall	04.64	1964–71	180	8	24	(F)
NEIL, William M.	Lanark	20.04.24	Morton	Bradford P.A.	12.47	1947	3		0	
				Workington	07.53					
				Bradford P.A.	11.57					
NEILL, Terry W.J.	Belfast	08.05.42	Bangor	Arsenal	12.59	1960–69	240	1	8	(CH) NI–59/NI U23-4/
			TR	Hull C.	07.70	1970–72	103	/	4	NI.SCH.INT.●
NEILL, Tom K.	Methill	03.10.30	R.A.F.Wharton	Bolton W.	09.50	1952–56	40		2	(WH)
			TR	Bury	12.56	1956–59	90		9	
			TR	Tranmere Rov.	10.60	1960–62	79		2	
NEILL, Warren A.	Acton	21.11.62	APP	Q.P.R.	09.80	1980-83	94	1	3	(D)
NEILSON, Gordon	Glasgow	28.05.47	Glasgow U.	Arsenal	06.64	1965–66	14	/	2	(W)
			TR	Brentford	10.68	1968–71	80	11	15	
NEILSON John C.	Hamilton	02.08.21	Clyde	Bradford C.	10.47	1947–48	29		11	
			TR	Wrexham	10.48					
NEILSON, Norman F.	S.Africa	06.11.28	S.Africa	Charlton Ath.	07.49	1949	1		0	(CH)
			TR	Derby Co.	09.51	1951–53	57		1	
			TR	Bury	05.54	1954–56	100		5	
			TR	Hull C.	04.57	1956–57	25		0	
NEILSON, Steve	Newtongrange	25.04.31		Rotherham U.	07.55	1956	9		0	
NEILSON, Tom	Armadale	28.07.22		Ipswich T.	05.48	1948	1		0	
NEKREWS, Tom J.	Chatham	20.03.33	Chelsea(AM)	Gillingham	09.53	1953–57	47		0	(CH)
			TR	Watford	07.58					
NELMES, Alan V.	Hackney	20.10.48	JNRS	Chelsea	10.65					(WH)
			TR	Brentford	07.67	1967–75	311	5	2	
NELSON, Andy	Custom House	05.07.35	JNRS	West Ham U.	12.53	1957–58	15		1	(CH)
			TR	Ipswich T.	06.59	1959–64	193		0	
			TR	Orient	09.64	1964–65	43	/	0	
			TR	Plymouth Arg.	10.65	1965–67	93	/	1	
NELSON, Anthony J.	Newport	12.04.30		Newport Co.	06.52	1951–53	19		6	(CH) Son of pre-war player/
			TR	Bristol C.	05.54					W.AMAT.INT.
			TR	Bournemouth	06.56	1956–64	195		1	
NELSON, Colin A.	Boldon	13.03.38	Unsworth Col	Sunderland	03.58	1958–64	146		2	(FB)
			TR	Mansfield T.	03.65	1964–65	38	/	0	
NELSON, David	Douglas Water	03.02.18	St. Bernards	Arsenal	*	1946	10		0	(WH)
			TR	Fulham	12.46	1946	24		3	
			TR	Brentford	08.47	1947–49	106		5	
			TR	Q.P.R.	02.50	1949–50	31		0	
			TR	Crystal Palace	03.52	1951–52	12		0	
NELSON, Dennis	Edinburgh	25.02.50	Dunfermline	Crewe Alex.	07.74	1974-75	65	6	18	(F)
			TR	Reading	03.76	1975-77	53	6	6	
			TR	Crewe Alex.	07.78	1978-80	97	10	15	
NELSON, Gary P.	Braintree	16.01.61	JNRS	Southend U.	07.79	1979-82	106	23	17	(M)
			TR	Swindon T.	08.83	1983	35	1	4	

Players Names	Birthplace	Date	Previous Club	League Club	Date Signed	Seasons Played	Apps	Sub	Gls	
NELSON, George	Mexborough	05.02.25	Sheffield U.(+)	Lincoln C.	09.46	1946	1		0	(IF)
NELSON, James F.	Newcastle	04.11.43		Sunderland	08.62					(FB)
			TR	Ipswich T.	07.63					
			TR	Barrow	01.65	1964–65	15	/	0	
NELSON, Sammy	Belfast	01.04.49	JNRS	Arsenal	04.66	1969–80	245	10	10	(D) NI-51/NI.U23-1
			TR	Brighton & H.A.	09.81	1981–82	40	/	1	
NELSON, Sammy E.	Belfast	26.05.24	Linfield	Blackpool	10.46	1946–47	14		0	(OR)NI.SCH.INT.
			TR	Luton T.	01.48	1947–48	4		1	
NELSON, William E.	Silvertown	20.09.29		West Ham U.	10.50	1954	2		0	(WH)
			TR	Q.P.R.	07.55	1955	9		0	
NESBITT, Edward	Boldon	12.10.51	Longbenton J.	Hartlepool U.	AM	1971	1	/	0	(G)
NESBITT, John	Washington	24.09.33	Ashington	Newcastle U.	12.55	1957	3		0	(HB)
NESS, Hugh	Dunfermline	30.04.40	Cowdenbeath	Accrington St.	07.59	1959	14		1	
			TR	Halifax	07.60					
NETHERCOTT, Ken	Bristol	22.07.25	Cardiff C. (AM)	Norwich C.	04.47	1947–58	378		0	(G) E'B'–1
NETTLESHIP, Reg	Worksop	23.02.25	Sheffield U.(+)	Mansfield T.	07.46	1946	1		0	(F)
NETTLETON, Ernie	Sheffield	07.01.18		York C.	07.46	1946	7		2	(IL)
NEVILLE, David R.	Birmingham	08.01.29	Paget Rgrs.	Bournemouth	04.49					
			TR	Chelsea	07.50					
			Burton A.	Rochdale	08.55	1955	1		0	
			TR	Crewe Alex.	09.55					
NEVILLE, Steve F.	Walthamstow	18.09.57	APP	Southampton	10.75	1977	5	/	1	(F)
			TR	Exeter C.	09.78	1978–80	90	3	22	
			TR	Sheffield U.	10.80	1980–81	40	9	6	
			TR	Exeter C	10.82	1982–83	73	3	26	
NEVILLE, William	Cork	15.05.35	Wembley T.	West Ham U.	11.56	1957	3		0	(F) EI'B'–1
NEVIN, Pat K. F.	Glasgow	06.09.63	Clyde	Chelsea	07.83	1983	38	/	14	(W)S.YTH.INT.
NEVIN, Ridley W.	Liverpool	28.07.56	APP	Everton	05.74					(IF)
			TR	Workington	08.75	1975	3	1	0	
NEVINS, Laurie	Gateshead	02.97.20		Newcastle U.	+					
			TR	Brighton & H.A.	05.47	1947	5		0	
			TR	Hartlepool U.	03.48	1947–48	18		8	
NEW, Martin P.	Swindon	11.05.59	APP	Arsenal	03.77					(G) E.SCH.INT.
			TR	Mansfield T.	06.78	1978–79	21	/	0	
			TR	Barnsley	06.80	1980	24	/	0	
NEWALL, Danny J.	Newport	05.06.21	JNRS	Newport Co.	*	1946–54	232		4	(WH)
NEWBERRY, Peter	Derby	04.03.38	JNRS	Derby Co.	03.55	1958–60	5		2	(CF)
NEWBOLD, Alf	W. Hartlepool	07.08.21	Ouston W.	Huddersfield T.	+	1946	2		0	(RB)
			TR	Newport Co.	10.46	1946	22		0	
NEWBY, T. Geoff	Barrow	09.10.49	JNRS	Barrow	AM	1968	1	/	0	(WH)
NEWCOMBE, (Len) Bernard J.	Swansea	28.02.31	JNRS	Fulham	05.48	1951–54	23		3	(OL)
			TR	Brentford	04.56	1955–58	84		10	
NEWELL, Edgar	Swansea	17.04.20		Swansea C.	08.46	1947–50	24		0	(CH)
NEWELL, George	Rochdale	07.03.36		Rochdale	04.57	1957	1		0	
NEWELL, Mike C.	Liverpool	27.01.65		Crewe Alex.	09.83	1983	3	/	0	(F)
			TR	Wigan Ath.	10.83	1983	5	4	0	
NEWLANDS, Doug	Edinbrugh	29.10.31	Aberdeen	Burnley	03.55	1954–58	98		21	(OR)
			TR	Stoke C.	07.59	1959	32		8	
NEWLANDS, Malcolm	Glasgow	28.03.25	St. Mirren	Preston N.E.	07.48	1948–52	80		0	(G)
			TR	Workington	11.52	1952–59	251		0	
NEWLOVE, Peter	Bradford	27.12.47	APP	Bradford C.	01.66	1964–66	2	1	0	
NEWMAN, Albert	Lichfield	01.03.15	W.B.A.(*)	Walsall	*	1946–49	136		2	(WH) d. 1982
NEWMAN, Eric I.A.	Romford	24.11.24	Romford	Arsenal	10.46					(G)
			TR	Ipswich T.	09.50	1952	18		0	
NEWMAN, H. Mike	Canada	02.04.32	Dagenham	West Ham U.	12.57	1956–57	7		2	
NEWMAN, John H.G.	Hereford	13.12.33	JNRS	Birmingham C.	03.51	1951–57	59		0	(WH)●
			TR	Leicester C.	11.57	1957–59	61		2	
			TR	Plymouth Arg.	01.60	1959–60	298	/	9	
			TR	Exeter C.	11.67	1967–71	91	1	1	
NEWMAN, Keith	Farnham	20.11.49	APP	Aldershot	11.66	1966–69	19	4	0	(WH) E.SCH.INT
			TR	York C.	07.70	1970	3	1	0	
NEWMAN, Robert N.	Bradford-on-Avon	13.12.63	APP	Bristol C.	10.81	1981–83	86	8	7	(M)
NEWMAN, Ron	Pontypridd	01.05.33	Ynysybwl	Northampton T.	10.53	1954–55	18		5	(IF)
			TR	Coventry C.	03.56	1955–56	13		2	
			TR	Torquay U.	07.57	1957	5		0	
NEWMAN, Ron V.	Portsmouth	19.01.34	Woking	Portsmouth	01.55	1954–60	108		21	(W)
			TR	Orient	01.61	1960–61	14		1	
			TR	Crystal Palace	10.62	1962	6		0	
			TR	Gillingham	09.63	1963–65	90	3	20	

Players Names	Birthplace	Date	Previous Club	League Club	Date Signed	Seasons Played	Apps	Sub	Gls	
NEWSHAM, Stan	Farnworth	24.05.31		Bournemouth	06.52	1952–56	142		74	(IF)
			TR	Notts. Co.	08.57	1957–61	99		45	
NEWSOME, Robin	Hebdon Bridge	25.09.19	Congleton T.	W.B.A.	*					(OR)
			TR	Coventry C.	06.47	1947	7		2	
NEWTON, Ben	Grimsby	10.10.34		Grimsby T.	07.53	1953	3		0	
NEWTON, Eric	Worrall	21.06.32	Norton Woodseats	Halifax T.	12.54	1954	10		3	
NEWTON, Graham W.	Bilston	22.12.42	Wolverhampton W.(AM)	Blackpool	08.61					(IF)
			TR	Walsall	02.62	1962–63	30		10	
			TR	Coventry C.	01.64	1963	8		3	
			TR	Bournemouth	12.64	1964–66	27	1	3	
			Atlanta	Port Vale	11.68	1968	4	/	0	
			Atlanta	Reading	08.70					
NEWTON, Henry A.	Nottingham	18.02.44	JNRS	Nottingham F.	06.61	1963-70	281	/	17	(M) E.U23-4/E.F.LGE.REP.
			TR	Everton	10.70	1970-73	76	/	5	
			TR	Derby C.	09.73	1973-76	111	6	5	
			TR	Walsall	07.77	1977	16	/	0	
NEWTON, John	Edinbrugh	19.01.40	Craiglea Th.	Notts. Co.	10.57	1958–60	5		0	(FB)
			TR	York C.	08.61					
NEWTON, John L.	Bishop Auckland	25.05.25	Newcastle U.(+)	Hartlepool U.	05.46	1946–57	332		15	(WH)
NEWTON, Keith R.	Manchester	23.06.41	JNRS	Blackburn Rov.	10.58	1960-69	306	/	9	(D) E-27/E.U23-4/●
			TR	Everton	12.69	1969-71	48	1	1	E.F.LGE.REP
			TR	Burnley	06.72	1972-77	209	/	5	
NEWTON, Reg W.	Bow	30.06.26		Orient	04.48	1948	23		0	(G)
			TR	Brentford	07.49	1949–56	87		0	
NEWTON, Robert	Chesterfield	23.11.56	APP	Huddersfield T.	11.73	1973-76	37	5	7	(F)
			TR	Hartlepool U.	08.77	1977-82	150	/	48	
			TR	Port Vale	09.82	1982-83	48	/	22	
			TR	Chesterfield	10.83	1983	33	/	14	
NEWTON, Robert A.	Leicester	19.01.46	APP	Leicester C.	08.63	1964	2		0	(F)
			TR	Bradford C.	05.65	1965	19	1	4	
NIBLETT, Vic	Ash Vale	09.12.24	JNRS	Reading	+	1946–49	6		0	(CH)
			TR	West Ham U.	06.50					
			TR	Gillingham	08.51	1951–55	156		0	
NIBLOE, John	Sheffield	01.06.39		Sheffield U.	08.58	1958–60	25		4	(CF) d.1964
			TR	Stoke C.	10.61	1961–62	19		4	
			TR	Doncaster Rov.	10.62	1962–63	36		7	
			TR	Stockport Co.	07.64	1964	19		1	
NIBLOE, Joseph	Glasgow	10.12.26	Clydebank J.	Cardiff C.	03.48	1948	1		0	+ Sheffield Wed.
NICHOL, George W.	Bannockburn	20.07.23	Falkirk	Aldershot	08.51	1951	19		0	(G)
NICHOL, Robert W.	Carlisle	19.01.41	JNRS	Carlisle U.	AM	1958–59	3		1	
NICHOLAS, Anthony W.L.	West Ham	16.04.38.	JNRS	Chelsea	05.55	1956–59	46		13	(IF) E.YTH.INT.
			TR	Brighton & H.A.	11.60	1960–61	65		22	
			Chelmsford	Orient	06.65	1965	8	1	2	
NICHOLAS, Charlie	Glasgow	30.12.61	Glasgow Celtic	Arsenal	07.83	1983	41	/	11	(F)S.U'21-3/S-7
NICHOLAS, G. Brian	Aberdare	20.04.33	JNRS	Q.P.R.	05.50	1948–54	115		2	(WH) E.SCH.INT.
			TR	Chelsea	07.55	1955–57	39		6	
			TR	Coventry C.	02.58	1957–61	113		0	
NICHOLAS, Glyn	Dartmouth	02.12.46	APP	Plymouth Arg.	09.64	1964–65	2	/	0	(F)
			L	Crewe Alex.	03.66	1965	2	/	1	
			TR	Torquay U.	07.66					
NICHOLAS, John T.	Derby	26.11.10		Derby Co.	*	1946	9		0	(WH) W.SCH.INT./d.1977
NICHOLAS, Ken W.	Northampton	03.02.38	JNRS	Arsenal	05.55					(FB) E.SCH.INT./
			TR	Watford	05.59	1959–64	198		4	E.YTH.INT.
NICHOLAS, Peter	Newport	10.11.59	APP	Crystal Palace	12.76	1977–80	127	/	7	(M)W-31/W.U21-3/●
			TR	Arsenal	03.81	1980-82	57	3	1	W.SCH.INT.
			L	Crystal Palace	10.83	1983	25	/	3	
NICHOLL, Chris J.	Wilmslow	12.10.46	JNRS	Burnley	04.65					(D)NI-51●
			Witton A.	Halifax T.	06.68	1968-69	42	/	3	
			TR	Luton T.	08.69	1969-71	98	/	6	
			TR	Aston Villa	03.72	1971-76	210	/	11	
			TR	Southampton	06.77	1977-82	228	/	8	
			TR	Grimsby T.	08.83	1983	39	/	0	
NICHOLL, Jimmy M.	Canada	28.02.56	APP	Manchester U.	03.74	1974-81	188	9	3	(D)NI-61/N1.U21-1/
			L	Sunderland	12.81	1981	3	/	0	NI.SCH.INT.
			Toronto	Sunderland	09.82	1982	29	/	0	
NICHOLL, Terry	Wilmslow	16.09.52		Crewe Alex.	02.72	1971-72	46	/	7	(M) Brother of Chris
			TR	Sheffield U.	03.73	1973-74	12	10	1	
			TR	Southend U.	05.75	1975-76	50	/	3	
			TR	Gillingham	10.76	1976-80	184	/	11	
NICHOLLS, Alan	Plymouth	10.02.63	APP	Bristol C.	02.80	1980-82	70	/	5	(D)
NICHOLLS, Brian A.	Dagenham	30.05.45	APP	Fulham	07.63	1965–67	50	1	1	(FB)
			TR	Millwall	07.68	1968–69	9		0	

Players Names	Birthplace	Date	Previous Club	League Club	Date Signed	Seasons Played	Apps	Sub	Gls	
NICHOLLS, James	Coseley	27.11.19		Bradford P.A.	05.46	1946–49	36		0	(G)
			TR	Rochdale	08.51	1951–52	50		0	
NICHOLLS, Johnny	Wolverhampton	03.04.31	Heath T.	W.B.A.	08.51	1951–56	131		58	(IF) E.2/E.U23–1
			TR	Cardiff C.	05.57	1957	8		2	
			TR	Exeter C.	11.57	1957–58	56		23	
NICHOLLS, Philip R.	Bilston	22.06.52	APP	Wolverhampton W.	07.70					(D)
			TR	Crewe Alex.	09.72	1972-76	155	8	8	
			TR	Bradford C.	03.77	1976-77	19	2	2	
			TR	Crewe Alex.	08.78	1978	10	3	0	
NICHOLLS, Ray I.	Fletton	07.04.65	APP	Cambridge U.	08.82	1981-83	18	5	1	(M)
NICHOLLS, Ron B.	Sharpness	04.12.33	Fulham(AM)	Bristol Rov.	11.54	1955–57	71		0	(G) Glouc. Cricketer
			TR	Cardiff C.	08.58	1958–60	51		0	
			TR	Bristol C.	07.61	1961–63	39		0	
NICHOLLS, Ron H.	Cannock	18.10.35	JNRS	W.B.A.	11.52					
			TR	Walsall	08.53	1953	2		0	
NICHOLLS, Wayne K.	Leicester	21.10.52	Leicester C.(APP)	Workington	08.71	1971–72	21	12	1	(CF)
NICHOLS, Adam A.	Ilford	14.09.62	APP	Ipswich T.	10.79					(D)
				Colchester U.	N/C	1983	4	2	1	
NICHOLS, David	Bradford	03.11.56	APP	Huddersfield T.	11.73					(CH) E.SCH.INT
			TR	Bradford C.	N/C	1975	0	4	0	
NICHOLSON, Derek	Chertsey	08.04.36	Chertsey	Orient	11.53	1957	5		0	(CF)
NICHOLSON, G. Harry	Carlisle	25.01.32	Carlisle U. (AM)	Grimsby T.	08.52	1953	17		0	(G)
			TR	Nottingham F.	07.55	1955–56	72		0	
			TR	Accrington St.	03.58	1958	1		0	
			TR	Orient	03.59	1959	4		0	
			TR	Bristol C.	07.60	1960	1		0	
NICHOLSON, Gary A.	Newcastle	04.11.60	APP	Newcastle U.	11.78	1978-80	7	5	0	(F)
			TR	Mansfield T.	08.81	1981-83	112	6	21	
NICHOLSON, James J.	Belfast	27.02.43	JNRS	Manchester U.	02.60	1960–62	58		5	(WH) NI–41/NI.U23–4/
			TR	Huddersfield T.	12.64	1964–73	280	1	26	NI.B–1/NI.SCH.INT.●
			TR	Bury	12.73	1973–75	79	4	0	
NICHOLSON, John P.	Liverpool	02.09.36		Liverpool	01.57	1959	1		0	(CH)d.1966
			TR	Port Vale	08.61	1961–65	184	/	1	
			TR	Doncaster Rov.	09.65	1965–66	41	/	0	
NICHOLSON, John R.	Harrington	23.06.28	Frizzington	Barrow	05.49	1949	4		1	(OL)
			TR	York C.	10.50					
NICHOLSON, Peter	Cleator Moor	12.01.51	Carlisle U.(APP)	Blackpool	08.69	1970	3	3	0	(D)
			TR	Bolton W.	06.71	1971-81	303	15	12	
				Rochdale	N/C	1982	7	/	0	
				Carlisle U.	N/C	1982-83	1	2	0	
NICHOLSON, Peter W.	Hull	11.12.36		Hull C.	AM	1960	1		0	(CF)
NICHOLSON, Reece	Bircotes	04.04.36	JNRS	Doncaster Rov.	09.53	1954–57	28		8	(IF)
NICHOLSON, Stan	Middlesbrough	20.08.31	South Bank	Middlesbrough	05.49					(IF)
			TR	Leeds U.	08.51					
			Horden C.W.	Hartlepool U.	07.58	1958	7		1	
NICHOLSON, William E.	Scarborough	26.01.19	JNRS	Tottenham H.	*	1946–54	306		6	(WH) E–1/E'B'–3/ E.F.LGE.REP.
NICKALLS, Jim	Amble	29.05.34		Sunderland	04.53					(CH)
			TR	Darlington	05.54	1954	18		0	
NICKEAS, Mark	Southport	20.10.56	APP	Plymouth Arg.	07.74					(D)
			TR	Chester C.	08.75	1975-78	58	2	1	
NICKLAS, Charles	Sunderland	26.04.30	Silksworth J.	Hull C.	12.50	1951	6		1	(WH)
			TR	Darlington	05.53	1953	17		6	
NICOL, Bennett	Glasgow	10.03.21		Bolton W.	11.46					
				Rochdale	07.49	1949	5		1	
NICOL, Robert B.M.	Edinburgh	11.05.36	Hibernian	Barnsley	08.62	1962–63	37		1	(HB) S.SCH.INT
NICOL, Steve	Irvine	11.12.61	Ayr U.	Liverpool	10.81	1982-83	21	6	5	(D)S.U'21-10
NIEDZWIECKI, Eddie	Bangor	03.05.59	JNRS	Wrexham	07.76	1977-82	111	/	0	(G) W.SCH.INT.
			TR	Chelsea	06.83	1983	42	/	0	
NIEUWENHUYS, Benny	S. Africa	05.11.11	S. Africa	Liverpool	*	1946	15		5	(OR)
NIGHTINGALE, Albert	Thrybergh	10.11.23		Sheffield U.	+	1946–47	62		14	(IF)
			TR	Huddersfield T.	03.48	1947–51	119		20	
			TR	Blackburn Rov.	10.51	1951–52	35		5	
			TR	Leeds U.	10.52	1952–56	130		48	
NIGHTINGALE, David R.	Liverpool	15.08.27		Tranmere Rov.	09.46	1946	3		0	(RB)
NIGHTINGALE, Mark	Salisbury	01.02.57	APP	Bournemouth	07.74	1974-75	44	5	4	(D) E.YTH.INT.
			TR	Crystal Palace	06.76					
			TR	Norwich C.	07.77	1977-81	28	7	0	
			Bulova H.K.	Bournemouth	09.83	1982-83	70	2	4	
NIGHTINGALE, Ron	Blackburn	27.01.37		Accrington St.	07.57	1958–60	13		0	(WH)
			TR	Tranmere Rov.	08.61					
NIKOLIC, Dusan	Yugoslavia	23.01.53	Red Star	Bolton W.	10.80	1980-81	22	/	2	(M) YUGOSLAV. INT.

Players Names	Birthplace	Date	Previous Club	League Club	Date Signed	Seasons Played	Career Record Apps	Sub	Gls	
NIMMO, Ian W.	Boston	23.01.58	APP	Sheffield Wed.	01.76	1975-78	26	19	10	(F)
			L	Peterborough U.	01.77	1976	4	/	1	
			TR	Doncaster Rov.	06.79	1979-81	77	9	29	
NIMMO, William B.	Lanark	11.01.34	Alloa Ath.	Leeds U.	02.56	1957	1		0	(G)
			TR	Doncaster Rov.	03.58	1957-61	182		0	
			TR	Mansfield T.	07.62					
NISBET, Gordon	Wallsend	18.09.51	JNRS	W.B.A.	09.68	1969-75	136	/	0	(M) E.U23-1/1 app. in
			TR	Hull C.	09.76	1976-80	190	3	1	goal for W.B.A.
			TR	Plymouth Arg.	12.80	1980-83	154	/	9	
NISH, David	Burton	26.09.47	Measham Imp.	Leicester C.	07.66	1966-72	228	/	25	(D) E-5/E.U23-10/
			TR	Derby Co.	08.72	1972-78	184	4	10	E.F.LGE.REP./E.YTH.INT.
NIX, Peter	Rotherham	25.01.58	JNRS	Rotherham U.	08.76	1977-79	22	/	2	(M)
NIXON, John C.	Preston	20.01.48	JNRS	Derby Co.	09.65					(F)
			Ikeston T.	Notts. Co.	01.70	1969-74	167	12	32	
			TR	Peterborough U.	09.74	1974-76	104	6	16	
			TR	Shrewsbury T.	08.77	1977	21	2	3	
			TR	Barnsley	03.78	1977	6	3	0	
			TR	Halifax T.	06.78	1978	12	7	1	
NIXON, Tom J.	Backworth	25.05.31	Newcastle U.(AM)	Darlington	AM	1951	1		0	(LH)
NIXON, William J.	Ballynahinch	28.09.41	Distillery	Norwich C.	03.61	1961	1		0	(F) NI.SCH.INT
			TR	Shrewsbury T.	03.62	1961-64	17		1	
NOAKE, David J.	Dorchester	09.06.40	Dorchester T.	Luton T.	11.59	1959-60	17		0	(F)
			TR	Bristol C.	06.61	1961	11		3	
NOAKES, Alf G.	Stratford	14.08.33	JNRS	West Ham U.	08.50					(FB)
			TR	Crystal Palace	06.55	1955-61	195		14	
			TR	Portsmouth	07.62	1962-63	13		0	
NOBBS, Keith A.	B. Auckland	19.09.61	APP	Middlesbrough	09.79	1980	1	/	0	(D)
			TR	Halifax T.	08.82	1982-83	87	/	1	
NOBLE, Alf W.T.	Hackney	18.09.24	Briggs Spts.	Colchester U.	AM	1955	1		0	(IF) E.AMAT.INT
NOBLE, Barry	Stockton	05.06.51	JNRS	Hartlepool U.	AM	1971	1		0	(G)
NOBLE, Frank	Sheffield	26.10.45	JNRS	Sheffield Wed.	05.63	1963-65	2	/	0	(FB)
			TR	Peterborough U.	07.67	1967-71	205	2	1	
NOBLE, John	Manchester	20.05.19	Warte Villa	Stockport Co.	*	1946	1		0	(WH)
NOBLE, Norman	Barnsley	08.08.23	Huddersfield T.(+)	Bradford C.	+					(FB) d.
			Ransome & M	Rotherham U.	05.48	1948-57	326		21	
NOBLE, Peter	Newcastle	19.08.44	Consett	Newcastle U.	11.64	1965-67	22	3	7	(M)
			TR	Swindon T.	01.68	1967-72	212	4	62	
			TR	Burnley	06.73	1973-79	241	2	63	
			TR	Blackpool	01.80	1979-82	92	5	14	
NOBLE, Robert	Newcastle	25.05.49	APP	Newcastle U.	04.67					(D)
			L	Barrow	08.69	1969	19	/	3	
			TR	Bury	08.70	1970	6	/	0	
			TR	Barrow	10.70	1970-71	72	1	5	
			TR	Colchester U.	08.72	1972	25	2	0	
			TR	Southport	03.73	1972-74	61	2	6	
			TR	Darlington	08.75	1975-76	54	/	3	
NOBLE, Robert	Manchester	18.12.45	APP	Manchester U.	12.62	1965-66	31	/	0	(FB) E.YTH.INT
NOLAN, George	Liverpool	09.12.25	A.I. Control FC	Southport	06.46	1946	3		0	(LH)
NOLAN, Mike	Dublin	08.07.50	APP	Oldham Ath.	08.67	1966-67	2	/	0	(FB)
NOLAN, Phil	Edmonton	29.12.23	Hayes	Watford	10.47	1947-54	91		8	(CH)
NOLAN, Terry S.	Whiston	16.03.56	Prescot Cables	Southport	N/C	1977	0	1	0	(F)
NOON, Harry	Sutton-in Ashfield	06.10.37	Bentinck Meth.	Notts. Co.	05.55	1957-61	122		0	(FB)
			TR	Bradford C.	07.62	1962	1		0	
NORCROSS, William	Preston	29.12.37	Chorley	Southport	AM	1959	1		0	(CF)
NORMAN, Anthony J.	Mancot	24.02.58	JNRS	Burnley	08.76					(G)
			TR	Hull C.	02.80	1979-83	177	/	0	
NORMAN, Derek	Birmingham	11.02.46	Alvechurch	Southampton	01.64					(F) E.YTH.INT
			TR	Aldershot	05.65	1965	22	1	0	
NORMAN, Griffith A.	Cardiff	20.02.26		Cardiff C.	04.50	1951	1		0	(WH)
			TR	Torquay U.	10.52	1952-57	216		6	
NORMAN, Malcolm A.	Cardiff	24.10.34	Cardiff Corries	Bristol Rov.	05.58	1958-61	69		0	(G)
NORMAN, Maurice	Mulbarton	08.05.34	Wymondham O.B.	Norwich C.	09.52	1954-55	35		0	(CH) E-23/E.U23-3/
			TR	Tottenham H.	11.55	1955-65	357	/	15	EF.LGE.REP.
NORMAN, Richard	Newcastle	05.09.35	Horden C.W.	Leicester C.	11.58	1959-67	303	/	2	(FB)
			TR	Peterborough U.	07.68	1968	9	1	0	
NORMANTON, Graham S.	Hartlepool	13.11.59	Middlesbrough (APP)	Hartlepool U.	07.78	1979-80	17	1	0	(D)
NORMANTON, Sid	Barnsley	20.08.26	Barnsley M.C.W.	Barnsley	+	1947-53	123		2	(WH)
			TR	Halifax T.	07.54	1954	14		0	
NORRIE, Craig T.	Hull	22.07.60	APP	Hull C.	08.78	1978-81	22	9	4	(F)
NORRIS, Derek	Beighton	19.06.35	Gainsborough	Peterborough U.	N/L	1960	5		0	(HB)

Players Names	Birthplace	Date	Previous Club	League Club	Date Signed	Seasons Played	Apps	Sub	Gls	
NORRIS, George A.	Aldershot	19.09.35	Farnborough	Aldershot	12.58	1958–63	106		58	(CF)
NORRIS, Graham J.	Hampton Court	08.02.54	APP	Crystal Palace	02.72					(W)
			L	Southend U.	03.73	1972	1	/	0	
NORRIS, Mike	Retford	27.02.57	APP	Scunthorpe U.	02.75	1973–75	25	/	0	(G)
NORRIS, Ollie P.	Londonderry	01.04.29	JNRS	Middlesbrough	07.48	1951–53	12		2	(CF)
			TR	Bournemouth	07.55	1955–58	96		34	
			TR	Northampton T.	09.58	1958	14		1	
			Ashford T.	Rochdale	01.61	1960	2		1	
NORRIS, Ray G.	Bristol	15.07.22	Bedminster	Bristol C.	05.47	1947	3		0	(CH)
NORTH, Eric	Halifax	06.10.23	Lee Mount FC	Halifax T.	AM	1948	1		0	(OL)
NORTH, Stacey S.	Luton	25.11.64	APP	Luton T.	08.82	1983	1	/	0	(D)
NORTH, Tom W.	Barrow-on-Soar	31.10.19	Banbury	Nottingham F.	+	1946	1		0	(IF)
NORTHCOTT, George E.	Torquay	07.05.35	JNRS	Torquay U.	10.52	1954–61	164		2	(WH)
			Cheltenham	Exeter C.	08.63	1963	1		0	
NORTHCOTT, Tommy T.	Torquay	05.12.31	JNRS	Torquay U.	12.48	1948–52	60		10	(IF) E.YTH.INT./●
			TR	Cardiff C.	10.52	1952–54	71		13	Brother of George
			TR	Lincoln C.	07.55	1955–57	94		34	
			TR	Torquay U.	11.57	1957–65	347	2	125	
NORTHOVER, Stan O.	Weymouth	03.07.26	Weymouth	Luton T.	AM	1949	1		0	(IF)
NORTON, David J.	Gateshead	24.01.57	Whickham	Hartlepool U.	12.78	1978-79	14	3	1	(M)
NORTON, Peter	Manchester	11.11.47	JNRS	Bournemouth	11.66	1966–67	18	/	1	(FB)
			TR	Crewe Alex.	07.68					
NORTON, Ralph	Aylesham	11.10.42	JNRS	Reading	10.59	1960–65	99	1	9	(IF)
			TR	Bournemouth	07.66	1966–67	44	4	4	
NOVACKI, Jan	Manchester	04.12.58	APP	Bolton W.	07.77					(F) E.YTH.INT.
			L	York C.	12.77	1977	24	1	3	
NOWAK, Tadeusz	Poland	28.11.48	Legia	Bolton W.	03.79	1978-80	22	2	1	(M) POLISH INT.
NUGENT, Arthur	Glasgow	30.05.26	Canterbury	Darlington	06.56	1956	5		0	(RB)
NUGENT, W. Cliff	Stoney Middleton	03.03.29	Headington	Cardiff C.	01.51	1951–58	117		19	(OL)
			TR	Mansfield T.	11.51	1958–59	51		7	
NULTY, Geoff	Prescot	13.02.49	JNRS	Stoke C.	07.67					(M)
			TR	Burnley	07.68	1969-74	123	7	20	
			TR	Newcastle U.	12.74	1974-77	101	/	11	
			TR	Everton	07.78	1978-79	22	6	2	
NUNDY, Jeff	Hull	29.11.35		Huddersfield T.	12.53					(HB)
			TR	Bradford C.	07.57	1957–59	32		0	
NUNN, Walter	Deptford	16.01.20	Bexley & W	Charlton Ath.	+					(HB) d. 1965
			TR	Swindon T.	06.47	1947	4		0	
NURSE, Mel T.G.	Swansea	11.10.37	JNRS	Swansea C.	06.55	1955–62	158		9	(CH) W–12/W.U23–2/●
			TR	Middlesbrough	10.62	1962–65	111	/	9	W. SCH.INT
			TR	Swindon T.	09.65	1965–67	122	1	10	
			TR	Swansea C.	06.68	1968–70	97	1	2	
NUTE, Steve L.R.	Plymouth	18.04.62	APP	Exeter C.	04.80	1980	5	/	0	(G)
NUTLEY, Robert	Paisley	10.09.16	Hibernian	Portsmouth	08.46	1946	9		1	(OL)
NUTT, Gordon E.	Birmingham	08.11.32	JNRS	Coventry C.	11.49	1951–54	76		13	(W)
			TR	Cardiff C.	12.54	1954–55	17		4	
			TR	Arsenal	09.55	1955–59	49		10	
			TR	Southend U.	10.60	1960	16		2	
NUTT, Philip J.	London	18.05.58	APP	Q.P.R.	07.75	1975-76	0	4	1	(F)
NUTTALL, Jim	Liverpool	14.10.29	Skelmersdale	Southport	05.50	1950–52	67		29	(CF)
NUTTALL, Martin	Oldham	12.09.61	APP	Oldham Ath.	09.79	1980-81	8	5	1	(F)
			TR	Halifax T.	08.82	1982-83	39	11	10	
NUTTALL, William	Preston	07.12.20		Preston N.E.	07.46	1946	2		0	(FB)
			TR	Barrow	08.48	1948–50	65		0	
NUTTON, Mike W.	St Johns Wood	03.10.59	APP	Chelsea	08.78	1978-82	77	2	0	(D)
			L	Reading	02.83	1982	6	/	0	
			TR	Millwall	03.83	1982-83	53	/	3	
NWAJIOBI, Chukwuemeka	Nigeria	25.05.59	Dulwich H.	Luton T.	12.83	1983	2	2	1	(F)

TERRY McDERMOTT (Bury/Newcastle U./Liverpool & England/Newcastle U.)
McDermott came to the fore with Bury after serving as an apprentice at Gigg Lane, before Newcastle United took more than a passing fancy when signing him in February 1973. Roughly 18 months later, McDermott was transferred to Liverpool and by 1976/7 had become a regular in the side. The transformation was complete, and he became a master of his trade, with classical passing and long range shooting his forte, resulting in the winning of the 1980 footballer of the year award. Club honours include four Championships, three European Cup and three Football League Cup winners medals to make up for two losing F.A. Cup Final appearances, one for Newcastle, the other for the "Reds", along with several England caps. Transferred back to Newcastle in September 1982 for £100,000 he re-established his partnership with Kevin Keegan, which was more than enough to enable the Geordies to return to the First Division by the end of the 1983/4 season.

MALCOLM MacDONALD (Fulham/Luton T./Newcastle U. & England/Arsenal).
MacDonald started out soccer life as a full back for Tonbridge, then was signed by Fulham who, although converting him to centre forward, allowed him to join Luton a year later in July 1969. His form in that position at Kenilworth Road was nothing short of sensational and after two seasons the "Hatters" were forced by economics to sell "Supermac" to Newcastle United for a club record fee of £185,000. Amazingly, in 14 England appearances he scored only on one occasion, but netted five times against Cyprus in that match. Arsenal signed this still dynamic sharpshooter in August 1976, but within three years injuries had forced him finally onto the sidelines, and later into soccer management with his first club Fulham. In a career of 269 League appearances, MacDonald notched up 191 goals, a great achievement by today's standards.

TED McDOUGALL (Liverpool/York C./Bournemouth/Manchester U./Norwich C. & Scotland/Southampton/Bournemouth/Blackpool).
Discovered by Liverpool, Ted McDougall signed for the "Reds", January 1966, but a year and a half later, in having not made an appearance, found himself transferred to York City. It was at Bootham Crescent that the well-made centre forward first struck up a twin striking partnership with Phil Boyer, who eventually followed Ted to other clubs in search of goals. When with Bournemouth he scored even more prolifically, once getting nine goals in an F.A. Cup tie, a record. At First Division level could never reach the same heights, although when at Norwich he showed up enough to gain seven Scottish caps.

ROY McFARLAND (Tranmere Rov./Derby Co. & England/Bradford C.)
A classic centre back, McFarland was likened by many to Neil Franklin of early post-war fame, and were it not for injury he would have played for England on many more occasions than his total of 28 caps. He started out with Tranmere Rovers, spending just one season there before Brian Clough saw in him a great future with Derby County, who were struggling to achieve First Division status. In his second season at the Baseball Ground a Second Division medal was attained and in 1971/2 the first of two League Championships were won.

BILL McGARRY (Port Vale/Huddersfield T. & England/Bournemouth)
A thoroughly sound if seemingly unspectacular wing half, but a very solid tackler when the occasion demanded, McGarry was discovered by Port Vale during the war and it cost Huddersfield £15,000 when they took him from the Potteries in March 1951. At one time he played 178 successive games for the Town before injury and was a member of the side that gained promotion from the Second Division 1952/3, famous for the fact that the whole defence in which McGarry had been prominent, was ever present. He played for his country four times to go with England "B" and Football League honours, before taking to Football League management.

JOHN McGOVERN (Hartlepool U./Derby Co./Leeds U./Nottingham F./Bolton W.)
A thoroughbred midfielder, McGovern came out with Hartlepool under Brian Clough and then followed his former manager to Derby County in September 1968, for a bargain fee of £7,000. Immediately he helped the "Rams" gain promotion as Second Division Champions, which followed closely on the heels of his part in Hartlepools climb out of the Fourth Division for the first time in the club's history the previous season. Settling in with Derby, John gained a Championship medal in 1971/2 and then in August 1974 made the mistake of signing for Leeds United, but six months later made the move to Nottingham Forest, which was to eventually bring him even more honours. Promotion to the First Division was followed by another Championship medal 1977/8, two Football League Cup, two European Cup and Super Cup winners medals. He is now with Bolton Wanderers.

KEVIN McHALE (Huddersfield T./Crewe Alex./Chester C.)
Thought by many to be the future star of English soccer when making his debut as a 16 year old with the Town, McHale was reckoned to be their finest post-war product but soon seemed to be in the shadows of the brilliant Denis Law, although amazingly he had played over 200 League games by 1962/3. He spent the whole of his Huddersfield career in the Second Division, before moving to Crewe, then finishing at Chester. As a boy prodigy, winning schoolboy International honours, he went on quickly to attain England youth status, but then drew a blank, settling down to become an efficient team member, and probably wondering where he went wrong.

JIMMY McILROY (Burnley, Stoke C. & N. Ireland/Oldham Ath.)
McIlroy made his mark with Glentoran as a highly skilled inside forward before being brought to Turf Moor by Burnley for £7,000. A marvellous scheming player, highly intelligent with great probing ability in opening up the opposition's defence, he had an almost telepathic partnership with Danny Blanchflower when playing for Ireland, which he did 55 times. He joined Stoke to mastermind their return to the top League in 1963, after gaining a League Championship medal with Burnley in 1959/60. He played for Great Britain versus Rest of Europe in 1955, which added to his reputation of being able to impart his personality at the highest level. He finished with Oldham Athletic in season 1967/8.

SAMMY McILROY (Manchester U., Stoke C. & N. Ireland)
Who will ever forget the goal the magical Sammy McIlroy scored for Manchester United against Arsenal at Wembley in the 1979 F.A. Cup Final, where United, after being pronounced dead and virtually buried, came back to the living with two goals in the remaining moments of the game. On his day he ranks with the best of traditional midfield players, often scoring invaluable goals as already stated and he has played many times for Northern Ireland since signing for the "Reds" in August 1971. He joined Stoke City in February 1982 for a fee of £350,000 and has become a key player in their First Division survival battles.

DAVE MACKAY (Tottenham H. & Scotland/Derby Co./Swindon T.)
One of the great swashbuckling heroes of modern soccer, indomitably surmounting serious injuries which threatened his future Mackay showed tremendous character throughout, finally being recognised as player of the year after joining Derby County. Really a player of several careers, his first was the one with Hearts where he first played for Scotland. Transferred to Spurs for a giveaway fee, he became the finest hard tackling wing half in Britain, picking up three F.A. Cup winners medals, a Championship medal from the "double" year and a European Cup Winners Cup medal from the destruction of Athletico Madrid 1963. His third career was with Derby County when Brian Clough signed him to lead the "Rams" back to the First Division. That being achieved, he later managed Derby to the First Division Title 1974/5.

BOB McKINLAY (Nottingham F.)
A highly dependable centre half of the day, well over 6ft tall, with strong build, McKinlay was recommended to the Forest by his uncle Billy, who had played pre-war at the City ground. Surprisingly he never played for Scotland, but was highly rated enough to be thought by many worthy of selection. As an ever present player, he was a major factor in Forest achieving promotion to the First Division as runners-up 1956/7 and two years later he was outstanding in the F.A. Cup Final win against Luton Town. Immensely powerful in the air, this great player went on to make 611, plus three substitute appearances, constituting a club record.

FRANK McLINTOCK (Leicester C., Arsenal & Scotland/Q.P.R.)
After signing for Leicester City from Shawfield juniors in January 1957, McLintock spent several seasons in the reserves before becoming a regular member of the club's half back line. He was an outstanding performer in gaining an F.A. Cup Final losers medal against the cock-a-hoop Spurs in 1961. Two years later the young Scot was back at Wembley for another losing F.A. Cup Final, this time against Manchester United. In October 1964, as a shrewd tactical wing half, he was signed by Arsenal for £80,000, where he later settled down as captain and eventual centre half, winning the coveted "Double" medals of 1970/1. On joining Q.P.R. he was instrumental in taking the club to its highest ever League position of second in the First Division 1975/6, before retiring gracefully. He represented Scotland on nine occasions and was footballer of the year 1971.

ALF McMICHAEL (Newcastle U. & N. Ireland)
A red-haired, dynamic left full back, McMichael, along with George Hannah, was transferred from Linfield to Newcastle United for a combined fee of £20,000 September 1949. This move followed sterling performances back home in the Irish League, but it was not until arriving at St. James' Park that the youngster was capped for his country, going on to become captain and collecting 40 full caps. He won an F.A. Cup winners medal from the game against Arsenal in 1952. Not terribly tall for a defender, he was tenacious in the tackle, very constructive when in possession and a highly regarded member of the United rearguard, making over 400 appearances during his stay with them.

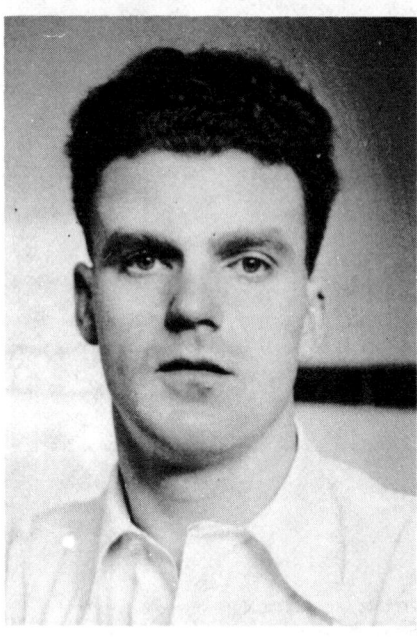

JIM McNAB (Sunderland/Preston N.E./Stockport Co.)
McNab was discovered by Sunderland when playing Scottish junior soccer, signing professional when 17, in June 1957. Within a season he had made his debut at Roker, becoming a regular in 1959/60, missing only 20 games in six seasons. Given the opportunity, he developed into a keen tackling half back in the best traditions of the club, and in 1963/4 helped the "Rokerites" achieve First Division status again, making 37 League appearances. Transferred to Preston in March 1967, he collected a Third Division medal in 1970/1, before going on to complete his career with Stockport County.

RICHARD McNEIL (Leicester C./Exeter C./Northampton T./Lincoln C./Hereford U./Wrexham/Hereford U.)
A much travelled, bustling, goalscoring centre forward known to all and sundry throughout the footballing fraternity as "Dixie", McNeil turned professional with Leicester City, but after 18 months without making his debut, moved to Exeter City in June 1966, later playing for Corby Town of the Southern League. Northampton Town spotted his potential, signing him in May 1969, and he responded with goals. He later moved to Lincoln City before being part of Hereford United's fight for higher Football League status, scoring 85 goals in three years. He finished his career still finding the net with Wrexham, and finally once again with Hereford.

JOHNNY McNICHOLL (Newcastle U./Brighton & H.A./Chelsea/Crystal Palace)
One of the unsung heroes of Chelsea's first League Championship win 1954/5, McNicholl was a typical Scottish inside forward, having great craft. He was constructive and could really shoot. Not making any appearances with Newcastle, he was transferred to Brighton for £5,000, quickly becoming one of the best ball players in the Third Division South, and when Ted Drake took over Chelsea, the first player he signed was McNicholl for £15,000. He had great perception, being an ideal team mate for Roy Bentley, and in the Title winning season played an invaluable 40 games for the "Blues". He was allowed to leave Stamford Bridge in March 1958, playing nearly 200 games for neighbours Crystal Palace before joining their non playing staff.

PETER McPARLAND (Aston Villa, Wolverhampton W. & Northern Ireland/Plymouth Arg.)
A powerful, hard shooting, direct left winger, McParland, after making his debut for Northern Ireland against Wales 1953/4, represented his country a further 33 times. Signed by Villa from Dundalk, he developed into a goalscoring winger, twice topping their scoring lists before being transferred to close rivals Wolves for £30,000 January 1962. He never settled at Molineux, and a year later was on the road to Plymouth before closing his career. He is remembered for Villa's winning goal against Manchester United in the 1957 F.A. Cup Final where he injured the keeper Ray Wood, who subsequently was carried off.

PAUL MADELEY (Leeds U. & England)
Leeds never regretted the day when they signed the upstanding defender-cum-utility player Paul Madeley as a professional in 1962. He became a highly valued member of Don Revie's club plans of the future, also going on to play 24 times for England as an accomplished master of the modern defensive game. Leeds born and bred, Paul collected many honours with his only club, including two championship medals, two U.E.F.A. Cup winners medals and an F.A. Cup winners medal against Arsenal 1972. He had the disappointment of an amazing run of near misses such as two other losing F.A. Cup Finals and Championship runners-up awards.

JOHN MAHONEY (Crewe Alex./Stoke C., Middlesbrough, Swansea C. & Wales)
A well-balanced skilful midfielder, Mahoney began with Crewe in 1965/6 and has since gone on to play more than 50 times for Wales. His flair and ability to control the middle of the park, quickly brought him to the notice of First Division neighbours Stoke City, who signed him in March 1967. He collected a Football League Cup winners medal as a sub in 1972 against Chelsea, before having a two year stint on Teeside, after signing for Middlesbrough for £90,000 in August 1977. He finally arrived in South Wales when Swansea brought him home for £100,000 in July 1979, playing a major part in the "Swans" drive to the First Division in 1980/1.

WILF MANNION (Middlesbrough & England/Hull C.)
Mannion was an inside forward who spent most of his career with Middlesbrough before being transferred to Hull City to spend his twilight years in the game. He developed through the South Bank nursery and really came to the fore after returning from war service with the Green Howards. He became a magnificent schemer, playing brilliantly for Britain versus Europe in 1947. He appeared to have come to stay, sturdy and fair haired, standing out from the crowd, but unfortunately he got himself dragged into permanent dispute with Middlesbrough, who would not release him. This hindered his career, costing him his England place.

PAUL MARINER (Plymouth Arg./Ipswich T., Arsenal & England)
A brilliant aerial player Mariner gets up remarkably well with resounding effect. He has played over 30 times for England since coming from Chorley to Argyle in July 1973 for £22,500. He scored so prolifically whilst at Home Park in helping the "Pilgrims" into the Second Division in 1974/5, that Ipswich Town paid £200,000 plus, to capture his services in September 1976. Ipswich were twice runners-up in the First Division during Paul's reign at Portman Road and he had great pleasure in gaining an F.A. Cup winners medal in 1977/8 from the game against Arsenal. Later in 1981 he added a U.E.F.A. Cup winners medal to his collection, before signing for the "Gunners" in February 1984.

LES MASSIE (Huddersfield T./Darlington/Halifax T./Bradford Pk. Av./Workington)
Massie was a skilful inside forward who came to the fore with the Town when Bill Shankly became manager in 1956/7, having previously been on the club's books for over three years. He made his debut that season with fellow Aberdonian Denis Law and the other boy wonder Kevin McHale, going on to play over 300 games at Leeds Road. Quite a goalscorer earlier on, he headed the lists for three seasons, but eventually settled into a wing half midfield role producing typical Scottish craft in his play, mixed with good distribution and control. After leaving Huddersfield he played out the rest of his footballing days in the lower reaches.

DON MASSON (Middlesbrough/Notts Co./Q.P.R., Derby Co. & Scotland/Notts Co.)
A little midfielder, Masson started out with Middlesbrough after starring in their junior side, but, on never becoming a regular, transferred to Notts County in September 1968, helping them from the Fourth to Second Division. During that period, Don scored over 80 League goals, an invaluable asset for a midfield player, showing himself to be adept at free kicks and other set pieces. He signed for Q.P.R. in December 1974 before going to Derby County for a brief sojourn. Capped for Scotland whilst at the Rangers and then Derby, he returned in August 1978 to Notts County to mastermind their battle to achieve First Division status, which was finally accomplished as runners-up to West Ham, in 1980/1.

STANLEY MATTHEWS (Stoke C., Blackpool & England/Stoke C.)
"The wizard of dribble" is one of the many superlatives used to describe football's greatest living legend, Stanley Matthews, who received a knighthood whilst still playing. Son of a professional boxer, he started with his home town side Stoke City as a brilliant schoolboy prodigy and swept all full backs off their feet as the most tantalising of outside rights. He was sensationally transferred to Blackpool in 1947 for £11,500 and after getting two Cup Final runners-up medals achieved a life time ambition by helping Blackpool beat Bolton in the 1952/3 F.A. Cup Final, known as the "Matthews Final". He went home to Stoke, assisting them back into the First Division and remarkably playing in that League past the age 50. The game's most mentioned personality, he will always be remembered for his ball control and body swerve, also as the greatest goal provider in the history of football.

EDDIE MAY (Southend U./Wrexham/Swansea C.)
May developed into a fine central defender with his 6ft 2in frame winning many an aerial battle, after joining Southend in January 1965 from Isthmian Leagers Dagenham. Quickly becoming a regular, he signed for Wrexham in the 1968 close season and in 1969/70 helped the club gain promotion into the Third Division as runners-up. In eight full seasons in North Wales he missed only 35 League games, mainly due to injury, before moving down to South Wales to join Swansea in August 1976. Eddie was an absentee on only two occasions over the next two seasons, before becoming the "Swans" coach, after the club had gained promotion to the Third Division in 1977/8. This success allowed the Londoner to concentrate off the field and reflect on a League career of over 500 matches, spent mainly in Wales.

TERRY MEDWIN (Swansea C., Tottenham H. & Wales)
When this brilliant player signed from Swansea for a fee of £18,000 in April 1956, the Spurs resolved their right wing problems of the previous season, when they used seven different men. The fair haired youngster had previously won a regular place at the Vetch field after gaining Welsh schoolboy honours and within two seasons he had added a full cap to his collection. He signed for Tottenham, predominantly because the "Swans" were using his skills at centre forward and, although being their leading scorer, he favoured the wing position. His career was unfortunately cut short by injuries, and Terry only played 14 times during the "double" season, but he did collect an F.A. Cup winners medal in 1962 against Burnley before leaving the game with 30 Welsh caps.

JIMMY MELIA (Liverpool & England/Wolverhampton W./Southampton/Aldershot/Crewe Alex.)
A brilliant scheming inside forward, Melia, after winning schoolboy International honours, signed professional for his native Liverpool in November 1954. He was on the verge of full honours, over a long period being in the shadow of the great Johnny Haynes, but eventually he was capped twice by England. With Liverpool he played a leading role in midfield, where he was instrumental in them coming back to the top flight as Second Division champions 1961/2. He had a short spell at Molineux, trying to revive a once great side, before moving on to Southampton November 1964, and a season later helped them into the top sphere for the first time in the club's history.

JOE MERCER (Everton & England/Arsenal)
Mercer was a really outstanding wing half with a biting tackle who read the game as well as any other. Joining Everton as a spindly legged youngster from Ellesmere Port, Joe had gained a Championship medal and established himself in the England side before the war clouds came. His many qualities helped in preserving a future which seemed doomed with a knee injury. In one of the great romance stories of the game, Tom Whittaker, Arsenal's ex physio and new manager, took Mercer to Highbury for £7,000, his captaincy being vital to the "Gunners" right up to 1954, when he broke a leg. In that period two League Titles, one winning, one losing F.A. Cup Final and a player of the year award were the bonuses of a man seen by many to be playing on borrowed time. Later he became a great manager, fondly remembered for his association with Malcolm Allison and Manchester City.

GIL MERRICK (Birmingham C. & England)
Merrick was the custodian of the Birmingham City goal immediately after the war, following the great Harry Hibbs. Later, Gil went on to emulate his idol by being capped for England in 1951/2 and then playing a further 22 times. Very cool and composed when on duty, he was very unfortunate to have been England's goalie during the 1953 thrashing handed out by the "marvellous Magyars", Hungary. Standing 6ft 1in, mustachioed and elegant, Gil really looked the part, and the City goal remained for long spells intact as positional sense saved the day time and again. Twice helping Birmingham to promotion, he was one of their most loyal servants.

VIC METCALFE (Huddersfield T. & England/Hull C.)
Vic was a direct, old fashioned outside left who always looked dangerous, especially after cutting inside the full back. He could make a fine left foot cross and Jimmy Glazzard benefited tremendously when regularly scoring in the Town's promotion drive from Division Two in 1952/3. The son of a Yorkshire rugby star, he joined Huddersfield during the war, making his debut immediately on resumption of the normal League programme. Surprisingly, he was capped only twice, but one has to remember the surfeit of class wingmen operating at that time. Finally, at the age of 36, he moved on to Hull City to complete within a season or so, a fine career spent mainly at the highest level.

JACKIE MILBURN (Newcastle U. & England)
Known to thousands of Tynesiders as "Wor Jackie", Milburn had rocket-like shooting ability, coupled with tremendous acceleration, which was used to great advantage. The proud holder of three Cup winners medals, he used Wembley as his own stage – on which he excelled. He won his first cap in 1948, which was followed by a further 12 appearances. He is most remembered for his two Cup Final goals against Blackpool in 1950/1, along with a great headed goal against Manchester City in the 1954/5 Cup Final. He often played at outside right but was really effective down the middle of the pitch; he was a danger to the opposition wherever he played.

STAN MILBURN (Chesterfield/Leicester C./Rochdale)
Born and developed in Ashington with three famous footballing brothers – George, Jim and John Milburn, alongside cousin Jackie, it was hardly likely that anything but soccer would suffice for Stan Milburn. During his playing career, he tended to be a good clubman and is most probably the only player to obtain three testimonials from separate clubs. He toured Canada with the F.A. in 1950 and obtained a Division Two medal with Leicester City in 1954. He will be remembered as the full back who, in trying to clear the Leicester lines, collided with his own defender Jack Froggatt when between them they scored a unique double own goal. Always constructive, reliable in the tackle, he was unlucky not to progress beyond an England "B" cap and Football League representative honours.

LEN MILLARD (W.B.A.)
Signed as an amateur at the Hawthorns in 1939, turning pro in 1942 originally as a forward, Millard became a really reliable full back, missing very few games until retiring after breaking the immortal Jesse Pennington's Albion appearance record. The highlight of his career was in leading the "Throstles" to victory at Wembley in the 1953/4 F.A. Cup Final against Preston. Not a classy player, but a highly efficient one, he was an object lesson to any aspiring youngster in dedication and perseverance.

MICK MILLS (Ipswich T. & England/Southampton)
Mills settled down in the Ipswich Town defence as a stocky, naturally left-sided full back, having originally played in midfield after being released by Portsmouth in February 1966, when "Pompey" abandoned their youth policy. Mick went on to captain both Ipswich and England. Always likely to score the odd goal in forward surges, and a good safe tackler, seldom ruffled. Captained the Town in gaining an UEFA Cup Final medal and highlighted his career when he lead Ipswich to victory in the 1978 F.A. Cup Final against Arsenal. He was allowed to sign for Southampton in November 1982, and has showed no signs of being a spent force.

ARNOLD MITCHELL (Derby Co./Nottingham F./Notts. Co./Exeter C.)
Mitchell was a versatile clubman who joined Exeter City after being rejected by Derby County and both Nottingham clubs, although he did make an appearance for the County before going on to St. James' Park, July 1952. A hard working, enthusiastic, non-stop player who appeared in virtually every position for Exeter on his way to collecting a club appearance record of 495. He was at one time put on the "open to offer" transfer list, a mistake which was quickly rectified, and in 1963/4 Mitchell was instrumental in getting the "Grecians" promotion into the Third Division, the highlight of his career.

JIM MONTGOMERY (Sunderland/Birmingham C./Nottingham F./Sunderland)
Montgomery was one of the top class young goalkeepers of the 1960s who were kept out of the International team only by the brillance of Gordon Banks. Signing for his local team on his 17th birthday in October 1960, he went on to gain firstly England youth honours and then England under 23 caps, also helping the "Rokerites" out of the Second Division in season 1963/4. His greatest moment of glory came when, against all the odds as a Second Division side, Sunderland won the F.A. Cup Final against Leeds United with an Ian Porterfield goal in 1973. The game was highlighted by a memorable double save by the brilliant Jim Montgomery which effectively won the match. He moved on to Birmingham City in February 1977 and since then has understudied Peter Shilton at Nottingham Forest.

ALAN MOODY (Middlesbrough/Southend U.)
A Middlesbrough born central defender, Moody set out with his local club after an apprenticeship at Ayresome Park, making his debut in season 1968/9. He never became a regular player and was allowed to join Southend United in October 1972 for a fee of £15,000. He was in the side that was relegated to the Fourth Division in 1976, but two seasons later was an ever present as the "Shrimpers" were promoted by dint of a hard earned second place to Watford. Relegated again in 1980, the club came back in style the following season with Alan playing 30 games and gaining a Fourth Division winners medal. He has now made well over 400 League appearances at Roots Hall and scores important goals whenever the opportunity arises.

BOBBY MOORE (West Ham U. & England/Fulham)
A brilliant youthful prodigy in the central defender's position Moore was capped at Youth level after joining West Ham. He developed into one of the finest wing halves in England, captaining club and country through almost every level of soccer, culminating in 108 full caps. He collected an F.A. Cup winners medal against Preston in 1964, but when playing for Fulham in the twilight of career was on the losing side at Wembley in 1975 against his old team mates West Ham. Footballer of the year in 1964, and on retiring he had achieved over 650 League appearances with a world wide reputation as a master of his craft.

WILLIE MORGAN (Burnley, Manchester U. & Scotland/Burnley/Bolton W./Blackpool)
A tricky winger, fast and magical, Morgan later in his career operated more in midfield as a provider of chances for others. He turned professional with Burnley in October 1961, making his debut in 1962/3, and later being selected for Scotland, the first of 21 appearances coming in 1968 against Northern Ireland. Shortly after, he was transferred to Manchester United for a fee of £100,000 in August 1968. With United, he was a member of the team that was relegated, but made 32 appearances the following season in gaining a Second Division Championship medal as United returned at the first time of asking. After a short spell back at Burnley, Willie signed for Bolton where he won another Second Division medal in 1977/8, before moving on to Blackpool.

PETER MORRIS (Mansfield T./Ipswich T./Norwich C./Mansfield T.)
A midfield general who started out with Mansfield Town, signing professional in November 1960, Morris was associated in promotion struggles with all of his League sides. He made 33 appearances when Mansfield were promoted to the Third Division in 1962/3, and came to the attention of the many club scouts looking for his kind of talent. Eventually he moved on to Ipswich in March 1968 to finish the season in the First Division, when the Town gained promotion. He was transferred to fellow East Anglians, Norwich, in the 1974 close season and in his very first season with the "Canaries" reached the Football League Cup Final, only to lose to Aston Villa, although promotion was later achieved to the First Division in third place. Two seasons later however, Peter was back at the Field Mill Ground and immediately won a Third Division winners medal, prior to going into League management with Peterborough.

STAN MORTENSEN (Blackpool & England/Hull C.)
As an inside forward or centre forward, Mortensen was a great hero of many England games, especially against Italy in Turin 1948, where he achieved acclaim after a wonderful performance. Originally, he was nearly rejected for being too slow for the pro game, but he sharpened up during the war. Stan recovered from a Wellington air crash and proceeded to score four goals against Portugal on his debut for England. Being a superb opportunist and always imbued with great courage, he will forever be associated with battling fight backs and although the 1953 Cup Final is remembered as the "Matthews Final", "Morty" scored a "hat trick". Apart from that, he played in two others, not being so lucky, and he scored 24 goals in 25 Internationals.

BOB MORTON (Luton T.)
The closest this terrific clubman came to full International honours was as acting reserve, after representing the England "B" team. This was scant reward for a highly meritorious career spent wholly in the service of the "Hatters", for whom he played just short of 500 League games. A utility player he could play equally well at centre half, wing half, or centre forward, as he proved in 1954/5 with vital goals helping Luton's promotion drive to the First Division as runners-up, after Jesse Pye had been allowed to move on. He was a member of the side that lost to Nottingham Forest in the 1959 F.A. Cup Final.

ERNIE MOSS (Chesterfield/Peterborough U./Mansfield T./Chesterfield/Port Vale/Lincoln C./Doncaster Rov.)

A 6ft 1½in striker, Moss came to the club of his birthplace via Chesterfield Tube Works. At the age of 19, and in his first full season, 1969/70,. he played 44 games scoring 20 goals, to collect a Fourth Division winners medal. He gave Chesterfield excellent service, with his height always a menace to the oppositions' defence, before being sold to Peterborough for £16,000 in January 1976. He stayed with the "Posh" for less than a year before packing his bags *en route* to Mansfield. He arrived there in time to play out the rest of the 1976/7 season and ended up with a Third Division winners medal. He was later transferred back to Chesterfield, then he moved on to Port Vale, Lincoln City and Doncaster Rovers in that order. Promotion from the Fourth Division was achieved in 1983, his first season at the Belle Vue Ground and it was Ernie's goalscoring prowess that paved the way.

KEN MULHEARN (Everton/Stockport Co./Manchester C./Shrewsbury T./Crewe Alex)

A 6ft goalie from Merseyside Mulhearn failed to make the grade at Everton before having two seasons with Stockport County, where he gained a Fourth Division medal 1966/7. Manchester City had noted the young man's progress carefully, and signed him immediately following the County's promotion campaign. He was later transferred to Shrewsbury in March 1971, after not maintaining a regular place at Maine Road due to the advent of Joe Corrigan, but with the Town went on to gain a Third Division medal and also create a club record 370 League appearances. Later he moved on to Crewe Alexandra.

JIMMY MULLEN (Wolverhampton W. & England)

A brilliant, long-striding outside left, blessed with an extremely powerful shot, Mullen joined Wolves straight from school in 1937 after winning England schoolboy honours, and made his debut in 1939 when only 16. He played in two World Cups, as well as winning Football League and F. A. Cup medals. A perfect foil to Johnny Hancocks, his long time clubmate, with whom he helped destroy the foreign club invasions of the mid 1950s. He had retired from the hurly burly of League soccer by the end of the 1950s, being remembered as a great club servant.

ALAN MULLERY (Fulham/Tottenham H. & England/Fulham)

An accomplished wing half, complete with football brain and driving aggression, Mullery was capped by England 35 times whilst at White Hart Lane. He started out with Fulham as a junior, establishing himself in their promotion team in 1958/9 and making 14 appearances. He became a regular and collected England under 23 caps, before signing for Spurs in March 1964 in a £72,000 deal. At Tottenham, Alan slotted into the right half position vacated by Danny Blanchflower, naturally taking some time to stamp his own authority on the team, but still going on to collect an F.A. Cup winners medal from the all London Final against Chelsea 1967. He returned to Fulham before going into soccer management.

BARRY MURPHY (Barnsley)

A long serving full-back, Murphy signed for the "Tykes" in the 1962 close season and went on to play over 500 League games in their colours, before leaving the game at the end of the 1977/8 season. Between 1967/8 and 1972/3 he missed only half a dozen League games, a tremendous record of consistency, and even in his final season he made 43 appearances. His best season was 1967/8, when the Yorkshiremen gained promotion as runners-up from the Fourth Division. He still holds the Barnsley individual appearance record, which looks likely to last a few years yet, in an era where clubmen are a rarity.

BERT MURRAY (Chelsea/Birmingham C./Brighton & H.A./Peterborough U.)

Murray came to the fore at Stamford Bridge when replacing the brilliant Peter Brabrook at outside right, being commonly known to fans and players alike as "Ruby". He collected several England under 23 honours to add to schoolboy and youth International caps before Chelsea allowed the young winger, in a Tommy Docherty clear out, to be signed by Birmingham City. But it was with Peterborough that "Ruby" finally collected a League medal when helping the club climb out of the Fourth Division after being placed there in 1968/9, having had 19 points deducted for offering bonuses to players.

BOBBY MURRAY (Stockport Co.)
Murray was a long service wing half with the County after signing from Scottish juniors Inverurie in November 1951, going on to play 465 games before leaving Edgeley Park at the end of 1962/3. In that period he missed only 40 odd matches, mainly due to injury, consistently playing well and prompting the team. He had a rather less than auspicious start in the F.A. Cup third round 1952/3, when Stockport were beaten 2-1 by the Isthmian Leaguers Walthamstow Avenue, who came close in the next round to putting out the mighty Manchester United at Old Trafford.

JIMMY MURRAY (Wolverhampton W./Manchester C./Walsall)
Only 5ft 9in tall Murray was a centre forward who fitted in nicely to the Wanderers attacking pattern, replacing the injured Roy Swinburne as regular leader of the attack in 1955/6. He followed his friend Peter Broadbent to Molineux after being spotted by chief scout George Poyser when playing in Dover schools soccer. He became quite a prolific marksman, showing verve and dash. He collected two Championship medals plus an F.A. Cup Final medal from the win against Blackburn in 1960, before signing for Manchester City for £27,000 in November 1963. The holder of England under 23 honours, he also represented the Football League.

PHIL NEAL (Northampton T./Liverpool & England)
An excellent, consistent right back, Neal has won all the honours that the English club game has to offer, plus over 50 England caps to go on the sideboard. Starting out soccer life with Northampton Town as an apprentice, Phil went on to play nearly 200 League games for the "Cobblers" in the Fouth Division, before being brought to Anfield by Bill Shankly for a fee of £65,000 in October 1974. Since that auspicious date, he has collected seven League Championship, four Football League Cup, four European Cup, one U.E.F.A. Cup and Super Cup winners medals. Still firmly positioned in the "Reds" defence, he looks likely to add to his many honours.

DAVE NEEDHAM (Notts Co./Q.P.R./Nottingham F.)
At 6ft 1in tall, Needham was a reliable central defender who excelled at set pieces as a foil to regular goalscorers. He began with Notts County, playing well over 400 League games in their colours and gaining a Fourth Division winners medal in 1970/1. In 1972/3 assisted the "Magpies" when winning promotion to the Second Division as runners-up to Bolton Wanderers, before moving on to Q.P.R. in June 1977. Some six months and 18 games later, he was transferred to Brian Clough's Nottingham Forest, where success came quickly. He was a member of the squad that won the Championship that very season and later gained a Football League Cup Winners medal in 1979, before settling down to deputising for central defensive duties.

TERRY NEILL (Arsenal, Hull C. & N. Ireland)
A well built centre-cum-wing half, Neill signed for Arsenal from Bangor, Northern Ireland, December 1959. In the main he spent most of his career at Highbury as a utility player, although by 1965/6 he had gained a regular place alongside Ian Ure in the heart of the "Gunners" defence. In July 1970, Hull City provided the young man, who was then chairman of the Professional Footballers Association, with an opportunity to make his way into soccer management. Before going fully into the manager's chair he had played over 100 League games for the "Tigers" and had appeared 59 times for Northern Ireland.

JOHNNY NEWMAN (Birmingham C./Leicester C./Plymouth Arg./Exeter C.)
A tall sturdy defender, Newman in seven years at St. Andrews, made only 59 appearances, mainly acting as deputy to the brilliant Trevor Smith. Sensationally, on the eve of the 1956 F.A. Cup Final, Jack Badham was declared unfit and the youngster stepped up to collect a losers medal from the game against Manchester City. He was transferred to Leicester City before joining Plymouth Argyle in January 1960, going on to skipper the "Pilgrims" and playing just short of 300 appearances in their colours. He was steadfast and durable, ideally suited to the lower Divisions, where he could exert some influence over younger players before finishing his career with Exeter City.

KEITH NEWTON (Blackburn Rov., Everton & England/Burnley)
A cool, cultured full back with astute passing ability, Newton was inclined to use the ball to greatest advantage. He turned professional with Blackburn Rovers, starring in their F.A. Youth Cup side of 1959 alongside other youngsters such as Fred Pickering and Mike England. After playing over 300 League games for the Rovers, Keith signed for Everton in December 1969 in an £80,000 deal, just in time to collect a League Championship medal. After playing in the 1970 World Cup, but missing the Brazil match, he closed his England account with 27 caps. Transferred to Burnley in the summer of 1972, he was again in time to collect a Second Division medal.

PETER NICHOLAS (Crystal Palace, Arsenal & Wales)
A Newport-born midfield defensive player Nicholas displays great fighting qualities and has gained many caps for his native Wales since starting out as an apprentice at Selhurst Park. He really came to the fore when playing 37 games for the Palace and gaining a Second Division winners medal in 1978/9. Arsenal were happy to pay £400,000 to bring the Welshman to Highbury in March 1981, but to date his promise has not really shone in the red shirt, and a regular place in the side has not been forthcoming. He is currently on loan to his old club, Crystal Palace of the Second Division, where he has been for most of the 1983/4 season.

CHRIS NICHOLL (Burnley/Halifax T./Luton T./Aston Villa, Southampton, Grimsby T. & N. Ireland)
A 6ft 2in tall central defender, formerly the mainstay of Southampton's defence and currently that of Grimsby, Nicholl brings to the game a wealth of experience gained from playing in all four Divisions of the Football League. He started as a junior with Burnley before dropping out with Witton Albion of the Cheshire League. Halifax signed him in June 1968, and he spent a season there before joining Luton Town and then Aston Villa, achieving the first of many Northern Ireland International caps with parental qualification. His brother Terry has also played League soccer.

JIM NICHOLSON (Manchester U., Huddersfield T. & N. Ireland/Bury)
A brilliant United junior star Nicholson represented Northern Ireland versus Scotland in November 1960, when only 17 years, eight months old, and eventually played 41 times. That same season he made his United debut, but not until leaving for Huddersfield Town in December 1964 did he get regular first team soccer. In 1969/70 he led the Town back to the First Division, a brilliant achievement. He was a strong tackler, very sound, collecting 31 caps whilst at Leeds Road.

TOMMY NORTHCOTT (Torquay U./Cardiff C./Lincoln C./Torquay U.)
A Torquay discovery, who graduated through their junior ranks gaining England youth International honours, Northcott was transferred to Cardiff City, playing in most of their forward positions during their stay in the First Division, and then was signed by Lincoln City, who began to recognise his latent goalscoring touch. A chunky stocky forward with the ability to keep the line moving with accurate passes to both flanks, he finally came home again to Plainmoor in November 1957, and in his second spell with the club played 347 games scoring 125 goals, arguably one of the "Gulls" best products.

MEL NURSE (Swansea C., Middlesbrough & Wales/Swindon T./Swansea C.)
Another of the brilliant Swansea youngsters to come off their conveyor belt, Nurse signed professional in June 1955 after appearing for the Welsh schools. Nearly 6ft 2in, he made his debut very early, but not until 1958/9 did the young centre half gain a regular place, eventually playing over 150 games before being transferred to Middlesbrough for £25,000 in October 1962. When signing for the 'Boro Mel became the fourth player to do duty in the centre half position that season. He missed only a handful of games during the next three years, having a stabilising effect on the defence, but on getting restless came back south with Swindon Town *en route* to South Wales.

Players Names	Birthplace	Date	Previous Club	League Club	Date Signed	Seasons Played	Apps	Sub	Gls	
O'BERG, Paul J.	Hull	08.05.58	Bridlington	Scunthorpe U.	07.79	1979-83	117	13	22	(M)
O'BRIEN, Anthony	Liverpool	04.09.56		Southport	N/C	1974-76	17	3	1	(D)
O'BRIEN, Colin	Dunfermline	19.04.56	Swaythling	Bristol C.	11.77					(F)
			L	Hereford U.	12.78	1978	1	1	0	
O'BRIEN, George	Dunfermline	22.11.35	Dunfermline	Leeds U.	03.57	1956-58	44		6	(IF)●
			TR	Southampton	07.59	1959-65	243		154	
			TR	Orient	03.66	1965-66	17	/	3	
			TR	Aldershot	12.66	1966-67	38	3	8	
O'BRIEN, George	Liverpool	21.10.39	JNRS	Everton	02.59					(HB)
			TR	Southport	07.60	1960	3		1	
O'BRIEN, Gerry	Glasgow	10.11.49	Clydebank	Southampton	03.70	1969-75	66	12	2	(M)
			L	Bristol Rov.	03.74	1973	3	/	0	
			TR	Swindon T.	03.76	1975-76	24	3	0	
O'BRIEN, Joe	Dundalk	09.05.24	Dundalk	Luton T.	11.47	1947-48	11		3	
			TR	Ipswich T.	06.49	1949-50	50		12	
O'BRIEN, Noel W.	London	18.12.56	APP	Arsenal	01.74					(HB)
			TR	Mansfield T.	06.75	1975	7	/	0	
			TR	Halifax T.	07.76					
O'BRIEN, Ray	Shelbourne	21.05.51	Shelbourne	Manchester U.	05.73					(D) EI-4
			TR	Notts. Co.	03.74	1973-82	323	/	30	
			L	Derby Co.	09.83	1983	4	/	0	
O'BRIEN, William	Middlesbrough	26.01.29		Darlington	02.50	1950	2		0	(HB)
O'CALLAGHAN, Brendan	Bradford	23.07.55	JNRS	Doncaster Rov.	07.73	1973-77	184	3	65	(F) EI-10/E.U21-1
			TR	Stoke C.	03.78	1977-83	235	10	45	
O'CALLAGHAN, Kevin	London	19.10.61	APP	Millwall	11.78	1978-79	15	5	3	(F) EI-11
			TR	Ipswich T.	01.80	1979-83	62	38	3	
O'CONNELL, Brian, E.	Fulham	13.09.37	JNRS	Fulham	03.56	1958-65	150	/	26	(OL)
			TR	Crystal Palace	07.66	1966	20	1	2	
O'CONNELL, Seamus	Carlisle	01.01.30	Queens Pk.	Middlesbrough	AM	1953	3		2	(IF) E. AMAT.INT
			B. Auckland	Chelsea	AM	1954-55	16		11	
			Crook T.	Carlisle U.	AM	1957	4		2	
O'CONNOR, Doug	Barnsley	29.04.54	APP	Barnsley	08.69	1970-73	27	9	6	(M)
			TR	Mansfield T.	07.74	1974	11	6	2	
			TR	Scunthorpe U.	07.75	1975-76	28	3	9	
O'CONNOR, James K.	Lanark	27.06.51		Bury	07.70	1970	7	/	2	(W)
O'CONNOR, Mark A.	Rochford	10.03.63	APP	Q.P.R.	06.80	1981-82	2	1	0	(D)
			L	Exeter C.	10.83	1983	38	/	1	
O'CONNOR, Malcolm J.	Ashton	25.04.65	Ashton Curzon	Rochdale	N/C	1982-83	12	4	3	(F)
O'CONNOR, Mike	Romford	11.01.52	APP	Southend U.	APP	1969	1	/	0	(W)
O'CONNOR, Pat	Wishaw	01.05.34	Bellshill	Barrow	06.58	1958-59	20		4	(HB)
			TR	Carlisle U.	08.60					
O'CONNOR, Philip K.	Romford	10.10.53	Bexley U.	Luton T.	12.72	1972	1	1	0	(F)
			L	Lincoln C.	01.75	1974	4	/	1	
O'CONNOR, Robert T.	Gateshead	09.08.40	JNRS	Gateshead	AM	1958	2		0	(OL)
O'CONNOR, Turlough	Athlone	22.07.46	Bohemians	Fulham	05.66	1967	1	/	0	(F) E1-7/E1.AMAT. INT.
O'CONNOR, Vince J.	Durham	12.03.29	Middlesbrough (AM)	Hartlepool U.	12.47	1948	2		0	
O'DELL, Andy	Hull	02.01.63	APP	Grimsby T.	01.81	1981-82	18	2	0	(M)
			TR	Rotherham U.	08.83	1983	15	2	0	
O'DELL, Robert	Isle of Wight	10.12.34	JNRS	Reading	07.52	1953	2		0	(HB)
O'DONNELL, Brian F.	Glasgow	08.08.57	Bournemouth (APP)	Bristol Rov.	05.76					(M)
			Blacktown	Bournemouth	01.82	1981-82	9	5	0	
			TR	Torquay U.	N/C	1982	19	/	0	
O'DONNELL, Daniel	Dunbar	27.02.39	Kirkintilloch	Brentford	02.60	1960-61	11		0	(F)
O'DONNELL, Edward	Barrow	05.02.21		Barrow	09.46	1946-52	33		0	(FB)
O'DONNELL, Frank	Buckhaven	31.08.11	Aston Villa(*)	Nottingham F.	+	1946	11		5	(CF) S-6/d.1952/*Glasgow Celtic/Preston N.E./Blackpool
O'DONNELL, Hugh	Buckhaven	15.02.13	Preston N.E.(*)	Blackpool	*	1946	1		1	(OL) Glasgow Celtic
			TR	Rochdale	03.47	1946-47	40		14	Brother of Frank/
			TR	Halifax T.	03.48	1947-48	13		1	d. 1964
O'DONNELL, James	Methil	18.04.34		Blackburn Rov.	05.52					
			TR	Oldham Ath.	10.53	1954-55	15		3	
			TR	Leeds U.	01.57					
O'DONNELL, John	Leeds	21.03.54	APP	Leeds U.	03.71					(D)
			TR	Cambridge U.	07.73	1973-75	79	/	8	
			L	Colchester U.	08.75	1975	1	/	0	
			TR	Hartlepool U.	07.76	1976	30	1	1	
			TR	Scunthorpe U.	07.77	1977-79	60	/	0	
O'DONNELL, Neil	Glasgow	21.12.49	JNRS	Norwich C.	12.66	1967-73	31	19	2	(D)
			TR	Gillingham	08.74	1974-75	18	6	0	
			TR	Sheffield Wed.	10.75	1975-76	40	/	1	

Players Names	Birthplace	Date	Previous Club	League Club	Date Signed	Seasons Played	Apps	Sub	Gls	
O'DONNELL, Ralph	Cudworth	17.10.31	Upton Col	Sheffield Wed.	05.49	1951–61	171		3	(CH)
O'DONNELL, William	Clydebank	09.08.24	Partick Th.	Northampton T.	06.51	1951–53	104		43	(CF)
			TR	Shrewsbury T.	07.54	1954–57	130		46	
O'DONOGHUE, Mike G.	London	13.09.56	Wembley T.	Southampton	01.79					(F)
			L	Northampton T.	11.79	1979	4	/	1	
O'DOWD, Adrian G.	Solihull	16.09.59	APP	Aston Villa	08.77					(F)
			TR	Oxford U.	02.80	1979–80	8	2	1	
O'DRISCOLL, John	Cork	20.09.21	Cork	Swansea C.	05.47	1947–51	117		26	(F) E1–3/N1–3
O'DRISCOLL, Sean M.	Wolverhampton	01.07.57	Alvechurch	Fulham	11.79	1979–83	141	7	13	(M)EI–3
			L	Bournemouth	02.84	1983	19	/	1	
O'FARRELL, Frank	Cork	09.10.27	Cork	West Ham U.	01.48	1950–56	197		6	(WH) E1–9
			TR	Preston N.E.	11.56	1956–60	118		3	
O'FLANAGAN, Kevin	Dublin	10.06.19	Bohemians	Arsenal	AM	1946	14		3	(W)
			Barnet	Brentford	AM	1949	6		0	NI.AMAT.INT
O'GRADY, Mike	Leeds	11.10.42	JNRS	Huddersfield T.	10.59	1959–65	160	/	26	(OL) E–2/E.U23–3/
			TR	Leeds U.	10.65	1965–69	91	/	13	E.F.LGE.REP.
			TR	Wolverhampton W.	09.69	1969–72	28	4	6	
			L	Birmingham C.	02.72	1971	2	1	0	
			TR	Rotherham U.	11.72	1972–73	24	/	2	
O'HALLORAN, Neil	Cardiff	21.06.33		Cardiff C.	08.54	1955–56	10		4	(F)
			TR	Newport Co.	07.57	1957	14		2	
O'HANLON, Kelham G.	Saltburn	16.05.62	APP	Middlesbrough	05.80	1982–83	49	/	0	(G)
O'HARA, Daniel	Airdrie	28.09.37	Cork Celtic	Mansfield T.	06.61	1961	3		1	(F)
O'HARA, Edward A.	Glasgow	28.10.35	Falkirk	Everton	06.58	1958–59	29		2	(OL) S. U23–3/S. SCH.INT.
			TR	Rotherham U.	02.60	1959–60	20		3	
			Morton	Barnsley	07.62	1962–64	127		37	
O'HARA, Edward P.	Dalkey	22.02.27	Dundalk	Birmingham C.	11.49	1949–50	6		0	(F)
O'HARA, Gerry J.	Wolverhampton	03.12.56	APP	Wolverhampton W.	12.74	1975–76	7	2	0	(M)
			TR	Hereford U.	N/C	1978	1	/	0	
O'HARA, Mike J.	Belfast	30.08.44	APP	Luton T.	11.61	1960	2		0	(G)
			TR	Swindon T.	11.61	1961–62	30		0	
			TR	Bournemouth	09.63					
O'HARE, John	Renton	24.09.46	JNRS	Sunderland	10.63	1964–66	51	/	14	(F) S–13/S.U23–3
			TR	Derby Co.	08.67	1967–73	247	1	65	
			TR	Leeds U.	08.74	1974	6	/	1	
			TR	Nottingham F.	02.75	1974–79	94	7	14	
O'KAMBACK, Joe	Tottenham	13.03.15		Millwall	+	1946	1		0	(CF)
O'KANE, Liam	Londonderry	17.06.48	Derry C.	Nottingham F.	11.68	1968–75	186	3	0	(CH) N1–20
O'KANE, Vince	Stephney	29.11.52	APP	Charlton Ath.	12.70	1970–72	29	3	1	(WH)
O'KEEFE, Eamon	Manchester	13.10.53	Stalybridge	Plymouth Arg.	02.74					(M) EI–1
			Mossley	Everton	07.79	1979–81	26	14	6	
			TR	Wigan Ath.	01.82	1981–82	56	2	25	
			TR	Port Vale	07.83	1983	34	3	10	
O'KEEFE, J. Vince	Birmingham	02.04.57		Birmingham C.	07.75					(G)
			TR	Walsall	07.76					
			AP Leamington	Exeter C.	06.78	1978–79	53	/	0	
			TR	Torquay U.	02.80	1979–81	108	/	0	
			TR	Blackburn Rov.	08.82	1982–83	21	/	0	
			L	Bury	10.83	1983	2	/	0	
O'KELLY, Richard F.	W. Bromwich	08.01.57	Alvechurch	Walsall	10.79	1980–83	130	12	32	(F)
O'LEARY, Daniel	Cork	11.01.51	APP	Millwall	05.68					(F)
			TR	Fulham	07.69	1969	0	1	0	
O'LEARY, David A.	London	02.05.58	APP	Arsenal	07.75	1975–83	308	/	9	(D) EI–28●
O'LEARY, Donal	Limehouse	24.06.36		Blackburn Rov.	10.54	1955	6		1	
O'LINN, Sid	S. Africa	08.05.27	Clyde S.A.	Charlton Ath.	12.47	1947–56	187		32	(IF) Kent cricketer
O'LOUGHLIN, Nigel	Denbigh	19.01.54	Rhyl	Shrewsbury T.	08.72	1972–75	23	10	7	(M)
			TR	Rochdale	08.76	1976–81	242	3	17	
O'LOUGHLIN, William	Bolton	18.01.37	Rossendale	Oldham Ath.	02.60	1959–60	27		4	(F)
O'MAHONEY Frank	Aldershot	05.04.35		Swindon T.	04.57	1956–57	8		5	(F)
O'MAHONY, Matt	Mullinavat	09.01.13	Bristol Rov.(*)	Ipswich T.	+	1946–48	58		4	(CH) *Newport Co./ EI–6/NI–1
O'MARA, John	Bolton	19.03.47	Margate	Gillingham	10.65					(CF)
			Wimbledon	Brentford	03.71	1970–72	53	/	28	
			TR	Blackburn Rov.	09.72	1972–73	32	4	10	
			Chelmsford C.	Bradford C.	12.74	1974	3	/	1	
O'MEARA, Alan M.	Grantham	15.12.58	APP	Scunthorpe U.	07.76	1975–76	41	/	0	(G)
O'NEIL, Brian	Bedlington	04.01.44	JNRS	Burnley	01.61	1962–69	231	4	2	(WH) E.U23–1/E.F.LGE
			TR	Southampton	05.71	1970–74	148	1	16	REP.
			TR	Huddersfield T.	10.74	1974–75	60	1	3	

Players Names	Birthplace	Date	Previous Club	League Club	Date Signed	Seasons Played	Apps	Sub	Gls	
O'NEIL, Joe	Glasgow	15.08.31	Aberdeen	Southend U.	11.52	1952–53	24		11	(IF) on loan to Southend U.
			Aberdeen	Leicester C.	03.56	1957	5		2	
			TR	Northampton T.	10.57	1957–58	28		4	
O'NEIL, Tom	Glasgow	02.02.58	Ipswich T. (APP)	Cambridge U.	07.76	1976-82	96	20	8	(M)
			TR	Northampton T.	06.83	1983	43	/	6	
O'NEIL, Tom P.	St. Helens	25.10.52	APP	Manchester U.	11.69	1970-72	53	/	0	(M) E.SCH.INT.
			L	Blackpool	01.73	1972	7	/	0	
			TR	Southport	08.73	1973-77	192	5	16	
			TR	Tranmere Rov.	06.78	1978-79	74	/	10	
			TR	Halifax T.	08.80	1980-81	39	1	2	
O'NEILL, Alan	Leadgate	13.11.37	JNRS	Sunderland	02.55	1956–60	74		27	(IF)
			TR	Aston Villa	10.60	1960–62	23		3	
			TR	Plymouth Arg.	11.62	1962–63	40		14	
			TR	Bournemouth	02.64	1963–65	37	/	8	
O'NEILL, Frank S.	Dublin	13.04.40	Home Farm	Arsenal	04.59	1960	2		0	(WH) EI–20
O'NEILL, George			Ellesmere Port	Port Vale	AM	1948	5		0	(OL)
O'NEILL, George	Port Glasgow	26.07.42	Glasgow Celtic	Barrow	10.64	1964	7		0	(CH)
O'NEILL, James	Magheramine	24.11.41	JNRS	Sunderland	11.58	1961	7		6	(CF) NI–1/NI.U23–1/
			TR	Walsall	12.62	1962–64	38		13	NI.SCH.INT
			Hakoah	Darlington	10.67	1967	20	3	4	
O'NEILL, James A.	Dublin	13.10.31	Bulfin U.	Everton	05.49	1950–59	201		0	(G) EI–17
			TR	Stoke C.	07.60	1960–63	130		0	
			TR	Darlington	03.64	1963–64	32		0	
			TR	Port Vale	02.65	1964–65	39	/	0	
O'NEILL, James J. (Shaun)	Belfast	24.02.52	APP	Leeds U.	05.69					(D)
			TR	Chesterfield	07.74	1974-83	353	5	5	
O'NEILL, John	Dublin	08.09.35	Drumcondra	Preston N.E.	04.58	1958–62	50		0	(CH) EI–1
			TR	Barrow	07.63	1963	35		3	
O'NEILL, John P.	Lanark	11.03.58	Denny ABC	Leicester C.	02.79	1978-83	201	/	6	(D) NI-25/NI.U21-1
O'NEILL, Les	Blyth	04.12.43	Blyth Spartans	Newcastle U.	11.61	1963	1		0	(M)
			TR	Darlington	01.65	1964-69	178	1	35	
			TR	Bradford C.	03.70	1969-71	95	2	17	
			TR	Carlisle U.	05.72	1972-76	148	7	20	
O'NEILL, Martin	Kilrea	01.03.52	Derry C.	Nottingham F.	10.71	1971-80	264	21	48	(M) NI-62●
			TR	Norwich C.	02.81	1980	11	/	1	
			TR	Manchester C.	06.81	1981	12	1	0	
			TR	Norwich C.	01.82	1981-82	54	1	11	
			TR	Notts Co.	08.83	1983	37	1	4	
O'NEILL, Tom H.	Spennymoor	05.01.25	Spennymoor	Newcastle U.	+					
			TR	Newport Co.	04.48	1948	9		0	
O'NEILL, William	Glasgow	30.12.40	Glasgow Celtic	Carlisle U.	05.69	1969	15	/	0	(FB)
O'NEILL, William A.	Cork	29.12.19	Chelmsford	Burnley	06.49	1950	1		1	(IF)
			TR	Walsall	01.51	1950–51	55		16	
O'REAGAN, Kieran	Cork	09.11.63	Tramore Ath.	Brighton & H.A.	04.83	1982-83	31	1	1	(D)EI-2
O'REILLY, Gary M.	Isleworth	21.03.61	JNRS	Tottenham H.	09.79	1980-83	39	6	0	(D)EI.YTH.INT.
O'RILEY, Paul	Liverpool	17.10.55	APP	Hull C.	11.68	1968-73	19	11	2	(F)
			L	Scunthorpe U.	03.71	1970	11	/	4	
			TR	Barnsley	07.74	1974	11	3	2	
			TR	Southport	03.75	1974-76	19	11	4	
O'RIORDAN, Donal	Dublin	14.05.57	APP	Derby Co.	07.75	1976-77	2	4	1	(D)
			L	Doncaster Rov.	01.78	1977	2	/	0	
			Tulsa	Preston N.E.	10.78	1978-82	153	5	8	
			TR	Carlisle U.	08.83	1983	42	/	8	
O'ROURKE, James	Glasgow	17.10.48	Possilpark J.	Arsenal	10.65					(FB)
			TR	Carlisle U.	10.67	1967	0	1	0	
O'ROURKE, John	Northampton	11.02.45	Arsenal(AM)	Chelsea	04.62					(CF) E.U23-1/E..YTH.INT.●
			TR	Luton T.	12.63	1963-65	84	/	64	
			TR	Middlesbrough	07.66	1966-67	63	1	38	
			TR	Ipswich T.	02.68	1967-69	69		30	
			TR	Coventry C.	11.69	1969-71	52	2	16	
			TR	Q.P.R.	10.71	1971-72	33	1	12	
			TR	Bournemouth	01.74	1973-74	21	1	4	
O'ROURKE, Ken	Lambeth	08.12.49	Orient (APP)	Arsenal	02.67					
			TR	Ipswich T.	08.68					
			TR	Colchester U.	10.68	1968	1	/	0	
O'ROURKE, William J.	Nottingham	02.04.60	APP	Burnley	02.78	1979-82	14	/	0	(G)
			L	Blackpool	08.83	1983	6	/	0	
			TR	Chester C.	03.84	1983	5	/	0	
O'SHAUGHNESSY, Brian	Wednesbury	08.09.32		Walsall	03.54	1953	1		0	(IF)
O'SHAUGHNESSY, Mike, J.	London	15.04.55	APP	Orient	08.73	1973	1	/	0	(G)
O'SHEA, Danny E.	Stoke Newington	26.03.63	APP	Arsenal	12.80	1982	6	/	0	(D)
			L	Charlton Ath.	02.84	1983	9	/	0	
O'SULLIVAN, Cyril J.	Lewisham	22.02.20	Crown Villa	Reading	09.46	1946-47	36		0	(G)

Players Names	Birthplace	Date	Previous Club	League Club	Date Signed	Seasons Played	Career Record Apps	Sub	Gls	
O'SULLIVAN, John	Cork	30.05.22	Waterford	Swansea C.	01.48	1947	2		0	(W)
			Lovells Ath.	Aldershot	11.51					
O'SULLIVAN, Peter A.	Colwyn Bay	04.03.51	APP	Manchester U.	03.68					(M) W-3/W.U23-6/
			TR	Brighton & H.A.	04.70	1970-80	432	3	38	W.SCH.INT.
			TR	Fulham	06.81	1981-82	45	1	1	
			L	Charlton Ath.	10.82	1982	5	/	0	
			L	Reading	11.82	1982	9	/	0	
			Hong Kong	Aldershot	07.83	1983	13	1	0	
O'SULLIVAN, William	London	05.10.59	APP	Charlton Ath.	10.77	1976-77	1	1	0	(F)
OAKES, Alan	Winsford	01.09.42	JNRS	Manchester C.	09.59	1959-75	561	3	26	(M) E.F. LGE. REP.●
			TR	Chester C.	07.76	1976-81	211	/	15	
				Port Vale	N/C	1983	1	/	0	
OAKES, Dennis R.	Bedworth	10.04.46	APP	Coventry C.	08.64					(WH) Warwicks Cricketer 00
			TR	Notts. Co.	06.67	1967-70	108	12	0	
			TR	Peterborough U.	05.71	1971-72	84	1	5	
OAKES, Donald J.	Rhyl	08.10.28	Downend	Arsenal	07.46	1952-54	11		1	(WH) d.
OAKES, George	Orrell	18.10.18	Red Tr. Y.M.C.A.	Southport	+	1946	7		0	(CF)
OAKES, John	Hamilton	16.01.21	Q. of South	Rochdale	02.47	1946	1		0	(CF)
OAKES, John	Hamilton	06.12.19	Q. of South	Huddersfield T.	+					(OL) *Wolverhampton W.
			Q. of South	Blackburn Rov.	02.47	1946-47	35		9	Cousin of John
			TR	Manchester C.	06.48	1948-50	77		9	(Hamilton)
OAKES, John	Northwich	13.09.05	Aldershot(*)	Charlton Ath.	*	1946	8		0	(CH) *Chilton Col./
			TR	Plymouth Arg.	07.47	1947	36		0	Nottingham F./Southend U.
OAKES, Keith B.	Bedworth	03.07.56	APP	Peterborough U.	07.73	1972-77	48	13	2	(D)
			TR	Newport Co.	09.78	1978-83	232	/	27	
OAKES, Tom	Manchester			Manchester C.	05.47	1946	1		0	
OAKEY, Graham	Worcester	05.10.54	APP	Coventry C.	10.72	1974-77	87	1	0	(D)
OAKLEY, Ken	Rhymney	09.05.29	Ebbw. Vale	Cardiff C.	03.50	1950-53	7		0	(CF)
			TR	Northampton T.	07.54	1954	13		6	
OAKLEY, Norman	Stockton	04.06.39		Doncaster Rov.	04.57					(G)
			TR	Scunthorpe U.	07.58					
			TR	Hartlepool U.	09.58	1958-63	182		0	
			TR	Swindon T.	03.64	1963-64	21		0	
			TR	Grimsby T.	09.66	1966	15	/	0	
OAKLEY, Royston	Tipton	05.01.28		Southampton	11.50	1953-55	6		0	(FB)
OATES, Graham	Scunthorpe	04.12.43	APP	Blackpool	05.61	1961-68	118	3	26	(W)
			TR	Grimsby T.	10.68	1968-70	80	2	11	
OATES, Graham	Bradford	14.03.49		Bradford C.	02.70	1969-73	158	3	19	(M)
			TR	Blackburn Rov.	06.74	1974-75	76	/	10	
			TR	Newcastle U.	03.76	1975-77	26	10	3	
OATES, Robert A.	Leeds	26.07.56	Ashley Rd. F.C.	Scunthorpe U.	08.74	1974-82	306	9	17	(D) E.YTH.INT.
			TR	Rochdale	08.83	1983	42	/	1	
OBENEY, Harry	Bethnal Green	09.03.38	Briggs Spts.	West Ham U.	05.56	1956-60	25		12	(WH)
			TR	Millwall	06.61	1961-63	75		11	
			TR	Colchester U.	09.64					
OELOFSE, Ralph J.	S. Africa	12.11.26	Berea Park	Chelsea	10.51	1951-52	8		0	(WH)
			TR	Watford	07.53	1953	15		0	
OGBURN, Mike	Portsmouth	19.02.48	Portsmouth (APP)	Brentford	05.65	1966	12	/	0	(FB)
OGDEN, Alan	Thrybergh	15.04.54	APP	Sheffield Wed.	05.71	1971-73	6	6	0	(FB)
			TR	York C.	09.74	1974	7	/	0	
			TR	Huddersfield T.	07.75					
OGDEN, Chris	Oldham	03.02.53	JNRS	Oldham Ath.	07.71	1971-77	128	/	0	(G) Son of Fred
			TR	Swindon T.	08.78	1978-79	24	/	0	
			TR	Rotherham U.	11.79	1979	3	/	0	
OGDEN, Fred	Oldham	03.04.25	Edgelane B.C.	Oldham Ath.	+	1947-54	152		0	(G)
			TR	Chesterfield	06.55					
			TR	Oldham Ath.	03.56	1955	5		0	
OGDEN, Paul	Leek	18.12.46	Leek Castle	Port Vale	AM	1965	2	/	0	(W)
OGDEN, Trevor	Culcheth	12.06.45		Manchester C.	09.64	1964	9		3	(F)
			TR	Doncaster Rov.	06.65	1965-66	39	/	14	
OGHANI, George W.	Manchester	02.09.60	Hyde U.	Bolton W.	10.83	1983	1	2	0	(F)
OGILVIE, John F.	Motherwell	28.10.28	Hibernian	Sheffield U.	08.55					(FB)
			TR	Leicester C.	09.55	1955-58	82		2	
			TR	Mansfield T.	01.60	1959-60	24		1	
OGILVIE, John L.	Workington	20.12.43	Blackpool (AM)	Workington	07.63	1962-74	386	4	14	(FB)
OGLEY, Alan	Barnsley	04.02.46	APP	Barnsley	03.63	1962	9		0	(G)E.SCH.INT.
			TR	Manchester C.	07.63	1963-67	51	/	0	
			TR	Stockport Co.	09.67	1967-74	240	/	0	
			TR	Darlington	08.75	1975-76	80	/	0	

Players Names	Birthplace	Date	Previous Club	League Club	Date Signed	Seasons Played	Career Record Apps	Sub	Gls	
OGRIZOVIC, Steve	Mansfield	12.09.57	O.N.R.Y.C.	Chesterfield	07.77	1977	16	/	0	(G)
			TR	Liverpool	11.77	1977–80	4	/	0	
			TR	Shrewsbury T.	08.82	1982–83	84	/	0	
OGSTON, John	Aberdeen	15.01.39	Aberdeen	Liverpool	08.65	1966	1	/	0	(G) S.U23.–3
			TR	Doncaster Rov.	08.68	1968–70	70	/	0	
OLAH, Bela	Hungary	08.06.38	Bedford T.	Northampton T.	12.58	1958–60	41		8	(F)
OLDFIELD, Craig	Wortley	24.11.63		Colchester U.	03.83	1983	0	3	0	(F)
OLDFIELD, John E.	Helsby	13.07.18	Helsby F.C.	Port Vale	+	1946	1		0	(RH)
OLDFIELD, John S.	Lindrick	19.08.43	JNRS	Huddersfield T.	08.61	1963–68	152	/	0	(G)
			TR	Wolverhampton W.	12.69	1969–70	19	/	0	
			L	Crewe Alex.	11.71	1971	5	/	0	
			TR	Bradford C.	12.71	1971–72	31	/	0	
OLDFIELD, Terry J.	Bristol	01.04.39	Clifton St. Vincents	Bristol Rov.	02.58	1960–65	130	1	11	(WH)
			TR	Wrexham	07.66	1966	40	1	6	
OLDHAM, Eric	Newcastle	27.06.33	Seaton Delavel	Bolton W.	10.53					(FB)
			TR	Gateshead	07.56	1956–57	53		0	
				Hartlepool U.	06.59	1959	12		0	
OLDHAM, George	Tintwhistle	20.04.02		Stoke C.	*					(LB)
			TR	Newport Co.	09.46	1946–47	63		0	
OLDHAM, John	Oswaldwhistle	30.01.26		Accrington St.	08.50	1950–52	10		0	(FB)
OLDHAM, John	Nottingham	24.10.49		Mansfield T.	02.67	1966	0	1	0	(CF)
OLDRIDGE, A. Robert	Barton	17.11.57		Grimsby T.	01.76	1975–76	9	6	1	(F)
OLINYK, Peter	Bolton	04.10.53	APP	Bolton W.	07.72	1973–74	7	3	0	(F)
			TR	Stockport Co.	11.74	1974	4	/	0	
OLIPHANT, David	Carlisle	29.01.42	JNRS	Wolverhampton W.	06.59					(WH)
			TR	Carlisle U.	12.60	1960–64	109		11	
OLIVE, R. Les	Salford	27.04.28	JNRS	Manchester U.	AM	1952	2		0	(G)
OLIVER, Alan J.	Blyth	08.09.24	Croften C.W.	Derby Co.	10.46	1947–49	16		2	(OL)
			TR	Stockport Co.	08.50	1950–53	139		28	
			TR	Gateshead	07.54	1954–57	146		36	
OLIVER, Brian C.	Liverpool	06.03.57	Bury (APP)	Rochdale	03.75	1975	3	/	0	(G)
			L	Southport	12.75	1975	2	/	0	
OLIVER, Edmund A.	Manchester	17.03.61	APP	Rochdale	03.79	1977–79	19	3	1	(D)
OLIVER, Eric	Spennymoor	08.07.40	W. Auckland	Darlington	AM	1963	2		0	(G)
OLIVER, Gavin R.	Felling	06.09.62	APP	Sheffield Wed.	08.80	1980–83	5	5	0	(D)
			L	Tranmere Rov.	01.83	1982	17	/	1	
OLIVER, George				Halifax T.	+					
			TR	Gateshead	10.46	1946	13		1	
OLIVER, Harry S.	Sunderland	16.02.21	Hartlepool U.(*)	Brentford	*	1946–47	18		0	(CH)
			TR	Watford	05.48	1948–51	122		2	E.SCH.INT.
OLIVER, Howard D.	Sunderland	16.04.50	JNRS	Sheffield Wed.	04.67					(W)
			TR	Hartlepool U.	08.68	1968	0	1	0	
OLIVER, J.H. Ken	Loughborough	10.08.24	Brush Spts.	Sunderland	08.46	1947–48	9		1	(CH)
			TR	Derby C.	09.49	1949–57	184		1	
			TR	Exeter C.	01.58	1957–59	92		0	
OLIVER, James	Fern	13.01.58	Montrose	Wigan Ath.	08.80	1980	1	1	0	(M)
OLIVER, James	Uxbridge	28.08.49	APP	Crystal Palace	03.67	1967–69	3	/	0	(HB)
OLIVER, James R.	Falkirk	03.12.41	Falkirk	Norwich C.	08.62	1962–64	40		17	(OR) S.SCH.INT.
			TR	Brighton & H.A.	03.65	1964–67	37	6	5	
			TR	Colchester U.	02.68	1967–69	64	10	10	
OLIVER, John	Bradford	21.09.46	Bradford C. (AM)	Bradford P.A.	09.66	1965	1	/	0	(FB)
OLIVER, John	Redrow	06.10.20	Amble F.C.	Chesterfield	10.46	1946–47	24		5	(IL)
OLIVER, Ken	Pelton	26.11.38	Birtley R.O.F.	Sunderland	05.58					(IF)
			TR	Barnsley	02.60	1959–62	94		38	
			TR	Watford	07.63	1963–64	58		26	
			TR	Workington	02.65	1964–66	84		20	
			TR	Bournemouth	01.67	1966	14	/	4	
OLIVER, Peter F.R.	Cowdenbeath	18.08.48	Hearts	York C.	07.74	1974–75	41	/	0	(D)
			TR	Huddersfield T.	05.76	1976	41	/	1	
OLIVER, Ralph	Tredegar	30.03.34	Hereford U.	Shrewsbury T.	08.55	1955–57	8		0	(HB)
OLLERENSHAW, John	Stockport	03.04.25	Manchester C. (AM)	Arsenal	09.46					(FB)
			TR	Hartlepool U.	06.50	1950	2		0	
			TR	Oldham Ath.	03.51					
OLNEY, Kevin	Doncaster	12.02.59	JNRS	Doncaster Rov.	08.76	1976–78	65	1	1	(D)
OMAN, Alan J.	Northampton	06.10.52	APP	Northampton T.	02.71	1970–74	83	5	3	(FB)

Players Names	Birthplace	Date	Previous Club	League Club	Date Signed	Seasons Played	Career Record Apps	Sub	Gls	
ONSLOW, Les G.	Swindon	29.08.26		Swindon T.	+	1946–48	6		0	(IF)
ONSLOW, Roy	Swindon	12.09.28		Swindon T.	08.48	1948–55	139		24	(IF) Brother of Les
ONYEALI, Elkanah	Nigeria	07.06.39	Nigeria	Tranmere Rov.	08.60	1960	13		8	(IF)
			Holyhead T.	Newport Co.	08.62					
OOSTHUIZEN, Ron	S. Africa	16.03.36	S. Africa	Charlton Ath.	09.53	1955	1		0	
			Yeovil T.	Carlisle U.	09.59	1959	1		0	
ORAM, Dennis G.	Knowle	14.01.20	St. Pancras B.C.	Bristol C.	AM	1946	3		0	(CH)
ORD, Brian	Dunstan	21.06.39	Bleach Green	Charlton Ath.	11.57	1961–62	13		1	(FB)
ORD, Ken	Sth. Shields	21.09.39	Cleadon	Sunderland	11.57					
			TR	Chesterfield	06.61	1961	3		0	
ORD, Tommy	London	15.10.52	Erith & B.	Chelsea	12.72	1972	3	/	1	(IF)
ORGILL, Harry	Hucknall	01.10.20		Nottingham F.	04.47	1946	7		0	(G) d.1980
			TR	Notts.Co.	06.47	1947	2		0	
ORHAN, Yilhaz	Cyprus	13.03.55	Aveley	West Ham U.	10.75	1975-76	6	2	0	(F)
ORMANDY, Jack	Liverpool	25.01.12	Southend U.(+)	Oldham Ath.	07.46	1946	30		5	(OL)*Prescot Cables/
			TR	Halifax T.	07.47	1947	7		0	Bradford C./Bury
ORMOND, John L.	Larkhall	10.08.47	New Zealand	Barnsley	12.67	1968	1	/	1	(F)
ORMOND, William	Greenock	26.08.26	Partick Th.	Blackpool	10.47					(IF)
			TR	Oldham Ath.	12.49	1949-53	122		24	
			TR	Barrow	02.54	1953-57	139		31	
			TR	Scunthorpe U.	08.58	1958	3		0	
ORMROD, Leslie	Stockport	08.10.52	Everton(APP)	Stockport Co.	03.70	1969-73	103	5	0	(FB)E.SCH.INT
ORMSBY, Brendan T.	Birmingham	01.10.60	APP	Aston Villa	10.78	1978-83	69	2	2	(D)E.SCH.INT./E.YTH.INT.
ORMSTON, Alex	Stoke	10.02.19	JNRS	Stoke C.	*	1946-51	158		27	(W) E.F.LGE REP./d.
ORPHAN, Leslie	Newport	17.04.23	Girlings F.C.	Newport Co.	02.49	1948	1		0	(IL)W.AMAT.INT
ORR, Anderson	Glasgow	19.12.23	T. Lanark	Nottingham F.	08.51	1951-54	43		0	(WH)
ORR, Doug M.	Glasgow	08.11.37	Hendon	Q.P.R.	AM	1957	5		0	(W)S.AMAT.INT
ORR, Henry	Lisburn	31.10.36	Distillery	Sheffield U.	11.58	1958.62	10		1	(HB)
			TR	Peterborough U.	07.64	1964-66	47	1	0	
ORR, Neil I.	Greenock	13.05.59	Morton	West Ham U.	01.82	1981-83	61	6	1	(D)S.U'21-7
ORRITT, Brian	Caernarvon	22.02.37	Bangor C.	Birmingham C.	02.56	1956-61	100		23	(WH)W.U23-3
			TR	Middlesbrough	03.62	1961-65	115	3	21	
OSBORN, Ken G.	London	23.11.48	Q.P.R.(APP)	Gillingham	06.66	1968-69	2	/	0	
OSBORNE, Glyn	Crewe	23.08.54	APP	Crewe Alex.	APP	1970-71	2	5	0	(CF)
OSBORNE, Ian L.	Leicester	28.10.52	APP	Birmingham C.	10.70	1975	10	/	0	(D)
			TR	Port Vale	06.76	1976	14	1	0	
OSBORNE, John	Barlborough	01.12.40	JNRS	Chesterfield	09.60	1960-66	110	/	0	(G)E.SCH.INT./1 app.
			TR	W.B.A.	01.67	1966-76	250	/	0	on field for Chesterfield
			L	Walsall	02.73	1972	3	/	0	
OSBORNE, John	Renfrew	14.10.19		Leicester C.	+					(HB)
			TR	Watford	02.48	1947-48	34		13	
OSBORNE, Roger	Otley	09.03.50	Grundisburgh	Ipswich T.	07.72	1973-80	109	15	9	(M)
			TR	Colchester U.	02.81	1980-83	129	3	8	
OSCROFT, Harry	Mansfield	10.03.26	Mansfield Col.	Mansfield T.	04.47	1946-49	112		39	(OL)
			TR	Stoke C.	01.50	1949-58	326		100	
			TR	Port Vale	09.59	1959-60	47		12	
OSGOOD, Keith	Ealing	08.05.55	APP	Tottenham H.	05.72	1973-77	112	1	13	(D) E.YTH.INT./E.SCH.INT.
			TR	Coventry C.	01.78	1977-78	24	1	1	
			TR	Derby Co	10.79	1979-81	61	8	10	
			TR	Orient	12.81	1981-83	36	/	0	
OSGOOD, Peter	Windsor	20.02.47	JNRS	Chelsea	09.64	1965-73	276	3	103	(F) E-4/E.U23-6/
			TR	Southampton	03.74	1973-77	122	4	28	E.F.LGE.REP./E.YTH.INT.
			L	Norwich C.	11.76	1976	3	/	0	
			Philadelphia	Chelsea	12.78	1978-79	10	/	2	
OSMAN, Harry J.	Alton	29.01.11	Southampton(*)	Millwall	*	1946-47	27		3	(OL)*Poole/Plymouth Arg.
			TR	Bristol C.	10.47	1947	18		1	
OSMAN, Rex C.	Derby	04.04.32	JNRS	Derby Co.	07.49	1953-54	2		0	(FB)E.YTH.INT
OSMAN, Russell C.	Ilkeston	14.02.59	APP	Ipswich T.	03.76	1977-83	265	/	14	(D) E-11/E.U21-7/
										Son of Rex
OSMOND, Avery N.	Huddersfield	25.12.24	Peterborough U.	Southend U.	05.48	1948	2		0	
OSMOND, Colin A.	Whitchurch	15.05.37	JNRS	Portsmouth	05.54	1957	1	/	0	(HB)E.YTH.INT.
OSTERGAARD, John B.	Denmark	06.02.55	Ikast	Charlton Ath.	11.79	1979-80	8	4	1	(F)
OTTEWELL, Sid	Horsley	23.10.19	Holbrook C.W.	Chesterfield	*	1946	39		12	(IF)
			TR	Birmingham C.	06.47	1947	5		2	
			TR	Luton	12.47	1947	15		4	
			TR	Nottingham F.	07.48	1948-49	31		3	
			TR	Mansfield T.	01.50	1949-51	68		21	
			TR	Scunthorpe U.	03.52	1951-52	30		10	

Players Names	Birthplace	Date	Previous Club	League Club	Date Signed	Seasons Played	Career Record Apps	Sub	Gls	
OTTO, Heine M.	Holland	24.08.54	Twente	**Middlesbrough**	08.81	1981-83	122	2	20	(M)
OTULAKOWSKI, Anton	Dewsbury	29.01.56	Ossett Trin.	**Barnsley**	05.76	1975-76	42	/	2	(M)
			TR	**West Ham U.**	10.76	1976-77	10	7	0	
			TR	**Southend U.**	03.79	1978-82	161	2	8	
			TR	**Millwall**	03.83	1982-83	47	/	9	
OUTHWAITE, George	Ferryhill	19.05.28	Chilton Col.	**Oldham Ath.**	AM	1955	4		0	(G)
OVARD, Frank	Evesham	16.12.55	Maidstone U.	**Gillingham**	12.81	1981	4	2	0	(F)
OVER, Eric	Sheffield	05.07.33		**Sheffield U.**	11.54	1954	2		0	(F)
			TR	**Barrow**	11.56	1955-57	19		1	
			TR	**Oldham Ath.**	12.57	1957	21		2	
OVERFIELD, Jack	Leeds	14.05.32	Yorks Amats	**Leeds U.**	05.53	1955-59	159		19	(OL)
			TR	**Sunderland**	08.60	1960-62	65		5	
			TR	**Peterborough U.**	02.63	1962	1		0	
			TR	**Bradford C.**	07.64	1964	11		0	
OVERSON, Richard J.	Kettering	03.06.59	APP	**Burnley**	06.77	1977-79	5	1	0	(D) Brother of Vince
			TR	**Hereford U.**	05.80	1980-81	6	5	1	
OVERSON, Vince D.	Kettering	15.05.62	APP	**Burnley**	11.79	1979-83	137	4	5	(D)
OVERTON, John	Rotherham	02.05.56	APP	**Aston Villa**	01.74	1975	2	1	0	(M)
			L	**Halifax T.**	03.76	1975	14	/	2	
			TR	**Gillingham**	06.76	1976-80	177	1	10	
OVERTON, Paul H.	Soham	18.04.61	APP	**Ipswich T.**	07.78	1977	1	/	0	(G)
			TR	**Peterborough U.**	05.79					
			TR	**Northampton T.**	06.80					
OWEN, Aled W.	Caeysegamen	07.01.34	Bangor C.	**Tottenham H.**	09.53	1953	1		0	(OL)
			TR	**Ipswich T.**	07.58	1958-61	30		3	
			TR	**Wrexham**	07.63	1963	3		0	
OWEN, Brian E.	Harefield	02.11.44	APP	**Watford**	07.62	1962-69	148	5	17	(W)
			TR	**Colchester U.**	05.70	1970-71	11	2	2	
			TR	**Wolverhampton W.**	01.72	1972	4	/	0	
OWEN, Brian G.	Bath	07.07.42	Bath C.	**Hereford U.**	N/L	1972-73	46	8	13	(F)
OWEN, Bryn	Rochdale	25.04.39		**Rochdale**	08.60	1960-61	6		0	(FB)
OWEN, Derek W.	Shrewsbury	11.03.38	Coton Rov.	**Shrewsbury T.**	01.57	1956-57	12		3	(F)
OWEN, Gary A.	St. Helens	07.07.58	APP	**Manchester C.**	08.75	1975-78	101	2	19	(M) E.U21-22/E.YTH.INT.
			TR	**W.B.A.**	06.79	1979-83	168	/	19	
OWEN, Gordon	Barnsley	14.06.59	JNRS	**Sheffield Wed.**	11.76	1977-82	33	15	5	(W)
			L	**Rotherham U.**	03.80	1979	9	/	0	
			L	**Doncaster Rov.**	11.82	1982	9	/	0	
			L	**Chesterfield**	03.83	1982	6	/	2	
			TR	**Cardiff C.**	08.83	1983	38	1	14	
OWEN, J. Les	Hawarden	11.04.33		**Chester C.**	07.54	1956-58	2		0	(FB)
OWEN, John G.	Llanwonno	25.03.32	Pontypridd	**Exeter C.**	10.53	1953-54	13		0	(WH)
			TR	**Bournemouth**	09.56					
OWEN, L. Terry	Liverpool	11.09.49	APP	**Everton**	12.66	1967	2	/	0	(F)
			TR	**Bradford C.**	06.70	1970-71	41	11	6	
			TR	**Chester C.**	06.72	1972-76	161	15	40	
			TR	**Cambridge U.**	08.77	1977	1	/	0	
			TR	**Rochdale**	09.77	1977-78	80	3	21	
			TR	**Port Vale**	07.79	1979	14	4	3	
OWEN, Maurice	Abingdon	04.07.24	Abingdon	**Swindon T.**	12.46	1946-62	554		151	(CF)●
OWEN, Neil	Bury	14.10.59	APP	**Sheffield Wed.**	APP	1976	1	/	0	(M)
OWEN, R. David	Ellesmere Port	25.09.38	Ellesmere Port	**Chester C.**	AM	1958-60	7		0	(G)
OWEN, Robert	Farnworth	17.10.47	APP	**Bury**	08.65	1974-67	81	2	38	(F)
			TR	**Manchester C.**	07.68	1968-69	18	4	3	
			L	**Swansea C.**	03.70	1969	5	1	1	
			TR	**Carlisle U.**	06.70	1970-76	185	19	51	
			L	**Northampton T.**	10.76	1976	5	/	0	
			L	**Workington**	12.76	1976	8	/	2	
			L	**Bury**	02.77	1976	4	/	1	
			TR	**Doncaster Rov.**	07.77	1977-78	74	3	22	
OWEN, Robert G.	Sunderland	05.05.24	Murton C.W.	**Lincoln C.**	01.47	1946-54	246		4	(WH)+Huddersfield T.
OWEN, Sid W.	Birmingham	29.09.22		**Birmingham C.**	+	1946	5		0	(CH)E-3/E.F.LGE REP.●
			TR	**Luton T.**	06.47	1947-58	388		3	
OWEN, Trefor	Flint	20.02.33	Tooting & M.	**Orient**	01.58	1958-60	15		0	(CH)W.AMAT.INT
OWEN, William M.	Llanfairfechan	30.06.14	Tranmere Rov.(*)	**Newport Co.**	*	1946	4		0	(WH) d.1976
			TR	**Exeter C.**	10.46	1946	19		9	
OWENS, Leslie T.	Sunderland	17.10.19	Charlton Ath.(*)	**Doncaster Rov.**	*	1946-47	10		3	(IF) d.1974
			TR	**Southport**	12.47	1947-48	53		11	
			TR	**Hartlepool U.**	07.49	1949	28		12	
			TR	**Norwich C.**	03.50	1949-50	20		8	
			TR	**Reading**	07.51	1951	8		4	
			TR	**Brighton & H.A.**	06.52	1954	15		4	

Players Names	Birthplace	Date	Previous Club	League Club	Date Signed	Seasons Played	Career Record Apps	Sub	Gls	
OWER, Ian	Glasgow	02.01.39	St. Johnstone	Workington	03.62	1962-67	199	/	0	(G)
OWERS, Adrian R.	Chelmsford	26.02.65	APP	Southend U.	03.83	1982-83	10	5	0	(F)
OWERS, Philip	B. Auckland	28.04.55	JNRS	Darlington	06.73	1972-74	45	/	0	(G)
			TR	Gillingham	07.75	1975	2	/	0	
			TR	Darlington	07.76	1976-79	69	/	0	
OXFORD, Ken	Manchester	14.11.29	JNRS	Manchester C.	10.47	1947	1		0	(G)E.YTH.INT
			TR	Derby Co.	01.49					
				Chesterfield	06.50					
			TR	Norwich C.	07.51	1953-57	128		0	
			TR	Derby Co.	12.57	1957-62	151		0	
			TR	Doncaster Rov.	07.64	1964	16		0	
			TR	Port Vale	03.65	1964	3		0	
OXLEY, Albert	Gateshead	21.10.15	Windy Nook	Gateshead	*	1946	1		1	(IF)
OXTOBY, Richard	Chesterfield	05.09.39	JNRS	Bolton W.	01.57	1959	3		0	(HB)
			TR	Tranmere Rov.	07.63	1963	5		0	

Players Names	Birthplace	Date	Previous Club	League Club	Date Signed	Seasons Played	Career Record Apps	Sub	Gls	
PACE, Derek J.	Bloxwich	11.03.32	Bloxwich Strollers	Aston Villa	09.49	1950-57	98		37	(CF)●
			TR	Sheffield U.	12.57	1957-64	253		140	
			TR	Notts Co.	12.64	1964-65	29	/	15	
			TR	Walsall	07.66	1966	4	1	1	
PACEY, David	Luton	02.10.36	Hitchin T.	Luton T.	08.56	1957-64	246		16	(WH) E.U23-1
PACEY, Dennis F.	Feltham	27.09.28	Walton & H.	Orient	12.51	1951.54	119		71	(CF)
			TR	Millwall	10.54	1954-58	132		36	
			TR	Aldershot	09.58	1958-59	32		13	
PACK, Roy J.	Islington	20.09.46	APP	Arsenal	11.63	1965	1	/	0	(FB)
			TR	Portsmouth	07.66	1966-68	92	/	0	
			TR	Oxford U.	05.69					
PACKARD, J.Edgar	Mansfield	07.03.19	Clipstone Col.	Sheffield Wed.	*	1946-51	124		1	(CH)
			TR	Halifax T.	08.52	1952-53	85		0	
PACKER, Les J.	Sunderland	08.04.59		Doncaster Rov.	09.78	1978-79	5	2	2	(F)
PACKER, Mike D.	London	20.04.50	APP	Watford	04.68	1968-72	57	10	2	(D)
			L	Crewe Alex.	03.72	1971	12	/	0	
			TR	Colchester U.	07.73	1973-82	237	7	20	
PACKER, Norman J.	Ynysybwl	14.06.31		Exeter C.	07.55	1955-60	20		0	(HB)
PADDON, Graham C.	Manchester	24.08.50	APP	Coventry C.	05.68	1968-69	3	2	1	(M) E.U23-1
			TR	Norwich C.	10.69	1969-73	162	/	19	
			TR	West Ham U.	12.73	1973-76	115	/	11	
			TR	Norwich C.	11.76	1976-81	126	2	6	
			L	Millwall	12.81	1981	5	/	1	
PAGE, John	Frimley	21.10.34	JNRS	Southampton	10.51	1952-60	190		23	(WH)
PAGE, Malcolm E.	Knucklas	05.02.47	APP	Birmingham C.	09.64	1964-80	327	11	9	(D) W-28/W.U23-6/
			TR	Oxford U.	02.81	1980-81	14	/	1	W.SCH.INT.
PAGE, Ray M.	Swindon	26.09.30		Swindon T.	04.51	1950-54	32		0	(FB)
PAINE, Terry	Winchester	23.03.39	Winchester	Southampton	02.57	1956-73	709	4	160	(W) E-19/E.U23-4/●
			TR	Hereford U.	08.74	1974-76	106	5	8	E.F.LGE. REP.
PAINTER, Edward G.	Swindon	23.06.21		Swindon T.	*	1946-50	77		0	(HB)
PAINTER, Ian J.	Womborne	28.12.64	APP	Stoke C.	12.82	1982-83	52	4	12	(F)
PAINTER, Trevor A.	Norwich	02.07.49	APP	Norwich C.	07.67	1967	2		0	(F)
			TR	Colchester U.	05.70	1970	1	/	0	
PAISLEY, Robert	Hetton	23.01.19	B. Auckland	Liverpool	+	1946-53	252		10	(WH)
PALETHORPE, Chris G.	Maidenhead	06.11.42	JNRS	Reading	11.59	1960-62	55		10	(OR)
			TR	Aldershot	06.63	1963-64	56		5	
PALFREYMAN, George	Sheffield	13.03.33	Sheffield F.C.	Halifax T.	AM	1953	1		0	(G)
PALIN, Grenville	Doncaster	13.02.40	JNRS	Wolverhampton W.	03.57					(CH)
			TR	Walsall	07.60	1960-63	129		10	
PALIOS, Mark	Birkenhead	09.11.52	JNRS	Tranmere Rov.	07.73	1973-79	177	13	25	(M)
			TR	Crewe Alex.	01.80	1979-82	114	4	23	
			TR	Tranmere Rov.	03.83	1982-83	32	3	4	
PALLISTER, Gordon	Howden	02.04.17	Bradford C.(*)	Barnsley	*	1946-51	210		3	(FB)E.F.LGE. REP.
PALMER, Calvin I.	Skegness	21.10.40	Skegness T.	Nottingham F.	03.58	1958-63	90		14	(WH)
			TR	Stoke C.	09.63	1963-67	165	/	24	
			TR	Sunderland	02.68	1967-69	35	5	5	
				Crewe Alex.	10.71	1971	2	/	0	
PALMER, Charles A.	Aylesbury	10.07.63	APP	Watford	07.81	1983	10	/	1	(D)
PALMER, David J.	Bristol	10.04.61	APP	Bristol Rov.	01.79	1978	1	/	0	(D)
PALMER, Des	Swansea	23.09.31		Swansea C.	04.50	1952-58	83		37	(IF)W-3
			TR	Liverpool	03.59					
			Durban C.	Derby Co.	06.61	1961	18		6	
PALMER, Frank	Sunderland	29.10.23	B. Auckland	Gateshead	AM	1950	2		1	(OL)
PALMER, Fred W.	Barrow	23.10.22		Crewe Alex.	+	1946	1		0	(WH)
PALMER, Geoff	Cannock	11.07.54	APP	Wolverhampton W.	08.72	1973-83	381	5	13	(D) E.U23-2
PALMER, Geoff	Barnsley	12.11.40	Doncaster Rov.(AM)	Bristol C.	08.58	1961	1		0	(FB)
PALMER, John N.	Bristol	01.07.58	Weston S.M.	Bristol C.	03.83	1982	2	6	0	(M)
PALMER, Leslie	Barrow	16.12.23	Holker C.O.B.	Barrow	10.49	1949	1		0	(WH)
PALMER, Mike J.	Norwich	06.01.47	APP	Norwich C.	01.65	1965	1	/	0	(G)
PALMER, Roger N.	Manchester	30.01.59	APP	Manchester C.	03.77	1977-80	22	9	9	(F)
			TR	Oldham Ath.	11.80	1980-83	140	2	41	
PAMMENT, Mike I.	Huddersfield	12.05.45	JNRS	Bradford C.	AM	1964	1		0	(CF)E.YTH.INT.
PANES, Simon M.	Almondsbury	22.02.60	Melksham T.	Bristol C.	08.82	1982	2	2	0	(F)
PANTER, Derek	Blackpool	22.11.43	W.B.A.(AM)	Manchester C.	08.62	1963	1		0	(F)
			TR	Torquay U.	05.64	1964	5		1	
			TR	Southport	07.65					
PAPE, Andy	Hammersmith	22.03.62	JNRS	Q.P.R.	07.80	1979	1	/	0	(G)
PARDOE, Glyn	Winsford	01.06.46	APP	Manchester C.	06.63	1961-74	303	2	16	(FB)E.U23-4/E.SCH.INT.

Players Names	Birthplace	Date	Previous Club	League Club	Date Signed	Seasons Played	Apps	Sub	Gls	
PARFITT, Henry E.	Cardiff	26.09.29		Cardiff C.	05.49	1953	1		0	(FB)
			L	Torquay U.	10.52	1952-53	58		0	
PARK, Colin S.J.	Swansea	08.02.45	JNRS	Swansea C.	09.63	1963	1		0	(G)
PARK, Robert	Douglas	07.04.30		Plymouth Arg.	11.54					(G)
			Airdrie	Crewe Alex.	08.55	1955-56	61		0	
PARK, Robert C.	Edinburgh	03.07.46	APP	Aston Villa	07.63	1964-68	60	13	7	(IF)
			TR	Wrexham	05.69	1969-71	98	4	8	
			TR	Peterborough U.	06.72	1972	15	3	1	
			TR	Northampton T.	02.73	1972-73	21	3	0	
			TR	Hartlepool U.	07.74	1974	14	3	0	
PARK, Robert	Coatbridge	05.01.52	JNRS	Sunderland	01.69	1969-71	50	15	4	(WH)
PARK, Terry	Liverpool	07.02.57	JNRS	Wolverhampton W.	03.74					(M)
				Stockport Co.	07.76	1976-79	87	3	8	
			Minnesota Kicks	Stockport Co.	03.81	1980-82	72	/	7	
			L	Manchester C	01.83	1982	0	2	0	
			TR	Bury	07.83	1983	18	3	1	
PARK, William	Gateshead	23.02.19	Felling Red Star	Blackpool	*					(CH)Nephew of C. Veitch–
			TR	York C.	09.46	1946	22		1	Pre-War Int.
PARKE, John	Belfast	06.08.37	Hibernian	Sunderland	11.64	1964-67	83	2	0	(FB)N.I.-14
PARKER, Albert E.	Liverpool	13.09.27	Sth. Liverpool	Crewe Alex.	12.48	1948-51	111		0	(FB)
			TR	Wrexham	51.11	1951-58	216		1	
PARKER, Alex H.	Irvine	02.08.35	Falkirk	Everton	06.58	1958-64	199		5	(FB)S-15/S.U23-6/
			TR	Southport	09.65	1965-67	76	/	0	S.F.LGE REP.
PARKER, Brian T.	Chorley	04.08.55		Crewe Alex.	08.72	1973	26	/	0	(G)
			TR	Arsenal	08.75					
PARKER, Cliff H.	Denaby	06.09.13	Doncaster Rov.(*)	Portsmouth	*	1946-50	68		7	(OL)*Denaby U./d.1983
PARKER, Derek	Colchester	23.06.26	Grays Ath.	West Ham U.	+	1946-56	199		10	(WH)
			TR	Colchester u.	03.57	1956-60	130		1	
PARKER, Gary S.	Oxford	07.09.65	APP	Luton T.	05.83	1982-83	14	/	2	(F)
PARKER, Graham S.	Coventry	23.05.46	APP	Aston Villa	05.63	1963-67	16	1	1	(FB)
			TR	Rotherham U.	12.67	1967	3	1	0	
			TR	Lincoln C.	07.68	1968	4	1	0	
			TR	Exeter C.	03.69	1968-73	180	2	12	
			TR	Torquay U.	05.74	1974-75	41	2	3	
PARKER, H. Derrick	Wallsend	07.02.57	APP	Burnley	02.74	1974-75	5	1	2	(F)
			TR	Southend U.	02.77	1976-79	129	/	43	
			TR	Barnsley	02.80	1979-82	104	3	33	
			TR	Oldham Ath.	08.83	1983	22	3	2	
PARKER, Harry	Blackburn	08.02.33		Blackburn Rov.	08.51	1951	3		0	
PARKER, John W.	Birkenhead	05.07.25		Everton	12.48	1950-55	167		81	(IF)
			TR	Bury	05.56	1956-58	81		43	
PARKER, Neil	Blackburn	19.10.57	APP	Leeds U.	10.75	1977	0	1	0	(D)
PARKER, Pat J.	Bow. Devon	15.07.29	Newton Abbot	Southampton	08.51	1951-58	132		0	(CH)
PARKER, Paul A.	London	04.04.64	APP	Fulham	04.82	1980-83	43	13	0	(D)
PARKER, Ray D.	Doncaster	27.01.25		Chesterfield	+	1947	14		0	(CH)
			TR	Sheffield Wed.	04.48	1948	1		0	
			Buxton	Bradford C.	06.51	1951-52	41		1	
PARKER, Reg. E	Pontyclun	10.06.21		Cardiff C.	11.46	1947	2		0	(CF)
			TR	Newport Co.	08.48	1948-53	201		99	
PARKER, Robert	Coventry	11.11.52	APP	Coventry C.	05.70	1969-73	78	3	0	(D) E.YTH.INT.
			TR	Carlisle U.	06.74	1974-83	373	2	6	
PARKER, Robert W.	Seaham	26.11.35	Murton C.W.	Huddersfield T.	06.54	1959-64	65		0	(FB)
			TR	Barnsley	07.65	1965-68	108	/	0	
PARKER, Sam	Liverpool	05.04.24	Marine Crosby	Accrington St.	07.48	1948	12		6	(CF)
			TR	Barnsley	12.48					
			TR	Accrington St.	09.49	1949-50	36		6	
			TR	Crewe Alex.	11.50	1950-51	43		5	
PARKER, Stan F.	Worksop	31.07.20		Ipswich T.	05.46	1946-50	126		48	(IF)
			TR	Norwich C.	08.51					
PARKER, Stuart J.	Preston	16.02.54	APP	Blackpool	04.72	1972-74	10	6	2	(F)
			TR	Southend U.	07.75	1975-76	62	2	23	
			TR	Chesterfield	02.77	1976-77	30	4	8	
			Sparta Rotterdam	Blackburn Rov.	07.79	1979	5	4	1	
			Frecheville C.	Bury	09.82	1982	26	8	10	
			R. C. Mechelen	Chester C.	N/C	1983	9	/	5	
			TR	Stockport Co.	N/C	1983	0	1	0	
PARKER, Stuart K.	Nantwich	13.04.63	JNRS	Wrexham	08.81	1982-83	10	/	0	(G)
PARKER, Tom R.	Hartlepool	13.02.24		Ipswich T.	08.46	1946-56	428		79	(WH)
PARKER, Walter	Doncaster	28.06.29	JNRS	Hull C.	08.47					(FB)
			TR	Crewe Alex.	08.51	1951-55	56		0	

Players Names	Birthplace	Date	Previous Club	League Club	Date Signed	Seasons Played	Apps	Sub	Gls	
PARKER, William	Liverpool	15.08.25	Runcorn	Reading	06.50	1950-52	32		5	(W)
			TR	Swindon T.	02.53	1952	10		0	
			TR	Exeter C.	07.53	1953	18		2	
PARKER, William F.	Liverpool	29.03.32	Burscough	Liverpool	04.53					(HB)
				Blackburn Rov.	12.57					
			Shelbourne	Southport	07.59	1959	9		0	
PARKER, William T.	Bolsover	06.10.20		Crewe Alex.	05.48	1947-48	17		0	(G) d.1953
PARKES, Alan	Hartlepool	12.01.29	Murton C.W.	Charlton Ath.	10.49					(CF)
				Darlington	03.55	1954	1		0	
PARKES, Anthony	Sheffield	05.05.49	Buxton	Blackburn Rov.	05.70	1970-80	345	5	38	(M)
PARKES, Barry J.	Hartlepool	21.01.40		Hartlepool U.	11.60	1960-62	27		9	(F)
				Reading	10.63					
PARKES, Harry A.	Birmingham	04.01.20	Boldmere St.M.	Aston Villa	+	1946-54	320		3	(CH)
PARKES, Phil	W. Bromwich	14.07.47	JNRS	Wolverhampton W.	09.64	1966-77	303	/	0	(G)
PARKES, Phil B.	Sedgley	08.08.50	JNRS	Walsall	01.68	1968-69	52	/	0	(G) E-1/E.U23-6/●
			TR	Q.P.R.	06.70	1970-78	344	/	0	E.U21-1
			TR	West Ham U.	02.79	1978-83	223	/	0	
PARKES, Sid	Hartlepool	20.09.19	Hetton U.	Hartlepool U.	08.46	1946-47	6		0	(G)
PARKHILL, James	Belfast	27.07.34	Cliftonville	Exeter	09.63	1963	1		0	(G)
PARKHOUSE, Richard R.	Calne	13.08.14	Calne	Swindon T.	*	1946	1		0	(CH)
PARKIN, Albert G.	Mansfield	11.04.28	JNRS	Derby Co.	05.46	1949	9		0	
PARKIN, Brian	Birkenhead	12.10.65		Oldham Ath.	03.83	1983	5	/	0	(G)
PARKIN, Derek	Newcastle	02.01.48	JNRS	Huddersfield T.	05.65	1964-67	60	1	1	(D) E.U23-5/E.F.LGE.REP.●
			TR	Wolverhampton W.	02.68	1967-81	500	1	6	
			TR	Stoke C	03.82	1981-82	40	/	0	
PARKIN, Herbert B.	Sheffield	10.04.20		Sheffield U.	+	1947-50	35		0	(FB)
			TR	Chesterfield	08.51	1951-52	56		0	
PARKIN, Ken	Wigan	21.04.31		Bradford P.A.	07.54	1954	1		0	
PARKIN, Maurice	Sheffield	08.09.49	APP	Leeds U.	10.67					(FB)
			TR	Shrewsbury T.	07.68	1968	4	2	0	
			TR	Barrow	11.69					
			TR	Bradford P.A.	01.70					
PARKIN, Steve J.	Mansfield	07.11.65	APP	Stoke C.	11.83	1982-83	3	/	0	(D)
PARKIN, Tim J.	Penrith	31.12.57	APP	Blackburn Rov.	03.76	1976-78	13	/	0	(D)
			Malmo	Bristol Rov.	09.81	1981-83	119	1	7	
PARKIN, Tom A.	Gateshead	01.02.56	APP	Ipswich T.	12.73	1977-83	32	10	0	(M)
			L	Grimsby T.	03.76	1975	6	/	0	
			L	Peterborough U.	07.76	1976	3	/	0	
PARKINSON, Alf A.	Camden Town	30.04.22		Q.P.R.	+	1946-50	77		2	(WH)
PARKINSON, Alan	Normanton	05.05.32	JNRS	Bradford P.A.	10.50	1951-54	11		0	(F)
PARKINSON, Alan	Dagenham	12.04.45	Aveley F.C.	Orient	AM	1966	1	/	0	(G)
PARKINSON, Alan A.	Longton	19.07.33	Leyland M.	Southport	08.53	1953-58	106		0	(FB)
PARKINSON, Andy J.	S. Africa	05.05.59	Dynamo U.	Newcastle U.	03.78	1977-78	0	3	0	(F)
			TR	Peterborough U.	08.79	1979	12	1	5	
PARKINSON, Eric	Longridge	14.12.30	JNRS	Preston N.E.	02.51					(HB)
			TR	Southport	06.56	1957	4		0	
PARKINSON, John	Trimdon	02.06.53	Trimdon J.	Hartlepool U.	AM	1971	1	/	0	(WH)
PARKINSON, Keith J.	Preston	28.01.56	APP	Leeds U.	02.73	1975-80	25	6	0	(D)
			L	Hull C.	11.81	1981	0	1	0	
			TR	Doncaster Rov.	N/C	1981	5	/	0	
PARKINSON, Noel	Hull	16.11.59	APP	Ipswich T.	12.76					(M)
			L	Bristol Rov.	11.79	1979	5	/	1	
			L	Brentford	02.80	1979	9	1	0	
			TR	Mansfield T.	07.80	1980-81	66	4	13	
			TR	Scunthorpe U.	08.82	1982-83	39	2	7	
PARKS, Albert				Notts. Co.	+	1946-47	28		4	(IF)
PARKS, Anthony	Hackney	28.01.63	APP	Tottenham H.	09.80	1981-83	19	/	0	(G)
PARKS, John A.	Wath	14.09.43	APP	Sheffield U.	11.60	1963	1	/	0	(F)
			TR	Halifax T.	09.66	1966-67	40	/	14	
PARLANE, Derek J.	Helensburgh	04.04.42	Glasgow Rangers	Leeds U.	03.80	1979-82	45	5	10	(F) S-12/S.U21-1/S.U23-5
			TR	Manchester C.	08.83	1983	40	1	16	
PARMENTER, Terry L.	Romford	21.10.47	APP	Fulham	11.64	1964-68	17	/	1	(W)
			TR	Orient	02.69	1968-70	34	3	3	
			TR	Gillingham	08.71	1971-72	48	1	0	
PARNABY, Tom W.	Sth. Shields	06.01.22	Sunderland(*)	Plymouth Arg.	+					(OL)
			TR	Oldham Ath.	02.47	1947	7		1	
PARNELL, Dennis R.	Farnborough	17.01.40	W.B.A.(AM)	Aldershot	08.58	1958-60	66		11	(W) E.YTH.INT
			TR	Norwich C.	07.61	1961	2		0	
PARNELL, Frank W.	Tranmere	04.11.35		Tranmere Rov.	01.56	1955-56	4		3	(F)

Players Names	Birthplace	Date	Previous Club	League Club	Date Signed	Seasons Played	Apps	Sub	Gls	
PARNELL, Roy	Birkenhead	08.10.43	JNRS	Everton	10.60	1960-63	3		0	(FB)
			TR	Tranmere Rov.	08.64	1964-66	105	/	2	
			TR	Bury	02.67	1966-69	97	/	2	
PARODI, Leslie	Lambeth	01.04.54	Slough T.	Bournemouth	09.73	1973-74	45	4	2	(FB)
PARR, Gordon	Bristol	06.12.38	JNRS	Bristol C.	02.57	1957-71	278	6	5	(WH)
PARR, Henry	Newark	23.10.15	Orient(AM)	Lincoln C.	AM	1946-49	112		14	(WH)E.AMAT.INT
PARR, Jack	Derby	21.11.20	Eaton St P.	Derby Co.	*	1946-52	113		0	(FB)
			TR	Shrewsbury T.	07.53	1953-55	112		0	
PARR, John B.	Weston-Super-Mare	23.11.42		Nottingham F.	11.62	1963	1		0	(G)
PARR, Steve V.	Preston	22.12.26	Farrington V.	Liverpool	05.48	1951-52	20		0	(FB)
			TR	Exeter C.	05.55	1955-56	8		0	
			TR	Rochdale	12.56	1956-57	16		1	
PARRISH, Don A.	Bilston	22.11.44	JNRS	Wrexham	06.63	1962-65	4	/	0	
PARROTT, John F.	Scunthorpe	05.06.34		Scunthorpe U.	12.55	1955	1		0	(F)
PARRY, Anthony J.	Burton	08.09.45	Burton A.	Hartlepool U.	11.65	1965-71	181	6	5	(WH)
			TR	Derby Co.	01.72	1972	4	2	0	
			L	Mansfield T.	01.74	1973	0	1	0	
PARRY, Colin	Stockport	16.02.41	Vernon Park	Stockport Co.	07.62	1962-67	132	1	0	(CH)
			L	Bradford C.	09.65	1965	5	/	0	
			TR	Rochdale	07.68	1968-71	154	2	1	
PARRY, Cyril	Derby	13.12.37	Derby Co.(AM)	Notts.Co.	05.55	1957-58	12		2	(F)E.SCH.INT
PARRY, David E.	Southport	11.02.48	APP	Blackpool	12.65					(F)
			TR	Tranmere Rov.	07.67	1967	3	/	0	
			TR	Halifax T.	09.68	1968	2	/	0	
PARRY, Glyn E.	Derby	02.11.33	JNRS	Derby Co.	04.51	1951	3		0	Brother of Ray/
			TR	Bolton W.	07.55					Jack/Cyril
PARRY, Jack	Derby	29.07.31	JNRS	Derby Co.	07.48	1948-65	478		105	(WH)●
PARRY, Jack B.	Swansea	11.01.24	Clydach	Swansea C.	09.46	1946-50	98		0	(G)W-1
			TR	Ipswich T.	08.51	1951-54	138		0	
PARRY, John E.	Flint	04.09.39	JNRS	Liverpool	09.56					(FB)
			TR	Doncaster Rov.	09.61	1961	14		0	
PARRY, Leslie I.	Wallasey	13.11.53	JNRS	Tranmere Rov.	09.72	1972-83	254	4	4	(D)
PARRY, Oswald	Dowlais	16.08.08	Crystal Palace(*)	Ipswich T.	*	1946-48	62		0	(FB)*Wimbledon
PARRY, Ray A.	Derby	19.01.36	JNRS	Bolton W.	01.53	1951-60	270		68	(IF)E-2/E.U23-4/●
			TR	Blackpool	10.60	1960-64	128		27	E.F.LGE REP./E.YTH.INT.
			TR	Bury	10.64	1964-71	136	10	17	E.SCH.INT.
PARRY, Steve	Wakefield	11.12.56	APP	Barnsley	12.74	1973-74	5	/	0	(G)
PARRY, William	Blaenau	18.02.33		Tottenham H.	09.53					(FB)
			TR	Gillingham	07.55	1955-60	199		4	
PARSLEY, Norman N.	Shildon	28.11.23	Shildon Wks.	Darlington	+	1946-52	161		14	(WH)
PARSONS, Dennis R.	Birmingham	29.05.25	B.S.A. Cycles	Wolverhampton W.	+	1948-51	23		0	(G) d.1980
			Hereford U.	Aston Villa.	09.52	1952-54	36		0	
PARSONS, Derek J.	Hammersmith	24.10.29		Q.P.R.	02.50	1952	2		1	(IF)
PARSONS, Edward J.	Bristol	22.03.28	Frome T.	Bristol Rov.	08.49	1949	5		2	(F)
PARSONS, Eric G.	Worthing	09.11.23	JNRS	West Ham U.	+	1946-50	145		34	(OR) E'B'-2
			TR	Chelsea	12.50	1950-56	158		37	
			TR	Brentford	11.56	1956-60	119		18	
PARSONS, Frank R.	Amersham	29.10.47	JNRS	Crystal Palace	07.65	1966	4	/	0	(G)
			TR	Cardiff C.	08.70	1970-72	17	/	0	
				Fulham	01.74					
			TR	Reading	09.74	1974	1	/	0	
PARSONS, Geoff	Belper	02.08.31	JNRS	Mansfield T.	05.51					(OL)
			TR	Chesterfield	07.52	1952	1		0	
PARSONS, John S.	Cardiff	10.12.50	APP	Cardiff C.	12.68	1970-72	7	8	6	(M) W.SCH.INT.
			TR	Bournemouth	02.73	1972-74	7	1	1	
			TR	Newport Co.	03.75	1974-76	57	3	22	
PARSONS, Lindsay W.	Bristol	20.03.46	APP	Bristol Rov.	04.64	1963-76	354	6	0	(D)
			TR	Torquay U.	08.77	1977-78	56	/	0	
PARSONS, Steve	London	07.10.57	Walton & Hersham	Wimbledon	12.77	1977-79	91	3	19	(F)
			TR	Orient	03.80	1979-80	36	/	6	
PARSONS, Stuart	Staveley	24.05.48	JNRS	Chesterfield	08.67	1966	1	/	0	(WH)
PARTON, Jeff J.	Swansea	24.02.53	APP	Burnley	03.70	1971-73	3	/	0	(G) W.U23-3/W.SCH.INT.
			TR	Northampton T.	07.75	1975-77	25	/	0	
PARTRIDGE, Brendan	Manchester	17.09.41		Stockport Co.	05.61	1960-61	31		6	(F)
			TR	Darlington	07.62	1962	3		0	
PARTRIDGE, Cyril	York	12.10.31		Q.P.R.	08.54					(OL)
				Rotherham U.	08.57	1957	7		2	
PARTRIDGE, Don	Bolton	22.10.25	Farnworth	Rochdale	+	1946-55	101		2	(HB)

Players Names	Birthplace	Date	Previous Club	League Club	Date Signed	Seasons Played	Apps	Sub	Gls	
PARTRIDGE, John T.	Chesterfield	14.09.62	APP	Chesterfield	09.80	1981-82	34	4	0	(D)
			L	Mansfield T.	09.83	1983	1	/	0	
PARTRIDGE, Malcolm	Chesterfield	28.08.50	APP	Mansfield T.	09.68	1967-70	67	2	20	(F)
			TR	Leicester C.	09.70	1970-73	25	11	4	
			L	Charlton Ath.	01.72	1971	1	1	0	
			TR	Grimsby T.	03.75	1974-78	134	4	24	
			TR	Scunthorpe U.	07.79	1979-81	91	6	21	
PARTRIDGE, Maurice	Birmingham	20.02.41	JNRS	Birmingham C.	03.58					(HB)
			TR	Walsall	07.61	1961-62	3		0	
PASCOE, Colin J.	Aberavon	09.04.65	APP	Swansea C.	04.83	1982-83	33	6	3	(F)W.YTH.INT./W.U'21-3
PASHLEY, Robert	Sheffield	09.09.37	Sheffield Wed.(AM)	Sheffield U.	01.56					(HB)
			TR	Rotherham U.	07.58					
			Gainsborough	Scunthorpe U.	05.59	1959	3		1	
			TR	Barrow	06.60	1960	26		2	
PASHLEY, Terry	Chesterfield	11.10.56	APP	Burnley	10.73	1975-77	16	2	0	(FB)E.SCH.INT.
			TR	Blackpool	08.78	1978-82	201	/	7	
			TR	Bury	08.83	1983	40	/	0	
PASSEY, Peter T.J.	Birmingham	13.07.52	APP	Birmingham	08.70					(FB)E.YTH.INT.
			TR	Newport Co.	01.72	1971-75	136	/	2	
PASSMOOR, Tom	Chester-le Street	12.02.37	JNRS	Sunderland	05.54					(CH)
			Sth.Shields	Scunthorpe U.	05.59	1959-63	27		0	
			TR	Carlisle U.	12.63	1963-69	242	2	0	
PASSMORE, Ernie	Moorsley	28.04.22	Portsmouth(+)	Swansea C.	+	1946	6		2	(CF)
			TR	Gateshead	04.47	1946-49	41		26	
PATCHING, Martin	Rotherham	01.11.58	APP	Wolverhampton W.	03.76	1975-79	78	12	10	(IF)E.YTH.INT./
			TR	Watford	12.79	1979-83	24	1	3	E.SCH.INT.
			L	Northampton T.	01.83	1982	6	/	1	
PATE, Alex	Lennox	15.08.44	Renfrew	Watford	03.65	1964-66	14	/	0	(D)
			TR	Mansfield T.	10.67	1967-77	412	1	2	
PATERSON, Alex	Hardgate	18.03.22	Alloa Ath.	New Brighton	07.46	1946-47	65		10	(WH)
			TR	Stockport Co.	03.48	1947-52	160		7	
			TR	Barrow	08.53					
			TR	Halifax T.	09.54					
PATERSON, George D.	Denny	26.09.14	Glasgow Celtic	Brentford	10.46	1946-49	62		0	S-1/S.F.LGE REP.
PATERSON, George L.	Aberdeen	19.12.16		Liverpool	+					
			TR	Swindon T.	10.46	1946-49	53		5	
PATERSON, Steve W.	Elgin	08.04.58	Nairn Co.	Manchester U.	07.75	1976-79	3	3	0	(D)
PATERSON, Tom	Newcastle	30.03.54	Leicester C.(AM)	Middlesbrough	09.74	1974	1	/	0	(F)
			TR	Bournemouth	04.76	1976-77	45	12	10	
			TR	Darlington	06.78	1978	6	1	2	
PATERSON, Tom A.	Lochore	03.04.27	Lochgelly Violet	Leicester C.	03.48	1948-49	17		4	(CF)
			TR	Newcastle U.	06.50	1950-51	2		0	
			TR	Watford	07.52	1952-54	45		7	
PATERSON, William			Morton	Accrington St.	08.49	1949	1		0	
PATERSON, William A.K.	Lochleven	25.02.30	Ransome & M.	Doncaster Rov.	03.50	1950-54	113		0	(CH)S'B'-1
			TR	Newcastle U.	10.54	1954-57	22		1	
PATES, Colin G.	Carshalton	10.08.61	APP	Chelsea	07.79	1979-83	150	/	6	(CH)E.YTH.INT.
PATON, David S.	Saltcoats	13.12.43	St. Mirren	Southampton	07.63	1963-67	13	/	0	(HB)
			TR	Aldershot	11.69	1969-70	31	/	0	
PATON, John A.	Glasgow	02.04.23	Glasgow Celtic	Chelsea	11.46	1946	18		3	(OL)
			Glasgow Celtic	Brentford	09.49	1949-51	90		14	
			TR	Watford	07.52	1952-54	84		16	
PATON, Robert	W. Calder	27.01.36	Hearts	Oxford U.	07.64	1964	2		1	(IF)
PATON, Tom G.	Saltcoats	22.12.18	Swansea C.(*)	Bournemouth	*	1946-47	29		6	
			TR	Watford	01.48	1947-51	141		1	
PATRICK, Alf	York	25.09.21	Cooks F.C.	York C.	09.46	1946-52	234		111	(CF)
PATRICK, Bert	Kelsut	26.04.46	JNRS	Preston N.E.	08.63	1964-69	50	/	1	(FB)
			TR	Barrow	07.71	1971	34	/	1	
PATRICK, Matt	York	13.06.19	Cowdenbeath	York C.	+	1946-53	244		46	(OL)Brother of Alf
PATRICK, Roy	Overseal	04.12.35	JNRS	Derby Co.	02.52	1952-55	49		0	(FB)
			TR	Nottingham F.	05.59	1959-60	57		0	
			TR	Southampton	06.61	1961-62	31		0	
			TR	Exeter C.	03.63	1962-64	50		0	
PATRICK, William C.G.	Lochgelly	12.03.32	Snowdon Col.	Coventry C.	11.54	1955-57	44		6	(FB)
			TR	Gillingham	06.58	1958-59	47		15	
PATTERSON, George T.	Castleton	15.09.34	Silksworth J.	Hull C.	10.52	1954-55	7		1	(HB)
				Darlington	12.56					
			Sth. Shields	York C.	05.57	1957-59	56		4	
			TR	Hartlepool U.	06.60	1960	18		1	
PATTERSON, John G.	Cramlington	06.07.22	Nth. Shields	Blackburn Rov.	+	1948-56	107		0	(G)
PATTERSON, Mark A.	Darwen	24.05.65	APP	Blackburn Rov.	06.83	1983	27	2	7	(F)

Players Names	Birthplace	Date	Previous Club	League Club	Date Signed	Seasons Played	Career Record Apps	Sub	Gls	
PATTERSON, Robert A.	Newcastle	12.03.35	Stanley U.	Gateshead	03.59	1958-59	26		0	(G)
PATTERSON, Ron L.	Gateshead	30.10.29		Middlesbrough	06.49	1951	1		0	(FB)
			TR	Northampton T.	06.52	1952-61	301		5	
PATTISON, Frank M.	Barrhead	23.12.30	Alloa Ath.	Barnsley	12.51	1951-54	30		5	(F)
PATTISON, John M.	Glasgow	19.12.18		Q.P.R.	*	1946-49	73		16	(OL)
			TR	Orient	02.50	1949-50	42		10	
PATTISON, John W.P.	Portsmouth	23.02.25	Portsmouth C.S.	Reading	+	1946	2		0	(RH)
PAUL, David D.	Kirkcaldy	19.02.36	JNRS	Derby Co.	02.53	1953-55	2		0	(G)S.SCH.INT.
PAUL, Ian K.	Wolverhampton	23.01.61	APP	Walsall	08.78	1977-80	68	2	9	(D)
PAUL, Roy	Ton Pentre	18.04.20		Swansea C.	+	1946-49	160		14	(WH)W-33/Uncle of
			TR	Manchester C.	07.50	1950-56	270		9	Alan Curtis●
PAUL, Tom	Grimsby	14.05.33		Grimsby T.	05.55	1955-58	3		0	(F)
PAUL, Tony G.	Isleworth	06.04.61	APP	Crystal Palace	04.78	1980	0	1	0	(M)
PAVITT, William E.	W. Ham	30.06.20	JNRS	Fulham	06.48	1949-52	49		1	(CH)
			TR	Southend U.	05.53	1953-54	80		0	
PAWSON, Anthony H.	Chertsey	22.08.21	Pegasus	Charlton Ath.	AM	1951-52	2		1	(W)E.AMAT.INT./ Kent Cricketer
PAXTON, John W.	Wolverhampton	24.03.28	JNRS	Wolverhampton W.	+					(FB)
			TR	Notts. Co.	05.50	1950	2		0	
PAYE, Mike C.	London	30.07.66	APP	Charlton Ath.	APP	1983	2	/	0	(D)
PAYNE, Albert C.	Liverpool	11.11.23		Tranmere Rov.	08.46	1946-48	13		0	
PAYNE, Brian	Altrincham	04.11.37		Huddersfield T.	10.55					(F)
			TR	Gillingham	07.57	1957-59	36		3	
PAYNE, Clive E.	Burgh	02.03.50	APP	Norwich C.	03.68	1968-73	122	3	0	(FB)
			TR	Bournemouth	12.73	1973-75	101	/	3	
PAYNE, David R.	Croydon	25.04.47	APP	Crystal Palace	11.64	1964-72	281	3	9	(D) E.U23-1
			TR	Orient	08.73	1973-77	88	5	0	
PAYNE, Don	Swansea	18.11.50	JNRS	Swansea C.	12.70	1971	11	/	0	(G)
			TR	Torquay U.	06.72					
			TR	Newport Co.	08.73	1973-74	32	/	0	
PAYNE, Frank E.	Ipswich	18.03.26	Ollerton Col.	Derby Co.	10.47					
			TR	Hull C.	08.48					
			TR	Lincoln C.	08.49	1949	5		0	
PAYNE, George H.	Liverpool	22.08.21		Tranmere Rov.	04.47	1946-60	435		0	(G)
PAYNE, Irving E.H.	Briton Ferry	29.06.21	JNRS	Swansea C.	*	1946-48	53		10	(IF)
			TR	Newport Co.	10.49	1949	12		1	
			TR	Scunthorpe U.	07.50	1950	18		1	
			TR	Northampton T.	08.51	1951	32		5	
PAYNE, Jess	London	07.03.58	JNRS	Leicester C.	07.76					(D)
			TR	Torquay U.	12.77	1977-78	25	/	1	
PAYNE, Jim	W. Bromwich	25.05.36		Walsall	08.56	1955	1		0	
PAYNE, Jim B.	Liverpool	10.03.26	Bootle A.T.C.	Liverpool	+	1948-55	222		38	(OR)E'B'-3
			TR	Everton	04.56	1955-56	5		2	
PAYNE, Joe	Bolsover	17.01.14	Luton T.(*)	Chelsea	*					(CF)*Biggleswade T./
			TR	West Ham U.	12.46	1946	10		6	d.1975
			TR	Millwall	09.47					
PAYTON, Cliff	Brighton	16.10.35	Wisbech	Accrington St.	07.56					(F)
			Tonbridge	Gillingham	03.59	1958-59	24		6	
PEACH, David S.	Bedford	21.01.51	APP	Gillingham	09.69	1979-73	186	1	30	(D) E.U21-3/E.U23-8
			TR	Southampton	01.74	1973-79	221	3	34	
			TR	Swindon T.	03.80	1979-81	52	1	2	
			TR	Orient	03.82	1981-82	47	/	6	
PEACH, Geoff L.	Plymouth	11.10.32	Millwall(AM)	Plymouth Arg.	07.56	1956	1		0	(F)
PEACH, Jack	Barnsley	04.04.23	York C.(+)	Barnsley	+					(IF)
			TR	Hull C.	10.46	1946-47	19		2	
			TR	Q.P.R.	09.47					
PEACHEY, John M	Cambridge	21.07.52	Hillingdon Bor.	York C.	08.73	1973-74	6	2	3	(F)
			TR	Barnsley	11.74	1974-78	116	10	31	
			L	Darlington	12.75	1975	5	1	3	
			TR	Darlington	03.79	1978-79	16	4	6	
			TR	Plymouth Arg.	07.80	1980	1	2	0	
PEACOCK, Alan	Middlesbrough	29.10.37	JNRS	Middlesbrough	11.54	1955-63	218		126	(CF) E-6/E.YTH.INT.●
			TR	Leeds U.	02.64	1963-66	55	/	26	
			TR	Plymouth Arg.	10.67	1967	11	/	1	
PEACOCK, Dennis M.	Lincoln	19.04.53	APP	Nottingham F.	07.72	1972-74	22	/	0	(G)
			L	Walsall	03.73	1972	10	/	0	
			TR	Doncaster Rov.	07.75	1975-79	199	/	0	
			TR	Bolton W.	03.80	1980-81	16	/	0	
			TR	Doncaster Rov.	08.82	1982-83	77	/	0	
PEACOCK, Ernie	Bristol	11.12.24	Syston	Notts.Co.	+					(WH)
			TR	Bristol C.	10.46	1946-58	343		7	

Players Names	Birthplace	Date	Previous Club	League Club	Date Signed	Seasons Played	Apps	Sub	Gls	
PEACOCK, Ernie A.	Renfrew	10.08.42	Falkirk	Workington	01.64	1963	1		0	(WH)
PEACOCK, Frank E.	Bolton	17.05.45	Blackburn Rov.(AM)	Stockport Co.	11.64	1964	5		0	(HB)
PEACOCK, George	Pontypool	10.02.24	Newport Co.(+)	Bristol Rov.	05.46	1946	7		0	(FB)
PEACOCK, John C.	Leeds	27.03.56		Scunthorpe U.	08.74	1974-79	185	5	1	(D)
PEACOCK, Keith	Barnhurst	02.05.45	JNRS	Charlton Ath.	07.62	1962-78	511	21	92	(M)
PEACOCK, Mike R.	Fishburn*	28.09.40	Shildon	Darlington	08.60	1960-62	46		0	(G)
PEACOCK, Robert J.	Rushden	18.12.37	Rushden	Northampton T.	02.57	1957	2		0	(HB)
PEACOCK, Terry	Hull	18.04.35	JNRS	Hull C.	12.52	1955	2		0	(F)
			TR	Q.P.R.	08.56	1956-57	17		4	
PEAKE, Andy M.	Market Harborough	01.01.61	APP	Leicester C.	01.79	1978-83	120	6	12	(M)E.YTH.INT./E.U'21-1
PEAKE, Dudley J.	Swansea	26.10.34	Tower U.	Swansea C.	05.56	1955-57	57		2	(CH)
			TR	Newport Co.	06.58	1958-62	129		0	
PEAKE, Trevor	Nuneaton	10.02.57	Nuneaton Bor.	Lincoln C.	06.79	1979-82	171	/	7	(D)
			TR	Coventry C.	07.83	1983	33	/	3	
PEAPELL, Fred D.	Swindon	16.11.45	APP	Swindon T.	11.63	1964	2		0	(F)
			TR	Exeter C.	07.65	1965	24	1	1	
PEARCE, Alan J.	Middlesbrough	25.10.65	JNRS	York C.	10.83	1983	17	1	5	(F)
PEARCE, Chris L.	Newport	07.08.61	Wolverhampton W.(APP)	Blackburn Rov.	10.79					(G)W.SCH.INT.
			L	Rochdale	08.80	1980	5	/	0	
			TR	Rochdale	08.82	1982	36	/	0	
			TR	Port Vale	06.83	1983	7	/	0	
PEARCE, David	Northolt	07.12.59		Millwall	02.78	1977	1	/	0	(F)
PEARCE, David G.	Scunthorpe	19.12.34		Scunthorpe U.	07.56	1958	2		0	(HB)
PEARCE, Graham	London	08.07.59	Barnet	Brighton & H.A.	01.82	1982-83	31	1	1	(D)
PEARCE, James J.	Tottenham	27.11.47	APP	Tottenham H.	05.65	1968-72	108	33	21	(IF)E.SCH.INT
PEARCE, John	Watford	12.12.50	JNRS	Watford	07.69	1970	0	1	0	(FB)
PEARCE, John A.	Grimsby	29.02.40	JNRS	Grimsby T.	12.58	1958-61	48		0	(HB)
PEARCE, Reg S.	Liverpool	12.01.30	Winsford	Luton T.	11.54	1954-57	75		6	(WH)E.F.LGE REP.
			TR	Sunderland	02.58	1957-60	61		4	
			Cambridge C.	Peterborough U.	08.63	1963	28		2	
PEARCE, Stuart	London	24.04.62	Wealdstone	Coventry C.	10.83	1983	23	/	0	(D)
PEARCE, Trevor	Canterbury	30.05.49	Folkestone	Arsenal	02.70					(F)
			TR	Aldershot	05.71	1971-72	19	6	2	
PEARS, Jeff	Acomb	14.06.20		York C.	09.47	1947-48	3		0	(G)
PEARS, Steve	Brandon	22.01.62	APP	Manchester U.	01.79					(G)
			L	Middlesbrough	11.83	1983	12	/	0	
PEARSON, Andy J.	Newmarket	19.11.60	APP	Luton T.	11.78	1979	1	1	0	(F)
PEARSON, David A.J.	Shotton	13.10.47	APP	Everton	10.65					(FB)W.SCH.INT./
			TR	Southport	08.67	1967-69	91	2	0	W.U'23-1
			TR	Rochdale	09.70	1970	3	/	0	
PEARSON, David T.	Dunfermline	09.11.32	JNRS	Blackburn Rov.	11.49					(CF)
			TR	Ipswich T.	05.54					
			TR	Oldham Ath.	08.56	1956	25		11	
			TR	Rochdale	03.57	1956-57	32		17	
			TR	Crewe Alex.	05.58	1958	9		2	
PEARSON, Don J.	Swansea	14.03.30		Swansea C.	06.50	1952-57	50		1	(WH)
			TR	Aldershot	07.58	1958	31		2	
PEARSON, Ian T.	Leeds	18.09.50	Goole T.	Plymouth Arg.	07.74	1974-75	6	6	0	(F)
			Wycombe W.	Millwall	08.77	1977-78	41	3	9	
			TR	Exeter C.	11.78	1978-80	67	2	10	
			Bideford	Plymouth Arg.	08.83	1983	5	3	1	
PEARSON, Jim F.	Falkirk	24.03.53	St. Johnstone	Everton	07.74	1974-77	76	21	15	(M) S.U23-6
			TR	Newcastle U.	08.78	1978-79	11	/	3	
PEARSON, John	Wigan	18.10.46	APP	Manchester U.	11.63					(F)E.SCH.INT
			TR	York C.	07.65	1965	14	1	4	
PEARSON, John	Ferryhill	08.05.51	Ferryhill Ath.	Hartlepool U.	AM	1968	1		0	(IF)
PEARSON, John A.	Isleworth	23.04.35	JNRS	Brentford	11.52	1955-56	5		0	(F)
			TR	Q.P.R.	06.58	1958-59	21		9	
PEARSON, John G.	Gateshead	10.04.31		Hartlepool U.	04.53	1952	1		0	
PEARSON, John S.	Sheffield	01.09.63	APP	Sheffield Wed	05.81	1980-83	61	35	21	(F)
PEARSON, Mark	Sheffield	28.10.39	JNRS	Manchester U.	05.57	1957-62	68		12	(F)E.YTH.INT./E.SCH.INT
			TR	Sheffield Wed.	10.63	1963-64	39		9	
			TR	Fulham	05.65	1965-67	53	5	7	
			TR	Halifax T.	03.68	1968	2	3	0	
PEARSON, Mike	Bilston	05.12.42	JNRS	Manchester C.	12.59					(F)
			TR	Walsall	05.62	1962	3		1	
PEARSON, Nigel G.	Nottingham	21.08.63	Heanor T.	Shrewsbury T.	11.81	1982-83	65	/	1	(D)
PEARSON, Richard J.	Portsmouth	14.06.31	Gosport Bor.	Portsmouth	05.49	1953	4		1	(F)

Players Names	Birthplace	Date	Previous Club	League Club	Date Signed	Seasons Played	Apps	Sub	Gls	
PEARSON, Stan C.	Salford	11.01.19	Adelphi B.C.	Manchester U.	*	1946-53	292		124	(IF)E-8/E.F.LGE REP.●
			TR	Bury	02.54	1953-57	122		56	
			TR	Chester C.	10.57	1957-58	56		16	
PEARSON, Stuart J.	Hull	21.06.49	JNRS	Hull C.	07.68	1969-73	126	3	44	(F) E-12/E.U23-1
			TR	Manchester U.	05.74	1974-77	138	1	55	
			TR	West Ham U.	08.79	1979-81	29	5	6	
PEARSON, Tommy U.	Edinburgh	06.03.13	Murrayfield Ath.	Newcastle U.	*	1946-47	59		7	(OL)S-2/S.F.LGE REP.
PEARSON, Trevor	Sheffield	04.04.52	Woodseat W.M.C.	Sheffield Wed.	AM	1971	4	/	0	(G)
PEARSON, Walter	Ottershaw	13.11.28	Tooting & M.	Aldershot	AM	1960	1		0	(G)
PEARSON, William G.A.	Clonmel	23.10.21		Grimsby T.	+	1946-48	35		8	(W)
			TR	Chester C.	06.49	1949	12		3	
PEART, Robert C.	Swindon	17.12.26	Burnley(AM)	Swindon T.	04.48	1949-51	12		5	(F)
PEART, Ron	Brandon	08.03.20	Hartlepool U.(*)	Derby Co.	*	1946	1		0	
			TR	York C.	06.48	1948	5		0	
PEAT, James L.	Birmingham	19.05.51	Cadburys	Workington	08.73	1973	0	1	0	(OL)
PEAT, John				Workington	10.53	1953	1		0	
PEAT, W. Arthur	Liverpool	01.09.40	JNRS	Everton	04.59					(WH)
			TR	Southport	07.61	1961-71	401	/	27	
			TR	Crewe Alex.	07.72	1972-73	82	/	5	
PECK, Trevor D.	Llanelli	25.05.38	Llanelli	Cardiff C.	02.58	1959-64	42		0	(HB)
PEDDELTY, J. Maurice	Carlisle	23.5.50	APP	Carlisle U.	12.67	1968-70	9	5	1	(IF)
			TR	Darlington	07.70	1970-71	51	5	1	
PEDDELTY, John	B. Auckland	02.04.55	APP	Ipswich T.	01.73	1972-76	44	/	5	(D) E.YTH.INT
			TR	Plymouth Arg.	10.76	1976-77	30	3	1	
PEDEN, George	Rosavell	12.04.43	Hearts	Lincoln C.	04.67	1966-73	223	2	15	(FB)
PEEBLES, Richard	Glasgow	30.08.23	St. Johnstone	Swindon T.	05.50	1950	13		1	(F)
PEEK, Jim	Hartlepool	07.07.33	Fosten W.	Hartlepool U.	AM	1959	7		0	(RB)
PEEL, Ken	Manchester	08.01.22	Rudholme	Crewe Alex.	09.46	1946	1		0	(IR)
PEEL, Trevor	Huddersfield	25.10.45	Huddersfield T.(AM)	Bradford P.A.	04.67	1966-67	11	/	0	(FB)
PEGG, David	Doncaster	20.09.35	JNRS	Manchester U.	09.52	1952-57	127		24	(OL)E-1/E.U23-3/E'B'-1/ E.SCH.INT./d.1958
PEGG, James K.	Salford	04.01.26	JNRS	Manchester U.	11.47	1947	2		0	(G)
			TR	Torquay U.	08.49	1949	2		0	
			TR	York C.	08.50	1950	1		0	
PEJIC, Mel	Newcastle-under-Lyme	27.04.59	JNRS	Stoke C.	07.77	1979	1	/	0	(D) Brother of Mike
			TR	Hereford U.	06.80	1980-83	129	/	1	
PEJIC, Mike	Chesterton	25.01.50	APP	Stoke C.	01.68	1968-76	274	/	6	(D) E-4/E.U23-8
			TR	Everton	02.77	1976-78	76	/	2	
			TR	Aston Villa	09.79	1979	10	/	0	
PELL, Dennis	Normanton	19.04.29	Methley	Rotherham U.	05.52	1952-55	12		3	(IF)
			TR	Grimsby T.	10.55	1955-56	3		1	
PEMBERTON, James H.A.	Wolverhampton	30.04.16	Brownhills	W.B.A.	*	1946-50	162		0	(FB)
PEMBERTON, James T.	Birmingham	14.11.25	Round Oak F.C. Stourbridge	W.B.A.	+					(OL)
				Luton T.	11.47	1950-56	92		8	
PEMBERTON, Selwyn R.	Cardiff	13.10.28		Newport Co.	03.52	1952	1		0	(RB)
PEMBERY, Gordon D.	Cardiff	10.10.26	Cardiff Nomads	Norwich C.	01.47	1946	1		0	(WH)
				Cardiff C.	08.48	1949	1		0	
			TR	Torquay U.	06.50	1950-51	51		7	
			TR	Charlton Ath.	01.52	1951-55	18		1	
			TR	Swindon T.	06.56	1956	37		2	
PENDER, John P.	Luton	19.11.63	APP	Wolverhampton W.	12.81	1981-83	81	/	2	(D)EI.YTH.INT.
PENDERGAST, William J.	Pen-y-groes	13.4.15	Chester C.(*)	New Brighton	08.46	1946-47	69		26	(F)*Bristol Rov.
PENDLEBURY, Keith D.	Stockport	22.01.34	JNRS	Stockport Co.	03.51	1953	2		0	(HB)
PENDREY, Gary J.S.	Birmingham	09.02.49	APP	Birmingham C.	10.66	1966-78	287	17	4	(D)
			TR	W.B.A.	08.79	1979	18	/	0	
			TR	Torquay U.	08.81	1981	12	/	0	
			TR	Bristol Rov.	12.81	1981	1	/	0	
			TR	Walsall	08.82	1982	8	/	1	
PENFOLD, Mark	Woolwich	10.12.56	APP	Charlton Ath.	04.74	1973-78	65	5	0	(D)
			TR	Orient	07.79	1979	3	/	1	
PENFORD, Dennis H	Reading	31.08.31		Reading	05.52	1953-58	101		4	(FB)
			TR	Torquay U.	06.59	1959-61	77		0	
PENGELLY, Richard N.	Looe	06.10.19	Looe	Plymouth Arg.	05.47	1947-49	9		0	
PENK, Harry	Wigan	19.7.34	Wigan Ath.	Portsmouth	09.55	1955-56	9		2	(W)
			TR	Plymouth Arg.	06.57	1957-59	103		14	
			TR	Southampton	07.60	1960-63	52		6	
PENMAN, Chris	Durham	12.09.45	Preston N.E.(APP)	Darlington	12.62	1962-63	30		0	(G)

Players Names	Birthplace	Date	Previous Club	League Club	Date Signed	Seasons Played	Career Record Apps	Sub	Gls	
PENMAN, Willie	Fife	07.08.39	Glasgow Rgrs.	Newcastle U.	04.63	1962-65	62	1	18	(IF)
			TR	Swindon T.	09.66	1966-69	87	13	17	
			TR	Walsall	08.70	1970-72	118	5	6	
PENN, Don J.	Smethwick	15.03.60	Warley C.B.	Walsall	01.78	1977-82	132	9	54	(F)
PENN, Frank R.	Edmonton	15.04.27	Fulham(AM)	Crystal Palace	AM	1949	1		0	
PENNEY, Steve	Ballymena	16.01.64	Ballymena	Brighton & H.A.	11.83	1983	22	3	1	(W)
PENNICK, Ray	Ferryhill	30.11.46	Willington	York C.	AM	1968	0	1	0	(IF)
PENNINGTON, James	Golborne	26.04.39	JNRS	Manchester C.	08.56	1958	1		0	(OR)
			TR	Crewe Alex.	03.61	1960-62	34		2	
			TR	Grimsby T.	04.63	1962-64	89		8	
			TR	Oldham Ath.	07.65	1965	24	/	0	
			TR	Rochdale	07.66	1966	14	/	0	
PENNINGTON, James	Warrington	13.11.28		Huddersfield T.	08.49					(IL) d.1976
			TR	Southport	07.51	1951-53	55		11	
PENNINGTON, John	Marsden	12.09.28	Marsden	Halifax T.	11.53	1953-54	7		2	(CF)
PENNY, John	Plymouth	19.08.38	JNRS	Plymouth Arg.	11.55	1957-59	8		0	(F)
PENNY, Shaun	Bristol	24.09.57	APP	Bristol C.	09.74					(F)E.SCH.INT.
			TR	Bristol Rov.	08.79	1979-81	57	3	13	
PENNYFATHER, Glen J.	Billericay	11.02.63	APP	Southend U.	02.81	1980-83	96	5	9	(M)
PENROSE, Colin R.	Bradford	01.11.49	Sedbergh Y.C.	Bradford P.A.	AM	1968	6	/	1	(IF)
PENROSE, Norman	Consett	10.03.22	JNRS	Grimsby T.	+	1946-47	9		0	E.SCH.INT.
PENTECOST, Mike	Hounslow	13.04.48	Sutton U.	Fulham	08.66	1966-72	81	6	0	(FB)
PEPLOW, Ron	Willesden	04.05.35	Southall	Brentford	08.55	1955-60	61		5	(IF)
PEPLOW, Steve T.	Liverpool	08.01.49	APP	Liverpool	01.66	1969	2	/	0	(W)
			TR	Swindon T.	05.70	1970-72	37	3	11	
			TR	Nottingham F.	07.73	1973	3	/	0	
			L	Mansfield T.	12.73	1973	4	/	3	
			TR	Tranmere Rov.	01.74	1973-80	232	16	44	
PEPPITT, Sid	Stoke	08.09.19	JNRS	Stoke C.	*	1946-49	80		23	(OR) E.SCH.INT.
			TR	Port Vale	05.50	1950	11		3	
PERCIVAL, John	Patrington	16.05.13	Durham C.	Manchester C.	*	1946	16		0	(WH)
			TR	Bournemouth	05.47	1947-48	52		1	
PERCIVAL, Ron F.J.	London	19.04.24	Tunbridge Wells	Huddersfield T.	02.48	1947-49	8		0	(HB)
			TR	Chesterfield	05.50	1950	6		0	
PERKINS, Eric	W. Bromwich	19.08.34	JNRS	W.B.A.	06.52	1955	2		0	(OL)
			TR	Walsall	06.56	1956-58	67		1	
PERKINS, Glen S.	Little Billing	12.10.60	APP	Northampton T.	10.78	1978	0	1	0	(M)
PERKINS, Steve A.	London	03.10.54	APP	Chelsea	11.71					(D)
			TR	Q.P.R.	06.77	1977	2	/	0	
			TR	Wimbledon	10.78	1978-80	52	/	0	
PERRETT, George R.	Kenilworth	02.05.15	Huddersfield T.(*)	Ipswich T.	*	1946-49	115		4	
PERRIN, Steve	London	13.02.52	Wycombe W.	Crystal Palace	03.76	1976-77	45	3	11	(F)
			TR	Plymouth Arg.	03.78	1977-79	34	1	6	
			TR	Portsmouth	11.79	1979-80	18	10	3	
			Hillingdon Bor.	Northampton T.	N/C	1981-82	22	/	5	
PERRY, Arthur	Doncaster	15.10.32		Hull C.	12.50					(FB)
			TR	Bradford P.A.	07.56	1956-57	60		0	
			TR	Rotherham U.	07.58	1958	2		0	
PERRY, Fred, N.	Cheltenham	30.10.33	Worthing	Liverpool	07.54	1955	1		0	
PERRY, Len	Walsall	14.05.30	JNRS	Walsall	10.50	1953	3		0	(FB)
PERRY, Mick A.	Wimbledon	04.04.64	APP	W.B.A.	02.82	1982-83	14	6	5	(F)
PERRY, Peter	Rotherham	11.04.36		Rotherham U.	07.56	1957-61	97		12	(FB)
			TR	York C.	07.62	1962	23		0	
PERRY, William	S. Africa	10.09.30	Johannesburg	Blackpool	11.49	1949-61	394		120	(OL)E-3/E'B'-2/E.F.LGE
			TR	Southport	06.62	1962	26		0	REP.
PERRYMAN, Gerry	W. Haddon	03.10.47	JNRS	Northampton T.	09.66	1966	1	/	0	(FB)
			TR	Colchester U.	07.68	1968	1	1	0	
PERRYMAN, Steve J.	Ealing	21.12.51	APP	Tottenham H.	01.69	1969-83	589	1	29	(M) E-1/E.U23-17/E.YTH INT./E.SCH.INT.
PETCHEY, George W.	London	24.06.31	JNRS	West Ham U.	08.48	1952	2		0	(WH)
			TR	Q.P.R.	07.53	1953-59	255		22	
			TR	Crystal Palace	06.60	1960-63	143		12	
PETERS, Alan G.	Newport	14.10.58	Aston Villa (APP)	Hereford U.	06.76	1976	1	/	0	(M)
			TR	Newport Co.	08.77					
PETERS, Gary D.	Carshalton	03.08.54	Guildford C.	Reading	05.75	1975-78	150	6	7	(D)
			TR	Fulham	08.79	1979-81	57	7	2	
			TR	Wimbledon	07.82	1982-83	83	/	7	
PETERS, Jeff	Wideopen	07.03.61	APP	Middlesbrough	03.79	1979	6	/	0	(D)

Players Names	Birthplace	Date	Previous Club	League Club	Date Signed	Seasons Played	Apps	Sub	Gls	
PETERS, Martin S.	Plaistow	08.11.43	APP	West Ham U.	11.60	1961-69	302	/	80	(M) E-67/E.U23-5/●
			TR	Tottenham H.	03.70	1969-74	189	/	46	E.F.LGE.REP./E.YTH.INT./
			TR	Norwich C.	03.75	1974-79	206	1	44	E.SCH.INT.
			TR	Sheffield U.	08.80	1980	23	1	4	
PETERS, Roger D.	Cheltenham	05.03.44	APP	Bristol C.	03.61	1960-67	158	/	26	(F)E.YTH.INT.
			TR	Bournemouth	06.68	1968-69	35	2	3	
PETERS, Tom J.	Droylsden	22.10.20		Doncaster Rov.	+					
			TR	Bury	12.46	1947	10		1	
			TR	Leeds U.	08.48					
			TR	Mansfield T.	03.49	1948	6		2	
			TR	Accrington St.	10.49	1949	4		2	
			TR	Brighton & H.A.	01.50					
PETERSON, Brian	S. Africa	20.10.36	Berea Pk.	Blackpool	10.56	1956-61	103		16	(IF)
PETERSON, Frank	London	03.04.51	APP	Millwall	02.69	1968-69	3	1	0	(F)
PETERSON, Paul W.	Luton	22.12.49	APP	Leeds U.	12.66	1969	3	/	0	(FB)
			TR	Swindon T.	06.71	1971	1	/	0	
PETHARD, Fred J.	Glasgow	07.10.50	Glasgow Celtic	Cardiff C.	08.69	1971-78	161	10	0	(D) S.SCH.INT.
			TR	Torquay U.	08.79	1979-81	104	1	0	
PETHERBRIDGE, George	Devonport	19.05.27	JNRS	Bristol Rov.	*	1946-61	457		86	(W)●
PETROVIC, Vladimir	Yugoslavia	01.07.55	Red Star Belgrade	Arsenal	12.82	1982	10	3	2	(M)
PETTIT, Ray J.	Hull	11.12.46	APP	Hull C.	12.64	1966-71	78	1	0	(CH)
			TR	Barnsley	09.72	1972-73	49	2	1	
PETTS, John	Edmonton	02.10.38	JNRS	Arsenal	05.56	1957-61	32		0	(WH)E.YTH.INT.
			TR	Reading	10.62	1962-64	34		0	
			TR	Bristol Rov.	07.65	1965-69	88	4	5	
PETTS, Paul A.	Hackney	27.09.61	APP	Bristol Rov.	06.79	1978-79	12	1	0	(M) E.YTH.INT.
			TR	Shrewsbury T.	08.80	1980-83	108	9	14	Son of John
PEVERELL, John	W. Gilling	17.09.41	Ferryhill Ath.	Darlington	09.59	1961-71	418	1	13	(RB)
PEYTON, Gerry	Birmingham	20.05.56	Atherstone	Burnley	05.75	1975-76	30	/	0	(G) EI-20
			TR	Fulham	12.76	1976-83	277	/	0	
			L	Southend U.	09.83	1983	10	/	0	
PEYTON, Noel	Dublin	04.12.35	Shamrock Rov.	Leeds U.	01.58	1957-62	105		16	(IF)EI-6/EI'B'-1
			TR	York C.	07.63	1963-64	37		4	
PEYTON, Robert A.	Birmingham	01.05.54	Chelmsley T.	Port Vale	07.72	1971	1	/	0	(HB)
PHELAN, Albert	Sheffield	27.04.45		Chesterfield	07.64	1974-74	384	4	14	(D)
			TR	Halifax T.	10.74	1974-76	118	4	4	
PHELAN, Mike C.	Nelson	24.09.62	APP	Burnley	07.80	1980-83	123	2	8	(D)
PHILIP, Ian	Dundee	14.02.51	Dundee	Crystal Palace	09.72	1972-73	35	/	1	(FB)S.U23-1/S.F.LGE REP./S.SCH.INT.
PHILLIBEN, John	Stirling	14.03.64	Stirling A.	Doncaster Rov.	03.84	1983	12	/	0	(D)
PHILLIPS, Ben	Hazel Grove	09.06.60	Macclesfield	Bury	09.80	1980	14	/	0	(D)
PHILLIPS, Brendan	W. Indies	16.07.54	Leicester C.(APP)	Peterborough U.	10.73	1973	1	/	0	(M)
			Boston U.	Mansfield T.	08.80	1980	17	/	0	
PHILLIPS, Brian J.	Manchester	09.11.31		Bury	06.53					(CH)
			Altrincham	Middlesbrough	06.54	1954-59	121		2	
			TR	Mansfield T.	06.60	1960-62	101		3	
PHILLIPS, Cornelius	Liverpool	10.05.38	JNRS	Liverpool	06.55					(F)
			TR	Southport	07.57	1957	19		6	
PHILLIPS, David O.	W. Germany	29.07.63	APP	Plymouth Arg.	08.81	1981-83	65	8	15	(M)W-2/W.U'21-3
PHILLIPS, Don	Llanelli	03.03.33	Llanelli	Swansea C.	12.56	1956-57	3		0	(F)
PHILLIPS, Edward J.	Leiston	21.08.33	Leiston	Ipswich T.	12.53	1953-63	269		160	(IF)●
			TR	Orient	03.64	1963-64	36		17	
			TR	Luton T.	02.65	1964	12		8	
			TR	Colchester U.	09.65	1965	32	/	13	
PHILLIPS, Ernie	Nth. Shields	29.11.23		Manchester C.	06.47	1948-51	80		0	(FB)
			TR	Hull C.	11.51.	1951-53	42		0	
			TR	York C.	06.54	1954-57	164		1	
PHILLIPS, Gordon	Hayes	17.01.46	Hayes	Brentford	11.63	1964-72	206	/	0	(G)
PHILLIPS, Ian A.	Edinburgh	23.04.59	Ipswich T.(APP)	Mansfield T.	08.77	1977-78	18	5	0	(D)
			TR	Peterborough U.	08.79	1979-81	97	/	3	
			TR	Northampton T.	08.82	1982	42	/	1	
			TR	Colchester U.	09.83	1983	43	/	5	
PHILLIPS, Jim N.	Bolton	08.02.66	APP	Bolton W.	08.83	1983	0	1	0	
PHILLIPS, John E.	Portsmouth	04.03.37	JNRS	Portsmouth	05.55	1955-59	76		0	(WH)
PHILLIPS, John T.S.	Shrewsbury	07.07.51	APP	Shrewsbury T.	11.68	1968-69	51	/	0	(G)W-4/W.U23-4
			TR	Aston Villa	10.69	1969	15	/	0	
			TR	Chelsea	08.70	1970-78	125	/	0	
			L	Crewe Alex.	08.79	1979	6	/	0	
			TR	Brighton & H.A.	03.80	1980	1	/	0	
			TR	Charlton Ath.	07.81	1981	2	/	0	
			TR	Crystal Palace	01.83					

Players Names	Birthplace	Date	Previous Club	League Club	Date Signed	Seasons Played	Apps	Sub	Gls	
PHILLIPS, Joseph R.W.	Cardiff	08.07.23	Cardiff Corries	Cardiff C.	+	1946	2		0	(FB)
PHILLIPS, Leighton	Briton Ferry	25.09.49	APP	Cardiff C.	04.67	1967-74	169	11	11	(M) W-58/W.U23-4/
			TR	Aston Villa	09.74	1974-78	134	6	4	W.U.21-1/W.SCH.INT.
			TR	Swansea C.	11.78	1978-80	97	/	0	
			TR	Charlton Ath.	08.81	1981-82	45	/	1	
			TR	Exeter C.	N/C	1982	10	/	0	
PHILLIPS, Les M.	Lambeth	07.01.63	APP	Birmingham C.	08.80	1981-83	36	8	3	(M)
			TR	Oxford U.	03.84	1983	2	4	0	
PHILLIPS, Len H.	Hackney	11.09.22	Hillside Y.C.	Portsmouth	+	1946-54	245		48	(WH)E-3/E.F.LGE REP.
PHILLIPS, Lionel R.	Much Dewchurch	13.12.29	Yeovil T.	Portsmouth	02.53	1953	3		1	(F)
PHILLIPS, Mike S.	Cumnock	18.01.33	Cumnock J.	Grimsby T.	01.55	1954	6		1	(CF)
PHILLIPS, Nick	W. Ham	19.11.60	APP	Coventry C.	08.78	1979	4	1	0	(M)
PHILLIPS, Peter S.	Wellington	19.06.46	Bishops Stortford	Luton T.	06.69	1969	2	3	0	(CF)E.AMAT.INT.
			L	Torquay U.	01.71	1970	2	/	1	
			TR	Cambridge U.	03.71	1970-72	40	13	13	
PHILLIPS, Ralph	Durham	09.08.33		Middlesbrough	05.54					(FB)
			TR	Northampton T.	08.58	1958-60	83		1	
			TR	Darlington	06.61	1961-62	29		2	
PHILLIPS, Reg R.	Llanelli	09.03.21	Shrewsbury	Crewe Alex.	05.49	1949-51	64		35	(CF)
PHILLIPS, Ron D.	Worsley	30.03.47	JNRS	Bolton W.	10.65	1966-74	135	10	17	(M)
			L	Chesterfield	01.75	1974	5	/	0	
			TR	Bury	06.75	1975-76	68	4	5	
			TR	Chester C.	09.77	1977-80	128	2	21	
PHILLIPS, Russell, G.T.	Exeter	22.06.16	Millwall(+)	Torquay U.	+	1946	30		3	
PHILLIPS, Steve E.	Edmonton	04.08.54	APP	Birmingham C.	08.71	1971-75	15	5	1	(F) E.YTH.INT.
			L	Torquay U.	12.74	1974	6	/	0	
			TR	Northampton T.	10.75	1975-76	50	1	8	
			TR	Brentford	02.77	1976-79	156	1	65	
			TR	Northampton T.	08.80	1980-81	75	/	29	
			TR	Southend U.	03.82	1981-83	102	/	43	
PHILLIPS, Stuart G.	Halifax	30.12.61	JNRS	Hereford U.	06.78	1977-83	152	6	46	(F)
PHILLIPS, Trevor	Rotherham	18.09.52	APP	Rotherham U.	03.70	1969-78	289	33	81	(F) E.YTH.INT.
			TR	Hull C.	06.79	1979	22	/	3	
			TR	Chester C.	03.80	1979-81	57	7	11	
			TR	Stockport Co.	03.82	1981-82	49	2	13	
			TR	Chester C.	N/C	1983	9	1	2	
PHILLIPSON, William E.	Barrow	04.04.17	Holker C.O.B.	Barrow	*	1946-47	14		0	(G) d.1974
PHILLIPSON-MASTERS, Forbes E.	Bournemouth	14.11.55	APP	Southampton	06.74	1976-77	9	/	0	(D)
			L	Exeter C.	09.76	1976	6	/	0	
			L	Bournemouth	09.77	1977	7	/	2	
			L	Luton T.	03.79	1978	10	/	0	
			TR	Plymouth Arg.	08.79	1979-82	119	/	0	
			TR	Bristol C.	11.82	1982-83	69	/	3	
PHILLISKIRK, Anthony	Sunderland	10.02.65	JNRS	Sheffield U.	08.83	1983	20	1	8	(F)
PHILPOTT, Alan	Stoke	08.11.42	JNRS	Stoke C.	11.59	1960-67	41	4	1	(HB)
			TR	Oldham Ath.	11.67	1967-68	28	3	1	
PHILPOTTS, David R.	Bromborough	31.03.54	APP	Coventry C.	10.71	1973	3	/	0	(D)
			L	Southport	01.74	1973	8	/	0	
			TR	Tranmere Rov.	09.74	1974-77	174	1	5	
			TR	Tranmere Rov.	10.83	1983	34	/	6	
PHIPPS, Harold J.	Dartford	15.01.16	Middx. Reg't.	Charlton Ath.	+	1946-50	185		2	(CH)
			TR	Watford	06.52	1952-53	47		0	
PHOENIX, Eric W.	Manchester	20.01.32	Hastings U.	Gillingham	07.54	1954-57	17		2	(IF) Brother of
			TR	Exeter C.	07.56	1956	5		0	Ron J.
PHOENIX, Peter P.	Manchester	31.12.36		Oldham Ath.	02.58	1957-62	161		26	(OL)
			TR	Rochdale	10.62	1962-63	36		4	
			TR	Exeter C.	10.63	1963	15		1	
			TR	Southport	01.64	1963	10		0	
			TR	Stockport Co.	07.64	1964	19		1	
PHOENIX, Ron J.	Stretford	30.06.29	Humphrey Pk.	Manchester C.	03.50	1951-58	52		2	(WH)
			TR	Rochdale	02.60	1960-61	64		0	
PHOENIX, W. Brian	Tyldesley	10.12.37	Boothstown	Southport	12.57	1957-58	15		3	(F)
PHYTHIAN, Ernie	Farnworth	16.07.42	JNRS	Bolton W.	07.59	1959-61	10		2	(CF)E.YTH.INT.
			TR	Wrexham	03.62	1961-64	134		44	
			TR	Hartlepool U.	06.65	1965-67	124	/	50	
PICKARD, Len J.	Barnstaple	29.11.24	Barnstaple	Bristol Rov.	01.51	1951	4		1	(CF)
			TR	Bristol C.	05.53					
			TR	Bradford P.A.	10.53	1953-55	77		33	
PICKERING, Fred	Blackburn	19.01.41	JNRS	Blackburn Rov.	01.58	1959-63	123		59	(CF)E-3/E.U23-3●
			TR	Everton	03.64	1963-66	97	/	56	E.F.LGE REP
			TR	Birmingham C.	08.67	1967-68	74	/	27	
			TR	Blackpool	06.69	1969-70	48	1	24	
			TR	Blackburn Rov.	03.71	1970	11	/	2	
			TR	Brighton & H.A.	03.72					

Players Names	Birthplace	Date	Previous Club	League Club	Date Signed	Seasons Played	Career Record Apps Sub Gls		
PICKERING, John	High Green	18.12.08	JNRS	Sheffield U.	*	1946-47	2		1	(IF)E-I/E.F.LGE REP.
PICKERING, John	Stockton	07.11.44	Stockton	Newcastle U.	07.63					(HB)
			TR	Halifax T.	09.65	1965-73	364	3	5
			TR	Barnsley	07.74	1974	42	1	2
PICKERING, Mike J.	Huddersfield	29.9.56		Barnsley	10.74	1974-76	100	/	1	(D)
			TR	Southampton	06.77	1977-78	44	/	0
			TR	Sheffield Wed.	10.78	1978-82	106	4	1
			L	Norwich C.	09.83	1983	0	1	0
			L	Bradford C.	11.83	1983	4	/	0
			L	Barnsley	12.83	1983	3	/	0
			TR	Rotherham U.	01.84	1983	24	/	0
PICKERING, Nick	Newcastle	04.08.63	APP	Sunderland	08.81	1981-83	118	/	11	(D) E.YTH.INT./E-1/E.U'21-7
PICKERING, Peter B.	York	24.03.26	Earswick	York C.	+	1946-47	49		0	(G) Northants. cricketer
			TR	Chelsea	05.48	1948-50	27		0
			Kettering	Northampton T.	07.55	1955-57	86		0
PICKERING, William H.	Sheffield	10.02.19	JNRS	Sheffield Wed.	*					(FB) d.1983
			TR	Oldham Ath.	07.48	1948-49	78		0
PICKETT, Reg A.	India	06.01.27	Weymouth	Portsmouth	03.49	1949-56	123		2	(IF)
			TR	Ipswich T.	07.57	1957-62	140		3
PICKRELL, Anthony D.	Neath	03.11.42	JNRS	Cardiff C.	09.60	1960-61	18		4	(F)
PICKUP, John A.	Wakefield	03.12.31	Frickley Col.	Bradford P.A.	09.55	1955	2		0	(IL)
PICKUP, Reg J.	Stoke	06.09.29	JNRS	Stoke C.	08.49	1949	1		0	(WH)
PICKWICK, Don H.	Rhondda	07.02.25	Cardiff C.(AM)	Norwich C.	08.47	1947-55	224		9	(WH)
PIDCOCK, Fred C.	Canada	29.06.33	Moor Green	Walsall	AM	1953	1		0	(G)
PIEKALNIETIS, John	Penrith	23.09.51	JNRS	Nottingham F.	03.69					(HB)E.YTH.INT.
			TR	Southend U.	04.71	1970	1	/	0
PIERCE, Barry J.	Liverpool	13.08.34	Truro C.	Crystal Palace	08.55	1955-58	85		23	(F)
			TR	Millwall	05.59	1959-60	47		17
			TR	York C.	07.61	1961	12		5
			TR	Exeter C.	07.62	1962	28		5
PIERCE, Gary	Bury	02.03.51	Mossley	Huddersfield T.	02.71	1971-72	23	/	0	(G)
			TR	Wolverhampton W.	08.73	1973-78	98	/	0
			TR	Barnsley	07.79	1979-82	81	/	0
			TR	Blackpool	08.83	1983	27	/	0
PIKE, Geoff A.	Clapton	28.09.56	APP	West Ham U.	09.74	1975-83	225	15	30	(M)
PIKE, Martin R.	South Shields	21.10.64	APP	W.B.A.	10.82					(M)
			TR	Peterborough U.	08.83	1983	28	7	2
PILGRIM, Alan J.	Billingborough	20.07.47	Billingborough	Lincoln C.	07.66	1965-71	20	3	1	(HB)
PILKINGTON, Brian	Leyland	12.02.33	Leyland M.	Burnley	04.51	1952-60	300		65	(OL)E-1/E'B'-2/E.F.LGE REP.
			TR	Bolton W.	03.61	1960-63	82		10
			TR	Bury	02.64	1963-64	19		0
			TR	Barrow	02.65	1964-66	86	1	9
PILKINGTON, George	Hemsworth	03.06.26	Gt. Houghton	Rotherham U.	11.48	1949	1		0	(IF)
			TR	Chester C.	07.52	1952	16		0
			TR	Stockport Co.	05.53	1953-55	77		4
PILKINGTON, Leslie	Darwen	23.06.25	Darwen Corries	Arsenal	03.48					(IF)
			TR	Watford	03.50	1949-50	5		0
PILLING, John J.	Peasley Cross	04.06.13	Liverpool(+)	Southport	+	1946	9		0	(LH)*Sth.Liverpool
PILLING, Stuart	Sheffield	26.03.51	Preston N.E.(AM)	Hull C.	07.70					(D)
			TR	Scunthorpe U.	05.73	1973-81	246	16	26
PILLING, Vince J.	Bolton	08.01.32	Lomax's	Bolton W.	10.52	1952-54	7		0	(F)
			TR	Bradford P.A.	08.55	1955	9		1
PIMBLETT, Frank	Liverpool	12.03.57	APP	Aston Villa	10.74	1974-75	9	/	0	(F) E.SCH.INT.
			L	Newport Co.	03.76	1975	7	/	0
			TR	Stockport Co.	07.76	1976	0	1	0
				Hartlepool U.	03.80	1979	3	/	0
PIMBLEY, Doug W.	Kings Norton	19.06.17	Stourbridge	Birmingham C.	07.46	1946	2		0	(WH)
			TR	Notts. Co.	03.48	1947-49	23		2
PIMLOTT, John G.	Radcliffe	21.01.39		Bury	12.57					(F)
			TR	Chester C.	08.59	1959-60	41		11
PINCHBECK, Cliff B.	Cleethorpes	20.01.25	Scunthorpe U.	Everton	12.47	1947	3		0	(CF)
			TR	Brighton & H.A.	08.49	1949	14		5
			TR	Port Vale	11.49	1949-51	69		34
			TR	Northampton T.	12.51	1951	3		3
PINCOTT, Fred	Bristol	19.03.13	Gravesend	Newport Co.	07.47	1947	14		0	(CH)*Wolverhampton W./ Bournemouth
PINDER, Jack J.	Acomb	01.12.12	JNRS	York C.	*	1946-47	50		4	E.SCH.INT.
PINKNEY, Alan J.	Battersea	01.01.47	St. Lukes College	Exeter C.	AM	1967-68	7	/	1	(IF)
			TR	Crystal Palace	07.69	1969-73	19	5	0
			L	Fulham	01.73	1972	11	1	0

Players Names	Birthplace	Date	Previous Club	League Club	Date Signed	Seasons Played	Career Record Apps	Sub	Gls	
PINNER, Mike J.	Boston	16.02.34		Aston Villa	AM	1954-56	4		0	(G)E.AMAT.INT.
				Sheffield Wed.	AM	1957-58	7		0	
				Q.P.R.	AM	1959	19		0	
				Manchester U.	AM	1960	4		0	
				Chelsea	AM	1961	1		0	
				Swansea C.	AM	1961	1		0	
			Pegasus	Orient	10.63	1962-64	77		0	
PIPER, Gilbert H.	Northfleet	21.06.21	Tottenham H.(+)	Gillingham	N/L	1950	4		0	(HB)
PIPER, Norman J.	Nth. Tawton	08.01.48	APP	Plymouth Arg.	02.65	1964-69	215	/	35	(M) E.U23-4/E.YTH.INT.
			TR	Portsmouth	05.70	1970-77	310	4	51	
PIPER, Ron D.	Lowestoft	16.03.43	Arsenal(AM)	Tottenham H.	10.60	1962	1		0	(F)
PIPER, Steve	Brighton	02.11.53	JNRS	Brighton & H.A.	09.72	1972-77	160	2	9	(D)
			TR	Portsmouth	02.78	1977-78	27	2	2	
PIRIE, Fred W.	Perth	19.01.34	Coupar Angus	Accrington St.	01.54	1954-59	17		0	(FB)
PITT, Jack H.	Wilklenhall	20.05.20	W.B.A.(AM)	Bristol Rov.	05.46	1946-57	467		17	(W.H.)●
PITT, Richie E.	Ryhope	22.10.51	JNRS	Sunderland	11.68	1968-73	125	/	7	(CH)E.SCH.INT.
PITT, Steve W.	Willesden	01.08.48	APP	Tottenham H.	08.65	1965	1	/	0	(F)
			TR	Colchester U.	06.69	1969	4	2	0	
PLACE, Charlie A.	Ilkeston	26.11.37	JNRS	Derby Co.	11.54	1955	2		0	(OL)
PLANT, Ken G.	Coventry	15.08.25	Nuneaton	Bury	02.50	1949-53	119		55	(CF)
			TR	Colchester U.	01.54	1953-58	190		82	
PLATNAUER, Nick R.	Leicester	10.06.61	Bedford T.	Bristol Rov.	08.82	1982	21	3	7	(F)
			TR	Coventry C.	08.83	1983	29	5	6	
PLATT, Edward H.	Romford	26.03.21	Colchester U.	Arsenal	*	1946-52	53		0	(G)
			TR	Portsmouth	09.53	1953-54	30		0	
			TR	Aldershot	08.55	1955	16		0	
PLATT, James A.	Ballymoney	26.01.52	Ballymena	Middlesbrough	05.70	1971-82	401	/	0	(G) NI-22/NI.AMAT.INT.
			L	Hartlepool U.	08.78	1978	13	/	0	
			L	Cardiff C.	11.78	1978	4	/	0	
PLATT, John R.	Ashton	22.08.54	Ashton U.	Oldham Ath.	03.74	1975-80	109	/	0	(G)
			TR	Bury	08.81	1981-82	20	/	0	
			TR	Bolton W.	07.83	1983	10	/	0	
PLATT, John S.	Bermondsey	29.06.42	Brookhill B.C.	Charlton Ath.	06.61	1961	2		0	(OR)
PLATTS, Lawrie	Worksop	31.10.21	JNRS	Nottingham F.	+	1946-49	7		0	(G)
			TR	Chesterfield	07.51	1951	11		0	
			TR	Stockport Co.	02.53	1952-53	28		0	
PLATTS, Peter	Dinnington	14.01.28		Scunthorpe U.	AM	1951	2		2	(CF)
PLAYER, Roy I.	Portsmouth	10.05.28	Portsmouth(AM)	Grimsby T.	12.53	1952-58	57		0	(WH)
			TR	Oldham Ath.	06.59	1959	2		0	
PLEAT, David J.	Nottingham	15.01.45	JNRS	Nottingham F.	03.62	1961-63	6		1	(W)E.SCH.INT./
			TR	Luton T.	08.64	1964-66	67	3	9	E.YTH.INT.
			TR	Shrewsbury T.	07.67	1967	10	2	1	
			TR	Exeter C.	07.68	1968-69	66	2	14	
			TR	Peterborough U.	07.70	1970	28	/	2	
PLENDERLEITH, Jackie B.	Belshill	06.10.37	Hibernian	Manchester C.	07.60	1960-62	41		0	(CH)S-1/S.U23-5/ S.SCH.INT.
PLLU, Charles	Saltcoats	28.02.34	Scarborough	Sheffield Wed.	12.56	1956-57	19		0	(G)
PLUCKROSE, Alan	Southwater	03.07.63	Falmouth	Torquay U.	N/C	1982	3	/	0	(D)
PLUMB, Richard K.	Swindon	24.09.46	APP	Swindon T.	12.63					(CF)
			TR	Bristol Rov.	04.65	1965-68	40	/	9	
			Yeovil T.	Charlton Ath.	09.70	1970-71	32	11	10	
			TR	Exeter C.	08.72	1972-73	59	/	17	
PLUME, Richard W.	Tottenham	10.06.49	APP	Millwall	03.67	1966-68	12	3	0	(HB)
			TR	Orient	05.69	1969-70	12	5	1	
PLUMLEY, Gary E.	Birmingham	24.03.56	APP	Leicester C.	12.74					(G)
			TR	Newport Co.	06.76	1976-80	182	/	0	
			TR	Hereford U.	N/C	1982	13	/	0	
			TR	Newport Co.	12.82	1982	2	/	0	
			TR	Cardiff C.	08.83	1983	1	/	0	
PLUMMER, Calvin A.	Nottingham	14.02.63	APP	Nottingham F.	02.81	1981-82	10	2	2	(M)
			TR	Chesterfield	12.82	1982	28	/	7	
			TR	Derby Co.	08.83	1983	23	4	3	
			TR	Barnsley	03.84	1983	1	1	1	
PLUMMER, Norman L.	Leicester	12.01.24	Leicester A.T.C.	Leicester C.	+	1947-51	66		1	(CH)
			TR	Mansfield T.	07.52	1952-55	166		5	
PLUNKETT, Sid E.	Norwich	02.10.20	Wolverhampton W.(*)	Norwich C.	*	1946	28		7	(W)*Norwich C.
PODD, Cyril (Cec)	St. Kitts	07.08.52		Bradford C.	08.70	1970-83	494	8	2	(D)
PODMORE, Edgar V.	Fenton	21.04.18		Crewe Alex.	08.47	1947	1		0	(G)+Stoke C.
POINTER, Keith C.	Norwich	16.02.51		West Ham U.	06.68					(F)
			TR	Cambridge U.	03.72	1971-72	6	2	2	

Players Names	Birthplace	Date	Previous Club	League Club	Date Signed	Seasons Played	Career Record Apps	Sub	Gls	
POINTER, Ray	Cramlington	10.10.36	Dudley Welf	Burnley	08.57	1957-64	222		118	(CF)E-3/E.U23-5/●
			TR	Bury	08.65	1965	19	/	17	E.F.LGE REP.
			TR	Coventry C.	12.65	1965-66	26	/	13	
			TR	Portsmouth	01.67	1966-72	149	4	31	
POINTER, Reg E.	Norwich	28.01.35	C.N.S.O.B.U.	Norwich C.	AM	1956	11		0	(CH)
POINTON, Neil G.	Church Warsop	28.11.64	APP	Scunthorpe U.	08.82	1981-83	96	/	2	(D)
POINTON, Ray E.	Birkenhead	06.11.47	APP	Tranmere Rov.	11.65	1967-70	41	5	0	(HB)
POINTON, William J.	Hanley	25.11.20		Port Vale	+	1946-48	74		26	
			TR	Q.P.R.	01.49	1948-49	26		6	
			TR	Brentford	02.50	1949-50	16		2	
POLAND, George	Penarth	21.9.13	Liverpool(+)	Cardiff C.	08.46	1946	2		0	(G)*Cardiff C./ Wrexham/W-2
POLE, Harry E.	Kessingland	25.03.22		Ispwich T.	10.46	1946-50	39		12	(F)
			TR	Orient	07.51	1951-52	12		0	
POLK, Stan	Liverpool	28.10.21	Sth. Liverpool	Liverpool	+	1946-47	13		0	(WH)
			TR	Port Vale	07.48	1948-51	159		14	
POLLARD, Brian	York	22.05.54	JNRS	York C.	03.72	1971-77	151	12	34	(F) E.YTH.INT.
			TR	Watford	11.77	1977-79	68	3	8	
			TR	Mansfield T.	01.80	1979-80	45	9	5	
			TR	Blackpool	08.81	1981	0	1	0	
			TR	York C.	09.81	1981-83	98	4	26	
POLLARD, Gary	Staveley	30.12.59	JNRS	Chesterfield	07.77	1977-82	83	4	1	(D)
			TR	Port Vale	06.83	1983	17	1	0	
POLLARD, James R.	Liverpool	04.06.20	Tredomen	Newport Co.	05.46					(OL)
				Tranmere Rov.	11.47	1947-48	24		1	
POLLITT, Jack	Farnworth	29.03.37	JNRS	Bolton W.	12.54					(F)
			TR	Bury	08.58	1958	4		0	
			TR	Accrington St.	03.60	1959	3		1	
			TR	Rochdale	08.60	1960	6		1	
POLLOCK, Maitland	Dumfries	31.10.52	Nottingham F.(APP)	Walsall	07.73	1973	1	1	0	(F) S.SCH.INT.
			Burton A.	Luton T.	03.74	1975	3	3	0	
			TR	Portsmouth	07.76	1976-77	50	4	10	
POLLOCK, Stewart	Bellshill	25.09.33	Motherwell	Gillingham	07.56	1956	10		0	
POLLOCK, William			Manchester U.(AM)	Oldham Ath.	07.47	1947	4		0	
POLYCARPOU, Andy	Islington	15.08.58		Southend U.	09.76	1976-80	43	20	10	(F)
			TR	Cambridge U.	08.81	1981	1	4	0	
			TR	Cardiff C.	04.82	1981	7	/	0	
POMPHREY, Edric A.	Stretford	31.05.16	Notts.Co.(+)	Rochdale	+	1946	9		0	(FB) Hyde U.
PONTE, Raimondo	Switzerland	04.04.54	Grasshoppers	Nottingham F.	08.80	1980	17	4	3	(F) SWISS. INT.
PONTIN, Keith	Pontyclun	14.06.56	APP	Cardiff C.	05.74	1976-82	193	/	5	(D)W-2/W.U21-1
POOK, David C.	Plymouth	16.01.55	APP	Torquay U.	01.73	1971-72	13	3	1	(W)
POOLE, Andy J.	Chesterfield	06.07.60	Mansfield T.(APP)	Northampton T.	07.78	1978-81	141	/	0	(G)
			TR	Wolverhampton W.	08.82					
			TR	Port Vale	03.83	1982	2	/	0	
			TR	Gillingham	03.83					
POOLE, Cyril J.	Mansfield T.	13.03.21	Gillingham	Mansfield T.	+	1950-51	16		0	(IF)Notts/England Cricketer
POOLE, Harry	Stoke	31.01.35	Oxford C.	Port Vale	04.56	1955-67	449	1	73	(WH)●
POOLE, John A.F.	Stoke	12.12.32		Port Vale	09.53	1955-60	32		0	(G)
POOLE, Joseph	Huddersfield	25.05.23		Huddersfield T.	+	1946	2		0	(OR)
			TR	Bradford C.	02.47	1946-48	56		6	
POOLE, Ken J.	Blaencwm	02.07.33	JNRS	Swansea C.	11.53					(FB)
			TR	Northampton T.	06.56	1956	4		0	
POOLE, Mick D.	Morley	23.04.55	Coventry C.(APP)	Rochdale	09.73	1973-77	192	/	0	(G)
			Fortland Timbers	Rochdale	08.81	1981	27	/	0	
POOLE, Richard J.	Heston	03.07.57	APP	Brentford	07.75	1973-75	12	9	1	(F)
			TR	Watford	07.76	1976	3	4	1	
POOLE, Roy	Sheffield	02.12.39	JNRS	Wolverhampton W.	01.57					(F)
			TR	Rotherham U.	07.58					
			TR	Chesterfield	07.61	1961-63	49		14	
POOLE, Terry	Chesterfield	16.12.49	JNRS	Manchester U.	02.67					(G)Brother to Andy
			TR	Huddersfield T.	08.68	1968-76	207	/	0	
			TR	Bolton W.	01.77	1980	29	/	0	
			TR	Sheffield U.	03.80	1979	7	/	0	
POOLE, Terry	Sheffield	08.12.37	JNRS	Sheffield Wed.	04.55					(HB)
			TR	Darlington	07.59	1959-60	41		3	
POPE, David W.	London	08.01.36	JNRS	Crystal Palace	09.53					(FB)
				Swansea C.	09.56	1957	4		0	
POPE, Terry J.	Newport	27.01.26	Bargoed	Newport Co.	07.50	1950-54	83		0	(G)
POPELY, Peter	York	07.04.43	Cliftonville	York C.	08.63	1962-66	24	1	0	(FB)

Players Names	Birthplace	Date	Previous Club	League Club	Date Signed	Seasons Played	Career Record Apps Sub Gls		
POPPITT, John	W. Sleekburn	20.01.23	W. Sleekburn	Derby Co.	+	1946-49	16		0	(FB)
			TR	Q.P.R.	09.50	1950-53	106		0	
POPPY, Arthur	Yeovil	06.01.61	APP	Northampton T.	APP	1977	1	/	0	(D)
PORRITT, William	Heckmondwike	19.07.14	Huddersfield T.(*)	York C.	*	1946	15		2	(IL)
PORT, Bernard H.	Burton	14.12.25	Newhall F.C.	Hull C.	09.50					(G)
			TR	Chester C.	08.51	1951-52	9		0	
PORTEOUS, Joseph	Shildon	20.04.25	Chesterfield(AM)	York C.	08.46	1946	23		0	(LH)
PORTEOUS, John R.	Motherwell	05.12.21	Alloa Ath.	Plymouth Arg.	07.49	1949-55	215		13	(WH)
			TR	Exeter C	03.56	1955-56	37		0	
PORTEOUS, John R.	India	12.01.33	Alton T.	Aldershot	02.56	1955	1		0	(IF)
PORTEOUS, Trevor	Hull	09.10.33	JNRS	Hull C.	10.50	1951-55	61		1	(WH)
			TR	Stockport Co.	06.56	1956-64	336		9	
PORTER, Andy	Ayr	21.01.37	Darvel	Watford	06.59	1959-62	72		4	(F)
PORTER, Chris J.	Petherton	30.04.49	Bridgwater	Swindon T.	11.69	1970-73	33	3	4	(W)
PORTER, Derek	Ulverston	22.06.36	Dalton T.	Barrow	05.57	1957-58	15		1	(OL)
PORTER, Gary	Sunderland	06.03.66	APP	Watford	03.84	1983	1	1	0	(M)
PORTER, George	Chirk	05.02.35	Chirk A.A.A.	Wrexham	AM	1959	1		0	(OL)
PORTER, Leslie	Gateshead	05.05.23	Redheaugh Wks.	Newcastle U.	+					(HB)
			TR	York C.	03.49	1948-53	37		1	
PORTER, Mike R.	Stoke	19.05.45	JNRS	Port Vale	07.62	1963-64	13		2	(HB)
PORTER, Trevor J.	Guildford	16.10.56	APP	Fulham	05.74					(G)
			Slough T.	Brentford	08.78	1978-79	15	/	0	
PORTER, William	Durham	23.11.23	Horden C.W.	Hartlepool U.	+	1946	2		0	(OL) d.1975
PORTERFIELD, Ian	Dunfermline	11.02.46	Raith Rov.	Sunderland	12.67	1967-75	217	12	17	(M)
			L	Reading	11.76	1976	5	/	0	
			TR	Sheffield Wed.	07.77	1977-79	103	3	3	
			TR	Rotherham U.	01.80					
PORTWOOD, Cliff,	Salford	17.10.37	Manchester Ath.	Preston N.E.	02.55					(IF)
			TR	Port Vale	08.59	1959-60	61		32	
			TR	Grimsby T.	07.61	1961-63	92		35	
			TR	Portsmouth	05.64	1964-68	95	3	28	
POSKETT, Malcolm	Middlesbrough	19.07.53	South Bank	Middlesbrough	04.73	1973	0	1	0	(F)
			Whitby T.	Hartlepool U.	11.76	1976-77	50	1	20	
			TR	Brighton & H.A.	02.78	1977-79	33	12	16	
			TR	Watford	01.80	1979-80	57	6	17	
			TR	Carlisle U.	08.82	1982-83	77	/	31	
POSKETT, Tom W.	Esh. Winning	26.12.09	Tranmere Rov.(*)	Crewe Alex.	*	1946	15		0	(G)*Grimsby T./Notts.Co./ d.1972
POSSEE, Derek J.	London	14.02.46	APP	Tottenham H.	03.63	1963-65	19	/	4	(W)
			TR	Millwall	08.67	1967-72	222	1	79	
			TR	Crystal Palace	01.73	1972-73	51	2	12	
			TR	Orient	07.74	1974-76	77	3	11	
POSTLEWHITE, Dennis	Birkenhead	13.10.57	APP	Tranmere Rov.	07.76	1976-78	31	2	1	(D)
POTRAC, Anthony J.	Victoria	21.01.53	APP	Chelsea	03.71	1971	1	/	0	(IF)
POTTER, Fred	Cradley Heath	29.11.40	JNRS	Aston Villa	07.59	1960	3		0	(G) 1 app. on field
			TR	Doncaster Rov.	07.62	1962-65	123	/	0	for Doncaster Rov.
			Burton A.	Hereford U.	N/L	1972-73	10	/	0	
POTTER, Gary C.	Chester	06.08.52	JNRS	Chester C.	07.73	1973-74	11	/	0	(CH)
POTTER, George R.	Arbroath	07.10.46	Forfar Ath.	Luton T.	03.687	1967-68	3	4	0	(D)
			TR	Torquay U.	07.69	1969-70	32	6	0	
			TR	Hartlepool U.	07.71	1971-76	211	2	4	
POTTER, Harry	Tyldesley	20.05.23	Winsford U.	Shrewsbury T.	N/L	1950-51	67		0	(FB)
			TR	Rochdale	06.52	1952-53	52		0	
POTTER, James	Belfast	20.11.41	JNRS	Sunderland	11.58					(WH)
			TR	Darlington	09.63	1963	19		1	
POTTER, Ray J.	Beckenham	07.05.36	JNRS	Crystal Palace	05.53	1953-57	44		0	(G)
			TR	W.B.A.	06.58	1958-66	217	/	0	
			TR	Portsmouth	05.67	1967-69	3	/	0	
POTTER, Ron C.	Wolverhampton	05.12.48	APP	W.B.A.	12.66	1968-69	8	1	0	(CH)
			TR	Swindon T.	11.70	1970-74	84	2	0	
POTTER, Steve D.	Belper	01.10.55	APP	Manchester C.	10.73					(G)
			TR	Swansea C.	08.74	1974-77	118	/	0	
POTTS, Brian	Sunderland	03.09.48	APP	Leicester C.	09.65	1967-68	9	1	0	(FB)
			TR	Peterborough U.	07.69	1969-70	49	1	0	
POTTS, Eric	Liverpool	16.03.50	Oswestry	Sheffield Wed.	12.69	1970-76	143	17	21	(W)
			TR	Brighton & H.A.	06.77	1977	19	14	5	
			TR	Preston N.E.	08.78	1978-80	50	7	5	
			TR	Burnley	09.80	1980-81	48	8	5	
			TR	Bury	10.82	1982-83	46	5	7	

Players Names	Birthplace	Date	Previous Club	League Club	Date Signed	Seasons Played	Apps	Sub	Gls	
POTTS, Harry	Hetton	22.10.20	JNRS	Burnley	*	1946-50	165		47	(IF)
			TR	Everton	10.50	1950-55	59		15	
POTTS, Henry J.	Carlisle	23.01.25	Pegasus	Northampton T.	AM	1950	9		0	(OL)E.AMAT.INT.
POTTS, Reg	Stoke	31.07.27	Stoke C.(AM)	Port Vale	+	1948-56	277		3	(FB)
POTTS, Victor E.	Birmingham	20.08.15	Doncaster Rov.(*)	Aston Villa	+	1946-47	62		0	*Tottenham H.
POULTON, George H.	Holborn	23.04.29		Gillingham	N/L	1951	5		1	(OL)
			TR	Orient	07.52	1952-54	61		24	
POUND, Ken	Portsmouth	24.08.44	Yeovil T.	Swansea C.	07.64	1964-65	27	2	4	(W)
			TR	Bournemouth	08.66	1966-68	102	/	24	
			TR	Gillingham	07.69	1969-70	62	10	11	
POUNDER, Albert W.	Charlton	27.07.31	Harveys Spts.	Charlton Ath.	02.50	1952	1		0	(OR)
			TR	Q.P.R.	02.54	1953-55	52		6	
POUNDER, John A.	Sheffield	16.03.35	Atlas Spts.	Luton T.	12.55	1955-56	3		0	(OR)
			TR	Coventry C.	06.57	1957	6		1	
			TR	Crewe Alex.	12.57	1957-58	29		6	
POUNTNEY, Dave	Baschurch	12.10.39	Myddle	Shrewsbury T.	09.57	1957-63	176		11	(WH)
			TR	Aston Villa	10.63	1963-67	109	6	7	
			TR	Shrewsbury T.	02.68	1967-69	54	4	1	
			TR	Chester C.	06.70	1970-72	135	/	1	
POUNTNEY, Ron A.	Bilston	19.03.55	JNRS	Walsall	07.73	1972	1	/	0	(M)
			TR	Port Vale	10.73					
			Bilston	Southend U.	01.75	1974-83	295	16	25	
POVEY, Vic R.	Wolverhampton	16.03.44	JNRS	Wolverhampton W.	07.61					(F)
			TR	Notts.Co.	08.63	1963-64	35		3	
POVEY, William	Billingham	11.01.43	JNRS	Middlesbrough	05.60	1962	6		0	(F)
			TR	York C.	03.64	1964	3		0	
POWELL, Andy	Plymouth	27.06.65	JNRS	Hereford U.	N/C	1982	4	/	0	(G)
POWELL, Anthony	Bristol	11.02.47	Bath C.	Bournemouth	04.68	1968-73	214	5	10	(D)
			TR	Norwich C.	08.74	1974-80	235	2	3	
POWELL, Aubrey	Swansea	19.04.18	Swansea(AM)	Leeds U.	*	1946-47	74		19	(IF)W-8
			TR	Everton	07.48	1948-49	35		5	
			TR	Birmingham C.	08.50	1950	15		0	
POWELL, Baden	Hebburn	17.06.31	Sth. Shields	Darlington	10.50	1950-53	9		0	(OR)
POWELL, Barry I.	Kenilworth	29.01.54	APP	Wolverhampton W.	01.72	1972-74	58	6	7	(M) E.U23-4
			TR	Coventry C.	09.75	1975-79	162	2	28	
			TR	Derby Co	10.79	1979-81	34	/	7	
POWELL, Brian J.	York	10.03.36	Cliftonville	York C.	09.56	1956-59	27		5	(F)
POWELL, Colin D.	Hendon	07.07.48	Barnet	Charlton Ath.	01.73	1972-78	230	14	22	(W)
			N. Eng. Teamen	Charlton Ath.	08.79	1979-80	71	6	8	
			TR	Gillingham	08.81	1981-82	54	1	1	
POWELL, Dai M.	Swansea	19.01.35		Blackpool	12.52					(LH)
			TR	Rochdale	07.58	1958-60	76		1	
POWELL, Dave	Dolgarrog	15.10.44	Gwydyn Rov.	Wrexham	05.63	1962-68	132	2	4	(WH)W-11/W.U23-4
			TR	Sheffield U.	09.68	1968-70	89	/	2	
			TR	Cardiff C.	09.72	1972-74	36	/	1	
POWELL, George R.	Fulham	11.10.24	Fulham(AM)	Q.P.R.	12.46	1947-52	125		0	(FB)
POWELL, Ivor V.	Bargoed	05.07.16	Bargoed	Q.P.R.	*	1946-48	103		2	(WH)W-8
			TR	Aston Villa	12.48	1948-50	79		5	
			TR	Port Vale	08.51	1951	6		0	
			TR	Bradford C.	06.52	1952-54	83		9	
POWELL, Ken	Mansfield	02.03.20	Mansfield C.W.S.	Derby Co.	+	1946	13		0	(OL) d.1976
			TR	Southport	06.47	1947-50	90		18	
POWELL, Ken L.	Chester	25.09.24		Cardiff C.	09.47					(CH)
			TR	Exeter C.	06.48	1948-49	22		1	
			TR	Bristol Rov.	. 07.51	1951	4		0	
POWELL, Mike J.	Newport	26.04.51	Newport YMCA	Newport Co.	N/C	1975-77	7	2	0	(D)
POWELL, Mike P.	Slough	18.04.33	JNRS	Q.P.R.	01.51	1951-58	123		0	(CH)
POWELL, Neville D.	Flint	02.09.63	APP	Tranmere Rov.	08.81	1980-83	75	10	4	(M)
POWELL, Ray	Swansea	05.08.24	Haverfordwest	Swansea C.	05.47	1947-50	17		5	(CF)
			TR	Scunthorpe U.	08.51	1951	31		14	
POWELL, Ron W.H.	Knighton	02.12.29		Manchester C.	11.48	1949	12		0	(G)●
			TR	Chesterfield	06.52	1952-54	471		0	
POWELL, Steve	Derby	20.09.55	APP	Derby Co.	11.72	1971-83	317	9	19	(D)E.U23-1/E.YTH.INT. E.SCH.INT./Son of Tommy
POWELL, Tommy	Derby	12.04.25	JNRS	Derby Co.	+	1948-61	381		58	(OR)Father of Steve
POWELL, Wayne	Caerphilly	25.10.56	APP	Bristol Rov.	10.74	1975-77	25	7	10	(F) W.YTH.INT.
			L	Halifax T.	10.77	1977	4	/	1	
			TR	Hereford U.	06.78	1978	6	/	2	
POWER, Mike D.	Stockport	03.10.61		Stockport Co.	12.81	1980-83	61	1	15	(F)
POWER, Paul	Manchester	30.10.53	JNRS	Manchester C.	07.75	1975-83	280	7	24	(M)

Players Names	Birthplace	Date	Previous Club	League Club	Date Signed	Seasons Played	Apps	Sub	Gls	
POWLING, Ritchie	Barking	21.05.56	APP	Arsenal	07.73	1973-77	50	5	3	(M) E.YTH.INT.
POWNEY, Bryan W.	Seaford	07.10.44	APP	Brighton & H.A.	11.61	1961-73	351	/	0	(G)
POWTON, Brian	Newcastle	29.08.29		Newcastle U.	10.50					(G)
			TR	Preston N.E.	08.51					
			TR	Hartlepool U.	07.52	1952	4		0	
POYNER, Robert C.	Newport	25.12.32	JNRS	Newport Co.	01.51	1950-51	2		0	
POYNTON, William	Shiremoor	30.06.44	JNRS	Burnley	07.61					(FB)
			TR	Mansfield T.	07.64	1964-65	20	/	0	
			Lockheed Leamington	Lincoln C.	10.66	1966	0	1	0	
POYSER, George H.	Stanton Hill	06.02.10	Brentford(*)	Plymouth Arg.	+	1946	3		0	(FB)*Wolverhampton W./ Stourbridge/Mansfield T./ Port Vale
PRAGG, Mike K.	Shrewsbury	08.10.41	JNRS	Shrewsbury T.	AM	1960-62	5		1	(IF)E.AMAT.INT.
PRANGLEY, Sam	Newport	30.09.24	Lovells Ath.	Newport Co.	11.46	1946	7		0	(WH)
PRASKI, Josef	France	22.01.26	Jeanfield Swifts	Notts.Co.	03.49	1948	3		0	(OR)
PRATLEY, Richard G.	Banbury	12.01.63	Banbury	Derby Co.	07.83	1983	1	1	0	(D)
			L	Scunthorpe U.	03.84	1983	10	/	0	
PRATT, John A.	Hackney	26.06.48	JNRS	Tottenham H.	11.65	1968-79	307	22	39	(M)
PRATT, John L.	Birmingham	01.03.43	Wycombe W.	Reading	07.69	1969-71	29	/	0	(G)
PRATT, Mike W.	Newport	15.01.66		Newport Co.	08.83	1983	3	3	2	(F)
PRATT, Ray E.	Merthyr Tydfil	11.11.55	Merthyr Tydfil	Exeter C.	03.80	1979-83	81	38	40	(F)W.YTH.INT.
PRATT, Wayne	Southampton	01.03.60	APP	Southampton	03.78	1980	1	/	0	(M)
PRECIOUS, Derek	Crewe	02.06.31		Crewe Alex.	09.55	1955-56	18		3	(F)
PREECE, Brian J.	Hereford	16.02.58	APP	Hereford U.	02.76	1974-76	5	1	0	(F)
			TR	Newport Co.	03.77	1976-77	38	6	12	
PREECE, David W.	Bridgnorth	28.05.63	APP	Walsall	07.80	1980-83	95	4	5	(M)
PREECE, Jack C.	Wolverhampton	30.04.14		Southport	+	1946	36		0	(FB)*Bristol Rov./
			TR	Swindon T.	06.47	1947	7		0	Bradford C.
PREECE, Paul W.	Penarth	16.05.57	APP	Newport Co.	06.75	1974-75	17	6	0	(W)
PRENDERGAST, Mike	Denaby	24.11.50	APP	Sheffield Wed.	11.67	1968-77	170	12	53	(F)
			TR	Barnsley	05.78	1977-78	12	6	2	
			L	Halifax T.	10.78	1978	4	/	1	
PRENTIS, John	Liverpool	22.03.39		Blackpool	10.62	1964-65	6	/	0	(FB)
				Stockport Co.	10.66	1966-67	16	3	0	
PRESCOTT, Frank S.	Birkenhead	19.08.22	St.Annes F.C.	Tranmere Rov.	10.47	1946	2		0	(CF) d.1969
PRESCOTT, Jim L.	Warington	02.11.30		Southport	03.54	1953-54	53		9	(IF)
			TR	York C.	06.55	1955	18		5	
			TR	Southport	10.56	1956	17		1	
PRESLAND, Edward R.	Waltham Cross	27.03.43	JNRS	West Ham U.	10.60	1964-65	6	/	1	(FB)
			TR	Crystal Palace	01.67	1966-68	61	/	0	Essex Cricketer
			L	Colchester U.	10.69	1969	5	/	0	
			TR	Orient	07.70					
PRESLEY, Derek C.	Warminster	08.03.30	Warminster T.	Bristol C.	03.50	1950-51	9		0	(WH)
			TR	Bristol Rov.	05.52					
PRESSDEE, Jim S.	Swansea	19.06.33	JNRS	Swansea C.	08.51	1953-55	8		0	(FB)Glamorgan Cricketer/ W.SCH.INT.
PRICE, Albert E.	Langwith	04.04.26	Creswell Col.	Crewe Alex.	12.46	1946	5		0	(G) d.1965
PRICE, Arthur				Leeds U.	+	1946	6		0	
PRICE, Bryan	Treorchy	15.11.36	Treorchy B.C.	Barnsley	05.55	1956-57	2		0	(HB)
PRICE, Cecil A.	Cardiff	02.12.19		Cardiff C.	09.48	1948	1		0	
			TR	Bradford C.	06.49	1949	7		0	
PRICE, Chris J.	Hereford	30.03.60	APP	Hereford U.	01.78	1976-83	245	3	18	(D)
PRICE, David J.	Caterham	23.06.55	APP	Arsenal	08.72	1972-80	116	10	16	(M) E.SCH.INT./
			L	Peterborough U.	01.75	1974	6	/	1	W.YTH.INT.
			TR	Crystal Palace	03.81	1980-81	25	2	2	
			TR	Orient	N/C	1982	10	/	0	
PRICE, Derek E.	Wellington	14.02.32	Donnington	Shrewsbury T.	02.53	1953-57	125		28	(OR)
			TR	Aldershot	07.58	1958-59	4		1	
PRICE, Dudley T.	Swansea	17.11.31		Swansea C.	04.50	1953-57	33		9	(IF)
			TR	Southend U.	01.58	1957-60	91		41	
			TR	Hull C.	09.60	1960-62	76		26	
			TR	Bradford C.	07.63	1963-64	62		21	
PRICE, Ernest	Easington	12.05.26		Darlington	12.48	1948-50	68		0	(WH) + Sunderland
			TR	Crystal Palace	07.51	1951-52	34		5	
PRICE, George	Crewe	02.12.29		Crewe Alex.	02.54	1953	4		0	
PRICE, John	Nantwich	28.04.60	Middlewich	Rochdale	01.78	1977-78	10	2	0	(M)

Players Names	Birthplace	Date	Previous Club	League Club	Date Signed	Seasons Played	Apps	Sub	Gls	
PRICE, John	Easington	25.10.43	Horden C.W.	Burnley	11.60	1963-64	20		2	(W)
			TR	Stockport Co.	05.65	1965-71	241	6	23	
			TR	Blackburn Rov.	09.71	1971-73	63	14	12	
			TR	Stockport Co.	03.74	1973-75	51	15	1	
PRICE, John	Shotton	29.08.18		Hartlepool U.	*	1946-48	54		9	
			TR	York C.	12.48	1948	1		2	
PRICE, John	Consett	14.04.47	APP	Leeds U.	05.65					(F)
			TR	Southport	07.66	1966	16	2	2	
PRICE, John D.	London	31.12.32	Eastbourne U.	Tottenham H.	09.54					(WH)
			TR	Aldershot	01.57	1956-58	85		1	
			TR	Watford	06.59	1959	22		0	
PRICE, John G.	Aberystwyth	22.11.36		Liverpool	10.54	1955	1		0	(FB)
			TR	Aston Villa	03.57					
			TR	Walsall	07.57					
			TR	Shrewsbury T.	07.58	1958-59	9		0	
PRICE, Ken E.	Ellesmere Port	25.03.39	W. Bromborough	Aston Villa	08.59					(F)
			TR	Tranmere Rov.	12.60	1960	3		2	
			TR	Hartlepool U.	07.61	1961	8		3	
			TR	Peterborough U.	08.62					
PRICE, Ken G.	Dudley	26.02.54	Dudley T.	Southend U.	05.76	1976	1	/	0	(F)
			TR	Gillingham	12.76	1976-82	247	8	79	
			TR	Reading	01.83	1982-83	34	3	6	
PRICE, Leslie E.	Consett	26.08.30		Sunderland	08.50					(OL)
			TR	Gateshead	07.52	1952-53	39		12	
PRICE, Neil	Hemel Hempstead	15.02.64	APP	Watford	02.82	1983	7	1	0	(D)
			L	Plymouth Arg.	02.84	1983	1	/		
PRICE, Paul T.	St. Albans	23.03.54	Welwyn G.C.	Luton T.	07.71	1972-80	206	1	8	(D) W-25/W.U21-1
			TR	Tottenham H.	06.81	1981-83	35	4	0	
PRICE, Peter	Yarbolton	26.02.32		Darlington	01.54	1953-54	3		0	
PRICE, Peter W.	Wrexham	17.08.49	APP	Liverpool	08.66					(F) W.U23-4
			TR	Peterborough U.	07.68	1968-71	114	5	62	
			TR	Portsmouth	06.72	1972-73	13	1	2	
			L	Peterborough U.	07.74	1974	2	/	0	
			TR	Barnsley	11.74	1974-77	72	7	28	
PRICE, Ray	Durham	18.05.44	JNRS	Norwich C.	07.63	1963	1		0	(FB)
			TR	Colchester U.	07.64	1964-66	15	2	0	
PRICE, Ray J.	Northampton	30.11.48	APP	Northampton T.	12.66	1966-67	7	/	0	(CF)
PRICE, Terry E.	Colchester	11.10.45	APP	Orient	08.63	1964-67	86	/	18	(W)
			TR	Colchester U.	09.67	1967-68	55	2	5	
PRICE, Trevor H.R.	Ellesmere Port	27.12.44		Workington	06.64	1964	2	1		(W)
PRICE, Walter B.	Neston	14.02.21		Tranmere Rov.	+	1946	3		0	
			TR	Rochdale	08.48	1948	1		0	
PRICE, William A.J.	Wellington	10.04.17	Wrockwardine	Huddersfield T.	*	1946-47	14		3	(CF)
			TR	Reading	10.47	1947-48	15		2	
			TR	Hull C.	01.49	1948	8		5	
			TR	Bradford C.	11.49	1949-51	54		28	
PRIDAY, Robert H.	S. Africa	29.03.25	S. Africa	Liverpool	+	1946-48	34		6	(W)
			TR	Blackburn Rov.	03.49	1948-50	44		11	
			TR	Accrington St.	12.52	1952	5		0	
			TR	Rochdale	08.53	1953	3		1	
PRIDDY, Paul	Isleworth	11.07.53	Walton & Hersham	Brentford	10.72	1972-76	121	/	0	(G)
			Tooting & Mitcham	Wimbledon	N/C	1978	1	/	0	
			Hayes	Brentford	08.81	1981	1	/	0	
PRIEST, Harry	Clay Cross	26.10.35	Clay Cross	Sheffield U.	02.54	1956	2		1	(F)
			TR	Halifax T.	01.58	1957-58	30		12	
PRIESTLEY, Derek	Queensbury	22.12.26		Halifax T.	10.50	1951-55	145		19	(OL)
			TR	Bradford P.A.	07.56					
PRIESTLEY, Gerald	Halifax	02.03.31		Nottingham F.	12.50					(W)
			TR	Exeter C.	06.53	1953-54	43		5	
			TR	Grimsby T.	06.55	1955-58	111		11	
			TR	Crystal Palace	11.58	1958-59	28		2	
			TR	Halifax T.	07.60	1960-62	105		23	
PRIESTLEY, Maurice	Bradford	27.10.22		Bradford P.A.	09.46					(F)
			TR	Halifax T.	01.48	1947-48	24		8	
PRIESTLEY, Royston M.	Kingston	26.11.48	JNRS	Barnsley	AM	1967	1	/	0	(CF)
PRINCE, Eric	Ipstones	11.12.24		Port Vale	+	1946	14		2	(IF)
PRINCE, Frank A.	Penarth	01.12.49	APP	Bristol Rov.	12.67	1967-79	360	2	23	(M) W.U23-4
			TR	Exeter C.	07.80	1980-81	27	4	2	
PRINCE, Harry	Stoke	04.12.21		Port Vale	+	1946-48	5		0	(G)
PRING, Dennis F.	Newport	08.11.40	Newport Y.M.C.A.	Southampton	02.59	1958	4		0	(F)
PRING, Keith D.	Newport	11.03.43	JNRS	Newport Co.	11.61	1961-64	61		3	(F)W-3
			TR	Rotherham U.	10.64	1964-67	80	2	6	
			TR	Notts.Co.	12.67	1967-68	41	3	2	
			TR	Southport	07.69	1969-70	48	/	4	

Players Names	Birthplace	Date	Previous Club	League Club	Date Signed	Seasons Played	Apps	Sub	Gls	
PRINGLE, Brian	Chathill	12.03.49	Ainwick T.	Hartlepool U.	AM	1972	1	/	0	(IF)
PRINGLE, William A.	Liverpool	24.02.32	JNRS	Liverpool	08.49					(F)
			TR	Grimsby T.	05.54	1954	2		0	
PRIOR, George K.	Newcastle	13.10.32	Sunderland (AM)	Newcastle U.	03.52	1951-52	8		3	(OL) Son of pre-war
			TR	Millwall	05.54	1954-55	60		17	Sheffield Wed. player
			TR	Newcastle U.	07.56	1956	2		0	
PRISCOTT, Anthony	Portsmouth	19.03.41		Portsmouth	07.59	1959-61	36		6	(W)
			TR	Aldershot	08.62	1962-65	141	/	43	
			TR	Bournemouth	01.66	1965-66	60	1	6	
			TR	Aldershot	08.67	1967-70	126	12	26	
PRITCHARD, Alf V.	Chester	31.08.20	Dumbarton	Wrexham	08.46	1946-49	36		8	(IF)
PRITCHARD, Alan S.	Chester	24.08.43	JNRS	Chester C.	10.60	1960-63	19		6	(F)
PRITCHARD, Harvey J.	Meriden	30.01.18	Crystal Palace(*)	Manchester C.	*					
			TR	Southend U.	02.47	1946-51	72		8	
PRITCHARD, Howard	Cardiff	18.10.58	APP	Bristol C.	08.76	1978-80	31	7	2	(F)
			TR	Swindon T.	08.81	1981-82	59	6	11	
			TR	Bristol C.	08.83	1983	46	/	10	
PRITCHARD, Joe	Birkenhead	04.09.43	Liverpool(AM)	Tranmere Rov.	09.62	1962-69	177	3	29	(F)
PRITCHARD, Keith	Wallasey	20.10.19		New Brighton	AM	1946-47	25		8	(OL)
PRITCHARD, Philip J.	Wordsley	09.01.65	APP	Stoke C.	01.82					(G)
			L	Southend U.	03.84	1983	9	/	0	
PRITCHARD, Ray	Liverpool	23.06.54	Everton(APP)	Tranmere Rov.	02.73	1972-73	13	1	0	(FB)
			L	Southport	01.74	1973	3	/	0	
PRITCHARD, Roy T.	Dawley	09.05.25	JNRS	Wolverhampton W.	+	1946-54	202		0	(FB)
			TR	Aston Villa	02.55	1955-57	3		0	
			TR	Notts Co.	11.57	1957	18		0	
			TR	Port Vale	08.58	1958-59	23		0	
PRITCHETT, Darrol W.	Bentley	22.05.33	JNRS	Hull C.	01.51					(FB)
			TR	Walsall	05.54	1954	1		0	
PRITCHETT, Keith	Glasgow	08.11.53		Wolverhampton W.	04.72					(D)
			TR	Doncaster Rov.	07.73	1973	6	/	0	
			TR	Q.P.R.	01.75	1974	4	/	0	
			TR	Brentford	07.76	1976	11	/	1	
			TR	Watford	11.76	1976-81	133	7	9	
			TR	Blackpool	11.82	1982-83	36	1	1	
PRITTY, George	Birmingham	04.03.15	Aston Villa(*)	Nottingham F.	*	1946	28		1	(WH)*Newport Co.
PROBERT, Eric W.	Sth. Kirkby	17.02.52	APP	Burnley	02.69	1968-72	62	5	11	(M)E.YTH.INT.
			TR	Notts. Co	07.73	1973-76	122	/	14	
			TR	Darlington	07.78	1978-79	20	1	0	
			TR	Rochdale	07.80					
PROCTOR, David	Belfast	10.10.29	Portadown	Grimsby T.	01.49					(WH)
			TR	Blackpool	08.49					
			TR	Norwich C.	01.53	1952-53	17		0	
			Northwich	Barrow	10.54	1954-58	160		2	
			TR	Wrexham	08.59	1959	2		0	
PROCTOR, Harry M.	Ushaw Moor	10.07.12	Hartlepool U.(*)	Norwich C.	*	1946	5		0	(HB)
PROCTOR, Mark G.	Middlesbrough	30.01.61	APP	Middlesbrough	09.78	1978-80	107	2	12	(M) E.U21-2
			TR	Nottingham F.	08.81	1981-81	60	4	5	
			TR	Sunderland	03.83	1982-83	45	1	2	
PROLZE, Brian J.	Altrincham	11.04.32	Altrincham	Crewe Alex.	AM	1953	1		0	(CF)
PROPHETT, Colin	Crewe	08.03.47		Sheffield Wed.	06.68	1969-72	111	6	7	(D)
			TR	Norwich C.	06.73	1973	34	1	0	
			TR	Swindon T.	09.78	1974-77	158	2	10	
			TR	Chesterfield	09.78	1978-79	35	2	1	
			TR	Crewe Alex.	10.79	1979-80	79	/	1	
PROSSER, Neil A.	Edmonton	08.03.57	Harlow T.	Bournemouth	07.80	1980	1	1	0	(F)
			TR	Tranmere Rov.	N/C	1982	1	1	0	
PROUDLER, Arthur	Kingswinford	03.10.29	Halesowen T.	Aston Villa	12.47	1954	1	/		(WH)
			TR	Crystal Palace	06.56	1956-58	26		2	
PROUDLOCK, George T.	Stubswood	19.09.19	Amble	West Ham U.	*	1946-47	14		4	(IF)
PROUDLOVE, Andy G.	Buxton	15.01.55	APP	Reading	APP	1971	4	1	0	(F)
			Buxton	Sheffield Wed.	09.75	1975	10	5	0	
			TR	Norwich C.	02.76	1976	0	1	0	
			TR	Hereford U.	05.77	1977	6	5	0	
			TR	Port Vale	11.78	1978	5	/	0	
PROUTON, Ralph O.	Southampton	01.03.26	Romsey T.	Arsenal	08.49					(LH)Hants Cricketer
			TR	Swindon T.	08.52	1952	13		0	
PROVAN, Andy	Greenock	01.01.44	St. Mirren	Barnsley	05.63	1963	3		0	(F)
			TR	York C.	08.64	1964-68	159	1	49	
			TR	Chester C.	08.68	1968-69	77	3	19	
			TR	Wrexham	04.70	1970-71	49	2	10	
			TR	Southport	07.72	1972-73	82	1	28	
			TR	Torquay U.	08.74	1974-76	83	8	14	

Players Names	Birthplace	Date	Previous Club	League Club	Date Signed	Seasons Played	Career Record Apps	Sub	Gls	
PROVAN, Dave	Glasgow	11.03.41	Glasgow Rgrs.	Crystal Palace	06.70	1970	1	/	0	(FB)S-3/S.U23-1/
			TR	Plymouth Arg.	03.71	1970-74	128	1	10	S.F.LGE REP.
PROVERBS, Roy J	Wednesbury	08.07.32	Stratford T.	Coventry C.	05.56	1956	10		0	(HB)
			TR	Bournemouth	07.57					
			TR	Gillingham	02.58	1957-61	144		2	
PRUDHAM, C. Edward	Gateshead	12.04.52	JNRS	Sheffield Wed.	07.69	1970-74	14	5	2	(F)
			TR	Carlisle U.	11.74	1974-76	15	2	2	
			L	Hartlepool U.	09.76	1976	3	/	0	
			L	Workington	02.77	1976	15	/	6	
			TR	Stockport Co.	07.77	1977-79	80	7	22	
			TR	Bournemouth	05.80	1980	2	2	0	
PRUDHOE, Mark	Durham	11.11.63	APP	Sunderland	09.81	1982	7	/	0	(G)
			L	Hartlepool U.	11.83	1983	3	/	0	
PRYCE, Idris	Wrexham	24.02.41		Wrexham	09.59	1959	3		0	
PRYDE, David	Edinburgh	10.11.13	Margate	Arsenal	*					(WH)
			TR	Torquay U.	10.46	1946-49	64		0	
PRYDE, Robert I.	Methill	25.04.13	St.Johnstone	Blackburn Rov.	*	1946-48	117		2	(CH) E.F.LGE.REP.
PRYDE, William	Polmont	20.05.19	Bo'ness	Southend U.	07.47	1947-48	17		1	
PUCKETT, Dave C.	Southampton	29.10.60	APP	Southampton	11.78	1980-83	33	34	9	(F)
PUGH, Daral J.	Sunderland	05.06.61	APP	Doncaster Rov.	12.78	1978-82	136	18	15	(M)
			TR	Huddersfield T.	09.82	1982-83	28	28	6	
PUGH, David	Markham	22.01.47	JNRS	Newport Co.	04.64	1964-67	73	5	9	(M) W.U23-2/W.SCH.INT.
			TR	Chesterfield	12.67	1967-72	212	1	12	
			TR	Halifax T.	08.73	1973-75	91	5	3	
			TR	Rotherham U.	07.76	1976-78	57	1	0	
			TR	York C.	11.78	1978-80	73	4	2	
PUGH, Gary	Ramsgate	11.02.61	Dover	Bournemouth	01.81	1980	0	3	1	(M)
PUGH, J. Graham	Hoole	12.02.48	APP	Sheffield Wed.	02.65	1965-71	135	4	8	(M) E.U23-1
			TR	Huddersfield T.	05.72	1972-74	80	/	1	
			TR	Chester C.	02.75	1974-76	67	2	3	
			TR	Barnsley	10.76	1976-79	128	2	8	
			TR	Scunthorpe U.	01.80	1979-80	54	1	0	
PUGH, Kevin J.	Corbridge	11.10.60	APP	Newcastle U.	10.78	1981	0	1	0	(M)
			Gateshead	Darlington	09.83	1983	0	2	0	
PUGH, Steve J.	Wolverhampton	01.02.65	APP	Wolverhampton W.	12.82					(D)
			TR	Torquay U.	10.83	1983	37	1	1	
PUGSLEY, David G.	Merthyr Tydfil	15.08.31	Gloucester C.	Newport Co.	AM	1952	1		0	(G)
PULIS, Anthony R.	Newport	16.01.58	APP	Bristol Rov.	09.75	1975-80	78	7	3	(D)
			Happy Valley	Bristol Rov.	06.82	1982-83	44	1	2	
PULIS, Ray J.	Newport	21.11.64	APP	Newport Co.	11.82	1982	0	1	0	(F)
PULLAR, David H.	London	13.02.59	APP	Portsmouth	02.77	1975-78	84	9	4	(M)
			TR	Exeter C.	07.79	1979-82	124	6	22	
			TR	Crewe Alex.	07.83	1983	33	1	6	
PULLEN, Walter E.	Ripley	02.08.19		Orient	+	1946-50	116		36	(IF)
PULLEY, Gordon	Stourbridge	18.09.36	Oswestry	Millwall	09.56	1956-57	61		9	(W)
			TR	Gillingham	05.58	1958-65	205	/	46	
			TR	Peterborough U.	11.65	1965-66	16	1	4	
PUNTER, Brian	Bromsgrove	16.08.35	JNRS	Wolverhampton W.	09.53					(CF)E.YTH.INT.
			Bromsgrove	Leic.C.	05.58					
			TR	Lincoln C.	11.59	1959-63	75		21	
PUNTON, William	Morpeth	18.12.57	Gainsborough	Bradford C.	N/C	1975-76	7	/	0	(G)
PUNTON, William	Perth	09.05.34	Portadown	Newcastle U.	02.54	1953-57	23		1	(W)
			TR	Southend U.	07.58	1958	38		6	
			TR	Norwich C.	07.59	1959-66	219	3	24	
				Sheffield U.	11.66	1966-67	16	/	1	
			TR	Scunthorpe U.	01.68	1967-68	45	1	2	
PURCELL, Brian	Swansea	23.11.38	Tower U.	Swansea C.	01.58	1959-67	160	2	1	(FB) d.1969
PURCELL, Daniel	Chesterfield	15.09.48	JNRS	Chesterfield	AM	1965	0	1	0	(F)
PURDIE, Bernard C.	Wrexham	20.04.49	JNRS	Wrexham	10.67	1968-69	7	3	3	(F)
			TR	Chester C.	07.71	1971-72	54	9	14	
			TR	Crewe Alex.	07.73	1973-79	203	10	44	
			TR	Huddersfield T.	10.79	1979-81	37	9	1	
			TR	Crewe Alex.	08.82	1982	14	2	0	
PURDIE, Ian	Motherwell	07.03.53	Motherwell	Wigan Ath.	07.78	1978-79	54	1	12	(M) S.U23-1
			TR	Portsmouth	11.79	1979	4	1	1	
PURDIE, James J.	Berwick	24.05.18	Airdire	Millwall	+	1946-47	50		0	(G)
			Kilmarnock	Southport	02.49	1948	6		0	
			Tunbridge Wells	Aldershot	10.50	1950	16		0	
PURDON, Edward J.	S. Africa	01.03.30	Maritz Bros.	Birmingham C.	08.50	1951-53	64		27	(CF)
			TR	Sunderland	01.54	1953-56	90		40	
			TR	Workington	03.57	1956-57	33		9	
			TR	Barrow	03.58	1957-58	37		11	
			Bath C.	Bristol Rov.	08.60	1960	4		1	

Players Names	Birthplace	Date	Previous Club	League Club	Date Signed	Seasons Played	Career Record Apps	Sub	Gls	
PURDY, Wilf	Gateshead	08.10.30		Sunderland	09.50					
			TR	Chesterfield	08.51	1951	2		0	
PURSELL, Robert W.	Glasgow	28.09.19		Port Vale	+	1946-47	39		0	Son of Scots Int.
PURVES, Charles R.	High Spen	17.02.21	Spennymoor	Charlton Ath.	10.46	1946-49	46		4	(IF)
			TR	Southampton	06.51	1951-53	30		2	
PURVIS, Bartholomew	Gateshead	15.10.21	Nth.Shields	Everton	+					
			TR	Gateshead	10.46	1946	1		0	
			TR	Reading	03.47					
			TR	Plymouth Arg.	06.47					
			TR	Notts.Co.	05.48	1948-50	25		0	
			TR	Carlisle U.	08.51	1951	4		0	
			TR	Hartlepool U.	08.52					
PURVIS, William Y.	Berwick	14.12.38	Berwick Rgrs.	Grimsby T.	08.61	1961-62	8		2	(F)
			TR	Doncaster Rov.	12.62	1962	2		0	
PUTNEY, Trevor A.	Harold Hill	11.02.61	Brentwood & W.	Ipswich T.	09.80	1982-83	49	6	5	(M)
PYATT, John H.	Barnet	26.09.48	Chesham U.	Liverpool	07.67					(IF)
			TR	Peterborough U.	07.68	1968	15	1	1	
PYE, Fred	Stockport	11.03.28	Stalybridge	Accrington St.	09.48	1947-48	5		0	
PYE, Jesse	Rotherham	22.12.19	Sheffield U.(*)	Notts.Co.	+					(CF)E-1/E'B'-3
			TR	Wolverhampton W.	05.46	1946-51	188		90	E.F.LGE REP.
			TR	Luton T.	07.52	1952-54	60		32	d.1984
			TR	Derby Co.	10.54	1954-56	61		23	
PYE, William	St. Helens	08.11.30		Stockport Co.	08.49					(IF)
			TR	Chester C.	07.52	1953-55	28		11	
PYGALL, David A.	Watford	23.01.39	JNRS	Watford	01.56	1955-60	20		2	(F)
PYKE, Malcolm	Eltham	06.03.38	JNRS	West Ham U.	03.55	1956-57	17		0	(WH)
			TR	Crystal Palace	06.59	1959	2		0	
PYLE, Elijah S.	Chester-le-Street	22.09.18		York C.	11.47	1947-48	10		3	
PYLE, Steve	Nth. Shields	28.09.63	APP	Cambridge U.	07.81	1980-83	16	9	2	(M)
PYLE, Walter D.	Trowbridge	19.12.36	Trowbridge	Bristol Rov.	07.55	1956-61	141		0	(HB)
			TR	Bristol C.	07.62	1962	8		0	
PYM, Ernie	Torquay	23.03.35	St. Marychurch	Torquay U.	09.57	1957-64	283		86	(W)

ALAN OAKES (Manchester C./Chester C.)
Alan Oakes made his debut for Manchester City in 1959 and was still going strong 22 years later at Chester. His boundless enthusiasm with strength in pushing forward and precise passing made the tall blond young man one of the top players of the 1960s and 1970s. With City he was one of the cornerstones in the great side of Mercer and Allison, which during a four year period collected the Football League Championship, F.A. Cup, European Cup Winners Cup and the Football League Cup. He represented the Football League before joining Chester in July 1976 in a player-manager role.

GEORGE O'BRIEN (Leeds U./Southampton/Orient/Aldershot)
A small inside forward, O'Brien packed great shooting power in either boot. He became one of the ''Saints'' great bargains after not shining too brightly with Leeds United who had purchased him from Dunfermline, before allowing him to go to the Dell for a moderate fee in July 1959. He won a Third Division medal during his first season, scoring an invaluable 23 goals, and before transferring to Orient in March 1966 had scored 154 goals from 243 games. Whilst at the club he formed a great partnership with the effervescent Terry Paine.

DAVID O'LEARY (Arsenal & Eire)
A cultured central defender who loves to play out of defence rather than use the big boot, O'Leary came through the "Gunners" apprentice ranks before signing pro forms in July 1975. He has since gone on to play many times for Eire, and proved himself to be at the forefront of the Football League back four players. He was in the Arsenal team that beat Manchester United in the 1979 F.A. Cup Final, but has twice on other occasions been on the losing Arsenal side in a Cup Final. He collected a European Cup Winners Cup runners-up medal in 1980 when the "Gunners", after drawing 0-0 with Valencia at the end of extra time, eventually lost out 5-4 on penalties, which was a bitter pill to swallow.

MARTIN O'NEILL (Nottingham F., Norwich C., Manchester C., Norwich C., Notts Co. & N.Ireland)
O'Neill was signed by Nottingham Forest from Derry in October 1971 to facilitate their midfield – a job he did most effectively. Like many Forest players of that period, it was not until Brian Clough and Peter Taylor took hold of the helm that their success was achieved at club level. As a strong, tough, tackling terrier of a player he fitted directly into the new Forest plans, which culminated in promotion to the First Division 1976/7, and began a playing relationship with Archie Gemmill. The winning of the League Championship in 1977/8, was followed by two European Cup winning medals to add to many Irish International caps on his shelf. In February 1981 he was transferred to Norwich City to help in an unavailing bid to stave off relegation, before signing for Manchester City for a short spell. He rejoined Norwich for £150,000 in January 1982, helping them back to the First Division, but in the close season was again on the move when snapped up by Notts County.

JOHN O'ROURKE (Chelsea/Luton T./Middlesbrough/Ipswich T./Coventry C./Q.P.R./Bournemouth)
A speedy centre forward, O'Rourke was snapped up by Chelsea when freed by Arsenal, where he had been a junior. He never made a League appearance whilst at Stamford Bridge, although getting a League Cup debut in a losing game to Swindon. He was allowed to join Luton Town in December 1963, where in three years he scored 64 goals from 84 games. Joining the 'Boro in July 1966, he was second in the Third Division scoring charts with 27 goals, helping the ''Teesiders'' to attain promotion. Moving on in February 1968, he was able to assist Ipswich Town in returning to the top flight that season. He was not such a heavy goalscorer in the First Division, but possessed a more than useful record, being capped by England at under 23 level.

MAURICE OWEN (Swindon T.)
A blond centre forward, Owen was a wartime chindit in Burma under Wingate, and on demob came home to play for Abingdon, the local side. He was soon spotted by Swindon Town, signing professional in December 1946, and in making his debut against Watford on 11 January 1947, the new boy celebrated by scoring a hat trick. He became much sought after as a speedy opportunist with an eye for the goal and many transfer offers were refused. He never developed into an outstanding striker and later in his career he settled down in the centre of the defence, where his experience was invaluable.

SID OWEN (Birmingham C./Luton T. & England)
Owen was signed for a modest £1,500 from Birmingham City as a wing half in the summer of 1947, developing into one of the great stopper centre halves after being converted by the manager Dally Duncan, who saw in the young man tremendous possibilities. Tall, imposing and red headed, Sid became highly polished at the centre of the Town's defence where, upon reaching a peak in 1954, he was capped three times by England. Unfortunate in playing for his country when England conceded 12 goals without winning any of the three games, he never played again. He retired after having appeared in the losing F.A. Cup Final for Luton against Forest in 1959, going out whilst still at the top.

DEREK PACE (Aston Villa/Sheffield U./Notts Co./Walsall)
Nicknamed "Doc", and rather on the small side for a centre forward, Derek was signed from the Bloxwich Strollers. He was as hardy and tough a player as one could wish to see, a real problem for any defender to cope with, but opportunities were limited at Villa, although he scored on debut in 1951. After not getting selected for the Villa's 1957 F.A. Cup side, he moved on to Sheffield United in December 1957 and, beginning to show a real opportunist trait, scored 140 goals in 253 appearances. He was ever present when the club achieved First Division status again, scoring 26 goals, and was United's top scorer for six seasons before moving to Notts County and then Walsall.

TERRY PAINE (Southampton & England/Hereford U.)
Terry Paine became one of the finest wingmen in the land after being signed by Southampton from Winchester City in February 1957. He collected a Third Division medal with the Saints in 1960, prior to gaining the first of 19 England caps three years later, and as a key member of the Southampton side he helped them into the First Division for the first time in the club's history, 1965/6. Fast, tricky, and elusive, he was two footed and scored over 150 League goals, in addition to his invaluable goal making qualities. Signing as player-coach at Hereford in August 1974, the still elegant soccer artist played over 100 further League games before ending a long and meritorious career.

PHIL PARKES (Walsall/Q.P.R. and England/West Ham U.)
Often brilliant and always reliable, Parkes, a 6ft 3in tall goalminder, signed for Walsall in January 1968, quickly making a tremendous reputation in the Third Division, before joining Q.P.R. for just £15,000 in June 1970. With the Rangers he collected a full England cap and several of the under 23 variety, being one of the prime factors in the club's rise from the Second Division in 1972/3. Later West Ham saw him as the ideal last man for their defence and in an effort to climb out of the Second Division they purchased the gentle giant for £50,000 in February 1979. Promotion plus a Second Division winners medal was achieved as an ever present, Parkes conceding only 29 goals, with the club having a 13-point ascendancy over its nearest rivals. The season he moved to Upton Park, the F.A. Cup was captured against the Arsenal 1-0, and later on runners-up medals were collected in the Football League Cup and European Cup Winners Cup Finals.

DEREK PARKIN (Huddersfield T./Wolverhampton W./Stoke C.)
A left back who followed a long line of classic Huddersfield defenders, Parkin spent three seasons at Leeds Road before signing for the Wolves in February 1968, in an £80,000 deal, which was a record fee at the time for a full back. A very consistent player, he overcame suspected heart trouble in 1972 by immediately finding top form. He did not claim any of the game's major honours at Molineux, but he won two League Cup winners medals to add to representative honours for England at under 23 and Football League levels. When starting out at Huddersfield he formed a full back partnership with Chris Cattlin in following Ramon Wilson and Bob McNab. After reaching 500 League appearnces with the Wolves he was given a free transfer to the "Potteries" side in March 1982.

JACK PARRY (Derby Co.)
A "play anywhere" type, Jack Parry, elder brother of Ray, marked his 1948/9 Derby County debut with a goal. A really good clubman, locally born, he was equally effective at wing half. He never attained the heights of Ray's career, but went on to make 478 League appearances, a County record. He was a member of the "Rams" sides that were relegated from First to Third Division North within two years, but later gained a Third Division North medal in 1956/7. In the Title season, Jack scored 24 goals from 34 games – a most telling feature of the club's success.

RAY PARRY (Bolton W. & England/Blackpool/Bury)
An inside-cum-wing forward Ray Parry was a brilliant schoolboy star who had two brothers, Glyn and Jack, already in League football with Derby County. Another brother, Cyril, followed Ray into the England schools side, later playing for Notts County, but Ray preferred Bolton, signing professional in January 1953. He had made his debut as the youngest ever First Division player versus Wolves on 13 October 1951, aged 15 years 207 days. Having a skilful deceptive left foot, he gained two England caps to follow under 23 caps and youth caps, and also represented the Football League. He picked up an F.A. Cup winners medal in 1958 before being transferred to Blackpool in October 1960 for £25,000. He later moved to Bury where he became player-coach.

ROY PAUL (Swansea C., Manchester C., & Wales)
Many times capped Welsh international Roy Paul joined Manchester City for £25,000 at the age of 27 upon returning from the unsuccessful journey to Bogota in July 1950. Well built, compact and strong, a very constructive wing half, he had previously played for Swansea in a variety of positions. Whilst at Maine Road he had to curb his attacking tendencies to fit the Manchester City "deep lying centre forward plan", and became an inspiring skipper. He captained the City at Wembley two years running; in 1955 losing to Newcastle United; but a year later gaining a winners medal from the "Trautmann" Final, when the keeper played out the game with a broken neck.

ALAN PEACOCK (Middlesbrough & England/Leeds U./Plymouth Arg.)
A prolific goalscoring forward Peacock made his debut for the 'Boro in the same season as Brian Clough, later forming a double spearhead with him, but being rather overshadowed by the other man. In 1957/8 he began to play regularly and over the next four seasons the partnership produced 219 goals before Clough moved to nearby Sunderland. At 6ft tall, Allan was extremely effective and, on becoming leader of the "Teesiders" attack, scored a further 60 goals, also collecting England caps before being signed by Leeds United in February 1964 for £53,000. Unfortunately his career became dogged with injury, and although still scoring heavily, he played less than frequently, eventually leaving for Plymouth Argyle.

STAN PEARSON (Manchester U., & England/Bury/Chester C.)
A Manchester United starlet on the outbreak of war Pearson had to wait before winning his first England cap against Scotland in 1948. A notable opportunist with good distribution, also a great forager, Stan scored in the winning Cup Final of 1948 against Blackpool. An inside forward who, although unspectacular, was an important cog in the United machine, he won a Championship medal in 1952 before moving to Bury in 1954. Still playing nearly as well at the age of 35, Stan carried on until season 1958/9, finally in the colours of Chester. He played eight times for England, and also represented the Football League.

MARTIN PETERS (West Ham U. Tottenham H. & England/Norwich C./Sheffield U.)
Peters was one of the great talents of the modern game, of whom the England team manager Alf Ramsey said "he was ten years ahead of his time" Beginning as a West Ham apprentice, he soon came to the fore in the early 1960s, settling down brilliantly in midfield with fine passing skills, but known mainly for scoring many goals by ghosting into good forward positions. He was a valued member of the World Cup winning side before signing for Spurs in March 1970, becoming Britain's first £200,000 player. Later he gave valuable service to Norwich before going as player manager to Sheffield United in 1980. He never won a League medal but has picked up European Cup Winners Cup and UEFA Cup winners medals to add to 67 England caps.

GEORGE PETHERBRIDGE (Bristol Rov.)
A terrific little outside right only 5ft 4in tall, Petherbridge was extremely fast and dangerous. He could pack quite a shot for one so small, occasionally playing on the opposite flank. He gained a Third Division South medal in 1952/3 when playing 39 games, and helped the Rovers into the Second Division for the first time in the club's history. In 1950/1 the club reached the sixth round of the F.A. Cup, with a significant part being played by the dynamic winger, before going out to the eventual winners Newcastle United after drawing the first match at St. James' Park. He will be remembered at Eastville for his effervescence and great sportmanship.

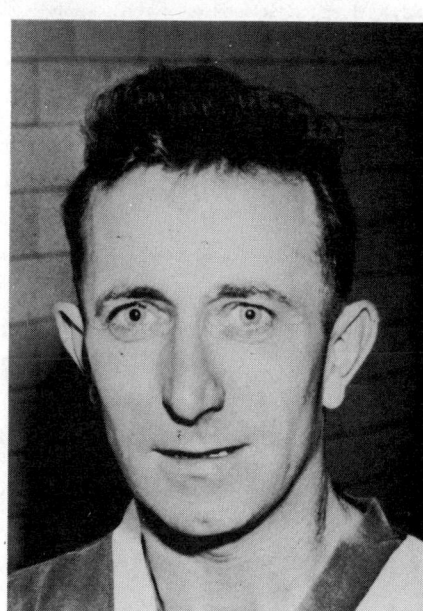

TED PHILLIPS (Ipswich T./Orient/Luton T./Colchester U.)
One of the most prolific goalscoring inside forwards of the post-war years, Phillips made his debut for Ipswich in 1953/4, but not until 1956/7 did the tall, strongly made player become a regular, scoring 41 goals in as many games. This sensational form was one of the significant factors in getting Alf Ramsey's team out of the Third Division South that term. Over the next two seasons Ted surprisingly did not play much, but in 1959/60 he came back "with a bang" and the next season scored 30 from 42 appearances, this time collecting a Division Two winners medal. Season 1961/2 brought Phillips 28 goals from 40 appearances and this time a Championship medal. In his career, Ted collected just short of 200 League goals with a 57% scoring rate.

FRED PICKERING (Blackburn Rov./Everton & England/Birmingham C./Blackpool/Blackburn Rov./Brighton & H.A.)
A tall, well made player Pickering came through the youth squad at Ewood Park as a full back, signing professional forms in January 1958, and making his debut the next season in the defence. The Rovers were well served in that department and opportunities for the youngster were limited, but on being switched to leader of the attack he was very successful. Transferred to Everton as the answer to their scoring problems in March 1964, the next season he collected 27 goals, the best by any Everton player in the First Division since Tommy Lawton hit 25 in 1938/9. Unfortunately he missed the 1966 F.A. Cup Final against Sheffield Wednesday owing to injury, but later went on to play for three further clubs, retiring on trial with Brighton.

JACK PITT (Bristol Rov.)
A highly polished, thoughtful wing half who in 11 post-war seasons missed only 37 games, Pitt was originally on the books of West Brom, but during the war appeared for Bath City, turning professional for the Rovers on the resumption of League football. He was skipper in 1955/6, having gained a Third Division South medal 1952/3 and having played in the Rovers' greatest ever F.A. Cup run two years previously. Enthusiastic in his quest to achieve success at Eastville, Jack was a tough tackler who could produce telling passes. Recognised not only as one of the club's most consistent players, he was also one of their greatest.

RAY POINTER (Burnley & England/Bury/Coventry C./Portsmouth)
A goalgetting, tireless, blond haired centre forward, Pointer was picked up by Burnley from Dudley Welfare in the North East after being turned down by Blackpool. Two months after joining the club in August 1957 Roy made his debut, winning a Championship medal in 1959/60 and going on to play in the losing 1962 F.A. Cup Final against the mighty Spurs. That same year he was given three England caps but by the next season was no longer a regular at Turf Moor, losing his England place into the bargain. Later, not settling with either Bury or Coventry, he moved to Portsmouth, playing more in a midfield role.

HARRY POOLE (Port Vale)
After playing for Oxford City in the Isthmian League whilst doing National Service, Harry went home to sign for Port Vale in April 1956. Appearing mainly at wing half in earlier games for the club, he later settled down at inside forward. He won a Fourth Division medal in 1958/9, making 35 appearances and scoring 17 goals. Later in his career he reverted back to wing half, playing over 450 League games.

RONNIE POWELL (Manchester C./Chesterfield)
Powell was a young Manchester City goalie up from Wales who signed professional November 1948. He played 12 games the next season following the retirement of Frank Swift, but was replaced when Bert Trautmann was discovered with St. Helens and was drafted into the City side immediately. Because it was obvious that the great German keeper was not going to be displaced, Powell was allowed to move to Chesterfield in June 1952, where he made an initial run of 284 League games without a break. Eventually he played 471 times for the "Spireites" before retiring. He was not very tall for a keeper but had great agility coupled with good handling.

Players Names	Birthplace	Date	Previous Club	League Club	Date Signed	Seasons Played	Apps	Sub	Gls	
QUAIRNEY, John	Girvan	07.01.27	Girvan J.	Rotherham U.	07.48	1948-59	260		0	(G)
QUATERMAIN, Pat	Oxford	16.04.37	JNRS	Oxford U.	N/L	1962-66	185	1	0	(FB)
QUEEN, Gerry	Glasgow	15.01.45	Kilmarnock	Crystal Palace	07.69	1969-72	101	7	24	(F)
			TR	Orient	09.72	1972-76	149	7	34	
QUESTED, Len W.	Folkestone	09.01.25	Folkestone T.	Fulham	08.46	1946-51	175		6	(WH)E'B-1
			TR	Huddersfield T.	11.51	1951-56	220		8	
QUIGLEY, Eddie	Bury	13.07.21	JNRS	Bury	+	1946-47	42		18	(IF)E'B'-2●
			TR	Sheffield Wed.	10.47	1947-49	74		50	
			TR	Preston N.E.	12.49	1949-51	52		17	
			TR	Blackburn Rov.	11.51	1951-55	159		92	
			TR	Bury	08.56	1956	10		3	
QUIGLEY, Gilbert	Ulverston	17.02.21	Vickers Spts.	Barrow	+	1946-48	27		0	(WH)
QUIGLEY, John	Glasgow	28.06.35	Ashfield J.	Nottingham F.	07.57	1957-64	236		51	(IF)
			TR	Huddersfield T.	02.65	1964-66	67	1	5	
			TR	Bristol C.	10.66	1966-67	66	/	7	
			TR	Mansfield T.	07.68	1968-70	104	/	2	
QUIGLEY, Tom	Mid Calder	26.03.32	Barry T.	Portsmouth	12.55					(F)
			TR	Q.P.R.	06.56	1956	16		7	
QUINLAN, Edward M.	Finsbury Park	15.08.31	Gt.Yarmouth	Tottenham H.	03.52					(F)
			TR	Reading	06.53	1953-55	51		11	
QUINLAN, Mike	Barnsley	04.12.41	Doncaster Rov.(AM)	Bristol C.	03.59	1960	2		0	(CH)
QUINN, Albert	Lanchester	18.04.20		Sunderland	11.46	1947	6		2	(F)
			TR	Darlington	05.48	1948-50	86		43	
QUINN, Anthony M.	Liverpool	24.07.59	Everton (N/C)	Wigan Ath.	01.79	1979-80	36	7	14	(F)
QUINN, Des	Co.Down	21.03.26		Blackburn Rov.	08.47	1947	1		0	(FB)
			TR	Millwall	06.49	1949-54	43		0	
QUINN, Gordon P.	London	11.05.32	Eastcote B.C.	Q.P.R.	08.52	1952-56	21		1	(IF)
			TR	Plymouth Arg.	09.56	1956-57	14		2	
QUINN, James	Kilsyth	23.11.47	Glasgow Celtic	Sheffield Wed.	11.75	1974-75	46	/	1	(FB)
QUINN, James M.	Belfast	18.11.59	Oswestry T.	Swindon T.	12.81	1981-83	34	15	10	(F)
QUINN, John D.	St. Helens	30.05.38	Prescot Cables	Sheffield Wed.	05.59	1959-67	165	8	19	(IF)
			TR	Rotherham U.	11.67	1967-71	114	/	7	
			TR	Halifax T.	07.72	1972-74	88	4	1	
QUINN, Mike	Liverpool	02.05.62	Derby Co. (APP)	Wigan Ath.	09.79	1979-81	56	13	19	(F)
			TR	Stockport Co.	07.82	1982-83	62	1	39	
			TR	Oldham Ath.	01.84	1983	14	/	5	
QUINN, Noel	Dublin	02.11.49	Manchester U.(AM)	Oldham Ath.	01.67	1967	4	/	0	(IF)
QUINN, Pat	Glasgow	26.04.36	Motherwell	Blackpool	11.62	1962-63	34		9	(IF)S-4/S.F.LGE REP.
QUINN, Pat	Croy	21.06.18	Ashfield J.	Halifax T.	07.46	1946	25		6	(RH) d.1979
QUINNEY, Henry J.	Rugby	15.10.22	Wolverhampton W.(AM)	Northampton T.	+	1946	3		0	(FB)
QUINNEY, John	Rugby	02.10.32	JNRS	Coventry C.	11.49	1952	3		0	
QUINTON, Walter	Anstow	13.12.17	Rotherham U.(*)	Birmingham C.	+	1947	8		0	
			TR	Brentford	04.49	1948-50	42		0	
			TR	Southend U.	08.52					
			TR	Shrewsbury T.	10.52	1952	3		0	
QUIRKE, David	Bedford	11.01.47	Bedford T.	Gillingham	07.66	1967-73	221	9	0	(HB)
QUIXALL, Albert	Sheffield	09.08.33	JNRS	Sheffield Wed.	08.50	1950-58	241		63	(IF)E-5/E.U23-1/
			TR	Manchester U.	09.58	1958-63	165		51	E.F.LGE REP./E'B'-3
			TR	Oldham Ath.	09.64	1964-65	37	/	11	E.SCH.INT.
			TR	Stockport Co.	07.66	1966	13	/	0	
QUOW, Trevor	Peterborough	28.09.60	APP	Peterborough U.	09.78	1978-83	127	10	13	(M)

Players Names	Birthplace	Date	Previous Club	League Club	Date Signed	Seasons Played	Career Record Apps	Sub	Gls	
RABJOHN, Chris	Sheffield	10.03.45	JNRS	Rotherham U.	07.63	1965-67	76	2	4	(HB)
			TR	Doncaster Rov.	02.68	1967-72	137	16	8	
RACKHAM, Derek	Norwich	14.06.28	Norman YC	Norwich C.	11.49	1951	8		2	(F)
RACKLEY, Robert W.	Teignmouth	15.03.40		Exeter C.	03.58					(F)
			TR	Bristol Rov.	07.60					
			TR	Oldham Ath.	10.60	1960	19		7	
RACKSTRAW, Charlie	Sheffield	23.04.38		Chesterfield	03.58	1958-63	172		48	(IF)
			TR	Gillingham	05.64	1964-66	93	1	25	
			TR	Bradford C.	01.67	1966-69	94	10	27	
RADCLIFFE, Mark	Hyde	26.10.19	Oldham Ath.(+)	Fulham	08.46	1946-47	11		0	(G)
			Wilton A.	Rochdale	11.52	1952	1		0	
RADCLIFFE, Vince	Manchester	09.06.45	APP	Portsmouth	06.63	1964-66	10	/	0	(HB)
			TR	Peterborough U.	07.67	1967	2	/	0	
			TR	Rochdale	07.68	1968	26	/	1	
RADFORD, Arthur	Rotherham	07.10.25		Huddersfield T.	+					
				Rotherham U.	05.47	1947-49	44		0	
			TR	Rochdale	06.51	1951	27		0	
			TR	Swindon T.	08.52	1952	15		0	
RADFORD, John	Pontefract	22.02.47	APP	Arsenal	03.64	1963-76	375	4	111	(F)E-2/E.U23-4/
			TR	West Ham U.	12.76	1976-77	28	/	0	E.F.LGE REP.
			TR	Blackburn Rov.	02.78	1977-78	36	/	10	
RADFORD, Ron	Sth. Elmsall	12.07.43	Sheffield Wed.(AM)	Leeds U.	10.61					(IF)
			Cheltenham	Newport Co.	07.69	1969-70	63	3	7	
			TR	Hereford U.	N/L	1972-73	61	/	6	
RADFORD, W. Howard	Abercynon	08.09.30	Penrhiwceiber	Bristol Rov.	08.51	1951-61	244		0	(G)
RAE, Alex	Glasgow	23.08.46	E.Fife	Bury	05.69	1969	10	1	0	(HB)
RAE, Ian J.	Grangemouth	19.01.33	Falkirk	Bristol C.	10.57	1957	12		0	(CH)S.U23-1/S'B'-1
RAE, Joe	Glasgow	06.03.25	Glasgow Celtic	Torquay U.	07.48	1948	20		4	
RAFFERTY, Bernard	Manchester	09.07.48		Bradford P.A.	10.69	1969	8	4	1	(F)
RAFFERTY, James	Manchester	07.11.30		Manchester C.	12.48					
			TR	Bradford P.A.	06.52	1952	2		0	
RAFFERTY, Kevin B.	Nairobi	09.11.60	APP	Crewe Alex.	12.78	1978-79	22	/	0	(G)
RAFFERTY, Pat T.	Stoke	28.11.25		Port Vale	01.49	1948-49	5		0	
RAFFERTY, Ron	Newcastle	06.05.34	Wycombe W.	Portsmouth	07.54	1954-56	23		5	(IF)●
			TR	Grimsby T.	12.56	1956-62	263		145	
			TR	Hull C.	07.63	1963-64	16		6	
			TR	Aldershot	07.66	1966-68	79	2	10	
RAFFERTY, Willie H.	Glasgow	30.12.50	Port Glasgow	Coventry C.	09.69	1969-72	27	/	3	(F)
			TR	Blackpool	10.72	1972-73	35	1	9	
			TR	Plymouth Arg.	03.74	1973-75	89	1	35	
			TR	Carlisle U.	05.76	1976-77	72	/	27	
			TR	Wolverhampton W.	03.78	1977-79	41	3	6	
			TR	Newcastle U.	10.79	1979-80	34	5	6	
			TR	Portsmouth	12.80	1980-82	98	4	40	
			TR	Bournemouth	02.84	1983	17	/	5	
RAFTER, Sean	Rochford	20.05.57	APP	Southend U.	06.75	1975-77	23	/	0	(G)
			TR	Leicester C.	01.78					
			TR	Orient	07.79	1980	2	/	0	
RAGGETT, Brian C.	Barnsley	11.01.49	APP	Barnsley	01.67	1966-71	57	7	0	(FB)
RAINE, David	Darlington	28.03.37		Port Vale	05.57	1956-61	144		0	(FB)
			TR	Doncaster Rov.	07.62	1962-64	107		2	
			TR	Colchester U.	06.65	1965-66	44	4	0	
RAINE, Robert R.	Chesterfield	17.11.27	Newbold Col.	Chesterfield	02.49	1949	1		0	(CF)
			TR	Aldershot	02.51	1950-53	48		20	
RAINEY, Hugh	Dumbarton	07.01.35	Renton Guild	Portsmouth	06.53					(HB)
			TR	Q.P.R.	06.55					
			TR	Aldershot	07.57	1957	8		0	
RAINFORD, John W.	London	11.12.30	JNRS	Crystal Palace	03.49	1948-52	64		8	(IF)
			TR	Cardiff C.	05.53	1953	3		1	
			TR	Brentford	10.53	1953-61	299		42	
RAINFORD, Ken S.	Saughall Massie	04.11.26	New Brighton Baptists	New Brighton	AM	1947	3		1	(F)
RAJKOVIC, Ante	Yugoslavia	17.08.52	Sarajevo	Swansea C.	03.81	1980-83	78	/	2	(D)YUGOSLAV INT.
RALSTON, Peter	Glasgow	31.01.29	Falkirk	Accrington St.	08.57	1957-58	6		0	(HB)
RALSTON, Walter	Glasgow	03.10.35	Partick Th.	Aldershot	06.58	1958	3		0	(HB) L Transfer
RAMAGE, Alan	Guisborough	29.11.57	APP	Middlesbrough	12.75	1975-79	67	4	2	(D)Yorks Cricketer
			TR	Derby Co.	07.80	1980-81	32	1	2	
RAMAGE, George M.	Newbattle	29.01.37	T. Lanark	Colchester U.	08.61	1962-63	38		0	(G)
			TR	Orient	07.64	1964	4		0	
			TR	Luton T.	11.65	1965	7	/	0	
RAMPLING, Dennis W.	Gainsborough	25.11.23		Fulham	+	1947	2		0	
			TR	Bournemouth	07.48	1948	24		4	
			TR	Brentford	05.49	1949	1		0	

Players Names	Birthplace	Date	Previous Club	League Club	Date Signed	Seasons Played	Career Record Apps Sub Gls		
RAMPLING, Edward	Wigan	17.02.48		Chester C.	03.67	1967	2	1	0 (F)
RAMSAY, George A.	Sunderland	24.04.23	Raith Rovers	Gateshead	11.46	1946	7		1 (OR)
RAMSBOTTOM, Neil	Blackburn	25.02.46	JNRS	Bury	07.64	1965-70	174	/	0 (G)
			TR	Blackpool	02.71	1970-71	13	/	0
			L	Crewe Alex.	01.72	1971	3	/	0
			TR	Coventry C.	03.72	1972-74	51	/	0
			TR	Sheffield Wed.	08.75	1975	18	/	0
			TR	Plymouth Arg.	07.76	1976	39	/	0
			TR	Blackburn Rov.	01.78	1978	10	/	0
			Miami	Sheffield U.	10.79	1979	2	/	0
			TR	Bradford C.	08.80	1980-82	73	/	0
			TR	Bournemouth	N/C	1983	4	/	0
RAMSCAR, Fred T.	Salford	24.01.19	Stockport Co.(AM)	Wolverhampton W.	+	1946	16		1 (IF)
			TR	Q.P.R.	10.47	1947-49	51		4
			TR	Preson N.E.	11.49	1949-50	19		4
			TR	Northampton T.	07.51	1951-54	139		56
			TR	Millwall	09.54	1954	30		5
RAMSDEN, Bernard	Sheffield	08.11.17		Liverpool	*	1946-47	33		0 (FB)
			TR	Sunderland	03.48	1947-48	12		0
			TR	Hartlepool U.	01.50	1949	13		0
RAMSEY, Alf E.	Dagenham	22.01.20	Portsmouth(AM)	Southampton	+	1946-48	90		8 (FB)E-32/E.F.LGE REP.●
			TR	Tottenham H.	05.49	1949-54	226		24
RAMSEY, Chris L.	Birmingham	28.04.62	Bristol C.(N/C)	Brighton & H.A.	08.80	1980-83	30	/	0 (D)
RAMSEY, Craig J.	Dunfermline	19.09.62	APP	Lincoln C.	09.80	1979-80	3	2	2 (F)
RAMSEY, Don	Manchester	27.09.28		Oldham Ath.	11.46	1949	2		0
RAMSEY, Paul	Londonderry	03.09.62	APP	Leicester C.	04.80	1980-83	84	2	2 (M)NI-3
RAMSEY, Robert	Sunderland	24.02.35	JNRS	Huddersfield T.	01.53				(FB)
			TR	York C.	05.58	1958-60	75		0
RANDALL, Ernie A.W.	Bognor Regis	13.01.26	Bognor	Chelsea	12.50	1951	3		1 (IF)
			TR	Crystal Palace	06.53	1953-54	22		12
RANDALL, Kevin	Ashton-under-Lyne	20.08.45	Droylsden	Bury	10.65	1965	4	/	0 (F)
			TR	Chesterfield	07.66	1966-71	258	/	97
			TR	Notts. Co.	08.72	1972-75	119	2	38
			TR	Mansfield T.	11.75	1975-77	62	4	20
			TR	York C.	10.77	1977-80	96	11	27
RANDALL, Maurice	Manchester	04.08.19	Droylsden	Crewe Alex.	02.47	1946-48	41		0 (LB) d.1976
RANDALL, Paul	Liverpool	16.02.58	Frome T.	Bristol Rov.	08.77	1977-78	49	3	33 (F)
			TR	Stoke C.	12.78	1978-80	38	8	7
			TR	Bristol Rov.	01.81	1980-83	111	13	41
RANDELL, Colin W.	Skewen	12.12.52	APP	Coventry C.	11.70				(M)W.U23-1/W.SCH.INT.
			TR	Plymouth Arg.	09.73	1973-76	137	2	9
			TR	Exeter C.	09.77	1977-78	78	/	4
			TR	Plymouth Arg.	07.79	1979-81	110	/	8
			TR	Blackburn Rov.	08.82	1982-83	42	1	4
			L	Newport Co.	03.84	1983	15	/	0
RANDLES, Tom	Blackpool	13.10.40	Ellesmere Port	Stoke C.	02.60	1961	2		0 (F)
RANKIN, Andy	Liverpool	11.05.44	JNRS	Everton	10.61	1963-70	85	/	0 (G)E.U23-1
			TR	Watford	11.71	1971-79	299	/	0
			TR	Huddersfield T.	12.79	1979-81	71	/	0
RANKIN, George	Liverpool	29.01.30	JNRS	Everton	08.48	1950-55	36		0 (FB)E.YTH.INT
			TR	Southport	07.56	1956-59	144		0
RANKIN, James	Gateshead	08.09.27	JNRS	Newcastle U.	+				
				Brighton & H.A.	08.49				
			TR	Grimsby T.	01.50	1949-50	5		1
RANKMORE, Frank	Cardiff	21.07.39	Cardiff Corries	Cardiff C.	12.57	1961-62	67		0 (CH)W-1/W.U23-2
			TR	Peterborough U.	08.63	1963-67	201	/	7
			TR	Northampton T.	06.68	1968-70	103	/	14
RANSHAW, Jack W.	Nettleham	19.12.16	Grantham	Lincoln C.	+	1946	3		0 (OL)
RANSON, Ray	St. Helens	12.06.60	APP	Manchester C.	06.77	1978-83	181	2	1 (D)E.U21-7/E.SCH.INT.
RAPER, Ken	Consett	15.05.56	APP	Stoke C.	06.73				(M)
			TR	Torquay U.	07.77	1977-78	51	1	8
RAPLEY, Peter	Portsmouth	24.10.36	Portsmouth(AM)	Exeter C.	06.57	1957-59	10		4 (WH)
RATCLIFFE, Barrie J.	Blackburn	21.09.41	JNRS	Blackburn Rov.	09.58	1959-63	36		4 (OL)
			TR	Scunthorpe U.	05.64	1964	26		7
			TR	Rochdale	07.65	1965	11	/	1
RATCLIFFE, Beaumont	Barmborough	24.04.09	Oldham Ath.(*)	Reading	05.46	1946-47	32		0 (CH)
			TR	Watford	05.48	1948	24		0
RATCLIFFE, David	Dewsbury	09.03.57	APP	Bradford C.	03.75	1974-77	17	11	1 (D)
RATCLIFFE, Don	Newcastle-U-Lyme	13.11.34		Stoke C.	05.53	1954-63	237		15 (IF)
			TR	Middlesbrough	09.63	1963-65	65	/	3
			TR	Darlington	02.66	1965-67	84	1	12
			TR	Crewe Alex.	01.68	1967-68	45	3	2

Players Names	Birthplace	Date	Previous Club	League Club	Date Signed	Seasons Played	Apps	Sub	Gls	
RATCLIFFE, Kevin	Mancot	12.11.60	APP	Everton	11.78	1979-83	114	1	1	(D)W-24/W.U21-2/ W.SCH.INT.
RATCLIFFE, Paddy C.	Dublin	31.12.19		Notts. Co.	+					(FB)
			TR	Wolverhampton W.	06.46	1946	2		0	
			TR	Plymouth Arg.	06.47	1947-55	236		10	
RATCLIFFE, Ray	St.Helens	03.11.29		Stockport Co.	08.49	1948	1		0	
RATHBONE, Graham C.	Newport	22.08.42	Merthyr Tydfil	Newport Co.	03.61	1960-66	190	/	6	(CH)
			TR	Grimsby T.	11.66	1966-72	232	1	11	
			TR	Cambridge U.	02.73	1972-73	35	1	0	
RATHBONE, Mike J.	Birmingham	06.11.58	APP	Birmingham C.	11.76	1976-78	17	3	0	(D)E.YTH.INT.
			TR	Blackburn Rov.	03.79	1978-83	162	2	2	
RATTRAY, Peter K.	Bannockburn	07.11.25	Dundee	Plymouth Arg.	09.50	1950-51	54		21	(F)
			TR	Norwich C.	06.52	1952-53	24		5	
RAWCLIFFE, Frank	Blackburn	10.12.21	Notts.Co.(+)	Newport Co.	06.46	1946	37		16	(F)
			TR	Swansea C.	05.47	1947	25		17	
			TR	Aldershot	07.48	1948	35		14	
RAWES, Herbert	Frizington	23.11.32		Carlisle U.	09.53	1953-54	11		1	
RAWLINGS, Charles J.	Coleshill	04.11.32	Erdington A.	W.B.A.	03.50					(WH)
			TR	Walsall	06.56	1956-62	201		5	
			TR	Port Vale	07.63	1963-64	31		2	
RAWLINGS, David	Llay	12.12.43		Wrexham	AM	1965	1	/	0	(OL)
RAWLINGS, James S.D.	Wombwell	05.05.13	Millwall(*)	Everton	+					(OR)*Preston N.E./
			TR	Plymouth Arg.	05.46	1946-47	56		20	Huddersfield T./W.B.A./ Northampton T./d.1956 Son of International
RAWLINGSON, John	Wallsen	07.04.44	Corinthian J.	Bury	07.62	1964	2		0	(HB)
			TR	Barrow	07.65	1965	19	/	2	
RAWSON, Colin	Shirebrook	12.11.26		Nottingham F.	*	1946	1		0	(WH)
			Peterborough U.	Rotherham U.	07.48	1949-52	113		12	
			TR	Sheffield U.	03.53	1953-55	70		1	
			TR	Millwall	10.55	1955-58	158		5	
			TR	Torquay U.	07.59	1959-61	86		2	
RAWSON, J.Ken	Nottingham	31.03.21		Nottingham F.	12.46	1947-49	6		0	
RAWSON, Ken	Ripley	18.09.31		Notts.Co.	05.53	1954-60	34		0	(HB)
RAY, Cecil H.	W.Grinstead	25.10.11	Lewes U.	Aldershot	*	1946	1		0	
RAY, John D.	Wolverhampton	07.11.46		Shrewsbury T.	01.65	1965	7	/	0	(F)
RAY, Philip	Wallsend	21.11.64	APP	Burnley	11.82	1982	1	/	0	(D)
			L	Hartlepool U.	10.82	1983	5	/	1	
RAYBOULD, Eric	Manchester	08.12.40		Chester C.	07.60	1960-61	10		0	(HB)
RAYBOULD, Philip E.	Caerphilly	26.05.48	Bridgend Th.	Swansea C.	07.68	1967-68	10	2	4	(IF)W.AMAT.INT./
			TR	Newport Co.	09.69	1969	5	1	1	W.SCH.INT
RAYMENT, Joe W.	W. Hartlepool	25.09.34	JNRS	Middlesbrough	10.51	1952-54	24		4	(OR)
			TR	Hartlepool U.	07.55	1955-57	63		17	
			TR	Darlington	07.58	1958-64	173		28	
RAYMENT, Pat J.	Peterborough	11.04.65	APP	Peterborough U.	04.83	1981-83	24	5	3	(D)
RAYNER, A. Edward	Salford	18.08.32	Northwich	Stoke C.	05.55	1956-59	4		0	(F)
RAYNER, Edward	Hemsworth	28.09.16	Scarborough	Halifax T.	+	1946-50	137		0	(G)
RAYNER, James P.	Cornsay	31.03.35	JNRS	Grimsby T.	05.52	1952-53	12		3	(HB)
				Hartlepool U.	11.54					
			TR	Bury	06.55					
			TR	Barrow	09.55	1955	11		1	
			Grantham	Peterborough U.	N/L	1960-62	119		12	
			Grantham	Notts.Co.	09.64	1964	32		13	
RAYNER, Warren A.	Bradford	24.04.57	APP	Bradford C.	04.75	1974-76	13	4	0	(M)
RAYNES, John	Sheffield	04.11.28	JNRS	Sheffield U.	+					(OL)
				Rotherham U.	03.49	1949	5		1	
			Worksop T.	Northampton T.	07.51					
RAYNES, William	Sheffield	30.10.64	Heanor T.	Rotherham U.	09.83	1983	11	3	1	(W)
RAYNOR, Paul E.	Chester	03.09.57	APP	Chester C.	07.76	1976-81	196	1	9	(D)
			Oswestry	Chester C.	N/C	1983	3	/	0	
RAYNOR, Robert	Nottingham	30.08.40		Nottingham F.	05.64					(G)
			TR	Halifax T.	08.65	1965-66	17	/	0	
REA, Ken W.	Liverpool	17.02.35	JNRS	Everton	06.52	1956-58	46		0	(WH)
REA, Wallace	Uddingston	21.08.35	Motherwell	Bradford C.	07.59	1959	11		2	(W)
READ, David P.	W. Bromwich	15.01.41	JNRS	Wolverhampton W.	10.58					(W)
			TR	Chester C.	10.62	1962-66	68	1	6	
READ, J. Anthony	Haydock	05.07.42	Wolverhampton W.(AM)	Sheffield W.	01.60					(G) 28 apps. on field
			TR	Peterborough U.	05.64	1964	2		0	for Luton T.
			TR	Luton T.	03.65	1964-71	196	2	12	
READER, Peter	East Ham	08.03.41	JNRS	West Ham U.	06.59					(G)E.YTH.INT.
			TR	Millwall	06.61	1961	1		0	

Players Names	Birthplace	Date	Previous Club	League Club	Date Signed	Seasons Played	Career Record Apps	Sub	Gls	
READFERN, T. Edward	Crook	09.07.44	JNRS	W.B.A.	08.61	1963	4		0	(CF)
REAGAN, C. Martin	York	12.05.24		York C.	09.46	1946	1		0	(OR)
			TR	Hull C.	04.47	1946-47	19		1	
			TR	Middlesbrough	02.48	1947-50	24		4	
			TR	Shrewsbury T.	08.51	1951-52	58		9	
			TR	Portsmouth	01.53	1952-53	6		0	
			TR	Norwich C.	06.54	1954-56	34		4	
REANEY, Paul	London	22.10.44	JNRS	Leeds U.	10.61	1962-77	550	6	6	(D)E-3/E.U23-5/●
			TR	Bradford C.	06.78	1978-79	37	1	0	E.F.LGE REP.
REAY, Edwin P.	Tynemouth	05.08.14		Q.P.R.	*	1946-49	23		0	
REDDIE, Tom M.	Stirling	05.10.26	Falkirk	Aldershot	07.51	1951-56	97		1	(HB)
REDDING, Tom R.	Grimsby	17.03.32	Brigg T.	Grimsby T.	07.54	1954-56	4		0	
REDFEARN, Brian	Bradford	20.02.35	JNRS	Bradford P.A.	08.52	1952-57	130		32	(OL)
			TR	Blackburn Rov.	12.57					
			TR	Darlington	06.59	1959-60	49		15	
			TR	Halifax T.	06.61	1961-62	67		10	
			TR	Bradford C.	07.63	1963	7		2	
REDFEARN, Neil D.	Dewsbury	20.06.65	Nottingham F.(APP)	Bolton W.	06.82	1982-83	35	/	1	(M)
			L	Lincoln C.	03.84	1983	10	/	1	
REDFERN, Edward	Liverpool	24.06.20	Unity Boys.	New Brighton	01.48	1947-49	20		0	
REDFERN, Fred	Hyde	28.09.14	Hyde U.	Stockport Co.	+	1946-47	36		0	(RB)
REDFERN, James	Kirkby	01.08.52	APP	Bolton W.	08.69	1969-72	19	5	2	(F)
			TR	Chester C.	08.73	1973-76	98	8	15	
REDFERN, Robert	Crook	03.03.18	Wolverhampton W.(*)	Bournemouth	*	1946	8		0	(OR)
			TR	Brighton & H.A.	08.47	1947	5		1	
REDHEAD, William S.	Newcastle	10.10.35	Fatfield J.	Newcastle U.	08.54	1956	1		0	(HB)
			TR	Gateshead	08.59	1959	19		0	
REDKNAPP, Harry J.	Poplar	02.03.47	APP	West Ham U.	03.64	1965-71	146	3	7	(W)E.YTH.INT.
			TR	Bournemouth	08.72	1972-75	96	5	5	
			TR	Brentford	09.76	1976	1	/	0	
			TR	Bournemouth	N/C	1982	1	/	0	
REDMAN, William	Manchester	29.01.28	JNRS	Manchester U.	11.46	1950-53	36		0	(FB)
			TR	Bury	06.54	1954-55	37		1	
REDMOND, Harry	Manchester	24.03.33	Tavistock	Crystal Palace	04.57	1957	2		0	(FB)
			TR	Millwall	05.58	1958-60	55		0	
REDROBE, W. Eric	Wigan	23.08.44	JNRS	Bolton W.	02.62	1963-65	4	/	1	(F)E.YTH.INT.
			TR	Colchester U.	07.66					
			TR	Southport	08.66	1966-72	186	6	55	
			TR	Hereford U.	10.72	1972-77	75	12	17	
REDWOOD, Barry K.	Torquay	11.09.46	APP	Exeter C.	09.64	1964	1		0	(CF)
REECE, Gil	Cardiff	02.07.42	JNRS	Cardiff C.	05.61					(W)W-29/W.SCH.INT.
			Pembroke Bor.	Newport Co.	06.63	1963-64	32	/	9	
			TR	Sheffield U.	04.65	1965-72	197	13	58	
			TR	Cardiff C.	09.72	1972-75	94	6	23	
			TR	Swansea C.	07.76	1976	0	2	0	
REECE, Tom S.	Wolverhampton	17.05.19	Wolverhampton W.(*)	Crystal Palace	*	1946-47	66		5	
REED, Barry R.F.	Huntingdon	24.11.37	St.Neots	Leicester C.	03.55					(FB)
			TR	Luton T.	05.61	1961	1		0	
REED, Frank N.	Seaham	12.10.33	Murton C.W.	Charlton Ath.	08.54	1955-62	29		/	(G)
REED, George	Normanton	16.07.38		Halifax T.	08.61	1962	2		0	(HB)
REED, Graham	Doncaster	24.06.61	APP	Barnsley	07.79	1978-79	3	/	0	(F)
REED, Graham	Kings Lynn	06.02.38	Kings Lynn	Sunderland	02.55	1957	5		0	(HB)
REED, Hugh D.	Alexandria	23.08.50	JNRS	W.B.A.	08.67	1968-70	5	3	2	(F)
			TR	Plymouth Arg.	11.71	1971-73	44	12	9	
			L	Brentford	10.73	1973	3	1	0	
			TR	Crewe Alex.	07.74	1974-75	38	9	9	
			TR	Huddersfield T.	09.76					
			TR	Hartlepool U.	10.76	1976	6	/	1	
REED, Kevin D.	Leicester	22.09.60	APP	Leicester C.	05.78	1978	0	1	0	(F)
REED, Steve E.	Doncaster	06.01.56	APP	Doncaster Rov.	01.74	1972-78	137	3	2	(D)
REED, Tom R.	Haltwhistle	04.10.34		Newport Co.	01.54	1953-54	2		0	(WH)
REED, William G.	Rhondda	25.01.28	Rhondda T.	Cardiff C.	07.47					(OR)W-2/W.AMAT.INT./
			TR	Brighton & H.A.	08.48	1948-52	129		39	W.SCH.INT.
			TR	Ipswich T.	07.53	1953-57	155		43	
			TR	Swansea C.	02.58	1957	8		0	
REES, Anthony A.	Merthyr Tydfil	01.08.64	APP	Aston Villa	08.82					(F)W.SCH.INT./W.U'21-1
			TR	Birmingham C.	07.83	1983	22	3	2	
REES, Barry G.	Rhyl	04.02.44	JNRS	Everton	09.61	1963-64	4		2	(F) d.1965
			TR	Brighton & H.A.	01.65	1964	12		1	
REES, Derek W.	Swansea	18.02.34		Portsmouth	05.54	1953-56	47		15	(OL)
			TR	Ipswich T.	05.57	1957-60	90		29	

Players Names	Birthplace	Date	Previous Club	League Club	Date Signed	Seasons Played	Apps	Sub	Gls	
REES, Doug C.	Slyne	12.02.23	Troedyrhiw	Ipswich T.	02.49	1948-58	356		0	(CH)W.AMAT.INT
REES, Graham J.	Pontypridd	28.08.37	Pontypridd YC	Exeter C.	09.54	1954-65	343	/	83	(W)
REES, Ian D.	Crosshands	21.09.43	Ammanford	Swansea C.	12.61	1964-68	2	2	0	(IF)
REES, John F.	Bedlinog	03.02.33	Troedyrhiw	Newport Co.	AM	1952	2		0	(CF)
REES, Maldwyn J.F.	Neath	21.04.24		Norwich C.	05.47					
				Brighton & H.A.	09.49	1949	2		0	
			TR	Scunthorpe U.	07.50	1950	18		1	
REES, Mark	Smethwick	13.10.61	APP	Walsall	08.79	1978-83	117	26	24	(F)E.SCH.INT.
REES, Nigel R.	Bridgend	11.07.53	JNRS	Cardiff C.	08.70	1970-72	21	6	1	(W)
REES, Peter N.	Machynlleth	05.05.32	Llanidloes	Tranmere Rov.	AM	1956	9		4	(F)
REES, R. Clive	Nantymoel	07.09.37		Newport Co.	AM	1962	4		0	(G)
REES, Ron R.	Ystradgynlais	04.04.44	APP	Coventry C.	05.62	1962-67	230	/	42	(OL)W-39/W.U23-7●
			TR	W.B.A.	03.68	1967-68	34	1	9	
			TR	Nottingham F.	02.69	1968-71	76	9	12	
			TR	Swansea C.	01.72	1971-74	88	1	5	
REES, William	Blaengarw	10.03.24	Carn Rov.	Cardiff C.	+	1946-48	101		33	(IF)W-4
			TR	Tottenham H.	06.49	1949	11		3	
			TR	Orient	07.50	1950-55	184		55	
REES, William	Swansea	31.09.37	JNRS	Swansea C.	10.54	1954-57	7		0	(IF)
			TR	Crystal Palace	05.59	1959	17		1	
REESON, M. Anthony	Rotherham	24.09.33		Rotherham U.	11.53	1954	4		1	(IF)
			TR	Grimsby T.	06.55	1955-57	75		20	
			TR	Doncaster Rov.	02.58	1957-58	21		6	
			TR	Southport	06.59	1959	42		9	
REEVE, Edward G.	Hounslow	03.12.47	APP	Brentford	12.65	1965-67	20	4	0	(IF)
REEVE, Fred W.	Clapton	01.05.18	Rochdale(*)	Grimsby T.	+	1946-47	48		1	(WH)*Ashford/Crystal Palace/
			TR	Reading	06.48	1948-49	34		1	Tottenham H.
REEVE, Ken E.	Grimsby	13.01.21	Humber U.	Grimsby T.	*	1946-47	22		4	(CF)
			TR	Doncaster Rov.	07.48	1948	30		12	
			TR	Mansfield T.	07.49	1949-53	139		62	
REEVES, Dennis J.	Dumfries	1.12.44		Chester C.	09.63	1963-66	139	/	0	(G)
			TR	Wrexham	10.67	1967-68	15	/	0	
REEVES, Derek B.	Parkstone	27.08.34	Bournemouth G.W.	Southampton	12.54	1954-62	273		145	(CF)●
			TR	Bournemouth	11.62	1962-64	35		8	
REEVES, Frank	Peckham	11.07.21	Sidcup	Millwall	02.47	1947-54	180		1	(WH)
REEVES, John C.	London	08.07.63	APP	Fulham	06.81	1981-83	9	1	0	(M)
REEVES, Kevin P.	Burley	20.10.57	APP	Bournemouth	07.75	1974-76	60	3	20	(F)E-2/E.U23-10/
			TR	Norwich C.	01.77	1976-79	118	1	37	E.YTH.INT.
			TR	Manchester C.	03.80	1979-82	129	1	34	
			TR	Burnley	07.83	1983	20	1	12	
REEVES, Mike R.	Saltash	13.01.43	Saltash	Plymouth Arg.	06.61	1962-69	107	2	0	(FB)
REEVES, Peter P.	Swansea	20.01.59	APP	Coventry C.	12.76					(M)
			TR	Swansea C.	07.78	1978	2	2	0	
REEVES, Peter J.	Eltham	07.02.49	APP	Charlton Ath.	02.66	1965-73	263	5	2	(HB)E.YTH.INT.
REEVES, Raymond H.	Reading	12.08.31		Reading	05.49	1952-60	284		29	(FB)E.YTH.INT.
			TR	Brentford	07.61	1961	5		0	
REEVES, T. Brian	Skelmersdale	18.02.39	Skelmersdale	Blackburn Rov.	08.60	1960-61	12		0	(G)
			TR	Scunthorpe U.	04.62	1962-64	38		0	
			TR	Southport	07.65	1965-68	143	/	0	
REGAN, Doug J.T.	Yeovil	03.06.22		Exeter C.	+	1946-52	204		62	(W)
			TR	Bristol C.	52.122	1952-55	37		12	
REGAN, James	Hemsworth	07.12.27	Moorthorpe C.	Rotherham U.	08.49	1951-52	12		0	(WH)
			TR	Bristol C.	06.53	1953-55	51		0	
			TR	Coventry C.	03.56	1955-56	26		0	
REGAN, John H.	Dalton	08.06.25	Swarthmoor	Barrow	01.48	1948-50	9		1	(OL)
REGAN, M.John	Worcester	18.06.44	JNRS	Birmingham C.	09.61	1962-63	5		2	(F)
			TR	Shrewsbury T.	10.64	1964-65	21	/	6	
			TR	Brentford	03.66	1965-66	14	/	5	
				Crewe Alex.	11.66	1966-68	48	3	17	
			TR	Doncaster Rov.	09.68	1968-70	91	4	25	
REGAN, Terry	Bradford	26.06.26	Salts	Bradford C.	AM	1948	1		0	(IL)
REGIS, Cyrille	Fr. Guyana	09.02.58	Hayes	W.B.A.	05.77	1977-83	226	4	81	(F)E.U21-5/E-4
REID, Alex D.	Glasgow	02.03.47	Dundee U.	Newcastle U.	10.71	1971-72	15	8	0	(F)
REID, David A.	Glasgow	03.01.23	Glasgow Perth	Rochdale	01.48	1947-50	36		2	(WH)
			TR	Bradford P.A.	09.50	1950-51	13		0	
				Workington	07.53	1953	8		1	
			TR	Crewe Alex.	08.54	1954	3		0	
REID, Doug J.	Mauchline	03.10.17	Stockport Co.(*)	Portsmouth	+	1946-55	309		129	(CF)
REID, Ernie J.	Merthyr Tydfil	25.03.14	Chelsea(+)	Norwich C.	+	1946	5		0	*Swansea C.

Players Names	Birthplace	Date	Previous Club	League Club	Date Signed	Seasons Played	Apps	Sub	Gls	
REID, Frank J.	Mauchline	16.06.20	Cumnock J.	Huddersfield T.	08.46	1946-48	7		0	(OR)
			TR	Stockport Co.	06.49	1949-50	23		0	
REID, James	Dundee	14.12.35	Dundee U.	Bury	01.57	1956-58	21		9	(F)
			TR	Stockport Co.	03.59	1958	11		2	
REID, John	Newmains	20.08.32	Hamilton	Bradford C.	12.57	1957-61	147		32	(IF)
			TR	Northampton T.	11.61	1961-63	85		14	
			TR	Luton T.	11.63	1963-65	109	2	7	
			TR	Torquay U.	06.66	1966	21	2	1	
			TR	Rochdale	07.67	1967	37	2	3	
REID, John	Edinburgh	23.07.35	Airdrie	Watford	12.56	1956	1		1	(F)
			Airdrie	Norwich C.	06.58					
			TR	Barrow	07.59	1959	20		4	
REID, John H.	Edinburgh	04.05.25	Hibernian	Torquay U.	05.49	1949-51	51		10	
REID, Mick J.	Wolverhampton	07.08.27		Wolverhampton W.	02.48					(CF)
			TR	Bournemouth	02.49	1948	5		2	
			TR	Portsmouth	07.50	1950	5		1	
			TR	Watford	12.52	1952	19		8	
REID, Nick S.	Urmston	30.10.60	APP	Manchester C.	11.78	1978-83	145	2	2	(D)E.U21-6
REID, Peter	Huyton	20.06.56	APP	Bolton W.	05.74	1974-82	222	3	23	(M)E.U21-6
			TR	Everton	12.82	1982-83	41	1	2	
REID, Robert	Hamilton	19.02.11	Brentford(*)	Sheffield U.	*	1946	1		0	(OL)S-2/S.F.LGE REP./
			TR	Bury	11.46	1946	17		1	*Hamilton Acds.
REID, Robert B.A.	Dundee	18.11.36	Downfield J.	Swansea C.	09.57	1957-59	17		0	(G)
REID, Ron E.	Liversedge	09.11.44		Chesterfield	07.67	1967	6	1	1	(CF)
REID, Shaun	Huyton	13.10.65		Rochdale	N/C	1983	17	/	0	(M)
REID, Tony J.	Nottingham	09.05.63	APP	Derby Co.	05.80	1980-82	27	3	1	(M)
			L	Scunthorpe U.	02.83	1982	6	/	0	
			TR	Newport Co.	03.83	1982-83	39	2	6	
REID, William D.	Ayr	13.01.20	Morton	Newport Co.	05.48	1949	9		0	(RH)
REILLY, Felix	Wallyford	12.09.33	E. Fife	Portsmouth	02.60					(F)Brother of Terry
			TR	Bradford P.A.	03.60	1959-61	31		12	
			TR	Crewe Alex.	12.61	1961	6		0	
REILLY, George G.	Bellshill	14.09.57	Corby T.	Northampton T.	06.76	1976-79	124	3	46	(F)
			TR	Cambridge U.	11.79	1979-82	136	2	36	
			TR	Watford	08.83	1983	27	/	8	
REILLY, Len H.	Rotherhithe	31.01.17	Diss T.	Norwich C.	*	1946	1		0	(CH)
REILLY, Terry	Culross	01.07.24	B'ness U.	Chesterfield	03.49					(FB)
			TR	Southport	08.50	1950-54	191		2	
			TR	Bradford P.A.	06.55	1955	14		0	
RELISH, John D.	Liverpool	05.10.53	APP	Chester C.	08.72	1972-73	10	1	1	(D)
			TR	Newport Co.	06.74	1974-83	286	16	8	
RENNIE, David	Edinburgh	29.08.64	APP	Leicester C.	05.82	1983	15	/	0	(D)S.YTH.INT.
RENSHAW, Derek	Gateshead	18.09.24		Sunderland	12.47					(FB)
			TR	Barrow	06.50	1950-54	150		0	
RENTON, William	Dunfermline	04.02.42	Dunfermline	Barrow	01.71	1970-71	23	1	2	(IF)
RENWICK, Craig	Lanark	22.09.58	E. Stirling	Sheffield U.	04.78	1978-79	8	1	0	(D)
RENWICK, Richard	Newcastle	27.11.42	JNRS	Grimsby T.	12.59					(FB)
			TR	Aldershot	07.63	1963-68	203	2	5	
			TR	Brentford	02.69	1968-70	96	/	5	
			TR	Stockport Co.	10.71	1971	30	/	1	
			TR	Rochdale	07.72	1972-73	48	1	0	
			L	Darlington	01.74	1973	19	/	0	
REVEL, Gordon H.	Mansfield	19.09.27		Mansfield T.	08.50	1952	1		0	(CH)
REVELL, Charles H.	Belvedere	05.06.19	Northfleet	Charlton Ath.	+	1946-50	104		15	(WH)*Callenders/
			TR	Derby Co.	03.51	1950-51	22		7	Tottenham H.
REVIE, Don	Middlesbrough	10.07.27	Middlesbrough Swifts	Leicester C.	+	1946-49	96		25	(CF)E-6/E'B'-1/●
			TR	Hull C.	11.49	1949-51	76		12	E.F.LGE REP.
			TR	Manchester C.	10.51	1951-56	163		37	
			TR	Sunderland	11.56	1956-58	64		15	
			TR	Leeds U.	12.58	1958-61	76		11	
REW, Roy E.	Belfast	26.05.24	Sea Mills	Exeter C.	02.49	1948-49	4		1	(CF)
REYNOLDS, A. Brayley	Monmouth	30.05.35	Lovells Ath.	Cardiff C.	05.56	1956-58	54		15	(IF)
			TR	Swansea C.	05.59	1959-64	151		58	
REYNOLDS, Graham E.A.	Newport	23.01.37	Brecon C.	Newport Co.	01.66	1956-66	47	1	12	(CF)W.AMAT.INT./ Glamorgan cricketer
REYNOLDS, Hugh	Wishaw	19.09.26	Morton	Torquay U.	05.48	1948	3		0	
REYNOLDS, Joe	Cleland	13.02.39		Crewe Alex.	08.60	1960	7		0	(HB)
REYNOLDS, Mark D.	Glapwell	01.01.66	APP	Mansfield T.	APP	1982	4	/	0	(D)
REYNOLDS, Richard J.	Looe	15.02.48	APP	Plymouth Arg.	02.65	1964-70	124	8	24	(CF)E.YTH.INT.
			TR	Portsmouth	07.71	1971-75	134	7	24	

Players Names	Birthplace	Date	Previous Club	League Club	Date Signed	Seasons Played	Career Record Apps	Sub	Gls	
REYNOLDS, Ron S.M.	Haslemere	02.06.28	JNRS	Aldershot	+	1946-49	115		0	(G)
			TR	Tottenham H.	07.50	1953-57	86		0	
			TR	Southampton	03.60	1959-63	91		0	
REYNOLDS, Tommy	Felling	02.10.22		Sunderland	07.46	1946-52	168		18	(OR)
			Kings Lynn	Darlington	12.54	1954-55	42		6	
RHOADES-BROWN, Peter	Hampton	02.01.62	APP	Chelsea	07.79	1979-83	86	10	4	(W)
			TR	Oxford U.	01.84	1983	19	1	4	
RHODES, Alan	Bradford	05.01.46	Salts	Bradford C.	AM	1964-65	7	/	0	(WH)
RHODES, Albert	Dinnington	29.04.36	Worksop T.	Q.P.R.	54.12	1955-56	5		0	(FB)
RHODES, Andy C.	Doncaster	23.08.64	APP	Barnsley	08.82	1983	31	/	0	(G)
RHODES, Anthony J.	Dover	17.09.46	JNRS	Derby Co.	10.63	1964-70	5	/	0	(D)
			TR	Halifax T.	11.70	1970-75	233	/	9	
			TR	Southport	08.76	1976	7	2	0	
RHODES, Brian W.	London	23.10.37	JNRS	West Ham U.	01.55	1957-62	61		0	(G)
			TR	Southend U.	09.63	1963	11		0	
RHODES, Mark N.	Sheffield	26.08.57	APP	Rotherham U.	08.75	1975-83	227	11	13	(M)
			L	Darlington	10.82	1982	14	/	0	
			L	Mansfield T.	03.83	1982	4	/	0	
RHODES, Stan	Sheffield	19.04.29		Leeds U.	05.48					(F)
			Worksop T.	Sheffield U.	11.51	1951	1		0	
RHODES, Trevor C.	Southend	09.08.48	APP	Arsenal	09.65					(HB)
			TR	Millwall	09.66	1966	4	/	0	
			TR	Bristol Rov.	07.68	1968	2	/	0	
RICE, Pat	Belfast	17.03.49	JNRS	Arsenal	03.66	1967-80	391	6	11	(D)NI-49/NI.U23-2●
			TR	Watford	11.80	1980-83	112	/	1	
RICE, Ron H.	Birkenhead	13.04.23	Huddersfield T.(AM)	Bradford C.	09.46	1946	1		0	(IL)
			TR	Tranmere Rov.	10.46	1946	4		1	
RICHARDS, Anthony W.	Birmingham	06.03.34	JNRS	Birmingham C.	12.51					(CF)●
			TR	Walsall	09.54	1954-62	334		184	
			TR	Port Vale	03.63	1962-65	60	4	30	
RICHARDS, Craig A.	Neath	10.10.59	APP	Q.P.R.	07.77					(M)
			TR	Wimbledon	06.79	1979	2	/	0	
			TR	Cardiff C.	08.80					
RICHARDS, Gary V.	Swansea	02.08.63	APP	Swansea C.	08.81	1981-83	48	2	1	(D)
RICHARDS, Geoff M.	Bilston	24.04.29	Albion Wks.	W.B.A.	08.46	1946-47	3		1	(OR)
RICHARDS, Gordon	Rhos	23.10.33	JNRS	Wrexham	05.52	1952-57	96		24	(OL)
			TR	Chester C.	01.58	1957-60	74		16	
RICHARDS, John B.	W. Bromwich	14.06.31		Swindon T.	09.56	1955-59	104		37	(F)
			TR	Norwich C.	12.59	1959	5		2	
			TR	Aldershot	10.60	1960	19		8	
RICHARDS, John P.	Warrington	09.11.50	JNRS	Wolverhampton W.	07.69	1969-82	365	20	144	(F)E-1/E.U23-6/
			L	Derby Co.	11.82	1982	10	/	2	E.U21-2/E.F.LGE REP.
RICHARDS, Lloyd G.	Jamaica	11.02.58	APP	Notts. Co.	02.76	1975-77	7	2	0	(M)
			TR	York C.	06.80	1980	17	1	1	
RICHARDS, Mike J.	Wolverhampton	26.05.39	Wellington	Oxford U.	N/L	1962-63	30		0	(G)
			TR	Shrewsbury	11.63					
RICHARDS, Peter (Pedro)	Edmonton	01.11.56	APP	Notts. Co.	11.74	1974-83	343	1	4	(D)
RICHARDS, Stan V.	Cardiff	21.01.17	Tufnell Pk.	Cardiff C.	+	1946-47	57		40	(CF)W-1
			TR	Swansea C.	06.48	1948-50	65		35	
RICHARDS, Steve C.	Dundee	24.10.61	APP	Hull C.	10.79	1979-82	53	3	2	(D)
RICHARDS, Tony	W.Houghton	09.06.44	APP	Mansfield T.	06.62	1961-63	3		0	(HB)
RICHARDS, Wayne	Scunthorpe	10.05.61	APP	Derby Co.	05.79	1979-81	16	3	0	(D)
RICHARDSON, Anthony F.	Cleethorpes	05.11.43	JNRS	Nottingham F.	11.60					(CF)
			Cheltenham	Bradford C.	AM	1962	2		1	
RICHARDSON, Anthony J.	Southwark	07.01.32	Slough S.C.	Q.P.R.	04.51	1951	2		0	(FB)
RICHARDSON, Brian	Sheffield	05.10.34		Sheffield U.	12.54	1955-64	291		9	(WH)
			TR	Swindon T.	01.66	1965	11	/	0	
			TR	Rochdale	07.66	1966	19	/	1	
RICHARDSON, Damien	Dublin	02.08.47	Shamrock Rov.	Gillingham	10.72	1972-80	314	9	91	(F)EI-3
RICHARDSON, David	Billingham	11.03.32	JNRS	Leicester C.	11.49	1954	2		0	(FB)
			TR	Grimsby T.	06.55	1955-59	175		1	
			TR	Swindon T.	06.60					
			TR	Barrow	07.61	1961-62	31		0	
RICHARDSON, Derek	London	13.07.56	APP	Chelsea	02.74					(G)E.YTH.INT.
			TR	Q.P.R.	04.76	1976-78	31	/	0	
			TR	Sheffield U.	12.79	1979-80	42	/	0	
			TR	Coventry C.	03.82					

Players Names	Birthplace	Date	Previous Club	League Club	Date Signed	Seasons Played	Career Record Apps	Sub	Gls	
RICHARDSON, Fred	Middlestone	18.08.25	B.Auckland	Chelsea	09.46	1946	2		0	(CF)
			TR	Hartlepool U.	10.47	1947-48	43		16	
			TR	Barnsley	10.48	1948-49	41		12	
			TR	W.B.A.	06.50	1950-51	29		8	
			TR	Chester C.	02.52	1951-52	23		6	
			TR	Hartlepool U.	11.52	1952-55	106		24	
RICHARDSON, Garbutt	Durham	24.10.38	JNRS	Huddersfield T.	10.55					(CH)
			TR	Preston N.E.	07.57	1959-60	15		1	
			TR	Accrington St.	07.61					
				Carlisle U.	07.62					
			TR	Halifax T.	11.62	1962-63	20		1	
			TR	Barrow	07.64	1964	30		5	
RICHARDSON, George	Worksop	12.12.12	Sheffield U.(*)	Hull C.	*	1947	16		5	(IR)*Huddersfield T./d.1968
RICHARDSON, Graham C.	Sedgefield	20.03.58	Darlington(AM)	Hartlepool U.	08.75	1975-80	89	/	0	(G)
RICHARDSON, Ian P.	Ely	09.05.64	APP	Watford	05.82	1983	4	3	2	(F)
			L	Blackpool	12.82	1982	4	1	2	
RICHARDSON, James R.	Ashington	08.02.11	Newcastle U.(*)	Millwall	*					(IF)*Blyth Spartans/
			TR	Orient	01.48	1947	15		0	Newcastle U./Huddersfield T. E-2/E.F.LGE REP./ E.SCH.INT./d.1964
RICHARDSON, John	Birkenhead	24.05.33	Canterbury	Southport	07.56	1956-59	103		0	(G)
RICHARDSON, John	Worksop	20.04.45	APP	Derby Co.	04.62	1962-70	118	/	4	(FB)
			TR	Notts.Co.	07.71	1971	0	2	0	
RICHARDSON, John P.	Ashington	05.02.49	APP	Millwall	APP	1965	1	/	0	(D)
			TR	Brentford	08.66	1966-69	83	2	7	
			TR	Fulham	08.69	1969-72	61	8	6	
			TR	Aldershot	07.73	1973-76	120	1	6	
RICHARDSON, Joseph A.S.	Sheffield	17.03.42	Winsford	Birmingham C.	09.59					(IF)d 1966
			TR	Sheffield U.	01.60					
			TR	Rochdale	10.60	1960-64	114		33	
			TR	Tranmere Rov.	07.65					
RICHARDSON, Kevin	Newcastle	04.12.62	APP	Everton	12.80	1981-83	64	11	9	(M)
RICHARDSON, Norman	Consett	15.04.15	Bolton W.(*)	New Brighton	*	1946-50	141		0	(FB)
RICHARDSON, Paul	Shirebrook	25.10.49	APP	Nottingham F.	08.67	1967-76	198	23	18	(M)E.YTH.INT.
			TR	Chester C.	10.76	1976	28	/	2	
			TR	Stoke C.	06.77	1977-80	124	3	10	
			TR	Sheffield U.	08.81	1981-82	35	1	2	
			L	Blackpool	01.83	1982	4	/	0	
			TR	Swindon T.	07.83	1983	7	/	0	
RICHARDSON, Rod K.	Hunstanton	01.10.42	Norwich C.(AM)	Torquay U.	07.62	1962-63	7		1	(F)
RICHARDSON, Russell	Sheffield	21.10.64		Scunthorpe U.	N/C	1983	2	/	0	(D)
RICHARDSON, Stan	Harrington	28.04.24		Workington	08.51	1951	8		1	(W)
RICHARDSON, Steve E.	Slough	11.02.62	APP	Southampton	02.80					(D)
			TR	Reading	07.82	1982-83	73	1	1	
RICHARDSON, Stuart	Leeds	12.06.38	Methley U.	Q.P.R.	11.56	1958	1		0	(HB)
			TR	Oldham Ath.	07.59	1959	22		0	
RICHARDSON, Tom	Reading	01.02.31		Middlesbrough	09.52					(HB)
			TR	Southport	05.54					
			TR	Aldershot	07.55	1955-57	41		9	
RICHARDSON, William	Bedlington	25.10.43	JNRS	Sunderland	60.10					(FB)
			TR	Mansfield T.	10.65	1965-67	61	2	0	
			TR	York C.	06.68	1968	24	/	0	
RICHLEY, Lionel	Gateshead	02.07.24	Tonbridge	Hartlepool U.	06.51	1951-53	72		0	(HB)
RICHMOND, John	Derby	17.09.38	Derby Corries	Derby Co.	01.56	1957-62	6		0	(HB)
RICKABY, Stan	Stockton	12.03.24	South Bank	Middlesbrough	07.46	1947-49	10		0	(FB)E-1/E.F.LGE REP.
			TR	W.B.A.	02.50	1949-54	189		2	
RICKARD, Derek B.P.	Plymouth	01.10.47	JNRS	Plymouth Arg.	12.69	1969-73	101	9	41	(IF)
			TR	Bournemouth	07.74	1974-75	22	10	6	
RICKARDS, Ken	Middlesbrough	22.03.29	Middlesbrough A.	Hull C.	05.47					(IR)
			TR	Darlington	01.50	1949	8		0	
RICKETT, Horace F.J.	Orsett	03.01.12	Orient(+)	Reading	06.46	1946-47	22		0	(G)*Chelmsford
RICKETT, Walter	Sheffield	20.03.17		Sheffield U.	+	1946-47	57		16	(OR)E'B'-1
			TR	Blackpool	01.48	1947-49	45		8	
			TR	Sheffield Wed.	10.49	1949-52	95		12	
			TR	Rotherham U.	09.52	1952	28		4	
			TR	Halifax T.	08.53	1953	31		2	
RICKETTS, Alan	Crawley	30.10.62	Wrexham (N/C)	Crewe Alex.	08.81	1981	14	3	2	(F)
RICKETTS, Graham A.	Oxford	30.07.39	JNRS	Bristol Rov.	08.56	1956-60	32		0	(WH)E.YTH.INT
			TR	Stockport Co.	07.61	1961-63	119		6	
			TR	Doncaster Rov.	07.64	1964-67	143	8	15	
			TR	Peterborough U.	03.68	1967-68	46	3	1	
RICKIS, Vic	Edinburgh	26.11.40	Dalkeith Th.	Millwall	12.59	1960	3		1	(F)

Players Names	Birthplace	Date	Previous Club	League Club	Date Signed	Seasons Played	Apps	Sub	Gls	
RIDDICK, Gordon	Langleybury	06.11.43	JNRS	Luton T.	04.61	1962-66	101	1	16	(M)
			TR	Gillingham	03.67	1966-69	114	/	24	
			TR	Charlton Ath.	11.69	1069-70	26	3	5	
			TR	Orient	10.70	1970-72	13	8	3	
			TR	Northampton T.	12.72	1972-73	28	/	3	
			TR	Brentford	10.73	1973-76	104	4	5	
RIDEOUT, Brian J.	Bristol	15.09.40		Bristol Rov.	02.59	1960	1		0	(FB)
RIDEOUT, Paul D.	Bournemouth	14.08.64	APP	Swindon T.	08.81	1980-82	90	5	38	(F)E.SCH.INT.
			TR	Aston Villa	06.83	1983	22	3	5	
RIDGE, Roy	Sheffield	21.10.34	Ecclesfield	Sheffield U.	11.51	1953-60	11		0	(FB)
			TR	Rochdale	08.64	1964-65	84	/	0	
RIDING, Alan	Tynemouth	19.11.34		Exeter C.	07.64	1965	1	/	0	(CF)
RIDLEY, Dave G.H.	Pontypridd	16.12.16	Bedford T.	Millwall	+					
			TR	Brighton & H.A.	07.46	1946	5		0	
RIDLEY, John	Consett	27.04.52	Sheffield Univ.	Port Vale	08.73	1973-78	149	7	3	(M)
			TR	Leicester C.	10.78	1978	17	7	0	
			TR	Chesterfield	08.79	1979-80	121	3	8	
			TR	Port Vale	08.82	1982-83	62	9	6	
RIDLEY, Robert M.	Reading	30.05.42	JNRS	Portsmouth	06.60					(F)
			TR	Gillingham	07.61	1961-66	71	2	8	
RIDYARD, Alf	Cudworth	05.03.08	W.B.A.(*)	Q.P.R.	*	1946-47	11		0	(CH)*Barnsley
RIGBY, Edward	Atherton	20.04.25		Manchester C.	02.48					
			TR	Barrow	07.49	1949	19		0	
RIGBY, Ernie	Kirkham	08.04.28	Blackpool(AM)	Accrington St.	02.51	1950-51	10		0	
RIGBY, Jack	Leigh	29.07.24		Manchester C.	12.46	1946-52	100		0	(CH)
RIGBY, Jon	Bury St. Edmunds	31.01.65	APP	Norwich C.	08.82	1983	3	2	0	(F)
RIGBY, Norman	Newark	23.05.23		Notts.Co.	+	1947-50	46		0	(CH)
			TR	Peterborough U.	N/L	1960-61	55		0	
RIGBY, William A.	Chester	09.06.21	JNRS	Chester	08.46	1946	1		0	(G) d 1979
RIGG, Tommy	Bedlington	20.02.20	Middlesbrough(+)	Watford	06.46	1946-48	80		0	(G)
			Ashington	Gillingham	08.51	1951-55	192		0	
RIGGS, Leslie J.	Portsmouth	30.05.35	JNRS	Gillingham	06.52	1953-57	152		3	(WH)
			TR	Newport Co.	06.58	1958-60	110		3	
			TR	Bury	06.61	1961	6		0	
			TR	Crewe Alex.	02.63	1962-63	67		6	
			TR	Gillingham	09.64	1964-65	17	1	1	
RILEY, Brian F.	Bolton	14.09.37	JNRS	Bolton W.	12.54	1956-58	8		1	(F)
RILEY, Chris J.	Rhyl	19.01.39	Rhyl	Crewe Alex.	03.58	1957-63	136		47	(IF)
			TR	Tranmere	07.64					
RILEY, David S.	Northampton	08.12.60	Keyworth U.	Nottingham F.	01.84	1983	0	1	0	(F)
RILEY, Glyn	Barnsley	24.07.58	APP	Barnsley	09.77	1974-81	103	27	16	(F)
			L	Doncaster Rov.	12.79	1979	7	1	2	
			TR	Bristol C.	08.82	1982-83	85	1	32	
RILEY, Howard	Leicester	18.08.38	JNRS	Leicester C.	08.55	1955-64	193		38	(W)E.U23-2/E.YTH.INT./
			TR	Walsall	01.66	1965	24	/	3	Son of County Cricketer
			U.S.A.	Barrow	07.68	1968	21	3	6	
RILEY, Hughen W.	Accrington	12.06.47		Rochdale	12.66	1967-71	79	12	12	(M)
			TR	Crewe Alex.	12.71	1971-74	116	5	9	
			TR	Bury	12.74	1974-75	47	4	4	
			TR	Bournemouth	04.76	1976-77	69	3	7	
RILEY, Ian	Tollesbury	08.02.47		Southend U.	11.67	1967-68	3	1	0	(FB)
RILEY, Joe			Stockton	Darlington	AM	1949	8		2	
RIMMER, Gilbert H.	Southport	14.07.32	Leyland Rd FC	Southport	AM	1955	2		0	Uncle played pre-war for Bolton W./E.AMAT.INT.
RIMMER, J. Jimmy	Southport	10.02.48	APP	Manchester U.	05.65	1967-72	34	/	0	(G)E-1
			L	Swansea C.	10.73	1973	17	/	0	
			TR	Arsenal	02.74	1973-76	124	/	0	
			TR	Aston Villa	08.77	1977-82	229	/	0	
			TR	Swansea C.	08.83	1983	14	/	0	
RIMMER, Ray	Marshside	06.08.38	Formby Dons	Southport	AM	1955-57	8		0	(OL)
RIMMER, Stuart A.	Southport	12.10.64	APP	Everton	10.82	1981-83	3	/	0	(F)
RIMMER, Warwick	Birkenhead	01.03.41	JNRS	Bolton W.	03.58	1960-74	462	6	17	(D)E.SCH.INT.●
			TR	Crewe Alex.	03.75	1974-78	114	14	0	Nephew of Ellis Rimmer
RIMMINGTON, Norman	Barnsley	29.11.23	Maplewell T.	Barnsley	+	1946	27		0	(G)
			TR	Hartlepool U.	12.47	1947-51	124		0	
RING, Mike P.	Brighton	13.02.61	APP	Brighton & H.A.	02.79	1981-83	1	4	0	(F)
RING, Tommy	Glasgow	08.08.30	Clyde	Everton	01.60	1959-60	27		6	(W)S-12/S.F.LGE REP.
			TR	Barnsley	11.61	1961-62	21		1	
RINGER, Walter A.	Stanley	07.10.41		Halifax T.	08.60	1959-60	6		0	(OL)
RINGSTEAD, Alf	Dublin	14.10.27	Northwich	Sheffield U.	11.50	1950-58	247		101	(W)E1-20
			TR	Mansfield T.	07.59	1959	27		3	

Players Names	Birthplace	Date	Previous Club	League Club	Date Signed	Seasons Played	Apps	Sub	Gls	
RINTANEN, Maund	Finland		Finland	Hull C.	AM	1956	4		0	(G)
RIOCH, Bruce D.	Aldershot	06.09.47	APP	Luton T.	09.64	1964-68	148	1	47	(M)S-24●
			TR	Aston Villa	07.69	1969-73	149	5	34	Brother of Neil
			TR	Derby Co.	02.74	1973-76	106	/	34	
			TR	Everton	12.76	1976-77	30	/	3	
			TR	Derby Co.	11.77	1977-79	40	/	4	
			L	Birmingham C.	12.78	1978	3	/	0	
			L	Sheffield U.	03.79	1978	8	/	1	
			Seattle Sounders	Torquay U.	10.80	1980-83	64	7	6	
RIOCH, Neil G.	Paddington	13.04.51	APP	Luton T.	07.68					(CH)E.YTH.INT.
			TR	Aston Villa	09.69	1969-74	17	5	3	
			L	York C.	02.72	1971	0	1	0	
			L	Northampton T.	03.72	1971	14	/	4	
			TR	Plymouth Arg.	05.75	1975	3	2	0	
RIPLEY, Keith A.	Normanton	10.10.54	Gainsborough	Huddersfield T.	08.78	1978	2	3	0	(D)
			TR	Doncaster Rov.	08.79	1979	5	/	0	
RIPLEY, S. Keith	Normanton	29.03.35	JNRS	Leeds U.	04.52	1954-57	68		15	(WH)
			TR	Norwich C.	08.58	1958	12		6	
			TR	Mansfield T.	11.58	1958-59	30		5	
			TR	Peterborough U.	07.60	1960-61	82		12	
			TR	Doncaster Rov.	08.62	1962-65	123	5	7	
RISDON, Stan W.	Exeter	13.08.13	Exeter C.(*)	Brighton & H.A.	*	1946	2		0	(WH)*St.Mary's Majors/d.1979
RISEBOROUGH, Cyril	Doncaster	22.02.33		Swindon T.	02.55	1954-56	26		1	
RIST, Frank H.	Leyton	30.03.14	Orient(*)	Charlton Ath.	*	1946	3		0	(CH)*Grays Ath./Essex Cricketer
RITCHIE, Andy T.	Manchester	28.11.60	APP	Manchester U.	12.77	1977-80	26	7	13	(F)E.SCH.INT./E.U'21-1
			TR	Brighton & H.A.	10.80	1980-82	82	7	23	
			TR	Leeds U.	03.83	1982-83	48	/	10	
RITCHIE, John	London	28.02.51	Slough T.	Arsenal	04.72					(CF)E.AMAT.INT.
			TR	Hereford U.	03.74	1973-74	19	3	4	
RITCHIE, John	Ashington	10.04.44	Whitley Bay	Port Vale	12.65	1965-66	49	/	3	(FB)E.AMAT.INT.
			TR	Preston N.E.	04.67	1966-71	93	/	5	
			TR	Bradford C.	03.72	1971-72	20	/	0	
RITCHIE, John	Fife	31.03.27	Crossgates	Accrington St.	06.49	1949	13		0	
RITCHIE, John B.	Auchterderran	12.06.47	Brechin C.	Bradford C.	07.71	1971-73	64	/	0	(G)
RITCHIE, John H.	Kettering	12.07.41	Kettering	Stoke C.	06.62	1962-66	110	/	64	(CF)●
			TR	Sheffield Wed.	11.66	1966-68	88	1	35	
			TR	Stoke C.	07.69	1969-74	151	9	71	
RITCHIE, Robert	Glasgow	01.02.20	Rickmansworth	Watford	02.48	1948	1		0	
RITCHIE, Steve K.	Glasgow	17.02.54	APP	Bristol C.	09.71	1972	1	/	0	(D)S.SCH.INT./
			Morton	Hereford U.	06.75	1975-77	102	/	3	Brother of Tom G.
			Aberdeen	Torquay U.	03.79	1978-79	58	/	2	
RITCHIE, Tom	Bangor	10.07.30	Bangor	Manchester U.	12.50					(OL)
			TR	Reading	02.53	1952-54	18		5	
			TR	Grimsby T.	08.58	1958	1		0	
			TR	Barrow	12.58	1958	16		6	
RITCHIE, Tom G.	Edinburgh	02.01.52	Bridgend Th.	Bristol C.	07.69	1972-80	308	13	77	(F)
			TR	Sunderland	01.81	1980-81	32	3	8	
			L	Carlisle U.	03.82	1981	14	1	0	
			TR	Bristol C.	06.82	1982-83	82	/	26	
RITCHIE, William S.	Dundee	13.11.32	Dundee	Bury	06.57	1957-58	13		7	(F)
			TR	Stockport Co.	03.59	1958-60	52		12	
RITSON, John A.	Liverpool	06.09.49	APP	Bolton W.	09.66	1967-77	321	3	9	(D)
			TR	Bury	09.78	1978-79	41	/	2	
RITSON, Ledger	Gateshead	28.04.21		Orient	+	1946-48	84		0	
RIVERS, Alan D.	Portsmouth	27.01.46	APP	Luton T.	01.64	1965-66	25	5	1	(D)
			TR	Watford	09.67	1967	0	2	0	
RIX, Graham	Doncaster	23.10.57	APP	Arsenal	01.75	1976-83	262	5	34	(M)E.U21-7/E-17
ROBB, David	Broughty Ferry	15.12.47	Tampa Bay	Norwich C.	09.78	1978	4	1	1	(F)S-5/S.U23-3
ROBB, George	Finsbury Park	01.06.26	Finchley	Tottenham H.	06.53	1951-58	182		52	(OL)E-1/E'B'-3/E.F.LGE REP./E.AMAT.INT.
ROBB, Ian	Doncaster	01.06.55	JNRS	York C.	02.73	1973-74	4	/	0	(IF)
ROBB, William L.	Cambuslang	23.12.27	Aberdeen	Orient	05.50	1950	5		0	(WH)
			Albion Rov.	Bradford C.	10.54	1954-57	127		4	
ROBBINS, Gordon	Barnsley	07.02.36	Wombwell	Rotherham U.	05.53					(HB)
			TR	Walsall	11.57					
			Goole T.	Crewe Alex.	12.58	1958	4		0	
ROBBINS, Robert	Newton Abbot	20.09.53		Torquay U.	N/C	1976	19	/	0	(G)
ROBER, H. Jurgen	W. Germany	25.12.53	Chicago Stings	Nottingham F.	12.81	1981	21	1	3	(M)
ROBERTS, Alan	Newcastle	08.12.64	APP	Middlesbrough	12.82	1982-83	7	1	1	(M)
ROBERTS, Alan	Bury	23.04.46	Mossley	Bradford P.A.	11.69	1969	15	/	0	(FB)
ROBERTS, Albert	Barnsley	27.01.07	Swansea C.(*)	York C.	07.46	1946	1		0	d.1957/*Southampton

Players Names	Birthplace	Date	Previous Club	League Club	Date Signed	Seasons Played	Apps	Sub	Gls	
ROBERTS, Brian L.F.	Manchester	06.11.55	APP	Coventry C.	05.74	1975-83	209	6	1	(D)
			L	Hereford U.	02.75	1974	5	/	0	
			TR	Birmingham C.	03.84	1983	11	/	0	
ROBERTS, Cledwyn	Colwyn Bay	12.08.47	Glan Conwy	Wrexham	08.65	1965	1	/	0	(WH)
ROBERTS, Colin	Castleford	16.09.33	Altofts	Bradford P.A.	10.51	1953-55	75		0	(WH)
			Frickley Col.	Bradford C.	06.59	1959-60	57		0	
ROBERTS, David A.	Birmingham	21.12.46	JNRS	Aston Villa	12.63	1965-67	15	1	1	(F)
			TR	Shrewsbury T.	03.68	1967-73	224	6	21	
			TR	Swansea C.	05.74	1974	32	5	1	
ROBERTS, David F.	Southampton	26.01.49	APP	Fulham	09.67	1968-70	21	1	0	(D)W-18/W.U23-4
			TR	Oxford U.	02.71	1970-74	160	1	8	
			TR	Hull C.	02.75	1974-77	86	/	4	
			TR	Cardiff C.	08.78	1978-80	40	1	2	
ROBERTS, David G.	Plymouth	08.05.44	APP	Plymouth Arg.	12.61	1961-63	11		0	(FB)
ROBERTS, Dennis	Bretton	05.02.18	Notts.Co.(*)	Bristol C.	*	1946-53	281		3	(CH)
ROBERTS, Don C.	Arlecdon	03.02.33	Whitehaven	Workington	07.52	1952-53	21		0	(IF)
			TR	Barrow	10.57	1957-58	22		2	
ROBERTS, Doug G.	Foleshill	30.05.25	Wolverhampton W.(+)	Northampton T.	+	1946-48	57		7	(W)
			TR	Brighton & H.A.	03.49	1948-49	17		3	
				Accrington St.	07.51	1951	39		10	
ROBERTS, Dudley E.	Derby	16.10.45	JNRS	Coventry C.	11.63	1965-67	11	1	6	(IF) son of Edward (Coventry)
			TR	Mansfield T.	03.68	1967-73	193	6	66	
			L	Doncaster Rov.	02.73	1972	7	/	0	
			TR	Scunthorpe U.	02.74	1973-75	56	3	17	
ROBERTS, Edward	Chesterfield	02.11.16	Derby Co.(*)	Coventry C.	*	1946-51	169		73	(CF)
ROBERTS, Edward	Liverpool	16.11.47		Tranmere Rov.	05.67	1968-69	7	/	0	(G)
ROBERTS, Eric			Altofts	Halifax T.	08.47	1947	5		1	(OL)
ROBERTS, Fred	Rhyl	07.05.16	Rhyl	Bury	*	1946	3		1	(OR)
			TR	Orient	11.46	1946	18		2	
ROBERTS, Gareth W.	Hull	15.11.60	APP	Hull C.	11.78	1978-83	192	2	29	(M)
ROBERTS, Gary P.M.	Rhyl	05.04.60	Wembley T.	Brentford	10.80	1980-83	138	7	33	(F)
ROBERTS, Geoff M.	Liverpool	29.12.49	APP	Bolton W.	01.67	1967-69	5	/	0	(FB)
ROBERTS, Gordon R.	Cardiff	30.12.46	APP	Wolverhampton W.	01.64					(F)W.SCH.INT.
			TR	Bury	09.65	1965	2	/	0	
ROBERTS, Graham P.	Southampton	03.07.59	Weymouth	Tottenham H.	05.80	1980-83	111	9	14	(D)E-6
ROBERTS, Griffith O.	Blaenau Ffestiniog	02.10.20	Blaenau Fest.	Nottingham F.	05.46	1946	9		0	(G)
ROBERTS, Harold	Liverpool	12.01.20	Harrowby FC	Chesterfield	+	1946-48	91		9	(OL)
			TR	Birmingham C.	11.48	1948-50	35		2	
			TR	Shrewsbury T.	06.51	1951-52	70		16	
			TR	Scunthorpe U.	07.53	1953-54	17		1	
ROBERTS, Ian M.	Colwyn Bay	28.02.61	JNRS	Wrexham	07.79	1978-79	2	4	0	(F)
ROBERTS, Ian P.	Glasgow	28.09.55	APP	Shrewsbury T.	09.72	1971-75	93	3	0	(D)
			TR	Crewe Alex.	07.76	1976-78	89	4	0	
ROBERTS, J. Dale	Newcastle	08.10.56	APP	Ipswich T.	09.74	1974-77	17	1	0	(D)E.YTH.INT.
			TR	Hull C.	02.80	1979-83	138	4	6	
ROBERTS, James N.	Stirling	12.06.23		Ipswich T.	09.49	1949-51	73		15	
			TR	Barrow	07.52	1952	11		2	
ROBERTS, Jeremy	Middlesbrough	24.11.66		Hartlepool U.	N/C	1983	1	/	0	(G)
ROBERTS, John D.	Wrexham	22.07.28	Brymbo S.Wks.	Wrexham	AM	1950	1		0	(F)
ROBERTS, John G.	Swansea	11.09.46	Abercynon A.	Swansea C.	07.64	1965-67	36	1	16	(D)W-22/W.U23-5/
			TR	Northampton T.	11.67	1967-68	62	/	11	W.U21-1
			TR	Arsenal	05.69	1969-72	56	3	4	
			TR	Birmingham C.	10.72	1972-75	61	5	1	
			TR	Wrexham	08.76	1976-79	145	/	5	
			TR	Hull C.	08.80	1980	26	/	1	
ROBERTS, John H.	Swansea	30.06.18		Bolton W.	*	1946-50	144		11	(FB)W-1
			TR	Swansea C.	09.50	1950	16		1	
ROBERTS, John T.	Australia	24.03.44	Leichardt	Chelsea	01.66					(G)
			TR	Blackburn Rov.	04.66	1965-66	3	/	0	
			L	Chesterfield	08.67	1967	46	/	0	
				Bradford C.	08.68	1968-70	44	/	0	
			TR	Southend U.	01.71	1970-71	47	/	0	
			TR	Northampton T.	07.72	1972	13	/	0	
ROBERTS, Ken	Crewe	10.03.31	Crewe Villa	Aston Villa	08.51	1951-53	42		7	(OR)
ROBERTS, Ken O.	Cefn-mawr	27.03.36	JNRS	Wrexham	AM	1951	1		0	(OR)
			TR	Aston Villa	05.53	1953-57	38		3	
ROBERTS, Kevin J.	Bristol	25.07.55	Welton Rov.	Swindon T.	03.77	1977	1	/	0	(G)
ROBERTS, Lee J.	Market Drayton	23.03.57	APP	Shrewsbury T.	01.75	1973-77	9	6	1	(D)
			L	Exeter C.	03.77	1976	5	2	0	
			TR	Exeter C.	09.77	1977-82	135	9	12	

Players Names	Birthplace	Date	Previous Club	League Club	Date Signed	Seasons Played	Apps	Sub	Gls	
ROBERTS, Maurice E.S.	Bristol	05.07.22		Brentford	08.46	1946	10		0	
			TR	Bristol C.	05.47					
ROBERTS, Mike J.	Birmingham	21.05.60		Shrewsbury T.	07.78	1978	0	1	0	(M)
ROBERTS, Owen J.	Maerdy	16.02.19	Aberaman	Swansea C.	+	1946-47	24		0	(G)*Plymouth Arg.
			TR	Newport Co.	08.48	1948	7		0	
ROBERTS, Paul	London	27.04.62	APP	Millwall	04.79	1978-82	142	4	0	(D)
			TR	Brentford	09.83	1983	34	/	0	
ROBERTS, Peter	Chesterfield	21.07.55	JNRS	Chesterfield	N/C	1974-75	2	/	0	(W)
ROBERTS, Peter L.	Durham	16.07.25		Leeds U.	09.46					
			TR	New Brighton	07.48	1948	3		0	
ROBERTS, Philip S.	Cardiff	24.02.50	APP	Bristol Rov.	11.68	1969-72	175	1	6	(D)W-4/W.U23-6
			TR	Portsmouth	05.73	1973-77	152	1	1	
			TR	Hereford U.	07.78	1978	3	/	0	
			TR	Exeter C.	02.79	1978-81	103	2	0	
ROBERTS, Robert	Edinburgh	02.09.40	Motherwell	Leicester C.	09.63	1963-69	224	5	26	(WH)S.U23-1/S.F.LGE
			TR	Mansfield T.	70.9	1970-71	76	4	3	REP.
			Coventry C (coach)	Colchester U.	07.73	1972	0	2	0	
ROBERTS, Ron	Wrexham	14.09.42	JNRS	Wrexham	04.60	1959-62	68		4	(OL)W.U23-2
			TR	Tranmere Rov.	03.63	1962-63	56		2	
ROBERTS, Stan	Wrexham	10.04.21		Wrexham	09.46	1946-47	27		9	(F)
			TR	New Brighton	07.48	1948-50	105		25	
ROBERTS, Tom	Liverpool	27.12.45	APP	Everton	11.63					(F)
			TR	Stockport Co.	03.65	1964-65	20	/	0	
			TR	Southport	07.66	1966	4	/	1	
ROBERTS, Tom	Liverpool	28.07.27	Skelmersdale	Blackburn Rov.	12.51	1951-53	6		0	(FB)
			TR	Watford	12.54	1954	1		0	
			TR	Chester C.	02.56	1955	5		0	
ROBERTS, Tom W.G.	Reading	11.06.32		Birmingham C.	05.53					(F)
			TR	Barrow	10.55	1955-56	40		14	
ROBERTS, Trevor E.	Caernarvon	25.02.42	Liverpool Univ.	Liverpool	06.63					(G)W.AMAT.INT./
			TR	Southend U.	01.66	1965-69	171	/	0	d.1972
			TR	Cambridge U.	N/L	1970-71	36	/	0	
ROBERTS, Trevor L.	Southampton	09.05.61		Portsmouth	02.79	1978-79	1	2	0	(F)
ROBERTS, Walter	Wrexham	23.11.17		Wrexham	*	1946-47	59		1	
			TR	Bournemouth	07.48	1948-49	14		0	
ROBERTS, William E.	Flint	22.10.18		Rochdale	+	1946-48	43		0	(G)
ROBERTS, Winston	W.Hartlepool	05.07.39		Hartlepool U.	09.58	1958	3		0	(F)
ROBERTSON, A. Lammie	Paisley	27.09.47		Burnley	09.66					(M)
			TR	Bury	06.68	1968	3	2	0	
			TR	Halifax T.	02.69	1968-72	142	7	20	
			TR	Brighton & H.A.	12.72	1972-73	42	4	9	
			TR	Exeter C.	05.74	1974-77	132	1	25	
			TR	Leicester C.	09.77	1977	6	1	0	
			TR	Peterborough U.	08.78	1978	12	3	1	
			TR	Bradford C.	01.79	1978-80	41	2	3	
ROBERTSON, Alistair	Philpstoun	09.09.52	APP	W.B.A.	09.69	1969-83	447	2	8	(D)S.SCH.INT.
ROBERTSON, David	Bailliestown	12.01.45	Motherwell	Crewe Alex.	07.63	1963	10		2	(F)
ROBERTSON, Edward H.	Edinburgh	19.12.35	Linlithgow Rose	Bury	07.54	1956-62	196		5	(FB) d.1981
			TR	Wrexham	10.63	1963	24		0	
			TR	Tranmere Rov.	07.64	1964-68	143	4	1	
ROBERTSON, George	Bainsford	20.04.30	Gairdoch J.	Plymouth Arg.	01.50	1950-63	358		2	(WH)
ROBERTSON, James	Leith	07.07.40	Aberdeen	Newport Co.	07.61	1961	29		5	(IR)
ROBERTSON, James G.	Glasgow	17.12.44	St. Mirren	Tottenham H.	03.64	1963-68	153	4	25	(W)S-1/S.U23-4
			TR	Arsenal	10.68	1968-69	45	1	7	
			TR	Ipswich T.	03.70	1969-71	87	/	10	
			TR	Stoke C.	06.72	1972-76	99	15	12	
			TR	Walsall	09.77	1977	16	/	0	
			TR	Crewe Alex.	09.78	1978	32	1	0	
ROBERTSON, James W.	Falkirk	20.02.29	Dunipace Th.	Arsenal	06.48	1951	1		0	(W)
			TR	Brentford	09.53	1953-55	85		11	
ROBERTSON, John C.	Aberdeen	15.07.28	Ayr U.	Portsmouth	08.55	1955	12		4	(F)
			TR	York C.	06.57	1957	17		5	
			TR	Barrow	08.58	1958-61	156		48	
ROBERTSON, John N.	Uddingston	20.01.53	APP	Nottingham F.	05.70	1970-82	374	12	61	(W)S-28/S.SCH.INT.●
			TR	Derby Co.	06.83	1983	31	/	2	
ROBERTSON, Len V.	Middlesbrough	01.03.16	Hartlepool U.(+)	Watford	06.46	1946	6		2	(OR)
			TR	Bradford C.	03.47					
			TR	Hull C.	04.47	1946-47	8		2	
			TR	Accrington St.	07.48	1948	3		0	
ROBERTSON, Stuart	Glasgow	29.09.59	APP	Burnley	07.77	1978-81	30	2	0	(M)
			TR	Exeter C.	03.82	1981	5	1	0	
			TR	Doncaster Rov.	N/C	1982	25	/	0	

Players Names	Birthplace	Date	Previous Club	League Club	Date Signed	Seasons Played	Apps	Sub	Gls	
ROBERTSON, Stuart J.	Nottingham	16.12.46	JNRS	Nottingham F.	08.64					(D)
			TR	Doncaster Rov.	07.66	1966-71	225	3	8	
			TR	Northampton T.	05.72	1972-78	254	/	24	
ROBERTSON, Tom	Coventry	28.09.44	St. Mirren	Crystal Palace	10.66	1966	5	/	0	(W)
ROBERTSON, William G.	Glasgow	13.11.28	Arthurlie	Chelsea	07.46	1950-59	199		0	(G) d.
			TR	Orient	09.60	1960-62	47		0	
ROBERTSON, William G.	Glasgow	04.11.36	JNRS	Middlesbrough	11.53	1954	5		2	(F)
ROBERTSON, William H.	London	25.03.23	RAF Lossiemouth	Chelsea	+	1946-47	37		0	(G)d.
			TR	Birmingham C.	12.48	1948-51	2		0	
			TR	Stoke C.	06.52	1952-59	238		0	
ROBERTSON, William J.T.	Montrose	09.11.23	Montrose Roselea	Preston N.E.	+	1946-52	52		0	(HB)
			TR	Southport	07.55	1955	28		0	
ROBINS, Ian	Bury	22.02.52	APP	Oldham Ath.	02.70	1969-76	202	18	40	(F)
			TR	Bury	07.77	1977-78	49	/	5	
			TR	Huddersfield T.	09.78	1978-81	145	11	59	
ROBINSON, Alan	Grantham	02.12.55	APP	Sheffield Wed.	12.73					(IF)
				Scunthorpe U.	08.75	1975	1	/	0	
ROBINSON, Albert	Chester	01.06.48	JNRS	Chester C.	07.68	1967-68	5	1	0	(WH)
ROBINSON, Bernard C.	Cambridge	05.12.11	Kings Lynn	Norwich C.	*	1946-48	88		7	(WH)
ROBINSON, Brian T.A.	Paddington	02.04.46	APP	Peterborough U.	04.64	1964-65	8	/	0	(G)
ROBINSON, Colin R.	Birmingham	15.05.60	Mile Oak R.	Shrewsbury T.	11.82	1982-83	30	12	7	(F)
ROBINSON, Cyril	Nottingham	04.03.29	Mansfield T.(AM)	Blackpool	09.49	1951-54	22		2	(WH)
			Northwich	Bradford P.A.	06.56	1956-58	89		3	
			TR	Southport	07.59	1959	37		0	
ROBINSON, David	Cleveland	14.01.65		Hartlepool U.	08.83	1983	6	1	0	(D)
ROBINSON, David	Birmingham	14.07.48	APP	Birmingham C.	07.66	1968-71	111	2	2	(D)
			TR	Walsall	02.73	1972-76	164	1	3	
ROBINSON, David S.	Exeter	06.01.37		Exeter C.	12.54	1957-58	17		4	(F)
			TR	Oldham Ath.	07.59					
ROBINSON, David W.	Manchester	25.11.21		Shrewsbury T.	08.50	1950	10		0	
ROBINSON, Edward	Bywell	15.01.22		Gateshead	+	1946-52	90		7	(FB)
ROBINSON, Eric M.	Manchester	01.07.35	Altrincham	W.B.A.	03.57	1957	1		0	(F)
			TR	Rotherham U.	01.59	1958-59	14		1	
ROBINSON, Fred J.	Rotherham	29.12.54	APP	Rotherham U.	01.73	1973	4	/	0	(D)
			TR	Doncaster Rov.	10.75	1975-78	111	8	3	
			TR	Huddersfield T.	08.79	1979-80	72	/	2	
ROBINSON, George D.	Liverpool	28.05.37		Southport	02.59	1958	2		0	
ROBINSON, George F.	Melton Mowbray	17.06.25	Holwell Wks	Notts.Co.	+	1946	29		0	(FB)
ROBINSON, George H.	Marlpool	11.01.08	Sunderland(*)	Charlton Ath.	*	1946	7		0	(IF)*Ilkeston/d.1963
ROBINSON, Henry	Southport	14.09.47	APP	Blackpool	01.65					(OR)
			TR	Southport	02.66					
			TR	Burnley	09.66					
				Newport Co.	11.67	1967-68	39	1	3	
ROBINSON, Herbert			Barnoldswick	Accrington St.	12.46	1946	5		4	(CF)
ROBINSON, John	Chorley	18.04.36	Leyland M.	Bury	09.54	1954-59	120		21	(OR)
			TR	Oldham Ath.	07.61	1961	3		1	
ROBINSON, John	Middlesbrough	10.02.34		Middlesbrough	10.51	1953-54	3		0	(IF)
			TR	Hartlepool U.	06.59	1959	9		0	
ROBINSON, John	Lurgan	02.04.20	Glenavon	Wolverhampton W.	+					d.1981
			TR	Walsall	03.47	1946	4		0	
ROBINSON, John	Shiremoor	10.08.17	Shiremoor	Sheffield Wed.	*	1946	7		6	(IF)E-4/E.F.LGE REP
			TR	Sunderland	10.46	1946-48	82		31	d.
			TR	Lincoln C.	10.49	1949	8		5	
ROBINSON, John J.	Blackburn	23.04.18	Accrington St.(*)	Manchester C.	*	1946	1		0	(G)
			TR	Bury	11.46	1946	12		0	
			TR	Southend U.	08.47	1947	6		0	
ROBINSON, Joseph	Lanchester	14.11.18	Ouston U.	Norwich C.	*	1946	2		0	(WH)
ROBINSON, Joseph	Morpeth	04.03.19		Hartlepool U.	*					(G)
			TR	Blackpool	07.46	1947-48	25		0	
			TR	Hull C.	02.49	1948-52	70		0	
ROBINSON, Joseph N.	Middlesbrough	15.01.21	South Bank St.P.	Middlesbrough	*	1946-47	16		0	
			TR	Grimsby T.	06.48	1948	5		0	
ROBINSON, Joseph W.	Chester-le-Street	13.04.32	JNRS	Newcastle U.	09.51					(F)
			W. Stanley	Hartlepool U.	07.54	1955-57	43		6	
			TR	Gateshead	08.58	1958	22		4	
ROBINSON, Keith	Bolton	30.12.37		Oldham Ath.	09.58	1958-60	40		3	(F)
ROBINSON, Len J.	Nottingham	01.10.46	Nottingham F.(AM)	Notts.Co.	03.64	1963-64	4		0	(FB)
ROBINSON, Mark W.	Middlesbrough	22.10.61	APP	Middlesbrough	10.79					(M)
			Hull C. (N/C)	Hartlepool U.	01.83	1982-83	34	2	4	

Players Names	Birthplace	Date	Previous Club	League Club	Date Signed	Seasons Played	Career Record Apps	Sub	Gls	
ROBINSON, Martin J.	Ilford	17.07.57	APP	Tottenham H.	05.75	1975-77	5	1	2	(F)
			TR	Charlton Ath.	02.78	1977-83	213	9	56	
			L	Reading	09.82	1982	6	/	2	
ROBINSON, Maurice,	Newark	09.11.29		Leeds U.	04.49					(OL)
			Gainsborough	Doncaster Rov.	12.52	1953	18		7	
			Kettering	Northampton T.	06.57	1957	11		2	
ROBINSON, Mike J.	Leicester	12.07.58	APP	Preston N.E.	07.76	1975-78	45	3	15	(F)EI-16
			TR	Manchester U.	07.79	1979	29	1	8	
			TR	Brighton & H.A.	07.80	1980-82	111	2	37	
			TR	Liverpool	08.83	1983	23	1	6	
ROBINSON, Neil	Liverpool	20.04.57	APP	Everton	05.74	1975-78	13	3	1	(D)
			TR	Swansea C.	10.79	1979-83	108	9	7	
ROBINSON, Paul	Hampstead	05.01.63	APP	Millwall	01.80	1979-83	56	3	2	(D)E.SCH.INT./E.YTH.INT.
ROBINSON, Peter	Ashington	04.09.57		Burnley	06.76	1976-79	48	7	3	(D)
ROBINSON, Peter	Manchester	29.01.22	JNRS	Manchester C.	+	1946	1		0	(WH)
			TR	Chesterfield	10.47	1947-48	60		0	
			TR	Notts. Co.	02.50	1949-52	82		1	
ROBINSON, Peter J.	St.Ives	11.04.44	Cambridge U.	Southend U.	03.69	1968-69	1	4	0	(HB)
ROBINSON, Philip B.	Doncaster	21.11.42	Montrose Vic.	Huddersfield T.	04.60					(F)
			TR	Doncaster Rov.	08.61	1961-65	157	/	19	
			TR	Bradford P.A.	07.66	1966-68	108	8	8	
			TR	Darlington	07.69	1969	26	1	4	
ROBINSON, Ray M.	Durham	02.12.50	APP	Preston N.E.	12.68	1968	2	/	0	(IF)
ROBINSON, Richard	Whitburn	19.01.27	JNRS	Middlesbrough	+	1946-58	386		1	(FB)E.F.LGE REP.●
			TR	Barrow	06.59	1959-62	139		0	
ROBINSON, Robert	Ashington	23.06.21	Burnley(AM)	Sunderland	02.47	1947-51	31		0	(G)
			TR	Newcastle U.	08.52	1952	5		0	
ROBINSON, Spencer L.	Bradford	29.12.65	Nottingham F.(APP)	Huddersfield T.	N/C	1983	4	1	1	(F)
ROBINSON, Steve M.	Sheffield	14.06.64	APP	Chesterfield	07.82	1981-82	8	1	0	(F)
ROBINSON, Stuart A.	Middlesbrough	16.01.59	APP	Newcastle U.	07.77	1977-78	11	1	2	(F)
			TR	Aldershot	07.80	1980-82	71	6	10	
ROBINSON, Terry A.C.	Stewkley	24.03.54	APP	Luton T.	03.72					(F)
			L	Cambridge U.	09.72	1972	6	/	1	
			TR	Crewe Alex.	12.72	1972-73	7	4	1	
ROBINSON, Terry H.	Woodhams	08.11.29	Loughboro Coll.	Brentford	AM	1954-56	34		3	(FB)E.AMAT.INT.
			TR	Northampton T.	AM	1957	13		0	
ROBINSON, William	Manchester	17.11.25		Stockport Co.	08.49	1949	9		2	d. 1953
			TR	Accrington St.	12.50	1950-52	96		2	
ROBINSON, William	Whitburn	04.04.19	JNRS	Sunderland	*					(CF)
			TR	Charlton Ath.	46.5	1946-48	53		16	
			TR	West Ham U.	01.49	1948-51	101		60	
ROBLEDO, Edward O.	Chile	26.07.28	JNRS	Barnsley	+	1947-48	5		0	(WH) d.1970
			TR	Newcastle U.	02.49	1949-52	37		0	
			Cola Cola	Notts.Co.	09.57	1957	2		0	
ROBLEDO, George O.	Chile	14.04.26	Huddersfield T.(AM)	Barnsley	+	1946-48	105		44	(IF)CHILEAN INT.
			TR	Newcastle U.	01.49	1948-52	146		82	
ROBLEY, Keith	Cockermouth	03.06.44	Corinthian J.	Workington	AM	1965	2	/	0	(W)
ROBSHAW, Harry W.	Edmonton	10.05.27	JNRS	Tottenham H.	11.48	1951	1		0	(WH)
			TR	Reading	02.53	1952-53	20		1	
ROBSON, Albert P.	Crook	14.11.16	JNRS	Crystal Palace	*	1946-47	48		8	(CF)
ROBSON, Ben T.	Gateshead	31.01.22	Aberdeen	Southport	08.49	1949	2		0	(WH)
ROBSON, Bryan	Chester-le-Street	11.01.57	APP	W.B.A.	08.74	1974-81	193	4	39	(M)E-32/E.U21-7/E.YTH.INT./●
			TR	Manchester U.	10.81	1981-83	98	/	27	Brother of Gary
ROBSON, Bryan S. (Pop)	Sunderland	11.11.45	JNRS	Newcastle U.	11.62	1964-70	205	1	81	(F)E.U23-2/E.F.LGE REP.●
			TR	West Ham U.	02.71	1970-73	120	/	47	
			TR	Sunderland	07.74	1974-76	90	/	34	
			TR	West Ham U.	10.76	1976-78	107	/	47	
			TR	Sunderland	06.79	1979-80	49	3	23	
			TR	Carlisle U.	03.81	1980-81	48	/	21	
			TR	Chelsea	08.82	1982	11	4	3	
			L	Carlisle U.	03.83	1982	11	/	4	
			TR	Sunderland	08.83	183	7	5	3	
ROBSON, Charles L.	Sth.Shields	01.11.31	Nth.Hull J.	Hull C.	05.50	1951	3		1	(OR)
			TR	Darlington	05.53	1953-54	68		19	
			TR	Liverpool	07.55					
			TR	Crewe Alex.	01.56	1955	14		2	
ROBSON, Don J.	Winlaton	05.02.34		Doncaster Rov.	07.51					(F)
			TR	Gateshead	09.53	1953-56	34		11	
ROBSON, Gary	Durham	06.07.65	APP	W.B.A.	05.83	1982-83	5	4	0	(M)

Players Names	Birthplace	Date	Previous Club	League Club	Date Signed	Seasons Played	Apps	Sub	Gls	
ROBSON, James	Pelton	23.01.39	JNRS	Burnley	01.56	1956-64	204		80	(IF)E.U23-1
			TR	Blackpool	03.65	1964-67	60	3	13	
			TR	Barnsley	01.68	1967-69	87	/	15	
			TR	Bury	08.70	1970-72	100	3	3	
			TR	Burnley	05.73					
ROBSON, John D.	Consett	15.07.50	Birtley YC	Derby Co.	10.67	1967-72	170	1	3	(D)E.U23-7/E.F.LGE REP.
			TR	Aston Villa	10.72	1972-77	141	3	1	
ROBSON, John D.	Washington	20.07.42		Darlington	10.62	1962-64	33		0	(HB)
ROBSON, Keith	Hetton-le-Hole	15.11.53	JNRS	Newcastle U.	05.71	1972-73	14	/	3	(F)
			TR	West Ham U.	09.74	1974-76	65	3	13	
			TR	Cardiff C.	08.77	1977	21	/	5	
			TR	Norwich C.	02.78	1977-80	61	4	13	
			TR	Leicester C.	09.81	1981	8	1	0	
			L	Carlisle U.	03.83	1982	10	1	4	
ROBSON, Lance	Newcastle	27.12.39	H. Stannington	Newcastle U.	10.58					(F)
			TR	Darlington	07.60	1960-63	144		49	
				Darlington	07.68	1968-69	69	/	17	
			TR	Hartlepool U.	02.70	1969	8	/	2	
ROBSON, Matt	Easington	29.12.54	APP	Sunderland	01.72					(F)
			L	Darlington	03.75	1974	1	/	0	
ROBSON, Robert W.	Langley Park	18.02.33	Langley Pk.J.	Fulham	05.50	1950-55	152		68	(WH)E-20/E.U23-1/●
			TR	W.B.A.	03.56	1955-61	239		56	E.F.LGE REP.
			TR	Fulham	08.62	1962-66	193	/	9	
ROBSON, Ron	Sunderland	12.09.32	Albion SC	Gateshead	06.57	1957-58	7		0	(HB)
ROBSON, Stewart I.	Billericay	06.11.64	APP	Arsenal	11.81	1981-83	79	/	10	(M) E.YTH.INT./E.U'21-1
ROBSON, Tom	Sunderland	01.02.36	JNRS	Sunderland	09.57	1958-59	5		0	(WH)
			TR	Darlington	08.60	1960	1		0	
ROBSON, Tom H.	Gateshead	31.07.44	APP	Northampton T.	08.61	1961-65	73	1	20	(W)E.YTH.INT.●
			TR	Chelsea	12.65	1965	6	1	0	
			TR	Newcastle U.	12.66	1966-68	46	2	11	
			TR	Peterborough U.	11.68	1968-80	440	42	111	
ROBSON, Tom R.	Newcastle	11.08.28		Cardiff C.	02.49					(FB)
			TR	Bradford C.	07.50	1950-51	9		0	
			TR	Grimsby T.	06.52	1952-54	58		2	
ROBSON, Trevor	Stoke	04.01.59	APP	Port Vale	01.77	1975	0	1	0	(F)
ROBSON, William H.	Whitehaven	13.10.31	Kells	Workington	08.51	1951-59	130		55	(IF)
			TR	Carlisle U.	11.59	1959	10		1	
ROBY, Don	Wigan	15.11.33	JNRS	Notts.Co.	02.51	1950-60	226		37	(W)
			TR	Derby Co.	08.61	1961-62	70		6	
ROCHE, John A.	Poplar	18.05.32	Margate	Millwall	06.57	1957-58	24		13	(F)
			TR	Crystal Palace	05.59	1959	27		11	
ROCHE, Pat	Dublin	04.01.51	Shelbourne	Manchester U.	10.73	1974-81	46	/	0	(G)EI-7
			TR	Brentford	08.82	1982-83	71	/	0	
ROCHFORD, William	Newhouse	23.05.13	Cuckfield	Portsmouth	*					(FB)E.F.LGE REP./d.1984
			TR	Southampton	07.46	1946-49	128		0	
			TR	Colchester U.	07.50	1950	2		0	
ROCKETT, Trevor D.	Finchampstead	08.10.51	Fleet	Aldershot	07.76	1976-77	5	/	0	(G)
RODAWAY, William	Liverpool	26.09.54	APP	Burnley	09.71	1971-80	201	2	1	(D)E.SCH.INT.
			TR	Peterborough U.	07.81	1981-82	80	1	0	
			TR	Blackpool	08.83	1983	41	/	0	
RODDOM, Joe	Spennymoor	16.05.24	Blyth Spartans	Chesterfield	01.48					(WH)
			TR	Darlington	06.50	1950	6		0	
RODGER, Graham	Glasgow	01.04.67	APP	Wolverhampton W.	APP	1983	1	/	0	
RODGER, James M.	Cleland	15.09.33	St.Mirren	Newport Co.	02.57	1956-57	5		1	(F)
RODGER, Richard J.	Hemsworth	01.07.36	JNRS	Halifax T.	09.57	1954-56	15		3	(F)
RODGER, William	Dalkeith	24.06.47	Newton Grange	Bradford P.A.	04.65	1965-66	6	2	0	(F)
RODGERS, Alwyn	Chesterfield	29.05.38		Doncaster Rov.	11.56	1958	1		0	(FB)
RODGERS, Arnold W.	Rotherham	05.12.23	Wickersley	Huddersfield T.	+	1946-49	28		17	(IF)Father of David●
			TR	Bristol C.	10.49	1949-55	197		147	
			TR	Shrewsbury T.	06.56	1956	13		3	
RODGERS, Cliff F.	Rotherham	03.10.21	RAF Pocklington	York C.	+	1946	26		0	(LB)
RODGERS, David M.	Bristol	28.02.52	JNRS	Bristol C.	07.69	1970-81	190	2	15	(D)E.SCH.INT.
			TR	Torquay U.	02.82	1981	5	/	1	
			Forest Green R.	Lincoln C.	03.82	1981	3	/	0	
RODGERSON, Alan	Easington	19.03.39	JNRS	Middlesbrough	05.56	1958-60	13		3	(F)E.SCH.INT.
ROGERS, Kevin P.	Merthyr Tydfil	23.09.63	APP	Aston Villa	09.81					(M)
				Birmingham C.	04.83	1983	8	1	1	
RODI, Joe	Glasgow	23.07.13	Grimsby T.(+)	Rochdale	+	1946	9		3	(F)d.1965
RODON, Chris P.	Swansea	09.06.63	Pontadawe	Brighton & H.A.	01.83	1982	0	1	0	(F)
			L	Cardiff C.	08.83	1983	4	/	0	

Players Names	Birthplace	Date	Previous Club	League Club	Date Signed	Seasons Played	Apps	Sub	Gls	
RODON, Peter C.	Swansea	05.02.45	JNRS	Swansea C.	11.62					(F)
			TR	Bradford C.	07.64	1964-66	60	4	15	
RODRIGUES, Peter	Cardiff	21.01.44	JNRS	Cardiff C.	05.61	1963-65	85	/	2	(D)W-40/W.U23-5/
			TR	Leicester C.	01.66	1965-70	139	1	6	W.SCH.INT.
			TR	Sheffield Wed.	10.70	1970-74	162	/	2	
			TR	Southampton	07.75	1975-76	59	/	3	
RODWELL, Joe	Southport	13.10.28	Birkdale Ath.	Accrington St.	AM	1948	3		0	(W)
ROE, John	Broxbourne	07.01.38	W.Calder	Colchester U.	07.58	1959	2		0	(FB)
ROE, Len M.	Hayes	11.01.32	Ruislip Manor	Brentford	05.51	1954-56	7		0	(HB)
ROEDER, Glen V.	Woodford	13.12.55	APP	Orient	07.74	1974-77	107	8	4	(D)
			TR	Q.P.R.	08.78	1978-83	157	/	17	
			L	Notts. Co.	11.83	1983	4	/	0	
			TR	Newcastle U.	12.83	1983	23	/	0	
ROFE, Dennis	Fulham	01.06.50	APP	Orient	02.68	1967-72	170	1	6	(D)E.U23-1●
			TR	Leicester C	08.72	1972-79	290	/	6	
			TR	Chelsea	02.80	1979-81	58	1	0	
			TR	Southampton	07.82	1982-83	18	2	0	
ROFFEY, William R.	Stepney	06.02.54	APP	Crystal Palace	06.72	1972-73	24	/	0	(D)
			TR	Orient	10.73	1973-83	324	4	8	
			L	Brentford	03.84	1983	13	/	1	
ROFFI, Guido	Llanwono	06.03.24	Arsenal(AM)	Newport Co.	02.47	1946-50	112		27	(CF)
ROGAN, L. Mike	Fleetwood	29.05.48	APP	Workington	08.66	1966-76	390	/	0	(G)
			TR	Stockport Co.	06.77	1977-80	73	/	0	
			L	Crewe Alex.	03.79	1978	3	/	0	
ROGERS, Alan J.	Plymouth	06.07.54	APP	Plymouth Arg.	07.72	1973-78	107	10	5	(W)
			TR	Portsmouth	07.79	1979-83	156	7	15	
			TR	Southend U.	03.84	1983	13	/	0	
ROGERS, Alf	Eccleshall	10.04.21	Birley Carr	Sheffield Wed.	+	1946-49	30		8	(OR)
ROGERS, Alf H.	Willenhall	17.01.20	W.B.A.(AM)	Aldershot	05.46	1946-53	317		5	(FB)
ROGERS, Andrew	Chatteris	01.12.56	Chatteris	Peterborough U.	07.76	1975-77	25	4	1	(W)
			Hampton	Southampton	02.80	1979-81	0	5	0	
			TR	Plymouth Arg.	09.81	1981-83	120	1	13	
ROGERS, Dennis	Chorley	28.03.36	Netherfield	Accrington St.	03.59	1958	3		0	(G)
ROGERS, Don E.	Paulton	25.10.45	APP	Swindon T.	10.62	1962-72	400	/	148	(W)E.U23-2/E.F.LGE REP./
			TR	Crystal Palace	11.72	1972-74	69	1	28	E.YTH.INT.●
			TR	Q.P.R.	09.74	1974	13	5	5	
			TR	Swindon T.	03.76	1975-76	11	1	2	
ROGERS, Eamon	Dublin	16.04.47	APP	Blackburn Rov.	05.65	1965-71	159	6	30	(W)EI-19
			TR	Charlton Ath.	10.71	1971-72	37	2	3	
			L	Northampton T.	11.72	1972	4	/	1	
ROGERS, Ehud	Chirk	15.10.09	Swansea C.(+)	Wrexham	+	1946	1		0	(OR)W.AMAT.INT./
										*Oswestry/Wrexham/
										Arsenal/Newcastle U.
ROGERS, Graham R.	Newport	05.09.55	APP	Newport Co.	01.75	1974	0	4	0	(IF)W.SCH.INT
ROGERS, James R.	Wednesbury	31.12.29	Rubery OFC	Wolverhampton W.	05.48					(CF)
			TR	Bristol C.	05.50	1950-56	153		32	
			TR	Coventry C.	12.56	1956-58	76		27	
			TR	Bristol C.	12.58	1958-61	115		28	
ROGERS, John C.	Liverpool	16.09.50	Wigan Ath.	Port Vale	10.76	1976	25	1	6	(F)
			Altrincham	Wigan Ath.	08.82	1982	4	2	2	
ROGERS, Ken J.	Chatham	21.11.54	APP	Gillingham	11.72	1972-73	11	2	1	(F)
ROGERS, Martyn	Nottingham	26.01.60	APP	Manchester U.	01.77	1977	1	/	0	(D)E.SCH.INT.
			TR	Q.P.R.	07.79	1979	2	/	0	
ROGERS, Martyn	Bristol	07.03.55	APP	Bristol C.	03.74					(D)E.YTH.INT.
			Bath C.	Exeter C.	07.79	1979-82	120	2	5	
ROGERS, Peter P.	Bristol	22.04.53	Bath C.	Exeter C.	02.79	1978-83	194	11	37	(F)
ROGERS, William	Pennington	03.07.19	Preston N.E.(*)	Blackburn Rov.	*	1946-47	32		6	(W)
			TR	Barrow	10.47	1947-52	197		14	
ROLES, Albert G.	Southampton	29.09.21		Southampton	+	1948	1		0	
ROLFE, James	Liverpool	08.02.32	JNRS	Liverpool	07.52					(OR)
			TR	Chester C.	07.53	1953-54	51		3	
			TR	Crewe Alex.	08.55	1955-57	101		13	
			TR	Barrow	07.58	1958	12		4	
			TR	Southport	08.59					
ROLLINGS, Andy N.	Portishead	14.12.54	APP	Norwich C.	12.72	1973	4	/	0	(D)
			TR	Brighton & H.A.	04.74	1974-79	168	/	10	
			TR	Swindon T.	05.80	1980	11	1	1	
			TR	Portsmouth	08.81	1981-82	29	/	1	
			TR	Torquay U.	N/C	1983	2	/	0	
			TR	Brentford	N/C	1983	1	/	0	
ROLLINS, Kevin	Halifax	02.01.47	APP	Halifax T.	APP	1964	1		0	(FB)
ROLLO, Alex	Dumbarton	18.09.26	Dumbarton	Workington	06.57	1957-59	127		3	(FB)

Players Names	Birthplace	Date	Previous Club	League Club	Date Signed	Seasons Played	Apps	Sub	Gls	
ROLLO, James S.	Perth	16.11.37	Poole T.	Oldham Ath.	05.60	1960-62	59		0	(G)
			TR	Southport	07.63	1963	38		0	
			TR	Bradford C.	07.64	1964-65	37	/	0	
ROLPH, Gary L.	London	24.02.60	APP	Brentford	02.78	1976-78	8	4	1	(M)
RONALDSON, Ken	Edinburgh	27.09.45	Aberdeen	Bristol Rov.	07.65	1965-68	73	4	15	(IF)
			TR	Gillingham	11.69	1969-70	6	/	0	
RONSON, Brian	Durham	07.08.35	Willington	Fulham	03.53	1953	2		0	(G)
			TR	Southend U.	08.56	1956-58	30		0	
			TR	Norwich C.	08.59	1959	1		0	
			TR	Peterborough U.	07.61	1961-62	50		0	
RONSON, William	Fleetwood	22.01.57	APP	Blackpool	02.74	1974-78	124	4	12	(M)
			TR	Cardiff C.	07.79	1979-81	90	/	4	
			TR	Wrexham	10.81	1981	31	1	1	
			TR	Barnsley	08.82	1982-83	70	1	3	
ROOKE, Ron	Carlisle	12.12.26	Carlisle Yng.Libs.	Carlisle U.	AM	1949	1		0	(OR)
ROOKE, Ron L.	Guildford	07.12.11	Crystal Palace(*)	Fulham	*	1946	18		13	(CF)*Guildford C.
			TR	Arsenal	12.46	1946-48	88		67	
			TR	Crystal Palace	06.49	1949-50	45		26	
ROOKES, Phil W.	Dulverton	23.04.19	Bradford C.(*)	Portsmouth	*	1946-50	109		0	(FB)
			TR	Colchester U.	07.51	1951-52	68		0	
ROOKS, Richard	Sunderland	29.05.40	JNRS	Sunderland	06.57	1960-64	34		2	(CH)
			TR	Middlesbrough	08.65	1965-68	136	1	14	
			TR	Bristol C.	06.69	1969-71	97	/	4	
ROONEY, James	Dundee	10.12.45	Lochee Harp	Peterborough U.	07.65	1965-66	7	/	2	(F)
ROONEY, Robert	Glasgow	26.10.20	Falkirk	Orient	05.48	1948-50	66		2	(CH)S.SCH.INT.
			TR	Workington	06.51	1951	27		0	
ROONEY, Robert M.	Cowie	08.07.38	Clydebank	Sheffield U.	06.58	1958-59	14		3	(IF)
			TR	Doncaster Rov.	10.62	1962	5		1	
			TR	Lincoln C.	01.63	1962-63	28		3	
ROOST, William C.	Bristol	22.03.24	Stonehouse	Bristol Rov.	09.48	1948-56	177		49	(IF)
			TR	Swindon T.	05.57	1957-58	18		3	
ROPER, Alan J.	Tipton	21.05.39		Walsall	05.59	1962-64	53		2	(HB)
ROPER, David	Ilkley	26.09.44	Salts	Bradford C.	AM	1962	13		0	(G)E.YTH.INT.
ROPER, Don G.	Botley	14.12.22	Ditton Nomads	Southampton	+	1946	40		8	(W)E'B'-1/E.F.LGE REP./
			TR	Arsenal	08.47	1947-56	297		88	Hants Cricketer
			TR	Southampton	01.57	1956-58	80		32	
ROSARIO, Robert M.	Hammersmith	04.03.66		Norwich C.	12.83	1983	6	2	1	(F)
ROSCOE, Phil	Barnsley	03.03.34	JNRS	Barnsley	08.51					(FB)
			TR	Halifax T.	07.56	1956-63	257		5	
ROSE, Fred	Stannington	27.03.55	APP	Huddersfield T.	04.72					(F)
			TR	Workington	07.74	1974	0	2	2	
ROSE, Gordon	Sheffield	22.03.35		Sheffield U.	10.56					(F)
			TR	Halifax T.	07.58	1958	8		1	
ROSE, James	Clayton-le-Moor	04.03.18	Clayton Villa	Accrington St.	*	1946	12		0	(G)
ROSE, John	Sheffield	26.10.21		Q.P.R.	+	1946-47	18		0	
ROSE, John W.	Woolwich	12.08.20	Salisbury C.	Bournemouth	+	1946	1		0	(IF)
ROSE, Ken	Eckington	18.08.30		Chesterfield	11.50					
			TR	Exeter C.	06.52	1952	11		3	
			TR	Rochdale	07.53	1953	11		0	
			TR	Workington	06.54	1954	6		2	
ROSE, Kevin P.	Evesham	23.11.60	Ledbury T.	Lincoln C.	08.79					(G)
			TR	Hereford U.	03.83	1982-83	61	/	0	
ROSE, Mick J.	New Barnet	22.07.43	St.Albans	Charlton Ath.	07.63	1963-66	75	/	0	(G)
			TR	Notts. Co.	03.67	1966-69	109	/	0	
			L	Mansfield T.	08.70	1970	3	/	0	
ROSENTHALL, Abe	Liverpool	12.10.21	Liverpool(AM)	Tranmere Rov.	*	1946	26		8	(IF)Ice Cream Mfg
			TR	Bradford C.	04.47	1946-48	44		11	
			TR	Oldham Ath.	03.49					
			TR	Tranmere Rov.	08.49	1949-51	69		24	
			TR	Bradford C.	01.52	1952-53	63		32	
			TR	Tranmere Rov.	07.54	1954	21		3	
			TR	Bradford C.	07.55	1955	1		0	
ROSS, Alan	Ellesmere Port	17.02.33	B. Auckland	Oldham Ath.	AM	1956	3		0	(G)
			Blackburn Rov.(AM)	Accrington St.	AM	1958	1		0	
ROSS, Alan J.	Glasgow	26.05.42	Petershill	Luton T.	04.62					(G)
			TR	Carlisle U.	06.63	1963-78	465	1	0	
ROSS, Alex M.C.	Glasgow	17.12.23	Shawfield J.	W.B.A.	10.47					(IF)
			TR	Crystal Palace	08.48	1948-50	33		0	
ROSS, Bryce T.	Edinburgh	04.12.27		Carlisle U.	11.46	1946-47	3		0	(CF)+Newcastle/d.1969
ROSS, Colin	Dailly	29.08.62	APP	Middlesbrough	09.80	1980-82	37	1	0	(M)
			L	Chesterfield	03.83	1982	6	/	0	
			TR	Darlington	08.83	1983	7	/	0	

Players Names	Birthplace	Date	Previous Club	League Club	Date Signed	Seasons Played	Apps	Sub	Gls	
ROSS, Eric W.	Belfast	19.09.44	Glentoran	Newcastle U.	08.67	1967-68	2	/	0	(IF)N.I.-1/N.I.U23-1
			TR	Northampton T.	08.69	1969-71	51	7	5	
			L	Hartlepool U.	11.71	1971	2	/	0	
ROSS, George	Inverness	15.04.43	JNRS	Preston N.E.	04.60	1960-72	384	2	3	(FB)
			TR	Southport	11.72	1972-73	31	/	0	
ROSS, George A.	Deptford	01.11.20	Metro Gas	Millwall	+					(FB)
			TR	Carlisle U.	05.47	1947	9		0	
ROSS, Ian	Glasgow	26.11.47		Liverpool	08.65	1966-71	41	6	2	(D)
			TR	Aston Villa	02.72	1971-75	175	/	3	
			L	Notts. Co.	10.76	1976	4	/	1	
			L	Northampton T.	11.76	1976	2	/	0	
			TR	Peterborough U.	12.76	1976-78	112	/	1	
			TR	Wolverhampton W.	08.79					
				Hereford U.	N/C	1982	15	/	0	
ROSS, Louis A.	Dublin	19.09.20	Q.of South	Walsall	08.48	1948	8		0	(FB)
ROSS, Robert			Dumbarton	Watford	07.46	1946	33		6	
ROSS, Robert A.	Wishaw	25.05.27	Wolkington	Leeds U.	08.50	1951	5		0	(FB)
			TR	Stockport Co.	06.54	1954	9		0	
ROSS, Robert C.	Edinburgh	09.09.41	St.Mirren	Grimsby T.	06.65	1965-70	208	4	18	(F)
ROSS, Robert H.	Edinburgh	18.05.42	Hearts	Shrewsbury T.	06.63	1963-65	99	/	29	(IF)
			TR	Brentford	03.66	1965-72	288	2	59	
			TR	Cambridge U.	10.72	1972-73	57	8	14	
ROSS, Robert R.	Cowdenbeath	13.12.25	Dundee	Milwall	08.52	1952	1		0	(FB)
ROSS, Stewart	Woking	01.09.45		Wolverhampton W.	11.65	1967-68	1	2	0	(FB)
ROSS, Tom	Dundee	27.02.47	Lochee Harp	Peterborough U.	07.65	1965-66	5	2	2	(F)
			TR	York C.	06.67	1967-68	56	5	20	
ROSS, Trevor W.	Ashton-under-Lyne	16.01.57	APP	Arsenal	06.74	1974-77	57	1	5	(M)S.U21-1/E.SCH.INT.
			TR	Everton	11.77	1977-82	120	6	16	
			L	Portsmouth	10.82	1982	5	/	0	
			L	Sheffield U.	12.82	1982	4	/	0	
			AEK Athens	Sheffield U.	01.84	1983	4	/	0	
ROSS, William	Glasgow	02.05.19	Arbroath	Bradford C.	07.50	1950	4		2	(F)Father of Trevor
ROSS, William B.	Swansea	08.11.24		Cardiff C.	+	1946-47	8		0	(OR)
			TR	Sheffield U.	05.48	1948	3		1	
			TR	Southport	08.49	1949-50	46		13	
ROSSER, Doug R.	Swansea	08.09.48	JNRS	Swansea C.	05.67	1968-70	28	2	1	(CH)
			TR	Crewe Alex.	08.71	1971	28	1	0	
ROSSITER, Don	Strood	08.06.35	JNRS	Arsenal	06.52					(IF)E.YTH.INT./
			TR	Hartlepool U.	03.54					Loan to Walthamstow
			TR	Arsenal	07.55					(Amat.cup winners)
			TR	Orient	03.56	1956	1		0	1951/2
				Gillingham	07.57	1957	1		0	
ROSSITER, John D.	Kingsbridge	28.10.42		Torquay U.	07.61	1962-63	24		0	(FB)
ROSTRON, J. Wilf	Sunderland	29.09.56	APP	Arsenal	10.73	1974-76	12	5	2	(M)E.SCH.INT.
			TR	Sunderland	07.77	1977-79	75	1	17	
			TR	Watford	10.79	1979-83	160	6	13	
ROTHWELL, Edward	Atherton	03.09.17		Bolton W.	*	1946-48	21		1	(W)
			TR	Southport	08.49	1949-50	40		5	
ROTHWELL, George	Bolton	22.11.23	Chorley	Accrington St.	+	1946-51	202		10	
ROTHWELL, John	Farnworth	29.03.20	Walkden Heath	Southport	*	1946	17		6	(CF)
			TR	Birmingham C.	03.47					
			TR	Southport	08.49					
			TR	Crewe Alex.	10.49	1949	3		1	
ROTHWELL, Ron	Bury	10.07.20	Dunfermline	Rochdale	12.47	1946-51	48		0	(FB)
ROUND, Len	Wall Heath	21.05.28	Ayr U.	Hull C.	06.57	1957	17		0	(G)
ROUND, Paul G.	Blackburn	22.06.59	APP	Blackburn Rov.	08.77	1976-81	41	10	5	(D)
ROUND, Steve C.	Dudley	28.02.63	APP	Walsall	03.80	1981-82	5	19	3	(F)
ROUNSEVELL, Anthony	Liskeard	01.04.45	APP	Plymouth Arg.	12.62	1963-67	34	1	0	(FB)
ROUSE, Herbert	Doncaster	19.11.20		Doncaster Rov.	06.48	1948-54	35		0	(FB)
ROUSE, R. Vic	Swansea	16.03.36	JNRS	Millwall	03.53					(G)W-1/W.U23-1
			TR	Crystal Palace	08.56	1956-62	238		0	
			TR	Oxford U.	08.63	1963-64	22		0	
			TR	Orient	07.65	1965-66	40	/	0	
ROUTLEDGE, Ron	Ashington	14.10.37	JNRS	Sunderland	10.54	1956-57	2		0	(G)
			TR	Bradford P.A.	05.58	1958-61	39		0	
ROUTLEDGE, T. Alan	Wallsend	06.05.60	Bath Univ.	Bristol Rov.	10.80	1980	0	1	0	
ROWAN, Barry	Willesden	24.04.42	Watford(AM)	Brentford	10.60					(W)
			Dover	Millwall	07.64	1964-66	73	/	14	
			U.S.A.	Middlesbrough	09.68					
			TR	Colchester U.	11.68	1968	2	/	0	
			TR	Reading	08.69	1969	1	/	0	
			TR	Plymouth Arg.	09.69	1969	10	/	1	
			TR	Exeter C.	07.70	1970-72	76	5	14	

Players Names	Birthplace	Date	Previous Club	League Club	Date Signed	Seasons Played	Apps	Sub	Gls	
ROWAN, Brian	Glasgow	28.06.48		Aston Villa	04.69	1969	1	/	0	(FB)
			TR	Watford	10.71	1971	8	4	0	
ROWDEN, Len A.	Swansea	31.05.27	Clydach	Swansea C.	10.53	1953	1		0	(CH)
ROWE, Colwyn	Ipswich	22.03.56		Colchester U.	01.74	1973-74	4	8	2	(W)
			TR	Gillingham	07.75					
ROWE, Eric S.	Exeter	20.08.21		Exeter C.	10.47	1947-53	139		0	(FB)
ROWE, Graham E.	Southport	28.08.45	APP	Blackpool	07.63	1963-70	100	5	12	(CF)
			L	Tranmere Rov.	11.70	1970	6	1	0	
			TR	Bolton W.	05.71	1971	4	2	0	
ROWE, Mark T.	Bodmin	09.06.64	APP	Plymouth Arg.	09.81	1981-83	32	8	1	(M)
ROWE, N. Terry S.	Fulham	08.06.64	APP	Brentford	06.82	1981-83	62	3	1	(D)
ROWE, Norman	Halesowen	20.03.40		Walsall	03.59	1959-60	6		0	(F)
ROWE, V. Norman	Shouldham	14.02.26	Kings Lynn	Derby Co.	12.49	1951	2		0	
			TR	Walsall	08.52	1952	26		0	
ROWELL, Gary	Seaham	06.06.57	APP	Sunderland	07.74	1975-83	229	25	88	(F)E.U21-1
ROWELL, John F.	Dawdon	31.12.18		Bournemouth	+	1946-47	31		11	(F)Father of Gary
			TR	Wrexham	07.48	1948-49	41		4	
			TR	Aldershot	08.50	1950	5		0	
ROWLAND, Alf	Stokerlsey	02.09.20	Stockton	Aldershot	08.46	1946-48	93		0	
			TR	Cardiff C.	02.49	1948-49	3		0	
ROWLAND, Andrew A.	Derby	08.09.54	Derby Co.(AM)	Bury	08.74	1974-78	169	5	58	(F)E.YTH.INT.
			TR	Swindon T.	09.78	1978-83	222	1	75	
ROWLAND, David C.	Arlesey	12.09.40	Arlesey	Luton T.	01.58	1957	1		0	(F)E.SCH.INT.
ROWLAND, John D.	Ridings	07.04.41	Ironville	Nottingham F.	04.61	1960-61	26		3	(W)E.YTH.INT
			TR	Port Vale	08.62	1962-66	147	2	40	
			TR	Mansfield T.	09.66	1966-67	48	/	18	
			TR	Tranmere Rov.	07.68	1968	25	1	3	
ROWLAND, John O.	Newport	16.03.36	Lovells Ath.	Newport Co.	06.58	1958-68	462	1	9	(WH)W.U23-1●
ROWLAND, Len C.	Manchester	23.06.25	Mansfield T.(AM)	Wrexham	AM	1949-50	18		0	(HB)E.AMAT.INT.
			Ashton U.	Stockport Co.	12.52	1952-56	61		0	
ROWLANDS, John H.	Liverpool	07.02.45		Mansfield T.	10.67	1967	14	2	0	(F)
			TR	Torquay U.	06.68	1968	18	/	4	
			L	Exeter C.	01.69	1968	1	/	0	
			TR	Stockport Co.	08.69	1969-70	45	1	13	
			TR	Barrow	01.71	1970-71	52	2	6	
			TR	Workington	07.72	1972-73	50	1	11	
			TR	Crewe Alex.	11.73	1973-74	31	4	1	
			TR	Hartlepool U.	09.75	1975-76	47	2	10	
ROWLANDS, Trevor I.	Rhondda	02.02.22	Cardiff Nomads	Norwich C.	08.46	1947-49	10		2	(FB)W.SCH.INT./
			TR	Colchester U.	07.50	1950-52	46		5	d.
ROWLES, A. Eddie J.	Gosport	10.03.51	APP	Bournemouth	03.68	1967-70	58	8	12	(F)
			TR	York C.	07.71	1971-72	61	6	14	
			TR	Torquay U.	06.73	1973-74	54	5	13	
			TR	Darlington	08.75	1975-77	96	7	21	
			TR	Colchester U.	12.77	1977-81	79	12	17	
ROWLEY, Antonio C.	Porthcawl	19.09.29	Wellington	Birmingham C.	01.49					(IF)W-1
			Stourbridge	Liverpool	10.53	1953-57	60		37	
			TR	Tranmere Rov.	03.58	1957-60	100		47	
ROWLEY, Arthur	Liverpool	09.05.33	F.Melly B.C.	Liverpool	05.51	1952	11		0	(IF)
			TR	Wrexham	11.54	1954-56	54		8	
			TR	Crewe Alex.	02.57	1956-57	34		7	
			TR	Tranmere Rov.	09.58					
ROWLEY, G. Arthur	Wolverhampton	21.04.26	Wolverhampton W.(AM)	W.B.A.	+	1946-48	24		4	(IF)E'B'-1/E.F.LGE REP./●
			TR	Fulham	12.48	1948-49	56		26	Brother of John F.
			TR	Leicester C.	07.50	1950-57	303		251	
			TR	Shrewsbury T.	06.58	1958-64	236		152	
ROWLEY, John	Wolverhampton	23.06.44		Bradford P.A.	10.67	1967	35	/	0	(FB)
ROWLEY, John F.	Wolverhampton	07.10.20	Bournemouth(*)	Manchester U.	*	1946-54	317		163	(CF)*Wolverhampton W./
			TR	Plymouth Arg.	02.55	1954-56	56		14	E-6/E'B'-1/E.F.LGE REP.●
ROWLEY, Ken F.	Pelsall	29.08.26	Elkingtons	Wolverhampton W.	10.47	1949	1		0	(IF)
			TR	Birmingham	01.51	1950-54	40		17	
			TR	Coventry C.	11.54	1954	3		0	
ROXBURGH, Alex W.	Manchester	19.09.10	Manchester C.(AM)	Blackpool	*					(G)
			TR	Barrow	08.46	1946-47	69		0	
ROY, Andy	Tillicoultry	14.07.28	Dunfermline	Exeter C.	08.49	1949	2		0	(IF)
ROY, John R.	Southampton	23.03.14		Ipswich T.	+	1946	15		2	(OR)*Norwich C./Mansfield T./ Sheffield Wed./Notts.Co./ Tranmere Rov.
ROYLE, Joe	Liverpool	08.04.49	APP	Everton	08.66	1965-74	229	2	102	(F)E-6/E.U23-10/
			TR	Manchester U.	12.74	1974-77	98	1	23	E.F.LGE REP.
			TR	Bristol C.	11.77	1977-79	100	1	18	
			TR	Norwich C.	08.80	1980-81	40	2	9	
ROYSTON, Robert	Newcastle	01.12.15	Southport(*)	Plymouth Arg.	*	1946	36		0	(RB)*Sunderland

Players Names	Birthplace	Date	Previous Club	League Club	Date Signed	Seasons Played	Apps	Sub	Gls	
RUARK, Anthony	West Ham	23.03.33		Southend U.	05.56	1956	9		0	(HB)
RUDD, Edward	Wigan	07.01.29		Bolton W.	09.50					
			TR	Accrington St.	08.51	1951	2		0	
RUDD, John J.	Hull	25.10.19	Terenure Ath.	Manchester C.	*	1946	2		0	(OL)Uncle of William T.
			TR	York C.	03.47	1946-48	83		21	
			TR	Leeds U.	02.49	1948-49	18		1	
			TR	Rotherham U.	10.49	1949-51	75		10	
			TR	Scunthorpe U.	10.51	1951	32		5	
			TR	Workington	09.52	1952	17		1	
RUDD, William T.	Manchester	13.12.41	Stalybridge	Birmingham C.	10.59	1959-61	24		3	(M)
			TR	York C.	11.61	1961-65	193	/	30	
			TR	Grimsby T.	07.66	1966-67	59	1	9	
			TR	Rochdale	02.68	1967-69	108	/	8	
			TR	Bury	06.70	1970-76	174	15	18	
RUDGE, Dale A.	Wolverhampton	09.09.63	APP	Wolverhampton W.	08.81	1982-83	23	4	0	(M)
RUDGE, David H.	Wolverhampton	21.01.48	APP	Aston Villa	05.65	1966-69	49	6	10	(W)
			TR	Hereford U.	08.72	1972-75	75	7	8	
			TR	Torquay U.	12.75	1975-77	60	4	4	
RUDGE, John R.	Wolverhampton	21.10.44	JNRS	Huddersfield T.	11.61	1962-66	5	/	0	(F)
			TR	Carlisle U.	12.66	1966-68	45	5	16	
			TR	Torquay U.	01.69	1968-71	93	2	35	
			TR	Bristol Rov.	02.72	1971-74	50	20	17	
			TR	Bournemouth	03.75	1974-76	18	3	2	
RUDGE, Simon J.	Warrington	30.12.64	APP	Bolton W.	12.82	1982-83	48	7	10	(F)
RUDHAM, Doug	S.Africa	03.05.26	Johannesburg	Liverpool	08.55	1954-59	63		0	(G)S.AFRICAN AMAT.INT.
RUDKIN, Tom W.	Peterborough	17.06.19	Peterborough U.	Arsenal	01.47	1946	5		2	(OL)*Lincoln C./+Grimsby T.
			TR	Southampton	08.47	1947-48	9		0	
			TR	Bristol C.	05.49	1949-50	34		4	
RUDMAN, Harold	Whitworth	04.11.24		Burnley	+	1946-56	71		0	(FB)
			TR	Rochdale	07.57	1957	22		1	
RUECROFT, Jacob	Lanchester	01.05.15		Halifax T.	*	1946	25		1	(HB)
			Scarborough	Bradford C.	01.48	1947-48	43		0	
RUFFETT, Ray D.	Luton	20.07.24	JNRS	Luton T.	+	1948	1		0	(WH)
RUGGIERO, John S.	Stoke	26.11.54	APP	Stoke C.	05.72	1976	9	/	2	(F)
			L	Workington	01.76	1975	3	/	0	
			TR	Brighton & H.A.	06.77	1977	4	4	2	
			L	Portsmouth	12.77	1977	6	/	1	
			TR	Chester C.	04.79	1979	9	3	1	
RULE, Alan H.	Southampton	10.01.30	Winchester	Chelsea	11.52					(IF)
			TR	Norwich C.	09.56	1956	8		0	
			TR	Bournemouth	06.57	1957	25		0	
RUMBOLD, George	Alton	10.07.11	Orient(*)	Ipswich T.	05.46	1946-49	121		11	(FB)*Crystal Palace
RUMNEY, J. Edgar	Abberton	15.09.36	JNRS	Colchester U.	05.57	1957-64	50		0	(FB)
RUNDLE, Charles R.	Fowey	17.01.23	St.Blazey	Tottenham H.	+	1946-48	28		12	(IF)
			TR	Crystal Palace	06.50	1950-51	38		2	
RUNDLE, Sid S.K.	Fowey	19.10.21	St.Blazey	Plymouth Arg.	+	1946-52	53		1	(HB)Brother of Charles R.
RUSH, Ian J.	St. Asaph	20.10.61	APP	Chester C.	09.79	1978-79	33	1	14	(F)W-20/W.U21-2/
			TR	Liverpool	04.80	1980-83	114	1	73	W.SCH.INT.
RUSH, Jon	New Zealand	13.10.61	N. Zealand	Blackpool	11.79	1980	11	/	0	(G)
			TR	Carlisle U.	08.82					
RUSHBURY, David	Wolverhampton	20.02.56	APP	W.B.A.	07.74	1974-75	28	/	0	(D)
			TR	Sheffield Wed.	11.76	1976-78	111	1	7	
			TR	Swansea C.	07.79	1979-80	51	1	0	
			TR	Carlisle U.	08.81	1981-83	101	7	1	
RUSHBY, Alan	Doncaster	27.12.33		Doncaster Rov.	01.52	1952-53	2		0	(HB)
			TR	Mansfield T.	03.57	1956-57	20		0	
			TR	Bradford P.A.	11.57	1957-58	12		0	
RUSHFORTH, Peter	Carlisle	06.12.45		Workington	AM	1966	5	/	0	(FB)
RUSHTON, Brian W.E.	Dudley	21.10.43	APP	Birmingham C.	10.60	1962-63	12		0	(HB)
			TR	Notts.Co.	06.67	1967	1	2	0	
RUSHWORTH, Peter T.	Bristol	12.04.27	Cheltenham	Leicester C.	11.51					(WH)
			TR	Bournemouth	06.53	1953-56	88		1	
RUSLING, Graham	Keadby	04.04.48		Scunthorpe U.	01.67	1966-70	71	10	17	(CF)
RUSSELL, Alan	Aberdeen	16.11.53	Leicester C.(APP)	Peterborough U.	08.71	1971-72	7	8	1	(W)
RUSSELL, Alec C.	Bristol	17.04.25		Bristol C.	11.47	1947-48	3		0	
RUSSELL, Alex	Sth.Shields	21.02.44		Everton	12.61					(M)
			TR	Southport	11.63	1963-69	262	1	63	
			TR	Blackburn Rov.	08.70	1970	22	2	4	
			TR	Tranmere Rov.	07.71	1971-72	54	1	7	
			L	Crewe Alex.	10.72	1972	4	/	0	
			TR	Southport	11.72	1972-74	84	1	12	

Players Names	Birthplace	Date	Previous Club	League Club	Date Signed	Seasons Played	Apps	Sub	Gls	
RUSSELL, Colin	Liverpool	21.01.61	APP	Liverpool	04.78	1980	0	1	0	(F)
			TR	Huddersfield	09.82	1982-83	64	2	23	
			L	Stoke C.	03.84	1983	11	/	2	
RUSSELL, Eddie T.	Cranwell	15.07.28	St.Chads.Coll.	Wolverhampton W.	+	1948-50	30		0	(IF)
			TR	Middlesbrough	12.51	1952	20		1	
			TR	Leicester C.	10.53	1953-57	90		5	
			TR	Notts.Co.	08.58	1958	9		0	
RUSSELL, Hugh W.	Redcar	10.03.21		Gillingham	N/L	1950-51	61		8	(CF)
RUSSELL, James W.	Edinburgh	14.09.16	Sunderland(*)	Norwich C.	*	1946	4		2	
			TR	Crystal Palace	12.46	1946-47	44		6	
			TR	New Brighton	07.48	1948	24		1	
RUSSELL, John M.	Plymouth	22.04.38		Plymouth Arg.	01.59					(F)
			TR	Southport	07.60	1960	1		0	
RUSSELL, Malcolm	Halifax	09.11.45	APP	Halifax T.	03.63	1962-68	184	1	0	(FB)
			TR	Southport	09.68	1968-70	92	/	2	
			TR	Barrow	12.70	1970-71	64	/	2	
			TR	Stockport Co.	07.72	1972	11	/	0	
RUSSELL, Peter W.	Gornal	16.01.35	JNRS	Wolverhampton W.	10.52	1954-55	3		0	(HB)
			TR	Notts.Co.	03.56	1955-58	106		6	
RUSSELL, Ray J.	Walsall	09.03.30	JNRS	W.B.A.	05.48					(IF)
			Burton A.	Shrewsbury T.	05.54	1954-59	168		56	
			TR	Crewe Alex.	03.60	1959	13		4	
RUSSELL, Robert I.	Aberdour	27.12.19	Airdrie	Chelsea	+	1946	2		0	(WH)
			TR	Notts.Co.	08.48	1948	2		0	
			TR	Orient	10.48					
RUSSELL, Roger	Corby	20.11.57	JNRS	Northampton T.	N/C	1981	0	1	0	(F)
RUSSELL, Sid E.J.	Feltham	04.10.37	Jolly X	Brentford	08.56	1956-59	54		0	(FB)Middlesex/Gloucester Cricketer
RUSSELL, Steve	Stockton	20.07.32	Whitby	Middlesbrough	03.52	1951-52	9		0	(HB)
RUSSELL, William	Hounslow	07.07.35	Rhyl	Sheffield U.	11.57	1957-62	145		55	(IF)E.AMAT.INT.
			TR	Bolton W.	03.63	1962-64	22		2	
			TR	Rochdale	07.66	1966-67	63	1	8	
RUSSELL, William H.	Coatbridge	19.10.19		Hartlepool T.	05.46	1946-47	13		1	
RUSSELL, William M.	Glasgow	14.09.59	APP	Everton	07.77					(D)S.YTH.INT.
			Glasgow Celtic	Doncaster Rov.	07.79	1979-83	203	3	15	
RUSSO, Gary	Horsey	02.08.56	Ipswich T.(APP)	Bournemouth	07.75	1975	1	/	0	(FB)
RUSSON, Ron	Wednesbury	10.12.28	JNRS	Wolverhampton W.	+					(CH)d.1981
			Hednesford	Walsall	05.48	1948-54	141		1	
RUTHERFORD, Colin	High Hold	11.07.44	JNRS	Sunderland	07.61					(HB)
			TR	Barnsley	06.63	1963	1		0	
RUTHERFORD, Joe H.	Chester-le-Street	20.09.14	Southport(*)	Aston Villa	*	1946-51	137		0	(G)
RUTHERFORD, Robert	Sth. Shields	20.04.22	Newcastle U.(+)	Gateshead	+	1946-52	10		2	(HB)
RUTHERFORD, Robert A.	Carlisle	28.07.53	APP	Leeds.U.	08.70					(F)E.SCH.INT
			TR	Workington	11.72	1972	1	1	0	
RUTHERFORD, William J.	Bellshill	23.01.30	Stirling A.	Darlington	07.52	1952-58	253		3	(WH)d.1980
			TR	Southport	07.59	1959-63	176		7	
RUTLEY, Peter	Exeter	19.05.46	APP	Exeter C.	07.63	1962-64	16		0	(HB)
			TR	Leicester C.	08.65					
RUTTER, Brian D.	London	11.05.33	Cardiff C.(AM)	Crystal Palace	AM	1954	3		1	(IF)
RUTTER, Charles F.	London	22.12.27	Taunton T.	Cardiff C.	09.49	1950-57	118		0	(FB)E'B'-1/ Brother of Brian
			TR	Exeter C.	08.58					
RUTTER, Cyril H.	Leeds	21.02.33	JNRS	Portsmouth	07.51	1953-62	171		0	(CH)
RUTTER, John T.	Warrington	13.09.52	APP	Wolverhampton W.	01.71					(D)
			TR	Bournemouth	08.73	1973	2	2	0	
			TR	Exeter C.	07.74	1974-75	31	1	1	
			TR	Stockport Co.	08.76	1976-83	346	3	10	
RUTTER, Keith G.	Leeds	10.09.31	Methley U.	Q.P.R.	07.54	1954-62	340		1	(CH)
			TR	Colchester U.	02.63	1962-63	63		0	
RYALLS, Brian	Grimethorpe	07.07.32	Grimethorpe Col.	Sheffield Wed.	01.53	1953-57	41		0	(G)
RYAN, David P.	Manchester	05.01.57	APP	Manchester U.	07.74					(G)
			L	Port Vale	01.76	1975	1	/	0	
			TR	Southport	03.76	1975-76	23	/	0	
RYAN, Eric W.	Oswestry	06.01.33	Oswestry T.	Mansfield T.	05.51	1954-56	20		0	(FB)
RYAN, George	Glasgow	29.12.31	Hull C.(AM)	Sheffield U.	05.52					(CF)
			T. Lanark	Chesterfield	07.54	1954	3		0	
RYAN, Gerry J.	Dublin	04.10.55	Bohemians	Derby Co.	09.77	1977-78	30	/	4	(F)EI-15
			TR	Brighton & H.A.	09.78	1978-83	114	36	27	
RYAN, James	Stirling	12.05.45	Corrie Hearts	Manchester U.	01.63	1965-69	21	3	4	(F)
			TR	Luton T.	04.70	1970-76	172	12	21	

Players Names	Birthplace	Date	Previous Club	League Club	Date Signed	Seasons Played	Career Record Apps	Sub	Gls	
RYAN, James P.	Rhyl	06.09.42	Dulwich H.	Charlton Ath.	02.63	1962-64	16	/	8	(IF)W.U23-1
			TR	Millwall	02.65	1964-65	11	/	2	
			Hastings	Exeter C.	01.67	1966	20	/	5	
RYAN, John B.	Ashton	18.02.62	APP	Oldham Ath.	02.80	1981-82	77	/	8	(D)
			TR	Newcastle U.	08.83	1983	22	/	1	
RYAN, John G.	Lewisham	20.07.47	Maidstone U.	Arsenal	10.64					(M)
			TR	Fulham	07.65	1965-68	42	3	1	
			TR	Luton T.	07.69	1069-75	264	2	10	
			TR	Norwich C.	08.76	1976-79	113	3	26	
			Seattle Sounders	Sheffield U.	09.80	1980-81	56	/	2	
			TR	Manchester C.	01.82	1981	19	/	0	
			TR	Stockport Co.	N/C	1983	1	1	0	
			TR	Chester C.	N/C	1983	4	/	0	
RYAN, John J.	Alloa	16.10.30	Chippenham	Charlton Ath.	02.54	1954-58	61		32	(CF)
			TR	Newcastle U.	03.59					
			TR	Bristol C.	07.60	1960	3		0	
RYAN, John O.	Liverpool	28.10.44		Tranmere Rov.	08.64					(F)
			Wigan Ath.	Luton T.	10.67	1967-68	18	1	1	
			TR	Notts.Co.	05.69	1969	22	2	1	
RYAN, Ken	Accrington	20.09.36	Accrington Col.	Accrington St.	AM	1958	1		0	(G)
RYAN, Mike J.	Welwyn	14.10.30	Chertsey	Arsenal	07.48					(IF)
			TR	Lincoln C.	06.52	1952	7		0	
			TR	York C.	01.53	1952	4		0	
RYAN, Reg A.	Dublin	30.10.25	Nuneaton	W.B.A.	+	1946-54	234		28	(IF)EI-16/NI-1
			TR	Derby Co.	07.55	1955-58	133		30	
			TR	Coventry C.	09.58	1958-60	65		9	
RYAN, Tom S.	Windlesham	09.07.52	APP	Reading	09.70	1970	1	/	0	(HB)
RYDEN, Hugh	Renton	07.04.43	Yoker Ath.	Leeds U.	10.60					(W)
			TR	Bristol Rov.	06.62	1962	8		4	
			TR	Stockport Co.	07.63	1963	38		9	
			TR	Chester C.	06.64	1964-67	141	1	44	
			TR	Halifax T.	11.67	1967-69	54	1	6	
			TR	Stockport Co.	12.69	1969-72	112	12	15	
RYDEN, John J.	Alexandria	18.02.31	Alloa Ath.	Accrington St.	02.54	1953-55	80		0	(CH)
			TR	Tottenham H.	11.55	1955-58	63		2	
			TR	Watford	06.61	1961	24		1	
RYDER, Derek F.	Leeds	18.02.47	JNRS	Leeds U.	02.64					(FB)
			TR	Cardiff C.	06.66	1966	4	/	0	
			TR	Rochdale	07.68	1968-71	168	/	2	
			TR	Southport	07.72	1972-73	80	2	2	
RYDER, Robert	Bolton	11.07.43	Nantwich	Gillingham	01.65	1964-67	8	/	0	(FB)
RYDER, Terry R.	Norwich	03.06.28	Norwich St.M.	Norwich C.	09.46	1946-49	46		12	(IF)
			TR	Portsmouth	10.50	1950-51	15		4	
			TR	Swindon T.	07.52	1952	34		13	
RYECRAFT, Fred	Southall	29.08.39	Southall	Brentford	09.59	1962-63	33		0	(G)
RYLANDS, David R.	Liverpool	07.03.53	APP	Liverpool	03.70					(D)
			TR	Hereford U.	09.74	1974-75	22	/	0	
			L	Newport Co.	03.75	1974	3	/	1	
			L	Hartlepool U.	03.76	1975	11	/	0	
			TR	Halifax T.	06.76	1976	5	/	0	
RYMER, George H.	Ardsley	06.10.23	Ardsley Vic.	Barnsley	+	1946	3		0	(G)
			TR	Accrington St.	02.47	1946	8		0	

EDDIE QUIGLEY (Bury/Sheffield Wed./Preston NE./ Blackburn Rov./Bury)
A well travelled player Quigley at one time was the costliest, when being signed by Preston for a fee of £26,000 December 1949. A real general in midfield, he utilised the crossfield pass to supreme effect and with stocky build was difficult to shake off the ball, always probing the defence in looking for an opening. He first made a name with Bury, scoring five goals on his debut at centre forward, before joining Sheffield Wednesday for £12,000 and collecting 50 goals from 74 appearances whilst at Hillsborough. He never quite made it at Deepdale, quickly moving on to Blackburn Rovers, where he was again highly successful in finding the net, before going home to Bury. Effective in midfield, with tremendous goalscoring talent, Eddie unluckily achieved only England "B" honours.

RON RAFFERTY (Portsmouth/Grimsby T./Hull C./Aldershot)
Spotted by Portsmouth playing in the Isthmian League with Wycombe Wanderers, Ron joined the Fratton Park playing staff in July, 1954. He did not get many opportunites to shine in "Pompey's" attack and, although he had already impressed the fans as a quicksilver goal snatcher of the future, was allowed to join Grimsby in December 1956. During seven years with the "Mariners" he was a prolific scorer, and his 34 goals in 1961/2 helped the club back into Divison Two as runners-up to his old mates. The next season the goal touch dried up and he was transferred to Hull City for £10,000 in the summer of 1963, later playing for Aldershot.

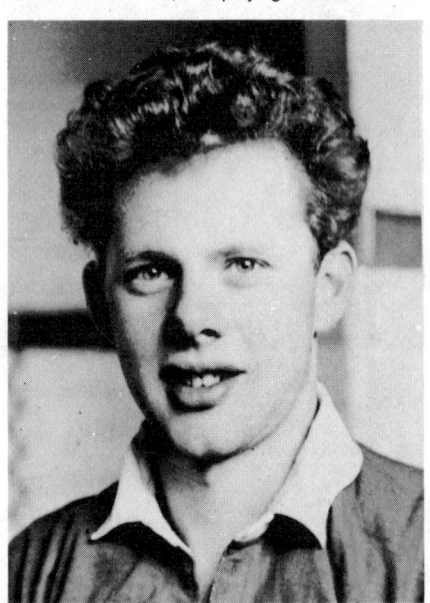

ALF RAMSEY (Southampton, Tottenham H. & England)
Nicknamed "The General," Ramsey was a strong, polished, distinguished right back, whose placing of the ball from defence to attack was meticulous. Capped by England 32 times, making his first appearance in 1948 when with Southampton, he played 28 consecutive games Internationally. Spurs acquired him in May 1949 for a fee of £21,000 and he responded by missing only three games in the two successive seasons, during which the Spurs won First and Second Division Titles. On retiring, he had a marvellous baptism into League management with little Ipswich, before taking the England job, which culminated in the winning of the World Cup 1966. Later he was knighted for services to soccer.

PAUL REANEY (Leeds U. & England/Bradford C.)
A small dark haired right full back Reaney served Leeds although being a Londoner, having signed professional in October 1961 after playing in the junior sides. A specialist in the art of overlap, possessing good positional sense with great powers of recovery, he was a perfect foil for full back partner Terry Cooper. He won two Championship medals and an F.A. Cup winners medal from the game against Arsenal in 1972. He played 550 League games for Leeds before leaving in June 1978 for fellow Yorkshiremen, Bradford City, with three England caps to his credit.

RONNIE REES (Coventry C., W.B.A., Nottingham F. & Wales/Swansea C.)
One of the outstanding discoveries of 1962/3 by Coventry City, Rees was selected for the Welsh under 23s after only ten League games, a natural outside left with plenty of flair, speed and a beautiful body swerve. He gained a Third Division medal in 1963/4 and a Second Division one in 1966/7, with the club going into the top Division for the first time in its history. The next season he transferred to W.B.A., but on being Cup-tied did not play in their F.A. Cup winning side and within a year had moved to Forest, later finishing in his native Wales with Swansea. He played 39 times for the Welsh International side and should have been one of the greats at club level.

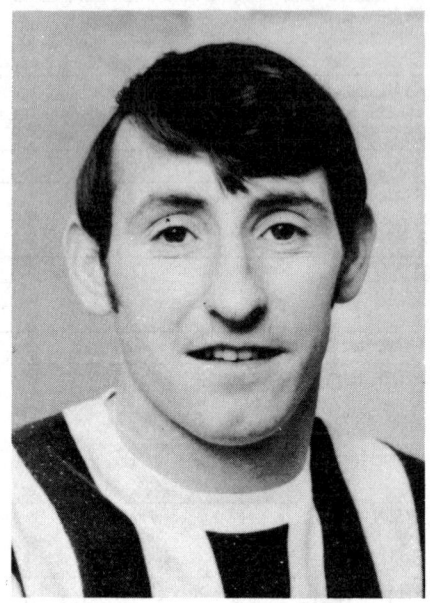

DEREK REEVES (Southampton/Bournemouth)
Reeves was holder of the Third Division post-war scoring record whilst at Southampton in 1959/60, collecting 39 goals from 46 ever present games as the "Saints" went nap in gaining promotion to the Second Division. Not very tall, he was a most prolific goalscorer after being picked up from the local Bournemouth Gasworks team in December 1954, making his debut before that season finished as an inside forward. Switching to centre forward, he topped the club's goal charts in four consecutive seasons and became explosive around the penalty area, picking up any half chance whatsoever. Goals then began to dry up, resulting in a transfer to near neighbours, Bournemouth, but Derek never found the net again with such regularity.

DON REVIE (Leicester C./Hull C./Manchester C. & England/Sunderland/Leeds U.)
Revie came to the fore as one of the vital links in Manchester City's "deep lying centre forward plan" of the mid 1950s, which really reflected the way the Hungarians were playing. Before that Don had begun with Leicester City, unfortunately missing the 1949 F.A. Cup Final against Wolves due to injury. From there the call came to help Raich Carter rejuvenate Hull City, before he went on to Maine Road in 1951. After a less than auspicious start, the advent of Bobby Johnstone from Hibs created the link needed to produce the "Revie Plan". One winning Cup Final medal against Birmingham City in 1956 compensated for a losers medal against Newcastle the year previous. Revie, after calling in on Sunderland, moved on again to became player-manager at Leeds United. Latterly he managed England but he left the post in unfortunate circumstances.

PAT RICE (Arsenal & N. Ireland/Watford)
Belfast born, Rice came through the Highbury Junior ranks, to turn professional in March 1966, later developing into an extremely capable right back. He went on to play nearly 400 League games for the "Gunners", and gained 49 caps for his country. Honours achieved at Arsenal include the double in 1970/1, plus another F.A. Cup winners medal in 1979 following the victory over Manchester United. When signing for Watford in November 1980 for a fee of £20,000, Pat could hardly have expected all the excitement of the club gaining promotion to the First Division in 1981/2 and then the next season finishing as runners-up in the Championship race, to Liverpool.

TONY RICHARDS (Birmingham C./Walsall/Port Vale)
Discarded by local side Birmingham City after signing professional in December 1951, Richards was snapped up by Walsall in the summer of 1954. Not tall for a centre forward, but strongly made, he went on to net more goals for Walsall than anyone had done previously, including the legendary Gilbert Alsop. Scoring goals consistently over a period of nine years was probably the biggest single factor in the club advancing its status from Division Four to the Second in 1960/1. Before leaving Port Vale, Tony had topped the scoring list six times and produced displays of the highest calibre in the art of finishing.

WARWICK RIMMER (Bolton W./Crewe Alex.)
Nephew of the famous England International Ellis Rimmer of Sheffield Wednesday fame, Warwick Rimmer picked up England schoolboy International honours before turning professional with Bolton Wanderers in March 1958. He became a regular member of the side by 1961, but unfortunately suffered all the problems associated with a once great club losing its way, later dropping into the Third Division. Before signing for Crewe Alexandra, his allegiance to one club was rewarded when, as an ever present in 1972/3, he collected a Third Division medal as Bolton began its climb in search of former glories. He played a career total of nearly 600 League matches.

BRUCE RIOCH (Luton T./Aston Villa/Derby Co., Everton, Derby Co. & Scotland/Torquay U.)
A strong shooting, left sided midfielder, Rioch first came into prominence when cracking in 24 goals from 44 games to collect a Fourth Division winners medal with Luton Town. He signed for Aston Villa in July 1969 for £100,000 and helped them to the losing Football League Cup Final against Spurs in 1970/1, but the following season gratefully picked up a Third Division winners medal. He moved on to Derby County in February 1974 in return for a fee of £200,000 and in his first full season with the club, won a Championship medal as an ever present. Another £300,000 took him to Everton in December 1976, but less than a year later, he was back at the Baseball Ground. Later he played for Seattle Sounders in the States before coming home to play for, and then manage, Torquay United.

JOHN RITCHIE (Stoke C./Sheffield Wed./Stoke C.)
A Stoke City bargain buy from Southern Leaguer's Kettering Town in June 1962, Ritchie took over as leader of their attack in October 1963, soon getting amongst the games leading scorers. Standing 6ft 1in, strong and purposeful, the young giant cracked in 64 goals before surprisingly being allowed to move to Wednesday for a fee of £70,000 in November 1966. He never really settled at Hillsborough, coming back to the "Potteries" in July 1969, although suspected of being past his best. A rejuvenated Ritchie was instrumental in helping Stoke beat Chelsea in the Football League Cup Final 1972, going on to score a further 71 League goals whilst at the Victoria ground.

JOHN ROBERTSON (Nottingham F., Derby Co. & Scotland)

A brilliant jinking, chunky left wingman, Robertson began with the Forest as a 17 year-old in May, 1970 and after a fairly inauspicious start eventually found his feet. In 1976/7 he helped the club into third place in the Second Division and the following season gained a Championship medal plus a Football League Cup winners medal. In 1978/9 Forest won the European Cup and the Football League Cup once again, as Brian Clough's men went on the march. Robertson played a major role in these many triumphs, and 1979/80 was no exception, as he gained yet another European Cup Winners medal when scoring the only goal of the match against SV Hamburg. The club also went on to lift the Super Cup. Transferred to Derby County in the 1983 close season, John once again joined up with Peter Taylor, this time at the Baseball Ground.

DICK ROBINSON (Middlesbrough/Barrow)

A product of Middlesbrough wartime junior sides, Dick soon made the grade in post-war soccer as a stylist with plenty of dash and stamina. One of the coolest of players, he formed a full back partnership at Ayresome Park with the great George Hardwick, captain of England, and many shrewd judges at the time reckoned he would follow his team mate in that direction, although he did collect Football League representative honours. He was a nephew of the North East's famous Smith brothers, Jack and Billy, who played for Portsmouth along with the great Seph of Leicester. He completed his career with Barrow, playing a total of 525 League games and finishing as a centre half.

BOBBY ROBSON (Fulham/W.B.A. & England/Fulham)

Robson first joined Fulham in 1950, later forming part of the brilliant trio with Johnny Haynes and Bedford Jezzard, for whom Newcastle once offered a record fee which was turned down. Constructive, sound and very stylish, he was great going forward, excelling either at wing half or inside forward. Transferred to the Albion for £25,000 in March 1956, he was capped two years later, playing 20 times for England before coming home to Fulham in August 1962 for a fee of £20,000. On retiring from League soccer he had made 584 appearances, and went on to become a highly successful manager with Ipswich Town, and then England.

BRYAN (POP) ROBSON (Newcastle U./West Ham U./Sunderland/West Ham U./Sunderland/Carlisle U./Chelsea/Sunderland)

A small stocky forward, Robson turned professional in November 1962 for Newcastle United, where he gained England under 23 honours before leaving for West Ham in February 1971, after playing over 200 League games and scoring 81 goals. He became known to the fans as "Pop", because of his shooting at the slightest chance of an opening. A prolific scorer, extremely quick on the turn and very difficult to mark, he was one of the top scorers of the day. He had two spells at both West Ham and Sunderland before, in his 35th year, again scoring regularly at Carlisle prior to joining Chelsea as player-coach. He is once again back at Sunderland, whom he joined in the summer of 1983.

BRYAN ROBSON (W.B.A., Manchester U. & England)

A brilliant midfield star Robson cost Manchester United £1,500,000 in October 1981, when they signed him from W.B.A. He started out as an apprentice at the Hawthorns, becoming a professional in August 1974, but it was not until 1978 that he gained a permanent place in the "Throstles" side, later going on to collect his first England cap in 1980. He began to show tremendous verve coupled with talent, often seen breaking up the oppositions' attack one moment and scoring himself the next. He scored twice as United beat Brighton in the F.A. Cup Final replay of 1983 and is currently the hottest property of English soccer. At the age of 27 Bryan has a great future with Manchester United and if able to remain injury free, will go on to claim a great many more honours as well as gaining even more adulation.

TOMMY ROBSON

(NorthamptonT./Chelsea/Newcastle U./Peterborough U.)

Robson, a veteran forward, although being born in the North East, started his career with Northampton Town in August 1961 as a direct down-the-line no nonsense type of winger. As the years rolled on, he developed distinct skills more in keeping with a midfielder. Signed by Chelsea in 1965, he never settled and went home to Newcastle, where again he could not keep a regular first team place, later signing for the "Posh" November 1968. In 450 League games he has scored over 100 goals and was still playing fairly regularly during the current season, well into his 35th year, an example to all youngsters taking the professional plunge.

ARNOLD RODGERS (Huddersfield T./Bristol C./Shrewsbury T.)
Rodgers made his debut at centre forward in the First Division for Huddersfield against Charlton Athletic, playing a further 28 times before joining Bristol City in October 1949. He formed a dynamic inside forward partnership with John Atyeo, and helped the "Robins" take the Third Division South Title in 1954/5. He moved on in 1956 to Shrewsbury Town, finishing the season before retiring. He is the father of David who later played for Bristol City, turning pro in 1969 after winning schoolboy honours.

DENNIS ROFE (Orient/Leicester C./Chelsea/Southampton)
A sturdy full back, fast in recovery and always ready to join in upfield forays, Rofe began at the age of 17 with Orient, and made a big impression, when picking up a Third Division winners medal in 1969/70 after playing all but eight games. Leicester City were soon alerted to this promising talent and signed the young Londoner for £112,000 against strong competition from other clubs. Dennis gained an England under 23 cap whilst at Filbert Street, and although the club had no real success, he was outstanding in their defence, playing nearly 300 League games. Later he joined Chelsea for an £80,000 fee, but after appearing only 58 times in their colours, was given a free transfer to Southampton.

DON ROGERS (Swindon T./Crystal Palace/Q.P.R./Swindon T.)
A hard running, natural outside left who signed for the Wiltshire side directly from school. Don Rogers turned professional in October 1962 and went on to collect England under 23 honours. He would surely have played for the full England side had he not passed the peak of his career whilst still in the lower Divisions. He was an exciting, two footed goalscoring favourite, who in 400 League games for the "Robins" netted just short of 150 goals. He will be remembered as the two goal destroyer of Arsenal in the 1969 League Cup Final at Wembley, where his ability to carry the ball was rewarded dramatically. He never really settled in London with Crystal Palace and Q.P.R., mainly due to injuries, and finally went back home.

JOHN O. ROWLAND (Newport Co.)
A tall, well made wing half, Rowland signed for the County in June 1958, following prominent displays for Lovells Athletic in the Welsh League. Within a season he had been selected for the Welsh under 23s against Scotland, only just qualifiying on birthdate. Consistency was the key factor in his football make up, for in a nine season spell until leaving the game at the end of 1968/9, Rowland only missed 18 games, a remarkable achievement. A thoughtful constructive defender he assisted others in scoring rather than putting his own name on the charts.

ARTHUR ROWLEY (W.B.A./Fulham/Leicester C./Shrewsbury T.)
Younger brother of Jack, of England fame, Arthur Rowley made his own reputation as the most prolific English goal scorer of all time, scoring a record 433 in a career stretching from 1946 to 1965. It is hard to understand why England "B" and Football League honours were not followed by a full cap. He played a leading role in getting first Fulham and then Leicester City into the First Division. Beginning as an outside left with the "Throstles," he did not show goalscoring possibilities to true effect until transferred to Fulham in exchange for Ernie Shepherd in December 1948 and converted to inside forward. Later he became player manager of Shrewsbury, still scoring prolifically.

JACK ROWLEY (Wolverhampton W./Bournemouth/Manchester U. & England/Plymouth Arg.)
Brother of Arthur, also of goalscoring fame, Rowley was prominent for the fact that in six England appearances he occupied all the forward positions except outside right. He rose to fame with Manchester United as a sharp shooter, being dubbed "Gunner" by his supporters who were delighted with Jack's net bulging practices. Without much finesse, but very direct, he was ideal for United's post-war requirements, and completed a brilliant attack. Before going to Argyle as player-manager in 1955, Jack had picked up a Championship medal and an F.A. Cup Final medal from the superlative 1948 defeat of Blackpool at Wembley.

Players Names	Birthplace	Date	Previous Club	League Club	Date Signed	Seasons Played	Career Record Apps	Sub	Gls	
SABELLA, Alex	Argentine	05.11.54	River Plate	Sheffield U.	08.78	1978-79	76	/	8	(M)
			TR	Leeds U.	06.80	1980	22	1	2	
SABIN, Arthur H.	Birmingham	25.01.39	JNRS	Aston Villa	01.57	1956-57	2		0	(G) d.1958
SADLER, David	Yalding	05.02.46	Maidstone	Manchester U.	02.63	1963-73	265	5	22	(D)E-4/E.U23-3/E.F.LGE.
			TR	Preston N.E.	11.73	1973-76	104	1	3	REP./E.AMAT.INT./ E.YTH.INT.
SADLER, George H.	Whitwell	07.05.15	Gainsborough	West Ham U.	*	1946	1		0	(FB)
SAGAR, Edward	Moorend	07.02.10	Thorne Col.	Everton	*	1946-52	164		0	(G)E-4/E.F.LGE REP.
SAGE, Frank R.	Chipping Sodbury	31.05.24		Cardiff C.	+					
			TR	Newport Co.	04.48	1947-48	3		0	
SAGE, Mel	Gillingham	24.03.64	APP	Gillingham	03.82	1981-83	44	6	2	(D)
SAILE, Mike A.	Heywood	31.12.50	APP	Bury	01.69	1968-72	92	1	0	(FB)E.YTH.INT.
SAINSBURY, Kim C.	Reading	21.09.57	APP	Reading	APP	1974	0	1	0	
ST.JOHN, Ian	Motherwell	07.06.38	Motherwell	Liverpool	04.61	1961-70	334	2	95	(CF)S-21/.U23-2/
			TR	Coventry C.	09.71	1971	18	/	3	S.F.LGE REP.
			TR	Tranmere Rov.	10.72	1972	9	/	1	
SAINTY, John A.	London	24.03.46	APP	Tottenham H.	07.63					(CF)E.SCH.INT.
			TR	Reading	08.67	1967-69	64	8	20	
			TR	Bournemouth	02.70	1969-73	111	7	21	
			L	Mansfield T.	11.72	1972	3	/	0	
			TR	Aldershot	08.74	1974-75	26	3	0	
SALATHIEL, Neil	Wrexham	19.11.62	Sheffield Wed. (N/C)	Wrexham	N/C	1980	4	/	0	(D) W.SCH.INT.
			TR	Crewe Alex.	06.81	1981-82	64	1	0	
			Arcadia Sheps.	Wrexham	01.84	1983	29	/	0	
SALES, Ron D.	Sth.Shields	19.09.20	Reyrolles	Newcastle U.	+					(CH)
			TR	Orient	05.47	1947-48	46		3	
			TR	Hartlepool U.	08.50	1950	3		0	
SALISBURY, Gareth	Caernarvon	11.03.41	JNRS	Wrexham	05.59	1959-61	11		0	(F)
			TR	Norwich C.	07.62					
			TR	Luton T.	07.63	1963	12		2	
			TR	Colchester U.	07.64	1964	15		2	
			TR	Chesterfield	07.65	1965	35	/	9	
SALMAN, Danis M.M.	Cyprus	12.03.60	APP	Brentford	08.77	1975-83	233	9	5	(D) E.YTH.INT.
SALMON, Len A.	W.Kirby	24.06.12	Burnley(+)	Tranmere Rov.	09.46	1946-47	30		1	
SALMON, Mike B.	Leyland	14.07.64	JNRS	Blackburn Rov.	10.81	1981	1	/	0	(G)
			L	Chester C.	10.82	1982	16	/	0	
			TR	Stockport Co.	03.83	1983	46	/	0	
SALMONS, Geoff	Mexborough	14.01.48	JNRS	Sheffield U.	02.66	1967-73	170	10	8	(M)
			TR	Stoke C.	07.74	1974-77	115	3	14	
			L	Sheffield U.	09.77	1977	5	/	0	
			TR	Leicester C.	10.77	1977	25	1	4	
			TR	Chesterfield	08.78	1978-81	119	1	15	
SALT, Sammy J.	Southport	30.12.38	JNRS	Blackpool	01.56	1960	18		0	(WH)
SALTER, Ken	Cullompton	16.11.33	JNRS	Exeter C.	11.50	1950	1		0	(G)
SALVAGE, Barry	Bristol	21.12.47	Eastbourne	Fulham	09.67	1967-68	7	/	0	(W)
			TR	Millwall	03.69	1968	1	1	0	
			TR	Q.P.R.	03.71	1970-72	16	5	1	
			TR	Brentford	02.73	1972-74	87	/	8	
			TR	Millwall	08.75	1975-76	43	12	9	
SAMBROOK, Ray	Wolverhampton	31.05.33	Wednesfield	Coventry C.	09.53	1954-57	96		26	(W)
			TR	Manchester C.	01.58	1957-61	64		13	
			TR	Doncaster Rov.	06.62	1962	8		0	
			TR	Crewe Alex.	01.63					
SAMMELS, John C.	Ipswich	23.07.45	APP	Arsenal	08.62	1962-70	212	3	39	(M) E.U23-9/E.F.LGE.
			TR	Leicester C.	07.71	1971-77	236	5	21	REP./E.YTH.INT.
SAMPLE, Jim	Morpeth	05.11.21		Bradford C.	08.47	1947-48	8		2	
SAMPSON, Peter S.	Pitsea	09.07.27	Devizes	Bristol Rov.	06.48	1948-60	340		4	(WH)Cousin of Les Stubbs
SAMPSON, Ray V.	Swindon	06.02.35	JNRS	Swindon T.	05.52	1953-58	64		10	(F)
SAMPSON, Tom W.	Lee	18.08.54	APP	Millwall	06.72	1972	0	1	0	(HB)
SAMUEL, Robert W.	Aberdeen	18.05.46	Aberdeen	Lincoln C.	07.67	1967	3	1	0	(IF)
SAMUELS, Les	Oldham	08.12.28		Burnley	12.49	1950	2		0	(IF)
			TR	Exeter C.	07.53	1953	12		1	
			TR	Wrexham	03.54	1953-54	26		11	
			TR	Crewe Alex.	11.54	1954-55	42		13	
			TR	Bradford C.	12.55	1955-57	85		38	
			TR	Stockport Co.	03.58	1957-58	25		5	
SANAGHAN, Joe	Motherwell	12.12.14	Bradford P.A.(*)	Bournemouth	*	1946-48	121		0	(FB)
			TR	Stockport Co.	08.49	1949-50	52		0	
SANCHEZ, John	London	21.10.40	JNRS	Arsenal	10.57					(WH)E.YTH.INT./
			TR	Watford	06.59	1959-60	19		0	E.SCH.INT.
SANCHEZ, Lawrie	Lambeth	22.10.59	JNRS	Reading	09.78	1977-83	234	13	26	(M)
SANDER, Chris A.	Swansea	11.11.62	APP	Swansea C.	11.79	1981-83	20	/	0	(G)

Players Names	Birthplace	Date	Previous Club	League Club	Date Signed	Seasons Played	Career Record Apps	Sub	Gls	
SANDERCOCK, Ken L.	Plymouth	31.01.51	APP	Torquay U.	01.69	1968-69	42	4	1	(FB)Brother of Phil
			TR	Leicester C.	11.69	1969	5	5	0	
			TR	Torquay U.	11.71	1971-74	113	6	5	
SANDERCOCK, Phil J.	Plymouth	21.06.53	APP	Torquay U.	09.71	1969-76	199	6	13	(D) Brother of Ken
			TR	Huddersfield T.	06.77	1977-78	81	/	1	
			TR	Northampton T.	09.79	1979-80	69	/	3	
SANDERS, Alan	Salford	31.01.34		Manchester C.	08.55					(FB)
			TR	Everton	07.56	1957-59	56		0	
			TR	Swansea C.	11.59	1959-62	92		0	
			TR	Brighton & H.A.	01.63	1962-65	80	/	0	
SANDERS, Alan J.	Newport	29.10.63	JNRS	Cardiff C.	11.81	1981	1	1	0	(M)W.SCH.INT.
SANDERS, James A.	Hackney	05.07.20	Charlton Ath.(+)	W.B.A.	+	1946-57	327		0	(G)+Longlands FC
			TR	Coventry C.	07.58	1958	10		0	
SANDERS, James C.F.	Marlborough	15.10.32		Bristol C.	11.51					(WH)
				Crystal Palace	03.55	1955-58	37		0	
			TR	Rochdale	10.60					
			Cheltenham T.	Exeter C.	08.62	1962	20		1	
SANDERS, Peter C.W.	Newport	07.09.42	JNRS	Newport Co.	10.59	1960	3		0	(F)
			TR	Gillingham	07.61	1961	2		0	
SANDERS, Roy J.	London	22.09.40	Romford	Northampton T.	05.62	1962	15		2	(OR)
SANDERSON, Eric	Chapeltown	10.11.21	Paramore	Rotherham U.	09.47	1947	2		1	(FB)
SANDERSON, Ian	Torquay	26.08.56		Torquay U.	N/C	1977	0	1	0	(F)
SANDERSON, John R.	Carlisle	05.02.18	Carlisle U.(*)	Wolverhampton W.	*					(LB)
			TR	Luton T.	05.46	1946	6		0	
SANDERSON, Keith	Hull	09.10.40	Bath C.	Plymouth Arg.	08.64	1964	29		2	(WH)
			TR	Q.P.R.	06.65	1965-68	98	6	11	
SANDERSON, Paul D.	Blackpool	16.12.66	APP	Manchester C.	11.83					(M)
			TR	Chester C.	02.84	1983	24	/	3	
SANDERSON, Phil	Barnsley	01.11.53	Worsboro Bridge	Barnsley	N/C	1974	2	/	1	(OL)
SANDIFORD, Ian R.	Chorley	26.02.46	APP	Blackburn Rov.	02.64					(F)
			TR	Stockport Co.	06.64	1964-65	47	/	9	
			TR	Crewe Alex.	01.66	1965-66	48	4	18	
SANDLANDS, Herbert	Nantwich	09.08.31	Nantwich	Crewe Alex.	AM	1954	1		0	
SANDY, Adam V.C.	Peterborough	22.09.58	Wolverton T.	Northampton T.	02.80	1979-82	88	16	7	(M)
SANDYS, Harry A.	Fulham	08.10.32	Yeovil T.	Torquay U.	08.54	1954	2		0	(IF)
SANFORD, Mark A.	London	10.09.63	JNRS	Aldershot	06.79	1979-82	72	12	23	(F)
SANKEY, John	Winsford	19.03.12	W.B.A.(*)	Northampton T.	+	1946-47	42		0	(WH)*Winsford U.
SANKEY, Martin A.	Wellington	04.05.64	APP	Shrewsbury T.	02.82	1982	0	5	0	(F)
SANSBY, Cliff P.	Peterborough	24.11.34	March T.	Peterborough U.	N/L	1960	1		0	(FB)
SANSOM, Ken G.	Camberwell	26.09.58	APP	Crystal Palace	12.75	1974-79	172	/	3	(D) E-41/E.U21-8/
			TR	Arsenal	08.80	1980-83	164	/	4	E.YTH.INT./E.SCH.INT.●
SANSOME, Paul E.	Addington	06.10.61	Crystal Palace (APP)	Millwall	04.80	1981-83	63	/	0	(G)
SAPHIN, Reg F.E.	Kilburn	08.08.16	Hayes	Q.P.R.	06.46	1946-50	34		0	(G)
			TR	Watford	07.51	1951-53	57		0	
SARGENT, Gary S.	Bedford	11.09.52	APP	Norwich C.	09.70	1971	0	1	0	(F)
			TR	Scunthorpe U.	07.72	1972	14	1	1	
			Bedford T.	Peterborough U.	07.77	1977-78	27	7	5	
			TR	Northampton T.	06.79	1979-80	41	2	4	
SARSON, Albert	Rossington	31.12.30	Mansfield T.(AM)	Doncaster Rov.	08.50	1949-50	2		0	(F)
SARTORI, Carlo	Italy	10.02.48	JNRS	Manchester U.	02.65	1968-71	26	12	4	(IF)
SATCHWELL, Ken R.	Birmingham	17.01.40		Coventry C.	09.58	1958-61	68		21	(F)
			Nuneaton	Walsall	01.65	1964-66	54	3	7	
SAUL, Frank L.	Canvey Island	23.08.43	JNRS	Tottenham H.	08.60	1960-67	112	4	37	(CF)E.YTH.INT
			TR	Southampton	01.68	1967-69	46	7	2	
			TR	Q.P.R.	05.70	1970-71	33	3	4	
			TR	Millwall	03.72	1971-75	85	11	4	
SAUNDERS, Carl S.	Marston Green	26.11.64	JNRS	Stoke C.	07.83	1982	0	1	0	
SAUNDERS, Dean N.	Swansea	21.06.64	APP	Swansea C.	06.82	1983	14	5	3	(F)
SAUNDERS, Dennis F.	Scarborough	19.12.24	Huddersfield T.(AM)	Newport Co.	AM	1946	7		0	(CH)E.AMAT.INT.
SAUNDERS, Derek W.	Ware	06.01.28	Walthamstow	Chelsea	07.53	1953-58	203		9	(WH)E.AMAT.INT.
SAUNDERS, George E.	Birkenhead	01.03.18		Everton	*	1946-51	133		0	
SAUNDERS, Glyn	Nottingham	16.06.56	APP	Nottingham F.	06.73	1976	4	/	0	(D)
SAUNDERS, John F.	Middlesbrough	24.08.24		Darlington	09.46	1946-47	67		0	(CH)
			TR	Chelsea	05.48	1949-53	52		0	
			TR	Crystal Palace	08.54	1954-56	68		0	
			TR	Chester C.	05.57	1957-58	67		3	

Players Names	Birthplace	Date	Previous Club	League Club	Date Signed	Seasons Played	Apps	Sub	Gls	
SAUNDERS, John G.	Worksop	01.12.50	APP	Mansfield T.	03.69	1969-72	90	/	2	(D)
			TR	Huddersfield T.	10.72	1972-75	121	/	1	
			TR	Barnsley	12.75	1975-78	149	/	7	
			TR	Lincoln C.	06.79	1979	25	1	1	
			TR	Doncaster Rov.	08.80	1980	27	1	2	
SAUNDERS, John H.	Maidenhead	18.12.43	JNRS	Charlton Ath.	08.62	1962	1		0	(F)
SAUNDERS, John T.	Newport	02.10.50	Birmingham C.(APP)	Newport Co.	08.69	1969-70	26	1	0	(FB)W.SCH.INT.
			TR	Leeds U.	07.71					
			TR	Walsall	10.72	1972-75	94	5	2	
SAUNDERS, Len J.	Liverpool	07.01.28		New Brighton	AM	1950	4		2	(F)
SAUNDERS, Paul B.	Watford	17.12.59	Watford (APP)	Northampton T.	07.78	1978-82	114	12	5	(D)
SAUNDERS, Robert C.	Poole	26.08.45	APP	Bournemouth	06.63	1965	2	1	0	(F)
SAUNDERS, Ron	Birkenhead	06.11.32	JNRS	Everton	02.51	1954	3		0	(CF)E.YTH.INT.●
			Tonbridge	Gillingham	05.57	1957-58	49		20	
			TR	Portsmouth	09.58	1958-64	234		139	
			TR	Watford	09.64	1964-65	39	/	18	
			TR	Charlton Ath.	08.65	1965-66	64	1	24	
SAUNDERS, Ron A.	Malmesbury	14.01.23		Swindon T.	AM	1947	1		0	(CH)
SAUNDERS, Roy	Salford	04.09.30	Hull C.(AM)	Liverpool	05.48	1952-58	134		1	(WH)E.YTH.INT.
			TR	Swansea C.	03.59	1958-62	95		3	
SAUNDERS, Steve J. P.	Warrington	21.09.64	APP	Bolton W.	09.82	1983	3	/	0	(M)
SAUNDERS, Wes	Sunderland	23.02.63	JNRS	Newcastle U.	06.81	1981-83	58	/	0	(D)
SAVAGE, John A.	Bromley	14.12.29		Hull C.	09.50	1950	4		0	(G)
			TR	Halifax T.	03.52	1951-53	57		0	
			TR	Manchester C.	11.53	1954-57	30		0	
			TR	Walsall	01.58	1957-58	51		0	
SAVAGE, Reg	Eccles	05.07.12	Q.of South	Nottingham F.	+	1946	20		0	(G)*Leeds U.
			TR	Accrington St.	08.47					
SAVAGE, Robert J.	Liverpool	08.01.60	APP	Liverpool	01.78					(M)
			L	Wrexham	10.82	1982	27	/	10	
			TR	Stoke C.	07.83	1983	5	2	0	
			TR	Bournemouth	12.83	1983	22	1	5	
SAVILLE, Andy V.	Hull	12.12.64		Hull C.	N/C	1983	1	/	0	(F)
SAVILLE, Peter W.	Dalbeattie	29.08.48		Carlisle U.	07.66	1967	1	/	0	(F)
			Hawick R.A.	Bradford P.A.	03.69	1968-69	31	/	1	
SAVIN, Keith A.	Oxford	05.06.29	Oxford C.	Derby Co.	05.50	1950-55	65		0	(FB)
			TR	Mansfield T.	05.57	1957-58	68		0	
SAVINO, Ray J.	Norwich	16.11.38	Thorpe Village	Norwich C.	02.57	1956-61	22		3	(W)
			TR	Bristol C.	07.62	1962-67	75	1	2	
SAWARD, Len R.	Aldershot	06.07.27	Beddington	Crystal Palace	03.49	1948-50	9		1	(IF)Brother of Pat
			TR	Newport Co.	01.54	1953-54	25		4	
SAWARD, Pat	Cork	17.08.28	Crystal Palace(AM)	Millwall	07.51	1951-54	120		14	(WH)EI-18
			TR	Aston Villa	08.55	1955-60	152		2	
			TR	Huddersfield T.	03.61	1960-62	59		1	
			TR	Coventry C.	10.63					
SAWBRIDGE, John	Wigan	20.09.20	Crossons	Oldham Ath.	*	1946-47	8		0	(G) d.1984
SAWYER, Brian	Rotherham	28.01.38	Rawmarsh	Rotherham U.	08.58	1957-62	92		31	(CF)
			TR	Bradford C.	12.62	1962-63	15		2	
SAWYER, Roy	Worsbrough Bridge	29.03.40	Worsbrough Bridge	Barnsley	05.58	1960-61	2		0	(HB)
SAWYERS, Keith	Banbury	14.06.60	Carlisle Spartans	Carlisle U.	01.78	1977-79	5	4	0	(D)
SAXBY, Gary P.	Mansfield	11.12.59	APP	Mansfield T.	12.77	1978	14	2	1	(D)
			TR	Northampton T.	08.80	1980-82	86	10	11	
SAXBY, Mick W.	Mansfield	12.08.57	APP	Mansfield T.	01.75	1975-78	76	3	5	(D) Brother of Gary
			TR	Luton T.	07.79	1979-81	82	/	6	
			L	Grimsby T.	03.83	1982	10	/	0	
			L	Lincoln C.	11.83	1983	10	/	1	
SAXTON, Robert	Doncaster	06.09.43	Denaby U.	Derby Co.	02.62	1965-67	94	2	1	(D)
			TR	Plymouth Arg.	02.68	1967-75	224	7	7	
			TR	Exeter C.	09.75	1975-77	92	/	3	
SAYER, Andy C.	Brent	06.06.66	APP	Wimbledon	APP	1983	2	/	0	(F)
SAYER, Peter A.	Cardiff	02.05.55	JNRS	Cardiff C.	07.73	1973-77	70	12	14	(W)W-7/W.U21-2
			TR	Brighton & H.A.	02.78	1977-79	46	9	6	
			TR	Preston N.E.	08.80	1980-83	42	3	6	
			L	Cardiff C.	09.81	1981	4	/	1	
SBRAGIA, Ricky	Lennoxtown	26.05.56	APP	Birmingham C.	06.74	1974-77	14	1	1	(D)
			TR	Walsall	10.78	1978-79	77	/	4	
			TR	Blackpool	07.80	1980-81	24	2	1	
			TR	York C.	08.82	1982-83	91	/	5	
SCAIFE, Robert H.	Northallerton	12.10.55	APP	Middlesbrough	10.72					(M)
			L	Halifax T.	01.75	1974	5	1	1	
			TR	Hartlepool U.	09.75	1975-77	77	3	10	
			TR	Rochdale	10.77	1977-79	95	3	9	

Players Names	Birthplace	Date	Previous Club	League Club	Date Signed	Seasons Played	Apps	Sub	Gls	
SCALES, George	Northwich	14.03.23	Manchester C.(AM)	Chester C.	+	1946-48	81		0	(G)
SCALES, Terry A.	West Ham U.	18.11.51	West Ham U.(APP)	Brentford	07.71	1971-76	212	/	5	(D)
SCANLON, Albert	Manchester	10.10.35	JNRS	Manchester U.	12.52	1954-60	115		34	(OL)E.U23-5/E.F.LGE
			TR	Newcastle U.	11.60	1960-61	22		0	REP./
			TR	Lincoln C.	02.62	1961-62	47		11	Nephew of Charles Mitten
			TR	Mansfield T.	04.63	1962-65	108		21	
SCANLON, Ian	Stirling	13.07.52	E. Stirling	Notts. Co.	07.72	1972-77	99	12	31	(W)
SCANNELL, Tommy	Goughal	03.06.25	Tilbury	Southend U.	12.49	1950-54	98		0	(G)EI-1
SCARBOROUGH, Brian	Ironville	11.12.41	JNRS	Derby Co.	01.59	1958-60	4		0	(F)
SCARBOROUGH, Jim A.	Nottingham	10.06.31		Darlington	09.51	1951-53	49		15	(CF)
SCARLETT, John E.	Wolverhampton	01.08.34		Walsall	03.52	1952-53	10		2	(IF)d.
SCARROTT, Alan	Malmesbury	22.11.44	Chippenham	W.B.A.	12.61					(F)
			TR	Bristol Rov.	06.64					
			TR	Reading	04.65	1965-67	90	/	7	
SCARTH, Jimmy W.	Nth.Shields	26.08.26	Percy Main	Tottenham H.	08.48	1949-51	7		3	(CF)
			TR	Gillingham	02.52	1951-54	138		24	
SCATTERGOOD, Eric	Worsbrough Bridge	09.09.29	JNRS	Barnsley	02.47	1949-51	11		0	
SCHIAVI, Mark A.	London	01.05.64	APP	West Ham U.	11.81					(M)
			L	Bournemouth	09.83	1983	10	/	0	
SCHOFIELD, A. Stewart	Blackburn	24.07.33	Blackburn Rov.(AM)	Southport	07.57	1957-58	36		9	(IF)
SCHOFIELD, Ernie				Bradford C.	+	1946	1		1	(IL)
SCHOFIELD, Gary P.	Barton	27.03.57		Stockport Co.	N/C	1977	0	1	0	(D)
SCHOFIELD, Graham	Manchester	18.12.50	JNRS	Oldham Ath.	08.69	1969	1	/	0	(HB)
SCHOFIELD, John R.	Atherstone	08.02.31	Nuneaton	Birmingham C.	02.50	1952-65	212	/	0	(G)
			TR	Wrexham	07.66	1966-67	52	/	0	
SCHOFIELD, Malcolm	Failsworth	08.10.18		Oldham Ath.	*	1946	7		0	(G)
SCHOFIELD, Mark A.	Wigan	10.10.66	APP	Wigan Ath.	APP	1983	0	1	0	
SCHOFIELD, Tom	Halifax	22.06.26	Boothtown	Halifax T.	AM	1952	1		0	(G)
SCHOLES, Martin	Barrow	28.01.54		Workington	N/C	1976	3	1	0	(D)
SCHROEDER, Nico	Holland	19.11.47	Holland	Swansea C.	07.76	1976	1	/	0	(G)
SCOTHORN, Gary	Hoyland	06.06.50	APP	Sheffield U.	06.67	1967	1	/	0	(G)
				Mansfield T.	08.74					
SCOTSON, Reg	Bensham	22.09.19	JNRS	Sunderland	*	1946-50	61		1	(WH)
			TR	Grimsby T.	12.50	1950-54	164		5	
SCOTT, Alex M.	Fife	17.11.22	Lochgelly Albert	Leicester C.	03.47	1947-49	31		1	(FB)
			TR	Carlisle U.	01.50	1949-55	203		3	
SCOTT, Alex S.	Falkirk	22.11.36	Glasgow Rgrs.	Everton	02.63	1962-66	149	/	23	(OR)S-16/S.U23-1/
										S'B'-2/S.F.LGE.REP.
SCOTT, Anthony J.	Huntingdon	01.04.41	JNRS	West Ham U.	05.58	1959-65	83	/	16	(W)E.YTH.INT.
			TR	Aston Villa	10.65	1965-67	47	3	4	
			TR	Torquay U.	09.67	1967-69	82	5	4	
			TR	Bournemouth	07.70	1970-71	59	2	6	
			TR	Exeter C.	06.72	1972-73	51	/	2	
SCOTT, August F.	Sunderland	19.02.21	Hylton Col.	Luton T.	+					(IF)
			TR	Southampton	07.47	1947-49	46		9	
			TR	Colchester U.	08.51	1951-53	120		11	
SCOTT, David P.	Belfast	06.06.18	Linfield	Northampton T.	+	1946-47	11		0	(G) d.1977
SCOTT, Derek E.	Gateshead	08.02.58	APP	Burnley	02.75	1974-83	250	7	23	(D) E.SCH.INT.
SCOTT, Don	Elland	20.10.22		Halifax T.	09.49	1948-49	20		5	
SCOTT, Fred H.	Fatfield	06.10.16	Bradford P.A.(*)	York C.	*	1946	2		0	(OR)*Bolton W./
			TR	Nottingham F.	09.46	1946-56	304		39	E.SCH.INT.
SCOTT, Geoff	Birmingham	31.10.56	Highgate U.	Stoke C.	04.77	1977-79	76	2	3	(D)
			TR	Leicester C.	02.80	1979-81	39	/	0	
			TR	Birmingham C.	02.82	1981-82	18	1	0	
			TR	Charlton Ath.	10.82	1982	2	/	0	
SCOTT, George W.	Aberdeen	25.10.44	APP	Liverpool	10.61					(F)
				Tranmere Rov.	11.68	1968-69	35	1	0	
SCOTT, James	Falkirk	21.08.40	Hibernian	Newcastle U.	08.67	1967-69	70	3	6	(W)S-1/Brother of Alex S.
			TR	Crystal Palace	02.70	1969-71	36	7	5	
SCOTT, James	Hetton	07.09.34	JNRS	Burnley	09.51	1954-60	3		0	(OL)E.SCH.INT.
			TR	Oldham Ath.	06.61	1961-63	76		0	
SCOTT, James A.	Newcastle	28.02.60	APP	Newcastle U.	03.78	1977-78	9	1	0	(F)
SCOTT, James D.	Dagenham	05.09.45	Chelsea(AM)	Orient	11.62	1963-65	22	1	6	(F)
SCOTT, James J.	Glasgow	26.12.27	Alloa Ath.	Workington	06.54	1954	6		1	(IF)
SCOTT, Joey	Plymouth	11.01.53	Falmouth	Bournemouth	06.78	1978	18	3	4	(F)
SCOTT, John	Normanton	02.01.42	JNRS	Bradford C.	08.60	1961-62	11		2	(F)
			TR	Chesterfield	07.63	1963	5		0	

Players Names	Birthplace	Date	Previous Club	League Club	Date Signed	Seasons Played	Apps	Sub	Gls	
SCOTT, John	Belfast	22.12.33	Ormond Star	Manchester U.	10.51	1952-55	4		0	(OL)NI-2/NI'B'-1
			TR	Grimsby T.	06.56	1956-62	241		51	
			TR	York C.	06.63	1963	21		3	
SCOTT, John A.	Workington	18.07.28	Workington	Leeds U.	05.50	1950-54	110		0	(G)
SCOTT, John M.	Edinburgh	21.08.53	Brechin C.	Workington	08.75	1975	1	1	0	(WH)
SCOTT, Joseph C.	Fatfield	09.01.30		Newcastle U.	04.49					(CF)
			Spennymoor	Luton T.	02.52	1952-53	13		2	
			TR	Middlesbrough	09.54	1954-58	93		26	
			TR	Hartlepool U.	01.59	1958-59	62		10	
			TR	York C.	06.60	1960	17		2	
SCOTT, Ken	Maltby	13.08.31	Denaby U.	Derby Co.	08.50	1950	2		0	(F)
			Denaby U.	Mansfield T.	08.52	1952	4		2	
SCOTT, Kevin A.	Lincoln	12.11.54	Sheffield Univ.	Lincoln C.	N/C	1973	1	/	0	(HB)
SCOTT, Laurie	Sheffield	23.04.17	Bradford C.(*)	Arsenal	*	1946-51	115		0	(FB)E-17/E'B'-4/
			TR	Crystal Palace	10.51	1951-52	28		0	E.F.LGE REP.
SCOTT, Lloyd E.	Stepney	13.10.61	APP	Orient	10.79					(G)
			TR	Blackpool	07.82	1982	2	/	0	
SCOTT, Malcolm E.	Sth.Shields	08.05.36	Cleadon J.	Newcastle U.	09.55	1956-59	25		2	(CH)Northants Cricketer
			TR	Darlington	10.61	1961-62	47		2	
			TR	York C.	10.63	1963	19		0	
SCOTT, Mel	Claygate	26.09.39	JNRS	Chelsea	11.56	1957-61	97		0	(CH)E.U23-4/E.YTH.INT.
			TR	Brentford	03.63	1962-66	156	/	2	
SCOTT, Mike R.	Gosforth	04.12.45	APP	Burnley	12.62					(F)
			TR	Hartlepool U.	07.64	1964	2		0	
SCOTT, Peter R.	London	01.10.63	APP	Fulham	10.81	1981-83	32	1	4	(M)
SCOTT, Peter W.	Liverpool	19.09.52	APP	Everton	07.70	1971-74	42	2	1	(D) NI-6/E.YTH.INT.
			L	Southport	01.74	1973	4	/	0	
			TR	York C.	12.75	1975-78	99	1	4	
			TR	Aldershot	03.79	1978-82	114	7	2	
SCOTT, Richard S.A.	Thetford	26.10.41	JNRS	Norwich C.	11.58	1960-62	29		1	(WH)
			TR	Cardiff C.	07.63	1963-64	37		5	
			TR	Scunthorpe U.	09.64	1964-65	47	/	8	
			TR	Lincoln C.	07.66	1966	9	1	1	
SCOTT, Robert	Bellshill	20.05.30	Alloa Ath.	Accrington St.	09.54	1954-58	149		32	(OL)
			TR	Wrexham	07.59	1959	2		0	
			TR	Oldham Ath.	10.59	1959	9		1	
SCOTT, Robert A.	Liverpool	29.10.13	Burnley(*)	Wolverhampton W.	*					(G)E.SCH.INT./ d
			TR	Crewe Alex.	08.47	1947-48	44		0	
SCOTT, Robert J.	Dundee	16.03.37	Dundee Violet	Cardiff C.	02.57	1957	3		0	(HB)
				Swindon T.	06.61					
			TR	Newport Co.	11.61	1961-62	18		0	
			TR	Southport	07.63	1963	3		0	
SCOTT, Robert W.	Liverpool	22.02.53	JNRS	Wrexham	07.71	1970-75	15	4	0	(D)
			L	Reading	01.75	1974	5	/	0	
			TR	Hartlepool U.	07.76	1976	37	/	0	
			TR	Rochdale	07.77	1977-78	71	/	3	
			TR	Crewe Alex.	08.79	1979-83	224	1	15	
SCOTT, Sam	Ashington	14.06.22	Ashington	Hartlepool U.	+	1946-47	49		17	(CF)
SCOTT, Stuart R.	Shrewsbury	31.03.46	JNRS	Shrewsbury T.	04.64	1963-65	18	/	2	(F)
SCOTT, Walter	Douglas	23.06.32	Dumbarton	Halifax T.	08.54	1954	13		0	(G)
SCOTT, William J.	Preston	14.06.21	JNRS	Preston N.E.	+	1946-53	207		0	(FB)
SCOTT, William R.	Willington	06.12.07	Middlesbrough(*)	Brentford	*	1946	12		0	(IF)E-1/
			TR	Aldershot	07.47	1947	21		0	d.1969
SCOTTING, Alan	Dartford	22.04.66		Gillingham	N/C	1983	2	/	0	(D)
SCOULAR, Jim	Livingston	11.01.25	Gosport Bor.	Portsmouth	+	1946-52	247		8	(WH)S-9● .
			TR	Newcastle U.	06.53	1953-60	247		6	
			TR	Bradford P.A.	01.61	1960-63	108		5	
SCREEN, Anthony L.	Swansea	09.05.52	APP	Swansea C.	05.70	1968-74	125	4	9	(FB)W.U23-1
SCREEN, William R.	Swansea	08.11.48	JNRS	Swansea C.	03.67	1967-71	131	9	14	(IF)W.U23-2/
			TR	Newport Co.	06.72	1972-75	137	5	7	Brother of Tony
SCRIMGEOUR, Brian	Dundee	11.08.59	Dundee	Chesterfield	07.83	1983	41	/	3	(M)
SCRIMSHAW, Stan	Hartlepool	07.08.15	Hartlepool T.(*)	Bradford C.	*	1946	2		0	(WH)
			Frickley Col.	Halifax T.	10.47	1947-49	52		0	
SCRINE, Frank H.	Swansea	09.01.25		Swansea C.	+	1947-53	142		45	(IF)W-2
			TR	Oldham Ath.	10.53	1953-55	78		21	
SCRINE, William H.	Swansea	03.12.34	JNRS	Swansea C.	12.51	1952	1		0	
SCRIVENS, Steve	London	11.03.57	APP	Fulham	03.75	1974-75	3	1	1	(F)
			L	Brentford	12.76	1976	5	/	0	
SCRIVENS, William	Rotherham	26.05.36		Rotherham U.	08.56	1956	3		0	(G)
SCRUGHAM, Robert	Cleator Moor	15.05.32	Cleator Moor	Workington	08.53	1953	3		0	(G)

Players Names	Birthplace	Date	Previous Club	League Club	Date Signed	Seasons Played	Career Record Apps Sub Gls			
SCULLION, Stewart	Bo'ness	18.04.46	Chesham U.	Charlton Ath.	03.65					(W)
			TR	Watford	02.66	1965-70	220	8	30	
			TR	Sheffield U.	05.71	1971-73	53	4	7	
			TR	Watford	12.73	1973-75	87	/	19	
SCURR, David W.	Netley	25.09.39		Southampton	04.58	1959-60	2		0	(FB)
SCURR, John T.	Nth.Shields	30.09.40	Nth.Shields BC	Arsenal	09.59					(F)
			TR	Carlisle U.	01.61	1960-61	15		1	
SEACOLE, Jason P.	Oxford	11.04.60	APP	Oxford U.	04.77	1976-81	104	16	22	(F) E.SCH.INT./E.YTH.INT.
SEAL, James	Pontefract	09.12.50	JNRS	Wolverhampton W.	03.68	1968	1	/	0	(F)
			L	Walsall	01.70	1969-70	40	/	14	
			TR	Barnsley	05.71	1971	43	/	12	
			TR	York C.	07.72	1972-76	152	9	43	
			TR	Darlington	11.76	1976-79	115	7	19	
			TR	Rochdale	11.79	1979-80	44	9	4	
SEALEY, Alan W.	Canning Town	22.04.42	Memorial Spts.	Orient	08.59	1960	4		1	(OR)Cousin of Les
			TR	West Ham U.	03.61	1960-66	107	/	22	
			TR	Plymouth Arg.	09.67	1967	4	/	0	
SEALEY, John A.	Wallasey	27.12.45	Warrington	Liverpool	12.63	1964	1		1	(F)
			TR	Chester C.	06.66	1966-67	4	1	0	
SEALEY, Les J.	Bethnal Green	29.09.57	APP	Coventry C.	03.76	1976-82	158	/	0	(G) Cousin of Alan
			TR	Luton T.	08.83	1983	42	/	0	
SEALY, Tony J.	London	07.05.59	APP	Southampton	05.77	1977-78	2	5	0	(F)
			TR	Crystal Palace	03.79	1978-80	16	8	5	
			L	Port Vale	02.80	1979	17	/	6	
			TR	Q.P.R.	03.81	1980-83	57	6	18	
			L	Port Vale	02.82	1981	6	/	4	
			L	Fulham	12.83	1983	5	/	1	
SEAMAN, David A.	Rotherham	19.09.63	APP	Leeds U.	09.81					(G)
			TR	Peterborough U.	08.82	1982-83	83	/	0	
SEAR, Cliff	Rhostyllen	22.09.36	Oswestry	Manchester C.	01.57	1956-65	248	/	1	(FB)W-1/W.U23-2
			TR	Chester C.	04.68	1968-69	49	1	1	
SEARGEANT, Steve G.	Liverpool	02.01.51	APP	Everton	07.68	1971-77	77	3	1	(D) E. SCH.INT.
SEARLE, Eric F.	Guildford	20.07.25		Aldershot	05.48	1947-49	12		0	(G)
SEARS, Doug R.	Eton	05.01.19	Grimsby T.(+)	Reading	05.46	1946	5		0	(IF)
			TR	Aldershot	06.47	1947-49	47		14	
SEARS, Gerry	Arkwright	13.01.35	JNRS	Chesterfield	01.52	1952-67	414	/	4	(FB)
SEARSON, Harold V.	Mansfield	03.06.24		Sheffield Wed.	08.46					(G)
			TR	Mansfield T.	06.47	1947-48	42		0	
			TR	Leeds U.	01.49	1948-51	104		0	
			TR	York C.	11.52	1952-53	62		0	
SEARY, Ray M.	Slough	18.09.52	APP	Q.P.R.	09.70	1971	0	1	0	(F)
			TR	Cambridge U.	03.74	1973-75	55	2	0	
SEASMAN, John	Liverpool	21.02.55	APP	Tranmere Rov.	02.73	1972-74	15	2	0	(F)
			TR	Luton T.	01.75	1974-75	7	1	2	
			TR	Millwall	02.76	1975-79	157	1	35	
			TR	Rotherham U.	08.80	1980-83	93	7	25	
SEATHERTON, Ray	Tiverton	20.05.32	Minehead	Bristol Rov.	02.55	1955	2		2	(F)
SEATON, Gordon	Wick	01.09.45	Rhyl	Chester C.	12.66	1966-67	45	3	2	(HB)
SEDDON, Andy J.	Worsley	23.11.59		Stockport Co.	N/C	1978-82	4	3	0	(D)
SEDDON, Ben	Liverpool	05.02.52	Formby	Tranmere Rov.	04.73	1973	1	/	0	(CH)
SEDDON, David A.	Rochdale	13.04.51	Stafford Rgrs.	Rochdale	07.74	1973-74	18	2	0	(FB)
SEDDON, Frank O.	Stockton	01.05.28		Notts.Co.	05.46					(CH)
				Hull C.	05.47	1949	3		0	
			TR	Halifax T.	01.51	1950-51	4		0	
SEDDON, Ian W.	Prestbury	14.10.50	APP	Bolton W.	06.69	1969-72	51	13	4	(M)
			TR	Chester C.	09.73	1973-75	62	11	7	
			L	Stockport Co.	11.75	1975	4	/	0	
			L	Chesterfield	01.76	1975	2	/	0	
			TR	Cambridge U.	02.76	1975-76	34	3	3	
			TR	Rochdale	07.77	1977	30	1	3	
			TR	Wigan Ath.	07.78	1978	1	/	0	
SEDDON, Tom	Rotherham	25.10.35		Rotherham U.	03.54	1958	1		0	(HB)
SEED, Trevance	Preston	03.09.23	JNRS	Preston N.E.	07.46					(CH)
			TR	Carlisle U.	12.46	1946-49	81		0	
			TR	Accrington St.	09.50	1950	1		0	
SEEMLEY, Ivor J.	Sheffield	30.06.29	JNRS	Sheffield Wed.	07.46	1953-54	15		0	(FB)
			TR	Stockport Co.	06.55	1955-56	81		0	
			TR	Chesterfield	06.57	1957-58	78		0	
SEIGEL, Arnold W.	Islington	21.03.19	Hendon	Orient	06.46	1946	9		0	(CF)
SEITH, Robert	Coatbridge	09.03.32	JNRS	Burnley	03.49	1953-59	211		6	(WH)
SELBY, Dennis	Broughton	15.10.20		Chester C.	AM	1946	5		1	(W)d.1969

Players Names	Birthplace	Date	Previous Club	League Club	Date Signed	Seasons Played	Apps	Sub	Gls	
SELF, Glen W.	Norwich	04.12.53	APP	Norwich C.	09.70	1970-72	4	1	2	(CF)
			L	Torquay U.	03.73	1972	3	/	0	
SELKIRK, Jack	Doncaster	20.01.23	Edlington	Rotherham U.	+	1946-56	427		12	(FB)●
SELLARS, Geoff	Stockport	20.05.30	Altrincham	Leeds U.	04.50					
			TR	Aston Villa	08.50	1950	2		0	
SELLARS, John	Stoke	28.04.24	JNRS	Stoke C.	+	1946-57	384		14	(WH)Son of pre-war player
SELLARS, Peter	Market Rasen	15.03.58	APP	Lincoln C.	APP	1975	0	1	0	(IF)
SELLARS, Scott	Sheffield	27.11.65	APP	Leeds U.	07.83	1982-83	20	/	3	(F)
SELLS, Charles E.	Paddington	24.09.39	Wealdstone	Exeter C.	08.62	1962	14		3	(IF)
SEMLEY, Alan	Barnsley	21.02.66	APP	Barnsley	02.84	1983	1	3	0	(F)
SENIOR, Alan G.	Dewsbury	29.09.30		Halifax T.	08.52	1952	1		0	
SENIOR, Colin	Deepcar	03.06.27	Stocksbridge	Huddersfield T.	+	1950	5		1	(WH)
			TR	Accrington St.	06.51	1951	27		1	
SENIOR, Philip M.	Darton	29.05.43	JNRS	Barnsley	06.61					(FB)
			TR	Southport	07.63	1963	2		0	
SENIOR, Roy V.	Barnsley	21.06.40		Doncaster Rov.	08.60	1960	13		5	(W)
			TR	Peterborough U.	07.61	1961-63	38		11	
			TR	Millwall	03.64	1963-64	15		3	
			TR	Barnsley	11.64	1964	20		4	
SENIOR, Steve	Sheffield	15.05.63	APP	York C.	05.81	1980-83	60	9	3	(D)
SENIOR, Stuart	Barnsley	26.10.53	APP	Barnsley	11.71	1972	1	1	0	(W)
SENIOR, Trevor	Dorchester	28.11.61	Dorchester T.	Portsmouth	12.81	1981-82	11	/	2	(F)
			L	Aldershot	03.83	1982	10	/	6	
			TR	Reading	08.83	1983	45	/	36	
SERELLA, David E..	Kings Lynn	24.09.52	APP	Nottingham F.	08.70	1972-74	65	3	0	(D)
			TR	Walsall	11.74	1974-78	265	2	12	
			TR	Blackpool	08.82	1982-83	34	1	3	
SERMANNI, Tom	Glasgow	01.07.54	Albion Rov.	Blackpool	03.78	1978	6	4	0	(F)S.SCH.INT.
			TR	Torquay U.	08.79	1979-82	83	6	12	
SETTERS, Maurice	Honiton	16.12.36	JNRS	Exeter C.	01.54	1953-54	10		0	(WH)E.U23-16/
			TR	W.B.A.	01.55	1955-59	120		10	E.YTH.INT./E.SCH.INT.
			TR	Manchester U.	01.60	1959-64	160		12	
			TR	Stoke C.	11.64	1964-67	87	/	5	
			TR	Coventry C.	11.67	1967-69	50	1	3	
			TR	Charlton Ath.	01.70	1969	8	/	1	
SEWARD, Bruce	Uxbridge	10.02.39	Yiewsley	Brighton & H.A.	05.57					(F)
			TR	Aldershot	07.59	1959	1		0	
SEWARD, Gary	Paddington	01.10.61	APP	Blackpool	11.79	1979	0	1	0	(F)
SEWELL, Arthur	W.Cornforth	15.07.34	B.Auckland	Bradford C.	AM	1954	1		0	(IL)
SEWELL, John	Whitehaven	24.01.27	Whitehaven	Notts.Co.	+	1946-50	179		97	(IF)E-6/E.F.LGE REP.●
			TR	Sheffield Wed.	03.51	1950-55	164		86	
			TR	Aston Villa	12.55	1955-59	123		36	
			TR	Hull C.	10.59	1959-60	44		8	
SEWELL, John D.	Brockley	07.07.36	Bexleyheath	Charlton Ath.	01.55	1956-63	185		5	(FB)
			TR	Crystal Palace	10.63	1963-70	228	3	6	
			TR	Orient	08.71	1971	5	2	0	
SEXTON, David J.	London	06.04.30	Chelmsford	Luton T.	06.51	1951-52	9		1	(IF)Son of Archie
			TR	West Ham U.	04.52	1952-55	73		27	(Boxing Middleweight)
			TR	Orient	06.56	1956-57	24		4	
			TR	Brighton & H.A.	10.57	1957-58	47		26	
			TR	Crystal Palace	05.59	1959	27		11	
SEYMOUR, Ian	Edenbridge	17.03.48	Tonbridge	Fulham	08.66	1966-70	64	/	0	(G)
			L	Brighton & H.A.	02.71	1970	3	/	0	
SHACKLETON, Alan	Padiham	03.02.34	JNRS	Burnley	05.54	1956-58	31		18	(CF)
			TR	Leeds U.	10.58	1958-59	30		16	
			TR	Everton	09.59	1959	26		10	
			Nelson	Oldham Ath.	08.61	1961	10		7	
SHACKLETON, Len E.	Bradford	03.05.22	Arsenal(AM)	Bradford P.A.	+	1946	7		4	(IF)E-5/E'B'-1/●
			TR	Newcastle U.	10.46	1946-47	57		25	E.SCH.INT./E.F.LGE REP.
			TR	Sunderland	02.48	1947-57	320		97	
SHADBOLT, William H.	Shrewsbury	04.08.32	Oswestry T.	Sheffield Wed.	01.53	1952	7		0	(OL)
			TR	Halifax T.	03.54	1953	3		1	
SHAKESPEARE, Craig R.	Birmingham	26.10.63	APP	Walsall	11.81	1982-83	70	7	10	(F)
SHANAHAN, Terry C.	Paddington	05.12.51	Tottenham H.(APP)	Ipswich T.	03.71	1970	3	1	0	(F)
			L	Blackburn Rov.	09.71	1971	6	/	2	
			TR	Halifax T.	11.71	1971-74	88	8	23	
			TR	Chesterfield	10.74	1974-75	56	4	28	
			TR	Millwall	04.76	1976	13	7	5	
			TR	Bournemouth	07.77	1977	14	4	1	
			TR	Aldershot	07.78	1978-79	16	/	4	
SHANKLAND, Andy J.	Stoke	08.04.64	APP	Port Vale	03.82	1981-83	13	10	1	(F)
SHANKLY, William	Glenbuck	02.09.13	Carlisle U.(*)	Preston N.E.	*	1946-48	79		11	(WH)S-5/d.1981

Players Names	Birthplace	Date	Previous Club	League Club	Date Signed	Seasons Played	Apps	Sub	Gls	
SHANKS, Don	London	02.10.52	Fulham(APP)	Luton T.	07.70	1971-74	89	1	2	(D) E.YTH.INT.
			TR	Q.P.R.	11.74	1974-80	176	4	10	
			TR	Brighton & H.A.	08.81	1981-82	45	1	0	
				Wimbledon	N/C	1983	1	/	0	
SHANKS, James	Barrow	31.10.18	Vickers Spts.	Barrow	+	1946	23		5	(OL)
SHANKS, Robert	Sunnyside	14.12.12	Crystal Palace(*)	Swindon T.	10.46	1946	1		0	(CH)*Swindon T.
SHANKS, Wally	Malta	01.05.23		Chelsea	10.46					(WH)
			TR	Luton T.	12.46	1946-56	266		6	
SHANNON, David L.	Liverpool	04.05.53	APP	Sunderland	05.70					(FB)Son of Les
			TR	Stockport Co.	07.73	1973	3	1	1	
SHANNON, Les	Liverpool	12.03.26	JNRS	Liverpool	+	1947-48	11		1	(WH)E'B'-3
			TR	Burnley	11.49	1949-58	263		39	
SHARDLOW, Paul	Stone	29.04.43	Northwich Vic.	Stoke C.	05.66	1966-67	3	/	0	(G) d.1968
SHARKEY, Dominic	Helensburgh	04.05.43	JNRS	Sunderland	05.60	1959-66	99	/	51	(CF)S.U23-2/S.SCH.INT.
			TR	Leicester C.	10.66	1966-67	6	/	5	
			TR	Mansfield T.	03.68	1967-69	67	2	17	
			TR	Hartlepool U.	07.70	1970-71	55	5	12	
SHARKEY, Pat G.	Omagh	26.08.53	Portadown	Ipswich T.	09.73	1975-76	17	1	1	(M) NI-1
			L	Millwall	11.76	1976	7	/	0	
			TR	Mansfield T.	08.77	1977	31	1	5	
			TR	Colchester U.	06.78	1978	5	1	0	
			TR	Peterborough U.	03.79	1978-79	15	/	0	
SHARMAN, Don W.	Rothwell	02.02.32	JNRS	Derby Co.	02.49	1950	2		0	(G)
			Gresley Rov.	Bradford C.	06.56					
SHARP, Duncan	Barnsley	16.03.33	JNRS	Barnsley	05.50	1953-61	213		0	(HB)
SHARP, Frank	Edinburgh	28.05.47	Hearts	Carlisle U.	03.67	1966-68	31	/	0	(W)
			TR	Cardiff C.	02.69	1968-69	13	1	1	
			TR	Barnsley	08.70	1970-72	125	/	7	
			TR	Grimsby T.	07.73	1973	26	3	2	
			TR	Port Vale	05.74	1974	17	7	2	
SHARP, George H.	Bedlington	20.07.35		Darlington	AM	1957	3		0	
			TR	Oldham Ath.	AM	1957	1		0	
SHARP, Graeme M.	Glasgow	16.10.60	Dumbarton	Everton	04.80	1979-83	96	8	36	(F)S.U'21-1
SHARP, John	Castleford	25.04.37	Fryston Col.	Halifax T.	01.55	1954-58	92		16	(OL)
SHARP, Len T.	Scunthorpe	29.11.32	JNRS	Scunthorpe U.	05.50	1951-61	186		3	(FB)
			TR	Hull C.	06.62	1962-65	58	/	4	
				Scunthorpe U.	03.67					
SHARP, Norman W.	Liverpool	26.11.19		Everton	*					
			TR	Wrexham	09.46	1946-49	122		17	
SHARP, Ron	Canada	22.11.32	Arbroath	Doncaster Rov.	10.58	1958-59	58		11	(F)
SHARP, Tom A.	Newmains	30.07.57	APP	Everton	08.75					(D)
			TR	Brentford	01.76	1975-76	4	12	1	
SHARPE, Fred A.				Wrexham	AM	1948	1		0	
SHARPE, Fred C.	London	11.11.37	JNRS	Tottenham H.	05.56	1958	2		1	(WH)
			TR	Norwich C.	07.63	1963-68	107	4	0	
			TR	Reading	07.69	1969-70	64	/	1	
SHARPE, Gerald R.	Gloucester	17.03.46	APP	Bristol C.	03.64	1964-70	149	4	48	(F)
SHARPE, John W.H.	Portsmouth	09.10.57	APP	Southampton	10.75	1976-77	21	/	0	(D)
			TR	Gillingham	09.78	1978-82	191	2	2	
SHARPE, Robert	Kirkcaldy	20.12.25	Raith Rov.	Darlington	08.52	1952	14		0	(RB)
SHARPLES, Brian	Bradford	06.09.44	APP	Birmingham C.	12.61	1962-68	60	1	3	(CH)
			TR	Exeter C.	12.68	1968-70	68	/	4	
SHARPLES, George F.	Ellesmere Port	20.09.43	JNRS	Everton	09.60	1960-63	10		0	(FB)E.SCH.INT./
			TR	Blackburn Rov.	03.65	1964-68	99	4	5	E.YTH.INT.
			TR	Southport	07.71	1971	23	2	1	
SHARPLES, John	Heath Town	08.08.34		Aston Villa	10.55	1958	13		0	(FB)
			TR	Walsall	08.59	1959-63	124		1	
SHARRATT, Harry	Wigan	16.12.29	Wigan Ath.	Blackpool	AM	1952	1		0	(G)E.AMAT.INT.
			B.Auckland	Oldham Ath.	AM	1955	1		0	
			B. Auckland	Nottingham F.	AM	1957	1		0	
SHARRATT, Stuart	Stoke	26.02.42	Oswestry	Port Vale	03.66	1965-71	143	/	0	(G)
SHARROCK, Anthony	Warrington	08.09.55		Southport	N/C	1973	1	/	0	(G)
SHAW, Alan	Preston	09.10.43	JNRS	Preston N.E.	10.60					(F)
			TR	Hull C.	08.61	1961-63	15		1	
SHAW, Alex				Crewe Alex.	+	1946	13		4	(IF)
SHAW, Arthur	Limehouse	09.04.24	Southall	Brentford	05.46	1946	4		0	(WH)
			TR	Arsenal	04.48	1949-54	57		0	
			TR	Watford	06.55	1955	3		0	
SHAW, Barry	Chilton	31.10.48	Crowboro Ath.	Darlington	AM	1967	1	/	0	(OL)
SHAW, Bernard	Selby	04.09.29	Buckley J.	Hull C.	05.48					(OR)
			Goole T.	Lincoln C.	10.53	1953-54	9		1	

Players Names	Birthplace	Date	Previous Club	League Club	Date Signed	Seasons Played	Apps	Sub	Gls	
SHAW, Bernard	Sheffield	14.03.45	APP	Sheffield U.	10.62	1962-68	135	1	2	(FB)E.U23-2/E.YTH.INT./
			TR	Wolverhampton W.	07.69	1969-72	113	3	2	Brother of Graham
			TR	Sheffield Wed.	06.73	1973-75	100	4	3	
SHAW, Cecil E.	Mansfield	22.06.11	Wolverhampton W.(*)	W.B.A.	*	1946	4		0	(FB)*Rufford Col./d.1977
SHAW, Chris J.	Bournemouth	23.08.65	JNRS	Bournemouth	06.83	1982-83	3	2	0	(F)
SHAW, Colin M.	St.Albans	19.06.43	JNRS	Chelsea	05.60	1961	1		0	(CF)E.YTH.INT.
			TR	Norwich C.	08.63	1963-64	3		0	
			TR	Orient	03.65	1965	7	/	0	
SHAW, David G.	Huddersfield	11.10.48	JNRS	Huddersfield T.	01.67	1966-68	23	2	2	(F)
			TR	Oldham Ath.	09.69	1969-72	155	/	69	
			TR	W.B.A.	03.73	1972-74	64	16	17	
			TR	Oldham Ath.	10.75	1975-77	55	4	21	
SHAW, Eric L.	Barnsley	12.02.47	APP	Barnsley	02.65	1964-65	2	1	0	(FB)
SHAW, Gary R.	Birmingham	21.01.61	APP	Aston Villa	01.79	1978-83	146	2	58	(F) E.U21-7
SHAW, Gordon	Wigan	05.05.27	Crompton Rec.	Southport	AM	1946	2		0	(RB)
SHAW, Graham L.	Sheffield	09.07.34	JNRS	Sheffield U.	07.51	1951-66	442	/	12	(FB)E-5/E.U23-5/E.F.LGE
			TR	Doncaster Rov.	09.67	1967	22	/	0	REP./Sch.Boxing ABA Champ.●
SHAW, Hugh	Clydbank	29.04.29	Rhyl	Tranmere Rov.	06.55	1955	3		0	
SHAW, John	Stirling	04.02.54	APP	Leeds U.	02.71					(G)
			TR	Bristol C.	05.74	1976-83	254	/	0	
SHAW, John S.	Doncaster	10.04.24		Rotherham U.	+	1946-52	262		124	(CF)
			TR	Sheffield Wed.	06.53	1953-57	56		21	
SHAW, Joseph	Marton	23.06.28	Upton Col.	Sheffield U.	+	1948-65	629	/	9	(CH)E.F.LGE REP.●
SHAW, Ken	Dukinfield	15.12.20		Stockport Co.	+	1946-47	41		18	
SHAW, Mark W.	St. Helens	15.10.64	JNRS	Wigan Ath.	N/C	1982	3	/	0	(F)
SHAW, Martin J.	Bristol	14.09.60	APP	Bristol Rov.	09.78	1978	1	1	0	(M)
SHAW, Peter K.	Northolt	09.01.56	Staines	Charlton Ath.	12.77	1977-80	100	5	5	(D)
			L	Exeter C.	11.81	1981	3	/	0	
			TR	Gillingham	02.82	1981-83	76	2	1	
SHAW, Ray	Walsall	18.05.13	Darlaston	Birmingham C.	*	1946	5		0	(WH)d.1980
SHAW, Ron	Bolton-on-Dearne	01.01.24	Harrow T.	Torquay U.	02.47	1946-57	384		99	(IF)
SHAW, Sam	Caverswell	14.09.34	Foley F.C.	Crewe Alex.	08.56	1956	19		3	
SHAW, Steve	Manchester	10.08.60	APP	Rochdale	APP	1977	6	/	0	(F)
SHAW, Stuart	Liverpool	09.10.44	JNRS	Everton	12.61	1964-65	3	/	0	(F)
			TR	Crystal Palace	12.66					
			TR	Southport	03.67	1966-68	66	1	6	
			TR	Port Vale	07.69	1969	1	2	0	
SHAWCROSS, David	Stretford	03.07.41	JNRS	Manchester C.	06.58	1958-64	46		2	(WH)E.U23-1/E.YTH.INT.
			TR	Stockport Co.	06.65	1965-66	59	1	14	
			TR	Halifax T.	03.67	1966-69	126	6	17	
SHEARD, Frank	Spilsby	29.01.22	Skegnes	Leicester C.	+					(CH)
			TR	Southend U.	05.46	1946-52	180		1	
SHEARER, David J.	Inverness	16.10.58	Inverness Clach.	Middlesbrough	01.78	1977-82	88	9	23	(F)
			L	Wigan Ath.	03.80	1979	11	/	9	
			TR	Grimsby T.	08.83	1983	1	3	0	
SHEARER, John M.	Dunfermline	08.07.17		Derby Co.	+					(F)
			TR	Bradford C.	10.46	1946-48	75		17	
			TR	Grimsby T.	02.49	1948-50	34		9	
SHEARING, Peter F.	Uxbridge	26.08.38	Hendon	West Ham U.	06.60	1960	6		0	(G)
			TR	Portsmouth	07.61	1961-63	17		0	
			TR	Exeter C.	06.64	1964-65	80	/	0	
			TR	Plymouth Arg.	06.66	1966-67	24	/	0	
			TR	Exeter C.	07.68	1968-70	79	/	0	
			TR	Bristol Rov.	02.71					
			TR	Gillingham	08.71	1971-72	39	/	0	
SHEAVILLS, James	Aylesham	28.07.40	JNRS	Leeds U.	09.57					(F)
			Holbeach	Peterborough U.	N/L	1960-62	30		8	
			TR	Barnsley	06.63	1963-64	65		6	
SHEEDY, Kevin M.	Builth Wells	21.10.59	APP	Hereford U.	10.76	1975-77	47	4	4	(M) EI.U21-1/NI.YTH.INT/
			TR	Liverpool	07.78	1980-81	1	2	0	EI-1
			TR	Everton	08.82	1982-83	68	/	15	
SHEEN, John	Airdrie	30.08.20	JNRS	Sheffield U.	*					
			TR	Hull C.	07.46	1946	5		1	
SHEFFIELD, Laurie	Swansea	27.04.39	JNRS	Bristol Rov.	07.56					(CF)W.SCH.INT.
			Barry T.	Newport Co.	04.62	1961-64	92		46	
			TR	Doncaster Rov.	08.65	1965-66	58		34	
			TR	Norwich C.	11.66	1966-67	27	/	16	
			TR	Rotherham U.	08.67	1967	19	/	7	
			TR	Oldham Ath.	12.67	1967	18	/	6	
			TR	Luton T.	07.68	1968-69	31	3	12	
			TR	Doncaster Rov.	10.69	1969	13	2	6	
			TR	Peterborough U.	08.70	1970	17	1	6	

Players Names	Birthplace	Date	Previous Club	League Club	Date Signed	Seasons Played	Career Record Apps Sub Gls		
SHELDON, Kevin J.	Stoke	14.06.56	APP	Stoke C.	06.73	1975-80	12	3	0 (M)
			TR	Wigan Ath.	08.81	1981-82	29	/	1
			L	Port Vale	08.82	1982	5	/	0
			TR	Crewe Alex.	N/C	1983	2	/	0
SHELL, Frank H.	Hackney	02.12.12	Barking	Aston Villa	*				(CF)
			TR	Birmingham C.	09.46				
			Hereford U.	Mansfield T.	06.47	1947	22		1
SHELLITO, Ken	E.Ham	18.04.40	JNRS	Chelsea	04.57	1958-65	114	/	2 (FB)E-1/E.U23-1
SHELTON, Garry	Nottingham	21.03.58	APP	Walsll	03.76	1975-77	12	12	0 (M)
			TR	Aston Villa	01.78	1978-81	24	/	7
			L	Notts Co.	03.80	1979	8	/	0
			TR	Sheffield Wed.	04.82	1981-83	87	2	10
SHELTON, John B.T.	Wollaston	09.11.12		Walsall	*	1946	3		0
SHEPHERD, Arthur L.	Liverpool	11.05.22		Liverpool	+				
			TR	New Brighton	08.49	1949-50	31		10
SHEPHERD, Brian A.	Leicester	29.01.35		Coventry C.	10.56	1957-59	29		0 (FB)
SHEPHERD, Ernie	Wombwell	14.08.19	Bradford Rov.	Fulham	*	1946-48	73		13 (OL)
			TR	W.B.A.	12.48	1948	4		0
			TR	Hull C.	03.49	1948-49	15		3
			TR	Q.P.R.	08.50	1950-55	219		51
SHEPHERD, James	Wigan	25.06.38		Blackburn Rov.	11.55				(F)
			TR	Everton	07.59				
			TR	Crewe Alex	06.60	1960-63	50		4
			TR	Southport	02.64	1963	13		6
SHEPHERD, J. Greig	Edinburgh	29.09.60	Musselburgh	Norwich C.	03.79	1979-81	13	3	2 (F)
			TR	Southend U.	08.83	1983	36	3	8
SHEPHERD, John A.	Rotherham	20.09.45		Rotherham U.	05.66	1965-67	21	2	2 (HB)
			TR	York C.	09.68	1968	5	/	0
			TR	Oxford U.	10.69	1969	9	2	0
			Hereford U.	Reading	09.71				
SHEPHERD, John H.	Kensington	29.05.32		Millwall	10.52	1952-57	150		64 (CF)
			TR	Brighton & H.A.	06.58	1958-59	45		19
			TR	Gillingham	02.60	1959-60	53		21
SHEPHERD, John W.	Liverpool	25.09.20	Elm Bank	Liverpool	+	1948-51	55		0 (FB)
SHEPHERD, Peter D.	Edrington	27.08.65	Plymouth Arg. (JNRS)	Exeter C.	N/C	1982	1	/	0 (G)
SHEPHERD, Trevor	Sutton-in-Ashfield	25.12.46	JNRS	Nottingham F.	12.63				(F)
				Coventry C.	10.66	1967-68	12	2	1
			L	Torquay U.	03.68	1967	14	/	6
			TR	Plymouth Arg.	06.69	1969-70	37	5	4
SHEPHERDSON, Harold	Middlesbrough	28.10.18		Middlesbrough	*	1946	3		0
			TR	Southend U.	05.47				
SHEPPARD, Hedley H.	E.Ham	26.11.09	West Ham U.(*)	Aldershot	*	1946-48	98		1 (FB)*Ilford
SHEPPARD, Richard J.	Bristol	14.02.45	APP	W.B.A.	02.63	1965-68	39	/	0 (G)
			TR	Bristol Rov.	06.69	1969-74	151	/	0
			L	Torquay U.	12.73	1973	2	/	0
SHEPPEARD, Howard T.	Ynysybwl	31.01.33		Sunderland	12.51	1953	1		0 (IF)
			TR	Cardiff	05.55				
			TR	Newport Co.	06.56	1956-57	31		6
SHERGOLD, Wilf F.	Swindon	18.09.43	JNRS	Swindon T.	10.60	1963-65	37	/	0 (WH)Son of William R.
			TR	Bradford C.	06.66	1966-67	22	6	2
SHERGOLD, William R.	Newport	22.01.23	B.Auckland	Newport Co.	07.47	1947-55	274		49 (W)W.AMAT.INT.
SHERIDAN, Alex	Motherwell	19.07.48	Queens Park	Brighton & H.A.	08.70	1970	12	4	2 (FB)
SHERIDAN, Frank M.	London	09.12.61	APP	Derby Co.	07.78	1980-81	41	2	5 (D)
			TR	Torquay U.	08.82	1982-83	24	3	3
SHERIDAN, George F.	Ince	30.10.29		Bolton W.	09.50				(CF)
			Colwyn Bay	Bradford C.	01.52	1951-52	12		1
SHERIDAN, John	Ramsgate	25.05.38	Linby Col.	Notts.Co.	07.55	1957-65	287	/	9 (WH)
			TR	Hartlepool U.	07.66	1966-69	117	3	1
SHERIDAN, John J.	Stretford	01.10.64	Manchester C. (JNRS)	Leeds U.	03.82	1982-83	38	/	3 (M)EI.YTH.INT.
SHERINGHAM, Edward P.	London	02.04.66	APP	Millwall	01.84	1983	4	3	1 (F)
SHERLOCK, Steve E.	Birmingham	10.05.59	Manchester C.(APP)	Luton T.	06.78	1978	2	/	0 (D)
				Stockport Co.	08.79	1979-83	182	5	7
SHERRATT, Brian	Stoke	29.03.44	APP	Stoke C.	04.61	1961	1	/	0 (G)
			TR	Oxford U.	08.65	1965-67	44	/	0
			L	Nottingham F.	10.68	1968	1	/	0
			TR	Barnsley	06.69	1969	15	/	0
			TR	Colchester U.	08.70	1970	9	/	0
SHERRATT, James A.	Warrington	24.12.21		Arsenal	12.46				(CF)
			TR	Hartlepool U.	12.48	1948	20		4
			TR	Orient	08.49	1949-51	37		7
			TR	Workington	08.52	1952-53	48		3
SHERRATT, John H.	Stoke	09.03.23		Port Vale	AM	1948	2		0

Players Names	Birthplace	Date	Previous Club	League Club	Date Signed	Seasons Played	Apps	Sub	Gls	
SHERWOOD, Alf T.	Aberaman	13.11.23	Aberaman	Cardiff C.	+	1946-55	353		15	(FB)W-41/W.SCH.INT.●
			TR	Newport Co.	07.56	1956-60	205		21	
SHERWOOD, Henry W.	Reading	03.09.13	JNRS	Reading	*					(IF)
			TR	Aldershot	09.47	1947-48	47		5	
			TR	Crystal Palace	07.49	1949	2		0	
SHERWOOD, Jeff	Bristol	05.10.59	Bath C.	Bristol Rov.	06.82	1982	16	2	0	(D)
SHERWOOD, Steve	Selby	10.12.53	APP	Chelsea	09.70	1971-75	16	/	0	(G) Brother of John
			L	Millwall	10.73	1973	1	/	0	(Olympic bronze medal
			L	Brentford	01.74	1973-74	62	/	0	athlete)
			TR	Watford	11.76	1976-83	189	/	1	Son of pre-war player.
SHIELDS, Duncan	Dumbarton	06.11.49		Workington	08.69	1969	7	1	0	(HB)
SHIELDS, James	Glasgow	28.11.31	Hibernian	Shrewsbury T.	05.56	1956	25		5	(F)
SHIELDS, Robert J.	Londonderry	26.09.31	Crusaders	Sunderland	03.54					(F)N.I.-1/IRISH LGE REP./
			TR	Southampton	07.56	1956-58	38		20	NI.AMAT.INT.
SHIELDS, Sam M.	Denny	21.03.29	Cowdenbeath	Liverpool	05.49	1949	1		0	(F)
			Airdrie	Darlington	06.52	1952	21		2	
SHIELS, Dennis P.	Belfast	24.08.38	Distillery	Sheffield U.	12.58	1958-63	32		8	(F)N.I.'B'-1
			TR	Peterborough U.	07.64	1964	12		4	
			TR	Notts.Co.	07.65	1965	28	1	7	
SHIELS, James M.	Derry	24.02.38	Waterside BC	Manchester U.	09.56					(FB)NI'B'-1
			TR	Southend U.	06.61	1961	25		0	
SHILTON, Peter L.	Leicester	18.09.49	APP	Leicester C.	09.66	1965-74	286	/	1	(G) E-60/E.U23-13/●
			TR	Stoke C.	11.74	1974-77	110	/	0	E.YTH.INT./E.F.LGE. REP./
			TR	Nottingham F.	09.77	1977-81	202	/	0	E.SCH.INT.
			TR	Southampton	08.82	1982-83	81	/	0	
SHIMWELL, Eddie	Matlock	27.02.20	Wirksworth	Sheffield U.	*	1946	14		0	(FB)E-1
			TR	Blackpool	12.46	1946-56	283		5	
			TR	Oldham Ath.	05.57	1957	7		0	
SHINER, Roy A.J.	Isle of Wight	15.11.24	Cheltenham	Huddersfield T.	12.51	1951-54	21		6	(CF)
			TR	Sheffield Wed.	07.55	1955-59	152		92	
			TR	Hull C.	11.59	1959	22		8	
SHINTON, Robert	W. Bromwich	06.01.52	Lye T	Walsall	03.72	1971-73	78	1	20	(F)
			TR	Cambridge U.	03.74	1973-75	99	/	25	
			TR	Wrexham	07.76	1976-78	128	/	37	
			TR	Manchester C.	07.79	1979	5	/	0	
			L	Millwall	02.80	1979	5	/	3	
			TR	Newcastle U.	03.80	1979-81	41	1	10	
			TR	Millwall	03.82	1981-82	29	5	4	
SHIPLEY, George M.	Newcastle	07.03.59	APP	Southampton	03.77	1979	2	1	0	(M)
			L	Reading	03.79	1978	11	1	1	
			TR	Lincoln C.	01.80	1979-83	199	/	35	
SHIPLEY, Mark E.	Hemsworth	11.02.59	APP	Blackburn Rov.	08.77					(G)
			TR	Doncaster Rov.	08.79	1979-80	6	/	0	
SHIPPERLEY, David	London	12.04.52	APP	Charlton Ath.	04.70	1970-73	93	8	8	(D)
			L	Plymouth Arg.	02.74	1973	1	/	0	
			TR	Gillingham	05.74	1974-77	144	/	11	
			TR	Charlton Ath.	02.78	1977-79	53	/	6	
			TR	Reading	09.79	1979-80	18	1	0	
SHIPWRIGHT, William K.	St.Pancras	22.12.32	Chesham	Watford	04.52	1953-58	146		0	(OR)
			TR	Aldershot	06.59	1959-62	123		0	
SHIRES, Alan J.	Leigh	29.06.48	APP	Southend U.	APP	1965	0	1	0	(F)
			TR	Colchester U.	07.66	1966-67	23	/	3	
SHIRLEY, Alex G.	Milngavie	31.10.21	Dundee U.	New Brighton	10.46	1946	18		3	
			TR	Bradford C.	08.47	1947	1		0	
			TR	Mansfield T.	08.48					
SHIRTLIFF, Paul R.	Barnsley	03.11.62	APP	Sheffield Wed.	11.80	1980-82	7	2	0	(M)
SHIRTLIFF, Peter A.	Chapeltown	06.04.61	APP	Sheffield Wed.	10.78	1978-83	132	/	5	(D)
SHOEMAKE, Kevin P.	Wickford	28.01.65	APP	Orient	01.83	1983	4	/	0	(G)
SHONE, George F.				Tranmere Rov.	12.46	1946	4		0	
SHORE, Andy W.	Kirby in Ashfield	29.12.55		Mansfield T.	07.74	1974	1	/	0	(HB)
SHORE, Brian	Huddersfield	01.02.35		Halifax T.	07.57	1956-57	9		3	
SHORE, Edward	Nuneaton	18.10.27		Port Vale	+	1947	3		0	
			TR	Coventry C.	07.48	1948-49	2		0	
SHORT, Alan J.M.	Plymouth	05.07.28	Tamerton	Exeter C.	08.50	1950	5		1	(OR)
SHORT, David	St.Neots	14.04.41	St.Neots	Lincoln C.	11.58	1958-59	4		0	(F)
SHORT, John	Barnsley	18.02.28	Wath W.	Wolverhampton W.	05.48	1950-53	98		0	(FB)
			TR	Stoke C.	06.54	1954-55	55		2	
			TR	Barnsley	10.56	1956-59	109		0	
SHORT, John D.	Gateshead	25.01.21		Leeds U.	*	1946-48	60		18	(WH)
			TR	Millwall	11.48	1948-55	243		19	

Players Names	Birthplace	Date	Previous Club	League Club	Date Signed	Seasons Played	Career Record Apps	Sub	Gls	
SHORT, Maurice	Middlesbrough	29.12.49	APP	Middlesbrough	02.67	1967-69	16	/	0	(G)
			TR	Oldham Ath.	06.70	1970	5	/	0	
			L	Grimsby T.	01.71	1970	10	/	0	
SHORTHOUSE, William	Bilston	27.05.22	St.Mirren O.B.	Wolverhampton W.	+	1947-56	344		1	(FB)
SHORTT, William	Wrexham	13.10.20	Chester C.(+)	Plymouth Arg.	+	1946-55	342		0	(G)W-12
SHOTTON, Malcolm	Newcastle	16.02.57	APP	Leicester C.	02.75					(D)
			Nuneaton Bor.	Oxford U.	05.80	1980-83	167	/	11	
SHOULDER, Alan	B. Auckland	04.02.53	Blyth Spartans	Newcastle U.	12.78	1978-81	99	8	35	(F)
			TR	Carlisle U.	08.82	1982-83	82	/	29	
SHOULDER, Jim	Durham	11.09.46	JNRS	Sunderland	02.64	1966	3	/	0	(FB)
			TR	York C.	08.69					
			Scarborough	Hartlepool U.	08.73	1973-74	62	1	3	
SHOWELL, George W.	Bilston	09.02.34	JNRS	Wolverhampton W.	08.51	1954-64	200		3	(FB)
			TR	Bristol C.	05.65	1965	9	3	0	
			TR	Wrexham	11.66	1966-67	48	/	1	
SHOWERS, Derek	Merthyr	28.01.53	JNRS	Cardiff C.	08.70	1970-76	76	7	10	(F) W-2/W.U23-6/
			TR	Bournemouth	07.77	1977-78	58	2	19	W.SCH.INT.
			TR	Portsmouth	02.79	1978-80	36	3	8	
			TR	Hereford U.	12.80	1980-82	87	2	13	
SHOWLER, Ken	Doncaster	03.02.33	Bentley C.W.	Chesterfield	11.52	1953	7		0	(F)
SHREEVE, John T.T.	Boldon	18.08.17	Boldon C.W.	Charlton Ath.	*	1946-50	93		0	(FB)
SHREEVES, Peter	Neath	30.11.40	Finchley	Reading	01.59	1958-65	112	1	15	(IF)
SHREWSBURY, Philip	Langley Moor	25.03.47	JNRS	Notts.Co.	09.65	1966	1	1	0	(HB)E.YTH.INT.
SHRUBB, Paul	Guildford	01.08.55	APP	Fulham	08.72	1972	1	/	0	(M)
			Helenic S.A.	Brentford	03.77	1976-81	170	12	8	
			TR	Aldershot	08.82	1982-83	66	6	1	
SHUFFLEBOTTOM, Frank	Chestefield	09.10.17		Nottingham F.	+	1946	2		0	*Ipswich T.
			TR	Bradford C.	10.46	1946-47	56		0	
SHUKER, John	Manchester	08.05.42		Oxford U.	N/L	1962-76	473	7	46	(D)
SHUTT, Steve J.	Barnsley	29.11.64	APP	Barnsley	12.82	1982	1	/	0	(F)
SHYNE, Chris	Rochdale	10.12.50	Dyers Arms	Rochdale	01.77	1976-78	20	/	0	(G)
			TR	Wigan Ath.	08.79	1979	10	/	0	
SIBBALD, Robert L.	Hebburn	25.01.48	JNRS	Leeds U.	01.65	1966-67	1	1	0	(D)
			TR	York C.	02.69	1968-70	74	5	7	
			TR	Southport	07.71	1971-76	240	/	13	
SIBLEY, Albert	Southend	06.10.19	JNRS	Southend U.	+	1946	21		3	(OR)
			TR	Newcastle U.	02.47	1946-49	31		6	
			TR	Southend U.	07.50	1950-55	193		37	
SIBLEY, Eric S.	Bournemouth	17.11.15	Bournemouth(*)	Blackpool	*	1946	37		0	(FB)*Tottenham H.
			TR	Grimsby T.	12.47	1947-48	23		0	
			TR	Chester C.	07.49	1949	7		0	
SIBLEY, Frank P.	London	04.12.47	APP	Q.P.R.	02.65	1963-70	147	3	3	(WH)E.YTH.INT.
SIBLEY, Tom I.	Porth	27.10.20	Ton Pentre	Birmingham C.	+					(OL)
			TR	Rochdale	03.47	1946-47	23		3	
SIDDALL, A. Barry	Northwich	02.05.30	Northwich	Stoke C.	02.51	1950-53	59		10	(IF)
			TR	Bournemouth	01.54	1953-56	86		14	
			TR	Ipswich T.	05.57	1957-60	58		6	
SIDDALL, Barry	Ellesmere Port	12.09.54	APP	Bolton W.	01.72	1972-76	137	/	0	(G)E.YTH.INT.
			TR	Sunderland	09.76	1976-81	167	/	0	
			L	Darlington	10.80	1980	8	/	0	
			TR	Port Vale	08.82	1982-83	72	/	0	
			L	Blackpool	10.83	1983	7	/	0	
SIDEBOTTOM, Arnold	Barnsley	01.04.54	JNRS	Manchester U.	02.72	1972-74	15	/	0	(D) Yorks Cricketer
			TR	Huddersfield T.	01.76	1975-77	56	5	5	
			TR	Halifax T.	10.78	1978	21	/	2	
SIDEBOTTOM, Geoff	Mapplewell	29.12.36	JNRS	Wolverhampton W.	09.54	1958-60	28		0	(G)
			TR	Aston Villa	02.61	1960-64	70		0	
			TR	Scunthorpe U.	01.65	1964-66	59	/	0	
			N.York R.	Brighton & H.A.	01.69	1968-70	40	/	0	
SIDLOW, Cyril	Colwyn Bay	26.11.15	Wolverhampton W.(*)	Liverpool	+	1946-50	149		0	(G)W-7/W.AMAT.INT./ *Llandudno
SIEVWRIGHT, George E.	Broughty Ferry	10.09.37	Dundee U.	Oldham Ath.	06.63	1963	37		4	(WH)
			TR	Tranmere Rov.	06.64					
			TR	Rochdale	07.65	1965	30	2	1	
SILK, George H.	Bootle	18.10.16	Southport(*)	Plymouth Arg.	*	1946-50	77		1	(FB) d.1969
SILKMAN, Barry	London	29.06.52	Barnet	Hereford U.	08.74	1974-75	18	19	2	(M)
			TR	Crystal Palace	08.76	1976-78	40	8	7	
			TR	Plymouth Arg.	10.78	1978	14	/	2	
			L	Luton T.	02.79	1978	3	/	0	
			TR	Manchester C.	03.79	1978-79	19	/	3	
			TR	Brentford	08.80	1980	14	/	1	
			TR	Q.P.R.	10.80	1980	22	1	2	
			TR	Orient	09.81	1981-83	91	7	11	

Players Names	Birthplace	Date	Previous Club	League Club	Date Signed	Seasons Played	Apps	Sub	Gls	
SILLE, Les T.	Liverpool	12.04.28	Tranmere Rov.(AM)	Bournemouth	AM	1946	1		0	(OL)
			Ipswich T.(AM)	Crystal Palace	AM	1948	3		0	
			TR	Tranmere Rov.	AM	1948	1		0	
SILLETT, John C.	Southampton	20.07.36	Southampton(AM)	Chelsea	04.54	1956-61	93		0	(FB)E.F.LGE REP./
			TR	Coventry C.	04.62	1961-65	108	1	1	Brother of Peter/
			TR	Plymouth Arg.	07.66	1966-67	37	1	1	Son of pre-war player
SILLETT, R. Peter	Southampton	01.02.33	JNRS	Southampton	06.50	1951-52	60		4	(FB)E-3/E.U23-3/E'B'-1/
			TR	Chelsea	06.53	1953-61	260		29	E.F.LGE REP./E.YTH.INT.
SILMAN, David A.	London	28.10.59	Wolverhampton W.(APP)	Brentford	02.78	1978	1	/	0	(F)
SILMAN, Roy	Rotherham	12.05.34	Edlington	Rotherham U.	04.52	1952-59	105		1	(FB)
			TR	Barnsley	07.60					
			TR	Bristol Rov.	09.61					
SILVESTER, Peter D.	Wokingham	19.02.48	APP	Reading	02.66	1965-69	76	2	26	(F)
			TR	Norwich C.	09.69	1969-73	99	1	36	
			L	Colchester U.	10.73	1973	4	/	0	
			TR	Southport	02.74	1973-76	79	2	32	
			TR	Reading	03.75	1974	2	/	0	
			L	Blackburn Rov.	10.76	1976	5	/	1	
			Washington Dips.	Cambridge U.	08.77	1977	2	2	1	
SIM, John	Glasgow	04.12.22	Kirkintilloch	Brighton & H.A.	10.46	1946-49	32		5	
			Chippenham	Plymouth	03.51					
SIMCOE, Ken E.	Nottingham	14.02.37		Nottingham F.	12.56	1957	2		1	(F)
			TR	Coventry C.	05.59	1959	8		1	
			TR	Notts.Co.	07.60	1960	2		0	
SIMM, John	Wigan	24.11.29		Bolton W.	10.47	1947	1		0	(OR)
			TR	Bury	05.51	1951-54	47		8	
			TR	Bradford C.	03.55	1954-58	95		22	
SIMMONDS, Chris K.	Plymouth	05.08.20	Barry T.	Millwall	05.47	1946-49	67		13	(IF)
			TR	Orient	06.50	1950	15		1	
			TR	Workington	06.51	1951-53	119		34	
SIMMONDS, Mel R.	Reading	20.12.51	Manchester U.(APP)	Reading	01.69					(F)E.SCH.INT.
			TR	Bournemouth	07.69	1969	4	2	0	
SIMMONITE, Gordon	Sheffield	25.04.57	Rotherham U. (APP)	Sheffield Wed.	08.75	1976	1	/	0	(D)
			Boston U.	Blackpool	09.80	1980-82	63	/	1	
			TR	Lincoln C.	11.82	1982-83	59	1	0	
SIMMONS, Anthony J.	Sheffield	09.02.65	APP	Sheffield Wed.	02.83	1981-82	1	3	0	(F)
			TR	Q.P.R.	11.83					
			L	Rotherham U.	03.84	1983	18	/	8	
SIMMONS, David J.	Gosport	24.10.48	APP	Arsenal	11.65					(CF)
			L	Bournemouth	11.68	1968	7	/	3	
			TR	Aston Villa	02.69	1968-70	13	4	7	
			L	Walsall	10.70	1970	5	/	2	
			TR	Colchester U.	12.70	1970-72	57	5	11	
			TR	Cambridge U.	03.73	1972-73	19	5	3	
			TR	Brentford	03.74	1973-75	47	5	17	
			TR	Cambridge U.	11.75	1975	16	1	5	
SIMMS, Gordon H.	Leamington Spa	20.12.36	Flavels	Coventry C.	AM	1957	1		0	(W)
SIMNER, Joe	Sedgley	13.03.23	Folkestone	Chelsea	10.47	1947	1		0	(F)
			TR	Swindon T.	07.49	1949-50	30		12	
SIMONSEN, Allan	Denmark		Barcelona	Charlton Ath.	11.82	1982	16	/	9	(F) DANISH INT.
SIMPKIN, Chris J.	Hull	24.04.44	APP	Hull C.	04.62	1962-71	284	1	19	(M)
			TR	Blackpool	10.71	1971-72	31	3	1	
			TR	Scunthorpe U.	10.73	1973-74	61	/	2	
			TR	Huddersfield U.	08.75	1975	25	/	0	
			TR	Hartlepool U.	12.76	1976-77	47	/	0	
SIMPKIN, Joe	Skelmersdale	26.09.21		Southport	+	1946-47	10		2	(CH) d.1969
SIMPKINS, Ken	Wrexham	21.12.43	JNRS	Wrexham	05.62	1962-63	4		0	(G)W.U23-1/5 apps. on
			TR	Hartlepool U.	03.64	1963-67	121	/	1	field for Hartlepool U.
SIMPSON, Alex	Glasgow	24.11.24	Benburb	Wolverhampton W.	01.47	1947-48	2		0	(WH)
			TR	Notts.Co.	10.49	1949-52	74		6	
			TR	Southampton	11.52	1952-54	68		1	
			TR	Shrewsbury T.	07.55	1955-57	99		4	
SIMPSON, Archie	Dundee	08.06.33	Dundee	Newcastle U.	07.55					(FB)S.SCH.INT.
			TR	Barrow	07.56	1956-58	76		1	
SIMPSON, Charles W.P.	Rochdale	11.07.54	APP	Rochdale	07.72	1972	1	/	1	(F)
SIMPSON, Cyril	Aylesham	18.08.42	JNRS	Gillingham	06.60	1959-61	18		0	(F)
SIMPSON, Dave	Glasgow	05.01.31	T.Lanark	Coventry C.	05.55	1955	4		1	(WH)
SIMPSON, Dennis E.	Coventry	01.11.19	JNRS	Coventry C.	+	1946-49	66		5	(OR)
			TR	Reading	05.50	1950-54	172		33	
			TR	Exeter C.	05.55	1955-56	31		5	
SIMPSON, Gary	Chesterfield	10.06.59	APP	Chesterfield	07.77	1976-80	36	7	8	(F)
			TR	Chester C.	08.81	1981-82	57	6	18	
SIMPSON, George L.	Shirebrook	03.12.33	JNRS	Mansfield T.	08.51	1952-53	8		0	(HB)
			Headington	Gillingham	08.56	1956	8		1	

Players Names	Birthplace	Date	Previous Club	League Club	Date Signed	Seasons Played	Career Record Apps	Sub	Gls	
SIMPSON, Harry	Ashton-u-Lyme	02.08.27	Fleetwood	Accrington St.	AM	1948	1		0	(OL)
SIMPSON, James	Clay Cross	08.12.23	Parkhouse C.W.	Chesterfield	+	1946	3		0	(IF)
SIMPSON, John	Hull	27.10.18	Bridlington	Huddersfield T.	+	1946	5		0	(FB)
			TR	York C.	03.48	1947-53	206		0	
SIMPSON, John L.	Kendall	05.10.33	Netherfield	Lincoln C.	03.57	1956	5		0	(G)●
			TR	Gillingham	06.57	1957-71	571	/	0	
SIMPSON, Ken	Sheffield	12.06.31	Ransome & M	Rotherham U.	09.55	1955-57	7		0	(F)
SIMPSON, Noel H.	Mansfield	23.12.22		Nottingham F.	+	1946-47	47		3	(WH)
			TR	Coventry C.	08.48	1948-56	254		8	
			TR	Exeter C.	02.57	1956-57	33		0	
SIMPSON, Owen	Stockfield	18.09.43		Rotherham U.	10.62	1964-66	6	/	0	(FB)
			TR	Orient	09.67	1967	36	/	4	
			TR	Colchester U.	08.68	1968	41	1	4	
			TR	Southend U.	08.69	1969-70	64	/	1	
			TR	Darlington	03.71	1970	11	/	0	
			TR	Grimsby T.	08.71	1971	6	1	0	
SIMPSON, Paul D.	Carlisle	26.07.66	APP	Manchester C.	08.83	1982	1	2	0	(M)
SIMPSON, Peter	York	06.11.31	JNRS	York C.	12.49	1950	1		0	
SIMPSON, Peter F.	Gt. Yarmouth	13.01.45	APP	Arsenal	04.62	1963-77	353	16	10	(D)
SIMPSON, Peter W.	Sunderland	21.09.40	JNRS	Burnley	11.57	1961-62	3		0	(F)E.SCH.INT.
			TR	Bury	08.63	1963	4		0	
SIMPSON, Reg				Preston N.E.	+	1946	4		0	
			TR	Carlisle U.	08.48	1948	36		0	
SIMPSON, Robert	B.Auckland	15.09.15	W.Auckland	Darlington	+	1946	30		0	(OL)
			TR	Hartlepool U.	07.47	1947	13		1	
SIMPSON, Ron	Carlisle	25.02.34	Holme H.Wks	Huddersfield T.	02.51	1951-57	110		25	(OL)Nephew of William
			TR	Sheffield U.	05.58	1958-64	203		45	
			TR	Carlisle U.	12.64	1964-65	45		6	
SIMPSON, Ron	Glasgow	11.10.30	T.Lanark	Newcastle U.	02.51	1951-59	262		0	(G)S-5/S'B'-2/S.F.LGE REP./S.AMAT.INT.
SIMPSON, Terry J.N.	Southampton	08.10.38		Southampton	06.57	1958-61	22		1	(WH)
			TR	Peterborough U.	06.62	1962	45		4	
			TR	W.B.A.	06.63	1963-66	71	1	3	
			TR	Walsall	03.67	1966-67	50	1	4	
			TR	Gillingham	07.68	1968	35	1	4	
SIMPSON, Tom	Airdrie	31.07.31	Dundee U.	Darlington	06.56	1956-57	4		0	(FB)
SIMPSON, William	Carlisle	02.10.19	Tottenham H.(AM)	Carlisle U.	08.46	1946	12	2		(IL)
SIMPSON, William G.	Glasgow	22.05.28	Trentside J.	Aston Villa	05.50					(F)
			TR	Crystal Palace	08.52	1952-54	38		13	
SIMS, Chris	Liverpool	06.12.39		Blackburn Rov.	04.59	1963-64	13		0	(FB)
SIMS, Frank	Lincoln	12.09.31	Ruston Spts.	Lincoln C.	08.51	1951-55	3		0	(CH)Father of Steve
SIMS, John	Belper	14.8.52	APP	Derby Co.	08.70	1972	2	1	0	(F)
			L	Luton T.	11.73	1973	3	/	1	
			TR	Oxford U.	09.74	1974	6	1	1	
			TR	Colchester U.	01.75	1974	2	/	0	
			TR	Notts. Co.	12.75	1975-77	48	13	13	
			TR	Exeter C.	12.78	1968-79	33	1	11	
			TR	Plymouth Arg.	10.79	1979-82	161	2	43	
			TR	Torquay U.	08.83	1983	30	/	8	
			TR	Exeter C.	02.84	1983	12	2	3	
SIMS, Nigel D.	Cotton-in-Elms	09.08.31	JNRS	Wolverhampton W.	09.48	1948-55	38		0	(G)E.F.LGE REP.
			TR	Aston Villa	03.56	1955-63	264		0	
			TR	Peterborough U.	09.64	1964	16		0	
SIMS, Steve F.	Lincoln	02.07.57	APP	Leicester C.	08.74	1975-78	78	1	3	(D) E.U21-10
			TR	Watford	12.78	1978-83	150	2	4	
SINCLAIR, Brian W.	Liverpool	02.08.58	Bury(N/C)	Blackpool	08.77	1977	0	2	0	(F)
			TR	Port Vale	08.78	1978	14	4	2	
SINCLAIR, Colin	Edinburgh	01.12.47	Raith Rov.	Darlington	06.71	1971-76	201	2	59	(M)
			TR	Hereford U.	10.76	1976-77	20	2	2	
			TR	Newport Co.	01.78	1977-78	29	1	5	
SINCLAIR, Dennis	Middlesbrough	20.11.31		Derby Co.	05.52					(F)
			TR	Mansfield T.	07.53	1953	1		0	
SINCLAIR, Harvey P.	Bournemouth	30.11.33	Bournemouth(AM)	Fulham	12.50					(G)
			Cambridge U.	Leicester C.	08.56	1956	1		0	
			Yeovil	Bristol Rov.	09.58	1958	1		0	
			Tonbridge	Fulham	07.59					
SINCLAIR, John E.	Dunfermline	21.07.43	Dunfermline	Leicester C.	05.65	1965-67	103	/	50	(W)S-1
			TR	Newcastle U.	01.68	1967-69	42	1	6	
			TR	Sheffield Wed.	12.69	1969-72	97	4	14	
			L	Chestefield	03.73	1972	10	/	3	
SINCLAIR, Mike J.	Grimsby	13.10.38		Grimsby T.	09.57	1957-60	6		1	(F)
SINCLAIR, Nick J.T.	Manchester	03.01.60		Oldham Ath.	06.78	1978-83	72	2	1	(D)

Players Names	Birthplace	Date	Previous Club	League Club	Date Signed	Seasons Played	Apps	Sub	Gls	
SINCLAIR, Robert D.	Winchburgh	29.06.15		Chesterfield	+					(OR)
			TR	Darlington	06.46	1946-47	69		11	
SINCLAIR, Ron M.	Stirling	19.11.64	APP	Nottingham F.	10.82					(G)
			L	Wrexham	03.84	1983	11	/	0	
SINCLAIR, Roy	Liverpool	10.12.44	Liverpool(AM)	Tranmere Rov.	10.63	1963-68	130	5	17	(W)
			TR	Watford	03.69	1968-71	29	12	3	
			L	Chester C.	12.71	1971	5	/	2	
			TR	Tranmere Rov.	07.72	1972	12	/	0	
SINCLAIR, Tommy	Ince	13.10.21	Gainsborough	Aldershot	+	1946-50	70		9	(OL)
			TR	Brentford	08.50	1950	16		5	
			TR	Bradford C.	08.51	1951	9		0	
SINCLAIR, William	Southport	11.09.20	High Pk.	Southport	+	1946	15		1	(W)d.1978
SINCLAIR, William I.	Glasgow	21.03.47	Morton	Chelsea	09.64	1964	1		0	(F)
SINCLAIR, William M.	Blairhall	14.10.34	Falkirk	Huddersfield T.	12.58	1958-59	15		5	(F)
			TR	Tranmere Rov.	06.60	1960	4		0	
			TR	Halifax T.	10.60	1960	21		3	
SINDALL, Mark	Shirebrook	03.09.64	Notts. Co. (APP)	Luton T.	08.82					(M)
			TR	Mansfield T.	07.83	1982-83	18	3	0	
SINGER, D.James	Gilfach Goch	30.08.37	Hengoed FDL	Newport Co.	05.56	1957-60	51		27	(IF)
			TR	Birmingham C.	09.60	1960-61	20		8	
			TR	Bournemouth	09.62	1962-63	59		22	
			TR	Newport Co.	07.64	1964	8		5	
SINGLETON, Anthony J.	Preston	30.03.36	JNRS	Preston N.E.	05.55	1960-67	286	1	0	(CH)
SINGLETON, Bernard	Conisbrough	14.04.24	Wolverhampton W.(+)	Exeter C.	+	1946-53	177		1	(G)
SINGLETON, Martin D.	Banbury	02.08.63	APP	Coventry C.	01.81	1981-83	18	3	1	(M)E.YTH.INT.
SINGLETON, Tom W.	Blackpool	08.09.40	JNRS	Blackpool	11.58					(FB)
			TR	Peterborough U.	06.62	1962-64	85		1	
			TR	Chester C.	06.65	1965-67	87	1	1	
			TR	Bradford P.A.	07.68	1968	32	/	1	
SINNOTT, Lee	Pelsall	12.07.65	APP	Walsall	11.82	1981-83	40	/	2	(D)
			TR	Watford	09.83	1983	19	1	0	
SINTON, Andy	Newcastle	19.03.66	APP	Cambridge U.	04.83	1982-83	45	2	11	(F)
SIRREL, Jimmy	Glasgow	02.02.22	Glasgow C.	Bradford P.A.	05.49	1949-50	12		2	(IF)
			TR	Brighton & H.A.	08.51	1951-53	55		15	
			TR	Aldershot	08.54	1954-56	33		2	
SISSONS, Graham J.	Chester-le-Street	10.05.34	Erdington	Birmingham C.	07.54	1956-62	91		0	(CH)
			TR	Peterborough U.	12.61	1962-64	68		0	
			TR	Walsall	11.64	1964-67	95	5	1	
SISSONS, John L.	Hayes	30.09.45	APP	West Ham U.	10.62	1962-69	210	3	37	(W)E.U23-10/E.YTH.INT./
			TR	Sheffield Wed.	08.70	1970-73	114	1	14	E.SCH.INT.
			TR	Norwich C.	12.73	1973	17	/	2	
			TR	Chelsea	08.74	1974	10	1	0	
SITFORD, J. Anthony	Crowborough	28.01.40		Brighton & H.A.	03.59	1960-61	22		2	(F)
SITTON, John E.	Hackney	21.10.59	APP	Chelsea	08.78	1978-79	11	2	0	(D)
			TR	Millwall	02.80	1979-80	43	2	1	
			TR	Gillingham	09.81	1981-83	97	5	6	
SIVELL, Laurie	Lowestoft	08.02.51	APP	Ipswich T.	02.69	1969-83	141	/	0	(G)
			L	Lincoln C.	01.79	1978	2	/	0	
SJOBERG, John	Aberdeen	12.06.41	Banks-of-Dee	Leicester C.	08.58	1960-72	334	1	15	(CH)S.SCH.INT.
			TR	Rotherham U.	06.73	1973	6	/	0	
SKEECH, H.Gordon	Warrington	15.05.34	Runcorn	Shrewsbury T.	11.54	1954-62	223		4	(FB)
SKEELS, Eric	Eccles	27.10.39	Stockport Co.(AM)	Stoke C.	12.58	1959-75	494	12	7	(D)●
			TR	Port Vale	09.76	1976	5	/	1	
SKEEN, George	Gateshead	04.08.20		Gateshead	10.46	1946-49	86		3	
SKEEN, Ken	Cheltenham	20.03.42	Trowbridge	Swindon T.	09.64	1964-66	13	/	4	(CF)
			TR	Oxford U.	07.67	1967-73	214	19	28	
SKEET, Stuart C.	Cheshunt	06.07.48	APP	Tottenham H.	12.65					(G)
			L	Northampton T.	03.69	1968	1	/	0	
SKEETE, Les	Liverpool	03.08.49	Ellesmere Port	Rochdale	04.73	1972-74	39	1	14	(CF)
SKELTON, George A.	Thurcroft	27.11.19	Thurcroft Welf.	Huddersfield T.	+	1946	1		0	(IL)
			TR	Orient	07.47	1947	3		0	
SKIDMORE, William	Barnsley	15.03.25	JNRS	Wolverhampton W.	+					
			TR	Walsall	05.46	1946-50	98		10	
SKILLEN, Keith	Cockermouth	26.05.48	Netherfield	Workington	12.73	1973-74	56	8	9	(IF)
			TR	Hartlepool U.	07.75	1975	4	2	1	
SKINGLEY, Brian G.	London	28.08.37	Ilfracombe	Bristol Rov.	01.55					(FB)
			TR	Crystal Palace	09.58	1958	11		0	
			TR	Q.P.R.	07.59					
SKINNER, George E.H.	Erith	26.06.17	Callenders	Tottenham H.	+	1946	1		0	(IF)
				Gillingham	Brighton & H.A.	02.48				

Players Names	Birthplace	Date	Previous Club	League Club	Date Signed	Seasons Played	Apps	Sub	Gls	
SKIPPER, Peter D.	Hull	11.04.58	Schultz Y.C.	Hull C.	02.79	1978-79	22	1	2	(D)
			L	Scunthorpe U.	02.80	1979	0	1	0	
			TR	Darlington	05.80	1980-81	91	/	4	
			TR	Hull C.	08.82	1982-83	92	/	5	
SKIRTON, Alan F.	Bath	23.01.39	Bath.C.	Arsenal	01.59	1960-66	143	1	53	(W)
			TR	Blackpool	09.66	1966-68	76	1	25	
			TR	Bristol C.	11.68	1968-70	76	3	14	
			TR	Torquay U.	07.71	1971	36	2	7	
SKIVINGTON, Glen	Barrow	19.01.62	Barrow	Derby Co.	07.80	1980-82	39	7	2	(M)
			L	Halifax T.	03.83	1982	4	/	0	
			TR	Southend U.	08.83	1983	2	2	0	
SKIVINGTON, Mike N.	Glasgow	24.12.21		Bury	06.47					(HB)L.O.I. REP.
			TR	Rochdale	01.48	1947	1		0	
			Dundalk	Orient	10.49	1949	5		0	
			TR	Gillingham	07.50	1950	7		0	
			TR	Brentford	09.51					
SKULL, John	Swindon	25.08.32	Swindon T.(AM)	Wolverhampton W.	06.50					(OR)E.YTH.INT.
			Banbury	Swindon T.	09.57	1957-58	33		11	
SLACK, Andy	Heywood	09.06.59	Bolton W.(APP)	Rochdale	01.78	1977-78	15	/	0	(G)
SLACK, Mel	B.Auckland	07.03.44	JNRS	Sunderland	03.61	1964	2		1	(HB)
			TR	Southend U.	08.65	1965-68	107	4	5	
			TR	Cambridge U.	N/L	1970	33	2	0	
SLACK, Roger C.	Morecambe	13.07.34		Stockport Co.	11.58	1958	8		1	(F)
SLACK, Rodney	Farcet	11.04.40		Leicester C.	09.58					(G)
			TR	Q.P.R.	03.61	1961	1		0	
SLACK, Trevor C.	Peterborough	26.09.62	APP	Peterborough U.	08.80	1980-83	121	/	11	(D)
SLADE, Robert F.	Hounslow	15.07.27	Acton T.	Millwall	AM	1948	1		0	(G)
SLATER, Fred	Burton	25.09.25	Burton A.	Birmingham C.	11.47	1948-49	5		1	(F)
			TR	York C.	06.51	1951	13		3	
SLATER, John	Heywood	08.05.17		Rochdale	+					(RH)
			TR	Crewe Alex.	08.46	1946	3		0	
SLATER, John B.	Sheffield	20.10.32		Sheffield Wed.	06.51	1952	3		0	(F)
			TR	Grimsby T.	07.54	1954	4		0	
			TR	Rotherham U.	09.55	1956	17		5	
			TR	Chesterfield	06.57	1957	15		3	
SLATER, Malcolm B.	Buckie	22.10.39	Montrose	Southend U.	11.63	1963-66	83		6	(F)
			TR	Orient	01.67	1966-69	111	/	4	
			L	Colchester U.	10.69	1969	4	/	0	
SLATER, Ray	Seaton Delaval	22.08.31	Sth.Shields	Chesterfield	06.56	1956	2		1	(CF)
			TR	Gateshead	10.56	1956	6		2	
SLATER, Robert	Musselburgh	05.05.36	Falkirk	Liverpool	05.59	1959-61	99		0	(G)S.U23-1
			Dundee	Watford	05.65	1965-68	134	/	0	
SLATER, William J.	Clitheroe	29.04.27	JNRS	Blackpool	AM	1949-51	30		9	(WH)E-12/E.AMAT.INT.●
			TR	Brentford	AM	1951	7		1	
			TR	Wolverhampton W.	02.54	1952-62	310		23	
			TR	Brentford	07.63	1963	5		2	
SLATTER, Les A.H.	Reading	22.11.31	M.Pleasant YC	Luton T.	03.49	1949	1		0	(OL)
			Crusaders	Aston Villa	08.53					
			TR	York C.	07.54	1954	13		0	
SLATTER, Neil J.	Cardiff	30.05.64	APP	Bristol Rov.	05.82	1980-83	110	1	2	(D) W.YTH.INT./W.U'21-3/W-1
SLATTERY, Clive J.	Swansea	21.07.46	North End	Swansea C.	10.69	1968-71	64	6	10	(W)
			TR	Hereford U.	07.72	1972	3	5	0	
SLATTERY, Joe W.	Newcastle	03.06.26	Hexham Hearts	Accrington St.	06.50	1950	13		2	(F)
SLEE, Carl D.	Swansea	30.11.47	JNRS	Swansea C.	01.66	1967-70	111	4	0	(FB)W.SCH.INT.
SLEEUWENHOEK, John	Wednesford	26.02.44	APP	Aston Villa	03.61	1960-67	226	/	1	(CH)E.U23-2/E.F.LGE
			TR	Birmingham C.	11.67	1967-70	29	1	0	REP./E.YTH.INT./
			L	Torquay U.	03.71	1970	11	/	0	E.SCH.INT.
			TR	Oldham Ath.	07.71	1971	2	/	0	
SLEIGHT, Geoff	Royton	20.06.43	JNRS	Bolton W.	08.61	1961	2		0	(F)
SLOAN, David	Lisburn	28.10.41	Bangor	Scunthorpe U.	11.63	1963-67	133	3	42	(W)N.I.-2/N.I.U23-1/
			TR	Oxford U.	02.68	1967-72	167	9	30	N.I.AMAT.INT.
			TR	Walsall	07.73	1973-74	44	5	3	
SLOAN, James	Newcastle	22.02.24	CA Parsons (Eng)	Newcastle U.	+					(F)
			TR	Hartlepool U.	10.46	1946-51	83		28	
SLOAN, Josiah W. (Paddy)	Lurgan	30.04.21		Tranmere Rov.	+					(CF)EI-2/NI-1
			TR	Arsenal	05.46	1946-47	33		1	
			TR	Sheffield U.	02.48	1947	12		2	
			Brescia	Norwich C.	12.51	1951	6		0	
SLOAN, Tom	Ballymena	10.07.59	Ballymena	Manchester U.	08.78	1978-80	4	7	0	(M) NI-3/NI.U21-1
			TR	Chester C.	08.82	1982	44	/	3	
SLOCOMBE, Mike	Bristol	03.05.41	JNRS	Bristol Rov.	06.61	1961-62	32		0	(HB)

Players Names	Birthplace	Date	Previous Club	League Club	Date Signed	Seasons Played	Career Record Apps	Sub	Gls	
SLOUGH, Alan P.	Luton	29.09.47	APP	Luton T.	05.65	1965-72	265	10	28	(D)●
			TR	Fulham	08.73	1973-76	154	/	13	
			TR	Peterborough U.	07.77	1977-80	104	1	10	
			TR	Millwall	06.81	1981	14	/	0	
SLYNN, Frank	Birmingham	10.02.24	L.Batchelors	Sheffield Wed.	09.46	1946-50	44		4	(WH)
			TR	Bury	12.50	1950-52	41		0	
			TR	Walsall	09.53	1953	10		0	
SMALE, Tom H.	Swansea	16.07.28	Derby Co.(AM)	Shrewsbury T.	N/L	1950-51	14		1	(FB)
			TR	Aldershot	08.52	1952	1		0	
SMALES, Ken	Hull	03.05.32	Brunswick Inst.	Hull C.	05.53	1956	1		0	(HB)
SMALL, David	Dundee	17.07.30	Dundee N.E.	Watford	06.50	1950-51	5		0	(W)
SMALL, John H.	Billingham	14.01.45		Hartlepool U.	AM	1965	2	/	0	(G)
SMALL, Martin L.	Gateshead	02.02.20		Gateshead	08.46	1946-51	96		29	(F)
SMALL, Mike A.	Birmingham	02.03.62		Luton T.	10.79	1981-82	0	4	0	(F) E.YTH.INT.
			L	Peterborough U.	10.82	1982	2	2	1	
SMALL, Peter V.	Horsham	23.10.24	Horsham T.	Luton T.	08.47	1947-49	27		5	(OL)
			TR	Leicester C.	02.50	1949-54	65		16	
			TR	Nottingham F.	09.54	1954-56	87		20	
			TR	Brighton & H.A.	07.57	1957	8		3	
SMALL, Sam J.	Birmingham	15.05.12	Birmingham C.(*)	West Ham U.	*	1946-47	53		10	(IF)*Bromsgrove
			TR	Brighton & H.A.	03.48	1947-49	38		0	
SMALLEY, Mark A.	Newark	02.01.65	APP	Nottingham F.	01.83	1982-83	0	2	0	(D)
SMALLEY, Tom	Kinsley	13.01.12	Norwich C.(*)	Northampton T.	+	1946-50	200		2	(FB)*Kirkby/E-1
SMALLMAN, David P.	Connahs Quay	22.03.53	JNRS	Wrexham	11.71	1972-74	100	1	38	(F) W-7/W.U23-5
			TR	Everton	03.75	1974-76	19	2	5	
SMALLWOOD, James W.	Bearpark	01.09.25	Spennymoor	Chesterfield	12.49	1949-60	347		15	(WH)
SMART, Jim	Dundee	09.01.47	Morton	Chelsea	02.65	1964	1		0	(IF)
SMART, Kevin G.	High Heaton	17.10.58	APP	Plymouth Arg.	10.76	1976-77	32	/	0	(D)
			TR	Wigan Ath.	07.78	1978-79	48	1	1	
SMART, Richard	B.Auckland	19.06.21	Stanley U.	Exeter C.	08.46	1946-51	103		34	(IF)
SMART, Roger W.	Swindon	25.03.43	JNRS	Swindon T.	05.60	1961-72	342	7	43	(IF)
			TR	Charlton Ath.	05.73	1973	30	1	1	
SMEDLEY, Laurie	Sheffield	07.05.22		Lincoln C.	+	1946-48	11		6	(IF)
SMEE, Roger	Reading	14.08.48	JNRS	Chelsea	03.66					(IF)
			TR	Reading	01.67	1966-69	49	1	16	
				Reading	07.73	1973	6	3	1	
SMELT, Lee A.	Edmonton	13.03.58	JNRS	Colchester U.	07.75					(G)
			Gravesend	Nottingham F.	06.80	1980	1	/	0	
			L	Peterborough U.	08.81	1981	5	/	0	
			TR	Halifax T.	10.81	1981-83	119	/	0	
SMETHURST, Derek	S.Africa	24.10.47	Durban U.	Chelsea	02.71	1970-71	14	/	4	(CF)
			TR	Millwall	09.71	1971-74	66	4	9	
SMETHURST, Edward	Doncaster	05.03.38	Denaby U.	Chesterfield	59.8	1959	19		0	(G)●
SMETHURST, Peter J.	S.Africa	08.08.40	Durban U.	Blackpool	02.60	1959	1		0	(F)Brother of Derek
				Tranmere Rov.	10.61					
			TR	Stoke C.	12.61					
SMEULDERS, John	Hackney	28.03.57	APP	Orient	07.74					(G)
			TR	Bournemouth	07.79	1979-80	14	/	0	
			Trowbridge T.	Bournemouth	01.84	1983	1	/	0	
SMILLIE, Andy	Ilford	15.03.41	JNRS	West Ham U.	06.58	1958-60	20		3	(IF)E.YTH.INT.
			TR	Crystal Palace	06.61	1961-62	53		23	
			TR	Scunthorpe U.	07.63	1963-64	13		2	
			TR	Southend U.	09.64	1964-68	163	/	29	
			TR	Gillingham	10.68	1968-70	88	6	7	
SMILLIE, Neil	Barnsley	19.07.58	APP	Crystal Palace	10.75	1976-78	71	12	7	(M)
			L	Brentford	01.77	1976	3	/	0	
			TR	Brighton & H.A.	08.82	1982-83	47	4	2	
SMILLIE, Ron D.	Grimethorpe	27.09.33	JNRS	Barnsley	12.50	1951-55	28		1	(OR)
			TR	Lincoln C.	06.56	1956-59	91		15	
			TR	Barnsley	07.60	1960-61	84		16	
SMIRKE, Alf H.	Pershore	14.03.17	S.P.P. FC	Southend U.	*	1946-47	59		13	(OL)E.SCH.INT.
			TR	Gateshead	03.48	1947	11		4	*Sheffield Wed.
SMITH, Alan				Hull C.	09.46	1946	1		0	
SMITH, Alan	Newcastle	15.10.21		Arsenal	05.46	1946	3		0	(OL)
			TR	Brentford	12.46	1946-48	13		4	
			TR	Orient	07.49	1949	6		1	
SMITH, Alan F.	Newport	03.09.49	JNRS	Newport Co.	09.66	1966-71	87	13	8	(IF)W.SCH.INT.
SMITH, Alan G.	Bromsgrove	07.04.36	Bromsgrove	Aston Villa	06.54	1955	1		0	(HB)
SMITH, Alan J.	Birkenhead	08.06.39	Port Sunlight	Torquay U.	08.56	1957-68	277	1	3	(CH)
SMITH, Alan M.	Harrogate	01.09.50	Harrogate R.I.	York C.	AM	1970	1	1	0	(OL)●

Players Names	Birthplace	Date	Previous Club	League Club	Date Signed	Seasons Played	Apps	Sub	Gls	
SMITH, Alan M.	Bromsgrove	21.11.62	Alvechurch	Leicester C.	06.82	1982-83	74	5	28	(F)
SMITH, Albert O.	Bargoed	18.10.23		Cardiff C.	+					(G)
			TR	Newport Co.	05.47	1946-47	27		0	
SMITH, Albert W.	Stoke	27.08.18		Q.P.R.	+	1946-48	63		3	
SMITH, Alex	Dundee	04.09.27		Blackpool	08.46					(CF)
			TR	Bradford P.A.	06.49	1949-50	5		0	
SMITH, Alex	Lancaster	29.10.38	Weymouth	Accrington St.	08.61					(G)
			TR	Bolton W.	03.62	1962-67	19	/	0	
			TR	Halifax T.	01.68	1967-75	341	/	0	
			TR	Preston N.E.	05.76	1976	8	/	0	
SMITH, Alex	Dewsbury	11.05.47	Ossett	Bradford C.	12.64	1965-67	91	2	2	(FB)
			TR	Huddersfield T.	03.68	1967-68	29	/	0	
			TR	Southend U.	04.70	1970-73	130	1	1	
			TR	Colchester U.	01.73	1973-74	51	/	1	
			TR	Halifax T.	02.75	1974-75	46	1	1	
SMITH, Alf				Walsall	10.53	1953	1		0	
SMITH, Anthony	Sunderland	31.12.43	Consett	West Ham U.	11.63					(F)
			TR	Watford	06.66	1966	3	/	0	
				Hartlepool U.	10.67	1967	2	/	1	
SMITH, Anthony	Sunderland	20.02.57	JNRS	Newcastle U.	07.75	1977	1	1	0	(D)
			TR	Peterborough U.	03.79	1978-81	68	/	5	
			TR	Halifax T.	08.82	1982-83	81	2	3	
SMITH, Archie N.	Larkhall	23.10.24	Hamilton	Exeter C.	05.48	1948-51	115		44	(CF)
				Carlisle U.	08.52	1952-53	31		8	
SMITH, Arthur E.	Whetstone	05.09.21	JNRS	Leicester C.	*	1946-47	17		3	(IF)
			TR	W.B.A.	06.48	1948-51	49		12	
			TR	Plymouth Arg.	08.52	1952-53	28		8	
			TR	Crewe Alex.	06.54	1954	4		0	
SMITH, Arthur E.	Bourne	13.02.22		Luton T.	+					(FB)
			TR	Aldershot	08.47	1947-48	2		0	
SMITH, Barrie A.	Colchester	03.03.53	JNRS	Colchester U.	07.71	1971-72	49	/	0	(G)
			TR	Sunderland	08.73					
			TR	Walsall	10.73					
SMITH, Brian	Bolton	12.09.55	APP	Bolton W.	09.73	1974-78	43	6	3	(M) E.YTH.INT.
			L	Bradford C.	10.77	1977	8	/	0	
			TR	Blackpool	08.79	1979	18	1	1	
			TR	Bournemouth	12.80	1980-81	40	/	2	
			TR	Bury	03.82	1981	6	/	0	
SMITH, C. Alan	Salford	07.06.40	Manchester C.(AM)	Stockport CO.	AM	1960	6	.	0	(G)
SMITH, C. Steve	Birmingham	13.01.61	Bromsgrove	Walsall	08.80	1980-81	17	2	3	(F)
SMITH, Charles				Accrington St.	AM	1950	1		0	
SMITH, Charles J.	Cardiff	26.08.15	Aberdeen	Torquay U.	+	1946	23		0	(OR)
SMITH, Colin R.	Ruddington	03.11.58	JNRS	Nottingham F.	10.81					(D)
			Hong Kong	Norwich C.	08.82	1982	2	2	0	
			Hong Kong	Cardiff C.	10.83	1983	34	/	2	
SMITH, Daniel	Armadale	07.09.21	Coltness	W.B.A.	+	1947	7		1	(OR)
			TR	Chesterfield	06.48	1948	17		4	
			TR	Crewe Alex.	08.49	1949-51	110		15	
SMITH, David	Thornaby	08.12.47	APP	Middlesbrough	12.64	1967	1	/	0	(M) E.SCH.INT.
			TR	Lincoln C.	07.68	1968-77	358	13	52	
			TR	Rotherham U.	07.78	1978-79	32	1	3	
SMITH, David	Durham	12.10.15	Sth.Shields	Northampton T.	+	1946-50	128		30	(OR)+Newcastle U.
SMITH, David	Frome	13.10.64	APP	Bristol Rov.	APP	1981	0	1	0	(D)
SMITH, David B.	Sheffield	11.12.50		Huddersfield T.	04.69	1971-73	27	7	7	(W)
			L	Stockport Co.	12.73	1973	7	1	0	
			L	Halifax T.	03.74	1973	12	1	4	
			TR	Cambridge U.	07.74	1974	15	2	3	
			TR	Hartlepool U.	02.75	1974-75	42	/	13	
SMITH, David B.	Dundee	22.09.33	JNRS	Burnley	09.50	1954-60	100		1	(FB)
			TR	Brighton & H.A.	07.61	1961	15		0	
			TR	Bristol C.	07.62	1962	3		0	
SMITH, David F.	Nottingham	11.03.56	APP	Notts. Co.	03.74	1975-77	45	5	0	(M)
			TR	Torquay U.	06.79	1979	20	3	1	
SMITH, David R.	Bristol	05.10.34	JNRS	Bristol C.	04.53	1955-58	20		1	(F)E.YTH.INT./
			TR	Millwall	09.59	1959	13		1	Glouc.Cricketer
SMITH, Dean	Leicester	28.11.58	APP	Leicester C.	12.76	1977	8	2	1	(F)
			TR	Brentford	10.78	1978-80	48	6	16	
SMITH, Dennis	Nelson	22.08.25	Frickley Col.	Hull C.	07.46	1946	15		0	(WH)
			TR	Accrington St.	10.47	1947-53	154		17	
SMITH, Dennis	Stoke	19.11.47	JNRS	Stoke C.	09.66	1968-81	406	1	30	(D)●
			L	York C.	03.82	1981	7	/	1	
			TR	York C.	N/C	1982	30	/	4	
SMITH, Dennis N.	Grimsby	23.12.32	JNRS	Grimsby T.	07.50	1952-53	5		0	(FB)

Players Names	Birthplace	Date	Previous Club	League Club	Date Signed	Seasons Played	Career Record Apps	Sub	Gls	
SMITH, Derek L.	Liverpool	05.07.46	APP	Everton	11.63	1965-66	3	1	0	(HB)
			TR	Tranmere Rov.	03.68	1967-69	78	5	21	
SMITH, Edward F.				Arsenal	*					(CF)
			TR	Aldershot	06.47	1947	7		2	
SMITH, Edward W.A.	London	23.03.29	Wealdstone	Chelsea	05.50					(CF)
			TR	Bournemouth	08.52					
			TR	Watford	07.53	1953-54	38		12	
			TR	Northampton T.	01.55	1954-55	53		8	
			TR	Colchester U.	06.56	1956	35		13	
			TR	Q.P.R.	07.57	1957	18		0	
SMITH, Edward W.J.	Grays	03.09.14	Barking	Millwall	*	1947	1		0	(FB)
SMITH, Edwin C.	Doncaster	03.03.36		Hull C.	01.57	1956-59	65		39	(F)
			TR	Rotherham U.	06.60	1960	9		3	
SMITH, Eric J.	Glasgow	29.07.34	Glasgow Celtic	Leeds U.	06.60	1960-65	66	/	2	(WH)S-2
SMITH, Eric T.H.	Tamworth	03.11.21	Castle Bromwich	Leicester C.	+	1946	5		0	(CH)
SMITH, Eric V.	Reading	20.03.28		Reading	04.49	1952-55	61		1	(HB)
SMITH, Frank A.	Colchester	30.04.36	Colchester Casuals	Tottenham H.	02.54					(G)
			TR	Q.P.R.	05.62	1962-65	64	/	0	
SMITH, Frank D.	Holymoorside	27.07.36	JNRS	Chesterfield	09.53	1953	7		0	(F)
				Mansfield T.	08.55	1955-56	31		4	
			TR	Derby Co.	07.57					
			TR	Coventry C.	11.57	1957-58	28		2	
SMITH, Fred A.	Aberdeen	14.02.26	Aberdeen	Hull C.	10.49	1949-50	17		1	(IF)
			TR	Sheffield U.	04.51	1950-52	40		12	
			TR	Millwall	01.53	1952-55	88		20	
			TR	Chesterfield	07.56	1956	6		1	
SMITH, Fred E.	Draycott	07.05.26	Draycott FC	Derby Co.	06.47	1947	1		0	(CF)
			TR	Sheffield U.	03.48	1947-51	53		17	
			TR	Manchester C.	05.52	1952	2		1	
			TR	Grimsby T.	09.52	1952-53	49		24	
			TR	Bradford C.	07.54	1954	9		3	
SMITH, Fred G.S.	W. Sleekburn	25.12.42	JNRS	Burnley	12.59	1963-69	83	/	1	(FB)
			TR	Portsmouth	07.70	1970-73	82	1	1	
			TR	Halifax T.	09.74	1974	3	/	0	
SMITH, Gary A.	Trowbridge	12.11.62	APP	Bristol C.	11.79	1980	7	7	0	(F)
SMITH, Gary M.	Greenford	04.11.55		Brentford	01.74	1974	3	/	0	(IF)
SMITH, Gavin	Cambuslang	25.09.17	Dumbarton	Barnsley	*	1946-53	257		35	(OR)
SMITH, Geoff	Cottingley	14.03.28	Rossendale U.	Bradford C.	07.53	1952-58	253		0	(G)
SMITH, George	Newcastle	07.10.45	APP	Newcastle U.	09.63					(M)
			TR	Barrow	03.65	1964-66	91	1	11	
			TR	Portsmouth	05.67	1967-68	64	/	3	
			TR	Middlesbrough	01.69	1968-70	74	/	0	
			TR	Birmingham C.	03.71	1970-72	36	3	0	
			TR	Cardiff C.	06.73	1973-74	43	2	1	
			TR	Swansea C.	05.75	1975-77	86	2	8	
			TR	Hartlepool U.	10.77	1977-79	81	4	2	
SMITH, George C.	Bromley	23.04.15	Charlton Ath.(*)	Brentford	+	1946	41		1	d.1983
			TR	Q.P.R.	06.47	1947-48	75		1	
			TR	Ipswich T.	09.49	1949	8		0	
SMITH, George C.B.	Portsmouth	24.03.19		Southampton	*	1946-48	86		1	(FB)
			TR	Crystal Palace	05.50	1950	7		0	
SMITH, George H.	Nottingham	13.04.36	Dale R.	Notts.Co.	07.53	1955-66	323	/	0	(G)
			TR	Hartlepool U.	07.67	1967-69	112	/	0	
SMITH, George R.	Fleetwood	07.02.21		Manchester C.	*	1946-51	166		76	(IF)
			TR	Chesterfield	10.51	1951-57	250		96	
SMITH, George T.				Walsall	AM	1953	1		0	
SMITH, Gerry	Huddersfield	18.11.39	JNRS	Huddersfield T.	05.58					(F)
			TR	Bradford C.	07.60	1960	7		0	
SMITH, Gordon D.	Kilwinning	29.12.54	Glasgow Rgrs.	Brighton & H.A.	06.80	1980-83	97	12	22	(F) S.U21-1
			TR	Manchester C.	03.84	1983	9	/	1	
SMITH, Gordon M.	Glasgow	03.07.54	St. Johnstone	Aston Villa	08.76	1976-78	76	3	0	(D)
			TR	Tottenham H.	02.79	1978-81	34	4	1	
			TR	Wolverhampton W.	08.82	1982-83	35	3	3	
SMITH, Graham	Wimbledon	07.08.51	Wimbledon	Brentford	08.74	1974	7	/	0	(WH)
SMITH, Graham L.	Pudsey	20.06.46	JNRS	Leeds U.	02.64					(D)
			TR	Rochdale	06.66	1966-73	316	2	3	
			TR	Stockport Co	07.74	1974-78	147	4	2	
SMITH, Graham W.C.	Liverpool	02.11.47	Loughborough U.	Notts.Co.	08.68	1968	10	/	0	(G)
			TR	Colchester U.	06.69	1969-71	95	/	0	
			TR	W.B.A.	12.71	1971-72	10	/	0	
			TR	Cambridge U.	01.73	1972-75	85	/	0	
SMITH, Granville	Bristol	04.02.37	APP	Bristol Rov.	05.57	1958-59	21		2	(W)
			TR	Newport Co.	06.60	1960-67	240	1	33	

Players Names	Birthplace	Date	Previous Club	League Club	Date Signed	Seasons Played	Apps	Sub	Gls	
SMITH, Harry A.	Ettingshall	10.10.32		Torquay U.	01.54	1953-60	188		0	(FB)
			TR	Bristol C.	07.61	1961	1		0	
SMITH, Harry S.	Chester	27.08.30		Chester C.	08.55	1953-57	73		8	(HB)
SMITH, Henry S.	Newburn	11.10.08	Darlington(*)	Bristol Rov.	+	1946	4		0	
SMITH, Herbert H.	Birmingham	17.12.22	Moor Green	Aston Villa	05.47	1949-53	51		8	(OR)
			TR	Southend U.	06.54	1954	5		0	
SMITH, Ian L.T.	Edinburgh	02.04.52	Queens Pk.	Birmingham C.	03.75	1974	0	2	0	(F)
SMITH, Ian R.	Rotherham	15.02.57	APP	Tottenham H.	04.74	1975	2	/	0	(D)E.YTH.INT.
			TR	Rotherham U.	06.76	1977	3	1	0	
SMITH, J. Barry	S.Kirkby	15.03.34	Farsley Celtic	Leeds U.	10.51	1952	2		2	(F)
			TR	Bradford P.A.	05.55	1955-56	64		38	
			TR	Wrexham	06.57	1957	18		10	
			TR	Stockport Co.	07.58	1958	17		5	
			Headington	Oldham Ath.	08.60	1960	1		0	
			TR	Southport	08.61					
			TR	Accrington St.	10.61					
SMITH, James			Burnley(+)	Orient	+	1946-47	22		3	(OR)
SMITH, James	Glasgow	20.01.47	Aberdeen	Newcastle U.	08.69	1969-74	124	5	13	(IF)S-4/S.U23-1/S.F.
										LGE REP.
SMITH, James A.	Coatbridge	09.09.25	Coatdyke J.	Walsall	06.48	1948	2		0	(OL)
SMITH, James A.G.	Arbroath	16.10.37	Arbroath Lads	Preston N.E.	10.55	1958-68	314	/	13	(FB)S.SCH.INT.
			TR	Stockport Co.	10.69	1969-70	78	/	2	
SMITH, James H.	Sheffield	06.12.30	Shildon	Chelsea	04.51	1951-53	19		3	(W)
			TR	Orient	07.55	1955-57	37		3	
SMITH, James M.	Sheffield	17.10.40		Sheffield U.	01.59					(WH)
			TR	Aldershot	07.61	1961-64	74		1	
			TR	Halifax T.	07.65	1965-67	112	1	7	
			TR	Lincoln C.	03.68	1967-68	54	/	0	
			Boston U.	Colchester U.	11.72	1972	7	1	0	
SMITH, Jeff.E.	Warren	08.12.35	JNRS	Sheffield U.	06.53	1956	1		0	(FB)
			TR	Lincoln C.	02.58	1957-66	318	/	2	
SMITH, John	Coatbridge	27.11.56	APP	Preston N.E.	11.74	1973-78	80	11	14	(F)
				Halifax T.	N/C	1979	26	2	6	
SMITH, John	Liverpool	14.03.53	APP	Everton	09.70	1973	2	/	0	(F) E.SCH.INT.
			TR	Carlisle U.	06.76	1976	4	1	0	
			L	Southport	02.77	1976	17	1	2	
SMITH, John	W.Hartlepool	24.04.36	JNRS	Hartlepool U.	05.53	1953-59	119		49	(CF)
			TR	Watford	07.60	1960	20		8	
			TR	Swindon T.	06.61	1961-63	97		37	
			TR	Brighton & H.A.	01.64	1963-66	88	/	33	
			TR	Notts.Co.	09.66	1966-68	74	4	12	
SMITH, John	Shoreditch	04.01.39	JNRS	West Ham U.	01.56	1956-59	125		20	(IF)E.U23-1/E.YTH.INT.
			TR	Tottenham H.	03.60	1959-63	21		1	
			TR	Coventry Co.	03.64	1963-65	34	1	1	
			TR	Orient	10.65	1965-66	38	1	3	
			TR	Torquay U.	10.66	1966-67	68	/	8	
			TR	Swindon T.	06.68	1968-70	79	5	9	
			TR	Walsall	06.71	1971-72	15	1	1	
SMITH, John	Stockbridge	15.09.10	Worksop	Sheffield U.	*	1946-49	94		0	(G)
SMITH, John	Wrexham	13.09.44	JNRS	Wrexham	05.63	1964-65	23	/	0	(FB)
SMITH, John	Batley	17.02.15	Manchester U.(*)	Blackburn Rov.	+	1946	30		12	(CF)*Newcastle U./
			TR	Port Vale	05.47	1946-47	29		11	Huddersfield T.
SMITH, John				Ipswich T.	+	1946	2		0	
SMITH, John E.	Romford	09.11.30	Barking	Millwall	04.56	1955-57	65		1	(FB)E.YTH.INT.
SMITH, John O.	Leicester	04.09.28		Northampton T.	09.49	1950-59	189		12	(WH)
SMITH, John T.	W. Stanley	08.09.19	Colchester U.	Watford	06.47	1947	10		0	(IF)*Charlton Ath./Fulham/
										Crystal Palace
SMITH, John T.	Birkenhead	21.12.27	Bromborough	Liverpool	03.51	1951-53	58		15	(CF)
			TR	Torquay U.	05.54	1954-57	65		16	
SMITH, John V.	Plymouth	12.11.27	Plymouth U.	Plymouth Arg.	07.50	1950-52	3		0	(FB)
			TR	Torquay U.	07.54	1954-59	164		0	
SMITH, John W.	St.Pancras	27.05.20		Bradford P.A.	+	1946-52	204		26	(OR)
SMITH, Keith W.	Woodville	15.09.40	JNRS	W.B.A.	01.58	1959-62	63		30	(CF)
			TR	Peterborough U.	06.63	1963-64	55		28	
			TR	Crystal Palace	11.64	1964-65	47	3	13	
			TR	Darlington	11.66	1966	17	/	2	
			TR	Orient	05.67	1966	3	/	0	
			TR	Notts.Co.	07.67	1967-69	85	4	7	
SMITH, Ken	Consett	07.12.27	Annfield Plain	Blackpool	04.49					(F)
			TR	Gateshead	08.52	1952-58	259		74	

Players Names	Birthplace	Date	Previous Club	League Club	Date Signed	Seasons Played	Apps	Sub	Gls	
SMITH, Ken	Sth.Shields	21.05.32	JNRS	Sunderland	08.49	1950-52	5		2	(CF)
			Headington	Blackpool	12.54	1954-57	6		4	
			TR	Shrewsbury T.	10.57	1957-58	44		20	
			TR	Gateshead	11.58	1958-59	41		16	
			TR	Darlington	12.59	1959	24		7	
			TR	Carlisle U.	07.60	1960	13		11	
				Halifax T.	10.61	1961	23		8	
SMITH, Ken G.	Norwich	22.04.36	Gothics	Norwich C.	09.55	1955-56	10		0	(FB)
SMITH, Kevan	Eaglescliffe	13.12.59	Stockton	Darlington	09.79	1979-83	206	3	9	(D)
SMITH, Kevin J.	Wallsend	20.04.65	APP	Cambridge U.	11.82	1982-83	28	8	4	(F)
SMITH, Kevin P.	St. Pauls Cray	05.12.62	APP	Charlton Ath.	08.80	1979-83	79	25	14	(M)
SMITH, Les	Manchester	02.10.20	Stockport Co.(AM)	Huddersfield T.	+	1946-47	37		0	(RH)
			TR	Oldham Ath.	07.49	1949-55	178		3	
SMITH, Les	Tamworth	16.11.21		Mansfield T.	+	1946-47	35		0	
SMITH, Leslie G.F.	Ealing	13.03.18	Brentford(*)	Aston Villa	+	1946-51	181		26	(OL)*Hayes/
			TR	Brentford	06.52	1952	14		1	E-1
SMITH, Leslie J.	Halesowen	24.12.27	JNRS	Wolverhampton W.	+	1947-55	88		15	(W)
			TR	Aston Villa	02.56	1955-58	114		24	
SMITH, Lindsay J.	Enfield	18.09.54	APP	Colchester U.	03.72	1970-76	185	27	16	(D)
			L	Charlton Ath.	08.77	1977	1	/	0	
			L	Millwall	09.77	1977	4	1	0	
			TR	Cambridge U.	10.77	1977-82	173	1	7	
			L	Lincoln C.	09.81	1981	5	/	0	
			TR	Plymouth Arg.	10.82	1982-83	76	/	5	
SMITH, Lionel	Mexborough	23.08.20	Yorks Tar.Dist.	Arsenal	+	1947-53	162		0	(FB)E-6/E.F.
			TR	Watford	06.54	1954	7		0	LGE REP.
SMITH, Malcolm	Stockton	21.09.53	APP	Middlesbrough	10.70	1971-75	32	24	11	(F)
			L	Bury	10.75	1975	5	/	1	
			L	Blackpool	01.76	1975	8	/	5	
			TR	Burnley	09.76	1976-79	82	3	17	
			TR	York C.	08.80	1980-81	28	7	6	
SMITH, Mark	Redruth	21.09.63	APP	Bristol C.	09.81	1981	1	4	0	(M)
				Plymouth Arg.	N/C	1983	3	/	0	
SMITH, Mark A.	Torquay	09.10.61		Torquay U.	N/C	1981-83	28	2	0	(D)
SMITH, Mark C.	Sheffield	21.03.60	APP	Sheffield Wed.	03.78	1977-83	216	1	14	(D)E.U'21-5
SMITH, Mark L.	Canning Town	10.10.61	APP	West Ham U.	10.79	1979	1	/	0	(D)
SMITH, Mark S.	Carlisle	04.04.62	APP	Orient	12.79	1978-79	3	/	0	(D) E.YTH.INT.
SMITH, Mike	Haddington	15.10.23	Aberaman	Plymouth Arg.	02.48	1947	1		0	(WH)
			TR	Chelsea	06.48					
SMITH, Mike	Sunderland	28.10.58	Lambton St B.C.	Lincoln C.	07.77	1977-78	20	5	0	(D)
			TR	Wimbledon	12.79	1979-83	150	2	11	
SMITH, Mike J.	Quarndon	22.09.35	JNRS	Derby Co.	10.52	1957-60	22		0	(FB)E.SCH.INT.
			TR	Bradford C.	06.61	1961-65	134	/	0	
SMITH, Nigel G.	Manchester	22.04.59	Blackburn Rov.(N/C)	Stockport Co.	08.79	1980-83	89	4	1	(D)
SMITH, Nigel K.	Bath	12.01.66	APP	Bristol C.	01.84.	1982	2	/	0	(M)
SMITH, Nigel P.	Banstead	03.01.58	Banstead	Brentford	03.75	1974-78	81	4	0	(D)
			TR	Cambridge U.	11.78	1978	0	1	0	
SMITH, Norman	Darwen	02.01.25	Darwen	Arsenal	07.47					(WH)
			TR	Barnsley	10.52	1952-58	156		14	
			TR	Shrewsbury T.	07.59					
SMITH, Norman	Boldon	23.11.19	Canley Std.Apps	Coventry C.	*	1946-47	9		0	(CF)
			TR	Millwall	12.47	1947	10		0	
SMITH, Norman H.	Burton	27.01.24	+	Accrington St.	+	1946-47	39		4	
			TR	Oldham Ath.	06.48	1948	1		0	
SMITH, Norman L.	Croydon	02.07.28	B.Auckland	Fulham	07.48	1952-56	60		0	(WH)E.AMAT.INT.
SMITH, Paul M.	Rotherham	09.11.64	APP	Sheffield U.	11.82	1982	7	/	0	(D)
SMITH, Paul W.	Doncaster	15.10.54	APP	Huddersfield T.	12.71	1972-73	1	1	0	(WH)
			TR	Cambridge U.	09.74	1974-75	35	3	3	
SMITH, Peter	Gosport	06.05.32	Gosport Bor.	Gillingham	11.54	1954-56	6		0	(CF)
SMITH, Peter A.	Islington	20.11.64	APP	Orient	11.82	1982	8	6	0	(D)
SMITH, Peter E.	Glascote Heath	02.02.36	Kingsbury Col.	Birmingham C.	02.54	1954	2		0	(HB)
SMITH, Peter J.	Balham	27.05.35	Tunbridge Wells	Gillingham	06.58	1958-59	39		2	(HB)
SMITH, Philip	Fleetwood	20.11.61	APP	Blackpool	11.79	1979	1	/	0	(F)
SMITH, R. Alex	Billingham	06.02.44	JNRS	Middlesbrough	12.61	1965-71	119	2	1	(FB)
			Bangor	Darlington	07.74	1974-75	43	/	0	
SMITH, Ray	Portadown	20.11.50	Glenavon	Oldham Ath.	01.68	1967	0	2	0	(F)
SMITH, Ray H.	Hull	13.09.34	JNRS	Hull C.	08.52	1954-55	23		2	(F)
			TR	Peterborough U.	07.60	1960-62	92		33	
			TR	Northampton T.	10.62	1962-63	23		7	
			TR	Luton T.	10.63	1963	10		1	

Players Names	Birthplace	Date	Previous Club	League Club	Date Signed	Seasons Played	Apps	Sub	Gls	
SMITH, Ray J.	Islington	18.04.43	Basildon	Southend U.	12.61	1961-66	150	/	55	(CF)
			TR	Wrexham	07.67	1967-71	161	11	62	
			TR	Peterborough U.	07.72	1972	22	/	8	
SMITH, Ray S.	Evenwood	14.04.29	Evenwood T.	Luton T.	02.50	1951-56	12		0	(HB)
			TR	Southend U.	08.57	1957-59	46		1	
SMITH, Robert	Barnsley	20.06.41	JNRS	Barnsley	06.60	1961-62	4		0	(HB)
SMITH, Robert	Dalkeith	21.12.53	Hibernian	Leicester C.	12.78	1978-83	132	5	20	(M)
			L	Peterborough U.	02.82	1981	5	/	0	
SMITH, Robert A.	Langdale	22.02.33	JNRS	Chelsea	05.50	1950-55	74		23	(CF)E-15●
			TR	Tottenham H.	12.55	1955-63	271		176	
			TR	Brighton & H.A.	05.64	1964	31		18	
SMITH, Robert G.J.	Bournemouth	15.12.41	JNRS	Portsmouth	05.59					(HB)
			TR	Gillingham	07.62	1962	7		0	
SMITH, Robert M.S.	Hull	25.04.50	APP	Hull C.	11.67					(IF)
			TR	Grimsby T.	09.71	1971	10	1	0	
			TR	Hartlepool U.	07.72	1972-75	141	11	4	
SMITH, Robert W.	Manchester	14.03.44	APP	Manchester U.	04.61					(IF)E.YTH.INT.
			TR	Scunthorpe U.	03.65	1964-66	82	/	12	
			TR	Grimsby T.	01.67	1966-67	48	3	1	
			TR	Brighton & H.A.	06.68	1968-70	72	3	2	
			TR	Chester C.	06.71	1971	2	/	0	
			TR	Hartlepool U.	10.71	1971-72	67	2	7	
			TR	Bury	08.73					
SMITH, Roger A.	Welwyn	03.11.44	APP	Tottenham H.	06.62					(F)
			TR	Exeter C.	06.66	1966	6	/	0	
SMITH, Roger W.	Tamworth	19.02.45	APP	Walsall	09.62	1962-66	52	1	2	(F)
			TR	Port Vale	08.65	1965	28	1	5	
			TR	Walsall	07.66	1966	8	1	0	
SMITH, Ron	Liverpool	07.06.36		Liverpool	12.57					(F)
			TR	Bournemouth	05.59	1959-60	36		6	
			TR	Crewe Alex.	07.61	1961-63	89		11	
			TR	Port Vale	10.63	1963-64	59		6	
			TR	Southport	07.65	1965-66	77	2	14	
SMITH, Ron	Aberystwyth	09.04.34	Maidenhead U.	Arsenal	07.54					(RB)
			TR	Watford	06.55	1955	2		0	
SMITH, Ron H.	York	25.11.29	Harrogate R.I.	York C.	05.54	1954	1		0	
SMITH, Roy H.	India	19.03.36	Woodford YC	West Ham U.	06.55	1955-56	6	1		(IF)
			Hereford U.	Portsmouth	01.62	1961-62	9		3	
SMITH, Roy L.	Shirebrook	22.09.16	Selby T.	Sheffield Wed.	*	1946-47	47		0	(G)d
			TR	Notts.Co.	12.48	1948-52	110		0	
SMITH, Roy P.	Haydock	18.06.36	Wigan Ath.	Southport	09.58	1958	23		4	(CF)d.1959
SMITH, Seph L.	Whitburn	15.03.12	Whitburn	Leicester C.	*	1946-48	81		3	(WH)E-1/E.F.LGE REP./E.SCH.INT.
SMITH, Stan J.	Kidsgrove	24.02.31	Stock C.(AM)	Port Vale	05.50	1954-56	59		14	(F)
			TR	Crewe Alex.	07.57	1957	28		6	
			TR	Oldham Ath.	03.58	1957	4		0	
SMITH, Stan W.	Coventry	24.02.25		Coventry C.	08.46	1946-48	30		0	
			Stafford Rgrs.	Swansea C.	08.50					
SMITH, Steve	Huddersfield	28.04.46	JNRS	Huddersfield T.	10.63	1964-76	329	11	29	(M)
			L	Bolton W.	12.74	1974	3	/	0	
			TR	Halifax T.	08.77	1977-78	78	3	4	
SMITH, Steve J.	Lydney	12.06.57	APP	Birmingham C.	07.75	1975	2	/	0	(G)
			TR	Bradford C.	03.78	1978-81	105	/	0	
			TR	Crewe Alex.	08.82	1982-83	54	/	0	
SMITH, Terry P.	Cheltenham	10.06.51	APP	Stoke C.	12.68	1970-71	4	1	0	(CF)
			L	Shrewsbury T.	02.73	1972	2	/	0	
SMITH, Terry V.	Rainworth	10.07.42	JNRS	Mansfield T.	04.60	1960	8		0	(HB)
SMITH, Thomas	Easington	02.02.23	Horden C.W.	Newcastle U.	+	1946-49	8		0	(CH)
SMITH, Tim C.	Gloucester	19.04.59	APP	Luton T.	05.76	1976-77	1	1	0	(M)
SMITH, Tom	Liverpool	05.04.45	APP	Liverpool	04.62	1962-77	467	/	36	(WH) E-1/E.U23-10/● E.YTH.INT./E.F.LGE. REP.
			TR	Swansea C.	08.78	1978	34	2	2	
SMITH, Tom E.	Wolverhampton	30.07.59	Bromsgrove	Sheffield U.	04.78	1978	2	1	1	(F)
			TR	Huddersfield T.	03.79	1978	0	1	0	
SMITH, Trevor	Brierley Hill	13.04.36	JNRS	Birmingham C.	05.53	1953-64	364		3	(CH)E-2/E.U23-15/ E'B'-2/E.F.LGE REP.
			TR	Walsall	10.64	1964-65	11	/	0	
SMITH, Trevor J.	Birmingham	07.05.54	APP	Coventry C.	05.71					(W)E.SCH.INT.
			TR	Walsall	08.72	1972	2	1	0	
SMITH, Trevor M.	Middlesbrough	04.04.49		Hartlepool U.	07.77	1976-78	27	6	1	(D)
			Whitby T.	Hartlepool U.	08.82	1982	30	2	2	
SMITH, Trevor R.	Lowestoft	12.08.46	APP	Ipswich T.	08.64	1964-65	22	1	0	(FB)
			TR	Crewe Alex.	08.68					
SMITH, Wilf	Manchester	20.01.35		Stockport Co.	02.57	1957-59	6		1	(F)

Players Names	Birthplace	Date	Previous Club	League Club	Date Signed	Seasons Played	Career Record Apps Sub Gls		
SMITH, Wilf S.	W. Germany	03.09.46	APP	Sheffield Wed.	09.63	1964-70	206	/	4	(D) E.U23-6/E.F.LGE
			TR	Coventry C.	08.70	1970-74	132	3	1	REP./
			L	Brighton & H.A.	10.74	1974	5	/	0	E.YTH.INT.
			L	Millwall	01.75	1974	5	/	0	
			TR	Bristol Rov.	03.75	1974-76	54	/	2	
			TR	Chesterfield	11.76	1976	26	1	2	
SMITH, William	Stoke	18.04.17		Port Vale	*	1946-48	27		0	
SMITH, William	Cumnock	12.10.42		Carlisle U.	03.63					(F)
				Sheffield U.	07.65	1966	2	/	1	
SMITH, William	Glasgow	06.12.43	Glasgow Celtic	Brentford	06.63	1963-65	25	/	0	(HB)
SMITH, William	London	29.09.48	Leatherhead	Wimbledon	08.77	1977	2	/	0	(D) E.AMAT.INT.
SMITH, William	Aberdeen	23.12.38	Raith Rov.	Darlington	07.63	1963	26		7	(IL)
SMITH, William A.	London	02.11.38	jNRS	Crystal Palace	12.56					(G)
			TR	Watford	08.57	1958	10		0	
SMITH, William C. (Conway)	Huddersfield	13.07.26	JNRS	Huddersfield T.	+	1947-50	36		4	(IF)Son of famous
			TR	Q.P.R.	03.51	1950-55	175		82	pre-war player
			TR	Halifax T.	06.56	1956-61	183		73	
SMITH, William H.	Plymouth	07.09.26	Plymouth U.	Plymouth Arg.	+					(WH)
				Reading	08.47	1947	3		0	
			TR	Northampton T.	07.48	1948	26		8	
			TR	Birmingham C.	02.50	1950-52	55		21	
			TR	Blackburn Rov.	12.52	1952-59	119		10	
			TR	Accrington St.	07.60	1960	34		3	
SMITH, William R.	Stafford	20.12.30		Crewe Alex.	12.55	1955-56	43		0	
SMITH, William V.	Pucklechurch	07.04.18		Bristol Rov.	*	1946	9		0	(FB)d.1968
			TR	Newport Co.	12.46	1946-47	9		0	
SMITHERS, Tim	Ramsgate	22.01.56	Nuneaton Bor.	Oxford U.	05.80	1980-82	95	4	6	(D)
SMITHIES, Mike H.	Hartlepool	18.09.62	St. James's	Hartlepool U.	08.83	1982-83	27	2	0	(D)
SMITHSON, Rod G.	Leicester	09.10.43	APP	Arsenal	10.60	1962	2		0	(WH)E.YTH.INT./
			TR	Oxford U.	07.64	1965-74	149	6	6	E.SCH.INT.
SMOUT, John	Newtown	30.10.14		Crystal Palace	08.65	1965	1	/	0	(G)
			TR	Exeter C.	06.66	1966-67	75	/	0	
SMYTH, Cecil	Belfast	04.05.41	Distillery	Exeter C.	08.62	1962-68	270	3	4	(FB)
			TR	Torquay T.	08.69	1969-70	22	2	0	
SMYTH, Gerry J.	Belfast	05.11.31		Cardiff C.	08.50					
			TR	Chester C.	07.51	1951	2		0	
SMYTH, Herbert R.	Manchester	28.02.21		Ipswich T.	+	1946-47	2		0	(HB)
			TR	Halifax T.	08.50	1950	2		0	
			TR	Rochdale	09.50	1950	3		1	
			TR	Accrington St.	01.51	1950	7		0	
SMYTH, Mike	Dublin	13.05.40	Drumcondra	Barrow	08.62	1962-63	8		0	(G)EI-1
SMYTH, Peter	Derry	03.12.24	Albion R.	Exeter C.	06.50	1950	5		0	(IF)
			TR	Southport	07.51	1951	5		0	
SMYTH, Sammy	Belfast	25.02.25	Linfield	Wolverhampton W.	07.47	1947-51	102		33	(IF)N.I.-9/IRISH
			TR	Stoke C.	09.51	1951-52	40		19	LGE REP.
			TR	Liverpool	01.53	1952-53	44		19	
SNAPE, John	Birmingham	02.07.17	Shirley T.	Coventry C.	*	1946-49	97		2	(RH)
SNEDDON, Charlie	W.Lothian	10.06.30	Stenhousemuir	Accrington St.	10.53	1953-60	213		3	(WH)
SNEDDON, David	Kilwinning	24.04.36	Dundee	Preston N.E.	04.59	1958-61	91		17	(IF)S.U23-1
SNEDDON, John D.	Bonnybridge	03.02.42	JNRS	Arsenal	02.59	1959-64	83		0	(CH)S.SCH.INT.
			TR	Charlton Ath.	03.65	1964-65	18	2	0	
			TR	Orient	07.66	1966-67	26	1	3	
			L	Halifax T.	11.67	1967	5	/	0	
SNEDDON, Tom	Livingstone	26.08.12	Q.of South	Rochdale	*	1946	2		0	(FB)
SNEDDON, William C.	Wishaw	01.04.14	Brentford(*)	Swansea C.	07.46	1946	2		0	(WH)*Falkirk
			TR	Newport Co.	10.46	1946	18		0	
SNELL, Albert E.	Dunscroft	07.02.31		Sunderland	08.49	1952-54	9		1	(WH)
			TR	Halifax T.	11.55	1955-56	25		0	
SNELL, Vic D.	Samford	29.10.27		Ipswich T.	+	1949-58	64		2	(FB)
SNODIN, Glyn	Rotherham	14.02.60	APP	Doncaster Rov.	10.77	1976-83	245	21	43	(M) Brother of Ian
SNODIN, Ian	Rotherham	15.08.63	APP	Doncaster Rov.	08.80	1979-83	140	7	17	(M)E.YTH.INT.
SNOOKES, Eric	Birmingham	06.03.55	APP	Preston N.E.	03.73	1972-73	20	/	0	(D)
			TR	Crewe Alex.	07.74	1974	33	1	0	
			TR	Southport	07.75	1975-77	106	4	2	
			TR	Rochdale	07.78	1978-82	183	/	1	
			TR	Bolton W.	07.83	1983	6	/	0	
SNOW, Simon G.	Sheffield	03.04.66	APP	Scunthorpe U.	N/C	1982-83	1	1	0	
SNOWBALL, Ray	Sunderland	10.03.32	Crook T.	Darlington	AM	1964-66	13	/	0	(G)

Players Names	Birthplace	Date	Previous Club	League Club	Date Signed	Seasons Played	Career Record Apps	Sub	Gls	
SNOWDON, Brian V.	B.Auckland	01.01.35		Blackpool	09.52	1955-59	18		1	(CH)
			TR	Portsmouth	10.59	1959-63	114		0	
			TR	Millwall	10.63	1963-66	128	/	0	
			Detroit Cougars	Crystal Palace	02.69	1968	1	4	0	
SODEN, Walter J.	Birmingham	22.01.21	Boldmere St.M.	Coventry C.	03.48	1947-48	2		0	
SOLAN, Ken	Middlesbrough	13.10.48		Middlesbrough	11.66					(F)d.
			L	Hartlepool U.	10.68	1968	5	/	1	
			L	Darlington	03.69	1968	8	/	1	
SOMERFIELD, Alf	Sth.Kirkby	22.03.18	Mansfield T.(*)	Wolverhampton W.	*					(OR)*Frickley Col.
			TR	Wrexham	06.47	1946	2		1	
			TR	Crystal Palace	09.47	1947	10		3	
SOMERS, Mick	Nottingham	27.02.45	Nottingham F.(AM)	Chelsea	11.62					(W)
			TR	Torquay U.	05.64	1964-65	40	1	3	
			TR	Hartlepool U.	07.66	1966-68	64	3	3	
SOO, Frank	Buxton	08.03.14	Stoke C.(*)	Leicester C.	+					(WH)*Prescot Cables
			TR	Luton T.	07.46	1946-47	71		4	
SORRELL, Dennis	Lambeth	07.10.40	JNRS	Orient	10.57	1958-60	37		1	(WH)
			TR	Chelsea	02.62	1961-63	3		0	
			TR	Orient	09.64	1964-66	74	/	3	
SOUNESS, Graeme J.	Edinburgh	06.05.53	APP	Tottenham H.	05.70					(M) S-40/S.U23-2/●
			TR	Middlesbrough	01.73	1972-77	174	2	22	S.SCH.INT.
			TR	Liverpool	01.78	1977-83	246	1	38	
SOUTAR, Tim J.	Oxford	25.02.46	JNRS	Brentford	07.63	1963	1		0	(F)
SOUTAR, William	Dundee	03.05.31		Burnley	12.53					(FB)
			TR	Chester C.	06.57	1957-59	51		1	
SOUTER, Don D.	Hammersmith	01.12.61	APP	Ipswich T.	01.79					(D)
			TR	Barnsley	08.82	1982	19	2	0	
			TR	Aldershot	08.83	1983	39	/	0	
SOUTH, Alex	Brighton	07.07.31	JNRS	Brighton & H.A.	03.49	1949-54	79		4	(CH)
			TR	Liverpool	12.54	1954	6		1	
			TR	Halifax T.	10.56	1956-64	302		12	
SOUTH, John A.	Bow	30.11.52	Orient(AM)	Colchester U.	07.72	1972	4	/	0	(CH)
SOUTH, John E.	London	08.04.48	Fulham(APP)	Brentford	11.66	1966	1	/	0	(CF)
SOUTH, William A.	Brighton	24.02.28	JNRS	Brighton & H.A.	08.51	1951	2		0	(HB)
SOUTHALL, Neville	Llandudno	16.09.58	Winsford U.	Bury	06.80	1980	39	/	0	(G)W-14
			TR	Everton	07.81	1981-83	78	/	0	
			L	Port Vale	01.83	1982	9	/	0	
SOUTHALL, Robert	Rotherham	10.05.22		Chesterfield	+	1947-52	126		11	(WH)
SOUTHAM, Jim H.	Willenhall	19.08.17	Shornhill Rec.	W.B.A.	+					(FB)
			TR	Newport Co.	05.46	1946	8		0	
			TR	Birmingham C.	11.46	1947	1		0	
			TR	Northampton T.	06.49	1949-54	144		1	
SOUTHEY, Peter C.	Putney	04.01.62	APP	Tottenham H.	10.79	1979	1	/	0	(D) d. 1983
SOUTHREN, Tommy	Sunderland	01.08.27	Peartree O.B.	West Ham U.	12.49	1950-53	64		3	(W)
			TR	Aston Villa	12.54	1954-58	63		7	
			TR	Bournemouth	10.58	1958-59	64		11	
SOUTHWELL, Aubrey A.	Grantham	21.08.21	Nottingham F.(AM)	Notts.Co.	+	1946-56	327		2	(FB)
SOWDEN, Maurice	Doncaster	21.10.54	APP	Scunthorpe U.	10.72	1972	3	/	0	(IF)
SOWDEN, Peter T.	Bradford	01.05.29	JNRS	Blackpool	06.47					(F)
			Bacup	Hull C.	09.48					
			TR	Aldershot	10.50	1950	4		0	
			TR	Hull C.	08.51					
			TR	Gillingham	08.52	1952-55	131		27	
			TR	Accrington St.	09.56	1956-57	54		13	
			TR	Wrexham	06.58	1958-59	38		4	
SOWDEN, William	Manchester	08.12.30		Manchester C.	04.49	1952-53	11		2	(CF)
			TR	Chesterfield	11.54	1954-56	97		59	
			TR	Stockport Co.	06.57	1957	15		7	
SOWERBY, William H.R.	Hull	31.08.32	Pilkington Rec.	Wolverhampton W.	05.50					(CF)
				Grimsby T.	01.54	1953-54	12		1	
SPACKMAN, Nigel J.	Romsey	02.12.60	Andover T.	Bournemouth	05.80	1980-82	118	1	10	(M)
			TR	Chelsea	06.83	1983	40	/	3	
SPALDING, William	Glasgow	24.11.26	Ballymena	Bristol C.	01.50	1949-50	10		0	(F)
SPARK, Alex	Stenhousemuir	16.10.49	JNRS	Preston N.E.	11.66	1967-75	207	18	6	(M)
			Motherwell	Bradford C.	12.76	1976-77	32	2	0	
SPARKS, Chris J.	Islington	22.05.60	APP	Crystal Palace	11.77					(D)
			L	Reading	08.79	1979	3	/	0	
SPARROW, Brian E.	London	24.06.62	APP	Arsenal	02.80	1983	2	/	0	(D)
			L	Wimbledon	01.83	1982	17	/	1	
			L	Millwall	12.83	1983	5		2	
			L	Gillingham	01.84	1983	5		1	

Players Names	Birthplace	Date	Previous Club	League Club	Date Signed	Seasons Played	Apps	Sub	Gls	
SPARROW, John P.	Bethnal Green	03.06.57	APP	Chelsea	08.74	1973-79	63	6	2	(D) E.YTH.INT./E.SCH.INT.
			L	Millwall	03.79	1978	7	/	0	
			TR	Exeter C.	01.81	1980-82	62	1	3	
SPAVIN, Alan	Lancaster	20.02.42	JNRS	Preston N.E.	08.59	1960-73	411	6	26	(M)
			Washington Dips	Preston & N.E.	11.77	1977-78	3	4	0	
SPEAKMAN, Sam	Huyton	27.01.34		Bolton W.	09.51					(OL)
			TR	Middlesbrough	07.53					
			TR	Tranmere Rov.	09.54	1954-55	68		9	
SPEARING, Anthony	Romford	07.10.64	APP	Norwich C.	10.82	1983	4	/	0	(D)
SPEARRITT, Eddie	Lowestoft	31.01.47	APP	Ipswich T.	02.65	1965-68	62	10	13	(M)
			TR	Brighton & H.A.	01.69	1968-73	203	7	22	
			TR	Carlisle U.	06.74	1974-75	29	2	1	
			TR	Gillingham	08.76	1976	19	/	1	
SPEARS, Alan F.	Amble	27.12.38	JNRS	Newcastle U.	02.56					(F)E.SCH.INT.
			TR	Millwall	06.60	1960-62	31		5	
			TR	Lincoln C.	07.63	1963	2		0	
SPECTOR, Miles D.	Hendon	04.08.34	JNRS	Chelsea	AM	1952-53	3		0	(OL)E.YTH.INT./
			Hendon	Millwall	AM	1956	1		0	E.AMAT.INT.
SPEDDING, Tom W.	Tynemouth	08.12.25		Doncaster Rov.	03.49	1948	1		0	
SPEED, Les	Wrexham	03.10.23	Llandudno	Wrexham	+	1946-54	211		0	(FB)
SPEEDIE, David R.	Glenrothes	20.02.60	JNRS	Barnsley	10.78	1978-79	10	13	0	(F)
			TR	Darlington	06.80	1980-81	88	/	21	
			TR	Chelsea	06.82	1982-83	66	5	20	
SPEIGHT, Mick	Upton	01.11.51	APP	Sheffield U.	05.69	1971-79	184	15	14	(M)
			TR	Blackburn Rov.	07.80	1980-81	50	1	4	
			TR	Grimsby T.	08.82	1982-83	35	3	2	
SPELMAN, Isaac	Newcastle	09.03.14	Tottenham H.(*)	Hartlepool U.	05.46	1946	26		0	(WH)*Southend U.
SPELMAN, Mike	Newcastle	08.12.50	Whitley Bay	Wolverhampton W.	11.69					(M) Son of Isaac
			TR	Watford	08.71					
			TR	Hartlepool U.	10.71	1971-76	115	6	4	
			L	Darlington	12.72	1972	4	/	0	
SPELMAN, Ron E.	Blofield	22.05.38	CNOSBU	Norwich C.	08.56	1957-60	2		0	(OR)
			TR	Northampton T.	11.60	1960-61	33		3	
			TR	Bournemouth	03.62	1961-63	28		4	
			TR	Watford	09.63	1963-64	40		3	
			TR	Oxford U.	05.65	1965	15	1	1	
SPENCE, Alan N.	Seaham	07.02.40		Sunderland	09.58	1957	5		1	(IF)E.YTH.INT.
			TR	Darlington	06.60	1960-61	24		10	
			TR	Southport	07.62	1962-68	225	5	98	
			TR	Oldham Ath.	12.68	1968-69	26	1	12	
			TR	Chester C.	12.69	1969	5	2	2	
SPENCE, Colin	Partick	07.01.60	APP	Crewe Alex.	N/C	1976-78	10	8	1	(F)
SPENCE, Derek W.	Belfast	18.01.52	Crusaders	Oldham Ath.	09.70	1971-72	5	1	0	(F) NI-29
			TR	Bury	02.73	1972-76	140	/	44	
			TR	Blackpool	10.76	1976	24	3	2	
			Olympiakos	Blackpool	08.78	1978-79	58	/	18	
			TR	Southend U.	12.79	1979-81	100	4	32	
			TR	Bury	08.83	1983	9	4	1	
SPENCE, Joe L.	Salford	13.10.25		Chesterfield	01.48					(HB)
			TR	York C.	07.50	1950-53	112		0	
SPENCE, Richard	Barnsley	18.07.08	Barnsley(*)	Chelsea	*	1946-47	39		7	(OR)*Thorpe Col./E-2
SPENCE, Ron	Tudhoe	07.01.27	Rossington	York C.	03.48	1947-58	281		25	(WH)
SPENCE, William J.	Hartlepool	10.01.26		Portsmouth	03.47	1949-50	19		0	(CH)
			TR	Q.P.R.	12.51	1951-53	56		0	
SPENCER, Derek	Coventry	10.01.31	Lockheed A.P.	Coventry Co.	12.51	1951-52	20		0	(G)
SPENCER, Harry	Burnley	30.04.19	JNRS	Burnley	*	1946-48	5		1	(HB)
			TR	Wrexham	07.50	1950	11		0	
SPENCER, John R.	Bradfield	20.11.34	JNRS	Sheffield U.	06.54	1954-56	24		10	(F)E.YTH.INT.
SPENCER, John S.	Bacup	24.08.20		Burnley	06.48	1949-50	36		8	(WH)
			TR	Accrington St.	06.51	1951	29		7	
SPENCER, Les	Manchester	16.09.36		Rochdale	01.58	1957-59	73		16	(F)
			TR	Luton T.	07.60	1960	7		1	
SPENCER, Ray	Birmingham	25.05.33	JNRS	Aston Villa	06.50					(CF)E.SCH.INT.
			TR	Darlington	03.58	1957-60	98		5	
			TR	Torquay U.	06.61	1961-63	59		1	
SPENCER, Tom H.	Glasgow	28.11.45	Glasgow Celtic	Southampton	07.65	1965	3	/	0	(D)
			TR	York C.	06.66	1966-67	54	3	20	
			TR	Workington	03.68	1967-71	167	/	10	
			TR	Lincoln C.	01.72	1971-73	67	7	10	
			TR	Rotherham U.	07.74	1974-77	137	1	10	
SPENCER, Tony R.	Chiswick	23.04.65	APP	Brentford	04.83	1981-83	17	1	0	(D)
SPERRIN, Martyn R.	Edmonton	06.12.56	Edgware T.	Luton T.	10.77	1977	0	1	0	(F)
SPERRIN, William T.	Wood Green	09.04.22	Finchley	Brentford	09.49	1949-55	90		28	(IF)

Players Names	Birthplace	Date	Previous Club	League Club	Date Signed	Seasons Played	Career Record Apps	Sub	Gls	
SPERRING, George B.	Epsom	30.04.35		Gillingham	AM	1955	1		0	(CF)
SPERTI, Franco	Italy	28.01.55	APP	Swindon T.	01.73	1973	1	/	0	(FB)
SPICER, Eddie	Liverpool	20.09.22	JNRS	Liverpool	+	1946-53	158		1	(FB)E.SCH.INT.
SPIERS, George	Belfast	03.09.41	Crusaders	Exeter C.	08.63	1963	5		0	(OL)
SPIERS, Richard A.	Benson	27.11.37	Chertsey	Reading	10.55	1955-69	451	1	3	(CH)●
SPINK, Antrhony A.	Doncaster	16.11.29		Sheffield Wed.	12.49					(F)
			TR	Chester C.	06.50	1951-52	14		3	
			TR	Workington	07.55					
			TR	Sunderland	12.55					
			TR	Tranmere Rov.	06.56	1956	7		3	
SPINK, Nigel P.	Chelmsford	08.08.58	Chelmsford C.	Aston Villa	01.77	1979-83	51	/	0	(G)E-1
SPINKS, Henry	Gt.Yarmouth	01.02.20	CEYMS	Norwich C.	AM	1946	2		1	(CF)
SPINNER, Terry J.	Woking	06.11.53	APP	Southampton	07.71	1972-73	1	1	0	(F)
			TR	Walsall	07.74	1974-75	10	6	5	
SPIRING, Peter	Glastonbury	13.12.50	JNRS	Bristol C.	06.68	1969-72	56	5	16	(M) E.YTH.INT.
			TR	Liverpool	03.73					
			TR	Luton T.	11.74	1974-75	12	3	2	
			TR	Hereford U.	02.76	1975-82	205	22	20	
SPITTLE, Paul D.	Wolverhampton	16.12.64	APP	Oxford U.	10.82					(M)
			TR	Crewe Alex.	08.83	1983	4	2	1	
SPOONER, Steve A.	London	25.01.61	APP	Derby Co.	12.78	1978-81	7	1	0	(M)
			TR	Halifax T.	12.81	1981-82	71	1	13	
			TR	Chesterfield	07.83	1983	20	/	3	
SPRAGGON, Frank	Marley Hill	27.10.45	APP	Middlesbrough	11.62	1963-75	277	3	3	(D)
			Minnesota Kicks	Hartlepool U.	11.76	1976	1	/	0	
SPRAGUE, Martyn	Risca	10.04.49	Lovells Ath.	Newport Co.	08.69	1969-73	155	1	1	(FB)
SPRAKE, Gary	Swansea	03.04.45	APP	Leeds U.	05.62	1961-72	381	/	0	(G)W-37/W.U23-5●
			TR	Birmingham C.	10.73	1973-74	16	/	0	
SPRATLEY, Alan S.	Maidenhead	05.06.49	APP	Q.P.R.	09.68	1968-72	29	1	0	(G)
			TR	Swindon T.	07.73	1973	7	/	0	
SPRATT, Graham	Leicester	17.07.39	JNRS	Coventry C.	12.56	1957-58	28		0	(G)
SPRATT, Tommy	Cambois	20.12.41	JNRS	Manchester U.	12.59					(IF)
			TR	Bradford P.A.	02.61	1960-63	118		45	E.YTH.INT./E.SCH.INT.
			TR	Torquay U.	07.65	1965-66	60	1	19	
			TR	Workington	01.67	1966-67	51	/	14	
			TR	York C.	03.68	1967-68	26	3	1	
			TR	Workington	03.69	1968-71	142	2	27	
			TR	Stockport Co.	06.72	1972-73	65	1	6	
SPRIDGEON, Fred A.	Swansea	13.07.35	JNRS	Leeds U.	08.52					(FB)
			TR	Crewe Alex.	07.56	1956	7		0	
SPRIGGS, Steve	Doncaster	16.02.56	APP	Huddersfield T.	02.73	1974	2	2	0	(M)
			TR	Cambridge U.	07.75	1975-83	319	5	46	
SPRING, Andy J.	Gateshead	17.11.65	APP	Coventry C.	11.83	1983	0	1	0	(F)
SPRINGETT, Peter J.	Fulham	08.05.46	APP	Q.P.R.	05.63	1962-66	139	/	0	(G) E.U23-6/E.YTH.INT.●
			TR	Sheffield Wed.	05.67	1967-74	180	/	0	
			TR	Barnsley	07.75	1975-79	191	/	0	
SPRINGETT, Ron D.	Fulham	22.07.37	Victoria U.	Q.P.R.	02.53	1955-57	89	/	0	(G)E-33/E.F.LGE REP.●
			TR	Sheffield Wed.	03.58	1957-66	345	/	0	
			TR	Q.P.R.	06.67	1967-68	45	/	0	
SPRINGTHORPE, Terry A.	Draycott	04.12.23	JNRS	Wolverhampton W.	+	1947-49	35		0	(FB)
			TR	Coventry C.	12.50	1950	12		0	
SPROATES, Alan	Hetton	30.06.44	JNRS	Sunderland	07.61					(IF)Brother of John
			TR	Swindon T.	08.63	1963-64	3		0	
			TR	Darlington	09.65	1965-73	305	11	17	
			TR	Scunthorpe U.	08.74	1974	19	5	0	
SPROATES, John	Houghton-le-Spring	11.04.43	W.Auckland	Barnsley	12.63	1963	2		0	
SPROSON, Phil J.	Trent Vale	13.10.59	JNRS	Port Vale	12.77	1977-83	226	4	16	(D) Nephew of Roy
SPROSON, Roy	Stoke	23.09.30	Stoke C.(AM)	Port Vale	07.49	1950-71	756	5	29	(FB)Uncle of Phil●
SPROSTON, Bert	Ellworth	22.06.15	Tottenham H.(*)	Manchester C.	*	1946-49	105		3	(FB)*Sandbach/Leeds U/E-11/E.F.LGE REP.
SPRUCE, George D.	Chester	03.04.23		Wrexham	10.48	1948-51	135		3	(CH)
			TR	Barnsley	05.52	1952-56	149		0	
			TR	Chester C.	07.58	1958-60	63		0	
SPRUCE, Phil T.	Chester	16.11.29		Wrexham	11.50	1951-55	23		0	(FB)
SPUHLER, John O.	Sunderland	18.09.17	Sunderland(*)	Middlesbrough	+	1946-53	216		69	(CF)
			TR	Darlington	06.54	1954-55	67		19	E.SCH.INT.
SPURDLE, William	Channel Islands	28.01.26	JNRS	Oldham Ath.	03.48	1947-49	56		5	(WH)
			TR	Manchester C.	01.50	1949-56	160		32	
			TR	Port Vale	11.56	1956	21		7	
			TR	Oldham Ath.	06.57	1957-62	144		19	

Players Names	Birthplace	Date	Previous Club	League Club	Date Signed	Seasons Played	Apps	Sub	Gls	
SQUIRE, Mike R.	Poole	18.10.63		Fulham	07.82					(F)
			Dorchester	Torquay U.	03.84	1983	12	1	3	
SQUIRES, Alan	Fleetwood	26.02.23		Preston N.E.	+					(LB)
			TR	Carlisle U.	12.46	1946-47	25		0	
SQUIRES, Barry	Birmingham	29.07.31	Wycombe W.	Birmingham C.	05.53	1953	1		0	(OL)
			TR	Bradford C.	06.54	1954	7		0	
SQUIRES, Frank	Swansea	08.03.21	JNRS	Swansea C.	*	1946-47	36		5	(IF)
			TR	Plymouth Arg.	10.47	1947-49	86		13	
			TR	Grimsby T.	07.50	1950	36		2	
SQUIRES, Robert	Selby	06.04.19	Selby T.	Doncaster Rov.	*	1947	21		0	(WH)
			TR	Exeter C.	07.49	1949	1		0	
STABB, George H.	Paignton	26.09.12	Port Vale(*)	Bradford P.A.	*	1946	2		1	(CF)*Torquay U.
STACEY, Steve D.	Bristol	27.08.44	APP	Bristol C.	11.61					(FB)
			TR	Wrexham	02.66	1965-68	101	3	6	
			TR	Ipswich T.	09.68	1968	3	/	0	
			L	Chester C.	12.69	1969	1	/	0	
			L	Charlton Ath.	01.70	1969	1	/	1	
			TR	Bristol C.	09.70	1970	9	/	0	
			TR	Exeter C.	07.71	1971-72	57	2	0	
STACEY, Terry J.	Mitcham	28.09.36	Carshalton	Plymouth Arg.	05.59	1959-61	22		0	(FB)E.AMAT.INT.
			TR	Watford	07.62					
			TR	Gillingham	08.63	1963-64	17		0	
STACK, William J.	Liverpool	17.01.48	JNRS	Crystal Palace	01.65	1965	2	/	0	(F)
STAFF, Paul	Hartlepool	30.08.62	APP	Hartlepool U.	09.80	1979-83	88	10	12	(F)
STAFFORD, Andy	Littleborough	28.10.60	Blackburn Rov.(N/C)	Halifax T.	01.79	1978-80	33	8	1	(F)
			TR	Stockport Co.	08.81	1981	21	4	1	
			TR	Rochdale	08.82	1982	1	/	1	
STAFFORD, Ellis	Sheffield	17.08.29	Scarborough	Peterborough U.	N/L	1960-62	17		0	(FB)
STAGG, William	Ealing	17.10.57	APP	Brentford	APP	1974	4	/	0	(IF)
STAINROD, Simon A.	Sheffield	01.02.59	APP	Sheffield U.	07.76	1975-78	59	8	14	(F) E.YTH.INT.
			TR	Oldham Ath.	03.79	1978-80	69	/	21	
			TR	Q.P.R.	11.80	1980-83	124	2	43	
STAINSBY, John	Stairfoot	25.09.37	Wolverhampton W.(AM)	Barnsley	12.55	1959-60	34		12	(CF)
			TR	York C.	07.61	1961-62	69		21	
			TR	Stockport Co.	07.63	1963	5		0	
STAINTON, Bryan E.	Slampton	08.01.42	Ingham	Lincoln C.	03.62	1961-64	25		0	(FB)
STAINTON, Jim K.	Sheffield	14.12.31		Bradford P.A.	04.53					(FB)
			TR	Mansfield T.	08.54	1955-56	9		0	
STAINWRIGHT, David P.	Nottingham	13.06.48	APP	Nottingham F.	08.65	1965-66	4	3	1	(F)
			TR	Doncaster Rov.	07.68	1968	1	/	0	
			TR	York C.	07.69	1969	6	1	1	
STALKER, Alan	Ponteland	18.03.39	B.Auckland	Gateshead	AM	1958	4		0	(G)
STALKER, John A.H.	Musselburgh	12.03.59		Leicester C.	07.79					(F)
			TR	Darlington	10.79	1979-82	107	9	36	
			TR	Hartlepool U.	01.83	1982	3	1	0	
STAMPER, Frank S.	W.Hartlepool	22.02.26	Colchester U.	Hartlepool U.	08.49	1949-57	301		25	(WH)
STAMPS, Jack D.	Maltby	02.12.18	New Brighton(*)	Derby Co.	*	1946-53	225		97	(CF)*Mansfield T.
			TR	Shrewsbury T.	12.53	1953	22		4	
STANBRIDGE, George	Campsall	28.03.20		Rotherham U.	*	1946-48	36		1	
			TR	Aldershot	06.49	1949	15		0	
STANCLIFFE, Paul I.	Sheffield	05.05.58	APP	Rotherham U.	03.76	1975-82	285	/	8	(D)
			TR	Sheffield U.	08.83	1983	43	/	1	
STANDEN, Jim A.	Edmonton	30.05.35	Rickmansworth	Arsenal	04.53	1957-60	35		0	(G)Worc.Cricketer
			TR	Luton T.	10.60	1960-62	36		0	
			TR	West Ham U.	11.62	1962-67	178	/	0	
			Detroit Cougars	Millwall	10.68	1968-69	8	/	0	
			TR	Portsmouth	07.70	1970-71	13	/	0	
STANDING, John	Walberton	03.09.43	Bognor	Brighton & H.A.	12.61	1961-62	10		0	(FB)
STANDLEY, Tom L.	Poplar	23.12.32	Basildon	Q.P.R.	05.57	1957	14		2	(WH)
			TR	Bournemouth	11.58	1958-64	159		5	
STANIFORTH, David A.	Chesterfield	06.10.50	APP	Sheffield U.	05.68	1968-73	22	4	3	(F)
			TR	Bristol Rov.	03.74	1973-78	135	18	31	
			TR	Bradford C.	06.79	1979-81	107	8	25	
			TR	Halifax T.	07.82	1982-83	66	3	21	
STANIFORTH, Gordon	Hull	23.03.57	APP	Hull C.	04.74	1973-76	7	5	2	(F) E.SCH.INT.
			TR	York C.	12.76	1976-79	128	/	33	
			TR	Carlisle U.	10.79	1979-82	118	8	33	
			TR	Plymouth Arg.	03.83	1982-83	47	3	12	
STANIFORTH, Ron	Manchester	13.04.24	Newton A.	Stockport Co.	10.46	1946-51	223		1	(FB)E-8/E'B'-3
			TR	Huddersfield T.	05.52	1952-54	110		0	
			TR	Sheffield Wed.	07.55	1955-58	102		2	
			TR	Barrow	10.59	1959-60	38		0	

Players Names	Birthplace	Date	Previous Club	League Club	Date Signed	Seasons Played	Apps	Sub	Gls	
STANLEY, Gary E.	Burton	04.03.54	APP	Chelsea	04.73	1975-78	105	4	15	(M)
			TR	Everton	08.79	1979-80	52	/	1	
			TR	Swansea	10.81	1981-83	60	12	4	
			TR	Portsmouth	01.84	1983	11	1	0	
STANLEY, Graham	Tinsley	27.01.38	JNRS	Bolton W.	10.55	1956-63	141		3	(WH)
			TR	Tranmere Rov.	07.65	1965	0	1	1	
STANLEY, Pat J.	Dublin	09.03.38	JNRS	Leeds U.	03.55					(HB)
			TR	Halifax T.	05.58	1958-62	119		1	
STANLEY, Terry J.	Brighton	02.01.51	Lewes U.	Brighton & H.A.	11.69	1969-70	16	6	0	(IR)
STANLEY, Tom	Hemsworth	07.12.62	APP	York C.	12.80	1980-82	14	4	0	(M)
STANNARD, James	London	06.10.62		Fulham	06.80	1980-83	34	/	0	(G)
STANNERS, Walter	Carriden	02.01.21	Bo'ness	Bournemouth	07.47	1947	3		0	(G)
			TR	Rochdale	08.49	1949	5		0	
STANSBRIDGE, Len E.	Southampton	19.02.19	JNRS	Southampton	*	1946-51	42		0	(G)
STANSFIELD, Fred	Cardiff	12.12.17	Grange A.	Cardiff C.	+	1946-48	106		1	(CH)W-1
			TR	Newport Co.	09.49	1949	21		0	
STANT, Philip	Bolton	13.10.62	Camberley	Reading	N/C	1982	3	1	2	(F)
STANTON, Brian	Liverpool	07.02.56	New Brighton	Bury	10.75	1976-78	72	11	14	(M)
			TR	Huddersfield T.	09.79	1979-83	189	4	43	
STANTON, Sidney H.	Dudley	16.06.23	Birmingham C.(+)	Northampton T.	07.46	1947-48	7		0	
STANTON, Tom	Glasgow	03.05.48	JNRS	Liverpool	05.65					(WH)S.SCH.INT.
			TR	Arsenal	09.66					
			TR	Mansfield T.	09.67	1967	37	/	1	
			TR	Bristol Rov.	07.68	1968-75	160	11	7	
STAPLES, Len E.	Leicester	23.01.26	JNRS	Leicester C.	07.47					(FB)E.SCH.INT.
			TR	Newport Co.	08.49	1949-56	164		2	
STAPLETON, Frank A.	Dublin	10.07.56	APP	Arsenal	09.73	1974-80	223	2	75	(F) EI-38●
			TR	Manchester U.	08.81	1981-83	124	/	40	
STAPLETON, Joe E.	London	27.06.28	Uxbridge T	Fulham	08.52	1954-59	96		2	(CH)
STARK, Roy	Nottingham	28.11.53	APP	Aston Villa	06.69	1973	2	/	0	(CH)
STARK, William R.	Glasgow	27.05.37	Glasgow Rgrs.	Crewe Alex.	08.60	1960-61	39		13	(W)
			TR	Carlisle U.	12.61	1961-62	35		17	
			TR	Colchester U.	11.62	1962-65	95	/	32	
			TR	Luton T.	09.65	1965	8	2	4	
			TR	Chesterfield	07.66	1966	31	1	16	
			TR	Newport Co.	07.67	1967	12	1	2	
STARKEY, Malcolm J.	Bulwell	25.01.36		Blackpool	08.54	1956-58	3		0	(IF)
			TR	Shrewsbury T.	06.59	1959-62	121		33	
			TR	Chester C.	04.63	1962-66	107	/	1	
STARLING, Alan W.	Barking	02.04.51	APP	Luton T.	04.69	1969-70	7	/	0	(G)
			L	Torquay U.	02.71	1970	1	/	0	
			TR	Northampton T.	06.71	1971-76	238	/	1	
			TR	Huddersfield T.	03.77	1976-79	112	/	0	
STARLING, Ron W.	Pelaw	11.10.09	Sheffield Wed.(*)	Aston Villa	*	1946	1		0	(IF)E-2/*Washington/ Hull C./Newcastle U.
STAROCSIK, Felix	Poland	20.05.20	T.Lanark	Northampton T.	07.51	1951-54	49		19	(W)
STATHAM, Derek	Wolverhampton	24.03.59	APP	W.B.A.	01.77	1976-83	224	1	4	(D)E.YTH.INT./E.U21-6/E-3
STATHAM, Terry	Shirebrook	11.03.40	JNRS	Mansfield T.	03.57	1956-59	27		0	(G)
STATON, Barry	Doncaster	09.09.38	JNRS	Doncaster Rov.	05.56	1955-61	85		0	(CH)E.YTH.INT./
			TR	Norwich C.	07.62	1962	23		1	E.SCH.INT.
STEAD, Kevin	West Ham U.	02.10.58	APP	Tottenham H.	04.76					(D)
			TR	Arsenal	07.77	1978	1	1	0	
STEAD, Mike J.	West Ham U.	28.02.57	APP	Tottenham H.	11.74	1975-77	14	1	0	(D) Brother of Kevin
			L	Swansea C.	02.77	1976	5	/	1	
			TR	Southend U.	09.78	1978-83	242	1	5	
STEEDMAN, Alex	Edinburgh	13.05.38		Barrow	09.64	1964	9	1		(CF)
STEANE, Nigel B.	Nottingham	18.01.63	APP	Sheffield U.	01.81	1979	0	1	0	(F)
STEBBING, Gary S.	Croydon	11.08.65	APP	Crystal Palace	08.83	1983	30	1	2	(M)
STEEDS, Cecil	Bristol	11.01.29	JNRS	Bristol C.	03.47	1949-51	9		0	(FB)
			TR	Bristol Rov.	05.52	1956	1		0	
STEEL, Alf	Glasgow	15.08.25	Petershill	Walsall	10.47	1948-49	2		0	(G)
			TR	Cardiff C.	01.50	1949	10		0	
STEEL, Barry	Felling	03.09.61	APP	Sheffield Wed.	09.79					(M)
			TR	Darlington	10.79	1980	7	2	0	
STEEL, Greg	Clevedon	11.03.59	Clevedon T.	Newport Co.	01.78	1977	3	/	0	(D)
STEEL, Richard	Ferryhill	13.03.30	Ferryhill Ath.	Bristol C.	06.53	1953-55	3		0	(FB)
			TR	York C.	07.56	1956-57	3		0	
STEEL, Ron	Newburn	03.06.29	B.Auckland	Darlington	01.50	1949-51	66		5	(WH)

Players Names	Birthplace	Date	Previous Club	League Club	Date Signed	Seasons Played	Apps	Sub	Gls	
STEEL, W. James	Dumfries	04.12.59	APP	Oldham Ath.	06.78	1978-82	101	7	24	(F)
			L	Wigan Ath.	11.82	1982	2	/	2	
			L	Wrexham	01.83	1982	9	/	6	
			TR	Port Vale	03.83	1982-83	27	1	6	
			TR	Wrexham	01.84	1983	21	/	0	
STEEL, William	Denny	01.05.23	Morton	Derby Co.	06.47	1947-49	104		27	(W)S-30/S.F.LGE REP.●
										d.1982
STEELE, Bennett J.	Seaton Delavel	05.08.39	Seaton Delavel	Everton	05.57					(F)
			TR	Chesterfield	05.58	1958	18		1	
			TR	Gateshead	08.59	1959	25		5	
STEELE, Eric G.	Newcastle	14.05.54	JNRS	Newcastle U.	07.72					(G)
			TR	Peterborough U.	12.73	1973-76	124	/	0	
			TR	Brighton & H.A.	02.77	1976-79	87	/	0	
			TR	Watford	10.79	1979-83	51	/	0	
			L	Cardiff C.	03.83	1982	7	/	0	
STEELE, Fred C.	Stoke	06.05.16	Downings	Stoke C.	*	1946-48	97		56	(IF)E-6/E.F.LGE REP./
			TR	Mansfield T.	06.49	1949-51	53		38	Uncle of David Steele
			TR	Port Vale	12.51	1951-52	25		12	(Cricketer)/d.1976
STEELE, Hedley	Barnsley	03.02.54		Exeter C.	07.74	1974	6	1	1	(FB)Son of pre-war player
STEELE, James	Edinburgh	11.03.50	Dundee	Southampton	01.72	1971-76	160	1	2	(D)
STEELE, John	Glasgow	24.11.16	Ayr U.	Barnsley	*	1946-48	9		4	(IL)
STEELE, Joseph M.	Blackridge	04.10.28	Bellshill	Newcastle U.	12.48					(OL)
			TR	Bury	05.50	1950	18		1	
			TR	Orient	08.51					
STEELE, Percy E.	Liverpool	26.12.23		Tranmere Rov.	+	1946-56	311		0	(FB)
STEELE, Simon P.	Liverpool	29.02.64	APP	Everton	03.82					(G)
			TR	Brighton & H.A.	06.83	1983	1	/	0	
			L	Blackpool	09.83	1983	3	/	0	
			TR	Scunthorpe U.	N/C	1983	5	/	0	
STEELE, Stan F.	Stoke	05.01.37	JNRS	Port Vale	05.55	1956-60	185		67	(IF)
			TR	W.B.A.	03.61	1960	1		0	
			TR	Port Vale	08.61	1961-64	148		23	
			South Africa	Port Vale	01.68	1967	2	/	0	
STEELE, William M.	Kirkmuirhill	16.06.55	APP	Norwich C.	06.73	1973-76	56	12	3	(M)
			L	Bournemouth	01.76	1975	7	/	2	
STEEN, Alan W.	Crewe	26.06.22	JNRS	Wolverhampton W.	*					(W)
			TR	Luton T.	05.46	1946	10		0	
			TR	Aldershot	06.49	1949	10		0	
			TR	Rochdale	06.50	1950-51	45		8	
			TR	Carlisle U.	12.51	1951	16		2	
STEEPLES, John	Doncaster	28.04.59	Pilkington Rec.	Grimsby T.	05.80	1980-81	4	3	0	(F)
			L	Torquay U.	09.82	1982	4	1	0	
STEFFEN, Willi	Switzerland	17.03.25	Switzerland	Chelsea	AM	1946	15		0	(FB)SWISS INT.
STEGGLES, Kevin P.	Ditchingham	19.03.61	APP	Ipswich T.	12.78	1980-83	38	/	1	(D)
			L	Southend U.	02.84	1983	3	/	0	
STEIN, Brian	S. Africa	19.10.57	Edgware T.	Luton T.	10.77	1977-83	237	10	83	(F)E.U'21-3/E-1
STEIN, Colin	Philipstoun	10.05.47	Glasgow Rgrs.	Coventry C.	10.72	1972-74	83	/	21	(CF)S-21/S.F.LGE
										REP./S.U23-1
STEIN, M. Eddie S.	S. Africa	29.01.66	JNRS	Luton T.	01.84	1983	1	/	0	(F)
STEINER, Geoff D.	Hackney	08.06.28		Watford	11.50	1951	3		0	(FB)
STELLING, Jack G.	Washington	23.05.24		Sunderland	+	1946-55	259		8	(FB)
STENHOUSE, Alec	Stirling	01.01.33	Dundee	Portsmouth	02.57	1956-57	4		1	(F)
			TR	Southend U.	11.58	1958-60	84		7	
STENNER, Arthur W.	Yeovil	07.01.34		Bristol C.	08.54					
			TR	Plymouth Arg.	08.55	1955	9		1	
			TR	Norwich C.	08.56	1956	6		0	
			TR	Exeter C.	12.56					
			TR	Oldham Ath.	04.57	1956	3		0	
STENSON, Gerard P.	Bootle	30.12.59	Everton(APP)	Port Vale	08.78	1978-79	11	1	0	(M)
STENSON, John A.	Catford	16.12.49	APP	Charlton Ath.	12.66	1967-68	3	6	0	(IR)E.YTH.INT./
			TR	Mansfield T.	06.69	1969-71	103	4	21	E.SCH.INT.
			L	Peterborough U.	01.72	1971	2	/	0	
			TR	Aldershot	07.72	1972-73	34	11	4	
STEPANOVIC, Dragoslav	Yugoslav	30.08.48	Wormatia	Manchester C.	08.79	1979-80	14	1	0	(M) YUGOSLAV. INT.
STEPHAN, Harold W.	Farnworth	24.02.24		Blackburn Rov.	+	1946-47	13		1	(IF)
			TR	Accrington St.	09.48					
STEPHEN, George A.	Ellon	21.09.27		Aldershot	08.48	1948	2		0	(FB)
STEPHEN, Jimmy W.	Fettercairn	23.08.22		Bradford P.A.	+	1946-48	94		1	(FB)S-2
			TR	Portsmouth	11.49	1949-53	99		0	
STEPHENS, Alan	Liverpool	13.10.52	APP	Wolverhampton W.	10.70					(FB)
			TR	Crewe Alex.	07.72	1972-73	30	3	0	

Players Names	Birthplace	Date	Previous Club	League Club	Date Signed	Seasons Played	Apps	Sub	Gls	
STEPHENS, Alf	Cramlington	13.06.19	E.Cramlington BW	Leeds U.	*					
			TR	Swindon T.	08.46	1946-47	16		2	
STEPHENS, Arnold E.	Ross-on-Wye	31.01.28	JNRS	Wolverhampton W.	+					d.1955
			Q.of South	Wolverhampton W.	07.48					
			TR	Bournemouth	12.48	1948-53	70		12	
STEPHENS, Arthur	Liverpool	19.05.54	Melksham	Bristol Rov.	08.81	1981-83	78	25	30	(F)
STEPHENS, Herbert J.	London	13.05.09	Brentford(*)	Brighton & H.A.	*	1946-47	22		4	(OL)*Ealing Ass'n
STEPHENS, John W.	Cramlington	13.06.19	E.Cramlington BW	Leeds U.	*					(CF)d.1974/
			TR	Swindon T.	07.46	1946-47	47		25	Brother of Alf (twin)
			TR	West Ham U.	12.47	1947-48	22		6	
			TR	Cardiff C.	11.50					
STEPHENS, Ken J.	Bristol	14.11.46	APP	W.B.A.	11.64	1966-67	21	1	2	(W)
			TR	Walsall	12.68	1968-69	5	2	0	
			TR	Bristol Rov.	10.70	1970-77	215	10	13	
			TR	Hereford U.	10.77	1977-79	56	4	2	
STEPHENS, Kirk W.	Coventry	27.02.55	Nuneaton Bor.	Luton T.	06.78	1978-83	226	1	2	(D)
STEPHENS, Malcolm K.	Doncaster	17.02.30		Brighton & H.A.	07.55	1954-56	29		14	(IF)
			TR	Rotherham U.	07.57	1957	12		3	
			TR	Doncaster Rov.	07.58	1958	11		2	
STEPHENS, Terry G.	Birkenhead	05.11.35		Tranmere Rov.	08.55	1955-56	15		5	(F)
STEPHENS, William J.	Cardiff	26.06.35	JNRS	Hull C.	08.53	1952-57	94		20	(OR)W.U23-1
			TR	Swindon T.	06.58	1958-59	18		2	
			TR	Coventry C.	02.60	1959	14		0	
STEPHENSON, Alan	Cheshunt	26.09.44	JNRS	Crystal Palace	02.62	1961-67	170	/	13	(CH)E.U23-7
			TR	West Ham U.	03.68	1967-71	106	2	0	
			L	Fulham	10.71	1971	10	/	0	
			TR	Portsmouth	05.72	1972-74	98	/	0	
STEPHENSON, George R.	Derby	19.11.42	JNRS	Derby Co.	09.60	1961-62	11		1	(F)Derby/Hants Cricketer/
			TR	Shrewsbury T.	06.64	1964	3		0	Son of pre-war international
			TR	Rochdale	07.65	1965-66	48	2	16	
STEPHENSON, Len R.	Blackpool	14.07.30	Highfield YC	Blackpool	11.48	1950-54	24		10	(CF)
			TR	Port Vale	03.55	1954-56	62		16	
			TR	Oldham Ath.	06.57	1957	8		0	
STEPHENSON, Peter	Ashington	02.05.36		Middlesbrough	08.55					
			Ashington	Gateshead	09.59	1959	35		6	
STEPHENSON, Ron	Barrow	13.04.48	APP	Barrow	05.66	1966-67	2	/	3	(HB)
STEPHENSON, Roy A.	Crook	27.05.32	JNRS	Burnley	06.49	1949-55	77		27	(OR)
			TR	Rotherham U.	09.56	1956-57	43		14	
			TR	Blackburn Rov.	11.57	1957-58	21		5	
			TR	Leicester C.	03.59	1958-59	12		0	
			TR	Ipswich T.	07.60	1960-64	144		20	
STEPNEY, Alex C.	Mitcham	18.09.44	Tooting & Mitcham	Millwall	05.63	1963-65	137	/	0	(G)E-1/E.U23-3/●
			TR	Chelsea	05.66	1966	1	/	0	E.F.LGE.REP.
			TR	Manchester U.	09.66	1966-77	433	/	2	
STEPNEY, Robin E.	Horsham	26.02.36	Redhill	Aldershot	09.58	1958-64	213		35	(WH)
STERLAND, Mel	Sheffield	01.10.61	APP	Sheffield Wed.	10.79	1978-83	123	4	11	(M)E.U'21-7
STERLING, Worrell R.	Bethnal Green	08.06.65	APP	Watford	06.83	1982-83	9	4	1	(F)
STEVEN, Trevor M.	Berwick	21.09.63	APP	Burnley	09.81	1980-82	74	2	11	(M)
			TR	Everton	07.83	1983	23	4	1	
STEVENS, Arthur H.	Battersea	13.01.21	Wimbledon	Fulham	+	1946-58	384		110	(OR)
STEVENS, Brian	Andover	13.11.33	Andover O.B.	Southampton	09.56	1956-57	12		0	(G)
STEVENS, Dennis	Dudley	30.11.33	JNRS	Bolton W.	12.50	1953-61	273		90	(IF)E.U23-2/E.F.
			TR	Everton	03.62	1961-65	120	/	20	LGE REP.
			TR	Oldham Ath.	12.65	1965-66	32	/	0	
			TR	Tranmere Rov.	03.67	1966-67	28	3	3	
STEVENS, Gary A.	Hillingdon	30.03.62	APP	Brighton & H.A.	10.79	1979-82	120	13	2	(D)E.U'21-7
			TR	Tottenham H.	06.83	1983	37	3	4	
STEVENS, Gary M.	Birmingham	30.08.54	Evesham	Cardiff C.	09.78	1978-83	138	12	44	(F)
			TR	Shrewsbury T.	09.82	1982-83	67	6	6	
STEVENS, Gregor	Glasgow	13.01.55	Motherwell	Leicester C.	05.79	1979	4	/	0	(D) S.U21-1
STEVENS, John M.	Forest	21.08.41		Swindon T.	10.63	1962-63	22		10	(F)
STEVENS, Keith H.	Merton	21.06.64	APP	Millwall	06.81	1980-83	50	1	0	(D)
STEVENS, Les W.J.	Croydon	15.08.20	JNRS	Tottenham H.	+	1946-48	54		5	(IF)
			TR	Bradford P.A.	02.49	1948-49	44		4	
			TR	Crystal Palace	08.50	1950	20		2	
STEVENS, M. Gary	Barrow	27.03.63	APP	Everton	04.81	1981-83	73	1	2	(D)E.U'21-1
STEVENS, Mark A.	Bristol	31.01.63	APP	Bristol C.	02.81					(G)
			TR	Swindon T.	06.81	1982	1	/	0	
STEVENS, Norman	Shoreham	13.05.38	JNRS	Brighton & H.A.	10.55	1958	1		0	(FB)
STEVENS, Paul D.	Bristol	04.04.60	APP	Bristol C.	04.78	1977-83	116	1	3	(D)
STEVENS, Sam B.	Rutherglen	02.12.35	Airdrie	Southampton		1958	14		0	(HB)

Players Names	Birthplace	Date	Previous Club	League Club	Date Signed	Seasons Played	Apps	Sub	Gls	
STEVENSON, Alan	Staveley	06.11.50	JNRS	Chesterfield	10.69	1969-71	104	/	0	(G) E.U23-11●
			TR	Burnley	01.72	1971-82	438	/	0	
			TR	Rotherham U.	08.83	1983	24	/	0	
STEVENSON, Alex E.	Dublin	09.08.12	Glasgow Rgrs.	Everton	*	1946-48	65		13	(IF)EI-7/NI-17
STEVENSON, Arthur	Lanchester	02.03.24	Denaby U.	Doncaster Rov.	+	1947-48	14		0	(RB)
STEVENSON, Byron W.	Llanelli	07.09.56	APP	Leeds U.	09.73	1974-81	85	7	4	(D) W.U21-3/W-15
			TR	Birmingham	03.82	1981-83	63	5	3	
STEVENSON, Ernie	Rotherham	28.12.23	JNRS	Wolverhampton W.	+	1947-48	8		0	(IF)
			TR	Cardiff C.	10.48	1948-49	50		15	
			TR	Southampton	02.50	1949-50	23		8	
			TR	Leeds U.	02.51	1950-51	16		5	
STEVENSON, Horace W.	Calow	06.09.16		Nottingham F.	+					
			TR	Ipswich T.	02.48	1947	3		0	
STEVENSON, Jim	Bellshill	04.08.46	Hibernian	Southend U.	07.67	1967	33	1	0	(WH) S.SCH.INT.
STEVENSON, Morris J.	Tranent	16.04.43	Morton	Luton T.	11.68	1968	1	/	0	(F)
STEVENSON, Nigel C.A.	Swansea	02.11.58	APP	Swansea	11.76	1975-83	189	9	14	(D)W.U'21-2/W-4
STEVENSON, Willie	Leith	26.10.39	Glasgow Rgrs.	Liverpool	10.62	1962-67	188	/	15	(WH)S.F.LGE REP.
			TR	Stoke C.	12.67	1967-72	82	12	5	
			TR	Tranmere Rov.	07.73	1973	20	/	0	
STEWART, Alan V.	Newcastle	24.07.22		Huddersfield T.	+	1946-48	13		0	(CH)
			TR	York C.	08.49	1949-56	208		1	
STEWART, Andrew C.	Letchworth	29.10.56	APP	Portsmouth	07.74	1973-75	14	5	3	(F)
STEWART, Arthur	Ballymena	13.01.42	Glentoran	Derby Co.	12.67	1967-69	29	1	1	(WH)NI-7
STEWART, David	Glasgow	11.03.47	Ayr U.	Leeds U.	10.73	1973-78	55	/	0	(G) S.U23-7/S-1
			TR	W.B.A.	11.78					
			TR	Swansea C.	02.80	1979-80	57	/	0	
STEWART, David C.	Belfast	20.05.58	APP	Hull C.	08.75	1974-78	46	5	7	(W) NI-1
			TR	Chelsea	05.79					
			TR	Scunthorpe U.	11.79	1979-81	88	9	19	
			Goole T.	Hartlepool U.	03.83	1982	6	2	0	
STEWART, Edward M.	Dundee	15.11.34	Dundee U.	Norwich C.	07.57	1957	13		0	(HB)
STEWART, George	Chirnside	18.10.20	Hamilton	Brentford	08.46	1946-47	24		3	(F)
			TR	Q.P.R.	03.48	1947-52	38		4	
			TR	Shrewsbury T.	01.53	1952	10		2	
STEWART, George S.	Larkhall	16.11.32	E.Stirling	Bradford C.	05.59	1959-60	22		0	(G)
STEWART, George T.S.	Buckie	17.02.27	St.Mirren	Accrington St.	09.54	1954-58	182		135	(CF)●
			TR	Coventry C.	11.58	1958-59	40		23	
			TR	Carlisle U.	06.60	1960	7		2	
STEWART, Gerry	Dundee	02.09.46	JNRS	Preston N.E.	09.63	1966-69	4	/	0	(G)
			TR	Barnsley	09.71	1971-74	138	/	0	
STEWART, Graham	Birkenhead	08.03.38		Sheffield U.	08.58					(F)
			TR	Chesterfield	05.59	1959	5		2	
STEWART, Henry	Wigan	28.04.25	Thorne Col.	Aldershot	07.48					
			TR	Huddersfield T.	08.48	1948-50	51		0	
STEWART, Ian	Belfast	10.09.61	JNRS	Q.P.R.	05.80	1980-83	47	7	2	(F) NI.SCH.INT./NI-16
			L	Millwall	03.83	1982	10	1	3	
STEWART, James G.	S.Africa	07.08.27	Parkhill FX	Leeds U.	10.51	1951-52	9		2	(IR)
STEWART, James M.	Perth	15.09.43		Swindon T.	08.64	1964	1		0	(G)
STEWART, Jim	Kilwinning	09.03.54	Kilmarnock	Middlesbrough	06.78	1978-80	34	/	0	(G) S-2/S.U21-3/S.U23-5
STEWART, John	Armadale	23.01.29	E.Fife	Walsall	06.57	1957	28		4	
STEWART, John B.	Middlesbrough	28.03.37	Whitby T.	York C.	09.56	1956	1		0	(F)
			TR	Darlington	12.57					
STEWART, John G.	Fife	04.09.21	Raith Rov.	Birmingham C.	01.48	1947-54	202		52	(F)
STEWART, Mike	Herne Hill	16.09.32	Corinthian Casuals	Charlton Ath.	10.56	1956-58	9		3	(IF)E.AMAT.INT./ Surrey/Essex Cricketer
STEWART, Paul A.	Manchester	07.10.64	APP	Blackpool	10.81	1981-83	83	13	20	(F) E.YTH.INT.
STEWART, Ray S.M.	Perth	07.09.59	Dundee U.	West Ham U.	09.79	1979-83	202	/	40	(D) S.U21-12/S-7/S.SCH.INT.
STEWART, Reg	Sheffield	30.10.25		Sheffield Wed.	+	1946	6		0	(CH)
			TR	Colchester U.	07.50	1950-56	256		0	
STEWART, Robert	Kirkcaldy	04.12.33	St.Mirren	Crewe Alex.	08.55	1955	22		3	S.SCH.INT.
STEWART, William	Clydebank	10.03.22	St.Mirren	Aldershot	06.51	1951-53	25		3	(IF)
STIFFLE, Nelson E.	India	30.07.28	Ashton U.	Chester C.	12.51	1951	7		2	(OR)
			Altrincham	Chesterfield	03.54	1954	38		9	
			TR	Bournemouth	05.55	1955-57	35		7	
			TR	Exeter C.	03.58	1957-59	94		17	
			TR	Coventry C.	07.60	1960	15		2	
STILES, Norbert P.(Nobby)	Manchester	18.05.42	JNRS	Manchester U.	06.59	1960-70	312	/	18	(WH)E-28/E.U23-3/●
			TR	Middlesbrough	05.71	1971-72	57	/	2	E.F.LGE REP./E.YTH.INT./
			TR	Preston N.E.	08.73	1973-74	44	2	1	E.SCH.INT.

Players Names	Birthplace	Date	Previous Club	League Club	Date Signed	Seasons Played	Apps	Sub	Gls	
STILL, John L.	W.Ham	24.04.50	JNRS	Orient	AM	1967	1	/	0	(CH)
STILL, Robert A.	Brinscall	15.12.12	Stockport Co.(*)	Crewe Alex.	+	1946	1		0	(WH)*Chorley
STILL, Ron G.	Aberdeen	10.06.43	Woodside	Arsenal	08.61					(F)
			TR	Notts.Co.	07.65	1965-66	46	/	15	
			TR	Brentford	07.67	1967	1	/	0	
STILLE, Giles K.	London	10.11.58	Kingstonian	Brighton & H.A.	05.79	1979-83	20	7	4	(M)
STILLYARDS, George	Lincoln	29.12.18	Botolph U.	Lincoln C.	+	1946-48	100		2	(RB)
STIMPSON, Barry G.	Billingham	08.02.64	APP	Hartlepool U.	02.82	1980-83	66	2	2	(D)
			TR	Chesterfield	11.83	1983	27	/	0	
STINSON, Hugh M.J.	Bacup	18.05.37		Accrington St.	05.55	1958	3		0	(F)
			TR	Gillingham	07.59	1959	1		0	
STIRK, John	Consett	05.09.55	APP	Ipswich T.	06.73	1977	6	/	0	(D)
			TR	Watford	06.78	1978	46	/	0	
			TR	Chesterfield	03.80	1979-82	54	2	0	
STIRLAND, Cecil J.	Ardwick	15.07.21	JNRS	Doncaster Rov.	*	1946-48	68		0	(WH)
			TR	New Brighton	01.50	1950	4		2	
			TR	Scunthorpe U.	08.51	1951	17		0	
STIRLING, James R.	Airdrie	23.07.25	Coltness U.	Bournemouth	07.47	1947-49	73		1	(CH)
			TR	Birmingham C.	06.50					
			TR	Southend U.	12.50	1950-59	218		1	
STITFALL, Albert E.	Cardiff	07.07.24	JNRS	Cardiff C.	11.48	1948-51	9		1	(FB)Brother of Ron
			TR	Torquay U.	03.52	1951-52	22		1	
STITFALL, Ron F.	Cardiff	14.12.25	JNRS	Cardiff C.	09.47	1947-63	400		8	(FB)W-2
STOBART, Barry	Doncaster	06.06.38	JNRS	Wolverhampton W.	12.55	1959-63	49		20	(CF)
			TR	Manchester C.	08.64	1964	14		1	
			TR	Aston Villa	11.64	1964-67	45	/	8	
			TR	Shrewsbury T.	10.67	1967-68	34	2	9	
STOBART, George C.	Pegswood	09.01.21	Netherfield	Middlesbrough	+					(F)
			TR	Newcastle U.	09.46	1946-48	66		21	
			TR	Luton T.	10.49	1949-51	107		30	
			TR	Millwall	08.52	1952-53	72		26	
			TR	Brentford	05.54	1954-55	57		18	
STOCK, Harry	Stockport	31.07.18		Stockport Co.	*	1946-47	18		6	(F)
			TR	Oldham Ath.	07.48	1948-50	36		10	
STOCKIN, Ron	Birmingham	27.06.31	W.B.A.(AM)	Walsall	01.52	1951	6		3	(IF)
			TR	Wolverhampton W.	02.52	1952-53	21		7	
			TR	Cardiff C.	06.54	1954-56	57		16	
			TR	Grimsby T.	06.57	1957-59	49		14	
STOCKLEY, Ken S.	Watford	24.11.26	JNRS	Luton T.	+					(IF)
			TR	Watford	07.48	1949	1		0	
STOCKS, David H.	Dulwich	20.01.43	JNRS	Charlton Ath.	01.62	1961-64	26		0	(D)
			TR	Gillingham	05.65	1965	45	/	0	
			TR	Bournemouth	06.66	1966-71	220	/	2	
			TR	Torquay U.	01.72	1971-76	150	/	3	
STOCKS, Joe R.	Hull	27.11.41	JNRS	Hull C.	12.58	1959-60	9		1	(WH)
			TR	Millwall	08.61	1961-63	32		1	
STODDART, Terry	Newcastle	28.11.31	JNRS	Newcastle U.	01.49					
			TR	Darlington	05.54	1954-55	8		0	
			TR	York C.	07.56	1956	3		0	
STOKES, Albert W.	Sheffield	26.01.33	Hampton Spts	Grimsby T.	02.54	1954-56	17		3	(CF)
			TR	Scunthorpe U.	07.57	1957	5		2	
			TR	Southport	02.59	1958	6		2	
STOKES, Alf F.	Hackney	03.10.32	Clapton	Tottenham H.	02.53	1952-58	65		40	(IF)E'B'-1/E.U23-1/
			TR	Fulham	07.59	1959	15		6	E.F.LGE REP.
			Cambridge U.	Watford	04.61	1961	14		0	
STOKES, Derek	Normanton	13.09.39	JNRS	Bradford C.	04.57	1957-59	94		44	(CF)E.U23-4
			TR	Huddersfield T.	06.60	1960-64	153		66	
			TR	Bradford C.	01.66	1965-66	31	1	11	
STOKES, Robert W.	Portsmouth	30.01.51	APP	Southampton	02.68	1968-76	194	24	40	(F) E.YTH.INT.
			TR	Portsmouth	08.77	1977	23	1	2	
STOKES, Wayne D.	Wolverhampton	16.02.65	Coventry C. (APP)	Gillingham	07.82	1982-83	2	1	0	(D)
STOKOE, Dennis	Blyth	06.06.25		Chesterfield	01.47					(WH)
			TR	Carlisle U.	07.48	1948-53	148		2	
			TR	Workington	10.53	1953-55	107		2	
			TR	Gateshead	08.56	1956	13		0	
STOKOE, Robert	Mickley	21.09.30	JNRS	Newcastle U.	09.47	1950-60	261		4	(CH)
			TR	Bury	02.61	1960-63	81		0	
STONE, David K.	Bristol	29.12.42	JNRS	Bristol Rov.	03.60	1962-67	144	3	6	(HB)
			TR	Southend U.	07.68	1968	6	/	0	
STONE, Edward L.	Aberdeen	05.01.42	JNRS	Charlton Ath.	08.59					(F)
			TR	Crystal Palace	05.61	1961	1		0	
STONE, Fred W.	Bristol	05.07.25		Bristol C.	06.47	1947-52	64		3	(FB)

Players Names	Birthplace	Date	Previous Club	League Club	Date Signed	Seasons Played	Apps	Sub	Gls	
STONE, Geoff	Mansfield	10.04.24	Beeston BC	Notts.Co.	09.48	1948-49	4		0	
			TR	Darlington	08.50	1950-51	31		0	
STONE, John G.	Saltburn	03.03.53	South Bank	Middlesbrough	07.70	1971	2	/	0	(D)
			TR	York C.	07.72	1972-75	86	/	5	
			TR	Darlington	07.76	1976-78	120	/	14	
			TR	Grimsby T.	07.79	1979-82	89	5	2	
			TR	Rotherham U.	09.83	1983	10	/	1	
STONE, Mike	Hucknall	23.05.38	Linby Col.	Notts.Co.	07.58	1958	7		0	(G)
STONE, Peter J.	Oxford	08.10.22	Oxford C.	Luton T.	AM	1951	1		0	(CH)
STONEHOUSE, Basil	Guisborough	27.10.52	APP	Middlesbrough	12.69					(W)
			L	Halifax T.	10.72	1972	1	1	0	
STONEHOUSE, Bernard	Manchester	23.12.34	Crewe Alex.(AM)	Rochdale	08.55	1955-56	19		1	(OL)
STONEHOUSE, Derek	Lingdale	18.11.32	Lingdale	Middlesbrough	05.51	1953-61	174		0	(FB)E.YTH.INT.
				Hartlepool U.	09.63	1963-64	34		0	
STONEHOUSE, Kevin	B. Auckland	20.09.59	Shildon	Blackburn Rov.	07.79	1979-82	77	8	27	(F)
			TR	Huddersfield T.	03.83	1982-83	20	2	4	
			TR	Blackpool	03.84	1983	13	/	5	
STONES, Gordon	Kearsley	18.11.34	Bury(AM)	Accrington St.	09.54	1955-60	109		1	(HB)
STOPFORD, Alan	Sheffield	20.11.46	Sheffield U.(AM)	Chesterfield	AM	1966	1	/	0	(OL)
STOPFORD, Les	Manchester	09.05.42	JNRS	Chester C.	06.60	1959-61	6		1	(F)
STORER, David M.	Lochgelly	16.10.33		Sheffield Wed.	02.51	1952	4		0	(OL)
STORER, Peter R.	Shoreditch	14.02.35	Berkhampstead	Watford	AM	1958	9		0	(G)
STORER, Stuart J.	Market Harborough	16.01.67	JNRS	Mansfield T.	N/C	1983	0	1	0	
STOREY, Jim	Rowlands Green	30.12.29	Spen B & W	Newcastle U.	05.48					(FB)
			TR	Exeter C.	06.53	1953	9		0	
			TR	Bournemouth	07.54					
			TR	Rochdale	06.55	1955-56	24		1	
			TR	Darlington	06.57	1957	6		0	
STOREY, Luke D.	Dawdon	17.12.20	Blackhall C.W.	Lincoln C.	09.47	1947-48	11		2	(OR)
STOREY, Peter E.	Farnham	07.09.45	APP	Arsenal	10.62	1965-76	387	4	9	(M) E-19/E.F.LGE.REP.
			TR	Fulham	03.77	1976-77	17	/	0	E.SCH.INT.
STOREY, Sid	Barnsley	25.12.19	Wombwell	York C.	05.47	1946-55	330		40	(IF)+Huddersfield T.
			TR	Barnsley	05.56	1956	29		4	
			TR	Accrington St.	10.57	1957-58	30		2	
			TR	Bradford P.A.	07.59	1959	2		0	
STOREY-MOORE, Ian	Ipswich	17.01.45	JNRS	Nottingham F.	05.62	1963-71	235	1	105	(W)E-1/E-U23-2/
			TR	Manchester U.	03.72	1971-73	39	/	11	E.F.LGE REP.
STORF, David	Sheffield	04.12.43	JNRS	Sheffield Wed.	12.60					(FB)
			TR	Rochdale	06.63	1963-66	138	/	19	
			TR	Barrow	07.67	1967-71	154	4	26	
STORRIE, Jim	Kirkintilloch	31.03.40	Airdrie	Leeds U.	06.62	1962-66	122	2	58	(CF)
			Aberdeen	Rotherham U.	12.67	1967-69	70	1	19	
			TR	Portsmouth	12.69	1969-71	43	/	12	
			L	Aldershot	03.72	1971	5	/	1	
STORTON, Stan E.	Keighley	05.01.39		Bradford C.	07.57	1959-63	111		5	(FB)Brother of Trevor
			TR	Darlington	01.64	1963	15		0	
			TR	Hartlepool U.	07.64	1964-65	72	/	0	
			TR	Tranmere Rov.	07.66	1966-69	113	7	2	
STORTON, Trevor	Keighley	26.11.49	JNRS	Tranmere Rov.	10.67	1967-71	111	7	9	(D)
			TR	Liverpool	08.72	1972-73	5	/	0	
			TR	Chester C.	07.74	1974-83	396	/	17	
STOTT, Ian	Wallingford	17.10.55	West Ham U.(AM)	Oxford U.	N/C	1977-79	27	/	3	(D)
STOTT, Keith	Atherton	12.03.44	Manchester C.(AM)	Crewe Alex.	10.64	1964-69	188	3	11	(HB)
			TR	Chesterfield	07.70	1970-74	140	1	4	
STOUTT, Steve	Halifax	05.04.64	Bradley Rgrs	Huddersfield T.	N/C	1983	3	/	0	(D)
STOWELL, Bruce	Bradford	20.09.41	JNRS	Bradford C.	12.58	1959-71	401	/	16	(IF)
			TR	Rotherham U.	07.72	1972	14	2	0	
STRAIN, Jimmy	Chesham	28.11.37	Chesham U.	Watford	11.55	1956	3		0	(HB)
			TR	Millwall	09.58	1958	5		0	
STRATFORD, Paul	Northampton	04.09.55	APP	Northampton T.	10.72	1972-77	169	3	58	(F)
STRATHIE, Jim W.	Beancross	12.02.13	Luton T.(*)	Northampton T.	+	1946	6		0	(CH)*St.Bernards/d.1976
STRATTON, Reg M.	Farnborough	10.07.39	Woking	Fulham	08.59	1959-64	21		1	(IF)E.AMAT.INT./
			TR	Colchester U.	06.65	1965-67	112	/	50	E.YTH.INT.
STRAUS, William H.	S.Africa	06.01.16	Aberdeen	Plymouth Arg.	07.46	1946-53	158		40	(OR)
STRAW, Ray	Ilkeston	22.05.33	Ilkeston T.	Derby Co.	10.51	1951-57	94		57	(CF)
			TR	Coventry C.	11.57	1957-60	143		79	
			TR	Mansfield T.	08.61	1961-62	44		12	
STREET, Jeff L.	Manchester	20.04.48	JNRS	Manchester C.	08.65					(CH)
			TR	Southport	08.67	1967	9	/	0	
			TR	Plymouth Arg.	07.68					
			Altrincham	Barrow	07.69	1969	11	/	1	

Players Names	Birthplace	Date	Previous Club	League Club	Date Signed	Seasons Played	Apps	Sub	Gls	
STREET, John	Sheffield	27.07.34	JNRS	Bradford C.	11.51	1951	1		0	
			TR	Lincoln C.	09.52					
STREET, John	Liverpool	30.05.28	Liverpool(AM)	Sheffield Wed.	+					(IF)
				Rotherham U.	07.47	1947	2		0	
				Southport	01.49	1948-49	7		1	
			Bootle	Reading	05.51					
			TR	Barrow	07.53	1953-54	30		5	
STREET, Terry E.	London	09.12.48	JNRS	Orient	12.66	1966	1	/	0	(WH)
STREETE, Floyd	W. Indies	05.05.59	Rivet Spts.	Cambridge U.	07.76	1976-82	111	14	19	(M)
STRETEN, Bernard	Gillingham	14.01.21	Shrewsbury T.	Luton T.	01.48	1946-56	276		0	(G)E-1/E.AMAT.INT.
STRETTON, Don	Clowne	04.09.20	Thorne Col.	Halifax T.	07.47	1947	10		5	(CF)d.1978
STRICKLAND, Derek	Stoneyburn	07.11.59	Glasgow Rgrs	Leicester C.	09.79	1979	4	3	2	(F)S.SCH.INT.
STRIDE, David R.	Lymington	14.03.58	APP	Chelsea	07.76	1978-79	35	/	0	(D)
			Memphis	Millwall	01.83	1982-83	55	/	3	
STRINGER, David R.	Gt. Yarmouth	15.10.44	Gorleston Minors	Norwich C	05.63	1964-76	417	2	19	(D) E.YTH.INT.
			TR	Cambridge U.	09.76	1976-80	153	4	1	
STRINGER, Edmund	Sheffield	06.02.25	Norton Woodseats	Oldham Ath.	07.49	1949	1		0	(F)
STRINGFELLOW, Mike D.	Nuncartgate	27.01.43	JNRS	Mansfield T.	02.60	1960-61	57		10	(OL)
			TR	Leicester C.	01.62	1961-74	292	23	82	
STRINGFELLOW, Peter	Walkden	21.02.39	Walkden T.	Oldham Ath.	12.58	1958-60	54		16	(F)
			TR	Gillingham	12.62	1962-63	35		2	
			TR	Chesterfield	08.64	1964	28		7	
STRODDER, Colin J.	Leeds	23.12.41		Huddersfield T.	04.60					(HB)
			TR	Halifax T.	07.61	1961-62	20		0	
STRODDER, Gary	Spenborough	01.04.65	APP	Lincoln C.	04.83	1982-83	26	4	1	(M)
STRONACH, Peter	Seaham	01.09.56	APP	Sunderland	09.73	1977	2	1	0	(F) E.SCH.INT.
			TR	York C.	06.78	1978-79	30	4	2	
STRONG, Geoff H.	Newcastle	19.09.37	Stanley U.	Arsenal	04.58	1960-64	125		69	(IF)
			TR	Liverpool	11.64	1964-69	150	5	30	
			TR	Coventry C.	07.70	1970-71	33	/	0	
STRONG, Jim G.	Morpeth	07.06.16	Walsall(+)	Burnley	+	1946-52	264		0	(G)*Hartlepool U./
										Chesterfield/Portsmouth
STRONG, Les	London	03.07.53	Crystal Palace (AM)	Fulham	06.71	1972-82	369	3	5	(D)
			L	Brentford	12.82	1982	5	/	0	
				Crystal Palace	N/C	1983	7	/	0	
STRONG, Steve	Bristol	17.04.62	APP	Hereford U.	02.80	1978-80	16	/	0	(D)
STROUD, Derek N.L.	Wimborne	11.02.39	Poole T.	Bournemouth	08.50	1950-52	78		17	(OR)
			TR	Grimsby T.	06.53	1953-54	71		13	
STROUD, Ken A.	London	01.12.53	APP	Swindon T.	03.71	1971-81	302	9	16	(M)
			TR	Newport Co.	08.82	1982-83	47	1	0	
			TR	Bristol C.	10.83	1983	34	/	3	
STROUD, Roy	Silvertown	16.03.25	Hendon	West Ham U.	11.53	1951-56	13		4	(OR)E.AMAT.INT./
										E.SCH.INT.
STROUD, William J.A.	London	07.07.19		Southampton	+	1946	28		4	(WH)
			TR	Orient	06.47	1947-49	65		1	
			TR	Newport Co.	06.50	1950-54	63		1	
STRUTT, Brian	Malta	21.09.59	APP	Sheffield Wed.	10.78	1979	2	/	0	(F)
STUART, Eddie	S.Africa	12.05.31	Rangers FC (S.A.)	Wolverhampton W.	01.51	1951-61	287		1	(FB)●
			TR	Stoke C.	07.62	1962-63	63		2	
			TR	Tranmere Rov.	08.64	1964-65	83	/	2	
			TR	Stockport Co.	07.66	1966-67	77	/	1	
STUART, Robert W.	Middlesbrough	09.10.13	South Bank	Middlesbrough	*	1946-47	31		0	(FB)E.SCH.INT.
			TR	Plymouth Arg.	10.47	1947	20		0	
STUBBINS, Albert	Wallsend	13.07.19	W & Monkseaton	Newcastle U.	*	1946	3		0	(CF)E.F.LGE REP.
			TR	Liverpool	09.46	1946-52	158		77	
STUBBS, Alf T.	West Ham U.	18.04.22		Crystal Palace	12.46	1947-48	3		0	
STUBBS, Barry	Stoke	05.10.47	APP	Port Vale	APP	1965	2	/	0	(FB)
STUBBS, Brian H.	Keyworth	08.02.50	Loughborough U.	Notts. Co.	09.68	1968-79	423	3	21	(D)
STUBBS, Charles F.	West Ham U.	22.01.20	Bamforths	Darlington	+	1946-47	41		17	(CF)Brother of Alf
STUBBS, Les	Great Wakering	18.02.29	Gt.Wakering	Southend U.	05.48	1949-52	84		40	(IF)
			TR	Chelsea	11.52	1952-58	112		34	
			TR	Southend U.	11.58	1958-59	22		3	
STUBBS, Robin	Birmingham	22.04.41	JNRS	Birmingham C.	04.58	1958-62	61		17	(CF)●
			TR	Torquay U.	08.63	1963-68	214	3	121	
			TR	Bristol Rov.	07.69	1969-71	90	3	32	
			TR	Torquay U.	02.72	1971-72	19	2	1	

Players Names	Birthplace	Date	Previous Club	League Club	Date Signed	Seasons Played	Apps	Sub	Gls	
STUCKEY, Bruce G.	Torquay	19.02.47	APP	Exeter C.	02.65	1965-67	37	1	6	(W)
			TR	Sunderland	11.67	1967-69	24	2	2	
			TR	Torquay U.	02.71	1970-73	70	18	6	
			TR	Reading	11.73	1973-76	92	5	7	
			L	Torquay U.	01.75	1974	4	/	0	
			L	Bournemouth	03.77	1976	5	/	0	
STURRIDGE, Mike A.	Birmingham	18.09.62	APP	Birmingham C.	06.80					(F)
			L	Wrexham	12.83	1983	3	1	0	
STURROCK, David	Dundee	22.02.38	Dundee U.	Accrington St.	07.60	1960	17		6	(F)
STUTTARD, J. Ellis	Burnley	24.40.20	Burnley(*)	Plymouth Arg.	*	1946	28		1	(WH)
			TR	Torquay U.	09.47	1947-50	82		0	
STYLES, Arthur	Liverpool	03.09.49	APP	Everton	08.67	1972-73	22	1	0	(D) E.YTH.INT./E.SCH.INT.
			TR	Birmingham C.	02.74	1973-77	71	3	3	
			TR	Peterborough U.	07.78	1978	32	/	1	
			TR	Portsmouth	07.79	1979	28	/	0	
STYLES, Arthur J.	Smethwick	29.10.39	JNRS	W.B.A.	11.56	1959	1		0	(WH)
			TR	Wrexham	03.60	1959-60	16		0	
SUART, Ron	Kendal	18.11.20	Netherfield	Blackpool	*	1946-49	104		0	(CH)
			TR	Blackburn Rov.	09.49	1949-54	175		0	
SUCKLING, Perry J.	Leyton	12.10.55	APP	Coventry C.	10.83	1982-83	27	/	0	(G)
SUDDABY, Donald	Brighouse	07.06.30	Chelsea(AM)	Halifax T.	08.51	1951	5		0	
			TR	Bradford P.A.	08.52					
SUDDABY, Peter	Stockport	23.12.47	Skelmersdale	Blackpool	05.70	1970-79	331	1	9	(D)E.AMAT.INT.
			TR	Brighton & H.A.	11.80	1979	21	2	0	
			TR	Wimbledon	11.81	1981	6	/	0	
SUDDARDS, Jeff	Bradford	17.01.29	Swan House	Bradford P.A.	03.49	1949-58	327		0	(FB)
SUDDICK, Alan	Chester-le-Street	02.05.44	APP	Newcastle U.	10.61	1961-66	144	/	41	(M) E.U23-2/E.YTH.INT.
			TR	Blackpool	12.66	1966-76	305	5	64	
			TR	Stoke C.	12.76	1976	9	/	1	
			L	Southport	08.77	1977	6	/	0	
			TR	Bury	09.77	1977	30	4	2	
SUGGETT, Colin	Washington	30.12.48	APP	Sunderland	01.66	1966-68	83	3	24	(M) E.YTH.INT./
			TR	W.B.A.	07.69	1969-72	123	5	20	E.SCH.INT.
			TR	Norwich C.	02.73	1972-77	200	3	21	
			TR	Newcastle U.	08.78	1978	20	3	0	
SUGRUE, Paul	Coventry	06.11.60	Nuneaton Bor.	Manchester C.	02.80	1979-80	5	1	0	(M)
			TR	Cardiff C.	08.81	1981	2	3	0	
			Kansas	Middlesbrough	12.82	1982-83	61	1	6	
SULLEY, Chris S.L.	Camberwell	03.12.59	APP	Chelsea	08.78					(D)
			TR	Bournemouth	03.81	1980-83	145	1	3	
SULLIVAN, Alan	Aberdare	12.11.53	APP	Swansea C.	08.71	1970-71	7	1	1	(W)W.SCH.INT.
SULLIVAN, Brian A.J.	Edmonton	30.12.41	JNRS	Fulham	05.59	1959	2		1	(F)E.YTH.INT./E.SCH.INT.
SULLIVAN, Colin J.	Saltash	24.06.51	APP	Plymouth Arg.	07.68	1967-73	225	5	7	(D) E.U23-2/E.YTH.INT.
			TR	Norwich C.	06.74	1974-78	154	3	3	
			TR	Cardiff C.	02.79	1978-81	61	2	1	
			TR	Hereford U.	N/C	1981	8	/	0	
			TR	Portsmouth	03.82	1981-83	94	1	0	
SULLIVAN, Cornelius H. (Con)	Bristol	22.08.28	Horfield OB	Bristol C.	05.49	1950-52	73		0	(G)
			TR	Arsenal	02.54	1953-57	28		0	
SULLIVAN, Derek	Newport	10.08.30	JNRS	Cardiff C.	09.47	1947-60	276		18	(WH)W-17
			TR	Exeter C.	06.61	1961	44		0	
			TR	Newport Co.	07.62	1962	23		0	
SUMMERBEE, George M.	Winchester	22.10.14		Preston N.E.	*					Uncle of Mike/
			TR	Chester C.	05.46	1946	9		0	d.
			TR	Barrow	06.47	1947-49	122		0	
SUMMERBEE, Mike G.	Cheltenham	15.12.42	Cheltenham	Swindon T.	03.60	1959-64	218	/	39	(W) E-8/E.U23-1/●
			TR	Manchester C.	08.65	1965-74	355	2	47	E.F.LGE.REP.
			TR	Burnley	06.75	1975-76	51	/	0	
			TR	Blackpool	12.76	1976	3	/	0	
			TR	Stockport Co	08.77	1977-79	86	1	6	
SUMMERFIELD, Kevin	Walsall	07.01.59	APP	W.B.A.	01.77	1978-81	5	4	4	(F)
			TR	Birmingham C.	05.82	1982	2	3	1	
			TR	Walsall	12.82	1982-83	42	12	17	
SUMMERHAYES, David M.	Cardiff	21.03.47	APP	Cardiff C.	03.65	1965-67	7	6	0	(HB)W.U23-1
SUMMERHAYES, Robert E.	Cardiff	08.01.51	APP	Cardiff C.	01.69					(WH)W.SCH.INT./
			TR	Newport Col.	08.72	1972-74	74	6	4	Brother of David
SUMMERHILL, Alan	Liss	25.11.50	JNRS	Bournemouth	07.68	1969	28	/	0	(WH)
			TR	Crewe Alex.	09.70	1970-71	46	4	1	
SUMMERILL, Phil E.	Birmingham	20.11.47	APP	Birmingham C.	12.64	1966-72	107	10	46	(F) E.YTH.INT.
			TR	Huddersfield T.	01.73	1972-74	48	6	11	
			TR	Millwall	11.74	1974-77	83	4	20	
			TR	Wimbledon	09.77	1977-78	27	4	4	
SUMMERS, George	Glasgow	30.07.41	Shawfield J.	Brentford	01.59	1960-64	71		25	(F)

Players Names	Birthplace	Date	Previous Club	League Club	Date Signed	Seasons Played	Career Record Apps	Sub	Gls	
SUMMERS, Gerry T.	Birmingham	04.10.33	JNRS	W.B.A.	08.51	1955-56	22		0	(WH)
			TR	Sheffield U.	05.57	1957-63	260		4	
			TR	Hull C.	04.64	1963-65	59	/	1	
			TR	Walsall	10.65	1965-66	39	2	1	
SUMMERS, John H.	London	10.09.27	JNRS	Fulham	02.47	1949	4		0	(F)d.1962●
			TR	Norwich C.	06.50	1950-53	71		33	
			TR	Millwall	05.54	1954-56	92		41	
			TR	Charlton Ath.	11.56	1956-60	171		100	
SUMMERSBY, Roy D.	Lambeth	19.03.35	JNRS	Millwall	03.52	1951-58	87		14	(WH)
			TR	Crystal Palace	12.58	1958-62	176		59	
			TR	Portsmouth	06.63	1963-64	12		1	
SUMMERSCALES, William	London	04.01.49	Leek T.	Port Vale	02.70	1969-74	126	3	4	(D)
			TR	Rochdale	07.75	1975-76	87	/	4	
SUMNER, Alan	Wrexham	18.04.49	JNRS	Stockport Co.	N/C	1978	3	2	0	(M)
SUMPNER, Richard A.	Leeds	12.04.47	JNRS	Bradford P.A.	01.67	1966	2	/	1	(F)
SUNDERLAND, Alan	Mexborough	01.07.53	APP	Wolverhampton W.	06.71	1971-77	139	19	29	(F)E.U23-1/E.J21-1/E-1
			TR	Arsenal	11.77	1977-83	204	2	55	
			L	Ipswich T.	02.84	1983	15	/	3	
SUNLEY, David	Skelton	06.02.52	APP	Sheffield Wed.	01.70	1970-75	121	12	21	(F)
			L	Nottingham F.	10.75	1975	1	/	0	
			TR	Hull C.	01.76	1975-77	58	11	11	
			TR	Lincoln C.	07.78	1978-79	36	5	6	
			TR	Stockport Co.	03.80	1979-81	79	4	7	
SURMAN, Les	Tamworth	23.11.47	APP	Charlton Ath.	11.65	1965	1	/	0	(G)
			TR	Rotherham U.	06.66	1966	1	/	0	
SURTEES, George H.	Gateshead	18.07.23	Murton C.W.	Southport	08.46	1946	3		0	(G)
SURTEES, Hubert	Durham	16.07.21		Watford	07.46	1947-48	14		1	(W)
			TR	Crystal Palace	08.49	1949	5		0	
SUSSEX, Andy R.	Islington	23.11.64	APP	Orient	11.82	1981-83	56	5	9	(M)
SUTCLIFFE, Fred	Brotherton	29.05.31		Birmingham C.	09.51					(F)
			TR	Chester C.	06.52	1952-54	49		2	
SUTCLIFFE, Fred W.J.	Fulham	29.07.23		Millwall	02.47	1947-48	12		3	
			TR	Walsall	07.50	1950	5		0	
SUTCLIFFE, Peter D.	Manchester	25.01.57	APP	Manchester U.	07.74					(W) E.YTH.INT.
			TR	Stockport Co.	12.75	1975-76	19	8	2	
			TR	Port Vale	03.77	1976-78	44	6	6	
			TR	Chester C.	12.78	1978-81	103	6	7	
			Bangor C.	Chester C.	N/C	1983	11	/	0	
			TR	Stockport Co.	N/C	1983	0	1	0	
SUTHERLAND, George B.	Glasgow	11.09.23	Partick Th.	Orient	08.49	1949-50	43		22	(CF)
SUTHERLAND, James S.	Armadale	06.08.18	Forth W.	Newport Co.	07.47	1947-48	32		0	(LB)
SUTHERLAND, John F.	Cork	10.02.32	Evergreen	Everton	05.50	1956	6		0	(FB)
			TR	Chesterfield	06.57	1957-58	47		0	
			TR	Crewe Alex.	11.58	1958-59	47		1	
SUTHERLAND, Hary R.	Salford	30.07.15		Leeds U.	*					
			TR	Exeter C.	05.47	1947	13		3	
			TR	Bournemouth	07.48					
SUTHERLEY, Charles E.	Chudleigh	30.03.20	JNRS	Exeter C.	*	1946	1		0	(OL)
SUTTLE, Ken G.	Hammersmith	25.08.28	Worthing	Chelsea	08.48					(W)Sussex Cricketer
			TR	Brighton & H.A.	07.49	1949	3		0	
SUTTON, Brian	Rochdale	08.12.34	Norden Y.C.	Rochdale	10.52	1952-55	13		0	(G)
SUTTON, David W.	Tarleton	21.01.57	APP	Plymouth Arg.	07.74	1973-77	60	1	0	(D)
			L	Reading	11.77	1977	9	/	0	
			TR	Huddersfield T.	03.78	1977-83	242	/	11	
SUTTON, Gary	Folkestone	02.02.62	APP	Gillingham	02.80	1980-81	11	/	0	(G)
SUTTON, James P.	Glasgow	06.09.49	Newcastle U.	Mansfield T.	07.70	1970	11	2	0	(IF)
SUTTON, Mel C.	Birmingham	13.02.46	Aston Villa (AM)	Cardiff C.	12.67	1968-71	135	3	5	(M)
			TR	Wrexham	07.72	1972-80	355	5	21	
			TR	Crewe Alex.	08.82	1982	13	/	1	
SUTTON, Mike J.	Norwich	05.10.44	JNRS	Norwich C.	09.62	1962-66	46	2	3	(HB)
			TR	Chester C.	05.67	1967-69	136	1	9	
			TR	Carlisle U.	06.70	1970-71	51	2	1	
SUTTON, Richard M.	Gravesend	21.08.65	APP	Peterborough U.	APP	1982	1	/	0	(D)
SUTTON, Steve J.	Derby	16.04.61	APP	Nottingham F.	09.80	1980-83	25	/	0	(G)
			L	Mansfield T.	03.81	1980	8	/	0	
SVARC, Robert L.	Leicester	08.02.46	APP	Leicester C.	03.63	1964-68	13	/	2	(F)
			TR	Lincoln C.	12.68	1968-71	40	5	16	
			L	Barrow	09.70	1970	15	/	3	
			Boston U.	Colchester U.	12.72	1972-75	116	/	59	
			TR	Blackburn Rov.	10.75	1975-76	42	8	16	
			L	Watford	09.77	1977	1	/	0	
SWAIN, Ken J.	Cardiff	31.12.54	APP	Newport Co.	08.73	1971-73	7	1	0	(FB)W.SCH.INT.

Players Names	Birthplace	Date	Previous Club	League Club	Date Signed	Seasons Played	Career Record Apps	Sub	Gls	
SWAIN, Kenny	Birkenhead	28.01.52	Wycombe W.	Chelsea	08.73	1973-78	114	5	26	(D)
			TR	Aston Villa	12.78	1978-82	148	/	2	
			TR	Nottingham F.	10.82	1982-83	73	/	2	
SWAIN, Malcolm	Windsor	02.02.52	APP	Reading	09.70	1970-71	37	3	2	(IF)
SWAIN, Robert	Ripon	26.03.44	JNRS	Bradford C.	09.61	1962	7		0	(F)
SWAIN, Sid	Liverpool	14.10.27		Halifax T.	07.51	1951	8		1	
SWAINE, Mark A.	Hammersmith	13.02.58	APP	Gillingham	APP	1974	1	/	0	(W)
SWALLOW, Barry E.	Doncaster	02.07.42	JNRS	Doncaster Rov.	07.59	1960-61	51		10	(CH)Son of Ernie●
			TR	Crewe Alex.	08.62	1962-63	14		0	
			TR	Barnsley	07.64	1964-66	97	/	1	
			TR	Bradford C.	02.67	1966-69	79	6	7	
			TR	York C.	10.69	1969-75	268	1	21	
SWALLOW, Ernie	Wheatley Hill	09.07.19	Bentley Col.	Doncaster Rov.	+	1946-47	50		0	(FB)d.1962
			TR	Barnsley	01.48	1947-49	35		0	
			TR	Oldham Ath.	08.50	1950	6		0	
SWALLOW, Ray	London	15.06.35	JNRS	Arsenal	12.52	1954-57	13		4	(WH)Derby Cricketer
			TR	Derby Co.	09.58	1958-63	118		21	
SWAN, Carl	Sheffield	12.12.57	Burton A.	Doncaster Rov.	12.80	1980-82	14	1	1	(D) Son of Peter
			L	Rochdale	10.82	1982	3	/	0	
SWAN, Maurice M.G.	Drumcondra	27.09.38	Drumcondra	Cardiff C.	07.60	1960-62	15		0	(G)EI-1
			TR	Hull C.	06.63	1963-67	103	/	0	
SWAN, Peter	Sth.Elmsall	08.10.36	JNRS	Sheffield Wed.	11.53	1955-72	273	2	0	(CH)E-19/E.U23-3/
			TR	Bury	08.73	1973	35	/	2	E.F.LGE REP./E.YTH.INT.
SWAN, Ron M.	Plean	08.01.41	E.Stirling	Oldham Ath.	05.64	1964-66	64	/	0	(G)
			TR	Luton T.	01.67	1966	13	/	0	
SWANKIE, Robert B.	Arbroath	25.02.32	Arbroath Y.C.	Burnley	07.50					(F)
				Darlington	01.54	1953	1		0	
SWANN, Gary	York	11.04.62	APP	Hull C.	05.80	1980-83	99	7	4	(D)
SWANN, Gordon	Maltby	07.12.37		Rotherham U.	07.57	1958-60	10		2	(F)
			TR	Barnsley	07.61	1961	2		0	
SWANNELL, John	Walton-on-Thames	26.01.39	Corinthian Cas.	Stockport Co.	AM	1959	1		0	(G)E.AMAT.INT.
SWEENEY, Alan	Glasgow	31.10.56	APP	Huddersfield T.	11.73	1974-77	65	1	1	(D)
			Emley T.	Hartlepool T.	09.79	1979-81	97	/	2	
SWEENEY, Andy	Oldham	15.10.51	JNRS	Oldham Ath.	02.71	1970-74	37	5	2	(W)
			L	Bury	03.73	1972	2	/	0	
			TR	Rochdale	07.75	1975	12	5	0	
SWEENEY, Gerry	Glasgow	10.07.45	Morton	Bristol C.	08.71	1971-81	396	10	22	(D)
			TR	York C.	02.82	1981	12	/	0	
SWEENEY, Tom J.	Luton	04.11.51	APP	Luton T.	APP	1968	0	1	0	
SWEENEY, William C.	St.Andrews	23.10.18	Clyde	Carlisle U.	01.48	1947-48	37		0	(G)
SWEENIE, Tom T.	Paisley	15.07.45	Johnstone Burgh	Leicester C.	06.63	1963-66	50	1	11	(F)
			TR	Arsenal	07.68					
			TR	Huddersfield T.	08.68					
			TR	York C.	10.68	1968	6	/	1	
SWEETZER, Gordon	Canada	27.01.57		Brentford	07.75	1975-77	68	4	40	(F)
			TR	Cambridge U.	04.78	1977-79	9	/	3	
			Toronto	Brentford	01.82	1981	8	1	1	
SWEETZER, James E.	Woking	08.01.60	APP	Oxford U.	02.77	1978	0	8	1	(F)
			TR	Millwall	11.79	1979	2	1	1	
SWIFT, Colin	Barnsley	23.12.33	JNRS	Barnsley	08.51	1955-61	239		0	(FB)
SWIFT, Frank V.	Blackpool	26.12.13	Fleetwood	Manchester C.	*	1946-49	107		0	(G)E-19/E.F.LGE REP./● d.1958
SWIFT, Humphrey M.	Sheffield	22.01.21	Lopham St.WMC	Sheffield Wed.	+	1946-50	181		0	(FB)E'B'-1/d.
SWIFT, John K.	Liverpool	26.07.28	JNRS	Liverpool	+					(F)
			TR	Southport	07.51	1951	5		0	
SWIFT, Trevor	Rotherham	14.09.48	JNRS	Rotherham U.	09.65	1967-74	283	4	21	(LH)
SWIGGS, Bradley	Plymouth	12.10.59		Plymouth Arg.	03.84	1983	1	1	0	(M)
SWIGGS, Robert	Plymouth	30.03.30	St.Blazey	Plymouth Arg.	01.56	1955-56	3		0	(CF)
SWINBOURNE, Roy H.	Denaby Moor	25.08.29	JNRS	Wolverhampton W.	09.46	1949-55	211		107	(CF)E'B'-1
SWINBURNE, Alan T.A.	Durham	18.05.46	APP	Oldham Ath.	09.63	1963	4		0	(G)Son of Tom A.
				Newcastle U.	06.64					
SWINBURNE, Tom A.	Fencehouse	09.08.15	Herrington Col.	Newcastle U.	*	1946	21		0	(G)
SWINBURNE, Trevor	E. Rainton	20.06.53	APP	Sunderland	06.70	1972-76	10	/	0	(G) Son of Thomas
			TR	Carlisle U.	05.77	1977-82	248	/	0	
			TR	Brentford	08.83	1983	21	/	0	

Players Names	Birthplace	Date	Previous Club	League Club	Date Signed	Seasons Played	Career Record Apps Sub Gls			
SWINDELLS, Jack	Manchester	12.04.37	Manchester C.(AM)	Blackburn Rov.	11.57	1957-59	9		1	(CF)E.YTH.INT.
			TR	Accrington St.	12.59	1959-60	65		28	
			TR	Barnsley	06.61	1961	14		8	
			TR	Workington	02.62	1961-62	61		19	
			TR	Torquay U.	07.63	1963	18		6	
			TR	Newport Co.	07.64	1964	23		3	
SWINDIN, George H.	Rotherham	04.12.14	Bradford C.(*)	Arsenal	*	1946-53	214		0	(G)
SWINDLEHURST, David	Edgware	06.01.56	APP	Crystal Palace	01.73	1973-79	221	16	73	(F) E.U21-1/E.YTH.INT.
			TR	Derby Co.	02.80	1979-82	110	/	29	
			TR	West Ham U.	03.83	1982-83	44	1	16	
SWINFEN, Reg	Battersea	04.05.15		Q.P.R.	*	1946	1		0	(OR)
SWINSCOE, Terry	Shirebrook	31.08.34	Spalding U.	Stockport Co.	02.56					(F)
			TR	Mansfield T.	11.56	1956-58	14		0	
SWINSCOE, Tom W.	Mansfield	16.10.19		Chesterfield	+	1946-47	43		13	(CF)
			TR	Stockport Co.	02.48	1947-49	73		30	
SWORD, Alan	Bywell	05.07.34	JNRS	Newcastle U.	08.51					(F)
			TR	Exeter C.	09.53	1955	9		4	
SWORD, Thomas W.	Newcastle	12.11.57	B. Auckland	Stockport Co.	11.79	1979-83	153	1	26	(D)
SYDENHAM, John	Southampton	15.09.39	JNRS	Southampton	04.57	1956-69	341	2	36	(OL)E.U23-2/E.YTH.INT.
			TR	Aldershot	03.70	1969-71	53	5	4	
SYKES, John	Huddersfield	02.11.50	APP	Bradford P.A.	11.68	1968	1	/	0	(F)
			TR	Wrexham	01.69	1968	1	/	0	
SYKES, Ken	Darlington	29.01.26		Darlington	05.46	1946	6		2	
			TR	Middlesbrough	06.47					
			TR	Hartlepool U.	09.49	1949	1		0	
SYKES, Norman	Bristol	16.10.36	JNRS	Bristol Rov.	10.53	1956-63	214		5	(WH)E.YTH.INT./
			TR	Plymouth Arg.	09.64	1964	3		0	E.SCH.INT.
			TR	Stockport Co.	09.65	1965-66	52	/	8	
			TR	Doncaster Rov.	02.67	1966	15	/	0	
SYME, Colin	Rosyth	23.01.24	Dunfermline	Torquay U.	12.46	1946	1		0	(OR)
SYMM, Colin	Dunstan	26.11.46	Gateshead	Sheffield Wed.	05.65	1966-68	16	4	1	(RH)
			TR	Sunderland	06.69	1969-71	9	5	0	
			TR	Lincoln C.	06.72	1972-74	60	9	7	
SYMMONS, Iorwerth	Swansea	03.02.30	Hafod FC	Swansea C.	05.48	1950-51	15		0	(FB)
SYMONDS, Anthony	Wakefield	10.11.44	Gt.Preston	Bradford P.A.	07.62	1964-66	28	1	2	(HB)
			TR	Fulham	07.67					
SYMONDS, Calvin R.	Pembroke	29.03.32	Bermuda	Rochdale	10.54	1955	1		0	
SYMONDS, Richard	Langham	21.11.59	APP	Norwich C.	08.78	1978-82	55	4	0	(D)
SYRETT, Dave K.	Salisbury	20.01.56	APP	Swindon T.	11.73	1973-76	110	12	30	(F) E.YTH.INT.
			TR	Mansfield T.	08.77	1977-78	65	/	20	
			TR	Walsall	03.79	1978	11	/	3	
			TR	Peterborough U.	08.79	1979-81	75	4	24	
			TR	Northampton T.	06.82	1982-83	42	2	13	
SZABO, Tibor	Bradford	28.10.59	APP	Bradford C.	05.78	1978	8	5	1	(F)

Players Names	Birthplace	Date	Previous Club	League Club	Date Signed	Seasons Played	Career Record Apps	Sub	Gls	
TABB, Ray	Brixham	29.05.31		Derby Co.	08.48	1948	1		0	
TADMAN, Maurice R.	Rainham	28.06.21	Bexleyheath	Charlton Ath.	*	1946	3		0	(CF)Brother of pre-war
			TR	Plymouth Arg.	08.47	1947-54	240		107	Charlton Ath. Player
TAFT, Doug	Leicester	09.03.26		Derby Co.	11.47	1948	5		0	
			TR	Wolverhampton W.	07.49					
TAGG, Anthony P.	Epsom	10.04.57	APP	Q.P.R.	03.75	1975	4	/	0	(D)
			TR	Millwall	07.77	1977-81	130	3	9	
			TR	Wimbledon	07.82	1982	14	/	0	
TAGG, Ernie	Crewe	15.09.17	Wolverhampton W.(*)	Bournemouth	+	1946-48	80		8	*Crewe Alex.
			TR	Carlisle U.	11.48	1948	5		1	
TAGGART, Robert	Torbush	10.03.27	Coltness U.	Cardiff C.	05.49	1949	2		0	
			TR	Torquay U.	06.50	1950	14		2	
			TR	Aldershot	08.51	1951	16		2	
TAINTON, Trevor K.	Bristol	08.06.48	APP	Bristol C.	09.65	1967-81	457	30	25	(M)E.SCH.INT.
			TR	Torquay U.	02.82	1981	19	/	1	
TAIT, Alex	Bedlington	28.11.33	JNRS	Newcastle U.	09.52	1954-59	27		7	(CF)E.YTH.INT.
			TR	Bristol C.	06.60	1960-63	117		37	
			TR	Doncaster Rov.	06.64	1964	19		7	
TAIT, Barry S.	York	30.06.38	Doncaster Rov.(AM)	York C.	09.58	1958-60	18		6	(IF)
				Peterborough U.	08.61					
			TR	Bradford C.	11.61	1961	20		10	
			TR	Halifax T.	07.62	1962-63	36		21	
			TR	Crewe Alex.	09.63	1963	9		2	
			TR	Notts.Co.	07.64	1964	3		0	
TAIT, Mick P.	Wallsend	30.09.56	APP	Oxford U.	10.74	1974-76	61	3	23	(M)
			TR	Carlisle U.	10.77	1976-79	101	5	20	
			TR	Hull C.	09.79	1979	29	4	3	
			TR	Portsmouth	06.80	1980-83	150	3	27	
TAIT, Peter	Bishopshorpe	17.10.36	JNRS	York C.	AM	1955	3		1	(CF)
TAIT, Robert J.	Edinburgh	04.10.38	Aberdeen	Notts.Co.	07.64	1962-63	60		11	(IF)
			TR	Barrow	07.64	1964-65	78	1	27	
			TR	Chesterfield	07.66	1966	28	/	2	
TALBOT, Brian E.	Ipswich	21.07.53	APP	Ipswich T.	08.72	1973-78	177	/	25	(M)E-6/E.U21-1
			TR	Arsenal	01.79	1978-83	208	5	30	
TALBOT, Ernie	Workington	13.11.32		Workington	08.51	1952-57	19		7	(F)
TALBOT, F. Leslie	Hednesford	03.08.10	Cardiff C.(*)	Walsall	+	1946	18		5	(IF)*Hednesford/Blackburn Rov.
TALBOT, Gary	Blackburn	15.12.37		Chester C.	09.63	1963-66	110	1	61	(F)
			TR	Crewe Alex.	07.67	1967	35	/	20	
			TR	Chester C.	06.68	1968	43	/	22	
TALBUT, John	Oxford	20.10.40	JNRS	Burnley	10.57	1958-66	138	/	/	(CH)E.U23-7/
			TR	W.B.A.	12.66	1966-70	143	1	0	E.SCH.INT.
TALKES, Wayne P.	London	02.06.52	APP	Southampton	07.69	1971-73	7	2	0	(IF)
			L	Doncaster Rov.	12.73	1973	3	1	0	
			TR	Bournemouth	07.74	1974	5	/	0	
TAMBLING, Robert	Storrington	18.09.41	JNRS	Chelsea	09.58	1958-69	298	4	164	(F)E-3/E.U23-13/●
			TR	Crystal Palace	01.70	1969-73	67	1	12	E.SCH.INT.
TANNER, Graham G.	Bridgewater	04.09.47	APP	Bristol C.	09.64					(HB)
			TR	Bradford P.A.	10.67	1967-68	44	/	2	
TANNER, John D.P.	Harrogate	02.07.21	Yorks Amats	Huddersfield T.	AM	1948	1		1	(CF)E.AMAT.INT.
TANNER, Tom W.	Devonport	24.06.22	Plymouth U.	Torquay U.	AM	1946	1		0	(IF)
TANSEY, Gerrard	Liverpool	15.10.33	JNRS	Everton	10.51					(F)Brother of Jim
			TR	Tranmere Rov.	07.55	1955	3		1	
TANSEY, James	Liverpool	29.01.29		Everton	05.48	1952-59	133	/		(FB)
			TR	Crewe Alex.	06.60	1960	9		0	
TAPKEN, Norman	Wallsend	21.02.13	Newcastle U.(*)	Manchester U.	*					(G)*Wallsend
			TR	Darlington	04.47	1946-47	31		0	
TAPLEY, Reg	Nantwich	02.11.32		Crewe Alex.	09.53					
			TR	Rochdale	19.56	1956	1		0	
TAPLEY, Steve	London	03.10.63	APP	Fulham	10.81	1983	1	/	0	(D)
TAPPING, Fred. H.	Derby	29.07.21		Blackpool	+					(RH)
			TR	Chesterfield	11.47	1947	1		0	
TAPSCOTT, Derek R.	Barry	30.06.32	Barry T.	Arsenal	10.53	1953-57	119		61	(IF)W-14
			TR	Cardiff C.	09.58	1958-64	194		79	
			TR	Newport Co.	07.65	1965	12	1	1	
TAPSCOTT, Eli J.	Plymouth	29.04.28		Leeds U.	03.50					(WH)Cousin of Derek
			TR	Wrexham	05.50	1950-55	172		4	
TARANTINI, Alberto	Argentine	03.12.55	Boca J.	Birmingham C.	10.78	1978	23	/	1	(D)ARGENTINE INT.

Players Names	Birthplace	Date	Previous Club	League Club	Date Signed	Seasons Played	Career Record Apps	Sub	Gls	
TARBUCK, Alan D.	Liverpool	10.10.48	APP	Everton	08.66					(W)
			TR	Crewe Alex.	06.67	1967-69	80	5	18	
			TR	Chester C.	10.69	1969-71	70	/	22	
			TR	Preston N.E.	09.71	1971-72	42	6	17	
			TR	Shrewsbury T.	03.73	1972-75	107	17	17	
			TR	Rochdale	07.76	1976-77	48	/	1	
TARGETT, Haydn R.	Shepton Mallet	01.07.28		Torquay U.	10.49	1950	1		0	(FB)
TARRANT, Brian L.	Stainforth	22.07.38	JNRS	Leeds U.	08.55					(F)Brother of John E.
			TR	Mansfield T.	07.60	1960	3		0	
TARRANT, John E.	Stainforth	12.02.32	JNRS	Hull C.	02.49	1950-53	30		2	(WH)
			TR	Walsall	12.53	1953-57	103		13	
TARTT, Colin	Liverpool	23.11.50	Alsager Col.	Port Vale	07.72	1972-76	171	4	7	(M)
			TR	Chesterfield	03.77	1976-81	185	1	7	
			TR	Port Vale	10.81	1981-83	104	1	8	
TATE, Geoff M.	Leicester	16.12.37	JNRS	Derby Co.	08.55	1955	1		1	(F)E.YTH.INT./E.SCH.INT.
TATE, Jeff	Blyth	11.05.59	JNRS	Burnley	08.78	1979	5	/	1	(M)
TAVENER, Colin R.	Trowbridge	26.06.45	Trowbridge	Hereford U.	N/L	1972-73	50	1	3	(LH)
TAWSE, Brian	Ellon	30.07.45	King St.A.	Arsenal	04.63	1964	5		0	(F)
			TR	Brighton & H.A.	12.65	1965-69	97	3	14	
			TR	Brentford	02.70	1969-70	19	2	1	
TAYLOR, Alan	Thornton	17.05.43		Blackpool	10.63	1965-70	94	/	0	(G)
			L	Oldham Ath.	12.69	1969	2	/	0	
			L	Stockport Co.	08.70	1970	5	/	0	
			TR	Southport	07.71	1971-73	102	/	0	
TAYLOR, Alan D.	Hinkley	14.11.53	Morecambe	Rochdale	05.73	1973-74	55	/	7	(F)
			TR	West Ham U.	11.74	1974-78	88	10	25	
			TR	Norwich C.	08.79	1979	20	4	5	
			Vancouver	Cambridge U.	10.80	1980-81	17	1	4	
				Hull C.	N/C	1983	13	1	3	
TAYLOR, Alan F.	Derby	07.03.54	Alfreton	Chelsea	10.72					(OL)
			TR	Reading	05.74	1974	13	8	4	
TAYLOR, Albert H.	Worksop	02.05.24		Bury	+	1946-47	4		0	(G)
			TR	Sheffield U.	05.48					
			TR	Halifax T.	07.51	1951	8		0	
TAYLOR, Alex	Menstrie	25.12.16	Stirling A.	Carlisle U.	*	1946	16		0	(CH)
TAYLOR, Andy	Stratford-on-Avon	04.04.63	Aston Villa (APP)	Northampton T.	06.81	1981	17	/	0	(D)
TAYLOR, Anthony	Glasgow	06.09.46	Morton	Crystal Palace	11.68	1968-73	192	3	8	(D)
			TR	Southend U.	08.74	1974-75	56	/	1	
			TR	Swindon T.	08.76	1976	20	6	0	
			TR	Bristol Rov.	09.77	1977	12	/	0	
			TR	Portsmouth	02.78	1977	17	/	0	
				Northampton T.	N/C	1979	4	/	0	
TAYLOR, Archie	Glasgow	04.10.18		Reading	+	1946-47	15		2	
			TR	Orient	08.48	1948-50	46		2	
TAYLOR, Arthur A.	Lambeg	05.04.31	Glentoran	Luton T.	07.50	1952-55	8		0	
TAYLOR, Arthur M.	Doncaster	07.11.39	Doncaster Rov.(AM)	Bristol C.	05.58	1959-60	12		2	(F)
			TR	Barnsley	07.61	1961	2		0	
			TR	Mansfield T.	11.61					
			Goole T.	Hull C.	05.62	1962	1		0	
			TR	Halifax T.	07.63	1963-67	173	/	18	
			TR	Bradford C.	12.67	1967	10	1	0	
			TR	York C.	10.68	1968-70	93	3	8	
TAYLOR, Arthur S.	Birmingham	14.03.25	Handsworth W.	W.B.A.	+	1947	4		4	(CF)
TAYLOR, Ashley	Conisborough	11.12.59	APP	Rotherham U.	12.77	1979-81	21	1	0	(D)
TAYLOR, Brian	Hodthorpe	12.02.54	APP	Middlesbrough	07.71	1972-75	14	4	1	(D)
			TR	Doncaster Rov.	12.75	1975-78	118	1	12	
			TR	Rochdale	12.78	1978-82	152	2	10	
TAYLOR, Brian	London	02.07.44	JNRS	Q.P.R.	03.62	1962-65	50	/	0	(FB)
TAYLOR, Brian	Manchester	29.06.42	JNRS	Rochdale	03,62	1963-67	130	1	7	(HB)
TAYLOR, Brian J.	Walsall	24.03.37	JNRS	Walsall	09.54	1954-57	75		19	(OL)
			TR	Birmingham C.	06.58	1958-61	54		7	
			TR	Rotherham U.	10.61	1961-62	44		5	
			TR	Shrewsbury T.	08.63	1963-64	73		8	
			TR	Port Vale	08.65	1965-66	44	2	2	
			TR	Barnsley	06.67	1967	24	0	2	
TAYLOR, Brian J.	Gateshead	02.07.49	Durham C.	Coventry C.	07.70					(D)
			TR	Walsall	05.71	1971-77	204	12	25	
			TR	Plymouth Arg.	10.77	1977-78	34	1	5	
			TR	Preston N.E.	10.78	1978-81	93	6	1	
			L	Wigan Ath.	03.82	1981	7	1	0	
TAYLOR, Carl W.	Penrith	20.01.37	Penrith	Middlesbrough	01.56	1957-59	11		1	(F)
			TR	Aldershot	06.60	1960-62	78		13	
			TR	Darlington	09.62	1962	18		1	

Players Names	Birthplace	Date	Previous Club	League Club	Date Signed	Seasons Played	Career Record Apps	Sub	Gls	
TAYLOR, Colin	Stourbridge	24.08.40	Stourbridge	Walsall	02.58	1958-62	213		93	(OL)●
			TR	Newcastle U.	06.63	1963-64	33		7	
			TR	Walsall	10.64	1964-67	148	/	52	
			TR	Crystal Palace	05.68	1968	32	2	8	
			TR	Walsall	09.69	1969-72	86	11	24	
TAYLOR, David	Rochester	17.09.40	JNRS	Gillingham	09.57	1957-58	20		3	(F)
			TR	Portsmouth	06.59	1959	2		0	
TAYLOR, Derek M.	Bradford	06.06.27	Bradford P.A.(AM)	Halifax T.	AM	1948	2		0	(OR)
TAYLOR, Doug	Wolverhampton	20.04.31	W.B.A.(AM)	Wolverhampton W.	10.49	1954	3		0	(CF)
			TR	Walsall	11.55	1955-56	38		8	
TAYLOR, Edward K.	Irvine	17.05.56	Ipswich T.(APP)	Scunthorpe U.	08.74	1974	7	/	0	(IF)
TAYLOR, Ernie	Sunderland	02.09.25	Hylton Col.	Newcastle U.	+	1947-51	107		19	(IF)E-1/E'B'-1
			TR	Blackpool	10.51	1951-57	217		53	
			TR	Manchester U.	02.58	1957-58	22		2	
			TR	Sunderland	12.58	1958-60	68		11	
TAYLOR, Francis G.	Magherafelt	02.01.23	Bangor	Leeds U.	07.49	1949	3		0	
TAYLOR, Fred	Burnley	24.02.20		Burnley	*	1946	1		0	
			TR	New Brighton	07.48	1948-49	55		10	
TAYLOR, Fred R.	Doncaster	28.10.43	JNRS	Doncaster Rov.	07.61	1961-64	34		2	(F)
TAYLOR, G. Barry	Sheffield	03.12.39		Sheffield U.	05.57					(FB)
			TR	Oldham Ath.	06.63	1963	40		0	
			TR	Chesterfield	08.64	1964-65	34	/	2	
TAYLOR, Geoff A.	Henstead	22.01.23	CNSOBU	Norwich C.	08.46	1946	1		0	(W)
			TR	Reading	03.47	1946	1		0	
			TR	Lincoln C.	08.47	1947	1		0	
			St.Rennais	Brighton & H.A.	08.48	1948	2		0	
				Bristol Rov.	09.51	1951	3		0	
				Q.P.R.	11.53	1953	2		0	
TAYLOR, George A.	King Edward	09.06.13	Aberdeen	Plymouth Arg.	08.48	1948-49	48		2	d.1982
TAYLOR, George E.	Doncaster	21.03.20	Gainsborough	West Ham U.	*	1946-55	115		0	(G)
TAYLOR, George J.	Dundee	23.10.48	JNRS	Grimsby T.	11.65	1965	0	1	0	(F)
TAYLOR, George L.	Edinburgh	11.05.26	Hamilton	Aldershot	06.53					(G)
			TR	Hartlepool U.	11.53	1953-54	34		0	
TAYLOR, George Mc.	Edinburgh	12.12.37	Hamilton	Aldershot	07.52	1952	8		2	(OR)
TAYLOR, Gerry W.	Hull	15.08.47	JNRS	Wolverhampton W.	11.64	1966-75	151	3	1	(FB)
			L	Swindon T.	10.75	1975	19	/	0	
TAYLOR, Gordon	Ashton	28.12.44	JNRS	Bolton W.	01.62	1962-70	253	5	41	(W)Now Secretary of P.F.A.●
			TR	Birmingham C.	12.70	1970-75	156	10	9	
			TR	Blackburn Rov.	03.76	1975-77	62	2	3	
			TR	Bury	06.78	1978-79	58	2	2	
TAYLOR, Gordon S.	W.Stanley	10.06.36	W.Stanley	Gateshead	02.57	1957	3		0	(G)
TAYLOR, Graham	Worksop	15.09.44	JNRS	Grimsby T.	07.62	1963-67	189	/	2	(FB)
			TR	Lincoln C.	07.68	1968-72	150	2	1	
TAYLOR, Granville R.	Worksop	28.07.50	APP	Mansfield T.	APP	1968	1	/	0	
TAYLOR, Henry J.	Tyton-on-Tyne	06.10.35	JNRS	Newcastle U.	11.52	1954-56	7		1	(F)
			L	Fulham	02.57	1957	4		0	
			TR	Newcastle U.	11.57	1958-59	21		4	
TAYLOR, J. Brian	Doncaster	07.10.31	Sheffield Wed.(AM)	Doncaster Rov.	03.49					(G)
			Worksop T.	Leeds U.	05.51	1951	11		0	
			Kings Lynn	Bradford P.A.	06.54	1954-55	66		0	
TAYLOR, James	Salford	02.11.36	JNRS	Bolton W.	12.54					(F)
			TR	Southport	07.59	1959	29		0	
TAYLOR, James	Newton-in-Moor	07.04.25		Manchester C.	+					(F)
			TR	Crewe Alex.	06.47	1947-48	48		8	
TAYLOR James	Tonbridge	13.05.34	Tonbridge	Charlton Ath.	08.54					(F)
			TR	Gillingham	08.56	1956-57	30		16	
			TR	Watford	07.58						
TAYLOR, James G.	Hillingdon	05.11.17	Yiewsley	Fulham	*	1946-52	228		5	(CH)E-2/E.F.
			TR	Q.P.R.	04.53	1953	41		0	LGE REP.
TAYLOR, Jeff N.	Huddersfield	20.09.30	JNRS	Huddersfield T.	09.49	1949-51	68		28	(CF)
			TR	Fulham	11.51	1951-53	67		14	
			TR	Brentford	08.54	1954-56	94		34	
TAYLOR, John	Barnsley	15.02.14	Wolverhampton W.(*)	Norwich C.	*	1946	16		0	d.1978
			TR	Hull C.	07.47	1947-49	72		0	
TAYLOR, John	Cresswell	11.01.39	Marston Moor	Mansfield T.	05.57	1959	5		2	(F)
			TR	Peterborough U.	07.60	1960	1		0	
TAYLOR, John			Kilmarnock	Bradford C.	09.46	1946	2		2	
TAYLOR, John E.	Newcastle	11.09.24	Stockton	Luton T.	02.49	1948-51	85		29	(CF)E'B'-1
			TR	Wolverhampton W.	06.52	1952	10		1	
			TR	Notts.Co.	02.54	1953-56	53		19	
			TR	Bradford P.A.	07.57	1957	12		6	

Players Names	Birthplace	Date	Previous Club	League Club	Date Signed	Seasons Played	Career Record Apps	Sub	Gls	
TAYLOR, John J.	Manchester	12.10.28		Blackpool	09.49					(OR)
			TR	Accrington St.	07.52	1952	15		0	
TAYLOR, John L.	Birmingham	25.06.49	Pwllheli	Chester C.	07.70	1970-73	70	/	0	(G)
			L	Rochdale	10.74	1974	3	/	0	
				Stockport Co.	11.75	1975	1	/	0	
TAYLOR, John W.R.	Durham	10.07.26	Leytonstone	Crystal Palace	AM	1948	2		0	(IF)
TAYLOR, Ken	Huddersfield	21.08.35	JNRS	Huddersfield T.	09.52	1953-64	250		14	(CH)Brother of Jeff/
			TR	Bradford P.A.	02.65	1964-65	51	/	1	Yorks Cricketer
TAYLOR, Ken	Portmadoc	05.06.52	JNRS	Wrexham	05.70	1970	1		0	(FB)
TAYLOR, Ken G.	Sth.Shields	15.03.31	Nth.Shields	Blackburn Rov.	01.50	1954-63	200		0	(FB)
TAYLOR, Ken V.	Manchester	18.06.36	Manch.Transp.	Manchester C.	08.54	1957	1		0	(FB)
TAYLOR, Kevin	Wakefield	22.01.61	APP	Sheffield Wed.	10.78	1978-83	118	7	22	(M)
TAYLOR, Larry D.	Exeter	23.11.47	APP	Bristol Rov.	12.65	1966-69	90	/	0	(G)
TAYLOR, Les	Nth. Shields	04.12.56	APP	Oxford U.	12.74	1974-80	219	/	15	(M)
			TR	Watford	11.80	1980-83	128	4	10	
TAYLOR, Mark	Hartlepool	05.12.62	Heary Smiths	Hartlepool U.	N/C	1982-83	6	/	0	(D)
TAYLOR, Paul	Leith	20.12.66	JNRS	Mansfield T.	N/C	1983	3	/	0	(D)
TAYLOR, Paul A.	Sheffield	03.12.49		Sheffield Wed.	06.71	1971-72	5	1	0	(M)
			TR	York C.	07.73	1973	4	/	0	
			L	Hereford U.	01.74	1973	0	1	0	
			TR	Colchester U.	03.74	1973	6	3	0	
			TR	Southport	07.74	1974-76	95	/	16	
TAYLOR, Peter J.	Southend	03.01.53	APP	Southend U.	01.71	1970-73	57	18	12	(W)E.U23-4/E-4
			TR	Crystal Palace	10.73	1973-76	122	/	33	
			TR	Tottenham H.	09.76	1976-80	116	7	31	
			TR	Orient	11.80	1980-82	49	7	11	
			L	Oldham Ath.	01.83	1982	4	/	0	
			Maidstone U.	Exeter C.	10.83	1983	8	/	0	
TAYLOR, Peter M. R.	Hartlepool	20.11.64		Hartlepool U.	N/C	1983	1	/	0	(M)
TAYLOR, Peter T.	Nottingham	02.07.28	Nottingham F.(AM)	Coventry C.	05.46	1950-54	86		0	(G)
			TR	Middlesbrough	08.55	1955-59	140		0	
			TR	Port Vale	06.61	1961	1		0	
TAYLOR, Philip A.	Sheffield	11.07.58	APP	York C.	07.76	1974-77	14	7	1	(F)
			TR	Darlington	07.78	1978-79	18	8	2	
TAYLOR, Philip H.	Bristol	18.09.17	Bristol Rov.(*)	Liverpool	*	1946-53	223		7	(WH)E-3/E'B'-2/E.F.
										LGE REP./E.SCH.INT./
										Glouc.Cricketer
TAYLOR, Ray J.	Doncaster	01.03.30	Wath W.	Huddersfield T.	09.49	1949	2		0	(OL)
			TR	Southport	08.53	1953-54	51		7	
			TR	Chesterfield	02.55					
			TR	Mansfield T.	08.55					
TAYLOR, Richard E.	Wolverhampton	09.40.18	JNRS	Grimsby T.	*	1946-47	34		0	(CH)
			TR	Scunthorpe U.	N/L	1950-53	131		2	
TAYLOR, Richard H.	Huddersfield	24.01.57	APP	Huddersfield T.	01.74	1973-81	105	/	0	(G)E.YTH.INT.
			L	York C.	03.80	1979	2	/	0	
TAYLOR, Richard M.	Oldham	21.08.28		Everton	06.51					(G)
				Southport	08.54	1954	1		0	
TAYLOR, Richard W.	Silskworth	20.06.51	APP	Sunderland	10.68	1971	0	1	0	(OL)
			TR	York C.	07.72	1972	26	2	2	
TAYLOR, Robert J.	Croydon	16.03.36	Fulham(AM)	Crystal Palace	AM	1954	2		0	(F)
			TR	Gillingham	09.56	1956-58	31		5	
			TR	Millwall	08.59	1959	2		1	
TAYLOR, Rodney V.	Corfe Castle	09.09.43	JNRS	Portsmouth	05.61					(HB)
			TR	Gillingham	07.63	1963-65	9	2	0	
			TR	Bournemouth	02.66	1965-66	29	1	0	
TAYLOR, Roy	Elsecar	02.04.33	Denaby U.	Scunthorpe U.	01.53	1952	2		0	(G)
TAYLOR, Royston	Blackpool	28.09.56	APP	Preston N.E.	10.74	1975	3	/	0	(M)
				Blackburn Rov.	11.76	1978	3	/	1	
TAYLOR, Sam M.	Glasgow	23.09.3	Falkirk	Preston N.E.	06.55	1955-60	149		40	(OR)
			TR	Carlisle U.	06.61	1961-63	93		12	
			TR	Southport	07.64	1964	36		3	
TAYLOR, Stan	Southport	17.11.32	Fleetwood Hesketh	Southport	02.56	1955	2		0	(OL)
TAYLOR, Stephen J.	Royton	18.10.55	APP	Bolton W.	07.74	1974-77	34	6	16	(F)
			L	Port Vale	10.75	1975	4	/	2	
			TR	Oldham Ath.	10.77	1977-78	45	2	25	
			TR	Luton T.	01.79	1978	15	5	1	
			TR	Mansfield T.	07.79	1979	30	7	7	
			TR	Burnley	07.80	1980-82	80	6	37	
			TR	Wigan Ath.	08.83	1983	29	1	7	
			TR	Stockport Co.	03.84	1983	12	/	6	
TAYLOR, Stewart R.	Owston	06.04.46		Scunthorpe U.	08.65	1965-68	64	3	0	(FB)
TAYLOR, Stuart	Bristol	18.04.47	JNRS	Bristol Rov.	01.66	1965-79	545	/	27	(D)●

Players Names	Birthplace	Date	Previous Club	League Club	Date Signed	Seasons Played	Apps	Sub	Gls	
TAYLOR, Thomas	Barnsley	29.01.32	JNRS	Barnsley	07.49	1950-52	44		26	(CF)E-19/E'B'-2/
			TR	Manchester U.	03.53	1952-57	168		112	E.F.LGE REP./d.1958
TAYLOR, Thomas F.	Hornchurch	26.09.51	APP	Orient	10.68	1967-70	112	2	4	(D)E.U23-11/E.YTH.INT./
			TR	West Ham U.	10.70	1970-78	340	/	8	E.SCH.INT.
			TR	Orient	05.79	1979-81	116	/	5	
			Beerschot	Charlton	08.83					
TAYLOR, Thomas W.J.	Wandsworth	10.09.46		Portsmouth	04.64					(F)
			TR	Gillingham	05.65	1965	19	1	0	
			TR	Bournemouth	06.66	1966-67	26	/	8	
TAYLOR, Walter B.	Kirkton	30.10.26	Hibaldstow	Grimsby T.	+	1949-50	21		0	(FB)
			TR	Southport	07.51	1951-57	269		1	
			TR	Oldham Ath.	07.58	1958-59	50		0	
TAYLOR, William	Edinburgh	31.07.39	Bonnyrigg Rose	Orient	08.59	1960-62	23		0	(FB)d.1981
			TR	Nottingham F.	10.63	1963-68	10	9	1	
			TR	Lincoln C.	05.69	1969-70	74	5	6	
TAYLOR, William	Keldholm	03.06.38	Partick Th.	Luton T.	12.67	1967-68	6	/	0	(G)
TEAGUE, William E.	Gloucester	26.09.37	Gloucester C.	Swindon T.	03.61	1960-61	3		0	(G)
			TR	Bristol C.	08.62					
TEALE, Richard	Millom	27.02.52	Walton & Hersham	Q.P.R.	07.73	1974	1	/	0	(G)
			TR	Fulham	08.76	1976	5	/	0	
			TR	Wimbledon	08.77	1977	15	/	0	
TEARSE, David J.	Newcastle	07.08.51	N.Kenton BC	Leicester C.	10.69	1969-70	7	1	1	(IF)
			TR	Torquay U.	11.71	1971-74	77	/	23	
			L	Reading	01.75	1974	2	/	0	
TEASDALE, Jack G.	Rossdale	15.03.29		Doncaster Rov.	10.49	1950-55	113		0	(WH)
TEASDALE, John	Glasgow	15.10.62	Nairn Co.	Wolverhampton W.	12.80	1980-81	6	2	0	(F)
			TR	Walsall	03.82	1981-82	13	/	3	
				Hereford U.	01.83	1982	5	/	1	
TEASDALE, Tom				Hull C.	AM	1946	1		0	
TEBBUTT, Robert S.	Irchester	10.11.34		Northampton T.	10.56	1956-59	56		21	(IF)
TEDDS, William H.	Bedworth	27.07.43	JNRS	Coventry C.	09.60	1961-64	8		0	(FB)
TEDESCO, John J.	Modbury	07.03.49	APP	Plymouth Arg.	05.66	1966-69	35	8	4	(F)
			TR	Bristol Rov.	07.70					
TEECE, David A.	Middleton	01.09.27	Hyde U.	Hull C.	02.52	1953-55	25		0	(G)
			TR	Oldham Ath.	06.56	1956-58	91		0	
TEER, Kevin	London	07.12.63	APP	Brentford	12.81	1980	0	1	0	(D)
TEES, Matt	Airdrie	13.10.39	Airdrie	Grimsby T.	07.63	1963-66	113	/	51	(CF)
			TR	Charlton Ath.	02.67	1966-69	88	1	32	
			TR	Luton T.	08.69	1969-70	33	2	13	
			TR	Grimsby T.	11.70	1970-72	83	/	42	
TELFER, George A.	Liverpool	06.07.55	APP	Everton	08.72	1973-80	81	18	20	(F)
			San Diego	Scunthorpe U.	12.81	1981-82	34	2	11	
			Altrincham	Preston N.E.	N/C	1983	0	2	0	
TELFORD, William A.	Carlisle	05.03.56		Manchester C.	08.75	1975	0	1	0	(CF)
			TR	Peterborough U.	09.75	1975	3	1	2	
			L	Colchester U.	01.76	1975	1	1	1	
TELLING, Maurice W.	London	05.08.19	Berkhampstead	Millwall	10.46	1946	1		0	(CF)d.1973
TEMBY, William	Dover	16.09.34	Rhyl	Q.P.R.	02.55	1955-56	6		3	(F)
TEMPEST, Dale M.	Leeds	30.12.63	APP	Fulham	01.82	1980-83	25	9	6	(F)
TEMPLE, Derek	Liverpool	13.11.38	JNRS	Everton	08.56	1956-67	231	1	72	(W)E-1/E.F.LGE REP./
			TR	Preston N.E.	09.67	1967-69	75	1	14	E.YTH.INT./E.SCH.INT.
TEMPLE, William	Barlow	12.12.15	Grimsby T.(*)	Gateshead	05.46	1946	10		0	(IF)*Aldershot/Carlisle U.
TEMPLEMAN, John H.	Yapton	21.09.47	Arundel T.	Brighton & H.A.	07.66	1966-72	219	7	16	(D)
			TR	Exeter C.	05.74	1974-78	205	1	7	
			TR	Swindon T.	07.79	1979-80	20	1	0	
TENNANT, Albert E.	Ilkeston	29.10.17	Stanton I.Wks	Chelsea	*	1946-48	2		0	(WH)
TENNANT, David	Walsall	13.06.45	JNRS	Walsall	08.63	1963-64	19		0	(G)
			Worcester C.	Grimsby	08.66					
			TR	Lincoln C.	09.66	1966-68	40	/	0	
			TR	Rochdale	08.69	1970	16	/	0	
TENNANT, David	Whitletts	22.01.30	Annbank U.	Ipswich T.	07.52	1952	4		0	(W)
TENNANT, Des W.	Cardiff	17.10.25	JNRS	Cardiff C.	+					(FB)
			Barry T.	Brighton & H.A.	07.48	1948-58	400		40	
TENNANT, John G.	Darlington	01.08.39		Darlington	05.57	1956-57	8		0	(G)
			TR	Chelsea	08.59					
			TR	Southend U.	10.59	1960-62	2		0	
TENNANT, Roy F.	S.Africa	12.09.36		Brighton & H.A.	08.57					(F)
			TR	Workington	07.58	1958-61	152		1	
TENNANT, S.D. Keith	Newport	06.06.34	JNRS	Newport Co.	01.55	1955-57	39		1	(WH)

Players Names	Birthplace	Date	Previous Club	League Club	Date Signed	Seasons Played	Apps	Sub	Gls	
TERNENT, F. Stan	Gateshead	16.06.46	APP	Burnley	06.63	1966-67	5	/	0	(RH)Brother of Ray
			TR	Carlisle U.	05.68	1968-73	186	2	5	
			TR	Sunderland	05.74					
TERNENT, Ray	Blyth	09.09.48	APP	Burnley	09.65	1966-70	13	1	0	(D)
			TR	Southend U.	06.71	1971-72	82	/	1	
			TR	Doncaster Rov.	08.73	1973-76	78	6	3	
TERRIS, James	Chippenham	25.07.33	Chippenham	Bristol C.	10.5	1956-57	4		0	(FB)
			TR	Carlisle U.	04.59	1959-60	28		1	
TERRY, Pat A.	Lambeth	02.10.33	Eastbourne	Charlton Ath.	03.54	1953-54	4		1	(CF)●
			TR	Newport Co.	05.56	1956-57	55		30	
			TR	Swansea C.	02.58	1957-58	17		9	
			TR	Gillingham	10.58	1958-60	109		60	
			TR	Northampton T.	07.61	1961	24		10	
			TR	Millwall	02.62	1961-63	97		41	
			TR	Reading	08.64	1964-66	99	/	41	
			TR	Swindon T.	02.67	1966-67	60	1	23	
			TR	Brentford	06.68	1968	29	/	12	
TERRY, Steve G.	Clapton	14.06.62	APP	Watford	01.80	1979-83	57	/	4	(D)
TESTER, Paul L.	Stroud	10.03.59	Cheltenham	Shrewsbury T.	07.83	1983	6	2	0	(F)
TETHER, Colin	Halesowen	11.08.38	JNRS	Wolverhampton W.	08.55	1956	1		0	(FB)E.YTH.INT.
			TR	Oxford U.	N/L					
TEWLEY, Alan B.	Leicester	22.01.45	APP	Leicester C.	03.62	1966-68	15	3	5	(OR)
			TR	Bradford P.A.	11.69	1969	28	/	4	
			TR	Crewe Alex.	10.70	1970-72	57	11	13	
THARME, Derek	Brighton	19.08.38	Whitehaven	Tottenham H.	10.56					(FB)
			TR	Southend U.	05.62	1962	7		0	
THEAKER, Clarence A.	Spalding	08.12.12	Grimsby T.(*)	Newcastle U.	*	1946	1		0	(G)
			TR	Hartlepool U.	06.47	1947	14		0	
THEAR, Anthony C.	London	04.02.48	JNRS	Arsenal	02.65					(F)
			TR	Luton T.	07.66	1966	12	2	5	
			TR	Gillingham	02.67	1966-68	7	/	1	
THIJSSEN, Frans J.	Holland	23.01.52	F.C. Twente	Ipswich T.	02.79	1978-82	123	2	10	(M)DUTCH INT.
			Vancouver W.	Nottingham F.	10.83	1983	17	/	3	
THOM, Lewis M.	Stornaway	10.04.44	Dundee U.	Shrewsbury T.	09.65	1965-66	48	1	5	(OL)
			TR	Lincoln C.	05.67	1966-68	45	2	4	
			TR	Bradford P.A.	06.69	1969	30	/	1	
THOMAS, Andy M.	Oxford	16.12.62	APP	Oxford U.	12.80	1980-83	76	19	29	(F)
			L	Fulham	12.82	1982	3	1	2	
			L	Derby Co.	03.83	1982	0	1	0	
THOMAS, Barrie	Merthyr Tydfil	27.08.54	JNRS	Swansea C.	AM	1971	2	/	0	(D)
				Bournemouth	08.79	1979	3	/	0	
THOMAS, Barrie E.	Measham	19.05.37	JNRS	Leicester C.	07.54	1954-55	7		3	(CF)E.YTH.INT.●
			TR	Mansfield T.	06.57	1957-59	72		48	
			TR	Scunthorpe U.	09.59	1959-61	88		67	
			TR	Newcastle U.	01.62	1961-64	73		48	
			TR	Scunthorpe U.	11.64	1964-66	52	/	26	
			TR	Barnsley	11.66	1966-67	43	/	19	
THOMAS, Brian H.	Carmarthen	28.06.44	JNRS	Swansea C.	08.62	1964	4		0	(WH)
THOMAS, Bryn	Coventry	13.12.32	Longford Rov.	Coventry C.	09.50	1952-53	12		1	(F)
THOMAS, Cedric D.	Heponstall	19.09.36	Heponstall	Halifax T.	07.57	1957-59	20		5	(F)
			TR	Southport	07.60					
THOMAS, D. Gwyn	Swansea	26.09.57	APP	Leeds U.	07.57	1974-83	79	10	3	(M)W.U21-2/W.SCH.INT.
			TR	Barnsley	03.84	1983	13	/	0	
THOMAS, Danny J.	Worksop	12.11.61	APP	Coventry C.	12.78	1979-82	103	5	5	(D)E.U21-7/E.SCH.INT./E-2
			TR	Tottenham H.	06.83	1983	26	1	0	
THOMAS, David	Kirkby	05.10.50	APP	Burnley	10.67	1966-72	153	4	19	(W)E-8/E.U23-11/
			TR	Q.P.R.	10.72	1972-76	181	1	29	E.YTH.INT.
			TR	Everton	08.77	1977-78	71	/	4	
			TR	Wolverhampton W.	10.79	1979	10	/	0	
			Vancouver W.	Middlesbrough	03.82	1981	13	/	1	
			TR	Portsmouth	07.82	1982-83	21	6	0	
THOMAS, David A.	Port Talbot	01.08.26	Abergregon	Swansea C.	08.48	1949-59	298		16	(IF)W-2
			TR	Newport	07.61	1961-62	58		1	
THOMAS, David S.	Machynlieth	12.11.19	Treharris	Fulham	*	1946-49	57		4	(W)W-4
			TR	Bristol C.	06.56	1950	13		1	
THOMAS, David S.L.	Swansea	19.09.20		Swansea C.	+					(F)W.SCH.INT.
			TR	Brighton & H.A.	06.47	1947	13		4	
THOMAS, David W.J.	Stepney	06.07.17	Romford	Plymouth Arg.	*	1946-47	51		22	(CF)Brother of Robert A.
			TR	Watford	02.48	1947-50	105		39	
			TR	Gillingham	10.50	1950-52	80		42	
THOMAS, Dean	Bedworth	19.12.61	Nuneaton	Wimbledon	07.81	1981-83	57	/	8	(D)
THOMAS, Dennis	Hebburn	02.02.26		Bury	01.49	1949	3		0	
			TR	Accrington St.	07.50	1950	34		5	

Players Names	Birthplace	Date	Previous Club	League Club	Date Signed	Seasons Played	Apps	Sub	Gls	
THOMAS, Edward	Newton-le-Willows	23.10.33	JNRS	Everton	10.51	1956-59	86		39	(IF)
			TR	Blackburn Rov.	02.60	1959-61	37		9	
			TR	Swansea C.	07.62	1962-64	68		21	
			TR	Derby Co.	08.64	1964-67	102	3	44	
			TR	Orient	09.67	1967	11	/	2	
THOMAS, Edwin H.C.	Swindon	09.11.32		Southampton	05.51	1951	8		0	(G)
THOMAS, Geoff	Swansea	18.02.48	APP	Swansea C.	02.66	1966-75	346	15	52	(HB)W.U23-3
THOMAS, Geoff P.	Bradford	12.03.46	APP	Bradford P.A.	03.63	1963-65	53	/	0	(FB)
THOMAS, Geoff R.	Manchester	05.08.64	Littleborough P.	Rochdale	N/C	1982-83	10	1	1	(F)
			TR	Crewe Alex.	03.84	1983	5	3	1	
THOMAS, Geoff S.	Derby	21.02.26	JNRS	Nottingham F.	+	1946-59	404		0	(FB)●
THOMAS, Geoff V.	Cardiff	25.06.30		Cardiff C.	05.49					
			TR	Newport Co.	07.53	1953-58	137		0	
THOMAS, Jeff	Newport	18.05.49	JNRS	Newport Co.	05.66	1965-72	206	5	34	(F)W.U23-1
THOMAS, John	Poole	28.05.36		Bournemouth	05.58	1958	4	/	0	(G)
THOMAS, John C.	W.Hougton	22.09.32	Wath W.	Wolverhampton W.	08.51					(FB)
			TR	Barnsley	06.52	1952-57	135		0	
			TR	Mansfield T.	03.58	1957-58	41		0	
			TR	Chesterfield	07.59	1959	6		0	
THOMAS, John E.	Walsall	15.07.22	Bournemouth(+)	W.B.A.	07.46					(F)
			TR	Crystal Palace	10.48	1948-51	52		17	
THOMAS, John W.	Wednesbury	05.08.58		Everton	07.78					(F)
			L	Tranmere Rov.	03.79	1978	10	1	2	
			L	Halifax T.	10.79	1979	5	/	0	
			TR	Bolton W.	06.80	1980-81	18	4	6	
			TR	Chester C.	08.82	1982	44	/	20	
			TR	Lincoln C.	08.83	1983	31	6	13	
THOMAS, John W.	Liverpool	23.12.26		Everton	12.48					(OR)
			TR	Swindon T.	02.49	1950-51	16		3	
			TR	Chester C.	07.53	1953	29		4	
			TR	Stockport Co.	07.54	1954	6		0	
THOMAS, Kevin A.	Prescot	13.08.45	Prescot Cables	Blackpool	06.66	1966-68	12	/	0	(G)
			TR	Tranmere Rov.	09.69	1969-70	18	/	0	
			TR	Oxford U.	07.71	1972	5	/	0	
			TR	Southport	07.74	1974-75	67	/	0	
THOMAS, Martin R.	Senghenydd	28.11.59	APP	Bristol Rov.	09.77	1976-81	162	/	0	(G)W.U21-2/W.YTH.INT.
			L	Cardiff C.	07.82	1982	15	/	0	
			L	Southend U.	02.83	1982	6	/	0	
			TR	Newcastle U.	03.83	1982-83	26	/	0	
THOMAS, Mickey R.	Mochdre	07.07.54	JNRS	Wrexham	04.76	1971-78	217	13	33	(M)W-42/W.U23-2
			TR	Manchester U.	11.78	1978-80	90	/	11	
			TR	Everton	08.81	1981	10	/	0	
			TR	Brighton & H.A.	11.81	1981	18	2	0	
			TR	Stoke C.	08.82	1982-83	57	/	14	
			TR	Chelsea	01.84	1983	17	/	4	
THOMAS, Mitchell A.	Luton	02.10.64	APP	Luton T.	08.82	1982-83	30	/	0	(D)
THOMAS, Patrick A.	Sidmouth	07.03.65	JNRS	Exeter C.	N/C	1982	0	1	0	
THOMAS, Peter J.	Coventry	20.11.44		Coventry C.	10.66	1966	1	/	0	(G)
THOMAS, Peter J.	Cardiff	18.10.32		Cardiff C.	03.53	1953	5		1	(OR)
			TR	Exeter C.	12.54	1954-55	29		4	
			TR	Newport Co.	07.56	1956-57	7		1	
THOMAS, Phil L.	Sherborne	14.12.52	APP	Bournemouth	07.71					(IF)
			TR	Colchester U.	05.72	1972-75	103	5	8	
THOMAS, Rees	Aberdare	03.01.34	JNRS	Cardiff C.	01.51					(RB)
			L	Torquay U.	08.53	1953	1		0	
			TR	Brighton & H.A.	09.56	1956-57	31		1	
			TR	Bournemouth	01.58	1957-58	48		0	
			TR	Portsmouth	07.59	1959-60	31		0	
			TR	Aldershot	07.59	1961-63	103		2	
THOMAS, Robert A.	London	02.08.19	Brentford(+)	Plymouth Arg.	+	1946	41		17	(IF)
			TR	Fulham	06.47	1947-51	168		55	
			TR	Crystal Palace	09.52	1952-54	96		31	
THOMAS, Rod J.	Glyncorrwg	11.01.47	Gloucester C.	Swindon T.	07.64	1965-73	296	/	5	(D)W-47/W.U23-6
			TR	Derby Co.	11.73	1973-77	89	/	2	
			TR	Cardiff C.	11.77	1977-81	89	7	0	
			TR	Newport Co.	03.82	1981	3	/	0	
THOMAS, Steven J.	Batley	29.01.57	JNRS	Swansea C.	AM	1973-74	10	/	0	(FB)
THOMAS, Valmore	Worksop	30.04.58	APP	Coventry C.	03.76					(D)Brother of Danny
			TR	Hereford U.	03.79	1978-80	31	1	1	
THOMAS, Walter K.	Oswestry	28.07.29	Oswestry T.	Sheffield Wed.	09.50	1950-51	10		1	(OR)
			TR	Cardiff C.	07.52	1952-53	9		4	
			TR	Plymouth Arg.	11.53	1953-55	35		8	
			TR	Exeter C.	03.56	1955-56	46		6	
THOMAS, William P.	Glyn-Neath	28.10.23	Merthyr Tydfil	Torquay U.	09.47	1947-54	90		17	(OL)

Players Names	Birthplace	Date	Previous Club	League Club	Date Signed	Seasons Played	Career Record Apps	Sub	Gls	
THOMAS, Wilson G.	Derby	18.11.18	Matlock T.	Bristol C.	+	1946-49	76		18	
THOMPSON, Alan	Goole	02.09.31	Westpark J.	Luton T.	12.49	1956	1		0	(FB)
THOMPSON, Alan W.	Liverpool	20.01.52	APP	Sheffield Wed.	01.69	1970-75	150	6	3	(D)
			TR	Stockport Co.	08.76	1976-78	93	1	17	
			Portland Timbers	Bradford C.	01.80	1979-81	31	/	0	
			TR	Scunthorpe U.	03.82	1981	11	/	0	
THOMPSON, Alex	Sheffield	08.12.17	Sheffield Wed.(*)	Lincoln C.	+	1946-47	34		1	(RB)
			TR	Tranmere Rov.	06.48	1948	2		0	
THOMPSON, Arthur	Desbury	15.06.22	Thornhill E.	Huddersfield T.	+	1946-48	25		5	(IF)
THOMPSON, Brian	Brierley Hill	09.02.50	APP	Wolverhampton W.	02.67					(LH)
			TR	Oxford U.	10.69	1969-72	50	5	4	
			L	Torquay U.	03.73	1972	9	/	1	
THOMPSON, Charles M.	Chesterfield	19.07.20	Bolsover Col.	Sheffield U.	*	1946	17		3	(CF)
THOMPSON, Chris D.	Walsall	24.01.60	APP	Bolton W.	07.77	1979-82	66	7	18	(F)E.YTH.INT.
			L	Lincoln C.	03.83	1982	5	1	0	
			TR	Blackburn Rov.	08.83	1983	31	2	8	
THOMPSON, Cyril A.	Southend	18.12.18		Southend U.	+	1946-47	67		35	(CF)
			TR	Derby Co.	07.48	1948-49	16		3	
			TR	Brighton & H.A.	03.50	1949-50	41		16	
			TR	Watford	03.51	1950-52	78		34	
THOMPSON, David	Middlesbrough	26.02.45		Lincoln C.	06.64	1964	3		1	(CF)
THOMPSON, David S.	Manchester	27.05.62	JNRS	Rochdale	N/C	1981-83	83	5	10	(F)
THOMPSON, David S.	Scotton	12.03.45	JNRS	Wolverhampton W.	04.62	1964	8		1	(OR)
			TR	Southampton	08.66	1966-70	21	3	0	
			TR	Mansfield T.	10.70	1970-73	129	2	24	
			TR	Chesterfield	12.73	1973	14	/	3	
THOMPSON, Dennis	Sheffield	02.06.25	JNRS	Sheffield U.	+	1946-50	96		20	(OR)E.SCH.INT.
			TR	Southend U.	07.51	1951-53	49		11	
THOMPSON, Dennis	Shuttland	19.07.34	JNRS	Chesterfield	07.51	1950-52	24		0	
			TR	Scunthorpe U.	07.55	1955	3		0	
THOMPSON, Dennis	Whitburn	10.04.24	Whitburn Welf.	Hull C.	04.47	1946-47	9		8	(IF)
THOMPSON, Des	Southampton	04.12.28	Gainsborough	York C.	01.51	1950-52	80		0	(G)Brother of George H.
			TR	Burnley	11.52	1952-54	62		0	
			TR	Sheffield U.	05.55	1955-63	25		0	
THOMPSON, Fred N.	Swindon	24.11.37		Swindon T.	09.55	1954-60	21		1	(HB)
THOMPSON, G. Brian	Ashington	07.08.52		Sunderland	06.71					(D)
			L	York C.	03.73	1972	4	2	0	
			Yeovil T.	Mansfield T.	11.79	1979	9	/	0	
THOMPSON, Gary L.	Birmingham	07.10.59	APP	Coventry C.	06.77	1977-82	127	7	38	(F)E.U21-6
			TR	W.B.A.	02.83	1982-83	49	/	20	
THOMPSON, George			Sligo Rgrs.	Huddersfield T.	*					(IF)
			TR	Exeter C.	06.46	1946-47	64		4	
			TR	Rochdale	07.48					
THOMPSON, George H.	Maltby	15.09.26		Chesterfield	06.47					(G)
			TR	Scunthorpe U.	06.50	1950-52	92		0	
			TR	Preston N.E.	10.52	1952-55	140		0	
			TR	Manchester C.	06.56	1956	2		0	
			TR	Carlisle U.	06.57	1957-61	202		0	
THOMPSON, Harry	Mansfield	29.04.15	Sunderland(*)	York C.	+					(IF)*Mansfield T./
			TR	Northampton T.	11.46	1946-48	38		2	Wolverhampton W.
THOMPSON, Henry	Sth.Shields	21.02.32		Gateshead	08.51	1951-55	23		4	(F)
THOMPSON, Ian P.	Dartford	08.06.58	Salisbury	Bournemouth	07.83	1983	42	2	12	(F)
THOMPSON, J. Trevor	Newcastle	21.05.55	APP	W.B.A.	01.74	1973-75	20	/	0	(D)
			TR	Newport Co.	08.78	1978-79	32	3	2	
			TR	Lincoln C.	12.79	1979-81	80	/	1	
THOMPSON, James	Chadderton	26.11.35		Oldham Ath.	01.54	1953-58	110		19	(WH)
			TR	Exeter C.	12.58	1958-60	104		9	
			TR	Rochdale	03.61	1960-65	199	/	15	
			TR	Bradford C.	12.65	1965	23	1	1	
THOMPSON, James B.	Gateshead	07.01.43	St.Mary's BC	Grimsby T.	09.61	1962-66	158	/	2	(FB)
				Watford	11.68					
			S.Africa	Cambridge U.	N/L	1970-72	116	1	0	
THOMPSON, Joe P.	Dawdon	15.11.27	Electrolux	Luton T.	05.46					(FB)
			TR	Shrewsbury T.	07.51	1951	7		0	
THOMPSON, John	Cramlington	21.03.15	Sheffield Wed.(*)	Doncaster Rov.	05.46	1946-47	59		17	(CF)
			TR	Chesterfield	07.48	1948-52	82		8	
THOMPSON, John H.	Newcastle	04.07.32	JNRS	Newcastle U.	09.50	1954-55	8		0	(G)
			TR	Lincoln C.	05.57	1957-59	42		0	
THOMPSON, Keith A.	Birmingham	24.04.65	APP	Coventry C.	01.83	1982-83	8	3	0	(F)
			L	Wimbledon	10.83	1983	0	3	0	

Players Names	Birthplace	Date	Previous Club	League Club	Date Signed	Seasons Played	Apps	Sub	Gls	
THOMPSON, Ken H.	Wearmouth	24.04.26		Middlesbrough	+					
			L	Gateshead	11.46	1946	9		0	
			TR	York C.	07.50	1950-51	21		0	
THOMPSON, Ken J.	Ipswich	01.03.45	APP	Ipswich T.	03.62	1964-65	11	/	0	(WH)
			TR	Exeter C.	06.66	1966	38	1	1	
THOMPSON, Kevan	Middlesbrough	08.09.48	Fred Halls	Hartlepool U.	AM	1970	5	/	1	(CF)
THOMPSON, Malcolm G.	Beverley	19.10.46	Goole T.	Hartlepool U.	11.68	1968-69	42	1	9	(F)
			TR	Gillingham	06.70					
THOMPSON, Max S.	Liverpool	31.02.56	APP	Liverpool	01.74	1973	1	/	0	(D)
			TR	Blackpool	12.77	1977-80	92	7	6	
			TR	Swansea C.	09.81	1981-82	25	1	2	
			TR	Bournemouth	08.83	1983	9	/	0	
			L	Port Vale	11.83	1983	2	/	0	
THOMPSON, Neil	Beverley	02.10.63	Nottingham F. (APP)	Hull C.	08.82	1981-82	29	2	0	(M)
THOMPSON, Nigel	Leeds	01.03.67	APP	Leeds U.	APP	1983	1	/	0	(D)
THOMPSON, Pat A.	Exeter	11.02.32	Topsham	Brighton & H.A.	01.51	1950	1		0	
THOMPSON, Peter	Carlisle	27.11.42	JNRS	Preston N.E.	11.59	1960-62	121		20	(W)E-16/E.U23-4/●
			TR	Liverpool	08.63	1963-71	318	5	42	E.SCH.INT.
			TR	Bolton W.	11.73	1973-77	111	6	2	
THOMPSON, Peter	Blackhall	16.02.36	Blackhall C.W.	Wrexham	AM	1955-56	42		21	(CF)E.AMAT.INT.
			TR	Hartlepool U.	07.58	1957-58	47		17	
			TR	Derby Co.	11.58	1958-61	52		19	
			TR	Bournemouth	01.62	1961-62	39		14	
			TR	Hartlepool U.	09.63	1963-65	91	/	34	
THOMPSON, Peter C.	Mombasa	25.07.42	Grantham	Peterborough U.	03.64	1963-68	79	6	15	(F)
THOMPSON, Phil B.	Liverpool	21.01.54	APP	Liverpool	02.71	1971-82	337	3	7	(D)E-42/E.U23-2/●
										E.F.LGE REP.
THOMPSON, Ray	B.Auckland	21.10.25		Sunderland	+					(FB)
			TR	Hartlepool U.	01.47	1946-57	396		2	
THOMPSON, Robert E.	Mexborough	03.12.44	Leeds U.(APP)	Doncaster Rov.	07.62	1962	9		0	(CH)
THOMPSON, Ron	Carlisle	20.01.32		Carlisle U.	07.51	1951-63	374		12	(WH)
THOMPSON, Ron	Sheffield	24.12.21		Sheffield Wed.	+					(IF)
			TR	Rotherham U.	05.47	1947-48	30		11	
			TR	York C.	06.49	1949	8		0	
THOMPSON, Sid	Bedlington	14.07.28		Nottingham F.	09.47	1952-54	22		8	(F)
			TR	Scunthorpe U.	08.55					
THOMPSON, Steve J.	Plymouth	12.01.63	JNRS	Bristol C.	07.81	1981-82	10	2	1	(M)
			TR	Torquay U.	N/C	1982	0	1	0	
THOMPSON, Steve J.	Oldham	02.11.64	APP	Bolton W.	11.82	1982-83	43	/	3	(M)
THOMPSON, Steve P.	Sheffield	28.07.55	Boston U.	Lincoln C.	04.80	1980-83	112	1	7	(D)
THOMPSON, Stuart C.	Littleborough	02.09.64	APP	Rochdale	09.82	1982-83	23	8	7	(F)E.SCH.INT.
THOMPSON, Terry W.	Barleston	25.12.46	APP	Wolverhampton W.	01.64					(HB)
			TR	Notts.Co.	03.66	1965-67	66	/	3	
THOMPSON, Thomas	Fencehouses	10.11.28	Lumley YMCA	Newcastle U.	08.46	1946-49	20		6	(IF)E-2/E'B'-1/●
			TR	Aston Villa	08.50	1950-54	148		67	E.F.LGE REP.
			TR	Preston N.E.	07.55	1955-60	188		117	
			TR	Stoke C.	06.61	1961-62	42		18	
			TR	Barrow	03.63	1962-63	44		16	
THOMPSON, Thomas W.	Stockton	09.03.38	Stockton	Blackpool	08.61	1961-68	154	1	1	(FB)E.AMAT.INT.
			TR	York C.	07.70	1970	4	/	0	
THOMPSON, William			Leeds U.(+)	Watford	08.46	1946	9		0	(G)
THOMPSON, William	Ashington	23.12.21		Gateshad	+	1946-47	3		0	
THOMPSON, William	Bedlington	05.01.40	JNRS	Newcastle U.	01.57	1960-66	79	1	5	(CH)
			TR	Rotherham U.	06.67	1967	8	/	0	
			TR	Darlington	01.68	1967-69	30	/	5	
THOMPSON, William G.	Glasgow	10.08.21		Portsmouth	+	1948-52	40		2	(WH)
			TR	Bournemouth	01.53	1952-53	45		0	
THOMSON, Arthur C.	Edinburgh	02.09.48	Hearts	Oldham Ath.	01.70	1969-70	27	1	1	(CH)S.U23-3
THOMSON, Brian L.	Paisley	01.03.59	Morecambe	West Ham U.	01.77					(F)
			TR	Mansfield T.	08.79	1979-81	54	9	1	
THOMSON, Charles R.	Perth	02.03.30	Clyde	Chelsea	10.52	1952-55	46		0	(G)
			TR	Nottingham F.	08.57	1957-60	121		0	
THOMSON, David L.	Bothkennar	02.02.38	Dunfermline	Leicester C.	08.61	1961	1		1	(F)
THOMSON, George M.	Edinburgh	19.10.36	Hearts	Everton	11.60	1960-62	73		1	(FB)S.F.LGE REP.
			TR	Brentford	11.63	1963-67	160	2	5	
THOMSON, Harry W.	Edinburgh	25.08.40	Bo'ness U.	Burnley	08.59	1964-68	117	/	0	(G)
			TR	Blackpool	07.69	1969-70	59	/	0	
			TR	Barrow	08.71	1971	40	/	0	
THOMSON, Herbert	Glasgow	18.02.29	Yeovil T.	Rochdale	06.58	1958-59	54		1	(HB)

Players Names	Birthplace	Date	Previous Club	League Club	Date Signed	Seasons Played	Apps	Sub	Gls	
THOMSON, James	Glasgow	01.10.46	Provenside Hibs.	Chelsea	0165	1965-67	33	6	1	(D)
			TR	Burnley	09.68	1968-80	294	3	3	
THOMSON, James A.	Glasgow	28.06.48	Petershill	Newcastle U.	08.68	1969	4	1	0	(RH)
			L	Barrow	12.70	1970	2	/	0	
			TR	Grimsby T.	07.71	1971	23	3	4	
THOMSON, James D.	Govan	17.03.31	Raith Rov.	Southend U.	05.56	1956-58	40		10	(F)
THOMSON, John	Newcastle	03.12.54	APP	Newcastle U.	12.72					(D)
			TR	Bury	11.73	1973-77	92	11	8	
THOMSON, John B	Glasgow	22.10.34	Hearts	Workington	05.58	1958	11		1	(FB)
THOMSON, Ken G.	Aberdeen	25.02.30	Aberdeen	Stoke C.	09.52	1952-59	278		6	(CH)
			TR	Middlesbrough	12.59	1959-62	84		1	
			TR	Hartlepool U.	10.62	1962	28		0	
THOMSON, Lawrie J.	Menstrie	26.08.36	Partick Th.	Carlisle U.	01.60	1959	12		1	(F)
THOMSON, Richard C.	Edinburgh	26.06.57	APP	Preston N.E.	06.75	1974-79	60	11	20	(F)
THOMSON, Robert	Glasgow	21.03.55	Morton	Middlesbrough	09.81	1981	18	2	2	(M)
THOMSON, Robert	Menstrie	21.11.39	Partick Th.	Liverpool	12.62	1962-63	7		0	(FB)
			TR	Luton T.	08.65	1965-66	74	/	0	
THOMSON, Robert A.	Smethwick	05.12.43	APP	Wolverhampton W.	07.61	1961-68	277	/	3	(D)E-8/E.U23-15/
			TR	Birmingham C.	03.69	1968-70	62	1	0	E.F.LGE REP.
			L	Walsall	11.71	1971	9	/	1	
			TR	Luton T.	07.72	1972-75	110	/	1	
			Hartford Cons.	Port Vale	10.76	1976	18	/	0	
THOMSON, Robert G.	Dundee	21.03.37	Airdrie	Wolverhampton W.	08.54	1956	1		1	(IF)
			TR	Aston Villa	06.59	1959-63	143		55	
			TR	Birmingham C.	09.63	1963-67	110	5	24	
			TR	Stockport Co.	12.67	1967	16	1	0	
THORBURN, Jim	Lanark	10.03.38	Raith Rov.	Ipswich T.	06.63	1963-64	24		0	(G)
THORLEY, Dennis	Stoke	07.11.56	JNRS	Stoke C.	07.76	1976-80	9	4	0	(D)
			L	Blackburn Rov.	03.80	1979	2	2	0	
THORNBER, Steve J.	Dewsbury	11.10.65		Halifax T.	N/C	1983	3	1	1	(F)
THORNE, Adrian	Brighton	02.08.37	JNRS	Brighton & H.A.	08.54	1957-60	76		38	(CF)
			TR	Plymouth Arg.	06.61	1961-63	11		2	
			TR	Exeter C.	12.63	1963-64	41		9	
			TR	Orient	07.65	1965	2	/	0	
THORNE, Terry	Kirton	02.02.47	Lincoln C.(AM)	Ipswich T.	08.64					(HB)
				Notts.Co.	06.66	1966	2	/	0	
THORNHILL, Dennis	Draycott	05.07.23	JNRS	Wolverhampton W.	+					
			TR	Southend U.	03.48	1948-49	11		0	
THORNHILL, Keith E.	Crewe	20.12.63	Nantwich	Crewe Alex.	N/C	1983	1	/	0	(F)
THORNHILL, Rodney	Reading	24.01.42		Reading	05.63	1963-69	188	4	18	(HB)
THORNLEY, Barry	Gravesend	11.02.48	Gravesend	Brentford	09.65	1965	7	/	0	(F)
			TR	Oxford U.	07.67	1967-68	22	1	4	
THORNS, John W.	Newcastle	10.07.28		Darlington	AM	1949	1		0	d.1975
THORPE, Adrian	Chesterfield	25.11.63		Mansfield T.	N/C	1982	0	2	1	(F)
THORPE, Andy	Stockport	15.09.60	JNRS	Stockport Co.	08.78	1977-83	251	2	3	(D)
THORPE, Arthur W.	Leeds	31.07.39	Ossett	Scunthorpe U.	09.60	1960-62	27		4	(F)
			TR	Bradford C.	07.63	1963-65	81	/	17	
THORPE, Ian R.	Blackheath	03.09.53		Gillingham	09.73	1973	5	/	0	(G)
THORPE, Len	Warsop	07.06.24	Nottingham F.(AM)	Mansfield T.	+	1946	5		0	(IF)
THORPE, Sam	Sheffield	02.12.20		Sheffield U.	+	1947-48	2		0	
THORUP, Borge	Denmark	04.10.43	Morton	Crystal Palace	03.69	1969	0	1	0	(HB)
THREADGOLD, Harry J.	Tottenhall	06.11.24		Chester C.	10.47	1950-51	83		0	(G)
			TR	Sunderland	07.52	1952	35		0	
			TR	Southend U.	07.53	1953-62	319		0	
THRELFALL, Joseph R.	Ashton	05.03.16		Bolton W.	+	1946	3		0	(FB)
				Halifax T.	10.47	1947	30		0	
THRELFALL, John	Little Lever	22.03.35		Bolton W.	12.54	1955-62	47		1	(FB)
			TR	Bury	11.62	1962-64	37		1	
THRESHER, Mike T.	Cullompton	09.03.31	Chard T.	Bristol C.	01.54	1954-64	378		1	(FB)
THRIPPLETON, Alan	Huddersfield	16.06.28	Rainham T.	Millwall	11.50	1950-54	27		4	(FB)
THROWER, Dennis	Ipswich	01.08.38	JNRS	Ipswich T.	08.55	1956-63	27		2	(HB)
THROWER, Nigel J.	Nottingham	12.03.62	APP	Nottingham F.	03.80					(D)
			L	Chesterfield	02.83	1982	4	/	0	
THURLOW, Alec C.E.	Depwade	24.02.22		Huddersfield T.	+					(G)d.1956
			TR	Manchester C.	09.46	1946-48	21		0	
THURLOW, Brian A.	Loddon	06.06.36	Loddon	Norwich C.	07.54	1955-63	193		1	(FB)
			TR	Bristol C.	07.64					
THURNHAM, Roy T.	Macclesfield	17.02.42	JNRS	Manchester C.	06.60					(HB)
			TR	Wrexham	06.61	1962	2		0	

Players Names	Birthplace	Date	Previous Club	League Club	Date Signed	Seasons Played	Apps	Sub	Gls	
THWAITES, Dennis	Stockton	14.12.44	APP	Birmingham C.	05.62	1962-70	79	4	18	(F)E.YTH.INT./E.SCH.INT.
THWAITES, Peter	Batley	21.08.36	Swillington	Halifax T.	AM	1960	2		0	(CF)
THYNE, Robert B.	Glasgow	09.01.20	Clydebank	Darlington	+	1946	7		0	(CH)
TIBBOTT, Les	Oswestry	25.08.55	APP	Ipswich T.	03.73	1975-78	52	2	0	(D)W.U21-2
			TR	Sheffield U.	03.79	1978-81	78	/	2	
TICKELL, Brian G.	Carlisle	15.11.39	JNRS	Huddersfield T.	11.56	1958	1		0	(CF)
			TR	Carlisle U.	05.59	1959	3		1	
TICKELL, E. Roy	Liverpool	25.04.24	St. Leonards	Exeter C.	+					(OR)
			TR	Southport	05.47	1947	6		1	
TICKRIDGE, Sid	Stepney	10.04.23	JNRS	Tottenham H.	+	1946-50	95		0	(FB)E.SCH.INT.
			TR	Chelsea	03.51	1950-52	61		0	
			TR	Brentford	07.55	1955-56	62		0	
TIDDY, Mike D.	Helston	04.04.29	JNRS	Torquay U.	11.46	1946-50	5		0	(OR)
			TR	Cardiff C.	11.50	1950-54	145		19	
			TR	Arsenal	09.55	1955-57	48		8	
			TR	Brighton & H.A.	10.58	1958-61	134		11	
TIERNEY, Jim M.	Ayr	02.05.40	Saltcoats Vic.	Bradford C.	01.60	1960	2		0	(F)
TIERNEY, Lawrie	Leith	04.04.59	Hibernian	Wigan Ath.	07.80	1980	4	3	0	(M)
TIGHE, John	Aghamore	13.03.23	Larkhall Th.	W.B.A.	+	1946	1		0	(G)
TIGHE, Terry W.	Edinburgh	12.08.34	Dunfermline	Accrington St.	06.57	1957-60	118		20	(HB)
			TR	Crewe Alex.	12.60	1960-62	86		5	
			TR	Southport	08.63	1963	36		3	
TILER, Brian	Whiston	15.03.43		Rotherham U.	07.62	1962-68	212	/	27	(WH)
			TR	Aston Villa	12.68	1968-72	106	1	3	
			TR	Carlisle U.	10.72	1972-73	51	1	1	
TILER, Ken D.	Sheffield	23.05.50		Chesterfield	09.70	1970-74	138	1	1	(D)
			TR	Brighton & H.A.	11.74	1974-78	130	/	0	
			TR	Rotherham U.	07.79	1979-80	45	1	1	
TILLEY, H. Rex	Swindon	16.02.29	Chippenham	Plymouth Arg.	03.51	1952-56	123		0	(WH)
			TR	Swindon T.	08.58	1958-59	31		0	
TILLEY, Kevin	Feltham	06.09.57	Q.P.R.(APP)	Wimbledon	N/L	1977	11	2	0	(D)
TILLEY, Peter	Lurgan	13.01.30	Witton A.	Arsenal	05.52	1953	1		0	(IF)
			TR	Bury	11.53	1953-57	86		12	
			TR	Halifax T.	07.58	1958-62	184		17	
TILLING, Harold K.	Warrington	06.01.18	Whitecross FC	Oldham Ath.	+	1947	3		0	(OL)
TILLOTSON, Maurice	Silsden	20.01.44	JNRS	Huddersfield T.	07.62					(FB)
			TR	Stockport Co.	10.64	1964-65	35	/	0	
TILSED, Ron W.	Weymouth	06.08.52	APP	Bournemouth	01.70	1969	2	/	0	(G)E.YTH.INT.
			TR	Chesterfield	02.72	1971	16	/	0	
			TR	Arsenal	09.72					
			TR	Portsmouth	03.73	1972-73	14	/	0	
			TR	Hereford U.	06.74					
TILSTON, Tom A.	Chester	19.02.26		Chester C.	+	1949-50	22		6	(IF)
			TR	Tranmere Rov.	06.51	1951	25		15	
			TR	Wrexham	03.52	1951-53	78		29	
			TR	Crystal Palace	02.54	1953-55	58		14	
TIMMINS, Arnold	Whitehaven	29.01.40	Low CA	Workington T.	07.61	1960-63	44		10	(IF)
TIMMINS, Charles	Birmingham	29.05.22	Jack Moulds	Coventry C.	09.46	1949-57	164		6	(FB)
TIMMINS, John	Brierley Hill	30.05.36	JNRS	Wolverhampton W.	06.53					(FB)
			TR	Plymouth Arg.	01.58	1957	5		0	
			TR	Bristol Rov.	09.58	1958-59	4		0	
TIMSON, David Y.	Leicester	24.08.47	APP	Leicester C.	09.64	1963-66	3	/	0	(G)
			TR	Newport Co.	08.67	1967	23	/	0	
TINDALL, Mike C.	Birmingham	05.04.41	JNRS	Aston Villa	04.58	1959-67	110	1	8	(IF)E.YTH.INT.
			TR	Walsall	06.68	1968	17	/	0	
TINDALL, Ron A.	Streatham	23.09.35	JNRS	Chelsea	04.53	1955-61	160		68	(CF)E.F.LGE REP./
			TR	West Ham U.	11.61	1961	13		3	Surrey Cricketer
			TR	Reading	10.62	1962-63	36		12	
			TR	Portsmouth	09.64	1964-69	160	2	7	
TINDILL, Herbert	Sth.Hindley	31.12.26	Sth.Hindley	Doncaster Rov.	+	1946-57	402		122	(IF)●
			TR	Bristol C.	02.58	1957-58	56		28	
			TR	Barnsley	03.59	1959-61	98		29	
TINGAY, Phillip	Chesterfield	02.05.50	Chesterfield Tube	Chesterfield	07.72	1971-80	181	/	0	(G)
			L	Barnsley	03.73	1972	8	/	0	
TINKLER, Luke	Chester-le-Street	04.12.23	W.B.A.(AM)	Plymouth Arg.	+	1946-47	24		4	
				Walsall	06.48	1948	18		0	
TINNEY, Hugh J.	Glasgow	14.05.44	Partick Th.	Bury	03.67	1966-72	235	3	3	(RB)S.U23-2
TINNION, Brian	Workington	11.06.48	JNRS	Workington T.	03.66	1965-68	93	5	24	(IF)E.YTH.INT.
			TR	Wrexham	01.69	1968-75	265	14	54	
			L	Chester C.	12.71	1971	3	/	0	
TINSLEY, Alan	Fleetwood	01.01.51	APP	Preston N.E.	01.69	1969	8	1	1	(IF)
			TR	Bury	08.70	1970-74	82	12	15	

Players Names	Birthplace	Date	Previous Club	League Club	Date Signed	Seasons Played	Apps	Sub	Gls	
TINSLEY, Colin	Redcar	24.10.35	Redcar B.C.	Grimsby T.	09.54	1954-57	23		0	(G)
			TR	Darlington	08.58	1958-60	79		0	
			TR	Exeter C.	07.61	1961-62	56		1	
			TR	Luton T.	08.63	1963-67	55	/	0	
TIPPETT, Mike F.	Bristol	11.06.30		Bristol Rov.	04.48	1949-51	8		2	(W)
TIPPETT, Tommy J.	Gateshead	04.08.24		Southend U.	05.46	1946-51	92		20	(OL)Nephew of pre-war
			TR	Bournemouth	09.51	1951-52	37		10	West Ham U. player
TOASE, Don V.	Darlington	31.12.29	Portsmouth(AM)	Newcastle U.	06.48					(RB)E.YTH.INT.
			TR	Darlington	08.51	1951	7		0	
TOBIN, Don J.	Liverpool	01.11.55	Everton (APP)	Rochdale	03.74	1973-75	46	2	5	(WH)
TOBIN, Maurice	Airdrie	30.07.20	L.Ringend Boys	Norwich C.	+	1946-50	102		0	(WH)
TOBIN, Robert	Cardiff	29.03.21	Cardiff Corries	Cardiff C.	+	1947	2		0	(IL)
			Barry T.	Newport Co.	10.49					
TOCKNELL, Brian T.	S.Africa	21.05.37	Berea Pk.	Charlton Ath.	07.59	1960-65	199	/	14	(WH)
TODD, Alex	Sth.Shields	07.11.29		Hartlepool U.	04.50	1952-53	4		0	(F)
				Southend U.	01.56					
TODD, Colin	Chester-le-Street	12.12.48	APP	Sunderland	12.66	1966-70	170	3	3	(D)E-27/E.u23-14/●
			TR	Derby Co.	02.71	1970-78	293	/	6	E.F.LGE REP./E.YTH.INT.
			TR	Everton	09.78	1978-79	32	/	1	
			TR	Birmingham C.	09.79	1979-81	92	1	0	
			TR	Nottingham F.	08.82	1982-83	36	/	0	
			TR	Oxford U.	02.84	1983	12	/	0	
TODD, Jim	Belfast	19.03.21		Blackpool	+					(WH)
			TR	Port Vale	10.46	1946-52	147		0	
TODD, Keith H.	Clydach	02.03.41	Clydach	Swansea C.	09.59	1960-67	196	3	76	(CF)W.U23-1
TODD, Ken	Butterknowle	24.08.57	APP	Wolverhampton W.	08.75	1976-77	4	1	1	(M)
			TR	Port Vale	08.78	1978-79	42	2	9	
			TR	Portsmouth	10.79	1979	1	2	1	
TODD, Kevin	Sunderland	28.02.58	Ryhope C.A.	Newcastle U.	08.81	1981-82	5	2	3	(F)
			TR	Darlington	02.83	1982-83	56	1	17	
TODD, Paul R.	Middlesbrough	08.05.20		Doncaster Rov.	+	1946-49	160		51	(IL)
			TR	Blackburn Rov.	07.50	1950-51	46		13	
			TR	Hull C.	10.51	1951-52	27		3	
TODD, Robert C.	Goole	11.09.49	Liverpool	Rotherham U.	03.68	1968	2	4	0	
			TR	Mansfield T.	11.68	1968	2	/	0	
			TR	Workington	07.69	1969	10	6	0	
TODD, Ron	Belshill	04.10.35	Lesmahagow	Accrington St.	02.56	1959	5		0	(HB)
TODD, Sam	Belfast	22.09.45	Glentoran	Burnley	09.62	1963-69	108	8	1	(WH)NI-11/NI.U23-4
			TR	Sheffield Wed.	05.70	1970-72	22	2	1	
			L	Mansfield T.	02.74	1973	6	/	0	
TODD, Tom B.	Stonehouse	01.06.26	Hamilton	Crewe Alex.	08.55	1955	13		3	
			TR	Derby Co.	11.55	1955	4		3	
			TR	Rochdale	05.56	1956	5		1	
TOLCHARD, Jeff G.	Torquay	17.03.44		Torquay U.	03.64	1963-64	11		4	(F)Leic.Cricketer
			TR	Exeter C.	07.65	1965	1	/	0	
TOLLIDAY, Stan A.	Hackney	06.08.22		Orient	12.46	1946-48	64		0	(G)d.1951
			TR	Walsall	06.50					
TOLMIE, Jim	Glasgow	20.11.60	Lokeren	Manchester C.	08.83	1983	38	3	13	(F)S.U'21-1
TOLSON, Max	Australia	18.07.45	Sth.Coast U.	Workington	02.66	1965-66	29	2	6	(F)
TOLSON, William	Rochdale	29.03.31	St.Albans (B.C.)	Rochdale	10.53	1953-54	10		0	(IF)
TOM, Steve	London	05.02.51	APP	Q.P.R.	02.69					(IF)
			TR	Brentford	06.71	1971	13	5	1	
TOMKIN, Cyril J.	Barrow	18.11.18	Dumbarton	Barrow	03.48	1946-47	3		0	(CF)
TOMKINS, Len A.	Isleworth	16.01.49		Crystal Palace	04.67	1967-69	18	2	2	(F)E.YTH.INT.
TOMKINSON, Derek	Stoke	06.04.31		Port Vale	12.52	1952-54	29		5	(IR)
				Crewe Alex.	08.56	1956	17		1	
TOMKYS, Mike G.	Kensington	14.12.32	Fulham(AM)	Q.P.R.	11.51	1951-58	91		15	(OR)E.YTH.INT.
TOMLEY, Fred W.	Liverpool	11.07.31	Litherland	Liverpool	09.53	1954	2		0	
			TR	Chester C.	07.55	1955	1		0	
TOMLIN, David	Nuneaton	09.02.53	APP	Leic. C.	10.71	1971-75	19	7	2	(F)
			TR	Torquay U.	04.77	1976-77	37	1	2	
			TR	Aldershot	08.78	1978-80	24	6	2	
TOMLINSON, Ashley D.	Doncaster	28.09.66	JNRS	Doncaster Rov.	N/C	1983	2	2	0	(F)
TOMLINSON, Charles	Sheffield	02.12.19	Bradford P.A.(+)	Sheffield Wed.	+	1946-50	68		7	(OL)d.
			TR	Rotherham U.	03.51	1950-51	32		12	
TOMLINSON, Frank	Manchester	05.01.26	Stalybridge	Halifax T.	11.50	1950	14		4	(F)
TOMLINSON, Frank	Manchester	23.10.25	Goslings	Oldham Ath.	11.46	1946-51	116		29	(W)
			TR	Rochdale	11.51	1951	20		2	
			TR	Chester C.	08.52	1952	11		0	
TOMLINSON, Harry	Devonport	26.10.22		Doncaster Rov.	+	1946-48	58		0	(FB)

Players Names	Birthplace	Date	Previous Club	League Club	Date Signed	Seasons Played	Apps	Sub	Gls	
TOMLINSON, John F.	Birkenhead	26.06.34	JNRS	Everton	06.52	1956	2		0	(F)
			TR	Chesterfield	06.57	1957-58	47		5	
TOMLINSON, Paul A.	Brierley Hill	22.02.64	APP	Sheffield U.	06.83	1983	30	/	0	(G)
TOMLINSON, Robert W.	Blackburn	04.06.24	Feniscowles	Blackburn Rov.	+	1946-47	25		0	(FB)
			TR	Halifax T.	06.51	1951	9		0	
TOMPKIN, Maurice	Countesthorpe	17.02.19	Leicester C.(*)	Bury	+					d.1956/
			TR	Huddersfield T.	09.46	1946	10		1	Leicester Cricketer
TONER, Jim	Glasgow	23.08.24	Dundee	Leeds U.	06.54	1954	7		0	
TONER, Willie	Glasgow	18.12.29	Dundee	Sheffield U.	05.51	1951-53	55		2	(CH)S.F.LGE REP.
TONES, John D.	Silksworth	03.12.50	APP	Sunderland	05.68	1972	2	4	0	(CH)
			TR	Arsenal	07.73					
			L	Swansea C.	09.74	1974	7	/	0	
			L	Mansfield T.	10.74	1974	3	/	0	
TONG, David J.	Blackpool	21.09.55	APP	Blackpool	09.73	1974-78	70	8	7	(M)
			TR	Shrewsbury T.	09.78	1978-81	156	4	8	
			TR	Cardiff C.	08.82	1982-83	85	1	2	
TONG, Ray	Bolton	03.02.42		Blackburn Rov.	07.62					(F)
			TR	Bradford C.	06.63	1963-64	20		2	
TONGE, Geoff	Gorton	05.05.42	Droylsden	Bury	03.60	1959	1		0	(F)
TONGE, Keith A.	Edmonton	06.11.64	APP	Brentford	11.82	1981	0	1	0	
TOON, Colin	Houghton	26.04.40	JNRS	Mansfield T.	07.57	1957-65	213	/	1	(FB)
TOOTILL, George A.	Walkden	20.10.13	Plymouth Arg.(*)	Sheffield U.	*					(CH)*Chorley
			TR	Hartlepool U.	07.47	1947	18		0	
TOOZE, Dennis G.	Swansea	12.10.17	Redditch T.	Coventry C.	*	1946-48	36		0	(FB)
TOOZE, Robert W.	Bristol	19.12.46	JNRS	Bristol C.	07.65					(G)
			TR	Shrewsbury T.	03.69	1968-72	73	/	0	
			L	Gillingham	03.72	1971	7	/	0	
TOPPING, Chris	Selby	06.03.51	APP	York C.	03.69	1968-77	410	2	11	(D)
			TR	Huddersfield T.	05.78	1978-80	43	/	11	
TOPPING, David	Shotts	09.03.26	Clyde	Torquay U.	05.48	1948-52	151		3	(FB)
TOPPING, Henry W.	Kearsley	21.09.13	New Brighton(*)	Stockport Co.	*					(RB)*Manchester U./Barnsley/
			TR	N.Brighton & H.A.	07.46	1946-47	67		0	Exeter C.
TORRANCE, Andy	Glasgow	08.04.34	Yeovil	Barrow	05.58	1958	29		2	(F)
TORRENCE, George S.	Glasgow	27.11.35	Thorniewood	Leicester C.	07.54					(G)
			TR	Oldham Ath.	08.56	1956	4		0	
			TR	Rochdale	09.57	1957	2		0	
TOSELAND, Geoff V.	Kettering	31.01.31		Sunderland	12.48	1952	6		1	
TOSER, Ernie W.	London	30.11.13	Dulwich H.	Millwall	*					(CH)E.SCH.INT.
			TR	Notts.Co.	09.46	1946	2		0	
TOSHACK, John B.	Cardiff	22.03.49	APP	Cardiff C.	03.66	1965-70	159	3	75	(F)W-40/W.U23-3/W.SCH.INT.●
			TR	Liverpool	11.70	1970-77	169	3	74	
			TR	Swansea C.	03.78	1977-83	58	5	25	
TOULOUSE, Cyril H.	Acton	24.12.23		Brentford	05.46	1946-47	13		0	d.1980
			TR	Tottenham H.	12.47	1948	2		0	
TOVEY, Ron A.	Bristol	24.09.30		Bristol C.	01.53	1952-53	12		0	(IF)
TOVEY, William J.	Bristol	18.10.31	JNRS	Bristol C.	12.48	1948-52	57		1	(WH)
TOWERS, Anthony M.	Manchester	13.04.52	APP	Manchester C.	04.69	1968-73	117	5	10	(M)E-3/E.U23-8/
			TR	Sunderland	03.74	1973-76	108	/	18	E.SCH.INT./E.YTH.INT.
			TR	Birmingham C.	07.77	1977-79	90	2	4	
TOWERS, Edwin J.	Shepherds Bush	15.04.33	JNRS	Brentford	05.51	1954-60	262		153	(CF)●
			TR	Q.P.R.	61.5	1961	27		12	
			TR	Millwall	08.62	1962	19		7	
			TR	Gillingham	01.63	1962	8		6	
			TR	Aldershot	07.63	1963	28		11	
TOWERS, Ian J.	Blackhill	11.10.40	JNRS	Burnley	10.57	1960-65	44	1	12	(W)
			TR	Oldham Ath.	01.66	1965-67	92	1	43	
			TR	Bury	07.68	1968-70	44	5	7	
TOWERS, John	Willington	21.12.13	Willington	Darlington	AM	1946	13		0	(WH)d.1979
TOWERS, William H.	Leicester	13.07.20		Leicester C.	+	1946	4		0	(WH)
			TR	Torquay U.	10.46	1946-55	274		0	
TOWNEND, Gary A.	Kilburn	01.04.40	Redhill	Millwall	08.60	1960-63	50		20	(IF)
TOWNER, Anthony J.	Brighton	02.05.55	APP	Brighton & H.A.	01.73	1972-78	153	9	24	(W)
			TR	Millwall	10.78	1978-79	68	/	13	
			TR	Rotherham U.	08.80	1980-82	108	/	12	
			L	Sheffield U.	03.83	1982	9	1	1	
			TR	Wolverhampton W.	08.83	1983	25	6	2	
TOWNSEND, Chris G.	Carleon	30.03.66	JNRS	Cardiff C.	N/C	1983	2	3	0	(F)
TOWNSEND, Don E.	Swindon	17.09.30	Trowbridge	Charlton Ath.	07.50	1954-61	249		1	(FB)
			TR	Crystal Palace	07.62	1962-64	77		0	
TOWNSEND, George E.	Ashton	29.07.5	APP	Rochdale	07.75	1974-75	31	1	0	(LB)

Players Names	Birthplace	Date	Previous Club	League Club	Date Signed	Seasons Played	Career Record Apps	Sub	Gls	
TOWNSEND, Jim	Greenock	02.02.45	St.Johnstone	Middlesbrough	02.64	1963-65	65	2	6	(HB)
TOWNSEND, Len F.	Brentford	31.08.17	Hayes	Brentford	*	1946	29		8	
			TR	Bristol C.	06.47	1947-48	74		43	
			TR	Millwall	07.49	1949	5		1	
TOWNSEND, Martin V.	Romford	15.06.46	APP	Fulham	APP	1963	2		0	(G)
TOWNSEND, Neil R.	Long Buckby	01.02.50	JNRS	Northampton T.	09.68	1968-71	65	2	1	(D)E.YTH.INT.
			Bedford T.	Southend U.	07.73	1973-78	156	1	7	
			Weymouth	Bournemouth	07.79	1979-80	34	/	2	
TOWNSEND, Russell	Reading	17.01.60	Barnet	Northampton T.	09.79	1979	12	1	0	(M)
TOWNSEND, William	Bedworth	27.12.22	Nuneaton	Derby Co.	+	1946-52	80		0	(G)
TOWSE, Gary	Dover	14.05.52	Folkestone	Crystal Palace	01.72					(G)
			TR	Brentford	06.73	1973	5	/	0	
TOZE, Edward	Manchester	06.03.23		Halifax T.	08.50	1950	5		0	
TRACEY, Mike C.	Durham	14.02.35	Crook T.	Luton T.	11.59	1959-60	24		3	(CF)E.AMAT.INT.
			TR	Lincoln C.	07.61	1961	21		5	
TRAFFORD, Stan J.	Leek	02.12.45	APP	Port Vale	10.64	1964	12		1	(W)
TRAIL, Derek	Edinburgh	02.01.46	Falkirk	Workington	07.67	1967-68	39	5	5	(F)
			TR	Hartlepool U.	07.69	1969	36	3	2	
TRAILOR, Cyril H.	Merthyr Tydfil	15.05.19	JNRS	Tottenham H.	*	1946-47	11		0	(WH)W.SCH.INT.
			TR	Orient	08.49	1949-50	39		0	
TRAIN, Ray	Nuneaton	10.02.51	APP	Walsall	11.68	1968-71	67	6	11	(M)
			TR	Carlisle U.	12.71	1971-75	154	1	8	
			TR	Sunderland	03.76	1975-76	31	1	1	
			TR	Bolton W.	03.77	1976-78	49	2	0	
			TR	Watford	11.78	1978-80	91	1	3	
			TR	Oxford U.	03.82	1981-83	49	1	0	
			L	Bournemouth	11.83	1983	7	/	0	
TRAINER, Jack	Glasgow	14.07.52	Cork Hibs.	Halifax T.	08.76	1976-78	101	4	5	(D)
			Hong Kong	Bury	09.80	1980	1	/	1	
				Rochdale	N/C	1982	7	/	0	
TRAINOR, Danny	Belfast	12.07.44	Crusaders	Plymouth Arg.	08.68	1968	18	1	3	NI-1/NI'U'23-1/ NI.AMAT.INT.
TRAINOR, Peter	Workington	02.03.15	Preston N.E.(*)	Brighton & H.A.	*	1946-47	37		4	(CH)d.1979
TRANTER, George H.	Yardley	11.09.15	Solihull T.	W.B.A.	+	1946	16		0	(RB)
TRANTER, Wilf	Pendlebury	05.03.45	APP	Manchester U.	04.62	1963	1		0	(WH)
			TR	Brighton & H.A.	05.66	1965-67	46	1	1	
			Baltimore	Fulham	01.69	1968-71	20	2	0	
TRAUTMANN, Bert C.	W.Germany	22.10.23	St.Helens	Manchester C.	11.49	1949-63	508		0	(G)E.F.LGE REP.●
TRAVERS, Mike J.	Camberley	23.06.42	JNRS	Reading	10.60	1960-66	156	2	34	(WH)
			TR	Portsmouth	07.67	1967-71	74	9	5	
			TR	Aldershot	07.72	1972	29	1	2	
TRAVIS, Don	Manchester	21.02.24	Blackpool(AM)	West Ham U.	+	1946-47	5		0	(IF)
			TR	Southend U.	05.48	1948	1		0	
			TR	Accrington St.	12.48	1948-50	71		35	
			TR	Crewe Alex.	11.50	1950-51	36		11	
			TR	Oldham Ath.	10.51	1951	4		1	
			TR	Chester C.	02.52	1951-53	99		45	
			TR	Oldham Ath.	08.54	1954-56	109		59	
TRAYNOR, Tommy J.	Dundalk	22.07.33	Dundalk	Southampton	06.52	1952-65	434	/	7	(FB)EI-8
TREACY, Frank	Glasgow	14.07.39	Johnstone Burgh	Ipswich T.	03.61	1963-65	17	1	5	(F)
TREACY, Ray C.	Dublin	18.06.46	APP	W.B.A.	06.64	1966-67	2	3	1	(F)EI-38
			TR	Charlton Ath.	02.68	1967-71	144	4	43	
			TR	Swindon T.	06.72	1972-75	55	/	16	
			TR	Preston N.E.	12.73	1973-75	54	4	11	
			L	Oldham Ath.	03.75	1974	3	/	1	
			TR	W.B.A.	08.76	1976	20	1	6	
TREBILCOCK, Mike	Gunnislake	29.11.44	Tavistock	Plymouth Arg.	12.62	1962-65	71	/	27	(CF)
			TR	Everton	12.65	1965-67	11	/	3	
			TR	Portsmouth	01.68	1967-71	99	10	32	
			TR	Torquay U.	07.72	1972	23	1	10	
TREHARNE, Colin	Bridgend	30.07.37		Mansfield T.	12.60	1961-65	191	/	0	(G)
			TR	Lincoln C.	07.66	1966	19	/	0	
TREHARNE, Cyril A.	Wellington	12.03.28		Shrewsbury T.	11.50	1950	4		1	
TRENTER, Ron H.	Ipwich	13.12.28	Wilton U.	Ipswich T.	+					(OR)
			Clacton	Ipswich T.	06.51	1951	28		0	
TREVIS, Derek	Birmingham	09.09.42		Aston Villa	06.62					(IF)
			TR	Colchester U.	03.64	1963-68	196	/	13	
			TR	Walsall	09.68	1968-69	63	2	6	
			TR	Lincoln C.	07.70	1970-72	100	8	18	
			TR	Stockport Co.	09.73	1973	33	2	2	
TREWICK, Alan	Blyth	27.04.41		Gateshead	09.59	1959	10		1	
TREWICK, George	Stakeford	15.11.33	W.Sleekburn	Gateshead	04.53	1956-59	111		0	(HB)

Players Names	Birthplace	Date	Previous Club	League Club	Date Signed	Seasons Played	Career Record Apps	Sub	Gls	
TREWICK, John	Bedlington	03.06.57	APP	W.B.A.	07.74	1974-80	84	12	11	(M)E.YTH.INT./
			TR	Newcastle U.	12.80	1980-83	76	2	8	E.SCH.INT.
			L	Oxford U.	01.84	1983	3	/	0	
TRIGG, Cyril	Meacham	08.04.17	Bedworth	Birmingham C.	*	1946-53	162		66	(CF)
TRIM, Reg F.	Portsmouth	01.10.13	Nottingham F.(*)	Derby Co.	+					(FB)*Bournemouth/
			TR	Swindon T.	07.46	1946	15		0	Arsenal/E.SCH.INT.
TRINER, Don A.	Sanford Hill	21.08.19	Downings	Port Vale	*	1946-47	22		7	(OR)
TRISE, Guy G.	Portsmouth	22.11.33	JNRS	Portsmouth	05.53					
			TR	Aldershot	08.54	1954	1		0	
TROLLOPE, N. John	Wroughton	14.06.43	JNRS	Swindon T.	07.60	1960-80	767	3	22	(D)●
TROOPS, Harry	Sheffield	10.02.26	Hadfield Wks.	Barnsley	12.46	1948	3		1	(OR)
			TR	Lincoln C.	08.49	1949-57	295		33	
			TR	Carlisle U.	06.58	1958-59	60		1	
TROUGHTON, Sam E.	Lisburn	27.03.64	Glentoran	Wolverhampton W.	12.83	1983	17	/	2	(F)NI.YTH.INT.
TRUETT, Geoff	Wycombe	23.05.35	Wycombe W.	Crystal Palace	06.57	1957-61	38		5	(IF)
TRUSLER, John W.	Shoreham	07.06.34	Shoreham	Brighton & H.A.	08.54	1954	1		0	
TRUSSON, Mike S.	Northolt	26.05.59	APP	Plymouth Arg.	01.77	1976-79	65	8	15	(M)
			TR	Sheffield U.	07.80	1980-83	125	1	31	
			TR	Rotherham U.	12.83	1983	25	/	2	
TUCK, Peter G.	Plaistow	14.05.32	JNRS	Chelsea	06.51	1951	3		1	(IF)
TUCKER, Barry W.	Swansea	28.08.52	APP	Northampton T.	08.70	1971-77	209	5	3	(D)
			TR	Brentford	02.78	1977-82	168	1	5	
			TR	Northampton T.	10.82	1982-83	62	1	5	
TUCKER, Keith	Deal	25.11.36	Bettshanger	Charlton Ath.	02.54	1954-60	3		0	(F)
TUCKER, Ken	London	02.10.25	Finchley	West Ham U.	08.46	1947-56	83		31	(OL)
			TR	Notts.Co.	03.57	1956-57	28		5	
TUCKER, Ken J.	Merthyr Tydfil	15.07.35	Aston Villa(AM)	Cardiff C.	10.55	1956-57	13		0	(W)
			TR	Shrewsbury T.	02.58	1957-59	46		8	
			TR	Northampton T.	03.60	1959-60	9		3	
TUCKER, Malcolm	Cramlington	12.04.33	Newcastle U.(AM)	Grimsby T.	11.50	1953-57	39		0	(CH)
TUCKER, William	Kidderminster	17.05.48	Kidderminster H.	Hereford U.	07.72	1972-76	135	2	12	(D)
			TR	Bury	12.76	1976-78	96	/	8	
			TR	Swindon T.	06.79	1979	35	/	4	
TUDDENHAM, Anthony	Reepham	28.09.56	West Ham U.(APP)	Cambridge U.	05.76	1975-76	11	1	0	(D)
TUDOR, Edward T.	Liverpool	15.03.35		Gillingham	04.58	1958	1		0	(F)
TUDOR, John	Ilkeston	25.06.46	Ilkeston T.	Coventry C.	01.66	1966-68	63	6	13	(F)
			TR	Sheffield U.	11.68	1968-70	64	7	30	
			TR	Newcastle U.	01.71	1970-76	161	3	53	
			TR	Stoke C.	09.76	1976	28	2	3	
TUDOR, William H.	Shotton	14.02.18	Lavender FC	W.B.A.	*					(CH)W.SCH.INT.
			TR	Wrexham	05.46	1946-48	56		2	
TUEART, Dennis	Newcastle	27.11.49	JNRS	Sunderland	08.67	1968-73	173	5	46	(F)E-6/E.U23-1/
			TR	Manchester U.	03.74	1973-77	139	1	59	E.F.LGE REP.
			N. York Cosmos	Manchester C.	02.80	1979-82	77	7	27	
			TR	Stoke C.	08.83	1983	2	1	0	
			TR	Burnley	12.83	1983	8	7	5	
TUGMAN, James	Workington	14.03.45		Workington	07.64	1965-67	32	12	0	(FB)
TULIP, William E.	Gateshead	03.05.33		Newcastle U.	06.51					(CF)
			TR	Darlington	05.56	1956-57	44		34	
TULLOCH, Roland	S.Africa	15.07.32	S.Africa	Hull C.	12.53	1954	2		0	(WH)
TULLOCH, Ron T.	Haddington	05.06.33	Hearts	Southend U.	05.56	1956	11		4	(F)
			TR	Carlisle U.	07.57	1957-59	73		22	
TULLY, Kevin	Manchester	18.12.52	Prestwich Heys	Blackpool	11.72	1972-73	10	1	0	(F)
			TR	Cambridge U.	07.74	1974-75	40	4	8	
			TR	Crewe Alex.	01.76	1975-78	81	5	4	
			TR	Port Vale	10.78	1978-79	7	6	2	
			Chorley	Bury	08.80	1980	7	3	1	
TUMBRIDGE, Ray A.	London	06.03.55	APP	Charlton Ath.	03.73	1972-74	43	3	0	(LB)
			L	Northampton T.	02.75	1974	11	/	0	
TUNE, David	Reading	01.11.38	JNRS	Reading	11.55	1957	1		0	(HB)
TUNE, Mike G.	Stoke	28.02.62	Stoke C.(APP)	Crewe Alex.	06.79	1979	0	1	0	(M)
TUNKS, Roy W.	W. Germany	21.01.51	APP	Rotherham U.	03.68	1968-73	138	/	0	(G)
			L	York C.	01.69	1968	4	/	0	
			TR	Preston N.E.	11.74	1974-80	277	/	0	
			TR	Wigan Ath.	11.81	1981-83	119	/	0	
TUNNEY, Edward	Wirrall	23.09.15	Everton(*)	Wrexham	*	1946-51	154		0	(FB)
TUNNICLIFFE, William	Stoke	05.01.20	Port Vale(*)	Bournemouth	*	1946	10		1	(OL)
			TR	Wrexham	06.47	1947-52	236		73	
			TR	Bradford C.	01.53	1952-54	89		20	
TUNSTALL, Eric W.	Hartlepool	02.11.50	APP	Hartlepool U.	11.68	1968	2	1	0	(HB)
			TR	Newcastle U.	01.69.					

Players Names	Birthplace	Date	Previous Club	League Club	Date Signed	Seasons Played	Apps	Sub	Gls	
TUOHY, Liam	Dublin	27.04.33	Shamrock Rov.	Newcastle U.	05.60	1960-62	38		9	(W)EI-8/EI'B'-2
TUOHY, Mike P.F.	W. Bromwich	28.03.56	JNRS	Walsall	07.74					(F)
			Redditch T.	Southend U.	06.79	1979	20	1	4	
TURBITT, Peter	Keighley	01.07.51		Bradford C.	08.69	1969-70	5	3	0	(F)E.YTH.INT.
TURLEY, John W.	Bebbington	26.01.39	Ellesmere Port	Sheffield U.	05.56	1957	5		3	(W)
			TR	Peterborough U.	07.61	1961-63	32		14	
			TR	Rochdale	05.64	1964	22		5	
TURLEY, Mike D.	Rotherham	14.02.36	JNRS	Sheffield Wed.	03.53	1954	3		0	(HB)
			TR	Burnley	10.56					
TURNBULL, Fred	Wallsend	28.08.46	Centre 64 FC	Aston Villa	09.66	1967-73	160	2	3	(CH)
			L	Halifax T.	10.69	1969	7	/	0	
TURNBULL, George F.	Gateshead	04.02.27	Alnwick T.	Grimsby T.	08.50	1950	2		0	(G)
			TR	Accrington St.	09.51	1951	33		0	
			TR	Gateshead	07.52	1952	3		0	
TURNBULL, Ron W.	Newbiggin	18.07.22	Dundee	Sunderland	11.47	1947-48	40		16	(CF)d.
			TR	Manchester C.	09.49	1949-50	30		5	
			TR	Swansea C.	01.51	1950-52	67		35	
TURNBULL, Roy	Edinburgh	22.10.48	Hearts	Lincoln C.	09.69	1969	0	2	0	(IF)
TURNBULL, Terry M.	Stockton	18.10.45	Crook T.	Hartlepool U.	N/C	1976	13	/	3	(F)
TURNER, Adam E.	Glasgow	13.03.34	Dunfermline	Sheffield Wed.	01.56					
			Dunfermline	Gateshead	10.58	1958	6		0	
TURNER, Alan	Hull	05.07.43	Scunthorpe U.(AM)	Coventry C.	03.62	1961-65	4	/	0	(F)
			TR	Shrewsbury T.	07.66	1966	14	2.	4	
			TR	Bradford P.A.	05.67	1967	30	2	4	
TURNER, Alan	Sheffield	22.09.35		Sheffield U.	09.57					(F)
			TR	Halifax T.	07.58	1958	7		0	
TURNER, Alfred T.	U.S.A.	26.12.29	Port Sunlight	New Brighton	AM	1950	4		0	(CF)
TURNER, Arthur	London	22.01.22	Charlton Ath.(AM)	Colchester U.	N/L	1950-51	45		14	(IF)
TURNER, Arthur	Stoke	01.04.09	Stoke C.(*)	Birmingham C.	*	1946	27		0	(CH)*Woolstanton
			TR	Southport	02.48	1947-48	28		0	
TURNER, Brian	Whitlesey	27.08.25	March T.	Lincoln C.	AM	1947	5		0	(CF)
TURNER, Brian	Salford	23.07.36	Bury Amats.	Bury	02.57	1957-69	451	3	4	(WH)●
			TR	Oldham Ath.	08.70	1970	10	1	0	
TURNER, Brian A.	N.Zealand	31.07.49	Eden FC	Chelsea	05.68					(RH)
			TR	Portsmouth	06.69	1969	3	1	0	
			TR	Brentford	01.70	1969-71	88	4	7	
TURNER, Charles J.	Newport	01.07.19		Newport Co.	05.46	1946-47	36		0	(G)*Newport Co.
			TR	Swansea C.	08.48	1948	2		0	
TURNER, Chris J.	St. Neots	03.04.51	JNRS	Peterborough U.	11.69	1969-77	308	6	37	(D)
			TR	Luton T.	07.78	1978	30	/	5	
			N. Eng. Teamen	Cambridge U.	09.79	1979	15	4	0	
			N. Eng. Teamen	Swindon T.	09.80	1980	0	3	0	
			TR	Cambridge U.	10.80	1980-83	68	3	3	
			TR	Southend U.	10.83	1983	22	/	1	
TURNER, Chris R.	Sheffield	15.09.58	APP	Sheffield Wed.	08.76	1976-78	91	/	0	(G)E.YTH.INT.
			L	Lincoln C.	10.78	1978	5	/	0	
			TR	Sunderland	07.79	1979-83	153	/	0	
TURNER, David	Derby	26.12.48	APP	Everton	10.66	1967	1	/	0	(RB)
			TR	Southport	05.70	1970-72	69	2	0	
TURNER, David J.	Retford	07.09.43	APP	Newcastle U.	10.60	1961-62	2		0	(WH)
			TR	Brighton & H.A.	12.63	1963-71	292	8	28	
			TR	Blackburn Rov.	08.72	1972-73	23	2	0	
TURNER, Eric	Huddersfield	13.01.21	Wooldale W.	Halifax T.	+	1946	7		0	
TURNER, Fred A.	Southampton	28.02.30	JNRS	Southampton	02.50					(RB)d.1955
			TR	Torquay U.	08.51	1951	1		0	
			TR	Southampton	03.53	1953-54	19		0	
TURNER, Gordon R.	Hull	07.06.30		Luton T.	03.50	1950-63	406		243	(CF)E.F.LGE REP./d.1976/●
										Son of pre-war player
TURNER, Graham J.	Ellesmere Port	05.10.47	JNRS	Wrexham	07.65	1964-67	77	/	0	(D)E.YTH.INT.●
			TR	Chester C.	01.68	1967-72	215	3	5	
			TR	Shrewsbury T.	01.73	1972-83	342	13	22	
TURNER, Herbert	Brithdis	19.06.09	Brithdis	Charlton Ath.	*	1946	11		0	(FB)W-8/d.1981
TURNER, Hugh	Southbank	12.05.17	Middlesbrough(*)	Darlington	+	1946	6		0	(FB)
TURNER, Ian	Middlesbrough	17.01.53	South Bank	Huddersfield T.	10.70					(G)
			TR	Grimsby T.	01.72	1971-73	26	/	0	
			L	Walsall	02.73	1972	3	/	0	
			TR	Southampton	03.74	1973-77	77	/	0	
			L	Newport Co.	03.78	1977	7	/	0	
			L	Lincoln C.	10.78	1978	7	/	0	
			TR	Walsall	01.79	1978-80	39	/	0	
			L	Halifax T.	01.81	1980	5	/	0	

Players Names	Birthplace	Date	Previous Club	League Club	Date Signed	Seasons Played	Apps	Sub	Gls	
TURNER, John G.A.	Peterlee	23.12.54	APP	Derby Co.	07.73					(G)
			L	Doncaster Rov.	02.74	1973	4	/	0	
			L	Huddersfield T.	03.75	1974	1	/	0	
			TR	Reading	05.75	1975-77	31	/	0	
			TR	Torquay U.	08.78	1978-79	76	/	0	
			TR	Chesterfield	02.80	1979-82	132	/	0	
			TR	Torquay U.	08.83	1983	34	/	0	
TURNER, Joseph	Barnsley	21.03.31	Denaby U.	Stockport Co.	07.54	1954-56	79		0	(G)
			TR	Darlington	12.57	1957-59	68		0	
			TR	Scunthorpe U.	06.60	1960-61	22		0	
			TR	Barnsley	11.61	1961	7		0	
TURNER, Keith J.	Coventry	09.04.34		Nottingham F.	06.54	1954	1		0	
TURNER, Ken	Barnsley	22.04.41	JNRS	Huddersfield T.	10.58	1961	5	/	0	(FB)
			TR	Shrewsbury T.	07.63	1963-65	64	/	1	
			TR	York C.	06.66	1966-67	88	/	2	
TURNER, Mark B.	Stockport	19.09.56	Everton(APP)	Stockport Co.	08.75	1975	8	/	0	(FB)
TURNER, Mike G.	Bridport	20.09.38	Dorchester	Swindon T.	12.61	1961-63	75		0	(G)E.YTH.INT.
			TR	Torquay U.	07.64	1964-65	14	/	0	
TURNER, Neil	Blackpool	15.03.42	JNRS	Blackpool	12.59	1963-66	10	1	1	(LH)
			TR	Crewe Alex.	07.68	1968-71	80	6	4	
TURNER, Paul	Barnsley	08.07.53	APP	Barnsley	07.71	1970-74	27	8	1	(RB)
TURNER, Peter A.	Leicester	14.08.31		Crewe Alex.	03.54	1954-55	23		4	
TURNER, Philip	Sheffield	12.02.62	APP	Lincoln C.	02.80	1979-83	160	2	12	(M)
TURNER, Philip S.	Chester	20.02.27	JNRS	Chester C.	07.46	1946-47	27		6	(IF)
			TR	Carlisle U.	09.48	1948-50	79		23	
			TR	Bradford P.A.	06.51	1951-53	55		24	
			TR	Scunthorpe U.	06.54	1954	5		2	
			TR	Accrington St.	10.55	1955-56	13		1	
			TR	Chester C.	11.56	1956	16		3	
TURNER, Robin D.	Carlisle	10.09.55	APP	Ipswich T.	04.73	1975-83	22	26	2	(F)E.YTH.INT.
TURNER, Stan F.	Wokingham	31.05.41	JNRS	Reading	12.58	1960	3		0	(IF)
TURNER, Stan S.	Bucknall	21.10.26		Port Vale	03.49	1950-56	227		0	(FB)
TURNER, Wayne L.	Luton	09.03.61	APP	Luton T.	04.78	1978-83	58	2	2	(D)
			L	Lincoln C.	10.81	1981	16	/	0	
TURNEY, Jim A.	Cramlington	08.07.22		Darlington	08.48	1948-49	40		3	
TURPIE, Robert P.	London	13.11.49	APP	Q.P.R.	11.67	1969	1	1	0	(FB)
			TR	Peterborough U.	07.70	1970-71	31	6	3	
TURTON, Cyril	Kirkby	20.09.21	Frickley Col.	Sheffield Wed.	+	1946-53	146		0	(CH)
TUTIN, Hary	Silksworth	06.06.19		Southport	AM	1946	2		0	
TUTT, Graham	London	27.08.56		Charlton Ath.	03.74	1973-75	65	/	0	(G)
			L	Workington	09.74	1974	4	/	0	
TUTTY, Paul	Manchester	22.02.52	Manchester U.(AM)	Stockport Co.	AM	1970	1	/	0	(CH)
TUTTY, Wayne K.	Oxford	18.06.63	Banbury U.	Reading	08.83	1982-83	11	2	4	(D)
TWAMLEY, Bruce	Canada	23.05.52		Ipswich T.	03.71	1973-74	2	/	0	(FB)
TWEEDY, George J.	Willington	08.01.13	Willington	Grimsby T.	*	1946-52	124		0	(G)E-1
TWELL, Terry	Doncaster	21.02.47	Bourne T.	Birmingham T.	10.64	1967	2	/	0	(G)
TWENTYMAN, Geoff	Liverpool	10.03.59	Chorley	Preston N.E.	08.83	1983	25	3	2	(D)
TWENTYMAN, Geoff	Carlisle	19.01.30	JNRS	Carlisle U.	02.47	1946-53	149		2	(CH)
			TR	Liverpool	12.53	1953-59	170		18	
			Ballymena	Carlisle U.	06.63	1963	10		0	
TWIDLE, Ken G.	Brigg	10.10.31	Retford T.	Rotherham U.	12.57	1957-58	24		6	(F)
TWIGG, Richard L.	Barry	10.09.39	Barry T.	Notts.Co.	11.57	1958	3		0	(G)
TWISSELL, Charles H.	Singapore	16.12.32		Plymouth Arg.	04.57	1955-57	41		9	(W)E.AMAT.INT.
			TR	York C.	11.58	1958-60	53		8	
TWIST, Frank	Liverpool	02.11.40	JNRS	Liverpool	08.58					(F)E.YTH.INT.
			Prescot Cables	Bury	10.61	1961-62	8		0	
			TR	Halifax T.	07.63	1963-64	64		11	
			TR	Tranmere Rov.	07.65	1965	7	/	3	
TWITCHIN, Ian R.	Teignmouth	22.01.52	JNRS	Torquay U.	01.70	1969-80	374	29	14	(D)E.YTH.INT.
TWOMEY, James F.	Newry	13.04.14	Newry T.	Leeds U.	*	1946-48	60		0	(G)NI-2/IRISH LGE REP.
TYDEMAN, Richard	Chatham	26.05.51	APP	Gillingham	09.69	1969-76	293	2	12	(M)
			TR	Charlton Ath.	12.76	1976-80	158	/	7	
			TR	Gillingham	08.81	1981-83	75	1	2	
			TR	Peterborough U.	10.83	1983	29	/	0	
TYLER, Dudley	Salisbury	21.09.44	Hereford U.	West Ham U.	06.72	1972-73	29	/	1	(M)
			TR	Hereford U.	11.73	1973-76	97	5	10	
TYLER, Len V.	Rotherhithe	07.01.19	Redhill	Millwall	+	1946-49	89		0	(LB)
			TR	Ipswich T.	07.50	1950-51	47		0	

Players Names	Birthplace	Date	Previous Club	League Club	Date Signed	Seasons Played	Career Record			
							Apps	Sub	Gls	
TYNAN, Robert	Liverpool	07.12.55	APP	Tranmere Rov.	07.73	1972-77	193	2	25	(M)E.YTH.INT.
			TR	Blackpool	07.78					
TYNAN, Tom E.	Liverpool	17.11.55	APP	Liverpool	11.72					(F)
			L	Swansea C.	10.75	1975	6	/	2	
			TR	Sheffield Wed.	09.76	1976-78	89	2	31	
			TR	Lincoln C.	10.78	1978	9	/	1	
			TR	Newport Co.	02.79	1978-82	168	15	66	
			TR	Plymouth Arg.	08.83	1983	35	/	12	
TYRELL, Joe J.	London	21.01.32	Bretforten OB	Aston Villa	05.50	1953-55	7		3	(IF)
			TR	Millwall	03.56	1955-56	36		19	
			TR	Bournemouth	06.57	1957-58	3		1	
TYRER, Alan	Liverpool	08.12.42	JNRS	Everton	12.59	1959-61	9		2	(F)
			TR	Mansfield T.	07.63	1963-64	41		5	
			TR	Arsenal	08.65					
			TR	Bury	08.67	1967	2	/	0	
			TR	Workington	07.68	1968-75	228	15	18	
TYRER, Arthur	Liverpool	14.10.34	St.Helens	Crewe Alex.	03.58	1957	6		3	(F)
TYRER, Arthur S.	Manchester	25.02.31	Mossley	Leeds U.	09.50	1951-53	39		4	(WH)
			TR	Shrewsbury T.	06.55	1955	24		3	
			TR	Aldershot	06.56	1956-63	235		9	
TYSON, Jack	Barrow	19.11.35		Barrow	04.54	1953-56	8		0	(F)

KENNY SANSOM (Crystal Palace, Arsenal & England)
A brilliant left-sided full back, Sansom makes up for a distinct lack of inches by his tremendous positional play and terrific speed in recovery. He excels also at overlaps way into opponents' territory, another facet of the makeup which has brought him many England caps since he made his debut with the Palace in December 1975. Kenny gained a Second Division winners medal in 1978/9, whilst still at Selhurst Park, but in the 1980 close season an £800,000 fee took him to Arsenal, where he is still waiting to win a major club honour. He looks set to be around for a long time yet in an International shirt, and must surely be one of the first players the team manager would look to if England is going to be a power in World soccer again.

RON SAUNDERS
(Everton/Gillingham/Portsmouth/Watford/Charlton Ath.)
Saunders was a brilliant junior at Everton when attaining England youth honours but never achieved stardom, playing only a handful of matches over five years before going out of the League with Harry Leyland to Tonbridge in 1956. Gillingham plucked the sturdily built centre forward from the Southern League and he responded by hitting the net regularly. Portsmouth then brought him to Fratton Park in September 1958 where Ron scored 139 goals in 234 appearances as a busy, chasing, goalscoring type. On leaving Charlton Athletic, he made his way towards Football League management.

JIMMY SCOULAR (Portsmouth & Scotland/Newcastle U./Bradford Pk Av.)
Scoular joined Pompey from Gosport in 1945 after service in the Royal Navy, soon being ranked amongst the First Division's most accomplished wing halves as a relentless tackler, tireless and a shrewd passer of the ball. He did not win his first Scottish cap until 1951 versus Denmark, an error soon rectified, as he was selected a further eight times. He won two League Championship medals in succession at Fratton Park and then surprisingly was transferred to Newcastle in the summer of 1953 for a fee of £26,000. In 1955 he led United in winning the F.A. Cup against Manchester City, and before becoming manager of Park Avenue had played just over 600 League games in a career spanning 18 years.

JACK SELKIRK (Rotherham U.)
A tall, well built full back, Selkirk became a great favourite at Millmoor after signing in 1944, winning a Third Division North medal in 1950/1. He was also a member of the side which in the Second Division in 1954/5 shared equal points with the Champions and runners-up. A regular choice for 11 seasons, sure footed and dependable, Jack was a key factor in Rotherham's finest Cup run to the fifth round in 1952/3. He was ever present in the 1950/1 promotion winning side, waiting until the last game before scoring his first goal direct from a free kick.

JACKIE SEWELL (Notts. Co./Sheffield Wed. & England/Aston Villa/Hull C.)
At one time Britain's most expensive player, after Sheffield Wednesday had paid Notts County £34,500 in March 1951, Sewell won his first England cap almost immediately as a direct inside forward of thrusting penetration and speed. He became a really dangerous opportunist helping to get Wednesday back in the top sector as Second Division Champions in 1951/2. Transferred to the Villa in December 1955 for £17,000, he collected an F.A. Cup winners medal against Manchester United in 1956/7. Hull City was Jackie's last club before leaving for Rhodesia to coach. He was capped six times in all as well as playing for the Football League.

LEN SHACKLETON (Bradford Pk Av./Newcastle U./Sunderland & England)
The "clown prince of soccer", Shackleton was a live entertainer whose total belief in enjoyment on the field interrupted what would have been a long International future. He began with Park Avenue after supposedly being rejected by the "Gunners" on the outbreak of war, and was very quickly transferred to Newcastle for £13,000. United, having a surfeit of forwards, then allowed the ball-playing genius to move to close neighbours Sunderland in February 1948 for £20,000. Shackleton's career was often held up by dislike of authority. Nevertheless the crowds loved him for giving great value as a "box o' tricks" magical entertainer, before Len retired with an old ankle injury in 1958.

GRAHAM SHAW (Sheffield U. & England/Doncaster Rov.)
A classy left back of the highest order, Shaw came through the Sheffield United nursery on leaving school. Whilst at school he gained a reputation as an outstanding all round sportsman when winning an England Junior A.B.A. boxing title and playing cricket for Yorkshire Colts. He made his debut at Bramall Lane March 1952, almost immediately becoming a regular until 1965, thereafter playing only sporadically. He formed a longstanding defensive partnership with Cecil Coldwell, during which time he gained a Second Division medal in 1952/3. He also played for England on five occasions after representing the Football League and playing for the under 23s. His younger brother Bernard was also a prominent United defender and at one time they partnered each other at the back.

JOE SHAW (Sheffield U.)
No relation to Graham, Joe Shaw was a long term "Blades" stalwart at centre half, turning professional during the war, but not making his debut until 1948, and then playing until 1965/6, appearing 629 times for the one club. Not very tall for a central defender, he made up for lack of inches with terrific recuperative powers; he also got up well, but above all was brilliant positionally and utterly dependable. He collected Football League representative honours to go with a Second Division winners medal 1952/3.

ALF SHERWOOD (Cardiff C., Newport Co. & Wales)
A great clubman who always seemed to rise to the heights when pulling on a Welsh jersey, Sherwood joined Cardiff City during the war, and went on to play 41 times for Wales as a fiery, tigerish full back who could use the ball constructively when the situation arose. Even after leaving Cardiff for Newport County in 1956, Alf still managed over 200 League games, also being further selected for the National side even when nearing the end of a long career.

PETER SHILTON (Leicester C., Stoke C., Nottingham F., Southampton & England)
A brilliant schoolboy star keeper, one of the few to mature into greatness at senior level, Shilton displaced the famous Gordon Banks whilst still a teenager at Filbert Street. Commanding and extremely agile, with a terrific physique, he is a specialist in cutting down shooting angles and has very safe hands. Transferred to Stoke City in November 1974, once again following in Gordon Banks' footsteps, he stayed three years before becoming the most important cog in the Forest rebuilding cycle. With Forest, Peter collected League and European Cup winners medals to go with a large collection of English caps, which would be more, but for shared duties with Ray Clemence. He signed for Southampton for a fee of £325,000 in August 1982, and his brilliant form has helped the "Saints" climb to the heights.

JOHN SIMPSON (Lincoln C./Gillingham)
A 6ft 1in tall, commanding keeper, Simpson was spotted by Lincoln scouts playing for Netherfield in the Lancashire Combination. He took the plunge and signed full time professional in March 1957, but after playing only five games for the "Red Imps," moved on to Gillingham that summer. He became the club's most outstanding goalkeeper ever when making 571 appearances in all, a club record, and settling down to produce tremendous form over nearly 15 years. In 1963/4 he was an ever present when winning a Fourth Division medal, conceding only 30 goals, the best defensive record in the country.

ERIC SKEELS (Stoke C./Port Vale)
For many seasons this strong tough tackling defender played in the number six shirt, but he was equally effective on either flank or at full back if needed. He played 38 times in Stoke's promotion challenge of 1962/3 when gaining a Second Division winners medal in the very same season that Stan Matthews appeared and the "Potters" became known as the team of "old crocks". He played over 500 games, if one takes into account substitute performances, before leaving the Victoria Ground in September 1976, bound for close neighbours Port Vale. Eric's great experience held him in good stead at the back of the defence when required.

BILL SLATER
(Blackpool/Brentford/Wolverhampton W. &
England/Brentford)
A fine composed wing half, Slater played as an
amateur for Blackpool and Brentford whilst at
Leeds University. After gaining amateur
International honours, he turned pro with Wolves in
February 1954, going on to play in 12 full
Internationals for England. He gained three
Championship medals at Molineux, and an F.A.
Cup winning medal in 1959/60 when Wolves beat
Blackburn, thus making up for a losing one, when
an amateur with Blackpool in the 1950/1 Final
against Newcastle. Never a full time professional
due to his University career, he was still highly
effective as a classic and cultured wing half good
enough to play for his country.

ALAN SLOUGH (Luton T./Fulham/Peterborough
U./Millwall)
A well-built defensive player, Slough on serving an
apprenticeship with Luton Town, turned
professional in 1965 and later played over 250
games in their colours. In 1967/8 he gained a
Fourth Division winners medal after appearing in
32 League matches, and in 1969/70 assisted the
"Hatters" into the Second Division as runners-up
when missing only one match. Transferred to
Fulham in August 1973, less than two years later
he stepped out at Wembley only to be awarded a
losers medal after the "Cottagers" had been
beaten by West Ham. He moved on to
Peterborough United in July 1977, later playing for
Millwall before signing off his League career.

BOBBY SMITH (Chelsea/Tottenham H. &
England/Brighton & HA.)
Smith was one of the first youngsters produced
from Chelsea's newly formed youth team, signing
professional at 17 for the "Pensioners" in May
1950, and reckoned by many at the time to be
England's greatest centre forward discovery.
Somehow he lost his way at the Bridge after a
terrific start in League soccer, becoming
overweight and sluggish, and he was transferred to
Spurs for £18,000 in December 1955. There he
transformed into a slimline bustling, brave goal
grabber of the highest order scoring 28 League
goals in the fabulous "double" season and also
playing for England on 15 occasions, netting 13
times. He scored in both winning Cup Finals, but
seemed to lose the goal touch temporarily until
being recalled in 1963/4 by club and country,
before finishing at Brighton.

DENNIS SMITH (Stoke C.)
Close on 6ft tall, a raw boned central defender,
Smith signed in September 1966 for Stoke City and
by 1969 was the regular lynch pin of the "Potter's"
defence. A throwback to the old time centre half,
Dennis was outstanding, especially in the 1971/2
Football League Cup Final win over Chelsea, when
Stoke came into the match as the underdogs. His
timely interceptions were crucial to the club's
success that day and were just as positive when
Stoke climbed out of the Second Division as third
placed in 1978/9. Following a period on loan to
York City, he moved to Bootham Crescent
permanently to become their manager and
occasionally play the odd game when required.

TOMMY SMITH (Liverpool & England/Swansea
C.)
A tough, battling wing half straight from the Bill
Shankley mould, Smith was tenacious and
extremely hardy; it was said in jest that the young
man had been quarried, not born. Signed for the
Pool, the team of his birthplace, on his 17th
birthday in April 1962, he was a member of the mini
World Cup team that carried off the trophy at
Wembley. He won only one England cap, probably
due to his toughness, which frightened officials as
well as players, but he collected many club
honours including four League Championships
two F.A. Cups and a European Cup winners
medal, before helping Swansea out of Division
Three in 1978/9, his final season of League soccer.

GRAEME SOUNESS (Tottenham
H./Middlesbrough, Liverpool & Scotland)
Souness came from Edinburgh as an apprentice
midfielder with the Spurs, and although turning
professional on his 17th birthday, could never
settle in London. Without ever appearing in the
League side he was sold to Middlesbrough for
£30,000 in January 1973. A season later he
collected a Second Division winners medal and
during his stay at Ayresome Park won the first of
many Scottish International caps. A sum of
£350,000 changed hands in January 1978 when
Liverpool persuaded him to transfer his allegiance
to their red shirt and impress upon the "Kop" his
silky skills, allied to surging drives in support of the
forwards. Honours to date have been plentiful,
including five Championship, four Football League
Cup, three European Cup and Super Cup winners
medals. As the club captain he is an inspirational
leader of the highest quality.

DICK SPIERS (Reading)
Spiers was a dependable centre half who played the whole of his Reading career in the Third Division after signing on at Elm Park in October 1955 and went to play over 450 times, breaking the club appearance record. Not spectacular but effective, over 6ft tall, he became a regular on returning from National Service. His dominant displays in the heart of the defence endeared him to the locals.

GARY SPRAKE (Leeds U., Birmingham C. & Wales)
A brilliant blond haired 6ft goalie, Sprake was discovered by Leeds after playing for Swansea schools, later becoming the youngest ever goalkeeper to appear for Wales when making his International debut at the age of 18 versus Scotland in November 1963. Earlier he had made his debut for Don Revie's side, being called in at the last minute to fly down to Southampton as a 16 year old to play in the club's Second Division match. Whilst at Elland Road in a 12 year career he picked up a League Championship medal, Second Division Title, and F.A. Cup runner-up medal along with numerous other honours before going to Birmingham City in October 1973. In the top flight of keepers, he was extremely acrobatic, with good handling and excellent judgement.

PETER SPRINGETT (Q.P.R./Sheffield Wed./Barnsley)
Not tremendously tall for a goalkeeper, young Peter Springett followed in the illustrious footsteps of his famous brother Ron, who also started out as custodian of the Rangers goal. Showing the same agility, the young Springett turned professional in May 1963, becoming the regular netminder by 1965/6. In 1966/7, probably the most notable season in the club's history, Peter was an ever present as Q.P.R. did the "double" – Third Division Champions and Football League Cup winners. At the end of the season he was exchanged for his brother Ron and made the journey to Sheffield Wednesday, where he stayed until July 1975. Barnsley then took him to Oakwell and before leaving the game he made 44 appearances for the side that gained promotion from the Fourth Division in 1978/9.

RON SPRINGETT (Q.P.R./Sheffield Wed. England/Q.P.R.)
A brilliant goalkeeper with cat-like reactions, great anticipation and utterly dependable, Springett was much sought after by the bigger clubs when attracting attention playing in Q.P.R.'s Third Division South side, resulting in Sheffield Wednesday paying a fee of £10,000 in March 1958 for his services. He was a star in the Wednesday promotion team the next full season when the club regained First Division status, making his debut for England November 1959 and playing in all but one of the next 29 games. In June 1967 he was traded in an exchange deal involving his younger brother Peter, also a Rangers keeper, and returned to Loftus Road. In his first season back, he helped the club gain promotion to the top Division for the first time in its history, conceding only 36 goals – the lowest in the League.

ROY SPROSON (Port Vale)
In July 1949, Sproson a young Stoke City amateur, joined Port Vale, then managed by Gordon Hodgson the former Liverpool and Aston Villa marksman. He became known in later years as "Mr. Loyalty"; before retiring Roy played for the "Valiants" in well over 700 games. Starting as a wing half, later settling down at full back, he even moved grounds with the club from the old Rec. to the new Vale Park. The great highlight of his career was the 1953/4 F.A. Cup in which the Vale finally went out in the semi-final to eventual winners W.B.A. from a penalty scored by their old player Ronnie Allen. League medals for the Third Division North, 1953/4 and Fourth Division, 1958/9 are amongst "Mr. Loyalty's" proudest possessions.

FRANK STAPLETON (Arsenal, Manchester U. & Eire)
A Dublin-born striker, Stapleton started out through the Arsenal apprentice ranks before signing professional in September 1973, where his play soon became a revelation. Frank scored in the F.A. Cup Final of 1979 versus Manchester United to gain a winners medal, but had to be satisfied with runners-up medals from the Finals against Ipswich and West Ham. Following the losing European Cup Winners Cup Final against Valencia, Frank signed for Manchester United when a £900,000 cheque changed hands. He scored the "Red Devils" first goal in the Cup Final against Brighton at Wembley in 1983, where a second game was needed before another winners medal was duly attained. He has played many times for the Republic, assisting in making chances for other forwards by his ability to manoeuvre central defenders out of position, and has scored well over 100 First Division goals himself.

BILLY STEEL (Derby Co. & Scotland)
Derby Country paid £15,000 to Morton of the Scottish League in June 1947 for the comparatively unknown Steel. His debut for Scotland was against the "ould enemy" at Wembley in April 1947 and so impressive was he that, a month later, he was picked at inside left for Great Britain against the Rest of Europe. Only 5ft 6in tall, and lightning-quick off the mark, getting into shooting positions was his speciality. Billy played just over the 100 game mark for Derby before being lifted back north of the border by Dundee for the then record transfer fee of £23,000 paid by a Scottish club. He emigrated to the U.S.A. in 1958 after representing his country 30 times.

ALEX STEPNEY (Millwall/Chelsea/Manchester U. & England)
Brought out of Isthmian League soccer with Tooting and Mitcham by Millwall in May 1963, Stepney made a real impact with the "Lions" when they created a record run of home games without defeat, which took the club from Fourth to Second Division in successive seasons. A highly consistent if unspectacular keeper, Chelsea sought his signature as cover for "The Cat", Peter Bonetti, but after only three months and one match played, Alex was transferred to Manchester United in September 1966, winning a Championship medal in his first season. The highlight of his career was the winning of the European Cup Final 1968 against the then mighty Benefica. He played for England on just one occasion against Sweden at Wembley in 1968.

ALAN STEVENSON
(Chesterfield/Burnley/Rotherham U.)
Stevenson is another of the long line of great Chesterfield goalies who seem to be mass produced. Safe as houses and as sound, he made his debut in the 1969/70 season for the "Spireites" and played 35 times in that first season to gain a Fourth Division winners medal. He moved to Burnley for £50,000 in January 1972 and went on to gain 11 England under 23 caps. In his first full season at Turf Moor he conceded only 35 League goals as the "Clarets" stormed back to the big time with the Second Division Champions tag firmly in position. Again in 1981/2 he was an ever present when collecting a Third Division winners medal and conceding only 45 goals throughout the duration. He signed for Rotherham United in August 1983.

GEORGE T. STEWART (Accrington St./Coventry C./Carlisle U.)
Stewart moved from St. Mirren to Accrington Stanley in the summer of 1954 to take up centre forward duties for the then Third Division North side after heading the Scottish club's scoring charts. In that first season he scored 28 goals from 33 games, helping to push the Lancashire side up to second in the table, and becoming the top scorers in the Division. For the next three seasons the club was placed in the top three with George getting a further 94 goals before being sold to Coventry City November 1958. He helped that club into a higher placing in the Fourth Division than Accrington, who in 1961/2 resigned from the League on financial grounds. In his English career the bustling forward scored 160 League goals.

NOBBY STILES (Manchester U. & England/Middlesbrough/Preston NE.)
Stiles became a National hero, mainly due to the T.V. coverage of the 1966 World Cup exploits of the winning England team which included the indomitable "Nobby" (real name Norbert) of the toothy grin and unquenchable "never say die" spirit. He developed through the United juniors as a "Busby Babe" maturing at wing half; in the shadow of so many great players he took a long time to attain a regular place in the side. He gained two Championship medals, and a winners medal from the game against Benfica in the 1968 European Cup Final, before moving on to pastures new, eventually going into League management.

EDDIE STUART (Wolverhampton W./Stoke C./Tranmere Rov./Stockport Co.)
A strapping 6ft South African, Stuart joined the Wolves in January 1951, from Rangers F.C. Johannesburg, where he had played representative football. Signed as a centre half, he actually made his debut at centre forward in April 1952 before settling down as a regular in the defence at full back. He collected two League Championship medals in consecutive seasons, only missing six games, then moved to Stoke City in the summer of 1962, playing 40 games and getting a Second Division medal with the "Potters". He finished his career in the lower reaches after playing 150 League games.

ROBIN STUBBS (Birmingham C./Torquay U./Bristol Rov./Torquay U.)
A beautifully built young centre forward, Stubbs began with Birmingham City and was seen to be a future International prospect by a good many shrewd judges. Somehow he did not utilise the natural talent in his keeping whilst in the First Division and was eventually transferred to Torquay United in August 1963. He scored consistently at Plainmoor over a six-year period, collecting 121 goals from 214 appearances before leaving for Bristol Rovers in July 1969, later to return to Torquay.

MIKE SUMMERBEE (Swindon T./Manchester C. & England/Burnley/Blackpool/Stockport Co.)
A striking, hard running outside right, Summerbee was rather old fashioned in approach but highly effective. The son of a former League player who was signed by Swindon Town from Cheltenham in March 1960, Summerbee was highly sought after as one of the many brilliant young players being groomed by Bert Head at Swindon, and in August 1965 Manchester City paid £30,000, a bargain fee by today's standards. He immediately helped City out of the Second Division, later winning League Championship, F.A. Cup, League Cup and European Cup Winners Cup medals in the most prolific spell of City's history. He also played eight times for England before finishing as a player manager at Stockport County.

JOHNNY SUMMERS (Fulham/Norwich C./Millwall/Charlton Ath.)
A whole hearted, tough, hard running, power shooting left winger, Summers could never be left unattended near the opposition's penalty area, always getting amongst the goals in a career that was tragically cut short by a long illness, resulting in his early death. A Londoner, he started out with Fulham as a winger, moving to Carrow Road in June 1950, before leaving for Millwall in May 1954. At the Den he scored consistently, but it was with his next club, Charlton, that he really made the headlines. Twice whilst at the Valley he scored five goals in a match from the wing, the most famous being against Huddersfield Town on 21 December 1957, in a sensational high scoring match.

BARRY SWALLOW (Doncaster Rov./Crewe Alex./Barnsley/Bradford C./York C.)
A 6ft 2in tall defender, Doncaster born, Swallow made his debut with the Rovers, being produced through their junior sides. The son of an early post-war Doncaster player, who also played for Barnsley, he did not make a mark until signing for York City in October 1969, settling into their defence at centre half and becoming a key player in the club's future plans. Promotion was achieved to the Third Division 1970/1 and to the Second 1973/4, and in those seasons, Swallow missed only two games.

FRANK SWIFT (Manchester C. & England)
The footballing world was shocked when, in February 1958, the sensational news of the Munich air disaster, also uncovered the fact that the "genial giant" Frank Swift, who was travelling as a reporter, had also been killed. As a 19 year old, he had collapsed at Wembley in a faint after helping City to win the 1934 Cup Final against Portsmouth. He became a great showman extremely popular on the terraces. Possessing tremendous ability between the posts, Frank even went on to captain England from that position. Held in great esteem, he undoubtedly ranks as one of the finest goalminders ever. At the age of 36 Frank bowed out of the game he had for so long graced meritoriously.

BOBBY TAMBLING (Chelsea & England/Crystal Palace)
One of the famous "Drake's Ducklings", Bobby came straight out of the Chelsea star-studded junior side after gaining schoolboy International honours. He replaced the legendary Jimmy Greaves when the latter went to Italy. A winger, he converted into an inside right of terrific power, able to contend with a heavy work rate, and had the ability to get on the end of goal chances with a rocket like left foot. He once scored five goals from the left wing against Villa in 1966 and amassed 164 League goals at the Bridge before leaving for Crystal Palace. He represented England on three occasions and collected an F.A. Cup losers medal from the all London Final against Spurs in 1967.

COLIN TAYLOR (Walsall/Newcastle U./Walsall/Crystal Palace/Walsall)
A powerful shooting outside left, with one of the hardest shots in League soccer, Taylor developed into one of the highest scoring wingmen of the post-war game with speed and an ability to cut inside the full back. Before being transferred to Newcastle for £10,000 in June 1963, he had missed only two games in the five years since his debut, scored 93 goals, collected a Fourth Division winners medal and helped the club a season later into the Second Division as runners-up. He couldn't seem to stay away from Fellows Park for long and signed for Walsall on three separate occasions, having failed to settle in the colours of his other teams.

GORDON TAYLOR (Bolton W./Birmingham C./Blackburn Rov./Bury)
A fine midfield clubman, Taylor's career in the League spanned nearly 20 years, before he later became the Secretary of the Professional Footballers Association when succeeding Cliff Lloyd. He turned professional on reaching his 17th birthday with Bolton, following many excellent performances in the junior sides, and he played over 250 League games for the Wanderers mainly in the Second Division as the once great "Trotters" struggled to recapture their former glories. Transferred to Birmingham, Gordon finally made it back into the First Division when the City attained promotion as runners-up in 1971/2 and he later saw service with both Blackburn Rovers and Bury.

STUART TAYLOR (Bristol Rov.)
A 6ft 4½in centre half, Taylor lent his commanding leadership totally to Bristol Rovers in a career stretching over 15 seasons and nearly 550 appearances in all. He turned professional in January 1966 following service as an amateur in the club's colours and in 1968/9 formed a terrific defensive partnership with Larry Lloyd, where between them they missed only four games. He was an ever present in 1973/4 when the Rovers gained Second Division status as runners-up to Oldham Athletic, a position they finally lost in 1981, long after Stuart had departed from first team service.

PAT TERRY (Charlton Ath./Newport Co./Swansea C./Gillingham/Northampton T./Millwall/Reading/Swindon T./Brentford)
A much travelled centre forward, tall, well built and with an eye for the goal, Terry arrived at Charlton from Eastbourne and went on to play in all four Divisions, scoring over 200 League goals. Only on one occasion did he play in a side that gained promotion, when with Millwall in 1961/2, after being signed from Northampton Town to score valuable goals – which he did, netting 13 from 17 appearances. In a career of 15 seasons with nine clubs, the longest period spent was where he collected 60 goals in just under three seasons at Gillingham.

BARRIE THOMAS (Leicester C./Mansfield T./Scunthorpe U./Newcastle U./Scunthorpe U./Barnsley)
A natural goalscorer even when with Leicester City, where he gained England youth honours, Thomas was allowed to leave for Mansfield Town, because of Bill Gardiner's consistent scoring. This turned out to be a costly mistake, for after two seasons with that club and a further two with Scunthorpe United, he had scored 115 League goals and was transferred to Newcastle United in January 1962 for a fee of £40,000. At Newcastle he suffered from injury, which restricted his first team appearances, before being transferred back to his old club Scunthorpe, later moving to Barnsley. As a tough, hard running, bustling, centre forward Barrie scored over 200 League goals.

GEOFF THOMAS (Nottingham F.)
Thomas was a full back who played for Derby schools before joining Forest as a 15 year old, making his League debut at the age of 17. Originally a wing half, he settled down well at the back before playing over 400 games for his only club. He won a Third Division South medal in 1950/1, followed by promotion with Forest to the First Division as runners up in 1956/7. He played his last League game in 1959/60, a year after not being selected for the winning Cup Final team that beat Luton Town at Wembley.

PETER THOMPSON (Preston NE/Liverpool & England/Bolton W.)

Schoolboy International star Peter Thompson made his debut with Preston, where he caused a stir with his skill and speed down either flank, culminating with pin point crosses into the area. Bill Shankly saw the flashing wingman as a key asset in the Liverpool rebuilding plans, taking him to Anfield in August 1963, where he immediately won a Championship medal, followed by another in 1965/6. Unfortunately, due to Alf Ramsey's policy of wingless International sides, this highly polished player only managed 16 full caps before dropping into the Second Division with Bolton Wanderers.

PHIL THOMPSON (Liverpool & England)

An outstanding member of the great Liverpool machine of the 1970s, Thompson is the proud possessor of 42 full England caps, to go with under 23 caps plus Football League representations. A cool, confident and constructive central defender, Phil was a key player in the club's great successes during this period, gaining six Championship, one F.A. Cup, two Football League Cup, two European Cup and U.E.F.A. Cup winners medals. His career was unfortunately brought to an end by injury, but by then he had collected all the game's major honours, along with the admiration of fellow professionals.

TOMMY THOMPSON (Newcastle U./Aston Villa/Preston NE. & England/Stoke C./Barrow)

Known as "toucher" to his team mates, Thompson was developed by Newcastle after the war and transferred to Villa in 1950, very quickly being capped for England. A diminutive (5ft 5in) scheming, probing inside forward, a specialist in the sharp break through to boot, he became quite a prolific goalscorer, especially after signing for Preston North End in 1955 where he formed a great partnership with the legendary Tom Finney, despite being troubled by an old cartilage operation, which hampered him considerably throughout his career. Again capped in 1957 he later assisted the Stoke City veterans to climb back to the First Division in 1962/3, after which he moved on to Barrow to end his footballing days.

BERT TINDILL (Doncaster Rov./Bristol C./Barnsley)

A great clubman for Doncaster Rovers, Tindill could operate on either wing or inside to great effect and scored quite consistently for a scheming clever player with general midfield skills. He was picked up during the war and blossomed under the guidance of the legendary Peter Doherty, later becoming skipper of the side. He collected a Third Division North winners medal 1949/50 and missed less than a dozen games over the next seven seasons, being one of the Rovers' most consistent post-war players. He later went on to play for Bristol City, then Barnsley.

COLIN TODD (Sunderland/Derby Co. & England/Everton/Birmingham C./Nottingham F./Oxford U.)

A great defender, Todd is a sure tackler who does not give the ball away too readily. Although making his debut for Sunderland in 1966/7, he did not get the first of his 27 England caps until Derby County had splashed out £170,000 in February 1971 to take the 22-year-old to the Baseball Ground. A key member of Brian Clough's side, he formed a brilliant centre back partnership with Roy McFarland, at International as well as at club level. He gained a Championship medal in his first season and collected another in 1974/5. Later he performed valuable service at Birmingham City after not really settling down with Everton when at Goodison Park, before going back to Nottingham Forest to bolster up a sagging defence. He is now with Oxford United whom he joined just in time to help add the finishing touches to their promotion from the Third Division as Champions.

JOHN TOSHACK (Cardiff C., Liverpool., Swansea C. & Wales)

A tall, powerful centre forward, Toshack began with his native Cardiff City, turning professional in March 1966 and giving them nearly five years great service before joining Liverpool as their then costliest signing at £110,000. A specialist in netting with far post headers, before leaving Liverpool for Swansea as player-manager, he had scored 74 League goals, collecting three League Championships and an F.A. Cup winners medal. He was one of Bill Shankly's shrewdest signings, benefiting fully from the lessons at his disposal and he used them to maximum advantage at the Vetch Field, where he guided Swansea into the First Division for the first time in the Club's history.

EDDIE TOWERS
(Brentford/Q.P.R./Millwall/Gillingham/Aldershot)
Another journeyman centre forward that the lower Divisions seem to produce in abundance, Thomas was a powerful and direct hustler who spelt danger to all opposing goalies. It was really at Brentford that he made his mark, being a product of the junior sides, and he developed into their record goalscorer. He set up a remarkable partnership with George Francis and together they came to be known as the "terrible twins." In six full seasons before Eddie transferred to Q.P.R. in May 1961, these two scored 244 goals between them for the "Bees." Again in January 1963, when signing for Gillingham, the duo paired up again, but only until the end of that season when Eddie again moved, this time to Aldershot.

BERT TRAUTMANN (Manchester C.)
The footballer of the year title for Trautmann was followed by a wonderful display in the 1956 winning F.A. Cup Final against Birmingham City, when the blond goalie sustained a broken neck in the cause of Manchester City and insisted on completing the match. The winners medal from that match was sufficient recompense for the loss at the hands of Newcastle United a season earlier. He made a meteoric rise to fame as a League goalie when signed by the City from St. Helens, November 1949, to replace the illustrious Frank Swift. The tall powerful keeper had been a German para and was in a P.O.W. camp when spotted by the Non-League side. The only German to represent the Football League, he played over 500 games whilst at Maine Road.

JOHN TROLLOPE (Swindon T.)
A long serving single clubman, Trollope made his debut back in 1960, before going on to play 770 League games for the Town, a record that may never be beaten. A very consistent full back of some quality, he was tall, well built, and an outstanding member of the Swindon glory side of the late 1960s. The highlight of a meritorious career spanning 20 years came with a League Cup winners medal from the 1968/9 Wembley epic, where the little Third Division side beat the mighty Arsenal in a game that will be long talked about. He was an object lesson to any youngster in the importance of sportsmanlike qualities.

BRIAN TURNER (Bury/Oldham Ath.)
Turner was a long service member of Bury, turning professional in February 1957 before going on to play over 450 League games for the "Shakers" by August 1970. Tall and well built, he gave consistent displays in the half back line throughout his career, the finest moment coming when winning a Third Division medal in 1960/1. Again in 1967/8 he was a member of the side that regained Second Division status, having lost it only a season earlier, once again an ever present. He played less than a dozen games for Oldham before leaving League soccer.

GORDON TURNER (Luton T.)
A goalscoring inside forward, Turner was the son of a former Hull City star who had played alongside Dally Duncan, the manager of Luton Town, who wasted no time in signing up Gordon in March 1950. Before retiring he had become Luton's record goalscorer with a total of 243. Well built, very quick off the mark, he was a real sharpshooter with either boot, netting 32 goals when the Town attained promotion to the First Division 1954/5. His best season was 1957/8 when scoring 33 and helping the Hatters to their then highest ever First Division placing, eighth. He did not play in the losing F.A. Cup Final against Forest 1959, a great disappointment, but represented the Football League on one occasion.

GRAHAM TURNER (Wrexham/Chester C./Shrewsbury T.)
Hard working, strong in recovery, Turner can play in the middle of the field, but his tenacious qualities have been seen to better effect certainly at Shrewsbury in a defensive role. He started out soccer life playing in North Wales, first for Wrexham and then for Chester, eventually coming to Gay Meadow for a then club record fee of £30,000 in January 1973. He played in all but two games in 1974/5 as the Town gained promotion from the Fourth Division as runners-up, but his greatest achievement came when winning a Third Division league medal in 1978/9. As the player-manager he has made a most valuable contribution to the fortunes of Shrewsbury Town in enabling them to maintain their Second Division status.

Players Names	Birthplace	Date	Previous Club	League Club	Date Signed	Seasons Played	Apps	Sub	Gls	
UFTON, Derek G.	Crayford	31.05.28	Bexleyheath	Charlton Ath.	09.48	1949-59	263	.	0	(CH)E-1/Kent Cricketer
UGOLINI, Rolando	Italy	04.06.24	Glasgow Celtic	Middlesbrough	05.48	1948-55	320		0	(G)
			TR	Wrexham	06.57	1957-59	83		0	
UNDERWOOD, Dave E.	London	15.03.28	Edgware T.	Q.P.R.	12.49	1951	2		0	(G)
			TR	Watford	02.52	1951-53	52		0	
			TR	Liverpool	12.53	1953-55	45		0	
			TR	Watford	06.56	1956	16		0	
			Dartford	Watford	04.60	1960-62	107		0	
			TR	Fulham	07.63	1963-64	18		0	
UNDERWOOD, George	Sheffield	06.09.25		Sheffield U.	09.46	1949-50	17		0	
			TR	Sheffield Wed.	10.51					
			TR	Scunthorpe U.	06.53	1953	8		0	
			TR	Rochdale	06.54	1954	19		0	
UNDERWOOD, William K.	Brigg	28.12.21		Hartlepool U.	AM	1947	1		0	(OL)
UPHILL, E. Dennis	Bath	11.08.31	JNRS	Tottenham H.	09.49	1950-52	6		2	(IF)
			TR	Reading	02.53	1952-55	92		43	
			TR	Coventry C.	10.55	1955-56	49		17	
			TR	Mansfield T.	03.57	1956-58	83		38	
			TR	Watford	06.59	1959-60	51		30	
			TR	Crystal Palace	10.60	1960-62	63		17	
UPRICHARD, Norman	Moyraverty	20.04.28	Distillery	Arsenal	06.48					(G)NI-18
			TR	Swindon T.	11.49	1949-52	73		0	
			TR	Portsmouth	11.52	1952-58	182		0	
			TR	Southend U.	07.59	1959	12		0	
UPTON, Colin C.	Reading	02.10.60	APP	Plymouth Arg.	10.78	1978	2	1	0	(F)
UPTON, Frank	Ainsley Hill	18.10.34	Nuneaton	Northampton T.	03.53	1952-53	17		1	(WH)
			TR	Derby Co.	06.54	1954-60	224		12	
			TR	Chelsea	08.61	1961-64	74		3	
			TR	Derby Co.	09.65	1965-66	35	/	5	
			TR	Notts.Co.	09.66	1966	33	1	3	
			Worcester C.	Workington	01.68	1967	6	1	0	
UPTON, James E.	Coatbridge	03.06.40	Glasgow Celtic	Cardiff C.	08.63	1963	5		0	(FB)
UPTON, Robin P.	Lincoln	09.11.42	JNRS	Brighton & H.A.	11.59	1962-66	40	/	0	(WH)
URE, J. Ian	Ayr	07.12.39	Dundee	Arsenal	08.63	1963-69	168	/	2	(CH)S-11/S.U23-1/
			TR	Manchester U.	08.69	1969-70	47	/	1	S.F.LGE REP.
URQUART, William M.	Inverness	22.11.56	Glasgow Rgrs.	Wigan Ath.	11.80	1980	5	5	2	(F)
URQUHART, George S.	Glasgow	22.04.50	Ross Co.	Wigan Ath.	07.79	1979-80	63	5	6	(F)
URSEM, Loek	Holland	07.01.58	AZ Sportlaan	Stoke C.	07.79	1979-82	32	8	7	(M)
			L	Sunderland	03.82	1981	0	4	0	
URWIN, Graham E.	Sth.Shields	15.02.49		Darlington	08.67	1967	1	/	0	(OR)
USHER, Brian	Belmont	11.03.44	JNRS	Sunderland	03.61	1963-64	60		5	(OR)E.U23-1
			TR	Sheffield Wed.	06.65	1965-67	55	1	2	
			TR	Doncaster Rov.	06.68	1969-72	164	6	6	
USHER, John A.G.	Hexham	06.09.18		Watford	05.46	1946-47	23		4	(WH)
UYTENBOGAARDT, Albert	S.Africa	05.03.30	Clyde S.A.	Charlton Ath.	10.48	1948-52	6		0	(G)
UZELAC, Steve	Doncaster	12.03.53	JNRS	Doncaster Rov.	06.71	1971-76	182	3	9	(D)
			L	Mansfield T.	02.76	1975	2	/	0	
			TR	Preston N.E.	05.77	1977-78	9	/	0	
			TR	Stockport Co.	03.80	1979-81	31	/	2	
UZZELL, John E.	Plymouth	31.03.59	APP	Plymouth Arg.	04.77	1977-83	199	2	4	(D)

Players Names	Birthplace	Date	Previous Club	League Club	Date Signed	Seasons Played	Apps	Sub	Gls	
VAESSEN, Leon H.	New Cross	08.11.40	Chelsea(AM)	Millwall	01.58	1957-60	26		2	(WH)E.SCH.INT./
			TR	Gillingham	08.61	1961-62	29		0	Father of Paul
VAESSEN, Paul L.	Gillingham	16.10.61	APP	Arsenal	07.79	1978-81	23	9	6	(F)
VAFIADIS, Odysseus	London	08.09.45	Chelsea(APP)	Q.P.R.	11.62	1963	15		4	(W)
			TR	Millwall	09.64	1964	4		0	
VAIREY, Roy H.	Sth.Elmsall	10.06.32		Stockport Co.	09.51	1956	5		0	(G)
VALENTINE, Carl	Manchester	04.07.58		Oldham Ath.	01.76	1976-79	75	7	8	(F)
VALENTINE, Peter	Huddersfield	16.04.63	APP	Huddersfield T.	04.80	1981-82	19	/	1	(D)
			TR	Bolton W.	07.83	1983	42	/	1	
VALLANCE, Tom H.W.	Stoke	28.03.24	Torquay U.(AM)	Arsenal	07.47	1948-49	15		2	(OL)
VALLARD, Len G.H.	Sherborne	06.07.40	Yeovil T.	Reading	05.58	1959-61	37		2	(HB)
VAN BREUKELEN, Hans	Holland	04.10.56	Utrecht	Nottingham F.	09.82	1982-83	61	/	0	(G)
VAN DEN HAUWE, Pat	Belgium	16.12.60	APP	Birmingham C.	08.78	1978-83	113	4	1	(D)
VAN DER ELST, Francois	Belgium	01.12.54	N. York Cosmos	West Ham U.	12.81	1981-82	61	1	14	(M) BELGIAN INT.
VAN GOOL, Roger	Belgium	01.06.50	FC Cologne	Coventry C.	03.80	1979-80	17	/	0	(F) BELGIAN INT.
VAN MIERLO, Tony W.M.	Holland	24.08.57	Willem II	Birmingham C.	08.81	1981-82	44	/	4	(F) DUTCH INT.
VAN WIJK, Dennis J.	Holland	16.02.62	Ajax	Norwich C.	10.82	1982-83	53	3	2	(M)
VANDERMOTTEN, William	Glasgow	26.08.30	T.Lanark	Bradford P.A.	03.53	1952	1		0	(FB)d.1979
VANSITTART, Tom	Merton	23.01.50	APP	Crystal Palace	04.67	1967-69	10	1	2	(FB)
			TR	Wrexham	02.70	1969-74	86	2	1	
VARADI, Imre	Paddington	08.07.59	Letchworth	Sheffield U.	04.78	1978	6	4	4	(F)
			TR	Everton	03.79	1979-80	22	4	6	
			TR	Newcastle U.	08.81	1981-82	81	/	39	
			TR	Sheffield Wed.	08.83	1983	35	3	17	
VARNEY, John F.	Oxford	27.11.29	Oxford C.	Hull C.	12.49	1950	9		0	(FB)
			TR	Lincoln C.	05.51	1951-52	20		4	
VARTY, Tom H.	Hetton	02.12.21		Darlington	+	1946-49	162		31	(IF)
			TR	Watford	09.50	1950	34		6	
VASPER, Peter J.	Bromley	03.09.45		Orient	11.63					(G)
			Guildford C.	Norwich C.	02.68	1967-69	31	/	0	
			TR	Cambridge U.	09.70	1970-73	136	/	0	
VASS, Steve	Leicester	10.01.54		Hartlepool U.	10.79	1979	4	/	0	(D)
			TR	Huddersfield T.	01.81					
VASSALLO, Barrie E.	Newport	03.03.56	APP	Arsenal	05.73					(M) W.SCH.INT.
			TR	Plymouth Arg.	11.74	1974-75	6	7	2	
			TR	Aldershot	07.76					
			Barnstaple	Torquay U.	03.77	1976-78	44	2	4	
VAUGHAN, Charles J.	London	23.04.21	Sutton U.	Charlton Ath.	01.47	1946-52	226		91	(CF)E'B'-1/E.AMAT.INT.
			TR	Portsmouth	03.53	1952-53	27		14	
VAUGHAN, Ian	Sheffield	03.07.61	APP	Rotherham U.	07.79	1979-80	4	/	0	(D)
			L	Stockport Co.	12.81	1981	2	/	1	
VAUGHAN, N.Glyn	Llandidloes	25.08.21	Oldham Ath.(AM)	Exeter C.	05.46	1946-47	6		0	(IF)
VAUGHAN, Nigel M.	Newport	20.05.59	APP	Newport Co.	06.77	1976-83	215	9	34	(M)W.U'21-2/W-7
			TR	Cardiff C.	09.83	1983	36	/	8	
VAUGHAN, Terry	Ebbw Vale	22.04.38		Mansfield T.	06.57	1958	6		0	
VEACOCK, James	Liverpool	05.09.19	Marine	Southport	11.47	1947	10		0	(CF)
VEALL, Ray	Skegness	16.03.43	Skegness	Doncaster Rov.	03.61	1960-61	19		6	(OL)
			TR	Everton	09.61	1962	11		1	
			TR	Preston N.E.	05.65	1965	11	/	0	
			TR	Huddersfield T.	12.65	1965-66	12	/	1	
VEARNCOMBE, Graham	Cardiff	28.03.34	JNRS	Cardiff C.	02.52	1952-63	208		0	(G)W-2
VEART, Robert	Hartlepool	11.08.44	Whitby T.	Hartlepool U.	07.71	1970-72	58	12	11	(IF)E.AMAT.INT.
VECK, Robert	Southampton	01.40.20		Southampton	+	1946-49	23		2	(CF)
			TR	Gillingham	07.50	1950	36		12	
VEITCH, George H.	Sunderland	18.01.31	Silksworth CJ	Hull C.	08.51		95			(FB)
			TR	Millwall	06.52	1952-57			0	
VEITCH, Tom	Edinburgh	16.10.49	Hearts	Tranmere Rov.	07.72	1972-74	76	3	5	(M)
			TR	Halifax T.	08.75	1975	20	2	0	
			TR	Hartlepool U.	08.76	1976	10	/	0	
VENABLES, Terry F.	Bethnal Green	06.01.43	JNRS	Chelsea	08.60	1959-65	202	/	26	(IF)E-2/E.U23-4/
			TR	Tottenham H.	05.66	1965-68	114	1	5	E.F.LGE REP./E.YTH.INT./
			TR	Q.P.R.	06.69	1969-74	178	1	19	E.AMAT.INT./E.SCH.INT.
			TR	Crystal Palace	09.74	1974	14	/	0	
VENISON, Barry	Stanley	16.08.64	APP	Sunderland	01.82	1981-83	94	4	1	(D) E.YTH.INT./E.U'21-2
VENNARD, Walter	Belfast	17.10.19	Crusaders	Stockport Co.	09.47	1947	5		0	(CH)
VENTERS, Alex	Cowdenbeath	09.06.13	T.Lanark	Blackburn Rov.	02.47	1946-47	25		7	(IF)S-3/S.F.LGE REP./d.1960
VENTOM, Eric G.	Hemsworth	15.02.20		Brentford	+	1947	1		0	

Players Names	Birthplace	Date	Previous Club	League Club	Date Signed	Seasons Played	Apps	Sub	Gls	
VERDE, Pedro	Argentina	12.03.52	Hercules Alicante	Sheffield U.	08.79	1979	9	1	3	(F)
VERITY, David A.	Halifax	21.09.49	APP	Scunthorpe U.	09.67	1966-67	3	2	0	(RB)Brother of Kevin
			TR	Halifax T.	09.68	1969-72	64	14	5	
VERITY, Kevin P.	Halifax	16.03.40	JNRS	Halifax T.	10.58	1958-59	13		6	(F)
VERNON, Jack	Belfast	26.09.18	Belfast Celtic	W.B.A.	02.47	1946-51	190		1	(CH)EI-2/NI-17
VERNON, John E.	S.Africa	02.03.56	JNRS	Stockport Co.	08.75	1974-75	4	2	0	(W)
VERNON, T.Roy	Hollywell	14.04.37	JNRS	Blackburn Rov.	03.55	1955-59	131		49	(IF)W-32/W.U23-2●
			TR	Everton	02.60	1959-64	176		101	
			TR	Stoke C.	03.65	1964-68	84	3	22	
			L	Halifax T.	01.70	1969	4	/	0	
VESEY, Kieron G.	Manchester	24.11.66	JNRS	Halifax T.	N/C	1983	2	/	0	(G)
VESSEY, Tony W.	Derby	28.11.61	APP	Brighton & H.A.	11.79	1980	1	/	0	(D)
VICKERS, Peter	Doncaster	06.03.34	JNRS	Leeds U.	03.51	1950-55	20		0	E.SCH.INT.
			TR	Lincoln C.	08.59					
			Wisbech T.	Northampton T.	02.60	1959	2		0	
VICKERS, Wilf	Wakefield	03.08.24		Brighton & H.A.	09.47	1947	5		1	
			TR	W.B.A.	05.48					
			TR	Aldershot	06.49	1949-51	14		1	
VICKERY, Paul W.	Chelmsford	20.05.53	APP	Southend U.	APP	1969	0	1	0	
VILJOEN, Colin	S. Africa	20.06.48	S. Africa	Ipswich T.	08.67	1966-77	303	2	46	(M)E-2
			TR	Manchester C.	08.78	1978-79	25	2	0	
			TR	Chelsea	03.80	1979-81	19	1	0	
VILLA, J. Ricardo	Argentina	18.08.52	Racing Club	Tottenham H.	07.78	1978-82	124	9	18	(M)ARGENTINE INT.
VILLARS, Anthony K.	Cwmbran	24.01.52	Cwmbran	Cardiff C.	06.71	1971-75	66	7	4	(F)W-3/W.U23-2
			TR	Newport Co.	07.76	1976	23	6	1	
VILLAZAN, Rafael	Uruguay	19.07.56	Huelva	Wolverhampton W.	05.80	1980-81	20	3	0	(D)URUGUAY INT.
VINALL, Albert	Birmingham	06.03.22	Southampton(AM)	Aston Villa	07.46	1947	5		1	(FB)Brother of Edward J.
			TR	Walsall	08.54	1954-55	79		0	
VINALL, Edward J.	Witton	16.12.10	Luton(*)	Walsall	07.46	1946	2		0	(CF)*Folkestone/Sunderland/Norwich C.
VINCENT, John V.	W.Bromwich	08.02.47	APP	Birmingham C.	02.64	1963-70	168	3	41	(IF)E.YTH.INT.
			TR	Middlesbrough	03.71	1970-72	37	3	7	
			TR	Cardiff C.	10.72	1972-74	58	8	11	
VINCENT, Norman E.	Prudhoe	03.03.09	Stockport Co.(*)	Grimsby T.	*	1946	15		2	(FB)*Spennymoor
VINCENT, Robert	Leicester	29.05.49	JNRS	Notts.Co.	AM	1965	1	/	0	(IR)
VINCENT, Robert	Newcastle	23.11.62	APP	Sunderland	11.79	1980	1	1	0	(M)E.SCH.INT.
			TR	Orient	05.82	1981-82	8	1	0	
VINE, Peter W.	Southampton	11.12.40	JNRS	Southampton	12.57	1958	1		0	(F)E.YTH.INT.
VINEY, Keith	Portsmouth	26.10.57	APP	Portsmouth	10.75	1975-81	160	6	3	(D)
			TR	Exeter C.	08.82	1982-83	76	/	4	
VINTER, Mick	Boston	23.05.54	Boston U.	Notts. Co.	03.72	1972-78	135	31	53	(F)
			TR	Wrexham	06.79	1979-81	90	12	25	
			TR	Oxford U.	08.82	1982-83	67	2	21	
VIOLLET, Dennis	Manchester	20.09.33	JNRS	Manchester U.	09.50	1952-61	259		160	(IF)E-2/E.SCH.INT.
			TR	Stoke C.	01.62	1961-66	181	1	59	
VIPHAM, Peter	Rawtenstall	09.09.42	JNRS	Accrington St.	06.61	1960	6		0	
VIRGIN, Derek E.	Bristol	10.02.34	Sth.Shields	Bristol C.	09.58	1955-60	21		4	(W)
VITTY, Jack	Windlestone	19.01.23	Boldon Villa	Charlton Ath.	11.46	1948	2		0	(FB)Brother of Ron
			TR	Brighton & H.A.	10.49	1949-51	47		1	
			TR	Workington	07.52	1952-56	196		3	
VITTY, Ron	Sedgfield	18.04.27	Boldon Villa	Charlton Ath.	09.47					
			TR	Hartlepool U.	08.49	1949	7		0	
			TR	Bradford C.	07.50					
			TR	Brighton & H.A.	08.51					
VIZARD, Colin J.	Newton-le-Willows	18.06.33	JNRS	Everton	09.51					(F)
			TR	Rochdale	05.57	1957-58	41		7	
VOWDEN, Geoff A.	Barnsley	27.04.41	Jersey DM	Nottingham F.	01.60	1959-64	90		40	(CF)
			TR	Birmingham C.	10.64	1964-70	214	8	80	
			TR	Aston Villa	03.71	1970-73	93	3	22	

Players Names	Birthplace	Date	Previous Club	League Club	Date Signed	Seasons Played	Apps	Sub	Gls	
WADDELL, Robert	Kirkcaldy	05.09.39	Dundee	Blackpool	03.65	1964-66	28	/	5	(F)
			TR	Bradford P.A.	11.66	1966	20	/	3	
WADDELL, William	Stirling	16.04.50	JNRS	Leeds U.	04.67					(IF)
			Kilmarnock	Barnsley	05.71	1971	17	1	4	
			TR	Hartlepool U.	03.72	1971-73	43	5	9	
			L	Workington	02.73	1972	1	2	0	
WADDINGTON, Anthony	Manchester	09.11.24	Manchester U.(AM)	Crewe Alex.	+	1946-52	179		7	(WH)
WADDINGTON, D. Paul	Oldbury	14.02.61	APP	Walsall	11.78	1978-81	14	5	1	(F)E.SCH.INT.
WADDINGTON, John	Darwen	16.02.52		Liverpool	05.70					(D)
				Blackburn Rov.	08.73	1973-78	139	9	18	
			TR	Bury	08.79	1979-80	46	1	0	
WADDINGTON, Steve	Crewe	05.02.56	APP	Stoke C.	06.73	1976-78	49	3	5	(M)
			TR	Walsall	09.78	1978-81	122	8	12	
			TR	Port Vale	08.82	1982	0	1	0	
			TR	Chesterfield	07.83	1983	14	4	1	
WADDLE, Alan	Wallsend	09.06.54		Halifax T.	11.71	1971-72	33	6	4	(F) Cousin of Chris
			TR	Liverpool	06.73	1973-74	11	5	1	
			TR	Leicester C.	09.77	1977	11	/	1	
			TR	Swansea C.	05.78	1978-80	83	7	34	
			TR	Newport Co.	12.80	1980-81	19	8	8	
			TR	Mansfield T.	08.82	1982	14	/	4	
			Hong Kong	Hartlepool U.	08.83	1983	12	/	2	
			TR	Peterborough U.	10.83	1983	33	/	12	
WADDLE, Chris R.	Gateshead	14.12.60	Tow Law	Newcastle U.	07.80	1980-83	134	/	33	(F)
WADDOCK, Gary P.	Kingsbury	17.03.62	APP	Q.P.R.	07.79	1979-83	141	12	7	(M)EI-11/EI.U21-1
WADE, Allen	Manchester	19.07.26		Notts.Co.	07.52	1952-55	10		0	(WH)
WADE, Don G.	Tottenham	05.06.26	Edgware T.	West Ham U.	12.47	1947-49	37		5	(IF)
WADE, S. Joe	London	07.07.21		Arsenal	+	1946-54	86		0	(WH)E.F.LGE REP.
WADSWORTH, Albert W.	Heywood	22.03.25	Mossley	Oldham Ath.	08.49	1949-51	33		8	(IF)
WADSWORTH, Mike	Barnsley	03.11.50	Gainsborough	Scunthorpe U.	08.76	1976	19	9	3	(F)
WAGSTAFF, Anthony	Wombwell	19.02.44	APP.	Sheffield U.	03.61	1960-68	140	3	19	(IF)Brother of Barry
			TR	Reading	07.69	1969-73	165	7	6	
WAGSTAFF, Barry	Brampton	28.11.45	APP	Sheffield U.	06.63	1964-68	105	10	5	(M) Brother of Tony
			TR	Reading	07.69	1969-74	198	6	23	
			TR	Rotherham U.	03.75	1974-76	42	3	1	
WAGSTAFF, Ken	Langworth	24.11.42	Woodland Imp	Mansfield T.	05.60	1960-64	181		96	(IF)●
			TR	Hull C.	11.64	1964-75	374	4	173	
WAGSTAFFE, David	Manchester	05.04.43	JNRS	Manchester C.	05.60	1960-64	143		8	(W)E.F.LGE●
			TR	Wolverhampton W.	12.64	1964-75	324	/	24	REP./E.YTH.INT./
			TR	Blackburn Rov.	01.76	1975-77	72	3	7	
			TR	Blackpool	08.78	1978	17	2	1	
			TR	Blackburn Rov.	03.79	1978	2	/	0	
WAIN, Les J.	Crewe	02.08.54	APP.	Crewe Alex.	08.72	1970-74	48	6	1	(OL)E.SCH.INT.
			TR	Southport	07.75	1975	3	2	0	
WAINMAN, W. Harry	Hull	22.03.47	Hull C.(AM)	Grimsby T.	07.64	1964-77	420	/	0	(G)E.YTH.INT.
			L	Rochdale	10.72	1972	9	/	0	
WAINWRIGHT, Edward	Southport	22.06.24		Everton	+	1946-55	207		69	(IF)E.F.LGE REP.
			TR	Rochdale	06.56	1956-58	100		27	
WAINWRIGHT, Lewis	Kirkton	15.12.30	Brigg T.	Scunthorpe U.	07.55	1951-55	3		0	(HB)
WAINWRIGHT, Robin K.	Luton	09.03.51	APP.	Luton T.	12.68	1971	15	1	3	(W)
			L	Cambridge U.	03.71	1970	1	/	0	
			TR	Millwall	11.72	1973	2	2	0	
			TR	Northampton T.	02.74	1973-74	23	9	5	
WAITE, John A.	Grimsby	16.01.42		Grimsby T.	11.60	1960-62	9		1	(F)E.YTH.INT.
WAITE, T.J. Aldwyn	Newport	03.08.28		Newport Co.	12.51	1951-53	57		1	(WH)
WAITE, William	Newport	29.1.17		Oldham Ath.	+	1946	4		4	(CF)d.1980
WAITERS, Anthony	Southport	01.02.37	Macclesfield	Blackpool	10.59	1959-66	257	/	0	(G)E-5/E.F.LGE REP./
			TR	Burnley	07.70	1970-71	38	/	0	E.AMAT.INT.
WAITES, George E.	Stepney	12.03.38	Harwich & P	Orient	12.58	1958-60	43		9	(W)
			TR	Norwich C.	01.61	1960-61	36		11	
			TR	Orient	11.62	1962	2		0	
			TR	Brighton & H.A.	12.62	1962-63	22		1	
			TR	Millwall	04.65					
WAKE, Geoff	Bristol	25.02.54	Barnstaple	Torquay U.	12.77	1977	9	/	0	(G)
WAKEFIELD, Albert J.	Pudsey	19.11.21		Leeds U.	+	1947-48	49		24	(CF)
			TR	Southend U.	08.49	1949-52	109		57	
WAKEFIELD, David	S. Shields	15.01.65	APP	Darlington	06.83	1982-83	7	15	0	(D)
			TR	Torquay U.	03.84	1983	10	/	1	
WAKEHAM, Peter	Kingsbridge	14.03.36	Kingsbridge	Torquay U.	10.53	1953-58	56		0	(G)
			TR	Sunderland	09.58	1958-61	134		0	
			TR	Charlton Ath.	07.62	1962-64	55		0	
			TR	Lincoln C.	05.65	1965	44	0	/	

Players Names	Birthplace	Date	Previous Club	League Club	Date Signed	Seasons Played	Apps	Sub	Gls	
WAKEMAN, Alan	Walsall	20.11.20	JNRS	Aston Villa	*	1946-49	6		0	(G)E.SCH.INT.
			TR	Doncaster Rov.	07.50	1950-51	5		0	
			Bloxwich Strollers	Shrewsbury T.	02.53	1952-53	6		0	
WAKENSHAW, Robert A.	Morpeth	22.12.65	APP	Everton	01.84	1983	1	/	1	(F)
WALDEN, Harry B.	Walgrave	22.12.40	Kettering T.	Luton T.	01.61	1960-63	96		11	(W)
			TR	Northampton T.	06.64	1964-66	76	1	3	
WALDEN, Richard F.	Hereford	04.05.48	APP	Aldershot	05.65	1964-75	401	4	16	(D)
			TR	Sheffield Wed.	01.76	1975-77	100	/	1	
			TR	Newport Co.	08.78	1978-81	151	/	2	
WALDOCK, Des H.	Northampton	04.12.61	APP	Northampton T.	11.79	1978-80	52	2	4	(D)
WALDOCK, Ron	Heanor	06.12.32	Loscoe Y.C.	Coventry C.	02.50	1952-53	26		8	(IF)
			TR	Sheffield U.	05.54	1954-56	52		10	
			TR	Scunthorpe U.	02.57	1956-59	97		45	
			TR	Plymouth Arg.	09.59	1959	18		5	
			TR	Middlesbrough	01.60	1959-61	33		7	
			TR	Gillingham	10.61	1961-63	67		14	
WALDRON, Alan	Royton	06.09.51	APP	Bolton W.	06.70	1970-77	127	13	6	(M)
			TR	Blackpool	12.77	1977-78	22	1	1	
			TR	Bury	06.79	1979-80	34	/	0	
			TR	York C.	09.81	1981	3	/	1	
WALDRON, Colin	Bristol	22.06.48	APP	Bury	05.66	1966	20	/	0	(D) Brother of Alan
			TR	Chelsea	07.67	1967	9	/	0	
			TR	Burnley	10.67	1967-75	308	/	16	
			TR	Manchester U.	05.76	1976	3	/	0	
			TR	Sunderland	02.77	1976-77	20	/	1	
			Atlanta Chiefs	Rochdale	10.79	1979	19	/	1	
WALDRON, Ernest	Birmingham	03.06.13	Bromsgrove	Crystal Palace	*	1946	4		1	(IL)
WALDRON, Malcolm	Emsworth	06.09.56	APP	Southampton	09.74	1974-82	177	1	10	(D)
			TR	Burnley	09.83	1983	16	/	0	
			TR	Portsmouth	03.84	1983	12	/	0	
WALES, Anthony	Doncaster	12.05.43	JNRS	Doncaster Rov.	05.60	1960-62	25		0	(FB)E.YTH.INT.
WALFORD, Steve J.	Highgate	05.01.58	APP	Tottenham H.	04.75	1975	1	1	0	(D)E.YTH.INT.
			TR	Arsenal	08.77	1977-80	64	13	3	
			TR	Norwich C.	03.81	1980-82	93	/	2	
			TR	West Ham U.	08.83	1983	41	/	2	
WALKDEN, Frank	Aberdeen	21.06.21	Bolton W.(AM)	Rochdale	AM	1946	1		0	(IF)
WALKER, Alan	Ashton-U-Lyne	17.12.59		Stockport Co.	08.78					(D)
			Telford U.	Lincoln C.	10.83	1983	32	1	2	
WALKER, Arnold	Haltwhistle	23.12.32	JNRS	Grimsby T.	05.50	1950-57	65		0	(HB)
			TR	Walsall	05.58	1958-59	7		0	
WALKER, Bruce A.	Newbury	27.08.46	JNRS	Swindon T.	12.63	1965-67	26	3	1	(F)
			TR	Bradford C.	03.68	1967-68	27	1	1	
			TR	Exeter C.	06.69	1969	22	3	2	
WALKER, Clive	Oxford	26.05.57	APP	Chelsea	04.75	1976-83	168	30	60	(F)E.SCH.INT./E.YTH.INT.
WALKER, Colin	Long Eaton	07.07.29	JNRS	Derby Co.	10.46	1948-54	25		0	(WH)
WALKER, Colin	Rotherham	01.05.58	Sutton T.	Barnsley	11.80	1980-82	21	3	11	(F)
			TR	Doncaster Rov.	02.83	1982	12	/	5	
WALKER, Cyril J.	Hitchin	24.02.14	Shorts Spts	Norwich C.	08.46	1946	3		2	(IF)*Watford/Gillingham/ Sheffield Wed.
WALKER, D. Clive A.	Leicester	24.10.45	APP.	Leicester C.	10.62	1963-65	17	/	0	(LB)E.SCH.INT.
			TR	Northampton T.	10.66	1966-68	72	/	1	
			TR	Mansfield T.	07.69	1969-74	223	6	7	
WALKER, David	Colne	15.10.41	JNRS	Burnley	05.59	1960-64	38		1	(LH)
			TR	Southampton	05.65	1965-73	189	8	1	
WALKER, Dean	Newcastle	18.05.62	APP	Burnley	05.80					(D)
				Scunthorpe U.	N/C	1981	1	/	0	
WALKER, Dennis A.	Northwich	26.10.44	APP.	Manchester U.	11.61					(WH)
			TR	York C.	04.64	1964-67	149	4	19	
			TR	Cambridge U.	N/L	1970-72	48	8	4	
WALKER, Dennis G.	Durham	05.07.48	APP	West Ham U.	05.66					(F)
			TR	Luton T.	08.67	1967	0	1	0	
WALKER, Des S.	Hackney	26.11.65	APP	Nottingham F.	12.83	1983	3	1	0	(D)
WALKER, Donald H.	Edinburgh	10.09.35	Tranent J.	Leicester C.	11.55	1957-58	32		1	(F)
			TR	Middlesbrough	10.59	1959-61	24		1	
			TR	Grimsby T.	09.63	1963	15		1	
WALKER, Fred	Stirling	07.04.29		Southport	10.51	1951-52	5		0	(FB)
WALKER, George H.	Aysgarth	20.05.16	Darlington(*)	Portsmouth	*	1946	11		0	(G)
			TR	Nottingham F.	04.47	1946-54	293		0	
WALKER, George W.	Sunderland	30.05.34	Chippenham T.	Bristol C.	07.57	1956-58	15		4	(IF)
			TR	Carlisle U.	03.59	1958-62	164		51	
WALKER, Greig G.	Dundee	11.10.63	Broughty A.	Chesterfield	10.83	1983	6	/	0	(F)
WALKER, J. Gordon	Sheffield	26.11.49	Stocksbridge Wks	Grimsby T.	11.68	1968-69	25	2	6	(F)

Players Names	Birthplace	Date	Previous Club	League Club	Date Signed	Seasons Played	Apps	Sub	Gls	
WALKER, J. Nick	Aberdeen	29.09.62	Elgin C.	Leicester C.	08.80	1981	6	/	0	(G)
WALKER, James	Belfast	29.03.32	Linfield	Doncaster Rov.	05.54	1954-56	46		14	(CF)NI-1
WALKER, James	Aberdeen	25.08.33	Aberdeen	Bradford P.A.	05.59	1959-63	144		2	(FB)
WALKER, James F.	Sheffield	01.07.31	JNRS	Sheffield U.	11.48	1949-53	4		0	(FB)
			TR	Huddersfield T.	08.55					
			TR	Peterborough U.	N/L	1960-64	125		0	
WALKER, James M.	Northwich	10.06.47	Northwich Vic.	Derby Co.	02.68	1967-73	35	7	3	(D)
			L	Hartlepool U.	03.70	1969	10	/	0	
			TR	Brighton & H.A.	09.74	1974-75	24	4	4	
			TR	Peterborough U.	10.75	1975-76	20	11	1	
			TR	Chester C.	11.76	1976-80	171	1	4	
WALKER, John	Rochford	10.12.58	APP	Southend U.	12.76	1977-82	38	13	0	(D)
WALKER, John H.	Glasgow	17.12.28	Camsie BW	Wolverhampton W.	07.47	1949-51	37		21	(IF)
			TR	Southampton	10.52	1952-57	169		47	
			TR	Reading	12.57	1957-64	286		24	
WALKER, Len	Darlington	04.03.44	Spennymoor	Newcastle U.	05.63	1963	1		0	(D)
			TR	Aldershot	07.64	1964-75	440	10	23	
			TR	Darlington	N/C	1976-77	10	/	0	
WALKER, Mike	Mexborough	08.03.52	APP	Bradford P.A.	03.70	1968-69	2	2	0	(FB)
WALKER, Mike J.	Harrogate	10.04.45	Sheffield W.(APP)	Doncaster Rov.	08.63					(W)
			Bourne T.	Bradford C.	10.64	1964-65	19	1	1	
			TR	Rotherham U.	03.66					
				Mansfield T.	03.69	1968	2	/	1	
				Stockport Co.	08.70	1970	1	1	0	
			TR	Chesterfield	09.70	1970	1	/	0	
WALKER, Mike S.G.	Colwyn Bay	28.11.45	JNRS	Reading	01.63					(G)W.U23-4●
			TR	Shrewsbury T.	06.64	1964-65	6	/	0	
			TR	York C.	06.66	1966-68	60	/	0	
			TR	Watford	09.68	1968-72	137	/	0	
			L	Charlton Ath.	03.73	1972	1	/	0	
			TR	Colchester U.	06.73	1973-82	451	/	0	
WALKER, Nigel S.	Gateshead	07.04.59	Whickham	Newcastle U.	07.77	1977-81	65	5	3	(M)
			San Diego	Sunderland	12.82					
			TR	Crewe Alex.	N/C	1982	20	/	5	
			TR	Sunderland	07.83	1983	0	1	0	
			L	Blackpool	03.84	1983	8	2	3	
WALKER, Pat J.	Dublin	20.12.59	APP	Gillingham	10.77	1977-80	34	17	3	(F)
WALKER, Paul E.	Hetton-le-Hole	26.02.58	Sunderland(APP)	Hull C.	05.76					(M)
			L	Doncaster Rov.	12.76	1976	4	/	0	
WALKER, Paul G.	Bradford	03.04.49		Wolverhampton W.	10.66	1968-71	16	11	0	(F)
			L	Watford	12.71	1971	2	1	0	
			L	Swindon T.	03.73	1972	2	3	0	
			TR	Peterborough U.	07.73	1973-74	75	3	3	
			TR	Barnsley	07.75	1975	11	2	0	
			TR	Huddersfield T.	11.76	1976	1	/	0	
WALKER, Paul J.	London	17.12.60	APP	Brentford	01.78	1976-82	53	18	5	(M)E.SCH.INT.
WALKER, Peter M.	Watford	31.03.33	Bushey U.	Watford	07.54	1954-61	169		36	(F)
WALKER, Phil	Sheffield	27.11.56	Sheffield U.(APP)	Cambridge U.	02.75	1974-75	19	/	0	(G)
			TR	Rotherham U.	09.77					
WALKER, Phil	London	24.08.54	Epsom & Ewell	Millwall	10.75	1974-78	143	3	16	(M)
			TR	Charlton Ath.	07.79	1979-82	80	9	14	
			L	Gillingham	11.82	1982	1	1	0	
WALKER, Phil A.	Kirkby	27.01.57	Belper	Chesterfield	12.77	1977-82	151	15	38	(F)
			TR	Rotherham U.	12.82	1982 -83	20	5	3	
			L	Cardiff C.	09.83	1983	2	/	0	
WALKER, R. Geoff	Bradford	29.09.26	JNRS	Bradford P.A.	+					(OL)
			TR	Middlesbrough	06.46	1946-54	239		51	
			TR	Doncaster Rov.	12.54	1954-56	84		15	
			TR	Bradford C.	06.57	1957	2		0	
WALKER, Ray	N. Shields	28.09.63	APP	Aston Villa	09.81	1982-83	6	3	0	(D) E.YTH.INT.
WALKER, Richard E.W.	Hackney	22.07.13	Park Rov.	West Ham U.	*	1946-52	190		2	(CH)
WALKER, Ricky P.	Northampton	04.04.59	APP	Coventry C.	03.77					(D)
			TR	Northampton T.	08.78	1978-80	50	3	0	
WALKER, Robert	Wallsend	23.07.42	Gateshead	Brighton & H.A.	05.62	1962	12		1	(FB)
				Hartlepool U.	08.64					
			Margate	Bournemouth	01.65	1965-66	10	/	0	
			TR	Colchester U.	07.67	1967	13	4	0	
WALKER, Robert M.	Glasgow	15.01.35	Redcar	Middlesbrough	08.52					(F)
			TR	Barrow	08.55	1955	11		1	
WALKER, Robert W.		1920	Aberdeen	Bournemouth	11.46	1946	2		2	(CF)
			TR	Wrexham	06.47	1947	2		0	
WALKER, Roger W.	Shrewsbury	17.02.44	JNRS	Shrewsbury T.	AM	1960	1		0	(W)
WALKER, Ron	Swansea	24.02.33		Shrewsbury T.	11.55	1955	1		0	

Players Names	Birthplace	Date	Previous Club	League Club	Date Signed	Seasons Played	Apps	Sub	Gls	
WALKER, Ron	Sheffield	04.02.32	Sunderland(AM)	Doncaster Rov.	05.50	1952-60	234		46	(OL)
WALKER, Ron L.	Wembley	02.09.52	APP	Watford	08.70					(D)
			TR	Workington	08.71	1971-75	143	10	3	
			TR	Newport Co.	08.76	1976-78	88	1	5	
WALKER, Ron W.	Westminster	10.40.30	Walthamstow	Watford	04.54	1954	5		0	(OL)
WALKER, Sam			Darwen	Oldham Ath.	08.47	1947	1		0	
WALKER, Shane	Pontypool	25.11.57	Arsenal(APP)	Hereford U.	03.75	1974-76	15	2	2	(D)
			Sligo	Newport Co.	08.77	1977	27	1	2	
WALKER, Steve	Sheffield	16.10.14	Sheffield U.(*)	Exeter C.	*	1946-49	110		3	(LH)
WALKER, Steve	Ilkeston	25.12.63		Halifax T.	01.82	1981	0	1	0	(M)
WALKER, Stuart	Tadcaster	09.01.51	Tadcaster A.	York C.	08.75	1976	2	/	0	(G)
WALKER, Terry	Poppleton	29.11.21		York C.	05.49	1949	16		9	(F)
WALKER, Thomas	Livingstone	26.05.15	Hearts	Chelsea	09.46	1946-48	97		23	(IF)S-20/S.F.LGE REP./S.SCH.INT.
WALKER, Thomas J.	Gosforth	20.02.52	APP	Stoke C.	07.69	1971	2	/	0	(IL)
WALKER, Thomas J.	Cramlington	14.11.23	Netherton	Newcastle T.	+	1946-53	183		35	(OR)
			TR	Oldham Ath.	02.54	1953-56	120		20	
			TR	Chesterfield	02.57	1956	14		1	
			TR	Oldham Ath.	07.57	1957-58	38		4	
WALKER, Vic	Kirkby	14.04.22		Nottingham F.	+					
			TR	Stockport Co.	06.46	1946-49	94		10	
WALL, Adrian A.	Clowne	25.11.49	APP	Sheffield Wed.	05.67	1967	3	/	0	(F)
			TR	Workington	08.69	1969	21	3	2	
WALL, T. Peter	Westbury	13.09.44	APP	Shrewsbury T.	09.62	1963-64	18		0	(D)
			TR	Wrexham	11.65	1965-66	15	7	1	
			TR	Liverpool	10.66	1967-69	31	/	0	
			TR	Crystal Palace	06.70	1970-77	167	10	3	
			L	Orient	12.72	1972	10	/	0	
WALL, William J.	London	28.10.39	JNRS	Chelsea	01.57					(W)
			TR	Southend U.	03.60	1959-62	57		5	
WALLACE, Barry D.	Plaistow	17.04.59		Q.P.R.	08.77	1977-79	17	8	0	(F)
WALLACE, Clive L.	Kirriemuir	06.01.32		Bury	03.59					
			TR	Stockport Co.	08.59	1959	13		4	
WALLACE, David L. (Danny)	London	21.01.64	APP	Southampton	01.82	1980-83	78	7	23	(W)E.U'21-8
WALLACE, George	Aberdeen	18.04.20		Scunthorpe U.	06.50	1951-52	33		9	(F)
WALLACE, Gordon H.	Lanark	13.06.44	APP	Liverpool	07.61	1962-64	20		3	(IF)
			TR	Crewe Alex.	10.67	1967-71	91	3	20	
WALLACE, Ian A.	Glasgow	23.05.56	Dumbarton	Coventry C.	08.76	1976-79	128	2	57	(F)S-3/S.U21-1
			TR	Nottingham F.	07.80	1980-83	128	6	36	
WALLACE, Ian R.	Hedley	12.09.48	APP	Wolverhampton W.	09.66	1966	0	1	0	(WH)
WALLACE, James	Kirkintilloch	17.02.33	Aberdeen	Northampton T.	05.55	1955	1		0	(CH)
WALLACE, James	Bridge of Allan	09.06.54	Dunfermline	Aldershot	07.75	1975-76	53	3	0	(D)S.U23-1
WALLACE, James	Bebbington	13.12.37		Stoke C.	10.55	1958-59	8		1	(F)
			Northwich V.	Doncaster Rov.	03.63	1962	14		1	
WALLACE, Jock M.	Deantown	13.04.11	Raith Rov.	Blackpool	*	1946-47	67		0	(G)d.1978/
			TR	Derby Co.	02.48	1947	16		0	Father of Jock M.B.
WALLACE, Jock M.B.	Wallyford	06.09.35	Blackpool(AM)	Workington	09.52	1952	5		0	(G)
			Airdrie	W.B.A.	10.59	1959-61	69		0	
WALLACE, John C.	Glasgow	11.01.36	St.Rochs	Rochdale	03.59	1957-58	7		0	(HB)
WALLACE, Joseph B.	Glasgow	28.12.33	RAOC(Donnington)	Shrewsbury T.	03.54	1954-62	337		3	(WH)
			TR	Southport	10.62	1962-64	79		0	
WALLACE, Ken	Workington	05.01.53	JNRS	Workington	N/C	1973-76	6	1	0	(D) Son of Ken (Snr)
WALLACE, Ken R.	Islington	08.06.52	JNRS	West Ham U.	09.70					(OL)
			L	Brentford	02.72	1971	3	/	0	
			TR	Hereford U.	07.72	1972	26	6	4	
			TR	Exeter C.	09.739	1973	8	2	1	
WALLACE, Ken(Snr)	Workington	14.01.32		Workington	07.51	1951-52	48		1	(FB)
WALLACE, Robert	Huddersfield	14.02.48	APP	Huddersfield T.	05.65	1966	4	/	0	(M)
			TR	Halifax T.	03.67	1966-71	190	11	16	
			TR	Chester C.	06.72	1972	41	/	9	
			TR	Aldershot	07.73	1973-76	70	6	1	
WALLACE, William B.	Kirkintilloch	23.06.41	Glasgow Celtic	Crystal Palace	10.71	1971-72	36	3	4	(IF)S-7/S.F.LGE REP.
WALLBANK, Bernard	Preston	11.11.43		Southport	08.62	1961	1		0	(CF)
WALLBANKS, Harold	Gateshead	27.07.21		Fulham	*	1946-47	33		1	(RH)Brother of Horace/Jim
			TR	Southend U.	10.49	1949-50	39		2	
			TR	Workington	08.52	1952	26		9	
WALLBANKS, James	Wigan	12.09.09	Millwall(*)	Reading	*	1946	18		1	(CH)*Barnsley/ Northampton T./Portsmouth/d.1979

Players Names	Birthplace	Date	Previous Club	League Club	Date Signed	Seasons Played	Career Record Apps	Sub	Gls	
WALLBANKS, W. Horace	Chopwell	04.09.18	Aberdeen	Grimsby T.	11.46	1946	9		1	(OR)
			TR	Luton T.	05.47	1946-47	4		1	
WALLBRIDGE, Trevor	Southampton	08.02.59	Totton	Bournemouth	N/C	1977	0	1	0	(F)
WALLER, David H.	Urmston	20.12.63		Crewe Alex.	12.82	1981-83	78	2	27	(F)
WALLER, Herbert	Ashington	20.08.17		Arsenal	*	1946	8		0	(WH)
			TR	Orient	07.47	1947	17		0	
WALLER, Phil	Leeds	12.04.43	JNRS	Derby Co.	05.61	1961-67	102	1	5	(WH)
			TR	Mansfield T.	03.68	1967-71	152	7	2	
WALLEY, Ernie	Caernarvon	19.04.33	JNRS	Tottenham H.	05.51	1955-57	5		0	(WH)
			TR	Middlesbrough	05.58	1958	8		0	
WALLEY, Keith J.	Weymouth	19.10.54	APP	Crystal Palace	08.73	1973	6	1	1	(IF)
WALLEY, Tom J.	Caernarvon	27.02.45	Caernarvon	Arsenal	12.64	1965-66	10	4	1	(M)W-1/W.U23-4/
			TR	Watford	03.67	1966-71	202	1	17	Brother of Ernie
			TR	Orient	12.71	1971-75	155	2	5	
			TR	Watford	06.76	1976	12	1	0	
WALLINGTON, Mark	Sleaford	17.09.52		Walsall	10.71	1971	11	/	0	(G)E.U23-2/E.YTH.INT.
			TR	Leicester C.	03.72	1971-83	401	/	0	
WALLIS, Derek R.	Hartlepool	06.10.37		Hartlepool U.	AM	1963	2		0	(CF)
WALLS, Arthur J.	Glasgow	15.01.31	Airdrie	Tranmere Rov.	06.54	1954-55	23		6	(F)
WALLS, David	Leeds	16.06.53	Leeds U.(APP	Lincoln C.	07.71	1971-72	9	/	0	(F)
WALLS, James P.	Crossgates	11.03.28	Crossgates	Charlton Ath.	+	1949-52	10		0	(CH)
			TR	Ipswich T.	05.54	1954	1		0	
WALLS, John	Seaham	08.05.32	JNRS	Barnsley	05.49	1952	7		0	(G)
			TR	Peterborough U.	N/L	1960-61	78		0	
WALMSLEY, Dennis	Southport	01.05.35	Crossens	Southport	AM	1954	4		0	(W)
WALSH, Alan	Hartlepool	09.12.56	Horden CW	Middlesbrough	12.76	1977	0	3	0	(F)
			TR	Darlington	10.78	1978-83	245	6	87	
WALSH, Colin D.	Hamilton	22.07.62	APP	Nottingham F.	08.79	1980-83	89	17	25	(M)
WALSH, David J.	Waterford	28.04.23	Linfield	W.B.A.	07.46	1946-50	165		94	(CF)EI-20/NI-9
			TR	Aston Villa	12.50	1950-54	108		37	
			TR	Walsall	07.55	1955	20		6	
WALSH, Frank	Wishaw	15.09.23	Glasgow Celtic	Southport	10.49	1949	5		3	(CF)
WALSH, Ian P.	St. Davids	04.09.58	APP	Crystal Palace	10.75	1976-81	101	16	23	(F)W-12/W.U21-1/
			TR	Swansea C.	02.82	1981-83	32	5	11	W.SCH.INT.
WALSH, J. Brian	Aldershot	26.03.32	JNRS	Arsenal	08.49	1953-55	17		0	(W)
			TR	Cardiff C.	09.55	1955-61	206		32	
			TR	Newport Co.	11.61	1961-62	27		4	
WALSH, James	Glasgow	03.12.30	Glasgow Celtic	Leicester C.	11.56	1956-62	176		79	(CF)S.U23-1
WALSH, James T.P.	London	20.11.54	APP	Watford	07.73	1973-77	60	5	0	(D)
			TR	York C.	06.78	1978-80	91	8	2	
WALSH, Kevin	Rochdale	11.02.28		Oldham Ath.	10.49	1949-50	3		0	(IL)
			TR	Southport	07.52	1952-53	67		1	
			TR	Bradford C.	07.54	1954-55	25		3	
			TR	Southport	08.56	1956	3		0	
WALSH, Mark	Preston	07.10.62	APP	Preston N.E.	10.80	1981-83	56	6	2	(D)
WALSH, Mick A.	Chorley	13.08.54	Chorley	Blackpool	10.72	1973-77	172	8	72	(F)EI-16
			TR	Everton	08.78	1978	18	2	1	
			TR	Q.P.R.	03.79	1978-80	13	5	3	
WALSH, Mick T.	Manchester	20.06.56	JNRS	Bolton W.	07.74	1974-80	169	8	4	(D) EI-5
			TR	Everton	08.81	1981-82	20	/	0	
			L	Norwich C.	10.82	1982	5	/	0	
			L	Burnley	12.82	1982	3	/	0	
			Fort Lauderdale	Manchester C.	10.83	1983	3	1	0	
			TR	Blackpool	02.84	1983	20	/	1	
WALSH, Paul A.	Plumstead	01.10.62	APP	Charlton Ath.	10.79	1979-81	85	2	24	(F)E.YTH.INT./E-2/E.U'21-7
			TR	Luton T.	07.82	1982-83	80	/	25	
WALSH, Peter	Dublin	18.10.22	Dundalk	Luton T.	08.49	1949	8		2	(F)EI.F.LGE REP.
			TR	Brighton & H.A.	08.50					
WALSH, Roy	Belfast	25.11.55	Glentoran	Swindon T.	03.80	1980	7	/	0	(D)
WALSH, Roy W.	Dedham	15.01.47	APP	Ipswich T.	01.65	1965	6	1	0	(F)
			TR	Southend U.	07.67					
WALSH, Steve	Fulwood	03.11.64	JNRS	Wigan Ath.	09.82	1982-83	73	/	1	(D)
WALSH, Wilf	Pontelottyn	29.07.17	Arsenal(*)	Derby Co.	+	1946	1		0	(CF)
			TR	Walsall	03.47	1946-47	33		4	d.1977
WALSH, William	Easington	04.12.23	JNRS	Sunderland	+	1946-52	98		1	(HB)
			TR	Northampton T.	07.53	1953	19		0	
			TR	Darlington	06.54	1954	28		4	
WALSH, William	Dublin	31.05.21		Manchester C.	*	1946-49	109		0	EI-9/NI-5

Players Names	Birthplace	Date	Previous Club	League Club	Date Signed	Seasons Played	Apps	Sub	Gls	
WALSHAW, Ken	Tynemouth	28.08.18	JNRS	Sunderland	+					(IF)
			TR	Lincoln C.	08.47	1947	17		6	
			TR	Carlisle U.	12.47	1947-49	50		15	
			TR	Bradford C.	08.50	1950	9		3	
WALSHAW, Philip D.	Leeds	16.04.29	JNRS	Halifax T.	AM	1946	6		1	(IF)Rugby League Player
WALTERS, George	Wolverhampton	21.06.35	Jenks & C.	Shrewsbury T.	02.57	1956-62	246		3	(RB)
			TR	Newport Co.	09.63	1963-65	80	/	2	
WALTERS, George A.	Glasgow	30.03.39	Clyde	Oldham Ath.	08.59	1959	13		2	(F)
WALTERS, Henry	Rotherham	15.03.25	JNRS	Wolverhampton W.	+					(WH)
			TR	Walsall	05.46	1946-52	253		2	
			TR	Barnsley	07.53	1953-59	159		4	
WALTERS, Mark	Birmingham	02.06.64	APP	Aston Villa	05.82	1981-83	51	9	9	(W) E.YTH.INT.
WALTERS, Mick	Banbury	17.11.39	JNRS	Coventry C.	12.56	1957	2		0	(FB)
			Rugby T.	Bradford C.	01.62	1961-62	19		0	
WALTERS, Peter L.	Wickham	08.06.52		Hull C.	08.70	1970-71	2	/	0	(G)
			L	Darlington	03.72	1971	16	/	0	
WALTERS, Robert J.	Glasgow	09.03.44	Winsford U.	Shrewsbury T.	12.62	1962	1		0	(CH)
WALTERS, Trevor B.	Aberdare	13.01.16	Wolverhampton W.(*)	Chester C.	*	1946-48	74		0	(CH)*Dundee/Hull C.
WALTERS, W.E.(Sonny)	Edmonton	05.09.24	JNRS	Tottenham H.	+	1946-55	209		66	(W)E'B'-1/
			TR	Aldershot	07.57	1957-58	66		11	d.1970
WALTON, Frank H.	Southend	09.04.18		Southend U.	*	1946-50	136		0	(FB)
WALTON, Harry				Southend U.	05.46	1946	1		0	
WALTON, Ian J.	Goole	17.04.58	APP	Grimsby T.	APP	1975	2	/	1	(F)
			TR	Scunthorpe U.	03.76	1976	1	/	0	
WALTON, John A.	Horwich	21.03.28		Bury	AM	1949-50	26		4	(IL)E.AMAT.INT.
			TR	Manchester U.	AM	1951	2		0	d.
			TR	Bury	02.54	1952-53	29		2	
			TR	Burnley	02.54	1954-55	18		2	
			TR	Coventry City	10.56	1956-57	13		0	
			Kettering	Chester C.	07.59	1959	1		0	
WALTON, Joseph W.	Manchester	05.06.25	JNRS	Manchester U.	+	1946-47	21		0	(FB)E.F.LGE REP.
			TR	Preston N.E.	03.48	1947-60	401		4	
			TR	Accrington St.	02.61	1960	18		0	
WALTON, Richard	Hull	12.09.24		Leicester C.	+					(FB)
			TR	Orient	07.48	1948-51	64		4	
			TR	Exeter C.	12.51	1951-55	135		6	
WALTON, Ron P.	Newcastle	12.10.45	Rotherham U.(AM)	Nothampton T.	09.63	1964	1		0	(W)
			TR	Crewe Alex.	10.65	1965	2	/	0	
			TR	Carlisle U.	01.66	1965	1	/	0	
			TR	Aldershot	08.66	1966-71	190	5	41	
			TR	Cambridge U.	11.71	1971-72	62	/	9	
			TR	Aldershot	07.73	1973-76	108	5	14	
WALTON, Roy	Crewe	19.07.28		Crewe Alex.	06.50	1950-51	12		0	(HB)
WALWYN, Keith I.	W. Indies	17.02.56	Winterton	Chesterfield	11.79	1980	3	/	2	(F)
			TR	York C.	07.81	1981-83	130	/	69	
WANDS, Alex M.D.	Cowdenbeath	05.12.22	Gateshead(AM)	Sheffield W.	+	1946	11		1	(LH)
			TR	Doncaster Rov.	05.47	1947	22		1	
WANKLYN, E. Wayne	Hull	21.01.60	APP	Reading	01.78	1977-80	47	7	3	(D)
			TR	Aldershot	08.81	1981	15	3	2	
WANN, Alex H.	Perth	20.12.40	Luncarty	Manchester C.	07.58					(HB)
			St.Mirren	Oldham Ath.	12.60	1960	19		0	
WANN, J. Dennis	Blackpool	17.11.50	APP	Blackpool	07.67	1969-71	11	6	0	(M)
			TR	York C.	01.72	1971-75	65	1	7	
			L	Chesterfield	11.75	1975	3	/	0	
			L	Hartlepool U.	01.76	1975	2	/	0	
			TR	Darlington	07.76	1976-78	119	2	13	
			TR	Rochdale	06.79	1979-80	66	1	7	
			TR	Blackpool	10.81	1981	13	6	0	
			TR	Chester	N/C	1983	2	1	0	
WANT, Anthony G.	London	13.12.48	APP	Tottenham H.	12.65	1967-71	46	4	0	(D)E.YTH.INT.
			TR	Birmingham C.	06.72	1972-77	98	3	1	
WARBOYS, Alan	Goldthorpe	18.04.49	APP	Doncaster Rov.	04.67	1966-67	38	1	11	(F)
			TR	Sheffield Wed.	06.68	1968-70	66	5	13	
			TR	Cardiff C.	12.70	1970-72	56	4	27	
			TR	Sheffield U.	09.72	1972	7	/	0	
			TR	Bristol Rov.	03.73	1972-76	141	3	53	
			TR	Fulham	02.77	1976-77	19	/	2	
			TR	Hull C.	09.77	1977-78	44	5	9	
			TR	Doncaster Rov.	07.79	1979-81	89	/	21	
WARBURTON, George	Brymbo	13.09.34		Wrexham	11.57	1958-59	22		0	(FB)
			TR	Barrow	08.60	1960	14		0	
WARBURTON, Ian T.	Haslingden	22.03.52		Bury	11.72	1972	6		2	(CF)
			TR	Southport	07.74	1974	5	2	1	

Players Names	Birthplace	Date	Previous Club	League Club	Date Signed	Seasons Played	Apps	Sub	Gls	
WARD, David(Dai)	Barry	16.07.34	Barry T.	Bristol Rov.	11.54	1954-60	174		90	(IF)W-2●
			TR	Cardiff C.	02.61	1960-61	35		18	
			TR	Watford	06.62	1962-63	59		31	
			TR	Brentford	10.63	1963-64	47	1	11	
WARD, David A.	Crewe	08.03.41	Taunton	Swansea C.	01.59	1960-65	45	1	0	(FB)
WARD, Dennis	Burton	25.10.24		Nottingham F.	08.47	1947	1		0	(G)
			TR	Stockport Co.	08.49	1949-52	52		0	
			Hastings U.	Bradford P.A.	08.55	1955-57	50		0	
WARD, Derek	Stoke	23.12.34	JNRS	Stoke C.	08.52	1952-60	54		8	(IF)
			TR	Stockport Co.	07.61	1961-63	81		21	
WARD, Gerry	London	05.10.36	JNRS	Arsenal	10.53	1953-62	95		10	(WH)E.AMAT.INT./
			TR	Orient	07.63	1963-64	43		2	E.YTH.INT./E.SCH.INT.
WARD, James	Shettleston	26.07.29	Queens Pk.	Crewe Alex.	AM	1956	11		0	(CF)
WARD, James S.	Frodsham	15.06.33		Crewe Alex.	AM	1956	2		0	
WARD, Joe	Glasgow	25.11.54	Clyde	Aston Villa	12.78	1978-79	2	1	0	(F)
WARD, John	Mansfield	18.01.48	APP	Notts.Co.	07.65	1965	5	/	0	(FB)
WARD, John P.	Lincoln	07.04.51	Adelaide Pk	Lincoln C.	03.71	1970-78	223	17	91	(F)
			L	Workington	09.72	1972	9	2	3	
			TR	Watford	07.79	1979-80	22	5	6	
			TR	Grimsby T.	06.81	1981	2	1	0	
			TR	Lincoln C.	03.82	1981	1	/	0	
WARD, John R.	Scunthorpe	16.09.40	JNRS	Scunthorpe U.	AM	1958	1		0	(IF)E.AMAT.INT.
			TR	Northampton T.	AM	1959-61	7		0	
			Tooting & M	Millwall	07.62	1962-63	12		3	
WARD, L. Whelan	Halifax	15.06.29	Ovenden	Bradford C.	08.49	1948-53	150		37	(IF)
			TR	Bradford P.A.	07.55	1955-58	108		31	
WARD, Mark W.	Huyton	10.10.62	APP	Everton	09.80					(M)
			Northwich Vic.	Oldham Ath.	07.83	1983	42	/	6	
WARD, Mike H.	Basford	30.08.20		Stockport Co.	10.48	1948	1		0	
WARD, Noel G.	Londonderry	08.12.52	Aberdeen	Wigan Ath.	N/L	1978-79	47	1	4	(D)
WARD, Patrick	Dumbarton	28.12.26	Hibernian	Leicester C.	09.55	1955-57	57		0	(WH)
			TR	Crewe Alex.	06.58	1958	31		1	
WARD, Paul T.	Sedgefield	15.09.63	APP	Chelsea	08.81					(D)
			TR	Middlesbrough	09.82	1982-83	37	6	1	
WARD, Peter	Derby	27.07.55	Burton A.	Brighton & H.A.	05.75	1975-80	172	6	79	(F)E-1/E.U21-2
			TR	Nottingham F.	10.80	1980-82	28	5	7	
			L	Brighton & H.A.	10.82	1982	16	/	2	
WARD, Peter	Rotherham	20.10.54	APP	Sheffield U.	10.72					(FB)
			TR	Workington	07.74	1974-75	39	4	2	
			TR	Huddersfield T.	07.76					
WARD, Ralph A.	Leicester	05.02.11	Bradford P.A.(*)	Tottenham H.	*					(FB)*Hinkley/
			TR	Crewe Alex.	08.46	1946-48	89		7	E.SCH.INT.
WARD, Robert	Glasgow	21.10.58	Glasgow Celtic	Newport Co.	01.80	1979-80	2	1	0	(M)
WARD, Robert A.	W. Bromwich	04.08.53	Imperial Star	W.B.A.	03.73	1974-76	9	/	0	(G)
			L	Northampton T.	02.77	1976	8	/	0	
			TR	Blackpool	09.77	1977-78	41	/	0	
			TR	Wigan Ath.	07.79	1980-81	46	/	0	
WARD, Ron	Altrincham	17.10.32		Stockport Co.	03.54	1953-55	16		4	(IF)
WARD, Ron	Killamarsh	10.02.35	JNRS	Chesterfield	02.52	1951-52	8		0	(G)E.SCH.INT.
WARD, Ron H.	Walthamstow	29.03.32		Tottenham H.	06.50					(G)
			Headington	Darlington	08.56	1956	26		0	
WARD, Sid	Dewsbury	26.11.23	Upton C.W.	Bradford C.	09.47	1947	2		0	(G)
WARD, Steve	Wortley	27.12.60	APP	Lincoln C.	05.79	1979	2	/	0	(D)
WARD, Steve C.	Derby	21.07.59	APP	Brighton & H.A.	10.76					(M)
			TR	Northampton T.	08.79	1979	13	2	2	
			TR	Halifax T.	06.80	1980-83	166	3	12	
WARD, Terry	Stoke	10.12.39	JNRS	Stoke C.	03.58	1959-62	43		0	(FB)
WARD, Thomas A.	Tow Law	06.08.17	Crook T.	Sheffield Wed.	*	1946-47	35		20	(CF)
			TR	Darlington	08.48	1948-53	119		32	
WARD, Tim V.	Cheltenham	17.10.18	Cheltenham	Derby Co.	*	1946-50	179		5	(WH)E-2
			TR	Barnsley	03.51	1950-52	33		0	
WARD, Wayne W.	Colchester	28.04.64	APP	Colchester U.	05.82	1981-82	17	2	0	(D)
WARD, William	Chester-le-Street	30.06.49		Hartlepool U.	02.73	1971-74	87	8	9	(W)
WARDLE, Ernie	Consett	13.06.30	Billingham	Middlesbrough	05.48					(FB)
			TR	York C.	01.55	1954-58	60		2	
WARDLE, Geoff	Trimdon	07.01.40	Houghton J.	Sunderland	01.58					(HB)
			TR	Lincoln C.	06.61	1961	1		0	

Players Names	Birthplace	Date	Previous Club	League Club	Date Signed	Seasons Played	Career Record Apps	Sub	Gls	
WARDLE, George	Kimblesworth	24.09.19	Middlesbrough(*)	Exeter C.	+	1946	38		6	(OR)
			TR	Cardiff C.	05.47	1946-48	40		11	
			TR	Q.P.R.	01.49	1948-50	53		3	
			TR	Darlington	08.51	1951-53	95		6	
WARDLE, Robert I.	Halifax	05.03.55	APP	Bristol C.	11.72					(G)
			TR	Shrewsbury T.	07.74	1977-81	131	/	0	
			TR	Liverpool	08.82					
			L	Wrexham	09.83	1983	13	/	0	
WARDLE, William	Hetton-le-Hole	20.01.18	Manchester C.(*)	Grimsby T.	+	1946-47	73		11	(OL)*Southport
			TR	Blackpool	05.48	1948-50	58		1	
			TR	Birmingham C.	09.51	1951-52	60		5	
			TR	Barnsley	11.53	1953-54	30		1	
WARDROBE, Mick	Newcastle	24.03.62	APP	Burnley	03.80	1980	0	1	0	(F)
			TR	Stockport Co.	08.81	1981-82	19	8	2	
WARE, Charles	York	09.03.31	JNRS	York C.	12.48	1953	8		0	(F)
WARHURST, Roy	Sheffield	18.09.26		Sheffield U.	+	1946-49	17		2	(WH)
			TR	Birmingham C.	03.50	1949-56	216		10	
			TR	Manchester C.	06.57	1957-58	40		2	
			TR	Crewe Alex.	03.59	1958-59	51		1	
			TR	Oldham Ath.	08.60	1960	8		0	
WARING, T. Alan	Preston	03.08.29		Burnley	08.48					(HB)
			TR	Halifax T.	07.54	1954	12		0	
WARK, John	Glasgow	04.08.57	APP	Ipswich T.	08.74	1974-83	295	1	94	(M)S.U21-8/S-28●
			TR	Liverpool	03.84	1983	9	/	2	
WARMAN, Philip R.	Bromley	18.12.50	JNRS	Charlton Ath.	03.68	1969-80	313	3	19	(D)E.YTH.INT.
			TR	Millwall	08.81	1981	27	/	1	
WARMINGTON, Peter	Birmingham	08.04.34	JNRS	Birmingham C.	12.51	1954-56	7		3	(F)
WARN, Keith D.	Watford	20.03.41	Croxley BC	Watford	04.59	1959	3		0	(G)
WARNE, Ray J.	Ipswich	16.06.29		Ipswich T.	10.50	1950-51	30		11	(CF)
WARNER, Dennis P.A.	Rotherham	06.12.30	Spurley Hill	Rotherham U.	03.50	1952-56	64		0	(FB)
			TR	Chesterfield	05.57	1957	8		0	
WARNER, John	Ashington	06.05.40		Luton T.	10.59	1959	1		0	(F)
WARNER, John	Tonyrefail	21.09.11	Swansea C.(*)	Manchester U.	*	1946-49	73		1	(WH)W-2
			TR	Oldham Ath.	06.51	1951	35		2	
			TR	Rochdale	07.52	1952	21		0	
WARNER, Les H.	Birmingham	19.12.18		Coventry C.	*	1946-53	192		18	(OR)d.1982
WARNER, Reg O.	Anstey	01.03.31	JNRS	Leicester C.	04.49	1952-53	7		0	(HB)E.YTH.INT.
			TR	Mansfield T.	03.55	1954-56	33		0	
WARNES, George	Sheffield	04.12.25		Rotherham U.	+	1946-49	98		0	(G)
			TR	Aldershot	06.50	1950-51	32		0	
WARNOCK, Neil	Sheffield	01.12.48		Chesterfield	07.68	1967-68	19	3	2	(F)
			TR	Rotherham U.	06.69	1969-70	46	8	5	
			TR	Hartlepool U.	07.71	1971-72	58	2	5	
			TR	Scunthorpe U.	02.72	1972-74	63	9	7	
			TR	Aldershot	03.75	1974-76	35	2	6	
			TR	Barnsley	10.76	1976-77	53	2	10	
			TR	York. C.	05.78	1978	1	3	0	
			TR	Crewe Alex.	12.78	1978	20	1	1	
WARREN, Derek B.	Colyton	23.05.23	Axminster	Exeter C.	01.48	1948-51	55		0	(RB)
WARREN, Ray R.	Bristol	23.06.18	Parson St.O.B.	Bristol Rov.	*	1946-55	381		26	(CH)
WARREN, Robert E.	Devonport	08.01.27	Plymouth U.	Plymouth Arg.	+	1946	3		0	(WH)
			TR	Chelsea	07.48	1948	1		0	
			TR	Torquay U.	08.51	1951	5		1	
WARRENDER, Robert	Leven	13.02.29	E.Fife	York C.	06.52	1952-53	24		5	(F)
WARRINER, Steve	Liverpool	18.12.58	APP	Liverpool	12.76					(D)
			TR	Newport Co.	07.78	1978-80	28	8	2	
			TR	Rochdale	08.81	1981-82	11	1	1	
			TR	Tranmere Rov.	02.83	1982	5	4	0	
WARRINGTON, Anthony	Ecclesfield	12.02.34		Lincoln C.	03.54	1953-55	2		0	(G)
WARSAP, John W.	Leytonstone	18.05.21		Gillingham	N/L	1950-52	9		1	(F)
WASILEWSKI, Adam		. .25		Rochdale	07.53	1953	4		1	d.1956
WASS, William	Ryehope	16.11.22	Middlesbrough(+)	Bradford C.	07.46	1946	7		1	(OR)
WASSALL, John C.	Birmingham	09.06.33	JNRS	Coventry C.	05.51	1955-56	16		0	(CH)
			TR	Southport	08.57	1957	4		0	
WASSALL, John V.	Shrewsbury	11.02.17	Wellington	Manchester U.	*					(IF)
			TR	Stockport Co.	10.46	1946-47	19		2	
WASSELL, Kim D.	Wolverhampton	09.06.57	W.B.A.(APP)	Northampton T.	09.77	1977-78	13	7	0	(F)
				Hull C.	N/C	1983	1	/	0	
WATERHOUSE, Ken	Orsmkirk	23.01.30	Burscough	Preston N.E.	12.48	1953-56	22		5	(IF)
			TR	Rotherham U.	05.58	1958-62	115		11	
			TR	Bristol C.	04.63	1962-63	16		1	
			TR	Darlington	08.64	1964	1		0	

Players Names	Birthplace	Date	Previous Club	League Club	Date Signed	Seasons Played	Apps	Sub	Gls	
WATERMAN, Derek	Guildford	12.04.39	Guildford C.	Exeter C.	06.57	1957	4		0	(IF)
WATERS, Joe W.	Limerick	20.09.53	APP	Leicester C.	12.73	1973-74	11	2	1	(M)EI-1
			TR	Grimsby T.	01.76	1975-83	356	1	65	
WATERS, Pat M.	Dublin	31.01.22	Glentoran	Preston N.E.	06.47	1947-49	64		0	(WH)
			TR	Carlisle U.	12.50	1950-57	261		0	
WATERS, Richard E.	Gateshead	18.05.45	Blyth Spartans	Darlington	AM	1964	2		0	(G)
WATERS, Sam	Croy	31.05.17	T.Lanark	Halifax T.	07.46	1946	26		9	(CH)d.
WATERS, William A.	Swansea	19.09.31		Blackpool	11.50					(G)
			TR	Stoke C.	09.52					
				Southend U.	11.53					
			TR	Swansea C.	08.54					
			TR	Wrexham	06.55	1955-58	99		0	
			TR	Millwall	07.60	1960	5		0	
WATFORD, Albert	Chesterfield	12.02.17		Chesterfield	*					
			TR	Lincoln C.	09.46	1946	14		0	
WATKIN, Alan J.	Felling	16.05.40		Gateshead	AM	1959	3		0	(OR)
WATKIN, Cyril	Stoke	21.07.26	JNRS	Stoke C.	+	1948-51	86		0	(FB)
			TR	Bristol C.	07.52	1952	3		0	
WATKIN, George	Chopwell	14.04.44	APP	Newcastle U.	04.62	1962	1		0	(CF)
			TR	Chesterfield	07.64	1964	7		1	
WATKIN, T. William S.	Grimsby	21.09.32	JNRS	Grimsby T.	10.49					(CF)E.SCH.INT.
			TR	Gateshead	12.52	1952-53	38		12	
			TR	Middlesbrough	03.54	1953-54	11		2	
			TR	Mansfield T.	06.55	1955	25		4	
WATKINS, Alan J.	Usk	21.04.22	Cardiff C.(+)	Plymouth Arg.	+	1946	4		1	Glamorgan/England
			TR	Cardiff C.	07.48					Cricketer
WATKINS, Charlie	Glasgow	14.01.21	Glasgow Rgrs.	Luton T.	09.48	1948-54	217		16	(WH)
WATKINS, John V.	Bristol	09.04.33	JNRS	Bristol C.	06.51	1953-58	95		17	(F)E.YTH.INT.
			TR	Cardiff C.	06.59	1959-60	65		17	
			TR	Bristol Rov.	02.61	1960-61	23		0	
WATKINS, Philip J.	Caerphilly	02.01.45	JNRS	Cardiff C.	09.62	1963	1		0	(HB)
WATKINS, Randall B.	Merthyr Tydfil	30.11.21	B.A.C.	Bristol Rov.	+	1946-54	118		7	(FB)
WATKINS, Robert S.	Bristol	20.12.45	Bristol C.(AM)	Bristol Rov.	07.65	1965	1	/	0	(OL)
WATKINSON, William	Prescot	16.03.22	Prescot Cables	Liverpool	+	1946-49	24		2	(CF)
			TR	Accrington St.	01.51	1950-54	105		49	
			TR	Halifax T.	09.54	1954-55	60		24	
WATKISS, Stuart P.	Wolverhampton	08.05.66	JNRS	Wolverhampton W.	N/C	1983	2	/	0	
WATLING, Barry J.	Walthamstow	16.07.46	APP	Orient	07.64					(G)
			TR	Bristol C.	07.65	1967-68	2	/	0	
			TR	Notts.Co.	07.69	1969-71	65	1	0	
			TR	Hartlepool U.	07.72	1972-75	139	/	0	
			L	Chester C.	09.75	1975	5	/	0	
			L	Rotherham U.	12.75	1975	5	/	0	
			TR	Sheffield Wed.	01.76	1975	1	/	0	
			TR	Charlton Ath.	10.76					
WATLING, John D.	Bristol	11.05.25	St.Andrews B.C.	Bristol Rov.	01.47	1947-61	319		19	(OL)
WATSON, Albert	Barmborough	01.06.18		Huddersfield T.	*	1946-47	10		0	
			TR	Oldham Ath.	07.48	1948-49	41		0	
WATSON, Andy	Aberdeen	03.09.59	Aberdeen	Leeds U.	06.83	1983	30	1	7	(M)
WATSON, Arthur E.	Sth.Hindley	12.07.13	Chesterfield(*)	Hull C.	+	1946	35		0	(FB)*Lincoln C.
WATSON, Charles R.	Newark	10.03.49		Notts.Co.	02.67	1967	1	/	0	(G)
WATSON, Clive E.	Dudley	28.11.47		Walsall	07.68	1968	1	/	0	(OR)
WATSON, David	Liverpool	20.11.61	JNRS	Liverpool	05.79					(D)E.U'21-7/E-3
			TR	Norwich C.	11.80	1980-83	131	/	8	
WATSON, David V.	Stapleford	05.10.46		Notts. Co.	01.67	1966-67	22	1	1	(D)E-65●
			TR	Rotherham U.	01.68	1967-70	121	/	20	
			TR	Sunderland	12.70	1970-74	177	/	27	
			TR	Manchester C.	06.75	1975-78	146	/	4	
			Werder Bremen	Southampton	10.79	1979-81	73	/	6	
			TR	Stoke C.	01.82	1981-82	59	/	5	
			Vancouver W.	Derby Co.	09.83	1983	34	/	1	
WATSON, Donald	Barnsley	27.08.32	Worsboro Bridge	Sheffield Wed.	09.54	1954	8		1	(IF)
			TR	Lincoln C.	12.56	1956-57	14		2	
			TR	Bury	11.57	1957-61	172		65	
			TR	Barnsley	01.62	1961	9		1	
			TR	Rochdale	07.62	1962-63	58		15	
			TR	Barrow	07.64	1964	17		1	
WATSON, Gary	Easington	02.03.61	APP	Oxford U.	11.78	1978-79	24	/	0	(D)
			TR	Carlisle U.	05.80	1980	17	1	0	
WATSON, Gary	Bradford	07.10.55	APP	Bradford C.	10.73	1972-83	246	17	28	(D)
			L	Doncaster Rov.	10.82	1982	13	/	0	

Players Names	Birthplace	Date	Previous Club	League Club	Date Signed	Seasons Played	Apps	Sub	Gls	
WATSON, Graham S.	Doncaster	03.08.49	APP	Doncaster Rov.	11.66	1966-67	47	1	11	(M)
			TR	Rotherham U.	02.68	1967-68	13	/	0	
			TR	Doncaster Rov.	01.69	1968-72	105	4	23	
			TR	Cambridge U.	09.72	1972-78	206	3	24	
			TR	Lincoln C.	09.78	1978-79	43	/	2	
			TR	Cambridge U.	03.80	1979	0	1	0	
WATSON, Ian	Hammersmith	07.01.44	JNRS	Chelsea	02.62	1962-64	5		1	(FB)
			TR	Q.P.R.	07.65	1965-73	197	6	1	
WATSON, Ian	Nth. Shields	05.02.60	APP	Sunderland	02.78	1978	1	/	0	(G)
			L	Rochdale	08.79	1979	33	/	0	
			TR	Newport Co.	04.82					
WATSON, James	Cowie	16.01.24	Motherwell	Huddersfield T.	06.52	1952-56	140		29	(IF)S-2/S.F.LGE REP.
WATSON, James M.	Birmingham	03.03.37		Walsall	05.55	1955	1		0	
			TR	Birmingham C.	08.57					
WATSON, John	Dewsbury	10.04.59	JNRS	Huddersfield T.	03.77					(G)
			TR	Hartlepool U.	03.79	1978-82	44	/	0	
WATSON, John	Wrexham	02.05.42	JNRS	Everton	05.59					(HB)W.SCH.INT.
			TR	Chester C.	08.60	1960-61	25		0	
			TR	Wrexham	08.62					
WATSON, John F.	Lanark	31.12.17	Bury(*)	Fulham	+	1946-47	71		2	(CH)
			R.Madrid	Crystal Palace	07.49	1949-50	61		1	
WATSON, Ken	Newcastle	08.09.34		Lincoln C.	05.52					(HB)
			TR	Aldershot	07.55	1957-59	29		1	
WATSON, Peter	Newcastle	18.03.35	Nth.Shields	Workington	11.62	1962-64	45		10	(CF)
WATSON, Peter F.	Stapleford	15.04.34	JNRS	Nottingham F.	05.55	1955-58	13		0	(CH)
			TR	Southend U.	07.59	1959-65	249	/	3	
WATSON, Stan	Darlington	17.03.37		Darlington	11.57	1957-58	27		0	(HB)
WATSON, T. Sidney	Mansfield	12.12.27	Palterton Welf.	Mansfield T.	01.49	1951-60	293		8	(IF)
WATSON, Thomas	Lanark	23.08.43	Stevenage	Peterborough U.	05.65	1965-67	75	/	20	(W)
			TR	Walsall	09.67	1967-69	82	3	17	
			TR	Gillingham	06.70	1970-71	42	7	7	
WATSON, Thomas D.	Boldon	03.02.36	Boldon C.W.	W.B.A.	11.53					(OR)
			TR	Gateshead	06.57	1957	21		5	
			TR	Grimsby T.	08.59					
WATSON, Thomas G.	Wolsingham	01.03.14		Everton	*	1946-48	34		0	
WATSON, Trevor P.	Gt.Yarmouth	26.09.38	JNRS	Fulham	07.56	1956-63	17		1	(F)
WATSON, Vaughan	Mansfield	05.11.31		Mansfield T.	04.52	1952-53	14		9	(F)
			TR	Chesterfield	05.54	1954	13		4	
WATSON, William	Sth.Hindley	29.05.16	Lincoln C.(*)	Chesterfield	*	1946-47	36		0	(RB)*Monkton Col./
			TR	Rochdale	06.48	1948-53	200		0	Brother of Arthur
WATSON, William	Bolton-on-Dearne	07.03.20	Huddersfield T.(*)	Sunderland	+	1946-53	211		15	(IF)E-4/E'B'-3/England,
			TR	Halifax T.	11.54	1954-55	33		1	Yorks, Leicester Cricketer. Son of pre-war player
WATSON, William	Motherwell	04.12.49	JNRS	Manchester U.	12.66	1970-72	11	/	0	(RB)
			TR	Burnley	08.73					
WATSON, William T.	Swansea	11.06.18		Preston N.E.	+	1946	15		0	(FB) d.1978
			TR	Cardiff C.	10.47	1947	1		0	
WATT,John	Hurlford	17.06.43	JNRS	Blackpool	08.60	1962	5		0	(F)
			TR	Stockport Co.	07.63	1963-64	55		3	
			TR	Southport	03.65	1964-65	17	1	2	
WATT, John G.	Airdrie	23.11.54	APP	Watford	03.73	1971	0	1	0	(HB)
WATT, William D.	Aberdeen	06.06.46	JNRS	Preston N.E.	06.63	1962-65	7	1	0	(F)
WATTERS, John				Stockport Co.	08.47	1947	5		1	
WATTON, James	Wolverhampton	01.11.36		Port Vale	09.62	1962	5		0	(HB)
			TR	Doncaster Rov.	07.64	1964-67	121	3	0	
WATTS, Derek	Leicester	30.06.52	APP	Leicester C.	03.72					(F)
			L	Northampton T.	10.73	1973	0	1	0	
WATTS, James A.	Cowes IOW	25.10.33		Gillingham	AM	1956	12		1	(CF)
WATTS, John W.	Birmingham	13.04.31	Saltley O.B.	Birmingham C.	08.51	1951-62	208		3	(WH)
WATTS, Mark R.	Welham Green	24.09.65	APP	Luton T.	01.83	1982	1	/	0	(F)
WAUGH, Keith	Sunderland	27.10.56	APP	Sunderland	07.74					(G)
			TR	Peterborough U.	07.76	1976-80	195	/	0	
			TR	Sheffield U.	08.81	1981-83	89	/	0	
WAUGH, Ken	Newcastle	06.08.33	Film Renters	Newcastle U.	08.52	1955	7		0	(FB)
			TR	Hartlepool U.	12.56	1956-61	194		0	
WAUGH, William L.	Edinburgh	27.11.21	Bathgate Th.	Luton T.	+	1946-49	135		9	(OL)
			TR	Q.P.R.	07.50	1950-52	76		6	
			TR	Bournemouth	07.53	1953	18		3	
WAY, Mike	Salisbury	18.05.50	Thame U.	Oxford U.	08.69.	1969-71	14	2	0	(FB)

Players Names	Birthplace	Date	Previous Club	League Club	Date Signed	Seasons Played	Apps	Sub	Gls	
WAYMAN, Charlie	B.Auckland	16.05.21	Spennymoor	Newcastle U.	+	1946-47	47		32	(CF)●
			TR	Southampton	10.47	1947-49	100		73	
			TR	Preston N.E.	09.50	1950-54	157		104	
			TR	Middlesbrough	09.54	1954-55	55		31	
			TR	Darlington	12.56	1956-57	23		14	
WAYMAN, Frank	B.Auckland	30.12.31		Preston N.E.	09.53					(F)Brother of Charlie
			TR	Chester C.	08.55	1955	30		2	
			Easington CW	Darlington	06.57	1957	1		0	
WEAKLEY, Bernard	Rotherham	20.12.32		Rotherham U.	08.55	1955	2		1	
WEALANDS, Jeff A.	Darlington	26.08.51	APP	Wolverhampton W.	10.68					(G)
			TR	Darlington	07.70	1971	28	/	0	
			TR	Hull C.	03.70	1971-78	240	/	0	
			TR	Birmingham C.	07.79	1979-81	102	/	0	
			TR	Manchester U.	02.83	1982-83	7	/	0	
			L	Oldham Ath.	03.84	1983	10	/	0	
WEALTHALL, Barry	Nottingham	01.05.42	JNRS	Nottingham F.	06.59	1960	2		0	(FB)
			TR	Grimsby T.	05.62	1961-62	9		0	
			TR	York C.	06.63	1963-66	75	/	0	
WEARE, Arthur J.	Newport	21.09.12	West Ham U.(*)	Bristol Rov.	+	1946-49	141		0	(G)*Lovells Ath./ Wolverhampton W.
WEARE, Len	Newport	23.07.34		Newport Co.	08.55	1955-69	526	/	0	(G)Son of Arthur●
WEARMOUTH, Mike	Barrow	16.05.44	JNRS	Barrow	06.62	1961-63	33		0	(HB)
			TR	Preston N.E.	03.64	1964-66	11	/	0	
WEATHERALL, Len	Middlesbrough	21.05.36	Redcar BC	Grimsby T.	04.55	1954-55	10		1	
WEATHERLEY, C. Mark	Canterbury	18.01.58	APP	Gillingham	12.75	1974-83	280	26	33	(D)
WEATHERSPOON, Charles	Newcastle	03.10.29	JNRS	Sunderland	08.47					(F)
			Annfield Plain	Sheffield U.	01.51	1950	1		0	
			TR	Hartlepool U.	08.52	1952	3		2	
WEAVER, Eric	Rhymney	01.07.43	Trowbridge	Swindon T.	05.62	1961-66	55	/	6	(F)
			TR	Nottingham F.	08.67	1967	16	1	4	
			TR	Northampton T.	12.67	1967-69	61	3	9	
WEAVER, John N.	Wrexham	26.11.24	JNRS	Wrexham	05.46	1946	2		0	
WEAVER, Sam	Pilsley	08.02.09	Chelsea(*)	Stockport Co.	+	1946	2		0	(WH)E-3/E.F.LGE REP./ *Sutton T./Hull C./ Newcastle U./ Somerset cricketer
WEBB, Alan R.	Wellington	01.01.63	APP	W.B.A.	01.80	1981-83	23	1	0	(D)
			L	Lincoln C.	03.84	1983	11	/	0	
WEBB, David	E. Ham	09.04.46	West Ham U.(AM)	Orient	05.63	1964-65	62	/	3	(D) 1 app. in goal for Chelsea●
			TR	Southampton	03.66	1965-67	75	/	2	
			TR	Chelsea	02.68	1967-73	230	/	21	
			TR	Q.P.R.	07.74	1974-77	116	/	7	
			TR	Leicester C.	09.77	1977-78	32	1	0	
			TR	Derby Co.	12.78	1978-79	25	1	1	
			TR	Bournemouth	05.80	1980-82	11	/	0	
WEBB, Doug J.	Stokenchurch	10.03.39		Reading	11.56	1956-66	178	2	83	(IF)
WEBB, James K.	warrington	06.07.38	Lymm Rgrs	Shrewsbury T.	04.56	1955-56	2		1	(F)
WEBB, John	Liverpool	10.02.52	APP	Liverpool	02.69					(RB)
			L	Plymouth Arg.	09.73	1973	4	/	0	
			TR	Tranmere Rov.	07.74	1974	17	3	0	
WEBB, Neil	Reading	30.07.63	APP	Reading	11.80	1979-81	65	7	22	(M) Son of Doug/E.YTH.INT.
			TR	Portsmouth	07.82	1982-83	82	/	18	
WEBB, Robert	Altofts	29.11.33	JNRS	Leeds U.	04.51	1953-54	3		0	(IF)
			TR	Walsall	03.55	1954	9		3	
			TR	Bradford C.	07.55	1955-61	208		59	
			TR	Torquay U.	07.62	1962-63	49		12	
WEBB, Ron C.T.	Brentford	13.03.25	Q.P.R.(+)	Crystal Palace	09.46	1946	3		0	
WEBB, Stan J.	Middlesbrough	06.12.47		Middlesbrough	07.67	1967-70	20	7	6	(F)
			TR	Carlisle U.	02.71	1970-72	16	10	5	
			TR	Brentford	10.72	1972-73	37	2	8	
			TR	Darlington	07.74	1974-75	69	5	21	
WEBB, William	Mexborough	07.03.32	Bohemians	Rochdale	05.51					(FB)
			TR	Leicester C.	06.51	1951-56	47		0	
			TR	Stockport Co.	06.57	1957-62	243		0	
WEBBER, Eric V.	Portslade	22.12.19	JNRS	Southampton	*	1946-50	182		0	(CH)
			TR	Torquay U.	10.51	1951-54	149		2	
WEBBER, George M.	Abercynon	28.06.25	Cardiff(AM)	Torquay U.	06.50	1950-53	118		0	(G)
			TR	Northampton T.	06.54	1954	13		0	
WEBBER, John V.	Blackpool	02.06.20	Hyde U.	Blackburn Rov.	02.47	1946-47	8		3	(CF)

Players Names	Birthplace	Date	Previous Club	League Club	Date Signed	Seasons Played	Apps	Sub	Gls	
WEBBER, Keith J.	Cardiff	05.01.43	Barry T.	Everton	02.60	1960-61	4		0	(CF) d.1983
			TR	Brighton & H.A.	04.63	1962-64	35		14	
			TR	Wrexham	09.64	1964-65	73	/	33	
			TR	Doncaster Rov.	07.66	1966-68	63	4	18	
			TR	Chester C.	06.69	1969-70	66	4	4	
			TR	Stockport Co.	07.71	1971	36	4	7	
WEBSTER, Alan J.	Melton Mowbray	03.07.48		Scunthorpe U.	· 07.66	1966-67	4	1	0	(HB)
WEBSTER, Andrew	Colne	18.03.47		Bradford C.	07.65	1965-66	10	2	1	(F)
WEBSTER, Colin	Cardiff	17.07.32		Cardiff C.	05.50					(CF)W-4
			TR	Manchester U.	05.52	1953-58	65		27	
			TR	Swansea C.	09.58	1958-62	159		65	
			TR	Newport Co.	03.63	1962-63	31		3	
WEBSTER, Colin	Halifax	05.03.30		Halifax T.	09.50	1950	16		1	
			TR	Rochdale	09.51					
WEBSTER, Eric	Manchester	24.06.31		Manchester C.	02.52	1952	1		0	
WEBSTER, Harry	Sheffield	22.08.30	JNRS	Bolton W.	10.48	1949-56	97		38	(IF)
			TR	Chester C.	06.58	1958-59	34		11	
WEBSTER, Ian A.	Norton	30.12.65	Leeds U. (N/C)	Scunthorpe U.	N/C	1982-83	9	1	0	(F)
WEBSTER, J. Barry	Sheffield	03.03.35	Gainsborough	Rotherham U.	05.56	1956-61	180		37	(OR)
			TR	Bradford C.	06.62	1962-63	53		9	
WEBSTER, Keith	Newcastle	06.11.45	Stockton	Newcastle U.	12.62					(F)
				Darlington	11.66	1966	8	1	0	
WEBSTER, Malcolm W.	Rossington	12.11.50	APP	Arsenal	01.68	1969	3	/	0	(G) E.YTH.INT./E.SCH.INT.
			TR	Fulham	12.69	1969-73	95	/	0	
			TR	Southend U.	01.74	1973-75	96	/	0	
			TR	Cambridge U.	09.76	1976-83	256	/	0	
WEBSTER, Richard	Accrington	06.08.19		Accrington St.	*	1946-50	186		3	(FB)
WEBSTER, Ron	Belper	21.06.43	JNRS	Derby Co.	06.60	1961-77	450	4	7	(D)
WEBSTER, Simon P.	Hinckley	20.01.64	APP	Tottenham H.	12.81	1982-83	2	1	0	(D)
			L	Exeter C.	11.83	1983	26	/	0	
WEBSTER, Terry	Eaton	27.09.41	JNRS	Sheffield U.	10.58					(HB)
			TR	Accrington St.	11.59					
			TR	Barrow	07.60	1960	4		0	
WEBSTER, Terry C.	Doncaster	09.07.30		Doncaster Rov.	06.48					(G)
			TR	Derby Co.	10.48	1948-57	172		0	
WEDDLE, Derek K.	Newcastle	27.12.35	JNRS	Sunderland	05.53	1955-56	2		0	(IF)
			TR	Portsmouth	12.56	1956-58	24		8	
			Cambridge C.	Middlesbrough	08.61	1961	3		1	
			TR	Darlington	06.62	1962-63	36		10	
			TR	York C.	07.64	1964-65	44	/	13	
WEDDLE, George D.	Ashington	24.02.19		Gateshead	06.47	1946-48	48		10	
WEEKS, Graham J.	Exeter	03.03.58	APP	Exeter C.	07.76	1976-77	49	4	1	(M)
			TR	Bournemouth	05.78	1978	3	/	0	
WEIGH, Ray E.	Flint	23.06.28	Shrewsbury	Bournemouth	03.49	1949-50	28		8	(OR)
			TR	Stockport Co.	07.51	1951-53	75		31	
			TR	Shrewsbury T.	06.54	1954-56	107		43	
			TR	Aldershot	07.57	1957	11		1	
WEIR, Alan	Sth. Shields	01.09.59	APP	Sunderland	05.77	1977	1	/	0	(D)E.YTH.INT.
			TR	Rochdale	06.79	1979-82	96	10	3	
			TR	Hartlepool U.	08.83	1983	9	1	0	
WEIR, Alex	Longridge	20.10.16	Preston N.E.(+)	Watford	+	1946	1		0	(IF)
			TR	Northampton T.	09.47					
WEIR, James	Glasgow	12.04.39	Clydebank	Fulham	07.57	1957	3		0	(OL)
			TR	York C.	06.60	1960-62	82		38	
			TR	Mansfield T.	09.62	1962	18		3	
			TR	Luton T.	08.63	1963	12		1	
			TR	Tranmere Rov.	07.64	1964	13		3	
WEIR, John B.	Fauldhouse	20.10.23	Hibernian	Blackburn Rov.	01.47	1946-47	23		7	(CF)
WELBOURNE, Don	Scunthorpe	12.03.49	APP	Scunthorpe U.	03.67	1966-75	250	7	5	(CH)
WELBOURNE, Duncan	Scunthorpe	28.07.40	Scunthorpe U.(AM)	Grimsby T.	08.57	1957-63	129		3	(WH)Brother of Don●
			TR	Watford	11.63	1963-73	404	77	22	
			TR	Southport	07.74	1974-75	52	1	2	
WELCH, Ron	Chesterfield	26.09.52	APP	Burnley	10.69	1970	1	/	0	(M)
			TR	Brighton & H.A.	12.73	1973-74	35	1	4	
			TR	Chesterfield	11.74	1974-76	17	7	1	
WELFORD, William	Newcastle	14.04.34		Hartlepool U.	11.58	1958	8		0	
WELLER, Chris W.	Reading	25.12.39	Reading(AM)	Bournemouth	09.59	1960-64	70		17	(F)
			TR	Bristol Rov.	07.65	1965	2	1	0	
			TR	Bournemouth	01.66	1965-66	39	2	9	
WELLER, Keith	Islington	11.06.46	JNRS	Tottenham H.	01.64	1964-66	19	2	1	(M)E-4/E.F.LGE REP.
			TR	Millwall	06.67	1967-69	121	/	38	
			TR	Chelsea	05.70	1970-71	34	4	14	
			TR	Leicester C.	09.71	1971-78	260	2	37	

Players Names	Birthplace	Date	Previous Club	League Club	Date Signed	Seasons Played	Career Record Apps	Sub	Gls	
WELLINGS, Barry	Liverpool	10.06.58	APP	Everton	06.76					(F)
			TR	York C.	06.78	1978-79	40	7	9	
			TR	Rochdale	07.80	1980-82	111	5	30	
			TR	Tranmere Rov.	02.83	1982	16	/	3	
				Tranmere Rov.	N/C	1983	9	/	0	
WELLS, Archie	Clydbank	04.10.20	Hibernian	New Brighton	07.46	1946-48	35		5	
WELLS, Peter A.	Nottingham	13.08.56	APP	Nottingham F.	10.74	1975-76	27	/	0	(G)
			TR	Southampton	12.76	1976-82	141	/	0	
			TR	Millwall	02.83	1982-83	33	/	0	
WELLS, W. David	Eccleston	16.12.40		Blackburn Rov.	05.62					(FB)
			TR	Rochdale	07.63	1963	8		0	
WELSH, Alan	Edinburgh	09.07.47	Bonnyrigg Rose	Millwall	07.65	1965-67	3	1	0	(IF)
			TR	Torquay U.	11.67	1967-71	140	8	45	
			TR	Plymouth Arg.	07.72	1972-73	64	2	14	
			TR	Bournemouth	02.74	1973-74	33	2	3	
			TR	Millwall	08.75	1975	5	4	1	
WELSH, Andy J.	Fleetwood	20.11.62	APP	Blackpool	08.80	1980	1	/	0	(F)
WELSH, Colin	Liverpool	09.06.45		Southport	10.63	1964	1		0	(F)
WELSH, Don	Manchester	25.02.11	Torquay U.(*)	Charlton Ath.	*	1946-47	29		13	(LH)E-3/E.F.LGE REP.
WELSH, Eric	Belfast	01.05.42	Distillery	Exeter C.	09.59	1959-65	105	/	18	(OR)NI-4/NI.U23-1
			TR	Carlisle U.	10.65	1965-68	73	2	17	
			TR	Torquay U.	06.69	1969-70	38	2	12	
			TR	Hartlepool U.	07.71	1971	13	2	2	
WELSH, James P.	Edinburgh	21.12.23	Tranent J.	Luton T.	09.46					
			TR	Aldershot	06.48	1948	5		0	
WELSH, Peter M.	Coatbridge	19.07.59	APP	Leicester C.	08.76	1976-81	24	17	4	(D)
WELTON, R. Pat	Eltham	03.05.28	Chislehurst FC	Orient	05.49	1949-57	263		0	(G)
			TR	Q.P.R.	03.58	1958	3		0	
WENT, Paul F.	Bromley-by-Bow	12.10.49	APP	Orient	10.66	1965-66	48	2	5	(D)E.YTH.INT./E.SCH.INT.
			TR	Charlton Ath.	06.67	1967-71	160	3	15	
			TR	Fulham	07.72	1972-73	58	/	3	
			TR	Portsmouth	12.73	1973-76	92	/	5	
			TR	Cardiff C.	10.76	1976-78	71	1	11	
			TR	Orient	09.78	1978-79	45	/	3	
WERGE, Eddie	Sidcup	09.09.36	Bexleyheath	Charlton Ath.	05.55	1957-60	44		19	(W)
			TR	Crystal Palace	05.61	1961-64	83		6	
			TR	Orient	11.66	1966-67	29	3	0	
WESSON, Robert W.	Thornaby	15.10.40		Coventry C.	11.58	1960-65	133	/	0	(G)
			TR	Walsall	09.66	1966-72	191	/	0	
			L	Doncaster Rov.	02.70	1969	5	/	0	
WEST, Alan	Hyde	18.12.51	APP	Burnley	12.68	1969-72	41	3	3	(M)E.U23-1
			TR	Luton T.	10.73	1973-80	272	13	16	
			TR	Millwall	07.81	1981-82	58	/	4	
WEST, Colin	Wallsend	13.11.62	APP	Sunderland	07.80	1981-83	68	11	10	(F)
WEST, Edward	Parbold	04.11.30		Doncaster Rov.	02.53					(FB)
			TR	Gillingham	07.54	1954-56	95		0	
			TR	Oldham Ath.	07.57	1957-60	117		0	
WEST, Gary	Scunthorpe	25.08.64	APP	Sheffield U.	08.82	1982-83	50	/	1	(D)
WEST, Gordon	Barnsley	24.04.43	JNRS	Blackpool	05.61	1960-61	31		0	(G)E-3/E.U23-3/
			TR	Everton	03.62	1961-72	335	/	0	
			TR	Tranmere Rov.	10.75	1976-78	17	/	0	
WEST, Thomas	Salford	08.12.16		Oldham Ath.	+					(F)*Stockport Co.
			TR	Rochdale	06.46	1946	4		2	
WEST, Trefor J.	Coventry	14.12.44	APP	W.B.A.	05.62					(FB)
			TR	Walsall	05.64	1964	12		0	
WESTAWAY, Kevin D.	Bristol	24.11.62	APP	Bristol Rov.	11.80	1980-81	2	/	0	(D)
WESTBY, Jack L.	Aintree	20.05.16		Liverpool	+					(FB)
			TR	Southport	08.47	1947	13		0	
WESTCOTT, Dennis	Wallasey	02.17.17	New Brighton(*)	Wolverhampton W.	*	1946-47	57		48	(CF)E.F.LGE REP./
			TR	Blackburn Rov.	04.48	1948-49	63		37	d.1960
			TR	Manchester C.	02.50	1949-51	72		37	
			TR	Chesterfield	06.52	1952	40		21	
WESTLAKE, Brian	Newcastle	19.09.43		Stoke C.	09.61					(F)
			TR	Doncaster Rov.	06.63	1963	5		1	
			TR	Halifax T.	01.64	1963-66	100	/	27	
			TR	Tranmere Rov.	09.66	1966	13	1	3	
			TR	Colchester U.	02.67	1966	14	1	5	
WESTLAKE, Frank A.	Bramborough	11.08.15	Thurnscoe Vic	Sheffield Wed.	*	1946-49	109		0	(FB)
			TR	Halifax T.	06.50	1950	2		0	
WESTLAND, James	Aberdeen	21.07.16	Aberdeen	Stoke C.	*					(IL) d.1972
			TR	Mansfield T.	11.46	1946	9		0	
WESTLEY, Shane L. M.	Canterbury	16.06.65	APP	Charlton Ath.	06.83	1983	8	/	0	(D)
WESTMORLAND, Joe E.	Carlisle	30.06.37		Carlisle U.	02.59	1958	3		0	(FB)

Players Names	Birthplace	Date	Previous Club	League Club	Date Signed	Seasons Played	Apps	Sub	Gls	
WESTON, Anthony D.	Maidstone	03.04.45	Maidstone U.	Gillingham	11.63	1964-69	162	/	2	(FB)
WESTON, Donald P.	Mansfield	06.03.36		Wrexham	06.59	1958-59	42		21	(CF)
			TR	Birmingham C.	01.60	1959-60	23		3	
			TR	Rotherham U.	12.60	1960-62	76		21	
			TR	Leeds U.	12.62	1962-65	69	/	24	
			TR	Huddersfield T.	10.65	1965-66	20	1	7	
			TR	Wrexham	12.66	1966-67	42	/	19	
			TR	Chester C.	08.68	1968	1	2	0	
WESTON, James	Whiston	16.09.55	Skelmersdale	Blackpool	01.74	1975-79	97	8	8	(M)
			TR	Torquay U.	06.80	1980-81	38	/	1	
			TR	Wigan Ath.	09.81	1981-82	63	3	2	
WESTON, Reg H.	Greenhithe	16.01.18	Northfleet	Swansea C.	+	1946-51	227		1	(CH)
			TR	Derby CO.	10.53					
WESTWELL, Simon	Clitheroe	12.11.61	APP	Preston N.E.	10.79	1980-82	63	/	1	(D)
WESTWOOD, Daniel	Dagenham	25.07.53	Billericay	Q.P.R.	07.74	1974	0	1	1	(F)
			TR	Gillingham	11.75	1975-81	201	10	74	
WESTWOOD, Eric	Manchester	25.09.17		Manchester C.	*	1946-52	218		3	(LB)E-2/E.F.LGE REP.
WESTWOOD, Gary M.	Barrow	03.04.64	APP	Ipswich T.	04.81					(G)
			L	Reading	09.83	1983	5	/	0	
WESTWOOD, R. William	Brierley Hill	14.04.12	Brierley Hill	Bolton W.	*	1946-47	40		4	(IF)E-6/E.F.LGE REP./
			TR	Chester C.	12.47	1947-48	38		13	d.1982
WETTON, Albert S.	Winlaton	23.10.28	Cheshunt	Tottenham H.	10.49					(CF)
			TR	Brighton & H.A.	06.51	1951-52	3		0	
			TR	Crewe Alex.	10.53	1953	2		0	
WETTON, Ralph	Rowland Green	06.06.27	Cheshunt	Tottenham H.	08.50	1951-54	45		0	(WH)Brother of Albert
			TR	Plymouth Arg.	06.55	1955	36		1	
			TR	Aldershot	11.56	1956-57	49		1	
WHALE, Ray	W.Bromwich	23.02.37	W.Bromwich C.A.	W.B.A.	12.54					(FB)
			TR	Southend U.	04.59	1959-60	29		0	
WHALEY, George D.	Darlington	30.07.20	Hearts	Gateshead	09.46	1946	6		0	(CF)
WHALEY, Ken	Leeds	22.06.35		Bradford P.A.	06.57	1958	1		0	(HB)
WHALLEY, Harold	Nelson	04.04.23	Barnoldswick	Accrington St.	12.46	1946	3		0	(FB)
WHALLEY, Herbert	Ashton-u-Lyme	06.08.12	Stalybridge	Manchester U.	*	1946	3			(LH) d.1958
WHALLEY, Jeff H.	Rossendale	08.02.52	APP	Blackburn Rov.	02.70	1969-70	2	/	0	(LH)
WHALLEY, Selwyn D.	Stoke	24.02.34		Port Vale	08.53	1956-65	178	/	22	(FB)
WHARE, William	Guernsey	14.05.24		Nottingham F.	05.47	1948-59	300		1	(FB) d.
WHARTON, Andy	Burnley	21.12.61	APP	Burnley	12.79	1980-83	63	2	6	(M)
			L	Torquay U.	11.83	1983	10	/	0	
			TR	Chester C.	02.84	1983	15	/	2	
WHARTON, Guy	Broomfield	05.12.16	Wolverhampton W.(*)	Portsmouth	*	1946-47	25		2	(WH)*Chester C.
			TR	Darlington	07.48	1948-49	39		2	
WHARTON, John E.	Bolton	18.06.20	Plymouth Arg.(*)	Preston N.E.	+	1946	25		7	(OR)
			TR	Manchester C.	03.47	1946-47	23		2	
			TR	Blackburn Rov.	06.48	1948-52	129		15	
			TR	Newport Co.	02.53	1952-54	74		10	
WHARTON, Ken	Newcastle	28.11.60	Grainger Pk B.C.	Newcastle U.	01.79	1978-83	140	14	14	(M)
WHARTON, Terry J.	Bolton	01.07.42	JNRS	Wolverhampton W.	10.59	1961-67	223	1	69	(OL)Son of John E.
			TR	Bolton W.	11.67	1967-70	101	1	28	
			TR	Crystal Palace	01.71	1970-71	19	1	1	
				Walsall	11.73	1973	1	/	0	
WHATLING, Keith R.	Worlingworth	01.11.47	JNRS	Ipswich T.	03.66					(F)
			TR	Exeter C.	07.67	1967-68	19	4	3	
WHATMORE, Neil	Ellesmere Port	17.05.55	APP	Bolton W.	05.73	1972-80	262	15	102	(F)
			TR	Birmingham C.	08.81	1981-82	24	2	6	
			L	Bolton W.	12.82	1982	10	/	3	
			TR	Oxford U.	02.83	1982-83	33	3	15	
			L	Bolton W.	03.84	1983	7	/	2	
WHEAT, Arthur B.	Nottingham	26.10.21	Montrose	Bradford P.A.	12.49	1950-51	22		3	(IF)
			TR	York C.	08.52	1952	4		0	
WHEATLEY, Barry	Sandbach	21.02.38		Liverpool	03.56					(IF)
			TR	Crewe Alex.	07.57	1957-65	242	/	49	
			TR	Rochdale	07.66	1966	13	/	4	
WHEATLEY, H. Joe	Eastham	09.05.20		Port Vale	*					
			TR	Shrewsbury T.	N/L	1950	7		0	
WHEATLEY, Roland	Nottingham	20.06.24	Beeston BC	Nottingham F.	06.46	1947-48	6		0	
			TR	Southampton	01.49	1948-50	10		1	
			TR	Grimsby T.	06.51	1951	5		0	
WHEATLEY, Steve J.	Durham	12.04.59	APP	Gillingham	04.77	1976-77	4	/	0	(G)
WHEATLEY, Steve P.	Hinckley	26.12.29	Hickley U.	Derby Co.	12.50	1951-52	4		0	(F)
				Boston U.	Chesterfield	07.55	1955	3		0	
WHEATLEY, Tom	Hebburn	01.06.29	Amble	Leeds U.	04.53	1953	6		0	(G)

Players Names	Birthplace	Date	Previous Club	League Club	Date Signed	Seasons Played	Career Record Apps	Sub	Gls	
WHEATLEY, William	Mansfield	05.11.20	Mansfield Col.	Mansfield T.	08.48	1948-49	38		3	(OR)
WHEATON, Gilbert J.	Newcastle	01.11.41	Mickley Col.	Grimsby T.	09.60	1962	7		0	(HB)
			TR	Chester C.	06.63	1963	1		0	
WHEELDON, Tom	Whiston	28.12.57	Runcorn	Torquay U.	N/C	1981	5	3	0	(D)
WHEELER, Alf J.	Fareham	06.04.22	Portsmouth(AM)	Blackburn Rov.	04.47	1947-48	21		5	(F)
			TR	Swindon T.	07.49	1949-50	23		4	
WHEELER, James	Reading	21.12.33		Reading	08.52	1952-66	405	1	147	(IF)
WHEELER, John E.	Liverpool	26.07.28	Carlton FC	Tranmere Rov.	+	1948-50	101		9	(WH)E-1/E'B'-5/
			TR	Bolton W.	02.51	1950-55	189		18	E.F.LGE REP.
			TR	Liverpool	09.56	1956-61	164		21	
WHEELER, William H.	Carlisle	27.09.20		Carlisle	10.46	1946	4		0	
WHEELER, William J.	Evesham	13.07.19	Cheltenham	Birmingham C.	*	1946-47	7		0	(G)
			TR	Huddersfield T.	08.48	1948-55	166		0	
WHELAN, Anthony G.	Dublin	23.11.59	Bohemians	Manchester U.	08.80	1980	0	1	0	(D)EI.U21-1
WHELAN, Anthony M.	Salford	20.11.52	APP	Manchester U.	12.69					(F)
			TR	Manchester C.	03.73	1972-73	3	3	0	
			TR	Rochdale	07.74	1974-76	124	/	20	
WHELAN, David	Bradford	24.11.36	Wigan B.C.	Blackburn Rov.	12.53	1956-59	78		3	(FB)
			TR	Crewe Alex.	01.63	1962-65	115	/	0	
WHELAN, Robert	Salford	09.11.30		Manchester C.	04.50					
			TR	Oldham Ath.	07.52	1952	1		0	
			TR	Accrington St.	07.53					
WHELAN, Ron A.	Dublin	25.09.61	Home Farm	Liverpool	10.79	1980-83	78	6	17	(M)EI.U21-1/EI-7
WHELAN, William A.	Dublin	01.04.35	Home Farm	Manchester U.	05.53	1954-57	79		43	(IF)EI-4/d.1958
WHENT, John R.	Darlington	03.05.20		Brighton & H.A.	08.47	1947-49	101		4	(WH)
			TR	Luton T.	08.50	1950	11		3	
WHIFFEN, Kingsley	Welshpool	03.12.50	APP	Chelsea	APP	1966	1	/	0	(G)
WHIGHAM, William	Airdrie	09.10.39	Falkirk	Middlesbrough	10.66	1966-71	187	/	0	(G)
			Dumbarton	Darlington	08.74	1974	4	/	0	
WHISTON, Don	Stoke	04.04.30	JNRS	Stoke C.	12.49	1949-56	30		4	(FB)
			TR	Crewe Alex.	02.57	1956-57	52		9	
			TR	Rochdale	05.58	1958	14		0	
WHISTON, Joe R.	Stoke	05.10.28		Crewe Alex.	09.51	1951-52	9		2	
WHITAKER, Colin	Leeds	14.06.32		Sheffield Wed.	11.51	1951-52	2		0	(OL)
			TR	Bradford P.A.	06.53	1953-55	49		10	
			TR	Shrewsbury T.	06.56	1956-60	152		59	
			TR	Q.P.R.	02.61	1960	8		0	
			TR	Rochdale	05.61	1961-62	54		10	
			TR	Oldham Ath.	10.62	1962-63	72		29	
			TR	Barrow	08.64	1964	12		0	
WHITAKER, Fred J.	Canada	12.10.23	Vancouver NS	Notts.Co.	08.46	1946	10		2	(CF)2 apps. in goal
WHITAKER, William	Chesterfield	07.10.23		Chesterfield	+	1946	13		0	(CH)E.F.LGE REP.
			TR	Middlesbrough	06.47	1947-54	179		1	
WHITAKER, William P.	Charlton	20.12.22	Kingstonian	Charlton Ath.	+	1946-48	28		0	(CH)E.AMAT.INT./
			TR	Huddersfield T.	11.48	1948-49	43		0	E.SCH.INT.
			TR	Crystal Palace	06.50	1950	35		1	
WHITBY, Brian	Luton	21.02.39	Hitchin T.	Luton T.	05.57	1957-58	7		1	(W)
WHITCHURCH, Charles H.	Grays	29.10.20	Portsmouth(AM)	Tottenham H.	+	1946	8		2	(F)E.SCH.INT.
			TR	Southend U.	07.47	1947	17		5	
WHITE, Alex	Lasswade	28.01.16	Bonnyrigg Rose	Chelsea	*	1946-47	17		0	(FB)
			TR	Swindon T.	07.48	1948-49	35		0	
			TR	Southport	07.50	1950	3		0	
WHITE, Andy C.J.	Newport	06.11.48	Caerleon	Newport Co.	08.69	1969-76	225	27	26	(F)
WHITE, Archie	Dumbarton	11.01.59	APP	Oxford	01.76	1976-79	10	14	1	(F)
WHITE, Arnold	Bristol	25.07.24	Soundwell	Bristol C.	03.47	1946-50	82		12	(IR)
			TR	Millwall	08.51	1951-52	14		0	
WHITE, Barry J.	Beverley	30.07.50	APP	Hull C.	08.68					(G)4 apps. on field
			TR	Halifax T.	11.70	1971-74	23	/	0	
WHITE, Dean	Hastings	04.12.58	Chelsea(APP)	Gillingham	07.78	1978-82	108	8	26	(M)
			TR	Millwall	03.83	1982-83	41	/	4	
WHITE, Dennis	Hartlepool	10.11.48		Hartlepool U.	11.67	1967-72	55	2	0	(FB)
WHITE, E. Winston	Leicester	26.10.58	APP	Leicester C.	11.76	1976-78	10	2	1	(F)
			TR	Hereford U.	03.79	1978-82	169	6	21	
			Hong Kong Rgrs	Chesterfield	N/C	1983	0	1	0	
				Port Vale	N/C	1983	0	1	0	
			TR	Stockport Co.	11.83	1983	4	/	1	
			TR	Bury	01.84	1983	29	/	1	
WHITE, Edward A.	Crewe	22.11.56		Crewe Alex.	N/C	1978	1	/	0	(F)
WHITE, Edward R.	Musselburgh	13.04.35	Falkirk	Bradford C.	10.59	1959	4		1	(F)Brother of Tom/John A.

Players Names	Birthplace	Date	Previous Club	League Club	Date Signed	Seasons Played	Apps	Sub	Gls	
WHITE, Fred	Wolverhampton	05.12.16	Everton(*)	Sheffield U.	*	1947-49	44		0	(G)
			TR	Lincoln C.	06.50	1950	42		0	
WHITE, Gwilym D.	Doncaster	23.02.36	Plymouth Arg.(AM)	Oldham Ath.	AM	1960	1		0	(FB)
WHITE, Howard K.	Timperley	02.03.54	APP	Manchester C.	05.71	1970	1	/	0	(HB)
WHITE, Ian S.	Glasgow	20.12.35	Glasgow Celtic	Leicester C.	05.58	1959-61	47		1	(WH)
			TR	Southampton	06.62	1962-66	62	2	5	
WHITE, James	Parkstone	13.06.42	JNRS	Bournemouth	AM	1957	1		0	(CF)E.YTH.INT.
			TR	Portsmouth	06.59	1958-61	33		6	
			TR	Gillingham	06.63	1963-65	65	/	1	
			TR	Portsmouth	07.66	1966-69	176	/	7	
			TR	Cambridge U.	12.70	1970-71	28	2	2	
WHITE, John	Doncaster	17.03.24		Aldershot	+	1946-52	209		24	(CH)Brother of Len R.
			TR	Bristol C.	10.52	1952-57	216		11	
WHITE, John A.	Musselburgh	28.04.37	Falkirk	Tottenham H.	10.59	1959-63	183		40	(IF)S-22/S.U23-1/ S.F.LGE REP./ E.F.LGE REP./d.1964
WHITE, Ken	Selby	15.03.22	Selby T.	Hull C.	12.47	1948	1		0	(RH)
WHITE, Kevin N.	Poole	26.06.48	APP	Bournemouth	08.66	1966-68	45	3	4	(W)
WHITE, Len R.	Skellow	23.03.30	Upton Col.	Rotherham U.	05.48	1950-52	43		14	(CF)E.F.LGE REP.●
			TR	Newcastle U.	02.53	1952-61	243		142	
			TR	Huddersfield T.	02.62	1961-64	105		39	
			TR	Stockport Co.	01.65	1964-65	53		22	
WHITE, Lewis	Stoke	02.08.27		Port Vale	10.48	1948	1		0	
WHITE, Malcolm	Sunderland	24.04.41	Wolves(AM)	Grimsby T.	08.58	1958-62	65		0	(G)
			TR	Walsall	08.63	1963	28		0	
			TR	Lincoln C.	07.64	1964	27		0	
			TR	Bradford C.	07.65	1965	9	/	0	
			TR	Halifax T.	11.65	1965-67	100	/	0	
WHITE, Mark I.	Sheffield	26.10.58	Sheffield U. (APP)	Reading	03.77	1977-83	191	5	3	(D)
WHITE, Maurice H.	Keadby	29.01.38		Doncaster Rov.	04.56	1957-60	56		0	(FB)
WHITE, Phil G.J.	Fineham	29.12.30	Wealdstone	Orient	07.53	1953-63	221		27	(OR)
WHITE, Ray	Brockley	05.02.41	JNRS	Millwall	08.58	1958	2		0	(HB)
			TR	Stoke C.	07.60					
WHITE, Ray B.W.	Bootle	13.08.18	Tottenham H.(+)	Bradford P.A.	05.46	1946-50	151		3	(WH)
WHITE, Ray S.	Rochford	14.01.48	APP	Southend U.	01.66	1963-65	6	/	0	(G)
			TR	Millwall	07.66					
			TR	Southend U.	10.66	1967	4	/	0	
			TR	Bristol Rov.	07.68	1968	3	/	0	
WHITE, Richard	Scunthorpe	18.08.31	Scunthorpe SC	Scunthorpe U.	N/L	1950-55	133		11	(CH)
			TR	Liverpool	11.55	1955-61	203		0	
			TR	Doncaster Rov.	07.62	1962-63	82		0	
WHITE, Ron T.	Bethnal Green	09.11.31	Maccabi Spts	Charlton Ath.	03.54	1953-61	165		8	(OL)
WHITE, Steve J.	Chipping Sodbury	02.01.59	Mangotsfield U.	Bristol Rov.	07.77	1977-79	46	4	20	(F)E.SCH.INT.
			TR	Luton T.	12.79	1979-81	63	9	25	
			TR	Charlton Ath.	07.82	1982	29	/	12	
			L	Lincoln C.	01.83	1982	2	1	0	
			L	Luton T.	02.83	1982	4	/	0	
			TR	Bristol Rov.	08.83	1983	38	5	9	
WHITE, Tom	High Hold	10.11.24	East Tanfield	Sunderland	+	1946	2		1	(IF)
WHITE, Tom	Musselburgh	12.08.39	Aberdeen	Crystal Palace	06.66	1966-67	37	2	13	(IF)Brother of John A.
			TR	Blackpool	03.68	1967-69	34	/	9	
			TR	Bury	06.70	1970-71	46	2	13	
			TR	Crewe Alex.	12.71	1971	4	/	0	
WHITE, William	Clackmannan	25.09.32	Motherwell	Accrington St.	08.53	1953	18		0	(G)
			TR	Mansfield T.	05.54	1954	3		0	
			TR	Derby Co.	08.55	1955	3		0	
			TR	Mansfield T.	09.55					
WHITE, William H.	Liverpool	13.10.36		Burnley	01.54	1957-59	9		4	(F)
			TR	Wrexham	03.61	1960	8		0	
			TR	Chester C.	07.61	1961	13		3	
			TR	Halifax T.	07.62					
WHITEAR, John M.	Isleworth	31.05.35	Walton & H.	Aston Villa	04.53					(F)E.YTH.INT.
			TR	Crystal Palace	05.56	1956	5		1	
WHITEFOOT, Geoff	Manchester	31.12.33	JNRS	Manchester U.	12.51	1949-55	92		0	(WH)E.U23-1/ E.SCH.INT.
			TR	Grimsby T.	11.57	1957	27		5	
			TR	Nottingham F.	07.58	1958-67	255	/	5	
WHITEHEAD, Alan	Bury	20.11.56		Bury	07.78	1977-80	98	1	13	(D)
			TR	Brentford	08.81	1981-83	101	1	4	
			TR	Scunthorpe U.	01.84	1983	15	/	0	
WHITEHEAD, Alan J.	Birmingham	03.09.51	APP	Birmingham C.	08.70	1971-72	4	/	0	(WH)
WHITEHEAD, Barry	Sheffield	03.12.46		Chesterfield	07.65	1965	5	1	1	(F)
WHITEHEAD, Clive	Birmingham	24.11.55	Northfield J.	Bristol C.	08.73	1973-81	209	20	10	(M)
			TR	W.B.A.	11.81	1981-83	77	1	3	

Players Names	Birthplace	Date	Previous Club	League Club	Date Signed	Seasons Played	Career Record Apps Sub Gls		
WHITEHEAD, Norman J.	Liverpool	22.04.48	Skelmersdale	Southport	12.67	1967	7	1	0 (F)
			TR	Rochdale	07.68	1968-71	153	2	11
			TR	Rotherham U.	03.72	1971-72	29	4	2
			TR	Chester C.	08.73	1973-75	66	8	5
			TR	Grimsby T.	08.76	1976	3	1	0
WHITEHEAD, Robert	Ashington	22.09.36	Fatfield Ath.	Newcastle U.	12.54	1957-59	20		0 (FB)
			TR	Darlington	08.62	1962-63	53		0
WHITEHEAD, William G.	Maltby	06.02.20	Maltby M.C.W.	Q.P.R.	+				(OL)
			TR	Aldershot	08.47	1947	6		1
WHITEHOUSE, Dean	Mexborough	03.10.63	APP	Barnsley	11.81	1983	1	1	0 (M)
WHITEHOUSE, Brian	W.Bromwich	08.09.35	JNRS	W.B.A.	10.52	1955-59	37		13 (CF)Brother of Jim A.
			TR	Norwich C.	03.60	1959-61	41		14
			TR	Wrexham	03.62	1961-63	45		19
			TR	Crystal Palace	11.63	1963-65	82	/	17
			TR	Charlton Ath.	03.66	1965	13	/	1
			TR	Orient	07.66	1966-67	52	/	6
WHITEHOUSE, Jim A.	W.Bromwich	19.09.34	JNRS	W.B.A.	11.54				(IF)
			TR	Reading	06.56	1956-61	202		61
			TR	Coventry C.	08.62	1962-63	46		12
			TR	Millwall	03.64	1963-64	38		13
WHITEHOUSE, Jim E.	W.Bromwich	19.09.24	W.Brom.Haw.	W.B.A.	05.48				(IF)
			TR	Walsall	06.49	1949	19		8
			TR	Rochdale	07.50	1950-51	46		13
			TR	Carlisle U.	10.51	1951-56	198		100
WHITEHURST, Walter	Manchester	07.06.34		Manchester U.	05.52	1955	1		0 (WH)
			TR	Chesterfield	11.56	1956-59	92		2
			TR	Crewe Alex.	07.60	1960	3		1
WHITEHURST, William	Thurnscoe	10.06.59	Mexborough	Hull C.	10.80	1980-83	118	17	20 (F)
WHITELAW, George	Paisley	01.01.37	St.Johnstone	Sunderland	02.58	1957-58	5		0 (CF)S.AMAT.INT.
			TR	Q.P.R.	03.59	1958-59	26		10
			TR	Halifax T.	10.59	1959-60	52		22
			TR	Carlisle U.	02.61	1960-61	34		10
			TR	Stockport Co.	01.62	1961-62	51		18
			TR	Barrow	08.63	1963	7		0
WHITELEY, Albert	Sheffield	13.07.32	Sheffield Wed.(AM)	Orient	11.52	1952-53	23		3 (OL)
WHITELEY, Andy M.	Sowerby Bridge	01.08.61		Halifax T.	08.79	1979-81	20	16	1 (F)
WHITELOCK, Arthur	Stockton	31.07.31	South Bank	Hartlepool U.	12.50	1950	6		0 (RB)
WHITELUM, Cliff	Farnworth	02.12.19	Bentley CW	Sunderland	*	1946-47	41		18 (F)
			TR	Sheffield U.	10.47	1947-48	41		15
WHITESIDE, Arnold	Garstang	06.11.11	Wood Plumpton	Blackburn Rov.	*	1946-48	35		0 (LB)
WHITESIDE, Charles W.	Liverpool	16.08.27		Swindon T.	12.48	1949	1		0
WHITESIDE, Edward K.	Liverpool	11.12.29	Brit.Eckna	Preston N.E.	05.52				(IF)
			Brit.Eckna	Chesterfield	05.53	1953	9		3
			TR	York C.	05.54	1954	8		0
			TR	Bournemouth	07.55	1955	1		0
WHITESIDE, Norman	Belfast	07.05.65	APP	Manchester U.	07.82	1981-83	70	8	19 (F) NI.SCH.INT./NI-15
WHITESIDE, William R.	Belfast	24.09.35	Portadown	Exeter C.	11.55	1955	3		1 (OR)
			Portadown	Scunthorpe U.	08.56	1956	2		0
			TR	Rotherham U.	12.56				
WHITFIELD, George A.	Penrith	10.02.34		Carlisle U.	11.55	1955-56	2		0
WHITFIELD, James	Hull	18.05.19	Humber U.	Grimsby T.	05.46	1946-48	29		7 (IR) d.1984
			TR	Scunthorpe U.	N/L	1950	16		6
			TR	Southport	08.51	1951	12		0
			TR	Scunthorpe U.	02.52	1951-54	103		20
WHITFIELD, John S.	Gateshead	10.06.38		Gateshead	07.59	1959	1		1 (FB)
WHITFIELD, Ken	Durham	24.03.30	Shildon Col.	Wolverhampton W.	12.47	1951-52	10		3 (IF)
			TR	Manchester C.	03.53	1952-53	13		3
			TR	Brighton & H.A.	07.54	1954-58	175		4
			TR	Q.P.R.	07.59	1959-60	19		3
WHITFIELD, Mike	Sunderland	17.10.62	APP	Sunderland	10.80	1982	3	/	0 (F)
			TR	Hartlepool U.	08.83	1983	15	1	0
WHITFIELD, Robert	Bywell	30.06.20	Prudhoe	Charlton Ath.	+				
			TR	Torquay U.	02.47	1946-49	11		1
WHITFIELD, Wilfred	Chesterfield	17.11.16	Bury(*)	Bristol Rov.	*	1946	16		0 (WH)*Birtley
				Torquay U.	08.49	1949-50	37		1
WHITHAM, Jack	Burnley	08.12.46		Sheffield Wed.	11.64	1966-69	54	9	26 (F)E.U23-1
			TR	Liverpool	05.70	1970-71	15	/	7
			TR	Cardiff C.	01.74	1973-74	12	2	3
			TR	Reading	07.75	1975	13	6	3
WHITHAM, Terry	Sheffield	14.08.35	JNRS	Sheffield Wed.	09.52	1956-58	4		0 (FB)
			TR	Chesterfield	06.61	1961-63	66		3
WHITLOCK, Mark	Portsmouth	14.03.61	APP	Southampton	03.79	1981-83	24	1	1 (D)
			L	Grimsby T.	10.82	1982	7	1	0
			L	Aldershot	03.83	1982	14	/	0

Players Names	Birthplace	Date	Previous Club	League Club	Date Signed	Seasons Played	Apps	Sub	Gls	
WHITLOCK, Phil J.	Cardiff	01.50.30		Cardiff C.	02.49					(WH)
			TR	Chester C.	08.50	1950-58	142		3	
WHITNALL, Brian	Doncaster	25.05.33	JNRS	Hull C.	06.50	1954	2		0	(FB)
			TR	Scunthorpe U.	05.56	1956-57	2		0	
			TR	Exeter C.	07.58	1958-61	37		0	
WHITTAKER, Ray H.	Bow	15.01.45	JNRS	Arsenal	05.62					(W)E.YTH.INT./
			TR	Luton T.	03.64	1963-68	169	1	40	E.SCH.INT.
			TR	Colchester U.	07.69	1969-70	41	2	6	
WHITTAKER, Richard	Dublin	10.10.34	St.Mary's BC	Chelsea	05.52	1955-59	48		0	(FB)EI-1/EI'B'-1
			TR	Peterborough U.	09.60	1960-62	82		0	
			TR	Q.P.R.	07.63	1963	17		0	
WHITTAM, Ernest A.	Wealdstone	07.01.11	Reading(+)	Rotherham U.	+	1946	1		0	(IF)*Huddersfield T./
				Leeds U.	12.47					Wolverhampton W./ Bournemouth
WHITTINGHAM, Alf	Altofts	19.06.14	Altofts	Bradford C.	*	1946	25		12	(CH)
			TR	Huddersfield T.	02.47	1946-48	67		17	
			TR	Halifax T.	03.49	1948-49	39		9	
WHITTINGHAM, Steve	Birkenhead	04.02.62	APP	Tranmere Rov.	02.80	1978-80	0	2	0	(F)
WHITTINGTON, Eric	Brighton	18.09.46	Chelsea(AM)	Brighton & H.A.	10.64	1965-67	26	6	8	(CF)E.YTH.INT.
WHITTLE, Alan	Liverpool	10.03.50	APP	Everton	07.65	1965-72	72	2	21	(F)E.U23-1/E.YTH.INT./
			TR	Crystal Palace	12.72	1972-75	103	5	19	E.SCH.INT.
			TR	Orient	09.76	1976-79	47	3	6	
			TR	Bournemouth	N/C	1980	8	1	0	
WHITTLE, Ernie	Durham	25.11.25		Newcastle U.	+					(OL)
			Seaham Col.	Lincoln C.	01.50	1949-53	145		63	
			TR	Workington	03.54	1953-56	112		45	
			TR	Chesterfield	11.56	1956	15		4	
			TR	Bradford P.A.	08.57	1957	18		6	
WHITTLE, Graham	Liverpool	30.05.53	JNRS	Wrexham	07.71	1970-80	288	18	91	(F) Brother of Alan
WHITTLE, Maurice	Wigan	05.07.48	APP	Blackburn Rov.	10.66	1968	5	2	0	(D)
			TR	Oldham Ath.	05.69	1969-76	307	5	39	
			Barrow	Wigan Ath.	03.80	1979-80	21	/	1	
WHITTON, Steve P.	London	04.12.60	APP	Coventry C.	09.78	1979-82	64	10	21	(F)
			TR	West Ham U.	07.83	1983	22	/	5	
WHITWORTH, George A.	Eckington	22.09.27	Stanton I.W.	Liverpool	03.50	1951	9		0	(FB)
WHITWORTH, Harry	Radcliffe	01.12.20		Bury	+	1946-50	112		14	(WH)
			TR	Rochdale	07.51	1951-52	70		9	
			Northwich V.	Southport	09.53	1953	33		6	
			TR	Crewe Alex.	07.54	1954	14		1	
WHITWORTH, Steve	Coalville	20.03.52	APP	Leicester C.	11.69	1970-78	352	1	0	(D)E-7/E.U23-6/●
			TR	Sunderland	03.79	1978-81	83	/	0	E.YTH.INT./E.SCH.INT.
			TR	Bolton W.	10.81	1981-82	67	/	0	
			TR	Mansfield T.	08.83	1983	41	/	0	
WHYKE, Peter	Barnsley	07.09.39	Smithies FC	Barnsley	01.58	1957-60	27		1	(F)
			TR	Rochdale	07.61	1961	5		0	
WHYMARK, Trevor	Burston	04.05.50	Diss T.	Ipswich T.	05.69	1969-78	249	11	74	(F)E.U23-6/E-1
			Sparta Rotherham	Derby Co.	12.79	1979	2	/	0	
			Vancouver	Grimsby T.	12.80	1980-82	83	10	16	
			TR	Southend U.	01.84	1983	19	/	3	
WHYTE, Chris A.	London	02.09.61	APP	Arsenal	06.80	1981-83	82	1	7	(D)E.U'21-4
WHYTE, David	Dunfermline	02.03.59	APP	Leeds U.	03.77	1976	1	1	0	(D)
			Bradford C. (N/C)	Barnsley	11.80					
WHYTE, Frank			Glasgow Celtic	Swindon T.	06.56	1956	7		0	(CH)
WHYTE, J. Archie	Falkirk	17.07.19	Armadale Th.	Barnsley	*	1946-49	91		2	(CH)
			TR	Oldham Ath.	08.50	1950-55	234		0	
WHYTE, James Mc.	Glasgow	19.01.30	T. Lanark	Southend U.	05.54	1954-56	33		8	(IF)
WHYTE, John N.	Calder	07.05.21	Falkirk	Bradford C.	08.50	1950-56	236		2	(FB)
WICKS, Alan H.	Henley	08.02.33		Reading	05.52	1955	1		0	(WH)
WICKS, Peter	Pontefract	14.05.48	APP	Sheffield Wed.	05.65	1964-69	13	/	0	(G)E.YTH.INT.
WICKS, Roger C.	Darlington	19.04.57	Netherfield	Darlington	08.81	1980-82	31	10	4	(F)
WICKS, Stan M.	Reading	11.07.28		Reading	08.48	1949-53	168		1	(CH)E'B'-1/
			TR	Chelsea	01.54	1954-56	71		1	E.F.LGE REP./d.1983
WICKS, Steve J.	Reading	03.10.56	APP	Chelsea	06.74	1974-78	117	1	5	(D)E.YTH.INT./E.U'21-1
			TR	Derby Co.	01.79	1978-79	24	/	0	
			TR	Q.P.R.	09.79	1979-80	73	/	0	
			TR	Crystal Palace	06.81	1981	14	/	1	
			TR	Q.P.R.	03.82	1981-83	54	/	3	
WIDDOP, Dennis	Keighley	14.03.31		Bradford C.	08.54	1954	1		0	
WIDDOWSON, J. Robert	Loughborough	12.09.41		Sheffield U.	07.59	1961-67	7	/	0	(G)
			TR	York C.	06.68	1968-69	30	/	0	
			L	Portsmouth	11.69	1969	4	/	0	

Players Names	Birthplace	Date	Previous Club	League Club	Date Signed	Seasons Played	Apps	Sub	Gls	
WIGG, Ron	Dunmow	18.05.49	Orient(APP)	Ipswich T.	04.67	1967-69	35	2	14	(F)
			TR	Watford	06.70	1970-72	91	6	20	
			TR	Rotherham U.	03.73	1972-74	65	/	22	
			TR	Grimsby T.	01.75	1974-76	51	12	11	
			TR	Barnsley	03.77	1976-77	14	4	5	
			TR	Scunthorpe u.	10.77	1977-78	48	2	6	
WIGGAN, Trenton A.	W. Indies	20.09.62	APP	Sheffield U.	08.80	1979-81	20	4	3	(F)E.SCH.INT.
WIGGETT, David J.	Sheffield	25.05.57	APP	Lincoln C.	06.75	1973-75	4	2	0	(D)d.1978
			TR	Hartlepool U.	10.76	1976-77	54	/	1	
WIGGIN, Ray	Rushall	13.09.42		Walsall	09.62	1962-63	19		6	(CF)
WIGGINTON, Clive A.	Sheffield	18.10.50	APP	Grimsby T.	10.68	1968-74	164	8	6	(D)
			TR	Scunthorpe u.	07.75	1975-76	88	/	7	
			TR	Lincoln C.	09.77	1977-78	60	/	6	
			TR	Grimsby T.	03.79	1978-81	122	/	2	
			L	Doncaster Rov.	03.82	1981	13	/	1	
			TR	Torquay U.	07.82	1982	9	/	0	
			TR	Doncaster Rov.	10.82	1982	18	/	0	
WIGGLESWORTH, Eddie	Burnley	12.02.23	Burnley G.S.O.B.	Burnley	+	1952	1		0	(WH)
WIGHTMAN, John R.	Duns	02.11.12	Huddersfield T.(*)	Blackburn Rov.	*	1946	23		1	(WH)*Scarborough/
			TR	Carlisle U.	08.47	1947	36		0	York C./Bradford P.A./d.1964
WIGLEY, Steve	Ashton-u-Lyne	15.10.61	Curzon Ashton	Nottingham F.	03.81	1982-83	27	12	1	(W)
WIGNALL, David A.	Liverpool	03.04.59	APP	Doncaster Rov.	07.76	1975-77	35	6	1	(M) Brother of Steve
			TR	Colchester U.	09.78					
WIGNALL, Frank	Chorley	21.08.39	Horwich RMI	Everton	05.58	1959-62	33		14	(CF)E-2/E.F.LGE REP.
			TR	Nottingham F.	06.63	1963-67	155	1	47	
			TR	Wolverhampton W.	03.68	1967-68	32	/	15	
			TR	Derby Co.	02.69	1968-71	29	16	15	
			TR	Mansfield T.	11.71	1971-72	50	6	15	
WIGNALL, Mark	Preston	06.12.62	APP	Wigan Ath.	12.80	1980-81	34	/	0	(M)
WIGNALL, Steve	Liverpool	17.09.54	Liverpool(AM)	Doncaster rov.	03.72	1972-76	127	3	1	(D)
			TR	Colchester U.	09.77	1977-83	279	2	22	
WILBERT, George N.	Dunston	11.07.24		Gateshead	+	1947-54	268		92	(CF)
WILBY, Edward	Wolverhampton			Wolverhampton W.	05.46					
			TR	Bradford C.	09.46	1946	3		0	
WILCOCK, Rod W.	Middlesbrough	28.02.56		Crewe Alex.	08.74	1974	2	2	0	(IF)
WILCOCKSON, Harold	Sheffield	23.07.43		Rotherham U.	07.63	1964-67	108	/	3	(FB)
			TR	Doncaster Rov.	02.68	1967-69	75	/	3	
			TR	Sheffield Wed.	12.69	1969-70	40	/	1	
			TR	Doncaster Rov.	05.71	1971-72	36	/	1	
WILCOX, Alex	Lossiemouth	05.11.23	Cowdenbeath	Hartlepool U.	07.51	1951	6		0	(CF)
WILCOX, Anthony	Rotherham	13.06.44		Rotherham U.	10.62					(G)
			TR	Barnsley	08.64	1964	8		0	
WILCOX, Caradoc	Merthyr Tydfil	08.11.23		Cardiff C.	05.49					(HB)
			TR	Newport Co.	07.52	1952-53	30		0	
WILCOX, Edward E.	Bridgend	24.03.27	Oxford C.	W.B.A.	05.48	1948-50	12		3	(CF)
WILCOX, Fred H.	St.Helens	23.10.22		Chester C.	07.47	1946	16		0	
WILCOX, George E.	Treeton	23.08.17	Denaby U.	Derby Co.	*	1946	3		0	(FB)
			TR	Rotherham U.	08.48	1948	1		0	
WILCOX, Ray	Merthyr Tydfil	12.04.21	Treharris	Newport Co.	+	1946-59	489		0	(CH)●
WILCOX, Russ	Hemsworth	25.03.64	APP	Doncaster Rov.	APP	1980	1	/	0	(M)
WILDON, Les E.	Middlesbrough	05.04.24		Hartlepool U.	12.47	1947-54	198		87	(CF)
WILE, John D.	Sherburn	09.03.47	Durham C.	Sunderland	06.66					(D)●
			TR	Peterborough U.	07.67	1967-70	116	2	7	
			TR	W.B.A.	12.70	1970-72	499	1	24	
			TR	Peterborough U.	N/C	1983	32	/	2	
WILEMAN, Richard A.	Breedon	04.10.47		Notts.Co.	07.66	1966	2	/	0	(HB)
WILKES, David A.	Barnsley	10.03.64	APP	Barnsley	03.82	1981-83	14	3	2	(M)
			L	Halifax T.	03.83	1982	4	/	0	
WILKIE, Arthur W.	Woolwich	07.10.42	JNRS	Reading	10.59	1961-67	170		2	(G)
WILKIE, Derek	Browney	27.07.39	JNRS	Middlesbrough	03.57	1959-60	4		0	(CH)
			TR	Hartlepool U.	09.61	1961-63	74		0	
WILKIE, John	Dundee	01.07.47	Ross Co.	Halifax T.	02.73	1972-73	29	8	8	(F)
			Elgin C.	Wigan Ath.	N/L	1978	3	1	0	
WILKIE, Robert	Dundee	07.10.35	Lochee Harp	Tottenham H.	12.56	1956	1		0	(F)
WILKINS, Alan J.	Treherbert	03.10.44		Swansea C.	05.63	1963-64	5		0	(IF)
WILKINS, Dean M.	Hillingdon	12.07.62	APP	Q.P.R.	05.80	1980-82	1	5	0	(M) Brother of Ray/Graham
			TR	Brighton & H.A.	08.83	1983	2	/	0	
			L	Orient	03.84	1983	10	/	0	

Players Names	Birthplace	Date	Previous Club	League Club	Date Signed	Seasons Played	Apps	Sub	Gls	
WILKINS, George E.	Hackney	27.10.17	Hayes	Brentford	*	1946	26		7	(IF)Father of Graham/Ray
			TR	Bradford P.A.	02.47	1946-47	27		7	
			TR	Nottingham F.	12.47	1947-48	24		6	
			TR	Leeds U.	09.49	1949	3		0	
WILKINS, Graham G.	Hillingdon	28.06.55	APP	Chelsea	07.72	1972-81	136	1	1	(D)
			TR	Brentford	07.82	1982-83	36	2	0	
			L	Southend U.	03.84	1983	3	/	0	
WILKINS, Ken	Salford	24.10.28		Southampton	10.49	1950	2		0	(F)
			TR	Exeter C.	10.51	1951	3		0	
			TR	Southampton	07.52	1952	1		0	
			TR	Fulham	07.53					
WILKINS, Len	Southampton	20.09.25	Cunliffe-Owen	Southampton	+	1948-57	259		2	(WH)
WILKINS, Len H.J.	Dublin	12.08.20	Guildford C.	Brighton & H.A.	07.50	1948-50	44		2	(FB)
WILKINS, Mike J.	Leeds	06.05.42	JNRS	Bradford C.	09.59	1959	1		0	(F)
WILKINS, Paul	Hackney	20.03.64	Tottenham H.(APP)	Crystal Palace	01.82	1981-83	9	4	3	(F)
WILKINS, Ray C.	Hillingdon	14.09.56	APP	Chelsea	10.73	1973-78	176	3	30	(M)E-59/E.U21-1●
			TR	Manchester U.	08.79	1979-83	158	2	7	E.U23-2/E.F.LGE REP.
WILKINS, Ray J.H.	Crossley	16.08.28	Moira U.	Derby Co.	01.50	1949-53	30		11	(CF)
			Boston U.	Wrexham	05.57	1957	3		1	
WILKINS, Ron	Treherbert	21.12.23	Gwynfi BC	Newport CO.	+	1946	1		0	(IL)
WILKINSON, Alan	Middlewich	05.06.35	Middlewich	Crewe Alex.	AM	1955	1		0	(IF)
WILKINSON, Albert	Barnsley	03.11.28		Bradford C.	AM	1950	2		0	(W)
			Denaby U.	Halifax T.	07.52	1952	14		2	
			TR	Rotherham U.	07.53					
			TR	Chesterfield	06.54					
WILKINSON, Barry J.	Lincoln	19.07.42	Ruston Spts.	Lincoln C.	12.63	1962-63	6		3	(CF)
WILKINSON, David L.	Sunderland	28.05.28		Blackburn Rov.	07.48	1948	1		0	(F)
			TR	Bournemouth	06.50	1950-51	8		3	
WILKINSON, Derek	Stalybridge	04.06.35	Dunkinfield	Sheffield Wed.	11.53	1954-64	212		54	(OR)E.F.LGE REP.
WILKINSON, Eric	Sheffield	06.03.31		Bradford C.	01.51					
			TR	Sheffield U.	08.53					
			TR	Bournemouth	07.55	1955	4		0	
WILKINSON, Eric	Stalybridge	04.06.35	Dunkinfield	Sheffield Wed.	03.58	1958	1		0	(F)Brother of Derek
WILKINSON, Ernest S.	Chesterfield	13.02.47	APP	Arsenal	02.64					(HB)
			TR	Exeter C.	06.66	1966-67	59	1	0	
			L	Rochdale	03.68	1967	9	/	0	
WILKINSON, G. Barry	B.Acukalnd	16.06.35	W.Auckland	Liverpool	06.54	1953-59	78		0	(HB)E.YTH.INT.
			Bangor C.	Tranmere Rov.	08.63	1963	3		0	
WILKINSON, Graham J.	Hull	21.10.34	JNRS	Hull C.	09.52	1958-59	3		0	(HB)
WILKINSON, Harry S.	Sunderland	20.03.26		Chelsea	06.46					(WH)
			TR	Exeter C.	05.50	1950	1		0	
			TR	Colchester U.	08.51	1952	1		0	
WILKINSON, Herbert	Sunderland	02.08.22		Lincoln C.	+	1946-50	39		0	.
WILKINSON, Howard	Sheffield	13.11.43	Sheffield U.(AM)	Sheffield Wed.	06.62	1964-65	22	/	3	(F)
			TR	Brighton & H.A.	07.66	1966-70	116	13	19	
WILKINSON, John	Middlewich	17.09.31	Witton A.	Arsenal	10.53	1954	1		0	(CF)Brother of Alan
			TR	Sheffield U.	03.56	1955-56	29		16	
			TR	Port Vale	06.57	1957-59	83		38	
			TR	Exeter C.	10.59	1959-60	49		25	
WILKINSON, John	Worksop	01.04.49	APP	Grimsby T.	04.66	1965-67	8	1	0	(FB)
WILKINSON, Joseph	Seaham	08.12.34	W.Auckland	Burnley	12.55					(G)
			TR	Bradford C.	03.59	1958-59	17		0	
			TR	Hartlepool U.	02.60	1959-61	74		0	
WILKINSON, Ken	Gateshead	09.05.24	JNRS	Huddersfield T.	+					
			TR	Hartlepool U.	04.47	1946-48	53		5	
WILKINSON, Neil	Blackburn	16.02.55	APP	Blackburn Rov.	02.73	1972-76	27	3	0	(D)
			S. Africa	Port Vale	07.78	1978	7	/	0	
			TR	Crewe Alex.	10.78	1978-80	68	7	0	
WILKINSON, Norman	Tantobie	09.06.10	Huddersfield T.(*)	Stoke C.	*	1948-51	41		0	(G)*Tanfield Lea
WILKINSON, Norman F.	Alnwick	16.02.31		Hull C.	AM	1953	8		3	(CF)
			TR	York C.	05.54	1954-65	354		125	
WILKINSON, Paul	Louth	30.10.64	APP	Grimsby T.	11.82	1982-83	39	2	13	(F)
WILKINSON, Paul I.	Themelthorpe	19.04.52	APP	Norwich C.	04.70					(F)
			L	Plymouth Arg.	01.71	1970	2	/	0	
WILKINSON, Roy J.	Hindley Green	17.09.41	JNRS	Bolton W.	02.60	1960-61	3		0	(HB)
WILKINSON, Steve J.	Halifax	06.08.46	JNRS	Halifax T.	AM	1963	2		0	(G)
WILKINSON, Tom	Blackhall	08.05.31		Hartlepool U.	09.52	1953-57	22		0	(WH)
WILKINSON, William	Stockton	24.03.43	Middlesbrough(AM)	Hull C.	05.62	1962-72	208	15	31	(M)
			TR	Rotherham U.	11.72	1972-73	25	1	0	
			Tacoma Tide	Southport	N/C	1976	10	/	0	

Players Names	Birthplace	Date	Previous Club	League Club	Date Signed	Seasons Played	Career Record Apps	Sub	Gls	
WILKS, Alan	London	05.10.46	APP	Chelsea	08.64					(CF)
			TR	Q.P.R.	05.65	1966-70	44	5	14	
			TR	Gillingham	07.71	1971-75	138	13	29	
WILLARD, Cecil T.	Chichester	16.01.24	Chichester	Brighton & H.A.	05.47	1946-52	190		23	(WH)
			TR	Crystal Palace	07.53	1953-54	46		5	
WILLDER, Fred	Lytham St. Annes	20.03.44	JNRS	Blackpool	05.62					(F)E.YTH.INT.
			TR	Preston & N.E.	08.63					
			TR	Chester C.	09.63	1964-65	1	1	0	
WILLDIG, Pat G.	Stoke	05.06.32	Stoke C.(AM)	Port Vale	05.50	1955	2		0	(F)
WILLEMSE, Stan B.	Brighton	23.08.24	JNRS	Brighton & H.A.	06.46	1946-48	91		3	(LB)E'B'-1/
			TR	Chelsea	07.49	1949-55	198		2	E.F.LGE REP./E.SCH.INT.
			TR	Orient	06.56	1956-57	59		2	
WILLETT, Ernie	Burslem	27.07.19	Stoke C.(AM)	Port Vale	+	1946	1		0	(CH)
WILLETT, Len	Ruabon	17.09.40		Wrexham	05.58	1959	1		0	(HB)W.SCH.INT.
WILLETTS, Joe	Shotton	12.07.24		Hartlepool U.	+	1946-55	239		20	(FB)
WILLEY, Alan E.	Exeter	16.09.41	Bridgwater	Oxford U.	07.62	1962-65	85	1	23	(IF)
			TR	Millwall	03.66	1965	6	/	0	
WILLEY, Alan S.	Houghton-le-Spring	18.10.56	APP	Middlesbrough	09.74	1974-77	27	23	7	(D)
WILLIAMS, A. Everton	Blackrod	01.02.57	JNRS	Wrexham	07.63	1975	1	1	0	(F)
WILLIAMS, Adrian D.	Bristol	04.08.43	APP	Bristol C.	08.60	1960	4		0	(F)E.YTH.INT./
			TR	Exeter C.	07.63					E.SCH.INT.
WILLIAMS, Alan	Bristol	03.06.38	JNRS	Bristol C.	09.55	1956-60	132		2	(CH)●
			TR	Oldham Ath.	06.61	1961-64	172		9	
			TR	Watford	07.65	1965-66	43	/	0	
			TR	Newport Co.	11.66	1966-68	63	/	3	
			TR	Swansea C.	10.68	1968-71	142	4	7	
WILLIAMS, Aled A.	Whitford	14.06.33	Rhyl	Burnley	10.52					(HB)
			TR	Chester C.	07.57	1957	33		1	
WILLIAMS, Alex	Manchester	13.11.61	APP	Manchester C.	11.79	1980-83	64	/	0	(G)E.YTH.INT.
WILLIAMS, Alf S.	S.Africa	01.05.19	Aberdeen	Plymouth Arg.	08.49	1949	35		4	(F)
WILLIAMS, Alvan	Penmon	21.11.32	Stalybridge	Bury	12.54	1955	2		1	(HB)
			TR	Wrexham	06.56	1956	13		6	
			TR	Bradford P.A.	06.57	1957-59	92		21	
			TR	Exeter C.	08.60	1960	18		1	
WILLIAMS, Ben F.	Lincoln	14.04.51	Lincoln U.	Grimsby T.	07.69	1969	2	/	0	(F)
WILLIAMS, Bert F.	Bilston	31.01.20	Walsall(*)	Wolverhampton W.	+	1946-56	381		0	(G)E-24/E'B'-1/● E.F.LGE REP.
WILLIAMS, Brian	Salford	05.11.55	APP	Bury	04.73	1971-76	148	11	19	(M)
			TR	Q.P.R.	07.77	1977	9	10	0	
			TR	Swindon T.	06.78	1978-80	89	10	8	
			TR	Bristol Rov.	07.81	1981-83	126	/	16	
WILLIAMS, Ceri	Toryrefail	16.10.65	JNRS	Newport Co.	06.83	1982-83	16	7	2	(F)
WILLIAMS, Charlie A.	Barnsley	23.12.28	Upton Col.	Doncaster Rov.	10.48	1949-58	158		1	(CH)Famous comedian
WILLIAMS, Chris R.	Brecon	25.12.55	Talgarth	Cardiff C.	12.77	1977	3	/	0	(F)
WILLIAMS, Clarence	Wardley	13.01.33	Doncaster Rov.(AM)	Grimsby T.	03.53	1952-59	189		0	(G)
			TR	Barnsley	03.60	1960-61	23		0	
WILLIAMS, Cyril E.	Bristol	17.11.21	JNRS	Bristol C.	+	1946-47	78		27	(IF)
			TR	W.B.A.	06.48	1948-50	71		19	
			TR	Bristol C.	08.51	1951-57	218		41	
WILLIAMS, D. Geraint	Cwmparc	05.01.62	APP	Bristol Rov.	01.80	1980-83	110	3	8	(M) W.YTH.INT.
WILLIAMS, D. Roley	Swansea	10.07.27	Milford Haven	Cardiff C.	02.49	1948-55	138		19	(IF)
			TR	Northampton T.	03.56	1955-56	15		0	
WILLIAMS, Danny T.	Rotherham	20.11.24	Silverwood Col.	Rotherham U.	+	1946-59	459		19	(WH)●
WILLIAMS, Darwell	Llanelli	04.11.26	Lougher FC	Swansea C.	05.46	1950-54	130		4	(WH)
WILLIAMS, David	Shafton	25.02.46		Doncaster Rov.	07.64	1964	1		0	(HB)
WILLIAMS, David	Sheffield	07.10.31	Beighton MW	Grimsby T.	03.53	1953	5		0	(WH)
WILLIAMS, David M.	Cardiff	11.03.55	Clifton Ath.	Bristol Rov.	12.75	1975-83	308	7	60	(M)W.U23-1 W.YTH.INT.
WILLIAMS, David S.	Newport	01.03.42	Nash.U.	Newport Co.	10.60	1960-72	303	4	2	(WH)
WILLIAMS, Derek	Mold	15.06.34	Mold Alex	Manchester C.	AM	1951	1		0	(G)W.AMAT.INT.
			Mold Alex	Wrexham	AM	1954	12		0	
			Mold Alex	Oldham Ath.	09.56	1956	28		0	
WILLIAMS, Derek	Wardley	28.01.37	Doncaster YMCA	Grimsby T.	01.57	1956-61	44		19	(F)
			TR	Bradford P.A.	08.62	1962	19		8	
WILLIAMS, Derek H.	Little Sutton	09.12.22	Little Sutton	Chester C.	+	1946	2		0	(HB)
				Oldham Ath.	08.51	1951	1		0	
WILLIAMS, Derek O.	Chirk	03.09.49	Oswestry	Shrewsbury T.	10.69	1969	1	/	0	(G)

Players Names	Birthplace	Date	Previous Club	League Club	Date Signed	Seasons Played	Career Record Apps	Sub	Gls	
WILLIAMS, Edgar	Sheffield	20.05.19		Rotherham U.	05.46					(G)
			TR	Nottingham F.	05.47					
			TR	Northampton T.	06.48	1948	3		0	
WILLIAMS, Edward M.L.	Chester	28.11.35	Everton(AM)	Aston Villa	08.53					
			TR	Wrexham	08.54	1954	1		0	
WILLIAMS, Elfyn	Barmouth	25.09.39	Portmadoc	Wrexham	03.58	1958	1		0	(F)
			TR	Crystal Palace	07.59					
WILLIAMS, Emlyn	Maesteg	15.01.12	Barnsley(*)	Preston N.E.	*	1946-47	62		0	
			TR	Barnsley	04.48	1947-48	17		0	
			TR	Accrington St.	12.48	1948	15		0	
WILLIAMS, Eric	Manchester	10.07.21	Brindle Hth.L.C.	Manchester C.	+	1946-49	38		0	(FB)
			Mossley	Halifax T.	10.51	1951-53	111		0	
WILLIAMS, Evan M.	Swansea	12.10.32	Penllegaer	Cardiff C.	03.50					(LB)
			TR	Exeter C.	05.54	1954	1		0	
			TR	Aldershot	07.55					
WILLIAMS, Evan S.	Dumbarton	15.07.43	T.Lanark	Wolverhampton W.	03.66	1967	13	/	0	(G)
			L	Aston Villa	08.69	1969	12	/	0	
WILLIAMS, Frank	Halifax	23.05.21	Boothstown	Halifax T.	AM	1947	4		0	(OL)
WILLIAMS, Gareth C.	London	30.10.41		Cardiff C.	06.61	1962-67	161	/	14	(WH)
			TR	Bolton W.	10.67	1967-70	108	1	11	
			TR	Bury	10.71	1971-72	39	3	4	
WILLIAMS, Gary	Wolverhampton	17.06.60	APP	Aston Villa	06.78	1978-83	146	5	0	(D)
			L	Walsall	03.80	1979	9	/	0	
WILLIAMS, Gary	Nantwich	14.05.59	JNRS	Tranmere Rov.	N/C	1976	1	/	0	(D)
			Djurgaarden	Blackpool	08.80	1980	30	1	2	
			TR	Swindon T.	08.81	1981	37	1	3	
			TR	Tranmere Rov.	02.83	1982-83	50	/	3	
WILLIAMS, Gary A.	Bristol	08.06.63	APP	Bristol C.	08.80	1980-83	98	2	1	(D)
WILLIAMS, Gary P.	Liverpool	08.03.54	Marine	Preston N.E.	04.72	1971-76	107	5	2	(D)
			TR	Brighton & H.A.	07.77	1977-81	158	/	7	
			TR	Crystal Palace	07.82	1982	10	/	0	
WILLIAMS, George	Ynysddu	19.05.14	Aldershot(*)	Millwall	*	1946	14		0	(FB)*Charlton Ath.
WILLIAMS, George R.	Wardley	18.11.32	JNRS	Rotherham U.	07.50	1953	4		2	(F)
			TR	Sheffield U.	05.54					
			Wisbech	Bradford C.	06.56	1956	6		0	
			TR	Mansfield T.	07.57	1957-61	154		5	
WILLIAMS, Gilbert	W.Bromwich	12.01.25	Harvills Hearts	W.B.A.	+	1947	7		0	(WH)
WILLIAMS, Glyn J.J.	Caerau	03.11.18	Caerau	Cardiff C.	08.46	1946-52	144		0	(RB)W-1
WILLIAMS, Gordon	Newcastle	22.02.29		Sheffield U.	09.49	1949	5		0	
			TR	Darlington	06.50	1950	5		1	
WILLIAMS, Gordon G.	Swindon	19.06.25		Swindon T.	+	1946-56	127		13	(WH)
WILLIAMS, Graham E.	Hellan	02.04.38	Rhyl	W.B.A.	04.55	1955-69	308	7	10	(LB)W-26/W.U23-2
WILLIAMS, Graham G.	Wrexham	31.12.36	Oswestry	Bradford C.	08.55	1955	8		2	(OL)W-5/
			TR	Everton	03.56	1955-58	31		6	W.U23-1/W.SCH.INT.
			TR	Swansea C.	02.59	1958-61	89		20	
			TR	Wrexham	07.64	1964	24		6	
			TR	Tranmere Rov.	08.66	1966-67	73	/	12	
			TR	Port Vale	07.68	1968	21	2	1	
WILLIAMS, Grenville R.	Swansea	30.06.21		Arsenal	+					
			TR	Norwich C.	06.46	1946-47	41		0	
			TR	Newport Co.	04.49	1949	5		0	
WILLIAMS, Harold	Britton Ferry	17.06.24	Ferry Ath.	Newport Co.	11.46	1946-48	75		16	(OR)W-4
			TR	Leeds U.	06.49	1949-55	209		32	
			TR	Newport Co.	03.57	1956	10		0	
			TR	Bradford P.A.	07.57	1957	15		0	
WILLIAMS, Henry G.	Salford	24.02.29		Manchester U.	05.49					(IF)
			Witton A.	West Ham U.	04.51	1951	5		1	
			TR	Bury	06.53	1953	2		0	
			TR	Swindon T.	06.54	1954	16		7	
WILLIAMS, Herbert J.	Swansea	06.10.40	JNRS	Swansea C.	05.58	1958-74	489	26	104	(WH)W-3/W.U23-5/● W.SCH.INT.
WILLIAMS, Herbert J.	Cwmbran	19.06.25	Westons	Newport Co.	AM	1948	2		1	(OL)W.AMAT.INT.
WILLIAMS, Horace O.	Maltby	04.10.21		Rotherham U.	+	1946-53	210		12	(HB)
WILLIAMS, Ivor	Scunthorpe	29.05.35		Scunthorpe U.	08.59	1959	8		0	(G)
WILLIAMS, James L.	Wolverhampton	08.05.53	Worcester C.	Walsall	03.79	1978-79	29	9	2	(F)
WILLIAMS, Jeff B.	Salford	01.01.33		Oldham Ath.	06.51	1951	1			
WILLIAMS, Jeremy S.	Didcot	24.03.60	APP	Reading	03.78	1976-83	168	17	9	(F)
WILLIAMS, John	Doncaster	14.04.20		Leeds U.	12.48	1948	1		0	
WILLIAMS, John	Greenock	21.11.25		Blackburn Rov.	06.47					
			TR	Southport	07.48	1948	2		0	
WILLIAMS, John D.	Pwllheli	22.08.65	JNRS	Wrexham	N/C	1982	0	1	0	

Players Names	Birthplace	Date	Previous Club	League Club	Date Signed	Seasons Played	Apps	Sub	Gls	
WILLIAMS, John D.	Treleurs	15.05.35		Everton	05.56					(F)
			TR	Crewe Alex.	06.57	1957	5		0	
WILLIAMS, John L.	Rhymney	27.01.36		Cardiff C.	05.53					(HB)
			TR	Plymouth Arg.	07.58	1958-61	34		0	
			TR	Torquay U.	06.62	1962-64	43		0	
WILLIAMS, John R.	Tottenham	26.03.47	APP	Watford	10.64	1964-74	371	4	6	(D)
			TR	Colchester U.	07.75	1975-77	107	1	1	
WILLIAMS, John S.J.	Plymouth	16.08.35	JNRS	Plymouth Arg.	10.52	1955-65	411	1	47	(WH)
			TR	Bristol Rov.	12.66	1966-68	67	3	11	
			TR	Plymouth Arg.	07.69					
WILLIAMS, John W.				Tranmere Rov.	AM	1946	1		0	
WILLIAMS, Keith D.	Burntwood	12.04.57	APP	Aston Villa	04.75					(M)
			TR	Northampton T.	02.77	1976-80	128	3	6	
			TR	Bournemouth	08.81	1981-83	78	3	1	
WILLIAMS, Keith M.	Liverpool	21.09.52	APP	Everton	07.70					(G)
			TR	Wrexham	08.73	1974	2	/	0	
WILLIAMS, Ken				Watford	01.47	1946	2		0	
WILLIAMS, Ken	Doncaster	07.01.27		Rotherham U.	09.48	1949	3		0	(FB)
			TR	York C.	07.51	1953	1		0	
WILLIAMS, Leslie	Thurcroft	27.03.35		Sheffield Wed.	07.53	1955-56	11		0	(G)
			TR	Swindon T.	01.57					
			TR	Rotherham U.	01.58					
WILLIAMS, Mark	Bangor	01.12.56		Wrexham	06.75	1975-77	7	/	0	(M)
WILLIAMS, Mark	Hereford	17.09.57	Arsenal(APP)	Newport Co.	08.76	1976-78	59	9	9	(M)
WILLIAMS, Mike	Mancot	06.02.65	APP	Chester C.	02.83	1981-83	30	4	3	(M)
WILLIAMS, Mike J.	Hull	23.10.44	APP	Hull C.	10.62	1962-65	88	/	0	(G)
			TR	Aldershot	07.66					
			TR	Workington	07.68	1968-69	15	/	0	
			TR	Scunthorpe U.	07.70	1970-73	28	/	0	
WILLIAMS, Mostyn	Cymfelinfach	02.10.28	Ynysddu Welf.	Newport Co.	12.49	1949-51	28		0	(RB)
WILLIAMS, Nigel J.	Canterbury	29.07.54	APP	Wolverhampton W.	08.72	1974-75	11	/	0	(M)
			TR	Gillingham	07.76	1976-78	51	2	1	
WILLIAMS, Oshor J.	Stockton	21.04.58	Middlesbrough(APP)	Manchester U.	08.76					(M)
			Gateshead	Southampton	03.78	1978-79	4	2	0	
			TR	Exeter C.	08.78	1978	2	1	0	
			TR	Stockport Co.	08.79	1979-83	179	1	24	
WILLIAMS, Paul J.	Lambeth	16.11.62	APP	Chelsea	07.80	1982	1	/	0	(D)
WILLIAMS, Paul S.	Newton Abbot	20.02.65	Ottery St. Mary	Bristol C.	03.83	1982-83	16	3	1	(F)
WILLIAMS, Peter J.	Nottingham	21.10.31	Sth.Normanton	Derby Co.	08.52	1952	2		0	
			Boston U.	Chesterfield	07.55	1955	13		3	
WILLIAMS, Peter S.H.	Plymouth	18.12.38		Exeter C.	04.60	1960	1		0	(HB)
WILLIAMS, Peter W.	Wrexham	17.05.60	JNRS	Wrexham	07.78	1978-80	4	1	1	(F)
WILLIAMS, Phil D.	Swansea	24.11.66	APP	Swansea C.	APP	1983	0	1	0	
WILLIAMS, Phil J.	Swansea	07.02.63	Arsenal (APP)	Blackpool	11.80					(M)W.SCH.INT.
			USA	Crewe Alex.	08.81	1981	39	/	3	
			TR	Wigan Ath.	08.82	1982-83	1	2	0	
			L	Chester C.	09.83	1983	6	1	1	
			TR	Crewe Alex.	12.83	1983	14	6	3	
WILLIAMS, Philip L.	Birkenhead	05.04.58	JNRS	Chester C.	07.76	1976	1	/	0	(F)
WILLIAMS, R. Brian	Liverpool	04.10.27	Sth.Liverpool	Liverpool	+	1948-52	31		5	(WH)
			TR	Crewe Alex.	05.54	1954-57	144		5	
WILLIAMS, R. Frank	Overton	12.03.17		Wrexham	08.46	1946-47	35		0	(G) d.1978
			TR	Halifax T.	08.48					
WILLIAMS, R.A. Keith	Eastham	14.01.37	JNRS	Everton	03.54					(F)
			TR	Tranmere Rov.	05.57	1957-60	161		88	
			TR	Plymouth Arg.	06.61	1961	10		4	
			TR	Bristol Rov.	01.62	1961-62	49		18	
WILLIAMS, Ray	Stoke	30.08.46	Stafford Rgrs.	Port Vale	08.72	1972-76	165	8	39	(F)
WILLIAMS, Ray	Wrexham	01.05.31	Holyhead	Wrexham	05.51	1951	12		0	(FB)
WILLIAMS, Reg F.	Watford	28.01.22	Watford(AM)	Chelsea	+	1946-51	58		13	(IF)
WILLIAMS, Robert F.	Chester	24.11.32	JNRS	New Brighton	AM	1949	1		0	(F)
				Chester C.	05.56	1951-59	37		3	
WILLIAMS, Robert G.	Bristol	17.02.40	JNRS	Bristol C.	05.58	1958-64	190		76	(IF)
			TR	Rotherham U.	02.65	1964-66	47	/	12	
			TR	Bristol Rov.	03.67	1966-68	27	2	5	
			TR	Reading	08.69	1969-70	60	3	20	
WILLIAMS, Robert R.	Liverpool	25.10.27	JNRS	Liverpool	+					
			TR	Wrexham	06.51	1951	7	/		
			TR	Shrewsbury T.	10.51	1951	5		0	
WILLIAMS, Ron A.	Swansea	12.09.49	JNRS	Swansea C.	09.68	1968	7	2	1	(FB)

Players Names	Birthplace	Date	Previous Club	League Club	Date Signed	Seasons Played	Career Record Apps	Sub	Gls	
WILLIAMS, Royston B.	Hereford	03.03.32	Hereford U.	Southampton	11.52	1952-54	44		7	(IF)
WILLIAMS, Sid F.	Bristol	21.12.19		Bristol C.	07.46	1946-51	100		12	(OR)
WILLIAMS, Steve C.	London	12.07.58	APP	Southampton	09.74	1975-83	263	1	17	(M)E.U21-14/E-3
WILLIAMS, Steve J.	Barry	27.04.63	APP	Bristol Rov.	04.81	1980	8	/	1	(F)W.YTH.INT.
WILLIAMS, Steve M.	Swansea	05.11.54		Swansea C.	03.76	1975	7	3	1	(OL)
WILLIAMS, Stuart G.	Wrexham	09.07.30	Victoria YC	Wrexham	AM	1947-49	6		0	(FB)W-43●
			TR	W.B.A.	02.51	1951-62	226		6	
			TR	Southampton	09.62	1962-65	147	2	3	
WILLIAMS, Thomas A.	Liverpool	01.08.29	JNRS	Tranmere Rov.	11.48	1946-56	53		2	(WH) d.1979
			TR	Southport	08.58	1958	17		0	
WILLIAMS, Thomas J.	London	10.02.35	Carshalton	Colchester U.	09.56	1956-60	151		30	(W)
			TR	Watford	06.61	1961	12		6	
WILLIAMS, Tommy E.	Leicester	18.12.57	APP	Leicester C.	06.76	1977-83	201	5	10	(D)
WILLIAMS, W. John	Liverpool	03.10.60	JNRS	Tranmere Rov.	10.79	1978-83	124	6	9	(D)
WILLIAMS, W. Ray	Bebbington	30.12.30		Tranmere Rov.	02.49	1951-58	195		12	(WH)
WILLIAMS, Wayne	Telford	17.11.63	APP	Shrewsbury T.	11.81	1982-83	82	/	4	(D)
WILLIAMS, William H.J.	Manchester	24.09.25		Bury	01.47	1946	1		0	
			TR	Rochdale	08.49	1949	8		3	
			TR	Aldershot	06.50	1950	6		4	
WILLIAMS, William R.	Littleborough	07.10.60	Ashe Labs.	Rochdale	08.82	1981-83	65	5	2	(D)
WILLIAMS, William T.	Esher	23.08.42	JNRS	Portsmouth	06.60	1960	3		0	(CH)E.YTH.INT./
			TR	Q.P.R.	07.61	1961-62	45		0	E.SCH.INT.
			TR	W.B.A.	06.63	1964	1		0	
			TR	Mansfield T.	01.66	1965-67	47	2	0	
			TR	Gillingham	09.67	1967-71	169	2	8	
WILLIAMSON, Arthur H.	Ardblae	26.07.30	Clyde	Southend U.	05.55	1955-61	269		2	(FB)
WILLIAMSON, Brian W.	Blythe	06.10.39	Seaton Delavel	Gateshead	10.58	1958-59	55		0	(G)
			TR	Crewe Alex.	07.60	1960-62	55		0	
			TR	Leeds U.	12.62	1962-64	5		0	
			TR	Nottingham F.	02.66	1967-68	19	/	0	
			L	Leicester C.	08.67	1967	6	/	0	
			TR	Fulham	11.68	1968-69	12	/	0	
WILLIAMSON, Charles	Glasgow	12.04.56	JNRS	Bristol C.	07.74					(D)
			L	Torquay U.	03.77	1976	5	/	0	
WILLIAMSON, Charles H.	Sheffield	16.03.62	APP	Sheffield Wed.	02.80	1979-83	61	1	1	(D)
			L	Lincoln C.	01.84	1983	5	/	0	
WILLIAMSON, Colin J.	Gretna Green	25.10.57	Liverpool(APP)	Workington	N.C.	1976	11	4	2	(OL)
WILLIAMSON, George	Newcastle	13.09.25		Middlesbrough	+					(IF)
			TR	Chester C.	07.47	1947-49	75		4	
			TR	Bradford C.	06.50	1950-56	222		31	
WILLIAMSON, Ian J.	Glasgow	14.04.39	Falkirk	Norwich C.	05.58	1958	10		1	(F)
			TR	Bradford P.A.	06.62	1962	17		0	
WILLIAMSON, John	Manchester	08.05.29	Newton Heath	Manchester C.	08.49	1949-54	59		18	(CF)
			TR	Blackburn Rov.	03.56	1955-56	9		3	
WILLIAMSON, Ken	Norton	07.08.28	B.Auckland	Darlington	AM	1952	13		3	(IF)
WILLIAMSON, Mike	Ashbourne	30.05.42	Ashbourne	Derby Co.	08.61	1961-63	12		0	(F)
			TR	Gillingham	07.64	1965	1	/	0	
WILLIAMSON, Phil J.	Macclesfield	19.09.62	APP	Blackburn Rov.	09.80	1981	0	1	0	(D)
WILLIAMSON, Robert	Midlothian	06.12.33	St.Mirren	Barnsley	08.63	1963-64	46		0	(G)
			TR	Leeds U.	06.65					
			TR	Rochdale	07.66	1966-67	36	/	0	
WILLIAMSON, Stuart H.	Seacombe	07.04.26		Tranmere Rov.	+	1946-52	96		23	(OL)
			TR	Swindon T.	06.53	1953-54	17		0	
WILLIAMSON, Tom	Salford	16.03.13	Northwich	Oldham Ath.	*	1946	36		0	(CH)
WILLINGHAM, C. Ken	Sheffield	01.12.12	Huddersfield T.(*)	Sunderland	+	1946	14		0	(CH)*Worksop T./E-12/
			TR	Leeds U.	03.47	1946-47	34		0	E.F.LGE REP./d.1975
WILLIS, Arthur	Denaby	02.02.20	Finchley	Tottenham H.	+	1946-53	144		1	(FB)E-1
			TR	Swansea C.	09.54	1954-57	95		0	
WILLIS, George	Newcastle	09.11.26		Wolverhampton W.	+					(IR)
			TR	Brighton & H.A.	02.48	1947-48	28		12	
			TR	Plymouth Arg.	05.49	1949-55	56		15	
			TR	Exeter C.	03.56	1955-56	25		2	
WILLIS, Graham	Bradwell	20.10.46	APP	Norwich C.	10.64	1964	1		0	(FB)
WILLIS, J. George	Shotton	25.07.33	Evenwood T.	Leeds U.	03.53	1953	3		0	(F)
			TR	Hartlepool U.	11.54	1954-58	25		6	
WILLIS, John L.	Boldon	28.05.34		Blackburn Rov.	08.54	1955	1		0	
			TR	Accrington St.	07.57					
			Mossley	Aston Villa	08.58	1958	1		0	

Players Names	Birthplace	Date	Previous Club	League Club	Date Signed	Seasons Played	Career Record Apps	Sub	Gls	
WILLIS, Ron I.	Romford	27.12.47	Coventry C.(AM)	Orient	01.66	1966-67	45	/	0	(G)E.YTH.INT.
			TR	Charlton Ath.	10.67	1967	1	/	0	
			L	Brentford	09.68	1968	1	/	0	
			TR	Colchester U.	10.68	1968-69	6	/	0	
WILLS, Gordon F.	W. Bromwich	24.04.32	W.B.A.(AM)	Wolverhampton W.	12.51					(OL)
			TR	Notts.Co.	08.53	1953-57	154		47	
			TR	Leicester C.	05.58	1958-61	111		30	
			TR	Walsall	06.62	1962-63	35		1	
WILLS, Len E.	London	08.11.27	Eton Manor	Arsenal	10.49	1953-60	181		4	(FB)
WILLSHAW, George J.	London	18.10.12	Bristol C.(*)	Orient	+	1946	12		2	(OL)*Walthamstow/Southend U.
WILMOT, Rhys J.	Newport	21.02.62	APP	Arsenal	02.80					(G)W.U'21-4/W.SCH.INT
			L	Hereford U.	03.83	1982	9	/	0	
WILMOTT, Gordon A.	Brinsley	26.05.29		Birmingham C.	05.47					(CH)
			TR	Stockport Co.	06.48	1948-58	206		1	
			TR	Crewe Alex.	03.59	1958-60	54		0	
WILSHAW, Dennis	Stoke	11.03.26	Packmoor BC	Wolverhampton W.	+	1948-57	210		105	(IF)E-12/E'B'-2
			L	Walsall	05.46	1946-48	74		27	
			TR	Stoke C.	12.57	1957-60	94		40	
WILSHAW, Steve E.	Stoke	11.01.59	APP	Stoke C.	01.77					(M)
			TR	Crewe Alex.	08.78	1978	20	2	1	
WILSON, Alan	Liverpool	17.11.52	APP	Everton	07.70	1971-72	2	/	0	(M)
			TR	Southport	07.75	1975-77	134	/	13	
			TR	Torquay U.	06.78	1978	38	4	2	
WILSON, Alan A.	Bathgate	10.01.45	Partick Th.	Scunthorpe U.	07.64					(G)
			TR	Mansfield T.	08.66	1966	5	/	0	
WILSON, Albert	Rotherham	28.01.15	Mansfield T.(*)	Crystal Palace	*					(F)
			TR	Rotherham U.	06.46	1946	38		19	
			TR	Grimsby T.	07.47	1947	17		1	
WILSON, Alex	Buckie	29.10.33	JNRS	Portsmouth	11.50	1951-66	348	4	4	(FB)S-1
WILSON, Alex	Stenhousemuir	03.07.38	Clyde	Rotherham U.	07.61	1961	5		0	(W)
WILSON, Ambrose M.	Lurgan	10.10.24	Glenavon	Swansea C.	09.50	1950	1		0	(FB)
WILSON, Andrew	Rotherham	27.09.40		Sheffield U.	01.60	1959-60	4		0	(W)
			TR	Scunthorpe U.	06.61	1961-64	112		14	
			TR	Doncaster Rov.	07.65	1965	20	1	0	
			TR	Chesterfield	07.66	1966-67	70	2	13	
			TR	Aldershot	07.68	1968	19	1	1	
WILSON, Andrew P.	Maltby	13.10.47		Rotherham U.	06.67	1967	12	4	3	(F)
			L	Notts.Co.	08.58	1968	1	/	0	
			TR	Scunthorpe U.	09.68	1968	23	1	4	
WILSON, Archie	Sth.Shields	04.12.24		Gateshead	+	1946	5		0	(G)
			Sth.Shields	Lincoln C.	04.51	1950-51	4		0	
WILSON, Bev	Stockport	11.04.53	APP	Stockport Co.	07.70	1969-73	59	2	1	(CH)
WILSON, Bev A.M.	Eccles	14.05.24		Wrexham	06.47	1947-50	98		0	(CH)
			TR	Barrow	03.51	1950-58	309		1	
WILSON, Brian	Newcastle	14.04.57	APP	Blackpool	05.74	1976-79	21	10	6	(D) (Married to a Nolan singing sister)
			TR	Torquay U.	11.79	1979-82	129	2	6	
WILSON, Carl A.	Consett	08.05.40	JNRS	Newcastle U.	02.58	1958	1		0	(F)Son of Joseph A.
			TR	Gateshead	01.60	1959	17		4	
			TR	Doncaster Rov.	07.60	1960	14		2	
			TR	Millwall	07.61	1961	9		1	
WILSON, Clive A.	Manchester	13.11.61	JNRS	Manchester C.	12.79	1981-83	14	1	0	(D)
			L	Chester C.	09.82	1982	21	/	2	
WILSON, Daniel	Wigan	01.01.60	Wigan Ath.	Bury	09.77	1977-79	87	3	8	(M)
			TR	Chesterfield	07.80	1980-82	100	/	13	
			TR	Nottingham F.	01.83	1982	9	1	1	
			L	Scunthorpe U.	10.83	1983	6	/	3	
			TR	Brighton & H.A.	11.83	1983	26	/	10	
WILSON, David	Glasgow	21.11.23		Manchester C.	07.47					
			TR	Bury	07.48	1948	2		1	
			TR	Torquay U.	08.49					
WILSON, David C.	Nelson	24.12.42	JNRS	Preston N.E.	04.60	1960-66	168	2	31	(W)E.U23-7/E.SCH.INT.
			TR	Liverpool	02.67	1966	1	/	0	
			TR	Preston N.E.	06.68	1968-73	99	12	10	
			L	Bradford C.	03.72	1971	5	/	0	
			L	Southport	10.73	1973	2	/	0	
WILSON, David E.J.	Wolverhampton	04.10.44	JNRS	Nottingham F.	10.61	1962-65	8	1	1	(W)
			TR	Carlisle U.	10.65	1965-66	54	1	23	
			TR	Grimsby T.	03.67	1966-68	63	/	23	
			TR	Walsall	09.68	1968-69	34	2	9	
			TR	Burnley	09.69	1969-70	12	4	0	
			TR	Chesterfield	06.71	1971-74	125	3	22	
WILSON, Dennis	Bebbington	30.04.36	JNRS	Wrexham	07.54					(FB)
			Rhyl	Stoke C.	08.59	1959-60	14		0	

Players Names	Birthplace	Date	Previous Club	League Club	Date Signed	Seasons Played	Career Record Apps	Sub	Gls	
WOOD, T. Les	Haslingden	20.12.32		Huddersfield T.	04.52					(G)
			TR	Barrow	08.55	1955	32		0	
			TR	Port Vale	06.56	1956	2		0	
			TR	Southport	01.58	1957	1		0	
WOOD, Terry L.	Newport	03.09.20	Newports Docks	Cardiff C.	AM	1946	4		0	(WH)W.AMAT.INT. W.SCH.INT.
WOOD, William	Barnsley	28.12.27	Sten J.	Sunderland	10.48	1949	1		0	(FB)
			TR	Hull C.	07.51					
			TR	Sheffield U.	06.52	1952	5		0	
WOOD, William R.	Manchester	11.11.25		Wrexham	11.49	1949	16		5	(F)
WOODALL, Arthur J.	Stoke	04.06.30	JNRS	Stoke C.	05.50	1953	1		0	(F)
WOODALL, Brian H.	Chester	06.06.48	APP	Sheffield Wed.	06.65	1967-69	19	3	3	(OR)
			L	Oldham Ath.	02.70	1969	3	/	1	
			TR	Chester C.	06.70	1970	11	2	2	
			TR	Crewe Alex.	03.71	1970	10	1	3	
WOODALL, John B.	Goole	16.01.49	Goole T.	York C.	02.67	1967	2	/	0	(IF)
			Gainsborough	Rotherham U.	03.74	1973-74	25	1	6	
WOODBURN, James	Rutherglen	29.01.17	Coltness U.	Newcastle U.	*	1946-47	36		4	(LH)
			TR	Gateshead	09.48	1948-51	132		10	
WOODCOCK, Anthony S.	Nottingham	06.12.55	APP	Nottingham F.	01.74	1973-79	125	4	36	(F)E-33/E.U21-2
			L	Lincoln C.	02.76	1975	2	2	1	
			L	Doncaster Rov.	09.76	1976	6	/	2	
			Cologne	Arsenal	07.82	1982-83	71	/	35	
WOODCOCK, Ernest	Salford	14.05.25	Blackburn Rov.(AM)	Bury	01.47	1946-47	18		3	
			TR	Oldham Ath.	06.48	1948-49	29		4	
			TR	Stockport Co.	09.50					
WOODCOCK, Harry	Darlington	18.09.28		Darlington	09.53	1952-53	5		0	
WOODCOCK, Tom	Chorley	19.03.26	Preston N.E.(AM)	Southport	AM	1946	1		0	(IF)
WOODFIELD, David	Leamington	11.10.43	JNRS	Wolverhampton W.	10.60	1961-69	250	3	13	(CH)
			TR	Watford	09.71	1971-73	14	1	0	
WOODFIELD, Terry	Nottingham	21.01.46	JNRS	Notts.Co.	07.63	1963	5		0	(HB)
WOODFORD, Robert M.	Keyworth	06.12.43	JNRS	Notts.Co.	03.61	1961	3		0	(HB)
WOODGATE, Terry J.	London	11.12.19	Becton	West Ham U.	*	1946-52	255		48	(OL)
WOODHEAD, Andy	Wallsend	12.07.66	APP	Gillingham	APP	1983	1	1	0	(M)
WOODHEAD, Dennis	Sheffield	12.06.25	Hillsboro BC	Sheffield Wed.	+	1946-54	214		71	(OL)
			TR	Chesterfield	09.55	1955	15		7	
			TR	Derby Co.	01.56	1955-58	94		24	
			L	Southport	02.59	1958	4		1	
WOODHEAD, Dennis	Huddersfield	02.09.24		Bradford C.	01.48					
			TR	Accrington St.	05.48	1948	7		0	
WOODHEAD, Simon C.	Dewsbury	26.12.62	JNRS	Mansfield T.	09.80	1980-83	87	11	4	(D)
WOODHOUSE, John	Middlesbrough	05.04.37	South Bank	Leeds U.	06.55					(F)
			TR	Gateshead	07.57	1957	2		0	
WOODIN, Steve	Birkenhead	06.01.55	JNRS	Tranmere Rov.	02.75	1974	1	2	0	(W)
WOODLEY, Derek G.	Isleworth	02.03.42	JNRS	West Ham U.	04.59	1959-61	12		3	(W)E.SCH.INT./ E.YTH.INT.
			TR	Southend U.	08.62	1962-66	159	2	23	
			TR	Charlton Ath.	06.67	1967	2	1	0	
			TR	Southend U.	10.67	1967	7	2	0	
			TR	Gillingham	01.68	1967-70	99	1	9	
WOODLEY, Vic R.	Slough	26.02.11	Chelsea(*)	Derby Co.	+	1946	30		0	(G)*Windsor & E/E-19/ E.F.LGE REP./d.1978
WOODROFFE, Lewis C.	Portsmouth	29.10.21		Manchester C.	+	1946	9		1	(OR)
			TR	Watford	08.47	1947-50	63		6	
WOODRUFF, Arthur	Barnsley	12.04.13	Bradford C.(*)	Burnley	*	1946-51	176		0	(CH)E.F.LGE REP./ d.1983
			TR	Workington	07.52	1952	11		0	
WOODRUFF, Robert J.	Wolverhampton	11.03.65	Cardiff C.(JNRS)	Newport Co.	08.83	1983	9	1	0	(F)Son of Robert W.
			L	Swindon T.	05.84	1983	1	1	0	
WOODRUFF, Robert W.	Highworth	09.11.40	JNRS	Swindon T.	05.58	1959-63	180		19	(WH)●
			TR	Wolverhampton W.	03.64	1963-65	59	/	18	
			TR	Crystal Palace	06.66	1966-69	123	2	48	
			TR	Cardiff C.	11.69	1969-73	141	9	22	
			TR	Newport Co.	08.74	1974-75	52	/	7	
WOODS, Alan E.	Doncaster	15.02.37	JNRS	Tottenham H.	02.54	1954	6		0	(WH)E.YTH.INT./ E.SCH.INT.
			TR	Swansea C.	12.56	1957-58	30		0	
			TR	York C.	07.60	1960-65	227	1	4	
WOODS, Charlie M.P.	Whitehaven	18.3.41	Cleator MC	Newcastle U.	05.59	1960-61	26		7	(IF)
			TR	Bournemouth	11.62	1962-64	70		26	
			TR	Crystal Palace	11.64	1964-65	49	/	6	
			TR	Ipswich T.	07.66	1966-69	66	16	5	
			TR	Watford	06.70	1970-71	40	2	3	
			L	Colchester U.	11.71	1971	3	/	0	
			TR	Blackburn Rov.	07.72					

Players Names	Birthplace	Date	Previous Club	League Club	Date Signed	Seasons Played	Apps	Sub	Gls	
WOODS, Chris C.E.	Boston	14.11.59	APP	Nottingham F.	12.76					(G)E.U21-6
			TR	Q.P.R.	07.79	1979-80	63	/	0	
			TR	Norwich C.	03.81	1980-83	136	/	0	
WOODS, Clive	Norwich	18.12.47	Gothic	Ipswich T.	06.69	1969-79	217	51	23	(F)
			TR	Norwich C.	03.80	1979-81	29	3	4	
WOODS, Dennis J.	Norwich	12.12.36	Cambridge U.	Watford	10.62	1962	13		2	(OR)
WOODS, Derek E.	Northampton	23.03.41	JNRS	Northampton T.	AM	1961	6		2	(F)E.AMAT.INT.
WOODS, Edward	Ton Pentre	29.07.51	Ferndale	Bristol C.	09.71	1972	1	1	0	(F)
			L	Scunthorpe U.	10.73	1973	4	/	2	
			TR	Newport Co.	09.74	1974-78	149	2	54	
WOODS, Maurice (Matt)	Skelmersdale	01.11.31	JNRS	Everton	11.49	1952-56	8		1	(CH)E.F.LGE REP.
			TR	Blackburn Rov.	11.56	1956-62	259		2	
			TR	Luton T.	07.65	1965	34	/	0	
			TR	Stockport CO.	07.66	1966-67	85	/	2	
WOODS, Neil S.	York	30.07.66	APP	Doncaster Rov.	08.83	1982-83	6	5	1	(M)
WOODS, Pat J.	Islington	29.04.33	JNRS	Q.P.R.	06.50	1952-60	304		16	(FB)
			Australia	Colchester U.	08.63	1963	36		0	
WOODS, Peter A.	Sale	21.01.50	APP	Manchester U.	04.67					(FB)
			TR	Luton T.	04.70					
			TR	Southend U.	02.72	1971-72	25	/	0	
			TR	Doncaster Rov.	07.73	1973-74	41	8	1	
WOODS, Ray	Peterborough	27.04.30	Peterborough U.	Southend U.	05.48	1950-51	3		1	(RH)
			TR	Crystal Palace	06.53	1953-54	18		0	
WOODS, Ray G.	Birkenhead	07.06.65	APP	Tranmere Rov.	06.83	1982-83	3	4	2	(F)
WOODS, William	Farnworth	12.03.26	Moss Grove	Rochdale	+	1946	15		1	(IF)
			TR	Bradford P.A.	01.47	1946	5		0	
			TR	Rochdale	01.49	1948-49	13		1	
			TR	Barrow	11.49	1949	16		4	
			TR	Crewe Alex.	07.50					
			TR	Accrington St.	11.50	1950	3		0	
WOODWARD, Alan	Chapeltown	07.09.46	APP	Sheffield U.	09.63	1963-78	537	2	158	(W)E.F. LGE● REP./E.YTH.INT.
WOODWARD, Alan	Stanton Hill	19.06.47	Alfreton T.	Grimsby T.	07.70	1970-71	54	/	12	(OL)
WOODWARD, Brian	Leeds	12.07.29	JNRS	Leeds U.						
			Hereford U.	York C.	08.50	1950	5		0	
WOODWARD, Harold G.	Bromley	29.08.19		Southend U.	05.46	1950-51	14		0	(FB)
WOODWARD, Horace J.	London	16.01.24	JNRS	Tottenham H.	05.46	1946-48	63		1	(CH)
			TR	Q.P.R.	06.49	1949-50	57		0	
			TR	Walsall	07.53	1953	5		0	
WOODWARD, John	Glasgow	10.01.49	Possilpark J.	Arsenal	01.66	1966	2	1	0	(M)
			TR	York C.	07.71	1971-77	152	15	6	
WOODWARD, John	Stoke	16.01.47	APP	Stoke C.	03.64	1964-66	10	1	1	(IF)
			TR	Aston Villa	10.66	1966-68	22	5	7	
			TR	Walsall	05.69	1969-72	116	10	23	
			TR	Port Vale	02.73	1972-74	88	11	30	
			TR	Scunthorpe U.	07.75	1975	16	3	5	
WOODWARD, Ken R.	Battersea	16.11.47	APP	Crystal Palace	12.65					(IF)
			TR	Orient	08.66	1966	1	/	0	
WOODWARD, Laurie	Troedyrhiw	05.07.18	Wolverhampton W.(*)	Bournemouth	+	1946-56	275		7	(WH)
WOODWARD, Tom	Horwich	08.12.17		Bolton W.	*	1946-49	121		14	(OR)
			TR	Middlesbrough	10.49	1949-50	20		6	
WOODWARD, Tom P.	Birmingham	06.07.34	Moor Green	W.B.A.	09.54					(G)
			TR	Walsall	08.58	1958	13		0	
WOODWARD, Vivien	Troedyrhiw	20.05.14	Folkestone	Fulham	*	1946	10		0	(IF)Brother of Laurie
			TR	Millwall	02.47	1946-47	42		13	
			TR	Brentford	07.48	1948-49	20		4	
			TR	Aldershot	02.50	1949-50	54		5	
WOOF, Cliff	Liverpool	20.09.56	JNRS	Liverpool	05.76					(F)
				Southport	N/C	1977	1	/	0	
WOOF, William	Gateshead	16.08.56	APP	Middlesbrough	08.74	1974-81	30	16	5	(F)
			L	Peterborough U.	03.77	1976	2	1	0	
			Blyth S.	Cardiff C.	09.82	1982	1	/	1	
			Gateshead	Hull C.	02.83	1982	9	2	3	
WOOKEY, Ken G.	Newport	30.12.46	JNRS	Newport Co.	01.64	1964-68	57	6	5	(CF)Son of Ken W.
			TR	Port Vale	07.69	1969	23	1	4	
			TR	Workington	07.70	1970	11	5	4	
WOOKEY, Ken W.	Newport	23.02.22	JNRS	Newport Co.	*	1946	14		2	(OR)W.SCH.INT.
			TR	Bristol Rov.	12.46	1946-48	53		10	
			TR	Swansea C.	11.48	1948-49	13		0	
			TR	Ipswich T.	10.50	1950	15		1	
WOOLCOTT, Roy A.	Leyton	29.07.46	Eton Manor	Tottenham H.	02.68	1969	1	/	0	(CF)
			L	Gillingham	02.72	1971	13	/	5	
WOOLDRIDGE, James	Rossington	28.09.18	Benburb FC	Doncaster Rov.	+	1946-47	30		0	(LB)

Players Names	Birthplace	Date	Previous Club	League Club	Date Signed	Seasons Played	Career Record Apps Sub Gls		
WILSON, Dennis F.	Farnham	06.09.29	JNRS	Norwich C.	09.46				
			TR	Aldershot	06.50	1950-51	5		0
				Crewe Alex.	10.55	1955-57	24		0
WILSON, Don	Heywood	04.06.30		Bury	05.51	1952-58	62		1 (RB)
WILSON, Eugene	Sheffield	11.09.32		Rotherham U.	05.53				(OL)
			TR	Stockport Co.	05.54	1954-61	224		41
WILSON, F. Peter	Newcastle	15.09.47		Middlesbrough	04.66	1967	1	/	0 (HB)
WILSON, Fred C.	Nottingham	10.11.18	Wolverhampton W.(*)	Bournemouth	*	1946-50	97		0
WILSON, Glen E.	Newcastle	02.07.29	Newcastle U.(AM)	Brighton & H.A.	09.49	1949-59	410		25 (WH)Brother of Joseph A.
			TR	Exeter C.	06.60	1960-61	37		2
WILSON, Harry	Hetton-Le-Hole	29.11.53	APP	Burnley	12.70	1971	10	/	0 (D)E.YTH.INT./E.SCH.INT.
			TR	Brighton & H.A.	12.73	1973-76	130	/	4
			TR	Preston N.E.	07.77	1977-79	38	4	0
			TR	Darlington	09.80	1980-82	82	3	0
			TR	Hartlepool U.	08.83	1983	16	/	0
WILSON, Ian G.	Fife	11.02.23	Forfar A.	Preston N.E.	11.46	1946-47	16		6 (OL)
			TR	Burnley	06.48	1948-49	19		1
			TR	Leicester C.	03.50	1949-50	12		2
			TR	Chesterfield	10.51	1951-52	77		19
			TR	Rotherham U.	05.53	1953-55	108		44
WILSON, Ian W.	Aberdeen	27.03.58	Elgin C.	Leicester C.	04.79	1979-83	170	6	11 (M)
WILSON, J. Robert	Liverpool	08.09.28	Burscough	Preston N.E.	04.50	1952-62	91		0 (RB)
			TR	Tranmere Rov.	09.62	1962-63	54		0
WILSON, James	Glasgow	19.12.29	Alloa A.	Leicester C.	07.54				
			TR	Mansfield T.	03.55	1954-55	18		1
WILSON, James	Newmains	20.04.42	Shotts BA	Newcastle U.	09.59	1960-61	12		2 (F)
WILSON, James A.	Musselburgh	28.06.22	Peterborough U.	Luton T.	07.47	1947-50	39		1 (FB)
			TR	Northampton T.	07.51	1951	23		0
			TR	Chesterfield	09.54				
WILSON, James M.	Saltcoats	19.03.23	Dundalk	Accrington St.	07.49	1949	4		0
WILSON, James T.	Middlesbrough	15.03.24	Gravesend	Chelsea	06.47				(IF)Son of Andy Wilson
			TR	Leeds U.	08.50				(pre-war)
			TR	Watford	11.50	1950-56	49		12
			TR	Southend U.	07.57				
WILSON, Jeff H.	S. Shields	07.12.64	APP	Darlington	09.83	1982-83	10	1	0 (D)
WILSON, John	Airdrie	29.10.16	Glasgow Celtic	Chesterfield	+	1946	16		2
			TR	Oldham Ath.	07.47	1947-48	29		2
			TR	Accrington St.	10.48	1948-49	26		1
WILSON, John A.	Jarrow	11.04.52	Consett	Darlington	09.71	1971-72	15	5	1 (W)
WILSON, John C.	Norwich	28.10.34	JNRS	Norwich C.	08.53	1953-58	47		0 (FB)
			TR	Chesterfield	07.59	1959	15		0
WILSON, Joseph	Workington	06.07.37	JNRS	Workington	01.56	1955-61	153		5 (FB)●
			TR	Nottingham F.	03.62	1961-64	85		1
			TR	Wolverhampton W.	03.65	1964-66	60	1	0
			TR	Newport Co.	05.67	1967	41	/	0
			TR	Workington	09.68	1968-72	168	1	4
WILSON, Joseph A.	W.Wylam	23.03.09	Newcastle U.(*)	Brighton & H.A.	*	1946-47	40		0 (IF)*Tanfield Lea
WILSON, Joseph H.	Manchester	17.05.25	JNRS	Manchester U.	+				
			TR	Accrington St.	10.46	1946-50	109		4
WILSON, Joseph W.	Newcastle	10.09.11	Reading(+)	Barnsley	05.46	1946	20		0 *Newcastle U./
									Southend U./Brentford
WILSON, Keith	Wallington	14.12.35	Andover	Southampton	07.59				(F)
			TR	Gillingham	07.61	1961	5		2
WILSON, Ken M.	Dumbarton	15.09.46	Dumbarton	Carlisle U.	09.72	1972	14	6	1 (IF)
			L	York C.	09.73	1973	2	/	0
			L	Workington	10.73	1973	4	1	0
WILSON, Kevin J.	Banbury	18.04.61	Banbury U.	Derby Co.	12.79	1979-83	93	16	22 (F)
WILSON, Les J.	Manchester	10.07.47	JNRS	Wolverhampton W.	09.64	1965-71	91	11	7 (RB)
			TR	Bristol C.	03.71	1970-72	42	1	1
			TR	Norwich C.	09.73	1973	6	/	0
WILSON, Paul A.	Norwich	19.06.56	APP	Norwich C.	07.74	1975	0	1	0 (HB)
WILSON, Philip	Hemsworth	16.10.60	APP	Bolton W.	10.78	1979-80	35	4	4 (M)
			TR	Huddersfield T.	08.81	1981-83	117	3	11
WILSON, Ramon	Shirebrook	17.12.34	Langwith J.J.	Huddersfield T.	08.52	1955-63	265		6 (FB)E-63/●
			TR	Everton	07.64	1964-68	115	2	0 E.F.LGE REP.
			TR	Oldham Ath.	07.69	1969	25	/	0
			TR	Bradford C.	07.70	1970	2	/	0
WILSON, Ray T.	Grangemouth	08.04.47	JNRS	W.B.A.	05.64	1965-75	230	2	3 (FB)S.U23-1
WILSON, Richard	Orpington	08.05.60	APP	Chelsea	08.78				(F)
			TR	Charlton Ath.	08.79	1979	16	1	1
WILSON, Robert	Motherwell		Stirling A.	Workington	12.52	1952	2		0 (LH)

Players Names	Birthplace	Date	Previous Club	League Club	Date Signed	Seasons Played	Career Record Apps	Sub	Gls	
WILSON, Robert J.	Birmingham	23.05.43	JNRS	Aston Villa	09.61	1963	9		0	(G)
			TR	Cardiff C.	08.64	1964-67	114	/	0	
			L	Bristol C.	10.69	1969	1	/	0	
			TR	Exeter C.	01.70	1969-75	205	/	0	
WILSON, Robert J.	Kensington	05.06.61	APP	Fulham	06.79	1979-83	129	7	23	(M)
WILSON, Robert P.	Chesterfield	30.10.41	Wolverhampton W.(AM)	Arsenal	03.64	1963-73	234	/	0	(G)S-2/E.SCH.INT.
WILSON, Robert S.W.	Musselburgh	29.06.34	Aberdeen	Norwich C.	05.57	1957-58	62		0	(HB)
			TR	Gillingham	06.60	1960	35		0	
			TR	Accrington St.	07.61					
			TR	Chester C.	04.62	1962	15		0	
WILSON, Robert W.	Oxford	29.05.44	Feltham	Brentford	AM	1966	1	/	1	(CF)
WILSON, Ron	Edinburgh	06.09.41	Musselburgh	Stoke C.	08.59	1959-63	11		0	(FB)
			TR	Port Vale	11.63	1963-70	261	3	5	
WILSON, Ron G.	Sale	10.09.24		West Ham U.	+	1946-47	3		0	(WH)
WILSON, Sam	Glasgow	16.12.31	Glasgow Celtic	Millwall	07.59	1959	23		11	(F)
			TR	Northampton T.	07.60					
WILSON, Thomas	Midlothian	29.11.40	Falkirk	Millwall	07.61	1961-67	200	/	15	(HB)
			TR	Hull C.	11.67	1967-69	60	/	1	
WILSON, Thomas	Bedlington	15.09.30	Cinderhill	Nottingham F.	04.51	1951-60	190		75	(CF)
			TR	Walsall	11.60	1960-61	53		19	
WILSON, Thomas B.	Ayr	25.07.33	Thornton Hibs.	Reading	03.56	1956	9		1	
			TR	Exeter C.	07.57	1957	22		2	
WILSON, Thomas F.	Southampton	03.07.30	Southampton(AM)	Fulham	08.50	1952-56	45		0	(FB)
			TR	Brentford	07.57	1957-61	148		0	
WILSON, William	Seaton Delavel	10.07.46	JNRS	Blackburn Rov.	09.63	1964-71	246	1	0	(D)
			TR	Portsmouth	01.72	1971-78	188	6	5	
WILSON, William J.R.	Portadown	23.09.36	Portadown	Burnley	09.55	1956-57	2		0	(HB)NI'B'-2
WILTON, Graham E.	Chesterfield	19.10.42	Chesterfield Tube	Chesterfield	AM	1961	1		0	(OR)
WILTSHIRE, David J.	Folkestone	08.07.54	Canterbury	Gillingham	03.74	1973-75	55	8	2	(D)
			TR	Aldershot	07.76	1976	5	/	0	
WILTSHIRE, Peter J.	Bristol	15.10.34	JNRS	Bristol Rov.	01.54	1953	1		0	(CF)
			TR	Bristol C.	06.55					
WIMBLETON, Paul P.	Havant	13.11.64	APP	Portsmouth	02.82	1981-83	5	5	0	(M)E.SCH.INT.
WIMSHURST, Ken	Sth.Shields	23.03.38	Sth.Shields	Newcastle U.	07.57					(WH)
			TR	Gateshead	11.58	1958-59	7		0	
			TR	Wolverhampton W.	11.60					
			TR	Southampton	07.61	1961-67	147	3	9	
			TR	Bristol C.	10.67	1967-71	146	3	9	
WINDLE, Charles	Barnsley	08.01.17	Bury(*)	Exeter C.	+					(OR)d.1975
			TR	Bristol Rov.	12.46	1946	7		1	
WINDLE, William H.	Maltby	09.07.20		Leeds U.	10.47	1947	2		0	(F)
			TR	Lincoln C.	02.48	1947-51	91		22	
			TR	Chester C.	10.51	1951-54	126		20	
WINDRIDGE, David H.	Atherstone	07.12.61	JNRS	Sheffield U.	01.79					(F)
			TR	Chesterfield	03.80	1980-82	66	12	14	
			TR	Blackpool	08.83	1983	32	2	6	
WINDROSS, Dennis	Guisborough	12.05.38		Middlesbrough	05.56	1959-60	4		1	(WH)
			TR	Brighton & H.A.	11.60	1960	18		2	
			TR	Darlington	06.61	1961	25		4	
			TR	Doncaster Rov.	06.62	1962-63	51		4	
WINDSOR, Robert	Stoke	31.01.26	JNRS	Stoke C.	+					
			TR	Lincoln C.	02.49	1948-49	11		1	
WINFIELD, B. John	Draycott	28.02.43	JNRS	Nottingham F.	05.60	1961-73	352	2	4	(FB)
			TR	Peterborough U.	07.74	1974	11	/	0	
WINFIELD, Philip	Denaby	16.02.37	Denaby U.	Lincoln C.	10.57	1957	1		0	(HB)
WINGATE, John	Budleigh Salterton	19.12.48		Plymouth Arg.	AM	1968	1		0	(W)
			Dawlish	Exeter C.	07.69	1968-73	187	14	32	
			TR	Bournemouth	07.74	1974	30	3	3	
			TR	Exeter C.	07.75	1975	44	1	2	
WINN, Steve	Thornaby	16.09.59		Rotherham U.	03.78	1978-80	17	7	3	(F)
			TR	Torquay U.	01.82	1981	12	2	2	
			Scunthorpe U.(N/C)	Hartlepool U.	N/C	1982	1	/	0	
WINSPEAR, Jack	Leeds	24.12.46		Leeds U.	10.64					
			TR	Cardiff C.	06.66	1966	1	/	0	
			TR	Rochdale	07.67	1967	15	1	3	
WINSTANLEY, Graham	Croxdale	20.01.48	APP	Newcastle U.	12.68	1966-68	5	2	0	(D)
			TR	Carlisle U.	08.69	1969-74	165	1	8	
			TR	Brighton & H.A.	10.74	1974-78	63	1	4	
			TR	Carlisle U.	07.79	1979	32	1	1	
WINSTANLEY, Eric	Barnsley	15.11.44	JNRS	Barnsley	05.62	1961-72	409	/	35	(D)E.YTH.INT.
			TR	Chesterfield	08.73	1973-76	100	1	7	
WINTER, Danny T.	Tonypandy	14.06.18	Bolton W.(*)	Chelsea	+	1946-50	131		0	(FB)

Players Names	Birthplace	Date	Previous Club	League Club	Date Signed	Seasons Played	Apps	Sub	Gls	
WINTER, John G.A.	Stoke Newington	06.03.28		Sheffield U.	11.48					(CF)
			TR	Walsall	01.51	1950-51	42		12	
WINTERBOTTOM, Dennis T.	Glossop	23.10.28	Stalybridge	Accrington St.	06.51	1951	12		0	(CH)
WINTERBURN, Nigel	Nuneaton	11.12.63	APP	Birmingham C.	08.81					(D)
			TR	Oxford U.	08.83	1983				
			TR	Wimbledon	09.83	1983	43	/	1	
WINTERS, Frank	Johnstone	30.10.23	Clyde	Torquay U.	05.49	1949-51	14		0	(WH)
WINTERS, Herbert R.	Chipping Sodbury	14.04.20		Bristol Rov.	09.46	1946-47	13		0	(CH)
WINTERS, Ian A.	Renfrew	08.02.21	N.Earswick	York C.	+	1946-47	27		10	(IF)
			Boston U.	Gateshead	12.48	1948-52	152		49	
			TR	Workington	07.53	1953	30		3	
WINTERS, John M.	Wisbech	24.10.60	APP	Peterborough U.	10.78	1980-82	60	/	3	(D)
WINTERSGILL, David	York	19.09.65	APP	Wolverhampton W.	06.83	1982-83	3	1	0	(D)
			L	Chester C.	03.84	1983	6	/	0	
WINTLE, Frank J.	Stoke	20.12.29		Port Vale	05.49	1956	1		0	(FB)
			TR	Crewe Alex.	06.57					
WINTON, Doug	Perth	06.10.29	Jeanfield Swifts	Burnley	09.47	1951-58	182		1	(FB)S'B'-1
			TR	Aston Villa	01.59	1958-60	37		0	
			TR	Rochdale	06.61	1961-63	120		0	
WIPFLER, Charles J.	Trowbridge	15.07.15	Hearts	Watford	*	1946	13		1	(IL)*Bristol Rov.
WISEMAN, George	E.Dereham	23.05.21	Notts Co.(+)	Norwich C.	09.46	1946	8		0	(G)
WITCOMBE, Doug F.	Ebbw Vale	18.04.18	Tottenham H.(AM)	W.B.A.	*	1946	26		1	(OR)W-3
			TR	Sheffield Wed.	03.47	1946-52	223		13	
			TR	Newport Co.	11.53	1953	25		0	
WITHAM, Richard	Bowburn	04.05.15	Blackpool(*)	Oldham Ath.	06.46	1946	5		0	(FB)*Huddersfield T.
WITHE, Chris	Liverpool	25.09.62	APP	Newcastle U.	10.80	1980	2	/	0	(D)Brother of Peter
			TR	Bradford C.	06.83	1983	45	/	1	
WITHE, Peter	Liverpool	30.08.51	Smiths Coggins	Southport	08.71	1970-71	3	/	0	(F)E-10
			TR	Barrow	12.71	1971	1	/	0	
			Arcadia Sheps	Wolverhampton W.	11.73	1973-74	12	5	3	
			TR	Birmingham C.	08.75	1975-76	35	/	9	
			TR	Nottingham F.	09.76	1976-78	74	1	28	
			TR	Newcastle U.	08.78	1978-79	76	/	25	
			TR	Aston Villa	05.80	1980-83	142	/	61	
WITHEFORD, James D.	Eccleshall	16.04.30	Norton Woodseats	Chesterfield	AM	1953	9		0	(OR)
WITHERS, Alan	Bulwell	20.10.30		Blackpool	07.49	1950-54	22		2	(IF)
			TR	Lincoln C.	02.55	1954-58	97		18	
			TR	Notts.Co.	01.59	1958-62	121		22	
WITHERS, Charlie F.	Edmonton	06.09.22	JNRS	Tottenham H.	10.47	1947-55	154		0	(FB)E'B'-1
WITHERS, Colin C.	Birmingham	21.03.40	W.B.A.(AM)	Birmingham C.	05.57	1960-64	98		0	(G)E.SCH.INT.
			TR	Aston Villa	11.64	1964-68	146	/	0	
			TR	Lincoln C.	06.69	1969	1	/	0	
WITHEY, Graham A.	Bristol	11.06.60	Bath C.	Bristol Rov.	08.82	1982	19	3	10	(F)
			TR	Coventry C.	08.83	1983	10	10	4	
WITHINGTON, Richard	Sth.Shields	08.04.21		Blackpool	*					(OR)
			TR	Rochdale	06.47	1947	32		6	
			TR	Chesterfield	06.48	1948	6		0	
WOAN, Alan E.	Liverpool	08.02.31	New Brighton	Norwich C.	12.53	1953-55	21		7	(IF)
			TR	Northampton T.	07.56	1956-59	120		69	
			TR	Crystal Palace	10.59	1959-60	41		21	
			TR	Aldershot	02.61	1960-63	108		44	
WOAN, Don	Liverpool	07.11.27	Bootle	Liverpool	10.50	1950	2		0	(F)Brother of Alan
			TR	Orient	11.51	1951-52	25		5	
			TR	Bradford C.	02.51	1952-53	21		4	
			TR	Tranmere Rov.	02.54	1952-54	27		2	
WOFFINDEN, Colin R.	Hove	06.08.47	Lewes T.	Brighton & H.A.	AM	1970	0	2	0	(CF)
WOJCIECHOWICZ, Steve	Lancaster	06.04.52	JNRS	Blackpool	08.70	1970	0	2	0	(F)E.YTH.INT.
WOJTCZAK, Edouard A.	Poland	29.04.21	Polish Army	York C.	AM	1946	8		0	(G)
WOLLEN, Terry L.	Swindon	30.07.43	JNRS	Swindon T.	08.60	1960-64	84		0	(FB)
WOLSTENHOLME, Ian A.	Bradford	12.01.43	St.Johns Coll.	York C.	AM	1963	2	/	0	(G)E.AMAT.INT.
WOLSTENHOLME, J. Trevor		18.06.43	JNRS	Birmingham C.	09.60					(HB)
			TR	Torquay U.	08.63	1963-65	82	/	2	
			TR	York C.	07.66	1966	11	/	0	
WOMACK, Albert R.	Denaby	20.09.34	Denaby U.	Derby Co.	10.57	1957	2		0	(F)
			TR	Southampton	05.59					
			TR	Workington	07.60	1960	9		1	
WOMBLE, Trevor	Durham	07.06.51	APP	Rotherham U.	10.68	1968-77	185	28	39	(F)
			L	Crewe Alex.	11.71	1971	4	/	1	
			L	Halifax T.	03.73	1972	9	1	2	
WOMERSLEY, Ernest	Hartshead	28.08.32	JNRS	Huddersfield T.	09.49	1950	2		0	(F)
			TR	Bradford C.	05.57					

Players Names	Birthplace	Date	Previous Club	League Club	Date Signed	Seasons Played	Apps	Sub	Gls	
WOOD, Alan E.	Gravesend	01.12.54	APP	Charlton Ath.	12.72	1972	1	/	0	(WH)
WOOD, Alf E.H.	Macclesfield	25.10.45	APP	Manchester C.	06.63	1962-65	24	1	0	(F) E.YTH.INT.
			TR	Shrewsbury T.	06.66	1966-71	257	1	64	
			TR	Millwall	06.72	1972-74	99	1	38	
			TR	Hull C.	11.74	1974-76	51	2	10	
			TR	Middlesbrough	10.76	1976	22	1	2	
			TR	Walsall	07.77	1977	26	3	2	
WOOD, Alf R.	Aldridge	14.05.15	Nuneaton	Coventry C.	*	1946-51	219		0	(G)
			TR	Northampton T.	12.51	1951-54	139		0	
			TR	Coventry C.	07.55	1955-58	13		0	
WOOD, Allen H.	Newport	13.01.41	Lovells Ath.	Bristol Rov.	10.62	1962	1		0	(HB)W.AMAT.INT.
			Merthyr Tydfil	Newport Co.	05.65	1965-72	149	5	5	
WOOD, Archie	Leven	18.03.26	Bowhill	Tranmere Rov.	08.49	1949	31	·	5	(F)
WOOD, Barrie W.	Doncaster	05.12.36	Wolverhampton W.(AM)	Doncaster Rov.	08.54	1955	2		0	(F)
			TR	Scunthorpe U.	07.58	1958	3		1	
			Sth.Shields	Barnsley	03.61	1960-61	5		0	
WOOD, Brian T.	Hamworthy	08.12.40	JNRS	W.B.A.	01.58					(CH)
			TR	Crystal Palace	05.61	1961-66	142	1	1	
			TR	Orient	12.66	1966-67	58	/	3	
			TR	Colchester U.	08.68	1969-69	71	/	1	
			TR	Workington	07.70	1970-75	202	2	9	
WOOD, Charles				Millwall	AM	1946	3		0	
WOOD, Chris C.	Pennistone	18.05.55	APP	Huddersfield T.	05.72	1972	7	/	0	(G)
			L	Barnsley	02.73	1972	1	/	0	
			L	Doncaster Rov.	07.74	1974	4	/	0	
WOOD, Darren T.	Scarborough	09.06.64	APP	Middlesbrough	07.81	1981-83	95	/	6	(D)E.SCH.INT.
WOOD, Edward J.	West Ham U.	23.10.19	Leytonstone	West Ham U.	*	1946-48	48		13	(OL)E.AMAT.INT.
			TR	Orient	10.49	1949	9		1	
WOOD, Eric	Bolton	13.03.20	Bolton W.(+)	Rochdale	+	1946-50	148		16	(WH)
WOOD, Frank	Manchester	17.08.24	Hulme	Bury	10.48	1950	1		0	(HB)
				Shrewsbury T.	10.52					
			TR	Exeter C.	01.53	1952	8		0	
			TR	Rochdale	08.53					
WOOD, Gary T.	Corby	02.12.55	Kettering	Notts. Co.	12.77	1977-80	7	4	0	(D)
WOOD, George	Douglas	26.09.52	E. Stirling	Blackpool	01.72	1971-76	117	/	0	(G)S-4
			TR	Everton	08.77	1977-79	103	/	0	
			TR	Arsenal	08.80	1980-82	60	/	0	
			TR	Crystal Palace	08.83	1983	42	/	0	
WOOD, Graham	Doncaster	10.02.33		Wolverhampton W.	09.50					(CF)
			TR	Halifax T.	06.53	1953-54	19		3	
WOOD, Harry	Barrow	31.12.11		Barrow	08.47	1947-48	11		1	
WOOD, Henry	Liverpool	08.04.27	Sth.Liverpool	Chesterfield	07.53	1953	9		1	(OR)
WOOD, Hugh S.	Bellshill	16.11.60	Grantham	Scunthorpe U.	09.80	1980	0	1	0	(D)
WOOD, Ian N.	Kirkby	24.05.58	APP	Mansfield T.	06.76	1975-81	135	14	9	(D)
			TR	Aldershot	08.82	1982	14	/	1	
WOOD, Ian T.	Radcliffe	15.01.48	Radcliffe Bor.	Oldham Ath.	07.66	1965-79	517	8	22	(D)
			TR	Burnley	05.80	1980	14	3	0	
WOOD, James H.	New Brighton	25.10.38	Burscough	Southport	05.58	1957	1		0	(G)
WOOD, Jeff R.	London	04.05.54	Harlow T.	Charlton ath.	11.75	1975-80	147	/	0	(G)
				Colchester U.	09.81					
WOOD, John	Royton	12.02.31		Aldershot	09.52	1952-54	39		1	(WH)
WOOD, John M.	Walsall Wood	09.09.48		Wrexham	07.66	1965-67	4	3	0	(FB)
WOOD, Kevin	Armthorpe	03.11.29		Doncaster Rov.	10.49					(F)
			Worksop T.	Grimsby T.	03.51	1950-51	3		0	
WOOD, Mike J.	Bury	03.07.52	APP	Blackburn Rov.	02.70	1969-77	140	7	2	(D)
			TR	Bradford C.	02.78	1977-81	143	3	9	
			TR	Halifax T.	08.82	1982-83	80	1	2	
WOOD, Norman				Oldham Ath.	AM	1946	1	/		(OR)
WOOD, Norman	Sunderland	10.08.32		Sunderland	05.54	1954	1		0	
WOOD, Paul A.	Saltburn	01.11.64	APP	Portsmouth	11.82	1983	7	1	1	(F)
WOOD, Ray E.	Hebburn	11.06.31	Newcastle U.(AM)	Darlington	09.49	1949	12		0	(G)E-3/E.U23-1/
			TR	Manchester U.	12.49	1949-58	177		0	E'B'-1/E.F.LGE REP.
			TR	Huddersfield T.	12.58	1958-64	207		0	
			TR	Bradford C.	10.65	1965	32	/	0	
			TR	Barnsley	08.66	1966-67	30	/	0	
WOOD, Robert	Elphinstone	15.02.30	Hibernian	Barnsley	07.51	1951-64	326		43	(IF)
WOOD, Royden	Wallasey	16.10.30	Clitheroe	Leeds U.	05.52	1953-59	197		0	(G)
WOOD, Steve	Bracknell	02.02.63	APP	Reading	02.81	1979-83	94	1	3	(D)

Players Names	Birthplace	Date	Previous Club	League Club	Date Signed	Seasons Played	Apps	Sub	Gls	
WOOD, T. Les	Haslingden	20.12.32		Huddersfield T.	04.52					(G)
			TR	Barrow	08.55	1955	32		0	
			TR	Port Vale	06.56	1956	2		0	
			TR	Southport	01.58	1957	1		0	
WOOD, Terry L.	Newport	03.09.20	Newports Docks	Cardiff C.	AM	1946	4		0	(WH)W.AMAT.INT. W.SCH.INT.
WOOD, William	Barnsley	28.12.27	Sten J.	Sunderland	10.48	1949	1		0	(FB)
			TR	Hull C.	07.51					
			TR	Sheffield U.	06.52	1952	5		0	
WOOD, William R.	Manchester	11.11.25		Wrexham	11.49	1949	16		5	(F)
WOODALL, Arthur J.	Stoke	04.06.30	JNRS	Stoke C.	05.50	1953	1		0	(F)
WOODALL, Brian H.	Chester	06.06.48	APP	Sheffield Wed.	06.65	1967-69	19	3	3	(OR)
			L	Oldham Ath.	02.70	1969	3	/	1	
			TR	Chester C.	06.70	1970	11	2	2	
			TR	Crewe Alex.	03.71	1970	10	1	3	
WOODALL, John B.	Goole	16.01.49	Goole T.	York C.	02.67	1967	2	/	0	(IF)
			Gainsborough	Rotherham U.	03.74	1973-74	25	1	6	
WOODBURN, James	Rutherglen	29.01.17	Coltness U.	Newcastle U.	*	1946-47	36		4	(LH)
			TR	Gateshead	09.48	1948-51	132		10	
WOODCOCK, Anthony S.	Nottingham	06.12.55	APP	Nottingham F.	01.74	1973-79	125	4	36	(F)E-33/E.U21-2
			L	Lincoln C.	02.76	1975	2	2	1	
			L	Doncaster Rov.	09.76	1976	6	/	2	
			Cologne	Arsenal	07.82	1982-83	71	/	35	
WOODCOCK, Ernest	Salford	14.05.25	Blackburn Rov.(AM)	Bury	01.47	1946-47	18		3	
			TR	Oldham Ath.	06.48	1948-49	29		4	
			TR	Stockport Co.	09.50					
WOODCOCK, Harry	Darlington	18.09.28		Darlington	09.53	1952-53	5		0	
WOODCOCK, Tom	Chorley	19.03.26	Preston N.E.(AM)	Southport	AM	1946	1		0	(IF)
WOODFIELD, David	Leamington	11.10.43	JNRS	Wolverhampton W.	10.60	1961-69	250	3	13	(CH)
			TR	Watford	09.71	1971-73	14	1	0	
WOODFIELD, Terry	Nottingham	21.01.46	JNRS	Notts.Co.	07.63	1963	5		0	(HB)
WOODFORD, Robert M.	Keyworth	06.12.43	JNRS	Notts.Co.	03.61	1961	3		0	(HB)
WOODGATE, Terry J.	London	11.12.19	Becton	West Ham U.	*	1946-52	255		48	(OL)
WOODHEAD, Andy	Wallsend	12.07.66	APP	Gillingham	APP	1983	1	1	0	(M)
WOODHEAD, Dennis	Sheffield	12.06.25	Hillsboro BC	Sheffield Wed.	+	1946-54	214		71	(OL)
			TR	Chesterfield	09.55	1955	15		7	
			TR	Derby Co.	01.56	1955-58	94		24	
			L	Southport	02.59	1958	4		1	
WOODHEAD, Dennis	Huddersfield	02.09.24		Bradford C.	01.48					
			TR	Accrington St.	05.48	1948	7		0	
WOODHEAD, Simon C.	Dewsbury	26.12.62	JNRS	Mansfield T.	09.80	1980-83	87	11	4	(D)
WOODHOUSE, John	Middlesbrough	05.04.37	South Bank	Leeds U.	06.55					(F)
			TR	Gateshead	07.57	1957	2		0	
WOODIN, Steve	Birkenhead	06.01.55	JNRS	Tranmere Rov.	02.75	1974	1	2	0	(W)
WOODLEY, Derek G.	Isleworth	02.03.42	JNRS	West Ham U.	04.59	1959-61	12		3	(W)E.SCH.INT./ E.YTH.INT.
			TR	Southend U.	08.62	1962-66	159	2	23	
			TR	Charlton Ath.	06.67	1967	2	1	0	
			TR	Southend U.	10.67	1967	7	2	0	
			TR	Gillingham	01.68	1967-70	99	1	9	
WOODLEY, Vic R.	Slough	26.02.11	Chelsea(*)	Derby Co.	+	1946	30		0	(G)*Windsor & E/E-19/ E.F.LGE REP./d.1978
WOODROFFE, Lewis C.	Portsmouth	29.10.21		Manchester C.	+	1946	9		1	(OR)
			TR	Watford	08.47	1947-50	63		6	
WOODRUFF, Arthur	Barnsley	12.04.13	Bradford C.(*)	Burnley	*	1946-51	176		0	(CH)E.F.LGE REP./ d.1983
			TR	Workington	07.52	1952	11		0	
WOODRUFF, Robert J.	Wolverhampton	11.03.65	Cardiff C.(JNRS)	Newport Co.	08.83	1983	9	1	0	(F)Son of Robert W.
			L	Swindon T.	05.84	1983	1	1	0	
WOODRUFF, Robert W.	Highworth	09.11.40	JNRS	Swindon T.	05.58	1959-63	180		19	(WH)●
			TR	Wolverhampton W.	03.64	1963-65	59	/	18	
			TR	Crystal Palace	06.66	1966-69	123	2	48	
			TR	Cardiff C.	11.69	1969-73	141	9	22	
			TR	Newport Co.	08.74	1974-75	52	/	7	
WOODS, Alan E.	Doncaster	15.02.37	JNRS	Tottenham H.	02.54	1954	6		0	(WH)E.YTH.INT./ E.SCH.INT.
			TR	Swansea C.	12.56	1957-58	30		0	
			TR	York C.	07.60	1960-65	227	1	4	
WOODS, Charlie M.P.	Whitehaven	18.3.41	Cleator MC	Newcastle U.	05.59	1960-61	26		7	(IF)
			TR	Bournemouth	11.62	1962-64	70		26	
			TR	Crystal Palace	11.64	1964-65	49	/	6	
			TR	Ipswich T.	07.66	1966-69	66	16	5	
			TR	Watford	06.70	1970-71	40	2	3	
			L	Colchester U.	11.71	1971	3	/	0	
			TR	Blackburn Rov.	07.72					

Players Names	Birthplace	Date	Previous Club	League Club	Date Signed	Seasons Played	Career Record Apps	Sub	Gls	
WOODS, Chris C.E.	Boston	14.11.59	APP	Nottingham F.	12.76			/		(G)E.U21-6
			TR	Q.P.R.	07.79	1979-80	63	/	0	
			TR	Norwich C.	03.81	1980-83	136	/	0	
WOODS, Clive	Norwich	18.12.47	Gothic	Ipswich T.	06.69	1969-79	217	51	23	(F)
			TR	Norwich C.	03.80	1979-81	29	3	4	
WOODS, Dennis J.	Norwich	12.12.36	Cambridge U.	Watford	10.62	1962	13		2	(OR)
WOODS, Derek E.	Northampton	23.03.41	JNRS	Northampton T.	AM	1961	6		2	(F)E.AMAT.INT.
WOODS, Edward	Ton Pentre	29.07.51	Ferndale	Bristol C.	09.71	1972	1	1	0	(F)
			L	Scunthorpe U.	10.73	1973	4	/	2	
			TR	Newport Co.	09.74	1974-78	149	2	54	
WOODS, Maurice (Matt)	Skelmersdale	01.11.31	JNRS	Everton	11.49	1952-56	8		1	(CH)E.F.LGE REP.
			TR	Blackburn Rov.	11.56	1956-62	259		2	
			TR	Luton T.	07.65	1965	34	/	0	
			TR	Stockport CO.	07.66	1966-67	85	/	2	
WOODS, Neil S.	York	30.07.66	APP	Doncaster Rov.	08.83	1982-83	6	5	1	(M)
WOODS, Pat J.	Islington	29.04.33	JNRS	Q.P.R.	06.50	1952-60	304		16	(FB)
			Australia	Colchester U.	08.63	1963	36		0	
WOODS, Peter A.	Sale	21.01.50	APP	Manchester U.	04.67					(FB)
			TR	Luton T.	04.70					
			TR	Southend U.	02.72	1971-72	25	/	0	
			TR	Doncaster Rov.	07.73	1973-74	41	8	1	
WOODS, Ray	Peterborough	27.04.30	Peterborough U.	Southend U.	05.48	1950-51	3	1	1	(RH)
			TR	Crystal Palace	06.53	1953-54	18		0	
WOODS, Ray G.	Birkenhead	07.06.65	APP	Tranmere Rov.	06.83	1982-83	3	4	2	(F)
WOODS, William	Farnworth	12.03.26	Moss Grove	Rochdale	+	1946	15		1	(IF)
			TR	Bradford P.A.	01.47	1946	5		0	
			TR	Rochdale	01.49	1948-49	13		1	
			TR	Barrow	11.49	1949	16		4	
			TR	Crewe Alex.	07.50					
			TR	Accrington St.	11.50	1950	3		0	
WOODWARD, Alan	Chapeltown	07.09.46	APP	Sheffield U.	09.63	1963-78	537	2	158	(W)E.F. LGE● REP./E.YTH.INT.
WOODWARD, Alan	Stanton Hill	19.06.47	Alfreton T.	Grimsby T.	07.70	1970-71	54	/	12	(OL)
WOODWARD, Brian	Leeds	12.07.29	JNRS	Leeds U.						
			Hereford U.	York C.	08.50	1950	5		0	
WOODWARD, Harold G.	Bromley	29.08.19		Southend U.	05.46	1950-51	14		0	(FB)
WOODWARD, Horace J.	London	16.01.24	JNRS	Tottenham H.	05.46	1946-48	63		1	(CH)
			TR	Q.P.R.	06.49	1949-50	57		0	
			TR	Walsall	07.53	1953	5		0	
WOODWARD, John	Glasgow	10.01.49	Possilpark J.	Arsenal	01.66	1966	2	1	0	(M)
			TR	York C.	07.71	1971-77	152	15	6	
WOODWARD, John	Stoke	16.01.47	APP	Stoke C.	03.64	1964-66	10	1	1	(IF)
			TR	Aston Villa	10.66	1966-68	22	5	7	
			TR	Walsall	05.69	1969-72	116	10	23	
			TR	Port Vale	02.73	1972-74	88	11	30	
			TR	Scunthorpe U.	07.75	1975	16	3	5	
WOODWARD, Ken R.	Battersea	16.11.47	APP	Crystal Palace	12.65					(IF)
			TR	Orient	08.66	1966	1	/	0	
WOODWARD, Laurie	Troedyrhiw	05.07.18	Wolverhampton W.(*)	Bournemouth	+	1946-56	275		7	(WH)
WOODWARD, Tom	Horwich	08.12.17		Bolton W.	*	1946-49	121		14	(OR)
			TR	Middlesbrough	10.49	1949-50	20		6	
WOODWARD, Tom P.	Birmingham	06.07.34	Moor Green	W.B.A.	09.54					(G)
			TR	Walsall	08.58	1958	13		0	
WOODWARD, Vivien	Troedyrhiw	20.05.14	Folkestone	Fulham	*	1946	10		0	(IF)Brother of Laurie
			TR	Millwall	02.47	1946-47	42		13	
			TR	Brentford	07.48	1948-49	20		4	
			TR	Aldershot	02.50	1949-50	54		5	
WOOF, Cliff	Liverpool	20.09.56	JNRS	Liverpool	05.76					(F)
				Southport	N/C	1977	1	/	0	
WOOF, William	Gateshead	16.08.56	APP	Middlesbrough	08.74	1974-81	30	16	5	(F)
			L	Peterborough U.	03.77	1976	2	1	0	
			Blyth S.	Cardiff C.	09.82	1982	1	/	1	
			Gateshead	Hull C.	02.83	1982	9	2	3	
WOOKEY, Ken G.	Newport	30.12.46	JNRS	Newport Co.	01.64	1964-68	57	6	5	(CF)Son of Ken W.
			TR	Port Vale	07.69	1969	23	1	4	
			TR	Workington	07.70	1970	11	5	4	
WOOKEY, Ken W.	Newport	23.02.22	JNRS	Newport Co.	*	1946	14		2	(OR)W.SCH.INT.
			TR	Bristol Rov.	12.46	1946-48	53		10	
			TR	Swansea C.	11.48	1948-49	13		0	
			TR	Ipswich T.	10.50	1950	15		1	
WOOLCOTT, Roy A.	Leyton	29.07.46	Eton Manor	Tottenham H.	02.68	1969	1	/	0	(CF)
			L	Gillingham	02.72	1971	13	/	5	
WOOLDRIDGE, James	Rossington	28.09.18	Benburb FC	Doncaster Rov.	+	1946-47	30		0	(LB)

Players Names	Birthplace	Date	Previous Club	League Club	Date Signed	Seasons Played	Apps	Sub	Gls	
WOOLDRIDGE, Steve J.	London	18.07.50	APP	Crystal Palace	07.67			/		(RB)
			TR	Plymouth Arg.	08.70	1970	20	/	0	
			TR	Colchester U.	06.72	1972	3	/	0	
WOOLER, Alan T.	Poole	17.08.53	Alton T.	Reading	11.71	1971-72	38	/	0	(D)
			TR	West Ham U.	08.73	1973-75	3	1	0	
			TR	Aldershot	04.76	1976-83	264	2	3	
WOOLER, M. Graham	Huddersfield	23.10.4		Huddersfield T.	08.64					(F)
			TR	Halifax T.	12.64	1964-67	51	7	8	
WOOLFALL, Alan F.	Liverpool	30.11.56		Bury	03.75	1974-78	46	11	11	(F)
			TR	Port Vale	08.79	1979-80	13	5	3	
WOOLFORD, Mike	Swindon	29.09.39	Swindon B.R.	Swindon T.	12.59	1959	3		0	(F)
WOOLGAR, J. Stuart	Chesterfield	21.09.52	APP	W.B.A.	10.69	1972	2	2	0	(WG)
			TR	Doncaster Rov.	07.74	1974	2	5	1	
WOOLGAR, Phil R.J.	Worthing	24.09.48	Wigmore Ath.	Brighton & H.A.	AM	1966	1	/	0	(G)
WOOLLARD, Arnold J.	Pembroke	24.08.30	Bermuda A.A.	Northampton T.	06.49	1950	3		0	(FB)
			TR	Newcastle U.	12.52	1952-55	9		0	
			TR	Bournemouth	06.56	1956-61	161		0	
			TR	Northampton T.	03.62	1961-62	28		0	
WOOLLETT, Alan H.	Leicester	04.03.47	APP	Leicester C.	08.64	1966-77	213	15	0	(D)
			TR	Northampton T.	07.78	1978	23	/	0	
WOOLLETT, Charles	Dawdon	25.11.20	Eppleton CW	Newcastle U.	+					
			TR	Bradford C.	08.46	1946-48	43		5	
			TR	York C.	02.49	1948	4		0	
WOOLLEY, Robert A.	Nottingham	29.12.47	APP	Notts.CO.	07.65	1963-65	9	/	2	(CF)d.1971
WOOLMER, Anthony J.	Norwich	25.03.46	JNRS	Norwich C.	12.65	1966-67	4	1	0	(CF)
			TR	Bradford P.A.	10.69	1969	30	/	7	
			TR	Scunthorpe U.	11.70	1970-71	35	5	3	
WOON, Andy	Bognor Regis	26.06.52	Bognor	Brentford	10.72	1972-74	42	8	12	(CF)
WOOSNAM, Phil A.	Caersws	22.12.32	Caersws	Manchester C.	AM	1952	1		0	(IF)W-17/
			Sutton U.	Orient	02.57	1954-58	108		19	W.AMAT.INT./
			TR	West Ham U.	11.58	1958-62	138		26	E.F.LGE REP./
			TR	Aston Villa	11.62	1962-65	111	/	23	W.SCH.INT.
WOOTTON, Len	Stoke	13.06.25		Port Vale	+	1946	10		1	(F)
			Q.of South	Wrexham	08.51	1951	20		2	
WORDLEY, Edward H.	Stoke	17.10.23	JNRS	Stoke C.	+	1946-49	11		0	
			TR	Bury	06.50					
WORKMAN, Ian P.	Liverpool	13.11.62	Southport	Chester C.	N/C	1982	3	/	0	(M)
WORLEY, Len F.	Amersham	27.06.37	Wycombe W.	Charlton Ath.	AM	1956	1		0	(OL)E.AMAT.INT./
			Wycombe W.	Tottenham H.	AM	1959	1		0	E.YTH.INT.
WORMLEY, Paul	Leeds	16.09.61	Yorks Amats.	Barnsley	10.79	1979	1	/	0	(F)
			TR	Huddersfield T.	08.80					
WORRALL, Fred J.	Warrington	08.09.10	Portsmouth(*)	Crewe Alex.	+	1946	7		1	(OR)*Nantwich/Oldham Ath.
			TR	Stockport Co.	09.46					E-2/d.1979
WORRALL, Gary G.	Salford	04.11.61	APP	Manchester U.	11.78					(F)
			TR	Peterborough U.	03.84	1983	18	1	2	
WORRALL, Harold	Northwich	19.11.18	Winsford U.	Manchester U.	+	1946-47	6		0	
			TR	Swindon T.	06.48					
WORRELL, Colin H.	Hitchin	29.08.43	JNRS	Norwich C.	11.61	1962-64	9		0	(FB)
			TR	Orient	09.64	1964-65	52	/	0	
WORSDALE, M. John	Stoke	29.10.48	APP	Stoke C.	11.65	1968	4	/	0	(W)
			TR	Lincoln C.	05.71	1971-73	55	12	9	
WORSMAN, Reg H.	Bradford	19.05.33		Bradford P.A.	10.53	1954-55	22		5	(IF)
			TR	Bradford C.	06.56	1956	1		0	
			Nelson	Darlington	06.60	1960	4		1	
WORSWICK, Mick A.	Preston	14.03.45	Chorley	Wigan Ath.	N/L	1978	0	1	0	(F)E.AMAT. INT.
WORTHINGTON, David	Halifax	28.03.45	JNRS	Halifax T.	04.62	1961-63	37		8	(RB)
			TR	Barrow	07.64	1964-65	60	1	7	
			TR	Grimsby T.	06.66	1966-72	292	1	14	
			L	Halifax T.	10.73	1973	5	/	0	
			TR	Southend U.	12.73	1973-75	92	3	0	
WORTHINGTON, Eric S.	Sheffield	29.12.25		Q.P.R.	09.47					
			TR	Watford	08.49	1949-50	24		4	
				Bradford C.	09.53	1953	2		1	
WORTHINGTON, Frank S.	Halifax	23.11.48	APP	Huddersfield T.	11.66	1966-71	166	5	42	(F)E-8/E.U23-2/●
			TR	Leicester C.	08.72	1972-77	209	1	72	
			TR	Bolton W.	09.77	1977-79	81	3	35	
			TR	Birmingham C.	11.79	1979-81	71	4	30	
			TR	Leeds U.	03.82	1981-82	32	/	14	
			TR	Sunderland	12.82	1982	18	1	2	
			TR	Southampton	06.83	1983	34	/	4	

Players Names	Birthplace	Date	Previous Club	League Club	Date Signed	Seasons Played	Apps	Sub	Gls	
WORTHINGTON, Fred	Manchester	06.01.24		Bury	07.47	1947-50	69		14	(IR)
			TR	Leicester C.	03.51	1950-54	55		9	
			TR	Exeter C.	07.55	1955	16		1	
			TR	Oldham Ath.	06.56	1956	10		1	
WORTHINGTON, Nigel	Ballymena	04.11.61	Ballymena U.	Notts Co.	07.81	1981-83	72	5	4	(D)NI-2/NI.YTH.INT.
			TR	Sheffield Wed.	02.84	1983	14	/	0	
WORTHINGTON, P. Robert	Halifax	22.04.47	APP	Halifax T.	05.65	1964	12	/	0	(LB)Brother of Frank/
			TR	Middlesbrough	08.66	1967	2	/	0	David
			TR	Notts.Co.	09.68	1968-73	230	2	1	
			TR	Southend U.	08.74	1974	20	/	1	
			L	Hartlepool U.	03.75	1974	6	/	0	
WOSAHLO, Roger F.	Cambridge	11.09.47	APP	Chelsea	12.64	1966	0	1	0	(W)E.SCH.INT.
			TR	Ipswich T.	07.67	1967	1	/	0	
			TR	Peterborough U.	07.68	1968	13	2	1	
			TR	Ipswich T.	07.69	1969	0	1	0	
WRAGG, Doug	Nottingham	12.09.34		West Ham U.	06.53	1956-59	16		0	(OR)E.SCH.INT.
			TR	Mansfield T.	03.60	1959-60	46		13	
			TR	Rochdale	07.61	1961-63	103		14	
			TR	Chesterfield	07.64	1964	17		4	
WRAGG, Peter	Rotherham	12.01.31	JNRS	Rotherham U.	05.48	1948-52	31		4	(IF)
			TR	Sheffield U.	01.53	1952-54	56		17	
			TR	York C.	08.56	1956-62	264		78	
			TR	Bradford C.	07.63	1963-64	73		5	
WRAITH, Robert	Largs	26.04.48	Glasgow Celtic	Southport	07.69	1969-70	28	/	0	(G)
WRAY, John G.	Mytholmroyd	07.07.41	Stainland A.	Halifax T.	11.64	1964	7	/	0	(G)
WREN, John	Bonnybridge	26.04.36	Hibernian	Rotherham U.	08.60	1960	1		0	(G)
WRIGGLESWORTH, John L.	Halifax	04.07.24	Watford(AM)	Halifax T.	07.46	1946	10		1	(FB)
WRIGGLESWORTH, William	Sth.Elmsall	12.11.12	Wolverhampton W.(*)	Manchester U.	*	1946	4		2	(OL)*Frickley Co./
			TR	Bolton W.	01.47	1946-47	13		1	Chesterfield
			TR	Southampton	10.47	1947	12		4	
			TR	Reading	06.48	1948	5		0	
WRIGHT, Alan G.	Birmingham	20.05.38		Walsall	05.58	1958	1		1	(F)
WRIGHT, Albert				Lincoln C.	10.46	1946	1		0	
WRIGHT, Alex M.	Kirkcaldy	18.10.25	Hibernian	Barnsley	08.47	1947-50	83		31	(CF)
			TR	Tottenham H.	09.50	1950	3		1	
			TR	Bradford P.A.	08.51	1951-54	132		25	
WRIGHT, Archie W.	Glasgow	23.11.24	Falkirk	Blackburn Rov.	05.51	1951-52	21		10	(IR)
			TR	Grimsby T.	07.53	1953	39		8	
			TR	Accrington St.	06.54	1954-56	80		26	
WRIGHT, Arthur W.	Burradon	23.09.19	JNRS	Sunderland	*	1946-54	259		14	(WH)E.SCH.INT.
WRIGHT, Barrie	Bradford	06.11.45	APP	Leeds U.	11.62	1962-63	4		0	(FB)E.YTH.INT./
			N.York Rgrs.	Brighton & H.A.	01.69	1968-69	8	2	0	E.SCH.INT.
			TR	Hartlepool U.	09.70					
WRIGHT, Barry A.	Wrexham	23.07.39		Wrexham	05.59	1959-61	11		0	(FB)
			TR	Chester C.	08.62	1962	1		0	
WRIGHT, Bernard A.	Derry	08.06.40	Sligo R.	Port Vale	09.62	1962	14		2	(OR)
WRIGHT, Bernard A.W.	Walthamstow	19.09.23		Notts.Co.	+	1946	3		0	(G)
WRIGHT, Bernard P.	Birmingham	17.09.52	Birmingham C.(AM)	Walsall	09.71	1971	15	/	2	(F)
			TR	Everton	02.72	1971-72	10	1	2	
			TR	Walsall	01.73	1972-76	145	7	38	
			TR	Bradford C.	02.77	1976-77	65	1	13	
			TR	Port Vale	06.78	1978-79	76	/	23	
WRIGHT, Brian R.	Leicester	09.01.37	JNRS	Leicester C.	02.54	1955	2		0	(F)E.YTH.INT.
			TR	Lincoln C.	01.59	1958-60	22		3	
WRIGHT, Charlie G.	Glasgow	11.12.38	Glasgow Rgrs.	Workington	06.58	1958-62	123		0	(G)●
			TR	Grimsby T.	02.63	1962-65	129	/	0	
			TR	Charlton Ath.	03.66	1965-70	195	/	0	
			TR	Bolton W.	06.71	1971-72	88	/	0	
WRIGHT, Dennis	Royton	09.01.30	JNRS	Oldham Ath.	08.51	1946-51	8		0	(FB)
WRIGHT, Dennis	Chesterfield	19.12.19	Clay Lane	Mansfield T.	*	1946-56	380		0	(G)
WRIGHT, G. Brian	Sunderland	19.09.39	JNRS	Newcastle U.	09.56	1959-62	45		1	(WH)
			TR	Peterborough U.	05.63	1963-71	291	2	9	
WRIGHT, Gary J.	Sunderland	15.09.64	APP	Hartlepool U.	N/C	1982	12	/	0	(G)
WRIGHT, Geoff D.	Countishorpe	01.03.30		Aston Villa	05.49					(CF)
			TR	Bournemouth	06.51					
			Rugby T.	Walsall	03.52	1952	16		1	
WRIGHT, George A.				Cardiff C.	+					
			TR	Hull C.	06.46	1946	4		1	
WRIGHT, George C.	Middlesbrough	18.10.44	APP	Middlesbrough	10.62					(F)
			TR	Hartlepool U.	06.64	1964-69	179	4	31	
			TR	Darlington	02.70	1969-70	16	/	4	

Players Names	Birthplace	Date	Previous Club	League Club	Date Signed	Seasons Played	Apps	Sub	Gls	
WRIGHT, George W.	Plymouth	10.10.19	Kitto Inst.	Plymouth Arg.	*	1946	4		0	(G)
			TR	Colchester U.	N/L	1950-54	151		0	
WRIGHT, George W.	Ramsgate	19.03.30	Margate	West Ham U.	02.51	1951-57	161		0	(FB)
			TR	Orient	05.58	1958-61	85		1	
			TR	Gillingham	07.62	1962	4		0	
WRIGHT, Glen M.	Liverpool	27.05.56	APP	Blackburn Rov.	APP	1973	1	/	0	(OL)
WRIGHT, Herbert M.	Shirebrook	29.05.31	Bolsover Col.	Leeds U.	10.51					(HB)
			TR	Stockport Co.	06.53	1953	1		0	
			TR	Chester C.	07.54	1954	21		4	
WRIGHT, Horace	Pontefract	06.09.18	Wolverhampton W.(*)	Exeter C.	+	1946-47	55		11	
WRIGHT, J. Mike	Ellesmere Port	25.09.46	APP	Aston Villa	09.63	1963-72	278	3	1	(FB)E.YTH.INT.
WRIGHT, J. William	Blackpool	04.03.31		Blackpool	05.50	1951-54	15		2	(IF)
			TR	Leicester C.	08.55	1956-57	25		10	
			TR	Newcastle U.	08.58	1958	5		3	
			TR	Plymouth Arg.	08.59	1959-60	42		9	
			TR	Millwall	08.61	1961	15		0	
WRIGHT, James F.	Whitfield	19.02.24	Bury Amats	Accrington St.	AM	1947	1		0	(G)
WRIGHT, Jeff	Alston	23.06.52	Netherfield	Wigan Ath.	N/L	1978-81	139	4	19	(M)
WRIGHT, John	Blackhall	30.01.25		Darlington	01.47	1946-48	17		0	(LH)
WRIGHT, John	Tyldesley	11.08.26	Mossley	Blackpool	06.46	1948-58	158		1	(FB)E'B'-1
WRIGHT, John B.	Sth.Shields	16.11.22	Tyne Dock U.	Hull C.	09.47	1947	1		0	(CH)
WRIGHT, John D.	Southend	29.04.17	Southend U.(*)	Newcastle U.	*	1946	30		0	(WH)E-1
			TR	Lincoln C.	12.48	1948-54	233		2	
WRIGHT, John F.D.	Aldershot	13.08.33		Colchester U.	11.54	1954-60	5		0	(G)
WRIGHT, Ken L.	Newmarket	16.05.22	Cambridge C.	West Ham U.	05.46	1946-49	51		20	(F)
WRIGHT, Mark	Dorchester on-Thames	01.08.63	JNRS	Oxford U.	08.80	1981	8	2	0	(D)E-1/E.U'21-4
			TR	Southampton	03.82	1981-83	71	/	3	
WRIGHT, Martin H.	Chesterfield	01.04.50	Alfreton T.	Chesterfield	08.69	1968-71	39	4	11	(OR)
			TR	Torquay U.	07.72	1972	8	5	3	
WRIGHT, Mike	Darlington	17.02.50		Darlington	07.69	1968-72	82	7	0	(FB)
WRIGHT, Mike E.	Newmarket	16.01.42	Newmarket	Northampton T.	11.59	1959-61	26		7	(F)
WRIGHT, Mike H.	Winsford	22.10.48	APP	Shrewsbury T.	APP	1965	0	1	0	(F)
			TR	Crewe Alex.	09.66					
WRIGHT, Pat D.	Oldbury	17.11.40	Springfield BC	Birmingham C.	11.59	1959-61	3		0	(FB)
			TR	Shrewsbury T.	09.62	1962-67	202	/	3	
			TR	Derby Co.	10.67	1967-68	13	1	0	
			L	Southend U.	03.70	1969	11	/	0	
			TR	Rotherham U.	09.70	1970	1	/	0	
WRIGHT, Peter B.	Colchester	26.01.34	JNRS	Colchester U.	11.51	1951-63	426		89	(OL)
WRIGHT, Ralph L.	Newcastle	03.08.47	Spennymoor	Norwich C.	07.68					(OL)
			TR	Bradford P.A.	10.69	1969	13	1	1	
			TR	Hartlepool U.	06.70	1970	24	1	3	
			TR	Stockport Co.	07.71	1971	19	2	0	
			TR	Bolton W.	02.72	1971-72	25	7	5	
			TR	Southport	12.72	1972-73	40	3	3	
WRIGHT, Richard	Mexborough	05.12.31		Leeds U.	05.49					(G)
			TR	Chester C.	08.51	1952-54	53		0	
			TR	Bradford C.	03.55	1955	1		0	
WRIGHT, Robert C.A.	Glasgow	20.02.16	Crook T.	Charlton Ath.	*	1946	9		0	(LH)
WRIGHT, Ron W.	Glasgow	06.12.40	Shettleston	Leeds U.	06.59	1960	1		0	(F)
WRIGHT, Steve P.	Clacton	16.06.59		Colchester U.	06.77	1977-81	112	5	2	(D) Son of Peter B.
			Lapfjard BK	Wrexham	04.84	1983	37	/	0	
WRIGHT, Terry I.	Newcastle	22.06.39	Nuneaton Bor.	Barrow	11.62	1962-64	10		1	(OL)
WRIGHT, Thomas	Bland Hill	20.01.28	Partich Th.	Sunderland	03.49	1948-54	167		51	(OR)S-3
			E.Fife	Oldham Ath.	03.57	1956	7		2	
WRIGHT, Thomas B.	Glossop	11.01.17	Altrincham	Hull C.	07.47					(WH)*Manchester C.
			TR	Accrington St.	10.47	1947-48	22		4	
WRIGHT, Thomas J.	Liverpool	21.10.44	JNRS	Everton	03.63	1964-72	307	1	4	(FB)E-2/E.U23-7
WRIGHT, Thomas K.	Stepps	11.01.25	Dunfermline	Aldershot	07.52	1952	17		1	(F)
WRIGHT, Tommy E.	Dunfermline	10.01.66	APP	Leeds U.	01.83	1982-83	26	3	9	(F)S.YTH.INT.
WRIGHT, Vince	Bradford	12.04.31		Derby Co.	09.51					E.YTH.INT.
			TR	Mansfield T.	07.52	1952	2		0	
WRIGHT, William	Wordsley	26.04.59	Birmingham C.(APP)	Lincoln C.	07.78	1978	3	/	0	(D)
WRIGHT, William	Liverpool	28.04.58	JNRS	Everton	08.74	1977-82	164	2	10	(D) E.U21-6/Nephew of Tommy
			TR	Birmingham C.	07.83	1983	40	/	5	
WRIGHT, William A.	Ironbridge	06.02.24	JNRS	Wolverhampton W.	+	1946-58	491		13	(CH)E-105/E.F.LGE REP.●
WRIGHT, William H.R.	Corbridge	04.11.62		Burnley	01.81					(F)
			L	Crewe Alex.	11.82	1982	3	/	1	
WRIGLEY, Wilf	Clitheroe	04.10.49	JNRS	Burnley	07.68	1968-69	6	/	1	(HB)

Players Names	Birthplace	Date	Previous Club	League Club	Date Signed	Seasons Played	Career Record Apps	Sub	Gls	
WYATT, George A.	Whitechapel	28.03.24		**Crystal Palace**	11.47	1948	7		0	d.1957
WYATT, Reg G.	Plymouth	18.09.32	Astor Inst.	**Plymouth Arg.**	08.50	1955-64	201		3	(CH)
			TR	**Torquay U.**	10.64	1964-66	80	/	6	
WYER, Peter W.	Coventry	10.02.37		**Coventry C.**	10.55	1955	1		0	(F)
			TR	**Derby Co.**	06.56	1956	2		1	
			TR	**Coventry C.**	07.58	1958	4		0	
WYLDE, Rodger J.	Sheffield	08.03.54	APP	**Sheffield Wed.**	07.71	1972-79	157	12	54	(F)
			TR	**Oldham Ath.**	02.80	1979-82	109	4	51	
WYLDES, Robert J.	Southport	06.10.28	Desborough	**Luton T.**	10.49	1949-51	26		8	(OL)
			TR	**Southend U.**	09.52					
WYLES, Harold	Melton Mowbray	28.10.22		**Leicester C.**	+					(FB)
			TR	**Gateshead**	03.48	1947-53	235		7	
WYLES, Tom C.	Dunsby Fen	01.11.19	Everton(*)	**Bury**	05.46	1946	2		0	(F)
			TR	**Southport**	11.46	1946-49	143		54	
WYLIE, John E.	Newcastle	25.09.36		**Huddersfield T.**	09.54					(WH)
			TR	**Preston N.E.**	05.57	1958-62	91		1	
			TR	**Stockport Co.**	11.62	1962-63	68		2	
			TR	**Doncaster Rov.**	08.64	1964-67	123	1	2	
WYLIE, Ron M.	Glasgow	06.08.33	Clydesdale	**Notts.Co.**	09.50	1951-58	227		33	(IF)S.SCH.INT.●
			TR	**Aston Villa**	11.58	1958-64	196		15	
			TR	**Birmingham C.**	06.65	1965-69	125	3	2	
WYLLIE, James	Saltcoats	15.10.27	Kilmarnock	**Southport**	07.50	1950	15		1	
			TR	**Wrexham**	12.50	1950	20		4	
WYLLIE, Robinson G.N.	Dundee	04.04.29	Dundee U.	**Blackpool**	05.53	1953-54	13		0	(G)
			TR	**West Ham U.**	05.56	1956	13		0	
			TR	**Plymouth Arg.**	07.58	1958	5		0	
			TR	**Mansfield T.**	10.59	1959-61	92		0	
WYNN, Ron W.	Wrexham	02.11.23		**Wrexham**	04.48	1947-55	183		11	(FB)

Players Names	Birthplace	Date	Previous Club	League Club	Date Signed	Seasons Played	Career Record Apps	Sub	Gls	
YALLOP, Frank W.	Watford	04.04.64	APP	Ipswich T.	01.82	1983	6	/	0	(D)
YARD, Ernie	Stranraer	03.05.41	Partick Th.	Bury	12.63	1963-64	45		13	(CF)
			TR	Crystal Palace	05.65	1965-66	35	2	3	
			TR	Reading	11.66	1966-68	101	3	6	
YARDLEY, George	Fife	08.10.42	Montrose	Luton T.	10.66	1966	1	/	0	(CF)
			TR	Tranmere Rov.	11.66	1966-70	123	/	69	
YATES, David	Barnsley	18.03.53	APP	Barnsley	03.71	1972-77	104	/	2	(D)
			L	Grimsby T.	03.77	1976	10	/	0	
YATES, Harry	Huddersfield	28.09.25		Huddersfield T.	+	1949	1		0	(F)
			TR	Darlington	05.50	1950-51	91		29	
YATES, John	Rotherham	18.11.29		Sheffield U.	06.50					
			TR	Chester C.	08.51	1951	2		0	
YATES, Richard	Queensferry	06.06.21		Chester C.	+	1946-47	52		37	(IF)
			TR	Wrexham	12.47	1947-48	31		19	
			TR	Carlisle U.	11.48	1948	16		9	
			TR	New Brighton	08.49	1949-50	42		14	
YATES, Steve	Burton	08.12.53	APP	Leicester C.	03.72	1973-76	12	7	0	(D)
			TR	Southend U.	11.77	1977-83	223	1	8	
			TR	Doncaster Rov.	12.83	1983	27	/	1	
YEATS, Ron	Aberdeen	15.11.37	Dundee U.	Liverpool	07.61	1961-70	357	1	13	(CH)S-2/S.SCH.INT.
			TR	Tranmere Rov.	12.71	1971-73	96	1	5	
YEATS, Tom B.	Newcastle	30.05.35	JNRS	Sunderland	02.53					(F)
			TR	Gateshead	08.54	1954	1		0	
YEATS, William	Hebburn	04.02.51		Newcastle U.	06.71					(CF)
			TR	York C.	03.72	1971-72	8	1	0	
			TR	Darlington	08.73	1973-74	22	3	7	
YEO, Brian G.	Worthing	12.04.44	JNRS	Portsmouth	05.61					(CF)
			TR	Gillingham	07.63	1963-74	345	10	135	
YEOMAN, Ray I.	Perth	13.05.34	St.Johnstone	Northampton T.	09.53	1953-58	168		4	(IF)
			TR	Middlesbrough	11.58	1958-63	210		3	
			TR	Darlington	06.64	1964-66	103	/	2	
YEOMANS, Kelvin	Nottingham	25.08.47	Beeston	Notts.Co.	AM	1967	1	/	0	(FB)
YEOMANSON, John	Margate	03.03.20	Margate	West Ham U.	02.47	1947-50	106		1	(FB)
YEULL, Jasper H.	Bilston	23.03.25	W.B.A.(AM)	Portsmouth	08.46	1946-51	31		0	(FB)
			TR	Barnsley	08.52	1952	19		0	
YORATH, Terry C.	Cardiff	27.03.50	APP	Leeds U.	04.67	1967-76	120	23	10	(M) W-59/W.U23-7/●
			TR	Coventry C.	08.76	1976-78	99	/	3	W.SCH.INT.
			TR	Tottenham H.	08.79	1979-80	44	4	1	
			Vancouver W.	Bradford C.	12.82	1982-83	21	3	0	
YORK, Alan	Newcastle	13.07.41	Gateshead	Bradford C.	02.65	1964-66	42	3	2	(FB)
			TR	Lincoln C.	07.67					
YOULDEN, Tom F.	London	08.07.49	APP	Arsenal	07.66					(D) E.SCH.INT.
			TR	Portsmouth	04.68	1968-71	82	8	1	
			TR	Reading	07.72	1972-76	161	2	3	
			TR	Aldershot	04.77	1976-80	118	5	1	
YOUNG, Alan F.	Kirkcaldy	26.10.55	JNRS	Oldham Ath.	07.74	1974-78	107	15	30	(F)S.SCH.INT.
			TR	Leicester C.	07.79	1979-81	102	2	26	
			TR	Sheffield U.	08.82	1982	23	3	7	
			TR	Brighton & H.A.	08.83	1983	25	1	12	
YOUNG, Alan R.	Hornsey	20.01.41	JNRS	Arsenal	04.59	1960	4		0	(CH)
			TR	Chelsea	11.61	1961-66	20	/	0	
			TR	Torquay U.	01.69	1968-71	59	/	1	
YOUNG, Albert E.	Caerleon	11.09.17		Arsenal	*					
			TR	Swindon T.	06.46	1946-49	123		1	
YOUNG, Alex	Loanhead	03.02.37	Hearts	Everton	11.60	1960-67	227	1	77	(IF)S-8/S.U23-6/
			Glentoran	Stockport Co.	11.68	1968	23	/	5	S.F.LGE REP.
YOUNG, Cecil R.	Bournemouth	22.07.25		Bournemouth	06.48	1948-49	18		0	
YOUNG, Charles F.	Cyprus	14.02.58	APP	Aston Villa	11.75	1976	9	1	0	(D)
			TR	Gillingham	03.78	1977-81	27	1	1	
YOUNG, Charles S.R.	Falkirk	23.08.29	Stalybridge	Sheffield U.	05.51	1951	3		0	(G)
YOUNG, Clarrie W.	Bow	23.02.20		Coventry C.	*	1946	1		0	
YOUNG, David	Newcastle	12.11.45	JNRS	Newcastle U.	09.64	1969-72	41	2	2	(D)
			TR	Sunderland	01.73	1972-73	24	6	1	
			TR	Charlton Ath.	08.74	1974-76	76	1	0	
			TR	Southend U.	09.76	1976-77	56	4	0	
YOUNG, David A.	Trimdon	31.01.65	APP	Darlington	08.83	1982-83	13	5	0	(D)
YOUNG, David J.	Birkenhead	27.04.62	Mossley	Wigan Ath.	N/C	1982	3	/	0	(F)
YOUNG, Doug	London	02.02.27	Walthamstow	Southend U.	06.53	1953-55	37		0	(FB)E.AMAT.INT.
YOUNG, Eric	Singapore	25.03.60	Slough T.	Brighton & H.A.	11.82	1983	30	/	4	(D)

Players Names	Birthplace	Date	Previous Club	League Club	Date Signed	Seasons Played	Apps	Sub	Gls	
YOUNG, Eric R.	Stockton	26.11.52	APP	Manchester U.	12.69					(F)E.YTH.INT.
			L	Peterborough U.	11.72	1972	24	1	2	
			L	Walsall	10.73	1973	8	/	0	
			TR	Stockport Co.	01.74	1973	16	/	0	
			TR	Darlington	07.74	1974-77	123	7	15	
YOUNG, George	Dundee	02.11.19	Hibernian	Watford	07.46	1946-48	43		5	(IF)
YOUNG, George R.	Newport	05.01.50	Cromwell J.	Newport Co.	07.68	1967-71	90	13	6	(IF)W.U23-1
YOUNG, Gerry M.	Sth.Shields	01.10.36	Hebburn Arg.	Sheffield Wed.	05.55	1956-70	307	2	13	(WH)E-1
YOUNG, John D.	Hartlepool	09.11.51	Newcastle U.(AM)	Hartlepool T.	AM	1968	3	/	0	(CH)
YOUNG, John R.				Gateshead	AM	1949	4		0	
YOUNG, Ken	Halifax	11.06.30		Halifax T.	09.50	1949	1		0	
YOUNG, Kevin	Sunderland	12.08.61	APP	Burnley	05.79	1978-83	114	6	11	(M)
			L	Torquay U.	11.83	1983	3	/	1	
			L	Port Vale	12.83	1983	28	/	4	
YOUNG, Len A.	W.Ham	23.02.12	West Ham U.(*)	Reading	*	1946-47	38		0	
			TR	Brighton & H.A.	02.48	1947-49	8		0	
YOUNG, Martin	Grimsby	09.04.55		Grimsby T.	03.74	1974-78	87	6	4	(D)
YOUNG, Neil J.	Manchester	17.02.44	APP	Manchester C.	02.61	1961-71	332	2	86	(IF)E.YTH.INT.
			TR	Preston N.E.	01.72	1971-73	67	1	16	
			TR	Rochdale	07.74	1974	8	5	4	
YOUNG, Noel J.	Derry	22.12.32	JNRS	Middlesbrough	04.50					
				Doncaster Rov.	01.55	1954	3		0	
YOUNG, Quintin	Irburne	19.09.47	Ayr U.	Coventry C.	07.71	1971-72	25	1	2	(W)S.U23-1
YOUNG, Ray G.	Derby	14.03.34	JNRS	Derby Co.	03.51	1953-65	252	/	5	(CH)E.SCH.INT.
YOUNG, Richard H.	Gateshead	17.04.18	Wardley C.W.	Sheffield U.	*	1946-48	59		0	(CH)
			TR	Lincoln C.	03.49	1948-53	100		2	
YOUNG, Richard	Felling	13.07.39	Unsworth J.	Newcastle U.	07.57					(F)
			Sth.Shields	Grimsby T.	03.62	1962-64	32		14	
			TR	Stockport Co.	05.65	1965	27	/	5	
YOUNG, Robert G.	Bournemouth	24.12.23	JNRS	Bournemouth	+	1947	1		0	(FB)
			TR	Crewe Alex.	06.48	1948-51	144		2	
YOUNG, Ron	Dunstan	31.08.45		Hull C.	08.63	1964-67	24	2	5	(F)
			TR	Hartlepool U.	09.68	1968-72	176	10	40	
YOUNG, Roy	Sheffield	02.10.50	Sheffield U.(AM)	Doncaster Rov.	07.70	1970	6	1	0	(FB)
YOUNG, T. Anthony	Urmston	24.12.52	APP	Manchester U.	12.69	1971-75	69	14	1	(M)
			TR	Charlton Ath.	01.76	1975-76	20	/	1	
			TR	York C.	09.76	1976-78	76	2	2	
YOUNG, Tom	Glasgow	24.12.47	Falkirk	Tranmere Rov.	06.72	1972-76	170	2	27	(F)
			TR	Rotherham U.	07.77	1977-78	11	4	1	
YOUNG, William J.	Glasgow	24.02.56	Arthurlie	Aston Villa	07.78	1978	3	/	0	(F)
			TR	Torquay U.	10.81	1981-82	35	3	0	
YOUNG, William D.	Edinburgh	25.11.51	Aberdeen	Tottenham H.	09.75	1975-76	54	/	3	(D)S.U23-5
			TR	Arsenal	03.77	1976-81	170	/	11	
			TR	Nottingham F.	12.81	1981-82	59	/	5	
			TR	Norwich C.	08.83	1983	5	1	0	
			L	Brighton & H.A.	03.84	1983	4	/	0	
YOUNGER, Tom	Edinburgh	10.04.30	Hibernian	Liverpool	06.56	1956-58	120		0	(G)S-24/S.F.LGE.REP/
			Falkirk	Stoke C.	03.60	1959	10		0	d.1984
			Toronto	Leeds U.	09.61	1961-62	37		0	
YOUNGER, William	Whitley Bay	22.03.40	Whitley Bay	Nottingham F.	05.57	1958-60	12		2	(IF)
			L	Lincoln C.	02.61	1960	4		0	
			TR	Walsall	06.61	1961	7		5	
			TR	Doncaster Rov.	12.61	1961	18		1	
			TR	Hartlepool U.	08.62	1962	37		3	

Players Names	Birthplace	Date	Previous Club	League Club	Date Signed	Seasons Played	Career Record Apps Sub Gls			
ZELEM, Peter R.	Manchester	13.02.62	APP	Chester C.	02.80	1980-83	109	5	11	(D)
ZENCHUK, Steve J.	Peterborough	20.11.56	JNRS	Peterborough U.	N/C	1983	1	/	0	(G)
ZONDERVAN, Romeo	Surinam	04.03.59	Twente Enschede	W.B.A.	03.82	1981-83	82	2	5	(M)
			TR	Ipswich T.	03.84	1983	8	/	2	

ROY VERNON (Blackburn Rov., Everton, Stoke C. & Wales)
A magical, skilful inside forward, Vernon was a Blackburn bred youngster, joining the ground staff from school. He developed along the right lines, making his debut in 1955/6, becoming a regular the next season. Transferred to Everton in February 1960 for £20,000, he was not with the Rovers when they reached Wembley for the F.A. Cup Final in May. Interestingly, Roy had declined to sign for Everton when leaving school. He gained a League Championship medal in 1962/3 before leaving for Stoke City in March 1965. A supreme architect of an inside forward he was very expressive, full of control, and ideal in taking over the City mantle from the great Jimmy McIlroy. He played for Wales 32 times.

KEN WAGSTAFF (Mansfield T./Hull C.)
A two footed, strongly made goalscoring centre/inside forward, Wagstaff in only his third season of League soccer, scored 34 goals from 44 appearances when assisting Mansfield Town to achieve Third Division status. Transferred to Hull City in November 1964, in his first full season with the "Tigers", he won a Third Division medal as an ever present with 27 goals to his credit. At Boothferry Park he struck up a great partnership with Chris Chilton and, in scoring 173 League goals on the completion of his career, closely rivalled Chilton as the greatest Hull City scorer of all time.

DAVE WAGSTAFFE (Manchester C./Wolverhampton W./Blackburn Rov./Blackpool/Blackburn Rov.)
A well built, fast, direct left winger, Wagstaffe could mesmerise the best of defences. He started out with local club Manchester City after coming through their junior ranks, following England schoolboy International honours. He was transferred to Wolves in December 1964, becoming a regular for the next ten years before leaving Molineux for Blackburn Rovers. He had a brief spell with Blackpool before rejoining the Rovers in March 1979 to seal a career which, through his choice of clubs, had not quite enabled this very good player to claim many of the game's honours. He played over 550 League games.

MIKE WALKER (Reading/Shrewsbury T./York C./Watford/Colchester U.)
An extremely competent goalie who has made nearly 700 League appearances since starting out with Reading in January 1963, Walker played for Shrewsbury and York City before coming to prominence with Watford, whom he joined in September 1968, immediately winning a Third Division medal when conceding only 34 goals. The following season he was one of the key factors in getting Watford to the F.A. Cup semi-final where the under-dogs were beaten 5-1 by eventual winners, Chelsea. He signed for Colchester United in June 1973, becoming a mainstay in the club alternating between Third and Fourth Divisions.

DAI WARD (Bristol Rov., Cardiff C. & Wales/Watford/Brentford)
Whilst with Bristol Rovers Ward gained a reputation as a goalscorer when following Geoff Bradford into the side, although having previously made his debut in 1954/5 after being signed from Barry Town. He was an instant success, equalling the "Pirates" record by scoring in eight consecutive games before signing for Cardiff City who paid £11,000 for his services in February 1961. He collected 90 goals from 174 League appearances. After settling in at Ninian Park, he got a second Welsh cap, having played for his country at centre and inside forward. Clever, with penetrating ability, Dai could have scored many more First Division goals if Cardiff had persevered with his thrusting play.

JOHN WARK (Ipswich T., Liverpool & Scotland)
A sharp-shooting midfielder, Wark specialises in long range efforts, and scores more goals than the majority of accomplished strikers. He signed for Ipswich in August 1974 after serving an apprenticeship at Portman Road and made his debut that coming season. The Town twice came within shooting distance of the Championship, with Wark missing only two of the matches and scoring 36 invaluable League goals from the 80 games he played. Capped many times for Scotland, his greatest club achievements have been the F.A. Cup winners medal in 1978 from the game against Arsenal and a U.E.F.A. Cup winners medal versus AZ 67 Alkmaar in 1981. He was transferred to Liverpool in March 1984 and immediately helped in another League Championship win.

DAVE WATSON (Notts Co./Rotherham U./Sunderland, Manchester C., Southampton, Stoke C. & England/Derby Co.)
A granite-like central defender Watson started soccer life as a forward at Notts County, joined Rotherham in January 1968, and under the management of Tommy Docherty, blossomed into a quality type utility player. He moved to Sunderland where he gained the first of many England caps, but is mainly remembered for the part played in the glorious F.A. Cup Final victory for the Second Division side over hot favourites Leeds United in 1973. His rugged qualities were just what Manchester City required, and he joined the "Citizens" in June 1975. He later had a short stay in the West German League with Werder Bremen. Southampton brought him back to England as part of their programme for gaining top honours, before he left to play in quick succession for Stoke City, Vancouver Whitecaps in the U.S.A. and currently Derby County.

CHARLIE WAYMAN (Newcastle U./Southampton/Preston NE./Middlesbrough/Darlington)
A diminutive goalscorer and creative centre forward, Wayman was a United discovery, but left after being dropped from the semi-final team. He went to Southampton for £19,000, but in 1950, because of his wife's health, was transferred to Preston where he continued to score freely. He played a great part in getting North End through to the 1954 Cup Final where they lost in a nail biting game to W.B.A., also earning the rare distinction of scoring in every round of the Cup including the Final itself. At the end of that season he was transferred to Middlesbrough, playing with the young Brian Clough. Finally, he moved to Darlington before retiring at the age of 36.

LEN WEARE (Newport Co.)
Nearly 6ft tall, well built, Weare was the talented custodian of the Newport County goal for over 15 seasons. He was the reserve keeper for Wales in the World Cup 1958, but because of the brilliant Jack Kelsey did not get a chance to play. Once highly rated enough to be considered by many to be worthy of First Division status, but he remained loyal to the needs of County which was nearly always having to stave off relegation one way or another. A fine servant who played 524 games, being ever present on four occasions.

DAVID WEBB
(Orient/Southampton/Chelsea/Q.P.R./Leicester C./Derby Co./Bournemouth) Webb started out as a crew-cut sturdy full back, signing for the "O's" after being rejected by West Ham. He was allowed to leave for Southampton, from where Chelsea signed him in February 1968, and became one of the great successes of the "Blues" Cup campaigns, powerfully scything his way upfield, chasing lost causes; the fans loved him. The greatest memory for him would surely be scoring the winning goal for Chelsea against Leeds in the 1970 F.A. Cup Final. In extra time of the first-ever replayed Final since 1912, this mightly player soared above all others to head home. After leaving Chelsea, David served three more clubs before going into soccer management with Bournemouth and gaining promotion to the Third Division in 1982/3.

DUNCAN WELBOURNE (Grimsby T./Watford/Southport)
Welbourne had five seasons with Grimsby Town, helping them regain Second Division status in 1961/2 before losing form and his first team place. He was transferred to Watford in November 1963, immediately gaining a regular place in the side at wing half. For five consecutive seasons he was an ever present player, a truly remarkable record, and was instrumental in the club's success when gaining a Third Division medal 1968/9. The next season, he was a valued member of the side that produced the greatest performance till then in Watford's history when reaching the semi-finals, losing gloriously to Chelsea, the eventual F.A. Cup winners. He finished his playing days at Southport.

LEN WHITE (Rotherham U./Newcastle U./Huddersfield T./Stockport Co.)
A sturdy forward, only 5ft 7in tall, very stocky and difficult to dispossess, White was crafty, with a great turn of speed. He began with Rotherham United, playing on the right wing, and was signed by Newcastle United in February 1953. He played sporadically at first, mainly in a forward utility role, but became a regular in 1954/5 gaining an F.A. Cup winners medal from the game against Manchester City where Jackie Milburn scored the first goal within seconds from his corner kick. When "Wor Jackie" retired, Len was moved to lead the attack with great success, scoring quite heavily and picking up Football League representative honours. Later he moved to Huddersfield Town, still effective, but used more at inside forward. He finished his career with Stockport County in the Fourth Division.

STEVE WHITWORTH (Leicester C. & England/Sunderland/Bolton W./Mansfield T.)
A tall, fast in recovery and constructive full back, Whitworth began with Leicester City in November 1969, after a successful apprenticeship at Filbert Street. He made his debut the following season, and missed only 14 games for the "Foxes" until transferring to Sunderland in March 1979, for a fee of £125,000. During his career at Leicester he was capped by England seven times and in his first season, 1970/1, gained a Second Division winners medal. At Roker Park, Steve did not have to wait long for success and as an ever present in 1979/80 he was instrumental in helping the "Rokermen" gain promotion to the First Division. He moved on to Bolton in October 1981 for £25,000, and later played for Mansfield Town.

RAY WILCOX (Newport Co.)
Wilcox was a constructive centre half signed during wartime by Newport County from his local club Treharris, the Welsh League side. Not very tall for a defender, he made up for distinct lack of inches with strong positional play befitting the pivot of the defence, with well placed passing allied to tough, strong tackling. From 1946 to 1960 Ray made 489 appearances, a record for the club, and was one of their greatest servants.

JOHN WILE (Sunderland/Peterborough U./W.B.A.)
A tall, consistent centre half Wile has played well over 500 League games since making his debut in the 1967/8 season for Peterborough. Prior to that he had been signed by Sunderland from Durham City, but had been allowed to leave a season later, not having made an appearance for the "Rokermen". Transferred to W.B.A. for a fee of £30,000 in December 1970, he succeeded John Talbut as the pivot of the defence, forming a solid reliable partnership with Ally Robertson. He was a key factor in helping Albion back into the First Division in 1975/6, where his superiority in the air was of immense value. He went into League management with Peterborough, making the odd appearance as a non-contract player into the bargain.

RAY WILKINS (Chelsea, Manchester U. & England)
Known as "Butch", Ray Wilkins comes from a large soccer family, with Dad George playing both sides of the war, and brothers Graham and Dean also currently playing League soccer. He was an England schoolboy star prior to turning professional for Chelsea in October 1973, and before he was transferred to Manchester United, had played for England at every level possible. He has been unfortunate with injuries whilst at Old Trafford and his form has obviously suffered, being reflected in International duties. He has brilliant midfield control when in possession, and could be outstanding, but tends to play short balls when the long forward pass is well within his scope and talent.

ALAN WILLIAMS (Bristol C./Oldham Ath./Watford/Newport Co./Swansea C.)
A strong, no nonsense centre half, Williams started out with native Bristol City, coming through their junior sides. He developed into a more than capable defender who was allowed to sign for Oldham Athletic June 1961 after spending six years at Ashton Gate. He became one of the "Latics" most consistent players, missing only 12 games in four seasons as the pivot of their defence, being ever present when promotion was attained to the Third Division 1962/3. He had short stays at Watford and Newport before signing for Swansea October 1968, going on to help the South Wales club achieve Third Division status in 1969/70 before hanging up his boots.

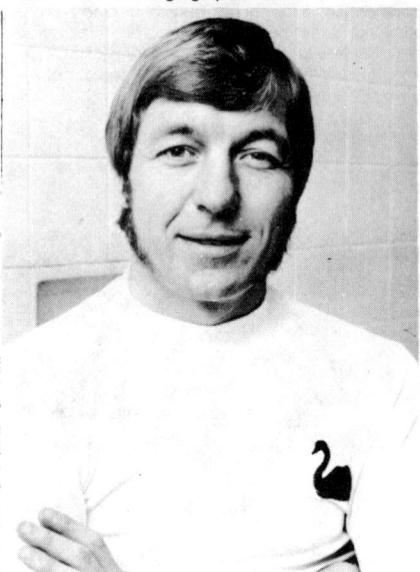

BERT WILLIAMS (Walsall/Wolverhampton W. & England)
Williams joined Wolves for a fee of £3,500 from Walsall in 1945, after shining in wartime football, where his goalkeeping agility stood out. Sometimes known as "the cat", Bert created a tremendous impression at International level when succeeding the great Frank Swift. The holder of Cup and League medals, he also won many sprint titles away from the soccer pitch. When superseded by Gil Merrick in the England side, the still not-too-old goalie had opened several sports shops in his native Bilston, paving the way for retirement. Recall to the National side came in 1955, the selectors once again opting for the spectacular, even at the age of 35. Then he quickly retired, leaving his Wolves jersey to the up-and-coming Nigel Sims who had understudied him for eight years.

DANNY WILLIAMS (Rotherham U.)
A great clubman, Williams later in life took those qualities into Football League management. A local signed from Silverwood Colliery during the war, he made his debut as an inside forward and played nearly 15 seasons in the "Merry Millers" colours, showing great consistency and settling down as a wing half before finally managing the club. He was originally a miner, like several of his team mates, and these dour professionals nearly gained Rotherham promotion to the First Division in 1954/5.

HERBIE WILLIAMS (Swansea C. & Wales)
Williams started out with his local club Swansea as an inside forward in May 1958, but soon converted to half back where his height was invaluable to defensive situations. Able to attack equally well, he was a highly constructive player who loved to break out of defence on surges upfield. He was rewarded with three Welsh full caps in recognition of outstanding club form, which followed several under 23 honours. Later in his career he played in various positions, scoring considerably for a midfield type, and but for talented competition would have played far more games for his country. A great wholehearted player, he always gave of his best.

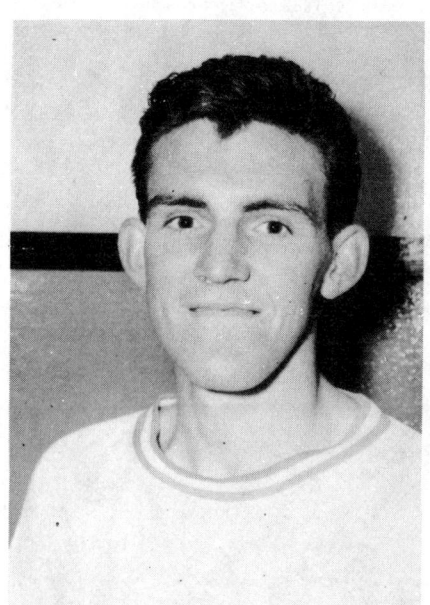

STUART WILLIAMS (W.B.A., Southampton & Wales)
The son of a Wrexham director, Williams started out as an amateur at that club, playing half a dozen games after the war until being signed professionally by the Albion in February 1951. After performing in several positions, he settled down as a very strong full back of some quality, being capped by Wales initially against Austria in May 1954, the first cap of 43. Difficult for any winger to master, he had a most tenacious recovery rate, also being an extremely tough tackler who didn't waste the ball often when in possession. Before retiring he joined Southampton where, in his last season of League soccer, he helped the "Saints" in their rise to the First Division for the first time in the club's history.

JOE WILSON (Workington/Nottingham F./Wolverhampton W./Newport Co./Workington)
Born in Workington, Wilson signed for his local club in January 1956. Settling down at full back and producing some great displays in their colours before Forest enticed him to the City ground in 1962. Not very tall, but stocky and very difficult to dispossess, Joe became a utility defender, later signing for the Wolves, then of the Second Division. After a season at Newport, only missing five games, he came back home to Workington, playing a further 168 League games before leaving soccer.

RAY WILSON (Huddersfield T., Everton & England/Oldham Ath./Bradford C.)
One of the most brilliant of home grown products, Wilson was considered by a great many experts to be the outstanding left back in the World after helping England beat Germany in that marvellous 1966 World Cup epic at Wembley. Surprisingly he started out with Huddersfield Town in August 1952 as an outside left, before being converted to full back with great success by Bill Shankly, then Town's Manager. Fancied by many a club, Roy was signed by Everton in July 1964, later collecting an F.A. Cup winners medal from the game against Sheffield Wednesday 1966, and before leaving Goodison had played for England 63 times. A great stylist, terrific tackler and very constructive when on the ball, he was unfortunately badly affected by injuries. Later he played for Oldham before becoming player coach to Bradford City.

BOBBY WOODRUFF (Swindon T./Wolverhampton W./Crystal Palace/Cardiff C./Newport Co.)
One of Swindon Town's great local discoveries of the late 1950s, Woodruff joined the club straight from school and impressed when making his debut as an attacking wing half with great flair. A member of the Town side that entered the Second Division for the first time in its history 1962/3, he became much sought after by the bigger clubs, eventually signing for Wolves. After spending nearly two years at Molineux, he rejoined former manager Bert Head, then at Crystal Palace where, in 1968/9, he achieved First Division status with that club. Later he played nearly 150 games with Cardiff City before ending up at Somerton Park with Newport County.

ALAN WOODWARD (Sheffield U.)
A long serving wingman Woodward played nearly 550 League games for his only club, and broke the United record in scoring 158 goals before finishing in 1978/9. Joining Sheffield United as an apprentice, Alan turned professional on his 17th birthday in September 1963. Strongly built and difficult to shake off the ball, he went on to become a regular. He was notable for heavy shooting from outside the penalty area, and the "Blades" relied on his ability. He was sorely missed as the club slipped conspicuously towards the Fourth Division. In his prime Woodward was honoured in representing the Football League, to supplement England youth honours achieved at an early age.

FRANK WORTHINGTON (Huddersfield T./Leicester C. & England/Bolton W./Birmingham C./Leeds U./Sunderland/Southampton)
A prolific free scoring, swashbuckling centre forward, Worthington brings enjoyment to some of the boring spectacles imposed on the public. Unfortunate brushes with authorities did not dim his belief that the game should be enjoyed by players and spectators alike, and his view was vindicated by his scoring some 170 goals. From a famous footballing family, Frank began with Huddersfield Town, winning a Second Division medal 1969/70. He signed for Leicester City in August 1972 for an £80,000 fee and whilst at Filbert Street he played for England on eight occasions. When playing for both Bolton and Birmingham City, he achieved First Division status at his first attempt with both clubs. Following spells in the U.S.A., "Worthy" returned to weave his magic spell with Leeds and Sunderland. Currently with Southampton, he still probes defensive weaknesses in style.

BILLY WRIGHT (Wolverhampton W. & England)
The fair haired star of the immediate post-war soccer scene, Billy Wright had begun with the Wolves straight from school, nearly being sent home for not being big enough. He became an inspiring captain for both club and country, making his International debut for England against Belgium in 1946 and going on to play a then record 105 appearances, including a run of 46 consecutive matches. Holder of three League Championship medals, he also captained Wolves in winning the 1949 Cup Final against Leicester City. Although only 5ft 8 in, he was converted to centre half, being a great success by keeping the ball on the ground to his advantage wherever possible. He was the player of the year in 1951/2, adding to his many honours.

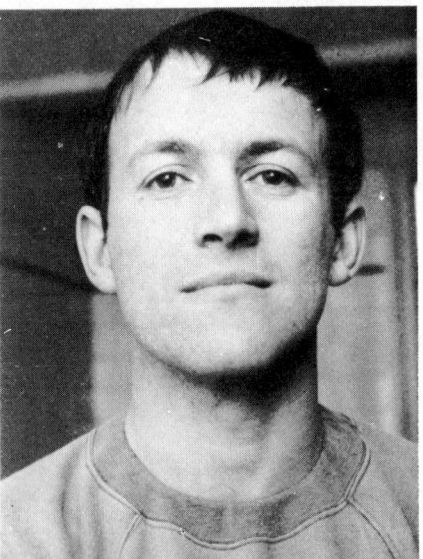

CHARLIE WRIGHT (Workington/Grimsby T./Charlton Ath./Bolton W.)
After playing 28 reserve games for the great Glasgow Rangers, Charlie Wright decided that a move south might benefit and, on his being granted a free transfer, Workington moved in for the young goalkeeper in June 1958. Upon National Service in 1960, Charlie actually played for Hong Kong while stationed there, saving a penalty against Peru and becoming their footballer of the year. On his return, he then was soon transferred to Grimsby and in March 1963 to Charlton Athletic. A real character, he was really appreciated at the Valley by fans who still remember the great Sam Bartram. By the time Charlie played his last game for Bolton Wanderers in 1972/3, he had amassed nearly 550 League games.

RON WYLIE (Notts Co./Aston Villa/Birmingham C.)
One of the cleverest of inside forwards, Ron Wylie was signed by Notts County from Clydesdale, the Scottish junior side, and made his debut at Doncaster in October 1951, aged 18. He remained eight years in the Second Division with County as their key player, very constructive and with great vision, before transferring to Aston Villa in November 1958, where he played just short of 200 League games. He collected a Second Division winners medal in 1959/60 and surely would have played for Scotland if he had moved to a top club when younger and at the height of his excellence. He finished with Birmingham City at the age of 36, after playing nearly 550 League games.

TERRY YORATH (Leeds U., Coventry C., Tottenham H. & Wales/Bradford C.)
A blond Welshman with midfield defensive duties instilled under Don Revie whilst serving Leeds United, Yorath was never assured of a first team place at Elland Road, spending nearly ten years in the wings, although being capped by Wales and later going on to play more than 50 times for the National side. In 1973/4 he appeared in more than half of the League campaign, helping Leeds win the Championship. He played more regularly until being transferred to Coventry City and then being transferred to Spurs, before going to the U.S.A. After a lengthy spell with Vancouver Whitecaps, he was welcomed back to Yorkshire by Bradford City in December 1982 as player-coach.